THE TEMPLE OF MAN

APET OF THE SOUTH AT LUXOR

R. A. Schwaller de Lubicz

Translated from the French by
Deborah Lawlor and Robert Lawlor

Illustrations by Lucie Lamy

Inner Traditions
Rochester, Vermont

Inner Traditions International
One Park Street
Rochester, Vermont 05767
www.InnerTraditions.com

First English language edition published by Inner Traditions International, Ltd. 1998
Originally published in French under the title *Le Temple de l'homme*
Copyright © 1957, 1993, 1998 by Éditions Dervy
Translation copyright © 1998 by Inner Traditions International

Library of Congress Cataloging-in-Publication Data
Schwaller de Lubicz, R. A.
[Temple de l'homme. English]
The temple of man : Apet of the South at Luxor / R. A. Schwaller de Lubicz ;
translated from the French by Deborah Lawlor and Robert Lawlor.
p. cm.
Includes bibliographical references and index.
ISBN 978-0-89281-570-8 (alk. paper)
1. Occultism—Egypt. 2. Temple of Luxor (Luxor, Egypt)—Miscellanea. I. Title.
BF1434.E3S3613   1998   97-21877
001.9—dc21   CIP

Volume 1 of two-volume slipcased edition
Printed in China

10 9 8 7 6

Text design by Virginia L. Scott and Peri Champine. Layout by Peri Champine.
This book was typeset in Adobe Caslon with Centaur as the display typeface.

Jacket and slipcase cover image: statue of Ramesses II, builder of the Ramesside court at Luxor.
Photograph by Georges and Valentine de Miré.
Hieroglyphs on jacket flaps, front cover stamp, and title pages
are the Egyptian words for *The Temple of Man.*
Endpapers are based on royal cartouches from the Eighteenth Dynasty.

THE

TEMPLE OF MAN

BOOKS BY R. A. SCHWALLER DE LUBICZ

The Egyptian Miracle

Esoterism and Symbol

Nature Word

Sacred Science

A Study of Numbers

Symbol and the Symbolic

The Temple in Man

The Temples of Karnak

To the Immortal Masters

of Ta-meri,

Earth, beloved of Heaven

CONTENTS

VOLUME 1

Part 2
MATHEMATICAL THOUGHT

Part 3
THE MASTER BUILDERS' GRID
PHARAONIC MATHEMATICS APPLIED

Part 4
THE ARCHITECTURE OF THE TEMPLE
THEMES

VOLUME 2

Part 5
THE PHARAONIC TEMPLE

Part 6
PLATES, LEGENDS, AND COMMENTARIES

Publisher's Preface

Does our search for meaning have a time and place best suited to a successful journey? Does this search still have a role to play in the modern world? Is it still important to search for meaning? If so, where do we search—in math, medicine, biology, the hard sciences, philosophy, religion, spirituality? Which discipline leads most surely to the truth? If we find truth, can it be meaningful? And finally, can any search for meaning be realized if it is not felt directly in our bodies? If truth is not *embodied* then where is it? If indeed the body is the temple, as our ancestors claim, then what use is a temple of stone?

Twenty-eight years ago I was standing in the aisle of Samuel Weiser's bookstore in New York City, consumed by these very questions. At that time Weiser's was the oldest and largest bookstore in the world specializing in Oriental philosophy, metaphysics, and the occult. Dissatisfied with my college major in physics, I had left mathematics and science behind and was now working at Weiser's. Physics as taught in school was no longer natural philosophy, and consequently I was searching for that natural and universal philosophy in the shelves of books on Hermeticism, alchemy, Buddhism, yoga, the kabbalah, and allied sacred sciences. Science, in its pure definition, is the search for knowledge, and it is sacred when directed at perfecting man. Man starts as an idea, becomes a seed, and only begins his gestation upon leaving the safe comfort of the womb. When science is not interested in making things for use in life, but rather in making man, it becomes truly sacred.

Early one morning Robert Lawlor entered the bookstore. Robert explained that he was on his way to India to live in the experimental community started by Sri Aurobindo in Pondicherry, South India. Robert told me that he had just left the home of André VandenBroeck, a student of R. A. Schwaller de Lubicz, with whom he had been studying sacred geometry. I myself had recently discovered the two *Her-Bak* titles of Isha Schwaller de Lubicz, the wife of R. A. Schwaller de Lubicz. These two books were the only expression of Schwaller de Lubicz's ideas in the English language at that time, and they had a great impact on my young mind. It was in Schwaller de Lubicz's ideas, as presented by his wife, that I found the source of sacred science. Robert suggested that I would be better served by reading Schwaller himself, and that André VandenBroeck, who was working on translating Schwaller de Lubicz's works from French into English,* could introduce me to the essence of his ideas. I told Robert I would do this and gave him, on his way out of Weiser's, a copy of *Theoretic Arithmetic of the Pythagoreans* by Thomas Taylor, the forgotten first English translator of Plato and source of inspiration for William Blake, Emerson, and others whom I was reading at the time. I felt sure that Taylor's work would find in Robert a receptive mind.

This encounter set in motion what would later become the publishing company Inner Traditions International, and the realization some twenty-plus years later of the publication of the complete opus of R. A. Schwaller de Lubicz, culminating in *The Temple of Man,* which you now hold in your hands. The works that André introduced me to so inspired me that I determined to start my own publishing house and to bring the work of R. A. Schwaller de Lubicz to the English-speaking world. André confided that he had promised Schwaller that *The Temple of Man* would find its way into English, and I took that vow unto myself, not knowing how or when I would be able to accomplish this mammoth task. Five years later I founded Inner Traditions and met with Robert and Deborah Lawlor in the south of France at the home of Lucie Lamy next to the Cistercian Abbey of Le Thorenet, a monument embodying the principles of sacred geometry as understood by medieval Europe. Robert and Deborah had begun the monumental task of translating R. A. Schwaller de Lubicz's *Le Temple de l'homme* in a grass hut in South India, surrounded by Tamil villagers. After three years of this endeavor they left India with a rough translation and were now working on the translation with Lucie, stepdaughter and collaborator of R. A. Schwaller de Lubicz. Lucie granted me the rights to publish her father's work, and thus began the practical work of bringing what is, in my view, this century's greatest natural philosopher's work to the English reader.

The work of R. A. Schwaller de Lubicz represents the most fundamental breakthrough in our understanding of Ancient Egypt since the discovery of the Rosetta stone. *The Temple of Man* proves in exact detail, as does no other contemporary work, how advanced the knowledge of the Ancients was. It is in geometry and number that the voices of our ancestors can most clearly be heard. After all, the square root of two has the same meaning today as it did five thousand years ago. The same cannot be said of words like *soul* and *spirit.* Schwaller de Lubicz shows through geometry and number that Egypt, not Greece, lies at the foundation of Western civilization. It was in Greece that what Schwaller de Lubicz called the "great deviation" to modern scientific materialism began and where the sacred science of the Temple that directed the great cultures of antiquity began to submerge.

The human body is the measure of the Temple and the Temple is the measure of man. Schwaller de Lubicz's colossal *The Temple of Man* offers those who search for meaning a view into the mind of Ancient Egypt, a mind whose expression has captured the imagination of people all over the world for millennia. It is in Egypt's temples that the realization of the "perfect man" was sought. And it is in *The Temple of Man* that we today can search for that very same and universal realization.

Ehud C. Sperling
July 7, 1998

* *Sacred Science,* 1982; *Egyptian Miracle,* 1985.

Translators' Acknowledgments

This translation of *Le Temple de l'homme* was accomplished through the tireless devotion, inspiration, and support given to the translators by Mlle. Lucie Lamy, the stepdaughter and longtime collaborator of R. A. Schwaller de Lubicz. Her vision and constant attention to every detail of the work was invaluable.

Gratitude must also be given to Dr. Getrude Englund of the Department of Egyptology, University of Uppsala, Sweden, who reviewed the entire translation, and to Ehud C. Sperling, publisher of Inner Traditions, for his long and ardent commitment to bringing this work to the English-speaking world.

Deborah Lawlor would like to thank Professor Anne Schlabach Burkhardt of Bennington College for her guidance on the disciplines of philosophy.

Robert Lawlor would like to extend appreciation to Dr. Ernest McClain, who edited the section relating to music and harmony.

We would further like to acknowledge and thank both Christopher Bamford and André VandenBroeck for their guidance in situating the thought of R. A. Schwaller de Lubicz within the Western esoteric and philosophic traditions.

We are also grateful to those who accomplished the final editing of the manuscript: the knowledgeable work of Lawrence Grinnell, who had been familiar with Schwaller de Lubicz's work for many years, and the sensitive and skillful editing of Cannon Labrie of Inner Traditions. Appreciation and thanks must also be given to the staff at Inner Traditions for the impeccable design and production of this complex book.

Translators' Preface

René Schwaller de Lubicz (1887–1961) was born in Strasbourg, the son of a pharmacist. In his early years, he was a student of the visual arts as well as of chemistry, physics, and mathematics. In 1910, at the age of twenty-three, he arrived in Paris initially to study painting with Matisse. Soon after he became fascinated with the study of European esotericism, Gothic and medieval symbolism, and alchemical philosophy. Schwaller's combined interests and acuity in the visual and esoteric arts brought him in contact with most of the intriguing groups and secret societies of the intelligentsia that converged upon Paris about the turn of the century.

In the arts, Jean Cocteau and Hans Arp were among his close associates, as well as a number of surrealists, who were directly influenced by the symbolist groups of which Schwaller was a leading force. Usually associated with psychological concepts, surrealism was also a vehicle for esoteric symbolism, both mathematical and mythological.

Paris at this time also attracted members of the European nobility, particularly from eastern Europe, who were escaping the turmoil and atrocities of Bolshevism. Among them was a Romanian prince, Matila Ghyka, who brought to light an original Renaissance text on ancient geometry called *The Divine Proportion,* authored by an Italian monk, Luca Paccioli, and illustrated by Leonardo da Vinci. This work verified what Schwaller had intuited from other sources: that a universal canon of proportions based on the laws of geometric form and musical harmony was the substructure of art and architecture, not only in Europe and the Middle East but in all known ancient cultures. It was recognized by Schwaller and others that the earliest and most profound source of this geometric knowledge and science was Ancient Egypt. Matila Ghyka and Schwaller established a detailed correspondence in which they both began to describe how this geometric key lay at the base of the unfoldment of human culture and intelligence.

Also in the early 1900s, the influence of the aristocracy on Parisian intellectual life saw the rise of interest in the royal art of alchemy. At this time, a renowned alchemical group formed around the legend-like figure of Fulcanelli and began publishing and inspiring alchemical philosophy. R. A. Schwaller de Lubicz's name has often been associated with the inner workings of this enigmatic group, and later, Schwaller was to confirm the initiatic character of his research by producing in a laboratory examples of alchemical glass—intense reds and blues obtained from the inherent mineral constituents with no added pigments, which, as the tradition also dictates, transform sunlight instantaneously into color and then again into white light.

During this period in Paris, Schwaller also lectured at the Theosophical Society, then at its zenith. This began for him the process of formulating and communicating his unusual and complex thought into a cohesive philosophy.

In World War I Schwaller served as a chemist in the French army. In 1917 he published his first book, *Études sur les nombres (A Study of Numbers)*, an essay on Pythagorean mathematical philosophy. Soon after Schwaller received the spiritual name of Aor, meaning "Light" or "Light of the Higher Intellect"—a name that served as a guide and impetus to all his future work. Schwaller established an intellectual exchange with the Lithuanian aristocrat and poet O. V. de Lubicz Milocz, who recognized in him a rare quality of intellectual refinement and spiritual intensity. In a formal ceremony, as an act of gratitude for Schwaller's attempt to persuade European governments to maintain the freedom and traditional culture of the poet's homeland, Milocz conferred the royal de Lubicz heraldic title upon Schwaller.

In the aftermath of World War I, Schwaller de Lubicz developed a social philosophy opposed to modernism, scientism, and industrialization, which he perceived as the substructure of this heinous militarism. Because of his exceptional ability to penetrate and articulate ancient metaphysics, particularly Hindu and Islamic, along with his profound understanding of the revolution in modern physics, Schwaller de Lubicz became the center of a group of prominent artists and scholars. He cofounded with Isha, his wife, a community at Saint-Moritz in the Swiss Alps. Their interests in occultism, herbal and homeopathic medicines, and traditional artisan crafts, in concert with their metaphysical involvements, forged the basis of this alternative community.

The diversity of Schwaller de Lubicz's intellectual interests again coalesced around the Hermetic, alchemical tradition and ultimately drew him away from this collective phase to more solitary research and contemplation, at first in Plan du Grasse, France, and later in Palma de Mallorca, Spain. In 1936 as the dark tempest of World War II gathered over Europe, Schwaller, Isha, and Isha's two children by her former marriage, Jean and Lucie Lamy, set sail with a small crew on a private yacht destined for Egypt, where they would stay for fifteen years. In preparing for the trip from Mallorca to Egypt, Schwaller applied his philosophy of geometric form and harmony and designed a model of the curvature of a boat's hull so that it caused the vortexes created by the boat's movement through water to spiral back against its surface and continually propel its forward momentum.

Their eventual arrival in Egypt had a revelatory impact on both Isha and Schwaller. They discovered that they possessed cultural affinities, linguistic and symbolic recognition, and skills which they had been unaware of before their setting foot in the land of the pharaohs. They also discovered that their previous research in symbolism and metaphysics was present, integrated, and complete in Egyptian architecture. For twelve years they lived in a hotel in Luxor, close to the Eighteenth Dynasty temple of Amun-Mut-Khonsu, where they conducted continuous research. Once again a group of collaborators gathered around Schwaller de Lubicz, including the respected Egyptologist Alexandre Varille and the archeologist Clément Robichon.

In addition to these specialists, Lucie Lamy, Schwaller de Lubicz's stepdaughter, emerged as his most important and indispensable lifelong collaborator. She executed exact-scale reproductions of nearly every bas-relief and inscription in the temple of Luxor and made many additional drawings from other temples and tombs. Lucie developed a masterful skill in rendering the delicate pharaonic images as well as an extraordinary hand for hieroglyphs. She became adept in the Egyptian system of measure, and her graphics provided the illustrative material for the books which Schwaller and Isha later published. These works by Schwaller include *Symbol and the Symbolic* (1949), *Esoterism and Symbol* (1960), *Sacred Science: The King of Pharaonic Theocracy* (1961), *Nature Word* (1961), *The Egyptian Miracle* (1963), and *The Temples of Karnak* (1982). Isha's works include a two-volume novel, *Her-Bak, Chick-Pea* (1954) and *Her-Bak, Egyptian Initiate* (1956); *Journey into the Light* (1960); and *The Opening of the Way* (1979).

The research at Luxor and its implications for interpreting the symbolic and mathematical processes of the Egyptians was first published as a thin volume in 1949 under the title of *Le Temple dans l'homme (The Temple in Man)*. The book was met with a disdainful silence from the academic Egyptologists and it required nearly another decade for Schwaller de Lubicz, working in France, to expand his geometric and mathematical explanations and to assemble the supporting data that he hoped would elicit a more open and investigative response. In so doing, Schwaller de Lubicz created one of the most theoretically conclusive and thoroughly researched documents in the annals of European esoteric philosophy: *Le Temple de l'homme (The Temple of Man)*, which was published in France in 1957 in a three-volume format. In this present English edition, the second and third volumes, containing the plates and their commentaries, have been combined into one.

The translators and editors have attempted to remain faithful to the original text in all its particulars, and additional notes and glosses have been kept to a minimum. Contrary to the original, we have favored a lowercase approach to many of the abstractions originally capitalized in the French. There are a number of terms, which the author considered as Causative Principles, which have retained capitalization as was conventional in the traditional philosophies to which he belonged. No attempt has been made to make Schwaller de Lubicz's rendering of Egyptian words consistent with the latest approaches to transliteration. Likewise, the dates assigned in the original text to the various dynasties have been preserved.

Part 1 sets up the general themes of pharaonic thought, the pivotal doctrine of the Anthropocosmos, and the way in which symbols operate in Egyptian language and thinking. Part 2 is preparatory to the actual study of temple geometry; it includes an exegesis of the Pythagorean science of number and a detailed examination of Egyptian mathematics based on the Rhind Papyrus. The chapters of part 3, the most technical section, are devoted to an elaboration of ancient trigonometry, the Egyptian canon for human proportions, the concept of volumetric thinking and calculation, the synthesis of various Egyptian cubits into a coherent system of measure in geodesics, the significance of the royal pharaonic apron, and the numerical basis of the various axes that govern the plan and construction of the temple. Chapter 7 in part 3 also includes a detailed appendix comparing the use of the inverse in Egyptian and Babylonian procedures of calculation.

Part 4 begins with a detailed study of the Edwin Smith Surgical Papyrus, throwing light on the Ancient Egyptians' knowledge of physiology. Then follow several chapters on the relationship of various parts of the temple to human anatomy and physiology. In volume 2, part 5 is prefatory to part 6, the presentation of the temple itself—its history, growth, dimensions, and bas-reliefs—in plates and commentaries.

In general, a condensation of all of the areas of knowledge and philosophy that constitute the infrastructure of this ancient monument are developed and woven together by the author in the first volume of this text. The second volume demonstrates how this corpus of knowledge applies to and appears in the images and architecture of the temple itself.

Historically, in many specialized branches of knowledge, it has been the nonspecialized, integrative minds that have made the ground-breaking innovations. Schwaller de Lubicz's multidisciplinary explanations of the Egyptian mentality and culture represent such an expansion of vision for the entire field of Egyptology. During his lifetime and for many years after, Schwaller de Lubicz's work was treated at best as radically innovative and controversial and at worst as an unfounded heretical fringe. These attitudes, however, began to change, gradually at first and more recently into a rapidly expanding circle of acknowledgment and recognition. In the early 1960s Dr. Alexander Badaway, a reputable American Egyptologist, utilized inspiration from Schwaller de Lubicz and published an influential thesis showing that harmonic principles governed the entire construction of Egyptian temples. This was the initial crack in the academic stone wall, but it was followed by more years of silence. Next, in 1972 author Peter Tompkins published his popular *The Secrets of the Great Pyramid.* It included the work of the renowned geodesic scientist Livio Stecchini, who conclusively verified what Schwaller de Lubicz had theorized decades previously: that the system of measure incorporated in Egyptian architecture was commensurate with the accurate measurements of the earth and its rotations and revolutions in the solar system. This was another turn in the gradual recognition of Schwaller de Lubicz's work.

Basing a decade of research on an early de Lubicz observation that the weathering of the body of the Sphinx in the Giza desert was caused by water erosion, independent researcher John Anthony West (*Serpent in the Sky,* 1979) finally procured exact scientific data which proved Schwaller de Lubicz's statement and, at the same time, induced a change in the dating of the construction of the Sphinx to perhaps as early as 10,500 B.C. This greater antiquity of Egypt had also been theorized decades before by Schwaller de Lubicz. The much publicized excavation of a boat and boat docks near the site of the Sphinx in 1998 points to the Sphinx having been in a lake at least 9000 years ago, adding further weight to the Schwaller de Lubicz/West theory of rain and water erosion and greater Egyptian antiquity.

In the early 1980s West skillfully utilized the media to awaken the world to the fact that the vast antiquity and meaning of Egyptian history was sometimes being obscured or distorted by the Egyptological establishment. Affirming this thrust, and also referencing Schwaller de Lubicz, Harvard professor of history Martin Bernal, in his book *Black Athena,* developed the theory that the academic rendition of Egyptian history was for the most part a politically motivated construct by a nineteenth-century white German and British academic elite.

Then in the 1990s came the work of Robert Bauvall and Graham Hancock who, in their widely recognized books and research, utilized techniques of archeo-astronomy and thus verified more of Schwaller de Lubicz's assertions: that the axes of Egyptian monuments and temples were oriented toward precise and intricate celestial movements and configurations.

Subsequently, many authors, researchers, and specialists in a diverse spectrum of fields of study are uniting in an attempt to overturn the orthodoxy and to reveal the existence of advanced civilizations and sophisticated spirituality and philosophy in prehistoric times. Within this widespread revisionist movement, the work of Schwaller de Lubicz has found growing acceptance. He stands as one of the courageous innovators and archiconoclasts. A distinctive quality in Schwaller de Lubicz's work is his view that the alignments and metrical concurrences of Egyptian architecture with celestial and geodesic data are not simply the result of refined methods of scientific observation among the Ancients, but are foremost an expression of the universal principles of organization and causation, which define not only the natural and cosmic creation but also the patterns and processes of the human mind and spirit.

The Temple of Man is many things in one: A book about the temple of Luxor and through it the world of the Eighteenth Dynasty; a synthesis of the mathematical, physiological, astronomical, geodetic, and mystical knowledge of the Ancients; a reading of Egyptian mythology that "re-members" Osiris and poses a challenge to contemporary Egyptological views; a work in the Pythagorean tradition of arithmology; a critique of Western scientism and rationalism; and finally, a work of natural philosophy.

The Temple of Man is a book or volumetric encyclopedia that one has to learn how to read.

Embodied in the temple is a code, by means of which is inscribed all the knowledge—practical and physical, spiritual and metaphysical—of the culture. Schwaller de Lubicz suggests that, like the cathedral of Chartres, Luxor was a center of learning, a university, and what was to be learned was inscribed or encoded in the physical volume of the temple building. This code consists in what he calls an architectural "grammar" in which the shapes of the stone blocks, the joints between them, the juxtapositions of symbols in the bas-reliefs by means of "transparencies" and "transpositions," and such things as the "finish of a carving or its rough aspect, the absence within a scene of essential parts—such as the eye or the navel—the reversal of right and left" hands and so forth, play the role of "accents, declensions, conjugations, and conjunctions." This interpretive strategy led directly to a synthetic view of the whole temple as symbolic of the genesis of Cosmic Man.

Schwaller de Lubicz adds another dimension to the methods and findings of Egyptology. He is asking Egyptology to open up to the presence in Ancient Egypt of a kind of analogical thinking common to many cultures of the ancient world, and still alive, for instance, in India today.

Schwaller de Lubicz sees in Egypt the source of the Pythagorean view of numbers as qualities in relationship with one another. The genesis of number, the movement from One to Many, is seen as a metaphor for cosmic genesis or becoming, just as are the creation myths of the various cultic centers. (And the gods of Egypt, the *neters*, are not merely divine personalities, but are anthropomorphized universal functions or activities—activities that are summarized within the human body: vision, digestion, assimilation, and so on.) The "Mysteries" of Heliopolis, Memphis, and Thebes, the dominant myths related to the cults of these temple-cities, each represent phases within the universal progression of spirit becoming matter, and returning again to spirit. Thus, the successive prominence of one center or another indicates an emphasis or exploration of one phase or another of genesis, one aspect or another of the myth. This is an alternative to the conventionally accepted scenario that the changing of the capital from one town to another was the result of various priesthoods battling each other for hegemony. Schwaller de Lubicz sees the three major mythic cycles as complementary rather than mutually exclusive. And curiously enough, the earliest of them, the myths coming from Heliopolis, form the basis for an integral universe by positing matter not as opposite but as part of spirit; matter as a resistance that is of the same nature as the light from which it comes.

While the sheer monumentality of *The Temple of Man* almost precludes attempts at a summary description, it is apparent that at the core of this text is a deep contemplation of the meaning and power of symbolic methods. Undoubtedly, one's inner reality or worldview is defined by the linguistic processes in which one participates. Pharaonic Egypt, standing on the threshold of the introduction of written language and inscribed symbols, as well as at the beginning of the dominant position of architectural enclosures and monuments in human surroundings, certainly realized that these innovations would profoundly intervene in humanity's perception of its environment and reality. The great challenge with the introduction of written symbols and glyphs was to assure that the original intuitive ways of direct knowing and perceiving were not interfered with by the extensive utilization of grammatical or structured symbolism.

Schwaller de Lubicz perceived that Egypt had confronted this issue through the complete integration of the four dual elements, upon which all human symbolizing methods are constructed. These components include images and glyphs in the visual realm, words and sounds in the auditory, numbers and mathematics in the purely conceptual, and geometric symmetries—both planar and volumetric—in the physical realm of architecture or the mental structuring of ideas. This integration was accomplished so that each symbolic creation could contain a reflection or representation of every other, as well as the entire system of which they are a part. This relational possibility—all parts proportional to each other and the whole—was the way Egyptian sages conceived the natural world to be ordered and, therefore, how their symbolic method was to be organized if it was to maintain human thought in harmony with creation. This same principle of proportion and relationship has a unique mathematical expression in an irrational constant (phi, ϕ) known as the golden mean and is the basis of an ancient philosophical doctrine, the Anthropocosmos, which Schwaller de Lubicz develops, in great detail, throughout the text. In this view the individual human organism in its form, function, and essence represents the ordering principles of the entire universe. The golden proportion not only has this philosophical and cosmological application but also contains the formula for analogical thought—the laws of correspondence—and is, therefore, at the foundation of symbolism itself.

It is this basis of Egyptian thought which allows for the interrelationship of the diverse fields of human activity represented by astronomy and music, mathematics and mythology, anatomy and architecture, physics and metaphysics, science and spirituality. In such a worldview the inner realms of the mind and the psyche are, through symbols, in direct transparency to the external world of the senses. An outgrowth of such disciplines and techniques of thought is a philosophy which considers that the processes of nature and the cosmos manifest the physical universe, parallel to the way mind and imagination manifest their creations through symbolism and language. Thus, symbolic methods are the instrument by which knowledge projects itself successively into generations and cycles of time. That is to say, it is the genetic material of consciousness and mind.

As such, symbols must contain in their grammatical and syntactical structuring a precise coded image of the entire body of knowledge they perpetuate. In addition to an informational code, symbolic language, like a seed, must possess the vital force, the fructifying impulse, which will enable it to attract and penetrate the mindfields of generations yet unborn. It is in this sense that R. A. Schwaller de Lubicz describes the ancient stones and remains of the temple of Luxor, a grammatical or symbolic seed of the entire corpus of Egyptian knowledge.

THE
TEMPLE
OF MAN

VOLUME 1

PREFACE

It was the "Temple of Man"—Apet of the South at Luxor—that allowed us to coordinate the elements that constitute our contribution to the study of pharaonic thought, the purpose of this book.

The fulfillment of this goal necessitated a long stay at the site; during the twelve years of continuous work my stepdaughter, Lucie Lamy, proved to be an invaluable collaborator, thanks to the meticulous precision she brought to the tasks under her care: the painstakingly exact survey of the entire temple, stone by stone; the drawing of the plans and axes of orientation; and the complete survey of the bas-reliefs (particularly in the covered temple), each figure of which had to be measured in detail and every hieroglyph and joint conscientiously verified and noted down. I can never thank her enough, both for her exhaustive work and for her careful collation of the texts that relate to the mathematical knowledge of the Ancients.

It is to my other understanding and dedicated collaborator, Clément Robichon, architect and archaeologist attached to the French Institute of Oriental Archaeology, Cairo, that I owe, with profound gratitude, the drawings of the plans as well as some of the figures and plates, which are as remarkable for their wonderful technique as for their clear understanding of the purpose of this book, to which he devoted his leisure time.

Although the guiding principle of this book has been to rely only on undisputed facts—such as the architecture and the bas-reliefs—certain texts have been used as guides. I am indebted for the study of these texts and the values of the hieroglyphs to Isha Schwaller de Lubicz, my wife and everlasting collaborator.

Doctor Jean Lamy supervised the anatomical drawings and checked the various statements regarding pathology and surgery.

In these times of misunderstanding between France and Egypt, I am very pleased to express my gratitude to the Egyptian government, whose kind hospitality we enjoyed from 1936 to 1952. It is thanks to our uninterrupted stay in Upper Egypt, in the seemingly living presence of those old pharaonic stones, that we were able to find the real significance of numerous details confirming the true meaning of the tradition that has always been my "Ariadne's thread," the indispensable safeguard from more or less romantic fantasies.[1]

I also wish to convey my special thanks to the Service des Antiquités, to Etienne Drioton, who was the director at the time, and to the department inspectors, his collaborators and our friends, Doctor Ahmed Fakhry, Labib Habachi, Zakaria Goneim, Professor Asfour, Mustapha el-Amir, and to the late architect Abu el-Naga.

We are also much obliged to the Chicago Institute of Egyptology, Luxor, for the use of the long ladders needed to survey the temple walls. I would like to express my thanks to the directors of that institution.

And how can I thank the kind population of Luxor, especially the faithful Sadi Abbas, whose help was so precious for the work at the temple?

Finally, I wish to express my gratitude to our great friend Alexandre Varille, who gave me a rapid introduction to the current state of affairs with regard to the artifacts and information amassed by the discipline of Egyptology. His erudition, and his special knowledge of the Amenhotep period, were indeed a valuable help when, in 1942, won over by the symbolist doctrine,* he became our daily collaborator in uncovering the evidence of a great pharaonic science. To my deep regret, the death of Alexandre Varille in a fatal accident in 1951 prevented him from taking part in the development of this new *Temple of Man,*† a book that demonstrates for our time the reality of this ancient knowledge, and in defense of which he dared to jeopardize his university career.

One month before his death he was still assuring us that we would be able to revive the methods and motives at the root of an empire founded many thousands of years ago. His clearsighted faith makes him still a partner in our work. Only the corporeal form decays; all ties are maintained by affinities of the spirit; our friend is living still.

I must clarify yet one more point. If I had not been led to the study of Ancient Egypt by "Ariadne's thread," valid for all knowledge [*Connaissance*], I would not have understood the thought of the Egyptian sages any better than standard Egyptology does, the efforts of which are all the more praiseworthy because it never had this guidance.

—∿∿—

The habit in pharaonic Egypt of treating the part only in relation to the spirit of the whole to which it belongs requires that we constantly refer to the general foundations of our study. Although this process may prove somewhat cumbersome, it is unavoidable in our time, lost as we are in detailed specialization and forgetful of the living bond that links all things.

---

[1] We are also indebted to our life in the pharaonic countryside—the Nile, the mountains and the fields where the country people (Coptic and Muslim) still retain old pre-Islamic customs—for Isha Schwaller de Lubicz's lively tales, *Her-Bak, Chick-Pea* [trans. C. E. Sprague (1954; reprint, Rochester, Vt.: Inner Traditions, 1978)] and *Her-Bak, Egyptian Initiate* [trans. R. Fraser (1967; reprint, Rochester, Vt.: Inner Traditions, 1978)].

* This is the notion that the hieroglyphs and monuments of Egypt represent an otherwise inexpressible vision. See chapter 2 and *Symbol and the Symbolic,* trans. Robert and Deborah Lawlor (1978; reprint, Rochester, Vt.: Inner Traditions, 1981).

† The results of Schwaller de Lubicz's studies of the temple of Luxor were initially published in a brief book, *The Temple in Man,* trans. Robert and Deborah Lawlor, illus. Lucie Lamy (1977; reprint, Rochester, Vt.: Inner Traditions, 1981). The present book elaborates those findings.

The exhaustive study of a single wall of a room within the covered temple would require a book in itself. The orientation axes that link the temple to cosmic influences, the stone joints that point to the physiological functions of the human body, the geometric functions that convey the numerical relationships appropriate to their locations in the temple, the dimensions of the figures, the offerings, the attributes, the placement of the hieroglyphs in relation to the images and their ritual meanings—all these are ideas to contemplate and coordinate. To this we must add the "transparencies" and "transpositions" connecting one side of a wall to what is conveyed on the opposite side in the adjoining room.

As much as possible, we have tried to trace through this maze the way to be followed for studying the teaching that the pharaonic sages—companions of the sages of all times—wanted to transmit to us. Here and there I have also introduced some notes concerning the guide that must be kept in view in order to clarify what is being communicated. This guide is also valuable for the study of the monuments of all eras that, up to our Gothic cathedrals, still hold knowledge.

Egypt is the school where the image speaks to us and tells us more and better than any other text could do. The image is a *synthesis* for which words are only an analysis, an analysis that offers us many opportunities to lose the guiding thread because we reject myth and theological thought, the axioms that are the "guardrails" on this dangerous path.

The world, bewildered by the extreme dispersal into details of scientific research, is perhaps more anxious than ever to find the bond that unites all aspects of existence. This bond can no longer reveal itself through the analytic mentality that predominates. We need to discover (or should I say rediscover) the ground of synthesis that summarizes or joins together these countless aspects into a single, white light. This is possible only through the anthropomorphization of the powers revealed to us by analysis, while absolutely excluding their humanization, against which our present mind-set, acquired through civilization, rebels.

Then the *symbolique* will speak (I did not say the "symbol," but the *symbolique**).

NOTES TO FACILITATE READING

The theme of this book being original,[2] a bibliography is unnecessary. Whenever a work is referred to, it is cited in a footnote. When reference is made to the plates, it is important to read the associated legends and commentaries in volume 2.[†]

In the parts dealing with mathematics, it is enough if the reader skims the more technical parts of the presentation and the various appendices to the chapters.

Some brief but important passages in this book are taken from *The Temple in Man* (*Le Temple dans l'homme,* published in Cairo in 1949) and from *Symbol and the Symbolic* (*Symbole et symbolique,* also published in Cairo in 1951, and almost entirely destroyed in the riot of January, 1952).

The temple of Luxor is called "Apet (or Ipet) of the Land of the South." The very word is already cabalistic. *Apet* is the name of the female hippopotamus,[3] symbol of the gestating womb.

---

[2] It is not the result of a compilation.

[3] The hippopotamus, or river horse, is the same symbol as the "horse of Poseidon" in the Hellenistic cabala.

* We will retain the French word when the author is referring either to an interconnected set of symbols or to the "concrete image of a synthesis" that cannot be otherwise expressed. See p. 21 and chapter 2.

[†] A complete list of works cited appears at the end of volume 2. The plates and commentaries, separate volumes in the French edition, are combined into one volume in this edition.

Moreover, Apet or Ipet derives from the root *ip,* which means "to count" or "to enumerate." Consequently, gestation, being a multiplication, is identified with the act of counting. As for the Land of the South, it is also the land of the white crown, therefore the land of the white phase in the work of gestation, south being the direction of realization or materialization (just as the earth's South Pole expels the continents, whereas the North Pole reabsorbs them).

INTRODUCTION

The purpose of this book is, first, to show the means of expression used by the Ancients to transmit knowledge, and to supply the evidence for it through the temple of Luxor—an exceptional work that actually represents man—and, second, to present an outline of the doctrine of the Anthropocosmos, the guide to the way of thinking of the sages.

In view of this purpose, two forces struggle within me. One is the awareness of my responsibility, and the other is the pessimism thrust upon me by the contemporary human attitude. Do I have the right to withhold what I have learned, little as it may be? This book may help those who are tormented by "holy anxiety," and it might also become a basis for those who are destined to go further than I.

Among the things I have learned there are some that are more dangerous than beneficial to divulge; but it is not possible for me to discriminate in this matter, for the preparedness of each individual, which opens or seals his or her eyes, must be the sole judge.

Pessimism suggests that as one draws nearer to the problem of knowledge, the necessity for material proof diminishes, "illumination" alone being of value. Why show that this unique temple represents man, in whom all the laws ordering the universe are inscribed? For these descriptions, which have cost us long years of work, may be read superficially. I can only answer that they have taught much to those who have gathered them. May the reader harvest the same fruit.

The casual reader will object to the fact that I have not developed the various subjects more fully, for he or she would like to read these things without effort, which in this field is impossible. He who cannot find within himself the link that ties together the various parts, which differ widely in material content, will see this work in the same light as the uninformed public sees African art or abstract painting; it may even disturb him, for we prefer a good, realistic picture that reminds us of what we already know.

Knowledge (or even elements of the knowledge) cannot be conveyed through writing alone; the symbolism of the image is indispensable. But always and above all it is through prayer, the prayer that springs from the joy of suffering, that innate knowledge (which is the divine word) reveals itself.

Esotericism

In order to avoid the all-too-frequent confusion between "esotericism" and "occultism," and to define the meaning of research based on the "implied idea," a brief explanation seems necessary.

Esotericism pertains to the immanent meaning, implied but inexpressible in words. The "implication" is not *esoteric,* a word that, etymologically, means "the inner meaning." Nor is the "implied meaning" by itself esoteric; it warrants the qualifier *immanent.*

The esoteric meaning is not addressed to cerebral understanding but solely to the functional character of the action, that is, to the state of consciousness (in the broadest sense of innate consciousness) that prepares and provides impulse to this action.

In numbers, for example, the Duality that is the expression and definition of Unity in the ternary ₁¹₁, includes the possibility of *continuity* by multiplication. This is arithmetically understandable, therefore exoteric, and it summarizes an *implied* meaning. Multiplication by two can be a continuous splitting into two (the Thotian principle: one, two, four, eight, equals one, as in the doubling of living cells and musical octaves), but it can also be the beginning of a geometric increase such as the multiplication of a surface (two multiplied by two, or four; four multiplied by four, or sixteen), which simultaneously generates volume and quantity (the Osirian principle). Such a function eludes the cerebral intelligence because the transition from the arithmetic unit to the geometric unit, from the value four to the square area, cannot be explained in words. *This reality is esoteric.* In order to approach this reality, we must resort to the *supposition* that unity is a mathematical point, therefore immaterial, without quantity, that can be both an arithmetic unit and a unit of square area—meaningless words! This "dissonance" required Euclid to use "circular reasoning" to define the point, and in the Gospel, Saint John did the same to describe the Original Verb.*

There must be no confusing, therefore, the "implied meaning" that makes the thought of the Ancients known to us through their works with the esotericism that appeals, within us, to a sense of synthesis located beyond our cerebral capabilities. The cerebral mind divides elements; in contrast, the Ancient Egyptians spoke of the "intelligence of the heart," later to be contested by the Greeks when cerebral analysis (metaphysics) began. Now, Reality reveals itself through the esoteric sense of synthesis, the vital link of which is broken and rejected by a cerebral analysis that only leaves parts isolated from each other, and from which it is impossible for mechanistic determinism to approach the secret of life.

Our study of the documents left by the Ancients, who honored the intelligence of the heart, can only be research into the implied idea, and we must attempt this, for if research into the thought of the Ancients were not the purpose of archaeology, it would have no profound meaning whatsoever.

That our personal research might be directed toward the esoteric, and that we encourage the development of the sense of synthesis—the intelligence of the heart—is a duty imposed upon us by the convictions we have acquired. But it is obvious that the question here is only one of invitation, whereas the explanations given in our writings and accounts can have bearing only on the knowledge and information implied in the observed fact.

---

* *Le Verbe originel* is conventionally rendered as "the Original" or "Divine Word" in English. The term *Verb* will be retained throughout this translation to convey the sense of the implicit, active power of the Word.

Standard Egyptology has been content with translating texts, many of which, among those carved on temple walls and steles, seem completely meaningless, because until now, it has not understood the method of architectural inscription. The pharaonic texts themselves, however, tell us that it is the temples and steles that carry the profound thought of their teaching.

ANTHROPOCOSMOS

In speaking of the Anthropocosmos, we have nothing to reveal. At issue here are truths as old as the world. They have been admirably expressed by the Ancients, but in a language we no longer understand.

Western thought, however, gets closer and closer to a concept of the unity of the world through the developing perception of the unity of the original substance of matter.

But this is as yet only an intuition, because the mechanistic mentality still prevails, and there is nothing to fill the gap between material form and its energetic cause, between body and spirit. Our only hope lies in the discovery, slow but sure, of the existence of another aspect of intelligence, which our mathematical "uneasiness" is now making evident to us. The important thing is not what we are now doing, but rather the acceptance of the discovery, forced upon us by logic and necessity, that *a phenomenon is the effect of a simultaneity of complements.* The "zero" (+ 0 −) of the decimal system, when "plus and minus" are cancelled, must be considered as a positive value, having, so to speak, an esoteric character. Between the past and the future there is a "present moment," cerebrally ungraspable but intuitively certain. This intuitive certainty is a nonobjectifiable—that is, esoteric—reality appealing to a synthesizing intelligence. This synthesizing intelligence cannot be the result of facts cerebrally defined in time and space, but itself must preside over any analysis of situation, and therefore must be an innate consciousness, a kind of knowledge subconscious to the cerebral.

In order to explain these things I am obliged to use words, which, though they define the idea, are by that very fact misleading. Indeed, to speak of the esoteric is necessarily to evoke the exoteric. In Nature, every thing, as well as every idea, has its complement. So, what can we do? We have to use words, but our aim is much higher; only the symbol can translate the synthetic sense of thought. It is a question of evoking that which can no longer be defined. It is thus a "feeling" that we must bring into being, an "unexpressed intuition," a "certainty" for which the word that would not limit it is lacking. We are not concerned here with a belief but with an intellectual certainty that we should then be able to verify experimentally, either by an *inexplicable phenomenon of synthesis,* or, after analysis, by means of complementary phenomena. The only true means of expression is the symbol and the hieroglyphic writing that can be inferred from it. If this writing is then expressed in language, it is made exoteric, whereas it speaks "without voice or tone" to the intellect (that is, to the subconscious awareness), evoking spatially "visualizable" sensations. Being unable to make use of this hieroglyphic means, we must circumscribe the idea. But the subject of the Anthropocosmos is so vast—and the available means of expression so poor—that unless we have recourse to transcription through myth, it would be necessary to go through all the essential parts of this science, its development, experiments, and hypotheses, which have led us to the point we have reached today. Since it is impossible to do this here, I will have to be content with summaries, and for a more detailed study, refer to the works that deal with these questions specifically. If we wish to get at the essence of things, we should first state the basic problems in all the aspects of this science; this way we can see what is undeniably real in our observations (in order to isolate what remains incomprehensible), but nonetheless logically immanent in the problems.

Anthropocentrism is a reality, a universal philosophical base. This subject, however, cannot be supported either by the exoteric or by the esoteric alone. In the first case, the vital essence will be found lacking; in the second, the spiritualistic character will not adapt itself to the mechanistic spirit of evolutionism.

Hence, as always, when we seek to *understand* the living phenomenon, we find oppositions, for in both camps or poles there is truth. Thus, there are certainties in biogenetic monism as well as in creative dualism. The defect does not lie in the logic or in the form of thought of the research—in the method—but in the state of consciousness of the one who applies it, that is, in man's present intellective faculty.

When positive, equational logic rejects feeling, it makes as great a mistake as when intuitive feeling rejects logical control.

Likewise, there are in us two intelligences that are complementary; one denies the other, and wisdom is knowing how to use them both simultaneously. Because everything is composed of units, that is, specific individualities, what our senses register is always only the statistically averaged phenomenon. This is true for the photon in light, the atom in matter, the wave in sound, the solid molecule in odor, and the liquid molecule in taste. Beyond this, nothing exists for the senses, that is, nothing capable of being looked upon as a fact. Even in mathematics we are condemned to build everything on "facts," such as logical proofs in arithmetic and the relationships and possibilities of relationships that figure in geometry. As soon as we depart from this sphere of learning (that is, from verifiable facts) through intellectual speculation, we enter into the sphere of logically true absurdities such as negative values, quantities that when subtracted are regarded as positive values.[1] Now, these absurd values exist for our *feeling of equilibrium or balance* of thought, similar to the feeling of equilibrium found in a quantitative algebraic equation. The absurd conclusion that results from the strict use of logic, instead of being the "wall of reflection" that demonstrates the solidity of practical facts, should, on the contrary, be considered an open door to another (and perhaps new) form of intelligence. The nature of this noncerebral (irrational) intelligence lies in its capacity to conceive of the simultaneity of the contradictory complements of a unity.

Our visual sense naturally accomplishes this absurdity by coordinating two views, each at a different angle, thus giving us the illusion of depth, or stereoscopic vision. *We have nothing to discover outside ourselves;* this is the axiom of the doctrine of the Anthropocosmos. There exists in us a unifying link that rationalism cannot explain, that quantitative, equational logic cannot grasp. This link enables us to see an object as a single image observed from different angles; to isolate *at will* different sounds heard simultaneously; to taste, that is, to coordinate flavor and odor; and to comprehend corporeality through touch. This is in no way a reasoned coordination, but a phenomenon of intelligence that resides in the synthesizing milieu, in other words, a faculty for canceling sensorial specifications.

It would be closer to reality to say that this synthesizing state always exists and that the senses are only instruments of *analysis,* an analysis that goes from the inner to the outer, and not from the outer, objective fact toward this center. We could even put it this way: at the center of the world, which is also man, there is a synthesis, an equilibrium of the six directions—that is, of the three spatial sections—*a neutral center.* These directions do not exist for the center but are defined as soon as there is an objective relation, that is, as soon as "the One becomes many." Such a relation, then, calls for a front-back, top-bottom, left-right analysis, that is, a projection of equilibrium through

---

[1] It is reasonable to say that the subtraction of a subtraction becomes a positive value: $(+a) - (-a) = a + a$; similarly, $(-a) \times (-a) = a^2$. The square root of a^2 is therefore $+a$ as well as $-a$.

the senses. When we look to the front, we feel that there is a behind. We cannot look in one direction without opposing to it a complementary pole, and although this pole is not sensorially observed, the awareness of it exists within us.

Exoteric, objective intelligence requires this polarization, in fact, exists only because of it, and is only possible through an intellective center of synthesis for which cerebral consciousness is no more than an analysis revealed by the senses. This synthesizing consciousness is innate in man and it must necessarily come from somewhere.

We can see that every animal is born with the consciousness appropriate to its own species. We also observe that the species loses some of its independence as its organism becomes more complex. The newborn mammal is dependent on its mother, and the nearer we come to the higher beings, the less capable the newborn is of living by itself. Is the independence of the newborn a sign of superiority? From the social point of view, it certainly is; from the point of view of consciousness, it certainly is not, because the innate consciousness, the "knowledge" that each individual brings with him, is limited all the more for his being born independent. His needs are limited, but they increase with the wealth of the acquired consciousness that the individual brings with him and, because of that, makes him more dependent at birth.

These observations would seem to favor the theory of the transformists, and yet experiments that seek to establish whether an artificially imposed habit can be passed on to descendants prove that this does not happen, and so it is concluded that transformism is mistaken. Now, our biologists forget that, first, if a habit is not in an animal's nature, it can have no effect on the animal; secondly, only what affects an animal emotionally can act upon it organically, that is, produce an impression on the seed it transmits. A mouse, for instance, if forced to take a complicated path to reach its food, will not be affected at all by this "habit," which will not be transmitted to its descendants. Only what affects the genes can cause a personal "hue" that the chromosome will pass on. Under these conditions, *there is something true in transformism*, but its cause is not material; it depends on a "transcendent" element that is "inseparable from the concrete," and this concreteness is then only an accident bounded in time and space, occurring within a continuous flux, a "granulation of genesis within a continuous creation," as I will later show in the chapter on the symbol.

———

From our observations we can always come to conclusions that correspond to what we are and to what we know today. We always run the risk of allowing our own mentality to cloud the consciousness necessary to feel and understand the mentality of the Ancients.

All imagination is made from fragments of ourselves.

Thus, the pharaonic "church" will be judged with the same cynicism as the present church. Pharaonic techniques will be judged by our own incapacities, which we remedy by mechanical means. The Ancients left us no evidence of having used machines, and because we cannot imagine that they were able to accomplish without machines the work to which their monuments attest, we suppose that they used extremely primitive methods. We can imagine these methods—sandheaps forming inclined planes so as to drag thirty- or forty-ton blocks to a height of twenty meters or more—but even the uninformed will realize the absurdity of such an operation. In Egypt there is a quantity of work the execution of which remains unexplainable to our way of seeing.

There is a world of energies whose existence we recognize—such as static electricity and electromagnetism—but it remains impenetrable to us because we want to penetrate it with our present consciousness, which thinks only of mechanics and mechanically, that is, believes solely in quantitative relationships between sensorially tangible sequences.

Yet it is obvious that each species of creature has its own world, its own "aesthetics," even its own "morality," its own "logic," finally, its own "mentality," whether we are talking about fish, insects, mammals—or human races. The snake finds the female in heat "beautiful" and desirable, and the spider as well as the praying mantis considers love—for it *is* a question of love—as being well worth the risk of death.

We judge these creatures in comparison to ourselves and thus their "secrets" elude us, such as, for example, the fascination that the snake exerts over the bird or over other animals it needs for food. We look at the bird's wings (are they really mechanical?) and declare that the bird can fly, although we know—mathematically—that the wings are not adequate to the task. But our mental fascination with the tangible object shuts the door to an identification that would give us knowledge, in this case, of what is evident to the creature that we observe. This creature, inferior to man in the chronological sense of genesis, cannot substitute its being for that of an individual of another species. Man has this ability, and herein lies his higher destiny, the destiny he demeans in order to idolize an artificial, mental science.

Modern man dreams and speaks of making his life comfortable. But who considers the effort, worry, risk, and discomfort he must undergo to acquire the resources that give him this comfort of which he is so proud? Transmutation of values? One must work with the sweat of one's brow to taste the coolness of an ice cube produced by a costly refrigerator.

Today man is enslaved by his machines, taking them for an end in themselves instead of regarding them only as a means of assistance and possible control; through pride man has removed himself from nature. By simple and natural means, it is possible to have cool water in sun-scorched lands and ice in midsummer. The firefly produces its own light and scoffs at dynamos. The falcon, the kingfisher, dive and make light of "mechanical" acceleration; they hover in the air and laugh at gravity. And how does the sparrow, speeding at sixty miles per hour, suddenly stop and fly off in the opposite direction? It has no brakes.

The Ancients stayed close to Nature, thought with her, and without extraordinary contrivances, they played with matter.

The West inevitably judges antiquity in the light of its own faculties, or more exactly, in the light of what it conjectures to be the case according to the intellective faculties it has cultivated so well, to the point that these faculties seem to be the only ones possible.

The problem of *intelligence*, however, remains unsolved. Besides the cerebral intelligence, we also have an emotional intelligence, considered by the cerebral consciousness to be an independent phenomenon.

We are willing to attribute intelligence to the animal, but we categorize this intellective complex under the term of instinct. Now, it is possible to communicate a spoken order to a household pet, provided that it has become accustomed to the meaning of such a command. A particular sound or word means that it should behave in a certain way. When spoken to by a child, or by an emotional person, as women are especially, the animal will understand the intention. In these cases, observation shows that speech is often unnecessary; the animal understands the felt intention, just as it forebodes earthquakes and other disasters, or understands when its masters are going for a walk or on a journey, or as it forebodes death.

The transmission of thought between humans must be put in the same category of intelligence. If a thought is experienced emotionally, it is communicated either to a person or to a crowd and the factor of distance is immaterial. There is also an *emotional* bond that remains between mother and child.

Our thought is always *descriptive;* it could be defined as visual. It is impossible for us to think anything without this thought presenting itself to us as images or as writing. Without speech, that is, without imaged or descriptive expression, there is no mental thought. The mind is constrictive, it narrows what we experience or observe into an image. Mental content tends toward the center, toward the definition of that which fixes; it is centripetal.

Emotion, on the other hand, could be defined as auditory; it dilates. The emotional sense (and not the emotion, which is a result) is a radiating substance. In man, emotion itself results from the effect of the dilating emotional intelligence on the constrictive solar plexus, as an intermediate reaction with thought, and creates the possibility of mental interpretation. In the animal, the feeling sense passes directly to the organizing center of action in the central nervous system.

Knowledge of this intellective source of the emotional center, in connection with the cerebral intelligence, can open our eyes to an altogether different way of thinking and acting that no longer excludes direct knowing, and that needs no physical or descriptive intermediary. Here the source of intuition resides, and this faculty can be cultivated to the point of enabling the communication of thought, with no outward signs, between sufficiently prepared people. This contact—a true personal identification—allows for the solving of problems of a technical and practical order where our mental, analytical method sees nothing but mechanical quantitative sequences.

—◠◠◠—

The immediate purpose of archaeology is to collect positive facts left by civilizations now extinct. Once all the information on physical and historical conditions, on architectural elements and recovered objects, has been put together, and, if possible, after study of the writings and the language, the work begins that really justifies archaeological effort: restoring the image and atmosphere of the period of human history that has left the evidence. This is a critical moment when mistakes can slip in and destroy the work already done. It is believed that comparisons based on the language, the writings, the nature of the objects, the techniques, and the art of that period of the past can be made with other, supposedly well-known civilizations, but valid conclusions can only be drawn insofar as the period and civilization in question are themselves truly and clearly known.

Greece has always been the chief source of reference for appraising the history of the peoples of the Near East. Authentic documents that have come down to us from ancient Greece, however, are rarer than those left to us by Babylonia and Egypt.*

After the Greek colonies of Alexandria and Cyrene, it was Rome, Byzantium, and then, after an obscure period, Islam and the Christianity of the Middle Ages that transcribed and passed on the major portion of our knowledge of Hellenic civilization. But legend was mixed with fact, and Greece became heir to that which it absolutely did not merit. As archaeology brings to light its findings in Babylonia and Egypt, our once golden image of the Greeks appears to be no more than a reflection.

Our conclusions are too exclusively founded on hearsay and on facts interpreted in the light of what we are and what we understand of ourselves; our judgments, therefore, whether they are favorable or unfavorable, are likely to be wrong. We seem to neglect a certain psychological ambiance that is as essential as the facts are tangible; this ambiance forms the typical character of a country that time can never efface.

---

* This is perhaps less the case now than when this was written.

In spite of the upheavals brought about by war and religious change, in spite of the intermingling of peoples and beliefs, the same soil always imposes the same influences: the land makes the people. One soil exalts the passions, another makes us patient; one river makes us quarrelsome, another makes us placid; one country makes men miserly, another makes them generous.

The qualities and defects of the Greeks in Pericles' time were in fact much the same as they are today: the lively—both rational and contradictory—intelligence, the patriotism of the islanders and highlanders, and the chauvinism that tends to exalt a nation's achievements at the expense of others. Passionate love of one's native soil is characteristic of peoples faced with a difficult life.

Certainly the expatriate Greeks in Egypt, Sicily, Asia Minor, and Babylonia changed their original character and absorbed the features of their new land. The fundamental character changes within three generations, but there are also inborn tendencies that never change.

Mentality can vary and adapt; racial essence never changes. The racial question is the concern of ethnologists, while the problem of mentality should concern the archaeologists, but unfortunately, they only rarely occupy themselves with it.

If we were to speak here, for example, of the "Djesireh"* civilizations, the Mesopotamian land washed by the Euphrates and the Tigris, we would have to study the "dualizing" mentality that the land of the two rivers gives to the Babylonians.

But in Egypt, we have the influence of Hapi, the Nile, a single river, calm, slow, and contemplative, which flows through a plain bordered by vast deserts. In the area known as Upper Egypt, which stretches from Cairo to Aswan, the Nile—the symbolic Physon of the Bible—washes the black earth *(kemit)* of Havilah, where gold can be found; here this marvelous river is single. The mentality of its riverside peoples differs from that of those in the area of the Delta, watered by the branches of a river divided. The riverside people are as simple, loyal to tradition, and religious by temperament as the peoples of the Delta are turbulent and subject to indecision.

The environment of the Nile country leads to envisioning and conceiving in large dimensions, a fact which, when people are unable to implement a project, tends to make them megalomaniacal. Everything is possible for the Egyptian people if they have wise, steadfast, and clear-sighted leaders. The mentality this country breeds does not allow for pettiness or stinginess.[2]

It is above all the country of the One God, and the majestic peace of the Nile is conducive to religiosity. In this land, no eye can gaze at a point on the horizon without being drawn to an unfathomable immensity. Such a mentality is not to be found among the highlanders of the small and tortured hills.

In order to study any past civilization, an archaeologist must always take into account the mentality that the geographical, and likewise the geological, environment imposes. He must dare to be something of a psychologist, instead of being merely a cold calculator.

—⁓—

Regarding our knowledge of Ancient Egypt, we must not oppose a favorable prejudice to the pejorative prejudice dominant in certain quarters. We must take facts as they are, as far as it is possible for us to establish them today.

In the religious domain, we must first of all admit that a system of theology illustrated by a symbolic myth easily turns to idolatry on the part of those people uninitiated into its profound, symbolic meaning, which is difficult enough to access.

---

[2] [In the French, *mesquinerie,*] from the Arabic, *meskin,* "poor."

* "Island."

This is a valid reason for preserving the historical character of Christianity.

Our present research, being particularly directed toward the esoteric meaning—that of the Temple—must not degenerate into generality and allow belief in a wisdom belonging to the general population. The people had their "gods," their fears, their superstitious expectations, and their "sorcery." The accusation of idolatry against the Egyptians by the people of Moses had its reasons, but it also showed bad faith in deliberately feigning ignorance of the knowledge preserved by the Egyptian Temple.[3] It also sheds light on the meaning of the religious faith Moses gave to his people: a form of abstract power, *accessible to all;* a retributive and vengeful God; a different form of symbolism, but of a popular character, no longer reserved for an elite. The deeper meaning is the same, but in its expression, it goes from one extreme to the other.

If we consider the essential, true, and invariable theological themes, which are the principles of reincarnation and redemption, we must recognize a profound wisdom in pharaonic theology.

Redemption is a promise, a divine grace, for the one moved by true—proven and unshakable—contrition. It is not a natural gift, realized in everyone. Christ—the unction of the Divine Verb—is the Redeemer for the one who realizes him in oneself. But when redemption is posed as an exclusive dogma, it calls forth a complementary damnation.

The other essential theme is reincarnation with its karmic consequences, which forms a "wheel" of exhaustion moving toward liberation. It is the law *for all.* Punishment is reincarnation, but reincarnation is also a divine mercy that allows one to make amends. Now, the principle of reincarnation is a reality *demonstrated by the fact of evolution,* which the observation of Nature imposes upon us. This is a true justice, without cruelty, without threat, a justice everyone can accept. It is also the *collective* form of religious government, just as, by contrast, the principle of redemption (which is personal) represents the *individual* form of religious rule. History shows that the groups and peoples who endured the longest were those governed by faith in reincarnation.

Now, pharaonic Egypt maintained the Osirian cult of renewal and reincarnation for the general population, but to the temple elite it taught the Horian principle, Horus the Redeemer. In the mystical sense, the elite is in fact composed of those whose every effort is directed toward liberation from successive incarnations, that is, toward an evolutionary end within the corporeal form. The Divine Verb is there at the Beginning, exactly as Saint John the Evangelist affirms it to be. By being "made flesh," the Verb manifests the Universe, Cosmic Man (the *puruṣa* of the Upaniṣads). The Divine Verb is at the origin of things and brings with it redemption because the separating, dividing cause necessarily brings with it the reuniting principle.

There is but one sole Truth, master of the Universe.

After the actual closing of the temples, the guardians of a very ancient science founded on knowledge (a few echoes of which were caught by the Greeks), the individual research known as gnosticism began. Gnosis, or knowledge, intrigues. In Egypt, as in Attica, the Temple was its domain. Now it is no longer forbidden to seek the keys. The quest for gnosis is a duty for those who love wisdom. Later, gnosticism became a type of doctrine opposed to the Church; it was no longer only the love of truth, a dangerous enough quest that all too easily—through mankind's inherent pride and fundamental vanity—leads to atheism.

---

[3] Although elsewhere the Bible acknowledges the pharaonic wisdom in which Moses was instructed.

In order to content oneself—and that says it all—with the simple and clear revelation of the Christic Passion—which tells us everything—it is necessary to have already had an intuition of its esotericism; the Osirian passion sublimated in Horus.

———∿∿∿∿———

The "*Neter-neteru*," the One and unknowable God, is, in pharaonic Egypt (as it is in India), ultimately a logical notion. Because present man is potentially Cosmic Man, his consciousness is undergoing an evolution that is leading him, through certain stages, toward universality. Compared to our present state, these stages represent powers of action (such as of saints and masters) far superior to ours, and, since there is evolution—verifiable in its lower stages—there must logically be a final stage of ultimate perfection.

This is still "mechanistic" reasoning, but it can help us understand the sage's position, because wisdom is indispensable here, since this "perfecting" of consciousness requires the knowledge of a *qualitative* widening, which has nothing to do with reason.

———∿∿∿∿———

In pharaonic Egypt, the king symbolizes human perfection for the cycle in which he is active. As such, he may sometimes be called a *neter*, but he is neither "god" nor *neter* in the sense of functioning as a "principle of Nature." The *neter*, or function, which can also be called one of the cosmic forces, is anthropomorphized, but *never humanized*. The *neter* represents one of the many functions or forces innate in man, one of the stages of his gestation into the human.

In contrast to Egypt, the Greek daimons and the gods of Olympus are humanized. Nothing prevents us from calling Apollo of Delphi whatever we like; no symbol sets him apart as being Apollo! This in no way diminishes the perfection of this work of "human" statuary.

Of course the same anthropocosmic directive presides over Hellenic myth, only contrary to the reality. The thought of Cosmic Man falls to earth. When this Cosmic Man—humanized—turns back over, it is not Olympus that is like man.

Man may be created in God's image, but this human figuration of the gods by the Greeks is the true indication of their mentality.

The pharaonic Temple designates its human representations of the *neters** either by the head or headdress, and by costume and attributes. *They have a name*, the name of one of the vital functions organically inherent in the actual human being.

———∿∿∿∿———

In Ancient Egypt, inhabited by people the Greeks said were the healthiest and most religious in the world, each person was chiefly preoccupied with the permanent moment of life. Stone was used for temple construction, but also—and above all—for building the eternal house, the tomb, which had to withstand time, and was thus built of long-lasting stone or hollowed out of rock.

Life's transient home was built of unbaked bricks, including the king's palace, which was "rebuilt" so the new king could live in his own house. Thus the pharaonic people remained consistent in daily life with their faith and convictions.

---

* The plural form of the word *neter* is *neteru*. We will, however, use the anglicized form, *neters*.

A member of our transitional civilization, mechanized and decadent, would not put up with this simple life, so much closer to Nature, if he or she suddenly had to go back to the way of living of the ancient peoples of the Nile, gathered around the Temple. Here was a small island of serenity and peace for people of goodwill.

We no longer know where this center of peace can be found, and it is likely that the majority would no longer know how to bear this serenity.

SYMBOL-EVOCATION

Let us put aside the deceptive symbol, that is, the word, image, or gesture that is merely a substitute for something else.

Let us look at each thing in its natural name. This name is written—it is the Symbol—but it cannot be uttered; it speaks for itself.

To explain the Symbol is to kill it, it is to take it only for its appearance, it is to avoid listening to it.

Who could dissect a living body?

The living thing is "self-similar." The branches of a tree develop in the image of its roots. The roots evoke the branches just as the Symbol evokes its Idea. In the Symbol, that which evokes is the soul that animates the thing, its life.

Let us look at the thing as it is, without decomposing it. In return it may evoke its own soul within us.

Pure and sublime love is the animating soul, hidden from animal love. Of such love the harlot yearns even to dream.

Form is what animates and characterizes, but form cannot be described when the thing is a Symbol.

By definition, the Symbol is magic; it evokes the form bound in the spell of matter. To evoke is not to imagine, it is to live; it is to live the form.

In order to speak of Heaven, we must describe Hell. Heaven cannot be described.

The spiritual evolution of earth is entering its final stage; we would therefore destroy the past. This is our mistake. We must look upon our earth as it is, a prison with all its illusions, so that we may call forth the future beyond this constraint.

Let us not try to describe the future. To describe it would be to deny it, would be to kill in ourselves the possibility of living this life, which is intangible, "undissectable."

To live is to grow and to keep growing in all directions at the same time. Evocation belongs to the sense of space; it is the vision and experience of volume with and within volumes.

But the evoking Symbol itself remains two-dimensional. It belongs to the senses and to the mental faculty, which is a surgeon.

Music evokes a state of being. The painter and the sculptor shape it, and then the "surgeon" arrives to dissect and analyze it.

Thus does man deny the magic of harmony. He could be other than this, but he is far more tempted to remain as he is and to go on loving what he habitually knows.

Form characterizes matter and makes a symbol of everything.

This is true, not only because it appears to be so to our senses but also because all the forms evoked by appearance are within us. The form-idea cannot be described; it must be felt and lived.

True poetry is magic, and magic is identification with form, body with body, Spirit with Spirit. The All in One, *Ecce homo,* is the symbol above all symbols; and man is not an image, a condensation of the Universe; man is the Universe.

What could I know, that is, what could I feel and experience of the stone, of light, of the animal, of you, if all these forms were not in me? You and I are not two. In the identity of form, in the origin and in the end, we are one.

I am responsible for your evil and your good, for your truth and your falsehood. I can do nothing to change you now, but I can improve you by improving myself.

This is moral magic.

Experience proves the truth, makes it certain, and drives falsehood away.

Part 1

THE DOCTRINE
OF THE
ANTHROPOCOSMOS

ELEMENTS

The mystery of the everyday: All the power of the father and of his fathers is in the *seed*. The genes in the chromosomes carry the father's whole heredity in form and substance, as well as all his characteristics. Then this seed fixes the heredity of the mother with the substance that provides its nourishment.

The seed, with no visible or tangible form, is the pattern, the Idea of what it engenders; it is a transcendent power. Around a bodiless pattern a formless substance coagulates into a living being, complete, complex, and thought by the power.

In the esoteric action from the Idea to the form—its finality—come the exoteric, transitory "finalities," the apparent, formal stages.

It is the wonder of the world: everything that is, all that exists has seed; just as will and thought are the seeds of mental creation.

One thought of the transcendent power compels *one* substance of the universal substance—passive, awaiting any seed—to become a specific product, an inheritor, a world that follows upon a world. *One sole power in one sole substance* works through all the transitory finalities toward the foreseen finality: man.

And at the end of humanity comes man without body, *substance within power.*

Not to be, then to be, and then to be no more is the pulsation that constitutes the apparent universe, the transitory finalities. Power-Idea, form-finality, powers without form, these are the vital alternations, the cosmic pulsations.

The law of genesis establishes the unvarying rhythm in the succession of stages—the transitory finalities—between the Idea and the thing. Also, the organs that assimilate (through air, liquids, and solids) as well as the organs that inform (through the intelligence and the senses) are the issue of an energy of the same nature as the object they assimilate or experience.

The indisputable reality of the evident mystery that makes visible the invisible and ponderable the imponderable is the Verb of wisdom. The invariance of the law of genesis is the basis of traditional philosophy. Any research undertaken without these guides leads to an impasse or to nothing.

Everything is either created or generated; what does it matter what is thus manifested? Knowledge is within that which creates and that which causes generation.

The ternary is at the beginning. For example, the impact of bodies makes a sound; there is an impulse, a resistance, and an effect. This process is repeated a third time with that which receives. The sound expands into volume, into concentric spheres of alternating density that determine the vertical axis and the two dimensions of the horizontal plane. Within itself the sound carries volume, the orientations, the prism of the octaves, the spirals of harmonics in the expansion of the layers of density into spherical spirals; also within it are the interferences and synchronisms of its numbers and tempos, the *specifications* of sound. They are materialized into the instruments that together make the ear.

The ear is not *made for* hearing. Could it be said that the riverbed and the shape of its banks are made for the river? Sound has made the ear; this is the reason that the ear detects sound.

Similarly, in the course of "evolution" the energies within the different states of matter have made the informing senses. The thought of the power creates the organ of a particular function, and thought is consciousness in action.

Thus the doctrine of the Anthropocosmos says: *Study the ear to know sound, study the eye to know light.*

—~~—

GESTATION bridges the gap between Idea, form, and matter. Breathing in and breathing out, pulsation and alternation, make up the other mystery of every moment—gestation. The regular, proportional relationship between different durations makes rhythm. The hour, the day, the month, the year, and the coincidences of the movements of the heavens are the containers of the rhythms of atoms, living cells, and all that exists.

And disorder creates the world and calls forth harmony; disorder scatters the parts, which come together again according to their affinities. Disorder, chaos; order, harmony: the alternation of rhythms.

Gestating is nothing but doing and undoing, creating and destroying, affirming and denying, contracting and dilating. What was is the seed of what will be; the destroyed form serves as the foundation of the form to be—*genesis*.

The finality for each phase of genesis is the innate consciousness of that which precedes it. For humanity, the finality of genesis is man; for wisdom, it is Cosmic Man liberated from the genesis of his elements: total, innate consciousness.

Thus the Universe is incarnate in man and is nothing but potential Man, Anthropocosmos. And man is the blueprint, the cosmographical map on which wisdom reads the Universe, the genesis, the functions.

—~~—

AN ANTHROPOCOSMIC FOUNDATION liberates philosophy from the limited ambit of simply speculating on ideas by offering it the object for experimental applications. It is a synthesis of art and science, of faith and reasoning, of thought and experience, of feeling and demonstration.

The causal energy becomes mineral, mineral becomes plant, plant becomes animal, animal becomes man, and man becomes Cosmic Man, the saint, Buddha, Jesus (Jehoshua). The mineral has suffered the scission from the Cause, the plant has suffered the mineral, the animal has suffered the plant, man has suffered the animal, and Cosmic Man will have suffered humanity. Vital suffering is consciousness undergoing the process of surpassing itself.

Genesis is the expansion of consciousness.

—⁓—

BELIEVING, LEARNING, AND KNOWING are the three gates of entry into the Temple.

"Learning" [*savoir*] is establishing, by means of the senses, the reality of what one believes; "believing" is having the conviction about the reality of that which cannot be demonstrated; but truth is the congruity of what one believes or learns—believes *and* learns—with that which is. This identification is knowledge, the gate leading beyond the Temple, being within Being.

We may believe in the Universe within man, we may study the Universe through man, because man is joined with the Universe in man. The identity of the Universe and man is the source of his faith, the source of his science, the promise of his deliverance; it is the knowledge of the "tree at the center" (Mosaic Genesis).

—⁓—

UNITY OF SOURCE, unity of purpose, and unity of function create a solidarity that give foundation to the superior person's morality. At any point whatsoever on the surface of the universal sphere, there bursts forth an imponderable particle of the causal energy. It projects innumerable sparks in all directions; the sparks travel at will, moving apart quickly or slowly, and they will all gather again at the antipole. Each of them was free, but the spherical surface conducts them.

The conditions of life belong to a cosmic order. Will and free will belong to an individual order and they can in no way affect the conditions of life. The conditions of life are "sacred" and relate to "wisdom." Knowledge alone comes near to wisdom. Purification, unction, and coronation are the rituals to be accomplished in order to gain the right to approach the "Holy of Holies."

—⁓—

THE MEANS OF REVEALING the particularity of one being to another is the *symbol*. It is a being's specification. Specifications are affinities and formal appearances in time, space, and motion. But knowledge requires no medium of transmission, for beings are not separate from Being. Man is not the symbol of the Universe; he is the Universe.

—⁓—

THE REIGN OF THE SPIRIT is the consciousness of Unity and the order governed by that certainty.

—⁓—

CONSCIOUSNESS is the identification of one nature with a similar nature, of a specified being with the specification of another being.

—⁓—

ENERGY is not mechanical. Mass is energy coagulated by seed; its *movement* is mechanical: it is the power of revolt, the liberating reaction against imprisonment.

—⁓—

REGENERATION is genesis as procreation is in the image of creation: form and universality; the mean, bearer of the Idea, and the Idea with no mean term. Man is the transition, the realized mean term that dissolves back into the Idea.

And man will have *eaten*, that is, returned to its source, all that the Universe knows, from mineral to animal. By means of the mineral, energy becomes a grain of wheat. The bread eaten by man becomes chyle, then lymph and blood. Together with the lymph, the blood makes flesh and bones.

By the cosmic ebb and flow, the channels draw the white and red solar energy through all the domains where the twelve powers, locked in the organs, lie dormant. Every hour of the night, each one of the twelve powers awakens once at the passage of Ra, sun of the blood, and then falls back to sleep. In the endocrine centers, the centers of transformation by "induction," the energy, borne by this flow, is liberated and then distributed by the medulla oblongata and spinal cord into a flow of nervous energy. Sensitivity is produced by the "self-inductions." But it is in the higher centers that the energy will again be depolarized, and nonpolarized energy is Spirit.

Only Spirit is conscious of Spirit.

This is genesis within regeneration.

THE ANTHROPOCOSMOS is a reality, an indisputable foundation. The Universe is neither an "imagination" nor a "will," but a "projection" of human *consciousness*.

The *man* within the human is the Colossus of the Universe. All that which can be recognized by man is within him or comes through him. The "logic" by which he is able to seek or construct all the edifices of thought is the result of his present position as a "sensitive being" face to face with that which impresses itself upon him within the present limits of his perception.

This "logic" is an equipoise between what is outside of him and at the same time inside him by way of his genesis. It varies according to his own genesis, the expansion of his consciousness. Man can bring himself to a vaster perception, but for him the world is what he himself is at each moment. In reality, the world is the totality of what man is in his finality. The present limit of this stage of human consciousness is contained as a lesser dimension within the seven possible dimensions. Man measures *his* world.

The present limit of his consciousness situates man intellectually inside the Universe, just as, for example, a smaller volume could be placed inside a greater volume that is logically derived from it. But factors of "extension" intervene here that no longer belong to a three-dimensional order. This "image" that we have is the *inverse* of that which is accomplished in the becoming and in the original scission: the vital division.

The "situation" in particular, and relationships in general, are the measure of the distance between two states of consciousness. It appears *quantitatively* through movement, and therefore mechanically in time and space.

SCIENCE AND THE ORDER OF LIFE that are founded on the "Man-Universe" are founded on bedrock. Otherwise, science and the order of life are founded on the quicksand of innumerable *suppositions*.

THE PHILOSOPHY that is friendship or love of wisdom is a *state*. But philosophy as dialectical research is a mistake, a blind alley. It is a legacy from the time when the void of knowledge was filled by faith, a faith imposed through ethical formulas that were a source of the revolutionary reaction that inevitably followed. Any constraint calls for movement, and movement is revolt.

Nowadays, this false philosophy is replaced by "the empiricism of scientific thought," that is, a research directed by successive discoveries, a mental process from start to finish. The ever growing complexity of the problems raised by this mentality leads to specialization and, *by reaction,* we are made aware of the need for a means of coordination.

The lack of a map showing the way to be followed, its contours, direction, and outcome, causes the anxiety felt by all those who have not been blinded by wearing the blinkers of overspecialization.

Furthermore, the purely ethical character of our religious doctrine no longer corresponds to the mentality of our present "learning," nor to the problems raised by this "learning." Promises of reward or punishment in the beyond no longer affect a humanity *that has no education with regard to a life greater than that of physical existence.*

We are born, we die, we come, we go. Who comes? Who goes? Answers to these questions are left to the domain of intellectual speculation. They are infinitely less persuasive than the mechanistic arguments of experimental rationalism.

The mystery, however, the basis of faith, the incomprehensible evidence, is *the mystery of the everyday,* and humanity itself is its revelation, its explanatory analysis.

From an anthropocosmic point of view, the symbols of bread and wine become an evocative reality, and humanity today has reached a state of consciousness that makes it capable of following this path—whatever its moral, and consequently its social, decadence, and no matter how serious its deviation in the search for truth.

True science moves not toward complexity but toward extreme simplicity, and Ancient Egypt shows us the way.

—∿∿—

A REASON FOR BEING exists only for what is created or born. Consequently, the Universe can only be the appearance of specificities potentially contained in the Unique, and nothing exists or takes place that is not an effect of this original seed or will, in which nothing can be arbitrary.

—∿∿—

What one can personally comprehend of knowledge is an individual matter. When one wishes to communicate and extend what one knows in this domain that escapes the rational (if only to fulfill the obligation of adding a small stone to the edifice of knowledge), one is faced with a lack of words and images needed to give one's thought a concrete form. Then, the temptation is very great to rely on the recent progress of atomic science and the disintegration of matter into energy in order to uphold the esoteric thesis.

BUT IT SHOULD BE WRITTEN IN LETTERS OF FIRE THAT, SCIENTIFICALLY, WE KNOW ONLY KINETIC ENERGY, WHEREAS VITAL ENERGY IS AT THE BASE, NOT AT THE END OF THINGS. IT IS NOT THE SAME ENERGY. HEREIN LIES THE KEY.

Causal energy is Spirit, *a latent fire,* without motion, that is, *a fire in time* (genesis) and not in space. The constituted body, having volume and therefore being itself space, is the only body capable of moving in space, thereby defining time and manifesting a kinetic energy.

The speed of light is a mechanical term of reference for mechanical equivalences in a mechanical system. Liberated intra-atomic energy, such as radioactivity, is kinetic energy, and not at all vital energy. By ricochet, intra-atomic energy can either mechanically destroy or vitalize the living organism, but it is not in itself a vitally causal energy. It can help a seed to grow more intensely (physicochemical action of the environment), but it can never cause this growth.

———

The explosive liberation of kinetic energy can only be associated with mechanical energy. *Only the splitting of the "neutron" could liberate vital energy; this can only come about by evolution and not by mechanical rupture. The reliberation of vital energy is accomplished ultimately by the living body's nerve energy, and even more so in human beings, even more so by the spiritual faculties of the intellect.*

The energetic disintegration of the neutron constitutes evolution through the widening of consciousness. This means that only the milieu of its origin can "dissolve" this "center-mass" of matter.

———

WHAT DISTINGUISHES THE NATURAL FROM THE SUPERNATURAL.[1] Everything materially corporeal, everything that goes under the name of "physics," and everything that is tangible, or can become so by means of artificial instruments, is called "natural." Everything commonly known as "miraculous" can be called "supernatural." The miracle, however, appeals to faith. Within the scope of the ideas treated in this work, I must try to explain what the supernatural is.

In this matter, we must again refer to the spirit of Ancient Egypt, which considered the sensorial *instrument* to be only of secondary importance, as a symbol, giving greater importance to the intellective faculty perceiving the phenomenon.

The sensorial instrument is a mean term between the phenomenon and a functional coincidence of this phenomenon, known in us. It is a question of a relationship, abstract in nature, not of a proportional relationship.

When we speak of proportion we are comparing two terms, but such a comparison requires a qualitative consciousness on our part (of size, color, form, and so on). We find it sufficient to put this consciousness in the category of mnesic functions. We have the memory of these qualities, of "lengths" for instance, and this enables us to observe a difference in length between two objects. Consciousness of length is not simple; it implies a consciousness of space (path) and of time (duration), in addition to the awareness of movement. This is indeed a complex "consciousness" (classified as social consciousness) that is automatic for us: such and such an object is longer, bulkier, and so forth, when compared objectively with another object. Because we are dealing with quantities, this seems *natural* to us.

But when we go from proportion to *relationship* the problem becomes more abstract. We may well speak of a "relationship of lengths," which will be a "relation," but at that moment we are evoking another consciousness: the relationship is a state and no longer a measure. At this moment the "intelligence" of proportion intervenes.

For example, the vibration of a taut string gives a sound; eight-ninths of this string length gives another sound; but it is the eight-ninths *relationship* of these sounds that creates the tone. The consciousness of this relationship between two sounds creates the *musical intelligence of the tone.* This intelligence is only possible because of a *coincidence that implies a possibility of identity.*

Identity between two natural objects does not and cannot exist because of the successive nature of phenomena and of natural causes. This identity, however, is the motive power of magic and of what is usually called miracle. The possibility of *relationship* is supernatural. It constitutes harmony as well as our intelligence of harmony. The possibility for human intelligence of harmony, in the

---

[1] There is a magnificent chapter in Basil Valentine's *Chymische Schriften* (Hamburg, 1677), p. 213, on this topic.

(sensorial) sensation, can be brought to an extreme sensitivity, and this speaks to a state within us that is not dependent on the physical senses. Every healthy human being can hear—or taste, see, and so on—the slightest nuance, but for all that, will not have the intelligence of harmonious relationship. This intelligence is directed toward a being within the person that is no longer physical, psychic-emotional, or mental, but a being in supernatural identity with its selfsame cosmic function.[2]

Absolute coincidence, or *identity,* makes for the intelligence of harmony. Mental, psychic-emotional, or physical effects follow this intelligence but do not cause it. Thus a supernatural means is available to guide us to the knowledge to be awakened in us, for the knowledge is not without, but within.

By believing in the popular traditions, which are both exoteric and naive, we generally judge "occultism" as wholly superstitious, the imagination of primitives. We only have to read the chapters where Paracelsus* inveighs against the absurd belief that planets and stars have a direct physical influence, which gave birth to popular astrology, to understand that in the minds of the masters, these questions are not within the grasp of everyone.

The functional coincidence that makes the consciousness of harmony possible belongs to a supernatural order that cannot be defined by the objectifiable limits of our concepts. It has nothing to do with a fourth or with an *n*th geometrical dimension, for we are dealing here with the principle of identity, which belongs to a world beyond our grasp. Still, this fact of identification is realized in us each time we experience the harmony of a relationship. It is also realized in nonorganized matter each time its own state is in functional harmony with its functional cosmic identity.

It is only in and because of this that the Temple becomes sacred when it is built from knowledge that includes all points of view: proportions and numbers, axes and orientations, choice of materials, harmony of figures, colors, lights, foundation deposits, and so on. It is this harmonious synthesis that creates the Temple, not a vulgar symbolization of the sky by the roof, of the earth by the floor, and other playthings of a childish symbolism.

The Magisterium of the master builder is the realization of this synthesis that consciously establishes the absolute coincidence between Earth and Heaven.

The most nearly perfect identity is found in the case of "identical" twins, or those born from the same cell. The Temple is conceived as the *mystic twin* of Heaven, in identity with the vital, cosmic moment of the position of the heavens, corresponding to the principle to which it is consecrated. The magical realization of the "mystic twins" is an age-old practice, still in use in black Africa. It always has the same magical purpose, the quest for the "miracle," the application of *supernatural* power by an act of identification.

Planetary and stellar influences must be considered in the same way: as a functional coincidence between that which is represented by number and time, the vital situations of the stars, and the vital situations of the person.

The meaning of these explanations will be better understood if we recall the "magic dances" of Native American hunters preparing to hunt buffalo. The hunter disguises himself as a buffalo and acts, behaves, defends himself, and attacks as if he were the animal he is about to fight. This ritual dance must continue until he obtains a sort of rapture of consciousness that enables him to know

---

[2] The "prototypical Idea" is already a formal restriction. We therefore insist here on the *function,* not on the Idea.

* For example, see Paracelsus, *Selected Writings,* ed. Jolande Jacobi, trans. Norbert Guterman, Bollingen Series 28 (Princeton: Princeton Univ. Press, 1979), pp. 151–56.

what the animal thinks and feels. One could give an infinite number of examples of "magical practices" of this kind.

On the other hand, "ghosts," spirit manifestations, and all psychic *phenomena* evoked as forms by the psychic influence—whether true visions or illusions, whether by projection or suggestion—*have nothing to do with the supernatural.* As soon as a state of functional confluence takes on a "tangible form," the supernatural *act* becomes natural. For example, the intelligence of harmony has a supernatural *nature* in that it is a coincidence of identities, but the resulting harmony of musical tones or feelings is for us perfectly natural.

The identity of an emotion, an imagination, or a thought with the same state in another person—which provokes the transmission of the thought—is a *supernatural state,* but the thought is again natural once it is received and formulated, even unconsciously. The supernatural is a state of identity, but the transcription of this state, however abstract, is natural. Mystic love, pure love, is supernatural.

—◦◦◦—

THE MARK OF A TRUE WORK OF ART is the suffering that is in it or around it. The unconscious knowledge that the poet strives to circumscribe, which opens the eye of the painter and guides his hand, the life that the sculptor would like to awaken in matter as a living blood—but which is better expressed by the poet than by the musician, by the musician better than the painter, and by the painter still better than the sculptor, because the nature of matter weighs him down as the form compels him and holds him back—this creates suffering.

If a painter could, with a brush, paint with the light that comes through the stained-glass window, draw its outlines with the (immaterial) line made of the rhythms and words of the poet, and give it volume with musical harmony, he could create a work without suffering.

This "consciousness of innate knowledge," of which the ordinary person is not yet cerebrally aware, is the supernatural force that is the signature of the work of art in the inspired moment of the artist, the present moment, without past or future.

—◦◦◦—

WHAT I UNDERSTAND BY *SYMBOLIQUE* is not an imaged representation of a concrete notion, but the concrete image of a *synthesis* that cannot be expressed in time or in comprehensible dimensions.

It is the potentiality of the finality within the original impulse (which in Nature is seminal) that is the synthesis. The effect (gestation and fruit) of this potentiality is the analysis (the concrete appearances) of this synthesis.

The concrete image is thus an analyzed moment of the synthesis that is evoked. This evoked synthesis is the real purpose of the *symbolique,* in other words, the symbol is the *writing of esotericism* that can only be experienced by this evocation, and can be described in no other way without falling from the *symbolique* into analysis, that is, into a symbol of the objectified notion.

In the hieratic *symbolique*—the only one that interests us here—all arbitrariness is excluded and conventionalism plays no part, either in the choice of symbols or in their interpretation.

Conventional symbolism leaves interpretation open to any kind of imagination. I do not accept symbolism in this sense, and I find it dangerous. It has nothing to do with the hieratic *symbolique* that addresses itself to the "intelligence of the heart" and not to cerebral intelligence.

The meaning of the *symbolique,* which is of utmost importance, can be better explained by an image. If we consider separately each part of a plant, for example, or the development of a fetus, or the living human body, each part thus distinguished from the whole can be used as a symbol. This symbol will be valid only insofar as it is a *functional* emphasis within the synthesis from which it is extracted, that is, that all the parts—whether they are named or implied by the whole to which the symbol belongs—are interrelated by the supernatural state called life, but for which one of the expressions—the function registered by the symbol—is meant more particularly.

For example, the hand, which receives with the palm turned upward or gives with the palm opened downward, is one aspect of the living human totality. It cannot be separated from this whole or considered as distinct from life without the meaning of the gesture being eradicated. Thus the gesture, the *function* symbolized by this hand, has a value extending beyond the mere fact of receiving or giving in its limited sense. It is the *action of receiving* and *the action of giving*, in general, that should be understood here, actions whose analysis would require a long explanation.

The concrete image of the hand and its gesture—thus an expression of life—evokes the abstraction that will be, in this case the universal function of giving and receiving, therefore of exchange, in other words, a polarization of action.

The opposite interpretation—to say that the giving and receiving of *something* is symbolized by these gestures of the hand—would be wrong. But this is the way that exotericism interprets symbols; we know, we define, we determine a thing quantitatively and we interpret it in figures instead of writing it in words. This is but a conventional writing and can be used for the transmission of ordinary thoughts.

But the hieratic symbol endeavors to transmit rather than transcribe knowledge, that is, the esoteric, undefinable moment of the supernatural impulse.

The masterpiece that is pharaonic hieroglyphs consists of the fact that both these interpretations are admitted, because the symbols were wisely chosen.

———

THE SPIRIT OF THE PROBLEMS. In the domain of rational determinism, one might say that a solution can be found to any problem that can be stated. Here the conditions are those of a determined and quantitative order, and therefore of a mechanical nature. Rational determinism is the sphere of antinomies and dialectics where complements compensate and cancel each other; it is the domain of collective science.

In the metaphysical and spiritual domain, the problem remains a question with no counterbalancing answer. Nothing can be opposed to an affirmation that becomes the expression of faith; that is the province of the individual who has exceptional gifts, or simply belief.

Thus, the individual believes in God without being able to demonstrate the reality of the object of his belief. As a philosopher or member of a religion, he adopts a formula defining his God, together with the moral or systematic conclusions that this formula reasonably and rationally implies. This is to resort once more to rational syllogism in order to justify an unproven affirmation that has been accepted collectively; the individual abdicates his independence to again become one with his kind.

The obscure, instinctive call to individual freedom that lives in every person is constantly denied by the fear of isolation. We think that by sharing our faith—or what we see and know, but cannot prove—we shall give these individual certainties a consistency that eludes doubt, for few people are capable of believing, or of being alone in their knowing, without doubting. This is what caused proselytism as well as the formation of doctrinal schools or personal religions. But this is also the cause of the dialectical philosophy that has reigned over the West ever since the Eleatic Greeks.

The only true, acceptable philosophy is the philosophy that exhibits, with no possible discussion, the chain of "becoming and return" *as demonstrated by facts.* This is then the knowledge that excludes doubt and therefore dialectics. All other forms are nothing but a quest founded on ignorance or uncertainty.

A number of elements allows us to suppose that such a knowledge was not only kept by, but was the essence of, the Temple in certain great ages of the past, among which is the age of pharaonic Egypt. If this supposition is well founded, it is certain that basic truths have sometimes been transmitted through the surviving legends. It might then be useful to seek the true spirit of the problems posed instead of accepting the way in which exotericism has claimed to understand them.

For example, the ancient Greeks tell us that there are three problems that have no answer: the squaring of the circle, perpetual motion, and the doubling of the cube. Now, our work has shown that the doubling of the cube is not only geometrically and arithmetically possible, but also very simple. It is only attainable, however, through a "geometric" mentality, that is, a *mode* of mathematical thought the West ignores. And this path opens the door to true knowledge of the laws of celestial mechanics, so that it is perfectly legitimate for us to think that solutions for the other two problems are related to the laws of genesis and *cosmic* mechanics, and that it should be said instead that these problems cannot be solved *with a deterministic, rational mentality* because they require another viewpoint.

Harmony results from disorder; if one could put the Universe in a box and shake it so everything would be in disorder, the order we know would necessarily return. This is because of affinities and the "age of the genetic states" of the various substances, through which the physical remains in affinity with the physical, the mental with the mental, and the spiritual with the spiritual. No electrical energy can remain unconnected from its magnetic pole; no psychic energy can remain unrelated to the corporeal form; no mental energy can remain unattached to a central nervous system. The satellites of the planets cannot exist beyond a certain state of genesis of planetary matter, and no planet can exist without its solar center, because one defines the other. No hydrogen atoms, for example, can be attached to copper without the agency of oxygen that links them together.

There is an inevitable law that says that *harmony-in-itself* is nothing other than that which is thrust upon us by what it is in itself. That our *individual sense* of harmony is related to our individual state of consciousness, and that the Universe can take on an altogether different aspect from that which it shows to the "collective consciousness"—this is another story.

The inevitable law means the ineluctable law. It therefore has a form, and this form can be apprehended and made into a general doctrine. All depends on our view of this form. Let us suppose that we have marked out a hexagon with six sticks of equal length. If we look sideways at this form, it will no longer be a hexagon but a line. If we then speak of a "form," this implies a fixed and definite angle of vision, and the doctrine drawn from it is open to dispute.

Therefore, the only indisputable doctrine is the doctrine that synthesizes all possible points of view around the basic "forms."[3] This simultaneity of vision is the essential quality to be developed, the only quality valid for the "spirit of the problems" of knowledge. A describable solution to a problem is only possible if none of its elements is *fixed* as an invariable form; the solution must adapt to all possibilities. This apparent instability still has its precise directives, and our aim in this book is to show its character with regard to the pharaonic mentality, the thinking of the Temple.

When a question is posed, it must never be tainted by the consciousness of its limits, to which the questioner unconsciously submits. The Christian who sees his God as a person, *similar to himself,* crucified on the charnel hill of Golgotha, in Palestine, east of the Mediterranean—a little sea

[3] It may be noted that first, hieroglyphic figures correspond to this principle in that for a double aspect they show the front view, and for a single aspect the profile; second, the sphere is a perfect form, for it is a perfect circle in all its aspects; and third, in pharaonic thought, geometry is not a drawing, a play of "forms," but the symbol of functions.

on the terrestrial globe, itself a particle in the solar system, again, a grain of dust in the galaxy—his faith has no more value than the negation of the atheist who, like him, sees God as something in his own measure.

The following story is told. A lecturing scientist had just finished leading his audience through all the astronomical features of nebulae in a universe measured in light-years. A troubled woman asked him, "If our earth is such an infinitely small thing in the universe, how can God be concerned with us?" She received the answer she deserved: "This, madam, depends on the size of the God in whom you believe."

It is very natural that each person should seek the answers to his questions within his own limited world, for he demands a comprehensible, limited, and circumscribed answer, a quantity that can be embraced by the senses.

Essential problems must not be approached in a deterministic, rational spirit, nor in a spirit of faith, but only in what I call a *functional spirit*, regardless of the "forms" involved in the function.

At the origin of the great movements of revealed knowledge, we always find an expression that is solely geometrical, to the complete exclusion of fixed "forms," whether in Egypt with the Pyramids, in India with the Brahmanic and Buddhist geometrical patterns, or in ancient China with its number games.

When figurations (forms) arrive afterward to specify the function, decadence begins, the fall of Reason into the rational. That is why, in order to penetrate the thought of the Ancients, we rely on the architecture and the geometry that guides it, rather than on descriptive texts.

It is the gesture that speaks and unveils.

———

HISTORICISM. Strangely enough, the historical aspect is the main concern of those who anxiously look into the great problems of the Spirit and the revelations that proclaim it. Now, the fact that one utterance has been given out before another, or that one revelation occurs on such and such a date, is a question of confluence and has no value in itself. To be, to have been, to become . . . One who wishes to find the light must know that it has nothing to do with time as we measure it on our scale.

An exact parallel can be drawn between the bases of the pharaonic myth and the dates of the Gospels, and also with the Hindu myth and pantheon.

We shall not draw a historical tableau of the fetal development of a man; we are concerned with what this man is and with what he can be or do. He was man in potential in the gene of the chromosome; he is man in actuality at his birth and in his detaching himself from his mother. This physical birth becomes the conception of physical consciousness.

Osirianism is indeed born of a seminal reality, and Christianity of the Osirian seed, just as the cells are born of spiritual substances, the organs are the issue of these cells, and the organized being the issue of these organs. There are no dates in time, there are stages of gestation; the end is in the beginning.

Truth is a word empty of meaning for our common intelligence. At the most, it is an abstraction from which we eliminate all our doubts; it is a negative reality. This Truth is One and indivisible; it has not "been" in order to be and to become; people have translated it according to the degree of their consciousness. We may pose a historicism of human consciousness, but we may not say, for example, that Christianity (that is, its true revelation) appeared as a light that did not exist before such and such a specific date. The Verb, redemptive when embodied, has always existed; but the yet unawakened consciousness only recognizes it at a given time, and it is this time that can be historically situated, exactly in the same way as we have always lived in the presence of electromagnetic waves, even before we suddenly discovered their detectors.

Job, for example, is always present; the dialogue between Kṛṣṇa and Arjuna is always present; these "truths" could not have existed in both the past and the present without having been in existence before the time of their entry into recorded history. Nothing is more vain than being concerned with the historical aspect of Reality. But, as surely as the same and unique Truth has appeared to human consciousness at certain fixed periods of its gestation, it is sure that today we are at the dawn of a new stage of consciousness, when the *same and unique Truth* will be known in a new light.

The gestation of a race, people, or empire is a different thing altogether; it is in the image of the cosmic gestation—inspired or conceived on a cosmic date whose nature and influence are known—and similar to the physical conception of a person. Within the "thing" that is this race, people, or empire, there are dates, there is a *history*, and each one of its stages will be in the *image* of the gestation of the consciousness of the whole. It is here that the empire of the pharaonic sages is so marvelously instructive, for it recounts the cosmic genesis and all the revelations of the spirit through its forms, names, and works—the *symbolique* of its existence. This empire is a book that speaks of the slightest nuances of thought, just as the ancient temples and our cathedrals are books that speak through their architecture and figurations.

How can the initiatory Christic Passion take on additional value if it is considered to be within human measure? What was initiatory becomes a story. And serious "overgrown children" attempt to place those historical events in the reign of Pontius Pilate, and the flight to Egypt in the reign of Herod Archelaus, which occurred (so they say) in A.D. 2 or 3, or later. It is a good way of slaying the great Christic teaching.

If this way of speaking about knowledge no longer corresponds to the requirements of consciousness today, it is not at all certain that it had more purpose for past humanity, which is alleged to have been more infantile, demanding images and objectifiable facts in conformity with its childish condition. We can ask ourselves if this way of presenting knowledge, making it enchanting through miracles, did not on the contrary keep humanity at an inferior level; if it did not make humanity stupid, instead of raising it up as the revelation of the redeeming, Divine Power should and could have. The gestation of the Christian revelation has been interrupted.

Historicism leads to idolatry, in other words, to true paganism, and to the revolt of those consciousnesses who aspire to the Light.

—⁓—

FOR THE CONCEPT OF THE "SACRED" we can accept the following definition: sacred is that which appears "causal" and has an immutable—or intangible, or indefinable—character, because of what we know or accept to be true, or to what we give our faith. For example, God, dogma, the sacraments; a commitment made under oath, by word, or by vows; filial respect, duty to one's children, to the fatherland, to tribal customs, caste, or place, to one's inherited name . . . In this sense there is also the "sacred triangle," the "Temple" as an entity of knowledge, the place consecrated to prayer. Also sacred will be the promise made to a dying person.

Such a definition is insufficient to specify the character of sacredness, not only because it is obviously incomplete but also because it does not get at the essence of the question. Because of the conditioning of the person who accepts them, faith, commitment, and form are relative, and by this very fact variable, elements. The following commandment, for example, can be taken as sacred: "Honor thy father and thy mother, in order to live long on earth." It is certain that the yogi, or in general, the person who is touched by the redeeming grace, in no way seeks to be reborn on earth (in this physical body). We can therefore question the obligations that such a person may or may not have toward his parents.

Nothing changeable, nothing destructible, can have a true, sacred character, whether it is a tangible fact, or an intellectual, or emotional fact. A commitment, a faith, once given, may be considered intangible or unchangeable, but there is nothing *sacred* in this except for the use of the word as a common expression underlining the absolute character that one wishes to give to one's faith or commitment.

This aspect does not interest us here, but the tendency to invoke "sacredness" demonstrates the existence of an intuition or the survival of a tradition that affirms "the sacred." As an example, and also as an answer to a question that puzzles certain people, I shall refer once more to Hermeticism. It is certain that neither the theory nor the practice of Hermeticism contains anything sacred in the absolute sense. But *that which will allow* the actual realization of what is proposed by the theory and sought by the practice—that is sacred.

The sacred is necessarily beyond time and space, it can only be the *function*, considered as Power in itself, beyond the object that manifests it. Thus the form, the definition, the specification—that is, the *symbols of the function*—evoke it and make it tangible to us, and this function, which we know only through evocation, *is sacred.*

The first Diophantine triangle, the 3 : 4 : 5, demonstrates, symbolizes, and evokes a function that is universal and invariable; it is *through this* that such a triangle is sacred, and not as a geometric figure. That which (within ourselves) awakens us to a faith without reasoning: this is sacred, not the faith that is expressed. That which allows a commitment within ourselves to the extent of absolute self-negation: this is sacred: not the commitment that one accepts.

Therefore, sacredness is *that which causes absolute certainty,* even if this certainty, should later undergo change; *that which causes unchangeable faith,* even if the object, formally or intellectually represented, should undergo variation; *that which causes forms and specifications,* even if these are transient, because that which causes certainty, faith, or form will always create it given the same conditions. Now, the function, that is, the defining power, is that which causes. It is therefore the function-power alone that is sacred: the *neter.*

—✺—

REALITY. There are too many meanings for the words *real* and *reality.* I shall call "real" that which is invariable, such as the "Unique," but also, for example, the invariability of the *genetic necessity that creates the vital chain of being.*

As for the word *genesis,* if it means the "becoming" that occurs between cause and effect, then an enumeration of discrete phases, a succession, is implied.

If from the rational point of view this succession is obvious, from the esoteric and vital point of view there is a bond linking cause and effect that cannot be cut up into phases. The Mosaic Genesis divides the becoming of the world into six or seven moments, in the same way that the musical scale locates six or seven tones in the scale between One and Two. These tones are "sensorial realities," indispensable to logical thought. But only the Unity of Becoming, beyond time considered as a measure, has value for the esoteric point of view, just as the harmony of a tone occurs precisely as the consciousness of a relationship without the elements of the relationship being taken into account. This is why I suggest the word *genharmony* instead of *genesis* when the term refers to the *genetic function in itself.*

On the other hand, the typical phases cut up into periods of time in the succession of a genesis (such as the *days* in biblical Genesis), represent the analysis of the potentialities of the Cause, making *sensorially real* the potential, *absolutely real* qualities immanent in the Cause. Symbolic philosophy—and not dialectical philosophy (Greek metaphysics)—will be based on the symbolic character of phenomenal reality in order to arrive directly at absolute reality, through the evocation of innate knowledge, which cannot be expressed by intellectual definition. In this way of thinking, one no longer opposes an intellectual fact to a phenomenal reality; one remains absolutely positive in the elements of research and expression, elements revealed by the symbols of the phenomenon, onto which one superimposes or into which one incorporates—through a sense no longer cerebral but belonging to "sensitive vision" or "vital proof"—the quantitative significance. Historical materialism is replaced by mythical history, a "theo-genesis." Theory is of no avail; experience tells everything and itself provides the new elements needed for the continuity of the experience.[4] It is sufficient in itself and for knowledge (not to be confused with learning), and it grasps abstractions directly without needing to define them in any way.

Any phenomenon left to itself, with no new influx of energy, is limited by the exhaustion of the impulse supplied by its cause. Moreover, any phenomenon, through reactivity, produces that which complements it, so that it destroys itself, just as an open flame burning in the air produces the water that could extinguish it. And lastly, the absolute (cosmic) phenomenon finds its cessation—therefore the exhaustion of the impulsive action considered to be absolute—in the overactivity of the product equalling, in reaction, the causal activity.

All phenomena have a beginning and therefore an end, but for the Universe this beginning cannot be situated, it does not exist, since we are dealing with the unique Phenomenon that is beyond time, in other words, *constant*. A phenomenal ending therefore always merges with a beginning, not of the phenomenon, but of its *identity*. This causes both the eternity of the Universe and its apparent granulation in time.

We therefore have no reason to concern ourselves with what is phenomenally real or nonreal, for it is merely a question of what position to take: the phenomenon being real in itself and absolutely unreal within the Reality of the unceasing cosmic genesis.

—⁓—

ANTHROPOCOSMIC MENTALITY. How difficult it is to make discernible what is tangible only for the spirit! It is not just a question of looking, but also of hearing, and above all, of feeling, of being aware; better still, of being in a state of consciousness different from the one that we exhibited only yesterday.

In general, our mentality is Cartesian. We seek the parts in order to understand the whole, we cut things up into what we think is their simplest expression, just as we look for the material atom to understand matter and then find that the atom of energy does not enable us to understand energy any more than the other—supposedly material atom—revealed to us the true nature of matter.

We are always playing the part of judge before Nature: we and it; at best, we ascribe to Nature what we are ourselves, like a man before his fiancée.

"I think, therefore I am. . . ."

[4] Any experience—whether carving a stone, combing one's hair, or realizing the spirit—engenders the consequences that guide the continuation of the experience. The theory that one would like to deduce from this, as our mentality conceives it, kills the possibility of *living* the experience, of being one with it and vitally *knowing* its conditions.

The creative act consists in self-recognition. But applied to the creature, this becomes the "separation" of the "thing-in-itself" from the ego, and poses the principle of antinomy, which is precisely that which the redemptive act necessarily surpasses.

With regard to our purpose, the liberation of consciousness from varying contingencies, the curiosity of knowing "if I am" is unwholesome because it divides the vital entity into opposites. For Western man, this curiosity has become such an obvious need that he is no longer capable of envisaging another way of life and thought.

As long as one of the two opposites wants to know itself through the other, which is typical of our mentality, it is impossible to find a resolution for our philosophical anxiety. We are forgetful of the mean term that summarizes the two opposites that define it.

When the Ancients solve problems in mathematics by an interplay of "inverses," they are showing us a path, whereas we see only a procedure of calculation. The goal proposed is *union,* where inverse elements are resolved and canceled.

"I am no longer the I who thinks," but Being. We oppose *beautiful* and *ugly,* but these opposites are only inverse elements, one of which contains a surplus of what is lacking in the other. Union is neither "beautiful" nor "ugly"; it is the supernatural sense of harmony.

Any resistance opposed to an activity is only the potential of the activity made concrete through inertia. The whole Universe is, in its form, the resistance to creative activity. Union is life, and in this Unity, the activity and the resisting form are but a harmonious interval.

Man considered as a natural finality is not in opposition to the Universe, he is the "mediety"* of the "inverse elements" that are the universal and the particular. In him, opposites are resolved and canceled; he is the All.

Therefore, the anthropocosmic mentality denies the mentality of dialectical philosophy. Inverse elements exist, this is the mark of Nature, but union is the sole Reality, the consciousness of Nature.

The comprehension of harmony, this innate and supernatural knowledge that produces the intuition of Unity and that we rationally translate as "the sense of balance," is the guide in the quest for this mean term, which is neither one nor the other of the opposing complements immanent in this state of union.

The senses inform us of the opposites that produce cerebrally graspable appearances, just as in music the ear gives us the knowledge of sound; but only innate knowledge can show us the tone of the sound.

Nothing in the Universe that is perceptible is so of itself. Everything has its opposite, its complement, that is, that which by comparison causes the other to appear. As long as our thought is founded on this duality, we shall never be able to infer a truth other than from the agreement or equating of the cerebral intelligence with an object, a relative truth. Invariable Truth is the equating of consciousness with Being.

But can we seek otherwise than through complements?

We may as well ask if it is possible to know light or harmony. If the sense of the simultaneity of opposites were not in us, we would still only be physically sensitive, emotive, and intelligent animals; but Spirit, the sense of the sacred, the call to become one, would not exist. The satisfactions of the body and the pleasures of the emotions would satisfy us; Art would have no meaning for us.

---

*As used by the author, "mediety" refers to the point of inversion, the crux. If proportion is the only way we can "make sense" of an experience in mathematical terms, then the mediety is the unitive point of crossing that a proportion as a whole represents. The various sorts of medieties (arithmetic, harmonic, and geometric) are specific cases of proportion. The dynamic, representational quality of the mediety should always be kept in mind.

THE MATHEMATICS OF INVERSE ELEMENTS, of "reciprocals," leads us from duality to Unity, this *root,* which, crossed with itself (multiplied by itself), gives the surface, or measure, of volumes.[5] This is starting from the variety of opposites, complementary with respect to each other (definitions), in order to arrive at the knowledge of Being. But genesis starts from this Being in order to arrive at the nature of the complements. Cosmic Man is, potentially, in the seed that is the original activity. That present man, the present culmination of one phase of the absolute formation of Cosmic Man, being himself definable by complements, does not deny the cosmic entity that is man, any more than the embryo, whether it is viable or not, ultimately denies, by the existence of its various phases of gestation, the entity that will be the final fruit; on the contrary, it affirms this finality for our measure.

The anthropocosmic mentality requires first of all that we consider the Being we want to know, that is, the being of the object, without intellectual definition. And *only the represented symbol* allows us to use this method. The outline of the object is sufficient to represent it if this object has the same appearance (represents the same *being*) from all three directions. The first is given by the outline as, for example, the outline of a round vase. This outline will no longer suffice for an object in the various aspects of its volume or its movement. Thus, the hieroglyph of the bird in flight will show it simultaneously from the side and from the front through its body and its wings.

The example of the symbol of a geometric volume makes this intent of the hieratic symbol of the being more tangible.

This mentality always requires us to consider as finished—that is, as Unity—the successive, completed moments intermediate in the genesis of the perfect result. This is one way of eliminating the analytical mistake of considering things intellectually, while satisfying the intellectual requirement that we observe the moments, or phases, in the study of the object. In a tree, for example, the trunk is one, the branches—as a function of branching out—are one, the bud is one, and so forth. These unities are always the starting points of a *new* state of being because the trunk becomes the root of the branches, the branches become the root of the buds, and so on. We have cut up the whole into separate entities, complete in themselves, and at the same time we have observed a succession of the kind cerebral intelligence (Nature) requires, but we have avoided a decomposing analysis. None of the parts of the whole has been separated from the life of the whole; in our example, that which creates the life of the tree trunk also creates the life of the branches and buds, for the same functions act in the growth and in the limitation of growth. The trunk puts out branches at a certain moment of its maturity, just as the branches, at an identical moment for them, as branches, give forth the bud.

This tree is above all a potential being; this potentiality becomes form through a genesis that functionally conforms to the universal law governing the concretization of the Idea or Spirit-substance. The Law, the hierarchy of stages, is unique, even if the ways and forms are various.

Thus, for the investigation of Nature, the method always consists in bringing back a finality of the phenomenon to Unity, that is, to *the origin of a becoming* that necessarily obeys the law of genesis. It is owing to the function of becoming in all moments, all phases, all forms, that everything in the Universe is interdependent.

[5] Cf. chapter 5, "The Root."

Chapter 1

CONSCIOUSNESS AND IRREDUCIBLE MAGNITUDES

CONSCIOUSNESS

The use of the term *consciousness* to denote a formative metaphysical power is inadequate in the usual philosophical sense that refers to psychological consciousness, specifically, "being conscious" or "being conscious of one's self" (in German, *Bewusstsein* and *Selbstbewusstsein*), that is, ego consciousness.

In any case, the "functional" meaning implied in "consciousness" or "being conscious" is "to put in relation." Now, when the term *consciousness* is used to mean a "formative metaphysical power," the possibility of relation is excluded, because multiplicity does not yet exist in the prephysical state (creation). The notion evoked by this meaning of the word implies, *potentially, the function of putting into relation* and therefore, that which *provokes* the original, creative scission—the number One, which *must* become Two.

The mystery of this scission remains unsolved—it cannot be solved for the psychological consciousness—but with the formative "consciousness-essence" as a starting point, cosmogonic philosophy is founded on "action" and therefore functionally situated. As it is, the formative "consciousness-essence" refers to a synthesis of "Being containing in itself its own opposition," which is the creative function, and which will appear later as a generating power throughout the becoming and transformations in all of Nature.

In this spirit, the material of form—from energy to the densest corporeal state—is nothing but a qualitative specification, an expression of the *consciousness that seeks itself,* through all its metamorphoses. Therefore, *quality is function.*

———

What we consider as psychological consciousness is now undergoing a modification of its foundation; its basis is no longer the specified thing, but the specification of the thing. The thing becomes symbol and the function becomes reality. The science of numbers (arithmology) loses in value what the function gains in terms of spatial geometry.

———

Science still holds on to a "shrinking" mentality, to a universe brought into the frame of our senses, requiring a quantitative basis, even when it knows that a chain of photons, without quantity, defines the extreme reference that is light. Everything appears as an alternation of *intensity,* thus of abstract functions.

———

If we admit a Cause-Source of the Universe, this source is necessarily unique. So, if reason imposes the idea of an indivisible unity—which is therefore without quantity—this concept of unity eludes our point of view as creatures who are part of the Universe, consequence of the unique Cause.

Such unity exists for us only if comparison is possible; but comparison means consciousness and duality. The whole process of creation thus occurs between the numbers One and Two; and duality is the fundamental character of the created Universe. This duality is the principle of sexuality. Duality implies comparison, and this succession of phenomena produces cerebral consciousness. Unity creates by "looking at itself"; this is the unfaithful angel of the Judeo-Christian tradition, another image of Adam's sin in Genesis. We can call this Unity God, or nonpolarized energy, in its aspect of indivisible Unity, and God the Creator, or polarized energy, in its aspect as *Unity-conscious-of-itself.*

Consequently, *the Universe is nothing but consciousness,* and in its appearance nothing but an *evolution of consciousness* from beginning to end, the end being a return to its cause. It is the purpose of all "initiatory" religions to teach the way that leads to this ultimate integration.

———

To exist means "to be" and "to persist." All that exists is specified and has its own qualities. The specificity of a thing places it in harmony or disharmony with other things, thus determining particular affinities. Affinity is selective. Selection by affinity (choice) is, through specificity, imposed on a thing, which by itself cannot modify it. This selecting disposition is distinguished from the psychological consciousness by the fact that the latter represents a certain power of control with regard to "choice."

In any case, affinity—selectivity through specificity—introduces a first form of consciousness, a fact that, historically, relates consciousness to the origin of things. Having reserved the term *consciousness* for psychological consciousness, we could refuse to use it to refer to the selective disposition in, for example, the chemical affinity of simple substances.

Functionally speaking, however, it is chemical affinity that represents the primary stage of what we call, psychologically, sympathy and antipathy, and that causes the phenomena of plant and animal symbiosis. Functionally, it is also the selective character of chemical affinity that represents the primary action of what we shall later call consciousness, for the nature of consciousness is *to distinguish.*

The chemical substance *does not realize* that it chooses among other substances the one to which it will prefer to attach itself. Its choice is conditioned both by its specificity and by the milieu. This chemical substance is not conscious of its choice, but the fact that a choice exists expresses the universal disposition that is consciousness. Therefore choice, through the affinity of specificities, appears as latent consciousness that will then become actual consciousness through the steps and stages of all the kingdoms up to man.

The organs of life are determined in the progression from the mineral to the human. The development of the organs is nothing but a progressive expansion, a widening of consciousness. In the plant kingdom, the rudiments of the essential organs, those of assimilation and reproduction, are formed. Assimilation organizes itself for the liquid, aerial, and solid states; and the organization of reproduction can take all possible forms, from the cryptogamic to separate sexes.

The "potential consciousness of the mineral" becomes vegetative in the plant kingdom. This is the passage from potentiality, or latent consciousness, to the consciousness of surroundings. For plant consciousness, the choice is larger and somewhat freer than for the mineral. Each new step in the expansion of consciousness plays, for the individual, the role of a finality.

This becomes more obvious in the animal kingdom, through which plant consciousness becomes instinctive consciousness. We find beings in this kingdom that are almost entirely a single organ: a mouth, a womb, a prehensile limb, an eye, ear, olfactory organ, and so on. Here plant consciousness has become innate in order to give complete importance to the new organ being developed in these animal beings of the organic becoming.

The sensory and motor central nervous system is concentrated in the cerebral organ, which, in mammals, has already attained *consciousness of the innate consciousness*. But the transition to human consciousness requires what can be called a "reversal" of consciousness, of which we will speak later on.

If the plausibility of a transition through "steps" can be demonstrated, this synoptic portrait of the expansion of consciousness is the true image of an *evolution*. It is not—as Bergson would have it—evolution that is creative, rather, it is the *continuity of the creative function* that causes evolution.

When consciousness is presented in this general sense, divided into latent and potential consciousness, then into plant, instinctive, and psychological consciousness, it appears as a *power* of life that seeks its final liberation through all possible expressions of Nature. It is a metaphysical power that potentially has all these forms within itself, and these forms of expression that fill up the Universe are then an *analysis* of all its possibilities. If this assertion has a foundation, evolution does exist, and one must find the proof for it.

The observable fact of succession in organic becoming, through an investigation of independence or organic "crystallization" of the functions indispensable for the maintenance of life, is what leads us to seek a law of evolution. But to base evolutionary theories exclusively on animal biology is to start from a given essential element and therefore to neglect the "reasons" for the becoming of that first living cell. To do this is to build an inadequate theory. Nevertheless, it is essentially the living cell's reasons for being that can guide the study of a sequence of lineages leading to humanity.

The origin of all things is mineral; without the mineral kingdom, no plant could exist, and the plant is the indispensable intermediary for animal life. The sequence of these three *kingdoms* is undeniable, but the transition from one to the other is unknown. In this area, evolutionary theories are nothing but hypotheses to which our observations lead us, but which mechanistic logic cannot follow without leaving serious gaps.

The Darwinian hypothesis according to which, generally, there is an adaptation of the organism, particularly through its struggle for survival, ends with the aphorism asserting that "the function creates the organ." We may admit that the word *creates* is inappropriately used for "develops." But it still remains to be known from where the organ comes. The theory of transformism (upon which the materialist Haeckel had, in the end, founded all his hopes) remains unproven and untenable, for it allows that the transmission of new organic functions occurs only *through the seed of the individual*.

An existing organ undoubtedly develops or atrophies because of exercise or inertia. Through adaptation, it may be modified by the environment, but "the function in relation to the exterior" requires first the presence of an organ. A reversal of the Darwinian aphorism, that is, "the environment creates the organ," can make this becoming more understandable. Without light, the eye is useless, but the absence of a visual organ leaves us unaware of light, and therefore the *desire* to observe light does not exist. The impulse to form a sensory organ can only originate in the living being *by reaction* to the energetic action of the environment, that is, from the energetic environment acting on it.[1] It is light that creates the mechanism of the eye, the sound vibration that creates the ear, the liquid environment that creates taste, terrestrial or corporeal emanation that creates the sense of smell, just as it is the corporeal obstacle that creates touch. This is what makes us see and hear and taste. Therefore, it is wrong to start from sight, hearing, and so forth, in order to find a reason for the development of the sense organs. I speak here only of the sensory instruments and not of the intellective functions.

Yet vibrations of infrared and ultraviolet light exist that our eye cannot perceive; but if we did perceive them, they would offer us, from the visual point of view, nothing more for the intelligence than the limited spectrum from red to violet does.

Our senses respond to five activities within the average limits of the necessities imposed by these activities. Consciousness is developed or expanded in relation to the general action of the environment, but it is not limited to *the reactive power of the senses* evoked and formed by this action.

Psychological consciousness misleads us. It generates *preconceptions* by the very fact of the limits of our perceptions, not because this perception is limited in itself, but because we cerebrally frame it into an intellectual definition. For example, the olfactory sensitivity of the dog by far surpasses our own, in the same way the bat's sensitivity to sound vibrations surpasses our hearing. Now, these forms of sensitivity are *innate in man,* and are limited only by his cerebral preconceptions. Proof of this is given when the cerebral presence is asleep and the sensitivity awake, as in the state of hypnosis or somnambulism, and even in certain cases of insanity; then the power of sensory acuity is increased to abnormal proportions, as seen in cases where muscular strength greatly surpasses what we normally expect in the way of endurance from sinews and organic fibers.

———∿∿∿———

In summary, consciousness is not the effect of a function, not the result of a relation, but a metaphysical power, a primary synthesis that potentially contains in itself the Idea of all particularities. If it were generally possible to define consciousness, I could be accused of playing with words. Now, *we are aware* of the existence of consciousness and yet are unable to define such a state.

The phenomenon of consciousness also exists in the animal, prior to human psychological consciousness. Memory, instinct, reasoning, emotional and psychic reactions, are terms that stand for extremely complex *functions* that all arise from the "mean state" I call consciousness. By basing evolution and the study of the phenomena of Nature on the metaphysical base of consciousness regarded as essence and energy or activity in general, we may build a perfectly coherent edifice.

———∿∿∿———

The evolution or *expansion of consciousness* manifests corporeally through the form and organism of the *individual.* In perpetuating himself, the individual does nothing but multiply the unit that he represents. The *adaptations* to the environment through the "struggle for survival" create the variations among groups of individuals, classified into races and species. This classification is made from below upward, from the individual to the general. It applies to the transmission of characteristics *through the seed of the individual.*

---

[1] For the origin of the visual organ, we can refer to the studies on comparative anatomy with regard to the pineal eye.

It is therefore in the individual himself that we must seek the movement of the development of consciousness, and *outside of all seminal proliferation. There is a reappraisal to be made regarding the possibilities of the transformation of specificities and their transmission.*

A precept as old as wisdom states: "A form cannot change into another form unless the first is completely decomposed into its essential component elements." A second precept from the same source affirms that "Every thing and every being contains a fixed nucleus that neither putrefaction nor fire can destroy." The fact that our biologists have ignored these principles has caused the failure of their attempts to elaborate a coherent theory of evolution, which is nevertheless imposed by natural facts.

If we leave aside the moral character that is usually associated with the word *soul* and retain only the sense of specificity denoted—although with some difficulty—by the word *psyche,* metempsychosis exists. Moreover, the legendary palingenesis of plants, based on the "fixed" residue contained in the ashes, is associated with the principle of metempsychosis.

By putrefaction, any substance, plant or animal, is reduced to two separable states, one volatile and the other a fixed residue. The latter, when dried, contains an alkaline salt.

Similarly, but more violently, combustion divides all plant and organic substances into volatile parts, with a residue of ash containing a fixed, alkaline salt. "Man, thou art ash and unto ash thou shalt return." All things are therefore essentially composed of a volatile part and a fixed part, a principle of generation that pharaonic theology, for example, summarizes in its teachings on *ba* and *ka.*

If the ashes of a burnt plant are sown in the soil together with a seed of the same plant, certain qualities of this plant can be exalted or its typical qualities modified. These same ashes can impede the growth of plants that are "complementary" to it. The legendary palingenesis of plants, as well as the phoenix legend, are initiatory traditions revealing a form of generation *that the "cellular" seed cannot achieve.*

Consequently, transformations can only be achieved *by and for the same individual,* the individual who, during his lifetime, has undergone a deep modification of his being. He must reincarnate because his *seed* cannot transmit these new characteristics to another being. Ignorance of this fact makes it impossible to establish a definitive law of heredity.

The fixed salt, which compared to the chromosome is extremely fixed or even indestructible, is the true carrier of the specificity of an individual, preserving in it all his *personal* characteristics, including those acquired during his life.

For the chemist, one living cell is equivalent to another, and one residual salt, whether from putrefaction or combustion, is equivalent to any other; but it is just as obvious that *from the vital point of view* there are some nuances, materially indiscernible, in the parts of each individual because this individual is always characterized. On a tree, one leaf is never identical to another; one individual—and its component parts—is never identical to another, except in those rare cases of twins born from the same egg.

For a "reincarnation" to occur, the *fixing* nucleus of an individual's psyche must be joined with the *organic* nucleus of a cell-seed. Of itself, the fixed nucleus cannot engender a new organized being, it cannot move backward in the evolutionary lineage to start the whole cycle that leads to organic life. A kinship between the two nuclei, the fixed mineral nucleus and the animal or plant cellular nucleus, is indispensable, and metempsychosis is the history of the reincarnations of this fixed nucleus in search of the living being that corresponds to its own rhythm.

This is the theme of many strange tales, such as "The Magician" from Egypt or certain Cambodian tales.[2] It is also the reason for many varieties of magical gestures, such as the black

---

[2] See *Contes Khmers,* trans. from the Cambodian by G. H. Menod (Högman, Mouans Sartoux, A.M.: Chitra Publications).

youth of the jungle who eats the eye of the great hunter who has just died to obtain the gift of swift and sharp sight.

In general, knowledge of the secret of psychic transmission—therefore of personal qualities and acquired, modifying experiences—is the foundation for many varieties of witchcraft, but also for true magical acts, including the theological precepts of burial methods.

The natural course of metempsychosis passes through the plant, for the plant is the first in evolution to reabsorb the fixed salt in the process of its growth. It is through food that the fixed salt returns to the individual carrier of the regenerating seed. It is here that we must seek one of the causes of genetic mutation.

In man the absolute fixed salt of his being is formed in the femur, the foundation and support of the physical body (the Egyptian *men.t*).

Coat of arms of Eze-sur-mer (A.-M.)[3]

The plant or animal cell-seed preserves the qualities typical of the species, including its adaptations; the fixed salt, on the other hand, carries over—often through very long periods of invisibility—the individual's *acquired consciousness,* which requires a modification of its form in order to give to his consciousness the means to express itself. The sudden appearance, apparently without transition, of new forms (gene mutation) is, in reality, a continuous sequence *in the evolution of consciousness.*

The regenerating seed is necessary to this succession; thus the plant remains confined to its own kingdom, and the animal to its; the mineral cannot pass on to the plant kingdom without the latter pre-existing. Now, in order to understand the transition from one kingdom to another, and therefore the expansion of consciousness, two essential principles must be taken into account. First is transmission of consciousness through reincarnation, therefore the prior destruction of a form; second is the energetic milieu that creates the organ.

---

[3] Cf. chapter 17.

For the sake of clarity, I use the words *fixed* and *volatile* here to represent the fixed and volatile *principles*. In nuclear science, one would generally speak of the nucleus and the negative electrons. The fixed salt is the neutral neutron in the fixed nucleus. Its alkaline and mineral character is nothing but the carrier of the energetic characteristics of the psyche. It has an energetic specificity, representing *a power that is consciousness.*[4]

With the destruction of the form, the fixed and the volatile are separated. This is what we call death. At the time of this separation, the energetic influences of the environment (such as light or sound) are able to act and create impressions, the form no longer being an obstacle.[5]

The rebirth of a form requires the rejoining of the volatile with the fixed. The fixed is determined, the volatile is feminine and undetermined, although having a general "rhythm" similar to the rhythm of its fixed element. The fixed element must refind its volatile element for reincarnation to occur in whatever form, whether physical or more subtle.

The carrier of the fixed element is paternal, that of the volatile is maternal. There is, at the same time as regeneration, a rejoining of the volatile with the fixed in a determined state.[6] It is at this moment that the influence of the environment intervenes to modify the *instrument* of the being's consciousness.

Such is the Hermetic thesis—so mysterious—that claims to show that the vital destruction of a mineral can render it vegetative and therefore capable of self-nourishment and self-multiplication. This principle is correct and verifiable in the plant and animal kingdoms, and there is adequate justification for the same claim with regard to the mineral. Further atomic research will perhaps confirm this fact and make the information generally accessible.

There is a transmission of the characteristics of the species as well as its preservation through the seed, and there is an evolutionary transformation and transmutation, and a transition from one kingdom to another, through the nucleus or fixed center.

Attempting to limit an evolutionary theory solely to biological evolution on earth is to neglect all the contingencies of life. If the part evolves from a simple and primitive to a complex organic state, it can only do so if its own particular milieu and the general milieu both evolve.

Now, observation shows that there are progressions and regressions that do not belong to the terrestrial or human evolutionary sequence. This is not incomprehensible if the evolutionary principle is extended to the planetary system on which all life as we know it depends.

The solar system becomes a living being if we disregard the only concept we have of it, which is mechanical. It is this living whole that is referred to in the sevenfold planetary system, similar to the sevenfold system of sound and of vibrations in general. The sevenfold principle is, moreover, found in the electronic layers of the atom.[7]

---

[4] With regard to psychological consciousness, this would be called a priori; it is not an *innate consciousness,* but an *innate function* that becomes the definition of a power.

[5] The separation of the elements *that belong to one another* creates the energetic milieu of the object. This energy is, so to speak, the "desire" for assemblage, affinity. (N.B.: This energy is made tangible in the "dilutions" used in homeopathic medicine.)

[6] If instead of the terms *ba* and *ka* of the pharaonic theory I use *volatile* and *fixed,* this is to avoid any misunderstanding as to the real meaning of *ba* and *ka.* To this day, standard Egyptology believes it must translate and explain these words. These are the basic principles of all traditional initiatory texts that aim at teaching the "avatars of a being" in its stages of transformation and purification prior to the rejoining, after the separation through the corporeal death of the two constituent principles.

This problem, posed in mysterious texts from all ages and climes, has given rise to a vast literature, which has all the more difficulty in making clear that each moment of the stages of transformation *has its own name,* a fact that necessarily produces confusions that can be avoided only by those initiated into the experience expressed in this teaching.

[7] Cf. chapter 5, "Harmony."

Energetic tension, the cause of life, is less intense at the periphery than at the center, and life on the outer spheres evolves more slowly than on the spheres nearest to the Sun, but each planet has its own limit, its own *frontier of life*. Thus, Saturn is mineral or *still* mineral, while Jupiter is already plant, and Mars, animal. At the same time, Earth is human life. It has lived through the mineral, the plant, and the animal, which have their own lineages on Saturn, Jupiter, and Mars, respectively. The animal-human lineage on Earth will come to an end when the plant and animal appear as *Saturnian plant and animal* on Saturn. They have existed on Earth like ghosts from another world, but they have no possible finality on this planet.[8] All environmental conditions on this terrestrial sphere, in its earthly aspect, are alien to them with regard to a more complete evolution, but human evolution had to be preceded by the planetary states of consciousness that came before it. This is the way what has been said here about a possible, eventual life on Saturn, Jupiter, and so on, must be understood.

In geology, the principle of stratification, with its upheavals, subsidences, and alluvia, is a mechanical system of reference that explains absolutely nothing about the origin of these minerals. The sudden appearance of Jurassic limestone on top of layers of silica and fluorite is a miracle if the possibility of an evolution of the mineral, such as that of the plant or animal, is excluded. Each one of these mineral evolutionary periods had its own life, which can be linked to the planetary principle in a scheme moving from Saturn, Jupiter, and Mars to Earth.[9]

The recent discoveries of nuclear science are already confirming the principle of the transition of one species to another by the fact of the transmutation of simple substances, thanks to the grouping of nuclei. The neutron represents the fixed salt typical of an *individual*. Seeing these transformations as solely the effect of the number of nuclei, however, would be to fall back into rational simplification. The electronic modifications accompanying these changes bring about modifications of "character." Specificities change and therefore "consciousness" is modified. It is consciousness, the metaphysical power, that presides over all transformation. It is the selective faculty that, through affinity, conditions transformation.

All the efforts causing these changes make up the "suffering" imposed upon the individual; it is suffering that causes the widening of consciousness. The moral suffering in the human individual is exactly of the same order, though not of the same nature, as the violence of energetic action produced artificially in the atom by our scientists.

For an individual to be able to *evolve* in the sense of a *transmutation*, and therefore change the characteristics belonging to his present species, both the milieu and the individual's reaction to that milieu would have *to make an impression* on him to the point of modifying one or the other of his vital dispositions. *This experience is his own.* These new vital dispositions require a new organic instrument that only the proper reincarnation can obtain.

[8] N.B. in this regard the so-called antediluvian animal and, in general, the characteristics of the various geological periods. The world of insects must be considered by itself; it belongs to the "Dwat," the world of transformations.

[9] In evolutionary theory, the duration by itself means nothing. It only has value through the change of influences from a cosmic place. There is a genesis of the parts within the genesis of the whole. At certain moments in the genesis of the whole, there exists a combination of conditions that bring the possibilities for modification within the genesis of the parts. In this way, the principle of genesis disclosed by the parts can acquaint us with the general character of the genesis. Within this "ever-growing" genesis there are moments of pause for the parts.

Only a *reincarnation* of the psyche of this individual, which reconstitutes *this same individual* after his corporeal destruction, can produce a new individual. Similarly, splitting the atoms of the individual mineral, for example, will liberate the energetic elements for a new reconstitution.

Evolution *summarizes* all adaptations and transmutations. It manifests through a progressive organization, expressive of specificity or consciousness. The organic instrument is not an end in itself. It is a momentary instrument in the service of the consciousness-power that, this way, is *finally able to recognize itself* in the human stage, thanks to the central, cerebral energetic system. This moment of human evolution constitutes an evolutionary reversal, that is, the end of the Becoming, signaling the beginning of *corporeal disintegration* or the Return.

The ultimate consciousness is the consciousness of negation. It constitutes the extreme possibility of comparison: to be and not to be. It is possible absence, nonbeing, which affirms being and produces the external appearance of reality in relation to the information brought by the senses.

Such is the exoteric path of the intellect. But when—by means of the senses—the Power informs the cerebral organ, then knowledge begins. Knowledge, then, appears at first as something innate. It is the long legacy of the innate functional powers that forms the treasure that the senses relate to the external, creating intuitive knowledge.[10] It is then that the intellect finds itself at a "fork" in the road: the result will be either rational knowledge, which requires analysis and serves dialectic, or functional knowledge, which is synthetic and categorical in nature.

Only functional consciousness can approach the corporeal abstraction that will be the liberation of consciousness from all physical contingencies, and allow for *existence without the physical body*. It is functional knowledge that allows for identification, the transmission of thought, divination and prophecy; it is this consciousness that brings forth certain dreams. . . .

If we call "meditation" the concentration of thought on a single object, excluding all distraction, then meditation on a thought of *directed* action can produce the effect of this action on the intended spot. Faith can move mountains. We call this a miracle; it is, however, only a natural effect and seems to be "outside of nature" only because of the common mistake of a misleading rational directive thrust upon knowledge. A variety of means, however, may be used to bring on this meditation—chants, litanies, dances, hypnosis, and so on—and these are either profane and impure or pure and sacred, according to the desired aim and the means employed.

IRREDUCIBLE MAGNITUDES AND CONSCIOUSNESS

Speed enters into all problems of a mechanicophysical nature. Speed is a notion that no quantity represents, but which is measurable and also measures. Thus, the speed of light is estimated at 300,000 kilometers per second, and serves, in its turn, as a reference for the definition of energy in relation to mass or quantity (Einstein). Being relative and qualitative, speed is a magnitude used *as* a quantitative value. It is a magnitude that can be reduced to its components, movement and path (time-path), and therefore to the movement that measures space in a given fraction of time. The

[10] Bergson: "Intuition is the direct vision of the spirit by the spirit. Intuition therefore means first of all an immediate consciousness, a vision barely distinguishable from the object, a knowledge that is consciousness and even coincidence." Now, this coincidence is the key. This great thinker's definition of intuition is perfect if we consider the reality of innate knowledge within the finality of natural genesis, represented at present by humanity.

elements of this analysis of the notion of "speed"—movement, time, and space—are in turn no longer analyzable; they are *irreducible magnitudes*, and, thus, two magnitudes are always necessary to define a third.

Similarly, any notion whatsoever, in order to be comprehended or rationally defined, is finally always determined as a third term by means of two others.

We can then speak of a "ternary" as the basis of all rational comprehension, with the result that this trinity of metaphysical elements represents the first physical unity. In principle, and therefore beyond all application or *specification*, this ternary is the creative Divine Principle that must not be confused with the metaphysical "Unity" incognizable in its nature as the absolute Divine Principle, the indivisible, irreducible Unity.

In contrast to traditional esoteric thought, Western thought considers these irreducible magnitudes only in their ternary groupings: movement is movement only because it measures a path through time. The fact that we analyze vital values rationally forces us to think only in terms of values that are objectifiable. This is, for the entire western Mediterranean, the application of Judeo-Christian thought in which Yod Hé Vau, and then Hé again, is transcribed by the Father, the Spirit, the Son, and then again as Unity, by the threefold creative Verb. Thought based on the "three-in-one" is the thought of the physicists and leads to rationalism: the starting point is something that is rationally admissible because it is reducible.[11]

As for the esoteric tradition, it is based on absolute Unity. A Westerner immediately interprets this assumption as being pure philosophical speculation, precisely because he thinks rationally. That this is an error is what I wish to try to demonstrate. Nowadays we know for certain that Egypt spoke of the "One God," and attempts have been made to draw a parallel between this monotheism and Christian deism. It is forgotten that if the One God exists in pharaonic theology, he is considered in his Unity, since the principle of the trinity is attributed to the *neters* that are the various aspects of creative power. If this metaphysics is not the pure speculation of thought, as rational analysis leads us to believe, there must be another way of thinking or another possible view of the problem.

The West looks upon the world from the exoteric side, that is, it objectively observes the forms of the body, and its investigation is nothing but an anatomical analysis of quantities, proceeding in similar fashion from the living cell to its chromosomes, and from chromosomes to their component genes. Western thought never "enters into" a body, does not see it from its living interior outward, from the perspective of its growth and the functional characteristic of its life. For example, the Westerner will look at the form of a tree—the form of its trunk, the form of its bark, the form of its branches, the

---

[11] The Christian dogma of the Mystery of the Trinity is neither contestable in itself, nor put in doubt here. As it is presented in the Gospels, however, it lends itself to being misinterpreted. The "Divine Son" speaks of his "Father" who is in heaven. This divine identity was the subject of the long "Byzantine" controversies and caused the separation of the eastern "monophysites" faithful to the intuitive tradition of the Unity. The "sacerdotal prayer" (Gospel of Saint John) is the affirmation of the unity of the Being, but not of the unity of existence. Indeed, existence is the separation between the ego and the self.

The Mystery of the Trinity, that is, the impossibility of understanding how three persons "spiritually" can actually be one person, is a reality that, because of the objectifying mentality inherent in the concept of multiplicity arising from Unity, was the basis for the development of an objectifying philosophy. The latter revolted against the spiritual intention of this affirmation, thus necessarily opposing rationality to faith.

"In principium erat verbum. . . ." This affirmation obviously puts the threefold Verb at the origin of things. Making this concession to mankind's limited faculties inevitably calls for a deviation, because one day mankind was bound to "slip" from the *rational absurdity* of the imposed faith and turn toward the misleading logic of mechanistic rationalism.

But it is certain that it is the "threefold Verb" that creates the Universe as we know it and that alone can become the "Redeemer" of this world. This being the purpose of the Christian revelation, the *concession* made to human nature in basing its philosophy on this threefold Verb is logically motivated, although esoterically it is a psychological error that was avoided by the pharaonic sages.

form of its leaves—and finally, he will study this object *through what is revealed to him by his senses,* which is a *cerebral,* quantitative view. On the other hand, Hindu and pharaonic *symbolique* show that the foliage of a tree, for example, is considered as the respiratory function, the lung of the plant. Then, under the general form of a leaf, foliage will serve as a symbol for respiration in general; the trunk around which the serpent is entwined will show the rising spiral of the life flux around the spinal column. The whole *symbolique* of traditional thought indicates the character of this thinking: the object that strikes our senses exoterically is the *consequence* of vital functions, that is, *we translate cerebrally into corporeal forms that which is in reality an interrelation of momentary specificities.* The relation is thus an identity between the state of consciousness of the thing and our own innate consciousness, that is, the consciousness that has already been lived and inscribed in our being. All of this happens as if, with the awakening of psychological consciousness, there occurred within us a "turning inside out," an exteriorization of our vital "interiority." It is an undeniable fact that everything in the Universe is alive, that is, moving from its *birth* as a specified being to its *death,* the transformation that allows it to acquire another form, until liberation from all specification and the return into nonpolarized energy, similar to the original energy. Our psychological consciousness—therefore the cerebral (or reversed) consciousness of our innate consciousness—identical to the specificities of objects outside ourselves, shows us specificity as an "object," varieties as "distance," growth or aging as "movement," and genesis as "time." We objectify living functions.

The irreducible magnitudes of mechanics are only rationally irreducible, but, regarded philosophically as vital functions, they can be reduced to the metaphysical functional essence that appears as activity, passivity, and reactivity.

By summarizing these irreducible magnitudes—movement, time, and space or path—under the magnitude that is "speed," then speed applied to a mass or quantity becomes force. Force annihilated by an obstacle appears as energy. But this energy is itself only movement—or speed of molecules and atoms—and it appears as heat, electricity, or light; light is a return to the original energy that produces movement. In this lower cycle (mass, energy, and force as irreducible magnitudes), mass turns out to be a body in motion. The Ancients would say that mass or quantity is not the basic element of this interaction, but on the contrary, it is the final result. The original, active principle finds its resistance and reaction in its own nature[12] and does not constitute a lower group of force-energy-mass; but conversely, it is the original, creative function that is genesis, or time, and its sequence of phases that is "movement"; and volume is the "thing" and the "mass."

Irreducible magnitudes applied to a moving object are measures; displacement within a given time is a force representing *a quantity* of energy. Such is Western or rationalistic thought. Traditional esoteric thought would apply those measures to these same magnitudes, but philosophically, as soon as there is genesis. Genesis means the sequence of phases from the cause to the predestined finality, in other words, from potentiality (as in a seed) to its finality (which is its fruit). Now, there is no time that can measure the sequence from potential to actual; the power that enables this sequence *is time.* It is in this spirit that we must understand the assertion according to which the Ancient Egyptians used the concrete symbol to know the abstract. Forms and all that affects psychological consciousness are only an appearance brought about by a *reversal* of the vital function of metaphysical magnitudes.

---

[12] This is the Original Mystery, the Heliopolitan theme. [See Lucie Lamy, *Egyptian Mysteries: New Light on Ancient Knowledge,* trans. Deborah Lawlor (London: Thames and Hudson, 1981).]

This reversal of consciousness—the consciousness that is in identity with the cosmic genesis and equally in identity with the specificity of a particular genesis—limits (that is, makes corporeal) this identification and gives rise to the notion of quantity and an apparent separation of objects.

Thus *identity* between natural objects no longer exists and it is only through "Art" that it can be sought; this accounts for magic, because identity is the source of all magic, given that two identical things are no longer separate, are no longer but one sole thing, and one must undergo what the other undergoes. It is therefore upon the knowledge of functional identity—the philosophy of the Unity—that the magic of religious rituals, the liturgy, and the perfect architecture of the temples are established. It is the vital function that is real, however metaphysical it might appear in contrast with the cerebral consciousness that we call physical.

Taking the grain or seed as an example, we see that the plant and the final fruit actually exist potentially in this seed where no tangible form exists for our cerebral or psychological consciousness. From this potentiality to the final effect, time marks the stages or typical phases that may be classified into seven or nine degrees. None of these phases is quantitatively separate from another; the one engenders and is found vitally in the other. When, following the initial putrefaction of the seed, it divides itself into root and germ, and the germ grows up at the same time as the root grows down, the potential, future fruit cannot be situated; it is as much in the germ as in the root. This power, "occult" for the cerebral consciousness, decides, *in conformity with the same cosmic power,* when leaves, branches, sexualized flowers, and new seeds and ovules for its proliferation will appear from the trunk. We objectively observe the effects of a marvelous vital function that eludes our understanding; cerebrally, we can only observe a time of growth, that is, of movement and specification of this occult power in the trunk, leaves, branches, and so on. We classify these appearances that are cerebrally objectified, that is, limited by our sensory capacity. Therefore, in order to be liberated from this obstacle we should learn to abstract ourselves from this mental illusion and to stop our mechanical reasonings on natural phenomena, for the sake of seeking and adopting the philosophical character of the values and magnitudes that reveal to us—that is, evoke—the symbol of Nature.

In summary: All specifications, which are the states of consciousness acquired during the human ontogeny, from the beginning of genesis to the present finality, place man in a relation of consciousness (although cerebrally unconscious) with the Universe. Because man is, in principle, the final term of all genesis (as present man he is still in a state of genesis moving toward this absolute end), the whole Universe appears to him to be populated by *residual* terms, but to which his innate consciousness is vitally related. His mind—his cerebral or psychological consciousness—consists of an objectification, a type of external projection of this innate consciousness that reveals time to him, time being the function of genesis, as a relative measure of duration, and it creates for him the illusion of movement by means of the *succession* of the phases within this genesis. The specificity of the phases is what distinguishes them and provides the mental illusion of the object. Exotericism, that is to say, the objective mental appearance, should serve as a guide for thought, but on the condition that it consider only the vital reality to be the philosophical magnitude that an object symbolizes. These philosophical magnitudes are metaphysical forces, or *neters,* that act, resist, or react.

This discussion leads us to the definition of the "Original Mystery." Are we dealing here with a supposition, a line of reasoning, that is, with speculation? The answer to this question would lead us deeper into Hermetic philosophy, to which a considerable amount of pharaonic evidence points us. We cannot commit ourselves to such a study here, however absorbing. It is by way of a path less probing but more accessible that we must attempt to answer the question raised by the mystery of the origin.

The chemical energies known as acidity and alkalinity show most clearly an application of the active and passive principles. *They are only known by their effects.* Moreover, Lavoisier's deadening formula, "Nothing is lost; nothing is created," which asserted that the world does, did, and will contain only a small number of simple substances that combine, decompose, recombine, and so on, has only recently received its final blow.[13] The atom is energy and its electronic layers emit photons, nonquantitative energy. The absurdity of Lavoisier, on which the materialism of the last century was founded, will be swept away, and microphysics will reveal a world of energy as the source of matter. For the time being, it is still only exotericism because the Western mentality is mechanistic; it needs a moving body, a carrier of energy. It appears, nevertheless, that negative and positive electrons exist and that one requires the presence of the other, just as the imaginary axis requires a north and a south pole. The physicist is unwilling to break the circle that opens the door to philosophy, but the evidence of activity with no material base will one day force him to do so.

In biology, the great mystery is the existence, in all living beings, of albumin or albuminoid (proteinaceous) matter. One albuminoid substance can be coagulated by heat (the white of an egg is of this type) and another cannot. The albuminoid substance carrying the spermatozoa is of this latter type. The albuminoid sperm cannot be coagulated because it carries the spermatozoa that coagulate the albuminoid substance of the female ovum. As soon as one spermatozoon has penetrated the ovum, this ovum coagulates on its surface, thus preventing any further penetration:[14] fertilization has occurred. The spermatozoon therefore plays the part of a "vital coagulating fire," just as common fire coagulates the feminine albumin. This is the *action* of a masculine fire in a cold, passive, feminine environment. Here also, there are always material carriers for these energies, but they manifest the existence of an energy with an active male aspect and a passive female aspect that submits. Ordinary fire brutally coagulates the white of an egg, but the spermatozoon gently coagulates it in specifying it into an embryo of its species. This image shows that the potentiality of the seed has a definite effect through the coagulation of a passive substance, similar to the action of an acid liquid in an alkaline liquid, which forms a specific salt. Now the sperm is no more acid than the male albumin, but it plays the same role as acid in the animal kingdom; ordinary fire is neither male nor acid and yet it has a type of male and acid action. This and other considerations incline the philosopher to speak of an Activity that is positive, acid, and coagulating, without material carrier, and of a Passivity, a substance that is negative, alkaline, and coagulable, also without material carrier. From their interaction results the initial, not-yet-specified coagulation, the threefold Unity, which is also called the "Creative Verb" because the Verb, as speech, only signifies the name, that is, the definition of the "specificity" of things. Before this emission there is no genesis, that is, there is no time. The source of this polarized energy is, logically, necessarily a nonpolarized energy that—because it is unique and not threefold—escapes all cerebral comprehension. This source, because it is the beginning and end of all things, is also the universal consciousness, for in it, necessarily and potentially, all possibilities are contained. Even if the mystery of the scission of this origin into Two and Three can be demonstrated experimentally, its comprehension—therefore its description—remains and always will remain impossible; for the cerebral intelligence, this is the impenetrable Mystery.

[13] For the physicist, this is not accurate. With the discovery of the energetic character of the atom, Lavoisier's axiom is not denied but sidestepped. Historical materialism is not affected, for the thought of the physicists has remained "quantitative." It is no prophecy, however, to foresee that it will be necessary to break the "quantitative" circle to open the door to philosophy.

[14] In reality, this impenetrability is not caused by a material obstacle, the solid shell, but by the fact that the two equal energetic polarities repel each other.

In order to illustrate the intangibility of this coagulating energy, the sages in all times have curiously used the same symbols.

1. In a Hermetic text that goes back to the Middle Ages entitled *A Dialogue between Mary and Aros,*[15] in which Mary plays the part of the feminine, original substance, Aros inquires: "O Prophetess, tell me . . . if one can make the Work from a single thing?" She replies: "Yes, and yet Hermes has not spoken of it because the root of Science is . . . [*sic*] and a venom . . . [*sic*] that coagulates Mercury by its 'odor.'"
2. In the hall of birth, called the "room of the theogamy" of the temple of Luxor,[16] it is said at the moment of fertilization: "and the odor of the god pervades the palace. . . ."
3. The step that leads to the altar of Amun's barque in room VI—the naos of Alexander—has a great slab at its base on which is chiseled the front portion of an ithyphallic Min whose shoulder, phallus, and foot are visible. This step is called "the step of the odor."
4. In the fifth key of the *Twelve Keys of Basil Valentine,* in order to explain the abstract character of this "Fire," Basil gives the symbol of an image reflected in a mirror: "One sees the image but cannot touch it."

It is difficult to speak of fortuitous coincidences when through millennia one finds the same images used to designate these abstractions. One is very much tempted to see here a science rather than pure speculation, a secret and sacred science that tends to show what words cannot convey.

Theoretically, it may seem unimportant whether a philosophy is founded on the Unique or on the threefold Unity. But the latter leads to a positivist and rational mentality, within which even dialectical materialism is found. In cerebral "objectivism," we will always find an argument "for or against," because it is the instrument of the world of complements and antinomies. The more the argument is founded on the apparent fact, the firmer it will be within this mentality, and the philosophy of the ternary itself thus creates its antagonist, because, in order to remain pure, it demands faith, a faith surrounded by rational arguments.

Thought founded on the Unique leads to a metaphysical and vitalist philosophy that does not take appearances for reality. It does not hesitate to speak of metaphysical "powers" and to aim at ultraphysical objectives. The function alone is important to it and not the functioning instrument. It gives all its attention to the intellective center of that which the exoteric senses show it, that is, the symbols that are the appearances. *And these centers of intelligence are the moments of identification between that which is innate in man during his becoming and that which cosmically surrounds him.*

In the pharaonic empire, with its single river, thinking governed by the Unique becomes one with this life, which for the mechanistic rationalist remains the insoluble mystery.

—∿—

Generation, whether metallic or human, whether "creation" or procreation through seed, represents a reduction into *volume* of an energy that is neither volume nor space. Volume alone is space. It is a quantity, a nonmaterial substance contracted into matter, just as at a lower level an albuminoid substance is coagulated by heat or by a seed. This means that at the origin there is a nonpolarized energy, an abstraction that can be called the indivisible Unity, the Unique.

---

[15] W. Salmon, ed., *Bibliothèque des philosophes alchimiques ou hermétiques* (Paris: Cailleau, 1741).

[16] Room IX of our plan.

The same energetic state finds its *analogues* at all the stages of the becoming of "volumes," but these volumes already have bodies that, in the end, will be animal albuminoids.

Such a genesis includes the magnitude time and is directly expressed in three dimensions. It therefore represents a time-volume unity. The first tangible product of genesis, starting from nonpolarized energy, includes a primary octave that, in numbers, represents the passage from the indivisible One to the first divisible unity, Two. These are the seven and the nine stages of *genharmony*,[17] expressing the *law of genesis*.

For genesis, the magnitudes time and space within volume are identical. Genesis is the transition from potentialities or possibilities to the present state. It is the function of qualification, or specification of the metaphysical moment into the physical moment, in other words—theologically and philosophically—*the Verb into tone*. (A parallel may be made with the breath that becomes speech.)

Any specification represents a disposition for or against another specification (an affinity); it is therefore a first expression of consciousness. Now, the first specification represents the manifestation of a state potentially contained within the Unique and formulated by genharmony. (This enables us to speak of an in-formation of consciousness when we are speaking of genesis.)

This becoming relates to the Creation and to the esoteric function of the Creation; it will govern the phenomenal function beginning with the number Two, the first space defined in volume, the first tone (following the first octave).

With the first tone, or volume, the exoteric, created world begins, volume entering into relationship with volume, which is only a scission between time and space. The scale then reveals the numbers and through them all possible functions, that is, all consciousness and all the internal relationships of matter.

This concerns the exotericism of the world and therefore the relation of quantities to each other, quantities for which time is separated from space, and for which new relations arise through movement.

Such are the two positions of consciousness: absolute consciousness, and *consciousness of consciousness,* which develops until the cerebral instrument is formed.

The existence of the exoteric world does not mean the cessation of the esoteric world, because the volume (the thing) grows old in itself, moving from its origin to its end. This aging is a continuation of the process of the corporification of energy, and therefore of consciousness, and therefore of the activity of this absolute, nonpolarized energy becoming polarized energy. This transformation—or the reduction of substance into matter—is a becoming into weight of energy, exoterically constituting the magnitude of matter we call mass. The limit of the internal becoming is determined by the cessation of the activity of the origin within this volume, its utmost energetic inertia. Then its reaction begins; the inertia throughout the body becomes reactively active. This is the return. This internal vitality also has its analogous image in the relationships of volumes to one another, that is, in the relative relations of quantities.

That which created time-volume unity was absolute energy; that which created weight was the extreme reabsorbtion of the energy. Likewise, the extreme movement that created time-space unity, and the slowing down of this speed, corresponds to the separation into time and space, just as its cessation produces extreme gravity in the relation of bodies to one another.

In vital (or esoteric) aging, perfect maturity (extreme corporification) is the moment of greatest weight. Then begins a new and last phase of aging, which is the return through reactivity. The

---

[17] Here this word means harmony and genesis, that is, harmony within genesis.

original activity is then in a *body* and has no more influence on *this* body. Now, it is the body that acts. This is the moment in which consciousness is integrally corporified and, paradoxically, in which it becomes independent of the body: the body itself becomes energy, being no longer the support of an energy, no longer the container but wholly the contents. Similarly, speed becomes inert mass and inertia becomes speed-energy. It no longer then has the same character as it had at the origin, for it contains time-space and movement, whereas, at the origin, it was simple nonpolarized energy.

The polarization of energy has made its potentialities actual, and this realization places these possibilities within its final activity.

Thus consciousness, which at the origin is a monad, becomes in the end a threefold unity through the experience of corporification.

EVOLUTIONISM

No hieratic text, no founding religious "revelation," no traditional text, speaks of evolution as it is understood in the West. Our evolutionary theories arise from purely exoteric observations of vital phenomena, from the juxtaposition of various individuals whose kinship we want to establish on a material basis: adaptation to the environment, transformation by heredity, and, finally, gene mutation. Mutation is also only an observation, and it explains nothing.

Now, corporeal evolution by itself must be excluded. Adaptations to the environment may modify the senses and the organs, but not transform them to the point of changing the species.

A transcendent cause is required to account for movement up the ladder in the hierarchy of beings. Atrophies are possible, but any transformation from the inert being to the organized being, from the primitive form to that of *Homo sapiens,* represents a *qualitative* transformation that corporeal nature refuses. These are transformations that require an energetic action, transcending the corporeal form, and having the same character as transubstantiation, which is acknowledged in the mystery of the Catholic Mass. Now, the variety of species and types of beings populating the Universe requires this incomprehensible reality of a qualitative transformation.

The materialistic mentality—that is, the thinking that supposes it can give a physicochemical (and therefore mechanical) explanation for phenomena and that, as a consequence, has put forward evolutionary theories—is now at an impasse: there is an energy at the origin of phenomena. This is still not a reason for a change of direction, but biologists are already straddling the province of mutation theory.

One can purify a metal or a chemical substance; one can select a pure race from a species; one has then isolated an existing quality, but has neither created nor increased it qualitatively.

The senses can be sharpened, the muscles and organic functions can be strengthened, sensitivity and even intuition can be cultivated; that which exists can always be improved, but nobody, no method, can *create* what Nature has not already given, except through syntheses and hybrids.

Everything that exists in time, all that was, is, and will be, necessarily exists, *potentially,* in a "pan-seminal," that is, unique, causal state.

It is this state of cosmic potentiality that I call *creative consciousness,* for which psychological consciousness is, in the end, only a phenomenon of the ego, through the cerebral organ. This cosmic consciousness does not have to *evolve,* but rather by "in-forming itself," it clothes itself in matter whose specificity—that is, its particular nature—is only a phenomenal manifestation of a particularity of the cosmic consciousness in the proc=ess of becoming innate consciousness. Thus the weight, density, hardness, color, chemical affinities, and so on, of inorganic matter are innate consciousness, as are all specific appearances of organic matter, and, in living beings, the organs and their functions. Innate consciousness does not think, does not want, and cannot make a mistake.

There is a guideline for this "materialization" or "incarnation" of the cosmic consciousness. It constitutes a directive that is the *genetic law* of the Universe. The stages of this genesis are invariably defined but offer with respect to each other innumerable possibilities for interaction, which does not affect the journey of the universal genesis, but interposes all possible varieties between the essential stages.

This incarnation is what I mean by the *evolution of consciousness*. In fact, the issue is one of successive phenomenal appearances of moments of consciousness, not of an evolution of consciousness itself.

Now, this succession juxtaposes individuals that are characterized by their own permanent specificities. For the individual to be able to move to the next higher stage, that is, to a widening of innate consciousness, thus creating a new instrument for its phenomenal expression, which represents a *qualitative evolution,* this individual's material form must be integrally brought back to its component energetic elements. This is the Hermetic thesis that applies to all Nature.

If we then look upon individuals in their variations presented by Nature, we see them as a "sequence of points" separated from one another, for which we seek vainly to understand the bond that unites them through their apparent forms. Corporeal evolution is discontinuous, but the phenomenal widening of cosmic consciousness, the fulfillment of its formal expression (genesis), is continuous.

Genesis is therefore the *evolution* of the phenomenal expression of cosmic consciousness.

Chapter 2

SYMBOLIQUE

THE MAGICAL CHARACTER OF THE SYMBOL

In a theological symbolique *the proliferation of symbols can veil the true implied meaning, but the symbol in itself is always revelatory. Every action depicted in the* symbolique, *every spontaneous or reasoned gesture, complies with an impulsion whose functional character is cosmic.*

Nothing is more difficult for human intelligence to access than natural simplicity. The everyday phenomenon is overlooked because of its banality and is made unintelligible to the complexities of thought.

This is why initiation in no way corresponds to the image we have of it, and once the moment of initiation into natural mysteries is over (whether for an individual, religious group, or, more generally, for an age), the imagination immediately comes in to weave fancy around fact. The fact being sacred, we would like its sacred character to be wrapped in an adorning literature; we cannot conceive of it in its simple and natural measure; we place it on a pedestal in order to exalt it, wishing to present it to the human imagination in its most precious aspect, that is, as a rare thing that pleases the senses.

And "around the empty hub we build the golden wheel." Those who are the guardians of knowledge and know it to be incommunicable are the first to gild the outer court that leads to the inaccessible sanctuary. Is it to guard? Is it to hide? Is it to teach? To guard is to preserve the treasure; to hide it is to control it; to teach is to open the way to the successors of the guardian caste, and it is also to select in order to find the one who—perchance—will rediscover "the lost word."

Such is the historic drama of all priesthoods, of all the clergy of the initiatory religions. Simple doctrine rapidly becomes complicated, analysis multiplies the imagery, this false symbolism that conceals under the pretext of teaching.

The most incomprehensible aspect of human nature is its search for the true understanding of natural things through substitutes. Why does man resort to symbolism? Is it possible for him not to want it? Symbolism both conceals and teaches, and the more complicated the teaching becomes, the more it conceals and removes one from knowledge: the effect runs contrary to its own purpose.

Yet whatever artifice is used to carry the symbolism, in some way or other it remains related to truth; literary complexity alone does not reveal this connection, for it is guided by a real link that compels recognition. Any symbol belonging to, or represented by, a myth can be chosen to illustrate this fact. Whether it be Wotan's staff, the wings outspread around Ra's solar disc, "Berthe au grand pied"* or Master Jacques, the cross, the falcon of Horus, each speaks clearly through its *functional* expression.

Every symbol, even one beyond interpretation, is in itself directly related to the thing that it expresses—that it is—that it represents perhaps, but certainly through that which it evokes. Thus wings can be nothing other than what evokes the fact of flying. That which flies can be nothing other than what rises and escapes the earth; this can be nothing other than the volatile principle, one of the principles of the original separation.

In this way, we finally see that there are several simple principles that, like archangels, preside over everything, shining forth with innumerable rays throughout the world. Each archangel is in that case one of these suns of primordial nature. It becomes impossible to *imagine* anything that does not come under their dominion, and the evocation of anything—image, word, or gesture—is at the same time the evocation of the principle and its momentary fixation, which at that instant is quite real. The symbol is thus the expression of a will; it is magic.

Every circle, as a circular movement, has a center. This center controls this continuous and regular curve, which is closed; it is attractive, just as the circumference is repellent (centrifugal). This center is an abstract power that rules the phenomenon of elliptical (or assimilated) movement if the curve is closed. If the curve is not closed but is superimposed, the center becomes a line or a figure, horizontal for a spiral, vertical for a helicoidal curve, and so on.

The center controls; it is the *will of the figure.* Three axes[1] of equal length, intersecting at 90°, are the *will* of the cube. The form of the movement and the form of the Euclidean volume are in the center and in its extension.

I say that the will of a rotating sphere is the magnetic axis, and its equator is the centrifugal electrical effect. Moreover, any magnetic effect is a contracting will that by reaction calls for the dilating, equatorial electrical effect. Conversely, every circular electric current provokes the magnetic axial effect. Will is esoteric; effect is exoteric.

But where, then, is the will of the "container" of the volume?

Its will is the seed, that is, the specification of the "contents," hence a genesis, that is, time, for time is none other than genesis; genesis appears to us as time.

Now, all will of movement and of form is a specification of energy. Will is thus identified with the seed, as the specifier, and, as genesis, appears as time or duration.

The seed ordains the volume, that is, space; the genesis of this space ordains time. Will is what Lao-tzu called "the empty hub of the wheel."[2]

---

[1] Lines of force.

[2] In the *Tao te Ching,* Lao-tzu, the magnificent sage, says (roughly): "The wheel has twelve spokes that meet at the center. Neither the rim nor the spokes make the wheel; it is the empty hub that makes the wheel." ["Thirty spokes unite at the hub but the ultimate use of the wheel depends on the part where nothing exists." From *The Book of Tao,* trans. Frank J. MacHovec (Mount Vernon, N.Y.: Peter Pauper Press, 1962).]

* Mother Goose.

The Absolute Will of the Origin includes all specifications. Everything that is naturally specified is a symbol and the expression of a will, hence of a specifying seed of nonobjectifiable energy—the container of nonpolarized Spirit-substance. The specifying will, the "Fire" of the seed, was called the "odor" by the Ancient Egyptians, the "odor of the *neter,*" that is, in an esoteric sense, that which is emanated by the *neter* like the fire of an ejected seed.

The contained will must always be sought in the symbol, when the symbol is chosen for an esoteric teaching. The character of this will is that which will always compel spirit—nonpolarized energy—to define itself in time and space, hence in the *form* of the symbol. This is the "magical" meaning of the symbol. With regard to Spirit, this magic operates as the Platonic Idea just as rhythm acts on our will of movement: we obey it in spite of and against everything, even when we do not give in.

SYMBOL-SYNTHESIS

The word *symbol,* derived and distorted from its usual Greek meaning signifying a sign of recognition or password, has become synonymous with the representation of a concept by means of a conventional sign. For example, the assemblage of the parts of a broken shard, which could also be represented by a torn-up note or calling card, meant—probably in a popular sense—the symbol or sign of recognition.

Nowadays any letter or image that is substituted for the development of an idea is called a symbol (such as a chemical symbol for simple or compound substances, an acronym used to denote a group, or a spokesperson or other figure for a trademark); but a single conventional letter in a mathematical operation (such as the coefficient π for the circle, h for Planck's constant, m for mass, or c for the speed of light, and so on) is also with each letter requiring a long elaboration to explain the meaning, *thus summarized.* Whether it is a natural or a compound image, or a conventional sign, *the property of the symbol is to be a summarizing representation, which is commonly called a synthesis.*

When, in chemistry, one wishes to represent a compound, the parts can be assembled in a static two- or three-dimensional form, and one has recourse to an image either in plane or in volume. These images are called symbols, that is, they are syntheses and not the true representation of the compound. They serve only as support (intuitively situated in the plane) for an essentially quantitative function that is probably indeterminable in time and space.

It is a property of thought to need a support, a hypothesis of a determined character that can be called an intuition-base, forming a scaffolding for the expression of learning through series and groups, implied ideas, surroundings, analogies—in short, all that radiates out from this symbol-synthesis.[3] Evolved thought, which is only a widening of consciousness, then rids itself of this support. It could be put this way: *The abstract Spirit needs a concrete support, which, by its nature, must be the synthesis—situated in space and time—of the form to be given to the Spirit so that it may have available the body necessary for experience. Later, this support will be cast off, leaving the new concept in its purity.*

We can distinguish three types of synthesis and three types of symbol. First is the *vital synthesis,* which is the natural symbol, and its expression (for example, tangible form, characteristic word or sound, and color) is the *pure symbol.* Second is the *action of synthesis* or *pseudosymbol,* such as the word, the vocable, replacing the image, defining the concept. Third is the *synthesizing effect*

---

[3] Until now in this chapter the word *synthesis* has been used in the sense of "combined group" and not as a true synthesis or potentiality of a cause.

of thought, or *psychological synthesis* represented by the *parasymbol,* through the conventional symbol summarizing a thought. All these aspects of "synthesis" are the *symbols* of the set of functions, and then of the *assemblage of the parts* that "synthesis," in the ordinary sense of the word, implies.

Thus, the symbol serves equally well for the objectification of thought as for a system of references; but in its esoteric sense it will act as a psychological synthesis when it evokes the functions, and thus the nonobjectifiable qualitative relationships through its determined form.

Today the new scientific thought should clearly appeal to two forms of intelligence, since experiment and observation require a deterministic position in time and space, while demonstrating the indeterminablility of the simultaneity imposed by the phenomenon. For the objective intelligence, it could be said that there is a past and a future, *but never a present,* and that, for (absolute) Reality, there is an eternal, invariable present, outside of time.

The important thing, however, is not the relative but the invariable truth. In this sense, the natural and objective symbol must not be considered as an invariable reality; it is not truth, but it is evocative of "reality." It is *objectively* determined in time and space but, as simultaneity (synthesis), it is outside of time. In its aspect of "authentic synthesis,"[4] the symbol is the eternal "present moment" because the same concurrence of conditions that brought about its becoming will always compel it to be again what it is; this prescribes the notion of identity, which is objectively inconceivable.

There is a reversal of positions for the two intelligences: for the objective intelligence, there is determinism, where for the unexpressed intelligence (innate knowledge), there is indeterminism. Moreover, what for the objective intelligence is the indeterminism of simultaneity, becomes the determined reality for the unformulated, intuitive intelligence.

The symbol acts as the link between the rational intelligence and the intelligence today called "surrational"; the latter can only be expressed in mathematical form. We are dealing here with a new consciousness or, epistemologically speaking, a new state of the power of thought. This power seems to have been well known and evident to the Ancient Egyptians, because everything they expressed is built on the knowledge of this dualism of intelligence, which tradition calls exotericism and esotericism.

The popular view of the Egyptian symbol reduces it to an elementary meaning that is arbitrary, utilitarian, and singular, whereas it is *in reality* a synthesis that requires great erudition for its *analysis* and a special culture for the esoteric knowledge that it implies—which does not exclude the necessity of being "simple" or of knowing how to "simply look" at the symbol.

INNATE KNOWLEDGE (A SUMMARY)

Each time an activity and its consequent reaction have produced a phenomenon by the total exhaustion of the energies involved, this phenomenon counts as one; that is, it constitutes an individuality. Egyptian calculation, by fractions, proceeds in this way just as, in another sense, our mathematics does. In relation to a new function, the symbol counts as one.

Thus, the symbol is the characteristic principle of Pythagorean number: there is "the enumerating number" and "the enumerable number" of ordinary arithmetic, and the "nonenumerable number" of the science of number, the new unity, an entity that results from the "vital linking-up" of the component numbers and not from a quantitative addition.

[4] In other words, as "seed or potential form about to be generated."

There is, for example, a trunk and its branches, constituting a tree. This tree, as such, has new qualities; it is a whole, a new individual. In another category, one can also say that a bouquet is a whole representing what each of the flowers composing it cannot be separately.

We count five fingers, and this number five is no longer an addition of five units, but *a hand* with new qualities and a particular power that no single finger alone can have. Thus, in the Pythagorean sense, each number is a unity in itself, an entity, an individuality, and as such it is nonenumerable.

Conclusions based on statistics, which serve the collective need, are in error with respect to the individual, because the group is "a whole," a new being; its energy is new, and its tendencies are different from those of its constituent units. Therefore, after research on the atom, it will be necessary to return to the study of the complex (the group), since—*for the rational, scientific method*—the simple is impenetrable.

In our symbolic approach it is understood that the individual is itself composed of a group, but through this group it has become an individuality, that is, a unity independent of other, similar unities. Thus each part of what composes it can no longer be regarded as an individuality, and can no longer even be objectified. Thus, one may only speak of qualitative or energetic "principles."[5]

The vital experience of the individuality becomes its own and can only affect the principles of its own constitution. It is this modification, introduced into the energetic whole constituting the individuality, that specifies the latter; the vital experience modifies its *specialization* in a constant manner, constituting its acquired experience, which then alone will influence the genes and their mutation—will create what I call "cerebrally unconscious consciousness," or *innate knowledge.*

Thanks to this innate knowledge we are able to *recognize;* through evocation, the sensorial observation of the symbol will cause the "Intellect," the living soul, to react.

THE PRINCIPLE OF THE
PRESENT MOMENT

Time is measured by movement. At each instant movement can only be completed or about to start. It cannot be otherwise, for it cannot be past and future "at the same time." The present moment cannot therefore be situated: it is outside of time, because it is outside measurable movement. It presents the conditions of an absolute.

It is from this absolute that we constantly draw our forces. The cell reproduces itself by dying. This passage from One to Two is its "present moment," which cannot be situated in time, even though the phases of karyokinesis succeed one another in order to generate a new cell. The present moment is "that which compels the nucleus to divide in two."

Each instant of life is negation and affirmation "at the same time," that is, absence of time. We can, by extension, speak of a duration as being the *present* hour or age, for example. But each moment of this hour or age is a "collision" between the impulsion of the past and the obstacle of the future.

Only by situating ourselves outside the continuity of time can we speak of a "presence." For example, a given person is present; he or she is not elsewhere, but here, in a definite space, that is, a movement arrested in time. Thus "presence" belongs to the past and not to the future. Presence is a symbol, a placement in time and space, *but the present moment is eternity.*

---

[5] The *neter* is a principle, but it was not used as a word meaning "principle" in Ancient Egypt. *Neter* is clumsily translated as "God," a word that in Judeo-Christian deism means the absolute Unity. The Greek *daimon* would be more suitable. But why not simply say *neter* to which, phonetically at least, the word *nature* is related? Natural principle = *neter.*

THE DISCONTINUOUS OBJECT IN THE CONTINUOUS PRESENT

In the vital phenomenon, genesis is the dynamic aspect;[6] any moment of the functional relationships that constitute genesis will be the vital moment. The vital moment can be objectively known only when it is stopped by death; this is then its static moment, signifying its negation. Therefore it is not the vital moment but only its effects, that is, its *fixed* effects, the stages of genesis, that can be known objectively.

Because of this contradiction, objective comprehension of "static-dynamic" simultaneity is impossible; but it is possible to juxtapose, or to compare, the intuitive (unexpressed) intelligence of the vital dynamism with the objective and static (situated) symbol of the vital moment, its current stage.

This state of comparison—that is, of juxtaposition of an objective state, unstable in time, with an ever present state of simultaneity—should not be confused with the juxtaposition of two worlds, or two "presences." In the present moment, everything mingles, including all the instants of the genesis of everything. The present moment is a nonobjectifiable dimension containing all volumes. From the point of view of space (or volume), it is *necessity* that compels being to exist in determined conditions; it is also, in the sense of time, the *possibility* immanent in each object at each instant. For esotericism, therefore, *creation* is constant, but for exotericism, it is situated: "In the beginning . . ."

The unexpressed comprehension of simultaneity is synthesis, and not synthesizing; it is the esoteric meaning, whereas exotericism is necessarily analytic. Consequently, in this sense, the symbol is the object, outside ourselves, that awakens innate knowledge through the senses. This creates our intuitive knowledge of the simultaneous, a continuity in which a discontinuity is situated.

For example, the image of a flying bird is the symbol of the flight of a winged animal. This image is a static moment (arrested in time) of this function of flight, its fixation. This symbol awakens in us not only what we have registered in our memory concerning the flight of birds but also our innate knowledge of flight, our *sensation of flight,* and we embody this knowledge in the image-symbol, which thus becomes a synthesis of *our* knowledge of the flight of the bird. What matters is not the image but the symbol-synthesis of the function of the vital moment.

The image is death, but the symbol of this image is life. In relation to life, death is nothing but a fixation in time, hence a false eternity. True eternity must be sought in the innate, unexpressed consciousness, which becomes the intuitive knowledge of simultaneity.

Now, it would require omniscience to be able to discern all the possibilities contained in a symbol, and that would imply "innate knowledge" of the whole Universe. Consequently, in order to make practical use of the symbol, a system consisting in a choice of the possibilities that are to be sought in it would appear inevitable. But to attempt to establish a rational system (which is possible, if need be) would be to fall back into an exoteric interpretation that would deprive the symbol of any possibility of speaking esoterically. *The choice must be made by the reader, solely in the light and to the degree of his own innate knowledge.*

It is sufficient to note the principles to which the symbols conform in order to learn, and then to seek in oneself, the summarized meaning of their synthesis. It is also necessary to know that, for example, the choice of an animal as a symbol was guided in Ancient Egypt by a profound knowl-

---

[6] The word *dynamic* is used here in the sense of an unspent impulse that engenders a vital sequence, or genesis, and not in the kinematic sense of displacement in space.

edge of the life of that animal, of its vital characteristics, its habits, its mode of assimilation, the length of its gestation, its mating patterns (the season and often the time of day), and so on.[7] *In the anthropocosmic doctrine, each animal is a stage of the universal gestation, the goal of which, for us, in the meantime, is humanity—present* Homo sapiens.

RELATIONSHIP IS THE SYMBOL OF BEING

Being, as existence, manifests only through relationship—that is, the interchange—between the two component complements of Being. We call complements the two specific qualities of a thing, one of which denies the other.

For instance, brightness and shadow make light. Without shadow, no object would be visible, so that if brightness were without shadow, we would no more know light than does a blind man. This proposition can also be reversed: the blind man is he who lives in a brightness without shadow, which is often true.

Another widely known example is that of complementary colors, such as red and green, yellow and purple, orange and blue. Superimposed (by subtraction), these complements annul all color and (theoretically) produce black; added together, they (theoretically) produce white light.

Complements do not exist separately, any more than the North Pole exists without the South Pole; they are the abstract components of Being; they are, essentially, the active and passive, male and female principles.[8] The mechanical passive state, which is merely a lesser activity, should not be confused with the vital passive principle.

In the vital state, the complements are the poles of a single axis and not a relative state, as would be the relationship between two bodies moving at different speeds. *The passive principle is an inverse activity.*[9] There is an interchange of activities, an exchange of energy; hence the possibility of addition and subtraction, of mutual annihilation or exaltation. This *relationship* is thus the symbol of Being: the thing.

The symbol links complements, demonstrates Being, implies positive and negative activities; it is the transient, phenomenal aspect between the causal abstraction and its negation. Thus the symbol must always be considered as a *relationship* between two abstract and complementary elements.

For example, the hare is not a symbol for the hunter, because he considers the hare in regard to other game animals: foxes, partridges, quails. The hare can only be a symbol in relation to itself, that is, as the resultant of the vital data that is "specifically hare." Consequently, the same food will produce a hare in the case of a hare, and a rabbit in the case of a rabbit. *To be a hare* means, above all, to be a specific ferment that transforms all energy it receives (the air it breathes and solid and liquid food) into hare. For this reason all the physical and psychical characteristics, as well as all the activities of this hare, will be manifest in this symbol. The hare-symbol, as a relationship between the principles of its specific seed, is a typal phase, situated embryologically (in the cosmic sense) within the becoming of the ultimate being toward which Nature tends. Its image can thus express the entire complex of this phase, and a nuance in its figuration can accentuate a principle of particular note.

---

[7] From among all the varieties of a type, the Egyptian *symbolique* never hesitated to choose the characteristic elements it wished to accentuate, thus creating a composite image that our scholars labor in vain to place in a schematic classification.

[8] The Chinese *yin* and *yang*.

[9] In this regard let us note that Spirit, or formless substance, is passive. It is the feminine cosmic principle. It is through the effect of the *odor*, which is the "acting Verb," that this Verb, through the feminine principle, falls into Nature. (For "odor," see p. 43.)

SYMBOLIQUE

The *symbolique* is the means of expression—the writing—of "vitalist" philosophy; the symbol is its vital argument or language. Because the symbol, as we have already said, is the static form of relationship between two moments incomprehensible in their simultaneity, the juxtaposition of symbols allows for the expression, without formulation, of identities in nature that can, moreover, manifest as opposed dualities.

It is evident that in a vitalist philosophy the symbol should act as the concept. But this concept has value only through the implied idea, since it is merely the relation between this idea and its complement. The symbol is thus the language of a logical function rather than a concept included in a quantitative syllogistic function.

This philosophy is that of the vital and "nonquantitative" play, that is, it relates functions only and not factors, and thus it cannot include an equational play of the syllogism, for which the facts—even when abstract—are made objectifiable through comparison. For instance, karyokinesis is in itself a nonobjectifiable function. It is comprehensible only in its static moments and not in its vital, dynamic moment. The essence of this function is the scission of a unity; the resulting duality confirms this for us. It is not this duality that is the scission; *this scission, inasmuch as it is will, is identical with the original scission, or Creation,* but is distinguishable from the latter by the fact that it works on something quantitatively divisible. In every function there is that moment that cannot be situated in time that I call the "present moment." It is this *esoteric* moment with which the *symbolique* is concerned; and the symbol plays in it the role of the language that conveys this implied functional idea. This indefinable idea can never be known except through the certainty of our innate knowledge, which assures us of this reality that is *necessarily implied* in the symbol. For instance, when a stone falls, this fact implies an attraction that we do not know in itself, but know only through a juxtaposition of the quantitative elements of an analysis that can be formulated into laws. We may speak of an attracting mass, but this tells us nothing more about what this attraction is.

The falling of the stone is an esoteric symbol if we consider it in terms of the implied idea, but if we regard this fall as being situated in time and space, it is only an *exoteric* fact, from a quantitative learning. Now, it is the "function of that which attracts," of the will to unite, that is the cosmic reality and not the actual attraction, which only acts as such within a certain aspect of matter, *as microphysics has recently revealed.*

Thus, vital philosophy, as expressed by the *symbolique,* is concerned with the eternal vital moment and not its accidental applications, in which it can always modify its appearance.

Can one reason, that is, construct a system of *vital logic,* under these conditions? Certainly, if one does not seek a conclusion arrested in time and space. It is life, dynamism in itself, that matters; the revelation of the symbol, then, is universal. This means that there is no difference in the vital moment with respect to the condition in which it manifests. For example, if a certain plant is aphrodisiac for the bull, there is in this plant the same functional state (we may recall here the Arcanum* of Paracelsus) as that which, for the bull, causes its sexual irritation. There is a functional identity. Moreover, if this plant (a static moment or symbol in the Universe) exists and likewise the bull exists (or even if this type of bull exists no more), the reality—or Idea—of this plant *is, was,* and always *will be;* it corresponds (as an analogue) to a phase of the cosmic genesis that will persist, because of the fact of constant creation.

---

* A Hermetically prepared medicine.

Herein lies a basis for the solution of the problem of original causality. When, through analysis, one arrives at the energetic origin of matter, the *principle of original causality* may be questioned insofar as one insists on seeing in the phenomenon only a quantitative sequence, and as long as life is regarded as a biophysicochemical (and today, of course, microphysical) effect. The border is pushed back; it is not crossed. This reduces the "cause" in general to a dynamic effect of quantity, a dynamism caused by the very nature of the energetic constitution of the atom. In this case, energy is seen only as polarized energy, that is, as an energetic *effect*, and not an original cause.

Einstein defines energy as an effect of mass and of the speed of its movement;[10] therefore, there is mass and there is movement, and thus there is also time and space, whatever subterfuge is used to set this fact aside, even if this mass is a state of energy.

Could we conceive of science without a system of reference? That would be a *Fiat lux*, hence a cause outside the system.

The problem, which we thought was definitely set aside at the end of the last century, arises again today, for we now find ourselves before an impasse. We resolve by acknowledging that everything is, in the end, light, the ultimate system of reference: c, the speed of the propagation of light. Now, is light a cause? If so, in what does it act? And if it is an effect, what is its cause? Does the coefficient c have the same value in all environments? Does it always have the same nature?

Insofar as we have not acknowledged the reality of the "present," posited as the incomprehensible moment in the phenomenal world, but which imposes itself even on the rational—as long as we do not posit the principle of the eternity of the present—the necessity for a duality, science and belief, remains; and "historians," in their interpretation of tradition, are, to a certain extent, right to distrust "symbolism."

This notion of the eternal present requires certain specifications. Exoterically we foresee that, under specific conditions, a certain cause will produce a certain effect. All know-how is based upon this foresight, which is the result of observation and constitutes a primary determination. Such empiricism enables the generalization that formulates the laws of science.

Now, philosophically, a cause is only cause at the moment it produces an effect, which is in no way certain. Under the same known conditions the same cause may fortuitously produce a very different effect. For instance, it is known today, at last, that certain influences (such as that of cosmic rays) can modify the effect of a chemical reaction.

Let us suppose a stone falls from the cornice of a house. It is too late to warn the passerby that this stone is about to kill him. We know that the stone will kill this man; we foresee this effect. What foresees? Our memory; it shows us the inevitability of this effect. This inevitability is in our imagination, created by our memory. For, in reality, this stone may be diverted from its course; or the man may move a little faster or more slowly, and the stone will miss him. In any event, the falling stone will only be the cause of the passerby being crushed (and hence will only produce its effect) if it finds in this man an obstacle to its fall. Before this point, it is not the cause.

---

[10] This speed is a limit represented by c^2 or the speed of light squared. Therefore, the mass $M = Ec^2$. In actual fact, the speed c^2 plays the role of the "mediety" that defines the equivalence between mass and energy. The real meaning of the mediety is made clear in chapter 5.

Cause and effect are not separated by any time. No chemical reaction can liberate the elements during the moment of their passage from one compound to another. Often it is gaseous bodies that *pass* thus, and no traces prove their existence in the free state.[11] Indeed, just as in biology, in the conjunction of the spermatozoon with the nucleus of the ovum,[12] as well as in the crystallization of a salt, the chemical reaction takes place *outside of time.* There are in the world, effects; but the interval of time between cause and effect does not exist. Creation is constant in the eternal present. Now, fertilization, that is, the vital moment of the conjunction, obeys the law of creation; this conjunction is instantaneous, as is, for example, the appearance of a crystal in its mother liquid. The same is true for the conjunction of chemical elements. It is always a question in this case (that is, between cause and effect) of a vital moment, which, even in inorganic matter, obeys the universal law of creation: *formless substance receives form,* since an activity is always compensated by an opposite activity, and activity signifies "dynamism in itself" before becoming mechanical (corporeal) dynamism. The effect is the neutralization of an activity, and this neutralization never occurs without the phenomenal reaction of resistance; it is simply a chain of activities, reaction being but a new activity of the first effect, hence the new cause. It is this "chain" that appears to us to be situated in time and space, whereas *it is a gestation* that is time; but between cause and effect there exists no time.[13]

The principle of the "present moment" is not a mystical doctrine, but it is a fact that has a mystical character. In exotericism one never demonstrates the cause outside of the system except *with* the system, hence in a duality one of whose poles is left to faith.

The symbol demonstrates the esotericism that, by means of the *symbolique,* unifies that which is divided and puts an end to the problem of causality. The cause, apparently outside of the system, is in it, eternally unified and present, and creation is constant. Such-and-such a phenomenon *was not;* it *is* always *in our innate knowledge,* upon which our psychological consciousness feeds and thus expands more and more with experience. Thus, light bears within itself that which acts and that in which it acts: the discontinuous within the continuous.

Light is, for true Light (the Mosaic Genesis), the symbol of the Presence that is absolute Cause-Effect. Succession, or time, as the distance between cause and effect, is a mental illusion and not a reality. This time is inconceivable, so why try to imagine it? Cause cannot be cause without producing an effect, which will be a new cause under the conditions suitable to its activity. Thus, there may be, in the sensorial appearance, a sequence of effects but never a sequence from cause to effect. Time as genesis—or genesis as time—moves in the direction of the effect becoming the new

[11] The following objections may be raised: first, the inertia of matter, and second, the fact that a chemical reaction takes place more rapidly under the effect of heat (cf. van't Hoff's laws). In the opposite direction, thermodynamics shows that at absolute zero (− 273°C), all chemical reaction must cease. Heat thus intervenes as a factor in the reaction by dispersing (liquifying) the molecular milieu, thus facilitating the reaction, but temperature in no way modifies its nature. Whether the reaction takes place rapidly or slowly, the present moment of the "passage" cannot be situated in time.

[12] Fertilization comprises the following phenomena: *(a)* Attraction of the spermatozoa by the ova; *(b)* penetration by the spermatozoon, formation of a defensive membrane, contraction of the protoplasm, and formation of a liquid between the two; *(c) division* of the center of the spermatozoon into two centrosomes, *before* the conjunction of the two pronuclei; *(d) conjunction* of the two pronuclei, while the two centrosomes separate; *(e) immediate division, which cannot be situated in time, of the new nucleus,* in which each group of chromosomes is attracted by one of the centrosomes.

[13] Let us note by this explanation that time thus becomes a quantity in "duration" through the juxtaposition of parts, a kind of granulation. These "parts" or "quantities" are the symbols of the Universe and constitute a chain that has an apparent (objective) beginning and an end.

cause. In this sense, the march of time is irreversible.[14] These are the dates of the cosmic genesis, the phases of which are the effects (the static, vital moment), the symbols—or "things"—surviving as individualities that in themselves are exhausted, *being finished as types* (the true symbols of esotericism) and no longer acting as causes.

Between the extreme original cause and the ultimate final cause (which we would like to call an effect) is the phenomenon, world, of which we know—in the different types of forms—all the "static moments," that is, the momentary corpses, which people the universe. *These are the symbols of the evolution of consciousness,* that is, of thought, through all its experiences. This is none other than the actual knowledge of the Self, still latent, in the accident of the "me."

There can be only one way in this despite the multitude of branchings. The goal is single; there is only one reality, and the most scattered, wildest, little branches send their sap to this heart.

The principle of the function being unique, there is necessarily a kinship and an analogy between the moments of the great cosmic cycles and small events on earth. For instance, if we find ourselves astronomically in the sign of Aries (in the precessional cycle), then the earth-event, in passing 2160 times through all twelve signs, will be under the influence of the "Aries vital moment," at work during each terrestrial vital moment of each sign, in Libra as much as in Leo, and so on, while *coloring* the Libra or Leo moment with its Aries temperament.

Secondary, tertiary, or even more distant (branched) events—that is, the "historic"—cannot exist independently from the *symbolique* of the moment. They become the symbol, the static synthesis-moment of cosmic life.

It is this life of the symbol, its esotericism, *identifying itself with this life,* that is Reality; it enables *that which was,* as a cosmic and historical event, actually to persist in us *from this moment forward,* because the life of the symbol is the experience of our consciousness: the consciousness of Cosmic Man who is in us and through whom we are all one.[15] And if this consciousness is particular to each person—since each individual, according to his or her faculties, may or may not recognize in it the state of the moment—it remains nonetheless universal, *present,* just as a universal container can hold all forms, just as the light-synthesis can manifest all appearances.

For esotericism, a problem of a situated, original causality does not exist. Nature, on the other hand, is the world of the creature; here everything is made dual for us in its cerebrally perceptible appearance. This is the exoteric world, the world that for us is projected outside of ourselves as "objective." Thus, as long as there is for us—as popularly expressed—the extreme aspects of God and the Devil, neither one nor the other is *real,* although they are relatively true.

Only that which is invariable and undivided is real: the present moment, which is eternal and indivisible, cerebrally incomprehensible, *but known through our innate consciousness.* This is the esoteric world, in which high and low, front and back, right and left, cease to be, making way for *spatial vision,* which, stemming from the center, can extend in all directions at once within the volume (space) that Spirit (energy) as it coagulates into matter.

---

[14] This principle of irreversibility may be contested. An effect of a genesis can be *artificially* brought back to its beginning point—therefore time, or genesis, is annulled, the *artificial* act reverses time. Now this act can be violent or supernatural, like grace or redemption or a transmutation. This is true, but it is always a question of para- or metaphysical conditions. The principle of irreversibility is therefore absolute only in the natural course of a natural genesis.

[15] For example, we can imagine that light, taking a certain time to reach a certain star 5000 light-years away from us, enables the star's inhabitants to see earth at the time of the construction of the Pyramid of Cheops. This is obviously pure fantasy, but it shows the "consciousness" or the "feeling" as well as the secret hope that an event will never be of the past, but that, in some fashion, it is always present.

This spatial becoming is our consciousness of the continuous (esoteric), and specified genesis (the becoming of time) is our consciousness of the discontinuous (exoteric) through the "situation" of the stages or phases.

CONCLUSION

A research without illumination is the character of modern, Western science. This indecision colors everything, art as well as social organization, and even, in many cases, faith.

The West is ignorant of that serenity of which all of Ancient Egypt bears the imprint. The tombs of the leaders of this people are consecrated to their profession of faith in the survival of the soul. For these men and women, death is the certainty of rebirth; terrestrial life is merely a passage; the mortal body is a temporary temple for the living soul.[16]

The West labels this attitude of wisdom a state of science that is "still mystical." But the Egyptian technique and their *symbolique* attest to a realistic sensibility and to faculties of reasoning, contradicting the view held of an age that is "primitive and mystical."

Our exoteric evolution, through the metaphysical or intellectualizing stages of the Greeks, which ends in our time at an exclusive rationalism, has given us, owing to the necessity for analysis, a "mentality of complexity" that today prevents us from seeing simply.

Cultivating simplicity of being and seeing in oneself is the first task of anyone wishing to approach the sacred *symbolique* of Ancient Egypt.[17] This is difficult because the obvious blinds us. One forgets, for example, that in sitting down to relax, all the fatigue goes to the thighs, the "support of the body." It is therefore worthwhile to study their role in the vital economy and the importance they have in terms of the *symbolique*. One forgets that in passing one's hand over one's forehead and particular parts of the skull, certain tired phrenological centers are thus magnetically vitalized. One forgets that in sleeping to restore one's energy, *the simple fact of eliminating cerebral consciousness* enables us to draw from the universal source of life, which might induce us to seek out (and find) its deeper cause.[18]

In order to know the true secrets of life, it is necessary to abandon the quite alluring but misleading arguments of science and learn how to look upon that which, by dint of our seeing, we no longer notice. Every day, at each instant, we apply "secrets" that, if we only knew how to become conscious of them, would unveil for us all the powers and all the Power that anthropocosmic man possesses.[19] There is absolutely no need to violate Nature in order to understand it, but, as the proverb says, "We do not see the forest for the trees."

In cultivating our own garden, we forget that plants grow toward the sky, that to vegetate means to rise up, and that to rise up means to make light that which is heavy, to annul gravity.

If the "group" has a new character of its own, it cannot draw it from anywhere other than from the abstract life of the individuals composing it, an abstract life that the isolated individual cannot

[16] We forget, or we are not aware, that our passage through this life is a school where consciousness must, through moral suffering, enrich itself with knowledge of all the higher states that Nature teaches us through its symbols. "Learning" is only the ABCs of the language that enables us to express ourselves so that communication among individuals becomes possible, but knowledge alone is a goal that justifies our existence and the misery of its contingencies.

[17] Simplicity here relates to the fact of "being simple" and of "seeing simply," not to "simple ideas." Seeing simply comprises two stages: first, observing, and second, accepting—observing what the symbol is without preconception, and accepting what it has to say just as it is said, adding to it neither supposition nor imagination.

[18] One can amuse oneself by seeking the reason for sleep in the elimination of toxins. This is the old habit of exotericism of moving the boundaries back instead of seeking to abolish them.

[19] Dr. Alexis Carrel had a premonition of this [in his *L'homme cet inconnu* (Paris: Plon, 1935)].

objectively reveal. For example, in Unity there is a male nature and a female nature, which are *unknowable*. The number-entity, composed of units, reveals, in the very first instance, this odd and even character.

In Nature everything is dualized, and the *high* reveals the nature of the *low*. The crown of the tree shows the nature of its roots; the bark and the nature of the wood show—without a microscope—the nature of the type of cell that makes up this tree, because, *in life, arithmetical statistics do not apply*. Doctor Carrel has shown that each cell of the heart is the heart, and beats as it does. Similarly, each cell of the liver is the liver, and so on. One could cite countless examples that cast a marvelous light on existence.

But pharaonic Egypt has summarized everything in a symbolic choice it has made from the elements of its environment, a choice so wise that we must bow low before it.[20]

Every natural type is a revelation of one of the natures and abstract functions that rule the world, a verb of the divine language, that is, of the entities or fully realized principles *(neters)*. They are fully realized in the sense that they are types or definite stages in the cosmic embryology of humanity.

Instead of starting from an imaginary construction, instead of relying on intellectual speculation, Ancient Egypt shows us the path of an infallible recognition of the forces and laws that govern the Universe, by beginning from its concrete results to seek in them the causal spirit, otherwise unknowable, because all philosophic speculation is vain if it is not confirmed by facts.

Pharaonic Egypt is essentially practical. It deals with Nature and works with natural means, in which it sees the symbols of spiritual states, knowable only intuitively. Intellectual definition, in the end, always leads to the necessity of choosing between the subjective and the objective; it resolves nothing, since it must consider everything within a situated duration, whereas Nature shows us the closed, Osirian cycle that renews itself spirally in progressing toward the liberation of consciousness.

Our mode of activity requires the prestated theory. Ancient Egypt, which is realistic, acts naturally, knowing that theory is a fixation that limits action. Thus, one could have believed it practiced a simple, empirical science, that is, a science of application without research into causes. One forgets that there is *a rigorous method dictated by myth and symbolic philosophy*.[21]

---

[20] The *symbolique* applies in all cases. Every gesture, every grimace, as well as the gleam in a person's eye, reveals his impulse or secret thought. His walk, his postures, and countless details of his behavior reveal a man's character; the aesthetic tendency of an age, the style, architecturally, and even the nature of the preferred material, are symbols of the character of a period or a people.

Thus, one can study the *symbolique* of any time and any people. If I prefer Ancient Egypt to the Maya, to India, China, Babylonia, or Greece, it is because this civilization is more accessible to us, by dint of the authentic "testimonies" it has left us, and because its entire "culture" is founded upon a symbolic form of writing. This attests to an unsurpassable wisdom, which dared found an empire on the purely symbolic expression of its writing. Any writing formed from an arbitrary, conventionally alphabetical system may in time be lost and become incomprehensible. On the other hand, the use of images as signs for the expression of thought leaves the meaning of this writing, five or six thousand years old, as clear and accessible as it was the day it was carved in the stone; for a chair, a falcon, a vulture, a piece of cloth, a placenta, a leg, or a human posture will not change as long as there are people on earth. This concerns sacred or hieroglyphic writing. As for grammatically constructed language, that is another matter and does not come within the scope of this account.

Let us also note that Egypt's flora and fauna include many species never used in the hieroglyphic *symbolique*. This shows a choice, hence a will to assemble the basic types of its environment that could be designated as "irreducible" for a *symbolique* necessary for a cosmic teaching (such as contained in the Osirian and Horian lunar and solar myths).

[21] This is why myth should be spoken of analytically. We cannot trust that we shall ever arrive at the mythical principle through the juxtaposition (syncretism) of dispersed elements, or that the myth might be a "poetic" construction, as Professor Alexander H. Krappe proposes (*La Genèse du mythe* [Paris: Payot, 1925]). There is no *Mythenbildung* (genesis of myth) in the mythic tenet; the latter is a revelation. Certainly, if one admits that the meaning of the myth is, as Professor Krappe believes, what he understands it to be in the light of his own science, then it is also admissible that this meaning may be purely individual fancy. But perhaps with a little modesty one could accept the existence of a meaning that goes beyond ordinary knowledge, as Mircea Eliade suggests in his *Patterns*

The directive of thought is provided by symbolic classification, that is, by the definition of the essential groups of a natural *symbolique*. All the functions of Nature are included in it; the thing, or being—that is, the symbol-type of a lineage—represents integrally, in a vital manner, all the nuances of the functions of this part of Nature that we can in fact know. We may well marvel at the choice of these symbol-types.

The following conclusions may be stated:

1. At each instant there is in the world a beginning and an end of genesis.
2. At each instant the procreative lineage may be interrupted by the creative act. This can bring an immediate end to the creature, by rejecting the sequence of procreation that might be called "accident," and by reducing to its predestined essence, which in the pure and primordial act is light, that light immanent in the creature from the beginning. This is the principle of Redemption.
3. Duration or procreation is not indispensable with respect to the original Cause, but it imposes itself upon the creature by "imitation"; it is the accident, and, in relation to the absolute order of *shadowless* light that is the self-contemplation of the causal consciousness, this duration or genesis is disorder and the fractioning of causal Unity into quantity.

The position taken in this study excludes the principle of a creation "making light" *within a chaotic state*. This "fact," cited in Genesis, takes on an explanatory, "unreal," exoteric character; this *explanation*, necessary for transmitting the teaching, aims to reveal *the reality of the Creation that is no longer situated in time*, but figures there always, without beginning or end.[22]

in Comparative Religion (Traité d'histoire des religions), trans. Rosemary Sheed (New York: Meridian, 1963), p. 417: ". . . indeed one whole series of myths, recording what gods or mythical beings did *in illo tempore,* discloses a level of reality quite beyond any empirical or rational comprehension."

Explanatory legends and changes in the names of the principles, adapted to the evolution of consciousness, may be devised, but the "functional" character of these *neters* is unchanging.

[22] This chapter on *symbolique* includes the most important passages from *Symbol and the Symbolic.*

Chapter 3

ANTHROPOCOSMOS

THE MEANING OF THE
ANTHROPOCOSMOS

In India the tradition of *vāstupuruṣamaṇḍala,* of basing the plan of a temple on Cosmic Man, is still alive. The model image for the cathedrals of the Middle Ages was Christ on the Cross. In Egypt, we know of at least one other temple patterned on the human figure; but whereas this figure is represented in a "ritual gesture," the Man of the Temple at Luxor is man *being born and growing*. We think that vestiges of such a temple are not to be found anywhere else.

If this temple were only an architectural curiosity, or a pious fantasy, or simply a way of showing respect to the royal principle, it would be of no interest to us. But all initiatory temples are founded on the principle of Anthropocosmos, that is, man as Universe, the anthropomorphization of divine thought, whether in its totality or in one of the cosmic functions innate in man, the ultimate product of Nature. Here, the principle of Anthropocosmos is not only a symbol but a doctrinal basis for all thought.

The rationalist tendency is to study the component part of a whole in light of the characteristics revealed by the whole. Common sense turns toward studying the component part, or at least toward observing this part in itself, in order then to study what becomes of the observed characteristic of the part in the composite or conglomerate, the new whole.

In the principle of *puruṣa,* or Anthropocosmos, there is an altogether different point of view: man is not the component part but the final product. He is not part of the Whole but the living expression of this Whole; and it is, on the contrary, the Universe that appears as a dispersal of the parts, each one separately alive, and although independent, analyzed with respect to the human Whole.

As an example, let us consider the atom and matter. The natural tendency is to study the atom by starting from what we have learned of matter, to understand matter by studying the atom. But this is a mistake: matter appears as a conglomerate in which atomic forces or energies are compensated, thus the characteristics of the living atom disappear or change, in the same way that colloidal particles, which in a living environment form Brownian movement, are made inert by coagulation. Contrary to this, stellar systems provide us with an image of the atom; in them, the matter of bodies in motion is organized into a living image, similar to the energetic elements of the atom. A nebula is certainly closer to the image of the atom than matter; that is, the nebula is a living whole, a symbol through which we can hope to know the composite nature of matter.

Thus, man is a living whole in which there are atoms as alive as he is, forming his matter, his organic components, which reveal (analyze) all the functional aspects of the Universe.

The Anthropocosmos appears as a basic doctrine-guide for knowledge, and as a rallying point for all aspects of thought, to which may be summoned all "philosophies," whether "materialist" or "spiritualist."

The foundations of this doctrine are *(a)* the fact that the Universe is necessarily limited by the characteristic specificities of the thing and of Being; *(b)* the fact that the variety of aspects and behaviors of all that forms the Universe is measured by consciousness; *(c)* the fact that there is in some way, biologically or mechanically, an evolution, that is, a sequence from the simpler to the more complex, and that the human being is at present a final, if not yet a perfect, effect. (If, in nature's becoming, we acknowledge thinking man as we presently know him, then a continuation of this natural becoming toward a more perfect man can be posited, since nothing proves that the limit of this becoming has been reached. It is impossible for us even to guess what future mankind, having reached the limit of natural becoming, will be like. Each moment of the becoming limits the Universe to the consciousness of that moment.) And, *(d)* every effect resulting from an impulse, such as the product of a seed, represents the corporification of specificities potentially immanent in that impulse, that is, in that seed.

As a final effect of the natural becoming, the human being represents the realization of the specificities immanent in the original cause, whatever this cause might be.

—∿∿—

Consciousness, or the measure of the Universe, appears in three essential aspects: *(a)* the specificity characterizing all substance and matter, determining affinities and repulsions; *(b)* the specificities functionally individualized into coordinated organs (these first two aspects represent an innate consciousness within the forms that constitute this Universe); and *(c)* the innate consciousness reflected by the cerebral organ (the cortex contained in the cerebral skullcap) constituting the (cerebral) intelligence.

Reason[1] is of the same nature as Being that is conscious of the three aspects of consciousness, just as the artist represents "reason" through his ability to contemplate and understand the work he has gestated through pure aesthetic sensibility.

---

[1] By "reason" I mean the first and pure apperception of complementation by the "essential" act of self-recognition (cf. the Heliopolitan Mystery). It is an "auto-insemination" of the spirit that results, finally, in the intellect through the reflection, the "inversion" of consciousness—a specifically human faculty.

Reason is therefore at the origin of the mental phenomenon, just as, in general principle, the *Fiat lux* is at the origin of Nature. Self-recognition is the dualization of the boundless consciousness (losing, on account of specificity, its cosmic character), which at first, becomes *intuition*. Intuition remains instinct as long as it cannot be directed by the intellect. From this may come either knowledge, and therefore the conscious mastery over direct apperception, or mental science, through the process of the objective reduction of the still intuitive "vision."

Reason is at the origin of the mental phenomenon. It constitutes the original pole of this phenomenon, which meets its definitive antipole when the innate consciousness in man (the natural, final form) mingles or remingles with the cosmic consciousness. Thus, reason is opposed to the process of becoming one or unification; between these two "poles" there is the Jehovian, natural being. The Christic unction can be considered as the gift of *royal irrationalization* for the natural being. Its image is found in the fact that the disciplined suppression of the cerebral mental presence (psychological consciousness) can provoke this mingling (communion).

Here, "Being" means the potentiality of all possible specificities, and thus consciousness without object. This is the metaphysical moment of the doctrine and the "stumbling block." "Philosophers" can accept or refuse this "reason" mentally, but this in no way changes the fact or the usefulness of the doctrine of the Anthropocosmos.

There is no function in the Universe that in its humanly energetic, psychological, psychic, and mental form cannot be observed and recognized by the human being. But the key is reason. This is why the pharaonic sages (and all the sages of the world) have attributed a *neter,* a cosmic principle, to each part of the human body, its organs and vital functions.

In order to make accessible to all this abstraction of unity that is the Anthropocosmos, the gnostics and the great theosophists of the Middle Ages presented it under the image of the microcosm.

THE PRINCIPLE OF THE MICROCOSM

In the esoteric sciences, the microcosm, as an anthropocentric doctrine, is intimately connected with geocentrism in astronomy. If the earth is the center of the moving Universe, it governs this Universe. If its center is the sun, then the earth is nothing but a planetary speck in the mechanics of the heavens.

In the latter case, the world would be a simple physical phenomenon obedient to mechanical laws founded on the law of gravitation. Today, however, this way of seeing is being questioned, for in approaching the atomic essence of matter, already we observe that at the heart of things, the quantitative laws of gravity give way to the forces of affinity.[2]

Moreover, it is obvious that the Universe, for man who sees the sky revolving around him, is what he is himself, for it is man who looks at it, studies it, and judges it. We could imagine this same man's life stripped bare of the physical body's contingencies; we could suppose him to be a kind of superman or saint, but it is impossible for us to represent such a being without body or form. Because this is so, in the eyes of present humanity, man must remain the summit of a biological evolution, and we can neither deny him nor substitute a superior concept for him without conferring our own characteristics on this concept.

This is the basic reasoning that necessarily and vitally places man at the center of the Universe, and justifies the esoteric concept of an anthropo- and geocentric system of the Cosmos.

In these conditions, we must remain consistent with this proposition. If man is, in principle, the summit, that is, the purpose of the Universe, this finalistic conception requires that he be the summation of all the elements and all the phases of the world's genesis: God created man in his own image.

The stellar Universe, therefore, can be none other than the essence of the form and vital functions of this man in his formal and final, present manifestation.

[2] We may note the fact that in order to fight against mechanistic thought and prevent the decline of anthropocentrism, which would open the door to a purely materialistic conception of the Universe and necessarily lead to rationalism, the Roman Catholic Church persecuted, *and with reason,* Galileo and Copernicus, just as, in his time, the Helladic Greek, ever faithful to traditionalism, persecuted Aristarchus of Samos. Aristarchus was threatened with a trial (by the Stoic Cleanthes) for his heliocentric theory, "so that, at the center of the earth, Vesta's peace might not be disturbed."

This may appear as a very "reactionary" way of seeing things, but it must not be forgotten that the conception of heliocentric astronomy was perfectly known to antiquity and in the temples, but remained reserved for initiates. Moreover, we see that in the footsteps of Copernicus, Kepler immediately undertook the truly inspired (and successful) study of the laws ordering planetary mechanics, and this, as he said himself, was done from ancient documents and on the basis of the five regular, Platonic bodies. His excuse was that because antiquity knew of the heliocentric system, why not teach it also? His age had already lost the meaning of the "Temple."

The geocentric system that was handed down to us through Ptolemy was certainly neither rational nor harmonious, but it answered to a mystical reasoning whereas the heliocentric system leads to mechanistic, analytical rationalism.

This form is actual and not eternal, it is neither definitive in its evolution nor absolute in its present possibilities. The actual form is transitory, but it represents all the potential possibilities of the awaited absolute state, when that which is mortal (variable) will be vanquished: Christ, in his Passion—*Ecce homo!*

Thus man is the Cosmos itself. We are not speaking here of the human individual, but of the Man who, in each person, in all people, forms the human vital principle.

The doctrine of the microcosm, the esoteric base of all religious and initiatory expression, is the doctrine of the principles and functions of life; their abstract character is made concrete in the functions of the corporeal economy, in the psychic functions of the emotional body, and in the functions of mental man's intelligence. Through the senses this mental man creates the relationship between innate knowledge, either acquired during this life or brought with him at birth, and the residual forms of *man's cosmic genesis* that fill the world.

There are an infinite number of places in the Universe where, through the cooperation and harmony of the stars, one same nonmaterial and energetic substance responds to different vibrations or influences. It is owing to this "resonant" substance that there exists the possibility of a sensorial relationship between man and his environment. These various aspects of the one same substance "coagulating" into cerebral matter enable us to have the *intelligence* of sight, hearing, smell, taste, and touch, through the *mechanism* of the senses.

The doctrine of the microcosm is not directly concerned with these mechanisms, such as the ear or eye; what pertains to it is localizing *the center capable of giving us the intelligence* of these perceptions, through coincidences between cosmic and particular events.

Now, these centers cannot be situated at random in the nervous and cerebral body; a harmonic relation must exist between Cosmic Man—who also contains the stellar world—and this incarnate man called Microcosm.[3]

The study of this harmony is the key to esotericism. There is thus an *esoteric science* because there is a projection of the Universe within the human body, a *body of experience* and, so to speak, an atlas of cosmic, spatial locations.

It is this science that gave the sages of all times the knowledge of the location of the *cakras* of Hindu yoga, and of the way to be followed in this process of rapid evolution. It is this science that revealed to the sages, among other things, the mystery of the transformations and transmutations of matter, of hereditary transmissions, of birth, and of the passing into supramaterial states.

In Ancient Egypt, as in China, the king embodies the Cosmos for his people and represents the *incarnation of the present state* of humanity's achievement; he is the Colossus.

That is why in Ancient Egypt the kings bear mystical names, and the dynasties evolve as embryological stages in the genesis of an empire, born on a date determined and known by the heavens, and therefore known in its becoming and end.

TOTEMISM AND HERALDRY

Each human being is a whole, each is in himself an assemblage of defined qualities. May the breath of the *herald* bestow the *coat of arms* that will be the *emblem,* the star one must follow, and

[3] The principle of harmonization can be defined as follows: Disharmony is always destructive. It dissociates the constituent elements of a state and these then freely reassociate to form a new, harmonious system by virtue of the natural affinity of the elements among themselves. Selective affinity is the source of harmony.

the *motto* that dictates the conduct to which one must conform.

Totemism has been greatly misunderstood, which is why the word *totem* leads to a misunderstanding of the esoteric sense of its real meaning. In the West, we have a heraldry that in its original "esoteric" sense is a form of totemism. There is an esoteric science of heraldry, a pure symbolism of the particular qualities of an individuality in, for example, *the tomb decorations of the nobles of the pharaonic empire.*

In Western chivalry (cabalary), the man who was distinguished among men used to receive for a shield a blank escutcheon bearing one of the seven (planetary) colors symbolically conforming to his nature. The great deeds or events *characteristic of his personality* were then inscribed on this escutcheon. The coat of arms became the emblem of this man and his descendants. He had to choose his motto himself, for example, *"Honny soit (qui) mal y pense,"** (for my intention will always be pure).

The human embryo passes through all the phases of animal genesis, and one more than any other of these phases influences the man's animal type. All Nature is in man, and a kinship between a man and a particular aspect of Nature marks him, that is, "specifies" him as an individuality among men.

This specification is not arbitrary. Various circumstances contribute to it, such as physical heredity, the astral moment, and the physical environment. These conditions, therefore, are necessarily those intimately related to the man and favorable to his activity. This man will always move—in spite of his free will—toward that atmosphere, toward that object, toward that aspect of life.

Knowing this kinship is knowing a person's totem; it is knowing his "arms." The *herald* is his consciousness, the breath; the *coat of arms* is his life; the *arms* are the symbols of his suitable environment and means; the *motto* dictates his chosen line of moral conduct.

—∿∿—

Nature, corporeal man, summarizes four elements and a quintessence: the organic trunk, the organic head, the organic reproductive organs, and the mobile limbs. The quintessence is thought, and the senses create a communion between the outer corporeal life and the inner noncorporeal life. *Analogically,* they correspond to Earth, Air, Fire, and Water, with the Archaeus, the life principle as the quintessence.

Three principles preside over existence: that which makes, that is, the Spirit; that which is made, that is, the body and its specificity; and that which joins the two, consciousness. From there come the two aspects or unequal parts: the masculine spirit-consciousness, and the feminine body-consciousness, both of which result from the Verb, the internal action whence all proceeds, the Unique.

The Verb creates appearances; it is the weaving (Neith). One becomes Two; the Verb is the root of Two, the supernatural harmony. This root is also called Heaven. The Earth is Two.

Both male and female exist in each human individual. Harmony is the scale of the phases of metabolic genesis, the activity of the Verb. Corporeal man, Nature, is Earth; noncorporeal man is Heaven. Man and life are One.

—∿∿—

There is the metabolism *in* man and there is the metabolism *of* man. Metabolism is the decomposing of what is composed, the separating of that which is pure and recombining of the pure,

* "Shame on him who evil thinks."

sublimating it and exalting its quality. The corporeal bread and the wine, spiritual blood, in the end become eternal life. From the corporeal, consciousness becomes nervous energy, then seed, thought, and undetermined, universal ferment.

The metabolism of man is metempsychosis, he has assumed and assumes all forms; one surpasses all the others: his personal lineage, the emblem of an ancestor's lineage. An accident.

—✴—

Being and the function of being produce the phenomenon that is the new first being, which in its function gives the new second being . . . seven and nine times: this is the scale that ranges from the potentiality of the Cause to the effect. This scale manifests the possibilities immanent, but not necessarily realized, in the Cause. From the *possibilities* come the deviations that are accidents. Accidents create definite types, arrested within the genesis of the perfect finality.

Finalities, on the way toward absolute finality, produce stones, plants, animals, colors, qualities. The limit of perceptions creates the possibility of the senses that inform us. What is informed is mankind's heaven, and this information is boundless for that which precedes *present* man in his becoming.

—✴—

The "sequence" of finalities, which is the fugitive appearance of a world, varied by sensorial information framed within limits, makes identities impossible. Yesterday, through today, has engendered tomorrow. No moment is identical with another. Only outside time and thus outside the series, and therefore only for consciousness, can one type of being be identified with one type of the genesis. The conditions and accidents defining this type are themselves constant within the possibilities of the constant genesis. The being of Cosmic Man includes all types because it includes all possibilities, potential or realized. But present man, specified by a type, evokes the conditions and accidents that have marked him and that place him within the rhythm of that type, that is, they endlessly evoke the accidents that have determined him.

This is the magical character of the particular totemic coat of arms: an identity. Essentially, it is through and in the gesture that identity can exist.

This is the rationale of the magic spell. But it is also said that one may treat a wound from a distance if one treats the unsheathed weapon, still stained with blood, that caused the wound. This is the magic of analogies. Seek not for explanations in causes that are outside ourselves, in "materialistic" explanations such as "astral" or psychic communications, which allow for a separation.

The Universe is man, man is the Universe, and if individualities are distinguished one from another, all are still in vital solidarity through the Universe. Identification creates magic and so-called miracles, and the human being possesses the faculty of identifying himself with anything whatsoever in the Universe.

The obstacle to this identification is the cerebral presence, the psychological consciousness that places a veil between the consciousness incarnate in man (his innate knowledge) and cosmic consciousness. Suppressing thought, even for a moment, ceasing to be sensorially aware of one's surroundings, is to merge with the living cosmic consciousness and draw from the source of life. In such a moment, the faculties are exalted beyond their normal limits. It is in this *meditation* that one must seek the knowledge of one's emblem. Also, in most so-called primitive societies, the boy, at puberty, is compelled to induce a trance state in himself in order to determine his totem, the image or object that is the emblem of his personal lineage and also the emblem of the tribe to which he belongs. His life will then be adapted to the rhythm of his totem, and he will know how to act and how to distinguish friend from foe.

In the West, the name given to a child, the name that is tied to a principle or to a patron saint, should play this role. Members of religious orders, more consciously, choose their models from among the saints.

It should be the first concern of parents to observe the characteristics of the tendencies and dispositions of their child so that they are able, during puberty, to guide him in his choice—without ever imposing it on him. Each child must recognize himself, and this is a delicate problem.

It is not difficult to choose a stone, a plant, or an animal toward which one feels more particularly drawn. But this does not mean anything, it is a rational choice. We have often seen people selecting a precious stone, but we have never come across anyone selecting pyrite or ochre, for example. Who will select the spider, the scorpion, the viper? And yet . . .

It is not a matter of choice among these things but of a state of being that must be "recognized." For Western man, it has become very difficult to discern the true from the false. And so he attaches all value to the product of his work, which, however, contributes absolutely nothing to his reality, that is, to the widening of his consciousness, the aim of his existence. He has forgotten that it is only the love that he puts into his work, only the quest to live at one with the life of the material he fashions, which can augment his humanness.

The totemic coat of arms is a state of being and a phase in the cosmic genesis, symbolized by that moment. This phase—this symbol—is represented by a mineral, a plant, an animal, and, at a higher level, by an organ and a function. Now, this specific animal is dependent upon the lineage of a plant, which in turn is tied to a phase of metallic genesis. The one is foundation for the becoming of the other.

The individuality of a human being is only the human "finality" of this particularly marked type, of this branch on the universal trunk of cosmic genesis. The animal does not have to become conscious of this moment of universal consciousness; it is itself the animal aspect of this moment. This turning back upon itself of consciousness, a repetition of creation's "self before itself," is the characteristic of man. He can thus see himself, and as a "cerebral" spectator, ascertain the aspect of being that he is amidst universal Being. This scission of consciousness that distinguishes good from evil, that is, delimits a fraction in time on the eternal thread of consciousness, is illusory appearance; but through this appearance cosmic consciousness experiments (that is, widens), recognizing itself in all these possibilities, being potentially immanent in them. This means that the corporification of the consciousness of the Unique is nothing other than genesis, through which, from the metal to the human being, consciousness descends into matter, and, at that moment, is turned back upon itself in order to return to its source as "conscious consciousness," by means of a liberating genesis that is nothing but a qualitative exaltation. *Cosmic Man, fallen to Earth, turns back over, facing toward Heaven.* This is the theological theme in all initiatory temples.

Not only is the totemic and heraldic particularity not an obstacle to this return, but its recognition, on the contrary, is an exceptional means of hastening this return. Indeed, any particularity ceases to be when it is universalized within its own character.

It is not sufficient then merely to recognize the symbol of one's lineage; more than that, one's life must be adapted to it, and above all, one must seek to live all its aspects throughout all of Nature.

I have spoken elsewhere about the distinction to be made between seminal incarnation, the continuity of the species, and individual reincarnation.* The totemic coat of arms relates only to the individuality and its reincarnation. That is why it should be noted that this individuality will only become incarnate in the social milieu and terrestrial place that conforms to its lineage and to the stage of consciousness already attained. Thus, for example, if during one of his lives, the totemic coat of arms of a man *living close to Nature* were to have been the eagle, one of the eagle's qualities (one of the more typical functions), such as the eye in general (or its rapacity) would later be his symbol. This eye will see colors, or contours and outlines better. Whether it is one or the other tendency, this disposition must "consciously" guide his life, and this individuality, if it wishes to go beyond itself, must seek to live all that is color, in art as in all Nature, for example, to the point of feeling the moment when genesis is expressed in color and through color. This example should not be taken literally, but only as a guide to thought. In reality, it is a question of dispositions and vital tendencies, not of exceptional faculties.

As an example of totemism, it is interesting to consider the tomb of an Egyptian princess of the Fifth Dynasty, the walls of which are entirely decorated with paintings representing all that can be linked to the tongue, from the creative Verb—speech—to Hermetic symbols, such as the hunter who catches a hippopotamus by the tongue with his lasso. This is an example of universalizing the particular, which is one of the great pharaonic lessons: the whole is always contained in the part.

Thus each temple, that is, each human individuality, is the Universe, seen not from a particular angle, but in one phase of its genesis, always situated within the total genesis, just as the *movement* of a child can be situated in the fourth month of its gestation.

And the totemic coat of arms is nothing but the symbol of one of these moments of the corporeal becoming (Nature) of consciousness on its way toward self-consciousness, in order finally to attain liberation from bodily contingencies.

MYSTICOMAGICAL SCIENCE

The notion of identity precludes separation while recognizing two beings. This duality within Unity, the incomprehensible truth of the Trinity, is the basis of all magic. We look upon this mystery with the eye of reason and that is why it overwhelms us and escapes us. On the contrary, if we consider it through the fact, it reveals to us the key to magical science.

Our senses—therefore our rational certainty—only apprehend the effect, but if from this effect we infer the quality of the metaphysical cause, we transfer the qualities of a lower stage to a higher stage by means of a supposition; logically, this is an error.

Were the metaphysical cause of the same quality as the effect, this effect would still be a similar cause. But it would only be capable of being a cause for a consequence belonging to its physical, and no longer its metaphysical, nature.

For a "return" to occur, it is necessary to go through the whole scale of concrete possibilities, up to the ultimate "coagulation." Facts indisputably show us only one thing: the necessity, and certainty, of a cause.

Certain geological aspects, certain plants, certain phenomena (such as products of fermentation), certain races and animal species, certain temperaments and vital dispositions among humans, demonstrate a bond between these effects and the place on earth and the propitious times at which

---

* For example, see chapter 1; also *Nature Word,* trans. Deborah Lawlor (Rochester, Vt.: Inner Traditions, 1990).

they occur. These are cosmic conditions that a God, knowing the cosmos, could explain—but the right and duty of ascertaining them is ours.

Without the power of the Trinity, not a blade of grass could exist, which is to say that an identity must preside over the vital phenomenon. We cannot master the reason for this identity, but we can become master of the knowledge of the circumstances and the measures to take in order to offer this knowledge the opportunity to act. This is magical science. And, by the fact that we appeal to a power superior to ourselves that cannot be grasped by our dualizing intelligence, we are dealing with a mystical science, that is to say, a science that causes the intervention of a hidden power, a power in which it is impossible for us not to believe.[4]

Man's pride is incommensurable, and our science simply postpones to the future what is unknown concerning the physical knowledge of causes. It is already known that the nuclear bombardment of "cosmic rays" transforms nitrogen into a certain carbon that plants on earth reduce to common coal. Is this an energetic effect on the atomic structure? We only have to discover how nitrogen comes to be, and prior to that, how simple energy, an unknown power, creates the atomic complex called hydrogen. We shall arrive there provided that the Tower of Babel does not collapse, and it will not collapse if the physical foundation holds; but, as the sage says: no stone will stand unless it is the triangular stone, the Trinity Power.

Every vital phenomenon, all life, is nothing but the effect of this identity.

In order to identify them, the principle of the Anthropocosmos invites us to seek in ourselves for sign of the characteristic moments. Thus the human being, in his organism, in his behavior, at the moments of identification or vital reaction in any sense, becomes the revealer that enables us to observe (to ascertain psychologically outside ourselves) the tangible conditions that the nature of the phenomenal surroundings, both terrestrial and astronomical, offer at that moment.

These identifications make up traditional science, which allows one to act with the knowledge of the cause and in the foreknowledge of the effects. This is the only true science. It is perfect and of a mysticomagical character.

GOD AND DETERMINISM

Knowledge is only possible if an invariable law orders the genesis of a finality implied in the potentiality of the original causal impulse. Logically, this imposes a determinism. But vital logic has nothing in common with the schematization of arithmetic series; it is motivated by the constant interchange of an absorbed action with a reaction or new activity, which is a constant double reversal. A thousand branchings are possible without deviating the course to the preconceived goal.

It is said, "The Verb was made flesh. . . ."

The creative impulse aims at ultimate form, potentially immanent in this cosmic seed. All accidents, all byways that appear in the process of realization, issue from the genesis toward the goal; all causes will have their effect-cause, but at some point they must reach exhaustion.[5]

Determinism thus concentrates on causes that are voluntarily or involuntarily engendered. But

[4] A good number of "recipes" unearthed in the "laboratory" of the temple at Edfu confirm this mysticomagical science. Professor Loret, for example, experimented in vain with these recipes, even though he strictly followed the prescribed procedures. Among these, the incense called *kephi* remains, and always will remain, a puzzle for the *uninitiated*.

[5] The principle of Hindu *karma* and the image of the karmic wheel.

cosmic determinism has nothing in common with the will or with possible "foresight"; it is called the "Will of God," but it is a will that has nothing of the arbitrary about it and that no longer acts reactively on the creative impulse.

The true God and our being are one. Every prayer to God is addressed to our own Being, but not to our ego, our person, our momentary forms of Being.

Now, our Being, as existence, is consciousness seeking itself, and its ultimate finality is this consciousness liberated from formal, limiting contingencies. Many stages mark this genesis, and these stages exist potentially within ourselves. Some beings, having reached stages higher than our present one, find in these stages, still potential within us, a fulcrum for their relation with our still limited consciousness. It is to these superior beings, who remain in "personal" contact with humans, that an appeal, a prayer, an "offering," can be addressed so that a modification can occur in the course of events related to the ego.

The "masters" and the "saints" exist potentially in each person, and it is to them that our prayer, our true sacrifice can go. It is childish to seek these powers outside ourselves, as if they were objects.

Determinism affects only the present moment, that is, what has a transient form. It does not exist for that which is indestructible. Prayer or sacrifice *for* one or another appeal can therefore be addressed only to this power, intermediate between the eternal and the present, whose vaster consciousness can guide us, inspire us, through ourselves.

God and the masters (or saints) are real from the moment there is an evolution of consciousness, that is, an expansion of the existing Being, for which our corporeal form serves as support, itself nothing but a concrete manifestation of the stage attained. No reasoning or intuition, however, can affirm that present humanity is the definitive stage of life.

But let us set aside the word *God,* so misunderstood, and set aside even the God that we call the Eternal, and call it the Unique instead, in whom the *neters,* the powers or functions of Nature, are merged and annihilated. The Unique *is,* but It ceases for us when we look upon the stages of consciousness in their perceptible aspects, that is, Nature.

By itself, Nature moves toward its disappearance into that of which it is made; this is the Osirian cycle, the constant renewal after death in the waters of the west. By itself, Nature cannot surpass itself because it is renewed only in the natural cycle; genesis may come to a halt, but it is irreversible.

It is with the reversal of consciousness, with consciousness of consciousness, the superior human state, that a break in the natural cycle may intervene in the form of Art, through the power of negation that marks this turning back of consciousness. To deny appearances, to deny polarity, to deny faith in sensorial reality, to descend voluntarily into the hells of destruction, in order to rise on the third day—all has been told to ears that hear not.

The way of knowledge, and thus of the Anthropocosmos, leads through a desert. One must dare to find this mystic desert. But he who lingers there as an atheist will die of thirst; he will not have dared to reject, with the devil, the "God" who is his counterpart; he will not have known how to perceive the Unique that alone can unite that which is separated, which alone can join the opposites and break the natural cycle of Ashaverus;* he will not have known how to find the fecundating member of Osirian Nature, voluntarily dissected, the center hidden in the essence of Nature, from which the Horian Light can be born.

---

* Or Ahasuerus, the Wandering Jew.

Only that which is naturally discordant can be separated. But does not the vital goal consist precisely in homogenizing that which is opposed? Is not the goal, sought after since the origin, the return to Unity?

Whoever would separate the north pole of a magnet from its south pole would destroy the magnet, whose intangible but indisputable reality is its "magnet force."*

It will not easily enter the mind of the "equationists," puffers, and quibblers that it is this Life-Unity that we must learn to see and consider without polarity.

We must learn to join that which is opposed in such a way that the elements thus joined cease to exist separately within the new Unity. Even in the human child, the father and mother remain disjunct, one contributing more to the physical, the other more to the psychological, corporeal, or mental makeup.

The corporeal carrier of quality divides quality into two antagonistic poles, from which arises the phenomenon.

---

*In French the word for "magnet" and "loving" is the same, *aimant.*

Chapter 4

PHARAONIC THOUGHT

ELEMENTS OF THE PHARAONIC
MENTALITY

We possess a great number of documents for the study of pharaonic thought or the pharaonic mentality, including papyri, carved inscriptions, ritual and common objects, tombs, and monuments.

The papyri contain proverbs, moral advice, hymns, allegorical tales, and the texts known as the "Book of the Dead," which should more appropriately be called the "Book of the Soul's Transmigrations," thus avoiding the confusion between the soul's liberation and Osirian metempsychosis. To these papyri we can also add therapeutic, surgical, and mathematical texts.

Egyptian grammar has been worked out mainly by using the allegorical tales.

We must never confuse the writing with the language, as is the case in standard Egyptology. Sacred (hieroglyphic) writing is composed of figurations, not conventional signs. The writing called "hieratic" consists of hieroglyphics transcribed into cursive writing. This writing leads to numerous simplifications, but, interestingly enough, it presents these characters in such a way that it retains the hieroglyph's essential "gesture." However simplified it may be, the sign is tied by a *gesture* to the hieroglyphic figure at its source.

Why did the pharaonic empire maintain, throughout millennia, a symbolic hieroglyphic writing instead of adopting an alphabetical writing of simple conventional signs? In Babylonia, the hieroglyph had long since become cuneiform, and Hebrew writing included a conventional alphabet. Standard Egyptology claims that the pharaohs did not have an alphabet, a fact that, as we know, is a serious error. But this alphabet—even as an ordered system of a limited number of letters—remains hieroglyphic. This system—similar to the Hebraic but far from being constructed on the same principles—constitutes a numerical and philosophical base of fundamental importance in the semantic construction of the writing.

The preservation of a hieroglyphic writing is an important indication for the study of pharaonic thought, for a transcription into conventional signs addresses itself to language, which creates a mental being that takes the place of the functional being that maintains the figured symbol.

In order to simplify their study of Egyptian writing and to transcribe hieroglyphic figures into letters, philologists have agreed to replace the symbol by adopting certain letters of our alphabet, refined by the added modifications of diacritical marks. One can eventually arrive at a language and progressively reconstitute a grammar in this way, but at some remove from the *intention* that caused the Ancients to keep a symbolic figure instead of a conventional sign.

The hieroglyph, or *medu-neter,* that is the "staff"[1] or *support* of the divine sign, is the only direct means of translating an esoteric meaning, which meaning cannot be quantitatively circumscribed.[2] The conventional *mental* sign can only transcribe the fact that is sensorially real, the fact that is defined only by comparison.

Academic Egyptologists commit the easily avoidable mistake of translating the meaning *(always imaged)* of the texts into the summarizing words of a European language. When it is said that a leader governs his nome "as far as its limit," only slight nuance is given by the usual transcription of "in its entirety." But when it is said that a supreme leader governs his nome "according to its character,"[3] it certainly does not refer to a geographic site, and we cannot transcribe this term by "in its entirety" when we know that each nome is consecrated to one *neter,* its patron, this *neter* being a principle. And if, for example, this *neter* is Anubis, the jackal, then it represents a *functional type,* the principle to which this nome is subject (its totem). To govern the nome "according to its character" means to maintain it vitally in a given rhythm.

One should at least respect the aspect figured in the phrases. We shall see with the mathematical papyrus that this (bad) habit of transcribing images into our own vocabulary has often hindered the understanding of the scribe's intentions.

Regarding the texts (which appear for the first time in the pyramids of the Fifth Dynasty) carved on temple walls, and on steles, Egyptologists admit that their meaning remains to a large extent incomprehensible, or else bafflingly banal. Here we draw near to secret Egypt, the aspect that will reveal to us the pharaonic mentality, the mode of thought of the masters of this empire. These masters gave utmost importance to the construction and to the inscriptions and figurations of the tombs (or mastabas, tombs hollowed out of rock). Their essential concern was the survival of the knowledge of the metaphysics of existence, the present incarnation being merely a passage.

Is this a matter of simple faith or of knowledge? If it is only a matter of faith—I mean on the part of the masters and not of the people—then there is need for a parallel, "mental" science. But if it is a matter of knowledge, then a science as rational as ours has no reason for being.

Now the fact of preserving the system of hieroglyphic writing—and this instead of the utilitarian facility offered by a conventional alphabet—shows that the pharaonic mentality rejected metaphysical and rational thought. The hieroglyphic form of writing makes the syllogistic system of such a rational science impossible. Pharaonic mathematics confirms this attitude.

There is no doubt that nothing made impossible the invention of a system of writing along the same lines as the Babylonian, Indian, or Hebrew systems. The refinement of Ancient Egyptian thought, which we see through their works, and which is substantiated by the study of the temple summarized in this book, allows for only one conclusion: this mode of writing, with all its consequences, was developed intentionally.

[1] Let us recall the runic staff.

[2] This does not exclude an alphabetical system founded on numbers for expressing an esoteric meaning. Isha Schwaller de Lubicz has oriented the reader's understanding toward this system, mostly by means of theological analysis and examples of interpretation in her *Her-Bak, Egyptian Initiate.*

[3] Cf. Gustave Lefebvre, *Grammaire de l'égyptien classique* (Cairo: I.F.A.O., 1955), § 189 a and b.

We are probably dealing with the knowledge that is an initiation into the secret of life, knowledge of the "key of life," the secret of the phenomenon, which precludes a science founded on the objective causes of phenomena.

The hieroglyphic *symbolique* is essentially practical. It selects its types from Nature or from the representative facts of a function, such as weaving, the bow, the arrow, or a seat. It represents the principles, the *neters*, not by abstractions (such as the eye of God the Father inside a triangle), but by human figures, even if the human head is replaced with an animal head, such as that of a cobra, scarab, or falcon.[4] The hieroglyphic determinative for the principle, *neter*, is set apart. Theology admits of only a single abstraction and nothing can represent it; it is the *Neter* of *neters*, the Unique, *that which is*, principle of all principles.

The pharaonic people, whose sole concern was the afterlife and who sacrificed everything to the life of the soul, which represents the immortal principle, were also extremely practical and very "down to earth" in all their expressions. Everything was for them a symbol of a *function* participating in the genesis of tangible Nature, an image of the genesis of immortality. This motivates the "stylization" of the scenes from daily life in the tombs of important figures, such as the field and livestock scenes at Saqqara, the wrestling scenes at Beni Hassan, or the various occupations, handicraft work, and family scenes depicted at Thebes.

Everything is symbolic: the choice of colors, and even the *technique of applying the colors*. All thought is expressed by gesture, not by words; and this is the mark of pharaonic "science," that is, a magical science (I am thinking here of "Trismegistus" and not of witchcraft). Although it is certain that a vast witchcraft flourished among the people, as much as in our early Middle Ages, it is the *thought* that interests us here, the directive of the behavior of the masters.

Of what does this "magical science" consist? It consists of *evocation*, not imaginary evocation, but of a "shock" intended to awaken the consciousness to the functional coincidence innate in man. This is the only possible explanation, which concurs with all that Ancient Egypt has left for us to know of her today. This is why theological images imbue the whole of life of this people, and what made them obey theological directives unfailingly and in all their acts. The Greeks said that the pharaonic people were the most pious of peoples. Would we say today that a people who are strictly scientific in all their acts is a pious people?

There is, however, a similarity in this loyalty, and in both cases there is a directing principle that is worshiped, but the two sides do not arrive at the same vital result. The pharaonic directive is cosmic, the scientific directive is desperately terrestrial, even though all its methods are abstract and imaginary, contrary to the pharaonic methods, which are practical and material.

From seed to fruit, from birth to death, among all individuals, throughout everything, there is the same "breath of life." From stone to man, all that exists, all that has tangible form, ages and reaches its maturity and its decrepitude. In a "functional" way, each individual is in relation with everything. The *possibility* of interaction with no material bond must therefore be admitted. Just as thought can be transmitted without tangible and physical support, there *must* exist a possibility for the will to act on matter. If the power of a solitary individual is insufficient, perhaps that of a circle of a certain number of people would be enough. We can observe that human beings, abstracted from cerebral control, can develop extreme muscular strength, just as they are capable of becoming insensitive, and even invulnerable, to pain.

---

[4] In this way the principle is anthropomorphized but not humanized.

Now, Egypt stressed the gesture. Movement is the symbol that carries the gesture, but since movement (the mechanical movement of the arm, for example) can only affect the corporeal, and the question here concerns a "vital movement," the Ancients could only evoke a "genesis" by the symbol of movement. This genesis is considered, then, as a *movement of becoming,* whether it is a realization or a destruction.

Our concept of gesture arises from an objective observation, but for the Ancients the concept of gesture is the synonym of a vital function, a power that animates in a determined direction. In other words, the vital function is a *determining function,* from which form and movement *result.*

Given these conditions, the object can be set aside when this determining function, the *neter,* is defined. For example, plant "nature" has a green color at the vegetating stage of its growth. This being generally the case, greenness relates to the idea of vegetative power. Even if this color does not exist visibly (as in the proliferation of animal cells), the color green, among others, will be the symbol of vegetation. There is a *verdant function* whose color is the tangible gesture.

This must be understood in the following spirit: the *functional power* is that which creates kinships and also allows for *identities.* It is therefore in this spirit that the Emerald Tablet, which affirms, "that which is above [cosmic] is as that which is below [particular]" must be understood. Then comes the conclusion, which is magic: ". . . that which is below, is as that which is above." Therefore, a *magical science,* pharaonic science, can only be formulated with the knowledge of cosmic conditions, through the functional identification of the parts with the whole within a single life or genesis.

We must therefore turn toward the known and present, final cosmic fruit—the human being—to know the forces of the environment from which he arises.

The tangible evokes the intangible, and this creates the character of the symbol; the visible gesture evokes the function, the animating power, and this produces "magical" power through identification, and will allow, through the accessible, the realization of the inaccessible.

If in a discursive explanation we can speak of a human microcosm, in the pharaonic spirit it can only be a question of *identity,* which I translate by Anthropocosmos, Man-Universe. Opposing microcosmic man to the Universe means breaking the philosophical condition allowing for a magical science, making null and void the very reason for accepting a microcosm.

As for the method and means of investigating such a "vital magical science," it is obvious that we should appeal to the *knowledge resulting* from this science so that we can have at our disposal the *true means* of investigation, that is, the key that gives life. This is why knowledge of the vital reason, that is, knowledge of the universal phenomenon, has the character of *revelation.*

Through revelation, the basis of the vitalist thesis remains mystical and renders all rational science useless. In its applications the directive, in principle, must apparently remain *empirical,* the reasons for the phenomenon being known only to certain initiates.

Thus the pharaonic empire presents itself. And this explains the reaction of the Greeks in Egypt, who, believing that they were confronted with a tradition of knowledge "emptied of the reasons" for its formulations, sought to find reasonable causes, a fact that gave birth to the dialectic philosophy that the West has found so seductive—as if intellectual arguments could substitute for knowledge of the cause of life.*

* For more on the "deviation" resulting from Greek rationalism, see the author's *Sacred Science: The King of Pharaonic Theocracy,* trans. André and Goldian VandenBroeck, illus. Lucie Lamy (Rochester, Vt.: Inner Traditions, 1982), chapter 2.

The study of the thought and achievements of Ancient Egypt, as seen through the Western mentality inherited from the Greek dialectical philosophers, leads nowhere and leaves us disappointed with the dissonance between this empire's gigantic achievement and the poverty of the deductions that standard Egyptology has drawn from it.

But if we let ourselves be guided in our research by the basic groundwork we have just presented, we can hope that a reconsideration of this research will be able to bring to light a mentality and a knowledge that today eludes us. Further advancement of our work should enable the completion of that which this "hypothesis-base" only partially presents.

It is in this spirit that we have tackled the study of a pharaonic temple, some of the results of which are summarized in this book. In order to avoid deviations, which may all too easily creep in because of our Western mental training, we must allow ourselves to be guided by the following principles:

1. The choice of symbols must be considered as having resulted from a rigorous selection process to find a *functional type.*
2. Consequently, every symbol is *evocative* of a "vital" function.
3. The "theory" of "magical science" is formulated by the myth; its principles are explained by the symbols of the *neters* and their attributes.
4. The theology is formulated by the themes of the myth and should guide all behavior in ordinary life, as well as practical applications in all fields.

With these principles in mind, let us follow the Egyptian mentality.

Man, or the human principle considered as an incarnation of cosmic functions, that is, Anthropocosmos, is the universal symbol to which everything relates. This Anthropocosmos, in its present human aspect, serves as support for the different vital functions and therefore provides the figurations for the *neters,* the vital principles constituting the characters of the *myth.* In order to represent the essential vital functions, the heads of the animals that incarnate these functions are often placed on the human body, and these animals are thus the living organic representatives of these functions. The crowns, costumes, and gestures complete and enlarge upon this significance.

Theology, which includes the doctrine of genesis, the teaching of the cause, aim, and end of living things, serves as the basis of all behavior, all thought, and even of the applied sciences and techniques; it is symbolized by the synthesis of the *neters* and the hieroglyphs. Respect for symbolic forms extends even to familiar objects.

Temples and funerary monuments built, or hollowed out, of rock never conform to any aesthetic purpose. Sculptures and inscriptions are never conceived as ornamental. The whole becomes beautiful because it is symbolically true, and conforms to the place and its surroundings: it is harmonious.

It must be noted that *the purpose is not didactic but becomes so,* because the work rigorously conforms to theological and philosophical rule. This observance ranges from the preparation of the ground at the site to the pinnacle of the monument, thus creating a magical and sacred ambiance.[5]

Every living function of the human being is but a symbol of an organically realized cosmic function. Swallowing, rejecting, assimilating, sleeping, sitting, talking, desiring, imploring, praying,

---

[5] Cf. Stella Kramrisch, *The Hindu Temple* (1946; reprint, Delhi, India: Motilal Banarsidass, 1991). See below, chapter 21.

and so forth, are nothing but incarnated cosmic functions. For example, swallowing and rejecting are the North and South Poles, but so are evening and morning and the solstices, that is, all that is taking and giving back in the function of assimilation. It is in this spirit that hieroglyphic, or sacred, *writing* must be studied. From among all the known animal and plant types of Egypt, a rigorous selection was made to determine which ones would serve as hieroglyphic symbols.

Mathematical thought is exclusively geometrical: a mathematical value is always proportional, never absolute. The notion of infinity does not exist and is therefore eliminated from mathematical functions. Space *is* volume, a volume *in* space does not exist. A volume or space is Spirit coagulated into matter more or less dense. The mathematical point is not an abstraction but the vertex formed by the intersection of at least three edges of three planes. Everything is volume, has volume. The plane is an aspect of a sectioned volume, but it does not exist in itself, whence the pharaonic concept of drawing the representation of a monument by showing both its plan and elevation.

Everything lives and therefore assimilates, grows, and reproduces, a fact that extends to monuments and statues conceived and executed on multiple axes simultaneously.

All pharaonic Egypt, from beginning to end and in all its achievements, is but a ritual gesture.

In what follows we shall show the application of these principles in some of the aspects we have covered thus far.

THE TECHNIQUE OF THOUGHT

Thought deals only with ideas, with more ideas as a consequence. Belief is addressed to an object.

Thought is expressed in writing, or in language, or in creation. Creation is thought in action, or the Verb.

Writing can leave the reader with the task of connecting the qualifying term to the subject; *spoken language* requires that we indicate the direction taken by an action. Thought without action does not exist.

On the other hand, it is certain that the basis of thinking is a self-contradictory condition, since everything is represented for us by a concept able "to be and not to be." Without this possibility of negation, reasoning would be impossible. The fact that there is a contradiction inherent in the concept is the first condition for a science of logic.

The conditions and bases of thought and method are *action* or *activity* and *negation*. Action conditions all qualification, and therefore all specification, and negation conditions all reasoning.

—⁓—

Action or activity creates the link between the two concepts of subject and attribute. But the concept itself is the result of an action (outside ourselves) and of a reaction (through cerebrally unconscious, innate, *functional knowledge,* which defines the form of our being). Without action, thought would not exist. The definition of the action creates idea and object; "definition," however, implies delimitation.

In the beginning, we are confronted with a nameless and boundless activity, the essence of function. It is nonpolarized energy, an abstraction for our psychological consciousness. Thus, all delimitation, or definition, is only a fractioning of this absolute Unity.

A delimitation requires a beginning and an end; it is a measure; for psychological consciousness, it is a quantity. Quantity therefore represents, from the absolute point of view, a cessation of the absolute activity. This can be admitted as the pure Idea of a metaphysical state, or it can be translated mathematically in relation to a given reference for a known extreme of the activity. From the philosophical point of view, we shall confine ourselves to the realm of pure Idea.

It follows that activity is the essence that presides over all and resides in all. The multitude included in this "all" is given by the delimitations, that is, the functional definitions, the fractions of the absolute activity.

Consequently, two possibilities present themselves for organizing thought with the goal of establishing a science: either we consider the Idea and defined object, or we consider the activity that creates the Idea or object. The first consideration leads to rationalism, the second to vital, or functional, thinking.

The first consideration supposes definition to be a *finality of action,* and designates it by a "word," a vocable, a stopped idea, embodied in the synthesis of the word.

The second consideration admits only the function, an activity that is characterized, but *without finality of action.* Thus, the Idea and the object can be designated only by symbols (diagrams or images) that summarize one or several *functions.* The subject is then only an assembly of functions. It is simultaneously *subject and attribute.*

Here the Idea, in its vital or *esoteric*—hieratic—expression, can be put in relation or concomitance with other Ideas and thus form a writing, composed of a single sequence of substantive roots.

This is the secret to the character of the early, initiatory texts. Pharaonic (traditional) thought remained faithful to this philosophy, and it acts according to the second consideration.

———

In sentence construction, the verb represents action and defines its nature, the function. The choice of the symbol thus will rest on the images that are roots, whether verbs, nouns, or adjectives. For example, a bird represents the noun *bird* and also *volatility* in general. It is thus the thing that holds itself up in the air, that rises and escapes the earth's attraction (a "centrifugation"); it is volatile or what can be made volatile (by heat, for example). It can also signify the Idea. The choice of a particular bird specifies other functions connected to the general function of volatility.

This constitutes the hieroglyph.

———

As we have seen, everything is either the consequence or the symbol of an activity. For example, we can say, "The basin contains water," and only the concept of the basin is retained; the word *basin* becomes the synthesis of all the notions related to it. We can also keep only the notion "capacity"; the action of containing characterizes the basin.

But there are many kinds of receptacles that can contain liquid, such as a vase, the heart, the fetal sac, and so on. Now, the basin contains and *keeps,* but the heart, as a vase, contains but does not keep what it contains. Each form can therefore correspond to one or several other functions as well, which no longer have anything in common with other, similar forms. Through the main function characterizing the basin, and in which the heart participates, there is a *functional kinship,* just as there is between all containers and the heart. There is also a certain kinship between the heart and a river. The basin dug into the earth *contains* and *keeps;* the heart *receives,* contains, and *sends back.* This example is cited here in its simplest form.

The functional definition remains a living one, and it manifests living kinships that can be represented in images by the hieroglyph, whereas the word can no longer be associated *in a living way* with other words. The word no longer evokes functions, the living qualities; it kills them.

The vitalist mode of thought leads to a philosophy with a *mystical* character. The main methods of action are considered as *abstract principles (neters)* that preside over characteristic lineages.

Every function has two aspects: *the action,* and *that which provokes the action,* the male (positive) aspect and the female (negative) aspect. Now, *that which provokes the action is not the thing itself but its reactivity.* The *thing* is the complemented and transitory natural effect.

For example, the action of *containing* also includes the reaction of giving form, and this totality defines the container. Another example is digestion in the stomach, considered as the *action of digesting,* includes *that which destroys homogeneity* as well as its reaction, which brings the action of digestion to a halt. The totality determines the digesting organ.

Each *neter* is thus a trinity that includes a masculine aspect, a feminine aspect, and the product: Amun-Mut-Khonsu. This is the esoteric sense of the Chinese *yin* and *yang,* exoterically represented by an emptiness and a fullness, which is misleading because the container does not have its masculine aspect within the contained, this latter being merely the complement given by *a thing* that is itself the consequence of an action and its own reaction.

Reaction is the reversal of the direction of the action, provoked by the resistance immanent in the nature of the activity, or "action in function."

In principle, reaction neutralizes action. The consequence is the *thing,* the object, a quantity, which is action (energy) defined.

The conclusion must be that the energetic complementation produces the (tangible) *appearance,* and the complementation of appearances in turn annuls definitions. This is expressed by the double crossing; an example is the double crossing of the scepters of the dead king.

Fig. 1. Sarcophagus of Tutankhamun, Valley of the Kings, Thebes

The scepters are the *hekat,* represented by a hook symbolizing the action, the seed, the ferment; and the *nekhakha,* which Egyptologists translate as "whip" or "flagellum," represented by a staff from which issues a triple flow: the effect of the resistance immanent in action, substance in its triple nature. Physically expressed, it is energy acting on substance in order to fix it, or that which acts and that which undergoes action. The *hekat* is held in the *left* hand, the receiving side, the north, the above; the *nekhakha* is held in the *right* hand, the returning, giving, and doing side, the south, the below. The *living* king is the active and reactive (mystical) power that creates Nature. The king will be dead when this power has produced body, quantity, determined form; this is the first crossing. But when the complementation of this appearance is realized in its turn—the second crossing of the scepters—then the appearance ceases and the creative power is liberated again *after having known form;* each scepter is back in its place, the *hekat* on the left, the *nekhakha* on the right (fig. 1).

In their hieratic aspect, the principle and the mode of pharaonic thought can be defined as follows:

The origin of all things being an active impulse, it is activity, or function, that characterizes all things. Activity, carrying its own resistance in itself, is represented in its triple nature: active-male-positive, passive-female-negative, and reactive-formed-neutral. Appearance is merely a passing *signature,* a *symbol* of the activity or incarnated function.

Through the *signature* the kinships (the analogues) of a characteristic lineage are distinguished, dominated and governed by a *neter,* a ternary and active (realized) power. The *neters* are cosmic, and everything that is related by its qualifying function to the lineage of a single *neter,* directly or collaterally, is cosmically interdependent.

Signatures or symbols chosen judiciously from among living natural products, or from among utilitarian objects that have invariable functions, constitute a set of glyphs that form a *writing* with an invariable meaning through all time, esoterically self-explanatory in the function.[6] *This is not a spoken language.*

All the essential functions can be summarized in a certain number of symbols and denoted by a *sound* whose pronunciation *affects the various physiological centers,* a fact that enables the alphabet of a sacred (mantric) language to be established. Certain determinatives point out the meaning of the indicated function. This, then, constitutes the writing of a *language,* made from words that refer to functional meanings. These words represent concepts that can then conform to a rational, syllogistic system.

In the *hieratic* spirit, we do not look for a concept of the function, but for an *identification of the self with the function that the* neter *represents.*

In this mode of thought, rationality has no place. What is called for is not a play of ideas that necessitate objectification, but a state of *functional consciousness,* superior to psychological consciousness. This state does not allow for the elaboration of a theoretical science, and neither is it any longer an empirical science, but in answering the question of *how* it also adds the possibility of answering the *why.* This mode of thinking is also valid in the applied arts and sciences.

FUNCTION, NUMBER, AND *NETER*

We call the *nature* of an activity a "function." It includes *an impulse, a goal,* and *a mode.* The impulse is undetermined and therefore invariable. It is the same in all cases, in the *Fiat lux* as well as in a mechanical impulse or any imperative whatsoever.

---

[6] For instance, weaving or the weaving tool, whether in its primitive or complex form. Likewise, the hoe or plowshare used for plowing, opening the earth, and making it attractive to the fertilizing dew.

The *goal* of the function is variable, by reason of the mode of activity. It is the mode that is complex. It includes an intensity, a milieu, and a rhythm. As a metaphysical principle, the milieu is indifferent, that is, unique. The mode is produced by the intensity and its variations, which create the rhythm.

The function, then, is essentially an impulse with a rhythmically varied intensity. The variation is number. If the intensity were invariable, there would be only one phenomenon, and the Cosmos would be mingled with its causal impulse. It is thus number that creates Nature.

The weakness of this "reasoning" lies in the impossibility of giving the impulse a name. We understand it only mechanically. It is always linked to movement, that is, to a displacement or a drop in potential. This means that something moves toward a place where this something or its like does not exist. The static *drop* relates to the gravitational characteristic of the environment—density; it is equally a drop toward the lower (solid) or toward the upper (gaseous fluid). Essentially, philosophically, the mechanical impulse, like any impulse, is given by negation in opposition to an affirmation: to be and "not to be," the mystery of the original scission.

"Mystery" means anything that eludes comprehension, but we can see the fact in the function without being able to name the impulse. (We could call it God, or nonpolarized energy, it does not matter; it is Reality par excellence.) We are led to this conclusion: There is a unique impulse, original and constant, and number reveals its modes to us through the varieties that make up Nature. Number is therefore the essential—but also the last—word explaining the Universe.

It is not a question here of calculation, but of the esotericism of number.

For example, the notion of space is characterized by extension, and volume is characterized by the *limit* of extension. Boundless extension can be *felt* by an aspect of our consciousness, but it cannot be understood cerebrally. The word *understand* (*verstehen* in German, *comprendre* in French) implies a limitation, a halt. Thus, in order to understand extension, the *principle of limitation* must intervene. This principle *(neter)* is independent of our will, our decision; it is immanent in the *principle of extension,* a *contracting* function, immanent in all *that is* (exists). Thus, being plays the part of a "sub-stance" that carries in itself its stypsis. We are always brought back to the same origin.

The principle, or *neter,* of extension is an abstraction, and the *neter* of limitation is what characterizes our *understanding,* the *concrete.* Now, extension is infinite, but limitation is relative; limitation is limited, and it enters into the category of *quantity.* It is because limit is not infinite that the laws defined by our science are relative and imaginary, and, in general, why science is opposed to knowledge (gnosis). Every object of science, everything "concrete," ceases to exist in its definition as soon as the limit of its limiting qualification is reached. The *qualifying function* is limitation and has *duration within the form,* but not when it is considered *as function,* because the concretizing, limiting, "styptic" action is immanent in *that which is,* and thus is *continuous.*

From these considerations, the following results can be drawn: for a volume to exist, there must be an action limiting the extension. In concrete things it is a ferment, a seed, in principle, a "fire." Nature serves us as a symbol of the knowledge of this original fact, since a concretization in a homogeneous milieu—such as the primordial milieu necessarily is—has its likeness in a *coagulation,* similar to the coagulation of a feminine, albuminoid substance. The white of an egg is an example of this. It coagulates either by the effect of heat or by the effect of the "fire" of the male spermatic ferment. In Egypt, the watery milieu out of which comes this coagulable substance (of a mysterious character) is represented by Amun, the great *neter* that the "king," the perfect creature, calls his father. Were it simply a question of expressing the fact we have just examined, this symbol represented by Amun would hardly have reason to exist. But it represents the anthropomorphization of a primordial activity with *universal ramifications,* and all the esoteric meanings and their keys are inscribed in various ways in this figure, open to interpretation by anyone able to hear it. *Through no other means can any explanation of these secrets be as precise and complete as it is in this symbolization.*

The limit of possibilities cannot be given by the passive milieu, but only by the intensity of the activity. This activity is originally expressed by a number, that is, the number results from the activity and therefore defines it.

The first volume is then necessarily spherical, being only extension, without orientation, and having only a radial measure; it is a contraction or first limitation by a "styptic," or coagulating, central fire. Primordial activity, source of all functions, is centripetal; it has the character of "placenta." Space is the nourishing, *amniotic milieu.*[7] By analogy, in pharaonic Egypt, this is Nun, represented as the cosmic ocean, the Hermetic *hyle.*

In order for the indefinite volume of the sphere to become *form,* at least three directions must be defined: the polar axis and the four directions of the equatorial cross. This is the reason for the whole of celestial mechanics, ordered by numbers that form a marvelous system and for which they are the key, and whose long development and special character are not within the scope of this book.

Exoterically, that is, from the outside, and therefore objectively, we see the world from the wrong side. We see the spherical stellar bodies turning, and their centrifugal force seems to us to be active, acting against the centripetal force that apparently plays a passive role. Seen vitally, from the inside, exactly the opposite is true. Nourishing space flows toward the center, not like a fluid toward a solid, but like the spiral currents of an immaterial sphere *that appears to be solid* at a certain degree of density defined by the central coagulating activity. These *falling* spirals occur according to the function of the golden number; they can be easily constructed on a $1 : \phi$ rectangle, as can the spirals of a snail's shell.

This determines two equatorial axes around a central point that forms the polar axis. The ternary axial system, *inevitable* as soon as the coagulating action occurs, is the Idea of the form in general, the Idea or *numerical* play *(numerus numerans)* that presides over the form or concrete appearance.

This (very simplified) description of the first Idea of the form is the *first limitation.* Since it is caused by the styptic (contracting) force, it thus ceases together with this action. Esoterically, it cannot exhaust itself since it is an original, causal power that nothing—except the very effect that it engenders—can annul. The following is a universal law: *The vital, natural cause reaches the end of its activity by excess of its effect.*

The fire that engenders and animates, ceases to engender and animate when it has burned up that which comes out of it; and that which comes of fire can become nothing but fire (just as the ash and ash salt are a "fire" we call caustic). Qualitatively, we can say: A cause reduces to itself that which it causes.

This further applies to the activity of the seed, which ceases when it has produced new seed of its own nature.[8] A grain of wheat or barley, for example, left to itself in dry conditions that prevent it from germinating or putrefying, burns itself, as demonstrated by the grains found in pharaonic tombs.

A limited, mechanical cause, that is, a moving object that has received a limited impulse, moves

---

[7] Physiology considers the placenta as the place of nourishment, since it is from here that the nutritive maternal vessels originate. Indeed, but in the functional spirit, this apparency is an error.

[8] The following well-known fact can be cited as an example: grape juice, when it is very rich in sugar, produces alcohol only up to a certain degree, after which, the very presence of this alcohol prevents the continuation of alcoholic fermentation, producing a sweet wine.

by "spending" this impulse. In reality, it reduces this impulse to its source, which is energy. According to the ancient axiom, everything finally resolves itself into that of which it is made.

The resistance that impedes the motion of an impulse can be measured. Here, number is reduced to the concept of "measure," that is, to a definition of "quantity." This removes number from its esoteric character, which resides in the *function* that it reveals, not in a measure that it specifies or counts.

The functional character of numbers is not relative or accidental, it is cosmic, the conscious revelation of our innate knowledge. We cannot better describe the absolute than by the number One, considered to be indivisible, since One, self-multiplied, reveals itself through the number Two.

With regard to the esoteric meaning of number, we must avoid the following mistake: Two is not One plus One; it is not a composite, it is the *multiplying power;* it is the *consciousness* of multiplication; it is the multiplying Work; it is the *notion* of the *plus* in relation to the *minus;* it is a new *unity;* it is sexuality; it is the origin of Nature, *physis,* the *neter* Two. It is the culmination (the separating moment of the full moon, for example); it is the line, the staff, movement, the way, Wotan, Odin, the *neter* Thoth, Mercury, Spirit.[9]

—◊◊◊—

The philosophy of number is based on the functional character of number. This character defines the functional "possibilities" whose application gives rise to our ideas. We do not attribute the notion of division to the number Two; it is the number Two that implies the dualizing function from which our notion of division derives.

Counting is not a faculty reserved to man, it is the first innate form of consciousness. Thus the elective affinity of the chemical molecule and its valence is already an innate consciousness of number.

The original scission, or polarization of energy, is the beginning of number, a first enumeration. For the human being, this becomes an a priori knowledge that imposes itself on our psychological consciousness. This psychological consciousness then classifies and names what number imposes upon it.

It is in this sense that the Pythagorean affirmation that "the Universe is nothing but number" must be understood. The "rationalist" thinkers who object to the "mystical" character attributed by the Pythagoreans to numbers as occult powers are wrong in finding in these gnostics a tendency to puerile mysticism. Number, as the very first manifestation of consciousness, is what specifies and characterizes everything.

That man then arrives with his psychological consciousness—the cerebral consciousness of innate consciousness—to name and to enumerate rationally, and therefore to reduce number to quantitative values, is merely a consequence that itself flows from number: an organic consciousness facing an innate consciousness, *two* forms of consciousness, scission and opposition.

NOTE

It seems useful to quote here the conclusions of the author of the most recent work on the history of mathematical knowledge, written in a spirit of neutrality, which is refreshing.

> To the extent that it is explanatory and ontological, science is a creation of the Greek genius (and if we consider these two aspects as essential, one can say that science is born in Greece). Indeed, Greek

[9] Cf. chapter 18.

science sought to give an account (λόγον διδόναι) of appearances, and it adhered to a metaphysics of the real (τὸ ὄν). Its disinterested ambition, its theoretical aims, and the astonishing rapidity of its progress, all make its superiority over Oriental science clear with no need to proceed to a minute comparison of their results. Greek science is separate from technology. It separated itself slowly from technology (as is shown by the slow semantic evolution of the term that denotes it), and each science in particular was to be for a long time intermingled with the art from which it originated. But an impetus has been given; a need—no doubt not entirely new, but for the first time entirely conscious—for rational explanation, which commits the human spirit to a path on which there is no going back.[10]

I am entirely in agreement with this author and with the generally accepted opinion that "science" is Greek if we consider science as "having need of the concept of the object, and investigating being"—as Meyerson is quoted by Michel—"it can foresee the phenomenon and is obstinately set upon explaining it."

To the extent that science can have a *concept of the object* and *foresee the phenomenon* and *explain it,* this science, which is derived from dialectical philosophy, is Greek. It is rational and can in no way lead beyond the *object,* which is to say that the *source of life,* inasmuch as it escapes mechanistic rationalism, is inaccessible to this science.

Nevertheless, the "mystery of the everyday," the potentiality of the seed realizing the corporeal form of the fruit, demands this irrational moment at the source of the phenomenon.

As long as there is a possibility of figuring (schematizing) a concept, even hypothetically, science can exist. This possibility ceases when the energy in question is depolarized, a fact that in the natural domain is impossible. Being unable either to conceive of this state of energy without polarity or to understand its action, but observing this reality in the fact, it must be represented by a supposition (such as the speed of light), or else pass from science to philosophy. Philosophy will then be speculative, therefore dialectical, as "the mode of inquiry" (the Greek way), or it will be replaced by the knowledge of the *secret* that "from the imponderable creates the ponderable."[11] Thus, science and philosophy no longer correspond to the definitions we have given them: as long as there is a *concept of the object,* there will be *technology,* that is, applied science. The description of the idea (in short, epistemology) can only be *symbolized* by the natural fact, the corporeal realization of the specificities immanent in the impulse and in the conditions of this realization. This creates the essential object of myth. We thus have *symbol* and *function* as elements for making predictions about the phenomenon and as a descriptive writing. "Understanding" will necessarily belong to the domain of a new state of consciousness that surpasses the "three-dimensional" state.

Now, the object of such a science is positive and the power of its application is "magic," in the sense that causes are no longer particular but cosmic, and the phenomenon is subject to a knowledge of cosmic conditions, neither more nor less so than for the sowing of a garden. In this way, science is knowledge.

Our science, born from Greek metaphysics, from dialectical philosophy, requires hypothetical representations, the stoppage or "fixation" of moments cut out of time.

[10] Paul-Henri Michel, *De Pythagore à Euclide: Contribution à l'histoire des mathématiques préeuclidiennes* (Paris: Belles-Lettres, 1950), p. 29.

[11] Ultimately, this "mode of formulation" was what the genius Albert Einstein sought in mathematical methods.

Every phenomenon has, by definition, a "finality," and this finality is the object of reasoned study. But if the phenomenon is arrested in its *gestation,* that is, in its vital movement, it becomes mental or corpselike in this artificial fixation. This scientific anatomy eliminates the possibility of a knowledge of the vital cause. Now this process has become so common that Western science is no longer aware of the error this mentality contains. It follows that our sciences necessarily concentrate on the concrete aspects of the object. Thus, medicine really becomes a science only in surgery, and all naturally effective therapeutics remain empirical. Mathematics is really a science only in algebra, and trigonometry only in geometry; these are fixed and generalized formulas, built upon hypothetical moments. All progress of thought in this sphere, such as the study of hyper-volumes or the geometry of curved surfaces, are only extensions constructed on concepts given by the "tangible," such as, for example, the fourth dimension conceived as a fourth section at right angles to the first three dimensions. But the planes of the sections, in general, are nothing but suppositions; the mathematical point is a supposition; the geometrical figure is a supposition; the circle is a supposition.

Only one thing is real—the *function*—and this *imposes itself* on our intelligence and on our senses. It is knowable only by its identity with the same vital function innate in ourselves. As soon as we want to define it, we "petrify" it; we make of it a "science." So that we can distinguish science from knowledge and knowingly use one or the other, it is enough to know this and always to be aware that science, in general, can be nothing but the science of the corpses of phenomena.

In this spirit, Ancient Egypt gives us no example of "science."[12] Everything we can learn of Ancient Egypt shows a thought founded on knowledge, a fact that places this civilization above a civilization founded on dialectical metaphysics, not below it. This disappoints us because we discover some "knowledge," repeated without an understanding of the causes and links to traditional applications, where we would like to find some "explanations." These explanations exist, but they do not correspond to our mentality. We have exploited our mentality to the full and are now able to evaluate it at its worth; it is quite disappointing with regard to life's big questions.

It is up to us to attempt to approach the mentality of the Ancients so as to detect the knowledge expressed by the traces they left behind.

We must not be too quick to object to the "traditionalism" of their civilization. It is the solid basis that preserves civilizations, the bony framework of nations. And when this traditionalism is founded on wisdom, even if this wisdom is transmitted only through ritual symbolism, the individual's "inner" progress is not hampered but sustained by it.

---

[12] This does not exclude the possibility of a strictly scientific observation of phenomena, as we shall see in the Edwin Smith Surgical Papyrus discussed in chapter 14.

Part 2

MATHEMATICAL
THOUGHT

Chapter 5

FOUNDATIONS OF PHARAONIC MATHEMATICS

THE MYSTICAL NUMBER

The number One is only definable through the notion of the number Two. Multiplicity is what reveals Unity to us; that is, our comprehension of things exists only through what we might call the original fractioning into parts and the comparison of these parts to one another, which is but the enumeration of the aspects of Unity. For this reason, a definition of the creative function is possible only when speaking in terms of fractioning, and in posing the hypothesis of the division of Unity, the cosmic source.[1]

If the original Unity were considered to be composed of parts, the results would then precede the cause. Now, our judgment, our intelligence—that is, our psychological attitude toward this problem—is precisely that of the result wanting to judge the cause.

Our inability to understand this uncompounded and therefore rationally indivisible Unity forces us to use an absurd formula to interpret that which must remain a mysterious phenomenon: the passage from One to Two, which is called the creative act.[2] We may describe it like this: An absolutely homogeneous milieu, *by the action of its own nature*, divides itself into two heterogeneous states. This phenomenon, functioning similarly, can be observed throughout all of living Nature that maintains itself by proliferating in like manner.

The concept of quantity only begins at the point of a dualization of what originally could only be a *quality* without quantity, a quality without definition.

---

[1] This is equivalent to

$$\overset{\frown}{\underset{\text{n n n}}{\ }} = \frac{\text{Unity}}{3} = \frac{\text{creative Verb}}{\text{natural multiplicity}}.$$

Cf. chapter 6, "The Egyptian Notation of Numbers."

[2] Creation is realized between the numbers One and Two, and located there in sevenths are all the scales, such as light and sound, that Plato, through Theon of Smyrna, called "the Soul of the World," which animates all. See chapter 8, appendix.

Time is genesis and genesis creates volume or space. At the beginning of things there is also *volume*, and neither plane nor line. The passage—the creation—from One to Two, the Soul of the World (Plato) is the becoming into volume. When we express it in numbers (octaves), we commit an error: sound, light, and all octaves are *volumes*.

We are dealing with a function that is the *numerating number*. This proliferating function, observable first in the plant kingdom, persists in all of Nature through the living cell, and must also be found at the basis of everything expressed in numbers.

Our science can only work backward from the effect—the *result*—to an eventual cause, by judging this cause from the point of view of the effect. Wisdom, on the contrary, begins with this cause and then works toward the result. That which speculative thought—and experience—show this cause and its consequences must be, sets out the conditions that applied philosophy must obey.

We see in pharaonic Egypt, as in almost all revealed religions, that theological philosophy was expressed through symbols in the form of "myths" or icons, that is, figurative symbols dramatized *in a historical guise*. We must remain consistent with the spirit behind these teachings; they express knowledge in the mentality of the sages of the time, for a specific era and a specific revelation, which the West, divided and "rationalized" by the exoteric debates of the Eleatic Greeks, was unable to do, as evidenced in its disregard of the myth of the Christic teaching.

We search for theories and explanations in Egypt, forgetting that the sages of those times conveyed all their thinking through their theology, in the form of myth, and in their hieratic monuments, by means of symbols. Similarly, a mathematics designed for profane needs must remain "respectfully" grounded upon hieratical principles of knowledge. To allow deviation from this discipline for "practical" reasons, or to make things "easier," is to deny its fidelity and connectedness to the esoteric tradition, and in doing so, allow it to perish.

The study of the science of numbers in the theological spirit of wise Kemit[3] must conform to the following general conditions:

1. Unity must appear as duality while retaining the essential nature of Unity. The question then is of an internal function, of the activity of a power immanent in Unity. This is the revelation of Heliopolis.
2. That which in relation to *the thing*, is as yet *nothing*, must become something, therefore must become a ternary, since we find this ternary to be the final result of any analysis. This is the revelation of Memphis.
3. That which results from the activity must be Two, that is, it must be able to multiply itself, since Two, or the dual principle, is the principle of multiplication, and everything is sustained by this principle. Thus, it is no longer only a question of pure quality, but also of a form, a quantified quality. This is the revelation of Hermopolis (Khemenu).
4. Consequently, the result must be at the same time a revelation of that which is both arithmetic—a quantitative relationship of things to each other—and geometric—the function of growth of the thing in itself. This is the Theban revelation.

These affirmations are *functional;* they have a vital, universal character. Their application or expression through numbers encourages us to regard them as denominators of active powers, not as arithmetic values. Proportions proceed from them but are not causal.

It is thus that the golden number, or sacred number (designated by the symbol ϕ),[4] is to be regarded as a creative or separating power; it is the power that *provokes* the scission, and consequently is not derived arithmetically from the root of 5, because the *power five* is not a cause but a result of this function ϕ.

[3] Kemit is a name for Ancient Egypt and means "black earth."
[4] It is customary to designate the golden number by the Greek letter ϕ.

The Heliopolitan revelation says: "Tum, immersed in the primordial water of Nun, by masturbating, created himself." This "irrationality" is represented in the temple of Luxor by the *kamutef*,
with the phallus located at the place of the navel, which in nature is the residuum of the attachment to the maternal medium and does not exist in this prenatural stage.

From our human and rational point of view we would say that the notion of activity implies
the notion of resistance, and from this the phenomenon results. Here we are dealing with a certainty that arises from the faculty of thinking itself.

Perceptible action and resistance are for us measured *values,* and from our point of view, it will
always be resistance that measures activity. It is indeed the character of Nature to be limited and
measurable, and thus everything within Nature is proportional. We are thus tempted to see in the
original scission two *equal* parts, each with the same value as the other, which, however, is impossible, since proportionality must result from this scission. Nature, the Cosmos, is *consequence,* not
cause, of this scission.

Thus Tum is, in and for life, the *coagulating* power of the formless substance, and, in numbers,
in the archetypal sense, *Tum is the power of* ϕ.[5] The "coagulation," the scission or "scissiparity," will
always occur as a function of ϕ, from which results the perfect proportion in Nature; we shall next
discover it in the pentagon as the geometrical key of numbers as functions.

It is in the nature of the function ϕ that we must search for the directives of a true numerical science, not in its applications. The applications of ϕ were brought to light again in the Renaissance,
and, in our own times, they have been studied very thoroughly by Matila C. Ghyka.[6] These studies are magnificent, but no research on this subject can be exhaustive.

One could infer from this a kind of "mysticism of numbers," but we must not lose sight of the
fact that, in the first place, ϕ *is the mystical number itself, the causal power in its numerating action.*

Numbers impose values that, with respect to each other, constitute certain invariable relationships that cannot be interpreted arbitrarily. This "power," which we must obey and which does not
obey us, leads us to speak of a mysticism of number. Accepting such a mysticism of number, however, creates an obstacle to the study of the true meaning of number.

There is an *esotericism* of number that proceeds from numbers seen as *functional symbols* (this
being the true meaning of Pythagoreanism), which is to say that the behavior of numbers with
respect to each other reveals, in their simplest expression, the functions that we see acting throughout all of Nature.

For this reason I do not accept a "mysticism of numbers," but I do see in the mysterious *function* ϕ a truly *mystical number* that presides over the harmony of Nature as the principle of the original scission, and by "presiding," I do mean an unceasing presence.

It is in the consequences of this acceptation that the mathematics of pharaonic Egypt becomes
clear. The first scission is always that of "Heaven from Earth." Heaven is Nut, unformed virginal
substance, which manifests through the germ of the seed as well as through the fetal amnion.

---

[5] In Memphis he becomes Ptah.

[6] It is to the works of Prince Matila C. Ghyka that we must always refer for the study of the golden number: *Le Nombre d'Or: Rites
et rythmes pythagoriciens dans le développement de la civilisation occidentale,* 2 vols. (Paris: Gallimard, 1931); *L'Esthétique des proportions
dans la nature et dans les arts* (Paris: Gallimard, 1927); *Philosophie et mystique du nombre* (Paris: Payot, 1952). It is since the appearance
of *Rites et rythmes* that everywhere we see all kinds of studies on the golden number and its applications. But it is to the work of
Ghyka that we must return for a perfect mathematical documentation of the question. [Books by Ghyka in English include *The
Geometry of Art and Life* (1946; reprint, New York: Dover, 1977) and *A Practical Handbook of Geometrical Composition and Design*
(London: Alec Tiranti, 1952).]

The Earth is always the first *form*, issuing from Nun, or the *punctal*, formless, unitary state of the Origin. Earth will also be the earth in general as Ptah, or Fire in earth, but also the placenta[7] and the visible root, and finally, the first *thing*, Atum or Adam.

We are dealing here with principles revealed by the action of ϕ within One; transcribed into numbers this reads $1/\phi + (1 - 1/\phi) = 1$. Now, $1 - 1/\phi = 1/\phi^2$, the first *form*, a negative square.

We thus obtain a classification including the *punctal numbers*—or *neters*—(the principles), the *linear* or *prime numbers*, then the *planar numbers*. The planar numbers result from multiplication and are therefore divisible, that is, they are the first values to appear as divisible quantities, for the former ones are not. Being divisible, planar numbers are necessarily, as products of a multiplication, composed of even numbers (feminine) and odd numbers (masculine). Thus $1/\phi$ is Heaven and $1 - 1/\phi$ is Earth, a divisible value because *it is the first square. The root of this Earth is Heaven.* Phi is the manifesting power provoking the original scission, but this creative *function* is written $\sqrt{2}$, which in relation to One reveals the first notion of duality, Heaven and Earth, whose elements are Nun $= 1$, and $\phi =$ coagulating action.

Mystically, and as a result of the action of ϕ, the number Two has the value ϕ^2, which is vitally true.

There are only two ways in which a line can be divided into two parts so that a proportional relationship between its two segments is formed, $1 : 1$ and $1 : \phi$.[8]

Let us note that the height of a newborn child is divided into two equal parts by the navel, which is the proportion $1 : 1$. In adulthood, the division of the body's height at the navel yields two parts that are to one another as $1 : \phi$.

One $+ \phi = \phi \times \phi = \phi^2$, that is, the second power of ϕ. If man, in the image of God (a ternary resulting from 2 to 1), is potentially the ultimate product of Nature, he is ϕ^2, which is true in pharaonic thinking, as we are going to see.[9]

And we shall proceed logically from this point on.

1. There exists only one irrational and incommensurable number and this is the punctal number, One. All other numbers denote quantity.
2. All the *numerated* numbers are, in principle, fractions of *One*, the totality, the numerator; and the fractions represent quantities.
3. All quantities expressed as whole numbers (except prime numbers) are, in the first place, surfaces, and, because they are composed of the multiplication of a number with itself or with one or more whole numbers,[10] their division can only be expressed by the number of multipliers of the whole numbers they contain.
4. The square root of a number that is not an exact square must be expressed through whole numbers of which, the plus and minus approximations being multiplied, give the absolute result.

---

[7] The films of Jean Painlevé show the male sea horse playing the nurturing role for the eggs that he receives from the female. This is not the only case in the animal kingdom where we find the male playing the role of placenta, which the female mammal carries in the womb. This is something to watch for when the hieroglyphs use the placenta as a symbol.

[8] Cf. Ghyka, *Esthétique des proportions*, p. 37: "With the two segments and the total length, one can establish six ratios. By establishing the equalities between two ratios, one obtains fifteen combinations, eight of which are impossible. Thus, seven are left, which reduces to four if one eliminates similar combinations. These four combinations reduce to two and their inverses."

[9] Cf. chapter 10.

[10] Decomposition into prime factors.

5. All vital functions are related to the separating action of ϕ and are described in terms of $\sqrt{2}$.[11]
6. Royal Man (perfect man) is ϕ^2, and all the units of measure derived from man are related to ϕ^2 and thus become cosmic measure.[12]

These are then the first conclusions issuing from the transcendental action that of *One* makes *Two.* These Two, like the Father and the Son in Christian dogma, as the First and the Third, are of the Universe with respect to their dual expression, which is the Spirit, Two. This *dual* nature is represented in Egypt by Shu and Tefnut coming between Nut (Heaven) and Geb (Earth) in the form of humidity and warmth.

Let us note here that Shu-Tefnut is represented in both single and double forms, and Shu with one knee on earth or standing, holding up Nut (Heaven) with both arms. Nut remains bound to the earth *by both feet and hands.* Nut is not "some thing," she is the place of gestation of all things, *the place from which the fire falls to earth,* that is, the materializing fire. Ordinary, visible fire is the act of marriage of this fire with the earth, the flame that burns the air and forms the water.

We see the circular zodiac of Dendera supported by four crossed Shu-Tefnuts, along with the double configuration of Heaven and Earth, all of these—the four single and four double elements—are in Nun, the primordial hyle.

Duality within Unity constitutes the essential mystical ternary. It is described in numbers by 1, $1/\phi$, $1/\phi^2$ (Father, Holy Spirit, and Son). These are the three mystical thirds of which Two have the value of One, of the whole or Unity from which they arise. There is no better way to explain the mystery of the Trinity. Among other reasons, it is out of respect for this mystery, and to recall this strange duality in three, that the numerical notation 2/3 was retained by the Ancients, the only case of a numerator of 2 among their fractions, which were always reduced to a numerator of 1.

As a mystical value, 2/3 equals 1, and in order to become 1 again arithmetically, it must be multiplied *by crossing* it with itself, $(2/3) \times (3/2) = 1$. Now, this unity will no longer be a punctal number but a surface, since $(2/3) \times (3/2)$ yields a quadrangle, a surface. In other words, the result of the division of the punctal Unity, multiplied with its reciprocal (complement), again becomes Unity, but a formal unity. This is obvious, but what is less so is the way by which we arrive at this result. What is revealed to us is *the inequality of the parts that form a whole,*[13] and also the *function of crossing,* which is something we find throughout all of Nature.

These principles are figured by 2/3, 𓂓 or 𓂓, which is composed of the mouth, *ra* 𓂋, and the sign *s* 𓋴. This is the acting function or the "cause" that divides, the Verb that from One creates the number Two, the divine ternary.

[11] See this chapter, "Harmony," and "Pharaonic Volumes."

[12] See chapter 10, "Measures and Cubits."

[13] The notation of 1/2 is 𓐛, two unequal quantities.

a) The first number, *One,* is all. It can just as well be the triangle as the square, male as well as female. Added to or subtracted from a number it modifies that number's functional value as male (odd) or female (even).

b) Any number divisible by whole numbers is a surface, which is the first notion of quantity since it is divisible.

A transcendental number, that is, an acting power, becomes a positive number when it responds to the demand that we make it cerebrally comprehensible. It must then become limited in time and space, hence, definable. The initial *temporal* definition is the surface, the transcendental square $1/\phi^2$, which we subsequently represent by the number 4, the first quantity that permits us to draw the square ¦ ¦. Here, each constituent unit is already positive and has undergone that which, conversely, only this way of thinking can make clear. Indeed, Unity is transcendent; it will only have a positive value through the number 4, and this number, in turn, only has a positive value when 1 is positive. Now, the notion *Four,* which implies all the functions that this number summarizes, includes One, Two, and Three, thus:

```
    |            1
   |  |          2
  |  |  |        3
 |  |  |  |      4
```

This is one of the justifications for the sacred tetraktys of the Pythagoreans, which originated in Egypt.

The transcendent Unity equals, in a positive or comprehensible number, Ten, and we should think "ten" in stating One. Then the first multiplied number, which is 4, the first square, has the value of *Forty* (the number of quickening in Nature), the first temporal measure, which is functionally $1/\phi^2$.

The tetraktys is a triangle because it is composed of the series of natural numbers increasing at the rate of 1, contained in the last number. Thus, *the triangle is the statement of the implicit values* that are made explicit by the values contained in a positive number.

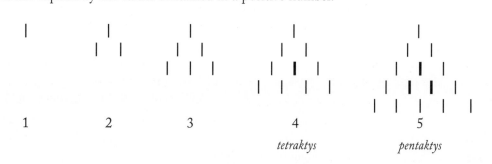

1	2	3	4	5
			tetraktys	*pentaktys*

The first *quantity* (temporal) is a square surface. The triangular number 4 plus the triangular number 5 is 10 + 15, which equals 25, the square of 5; thus

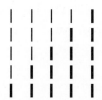

This is the throne of the world and the royal pharaonic throne, symbolized by a square divided into four, that is, 1 and 3 making 4, with one fourth being added to the four others to make the gnomon of 4 to 5 (fig. 2).

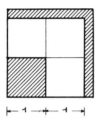 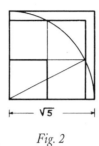 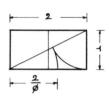

Fig. 2

The full side of this throne will be the square root of five. The square root of five less one unit equals $2/\phi$, if the side equals 2, or geometrically $\sqrt{5} - 1$; but if the side equals 1, we have the proportion $1/\phi$ or $(\sqrt{5} - 1)/2$ (fig. 3).

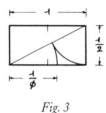

Fig. 3

All the positive numbers, all the possible functions, are thus summarized in the single symbol of the throne: the mystical function ϕ; the relationship $3 : 4 : 5$, the basis of trigonometry; the temporal value that presides over all gestation, the numbers One to Five, and which, by their triangular nature preside over time: the nine cosmic temporal principles and their twelve temporal zones in the heavens.

The tetraktys includes nine powers around the throne of unity; this is Semitic thinking. The pentaktys includes twelve zones (the Twelve Apostles around the unitary Trinity); this is Christian thinking.[14]

We are able to situate a temporal moment in space, but space as volume is only comprehensible to us through the plane, the surface that measures volume. The cerebral intelligence is *planar* and not spatial. *The intelligence of volume is what the Ancients called the "intelligence of the heart."* All imagination, all linear representation, all description, is planar. The parabolic line, for example, is the contour of a section of volume, as is the path traced by the movement of a comet. In this way we can consider all curves as sectional contours of a volume.

To demonstrate the esoteric sense we have only the symbol that, through architecture, speaks to us in volume.

Analysis shows us three directions within a volume, but in reality three planes will never, even in their displacement, reconstitute a volume. Displacement in the direction of a plane is only an addition of planes, which is pure supposition, because planes have no depth. The geometric

---

[14] From the tetraktys to the pentaktys we are going from Semitic to Christian consciousness, but wisdom brings them together in a single whole.

description of volume by the movement of planes is cinematography, an illusion. Our rationalistic mathematics is thus a mass of *suppositions* by which we bring back to the *lower stage* of our cerebral consciousness realities *experienced* a priori: the knowledge of the intelligence of the heart.

Pharaonic thought clearly guards against following this path of "reduction." The first *thing*, the first quantity, is a volume, a space defined within time. A sectioned volume appears as a plane, but in order to make a volume, one must assemble other volumes.

Moses said, "and God made the expanse." Now Moses was initiated in Egypt, and he took the knowledge with him.

While $1/\phi^2$ appears to us as a plane, the Unity in which ϕ acts is space. In numbers, the first square is 4 and the first volume is 8. The root of 4 is 2, and *half* of 4 is 2, and 2 is also the cube root of 8.

We write $1/\phi^2$ as 0.381966..., *half* of which is 0.19098.... The number 19.098..., which equals $6.180...^2/2$ (which we can round off as 19), is of the nature of ϕ. Now, this "pilot number" and the mystical number ϕ engender only those numbers that are functions of ϕ, and since the entire universe results from this function, all will be proportioned by this function, whether it be the human being, plant, or the genesis of the mineral, or time, or the sizes and distances of the stars.

Consequently, it is important to establish fundamental values in order to provide a solid foundation for the construction of this thought.

It is necessary to regard ϕ as the *numerical symbol* of the creative *function* and of procreation, and not as a quantity. It is this function that proportions things, distinguishes them, qualifies them, and situates them. It is the action of Tum; it is the Fire animating all life, the seed that specifies the indeterminate, nutritive substance, the male (solar) action of the spermatozoon, the ♄ of the Hermeticists, the Verb acting in God, the Verb of the Gospel of John.

The numbers 1, 2, 4, and 8 are the *names,* respectively, of the *point* and the *line* that is movement, the first divisible number, then the surface, that is, the enumerated number, and finally, the *volume,* that is, the space (One), limited in quantity.

Volume is space contracted, coagulated into its form, by the action of ϕ. Volume is thus Unity *temporally* situated in quality of space, that which makes *form.* We should rectify here the meaning of a notion: the geometric rendering of a form is an artifice, a reasoned numerical definition, not actually the form itself. The "form" is a *vital specification:* the mineral, the plant, the animal, and the human body are all real natural forms. Copper is a form; grasses and other specific plants are forms; and by the same token a cat and a dog are forms.

The action of ϕ within the human spermatozoon causes the human form, and its gestation is a coagulation of spatial substance into temporal situations, dividing itself into embryonic phases in a temporal relation with cosmic gestations.

Although the activity of ϕ is universal, it is *uniform.* Variety cannot be caused either by the coagulating substance or by the action of ϕ. Variety is produced by the succession of moments within a single genesis that, for us, has its finality in man. Thus, all forms are situated between a term that is the first, universal form and this final form having present man as its form. The first form is thus *potentially* man, and each moment of this genesis is a specificity that is contained and summarized in man, whether it be an atomic moment, or a geological, plant, or animal moment.

This succession, each moment of which has a *name,* constitutes the sequence of natural numbers: the nature, the character, the kinships, the relationships, and the proportions proper to these moments, the *things* contained in the human genesis.

The nine members of the tetraktys surrounding the Unity are the nine transcendental powers or numbers characterizing the modes of action. The twelve numbers around the original ternary in the fifth triangle define the twelve divisions of time.

The volume is the form, but the perfect sphere has no form; it is the amniotic sac containing all; it is the transcendental form for volumes just as Unity is the transcendental number for the numerated numbers. It represents the first expanse.

The surface, which appears to us as the limit of a form, or a sectioned form, is the *definition of the size of that form*. This definition is temporal, that is, present, and is not definitive. It is the (numerated) number itself, variable in time.

Essentially, number is triangular and remains so through all the forms that are composed of this triangular principle.[15]

Similarly, the volume-form can only be composed of volumes; the surface, being the measure of the sizes of the volume or form, can only be composed of surfaces. It is through the mystery of the Ternary that the transcendent Unity becomes actual, and it is by the Duality in the Ternary that the Unity becomes the measure of the thing, the surface $3 \times 3 \times 3$ defining the volume, and 2×2 defining the surface.

The first form or the first volume results from the action of ϕ within One and is written 1 to $1/\phi$ to $1/\phi^2$. We can also write it as $1/1 : 1/\phi : 1/\phi^2$, being the proportion $1 : \phi : \phi^2$. This corresponds to the squares of the sides of the triangle of the vertical half-section of the Pyramid of Cheops: the base equals 1; the height equals $\sqrt{\phi}$; the slope or apothem equals ϕ. Their squares are respectively $1, \phi, \phi^2$.

The first surface of the action of ϕ within One is the dualization of this Unity into $1/\phi$ and $1/\phi^2$. Now, the sum, as the product of ϕ and ϕ^2, is ϕ^3. In negative (or inverse) numbers the sum equals One and the product equals $1/\phi^3$.[16] Now, this is the sum that must make One, being like the addition of *two* parts of One.

With regard to the Pyramid of Cheops, the sum of the squares of the height and the hypotenuse of its triangle (vertical half-section) is also $\phi + \phi^2 = \phi^3$. Then the unity of the base is either $\phi^3/\phi^3 = 1$, as a positive number, or One, the transcendent number. One of these gives a positive number for the *cube*, the other a negative number for the Unity that is space.

In negative or "inverse" numbers, the square plus its root equals One. In positive numbers the square plus its root equals a cube. One materializes the other, giving it form. The surface measures the volume but has no volume itself.[17]

―――

[15] On this subject, the total number of units composing the triangle whose last term is n, is $n[(n+1)/2]$, and, since each number is triangular in its essence, if ϕ were a number and not a function, we should find for $\phi[(\phi+1)/2]$, a sum of ϕ, but instead we find $\phi^3/2$, half of a cube.

   If one does a summation of ϕ in the manner of triangular numbers, $\phi^{\phi^{\phi}}\phi$, the sum $n[(n+1)/2]$ applied to ϕ becomes $n: \phi[(n+1)/2]$.

[16] That is, $\phi + \phi^2 = \phi \times \phi^2 = \phi^3$.

[17] Here are some relationships: the functional value of the first square $= 0.381966...$, and the positive value of the first square $= \phi$. The root of $0.381966 = 1/\phi = 0.618034...$, and the root of $\phi^2 = \phi = 1.618034...$. The cube of $1/\phi = 0.236067...$, and the cube of $\phi = 4 + 0.236067... = 4.236$.

The *line,* the number-line, understood in its esoteric sense, is movement. In its exoteric sense, movement is a displacement in space and in a time. This is an objective analysis of that which is esoterically termed duration, or vital movement.[18]

Unity alone is absolute duration. Any other duration is conditioned by a beginning and an end; it is a fraction of absolute duration. The impulse of the beginning reaches its conclusion with the potentially implied finality, that is, *the seed of its species.*

Duration, the esoteric movement, is thus a continuity in and of itself, represented by the prime numbers: odd numbers (male) that are not formed by the multiplication of either male or female numbers, such as 1, 3, 5, 7, 11, 13, 17, 19, ... Each one of these numbers is comparable to a species that perpetuates itself through the individual. They are composed of units that are of the nature of the whole number. They form a continuity, a duration, by their own seed.

The number-line is the Father, and at the same time the Son, of surfaces measuring a volume. In a solid it is represented by the edge.[19]

Movement, in the sense of exoteric duration, is the complement, the opposition to the coagulating action of ϕ. The function ϕ reduces the Space (One) into *volume; movement fights this reduction* by trying to force apart again this contracted space.

In physics the activity ϕ appears thus as the centripetal magnetic force in opposition to the centrifugal electric effect. The centrifugal effect is equatorial; therefore, it is a plane delimited by a circuit.

The circle is not a line, neither is the disk a surface. The circle is a *circuit* and as such *is vitally never closed.* The linear function ϕ is represented as a spiral of the function ϕ progressively moving toward its own center, which determines a surface $\phi^2 = \phi + 1$, in opposition to $\phi^2 - 1 = \phi$ (fig. 4).

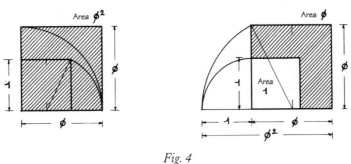

Fig. 4

This graphic representation is the opposite of the direction of the action in which $\phi + 1$ is a concentration, whereas $\phi^2 - 1$ is a dispersal.[20]

---

[18] How could we carve a duration out of eternity? Either eternity is an illusion formed of juxtapositions of "durations," or the duration is an apparent fraction of eternity appearing and disappearing as a form. Now, nothing allows the notion of duration, thus the appearance of an existence for a time, with a beginning and without end, which is precisely the notion of continuity. It imposes the consciousness of a "before" and an "after." The "irrational consciousness" of the eternal is what forms the psychological consciousness of duration. The eternal could then be symbolized as a thread assumed to be without beginning or end, forming *nodes* or temporary appearances, limited in duration, on the continuity. This is symbolized by the *chen,* the "cartouche," ⬭ the "set of initials" imprisoning the *ren,* the name.

[19] The number-line can serve as an example to demonstrate the "contradictory" character of the simultaneity of the complements and the exoteric and esoteric aspects.

[20] It is impossible to represent the function graphically without reversing it.

In plant genesis $\phi + 1$ causes the root, and in embryo genesis it causes the placenta. They have their complementary opposites in the germ of the seed and in the amnion. The alternation of these causes and effects gives the product that manifests life, which is the action of ϕ: the alternating concentration of the $\triangle$ (or Fire) of the Space (One).

—⁓—

The importance of defining the esoteric rationale for numbers—that is, the importance of considering the vital cause of enumeration in the Universe—consists in revealing the knowledge of the powers that create the genesis. Numbers are then no longer merely notations that designate quantities, but the expression of living functions. They become the names and terms of a language in which each number is a *personality* that has sympathies and antipathies, that arranges marriages and generates series, that divides and assembles.

Since each number is a characterized unity and a surface, it is best represented graphically. Mathematics is then geometrical; if it were not, it would open the door to all the "plays of the mind" that are based upon "suppositions."

As long as we deal with mechanical considerations, the mathematics of quantities, algebraic or not, has reason to exist. It becomes, on the other hand, cause for misunderstanding when it addresses itself to the vital function.

The function $(a + b)^2$ becomes tangible and clear when it is rendered graphically (fig. 5).

Fig. 5

The odd-numbered "gnomons" that separate each square from the following one in the series of natural numbers are obvious.

The triangular numbers ₁¹₁ are distinguished from square numbers ¦ ¦ and from hexagonal numbers ₁¦₁¦₁.

The diagonal *drawn* in a square with whole number sides is mathematically irrational and graphically finite, thus we must calculate in such a way that the number can be determined. A fractioned totality must be able to be reconstituted into a whole.

Because there is a creative function definable at the origin, everything should be able to be resolved again by that function. This, then, is the Theory of Number and the only true Philosophy. All the rest is but imaginary projection.

Everything in the Universe is *vitally* moving; thus, mathematics, insofar as it is a description of this Universe, must conform to this movement.

Man is the center of our Universe—made in the image of the creative power that is his *potentiality*—thus he must, by his being, his form, and his life, demonstrate all that we can think and know of this Universe. This is the foundation for the esotericism of number *born from the mystical number.*

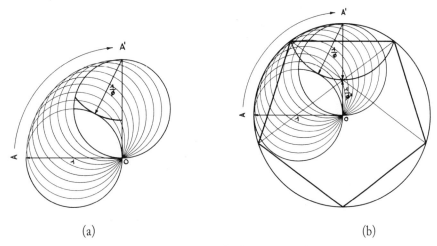

(a)   (b)

Fig. 6. Figure synthesis of the mystical function φ

(a) Following construction of a quarter arc, any diameter of a circle, equal to 1, when rotated around one of its ends will have its opposite end at a distance of $1/\phi$ from its original circumference. *(b)* The double square results from this function, whereas the usual demonstration of ϕ by a double square is but one geometrical resolution of the arithmetical proposition $(\sqrt{5}+1)/2$.

From this function, which is the result of the cycle, innumerable forms emerge.

THE IRRATIONAL

The first number, the line, can be regarded as an addition of supposed points. We can then say that the Universe is only number on the condition that we consider this Universe as being *composite*.

Now, the *composite* of the Universe is *vitally* made only by formed units, that is, by generated units, not assumed ones (such as the mathematical point). We are reasoning with the Pythagorean principle as materialists, whereas the Ancients reasoned as vitalists. For them—in the esotericism of the science of numbers—unity is not a stage, an arrested moment of a genesis (quantity), but a *state* of a gestation.

Thus, the number is a function and not the factor of a function. In this sense the study of the relationships of quantities would not be of interest to the sage. It would only be a play of quantitative relationships creating some possible (rational) ratios and some impossible (irrational) ratios "without name" (ἄλογον). The function alone is important, and if the statement (the logos, λόγος, and ⬦) is impossible, it does not relate to the function but only to a quantitative relationship.

In truth, squares are functionally only the surfaces (or sections) of cubes resulting from a number multiplied with itself. They are the only ones to have rational roots. All other surfaces are what we may call surfaces "by marriage" because they result from the multiplication of two unequal numbers whose root is a composite of the roots of each component.

If a number is not a surface, that is, not the result either of the multiplication of a number by itself or of the marriage of unequal numbers, then it is a prime number and will not have a rational root.

Thus we can only look for the surface number, smaller or larger, that is contained in this number or in the number immediately following it. If this married surface itself contains a number that is not a surface, we can then only search for approximations that never culminate in a rational result, and that can only be expressed in unresolvable fractions.

This irrational character results from *our mental desire for schematization*. We insist that a square root correspond to an exact square even if the components of this quadrangle are unequal. We *require* that the object conform to the rational character of the applied function.

It is a question here of a mental systematization that is absolutely contrary to the mentality of the Ancients.

For example, we say "the root of 10" without troubling ourselves as to whether this number is a square or a rectangle. We require that the number be composed of the multiplication of a rational number with itself, while the actual result is an irrational number that can no longer ever reconstitute this number 10. When we want to reconstitute a perfect square from what was an irregular quadrangle, we are satisfied with this type of conclusion, but the pharaonic mathematician would not be satisfied. For him, the divine Unity alone escapes our reason, whereas everything that is created is knowable, and any whole that is divided can be reconstituted with its fractions into a near unity.

On the other hand, the number is always reconstituted again through the procedure of the "inverse" or reciprocal. (It is a question here of the simultaneity of the component complements that create the phenomenon. This simultaneity is a crossing.) What is irrational for our mental concept is the indefinable vital moment of a genesis.

The notion of the inverse goes back to the furthest antiquity (as Thureau-Dangin has pointed out, this mode of calculation is already found in Sumerian mathematics). The use of the inverse is so prevalent in Egypt that it is not even mentioned, but is constantly applied (Rhind Papyrus).[21]

Obviously, we can always *substitute* a regular quadrangle for any surface (any numerating number is a surface), whether it be a triangle or a polygon, and state the value of its surface in the supposed square. But these are "mental games," "*jeux d'esprit*," if one can refer to the mental faculty with the word *esprit*. It is this predisposition of the Ancients that I would like to speak of here, leaving the explanation of procedure to the chapter on calculation.

The Egyptians were geometers and they thought as geometers, but at the same time they did not make the mistake of taking geometric figures for reality. Any figuration is a "mental" transposition of a function, a *symbol*. In the same way a numeral is a mental transposition of a number, that is, of the definition of a function.

The Egyptian mentality is not "scientific" in the Western sense of the word, it is *vital*. In fact, *for the pharaonic mathematician the problem of the rational and the irrational did not exist because of his certainty concerning the Unique Being who alone dominates the rational and by this fact escapes it. It is this Being who creates life.* The sage then would never succumb to the temptations of the facility of mechanistic rationalism. The phenomenon (here the result of a calculation) is an apparent moment of an action and the reaction of complementary components, which is the principle of the procedure of the inverse, the source of the Pythagorean (and Greek) *medieties*.

Any definitive edge given by a geometric (figured) symbolization, and standing as invariable law, is an embalmed corpse, the symbol, the support of an abstract life that is rationally indefinable. (In this light we can look upon all the objects and symbolic figurations added to the mummy and see that they were placed on it in precise locations in order to point to knowledge of "abstractions," the supraterrestrial or ultraphysical life.)

---

[21] For example, to divide a number by a fraction, you multiply it by the inverted fraction, or, according to the Babylonian expression, you multiply it by the reciprocal of the dividing fraction. Thus:

$$2 \div \frac{1}{3} = 2 \times \frac{3}{1} = 2 \times 3 = 6.$$

Based on this fundamental principle, we shall see that the scribe of the papyrus also operates by "direct division" and multiplies the dividing fraction by 1/3 to find the number 2. Moreover, this technique applies the law of proportion in which "the product of extremes equals the product of the means." The issue here is of a double inversion characteristic of pharaonic mathematics.

A geometric function in which an irrational number intervenes is in a state of gestation. In a geometric figuration, the irrational number always indicates the function. When we have a geometric figure in which all the givens are rational, such as a Diophantine triangle, we have an example of an arrested, finite form; with such figures we are not able to reconstitute an essential, living figure, as we can do with a simple square.

For example, if we take cylinders and put them next to each other in successive layers, they will pack together in such a way that all the empty spaces between them are filled and will form hexagonal prisms that will resemble a row of wax cells in a beehive. The first opening is a circle; the size of this circle will not vary but will become a hexagon each side of which has the value of $\pi/3$ for the radius of 1 of the original circle.

This irrationality is the functional expression of the action of carrying the same size, such as the circumference of a circle, from one form to another.

Now, this is the manner in which life operates in Nature.

Whether it was a question of spirit, life, cosmogony, theology, or geometry and mathematics in general, the pharaonic sages did not conceive of any separation in principle among these domains. They did not, as we do, cut the Universe into a thousand pieces, and put each part in a different pigeonhole.

—///—

The diagonal of a square whose side equals 1 will be the square root of 2. The square is a defined fact, thus the root of 2 is a defined fact, but an arrested moment of a movement, in reality, a stage of a gestation. Now, this square is the vertical section of a cube whose measures are the root of 2 and the root of 3, its diagonals. *The "functions" of the root of 2, the root of 3, and the root of 5 speak as numbers in the sanctuaries* (rooms I, V, and VII) *of the temple of Luxor.*[22] The "Holy of Holies" expresses the *function-keys* from which the living phenomenon results. This is said in "numbers" at the places on the human body where the glands of the encephalon, the centers of life, are located. But the procedure that allows for the calculation of these "roots" is precisely the revelation of the procedure of interchange of these endocrine glands, essential and "original" to organic life (fig. 7).

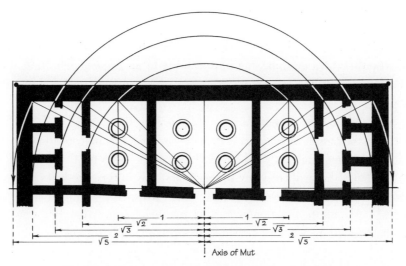

Fig. 7. The southern sanctuary of the covered temple of Luxor

[22] We will also find here the essential functions of the cycle and of volume.

Number is the definition of the functions, and it is in this sense only that the Universe is number.

With the root of 2, the root of 3, and the root of 5, all three of which are irrational to our mentality, it is possible to reconstitute all surfaces and all volumes.[23]

GOD AND THE IRRATIONAL

The rationalistic thinker would say: "God is a word designating an extrapolation that indicates everything we cannot understand." From his point of view, which seeks cerebral, therefore objectifiable understanding, he is correct. He is also correct in saying that this state called God is incomprehensible. But the rational thinker is wrong not to designate this state as the incomprehensible Being who, in the last analysis, is the Being of everything and that the comprehensible thing is only a momentary limitation of this One Being into a definable being, because all that which is defined necessarily comes out of an indefinable All.

Now, number exists in order to make this axiom evident to us when it shows us the irrationality of the relation between two numbers. The irrational number imposes itself through the reasoning of calculation. It takes on a finite appearance by means of the geometric figuration, but it is and always remains infinite. It is as irrational as God and as the ultimate formless substance that we call Spirit.

This is why the irrational *number* is an absurdity. We should speak of an irrational *value* made evident by a relation between two rational numbers, which, themselves, are accessible because they are arrested. Thus the root of 2 appears as an irrational value that creates the relationship between 1 and 2.

The characteristic by which we can recognize an irrational value is that its multiplication with itself produces a finite number. Yet it is incomprehensible that the infinite multiplied with the infinite could give the finite.

This is the mystery of the Origin, and it is also the mystery of the everyday, because there can be no becoming at all except through this strange function.

It is not possible for One to become Two without this mystical function that summarizes all the relationships of harmony in the world.

But with regard to the number Two and to all the numbers thus defined, they will always lack a *quantum,* no matter how minute, because of this impossibility of multiplying the infinite with itself.

In other words, numbers and their relations show us the real existence of an irrational being and they prove, by their own example, the impossibility of an *absolute* definition. Thus, irrational values must always be considered as being Spirit in its becoming toward a characterized, that is, specified, thing.

If the sages established the numerical schemes based on the roots of 2, 3, and 5 for the three secret sanctuaries in the temple of Luxor, it is necessary to look for their spiritual significance in the fixing of life in these three vital centers. One establishes the harmony, that is, the form, the other will make the substance that will corporify the seed, and this in turn produces the third.

There are essentially three aspects of the irrational: the function of the square $[\sqrt{2}]$; the function of the circle $[\sqrt{3}]$; and the function of ϕ $[\sqrt{5}]$, the dividing function. Before we pass on to the application of these functions we must consider the principle of harmony.

[23] Cf. chapter 7, "Functional Development of the Law of Right Triangles," and the construction of the octahedron.

ON HARMONY

HARMONY

It is not without reason that the Ancients placed the harmonic relation at the origin of their mathematics. But rather than seeing a numerical proportion as a foundation for calculating, we must see instead the numerical expression of a vital function.

Harmony presupposes a relationship and essentially includes a notion of equilibrium. This, however, cannot entirely express harmony because perfect equilibrium excludes movement, be it mechanical or vital, and does not represent concord any more than discord, the balanced elements together constituting a new state. It is only at the moment when the equilibrium ruptures that harmony or disharmony can manifest between the parts, which will be expressed by either their affinity or their repulsion. If the affinity again produces a state of equilibrium between the two natures or forces (or tendencies), we can no longer speak of a harmony. We must then circumscribe the notion of harmony with *a functional affinity*, more precisely, an affinity that is never complemented and that manifests only in response to a vital movement. Materially (in mechanics) or vitally, the harmonic moment will always be the *present moment*, between equilibrium and disequilibrium.

The sense of harmony in human beings is thus a supernatural sense. It can be applied to the five informing senses, but it is tangibly most evident to the ear in musical harmony.

Nature is the consequence of a rupture in the equilibrium of Unity, a disharmony of the original equanimity, which escapes us. The harmony of Nature becomes then the call to assemblage through affinity, and Nature, which seeks equilibrium (its inertia), allows for neither disharmony nor excess. But life constantly comes to disturb this repose; thus each rupture of the natural harmony dissociates anew the component elements that immediately will seek to reassemble themselves following their own affinities. This will once again be a harmony that can take on a new form.

Death is a dissociation of the bodily complex and a liberation of the consciousness, the mediety in its vital form. The body is then given to further dissociation into its mineral, plant, and animal components, with an immediate reassociation of the elements from these kingdoms into various "lives." But consciousness undergoes a similar dissociation because it is not yet an absolute Unity. Anesthesia or drunkenness or passionate excitement are cases of a similar dissociation of consciousness, where dispositions can appear that in a more disciplined life remain quite hidden.

The calculation of the Ancients using inverses and medieties is but an application of what in fact occurs in all of living Nature. Harmony and disharmony are the manifestations of vital alternation.

The sense of musical harmony is the sensitivity to Reality, a supernatural state, imponderable and thus indestructible, a relationship, a function. But we are educated to see only the exoteric aspect of the phenomenon. It is certainly the most difficult thing in the world to get rid of the "upside-down" consciousness that we have had to acquire in order to adapt to physical incarnation.

We ascertain sensorially that a shock or blow to a body, caused by whatever means and with the intention of breaking or separating it into parts, produces a sound. I will even go so far as to say that it is not the force employed that will cause the break but the particular sound. In a vacuum, this sound does not exist—for our ear—but it exists through its vibration. So the error is to believe that it is this vibration that produces the effect when, in reality, it is the *musical character* of the sound, that is, the harmonic or disharmonic relationship, that acts. There is a magic in sound, but it escapes the exoteric intelligence, this baneful deity that the West worships exclusively.

The Sense of Harmony

In order to facilitate understanding of the problem of musical numbers, a dry subject to the uninformed reader, here are some explanations.

A taut string, when vibrated (by either striking or plucking it), produces a sound. But this will not be a *tone*.[24] This sound will be arbitrary until there is a further development. If we now divide this same string into 3/4 of its length, this 3/4 will vibrate more rapidly than the 4/4. By itself, this vibration is still only a sound. But if we place the vibration of the 4/4 into relation with the vibration of the 3/4, thereby establishing a *ratio of vibrations of 4 to 3*, we will then have a harmonious musical consonance; in this case, it is the first harmonious relationship, the *fourth*.

Likewise, if we take 8/9 of the same string at the identical tension as the 9/9, we will have the first *tone* of this fourth. After we have gone through the various divisions (thus establishing the different possible ratios), we will come to the half-string, which will vibrate at the *octave* of the pitch of the whole string.

Thus, the starting point is physical through the vibration and arithmetical through the proportion. The *musical effect*, our *sensation* of harmony or disharmony, is a judgment related to our *vital* equilibrium. This has nothing in common with the physical and arithmetical, or mechanical, aspects of sound retransmitted by the mechanism of the ear, but is heard and understood by our vital living being without the intervention of reason. Now, this capacity of hearing is extremely sensitive, and, when retranslated into its mechanical aspect, it reveals to us the very slightest physical and arithmetical modifications.

Sound

The *sound* is the effect of a vibration. The *tone* is the effect of a relationship between vibrations. We use the string as an instrument to produce the sound and to measure the vibrations.

Sound spreads in spheres[25] and its intensity diminishes in inverse ratio to the square of the distance. The "pitch" of the sound is in inverse ratio to the length of the vibrating string. If we start with a string that produces sixteen vibrations per second, half of this string will give twice sixteen, or thirty-two, vibrations. Now the halved string gives the octave of the original sound. Thus a first octave lies between sixteen and thirty-two vibrations, that is, between one and one-half of the length of the string.

When the string is shortened by part of its length with a bridge, the ratio or interval between the sound of this length and that of the entire string, represented by whole numbers, forms the harmony. Thus, the ratio of length 3 to 4 will give the ratio of vibrations produced by 4 to 3, which forms the first consonant interval, called the fourth.

One needs to consider this phenomenon then from both the physical and the musical points of view. The two are related to one another but should not be confused. The phenomenon of the musical "interval" is of a purely *numerical* and functional kind; the phenomenon of "vibrations" is by nature physical and expressed in quantities: length, surface, and volume.

It is possible, therefore, to express a sound by a specific length; it is not possible to express tone except by a ratio of two lengths. Thus we recall that 8/9 of a string constitutes a tone in relation to

---

[24] Cf. Theon of Smyrna, *Le Nombre de Platon*, trans. J. Dupuis (Paris: Hachette, 1892), Part 2, §5, p. 83: "Dissonant and nonconsonant sounds are those sounds for which the interval is a tone or a half tone, because the tone and the half tone are the basis of harmony but not harmony itself." (Consonant intervals: octave, double octave, fifth, and fourth.)

[25] Sound *spreads in volume*, so there is a connection between sound and volume, as we shall see in the definition of pharaonic volumes.

the sound of the whole string, establishing one tone of the first scale formed by this whole string up to its halfway point, which is its octave. The complete octave comprises seven sounds; the eighth sound is the *analogue* of the first sound for the second octave.

There are three principles of simple and perfect harmony:

$$\text{the fifth } = \frac{2}{3} \quad \text{or} \quad \textbf{2 to 3}$$

$$\text{the fourth } = \frac{3}{4} \quad \text{or} \quad \textbf{3 to 4}$$

$$\text{the third } = \frac{4}{5} \quad \text{or} \quad \textbf{4 to 5}$$

The third was not considered, or at least *was not named,* by the Pythagoreans, who—for their initial demonstration—took into account only the simple ratios of the fourth, fifth, and the octave, the *tetrachord.* We can see immediately the relation of harmony to the tetraktys and to the sacred 3, 4, 5 triangle.

Let us note once more that this passage from one (the length of the string) to one-half (of this length), which makes up the octave—the passage from One to Two—includes seven fundamental stages.

TABLE 1

Ratios of String Length and Vibrations for a String with a Value of 1

Division of the string	Ratio of vibrations	Musical effect	= Interval	Geometric form
$\frac{1}{1}$	$\frac{1}{1} = 1$	a sound		unity
$\frac{8}{9}$	$\frac{9}{8}$	a tone	difference between a fifth and a fourth	
$\frac{3}{4}$	$\frac{4}{3}$	fourth	first harmonious interval	
$\frac{2}{3}$	$\frac{3}{2}$	fifth	second harmonious interval	
$\frac{1}{2}$	$\frac{2}{1} = 2$	octave	2 fourths + 1 tone 1 fourth + 1 fifth	the line
$\frac{3}{8}$	$\frac{8}{3}$		1 octave + 1 fourth	
$\frac{3}{9} = \frac{1}{3}$	$\frac{9}{3} = 3$		1 octave + 1 fifth	
$\frac{3}{12} = \frac{1}{4}$	$\frac{12}{3} = 4$	2 octaves	4 fourths + 2 tones 2 fourths + 2 fifths	the square
$\frac{3}{16}$	$\frac{16}{3}$		2 octaves + 1 fourth	
$\frac{2}{12} = \frac{1}{6}$	$\frac{12}{2} = 6$		2 octaves + 1 fifth	
$\frac{2}{16} = \frac{1}{8}$	$\frac{16}{2} = 8$	3 octaves	6 fourths + 3 tones 3 fourths + 3 fifths	the cube

The addition of the intervals is equal to the multiplication of the ratios of the vibrations:

Addition	Multiplication
1 fifth + 1 fourth = 1 octave	$\dfrac{3}{2} \times \dfrac{4}{3} = \dfrac{12}{6} = 2$
2 fifths + 2 fourths = 2 octaves	$\left(\dfrac{3}{2}\right)^2 \times \left(\dfrac{4}{3}\right)^2 = \dfrac{9}{4} \times \dfrac{16}{9} = 4$
3 fifths + 3 fourths = 3 octaves	$\left(\dfrac{3}{2}\right)^3 \times \left(\dfrac{4}{3}\right)^3 = \dfrac{27}{8} \times \dfrac{64}{27} = 8$

SPACE

THE MYSTICISM OF SPACE

This section concerns volume, which is space. A contracting power (Tum of the Mystery of Heliopolis, the Verb of Saint John), which we will indicate by the numerated function ϕ (the golden number), acts within the unformed substance called Spirit and contracts it into a volume that is determined space, and this space is none other than volume. Spirit is space but it does not appear as such without the determination into volume. This is the first and universal matter. It is spherical, that is, it is a chaos of forms that are all contained in the sphere.

This contracting, paternal power compels Spirit to become matter, but this is a creative act opposed to the nature of Spirit, which wants to free itself from this hold by a counteractivity, which is movement. Mechanical movement is the energy of despair, the revolt of Spirit against its imprisonment in determination.

Now, the contracting power is a Fire surpassing all other fires; neither movement nor anything else can vanquish it except its own excess, that is, it can dissolve itself into nonmatter only if it communicates its power to spirit, materialized space, in order to produce in it a Fire identical to itself, because the contracting materializing action ceases when the substance upon which it acts has become equal to it.

A power cannot act against itself; it needs an opposition. Thus the form of a volume results from a struggle between movement, the disaggregating revolt of matter, and the contracting power on Spirit; the appearance of this double effect is life, which we translate by the specific numbers of form-volumes, because it is this life that manifests through volumes. The five regular solids, like the four elements and their dodecahedral quintessence, are the symbol-bases for understanding. They are the hieroglyphs of number in form. They are not real (perceptible) as forms, but they are the reality defining the boundary numbers of the five phases of a genesis from the sphere, into forms, and then into their redispersal.

The nucleus of the extreme contraction ϕ is octahedral. It is "Eight," summarizing all numerical possibilities; it is the solid cosmic heart, resulting from the impulse of ϕ, but the function five will appear only later.[26] The octahedron has six vertices, eight faces, and twelve

---

[26] In the construction of the octahedron, we see the apothem divided into 1/3 and 2/3, giving us the most primitive proportion of the ϕ series: 1, **1, 2, 3, 5, 8**, etc. (Cf. chapter 7, "Functional Development of the Law of Right Triangles," and chapter 8.)

edges.[27] Its volume is *one-third* of the parallelepiped that contains it, as the inscribed sphere is *two-thirds* of the volume of the cylinder that contains it.

Number creates the basic kinship between the principal chaotic sphere and the corporeal octahedral nucleus (the mineral origin). In the mineral kingdom the function ϕ occurs only in its vegetative or growing action (that is, in the mine), and becomes apparent only in the visible vegetation of the plant kingdom.

Volume is space, in principle without form. Mystically, it must be reduced into form as 1, 2/3, 1/3. Space, having no form, in contracting itself into volume is reduced by 1/3, the sphere having 2/3 the volume, and in contracting itself into the octahedron is reduced by 2/3, the octahedron having 1/3 the volume (fig. 8).

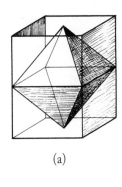
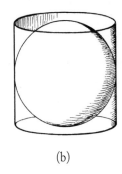

(a)   (b)

Fig. 8

(a) In a parallelepiped of volume 1, the octahedron is equal to 1/3. *(b)* In a cylinder of volume 1, the sphere is equal to 2/3.

The form is ordained (or desired) by a power, a seminal *potentiality*, which manifests through the elements, that is, the analysis of this potentiality. We can now know this potentiality as sphere and octahedron, the double pyramid. One of these pyramids is actual, the other is principial, its complementary stability, as with the sphere, where one side is "day" and the other is "night."

The perceptible form is nothing other than an action in six directions, or "axes," in equal proportions or varying in intensity. It is thus impossible to dissociate this action from that of these "axes" and orientations that define *our* space, that is, the volume of the world such as it appears to us, insofar as our senses are able to grasp it.

The difference between the sphere and volumes having straight edges is that the former results from a circuit such as that of the sun as it moves from day to night, and not from a circuit cut up into proportioned parts, our three-dimensional orientation imposes upon us.

The mysticism of volume has nothing in common either with our rational schematization that shows us a cube, for example, as made up of an agglomeration of atomic spheres, or with the axial system of crystallography.

---

[27] We see a relationship between the containing cube and octahedron in the number of their edges, faces, and vertices.

	Edges	Faces	Vertices	
Cube	12	6	8	(Eight is the harmonic mean
Octahedron	12	8	6	between 6 and 12.)

We are concerned here with powers, such as the inspiring north and the realizing south—given as the zenith and nadir for the body—and the four vital moments that define the surface, which are midday and midnight, morning and evening (we note this classification as a key).

We can rationalize this grouping and picture it as the axes, but vitally it does not conform to reality unless the edges were to constitute lines (necessarily imaginary) that extend between the ends of right axes or diagonals. Axes and diagonals are nothing more than graphic representations of a geometry of numbers, but the reality, the fact, is only accessible through the function and through the intelligence of the function.

The body as a whole is to be conceived as a moment of a body in revolution, thus in the *activity of the axes,* whether it is a crystal or any other *living* form. Crystalline forms, for example, are finalities (arrested phases) defining a type of mineral genesis, specifying that body.

As the basis of forms (numbers), geometry poses the three and the five regular solids, as in embryology we situate (set apart) the typical phases in the development of a human being. There is an analogy here because life and genesis both follow a unique order. The hierarchy is indicated by the approaches to the perfection of the finality, immanent in the causes, of minerals, plants, or animals, respectively. The dodecahedron is perfection for the regular forms, as gold is for the metal, the grape is for the plant, the human being is for the animal, Cosmic Man is for the human being.

We are giving undetermined space the name of Spirit and every form the name volume, that is, Spirit coagulated into determined space. The "coagulating," contracting power is consciousness. It persists in every form from its origin to its end. It is the spiritual salt, neutral and invariable.

The two-thirds of a container are the unity-form, the container being divisible by two and by three, because everything in the Universe is triple in principle and double in nature, and summarizes the four elementary qualities.

The evolution of forms consists in the specified expression of consciousness, the reduction in the Fire of the coagulating Salt, until *matter,* that is, space-volume, dissolves again into space-Spirit.

Thus, Spirit is at the same time substance and the contracting Fire, the Virgin Mother, the principle of Isis in Hathor—the house that contains and carries Hor. (With regard to the *symbolique,* note the four faces of the cubic capital on Hathorian columns.)

THE SYMBOL OF THE EYE

The eye is the only nerve that comes to the surface of the body, the only one we can observe in its living function. It blossoms into a sphere filled with a white crystalline liquid. It is sensitive to light, to the *effect of fire,* and it reacts to colors.

It is the sense that informs us directly of volume and that demonstrates the function of intelligence through *the crossing,* there being a unification and at the same time an exchange between the two eyes.

The eye is the "sense *du jour,*" that is, of the visible sun. The right eye is, as is the left side of the brain in man, sensitive to that which is positive and affirmative, while the left eye is related to the right side of the brain and is sensitive to that which is negative. There is a crossing between the left and right eyes and the right and left lobes of the brain. The center of the optical nerve is an empty channel that conducts the vital, nervous energy. These are already sufficient reasons to motivate us to use the eye as a symbol for, among other things, the capacity of volume. The animal with an optical brain is the bird, and among birds the falcon (in Egypt) corresponds best to the array of noble qualities that can be symbolized as "eye."

The two eyes are our *two luminaries.* While one is solar and the other is lunar in *function,* both eyes nevertheless belong to the sun, the left to the morning sun, the right to the evening sun (Hathor, in accord with the moon), and this by reason of their *natures.*

In the same way that touch informs us of matter, sight (the light) reveals volume, that is, space made concrete.

The constitution of the eye shows that the "fire" of light must be neutralized by the watery nature of the aqueous humor and the vitreous body, the Amunian aspect of life. The phenomenon of vision is a reaction to the light filtered by the iris; then the "fire," neutralized by the crystalline lens, strikes the complementary rods and cones of the retina. If this *reaction* did not occur, the phenomenon of light would never exist for the intellective optical center of the brain. Functionally, this complete process constitutes the "eye of Ra"; the *reactive* emanation from the retina is the true light. The electromagnetic vibration, or the photons, are the impulsive activity, the active mechanical energy, and the light that we see is the reactive vital energy. The physical and chemical effect of the light only exists through some similar reactive phenomena, but these effects are only visible (to the eye) after this vital genesis. It is thus that the sun, the eye of Ra (and not Aten, the solar disk) emanates an *invisible light* that nourishes the world; this invisible light—the luminous vital energy—makes possible our *intelligence* of the active, visible light, our *knowledge of the light.* This concerns the esotericism of the symbol of the eye. To these explanations is added the symbol of genesis represented by the eye and in which, as in all generation, the amniotic crystalline lens takes part. The myth says that it is from the *tears* of Ra, the salty Water evoked by solar Fire, that human beings were created.

PHARAONIC VOLUMES

It is the prejudice of our modern mentality to demand of pharaonic knowledge some explanatory writings, and this is the cause of our ignorance about the real learning of the Ancients. We have not understood until now the means of expression and the line of conduct of pharaonic thought.

The sages of that epoch have said all, but in figurations and applications, not in discursive writings, which only have research value for a rationalistic mentality. Thus, their system for measuring volumes is and remains an enigma for this mentality, whereas we see these measures explained through numbers. These numbers lead us infallibly toward the bases of musical harmony, which are known—traditionally—to be the same as those used by the Pythagoreans to explain the entire world system.

As the present representative of the Anthropocosmos, man offers through his body the units of measure such as the cubit, the hand, and the digit for linear units, the *remen* (the arm) for surface units, and the cubic cubit designating the volume of reference. These are elements of measure, but these measures are as alive as the whole human body itself. Now, life signifies rhythmic alternation, following the laws of harmony; this rhythmic alternation creates from these measures a *function* and a generation as phenomenon. Only numbers can express this because it is impossible to give expression to the interdependence of volume, time, and music in a schematization.

THE VOLUMES OF PHARAONIC EGYPT

The *cubit* measures the initial volume, which is a *cubic cubit.* The *khar* represents two-thirds of a cubic cubit. Let us recall here the principle of the relation of space and sphere. The *hekat,* a new unit (in time value), represents the thirtieth part of the cubic cubit; there are as many of these new units as there are days in the pharaonic month of the vague year ($360 \div 12 = 30$).

The *hekat,* considered as a unit of capacity for the measure of grains (thus of a lunar character), is subdivided into sixty-four parts. The symbols used to express these subdivisions are derived from the ancient myth according to which the eye of Horus 𓂀 was fragmented by Seth.

Later Thoth (Mercury, Hermes), symbolized by the ibis, miraculously "filled" or "completed"[28] the eye, bringing together its parts so that the eye reacquired its title "the whole eye," or "the healthy eye." Of the two eyes, it is then the lunar one that is identified with the measure of volume.[29]

The *hekat* is subdivided into 1/2, 1/4, 1/8, 1/16, 1/32, and 1/64. These fractions added together make 63/64 with 1/64 missing (fig. 9).

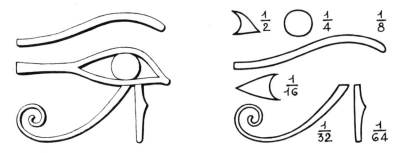

Fig. 9. The wedjat *eye and the subdivisions of the* hekat

The other subdivisions of the cubic cubit that are frequently mentioned in the calculations of the Rhind Papyrus are the quadruple *hekat,* that is, four months, or one of the three pharaonic seasons, and the *henw,* which is the tenth part of the *hekat.* The *hekat* and the *henw,* however, have different origins; the *henw* is not used as a fraction of the *hekat* but as a totally independent unit. The *hekat* was later divided into 320 parts, or *ro* (⌁ = fraction, part).

Table 2 summarizes the values and correspondences between these different measures of volume. This table suggests an incoherence in the relation between volumes and their functions. But this incoherence is only apparent, as our further study will demonstrate.

In this table the cubic cubit is symbolized simply by the cubit. In the Rhind Papyrus the cubic cubit is brought up several times, but we are unaware of the symbol that particularly designates it.

The Mode of Calculation

It is in the method of the calculation of volumes that we uncover the analogies with numbers that have musical relationships.

1. To calculate approximately the surface of a disk inscribed in a square, we take 8/9 of the diameter or the side of the square. We then square 8/9, which gives

$$\frac{64}{81} = \frac{\text{disk surface}}{\text{square surface}}.$$

[28] Translation of the explanation given by A. J. Gardiner, *Egyptian Grammar* (Oxford: Clarendon Press, 1927), §266, which emphasizes the use of the words *filled* or *completed* (*mḥ.*). The word *mḥ.* is used in the Rhind Papyrus in problems 35–38, which deal with the *hekat.*

[29] The problem of the meanings of the eyes is very complex and has been the subject of many Egyptological studies, the results of which remain inconclusive; however, it is undeniable that the "filling" of the eye here also constitutes its measure, and that this action, attributed to Thoth (Hermes), is a lunar action. This once again connects the principle of the measure of grain with what is lunar.

TABLE 2

Pharaonic Volumes

1 cubic cubit	$1\frac{1}{2}$	$7\frac{1}{2}$	30	300	9600
$\frac{2}{3}$	1 *khar*	5	20	200	6400
$\frac{2}{15}$	$\frac{1}{5}$	4 *hekat*	4	40	1280
$\frac{1}{30}$	$\frac{1}{20}$	$\frac{1}{4}$	1 *hekat*	10	320
$\frac{1}{300}$	$\frac{1}{200}$	$\frac{1}{40}$	$\frac{1}{10}$	1 *henw*	32
$\frac{1}{9600}$	$\frac{1}{6400}$	$\frac{1}{1280}$	$\frac{1}{320}$	$\frac{1}{32}$	1 *ro*

2. To calculate the volume of a cylinder, we multiply the surface area of the disk by the height, and if this height is equal to the diameter, that is, 9, the volume of the cylinder equals:

$$64 \times \frac{9}{81} \times 9 = \frac{576}{729} = \frac{\text{volume of the cylinder}}{\text{volume of the cube}} \quad \text{(see table 4).}$$

3. To change the capacity of the cylinder into a *khar*, which is 2/3 of a cubic cubit, the scribe multiplies the volume of the cylinder by the inverse of 2/3, that is,

$$\frac{3}{2} = \frac{864}{729} = \frac{32}{27} = \frac{\text{volume of the cylinder of } khar}{\text{volume of the cube in cubic cubits}} \quad \text{(see table 4).}$$

4. A second procedure consists in directly multiplying 8/9 by 3/2 to make a square, then multiplying this square by 2/3. This operation gives the following results:

$$\frac{8}{9} \times \frac{3}{2} = \frac{24}{18} \text{ or } \frac{4}{3}, \text{ the square of } \frac{4}{3} = \frac{16}{9}, \text{ and finally } \frac{16}{9} \times \frac{2}{3} = \frac{32}{27}.$$

The result is evidently the same, but the relationships that enter into play are very different.

We can compare the numbers revealed by this singular method of calculating imposed by ancient practice and the subdivisions of the measures of volume with the essential numbers of music. The tone, 9/8, the fifth, 3/2, the fourth, 4/3, are all functional numbers that one rediscovers in the

Chinese pipes, in the numbers of Plato, and in "the volumes" themselves. The analogies intimately tie them together (tables 3A, 3B, and 4).

The Numbers of Musical Harmony

We have already seen (in the section on harmony) the relationships between sound vibrations and the divisions of a string. We have seen as well that musical intervals are added together whereas their ratios are multiplied. We still have to consider how these relationships were originally established.

In explaining the formation of the Soul of the World, Plato divided the original formed "mixture" into seven parts, which are to one another as the terms of two progressions, one at a double rate, the other at a triple rate (1, 2, 4, 8, and 1, 3, 9, 27).[30] Then God "filled up" the intervals between the successive terms in both these geometric progressions by means of two medieties.

The first ratio is that of the octave in the double rate of 1 to 2. The intermediate ratios are found by dividing the octave into harmonious parts, and that is done by inserting two mean terms between 1 and 2, that is, an *arithmetic mean* and a *harmonic mean*, which together constitute musical proportion. The arithmetic mean, $(1+2)/2 = 3/2$, produces the relationship of the fifth. The harmonic mean, $2(1 \times 2)/(1+2) = 4/3$, produces the relationship of the fourth.

The fourth is equal to two tones and a half tone, the fifth to three tones and a half tone, so that the difference between them is one tone. The tone is thus formed in the following manner:

$$\text{one fifth minus one fourth} = \frac{3}{2} \div \frac{4}{3} = \frac{9}{8} = \text{one tone.}$$

To find the half tone (diesis or limma), it is necessary to subtract two tones from the fourth, which brings us again to the following calculations:

$$\text{Two tones} = \frac{9}{8} \times \frac{9}{8} = \frac{81}{64} = \text{a major third of our scale.}$$

$$\text{A fourth minus two tones} = \frac{4}{3} \div \frac{81}{64} = \frac{4 \times 64}{3 \times 81} = \frac{256}{243} = \text{the limma.}$$

Theon of Smyrna gives the following scheme:

$$
\begin{array}{cccc}
192 & 216 & 243 & 256 \\
\end{array}
$$

$$\text{tone} = \frac{9}{8} \qquad \text{tone} = \frac{9}{8} \qquad \text{limma} = \frac{256}{243}$$

$$\text{fourth} = \frac{4}{3}$$

Theon does not complete the full octave but gives again the same sequence by taking as a beginning the double of 192, which is 384, and the succession of the following numbers:

$$
\begin{array}{cccc}
384 & 432 & 489 & 512 \\
\end{array}
$$

$$\text{tone} = \frac{9}{8} \qquad \text{tone} = \frac{9}{8} \qquad \text{limma} = \frac{256}{243}$$

$$\text{fourth} = \frac{4}{3}$$

---

[30] Plato is quoted in the appendix of chapter 8. It is the *canevas,* as we present it, that gives us the complete solution for the principle of the "Soul of the World."

If we calculate all the possible numerical relations between 1 and 27 using the method indicated by Theon of Smyrna, we can establish the following ratios (see tables 3A and 3B), as well as their transcriptions into whole numbers, by taking as unity the number 384.

TABLE 3A

*Progression of Doubles**

	$1 = 384$	$2 = 768$	$4 = 1536$	$8 = 3072$	$16 = 6144$
	$\frac{9}{8} = 432$	$\frac{9}{4} = 864$	$\frac{9}{2} = 1728$	$9 = 3456$	$18 = 6912$
	$\frac{81}{64} = 486$	$\frac{81}{32} = 972$	$\frac{81}{16} = 1944$	$\frac{81}{8} = 3888$	$\frac{81}{4} = 7776$
Harmonic mean	$\frac{4}{3} = 512$	$\frac{8}{3} = 1024$	$\frac{16}{3} = 2048$	$\frac{32}{3} = 4096$	$\frac{64}{3} = 8192$
Arithmetic mean	$\frac{3}{2} = 576$	$3 = 1152$	$6 = 2304$	$12 = 4608$	$24 = 9216$
	$\frac{27}{16} = 648$	$\frac{27}{8} = 1296$	$\frac{27}{4} = 2592$	$\frac{27}{2} = 5184$	$27 = 10368$
	$\frac{243}{128} = 729$	$\frac{243}{64} = 1458$	$\frac{243}{32} = 2916$	$\frac{243}{16} = 5832$	
	$2 = 768$	$4 = 1536$	$8 = 3072$	$16 = 6144$	

*Tables 3A and 3B from Theon of Smyrna, *Le Nombre de Platon*, note 13, p. 348. In order to orient the investigation in this domain, let us mention that the complete series of triples (table 3B) from 1 to 27 has new notes (dieses) that cannot be found in the series of doubles.

Between 1 and 2, the harmonic mean equals 4/3; the arithmetic mean equals 3/2.

TABLE 3B

Progression of Triples

	$1 = 384$	$3 = 1152$	$9 = 3456$
	$\frac{9}{8} = 432$	$\frac{27}{8} = 1296$	$\frac{81}{8} = 3888$
	$\frac{81}{64} = 486$	$\frac{243}{64} = 1458$	$\frac{729}{64} = 4374$
	$\frac{4}{3} = 512$	$4 = 1536$	$12 = 4608$
Harmonic mean	$\frac{3}{2} = 576$	$\frac{9}{2} = 1728$	$\frac{27}{2} = 5184$
	$\frac{27}{16} = 648$	$\frac{81}{16} = 1944$	$\frac{243}{16} = 5832$
	$\frac{243}{128} = 729$	$\frac{729}{128} = 2187$	$\frac{2187}{128} = 6561$
Arithmetic mean	$2 = 768$	$6 = 2304$	$18 = 6912$
	$\frac{9}{4} = 864$	$\frac{27}{4} = 2592$	$\frac{81}{4} = 7776$
	$\frac{81}{32} = 972$	$\frac{243}{32} = 2916$	$\frac{729}{32} = 8748$
	$\frac{8}{3} = 1024$	$8 = 3072$	$24 = 9216$
	$3 = 1152$	$9 = 3456$	$27 = 10368$

Between 1 and 3, the harmonic mean equals 3/2; the arithmetic mean equals 2.

The transcription of each ratio into whole numbers is based on $128 \times 3 = 384$, the number 128 or the double of 64 being the smallest common multiple of all the denominators. We should recall here that the *wedjat* eye is divided into sixty-fourths.

The "Numbers of Plato," as well as those shown in table 4, are related to the numbers derived from the calculations and measures of pharaonic volumes, as well as to the numbers for the volumes of the octahedron and sphere, cube and cylinder.

TABLE 4

Harmony and Pharaonic Volumes

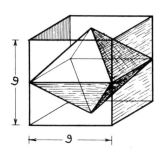

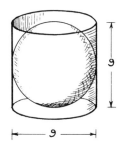

Octahedron
1/3 volume of the containing cube*

Sphere
2/3 volume of the containing cylinder

volume of cube with side $9 = \mathbf{729}$
volume of inscribed octahedron $= \mathbf{243}$

volume of cylinder $= 64 \times 9 = \mathbf{576}$
volume of inscribed sphere $= \mathbf{384}$
volume of cylinder in *khar* $= \mathbf{864}$

Notes	Intervals	Pharaonic ratios	Numbers from table 3
$Do = 1$	. . . .	. . . .	192 or **384**
$Re = \dfrac{9}{8}$	1 tone =	$\dfrac{\text{diameter of disk}}{\text{side of square}}$ **	216 or 432
$Mi = \dfrac{81}{64}$	2 tones =	$\dfrac{\text{area of square}}{\text{area of disk}}$ **	243 or 486
$Fa = \dfrac{4}{3}$	$2\dfrac{1}{2}$ tones =	$\dfrac{8}{9}$ diameter $\times \dfrac{3}{2}$ †	256 or 512
$Sol = \dfrac{3}{2}$	$3\dfrac{1}{2}$ tones =	$\dfrac{\text{cubic cubit}}{\text{volume of } khar}$	288 or **576**
$La = \dfrac{27}{16}$	$4\dfrac{1}{2}$ tones =	$\dfrac{9}{8} \times \dfrac{3}{2}$ ††	324 or 648
$Ti = \dfrac{243}{128}$	$5\dfrac{1}{2}$ tones =	$\dfrac{\text{volume of cube}}{\text{volume of sphere}} = \dfrac{729}{384}$	$364\dfrac{1}{2}$ or **729**
$Do = 2$	6 tones	. . . .	**384** or 768
$Re = \dfrac{9}{4}$	7 tones	. . . .	432 or **864**

*If the containing volume were equal for the sphere and the octahedron, this octahedron would be 1/2 the sphere. The containing volume of the cylinder is related to the containing volume of the cube as $8^2/9^2$.

** Rhind Papyrus

† Kahun Papyrus

†† Inverse of the calculation from Kahun Papyrus

APPENDIX:

NUMBERS AND RATIOS IN CHINESE MUSICAL PIPES

"The nine sections of the *Hong fan* were granted by Heaven to Yu whose body was strong and merited being taken as the standard of all measure, while his voice could serve as the diapason. . . . The pipe that gave the initial note could never be separated from the divinitory tool made from two small boards, one the image of Heaven, the other of Earth, superimposed upon one another as two magic squares."[31]

The building of the House of the Calendar rests on two fundamental elements: the roof represents Heaven, and the floor that supports it represents Earth. "Tradition says that the House of the Calendar in ancient times consisted of a square area (rectangular) that was covered by a circular roof of thatch (united by several columns)."[32]

Musical theory juxtaposes a classification of the twelve musical pipes, which can be used to construct a compass of twelve directions, with a classification of *five notes* forming a cross with a center, symbolizing the four seasons and the four directions.

The pipes generate each other by turns in what the Chinese called the lower and higher generations, done by alternately shortening or increasing the length of the preceding pipe in a rhythmically proportional way, by multiplying it successively by 2/3 and 4/3.[33] The generation of the Chinese musical pipes is as follows:

$$\text{first pipe} = 81, \quad \tfrac{2}{3} \text{ of which} = 54, \qquad \text{lower generation}$$

$$\text{second pipe} = 54, \quad \tfrac{4}{3} \text{ of which} = 72, \qquad \text{higher generation}$$

$$\text{third pipe} = 72, \quad \tfrac{2}{3} \text{ of which} = 48, \qquad \text{lower generation}$$

$$\text{fourth pipe} = 48, \quad \tfrac{4}{3} \text{ of which} = 64, \qquad \text{higher generation}$$

$$\text{fifth pipe} = 64, \quad \tfrac{2}{3} \text{ of which} = 42\tfrac{2}{3}, \qquad \text{lower generation}$$

$$\text{sixth pipe} = 42, \quad \tfrac{4}{3} \text{ of which} = 56, \qquad \text{higher generation}$$

$$\text{seventh pipe} = 57, \quad \tfrac{4}{3} \text{ of which} = 76, \qquad \text{higher generation}$$

$$\text{eighth pipe} = 76, \quad \tfrac{2}{3} \text{ of which} = 50\tfrac{2}{3}, \qquad \text{lower generation}$$

$$\text{ninth pipe} = 51, \quad \tfrac{4}{3} \text{ of which} = 68, \qquad \text{higher generation}$$

$$\text{tenth pipe} = 68, \quad \tfrac{2}{3} \text{ of which} = 45\tfrac{1}{3}, \qquad \text{lower generation}$$

$$\text{eleventh pipe} = 45, \quad \tfrac{4}{3} \text{ of which} = 60, \qquad \text{higher generation}$$

$$\text{twelfth pipe} = 60, \quad \tfrac{4}{3} \text{ of which} = 80, \qquad \text{higher generation}$$

[31] Marcel Granet, *La Pensée chinoise* (Paris: Renaissance du Livre, 1934), p. 209.

[32] Ibid., p. 250. Here we find the association again between the square and the disk, and thus also between the cube (block) and the sphere.

[33] Notice that the Chinese proceed by alternation [up a fifth and down a fourth].

Here are the essential points:

1. The pipes are generated by the successive multiplication of the preceding length by 2/3 and 4/3, which are the ratios of the fifth (3/2) and the fourth (4/3), but also of the arithmetic and harmonic mean terms (3/2 and 4/3) that come between 1 and 2, as in the proportional sequence of 1, 3/2, 4/3, 2, the "product of the mean being equal to the product of the extremes," that is, $3/2 \times 4/3 = 2$.

2. The initial pipe = 81. The first* pipe regenerated by the last = 80. The ratio 80/81 equals 0.987654320987654320..., which when stopped at the ninth decimal is 0.987654321..., and which multiplied again by 81 gives: $0.987654321 \times 81 = 80.00000001$.[34] The number 80/81 is related to the "comma" in music.

3. The twelve months are related to the twelve pipes.

$$\text{If the first pipe} = A, \text{ the second pipe} = \frac{2}{3}A = \text{the fifth}$$

$$\text{the third pipe} = \frac{2}{3}A \times \frac{4}{3} = \frac{8}{9}A = \text{the tone}$$

$$\text{the fourth pipe} = \frac{8}{9} \times \frac{2}{3} = \frac{16}{27}A = \text{the sixth}$$

$$\text{the fifth pipe} = \frac{16}{27} \times \frac{4}{3} = \frac{64}{81} = \text{the third}$$

$$\text{the sixth pipe} = \frac{64}{81} \times \frac{2}{3} = \frac{128}{243} = \text{the seventh}$$

$$\text{the seventh pipe} = \frac{128}{243} \times \frac{4}{3} = \frac{512}{729} = \text{the tritone.}$$

Thus . . . one and the same law governs the establishment of pharaonic volumes, the Chinese harmonic pipes, and the numerical system transmitted by Plato, inherited from Pythagoras, who was instructed in the temples of ancient Kemit.

And in ancient China, Yu is the Anthropocosmos, the Man who received everything from Heaven.

THE ROOT

What we call the square root of any number is a value that, multiplied by itself, gives that number. This implies two suppositions: that any number can be a surface; and that this surface is square, that is, has a base and height equal to and at right angles to each other, or a base and a cathetus of the same length on this base.

Thus $\sqrt{n}$ implies that $n = (\sqrt{n})^2$, but also that n cannot be other than a square, whether it is a square number by its nature, such as 4, 9, 16, ..., or a rectangular number such as 6, 8, 10, ...[35] We have already observed the consequences of these considerations in discussing the irrational.

---

[34] We can relate this to trigonometry with the angle 1/1, or 1/8 of the cycle of time, in other words:

$$\frac{360}{8} = 45 = \text{the sum of numbers 1 to 9, or } n\frac{(n+1)}{2}.$$

[35] Or a linear number, such as 3, 5, 7, ...

* That is, the "thirteenth" pipe.

It is the *function* that must interest us here, not the results. The multiplication of a number with itself implies an enumeration of that which is multiplied. It is thus a question of an addition, and not of a real multiplication, which would be a procreation.

When we state 4×4, we are actually adding $4 + 4 + 4 + 4$, and we obtain the *surface* 16. This necessarily supposes that 4 already symbolizes a surface. We *transpose* a number counted as unity without definition (a mathematical point) and accept that it becomes an area by this multiplication with itself; or we may also assume that 4 represents a line and, agreeing with Euclid, again suppose that, by moving, this line gives a surface. In obedience to our mentality, we can only transpose by supposition and not otherwise.

We speak of roots—both square and cube—comparing by this term the vegetative cause of a number's growth to its vegetal root (radix), which is also the vegetative cause of plants. Now, the vegetal root is never formed by itself, but forms a unity with the germ (fig. 10).

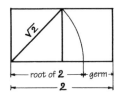

Fig. 10

Let us accept as a complement of the root of 2, its germ, which is, numerically stated, $2 - \sqrt{2}$.[36] We now have a parallel between the function ϕ and the root of 2 that will allow us to use $\sqrt{2}$ as a *symbol* in (enumerated) numbers of the generative function ϕ. It is the action of the root and its germ (that is, the root plus its complement) as it is applied to the first possible number, which is 2. Now, among whole numbers, 2 is the standard number for logarithms because in being added, it multiplies itself (fig. 11).

In this way it appears that the Unity (the original One), in order to become objective Unity, must undergo a division by ϕ, and that the root of this Unity will then be functionally $1/\phi$, its germ being $1/\phi^2$, creating thus the idea of the square.[37]

With the root-germ function through ϕ we have the functional demonstration because for results it gives only negative—thus principal—values with a positive relationship, but let us not forget that ϕ is a function and not a number.

The same root-germ function expressed by the root of 2 relates to a rational number, which is 2, and no longer to a function, which is ϕ; this is the reason why we can see this root-germ function of the root of 2 used in architecture and in numerical demonstrations.

---

[36] In this regard, let us recall what we have said about the mystical number, namely, that ϕ is the internal dividing function of Unity, while the number 2 is the quantified function of ϕ within Unity.

[37] The relationships given in fig. 11 are particular to ϕ and $\sqrt{2}$. For any other numbers of which the root can be expressed in whole numbers or in fractions, the germ is actually a rectangular *surface*, represented by "a square less its side." It is thus obvious that the relationship will always be in the form:

$$\frac{n - \sqrt{n}}{\sqrt{n} - 1} = \sqrt{n}, \quad \text{for example,} \quad \frac{361 - 19}{19 - 1} = \frac{342}{18} = 19.$$

It is important therefore to remember that the "germ," whatever it may be, will always necessarily be a *surface*, in the image of the first perfect *square*, produced by $1/\phi$ and $1/\phi^2$, which verifies the assertion that "one is Earth and the other is Heaven" (p. 91).

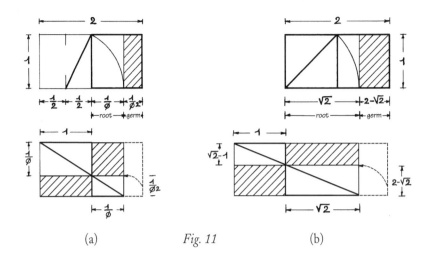

(a)   *Fig. 11*   (b)

(a) In the function ϕ, the root is 1 minus the germ.

$$1 : \text{root} :: \text{root} : \text{germ}$$

$$1 : 1 - \text{germ} :: \text{root} : \text{germ} = \text{root} + 1$$

$$1 : \frac{1}{\phi} :: \frac{1}{\phi} : \frac{1}{\phi^2} = \frac{1}{\phi} + 1 = \phi$$

The product of the means is a square. *(b)* In the function root of 2, the root is 2 minus the germ.

$$1 : 1 - \text{germ} :: \text{root} : \text{germ} = \text{root} + 1$$

$$1 : \sqrt{2} - 1 :: \sqrt{2} : 2 - \sqrt{2} = \sqrt{2} + 1$$

The product of the means is a rectangle.

In order to make the importance of the germ comprehensible, we must first recall the principle of harmony, or more specifically, the medieties. With the principle of the root and the germ, we have the function that we see applied in calculation with the medieties where we obtain arithmetic and harmonic results by addition on the one hand, and by multiplication on the other: root + germ = the number by addition; root × root = the number by multiplication.

———〰———

In reality, the "successive approximations" of roots of *n* are the expression of the vegetative principle, and it is thus that we will designate them from now on.

Vegetation demonstrates an astonishing phenomenon through its power of development. As long as we see in the plant only an addition of parts, such as the bringing out of new cells between the bark and the sapwood of the trunk of the tree, nothing exceptional will occur. But when we observe the expansion of a squash or a melon or a pomegranate, we see that the sap travels through the frail stems and fills and expands the fruits until they burst. This is evidently not caused by the mechanical pressure of the sap or by the growth from the simple addition of new cells under the bark. There is only one possible explanation: a rhythmic and synchronized alternation of influx and resorption forming the genesis of the central seed from the epidermis to the marrow (the germ of the seed in this case), and all of this leads us to the knowledge of volume.

Plus-minus follow one another, but it remains a question of qualitative, not quantitative, values, of harmonic, not arithmetic, relationships.

The problem posed by musical harmony consists in inserting between the initial sound 1 and its octave 2 the harmonic consonances from which will spring forth the scale. The problem posed by the root of 2 is also that of inserting between 1 and 2 its geometric mean, that is, the root of 2, so that the three numbers, 1, $\sqrt{2}$, 2, form a *geometric proportion* corresponding to the condition that *the square of the mean term be equal to the product of the extremes.* Now, the root of 2 is irrational.

Figure 12 shows the equality $2 : \sqrt{2} :: \sqrt{2} : 1$.

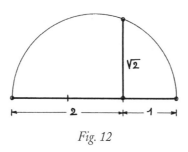

Fig. 12

Now, music is transcribed, as we have seen, by whole numbers, and *musical proportion* is made up of two medieties. As for the octave, it is thus a matter of inserting two mean terms between 1 and 2 whose product will equal 2, and this is accomplished by means of two proportions: the *arithmetic mediety,* in which the mean term is equal to half of the sum of the extremes, $(1+2)/2 = 3/2$, equivalent to the fifth, or $1\frac{1}{2}$ (fig. 13a); and the *harmonic mediety,* in which the mean term is equal to twice the product of the extremes divided by the sum of the extremes, $2(1 \times 2)/(1+2) = 4/3$, equivalent to the fourth, or $1\frac{1}{3}$ (fig. 13b). The product of the two mean terms is equal to $3/2 \times 4/3 = 12/6 = 2$, that is, the addition of a fifth and a fourth.

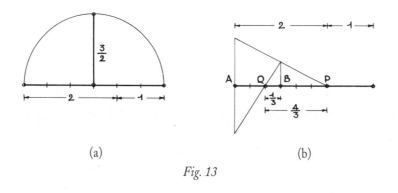

(a)   (b)

Fig. 13

Figure 13b shows that $PA/PB = QA/QB$, as $2/1 = (2/3)/(1/3)$. The mean term $PQ = PB + BQ = PA - QA$ as $2 - 2/3 = 1 + 1/3$.

When brought together in a single diagram (fig. 14), the three graphically obtained mean terms, of which only the latter two can be transcribed in whole numbers, give us the first possible relationships for transforming a rectangle whose sides AB and AD are to each other as 1 is to 2 into a rectangular parallelepiped $DEFG$ of the same surface area. It is evident that the geometric mean $\sqrt{2}$ is smaller than 3/2 or $1\frac{1}{2}$ (the arithmetic mean DE) and larger than 4/3 or $1\frac{1}{3}$ (the harmonic mean DG).

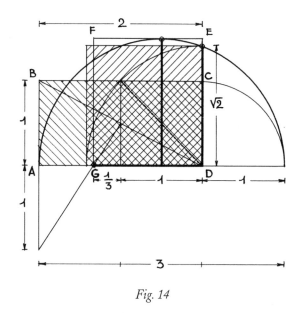

Fig. 14

The method of inquiry employed here is attributed to Archytas of Tarentum[38] under the name of "musical proportion." This procedure, by inserting again between $1\frac{1}{2}$ and $1\frac{1}{3}$ their arithmetic and harmonic means, allows us to determine the ratios that approach closer and closer to the perfect square; thus the next pair of ratios[39] will be $(17/12) \times (24/17)$.

We can, however, already observe that by taking any length whatsoever for the side of a rectangle that must have 2 for its surface area, the value of the other side will always be obtained by dividing 2 by the value of the first determined side. Thus this investigation of what we have called here the "harmonic mean," simply comes back to the division of 2 by the first "arithmetic mean" occurring between 1 and 2. In the system of fractional notation that was practiced in pharaonic Egypt, this operation was transcribed, for example, under the simple form, "Divide 2 by $1\frac{1}{2}$; the result $1\frac{1}{3}$."

The practice of this function is pharaonic, but its descriptive expression was passed on by the Pythagoreans.

———◊———

Despite the obvious similarity in the method of extracting roots with the arithmetic and harmonic "mean terms" inserted so that they approach closer and closer to the irrational geometric mean, and which takes the "musical proportion" for its point of departure, there are serious reasons to think that its origin is different.[40] But we must not forget that all these calculations are still exoteric, and there remains a "mystical function" that makes of One the quantity Two.

Theon of Smyrna has passed on to us the "lateral and diagonal numbers" beginning with unity, which, he says, contains in potentiality both the side and the diagonal.[41] This concept is quite probably much older and more in conformity with the mentality of its origin: the unity that is both the

[38] Paul Tannery, "Du rôle de la musique grecque dans le développement de la mathématique pure," *Mémoires scientifiques* (Paris: Gauthier Villars, 1915), 3:81–85.

[39] Cf. chapter 7, appendix 2, on the use of this coefficient for the root of 2.

[40] Tannery, *Mémoires scientifiques*, 3:85, arrives at the conclusion that we summarize here.

[41] Theon of Smyrna, *Le Nombre de Platon*, part 1, §31, p. 71.

side and the diagonal is for us an absurdity, but it accurately conforms to the mystical sense of Unity held by the Ancients.

Theon also said "That which the side can do twice, the diagonal can do once,"[42] and his procedure, as we shall see, consists in a sequence of successive *additions:*

the first side = 1, its diagonal = 1

$$\frac{\text{the second diagonal} = 2 \text{ sides } a + 1 \text{ diagonal } a}{\text{the second side} = 1 \text{ side } \ \ a + 1 \text{ diagonal } a} = \frac{3}{2}$$

$$\frac{\text{the third diagonal} = 2 \text{ sides } b + 1 \text{ diagonal } b}{\text{the third side} = 1 \text{ side } \ \ b + 1 \text{ diagonal } b} = \frac{4+3}{2+3} = \frac{7}{5}$$

$$\frac{\text{the fourth diagonal} = 2 \text{ sides } c + 1 \text{ diagonal } c}{\text{the fourth side} = 1 \text{ side } \ \ c + 1 \text{ diagonal } c} = \frac{10+7}{5+7} = \frac{17}{12}.$$

One can continue in this manner indefinitely and we can verify, as Theon says, that the square of the diagonal will always be twice the square of the side, but be alternately larger or smaller by one unit:

Side number	Square	Double square	Diagonal number	Square	Difference
1	1	2	1	1	2 − 1
2	4	8	3	9	8 + 1
5	25	50	7	49	50 − 1
12	144	288	17	289	288 + 1
					etc.[43]

The function cited here by Theon consists of adding the diagonal to the side of the square, thereby calling to mind the division in two of the angle.[44]

This process is a *growth by addition,* as will thus be demonstrated the *canevas** where we find the interaction between germ and root and the actual graphic description of this phenomenon of growth (fig. 15).

Figure 15 shows how each numbered diagonal, or *root* of 2, becomes the germ of the following pair.[45] With this growth by root-germ we thus have the living expression by the root of 2 of the function ϕ. It is through this form of growth by the root of 2 that all Nature proceeds.

We can indicate here the relationship that exists between the harmonic phenomenon expressed by the ratios of numbers and the "supernatural sense" of musical harmony.

---

[42] In other words: two times the square of the side is equal to one times the square of the diagonal. Cf. ibid., p. 73.

[43] This alternation plus one, less one, which we will also find elsewhere, is also related to the numbers 80 and 81 that we have just observed in the Chinese musical pipes. The old procedure reported by Theon leads to numbers that are always a little too large. We can be satisfied, however, by the argument of the calculation and the approximations, since precision can be obtained at will (architecture, astronomy).

[44] The process of dividing the angle in two is attributed to Hipparchus, however, problems 120 to 124 of the Babylonian tablets are established on this principle.

[45] If the side is equal to 5, the root of 2 = 7 and the germ = 3. If the side is equal to 12, the root of 2 = 17 and the germ = 7.

* Or "grid"; the French word has been retained because of its specific application. It derives from weaving and suggests the framework that allows the weaver to work out the design.

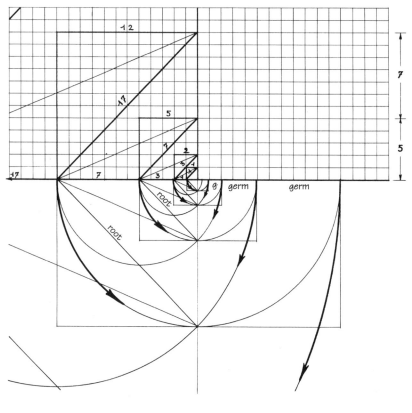

Fig. 15

The division of an angle formed by the diagonal of a square with side 1 into *two equal parts* divides the side, which in music is the vibrating string, into *two unequal parts* that are to each other as 1 is to the root of 2, that is, as 5 is to 7 in a square with a side of 12.

Musical harmony shows us that five half tones equals the fourth, or two and one-half tones, and seven half tones equal the fifth, or three and one-half tones. Their sum is twelve half tones, which equals the octave or six tones.[46] The perimeter of a square with a side of 6 is equal to $4 \times 6 = 24$ (total hours of the day).[47]

———

The successive ratios given by Theon for the root of 2 are found again in the monuments of Egypt and also in the division of the cubit.[48] In addition, we find in the Rhind Papyrus problems dealing with arithmetic and geometric progressions, and we shall have the opportunity to observe that the laws concerning the harmonic medieties constitute one of the essential bases of the pharaonic

[46] Cf. table 1, above.

[47] The surface area or section of a perfect cube will be $6 \times 6 = 36$. The volume of the cube will be $6 \times 36 = 216$ or 6^3; thus, the volume is equal to the total surface area of the cube. These are all numbers of time; more exactly, it is the cube of Six and its values that preside over the division of time, which is genesis, and genesis is spatial function.

[48] Cf. chapter 9, "Gnomonic Growth of Cubes and a Practical Method for Extracting a Cube Root."

method of calculation,[49] in such a way that all the elements serving to make up the "musical pro-portion" were perfectly known by the pharaonic mathematicians without their having to identify repeatedly the term (the word) that designates this proportion.

—⁓—

In order to approach the esoteric sense of the root function, let us recall the approximate calcula-tion given by the Rhind Papyrus for obtaining the surface area of a disk: a diameter is given the value 9, and 8/9 of this diameter, raised to the square, is equal to the area of the disk (fig. 16). Thus, for a disk of diameter 9, 8^2 or 64 is its area. It did not disturb them to take the *square* root of a *curved* surface in order to establish a principle.[50]

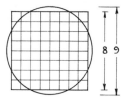
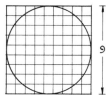

Fig. 16

Now, the ratio of vibrations of 9/8, or 8/9 of a string length, gives a major tone of the scale, as if the tone defined by the length of the string were related to the square root of the disk (surface area) of this string. Between the lengths 8 and 9, there is the same numerical relationship as between the root of the square and of the disk, but there is an equality between the surface areas of this square and this disk, that is, a new state that is a consequence of a relationship; its transcrip-tion will no longer be a sound, but a tone, which is the basis of the scale contained in half of this string length (radius or half-diameter).[51]

This coincidence between the sound and the length of the vibrating string (8/9) and the geo-metric problem (approximate, but quite sufficient) is noteworthy. For we have here the indication of a relationship between an arithmetic function and a geometric (logarithmic) function that is, in the end, similar to the function ϕ, through the absurdity of the square root of a disk.

The parallel with the function ϕ stands out: the addition of successive terms results in a geo-metric progression. Let us recall the preceding musical table:[52]

$$1 \text{ tone} + 1 \text{ tone} = 2 \text{ tones}$$
$$\frac{9}{8} \times \frac{9}{8} = \frac{81}{64}$$

---

[49] Cf. chapter 6, "The Rhind Papyrus," where the "Table of 2/n," appearing as a harmonic progression, turns out to be an inverted arith-metic progression.

[50] In chapter 21 we will summarize some elements of the Hindu temple canon; we will see an equal and constant evocation of this connection between 8 and 9 and of the disk and the square.

[51] Sixty-four represents the surface area of a disk inscribed in a square of side 9 (equal to the diameter of the circle) and an area of 81 (fig. 16), establishing the relation 64/81 = 0.790123... or $\pi/4$, where $\pi = 3.16049...$.

[52] Cf. table 4 above.

The musical effects are added; the vibrations (numbers) are multiplied. Let us look at this with respect to the functions of ϕ:

$$1/\phi + 1 = \phi = 1 \times \phi$$
$$1 + \phi = \phi^2 = \phi \times \phi = \phi + 1$$
$$\phi + \phi^2 = \phi^3 = \phi \times \phi \times \phi = \phi + 1 + \phi$$
$$\phi^2 + \phi^3 = \phi^4 = \phi \times \phi \times \phi \times \phi = \phi + 1 + \phi + 1 + \phi$$

With ϕ we have the two effects in one function. When we add, we have the geometric effect. Addition plays the role of the musical effect and multiplication (elevation to a power, the geometric effect) plays the numerical role. Thus $\phi + 1 + \phi = \phi^3$ is a volume that results from an addition.

Let us note here that the logarithmic function, that is, the addition of exponents corresponding to the geometric growth, stops with ϕ^3. For example, $1^1 + \phi^1 = \phi^2$, and $\phi^1 + \phi^2 = \phi^3$, again 1; but $\phi^2 + \phi^3 = \phi^4$, not ϕ^5. In the generating function, everything is accomplished with the cube, as we find in the saying of Thoth:

I am One (which is) transformed into Two;
I am Two (which is) transformed into Four;
I am Four (which is) transformed into Eight;
I am after this, One.[53]

Everything, then, occurs as if we were to consider One as being without definition, until it becomes One as a cube, that is, ϕ^3 equals One.[54]

SUMMARY

Transcribed into, or more exactly, *symbolized* by numbers, the roots of 2, 3, and 5 serve to trace out and describe all planes and volumes. The root of 2, as a numerating number, plays the *symbolic* role of the passage from 1 to 2, the vital characteristic of the function ϕ. Now, ϕ is the function of the *scission* of the Unique, which is traditionally recalled in speaking of the golden section. When ϕ, transcribed into (numerating) numbers, must define volume, *it acts* as the square root of 5. The root of 3 defines the plane for equilateral triangles, hexagons, and so on. These roots serve to define the five regular solids that are engendered from one another: the music of volumes.

Now the square, and in general all quadrangles, are the result of a *multiplication* and, *functionally*, are also the result of addition, while polygons other than quadrangles, as well as volumes, are the result of addition only and therefore, esoterically, of fractioning. The essence of surfaces is the triangle, the essence of the regular volumes is the octahedron, the double pyramid, a synthesis of triangle and square.

[53] The text written on the back of the boarding of the coffin of Petamun (Cairo Museum, no. 1160).

[54] The historical account of the knowledge of numbers in relation to music (which is the base of all mathematical knowledge) establishes the following progression: Pharaonic Egypt to Pythagoras, then from Pythagorus to Eudoxus, with the teaching of Eudoxus being passed on—but not explained—by Euclid.

The different ratios of the numbers of harmony have been preserved by the Greeks (Plato, Theon of Smyrna, etc.). For more on this question, cf. Tannery, *Mémoires scientifiques,* 3:68; and Michel, *De Pythagore à Euclide,* p. 396. We will see, in connection with the measures of the pharaonic volumes, that the origin of these musical relationships, of which no papyrus speaks explicitly, is actually Egyptian.

Phi is a function and not a number. This function is in the same relation to the numerating number as the harmonic interval is to the vibration.

In the same way that the octave is formed by two fourths and one tone, the ratios of sounds, in vibrations *add up* like this:

$$\frac{4}{3} \quad \times \quad \frac{4}{3} \quad \times \quad \frac{9}{8} = \frac{144}{72} = 2 \ = \text{one octave}$$

$$\text{a fourth } + \text{ a fourth } + \qquad \text{a tone} \qquad = \text{one octave.}$$

Addition is expressed in the musical interval; *multiplication* is expressed in vibrations, which equal numbers. The geometric expression, in numbers or in figured geometry, concerns *quantity*.

The addition of intervals, as the effect of the division of the string that increases the denominator by fractioning, relates to the function. It is the function that gives the sensorially perceptible effect, but which the sensorial instrument (not the intelligence or the consciousness) retransforms into number (vibrations).

When we adapt by our means of calculation the notion of the root of a number, accepting with it the irrationality of numbers, we are moving away from the synthetic thinking of the esoteric tradition. In order to remain orthodox, the root of a number must remain in a relationship that gives a square or a rectangle but allows that which forms the interval to remain in kinship with the function ϕ of the cosmic harmony, a *mediety*.

Thus the pharaonic method of calculation remains faithful to this directive: in reconstituting the square surface known by *multiplication* it allows for its construction by *addition*. This statement concerning the root leaves open the relationships of the medieties that are, as it were, the music of number.

—◦◦◦—

In pharaonic mathematics there is an interdependence between logical form, volume, and harmony, the vital link for which is given by the germ and the alternating function of the inverse.

Later on, in our discussion of the *canevas,* we shall see this vital concept of the interdependence between mathematics and harmony that Theon of Smyrna indicated without demonstrating the bond (which perhaps was already lost to him). He begins with the absurd: the side *one* is equal to the diagonal of the square, obeying the pharaonic principle that all comes from the Unique.

Until now we have summarized the different relationships and functions on the basis of the Pythagorean material passed on by the Greeks. Further on we shall approach, with trigonometry and the *canevas,* these same problems in the light of pharaonic thinking, because, however important these developments may be from a mathematical point of view, we should consider them valueless unless they constitute a perceptible, quantitative expression of an abstract and *real* function, thereby evoking knowledge, that is to say, an applied science in the vital domain.

Chapter 6

PHARAONIC CALCULATION

FUNDAMENTALS

Pharaonic mathematical thinking is governed by theological principles, a fact that makes research into the mathematical knowledge of the Ancients difficult for our mentality, which is algebraic and, with the introduction of zero, based on the decimal and algorithmic systems.

The Ancients used an abacist system of calculation. It was not until the twelfth century that the West accepted the decimal system with the zero that was brought from India by Islam. The abacist system was then placed in opposition to the system generally referred to as algorithmic, after al-Khwārizmī, the "Khwārizmian," who supposedly made this system known.

When, following the Egyptians, Plato and the Alexandrian Greeks affirmed that there is no mathematical science other than geometry, this axiom, because it was a warning, implied knowledge of the existence of a possible imaginary mathematics, a "play of the mind."

If our science and philosophy assumes that everything in the Universe has *quantity*, that everything is composed of quantities, however infinitesimal they may be, then we must reckon with these quantitative units by placing them in a space that is itself limited. Four-dimensional geometry does nothing to alter this disposition of the mind, but only further displays our "quantified" field of vision.

Paradoxically, this materialistic mentality ultimately leads to thinking with abstractions until there is no possibility of constructing a thought without bringing in terms for which there is no concept. By refusing the abstraction of the creative principle we are forced to call in an arbitrary abstraction, a "supposition" or hypothesis, at every moment.

It is thus obvious that if in the philosophical foundation there is a recognition of an original abstraction, and if a strict observance of this principle is respected, then all the resulting thought will be absolutely different from our own.

From the outset, two basic elements of our mathematics would be eliminated: *zero* and *infinity*. These words, which designate a negation and the unknowable, have no concept. What is unknowable is precisely the Original Cause, and this equals One: the Unique Absolute containing the whole Universe. With regard to the negation zero, it is pure imagination, and at the most can only indicate an *absence,* or a *level,* separating affirmation from negation.[1] Mathematics is not and should never become a "play of the mind," but rather an essential transcription—in numbers—of the concrete knowledge of the Universe.

The Causal Unity is All, and the Universe that results from it can only be composed of *fractions* of this Unity. The fractioning, the *original division,* as the Mystery of Heliopolis tells us, becomes the law, the *divine gesture* in whose image we must proceed. Thus, all pharaonic arithmology is founded on Unity and its fractions, then on the return to Unity.

For our mentality, the mathematical point is an indescribable supposition because this point is, in reality, the Unity from which everything *esoterically* issues forth. This abstraction would be of no use to the Ancients unless they too were to "fall" into a way of thinking founded on quantity, for the Universe would then be but an *addition* of points, which is in contradiction with their theological principles. Everything that emanates from the Unique does so by its fractioning and appears to us as *volume,* because the fraction is comprehensible, and all that is tangibly comprehensible to us is so through its volume. Volume is the starting point, defining the surface, with the edge defining the line, and the intersection of these edges defining the point. Here then are the geometric elements that by themselves do not exist, but that serve symbolically in the demonstration of the function.

Starting from volume, everything exists only with regard to another; it is qualified as a *thing,* and this qualification is only psychologically comprehensible to us through comparison. This comparison creates applied geometry, which—including trigonometry—can only consist of *proportional relationships.* With these principles are given the fundamental bases of pharaonic mathematical thought.

In order to understand Ancient Egypt, it is necessary never to deviate from theological facts. All that might give rise to a "materialistic" and mechanistic conception was pitilessly rejected, no matter how practical it might be. Thanks to this and to similar disciplines, this empire was able to endure for millennia, and all its invaders were absorbed, for they had nothing to contribute.

—∿—

Pharaonic mathematical thought, being purely geometrical, is thus essentially logical. From this fact, the conclusion (in the Greek mind) became, exoterically, the Euclidean system in which invariable elements, translated into theorems, eliminated that which formed the true character of pharaonic thought; in other words, a living, moving approach was rejected by the systematizing logic of the Greeks. What makes Euclid so respectable for present science is precisely what we find deplorable and what Egypt never accepted.

For the pharaonic mathematician, the distance from point *B,* located in the middle of the straight line *AC,* would not be invariable. Also, this separation into two absolutely *equal* parts, *AB* and *BC,* is excluded. A supposition of this type would be blasphemy to him, not because he is a "relativist," but because all—including the thought with which he defines things—is living, and life is for him a flux of "becoming." He would not conclude that there is a closed circuit, "a ray of light that returns to its source,"[2] but a spiraling growth and decline of the source itself, a genesis that enables all possibilities (states of consciousness) of form to return to the Cause.

The pharaonic mathematician remains a theologian. He accepts comparisons, but for the directive of his thought he accepts neither a "situated point," nor, mechanically, a speed (such as that of light); only the Unique and Unity will be his reference.

[1] Cf. below, problem 40 of the Rhind Papyrus, which presents the geometric solution of a clearly algebraic problem.
[2] As in the theory of relativity.

Now the Unique is indefinable. Although logically justified, this appears to us absurd in practice. It is no longer absurd, however, if we consider, with the Ancients, that *every finite moment* as a unity in the image of the Unique, as one of the phases of the gestation of the finality of this Unique.

"... and God created man in His own image...." (Gen. 1:27). Thus man, being the last creature, is a unity, an image of the Unique. And the violet of the field is equally a unity in the image of the Unique, who, Himself, is indefinable, save by all the unities (finite images) of all the possible types of the creation. The Ancients would not say, as we do today, that each finite moment is a *quantum*, but rather, that each unity is a new departure, a *new beginning*.

Let us illustrate this geometrically. A square with a side of 1 has a diagonal equal to the root of 2. But this unity of the side can be composed, we may say, of ten equal segments, and thus the diagonal would be $10\sqrt{2}$. Continuing in this way, we would have $100\sqrt{2}$, $1000\sqrt{2}$, and (because we remain logical) we would finally arrive at $\infty\sqrt{2}$ for a side ∞. The side will be irrational by infinity, but the diagonal, also irrational, will be infinitely the root of 2. To our reasoning this is absurd, but it is not absurd for pure thought, which authorizes the scientist to say "Where common sense ends, true science begins." Similarly, can we say for a heated body that dilates and increases in volume in three directions that this increase, occurring in a moment infinitely small, and in a quantity of no value, would be three aspects of nothing? Certainly nothing prevents us from thinking like this, and until recently, at least, we were able to, but the most recent analysis of the atom has shown that in reality the phenomenon is never continuous as we suppose, but that everything occurs through a sort of granulation by alternations. Thus, we do not grow in a regular way in all directions of height and thickness at once, but periodically, alternately.

When we accept a single intellectual truth and oppose it to perceptible reality (science against phenomenon), we create a hiatus in our thinking that permanently excludes knowledge, not of provisional definitions, but of the vital phenomenon. Now it is impossible to reconcile intellectual truth with the phenomenon unless we take a *vitalist* attitude; this excludes *tangible* reality, which is considered solely as a transitory appearance and only used in an intellectual way as a guide for research into that which is neither hypothesis nor definitive phenomenon.

The Occidental mentality is rigid; it seeks invariables. It regards the phenomenon as a definitive effect. This mental "facility" leads us to *believe* in the reality of the phenomenon and, consequently, to imagine a purely intellectual science with all doors open for the satisfaction of logic.

But neither actually nor vitally in the genesis of the effect does this "equational logic" exist. The reasons for this are metaphysical, the consequences are ephemeral effects, and in order to discern the laws of this life it is necessary, above all, to live them oneself. With a science of "intellectual truths" one can decompose and recompose that which is given by life, but one will never be able to approach the vital cause. Our science knows this, but it continues to believe in the possibility of attaining this goal to which, obviously, all research into knowledge is devoted. Its method is "easy," as Einstein or Poincaré understood it, and this convenience is satisfying.

To come back to the example of the square, we know that the diagonal of any supposedly perfect square is the root of 2. And this root represents a number that, although figuratively finite, is intellectually incommensurable, because we want to see in it a finite consequence instead of accepting it as a *function*. Now, the root of 2 is *this fact:* that any number multiplied by itself will form a square, and if the side of the square is *n,* the diagonal will be $n\sqrt{2}$. We can calculate this diagonal and attribute to it any value, but this will not modify the function expressed by the root of 2, which is *immanent in the notion of the square*.

One could never trace or draw a perfect square, an absolute square; it does not *exist,* it *is;* that is, it is one with the Unique.

We can respond to this by saying that this absolute square can only be "assumed" to exist. Obviously we can admit anything whatsoever, but does this make it a *truth?* We can calculate with squares as if they existed without being preoccupied about whether or not they are *real,* but we will have thereby neglected what this function can reveal to us, that is, the law that governs all genesis, because, in any case, nothing can exist without having become, without starting from a cause that necessarily obeys the scission that makes of One the number Two. For this profound reason pharaonic mathematicians make the *function* of the root of 2 the instrument of their definition of *becoming.*

What difference does it make whether the result is a perfect square or only an approximation, sufficient from every point of view? Its tangible reality is not important, but in remaining aware of its vital, functional character, we will not have "prostituted" the notion of an immutable and therefore sacred Reality. And we will not have further sacrificed this Reality to a hypothesis, to an imaginary construction, simply for the sake of "convenience."

Has not our science come to perceive that the atomic substance of bodies is moving? That all bodies, beginning with the most elementary ones, are subject to modifications, to aging, and that they are therefore living? On the day—which is already approaching—when we will have to revise our "philosophical thinking" in light of our newly acquired convictions, we shall most likely come nearer to the guiding knowledge of our pharaonic ancestors.

This conclusion imposes itself in studying the mathematical thought of pharaonic Egypt. We shall now explain its application to calculation as succinctly and clearly as possible.

———————

"'Number resides within all that is known. Without it, it would be impossible to reason or to know,' wrote the Pythagorean philosopher Philolaus. . . . 'They say,' the Platonist philosopher Proclus assures us, 'that the people who first divulged the secret of the irrational numbers perished in a shipwreck to the last man, because the inexpressible, the formless, must be kept absolutely secret; those who divulged it and depicted this image of life perished instantaneously and must be tossed about by the waves for all eternity.'"[3]

Can there be a better description of the error of "scholarly" thought?

GENERAL CONSIDERATIONS

This exposition of the method of pharaonic calculation, based on examples given in the mathematical papyri, especially the Rhind Papyrus, has the sole aim of clarifying *the mode of pharaonic thinking.*

The concern of the eminent mathematicians who have begun to study these papyri has naturally always been to relate the mathematical knowledge of the Ancient Egyptians to our own. They have been preoccupied with finding out whether the Egyptians knew algebra, the algorithmic decimal system, or binomials. In these studies, a prejudice either for or against a pre-Greek mathematical science is not uncommon, nevertheless, some do strive to remain neutral and to keep the search for truth as their major concern.

[3] F. Le Lionnais, *Great Currents of Mathematical Thought,* trans. R. A. Hall and Howard G. Bergman (New York: Dover, 1971), 1:68, 69.

The dread in universities regarding anything "philosophical" or anything that touches on the "mystical" is cause for a false and defective position in the study of the thought of the Ancients and of the methods they adopted. This research is further complicated by the fact that the papyri do not give *the rules that govern the operations,* yet these rules are employed in stating the proposed problems, thus requiring the student to discover the method of operation for himself. Obviously, if he succeeded in this difficult task—something not always accomplished by today's mathematicians—the student would undoubtedly be considered to have acquired the sense of the mathematics. It would also prove that he was *in the spirit of the philosophical tradition.* It was not therefore a merely childish enthusiasm that inspired the scribe Ahmose, the copyist of the papyrus found in the Rhind collection, when he wrote: "Herein is written all knowledge."

For these reasons I have found it necessary to preface this chapter with an exposition of the elements of the anthropocosmic theme. But to enter into the method of pharaonic calculation one must realize that it requires long practice, and above all, a particular aptitude for mental calculation.[4] Many of the operations are not mentioned in the papyrus because they were done mentally, and for the people of those times, they were self-evident. For the conversions of fractions, which often take long to calculate, there were prepared "tables" such as those we now use for trigonometry and logarithms.

The "crossing"[5] is one of the essential principles at the base of the thought of the Ancients, a principle that will become evident as soon as we set out their method of calculation. This element, among others, was neglected in the study of Egyptian mathematics until now, although the principle of the "reciprocal" was well known and applied in Babylonia, as well as in Egypt and Greece. There is, however, in the "principle of crossing" a more profound esoteric foundation for the reciprocal than would appear in its application.

It should never be forgotten that the theological directive is always piously respected, and that, above all, the play of thought *that has no geometric confirmation is excluded.* Nevertheless, it is not to this directive only that mathematical thought is confined. There is another mental disposition that is very difficult for us to understand today; it consists of a kind of alliance between a very *practical,* realistic sense, and the "feeling" I call "spatial vision."[6] It has to do with a kind of synthesis, *a planar vision of the three-dimensional,* because, for the pharaonic thinker, all is in motion, nothing is definitively stopped, as it is for us. Our mental disposition looks for "invariance," for the rigid, rational scheme upon which, taken as a firm foundation, we attempt the construction of our mental edifice. Pharaonic thought refuses to build on such an invariable base because life is moving and progressing. Destruction and death are likewise *moments of life;* they are transitions, and "tomorrow" contains the past. There is a simultaneity of time and appearance in the phenomenon; the phenomenon is a *trompe-l'oeil,* and because one knows it, and never forgets it, one can be practical and realistic without danger.[7] It is the conscious application of the reactive principle of life, which always calls forth its complementary reaction, in actual fact as well as in thought and psychology.

Thus for pharaonic mathematics and its applied, descriptive geometry, the irrational does not exist. One works with whole numbers or with fractions that can be brought back to whole numbers. One knows that the irrational is the *essence* of all visible things, and consequently, one can accept the appearance as momentarily real.

---

[4] The facility for mental calculation is still common today, especially with Semitic people, the people of black Africa, and the whole of the Orient.

[5] See chapter 19.

[6] The "intelligence of the heart" of the Ancients.

[7] This is the recognition, before the fact, of Heisenberg's "uncertainty principle." The pharaonic sages started with this reality, which excludes a deterministic science.

THE EGYPTIAN NOTATION OF NUMBERS

Here we shall attempt to explain the decimal system without zero.

The pharaonic mode of symbolizing numbers is typically abacist. For calculation, it considers numbers in enumerated form. It remains practical and is very easy for the calculator to use. Our transcription of figures in the "Arabic" system simplifies writing; it appeals to a convention that no longer represents the positive value, and puts a "total" in place of the enumeration. This, obviously, modifies the mentality of the calculator. The Arabic figures, which only go from 1 to 9, define the tens and the powers of ten. This makes for complexity in the mind of the calculator, while simplifying the practice.

We should recall here that our decimal system does not allow for an even division by three, since the total thus divided cannot be integrally reconstituted. The pharaonic calculator would not allow this weakness.

—⁓—

Egyptian mathematics combines a system of decimal notation with a method of multiplication based on successive duplications, which we will explain later on. Our present decimal system differs from that of the Ancients because of the introduction of zero, a notion totally excluded from pharaonic thinking.

The first nine numbers are figured by as many vertical strokes as there are units in the number.[8] The number 10 is represented by the sign ∩, which is drawn as many times as there are units of ten in the number. The other powers of ten, that is, hundreds, thousands, ten thousands, millions, each have their own special sign and are treated in the same manner:

    ℃ 100   𐎟 1,000   𐎟 10,000   𐎟 100,000   𐎟 1,000,000

Now, we must see in this system of notation the origin of the tradition handed down by the Pythagoreans that expresses the properties of numbers by means of *unit-points*. Any number can thus represent a figure, and can be either odd or even, linear, planar, or solid; it can be either product or sum, whichever is expressed by the different figures that the unit-points can form.

Knowing as we do that the Greeks wrote numbers by means of the letters of their alphabet, the unit-point system was thus a foreign concept to them, and since Pythagoras was instructed in Egypt where the unit-point system was used in the form of short vertical and horizontal strokes, we can begin the study of the pharaonic mathematical papyrus in light of the teaching that Theon of Smyrna has handed down to us as the heritage of the Pythagorean tradition.

Theon says, "The decad completes the series of numbers containing in itself the nature of both even and odd, of that which is in motion and of that which is still, of good and of evil."[9] Pythagoras considered number, in fact, as the universalized *function* immanent in the entity it represents. This warrants the moral qualification of number as good or evil.

Anatolius also says: "The Pythagoreans have reduced all numbers to ten, and there are no new numbers over ten. . . . It is the circle and it is the limit of all number because we turn around and come back to it, like the starting point the runners pass when they run twice around the stadium."[10]

---

[8] This representation of the number by units of 1, 10, 100, and so on, is strictly observed in the hieroglyphic inscription. In hieratic writing this principle is respected while adapting itself to fast writing by abbreviations. There are, however, certain numbers that are represented in this writing by symbols, such as the numbers 7, 70, 700, and 50.

[9] Theon of Smyrna, *Le Nombre de Platon*, part 2, §49, p. 175.

[10] Tannery, *Mémoires scientifiques*, 3:12, 24.

It is curious to compare the Greek stadium represented by the image ⟣ and the number 10, which the Egyptians represented by ⋂. The number 10 is read *mdj*, and one of the names for "headband," *mdjh*, is determined by the symbol ⟳. This example illustrates one of the aspects of this number. Also in this regard, we ought to point out that the curved roof (or ceiling) is not found in Egypt except when directly symbolizing cyclic movement, that is, the Osirian renewal.

Let us remember that the Pythagoreans kept ten principles or "oppositions" in mind: limited and unlimited, odd and even, one and many, right and left, male and female, rest and movement, rectilinear and curved, light and darkness, good and evil, square and oblong.

It thus appears that the decimal system originated from a different concept than the rather simplistic one based on the use of the ten fingers, as many have claimed.[11]

Finally, the number 10 is the sum of the numbers of the first quaternary: $1 + 2 + 3 + 4 = 10$. "Now, these numbers contain the consonance of the fourth (4/3) . . . , the fifth (3/2) . . . , that of the octave in the double ratio (2/1), and that of the double octave in the quadruple ratio (4/1), and in this way the immutable diagram is completed."[12]

EGYPTIAN CALCULATION

Before starting on the contents of the Rhind Papyrus, it seems necessary to define the four major mathematical operations as they were practiced in ancient Egypt, and to show, through the terminology by which they are defined, the meaning given to them by the Ancients.[13]

1. *Addition* is defined by several expressions derived from the preposition ⟳ *hr*, meaning "in addition to," a very ancient derivative from the literal meaning "over," or "on." For example:

$\frac{1}{4}$ its   over   its 1

"Its quarter over itself" (lit.).
"Plus one quarter" (c.t.).[14]

Put   you   100 over it

"You will place 100 over it" (lit.).
"You shall add 100" (c.t.).

Without going into all the nuances that this expression contains, we see that it expresses the *action* of adding, which is putting one thing on top of another, or of "piling up."

---

[11] I believe, rather, that two times five, or ten, fingers result in the number 10.

[12] Theon of Smyrna, *Le Nombre de Platon*, part 2, §37, p. 153.

[13] T. Eric Peet, in *The Rhind Mathematical Papyrus* (London: Hodder and Stoughton, 1923) [hereafter cited as *RMP*] provides the translation and the philological commentaries that are the basis of our summaries.

[14] We provide two possible translations here of the most common expressions, adapted from Peet, who also provides a literal rendering (lit.) and the generally accepted conventional translation (c.t.).

What we call the sum, or total, will also be determined in several ways. Sometimes "Whose fourth part added to it becomes *n*" is expressed, and sometimes one finds at the base of a long addition the mark ⌒, which is an abbreviation of the whole word �⌒, which means "total," and is derived from "to unite" or "to reunite."

2. *Subtraction* is also defined by several terms, the most common of which is the verb ⌒✕ *khbi*, determined by the two crossed sticks to which the sense of "breaking," "splitting," or "diminishing" is given. Here again the term used represents the *action* of subtracting. The notion of "difference" is expressed by what *remains* and is written ⌒ *djat*. For example, problem 41:

"You take away 1/9 of 9, to wit, 1; remainder 8" (lit.).
"You subtract 1/9 of 9, or 1, leaving 8" (c.t.).

To express difference there is also another word used in the *s'km* problems. The true meaning of this word is "to complete," or ⌒ *s'km*, and problem 21 is worded as follows:

"It is said to you, 'What completes 2/3 + 1/15 into 1?'" (lit.).
"It is said to you: 'What is the complement of 2/3 + 1/15 with regard to 1?'" (c.t.).

It is certainly a question here of looking for the *difference* between the given fractional expression and unity, which the scribe expresses through the term *complement*. Now, this notion of complement plays a major role in the calculation of fractions, where, in long additions of complicated fractions, we find ourselves continually obliged to look for a unit fraction* to add to complete the unity or the required number.

The word *s'km* is applicable to linear numbers as well as to planar and "solid" numbers, which remained misunderstood until recently.

3. *Multiplication*, which we define here as a "product of two numbers," consists of "repeating the first number as often as there are unities in the second." The Egyptian expression is thus (problem 41):

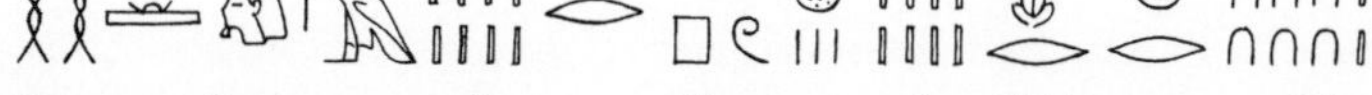

Put   first   8   times   8   will become   64

"Place 8 until 8 times, result 64" (lit.).
"Multiply 8 times 8, resulting in 64"; or "Count with 8, 8 times; it becomes 64" (c.t.).

The expression "8 times" corresponds exactly to our concept of multiplication, but in practice this operation follows a method that is invariably the same as what we call "duplication" (or "dichotomy" in the case of multiplication by fractions).

*A *quantième* in the French (and an *aliquot part* in Peet). We will translate *quantième* by the conventional term "unit fraction." A unit fraction is a fraction having 1 as its numerator; with the exception of 2/3, unit fractions are the only type of fractions found in Egyptian mathematics. See below, "Fractions."

We decompose the multiplier into tens and units with our decimal system; this decomposition of the multiplier can take any form we desire, and this question is worth our attention exactly because the procedure is so simple.

"But the simplicity is more often a point of arrival than a point of departure. It is the daughter of many trials and of long reflections that the careful person applies to a difficult problem to which our first concepts invariably respond—our mind is made so—with solutions that are unnecessarily complex,"[15] so we read with regard to the "cybernetic" movement that requires a return to the binary system.[16]

Thus, to explain Egyptian multiplication we are going to apply the essential principle to which our "progress" requires that we return: *Any number can be decomposed into a sum of powers of 2, plus unity.* Thus: $31 = 16 + 8 + 4 + 2 + 1 = 2^4 + 2^3 + 2^2 + 2^1 + 1$.

Without following this author in the applications of this to the machine, it is nevertheless interesting to note his comments on our decimal system:

> As long as man lived taking his organic impulses and constitutional tendencies as his only guide, that is, before the periods of the great civilizations that have made of him a being very nearly totally divorced from Nature, he had recourse to some system of nondecimal numeration. The most beautiful of his creations, perhaps, was the installation of the base 10 in his calculations. . . .
>
> Decimal arithmetic permanently conflicts with our natural tendencies. It accords badly with our disposition and has come into daily use only after having been compounded with octonary arithmetic. A. Mariage says on this point, and very rightly: "We should not have to do division to obtain the numbers; we ought to do numbers to arrive at division," and the natural divisions are 1/2, 1/4, and 1/8, because the natural multiplications are doublings, as 2, 4, 8.[17]

Thus, here we are back at the Egyptian system to which the Ancients remained scrupulously faithful, and it is ironic to see the multiplication that was practiced 5000 years ago being taken as an example today of the "notation of the future."

Thus "Put 8, 13 times," is written

$$/1 \text{ times } 8 = 8$$
$$2 \text{ times } 8 = 16$$
$$/4 \text{ times } 8 = 32$$
$$/8 \text{ times } 8 = 64$$

The scribe marks with a line the partial multipliers 1, 4, 8, of which the sum equals 13, making the sum of the partial products $8 + 32 + 64 = 104$. This method offers a great advantage in that each multiplier is double the previous one. Consequently, the partial products are also double each other.

---

[15] Cf. C. Laville, "Numérations non décimales," *La Nature* (January 1953).

[16] Regarding cybernetics and the senseless dreams that it has already given rise to, see P. Cossa, *La Cybernétique: Du cerveau humain aux cerveaux artificiels* (Paris: Masson, 1955), and the conclusion called for by the author: "If such a cybernetician sees so easily in the behavior of his small monster an image of free behavior, it is, in essence, because for him all behavior is determined and can only appear to be free. If others insist and confirm that the sensorial representation, the memory, relies on oscillating circuits, it is because, for him, sensorial consciousness and memory are only a material performance. We could multiply the examples—a good subject for meditation for those who are interested in the problem of unconscious motivations. We could even wonder if there isn't another even more profoundly unconscious element that interferes, a kind of machinist animism that involves making the machine a fetish to deify it."

These serious thoughts oddly remind us of the prophetic vision of G. de Pawlowski in his humorous *Voyage au pays de la quatrième dimension* (Paris: Eugène Fasquelle, 1923).

[17] Laville, "Numérations non décimales."

The operation, which is found exactly this way in all the papryi, is put even more simply than presented here for the reader's understanding. Thus, "Put 5, 15 times" is written

/1	5
/2	10
/4	20
/8	40
Total	75

Examining the form of this operation, we can see that it is presented in two columns of numbers that are each a geometric progression. The progression on the left has a ratio of 2 with unity for its first term, and the one on the right also has a ratio of 2 with the number n for its first term, which is the number to be multiplied.

Now, as we see in problem 79 of the Rhind Papyrus, these geometric progressions were not unknown to the Ancients. They form a part of the Pythagorean teaching that distinguishes continuous "proportions" of three terms from continuous or discontinuous proportions of four terms. The essential law that governs these proportions is: *The product of the extremes is equal to the product of the means* in the four-term proportion, and *the product of the extremes is equal to the square of the mean* in the three-term continuous proportion. Thus, in the progressions 1, 2, 4, 8, and 5, 10, 20, 40, $1 \times 8 = 2 \times 4$, as $5 \times 40 = 10 \times 20$ for four terms, and $1 \times 4 = 2 \times 2$, as $5 \times 20 = 10 \times 10$ for three terms.

Geometrically, the three-term proportion plays an immense role and is the basis of an essential function: the passage from the rectangle to the square, which is obtained geometrically in the following way, for example, in the proportion $2 : 4 : 8$ (fig. 17).

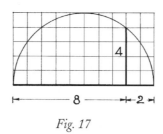

Fig. 17

Between 8 and 2, the geometric mean is 4, which is written as $8 : 4 : : 4 : 2$.

4. *Division* has the goal of finding the *quotient* of two whole numbers, which in our day is defined as "the number of times that one number contains the other." By this definition there is nothing to keep us from considering the greater number as the product of the smaller by a number that we have to find. Here, the unknown is the "number of times" that the smaller number has to be repeated to find the greater one. In practice, we can define division *as a multiplication*, but with the difference that the product is already known and that we must multiply the smaller number as many times as necessary to find the larger. Now, the scribe is going to operate in just this way, and the expression that he employs defines this operation exactly.

Thus for "Divide 15 by 5" the scribe writes

| Put | first | 5 | to | find | 15 |

"Put 5 to find 15" (lit.).
"Divide 15 by 5" (c.t.).

and he operates like this:

$$
\begin{array}{rr}
/1 & 5 \\
/2 & 10 \\
\text{Total} & 15
\end{array}
$$

The *quotient* sought is in the left-hand side of the operation. It is the sum of the partial multipliers $1 + 2 = 3$, which the scribe marks by a line. The scribe has effectively "Put 5 to find 15"; the answer is 3 times.[18]

We have just seen how the scribe accomplishes the *operation* of division. But while we only have one word to describe this notion, there are three distinct expressions in the papyrus that are translated indiscriminately as "divide *a* by *b*." These expressions taken in their literal sense should orient us toward the manner of thinking of the Ancients.

1. The action of dividing in the sense of cutting or splitting one quantity into several parts is expressed at the top of problem 1 of the Rhind Papyrus, where it is written, "Example of dividing [☐ *psch*] 1 [loaf] among 10 men." The scribe provides the result without making the division.

2. The notion of *ratio* between two whole numbers, for which one of the forms of transcription is a fraction, seems to be defined at the beginning of a table called the "division of 2 by odd numbers," where the scribe writes,

Call   2   before   3 $\frac{2}{3}$

"Call 2 in front of 3" (lit.).
"Divide 2 by 3" (c.t.).

Instead of placing the two numbers one *on top* of the other, as we do today, the scribe placed them one *in front* of the other as the Greeks have continued to do. This expression is used both when *a* is larger than *b* and when *a* is smaller than *b*. Thus we see, among other things, that in problem 66 the scribe writes: "You will call 3200 in front of 365; it will become . . ."[19] and gives the quotient immediately in fractions with no operation. He put it in the following way, as we would do today:

$$
3200 : 365 = 8 + \frac{2}{3} + \frac{1}{10} + \frac{1}{2190}.
$$

The *ratio* between the numbers 3200 and 365 is the *quotient*.

[18] The first part of the sentence is identical to that used in multiplication. We give it the meaning of "counting with," but we can also say "to put in," "to place," or even "to add," or rather, "to accumulate."

[19] Peet [*RMP*, p. 14] translates the first word, *nis*, by "call" or "summon," and the second, *khnt*, by "out of," while its current meaning is "in advance of," "before," "at the top of," "in front of," whence derives "presidio" [*préside*] and so on, which we can also translate as "overseer" [*préposé*]. G. Lefebvre, in *Tableau des parties du corps humain mentionées par les Egyptiens*, supplement aux Annales du Service des Antiquités de l'Egypte, notebook no. 17 (Cairo: I.F.A.O., 1952), pp. 13–14, gives "in front of" as the standard translation of the word *khnt*.

3. Finally, the operation. As we have seen from the preceding, the expression "Put 5 to find 15" determines the operation that consists of "repeating" 5 as many times as necessary to find 15.

In order to make the difference between multiplication and division in the pharaonic method more precise, let us compare them to each other:

Multiplication of 5 times 15		Division of 15 by 5	
"Put 5, 15 times"		"Call 15 in front of 5"	
		"Put 5 to find 15"	
/1	5		
/2	10	/1	5
/4	20	/2	10
/8	40		
Total	75	Total	15

The product is 75 and appears on the right. The quotient is 3 and appears on the left.

In division there is thus an "inversion": it is *the dividing number that takes the passive role and is multiplied.* This mode of operation is typical of the mentality of a people who continuously calculate with fractional expressions, and who, the same as in our present mathematics, transform division into multiplication, as we will see later on.

In fact, it appears that the pharaonic mathematician recognizes only one operation that corresponds to the original principle of division and that summarizes all four operations, since by the system of duplication one has equally division and multiplication, with the reading of the outcome done by addition and subtraction.

In these examples we have always used the same very simple numbers in order to demonstrate the method that invariably will be employed regardless of the complications and nuances required by fractional numeration with the numerator 1, of which we will now speak.

FRACTIONS

"If we divide unity into a certain number of equal parts and we take one or several of these formed parts, we have a fraction"; such is our teaching today. Now, in our fractions we distinguish the numerator and the denominator.

Ancient Egypt allowed only the numerator 1, with the single exception of 2 in the case of 2/3. Thus, we will always be dealing with fractions when we write $1/n$. Now, our way of transcribing with the term $1/n$ is still according to *our mentality,* but it is absolutely incorrect for the pharaonic mind; fractional numbers are always expressed by the sign of the *mouth,* under which the denominator is written.

For example, the pharaonic scribe writes 1/7 as ⤫. The hieroglyphic symbol ◯ is the letter *r,* which represents the mouth or the vocal cords "that emit the Verb." This is, symbolically, the *unitary Verb* that (in this case) *announces* seven as 1 1 1 plus 1 1 1 1.[20] It is also this same sign representing

---

[20] For ease of discussion, we shall keep to standard notation. We shall also be adding some remarks that the calculator did not express, but that it seems necessary to note for the unprepared reader, since these pages are addressed to the general public, and it is very important to follow closely the workings of the procedure.

the "mouth" that is used to write the name of Ra, the sun, the symbol of the emanation of the "Verb" that creates the Universe.[21]

This confirms the theological principle that presides over the pharaonic mentality, with respect to mystical principles. This reality is accentuated again in the hieroglyph designating "two-thirds" ⨍ , which we noted in relation to the mystical number ϕ. The "All" is ⬭ , from which, through scission, come the two unequal parts reconstituting this unity.[22]

In using this mode of transcription, the first characteristic of the Egyptian system of fractional notation is that all fractions, with the exception of 2/3, are considered to have 1 for the numerator.

The second characteristic, which derives from the first, is thus the impossibility of writing, for example, 2/7, which compels the scribe to transcribe this value into an appropriate form. Tables for transforming $2/n$ into fractional expressions with a numerator of 1 are found at the head of all mathematical papyri.

Regarding the division of whole numbers, it has been shown that the expression "Call a in front of b" can perhaps be transcribed as $a : b$, thereby establishing a ratio between the two numbers.

The art of the scribe consists in transforming this ratio (which we write a/b) into a new ratio in which one term is unity and the other must be expressed in fractions of unity, as, for example $4 : 3 :: 1 + 1/3 : 1$, which we write as $4/3 = 1 + 1/3 = 1.333$; or again $3 : 4 : : 1/2 + 1/4 : 1$, which we write as $3/4 = 0.75$.

Let us recall this sentence from chapter 5, "Multiplicity is what reveals Unity to us; that is, our comprehension of things exists only through . . . the original *fractioning* into parts and the *comparison* of these parts to one another. . . ."[23] In our current mathematics it is taught that if we divide a defined length into a certain number of equal segments, each segment is in a *common measure* with the unity.

The "common denominator" necessary for any addition or subtraction of fractions is this common measure. In the papyri, however, its method of calculation and its choice do not answer to a rational concept but, as we shall see later on, follow a form of thinking of which Theon of Smyrna appears to have passed on some vestiges.

> The number is a collection of monads or a progression of the multitude beginning from and returning to the monad (through the successive addition or subtraction of one unit). As for the monad, it is the determining quantity—the principle and element of numbers—that, when disentangled from the multitude by subtraction and isolated from all number, remains firm and fixed; it is impossible to push division any further. If we divide a tangible object into several parts, what was *one* becomes several, and if each part is then subtracted, it will terminate again at *one;* and if we again divide this *one* into several parts, the multitude will arise out of it. And in taking away each of these parts we will come back again to *one* in such a way that that which is *one,* as *one,* is without parts and indivisible.[24]

Notice here how the idea of infinity is left out because it would become confused with the indivisible Unity, that is, with the divine Original Cause.

[21] Numerous religious hymns support this idea.

[22] To this we can relate the following words: ⧈ *sp.t,* "the lip." By writing *sp.ty,* "the two lips," we designate the dual, which is the separation of the unitive Verb that symbolizes the mouth. ⧈ *sp.t,* "to enumerate" (to count the herd). ⬭ *sp,* "times," for example in "place *n* times."

[23] See p. 88.

[24] Theon of Smyrna, *Le Nombre de Platon,* part 1, §3, p. 29.

The translator perhaps sees here a "sophism" for our present mentality, but can we not see in this Greek reasoning, passed on in a later age, the remnants of the old Egyptian procedure for addition and subtraction of fractions? We shall put this into practice by recreating the division of a "tangible object," sentence by sentence.

Let us take a rod of a certain length and give it the value 1. We may call it, for example, 1 cubit.

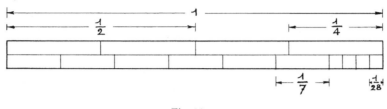

Fig. 18

If we divide this length into 7 parts, it becomes "several" parts, what we will call 7 "palms," each one of these representing a new unit, the palm. If we again divide each palm into 4 parts, we have 4×7 or 28 parts, forming another new unit that we will call a digit (fig. 18). If the scribe asks, in relation to the original "cubit," what the sum of the following fractions is,

$$\frac{1}{2} \quad + \quad \frac{1}{4} \quad + \quad \frac{1}{7} \quad + \quad \frac{1}{28}$$

$$14 \qquad 7 \qquad 4 \qquad 1,$$

he considers the smallest part as having the value of a new unity and puts the number **1** in red underneath.[25] Then, seeing that 7 is contained 4 times in 28, he puts the number **4** under the 1/7, then the number **7** under the fraction 1/4, and finally, the number **14** under the fraction 1/2.

Now if we compare the so-called sophism of Theon with this "technique" of calculation, we can conclude the following: The fractioning of the unity is a *multiplication* into as many units as there are parts, and *only one of these parts is taken to be the new unity*.[26] Thus the *sum* = **14 + 7 + 4 + 1 = 26**.

What we call the "common denominator," 28, is implied, but there is no need to mention it. If we ask how much is missing from this sum in order to recover the unity—1 cubit—equal to 28 (digits), the scribe would write, "Total 26, remaining 2" and for "the completion up to 1," he would know that he must still add 2 digits more, that is, 1/14.

If we wish to formulate this method of calculation we can express it as follows: To find the sum of fractions with numerators of 1 and with different denominators, take as unity the fraction with the largest denominator, and this denominator, considered as containing all the others, is the common denominator. Count how many times each of the other denominators is contained in it and write its respective value in red under each fraction. The sum of these values gives the result that was sought, written in whole numbers, without mentioning the common denominator (the largest one), which is always *implied* but never written.

The very simple example we have used in this demonstration has the advantage that all the denominators are multiples of each other; this favorable circumstance is not always the case, and this fact does not seem to have embarrassed the scribe. As we shall see in the problems of the papyrus, even the most difficult operations did not present an obstacle for him.

---

[25] We use boldface for what is marked in red in the papyrus.

[26] See chapter 5, "The Mystical Number."

In the table of the decomposition of $2/n$, we find but one case, 2/35, in which the common denominator is indicated. Mathematicians have long argued about whether or not the Ancients looked for the common denominator in calculations such as those we have shown. As we just saw, their procedure is disconcertingly simple in comparison with our method, which consists of: (1) decomposing each denominator into its prime factors; (2) looking for the smallest common multiple of the denominators by taking the product of all the factors that make up these numbers, using each one only once, with its largest exponent; and (3) dividing the smallest common multiple by each of the denominators and multiplying the two terms of each fraction by the corresponding quotient. As we have seen, the Egyptian procedure goes straight to the third operation and finds the total directly.

In some way, this method of multiplication or division is the inverse of a decomposition into prime factors in that the scribe, in the end, knew his numbers and their factors better than we. We shall have the opportunity to see in the $2/n$ table the extent of this knowledge of the "factors" that make up numbers.[27]

This procedure is infinitely more simple and quicker than ours, and we can again ask whether this simplicity that returns the function of calculation to its most direct method of operation is not conclusive proof of the power of thought that governed the establishment of these methods.

MULTIPLICATION

We have seen that the Ancients distinguished linear, planar, and solid numbers. It is undeniable that geometric thinking presided over this conception.[28] Among the planar numbers we principally distinguish the triangular numbers, which are the essence from which all the polygonal numbers, the square numbers, the rectangular numbers, and so on, are derived.

To clarify our explanation we can say that *when represented by unit-points, any planar number can be either a product or a sum.* Thus the number 4 can be the product of 2×2 or the sum of $2 + 2$ or of $1 + 3$.

Any triangular number is a sum, because it results from the summation of an arithmetic series, $1 + 2 + 3 + 4$, and so on.

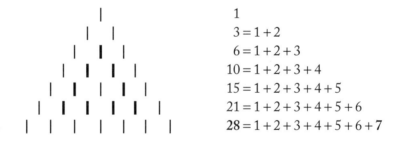

$$1$$
$$3 = 1 + 2$$
$$6 = 1 + 2 + 3$$
$$10 = 1 + 2 + 3 + 4$$
$$15 = 1 + 2 + 3 + 4 + 5$$
$$21 = 1 + 2 + 3 + 4 + 5 + 6$$
$$28 = 1 + 2 + 3 + 4 + 5 + 6 + 7$$

The triangular number **28** happens to be the seventh term of this series and the sum of the first seven numbers. As the ancient diagram shows, eighteen unit-points encircle the decad formed by the Great Ennead surrounding the central unity.

Moreover, 28 is a *perfect number* because it is equal to the sum of its factors, that is, $28 = 14 + 7 + 4 + 2 + 1$, a property that was considered to be a remarkable perfection in ancient times.[29]

---

[27] See these complete problems in the appendix to this section, p. 144.

[28] See chapter 5, "The Mystical Number."

[29] A tradition passed on by the Pythagoreans. The first three perfect numbers are 6, 28, and 496.

Now, it is not unimportant to mention in relation to this that the royal cubit contains 28 digits and that its origin is undeniably pharaonic; no other civilization of this period adopted this subdivision.[30]

The square numbers can be formed in different ways: first, *by the multiplication of two factors or equal sides;* second, *by the addition of two consecutive triangular numbers.* Thus, the triangular series added to itself, with a shift forward of one unity, has for its sum the natural series of perfect squares:

$$1 = 1$$
$$3 + 1 = 4$$
$$6 + 3 = 9$$
$$10 + 6 = 16$$
$$15 + 10 = 25, \text{etc.}^{31}$$

This can be demonstrated geometrically by means of unit-points in the following way:

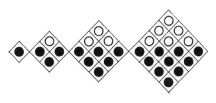

Fig. 19

A third way square numbers can be formed is *by the generation of a primary square to which is added a gnomon.* This generation of squares by the addition of a gnomon proceeds through a sort of growth by means of the primary square 1 and from the natural series of odd numbers, 3, 5, 7, 9, and so forth.

Unity is the first possible square, and the first gnomon is 3.

$$1 = 1 = 1 \times 1$$
$$1 + 3 = 4 = 2 \times 2$$
$$4 + 5 = 9 = 3 \times 3$$
$$9 + 7 = 16 = 4 \times 4$$
$$16 + 9 = 25 = 5 \times 5$$
$$25 + 11 = 36 = 6 \times 6, \text{etc.}$$

---

[30] The Babylonian cubit has 30 digits. For the "balance" Jābir takes the numbers 28 and 17 as the essential base. Cf. Paul Kraus, *Jābir ibn Hayyān: Contribution à l'histoire des idées scientifiques dans l'Islam,* Mémoires présentés à l'Institut d'Egypte 44–45, vol. 2 (Cairo: I.F.A.O., 1942). We will have an opportunity to speak again about the number 17 in the chapter on the *canevas* [see note on p. 236]. The number 28 draws its indisputable provenance from the qualities of which we just spoke.

[31] Egyptian knowledge of arithmetic progressions and the laws governing them is verified by problems 40 and 64 of the Rhind Papyrus. Particularly in the case of the latter, we will see that the theory concerning this subject was perfectly established. We find in the Babylonian tablets the important problems 149, 168, and 171 that also deal with arithmetic progressions. Problem 149 is in the form of a decreasing arithmetic progression the sum of which is known, as is the rate, 1, and the last term, 1. The unknown is the number of terms. The scribe solves this problem by the extraction of a square root, speculating on the fact that any square is the sum of two successive triangles; in the case of a progression at the rate of 1 and having 1 for the first term, the sum is a triangle. Twice this sum thus gives a "square plus its side." The unknown, the largest term (or side), can then be found by the following formula:

$$x = \sqrt{2s + \frac{1}{4}} - \frac{1}{2}, \quad \text{with } s = \text{the sum.}$$

This problem applies the theories regarding the addition of triangular numbers and gnomons.

If, no matter what its real value, we consider the initial square as always having the value 1, and the gnomon that is added to it as a fraction of unity, we arrive at pharaonic fractional multiplication.

To multiply $(1 + 1/3) \times (1 + 1/3)$ the scribe would write

$$
\begin{array}{cc}
1 & 1+\dfrac{1}{3} \\[2ex]
\dfrac{1}{3} & \dfrac{1}{3}+\dfrac{1}{9}
\end{array}
$$

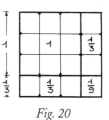

Fig. 20

The product will be $1+\dfrac{2}{3}+\dfrac{1}{9}$.

Now we can either keep the product we have found as it is or transform it by following the Egyptian mode of taking as a new unity the fraction with the largest denominator, 1/9, thus,

$$
1 + \frac{2}{3} + \frac{1}{9}
$$
$$
9 + 6 + 1 = 16
$$

We find here the origin of the squares and gnomons passed on by the Pythagoreans. To the initial square 9 is added 7 to make the next square, 16.

But there is another essential law at the base of this mode of calculation. Although the Ancients never used letters for numerical formulas, we allow ourselves to do this in order to make clearer the analogy between our binomial formula and the method of the scribe.

$$
(a+b)^2 = a^2 + 2ab + b^2
$$
$$
\left(1+\frac{1}{3}\right)^2 = 1 + \frac{2}{3} + \frac{1}{9}
$$

We know of no written demonstration of this formula either in Egypt or Babylonia, but we see it applied in both places. As we have just seen, this mode of operation requires not only knowledge of this formula but also knowledge of all the possible square and rectangular combinations that are derived from it, and the scribe does not go to the trouble of demonstrating this proof, as the Greeks did later on.[32]

Operating with our decimal system, of which we are so proud, such considerations as these do not occur to us since the multiplication of $(1 + 1/3) \times (1 + 1/3)$ becomes $1.3333...^2$, which equals 1.7777..., excluding any geometric idea. Likewise, in our fractional system, when we multiply 4/3 by 4/3, we find only that a new numerical ratio emerges between two square numbers, 16/9, but we lose the image of the original square and the addition of its gnomon, whereas, being obliged to write $(1 + 1/3)^2 = 1 + 2/3 + 1/9$, which we transcribe as $(a + b)^2 = a^2 + 2ab + b^2$, we are necessarily brought to essential laws, and *we are not allowed to forget them.*

Further on, we shall discuss the problem of the Berlin Papyrus, which is comparable in all points with numerous problems found in the Babylonian tablets based on the formula given above and its developments.

---

[32] This fact is noted, with regard to the Greeks, by Alexis-Claude Clairaut, *Eléments de géométrie* (Paris: Gauthier-Villars, 1920), p. xiii.

Let us summarize the formulas that apply to the multiplication of fractions as we currently phrase them:

1. *To multiply a fraction by a whole number we multiply its numerator by the whole number.* For example, $(2/3) \times 5 = 10/3$, which the scribe would write as $3 + 1/3$. The scribe would say: "Put 2/3, 5 times," and he works in the same way as in ordinary multiplication.

2. *To multiply a fraction by a fraction, we multiply them term by term.* This is exactly what we have done several times, except without formulating it. Thus the scribe writes in problem 37: "1/3 of this 1/3 is 1/9," which we write as $(1/3) \times (1/3) = 1/9$.

On account of fractions having a numerator of 1, a fractional expression is most often presented in the form of a series of fractions, and thus more particularly we have to verify the use of the following theorem:

3. *To multiply a number by a sum, we multiply it by each term of the sum and the partial products thus obtained are added.* The application of this formula represents one of the parts of the following general formula:

4. *The product of a sum multiplied by a sum is the sum of the products of all the terms of the first sum multiplied by each of the terms of the second.* Thus, $(a + b)(a + b) = aa + ab + ba + bb$, which makes a square, as we have developed above, or $(a + b)(c + d) = ac + ad + bc + bd$, which forms a rectangle and corresponds exactly to all the multiplications of fractional expressions that we find in the papyrus.

———

In order to illustrate one of the possibilities that permits this typically pharaonic mode of calculation, which always expresses a ratio, we will take the example of 5/4 and decompose it into several terms, which are here a unity and a unit fraction, $1 + 1/4$. We offer an example taken from the Berlin Papyrus 6619.[33]

The problem consists in dividing a square surface with side 10 into two squares of unknown sizes for which the sides are as 3 : 4. The scribe begins by "always making a rectangle of 1."* Then he takes "1/2 + 1/4 of 1" to establish the side of the other square. He adds these as the area of two squares and finds the value $1 + 1/2 + 1/16$ for their area. The scribe "takes the root" of this surface and finds $1 + 1/4$. He then divides 10 by $1 + 1/4$, and finds 8.

The rest of the papyrus is fragmented, but we can still understand that the scribe looks for 3/4 of 8 and finds 6. Here is a review of the essential facts:

1. The larger of the unknown squares is considered to have the value 1.
2. The smaller of the two unknown squares thus has for its side 3/4 of the other (because their sides are as 3 : 4).
3. The square containing the two preceding squares has a side of 5/4.

From the beginning, the problem defines the ratio 3 : 4. The conclusion that results is that the sum of $3^2 + 4^2 = 5^2$, because after finishing his calculations, the scribe finds the correct result, $1 + 1/4$, for the side of the containing square. The entire problem is based on the knowledge of the sacred 3, 4, 5 triangle.

[33] Cf. appendix to this section, p. 144.

* That is, a square of side 1.

Its final resolution is purely proportional, being $10:8::1+1/4:1$ and consequently $8:6::1:1/2+1/4$. We can, moreover, observe that the scribe applies in his calculations two essential formulas of our trigonometry: $a^2+b^2=c^2$ and $(a+b)^2=a^2+2ab+b^2$, or $(1+1/4)^2=1+1/2+1/16$, so we can translate geometrically these two associated formulas in the Berlin Papyrus by the following diagram:

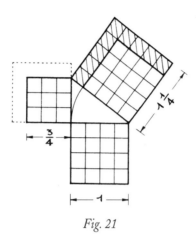

Fig. 21

It is thus evident that to approach their mathematical knowledge we must not lose sight of the fact that pharaonic methods are always and above all *geometrical,* something that our modern mathematicians do not take into account.

Appendix

. . . Pap. Berlin 6619, Pap. Kahun Pl. VIII, l. 40, and Pap. Moscow (unpublished) show that the idea of square root existed and that the technical term for it was *knbt,* literally "corner" or "angle," the idea presumably being that the original number, say 16, represented the area of a square, while the length of each of the two sides containing any corner of it was its square root, 4. The Egyptians were capable of taking the root of quantities involving simple fractions, the quantities whose root is taken in Berlin 6619 being $6\frac{1}{4}$ and $1\frac{1}{2}+\frac{1}{16}$.[34]

The determinative $\ulcorner$ for *knbt* ⌐⌐ is the very image of the gnomon, indicating by this the two sides of a quadrangle, that is, the elements for the process of finding the side of the square (the root).

Here is the commentary by the translator of the Berlin Papyrus:

The assignment is to understand that 100 square cubits are divided into two squares the sides of which are in the ratio of 1 to 3/4. The calculation now follows, which is developed in such a way that the lengths of the sides of the square in question are hypothetically posed as 1 cubit and 3/4. The two squares should together have a surface of $1+9/16$ or $25/16$ square cubits.

A square of this surface will have a side of 5/4 cubit, while the given surface of 100 square cubits corresponds to a square of 10 cubits to a side. Ten is therefore 8 times 5/4, hence the sides of the looked for square must be 8 times this length. They are therefore 8×1 and $8\times3/4$, or 8 and 6 cubits long. Thus, $8^2+6^2=64+36=100$.[35]

[34] Peet, *RMP,* p. 20.

[35] H. Schack-Schackenburg, *Der Berliner Papyrus 6619,* in *Zeitschrift für ägyptische Sprache,* no. 38, p. 135 et sqq.

DIVISION

The problems of the Rhind Papyrus are preceded by a table of division of $2/n$, since numerators larger than 1 (with the exception of 2/3) are not used in the calculation, and it is forbidden to decompose $2/n$ into two equal fractions.[36] The theological principles, which we always see respected, affirm that the Unique can only manifest by its own self-division into two unequal parts. Thus, the fraction $2/2a$ can never be decomposed into $1/a + 1/a$. This amounts to saying that the number 2 must be made up of two unequal parts in the proportion of $1/\phi$ to $1/\phi^2$. This table is indispensable to the calculator for resolving problems without having to enter into complicated operations. At least this is the way the table has been interpreted. Now, this division of $2/n$ presents some difficulties and requires the knowledge of the solution of all kinds of arithmetic problems appearing in the papyrus *before one can understand it,* and the scholars who have studied this document have caught enough of a glimpse of this to be passionately bent upon clarifying the procedure of this division. It is their work that has prepared the ground for our subsequent studies.

For our part, we have remained as faithful as possible to the fundamental conditions characterizing the pharaonic mentality, and we have recognized as our foundation the fact that even if an arithmetic division is presented as a play of quantities, it has nevertheless in its essence a vital character; in other words it is a question of a function of "scissiparity" for which the quantitative fractioning is only a symbol. Between One and Two there is an octave of phenomenal factors; thus, if the pharaonic mentality refuses the division into two equal parts and imposes the numerator One, its intent is for a proportional relationship in the spirit of a harmonic proportion.[37]

Moreover, we see a purely abacist method at the basis of the calculations of the Ancients, which our scholars at first recognize and later forget. The notation of numbers maintains an enumerating format. It is necessary to take into account this form of writing because it brings us straight to a geometrical representation of calculation through the magnificent transposition of the abacist conception into the *canevas.* Later on we will discuss the *canevas,* a veritable architecture of number by virtue of which the prime function, as proportionality, supersedes the mentality of a mathematics of quantities.

⸺⸻⸺

We must take up two essential questions: the notion of the *reciprocal of a number,* and that of the *crossing.* Pharaonic division is formulated in an identical way to multiplication, but in actual fact there is an "inversion" and a crossing. This method was used in Babylonia as well.

To divide one number by another, it is multiplied by the reciprocal of the dividing number. Thus in problem 63 of the Rhind Papyrus where 700 must be divided by $1 + 1/2 + 1/4$ (or 7/4), the scribe performs two operations. First, he divides 1 by $1 + 1/2 + 1/4$ (or 1 by 7/4) and obtains $1/2 + 1/14$ (or 4/7); then, he multiplies 700 by $1/2 + 1/14$, the result being 400.

---

[36] It is necessary to clarify that the division of a number by a number *greater* than it, for example 2 : 7, cannot be resolved, as in our system of numeration, by the fraction 2/7. In order to obtain the desired expression the smaller number must be divided into smaller and smaller parts through successive halvings. This fractioning is done, according to the case, by means of one of the following two fractional lineages: the lineage with 1/2 as its origin, 1/2, 1/4, 1/8, 1/16, etc.; and the lineage with 2/3 as its origin, 2/3, 1/3, 1/6, 1/12, etc. The lineage beginning with 2/3 has puzzled all the mathematicians who have studied pharaonic mathematics. Logically, from the point of view of calculation, it would have been simpler to first take 1/3 of a number and multiply it by 2, and then only if this were necessary. The cause of this anomaly has been sought for in vain.

[37] See in the $2/n$ table the sequence of the phrase beginning with the repetition of all twelve numbers seven times, starting from the number 17. The first reference is to the number 3. There is then an interval of fourteen (or seven odd numbers) between 3 and 17.

This brings us back precisely to the formula: *To divide a number by a fraction, multiply it by the inverted fraction.* This is the *inversion* (the reciprocal).

This notion of the reciprocal of a number is attested to in Egypt and in Babylonia through the calculations and through the very form of the expression; in the pharaonic cubit it is likewise applied.

In the phrase that we find at the beginning of the table of 2/n, "*nis 2 khnt 3*," "Call 2 in front of 3" (2 : 3), the word *khnt* 𓏏𓏤 —which originally designated the face or the forehead—is used here to mean "in front of."[38]

There is a striking analogy between this expression and that used by the Sumerians: *igi,* an abbreviation of *igi-gal,* which signifies "that which is in front of." Now, in Sumerian, 1/3 was expressed by *igi 3 gal.*[39] As Thureau-Dangin has judiciously remarked, contained here is the idea of opposition, of the reciprocal. Thus, 1/3 is the reciprocal of 3, as 1/2 is the reciprocal of 2, and so on. This word, however, would later lose its proper meaning in Babylonia where the same term would be used to designate "part" or "fraction."

When the Egyptian cubit marks its subdivisions by enumerating them from left to right, 1, 2, 3, 4, 5, etc., to 28, and sets down 1/2, 1/3, 1/4, 1/5, etc., to 1/16, from right to left, there exists the idea of the reciprocal in the very direction of the reading; if we place them end to end, we find the following:

$$\ldots \frac{1}{9}, \frac{1}{8}, \frac{1}{7}, \frac{1}{6}, \frac{1}{5}, \frac{1}{4}, \frac{1}{3}, \frac{1}{2}, 1, 2, 3, 4, 5, 6, 7, 8, 9, \ldots.$$

The series of whole numbers constitutes an *arithmetic progression,* and the series of reciprocals is a *harmonic progression.*[40]

Let us note here that Michel, guided by the locution used to denote the "harmonic proportion," a term that also includes the idea of a "progression," has investigated whether this progression was possible. He poses as a condition of the problem the finding of "a procedure that permits the formation of an unlimited series in which *three successive terms are always in harmonic proportion.*"

He observes that any construction with whole numbers is impossible, but that the Ancients expressed the harmonic mediety by means of fractional terms, and this suggested to him the idea of looking for a solution by means of the reciprocals. He concluded that "whatever may be the chosen numerator, the series of fractions obtained by taking for the denominator the series of whole numbers will form a harmonic progression *n/1, n/2, n/3, n/4,* etc., and finally, that the reciprocal numbers of any mediety or of any arithmetic progression make up a mediety or a harmonic progression."

Then he concludes, "Thus the 'harmonic progression' appears clearly as an inverse arithmetic progression, and the name ὑπεναντία originally attributed to the μεσότης ἁρμονίχη is justifiably the same."[41]

As a result, the table of 2/n at the beginning of the Rhind Papyrus (which has aroused much discussion) is in fact, among other things, the harmonic progression alluded to by the ancient word that defines it, ὑπεναντία, "opposed," or "contrary."

[38] Cf. Lefebvre, *Parties du corps humain,* pp. 13–14. "An ancient word indicating both a face and a forehead or the front part of the head, is *khnt.* . . . It has survived especially in the preposition *khnt* and *m khnt,* meaning "in front of."

[39] F. Thureau-Dangin, *Textes mathématiques babyloniens* (Leiden: E. J. Brill, 1938), p. xi, et sqq. [hereafter cited as *TMB*].

[40] See chapter 37, plate 64.

[41] Michel, *De Pythagore à Euclide,* pp. 394–95.

In developing the method of multiplication, we have accepted the product of two numbers as being a surface, determined by two sides, but we must not forget that any volume, whether parallelepipedal or cylindrical, is equally the product of a surface and a length. (Thus 8 is the cube of 2, but 8 can also be represented by 2 times the square of 2.)

While the product of two numbers stays the same regardless of the position of the factors, the quotient—what the Ancients call a "ratio between two numbers"—changes according to their position. Thus, division offers two possible ratios, one being the inverse of the other.

For example, the multiplication of 2×3 can be transcribed as

$$\begin{array}{ccc} | & | & | \\ | & | & | \end{array}$$

or as 3×2

$$\begin{array}{cc} | & | \\ | & | \\ | & | \end{array}$$

and the product will always be the same rectangular number 6; whereas with division, $2 \div 3 = 2/3$ or again $1/2 + 1/6$, and $3 \div 2 = 1 + 1/2$.

If we recall the law that governs all geometric proportions of three terms and the figure that demonstrates it, we see that any ratio and its inverse together with unity forms a geometric proportion, thus: $2/3 : 1 : : 1 : 1 + 1/2$. When transformed into whole numbers this gives $4 : 6 : : 6 : 9$, and it becomes easy to verify then that $4 \times 9 = 6 \times 6 = 36$. This is a continuous proportion of three terms.

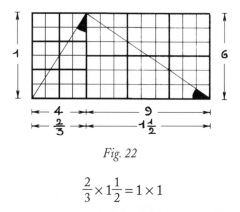

Fig. 22

$$\frac{2}{3} \times 1\frac{1}{2} = 1 \times 1$$

The continuous proportion of three terms is transcribed by the right triangle, inscribed in the half-circle with the altitude dropped onto the hypotenuse; this figure represents the case of the inversion of the terms $A : B : : B : C$, becoming $AC = B^2$ (fig. 23a). But in the case of a discontinuous proportion of four terms this single inversion is not sufficient, and we must call upon the crossing (fig. 23b).

We can arrange these in eight different ways:

$$A : B : : E : F$$
$$B : A : : F : E$$
$$A : E : : B : F$$
$$E : A : : F : B,$$

in which the product $E \times B$ is equal to $A \times F$. Figure 23 summarizes one of the essential laws governing proportion.

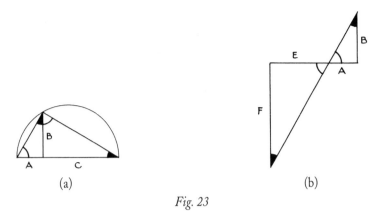

Fig. 23

We are now going to operate by following exactly the way the problem is stated by the pharaonic mathematicians. If, on the contrary, we were to translate these words into our present language and instead of saying "Call 2 in front of 3" and "Put 3 to find 2" use the term "divide,"[42] we would be neglecting the mentality of the pharaonic mathematician, who obeyed the function demonstrated by the geometric figure. In thus using two formulas for that which we call division, we can write "Call 1 in front of 2/3," and divide a horizontal line into two segments that are to each other as 1 : 2/3; next, we draw a perpendicular at each end, one rising, the other descending, thus *inversely* to each other (fig. 24). We then do the following operation:

"Put $\frac{2}{3}$ to find 1."

1	$\frac{2}{3}$
$\frac{1}{2}$	$\frac{1}{3}$
Total	1

$\left(\text{The quotient is } 1\frac{1}{2}\right)$

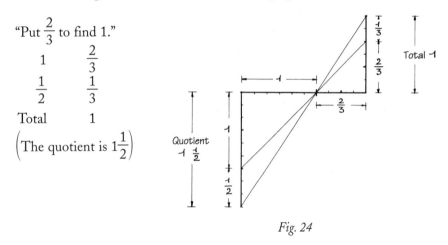

Fig. 24

On the lower vertical we mark 1 and extend the diagonal that passes through the point of crossing and determines 2/3 on the ascending vertical line; it is obvious that 1 : 1 : : 2/3 : 2/3. To equal a height of 1 the line lacks 1/3, that is, half of 2/3; therefore we take 1/2 of the lower vertical, corresponding to 1/3 of the ascending vertical, and we can easily verify that 1 + 1/2 : 1 : : 1 : 2/3.

We have not needed to convert the fractions into whole numbers. This also allows us to give the length called 1 the value that we want and to establish a true discontinuous proportion, as for example, 2 : 3 : : 6 : 9. In the diagram, as in the operation of the scribe, the product is read on the right and the quotient is read on the left.

---

[42] Peet gives the literal sense of the word *nis* as "call," "summon," "evoke" [*RMP*, p. 14]. It is also translated as "mark," "enumerate." The transcription "divide" is thus purely conventional and takes away the living character of the statement.

We see here how, in starting from a simple abacist calculation, the Ancients became geometers, whereas our way of dividing remains abacist: we count how many times a small number is contained in a larger one.

Figure 24 can represent any division that we find in the papyrus.

THE RHIND PAPYRUS

The Rhind Papyrus was discovered in two fragments, now in the British Museum,[43] and a few small pieces (coming from the missing part between the two) that belong to the New York Historical Society.* Together they originally made a single roll.

The two parts in the British Museum were purchased from Luxor in 1858 by A. H. Rhind. It is said that they were found in one of the rooms in a small building neighboring the Ramesseum along with other fragments that are listed in the catalog of the Egyptian Collection of the New York Historical Society with the description "265. Fragments of two or more papyri, containing numbers and quantities. Found with fragments of the Medical Papyrus and No. 262." The medical papyrus is the well-known Edwin Smith Papyrus, and no. 262 is a small fragment of hieratic writing containing the name of Tuthmosis I.

The fact that all these fragments were found together is extremely interesting, for as Peet has said, "We should infer that the Arabs found a cache of scientific documents dating, like the Rhind and the Edwin Smith, from the Hyksos Period, stored away not earlier than the reign of Tuthmosis I."[44]

DESCRIPTION OF THE PAPYRUS

The papyrus is divided into two pieces, originally measuring 543 centimeters long by 33 centimeters high, and was made up of fourteen sheets admirably glued together. It is written on both sides in deep black ink for most of the text and numbers, and in brilliant red ink for the titles and to emphasize certain numbers.

After the dedication, which is written in two vertical columns, the papyrus is laid out in six horizontal bands in which the problems are written. These bands cover the whole length of the paper.

The recto contains *(a)* the table of 2/*n*; *(b)* problems 1 to 40; and *(c)* after a blank space, problems 41 to 60. The verso contains what could be called a "miscellany" of all kinds of problems, which are numbered from 61 to 86. They appear to be complementary information for problems 1 to 60, which seem to be ordered in terms of increasing difficulty.

We are not making a study of the papyrus here; rather, we are using it to study the pharaonic mentality. In the section on division we entered fully into an explanation of the principles of proportion, which leads us first of all to discuss problems 24 to 38 in which these principles are

[43] Cf. *Facsimile of the Rhind Mathematical Papyrus* (London: British Museum, 1898).
[44] Peet, *RMP,* p. 2.
* These fragments are now in the Brooklyn Museum (no. 37.1784E).

applied. Subsequently, we shall follow the natural sequence of the function by choosing character-istic problems.[45]

PROPORTIONS AND THE RULE OF THREE,
PROBLEMS 24 TO 38

The statement of problems 24 to 27 can be transcribed as, "One quantity *(ahaw)* to which is added a fraction of itself becomes *n* (the given number); find this quantity." Problems 28 and 29 also consist of finding a quantity from which one or two fractions of itself are subtracted and afterward added. From the point of view of their solutions, these six problems form the first group of the problems of *ahaw*   .

Problems 31 to 34 can be transcribed in this way: "A quantity to which one adds several fractions of itself when added becomes *n*; find this quantity." Problems 35 to 38 introduce the measure of volume *(hekat)* and can be transcribed as follows: "I descend *n* times in 1 *hekat*, one (or several) fractions of myself are added to me; I return fully satisfied." These last problems (along with problem 30) are treated following a method generally called "direct division." According to their resolution, the problems of *ahaw* are classified into two categories.

The first category (problems 24 to 29) has aroused many comments among mathematicians who, in the end, can be divided into two camps: those who see algebraic exercises that correspond to a *first degree equation with one unknown,* and those who react violently against the idea of seeing algebra in these problems and recognize only a method of *false supposition.*

Peet sees in them a false supposition following from a proportion. Gillain, on the other hand, while fully acknowledging that these problems can be marvelously treated algebraically—since for their demonstration we are obliged to use *x*, which is never found in either Babylonia or Egypt—looks for the means of solving them arithmetically. He concludes that the first series is treated by the rule of three and the second by direct division.[46]

Let us take up these hypotheses:

1. *Equation of the first degree with one unknown,* because the first four problems can be written,

$$x + \left(\frac{1}{b}\right) x = n, \quad \text{or, for example,} \quad x + \frac{x}{4} = 15.$$

2. *False supposition,* because the scribe will always take *b*, the denominator, as the value of the supposed unity.

3. *Proportion,* because by this term we refer to an equality of two ratios, and because all the problems are effectively solved by establishing two ratios that contain an unknown term.

4. *The rule of three,* because when three terms of a proportion are known, the fourth can be calculated.

For example, let us take problem 26, which is located on the third line (from top to bottom) of the papyrus, third of this series in which the method is clearly presented from the first sentence (fig. 25).

---

[45] The reader not a specialist in mathematics need only read the conclusions given in this chapter. Without having either to read or verify the hieroglyphs and numerals one can familiarize oneself with the mentality of the Ancients. It is clear that here we are discussing only some typical problems chosen from among those that present the simplest numbers.

[46] Cf. O. Gillain, *La Science égyptienne: l'Arithmétique au Moyen Empire* (Brussels: Fondation Egyptologique Reine Elisabeth, 1927), pp. 208–50.

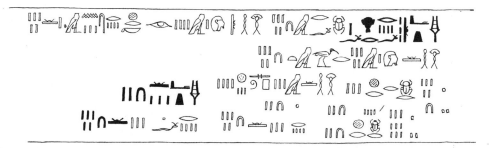

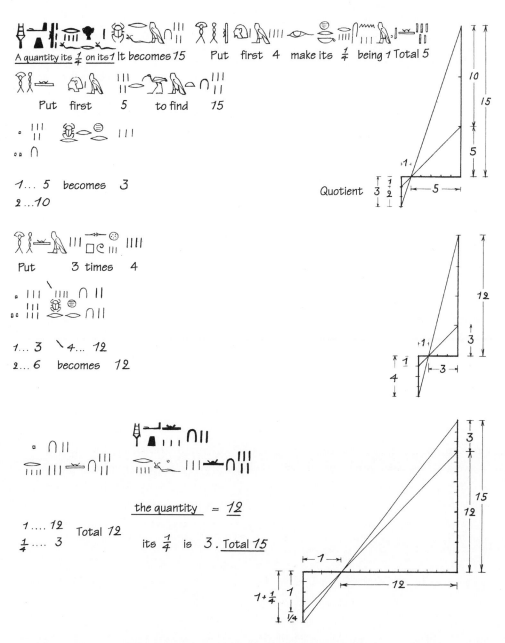

Fig. 25. Text, translation, and solution of problem 26

Above, the hieratic transcription in hieroglyphs, sign by sign, in the exact form of the facsimile and with its true reading, from right to left. *Below,* the translation of the reversed text into English, reading from left to right. The parts written in red by the scribe are in boldface.

"A quantity, one adds to it its quarter, it becomes 15. Put first 4, make its quarter, which is 1 [add it to 4]. The total is 5." In algebraic form, this statement would be $x + x/4 = 15$, from which $5x/4 = 15$. The scribe takes the denominator 4 as the value of the unknown and adds to it its quarter for a total of 5.

The second line says "Count with 5 to find 15," that is, divide 15 by 5. The result is 3, which represents the quarter of the unknown.

In the third line, it says to put 3 times 4, which gives 12, the value sought.

The fourth line is the proof showing that 12 plus its quarter is equal to 15.

The rule of three clearly appears in the sequence of operations that are transcribed by our formula as $(15 \times 4)/5 = 12$, and by the final proportion, $5 : 4 : : 15 : 12$.

This very peculiar method, in which we first put the unity in front of the number upon which we operate, invites us to present these operations in the appropriate geometric form. We can conclude that, most certainly, it is the function expressed geometrically that guides the thinking of the scribe in both the stating of the problem and in his way of working. Division and multiplication can be represented geometrically in the same manner and are based on the notion of proportionality.

Problems 24 through 27 are all treated in an identical way; with some nuances in the exposition and in their manner of solution, problems 28 and 29 can also be solved in the same way.

Starting with problem 30 the scribe adopts a method that is presented as a "direct division," and consists in solving similar equations in a single operation. Let us take, for example, problem 35 in which the first operation is very simple (fig. 26).

In the papyrus, the statement of this problem is characterized by the fact that it is divided horizontally into two parts that are to each other as 1 to ϕ, in addition to which it is marked by reference points that specify the ruled lines. The upper part comprises the actual problem and the lower part consists in transforming the result obtained into fractions of *hekat* and *ro*. The intention is thus to relate the function ϕ to volume and together relate them to harmony.[47]

In the first line the statement is thus phrased, "I have descended 3 times in 1 *hekat*; my third is added to me; I return fully satisfied. By whom is this said?"[48]

In algebraic form this problem would be written $3x + x/3 = 1$, which comes to $10x/3 = 1$. To solve this problem, which includes a fractional expression, the scribe could have proceeded as in problem 26 by transforming this expression into whole numbers: $1/3 = 1$, then $3 + 1/3 = 10$.

Instead of doing so, he keeps the fractional expression and opposes the unity to $3 + 1/3$, implying that the unity has the value of 10/10 opposite the dividing number, which has the value of 10/3. Thus, the procedure is indicated that can be applied to any fractional expression.

To solve this operation whereby 1 *hekat* is divided by 10/3, the modern formula is, "To divide a number by a fraction, multiply it by the inverted fraction." This notion of the reciprocal is obvious to the scribe, who looks directly for the 3/10, which he transcribes as $1/5 + 1/10$.[49]

The problems belonging to this category are all treated by "direct division," but with variations allowed for by this method.

---

[47] Cf. chapters 5 and 11.

[48] Peet suggests that the translation of "fully satisfied" be understood in the sense of "to pay in full." The best translation seems to be, "I am filled" or "I leave filled." This is the unknown, that is, the sought-for volume that speaks, although logically it would be that which "fills," and not that which "is filled." [*RMP*, p. 72.]

[49] Obeying the rule that requires the numerator be unity.

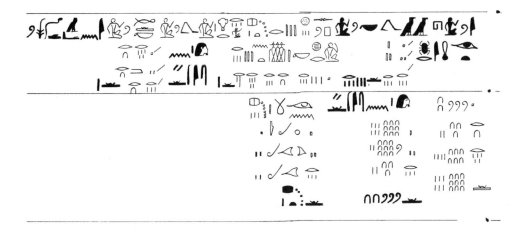

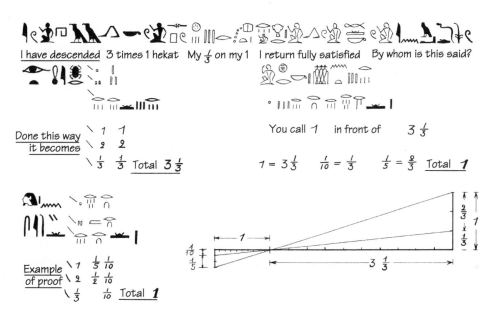

Fig. 26. Text, translation, and solution of problem 35

Above, the hieratic transcription in hieroglyphs, sign by sign, in the exact form of the facsimile and with its true reading, from right to left. *Below*, the translation of the reversed text into English, reading from left to right.

Conclusion

The very statement of the problem, "a quantity" that is to be sought, implies what we call today "the unknown *x*." Now, in our algebraic method we calculate by using this *x* as the balancing unknown value. The Egyptian would not do this. The unknown was for him a consequence and he would pose the problem as a rule of three, which implies the notion of proportionality.

The unknown that we would call *x* is in all cases already indicated by the character of the fraction, and it is the *denominator* that is viewed as having the value of this quantity, which corresponds to the method of pharaonic calculation. The remainder of the solution is a *proportion*, the operation being a rule of three for the first series and a "direct division" for the second, in which the principle of the inverse is applied.

When a problem is clearly stated, it contains all the elements for its solution. The Ancients have shown us how to use fractions by considering the denominator as unity, and we should therefore follow their way of thinking in all its applications.

The unknown x and the infinite ∞ are two notions that were systematically rejected. Only God is unknown and infinite.

—∿—

The problems of *ahaw* contain more than we have spoken about. Its symbol is a pile (heap). In what other way could a volume be represented, particularly when we have no recourse to an image in perspective, which is unknown in hieroglyphic symbolism? With this term we would be dealing not only with the notion of a quantity but also with the notion of a volume that implies a quantity.

Knowing as well that the Ancient Egyptians, like the Babylonians, always conceived of volume as resulting from the multiplication of a surface by a height, the calculation is reduced to a ratio between two numbers. For example, problem 32 of the Rhind Papyrus seeks to divide 2 by 19/12 (expressed in the form of unit fractions) and for the result finds 24/19, implying the division of the volume 2 by the cube root of 4, the result being the cube root of 2. It is thus easy to formulate our irrationals by an approximate but "finite" fractional expression.[50] Such an expression and its inverse always gives back the number without a remainder.

Moreover, the use of the *hekat* in problems 35 to 38 confirms again the idea of volume implied in these problems, of which we have only here studied the strictly proportional aspect.

Finally, we have to mention that problems 24 to 27 are based on the fundamental ratios $n + 1/n$, or 3/2, 5/4, 6/5, 8/7, as examples, and we recall the role that ratios of this type play in musical harmony, as well as their relation to the measures of pharaonic volumes.

Proportional Exchanges,
Problems 72 to 78

As part of the miscellany on the verso of the papyrus we find problems 72 to 78, which are undoubtedly problems of proportion. Their statements define a "proportional exchange" of n loaves of bread made at a certain rate a of flour against a number x of loaves made at another rate b. Except in one instance, their method of solution is similar to that of the first sequence of problems of the *ahaw*, that is, by the rule of three.

Problem 72, the first in this series, is given as an example *(tp)*; it is, however, treated in a completely different way because it plays on the differences, which obliges us to recall two of the properties that characterize proportions. First, *four numbers being given, if the product of two of them is equal to the product of two others, it is possible to arrange these numbers in eight different ways such that the four numbers of each of the eight obtained arrangements can be in proportion.*

And the second law, which the scribe combines with the preceding, is, *in every proportion the sum or the difference of the first two terms is to the second as the sum or the difference of the last two terms is to the fourth.*

---

[50] It is well known that the approaching values of these ratios are made into a series that we can develop with as much precision as we wish.

Problem 72

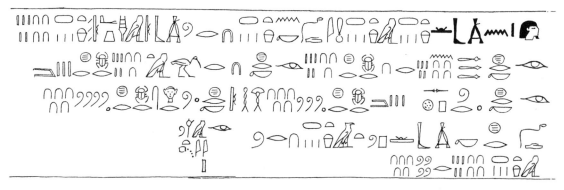

"An example of the exchange of loaves for loaves. If it is said to you, 100 loaves at rate 10 exchanged for a quantity of loaves at rate 45.

[*a*] You will take the excess of 45 over 10, result 35.
[*b*] You will take 10 to find 35, result $3\frac{1}{2}$ [$35 : 10 = 3\frac{1}{2}$].
[*c*] You will take 100 times $3\frac{1}{2}$, result 350.
[*d*] You will put 100 over that, result 450.

Then you shall say, it is the exchange of 100 loaves at rate 10 against 450 loaves at rate 45, making in flour [*wdjyt*] 10 *hekat*."[51]

The statement of this problem amounts to posing

$$\frac{100 \text{ loaves}}{\text{rate } 10} = \frac{x \text{ loaves}}{\text{rate } 45}$$

and it is clear that the result (450 loaves) is obvious without calculation. It is thus a problem of pure theory.[52]

Let us look again at the result sentence by sentence. In *(a)* and *(b)* the scribe finds the difference between the two rates and then divides by the smaller rate. This goes back to the application of the second law by virtue of which one can make the equivalence:

$$\frac{45 - 10}{10} = 3\frac{1}{2} = \frac{x - 100}{100}.$$

In *(c)* the multiplication $3\frac{1}{2} \times 100 = 350$ is made by virtue of the equality of the differences,

$$\frac{45 - 10}{10} = \frac{x - 100}{100}, \quad \text{that is,} \quad \frac{35}{10} = \frac{350}{100}.$$

In *(d)* having thus defined the quantity $x - 100 = 350$, the scribe adds 100 to 350 and finds the number he was looking for: 450 loaves. The conclusion defines in only one sentence what we would transcribe by the proportion 10 : 100 : : 45 : 450.

---

[51] The rate is the number of loaves that can be made from one *hekat* of wheat. The flour, *wdjyt*, is probably barley flour from Upper Egypt.

[52] The word *tp*, or profile of the face, written at the beginning means "example of the method of resolution."

It is well to stress that this process necessarily implies knowledge of the laws that we have stated, but that as always, these laws are simply applied without the slightest commentary. The resolution of this problem in the arithmetical way requires long explanations and the application of the formulas that we have presented in their present-day form.

Here now is the problem posed and resolved in pharaonic thinking based on geometry.

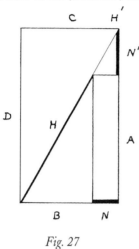

Fig. 27

Principles:

The ratio is the element of the proportion.

The general formula will be a description of the geometric gesture.

B is enlarged by *N*. In what proportion is *A* enlarged so that $A+N'$ will be proportional to $B+N$?

Draw the hypotenuse *H* extended to *H'*. The extension of *A* to $A+N'$ remains proportional to $B+N$. The given base is then expressed by the first proportion $A:B$. The result we seek will be $A:B::A+N':B+N$, or again, $A:B::D:C$.[53]

This problem can also be treated following the principle of the inverse and the crossing. Let us take as an example the way problem 72 is stated, choosing any numbers small enough for the sake of demonstration:

9 loaves at rate $3 = x$ loaves at rate 7.

1) Difference between the rates: $7-3=4$.

2) $\dfrac{\text{Difference}}{3} = \dfrac{4}{3} = 1\dfrac{1}{3}$.

3) Multiply $1\dfrac{1}{3}$ by $9 = \mathbf{12}$.

4) Add 9 and $12 = 21$

$$9:3::21:7.$$

The play of the "differences" establishes the relationships:

$$3:9::4:12 \quad \text{and} \quad 3:9::4+3:12+9.$$

Translated into our form:

$$3:9::7-3:21-9.$$

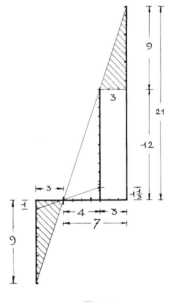

Fig. 28

---

[53] Geometrically, we know that

$$\frac{NA}{B} = N',$$

therefore the final result is

$$A:B::A+\frac{NA}{B}:B+N.$$

ARITHMETIC PROGRESSION,
PROBLEMS 39 AND 40

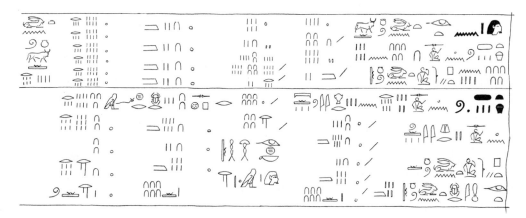

Here the way in which problems 39 and 40 are written and laid out on the papyrus should be noted. The two problems are inscribed one above the other and take up the two upper lines of the papyrus, while the four lower lines remain empty. These problems are also separated from the previous ones by a vertical line marking their beginning, and from the following ones by a blank space.

Problem 39 is to 40 as 1 is to ϕ by the line that separates them horizontally. This relates problem 40 to the principle of harmony, and problem 39, whose title begins with *tp*, the head, is an "example" of the method of resolution.[54]

Problem 40 is presented as a characteristic arithmetic progression. Now, remembering that any arithmetic progression when inverted becomes a harmonic progression, we see that its kinship with harmony becomes clear.[55] In seeming to give the method for the discovery of a *twnw*, problem 39 does not appear at first sight to be an arithmetic progression, which leads us to discuss problem 40 first.

Problem 40 (first part, beginning at the right of the hieroglyphic text)

"One hundred loaves for 5 men; 1/7 of the 3 who are above to the 2 men who are below.

	/1	23	
	/1	$17\frac{1}{2}$	
What is the *twnw*?	/1	12	
	/1	$16\frac{1}{2}$	
Make according to the becoming, *twnw* $5\frac{1}{2}$	/1	11	Total 60"

The problem presents itself as an arithmetic progression in which one is given the sum and the number of terms, and in which the two unknowns are the first term and the rate that is designated *twnw* .[56]

---

[54] It seems clear that the hieroglyph of the profile of the head, *tp*, signifies "This is the example of the method of resolution." Or said another way, "Here is the chief who commands the others."

[55] Cf. in this regard, below, study of problem 39.

[56] "The word *twnw* [pronounced *tewnew*] is unknown outside this papyrus. A verb *twn*, determined in the same way, occurs in Ebers Medical Pap., 101, 12–13, and in Pap. Harris Mag., 8, 6, but I am unable to seize its meaning in either passage. The ox persists even in the plant name *twn*, Hearst Med. Papyrus, 8, 4, and Brugsch, *Wörterbuch Supp.* 1315. Doubtless the same root is involved in the town-name *Mtwn* of Medum, Pl. XIX (determined by a lassoed ox)." Peet, *RMP,* p. 77. (We ask, is this ox not a bull?)

The master who poses this problem asks that it be resolved in such a way that it demonstrates the becoming[57] with this *twnw* of 5 + 1/2. To our mathematicians this poses an additional question: how has the master determined the value 5 + 1/2 for this *twnw?*

The solution of the first part of the problem becomes simple if we take it to be an arithmetic progression for which the sum and the rate are known, as well as the number of terms. It remains only to define the value of each term. The reply to the second question will not be possible for our modern mathematicians without the use of algebra, which uses plus and minus signs, and thus negative values.

Now the translator, in observing that the literal transcription employs the terms "the three higher" ("who are above") and "the two lower" ("who are below"), uses the terms "the first" and "the last,"[58] and in this way loses sight of the method of resolution implied by this form of expression, and of the geometrical vision that guides the thought.

In all arithmetic progressions, *the sum of the extreme terms is equal to the sum of the mean terms* in a series in which the number of terms is even, and equal to the double of the mean term in a series in which the number of terms is odd; this fact is demonstrated by taking, for example, the natural number series 1, 2, 3, 4, 5, in which 3 is the mean term and 1 and 5 are the extremes, or the natural series 1, 2, 3, 4, 5, 6, in which the mean terms are 3 and 4 and the extremes are 1 and 6.

Odd series				Even series		
1	2	3		1	2	3
5	4			6	5	4
6	6	3		7	7	7

But if we remain faithful to the statement of the problem and to the method of the Ancients, we must put the larger terms—that is, the higher—on the line above, and the smaller—that is, the lower—on the line below.[59] Here is the presentation suggested by this statement:

Odd series				Even series			
5	4	3		6	5	4	higher terms
1	2			1	2	3	lower terms
6	6	3		7	7	7	

Viewing the arrangement in this way lets us distinguish the terms "which are above" from the terms "which are below" as specified in the literal statement of the problem.

Now, problem 40, as well as problem 64, which we will study later on, offers this same feature.

[57] "The problem consists in dividing 100 loaves among 5 men in such a way that the shares are in arithmetical progression and that the sum of the two smallest parts is one-seventh the sum of the three greatest. The first of these two essential conditions is not mentioned in the problem as set by the Egyptian, but it is possible that it was implied by the mention of *twnw*. In dealing with no. 39 we found it difficult to believe that a special technical term should have been invented for the 'difference of share' in the very simple sense in which it occurs in that problem, and it is possible that the real technical meaning of *twnw* is that in which it is used here, namely the 'common difference' in an arithmetical series." Ibid, p. 78.

[58] "A hundred loaves to five men, one-seventh of the three first men to the two last. What is the difference of share? The doing as it occurs supposing the difference of share to be $5\frac{1}{2}$." Ibid.

[59] This form of expression was also used by Sumerian mathematicians. Cf. problem 169 in the Babylonian tablets.

The scribe established the largest share first and then obtained the others by successive subtractions. This method implies knowledge of the rule that we may state in the following way: *The nth term is equal to the first plus n − 1 times the rate.*

But the expression of the Ancients forces us to read in reverse because the progression is viewed as decreasing, and we can put the progression, as in problem 40, in the following form:

1 + 4 *twnw*	1 + 3 *twnw*	1 + 2 *twnw*	=	the three higher terms
1 *twnw*	1 + 1 *twnw*		=	the two lower terms
2 + 4 *twnw*	2 + 4 *twnw*	1 + 2 *twnw*		

Arranged in this way, it becomes obvious that there are five terms; the share of the higher term is equal to 1 + 4 *twnw*, taking the first term as equal to unity. With the *twnw* accepted as 51/2, the first term being 1, and following the directives of the above table, the scribe can establish the progression directly, starting from the largest term:

$$1 + 4 \;\; twnw = 1 + 22 = 23$$
$$1 + 3 \;\; twnw = 1 + 16\tfrac{1}{2} = 17\tfrac{1}{2}$$
$$1 + 2 \;\; twnw = 1 + 11 = 12$$

the three higher terms $= 52\tfrac{1}{2}$

$$1 + 1 \;\; twnw = 1 + 5\tfrac{1}{2} = 6\tfrac{1}{2}$$
$$1 = 1 = 1$$

the two lower terms $= 7\tfrac{1}{2}$

Total   **60** [60]

The sum of the shares of the two lower terms is actually contained seven times in the sum of the three higher, which fulfills one of the conditions of the problem. The sum of the five shares thus obtained is 60, so there are 100 loaves that must be divided among five men. The scribe established the ratio between 60 and 100, which is 1 + 2/3, and he multiplied each term of the progression by this number, knowing that *if the terms of an arithmetic progression are multiplied by the same number, they remain proportional with respect to each other,* as is shown at the end of the problem.

/1	60	times	23	will become	$38\tfrac{1}{3}$
/$\tfrac{2}{3}$	40		$17\tfrac{1}{2}$		$26\tfrac{1}{6}$
You will: put			12		20
at first $1\tfrac{2}{3}$			$6\tfrac{1}{2}$		$10\tfrac{2}{3} + \tfrac{1}{6}$
			1	total 60	$1\tfrac{2}{3}$ Total 100

The second question that remains to be clarified is, if the master who posed the problem gives the *twnw* the value of 5 + 1/2, answering the condition "1/7 of the three higher to the two lower," did he do it through calculation? If so, how?

---

[60] Here, in boldface, are the only numbers put down by the scribe; the elements of calculation we have written were done mentally by him.

The mathematicians who have studied this problem are very tempted to solve it with the algebraic method. There are two unknowns, the first term and the rate. Now if the first term is taken to be equal to unity, the *twnw*, or rate, can be established by again using the configuration already given above:

$$1 + 4 \ twnw \qquad 1 + 3 \ twnw \qquad 1 + 2 \ twnw \ = \ 3 + 9 \ twnw \ = \ 3 \text{ higher terms}$$
$$1 \qquad\qquad\qquad 1 + 1 \qquad\qquad\qquad\qquad\qquad = \ 2 + 1 \ twnw \ = \ 2 \text{ lower terms}$$

This presentation, which has already allowed us to establish the largest term directly, also permits us to calculate the sum of the three higher terms and the sum of the two lower ones. The statement specifies that the three higher numbers have the value of 7 times the two lower numbers. Thus, if we multiply the shares of the latter by 7, they will have a value equal to the three higher ones as follows: **14 + 7** *twnw* are equal to **3 + 9** *twnw*.

This is where our modern mathematicians must resort to algebra in order to deduce the value of the *twnw* of this equality. If we put together the numbers of shares on one side of the equation and the *twnw*'s on the other side, "changing their sign" following the algebraic method, we obtain[61] **14 − 3 = 9** *twnw* **− 7** *twnw*, from which we get **11 = 2** *twnw*, and consequently, 1 *twnw* = 5 + 1/2.

To explain this line of reasoning, we use the + and − signs, which did not exist for pharaonic mathematicians. Nevertheless, one observes that there are 9 *twnw* on one side and 7 *twnw* on the other side of the equation, and that there are 14 units on one side and 3 on the other, thus the difference between 14 and 3, that is, 11, is equal to the difference between 9 *twnw* and 7 *twnw*. It is a question of a play of *differences* here, and this must be resolved without changing signs.

But this line of reasoning is again algebraic. There is, however, a geometric solution. The *twnw* plays the role of the seed, or rather of a seminal power prior to determination, engendering a growth (which would explain the bull being the determinative of the *twnw*). We could object that this *twnw* has been obtained by trial and error and therefore by empiricism, *but the ratio 1 to 7 could not have been proven in this way.*

Geometric Solution

The question is one of demonstrating geometrically how the difference between the number of *twnw* of the three higher numbers is equal to the difference between the number of shares of the two lower numbers when these last are multiplied by 7 to establish the equality that we recall here: The three higher terms = 3 + 9 *twnw*; the two lower terms = 2 + 1 *twnw*, and times 7 = 14 + 7 *twnw*.

In figure 29, vertically, the value 14 + 7 *twnw* is decomposed into 3 + 11 + 7 *twnw*. Horizontally, the value 3 + 9 *twnw* is decomposed into 3 + 2 *twnw* + 7 *twnw*. We can verify that after the subtraction of 3 on the vertical and horizontal, there remains the intermediate fragment that has the value of 11 vertically and 2 *twnw* horizontally, demonstrating the equivalence of 11 with 2 *twnw*. Therefore the *twnw* = 5 + 1/2.[62]

---

[61] Cf. Gillain, *La Science égyptienne*, p. 251.

[62] The term *twnw* being written with a bull for the first problem plays the role of the seed. In the second problem it is only written with a hare, *wn*, which signifies "to be" or "to exist" in the sense of perpetuity. Now in the geometric resolution, the 7 *twnw* have no determination. Here the *twnw* is an indispensable continuity for the graphic expression, without being limited.

Putting the quantity 11 on the vertical over the quantity 2 *twnw* on the horizontal is equivalent here, geometrically, to "changing the sign," *which is the deeper sense of the inverse, without having the idea of negative values intervene, as in our algebraic system.*

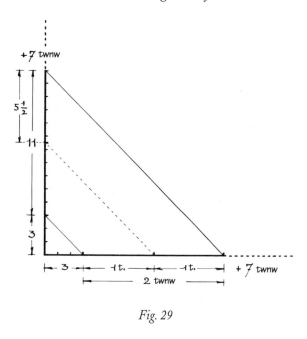

Fig. 29

Solution Implied in the Statement

Here we can see how it is possible to find the solution for the sought-for value of this *twnw* by virtue of the ancient arrangement that allows a direct reading of the essential functions of any arithmetic progression:

1 + 4 *twnw*	1 + 3 *twnw*	1 + 2 *twnw*	= 3 +	9 *twnw*
1	1 + 1 *twnw*		= 2 +	1 *twnw*
2 + 4 *twnw*	2 + 4 *twnw*	1 + 2 *twnw*	= 5 +	10 *twnw*

First, *(a)* the sum of the extremes is equal to the sum of the means; *(b)* the higher term is equal to the smallest term plus as many times the rate *(twnw)* as there are terms preceding it; *(c)* the sum of an arithmetic progression is equal to n times the lower term plus $n([n-1]/2)$ times the rate (n being the number of terms). Moreover, the presentation allows us to read the partial sums of the progression, and in the case of problem 40, establish directly the equivalence of $1:7$ required between the three higher terms and the two lower, which we must multiply by 7.

1 + 4 *twnw*	1 + 3 *twnw*	1 + 2 *twnw* =	3 + 2 *twnw* + 7 *twnw*
7	7 + 7 *twnw*	=	3 + 11 *twnw* + 7 *twnw*

From this we obtain the *twnw* $5 + 1/2$.

One can do conversions following this model in order to satisfy any other apportionment that is called for.

Characteristic Lesson

Problem 40 starts from the ratio $2:3$ among five men, and poses a proportion of $1:7$, which is a limit because under the same conditions for a ratio of $1:8$, the sum of 100 loaves would be surpassed and we would find ourselves dividing a smaller number by a larger one.

It appears then that a careful selection is involved in establishing these numbers, which motivates us to look for the intent behind this problem.

Problem 39

"Method for making a *twnw*. One hundred loaves for 10 men, 50 for 6, and 50 for 4. What is the *twnw?*"

In the first column the scribe divides 50 by $4 = 12\frac{1}{2}$.
In the second column the scribe divides 50 by $6 = 8\frac{1}{3}$.
In the third column he writes four times $12\frac{1}{2}$.
In the fourth column he writes six times $8\frac{1}{3}$.
He writes at the bottom the difference between $12\frac{1}{2}$ and $8\frac{1}{3}$, *twnw* $= 4\frac{1}{6}$.

Exactly below this problem, problem 40 is written, so that the progression with the sum of 60 is placed under the column of the four shares valued at $12 + 1/2$. Also, a progression with the sum of 100 is found under the column of six shares of $8 + 1/3$.

Does this problem actually give the method of finding the difference or "rate" by which we interpret the same word *twnw* in problem 40? In the way that the problem is written, the scribe does not carry out the arithmetic progression, and the fact that he stops the resolution of the problem at this point is because there must be, by virtue of the given *twnw*, a means for determining the sequence without calculation, that is, a geometric method.

The solution the scribe gives can be transcribed as follows: six equal shares each have a value of $8 + 1/3$, representing fifty loaves of bread, and four equal shares each have a value of $12 + 1/2$, whose sum is also fifty loaves. Their difference is the given *twnw*, $4 + 1/6$ (fig. 30a). The men are divided into two groups that can be designated as the four higher and six lower.

Each group of men forms an even series, and since in any even series the mean term is included between the middle terms, the two given mean shares will be located respectively, at $12 + 1/2$, mean share of the four higher terms, between the second and the third in *A* (fig. 30a), and $8 + 1/3$, mean share of the six lower terms, between the seventh and the eighth in *B* (fig. 30a).

The *diagonal drawn between A and B determines the angle of the slope that allows us to establish an arithmetic progression,* verifiable by calculation. There are five intervals between *A* and *B*, the *twnw* that is given represents therefore five differences, that is, $4 + 1/6 : 5 = 1/2 + 1/3 =$ the common difference.

Knowing that for ten men there are nine intervals, there remain two differences, $1/2$ between *B* and the lower term and $1 + 1/2$ between *A* and the higher term. The largest share is equal to $13 + 1/2 + 1/4$. The smallest share is equal to $6 + 1/4$.

The graphic transcription of this progression (fig. 30b) shows a kind of staircase in which the slope is defined by a ratio. In the present case, this ratio is as $4 + 1/6$ is to 5, defined by the given *twnw* and the number of intervals. Transcribed into whole numbers this ratio becomes 25 to 30, or 5 to 6.

In problem 39 the word *twnw* is determined by a bull; now, this problem does not include the arithmetic progression but gives the elements necessary to establish the progression by virtue of this seed *twnw* that the problem defines.

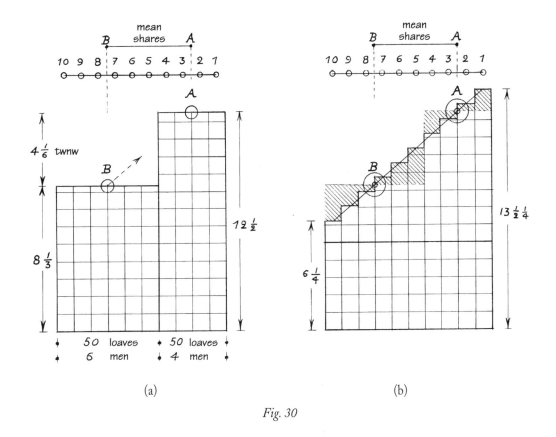

Fig. 30

On the other hand, problem 40 establishes an arithmetic progression, so the *twnw* is no longer determined by the bull, in other words, he is in full generation of his effect, and the difference is given under the name *twnw*. Nevertheless, it would appear that the *twnw* plays less the role of a difference than of a junction.[63]

The inversion of the initial construction determining the two mean shares *A* and *B* (fig. 30) is drawn in a square with 100 for its side on the condition of taking away fifty (5 × 10) loaves at the base.[64] The two figures are superimposed on each other so that their two mean shares, *A* and *B′* define a quantity that is equal to the "common difference." Joining the points *A′B* and *B′A* determines the angle of the slope that allows the progression to be established (fig. 31). This inversion allows one to verify that between *A* and *B* there are five differences, as there are between *A′* and *B′*, but that the overlapping leaves an empty rectangle in the center that is equal to the two bands between *A′* and *B* and between *A* and *B′*.

Thus the *twnw* given by problem 39 allows the determination of common differences by *crossing* and *inversion*.

The twnw *takes on great importance because as a seed it allows for the establishing of an arithmetic progression answering to the distribution of a given quantity between a certain number of terms divided into two groups, the mean shares of which must be in relation to each other in a fixed proportion.*

Problem 39 explains what the *twnw* is and what must be understood by this word, namely, a quantity that plays the role of a link while being a difference. This value presides over geometric growth through the effect of the pivoting squares, and also expresses itself as an angle (fig. 32).[65]

---

[63] The "common difference" will be designated in problem 64 by another word, *prw*.

[64] That is, half of the total sum of loaves.

[65] Cf. chapter 7, "Addition and Subtraction of Angles in Proportional Notation."

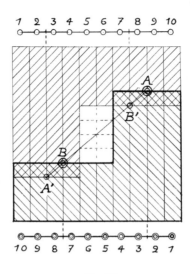

Fig. 31

The central square having 100 for its surface area (fig. 32) represents the total sum of loaves to be distributed among the ten men. The progression is proved geometrically by its inversion on the condition that we omit the fifty loaves at the base, which through this construction, leaves a definite square.

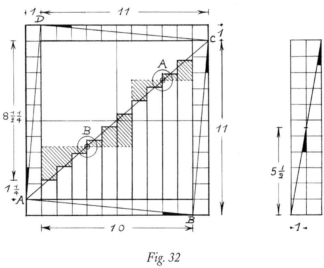

Fig. 32

Make a square with 12 for its side. Cut out 1, leaving 11, forming an inscribed square *ABCD*. Join the perpendicular and parallel lines between the points *A*, *B*, *C*, and *D*, which, when they cross each other, determine the central square of side 10 with 100 as a surface. The surface of the exterior square is 144, which is diminished by four rectangles of 1 by 11, the sum of the surfaces of which is 44. The diagonal *AC* defines the angle of the slope of the *twnw*, which is 5 in height to 6 at the base.

This geometric representation gives the *twnw* of the following problem, 5 + 1/2, taking half of the *ratio* 1 to 11 as defined by the four triangles surrounding the "pivoting square."

In the papyrus these two problems are arranged in such a way that the line that separates them determines between them a ratio of 1 to ϕ, and this arrangement seems to establish a ratio between an arithmetic progression and the function of ϕ.

The distribution suggested by problem 39 between the four higher and the six lower terms, using the series of natural numbers, leads to the following result:

$$
\begin{array}{llll}
\text{The four higher terms} & = 10 + 9 + 8 + 7 & = 34 = \phi \\
\text{The six lower terms} & = 1 + 2 + 3 + 4 + 5 + 6 & = 21 = 1 \\
\hline
\text{Their sum} & 11 + 11 + 11 + 11 + 11 & = 55 = \phi^2 \text{ (F series).}
\end{array}
$$

Through problem 39, the papyrus provides the way to establish a *twnw*, and in problem 40 the way to use it. It then leaves the following lines empty and does not continue to apply the principle. Now, the establishment and use of this *twnw* can only be done for certain numbers and proportions that have particular properties. This fact requires further investigation.

Thus, the complete progression from problem 39 distributes the shares of the four higher and six lower terms as 7 to 3, and it is precisely one-third of this ratio that is called for between the three higher and the two lower terms in the next problem.

Here is another example: If we are asked to distribute one-sixth of the three higher terms to the two lower, the *twnw* is 3, and if the sum is 100, the first term will be 2 + 6/7. The "reciprocal" *twnw* will be 2 (series of odd numbers), and the characteristic of this progression will be to divide the total sum 100 between the first five and the last five shares as 3 to 1 (75 and 25).

Problem 64 [66]

"Example of distributing differences [*prw*]. If it is said to thee, 10 *hekat* of barley to 10 men, the difference of each man over his neighbour being 1/8 of a *hekat* of barley.

"The mean share is 1/2 *hekat* (read 1 hekat). Take 1 from 10; the remainder is 9. A half of the common difference [*prw*] is taken, namely 1/16 *hekat*. Multiply it 9 times, result (1/2 + 1/16) *hekat*. Add to the mean share. You are now to subtract 1/8 *hekat* for ['on'] each man down to the last [until 'taking in the net he who is under the last.' Make according to the becoming.]"[67]

$1 \; \frac{1}{2} \; \frac{1}{16}$	$1 \; \frac{1}{4} \; \frac{1}{8} \; \frac{1}{16}$	$1 \; \frac{1}{4} \; \frac{1}{16}$	$1 \; \frac{1}{8} \; \frac{1}{16}$	$1 \; \frac{1}{16}$
$\frac{1}{2} \; \frac{1}{4} \; \frac{1}{8} \; \frac{1}{16}$	$\frac{1}{2} \; \frac{1}{4} \; \frac{1}{16}$	$\frac{1}{2} \; \frac{1}{8} \; \frac{1}{16}$	$\frac{1}{2} \; \frac{1}{16}$	$\frac{1}{4} \; \frac{1}{8} \; \frac{1}{16}$

[66] The word *tp* (profile of the face) written at the beginning of this problem indicates "example of the method of resolution." [Peet, *RMP*, pp. 107–8.]

[67] Peet, *RMP*, pp. 107–8.

The question here is of a decreasing arithmetic progression for which the rate of 1/8 is given as well as the number of terms, 10, and the sum 10. We still need to determine what each term is.

The word used to mean the "rate" or the "difference" is *prw* ⟨glyph⟩, which can be translated as "the going out." The term translated as "mean share" ⟨glyph⟩ corresponds exactly to the meaning we give to the phrase "the middle part." The operations proceed in the following way:

1. Establishing the mean share, 10 *hekat* for ten men equals 1 *hekat* for each, but the scribe writes 1/2 *hekat* knowing that the geometrical proof consists of superimposing and inverting the two identical progressions from which *half of the mean share* was subtracted (fig. 33a).[68]
2. Subtract one from ten men and there are nine men left.
3. Take half of the common difference and multiply it nine times, knowing that one *adds it to the mean share as many times the half-difference as there are terms in the progression minus one* (fig. 33a).
4. "Put" the result on the *mean share* to obtain the largest share (fig. 33b).
5. Subtract the difference "on" each man "until taking in the net he who is under the last" (fig. 33b).

Graphically transcribed, this arithmetic progression makes evident the compensation in the deficit under the mean share, *A*, by the excess of what is above this mean share, and shows the need to work with the half-mean share located on *A*, at the center of 10 *hekat*. The multiplication by 9 of the half-difference has 1/2 + 1/16 for its product (fig. 33a). We only have to "put" this result on the actual mean share, 1 *hekat*, and carry out the decreasing sequence by successive subtractions of 1/8 (fig. 33b).

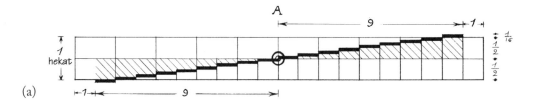

(a)

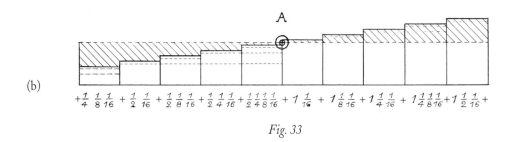

(b)

Fig. 33

Once again the geometric scheme has guided the statement of this problem and allowed us to understand why, in noting the mean share, the scribe writes 1/2 *hekat* while he is in the process of operating, and afterward correctly calculates his final result with the real mean share, which is 1 *hekat*.

---

[68] See this same procedure demonstrating the progression of problem 39, fig. 32.

The last sentence of the text, "subtract 1/8 on each man until taking in the net he who is under the last," greatly puzzles translators. What is the word *skht*, which signifies "taking with the net," doing in a mathematical problem when it is usually used in bird hunting scenes and also in weaving?[69]

A study of these "nets" will reveal that they are a geometrical demonstration and that *skht* can mean, among other things, "making two rectangular elements into a square." Indeed, the determinative of this word ⌐▱[70] is two rectangles crossed perpendicularly, evoking the image of a staircase. *Skht*, that is, "taking with the net" corresponds here to the idea of the crossing, which represents the staircase formed by any arithmetic progression and its inverse complement.

Thus, the irregularities of language are explained by the graphic demonstration: one actually takes away the difference *on* each man starting from the largest term, and descending until "he who is under the last,"[71] that is, under the half-*hekat* or the half-mean share. The difference between the *twnw* (problems 39 and 40) and the common difference *prw* appears through the comparison of these problems.

In problem 64 the progression is to be calculated with only one *mean term*, which is consequently central, "the part of the middle," and a "difference": "the going out," which directly establishes a continuous progression.

In the other problems, the *twnw* puts as an essential condition the distribution of a quantity into two definite parts to create a certain number of terms on one side and another number of terms on the other side. This determines *two mean shares* and *two centers* between which the *twnw* acts as a link to establish the final progression.

GEOMETRIC PROGRESSION

Problem 79

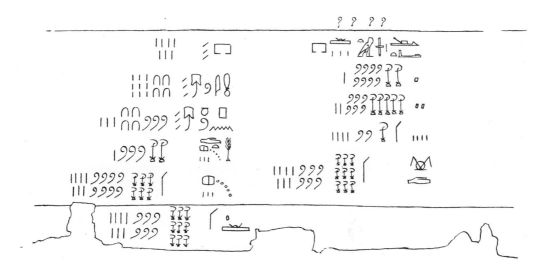

---

[69] Cf. Peet, *RMP,* p. 108, on *sekht:* "I can find no other examples of the figurative use of the verb in this sense. The metaphor must be either 'to weave in' the men one after the other, or 'to catch' them as in a net."

[70] Sign drawn from a bas-relief in the tomb of Ukhotep, chapter 37, plate 56.

[71] Peet translates this by "he who has the end," in other words, "the last," [*RMP,* p. 108] but the word-for-word translation is "he who is under the last," this word being written with the posterior of the lion and designating the end, the extremity, the rear.

An inventory of a household [?]

1	2801	7	houses
2	5602	49	cats
4	11204	343	mice
Total	19607	2301 [*sic*]	spelt
		16807	*hekat*
			Total 19607 [72]

The translation of the first sentence is very difficult because of the uncertainty about how to transcribe the hieratic signs. The operation on the left side amounts to the multiplication of the number 2801 by 7, giving a total of 19607. The operation on the right is the addition of the five first powers of 7, the total of which is equal to the preceding, that is, 19607.

Regarding this problem, Gillain says,

> After all, the strange inventory with which we are occupied is only really interesting in the association of the powers of 7 with a series of miscellaneous objects: houses, cats, mice, spelt, and *hekat*, which Rodet has explained in the following way:

> > In going through the *Liber abaci* of Leonard of Pisa to find some examples of problems analogous to those of *hau* of Ahmose, I fell upon the following statement, which is part of the explanation of calculating progressions. It is at the bottom of page 311 of the Boncompagni edition:

> > > Septum vetulae vadunt Romam; quarum quaelibet habet burdones 7; et in quolibet burdone sunt sacculi 7; et il quolibet sacculo panes 7; et quilibet panis habet cultellos 7; et quilibet cultellus habet vaginas 7. Quaeritur summa omnium praedictorum.

> > The similarity of the rate, 7 in both cases, caused me immediately to apply myself to this problem of the Egyptian progression. By one of those sudden deductions with which we are all familiar, I came at once to the conclusion that problem 79 of this papyrus was only the end of a problem and was written by Ahmose in an empty space. We have seen above that he wrote small auxiliary calculations of problems 31 and 33 far away from the presentation of these problems. The statement, which we do not have either because the scribe did not copy it or because it was previously written on a part of the papyrus that is now destroyed, should go something like this:

> > > Seven scribes each have seven cats. In a certain period of time (let us put *t*) each cat catches seven mice. In time *t* each mouse eats seven ears of spelt, which if planted in the earth, would have furnished in time *t* seven bushels of grain.

> > > The summation of all these heterogeneous terms is no more bizarre than that of the Italian problem that adds up knives with loaves of bread, loaves of bread with sacks of grain, and sacks of grain with old ladies.[73]

Rodet,[74] as well, notices a similarity between the calculations of the left side of problem 79 and the resolution of the problem called "squares of a chessboard" by the Arabian author Ibn al-Bannā.[75]

---

[72] Translated by Peet, *RMP*, p. 121. The inscriptions of the papyrus go from right to left, and the English transcription from left to right.

[73] From L. Rodet, "Les Prétendus problèmes d'algèbre du manuel du calculateur égyptien," *Journal asiatique* (1881), pp. 451–52.

[74] Ibid., p. 454–59.

[75] Manuscript 9512, Bibliothèque Nationale, Paris.

The goal of this problem is to calculate the sum of a geometrical progression in which the rate is 2 and the first term is given when we know the sum of a progression of the same rate, and beginning with unity.

In effect there is little missing, for then the text of the papyrus becomes very clear; it is simply a progression with a rate of 7 and beginning with 1.

Arranged like this

```
            1          1    2801        7
            7          2    5602        49
           49          4   11204        343
          343       Total  19607       2301  (2401)
      2301 (2401)                      16807
    Total 2801                      Total 19607
```

it would verify the characteristic quality of geometric progressions for which the following is the statement:

The sum of the terms of a geometric progression is equal to the product, by its first term, of the sum of the terms of a progression of the same rate and for which the first term is unity.[76]

Eric Peet, who also looked for the origins of the number 2801, for which the scribe does not give the source, reminds us of the modern expression for the sum of a geometric series and observes that the calculation established by following this formula shows exactly the numbers used by the Egyptians.[77]

Problem 79 is solved without indicating the procedure, but the use of the number 2801 suggests that the scribe had knowledge of the possibility of this solution. How did he find this number? Multiplication by duplication makes it clear that in a geometric progression of rate 2 beginning with 2, each term A is the double of the term a in the same row of the series that begins with unity.

The sum S is also the double of the sum s for the same number of terms. When applied to the progression of 7, this proportional function explains the multiplication of 2801 by 7. The addition of terms with the rate 1 is unnecessary, since the scribe can obtain it in the progression beginning with 7 by putting in unity.

Rate 2				Rate 7			
s	a	A	S	s	a	A	S
	1	2			1	7	
1			2	1			7
	2	4			7	49	
3			6	8			56
	4	8			49	343	
7			14	57			399
	8	16			343	2401	
15			30	400			2800
	16	32			2401	16807	
				2801			19607

[76] Gillain, *La Science égyptienne*, pp. 273–74.

[77] Cf. Peet, *RMP*, p. 122.

It is clear that the scribe let himself be guided by a simple geometric function, which has the characteristic of allowing him to read the result directly. Given his habit of multiplying by duplication, as shown at the left, *a* and *A*, the properties of the geometric progressions were familiar to him.

This problem is one of the miscellaneous items written on the verso of the papyrus, in the same place on the recto that the table of 2/*n* is given. The reductions that are in "transparency" with this geometric progression are those of 2/29 and 2/31, which present some irregularities in the course of their operations.[78]

Concerning the Supposed Error of the Scribe

Mathematicians who have studied this papyrus believe they must point out an error by the copyist Ahmose, who, in the geometric series, wrote 2301 instead of 2401, although the sum 19607 is correct.[79] We propose here an explanation for the number 100 that is missing from the number 2301.

With the added unity considered as necessary to complete the geometric series, its presentation would be the following:

$$7$$
$$49$$
$$343$$
$$\underline{2301}$$
$$2700$$
$$\underline{+101}$$
$$2801$$

The square of 49 is 2401 $\Big\}$
The number written is 2301 $\Big\}$ The difference is 100 *in surface.*
The root of 100 is 10, its half is 5.
Half of 49 is 24 + 1/2.

The surface 2301 is made up of four rectangles that have for their sides the half of the side of the largest square plus or minus the half-difference that is the half-side of the small center square (fig. 34).

$$24\frac{1}{2}\begin{cases}+5=29\frac{1}{2}\\[2mm]-5=19\frac{1}{2}\end{cases}$$

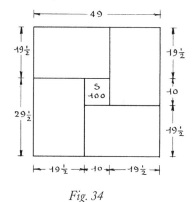

The surface of each rectangle $=29\frac{1}{2}\times19\frac{1}{2}=575\frac{1}{4}$.
The four rectangles = 2301.
The central square = 100.
The square of 49 = 2401.

Fig. 34

[79] Problem 79 is the hieroglyphic transcription of the hieratic text. If it is obvious that 100 cannot pass unnoticed in hieroglyphs, it can also be the case with the hieratic, where the number of hundreds is designated by the number of points beside the hundred sign. It remains to be discovered whether there was an oversight or accident afterward, or if it was intentional. Either way, the geometric explanation we give is valuable in itself.

TABLE OF FRACTIONS WITH THE
NUMERATOR 2

The 2/*n* table includes the resolution of the division of 2 by all the odd numbers from 3 to 101. The conditions for calculating posed for the division of 2 by *n* are the refusal to divide the fraction into two equal parts, and the exclusion of any fraction with a numerator greater than 1 except for 2/3. To these conditions are added the conclusions observed for the resolutions of this 2/*n* table: the number of terms of the decomposition should never exceed four; and the smallest possible denominators are sought for the fractions.

The observation of these four conditions for the resolution of 2/*n* has caused some arduous investigations, and our mathematics scholars have not always reached the same opinion regarding the procedures, but each of them (from Eisenlohr in 1877 until today) has added his stone to the edifice, and without all of these efforts combined, we would not have a definitive and coherent solution, especially regarding the justification for the choice of the first denominator by the scribe of the papyrus.[80]

The study of this table leads us to classify the odd numbers between 3 and 101 into prime and composite numbers. The composite numbers, after decomposition into their factors, are treated as multiples of one of the aliquot parts and give four essential types of decomposition, which can be known through the examples of 2/3, 2/5, 2/7, and 2/11.

Except for some particular instances, the study of the decomposition of 2/*n* is thus summarized by those prime numbers that can be distinguished from among the odd numbers between 3 and 101.

Is there a procedure that allows for the designation of these prime numbers without calculating? The sieve of Eratosthenes certainly does not give the solution because it requires elimination through calculation.[81]

Now, the distribution of the odd numbers on the papyrus reveals a simple and direct method that furnishes all the multiples of 3, 5, and 7 and constitutes a kind of "sieve" that allows all the prime numbers between 3 and 101 to appear.[82]

Immediately following the dedication, written vertically, and occupying the entire height of the papyrus, a double vertical line marks the beginning of the table of 2/*n*. Starting from this vertical line, the height of the papyrus is divided into six horizontal bands on which the odd numbers are distributed so that 3 and 5 occupy the beginning of the first band, 7 the second, and so on. In the third and sixth lines (counting from top to bottom) we find all the multiples of 3. When the diagonals are drawn, they pass through all the numbers ending with 5, thus eliminating all the multiples of 5. The diagonals pass through all the multiples of 7, eliminating them.

[80] This has caused people to say that the table of 2/*n* is not coherent, that it was made up "piecemeal."

[81] "'If there is,' as Bossuet says, 'an easy and comfortable method to find the prime numbers,' one must recognize that this method would require a lot of time and patience to extend Eratosthenes' method to higher numbers. Suppose that we use only a quarter of an hour to obtain all the prime numbers between unity and one thousand in this way. It would take 250 hours, that is, more than ten days of continuous work, to go up to one million. Unfortunately, no direct method has yet been found; all until now were limited to simple endeavors, such as that of Leibniz, who announced that 'every prime number is a multiple of six, increased or diminished by unity.' But this was, it did not take long to recognize, far from being true in a general way." P. Hoefer, *Histoire des mathématiques* (Paris: Hachette, 1874), p. 238.

[82] The continuation of the table following these principles allows the designation of the multiples of 11, 13, 17, 19, and so on, and the indefinite continuation of the sieve.

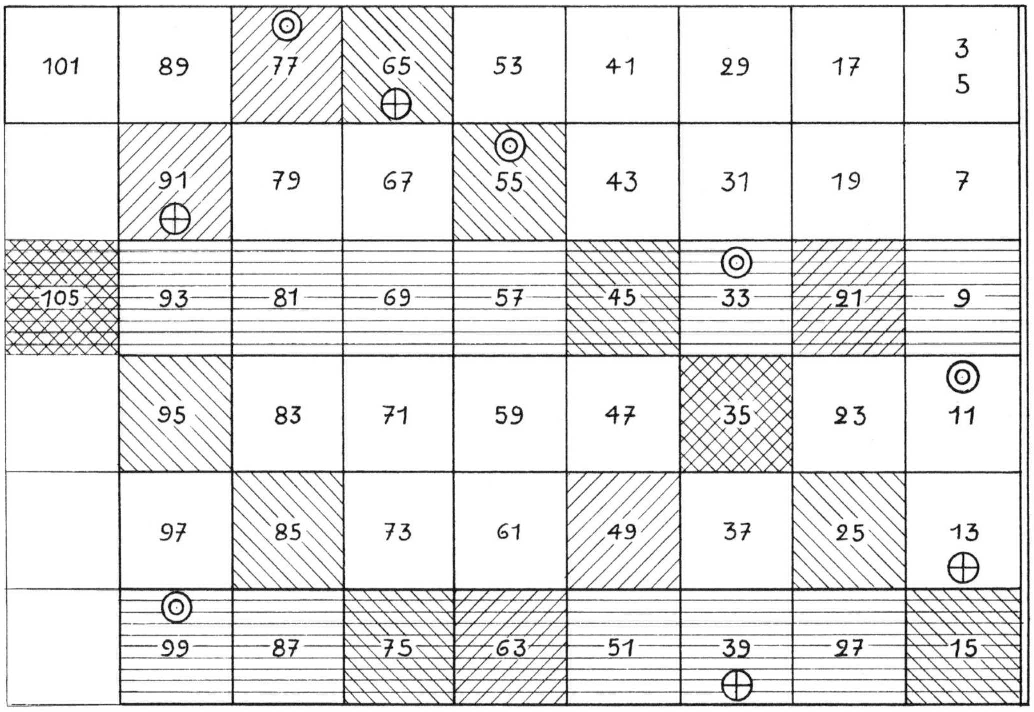

101	89	77	65	53	41	29	17	3 5
	91	79	67	55	43	31	19	7
105	93	81	69	57	45	33	21	9
	95	83	71	59	47	35	23	11
	97	85	73	61	49	37	25	13
	99	87	75	63	51	39	27	15

Fig. 35. The sieve of prime numbers, origin of the game of chess

The reading is done horizontally for the multiples of 3 (third and sixth bands) and diagonally for the multiples of 5 and 7 (those of 5 start at 15 and go upward; multiples of 7 start at 7 and go downward). For the multiples of 11 and 13 (marked by circles) we jump one square forward and then one diagonally. The multiples of 11 are found to go upward and those of 13 go downward. All the white squares are prime numbers.

These patterns parallel very exactly the movements of the pieces in the game of chess. The two lines of the multiples of 3 indicate the movement of the two rooks, and start at 9 and 15. The diagonals of the multiples of 5 and 7 are the movements of the two bishops. The "jumps" of the knights are given by 11 and 13. This leaves 3 and 5, the seed numbers, to the king and queen.

The fact that 3 and 5 are placed in the first square allows us to end the first column with 15, their multiple. This is essential, not for the establishment of the table, but for a correspondence with the laws of harmony, which govern the entire table.

This sieve is inspired by the arrangement of the odd numbers on the papyrus into six lines. The game of chess in question here is evidently not to be confused with the Egyptian game *men*, composed of only three rows of ten squares.

Thus, only the arrangement of odd numbers between 3 and 101, following the directive indicated by the papyrus, allows us to solve a problem that has remained without a solution until now—the sorting out of the prime numbers from among the odd numbers.

This table forms a grid made up of several arithmetic progressions: two progressions of the multiples of 3, for which the multipliers form an arithmetic progression at the rate of 4, and two progressions of the multiples of 5 and 7, for which the multipliers form an arithmetic progression at the rate of 2.

Put in this way, these progressions in the natural sequence of odd numbers allow them to be sorted without any calculation, and also allow the reading of the factors of the composite numbers.

Thirty-five marks the crossing of the diagonals formed by the progressions of 5 and 7 and will be treated by a singular procedure that confirms a perfect knowledge of the properties of numbers and of the laws of harmony.

Now, not only does the arrangement of these numbers on the papyrus reveal one of the essential keys directing their decomposition, but the proportions of the two upper lines, which are related to each other as 1 is to ϕ, teaches the function that presides over all harmonic proportions.

Between 1 and 2 there is an octave of phenomenal factors; thus, if the pharaonic mentality refuses the division into two equal parts and imposes the numerator 1, its intent is for a proportional relationship in the spirit of a harmonic proportion.[83]

Harmonic Proportion: The Model of ϕ

Division of a Line into Extreme and Mean Ratio

$$BB' = AA' = BA = 1$$

$$AQ = AM = \frac{1}{\phi}$$

$$BQ = \frac{1}{\phi^2}$$

$$PB = BM = BA + QA = \phi$$

$$PA = PB + BA = \phi^2$$

$$B'A' = \sqrt{5}$$

$$MO + OB = \frac{\sqrt{5}}{2} + \frac{1}{2} = \phi$$

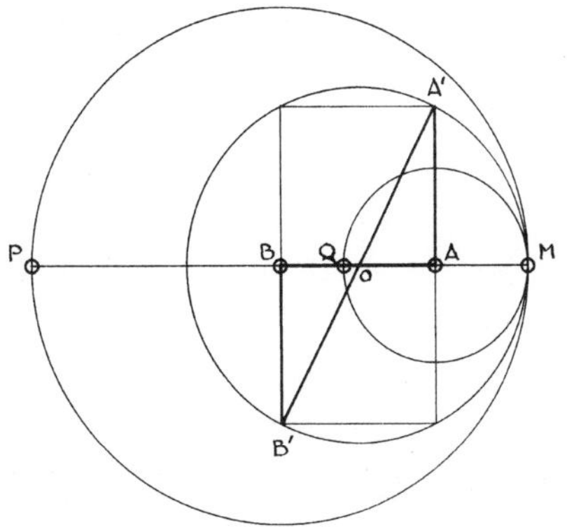

Fig. 36

If we let the line segment AB be divided into extreme and mean ratio by the point Q so that $AB/AQ = AQ/BQ$, we find that $AB/AQ = (AB + AQ)/AB = \phi$.

Point P is obtained by extending the length BM (being $AB + AQ$) from B in the opposite direction of BM. Point P has the advantage of being exactly analogous to point Q, that is, *its distance to point B is the proportional mean between its distance to point A and the straight line AB.* Point P is said to divide externally the straight line AB into extreme and mean ratio. $PA/PB = PB/BA = \phi$.

If we replace the letters with the symbol ϕ, we find the additive series: $BA = 1/\phi^2 + 1/\phi = 1$, then $PB = 1/\phi + 1 = \phi$, and finally, $PA = 1 + \phi = \phi^2$.

If we apply to this standard geometric scheme the principle of the inverse and transpose our triangles in reflection, we obtain the direct resolution in $2/n$ of the function ϕ, and thus all the odd and prime numbers, on the condition that we add or subtract a unity from the latter.

[83] Cf. above, p. 145.

Harmonic Proportion

Relationships of the triangles:

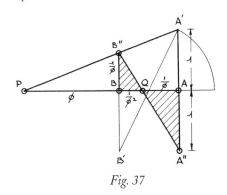

$$1 : \frac{1}{\phi} : : \frac{1}{\phi} : \frac{1}{\phi^2} = \phi$$

$$\phi^2 : 1 : : \phi : \frac{1}{\phi} = \phi^2$$

$$PQ = \phi + \frac{1}{\phi^2} = 2$$

$$PB + BA = \phi^2 = \phi + 1$$

Fig. 37

Beginning from the preceding construction, we extend the length AA' in the opposite direction to get A''. Joining the points P and A' and extending BB' in the opposite direction to BB'' until its junction with $A'P$, the diagonal $A''B''$ will cut AB in a harmonic proportion so that $PA/PB = QA/QB$, being $\phi^2/\phi = (1/\phi)/(1/\phi^2) = \phi$. The segment PQ will be the *harmonic mean* between PA and PB, corresponding to the conditions: $PA/PB = (PA - PQ)/(PQ - PB) = (\phi^2 - 2)/(2 - \phi) = \phi$. The harmonic division leads to the following fact: *The inverse of the distance PQ is the arithmetic mean of the inverses of the lengths PA and PB.* In this way we find

$$\frac{1}{PQ} = \frac{1}{2}\left(\frac{1}{PA} + \frac{1}{PB}\right) \quad \text{or} \quad \frac{2}{PQ} = \frac{1}{PA} + \frac{1}{PB}.$$

In the case of the function ϕ the values are demonstrative: $2/PQ = 2/2$, that is 1, thus $1 = 1/\phi + 1/\phi^2$.

It is very important to understand thoroughly this function as well as its inversion, because the divisions of $2/n$ will be made in such a way that $n = PQ$. *Consequently, n will be the "harmonic mean" between PA and PB, which will be the two chosen denominators for the two terms of the result.* Because of the inversion, $2/n$ is the arithmetic mean between $1/PA$ and $1/PB$.

Inversion of the Harmonic Proportion and the Function of the Crossing

In order to understand this inversion better, let us use musical proportion, in which we can insert the two means, arithmetic and harmonic (A.M. and H.M.) between 1 and 2, giving the first two musical relationships:

	note	H.M. fourth	A.M. fifth	octave
Ratio of vibrations	1	$\frac{4}{3}$	$\frac{3}{2}$	2
In whole numbers	6	8	9	12
In whole numbers	12	9	8	6
Length of the string	1	$\frac{3}{4}$	$\frac{2}{3}$	$\frac{1}{2}$
	note	fourth	fifth	octave
		A.M.	H.M.	

Here we see that as the ratio of the vibrations grows larger, the ratio of the string lengths grows smaller; one grows in the opposite direction to the other. The ratio between the extremes remains the same, $2 : 1 : : 1 : 1/2$, but the ratio of the means is inverted: *The harmonic mean term, 4/3, in the increasing series becomes the arithmetic mean term, 3/4, in the inverse series.*

There is an inversion and a crossing of functions so that 6, 8, and 12 are in harmonic proportion and their reciprocals, 1/6, 1/8, and 1/12, constitute an arithmetic proportion in which the mean term is half the sum of the extremes, $1/6 + 1/12 = 1/4$, an equality constantly used by the scribe of the papyrus.

The Essential Types of Decomposition for $2/n$

The first band of the table treats the numbers 3 and 5. The sixth band treats the number 15, that is, their multiple. Between these numbers are placed the decompositions of 7, 9, 11, and 13, which furnish the types applied to all their multiples, with the exception of 13.

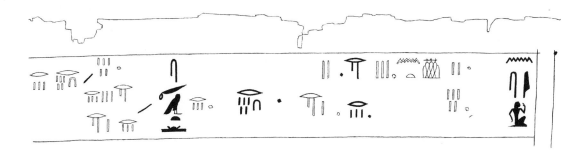

First line of the table. All the operations are translated in the following way:[84] "Call 2 in front of 3, **2/3**. 2." The scribe has written 2/3 with no other explanation and writes underneath:

. 5	$\frac{1}{3}$	$1\frac{2}{3}$	$\frac{1}{15}$	$\frac{1}{3}$	Directives	.	5
						$\frac{2}{3}$	$3\frac{1}{3}$
						$/\frac{1}{3}$	$1\frac{2}{3}$
						$/\frac{1}{15}$	$\frac{1}{3}$

Let us summarize the questions suggested by this arrangement:

1. The scribe has put a point in front of the number 5. Is the real significance of this point to indicate the repetition of the phrase at the beginning, as we have wanted to believe, in the same way that our quotation mark signifies "ditto"? Now, a point is also used to indicate 1.

2. The first line written immediately after the number 5 gives the final result, that is, the line shows the equivalence between the numbers marked in red, **1/3** and **1/15**, which gives a total of 2/5, and the numbers marked in black, $1 + 2/3 + 1/3 = 2$. The obvious conclusion is that the scribe already knew the result because he put it at the beginning. How did he obtain it?

3. The following group of numbers is the operation where the scribe notes the chosen fractions with a mark. Now, if the operation is meant to explain the process, we are forced to admit that it is only a repetition of the statement of the problem, which already gives the result.

Moreover, we have seen that all multiplication by fractions presents two lineages: the geometric series 1/2, 1/4, 1/8, 1/16, ..., and the series 2/3, 1/3, 1/6, 1/12, ...

Between these two lineages, 2 and 3, why has the scribe unhesitatingly chosen that of 3? And, following this, how did he determine with the same certainty the fraction 1/15, which nothing in his usual methods would justify?

---

[84] Cf. Peet, *RMP*, p. 38.

Let us then examine this operation: the scribe places at the very beginning 1   5, just as, graphically, we might draw a straight line and mark it •¹•┼┼⁵┼┼• . This very simple line directs us to the solution; in all multiplications or divisions, the scribe begins by putting *unity in front of the number on which he will operate.* Why? In the present case, this line has a value of 1 + 5. Its half is equal to (1 + 5)/2 = 3, the arithmetic mean between 1 and 5, which is the *first denominator chosen.*

As with musical proportion, this arithmetic mean term is called the harmonic mean, which is (1 × 5)/(1/2)(1 + 5), or 5/3, and *represents the first term of the decomposition.* This first term leads to the division of the first unity by 3, and the five original unities then have the value of 15.

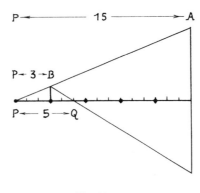

Fig. 38

Recalling the *function* stated with regard to the harmonic proportion established with ϕ and *its inversion,* it is shown without calculation that the decomposition of 2/5 corresponds to the formula $2/PQ = 1/PB + 1/PA$, or $2/5 = 1/3 + 1/15$. The knowledge of this law explains why the scribe inserts the results with no calculation.

The operation, written after the word translated as "directives," consists in transforming the two ratios we have found, 1/3 and 1/15, into their equivalents, $1 + 2/3$ and 1/3, the sum of which equals 2.

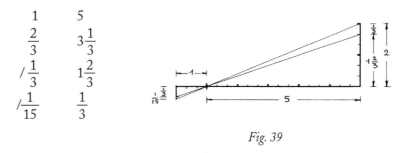

Fig. 39

The decompositions of 2/3, 2/5, 2/7, 2/11 are made following this functional law, which comes down to the following mathematical formula:

$$\frac{2}{n} = \frac{1}{\frac{n+1}{2}} + \frac{1}{\frac{n(n+1)}{2}},$$

and which finds its geometrical demonstration thanks to the harmonic proportion that, *inverted,* becomes an arithmetic proportion.

All the multiples of 3 are treated as if they had the value of 3, and it is in the ratio 2 : 9 that for the first time we meet the application of the model that corresponds to the following form:

$$\text{Arithmetic mean} = \frac{3+1}{2} = \text{first denominator.}$$

$$\text{Harmonic mean} = \frac{3}{2} \text{ or } 1\frac{1}{2} = \text{first term.}$$

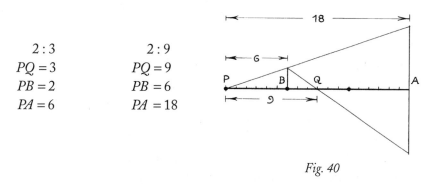

2 : 3	2 : 9
$PQ = 3$	$PQ = 9$
$PB = 2$	$PB = 6$
$PA = 6$	$PA = 18$

Fig. 40

This decomposition, which no longer conforms to the mathematical form $(n + 1)/2$, and which in this case comes to $(9 + 1)/2 = 5$, would have two drawbacks. First, the decomposition $2/9 = 1/5 + 1/45$ would cause the introduction of the number 5, which is not in the family of 3, whereas pharaonic decomposition obtains $2/9 = 1/6 + 1/18$, and consequently stays with numbers that are multiples of 3. Second, this last result has a denominator that is much smaller for the second term of the expression. Furthermore, the aforementioned formula, $2/PQ = 1/PB + 1/PA$, geometrically confirms this result.

All the multiples of 3 without exception are treated in this way, that is, 2 is broken down into two parts that are to each other as $1 + 1/2$ is to $1/2$. Still, the "model" is not given in the first band of the papyrus, which contains $2/3$ and $2/5$, because the development of the harmonic division employed for the number 5 also gives that of 15, and consequently, the model that will be adopted for 3.

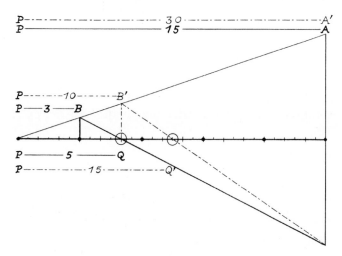

Fig. 41

$$\frac{2}{PQ} = \frac{1}{PB} + \frac{1}{PA} = \frac{2}{5} = \frac{1}{3} + \frac{1}{15} \quad \text{(solid lines).}$$

$$\frac{2}{PQ'} = \frac{1}{PB'} + \frac{1}{PA'} = \frac{2}{15} = \frac{1}{10} + \frac{1}{30} \quad \text{(dotted lines).}$$

In figure 41, the length *PA* is divided successively into five by the point *B*, into three by the point *Q* = *B′*, and into two by the point *Q′*. The numbers written in the first band of the table are 2, 3, and 5. The multiples of 5 that are not divisible by 3 can all be decomposed in the following way: 2 = 1 + 2/3 + 1/3. The only exception is 95, which equals 5 × 19, and is decomposed following the model of 19.

The multiples of 7 correspond similarly to a harmonic division that is stated (7 + 1)/2 = 4, which is the first denominator, so that the first term is 7/4 and the second term is 1/4. The sum of these two fractions is 8/4, which equals 2. Under the pharaonic form, 7/4 is equal to 1 + 1/2 + 1/4.

The final expression 2/7 = 1/4 + 1/28 is important because we find **1 + 1/2 + 1/4 + 1/4** frequently used, notably in the first problems of *s'km*.

Among the multiples of 7 only 7, 49, and 77 are treated in this way. Two remarkable exceptions are 35 and 91 because they demonstrate not only a faultless knowledge of numbers, but also the application of the harmonic proportion in the following form.

Decomposition of 2/35

$$35 \quad \frac{1}{30} \; 1\frac{1}{6} \qquad \frac{1}{42} \; \frac{2}{3}\frac{1}{6} \qquad /\frac{1}{30} \; 1\frac{1}{6}$$

$$6 \quad 7 \qquad\qquad 5 \qquad\qquad /\frac{1}{42} \; \frac{2}{3}\frac{1}{6}$$

This example is important from several points of view. First, *it is the only case in which there is mention of a "common denominator,"* 6, *marked in red under the number* 35. Second, by this same fact *it is the formal proof of the perfect knowledge of the harmonic proportion as the inverse of any arithmetic proportion.*

The number 6 is obtained by taking the arithmetic mean of the factors of 35. Here is the sequence of the problem: 35 = 7 × 5. The arithmetic mean between 5 and 7 is (7 + 5)/2 = 6.

There are thus three numbers that form an arithmetic proportion, 5, 6, and 7, of which 6 is the mean term. Recalling that the reciprocals of this sequence necessarily make a harmonic proportion, we get 1/5, 1/6, 1/7, the values of which, transcribed into whole numbers, are 42, 35, 30.

Thus, instead of decomposing 35 on the model of 5 or 7, the scribe has operated in a completely different way. He has directly obtained three numbers, very near to each other, of which 35 is the mean term of a harmonic proportion whose extremes are 30 and 42, corresponding to one of the essential conditions of these proportions and resting on the "differences." Thus, 30 + its sixth = 35, as 42 − its sixth = 35.

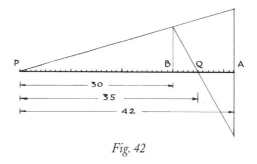

Fig. 42

Recalling that in all harmonic proportions the inverse of the mean is equal to the half-sum of the inverse of the extremes; thus, 2/35 = 1/30 + 1/42.

We discover here the application of the double inversion or double crossing of functions that corresponds to true pharaonic thinking and to its symbolism, which our mathematicians have tried to resolve in a numerical fashion.[85]

Is this example unique? No, another multiple of 7 will be constructed in an identical way, $91 = 7 \times 13$, and the chosen denominators, after establishing the arithmetic mean, will thus be $(7 + 13)/2 = 10$, the product of $7 \times 10 = 70$ and $13 \times 10 = 130$. From this the final decomposition will be $2/91 = 1/70 + 1/130$.[86]

A study of all the composite numbers reveals that 27, being 3×9, has 6 as its mean term with 18 and 54 for denominators. The number 75, being 15×5, has 10 as its arithmetic mean with 50 and 150 for denominators. These last two decompositions belong to the multiples of 3 coinciding with the decomposition of 2 into $1 + 1/2$ and $1/2$.

The Prime Numbers above 13

Beyond $2/3$, $2/5$, $2/7$, $2/11$, the decomposition $(n + 1)/2$, adopted previously, will give numbers for the second denominator that are too big to be used in practice.[87] This is the reason why the scribe looks for the first denominator to be a composite number that allows other denominators to be found. This choice has intrigued our mathematicians.

A prime number is neither a surface nor a volume because it is not the product of a multiplication. It cannot be a point either because it represents a sequence of unities. Therefore, it can only be a line, that is, a pathway considered to have the value of one.

The prime number as a pathway is harmonically decomposed directly, as shown by the first numbers of the table, whereas $(n + 1)/2$ is included among the factors of 12. Proceeding from these, each prime number must be treated following its particular characteristics; thus, a unity added or subtracted from this prime number can transform it into a surface that can be either square or rectangular; for example, $37 + 1 = 38$, which is a rectangle, and $37 - 1 = 36$, which is the square of 6 or the rectangle 4×9.

When the prime number $(n + 1)/2$ gives a square, it allows an excellent decomposition that contains three terms, the second two terms of which have the smallest possible denominators. Now only four prime numbers corresponding to these conditions are found between 3 and 101. They are 17, 31, 71, and 97.

---

[85] Gillain, *La Science égyptienne*, p. 182, gives the following numerical game:

$$\frac{2}{35} = \frac{7}{6 \times 7 \times 5} + \frac{5}{6 \times 5 \times 7} = \frac{1}{6 \times 5} + \frac{1}{6 \times 7},$$

and discusses this decomposition as a true masterpiece.

[86] Tannery, *Mémoires scientifiques*, 2:146, gives the following formula for these two cases:

$$\frac{2}{pq} = \frac{1}{\frac{p(p+q)}{2}} + \frac{1}{\frac{q(p+q)}{2}}.$$

[87] Applying the formula

$$\frac{1}{\frac{n+1}{2}} + \frac{1}{\frac{n(n+1)}{2}}$$

the last prime number is 23, from which is derived

$$\frac{2}{23} = \frac{1}{12} + \frac{1}{12 \times 23}.$$

The famous number 17, which antiquity has handed down to us through Jābir (Geber), falls between the square of 4 and the double of the square of 3: $17 - 1 = 16$, the square of 4; $17 + 1 = 18$, double the square of 3.

This case is unique because of the ratio between 3 and 4 that it provides. The scribe takes for the first denominator the product of 3×4, which is 12, and arranges the other two by means of 17×3 and 17×4. This decomposition can be considered a model of perfection and is presented in its ancient form as follows:

$$\frac{2}{17} = \frac{1}{12} \; 1\frac{1}{3}\frac{1}{12} + \frac{1}{3 \cdot 17}\frac{1}{3} + \frac{1}{4 \cdot 17}\frac{1}{4},$$

which we express in modern form by $17/12 + 4/12 + 3/12 = 24/12 = 2$.

The number 31 plus a unity is composed of two squares of 4 ($31 + 1 = 32 = 2$ times the square of 4).

The scribe forms his first denominator by means of 4 and $4 + 1$ and gets 20, which distinguishes it from the neighboring decompositions for which the preferred number is 24.[88]

For all numbers not corresponding to these conditions the difficulty—and the art of the scribe—consists in choosing a decomposable number with the largest quantity of simple continuous factors for the first denominator, such as 3, 4, 5, or 4, 5, 6 and so on, or the factors of 60. The method employed by the author of the papyrus is even more interesting to note, for it reveals the use of the number 60 in Egypt the same way it was used in Babylonia. It is the "abundant" number because it presents a large series of composing factors the sum of which, 108, is greater than itself. An example of the series is

	60	40	30	20	15	12	10	6	5	4	3	2
1		$\frac{2}{3}$	$\frac{1}{2}$	$\frac{1}{3}$	$\frac{1}{4}$	$\frac{1}{5}$	$\frac{1}{6}$	$\frac{1}{10}$	$\frac{1}{12}$	$\frac{1}{15}$	$\frac{1}{20}$	$\frac{1}{30}$

The scribe can then proceed following the standard method of pharaonic mathematics. This allows the arrangement of the various odd or prime numbers by means of 60 and its unit fractions, for example, for 2/83 the first term is 83/60.

/ 1	60	/ $\frac{1}{4}$	15
/ $\frac{1}{3}$	20	/ $\frac{1}{5}$	12
/ $\frac{1}{20}$	3	/ $\frac{1}{6}$	10
Total	83	Total	37

---

[88] Tannery, *Mémoires scientifiques*, 2:142 et sqq. "From the Egyptian point of view the decomposition of 2/17 thus offers a singularity worth mentioning. If $(p+1)/2 = m^2$, we have

$$\frac{2}{p} = \frac{1}{m(m+1)} + \frac{1}{mp} + \frac{1}{(m+1)p};$$

the two factors of p differ by only one unity. This decomposition applies effectively for $p = 31$ and for $p = 97$. In the first case we see the appearance of $m = 20$, then that $m = 24$ is preferred for the adjacent numbers; in the second case, we have $m = 7 \times 8$, which is outside the sexagesimal series, but on the other hand, the analogous decomposition $2/71 = 1/42 + 1/(6 \times 71) + 1/(7 \times 71)$ is not given although 42 is chosen for m in a less favorable case."

Necessarily, 120/60, therefore 120 − 83 = 37 is distributed into three terms. The answer will be

$$\frac{2}{83} = \frac{1}{60} \cdot \frac{1}{4\times83} \cdot \frac{1}{5\times83} \cdot \frac{1}{6\times83}.$$

The number 60 is chosen because its factors follow in such a way that it allows the formation, every time it is possible, of the three last unit fractions to be in harmonic proportion; the decomposition of 2/83 offers a good example of this.

But the choice of 60 and its factors does not represent a uniform system. Thus, after adopting the denominator 60 for all the prime numbers between 73 and 95, the scribe suddenly takes a smaller denominator for 97 outside of the sexagesimal series. The number 56 is this exception. This decomposition takes the following form: 2/97 = 97/56 + 15/56 = 112/56. In its Egyptian form this is 2/97 = 1/56 + 1/(7 • 97) + 1/(8 • 97).

The first group equals 97/56, which equals 1.7321...[89] in our decimal form and represents an already perfect approximation of the square root of 3: the triple square of 56 equals 9408 and the square of 97 equals 9409.

Since this ratio represents an irregularity in the table, and since it provides an excellent coefficient for the square root of 3, it cannot be by chance that it was chosen. Now this case is not unique; the groups 17/12, 29/24, 41/24, belong to the generative series of the square root of 2 and are transcribed as follows:

$$\frac{17}{12} = \frac{\sqrt{2}}{1}, \text{ and its inverse } \frac{24}{17} = \frac{2}{\sqrt{2}}$$

$$\frac{29}{24} = \frac{17+12}{24} = \frac{\sqrt{2}+1}{2}$$

$$\frac{41}{24} = \frac{17+24}{24} = \frac{\sqrt{2}+2}{2}$$

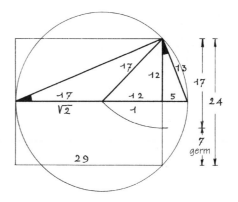

Fig. 43

The pairs of ratios that approach the square roots of 2 and of 3, respectively, are obtained by a generation that starts with the musical proportion composed of the arithmetic and harmonic mean terms. Now, since the three essential examples of the decomposition of 2/n rest upon this same functional origin and also associate an arithmetic mean term and its inverse, the harmonic mean term, it is not surprising that we again find these transcribable functions in the form of square "roots" in the 2/n table. Both come from a numerical series that has an essential function for its base.[90]

The modern transcription of formulas in which letters replace numbers causes one to lose sight of the different "series," each of which has its own character and does not allow any confusion. The

[89] $\sqrt{3}$ = 1.73205... .

[90] Cf. chapter 8.

Ancients remained faithful to the exploration of *harmonic proportion*, which is always functionally demonstrable through a geometric diagram.

We have already indicated that the study of this papyrus must not be confined only to investigating the methods of resolution of the problems posed (as has been done until today), but above all it is necessary to account for the way in which this series of problems is written, because a symbolic intention and a truly surprising knowledge of numbers and their families presides over their arrangement. This observation has led us to discover the method that the Ancients used to determine the prime numbers without any calculation.

Problems 1 to 23

The papyrus is at present torn into two pieces, one of which contains the 2/*n* table and the other the problems. This accidental tearing seems to divide the papyrus into two distinct parts that correspond to the real subdivision of the manuscript. Thanks to the discovery of two fragments that fit in between the two major parts, we can reestablish the general arrangement.

In the recovered fragments the decomposition of 2/101 occupies the first line directly following the table of 2/*n*, in which the last number is 2/99. Beneath 2/101 is a small table of the multiples of 1/10, that is, 2/10, 3/10, 4/10, etc., expressed in the form of fractional expressions with 1 for their numerators (in *A*, fig. 44),[91] and problem 1.

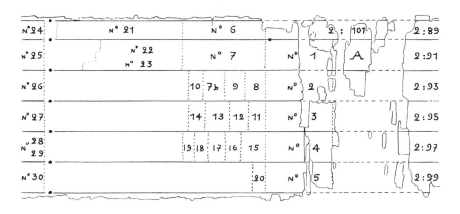

Fig. 44

Problems 1 to 6 consist in multiplying the fractional expressions given in table A by successive duplications, following the last decomposition in the table of 2/*n*.

Below problem 6, the last of this series, are problems 7 to 20, also multiplications of fractional expressions taken from the table. Finally, the three problems 21 to 23 are written in the first two upper intervals, leaving a blank space below, which seems to make a separation between this category of problems and that of *ahaw*, which comes next.

This arrangement allows us to consider problems 1 to 23, and also the small table A, as complements of the 2/*n* table, and to distinguish them from the following problems. This division of the papyrus (between problems 21 and 24) is made at half its length, that is, approximately 2.70 meters of the total restored length of 5.43 meters.

---

[91] *A*, figure 44, corresponds to fragment 6 of plate E in Peet, *RMP.*

Problem 6 (written on the first band)

"To make: 9 loaves for 10 men.

To make according to the becoming, you will at first put

$$\frac{2}{3} \quad \frac{1}{5} \quad \frac{1}{30} \quad \text{times 10} \qquad . \qquad \frac{2}{3} \quad \frac{1}{5} \quad \frac{1}{30}$$

$$/2 \qquad 1\frac{2}{3} \quad \frac{1}{10} \quad \frac{1}{30}$$

$$4 \qquad 3\frac{1}{2} \quad \frac{1}{10}$$

$$/8 \qquad 7\frac{1}{5}$$

The total is 9 loaves."

The first six problems, the last of which is given here as an example, consist in multiplying by successive duplications the fractional expressions given in the small table A preceding these problems.

This table A is already a table of multiplication of 1/10, and the first six problems constitute a proof that ten times the given expression reconstitutes the number of loaves, letting one, then two, six, seven, eight, and nine loaves be divided among ten men. These operations provide the occasion to work with the inverses of 5 and 15, the decompositions of which are found in the 2/n table.

Recalling that the divisions of 2 by 5 and 2 by 15 are made by following the principle of harmonic division, the exercises in question become the application of the following law: *When several numbers of a harmonic proportion are multiplied by the same number, the products are also in a harmonic proportion.*

Problem 6 consists in multiplying the expression represented by 9/10 by 10. The total must again give 9. Now it is obvious to the scribe that the product of his multiplication, namely, 8 + 2/3 + 1/5 + 1/10 + 1/30, is equal to 9; this is not immediately apparent to those who are not familiar with this form of calculation (fig. 45).

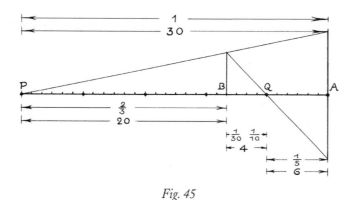

Fig. 45

These exercises suggest to the translator the following remark: "It is easy to understand the omission from the series of 4 loaves, for 4/10 is equivalent to 2/5, which by the preceding tables can be resolved at once into 1/3 + 1/15. But why omit the division of 3 loaves and include that of

1, the answer to which, 1/10, is already in the required form of an aliquot part? Here we are face to face with one of those anomalies which from time to time baffle all our attempts to see things with the mind of the Egyptian mathematician."[92]

Nevertheless, 3/10 represents for the calculator 1/5 + 1/10 and this is the anomaly that attracts our attention. This 3/10, however, is not forgotten by the scribe; when in problem 22 he is asked to "complete a quantity until 1," it is precisely this 3/10 lacking here that serves as the subject of the problem. Thus, we are led to study problems 21, 22, and 23 immediately after problem 6.

Problems 21 to 23

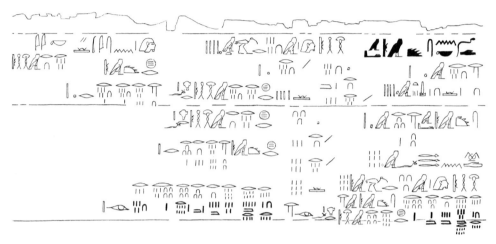

Problem 21 occupies the first band of the papyrus, following after problem 6. Problems 22 and 23 are written on the second band. Problem 23 is written in such a compressed way that the signs overlap each other and the final operation reaches up to the level of the results of the previous problem. There must have been an effort not to exceed the area assigned for these three problems because four bands remain free just below. Problem 21 is to the two following problems as 1 is to ϕ by the dimension of the intervals they occupy, so logically, one could approach the study of these three problems at the same time.

Problem 21

"If one says to you: 'What is the *s'km* of 2/3 + 1/15 within 1?'[93]

10 . . . 1, total 11, the remainder is 4."

The operation consists of "putting 15 to find 4," the result is 1/5 + 1/15, which represents the *s'km* completing the expression up to 1.

Problem 22

"What is the *s'km* of 2/3 + 1/30 within 1?   .

20   1, the total of the excess is 9."

[92] Peet, *RMP*, p. 50.

[93] Generally translated, "What is the *s'km* of 1/*a* + 1/*b* up to 1"; but "in 1" corresponds quite well to the idea of bringing everything into this unity, and is, moreover, the literal translation.

As in the preceding problem, the operation consists of "putting 30 to find 9." The result is 1/10 + 1/5, which completes the expression up to 1 (fig. 45).

Comparing these two problems, the first *s'km* represents 8/30 and the second 9/30, whereas the given numbers correspond to problems 22 and 21. Is there an effort here to recall the ratio of 8 to 9 of the musical tone, or of the diameter of a square to a disk? Moreover, the second *s'km* corresponds to the 3/10 lacking in the series of divisions of the loaves of bread. The ratio of the fractions to each other corresponds to the same harmonic division in both these categories of problems.

Problem 23, written on a single line and tightly compressed underneath the preceding one, contains no explanation.

$$\frac{1}{4} \qquad \frac{1}{8} \qquad \frac{1}{10} \qquad \frac{1}{30} \qquad \frac{1}{45} \quad \text{to complete "in"} \; \frac{2}{3}$$
$$11\frac{1}{4} \quad 5\frac{1}{2}\frac{1}{8} \quad 4\frac{1}{2} \quad 1\frac{1}{2} \quad 1$$

The answer is given immediately without calculation: "1/9 + 1/40 to put above himself, this makes 2/3." The end of the line of figures repeats the statement, adding to it the discovered *s'km*, then adding 1/3, which makes 1.

In the last problem, our attention is attracted to the largest denominator, 45, and to the *s'km* with denominators 9 and 40, which are found without calculation. The 1/40 and 1/45 of this problem are in the same ratio as that of 9 and 8 representing the two preceding *s'kms*. By taking *PA/PB* = 45/40 = 9/8 = *QA/QB*, this leads to the establishment of the harmonic decomposition relative to these numbers.

SYNTHESIS 1

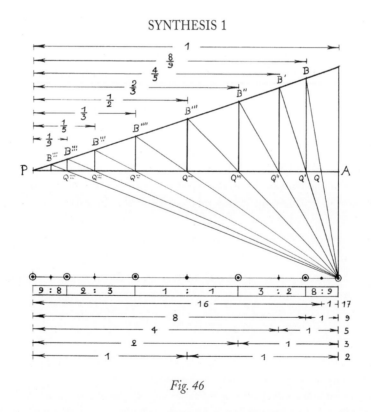

Fig. 46

The development of the harmonic decomposition (fig. 46), by taking successively *PB* = *PQ'*, then *PB'* = *PQ"*, and so on, leads to the division of the total length *PA* into segments that are to each other as 1 to 16, 1 to 8, 1 to 4, 1 to 2, and 1 to 1. Their total lengths represent, respectively, 17, 9, 5, 3, and 2. Beginning from 1 to 1, the series is inverted and is reflected exactly, in such a way that each half is divided into fragments that two by two define, with respect to each other, the ratios of the octave, the fifth, and the tone. Apparently, the fourth is missing, but it is the inverse of the fifth, and the study of this construction will reveal that the fourth is a direct result of it.

The transformation into whole numbers of all the relationships that are generated from one another leads us to establish the following formula (fig. 47):

$$\frac{PA}{PB} = \frac{QA}{QB} = \frac{a}{b}, \quad \text{for example, } \frac{a}{b} = \frac{3}{1}$$

$$\frac{PA}{PB} = \frac{a^2 + ab}{ab + b^2}, \quad \text{for example, } \frac{9+3}{3+1} = \frac{12}{4}$$

$$\frac{PQ}{AB} = \frac{2ab}{a^2 - b^2}, \quad \text{for example, } \frac{2 \times 3}{9 - 1} = \frac{6}{8} = \frac{3}{4}$$

Finally, $PA + PB - PQ = a^2 + b^2$.[94]

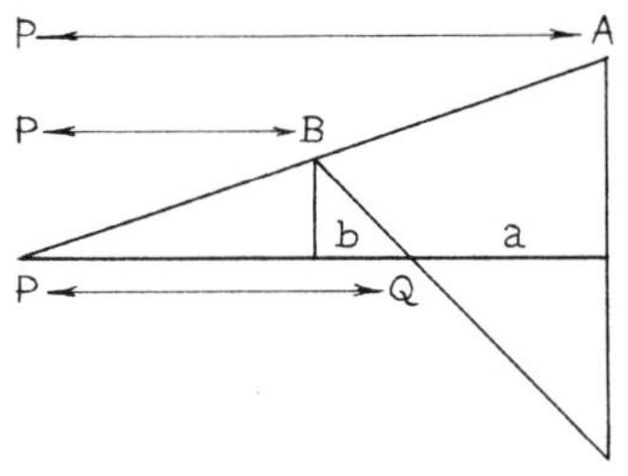

Fig. 47

Thus, the ratio of the fourth is implied in the harmonic decomposition of PA into 1/3 and 2/3, which requires the reading of these proportional functions with their inversion, which is given directly with their complements.

———₩₩———

The scribe poses problem 7 as being "*tp n s'km*," which is an "example of complementation." Now, considering the width of the bands on which problems 6 and 7 are written, which are related as 1 is to ϕ, it is remarkable to find that the harmonic decomposition at the foundation of problem 6 leads toward the ratios of musical harmony, and that those governing problem 7 lead to the functions of ϕ through the pentagon (fig. 48).[95]

Problems 21, 22, and 23 correspond to the same arrangement, confirming the intention of expressing the function ϕ, which governs all these problems.[96]

The decomposition of 2/7 from the table is equal to 1/4 + 1/28 and constitutes the object of problems 7 to 15. Now, the development of this decomposition (fig. 48) leads to the following results:

The first ratio, which generates the following ones, is 1/4. In the decreasing direction it generates 1/7, and the increasing direction it generates successively the ratios 2/5, then 4/7, then 8/11, and finally 16/19. Their complements are 3/4, 3/5, 3/7, 3/11, and 3/19.

This decomposition of 2/7 thus leads to all the fundamental numbers that govern the division of the cubit into 7 palms of 4 digits each, measuring a total of 28 digits. Its development generates the ratio 8/11, which represents the rectangle that governs the pentagon, adopted for the establishment of a naos drawn on papyrus and for the naos in the temple of Luxor.[97] Finally, the number 19 will appear as the number governing the pharaonic human canon.

[94] Cf. chapter 7, "Addition and Subtraction of Angles in Proportional Notation." The letters a and b used in fig. 47 are to be understood as values of the ratios between the lengths and not as real lengths.

[95] Syntheses 1 and 2 constitute the seeds of chains that develop in two directions and that cross each other.

[96] Note that in problem 23 the sum of the fractions whose complement we are looking for is 191/240 for 2/3 and 191/360 for unity. Now, 19.0983... represents the radius of a circle equal to 120 (with π resulting from $1.2 \times \phi^2$) and the inverse of the given ratio is 240/191 corresponding to 0.4π for π equal to 3.14136....

[97] Cf. plates 65 and 66 and chapter 37, "The Grid and the Architecture"; fig. 154.

SYNTHESIS 2

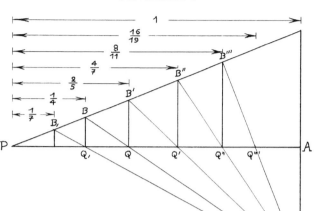

Fig. 48

The angles adopted in the temple of Luxor, 1/7, 8/11, and 3/19, also result from this figure, from which certain consequences will appear as we study pharaonic trigonometry.

CONCLUSION

Calculation is the science of assemblages and combinations of quantities designated by numbers. These intellectual "quantities," or numbers, always represent a notion that is quantitatively limited.

It is the *faculty* of assembling and of consciously combining that reveals the intellect. This latter belongs only to human beings and results from the *re-cognition* of the consciousness innate in us, and therefore from a mental faculty for the projection outside of ourselves of this consciousness.

Natural life, in the sense of corporeal continuity, is also only a calculation, or an assemblage of quantities, but these are never separated from each other by a delimitation in time and space; this delimitation appears only *after* the assemblage. The defined quantity precedes mental calculation and, on the contrary, it follows calculation (becoming and growth) in the natural phenomenon. The natural genesis is the reduction into rationality of an irrational "quantity."

Thus, calculation is only a play of the mind, a *jeu d'esprit* and has no spiritual or initiatory value, since it operates only with limited quantities.

It is only through the consciousness of proportionality that calculation comes alive. The limited quantity is a cadaver, reduced to being but a definitively arrested moment, while proportionality is a *function* that a finite quantity cannot arrest.

It is this discipline of pharaonic calculation, *of thinking only in terms of proportionality,* that formed the geometric mentality of the sages, and not an empirical turn of mind, as many people would like to think. Geometry is only a graphic symbolization of "relationships"; the defined quantity plays no role in it.

Our "scholarly" method of mathematics is able to approach natural phenomena only by introducing the "imaginary." Now, there is a kinship between $\sqrt{-1}$ and the principles of the inverse and the crossing combined in the pharaonic method, with this difference, that the function—inversion and crossing—conforms to the natural function, whereas our decimal system based on zero, and algebra with its negative values, remove us from living contact with the real phenomenon.

Infinitesimal calculus and "integrals" are only useful in mechanics; the search for the smallest possible quantity (the quantum) in the vital phenomenon is absurd. The beginning is *without limited quantity*, it is an *energetic state*, not an energy defined and limited by mass and speed.

There are two definite paths: the mechanistic path, useful but leading nowhere from the vital point of view, and the vitalist path, which requires research into the knowledge of the fundamental Phenomenon and serves all forms of knowledge.

———

With regard to the study of pharaonic mathematical problems, the Occidental mind is too obsessed with quantity, and therefore with the precise quantitative resolution, for example, of the distribution of various given values (*twnw*), or the completing (*s'km*) of one value.

Certainly there is a possible answer in this sense, but it really seems that the arithmetic and geometric solution is only the "exoteric" aspect of the question, and there exists another intent of "esoteric" character based on harmony. One does not look for quantities but for relationships.

The sense of harmony, thus the faculty of testing through our senses for harmonic disequilibrium, derives from something other than material things. This sense is, prior to the mental and reasoning faculties, an innate state in ourselves that puts us into communion with the "fatal" equilibrium of natural forces; it is a supernatural sense. We can establish proportional relationships that express this very subtle sense of equilibrium and disequilibrium and that are mentally translated through calculation, properly so called. But this is only a grossly material aspect of a vital reality.

The study of pharaonic mathematical knowledge has to be revised now that we know how everything in this science leads us toward harmonic proportion as a foundation, and how everything in the pharaonic world—measures, canon, *canevas*, trigonometry—issues forth from this synthesis-seed.

The Pythagorean tradition should have already guided us toward this aspect of thinking. We know now that the great sages of Hellenic antiquity drew their knowledge from the PHARAONIC TEMPLE.

I do not pretend that our analysis of the pharaonic mentality as applied to calculation presented here is exhaustive, nor that it will clarify all the nuances of their thinking. Nevertheless, it is unquestionable: the pharaonic mentality is proportionalist and remains, without fail, faithful to a given theological truth and to the anthropocosmic directive. Every moment and every defined state has a "countermoment," a "counterstate," the true "plus and minus" surrounding the living zero that is the present moment; this present moment is forever One, the indivisible Unity.

Part 3

THE MASTER BUILDERS' GRID

PHARAONIC MATHEMATICS APPLIED

Chapter 7

PHARAONIC TRIGONOMETRY

FUNDAMENTALS OF THE TRIGONOMETRY

THE KEY

Not a little evidence has escaped the sometimes too "positive" observations of Egyptologists. Thus one can imagine a serious professor who, preferring to ignore symbolism and remain "rational" and positive, would investigate assiduously how the Ancient Egyptians endeavored to capture birds with the *net* that they had taken the trouble to draw or sculpt on temple and tomb walls. He concludes, moreover, that the representation of the net, open or closed, does not conform to how it should be in a realistic depiction. (This already indicates that this image has a double meaning.)

We can see, among other bas-reliefs in the tomb of Ukhotep,[1] a net "for capturing birds" (but in fact, and more correctly, for capturing the spirit, or numbers and ideas) drawn on a *canevas* and surrounded by figures whose symbolic sense leaves no doubt: the *canevas* clearly specifies that it is concerned with numbers—about this there can be no mistake. We have studied this "net" and then looked for confirmation in other, similar nets. What we are dealing with here is a *description and demonstration of the trigonometric concept of pharaonic mathematics.*

Now, these sages believed in indestructible life; they lived and drew their knowledge and their science, and therefore also their symbolism, from the manifestations of life as it exists.

Our objective, rational, Euclidean thought holds that two straight lines meeting at a point make an angle. But what intrigues the Ancient Egyptian is the point of intersection and the two straight lines. He sees an *articulation*, therefore a *cause* of the dividing into two (fig. 49).

It is always the same problem: the dividing into two, the scission, is not made into two equal parts, and the articulation is the function of the scission. This is the philosophy of the mystical function ϕ *viewed in its trigonometric aspect,* as it may be in all aspects of Nature.

---

[1] Chapel tomb no. 2 at Meir. Cf. plate 56 and chapter 37.

190

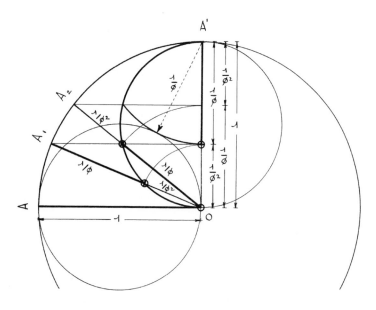

Fig. 49

By this fact, there is a kinship between the cause of branching out in the plant (blossom, leaf, branch, and so on) and the articulation of the elbow and knee in the human being.[2] There will be an inequality between the two lines thus engendered. One is "Heaven" and the other is "Earth." One is unitary, the other divisible, so that they are as arm and forearm (radius and ulna), or as femur and lower leg (tibia and fibula), or as elbow and knee in man; they are like the branch that always divides itself in two on the trunk of the tree, or the leaf (surface), or the fruit. If one of these parts is given the value 1, the other will be ϕ or $1/\phi$, or a function of ϕ, as in the length of the bones in the human body.

In principle, one of the branches of our angle will thus be 1 and the other ϕ. This is *the functional and mystical angle that presides over* cosmic mechanics. The distance between them will then be $\sqrt{\phi}$, the angle that we find in the Pyramid of Cheops, and its geometric application (represented by the Pyramid of Chephren) will be 3 : 5, the first actual "Fibonacci" ratio of 1 : ϕ. This opening, the measure of this angle, is geometrically 4 and mystically $\sqrt{\phi}$ (fig. 50).

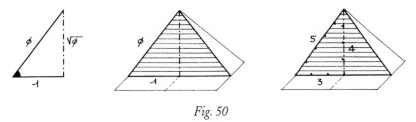

Fig. 50

Now, for the pharaonic mathematicians the circle remains a cycle measuring time and is not used for the measure of degrees, minutes, and seconds that an angle intercepts on an arc.[3] *Pharaonic trigonometry notates the angle by the proportion that defines the ratio between the large side and the cathetus of a right triangle.* The hypotenuse is given by *a sighting* toward the cathetus (the perpendicular)

[2] Cf. the Greek words γov and γωv, angle and knee.

[3] Tannery, *Mémoires scientifiques*, 3:256–68, confirms this and offers the opinion that the division of the circle was used for the division of time (the zodiac, e.g.), but not for the circle as a geometric drawing.

while assigning, for example, the value 1 to the large side (base) of the triangle. Through this sighting, the cathetus increases until it becomes equal to the length 1 of the large side, and this proportion is written $1 : n$ (fig. 51a).

In the system of notation $1 : n$, it is the base B of the triangle that is considered invariable, while in our system of reading by sines and cosines, it is the radius that remains invariable and the values A, A_1, A_2, and B, B_1, B_2 of the sines and the cosines that vary according to the angle (fig. 51b).

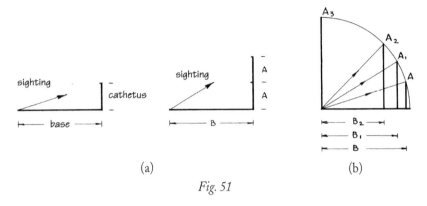

(a)   (b)

Fig. 51

The pharaonic notation of angles through ratios (without the intervention of the circle) presents several advantages and avoids the absurd notion of the infinity of the tangent at 90°. Our method of reading in tangents implies a tangent value ranging from zero to infinity. This notion of the infinity of a number is incompatible with theological concepts: only the Unique (or God) is infinite, indeterminable. Therefore, a tangent terminating in Euclidean parallels is inconceivable; it is not geometric. The pharaonic proportional angle is thus read from $1 : 0$ until $1 : 1$, necessarily passing through all $1 : n$ the fractions. The angle $1 : 1$ read in a horizontal sighting will be completed by the angle $1 : 1$ read in a vertical sighting. In this way, one avoids irrationals in practical calculations (fig. 52).

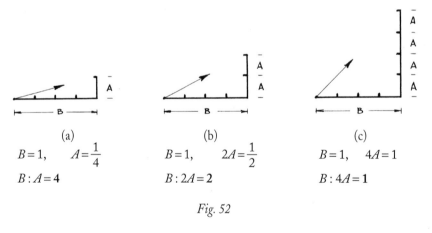

$$(a) \qquad\qquad (b) \qquad\qquad (c)$$
$$B=1, \quad A=\frac{1}{4} \qquad B=1, \quad 2A=\frac{1}{2} \qquad B=1, \quad 4A=1$$
$$B:A=4 \qquad\qquad B:2A=2 \qquad\qquad B:4A=1$$

Fig. 52

With this approach, when do we arrive at 1/1 (45°)? The Egyptian would say, "Make A grow to find 1" (or B), and thus we have the method of pharaonic fractional notation in which the fractions, compared to each other with respect to unity, are transcribed into whole numbers. For example,

$$\begin{array}{cccc} \dfrac{1}{4} & \dfrac{1}{2} & \dfrac{1}{2}+\dfrac{1}{4} & 1 \\[1em] 1 & 2 & 3 & 4 \end{array}$$

in which $1 = 4$ (quarters).

The ratio $1 : 1$ is what we call a 45° angle, in other words, one-eighth of a circle or half of a right angle. The proportionality that defines the designated angle thus refers to the sine as well as to the tangent and allows us to work with *whole numbers, although expressed in the form of ratios or fractions.*

In practice, in the problems concerned with calculating the slope of a pyramid, the scribe gives any ratio whatsoever between the base and the altitude. This ratio is then brought back to $1 : n$, which allows this ratio to be established in cubits or in palms, according to the case.[4]

One of the sides of the triangle is always brought back to unity, and the other side is transformed into a *part* of that unity. The squares of these parts are surfaces, a function of this angle, therefore the function of an angle becomes the passage from one surface to another (fig. 53).

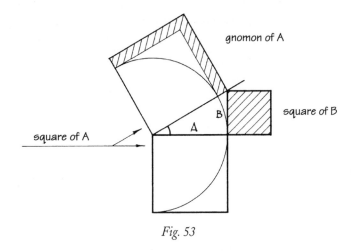

Fig. 53

The square of *B* is equal to the gnomon of *A*. The width of this gnomon is the difference between the hypotenuse and the base of the triangle, that is, between the sine and the tangent.

The advantage of this form of proportional notation $(1 : n)$ is as much its immediate application in architecture (through the *canevas,* which we will explain later) as well as its absolute precision in the definition of angles, read in "sines" or in "tangents" (fig. 54).

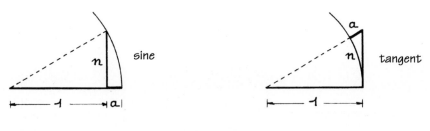

Fig. 54

If the hypotenuse (the sighting) represents the radius of a circle, the reading is equivalent to our "sine," whereas if the large side of the triangle represents the radius of the circle, the cathetus reads as the tangent. The value of this notation is constantly substantiated by its application in architecture. The temple of Luxor demonstrates the advantages of this approach.

Thus, the principles and practice of ancient trigonometry are made clear on the condition that we know how to add and subtract the angles expressed in proportional notation.

---

[4] Cf. problem 56 of the Rhind Papyrus.

FUNCTIONAL DEVELOPMENT OF THE LAW OF RIGHT TRIANGLES

The side of a square is to be seen as the hypotenuse of a right triangle. This hypotenuse is then the root of a square and is considered to have a value of 1. It is also the diameter of a semicircle any point of which connected to the ends of this diameter always forms a right triangle.

It is obvious that all the possible right triangles are inscribed on half the semicircle whose diameter is their hypotenuse. This then becomes the image that defines all right triangles. Now, dropping *the altitude of these right triangles onto the hypotenuse forms the geometric mean term between the extreme values,* that is, the two fractions determined on this hypotenuse (the diameter of the semicircle).

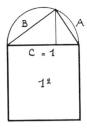
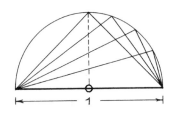

Fig. 55

The hypotenuse C, the diameter, always has a value of 1 and will be considered as being C^2 (fig. 55). The perpendicular dropped onto the hypotenuse defines two triangles that are similar to the initial triangle. The fact of always taking the hypotenuse C as 1, and as the side of a square of surface 1^2, will result in the following (fig. 56):

In the triangle ABC, the sides A and B are fractions of unity.

The perpendicular AB divides the hypotenuse C into two segments that are to each other as the squares of A and B, in such a way that we have here the geometrical demonstration of the theorem named for Pythagoras, $A^2 + B^2 = C^2$.

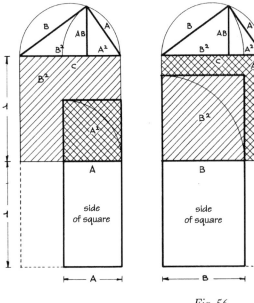
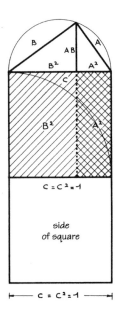

Fig. 56

The altitude *AB* is a rectangular number that is equal to the product of sides *A* and *B*. This altitude *AB* is the geometric mean between the small segment A^2 and the larger B^2, and the figure demonstrates that a rectangular number is always the geometric mean between the squares of the two numbers that compose it.[5]

The hypotenuse *C*, equal to 1, can be taken as a line representing either the side of a square or the edge of a cube equaling 1^2 or 1, respectively; but following the ancient conception, the "side" of a square can also signify one of the facets of a prism that always has 1 as its height and a square base of varying surface.

By adopting this way of seeing, the hypotenuse *C*, as the "side of the square," represents a surface equaling 1. In the same way the "sides of the square," *A* and *B*, will also be surfaces having 1 for height and *A* and *B*, respectively, for width. Thus, the two prisms defined by "the side of square *A*" and the "side of square *B*" have for their sum the cube determined by the "side of square *C*." Their sum comes to the same amount as that of the surfaces. Furthermore, the fact of always bringing the value of the hypotenuse back to unity allows for the display of all the forms that can be taken from the surfaces A^2 and B^2; the line, the band, and the gnomon (fig. 56).

If we draw four similar triangles in a square having the hypotenuse of 1 for a side, the extension of the four heights *AB* to their crossing points forms a square at the center (fig. 57) the side of which has the value of $B^2 - A^2$.

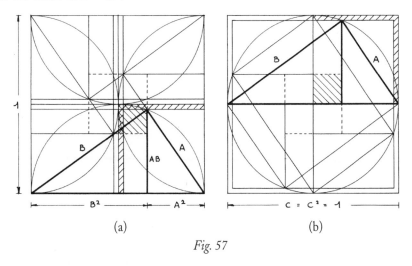

(a)   (b)

Fig. 57

The side of this central square is cut proportionally into two segments that are to each other as *A* and *B*, and a quarter of the surface of this central square (hachured) is equal to the gnomon of the square *AB* (also hachured) (fig. 57). This figure suggests the small square of the throne (see fig. 2) the surface of which is equal to its border in certain pharaonic figurations.[6]

The fact of bringing the hypotenuse of the triangle back to the value 1 allows for the treatment of surfaces as lines and, among other things, the establishment of a triangle the squares of whose sides are proportional to each other in a fixed ratio. For example, if we are asked to establish a triangle the squares of whose sides are to each other as 1, 2, 3, this triangle would have in positive values 1, $\sqrt{2}$, and $\sqrt{3}$ for sides, which necessitates a *construction*. On the other hand, if the hypotenuse $C = C^2 = 1$, it is sufficient to divide it into two fractions with the values of 1/3 and 2/3, respectively, to obtain the triangle we are looking for (fig. 58).

---

[5] This is a general rule, but applied here to $C = 1$, it necessarily produces fractions of unity.

[6] Cf. Babylonian problem 12 on p. 221, which was established following these principles.

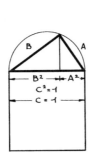
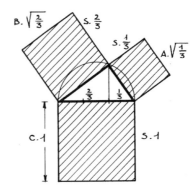

Fig. 58

If four triangles thus constructed are put together by taking their right angles for the center of the figure, one obtains the cross section of a regular octahedron whose apothem is represented by the hypotenuse equal to 1 (fig. 59).

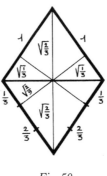

Fig. 59

Vertical cross section of a regular octahedron giving the three radii—of the inscribed sphere, of the sphere tangent to the edges, and of the circumscribing sphere—by its three diagonals.

ADDITION AND SUBTRACTION OF ANGLES IN PROPORTIONAL NOTATION

Compared to notation in degrees, minutes, and seconds of the circle, the proportional notation $1 : n$ presents a difficulty; it is easy to add degrees of whatever value, but is it possible to add or subtract angles notated by $1 : n$, knowing that we cannot treat them as simple fractions?

For example, take the addition of $\widehat{1/4} + \widehat{2/5}$ (fig. 60). The base AB common to the two triangles is equal to 1, and the perpendiculars of each are valued, respectively, as 1/4 and 2/5 (fig. 60a). Now the base AB must necessarily be subdivided into a number of parts equal to the product of the two denominators, $4 \times 5 = 20$ in this case. The perpendiculars become 5 and 8, respectively (fig. 60b).

In order to add together these two triangles DAB and BAC, we draw the perpendicular onto the hypotenuse of one of them, for example, BE (fig. 60b). This perpendicular divides the initial triangle BAC into two similar triangles (CEB and BAE). The parallel to this perpendicular drawn as DF forms a right triangle in which the angle DAF is the sum of the two given angles.

The length *OB* subtracted from the original length *AB* is inevitably 2, because the angular ratio $\widehat{2/5}$ equals *OB/BD*. Where the general formula is applied to the addition of any two angles (the denominators being larger than the numerators), then $\widehat{a/b} + \widehat{c/d} = (ad + bc)/(bd - ac)$, for example, $\widehat{1/4} + \widehat{2/5} = (5 + 8)/(20 - 2) = \widehat{13/18}$ (fig. 60b).

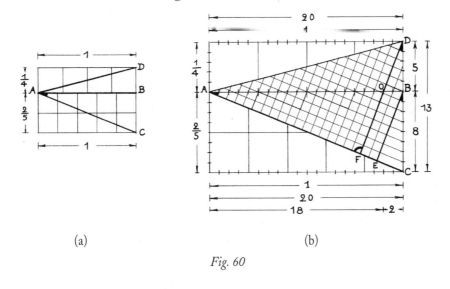

(a)   (b)

Fig. 60

The *subtraction* of any two angles rests on the same principles and on a similar graphic demonstration. Subtracting $\widehat{1/4}$, *BAC*, from $\widehat{3/4}$, *DAB* (fig. 61), the general formula is as follows: $\widehat{a/b} - \widehat{c/d} = (ad - bc)/(bd + ac)$, for example, $\widehat{3/4} - \widehat{1/4} = (12 - 4)/(16 + 3) = \widehat{8/19}$ (fig. 61).

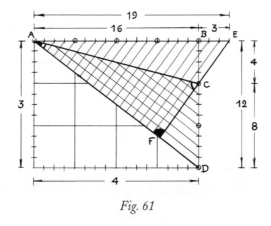

Fig. 61

To subtract the angle *BAC* = 1/4 from the angle *DAB* = 3/4, draw the perpendicular *CF* onto *AD* and extend *CE* to the extension of *AB*. The segment *BE* is equal to 3 because *BC* = 4. Therefore, the new triangle *CAF* has for a perpendicular 12 – 4 = 8, and for a base, 16 + 3 = 19.

The two formulas presented here can be applied to any addition or subtraction of angles expressed in the form of proportional notation. Furthermore, for the addition of two equal angles and for the difference between an angle of 45°, or 1/1, and an angle less than 45°, or 1/*n*, there are two demonstrations that play a very important part in ancient geometry.

ADDITION OF TWO EQUAL ANGLES

It is remarkable that any addition of two equal angles expressed in proportional notation creates a Diophantine triangle, a triangle whose three sides are composed of whole numbers. Now, the use of these triangles is attested to in pharaonic architecture as well as in the Babylonian tablets. The formula is as follows (a being larger than b):

$$\frac{\hat{b}}{a} + \frac{\hat{b}}{a} = \frac{2ab}{a^2 - b^2}, \qquad \text{the hypotenuse being equal to } a^2 + b^2.$$

By a very curious functional relationship, the harmonic proportion contains in its development all the elements of the formula mentioned above, in such a way that if $PB/PA = QB/QA = b/a$, the ratio $PQ/AB = 2ab/(a^2 - b^2)$. For example, $\widehat{2/5} + \widehat{2/5} = (10 + 10)/(25 - 4) = \widehat{20/21}$. The hypotenuse corresponds then to $(PA - \frac{1}{2}PQ) + (PB - \frac{1}{2}PQ) = a^2 + b^2$, for example, to $25 + 4 = 29$ in the above case.

Now, this hypotenuse is the mean term of the mediety called the *subcontrary to the harmonic*,[7] in which the mean term between PA and PB will be, for example, PO. This mean term is established so that the differences between the three terms are in an inverse ratio to the differences of the harmonic proportion. Thus, $(PA - PQ)/(PQ - PB) = 5/2$ in the harmonic proportion, and $(PA - PO)/(PO - PB) = 2/5$ in the subcontrary to the harmonic.

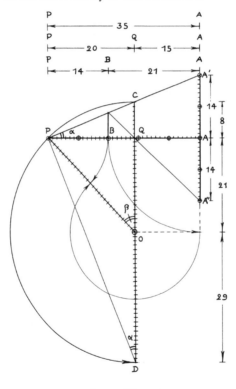

Fig. 62. The Bolt

$PA = 35$ and $PB = 14$, the harmonic mean $PQ = 20$. The length $AB = 21$, the vertical extension of AB determines with PQ the Diophantine triangle 20 to 21 in which the hypotenuse PO is the subcontrary mean term 29.

---

[7] Cf. Theon of Smyrna, *Le Nombre de Platon*, part 2, §58, p. 191: "The mean called 'subcontrary to the harmonic,' is the one in which the third term is to the first as the excess of the first (over the second) is to the excess of the second (over the third). Such is the mean formed by the numbers 6, 5, 3, in which 6 is greater than 5 by one unit, and 5 is greater than 3 by two units, and in which, finally, 3 is half of 6, as the unit, the excess of the first number (over the second) is half of 2, the excess of the second number over the third."

Applied to the example given above, the subcontrary mean term is formed by $PA - BQ$ or $35 - 6 = 29$, or again, $PB + AQ$ would be $14 + 15 = 29$, which the geometric construction of the harmonic proportion allows us to establish (fig. 62). Now, this number 29 corresponds to the sum of the squares of a and b.[8]

In order to demonstrate the mean of the harmonic proportion, the addition of two equal angles, and the formation of a Diophantine triangle, we must give to the height $AA' = AA''$—normally taken as being any height whatsoever—a value equal to PB so that the angle APA' is equal to the ratio b/a (fig. 62).

The geometric proof rests on the functional law of right triangles in which one of the consequences is that the angle β is the double of α.

SUBTRACTION OF A RATIO b/a FROM THE RATIO $1/1$

The angular subtractions of this form are based on the sum of two numbers and on their difference, and correspond to the formula (a being larger than b):

$$\frac{\hat{1}}{1} - \frac{\hat{b}}{a} = \frac{a-b}{a+b}.$$

By its constitution, the harmonic proportion contains the elements of this function, but only proportionally, because if $PB/PA = QB/QA = b/a$, the following relationships ensue: $PA - PB$ is as $a - b$, then $PA - PB = AB$; $QA + QB$ is as $a + b$, then $QA + QB = AB$, which result appears nonsensical because AB cannot be the sum and the difference at the same time.

Let us take, for example $\hat{1/1} - \hat{2/5} = (5-2)/(5+2) = \hat{3/7}$. The duplication of the ratio $\hat{2/5}$ previously established (fig. 62) provides the numbers that allow for the construction of the geometric proof and at the same time the duplication of $\hat{2/5}$ and its complement to 45°, that is, $\hat{3/7}$.

This demonstration has the "pivoting square" at its base, inclined at the angle α in which the diagonal is determined by its ratio to the vertical angle β complementary to 45°. Subsequently, the right angle is formed of twice α and twice β (fig. 63).

Again taking the numbers established for the duplication of $\hat{2/5}$ we find:

$$\frac{1}{1} - \frac{PB}{PA} = \frac{1}{1} - \frac{\hat{14}}{35} = \frac{35-14}{35+14} = \frac{\hat{21}}{49},$$
$$\frac{1}{1} - \frac{QB}{QA} = \frac{1}{1} - \frac{\hat{6}}{15} = \frac{15-6}{15+6} = \frac{\hat{9}}{21},$$

relationships in which the height 21 is the geometric mean between 9 and 49 (because $9 \times 49 = 21^2 = 441$).

[8] Michel, *De Pythagore à Euclide*, pp. 399–400, translates Theon's definition by the formula
$$\frac{a-b}{b-c} = \frac{c}{a}.$$
"The fourth mediety has the following properties: The mean multiplied by the sum of the extremes is equal to the sum of the squares of the extremes:
$$b(a+c) = a^2 + c^2, \quad \text{or} \quad b = \frac{a^2 + c^2}{a+c}."$$
This formula evidently applies to the demonstration given below, but we have not yet found a single example of the development of the harmonic proportion and its subcontrary related to the addition of two equal angles, expressed in proportional notation and determining a Diophantine triangle.

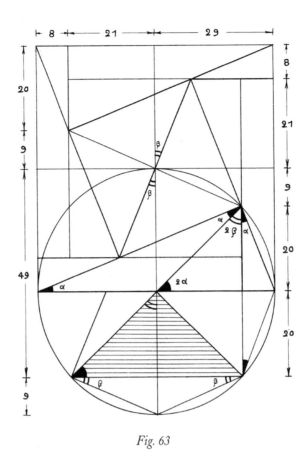

Fig. 63

Finally, a particular quality of the harmonic proportion should be noted in which the mean term *PQ* is equal to the smallest term *PB* increased by a fraction *of itself*, and is also equal to the larger term *PA* diminished by this same fraction *of itself*.

Recalling that in the established proportion *PB/PA* = 2/5, the sizes had become, respectively: *PB* = 14, and 14 plus *its* 3/7 = 20 = *PQ*; *PA* = 35, and 35 less *its* 3/7 = 20 = *PQ*, the "fraction of itself" that is added to the smaller number and subtracted from the larger to determine the mean term is precisely the difference between the ratio $\widehat{1/1}$ and $\widehat{2/5}$, which is $\widehat{3/7}$, as has just been demonstrated.

We emphasize "*its* fraction" because it is in this way that the scribe expressed himself in certain problems of the Rhind Papyrus. For example, "Its quarter on itself . . ." is terminology that comes from the search for the harmonic mean term, and this confirms that the mode of thought of the Ancients was governed by the functions we have just demonstrated.

Regarding this, it is now possible to understand one of the oddities of the inscription on the papyrus of the two problems of *twnw*, numbers 39 and 40. The *twnw* of the first was as 5/6, so the subtraction of $\widehat{1/1} - \widehat{5/6} = (6 - 5)/(6 + 5) = \widehat{1/11}$ (fig. 32), and the *twnw* of the following problem was 2/11, a ratio that is not double the *angle* $\widehat{1/11}$ but double the *ratio*, which permits exactly the distribution asked for. Now, the fact that these two problems are found under one another and are associated by the same numbers cannot be simply a coincidence.

Let us also recall that these two problems occupy the two upper bands of the papyrus, which are related to each other as 1 to ϕ, and that ϕ allows the perfect demonstration of harmonic proportion.

SUMMARY OF THE BOLT (FIG. 62)

On the line *PA*, divided into any number of parts, a perpendicular *A'AA''* is raised at one of its ends and then the hypotenuse *A'P* is drawn. From one of the units of the division in *B*, a perpendicular is raised to *PA'* that just touches the hypotenuse. From this point a new hypotenuse crosses *PA* at point *Q* and rejoins the vertical *A''* at the other end.

The point *Q* divides the length *AB* into two segments that are to each other as *a* is to *b*. This length *AB* is thus as *a + b*, whereas point *B* divides the length *PA* so that the difference *AB* is as *a − b*. This arrangement constitutes a harmonic proportion in which *PQ* is the mean term between *PA* and *PB*.

Harmonic proportion. The mean term *PQ* is equal to the smallest term increased by a fraction of itself and to the larger term diminished by the same fraction of itself; this fraction corresponds to $\widehat{1/1} - \widehat{b/a}$.

Inversion, arithmetic proportion. The inverse of *PQ*, or 1/*PQ*, is the arithmetic mean term between the inverse of *PA*, or 1/*PA*, and the inverse of *PB*, or 1/*PB*, such that 2/*PQ* = 1/*PA* + 1/*PB*.

Square numbers. To transcribe any harmonic proportion into whole numbers, *PA + PB* will always be a square number since it obeys the formula $a^2 + 2ab + b^2$.

Addition of two equal angles. Functionally, *PQ* will be the shorter side and *AB* the base of the sum of two equal angles given by the ratio *PB/PA = b/a*. The result is always a Diophantine triangle in which the hypotenuse is equal to (*PA + PB*) − *PQ*.

Geometric proportion. If instead of giving any size whatever to the vertical *A'A = AA''*, one gives it a definite value equal to *PB* in relation to *PA*, one gives to all the *principal functions* a concrete character, and one thus adds to the harmonic and arithmetic proportions the geometric proportion in which *PQ* becomes the geometric mean term between *QC* and *QD* (fig. 62), completing what we call the *bolt*, which offers all the possibilities of the three fundamental proportions of mathematics. These are the essential functions from which all trigonometry springs.

The Bolt in Relation
to the Pyramids of Dahshur

The bolt goes to and fro, and it opens and closes; it is opposite in both directions, but it is also itself. One would search Ancient Egypt in vain for a text demonstrating the bolt as we present it here, just as one cannot find a formula for the binomial in current algebraic form. One speaks of "squares" with regard to the binomial; the bolt is applied in solving mathematical problems, and it is explained through the monuments. Only a portion of the teaching, however, can be recalled here, because it must never be forgotten that the monument is a volume and that the Ancients thought in volumes, something that we no longer know how to do. The means by which they transmitted their science attests to this fact.

The monuments, as well as certain later texts, lend support to the supposition that the historic epoch of the pharaonic empire is the revelatory phase of a teaching reserved until then for a select circle of sages. It fulfills the historical work of a reality known and knowable by the spirit alone—an analysis that clarifies, for example, the cult of the ancient temple of Abydos.

The great monuments of the first historical dynasties are geometric, not "literary." With the pyramids of Cheops and Chephren in the Fourth Dynasty, a "decomposition" of geometric functions is inscribed—such as the relationships $1 : \sqrt{\phi} : \phi$ in Cheops and $3 : 4 : 5$ in Chephren—whereas, before them, Snefru, father of Cheops (Third Dynasty), gives us, through the pyramids of Dahshur, the principle of the bolt of mathematics, a synthesis.

A little south of Cairo, on the west side of the river, two great stone pyramids rise, both attributed to Snefru. The Northern Pyramid is nearly as large as Cheops', but its proportions give it a much flatter silhouette (fig. 64).

Fig. 64. The Northern Pyramid of Dahshur

The Southern Pyramid is also called the "Rhomboidal Pyramid" because of its irregular shape, which results from a sharp variation of the slope of the apothem such that the first part makes a base, formed from the trunk of a pyramid that supports another pyramid with a different slope (fig. 65). There is therefore an *ideal* pyramid indicated by the base and not terminated by the height, but supporting the upper part of a pyramid similar to the Northern Pyramid, which by this fact, becomes a headdress of the first, and together they form one pyramid with two slopes[9] (fig. 67).

Fig. 65. The Southern, Double "Rhomboidal" Pyramid of Dahshur

Geometric Study

The entirety of the measurements given by Perring[10] for the Southern or Rhomboidal Pyramid suggests the following geometric construction. The lower trunk portion of the pyramid has 54°14′46″ for the angle at the base. Now if one admits the possibility of an error of a few minutes,[11] the nearest function to this angle is, for a half-base of 1, an altitude or tangent equaling $1 + 1/\phi^2 =$ 1.381966..., which would bring the angle of the slope of the base back to 54°6′30″.

The complete pyramid *ABC* (fig. 66) corresponds to the continuation of the slope given by the trunk of the pyramid that forms the base of the Rhomboidal Pyramid of Snefru. But this pyramid *ABC* is not entirely built and its upper portion remains imagined; at a certain height of the building the slope changes and, according to Perring, becomes 42°59′26″.

---

[9] In 1947 our collaborator Alexandre Varille published a pamphlet suggestive of the *symbolique,* with some characteristic geometric indications about the two Dahshur pyramids attributed to Snefru (*A propos des Pyramides de Snefrou* [Cairo: Schindler, 1947]), from which some extracts are given in the appendix. The information that we have just given concerning the "bolt" of the mathematical thought of the Ancients makes possible a response that previously could not be made. Letters coming from diverse sources all pose an initial question: "What mathematical point determines the break of the slope that gives the Southern Pyramid this rhomboidal form?"

[10] J. S. Perring, *The Pyramids of Gizeh* (London: J. Fraser, 1839–42).

[11] The precision of this angle, given to the nearest second by Perring, demonstrates a method using triangulation. This angle is thus obtained by calculation. Our experience has shown that it is very difficult to establish an angle on the slope of a damaged monument to the nearest minute other than by establishing the average between the angular measures taken on the four faces and measuring several places on each. However, the angles given by Perring are those measured at only a few places on the slope.

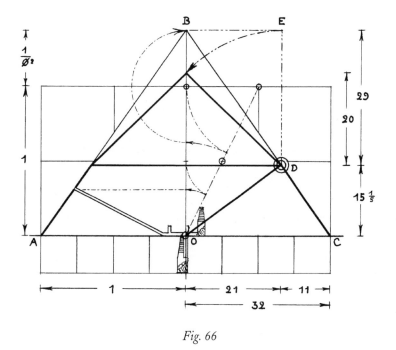

Fig. 66

Measurements given by Perring:

   length of the base = 187.96 meters

   perpendicular height of the lower body = 44.905 meters

   height of the upper part = 52.475 meters

   total present height = 97.38 meters

   total restored height = 102.33 meters

Measurements resulting from the geometric proposition:

   perpendicular height of the lower body = 44.63 meters

   perpendicular height of the upper body = <u>58.83 meters</u>

   total restored height   103.46 meters

   This interruption is explained by the development of the geometrical construction: the perpendicular to the hypotenuse *BC* of the imagined pyramid, drawn from the center *O*, determines point *D*, *the point where the change in the angle is made.* This new slope is defined by the rabattement of the height *DE* onto the vertical axis *OB* of the monument. The angle to the base of the small upper pyramid as thus defined will be 43°38′50″. Now, the topmost portion of the small pyramid, the pyramidion, is presently missing, and the remaining areas of damaged limestone facing are very small, allowing an approximation of this angle, but the estimate is yet to be verified.

   Furthermore, the Northern Pyramid of Dahshur has 43°36′ for a base angle, which corresponds within 2′ of arc to the angle proposed by the geometric construction. There should be a functional identity between the upper pyramid of the south and the large pyramid of the north. This latter is slightly less than 2 meters more than the vertical height of the Rhomboidal Pyramid, which means that the Southern would be able to fit into the Northern Pyramid.

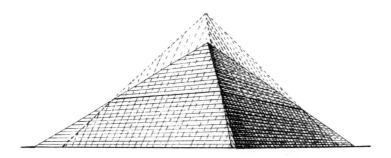

Fig. 67. Diagram of the Northern Pyramid enclosing the Southern

The transcription of these irrational functions into whole numbers by means of the ϕ series suggests the following simple numbers: if $1 = 21$, $1/\phi = 13$, $1/\phi^2 = 8$; thus, $1 + 1/\phi^2 = 29$.

The upper pyramid of the Rhomboidal Pyramid, the plane (base) of which is on a level with point D, will have a half-base of 21 and an apothem of 29. Its height of 20 is defined by the rabatement toward the central axis of the height 29 of the "imagined pyramid" having 21 for a half-base. Now, its vertical section is the Diophantine triangle, 20, 21, 29 (since $20^2 + 21^2 = 29^2$). Furthermore, this Diophantine triangle is generated by the duplication of the ratio 2/5 (figs. 62 and 63).

Finally, the length of the base of the Northern Pyramid, which is 219.27 meters, helps support these hypotheses because the half-base of the pyramid with this Diophantine triangle for its section is 21 and the total base is 42. Now 420 royal cubits = 219.91 meters. The height would then be 200 royal cubits, or 104.7 meters. The vertical height given by Perring is 104.5 meters. So the Northern Pyramid proves metrically the use of the Diophantine triangle transcribed into *numbers of royal cubits*. That these two pyramids are attributed to Snefru allows one to connect both of them to the same fundamental geometric function, one confirming the other: the irrational function ϕ of the origin transcribed into whole numbers.

The Rhomboidal Pyramid has a double character throughout its construction; not only does it have two slopes, but it also has two interior apartments, one at ground level and the other underground. There are two entrance passages, one for each apartment.

One of the entrances opens at the center of the north face around 10.60 meters above ground level. It descends toward the lower apartment at an angle that had apparently originally been 26°10′, but which because of settling is presently 28°38′ on a certain length.

The other passage has its entrance on the west face and descends toward the upper apartment forming an angle of 26°36′ with the horizontal. Now, this angle supports the following hypothesis for which the function ϕ is the starting point of the construction: the angle 1 to 2 is 26°33′55″, and this angle is at the origin of all ϕ construction.[12]

Finally, the underground chamber measures 24.38 meters high and its upper portion is just under ground level, so that it is possible to define the underground depth as being one-fourth of the half-base (around 23.50 m).

If these considerations were to be verified by precise measurements, they would consequently show the application of the harmonic decomposition whose originating model is ϕ, and its concretization through the harmonic proportion developed from the starting point of 1/4 (synthesis 2,

---

[12] Furthermore, the entrance of this passage is 29.76 m above ground, perpendicular to the base. Now, one-fourth of the pyramid's base multiplied by $1/\phi$ yields a height of 29.04 m.

fig. 48), in which this ratio 1/4 (shown underground) determines successively the ratios 2/5, then 4/7, 8/11, and finally 16/19. The duplication of $\widehat{2/5}$ defines the 20, 21, 29 Diophantine triangle corresponding to the vertical half-section of the Northern Pyramid and to that of the small upper Southern Pyramid. The ratio 21 to 29 between the base and the altitude defines the vertical section of the trunk of the lower pyramid in the Southern Pyramid and establishes it as an ideal pyramid. Finally, let us recall that $\widehat{8/11}$ defines the pentagon that results from the function ϕ and that 16/19 ties in with the pharaonic human canon.

In the double Southern Pyramid there is certainly not only the play of doubles, but also the affirmation of a genesis.

Cheops adopted a principle of construction analogous to that demonstrated by Snefru, his father. The vertical section of the Pyramid of Cheops is $\sqrt{\phi}$ high with a half-base of 1 and an apothem of ϕ. Now, to establish this triangle geometrically it is necessary to construct a triangle with ϕ for its altitude and 1 for its base. Then the altitude $\sqrt{\phi}$ is obtained by the rabattement of the altitude ϕ of the original triangle, so that it becomes the hypotenuse of the new triangle having $\sqrt{\phi}$ for its altitude, giving it the same function, if not the same numbers, as that of Snefru.

The Pyramid of Chephren is established on the sacred 3, 4, 5 Diophantine triangle and results from the duplication of $\widehat{1/2} + \widehat{1/2} = (2 + 2)/(4 - 1) = \widehat{4/3}$.

APPENDIX 1: EXCERPTS FROM *THE PYRAMIDS OF SNEFRU* BY ALEXANDRE VARILLE

The southern extremity of the necropolis of Memphis is distinguished by the Dahshur plateau. Lying at the edge of the desert, it supports the brick pyramids of Sesostris III and of Amenemhet II and probably Amenemhet III. These pyramids and their surroundings were explored by J. de Morgan in the course of his justifiably famous excavations.[13] Behind these three brick pyramids, rising in the open desert, are two gigantic stone pyramids, which as yet have been very insufficiently studied.

The most northern one, which is a perfect pyramid,[14] has a base almost as large as the Pyramid of Giza, but is not as high. The name of Snefru has not been found in the pyramid, although no serious excavation has ever taken place there. It has nevertheless been most often attributed to this king, based especially on the presence of an important necropolis of Snefru's courtesans in the neighborhood of the access ramp to the pyramid, and above all on the discovery, at the base of the ramp, of a charter of immunity for Pepi I, which was published by Borchardt, and called the "Burial Site of the Two Pyramids of Snefru.". . .

About 3 kilometers south of this pyramid stands one of the most impressive monuments left by the kings of the Old Kingdom. This is the so-called Rhomboidal Pyramid of Dahshur, the "Blunt Pyramid," which would be better named the "Pyramid of Two Slopes" or the "Double Pyramid."

According to the old measurements of Perring, the lower part rises at an angle of 54°14′ to 44.90 meters in height; at this point the angle changes and becomes 42°59′, the summit being 57.50 meters more. Large areas of the fine limestone facing of the pyramid are still intact. . . .

[13] J. de Morgan, *Fouilles à Dahchour (mars–juin 1895)* (Vienna: Adolphe Holzhausen, 1895); *Fouilles à Dahchour en 1894–1895* (1903).

[14] Lepsius gave this pyramid the number 49 and Perring gave it the number 29. Plan and sections in Perring, *Pyramids*, part 3, plate 14; Vyse, *Operations Carried on at the Pyramids of Gizeh in 1837* (London: J. Fraser 1840–42), part 3, plates facing pages 64 and 65.

So it is a monument that has been scientifically explored very little. The Antiquities Service renewed exploration there in 1946. . . .

The northern corridor descends to about 24 meters, becomes horizontal at this depth, then rises vertically in a kind of vestibule that enters into a chamber that, with the daring grandeur of its architecture, is one of the marvels of Egypt.

The walls of this rectangular chamber are made of beautiful blocks of white limestone; the lower ones are vertical while the upper ones on each of the faces come together gradually to form an arched ceiling. In the southeast corner of the room a passage opens that leads to a well on the axis of the pyramid. This well reaches into the depths of the rock, and above, it rises curiously like a chimney into the mass of the stone monument, crossing two trap doors that have never been lowered and extending up to two slabs at its summit that have never been displaced. . . .

Uncovering the exterior northeast angle of the pyramid revealed to us the existence of a cornerstone on which the ancient quarriers and architects had inscribed in red ink, in addition to the name of the river transport company and reference points for the construction of the edges, the titulary of "Horus Neb-maāt exalted (Shu) in the city of the double *djed.*"[15] The mention of the Horus name of Snefru, in addition to the one we found in the upper apartment in the very heart of the monument, leaves no doubt regarding the identity of the builder of the pyramid. It is the work of the powerful predecessor of Cheops, Snefru.

It is not my purpose to study here the architectural details of the Double Pyramid of Dahshur. I must, however, point out to the specialist several important facts that should be verified. The pyramid was intended from the very beginning of its construction to have two slopes. Everything about it expresses duality: two independent galleries lead to two apartments; in the lower apartment two trap doors open into the chimney of the well sealed with two slabs; and there are two sliding doors in the horizontal part of the high gallery. To these elements it is useful to add those on the exterior of the monument already listed by Jéquier. The pyramid is surrounded by two parallel enclosing walls that are separated by a narrow corridor; the access avenue arrives at a door with two leaves. Not far away there is a door that also has two leaves placed curiously a small distance behind the other, to which we cannot avoid giving a symbolic explanation. Everything is therefore double in this monument, so much so that we can inquire if, in spite of its spelling, the name Snefru might indicate the cabalistic possibility of the Egyptian root *sen,* "two."[16] This possibility appears less surprising if we remember that the famous tomb of the Theban prince Sen-nefer, represented with two hearts, one white and the other red, is composed of two apartments that are clearly distinct and placed successively one under the other. Now we know that the heart is part of the composition of the hieroglyph *nefer.* And moreover we have found on one of the blocks of masonry of the two-sloped pyramid in the proximity of its northeast corner, the newly certified Horus name Djefa-ab, "food of the heart," which could be applied to Snefru. . . .

To attribute many pyramids to the same King Snefru again raises a problem that has already caused much ink to flow: What is the meaning and what is the ultimate purpose of the pyramids? Alexandre Moret, one of the Egyptologists who has made great strides in the philosophical understanding of the problems arising from Ancient Egypt, has replied to these questions: "The pyramid is a work of faith," thus restating the idea of Michelet concerning the cathedral. In reality, we should say, "The pyramid is a work of faith and the expression of a knowledge."

It is sufficient to look, even superficially, at the effort represented by the construction of an edi-

---

[15] The "city of the double *djed* of Snefru" is mentioned in the Wetscar Papyrus 7, 1, and 10.

[16] First of all, we would think of a causative form of the root *nefer.*

fice such as the Double Pyramid of Dahshur to understand the absurdity of considering such a monument the result of a groping around by an architect who was only looking for the simple pyramidal form. This is as stupid as imagining an Imhotep propping up the columns of the gallery of Djoser (at Saqqara) to assure stability. The construction of this pyramid, whose two slopes were foreseen from the placing of the first stone, presented difficulties other than those met in the building of a regular pyramid; and moreover the beds of masonry are not horizontal, but the exact gradient of each bed is different.[17] A thousand details of this kind indicate in the edifice of Snefru the conscious technique of the master builder who conceived and executed it. Would it not then be prudent to reconsider the accepted ideas formulated on the subject of pyramids by our greatest archaeologists, Borchardt and Reisner in particular?

When a Borchardt, after having measured the Pyramid of Cheops with perfect scientific attention to detail, verifies that the directions of the lines of construction are of such astonishing precision that our modern architects could not surpass them, and then concludes that when all is said and done pharaonic science was at that point still in its childhood, that is something to cause astonishment.

The Egyptians have often affirmed that they knew the law of number. We also cannot deny that they jealously kept secret this key of knowledge. Hippolytus said, "Pythagoras learned number and measure from the Egyptians; and being struck by the plausible and difficult to communicate wisdom of the Egyptian priests, in a desire to emulate them, also prescribed the law of silence." It is therefore absolutely not in the texts that we must look for this law of measure, but rather in the monuments themselves.

APPENDIX 2: BABYLONIAN MATHEMATICS

Regarding the study of ancient thought, and more particularly that of the pharaonic people, it is interesting to glance at the Sumerian and Babylonian mathematical procedures so clearly set forth by Thureau-Dangin.[18] The constant communication between Egypt and Babylonia is known, and this makes the difference between their directives of thought more obvious. We find an identity of origin in mathematical procedures between pharaonic Egypt and ancient Sumer. We observe with the Babylonians, the heirs of the Sumerians living in Mesopotamia, the first indication of what we call here a decline in thinking, the "technical" and "geometric" form giving way to the "scholarly" form. This movement proceeded to influence the Asiatic Greeks, and finally, through them became the basis of Greek thought as it has come down to us, dominating the West until modern times.

This area had constant exposure to the theological foundations of the pharaonic empire with its one river, not two, its loyalty to the faith in the Unique, and also its fidelity to the directives of this faith, consistently refusing all "the easy ways" in order to keep thought from falling into a mechanistic mentality.

The large majority of the texts presented by Thureau-Dangin have been dated by the author as being from the Old Babylonian Period. They are estimated to be "contemporaneous with the First Dynasty or a little after";[19] the oldest would not be before the reign of Hammurabi (2500 B.C.). None of the tablets date from the New Babylonian or Persian eras and only two date from the Seleucids. The texts allocated to the Middle Babylonian Period would be from the second third of the second millennium.

---

[17] The beds of stone of the facing are not horizontal but are sloped toward the interior of the building. This gradient is not uniform; the upper part is generally at an angle of 3°30′ and the lower section varies from 6°30′ to 9°. (Note by Varille, from Perring, *Pyramids*.)

[18] Thureau-Dangin, *TMB* [see chapter 6, note 39].

[19] Compare with the Rhind Papyrus, the original of which goes back to the Twelfth Dynasty (ca. 1850 B.C.)

The originality of Babylonian mathematics resides for the most part in its system of numeration. It is a scholarly system of Sumerian origin entirely distinct from the system commonly used by the Babylonians. As a general rule, this system employed a decimal numeration, while using a sexagesimal numeration in mathematics. . . . This was not a pure sexagesimal system but one that used alternate factors of 10 and 6, whence the scale 1, 10, 60, 600, 3600, and so on. The scholarly system extends this scale of fractions, retaining only two signs: Ⲓ the sign of unity, which expresses not only unity itself but also any positive or negative powers of 60, and ⟨, the sign of tens, which expresses a collection of ten. It is thus in the scholarly system that an abstraction is made of the absolute order of the size of the number. When a number is formed of units of different orders, the relative order of size of the units is expressed by its position.[20]

The introduction of the medial zero dates from the Seleucids. It is represented either by an empty space or by a sign of separation.

The sexagesimals of the scholarly system certainly proceed from the Sumerian *gin*. The sixtieth part of the *mine*, the *gin* was employed by the Sumerians to designate the sixtieth part of unity.

In the scholarly system, 1/3 is expressed by 20, 1/4 by 15, etc., which was stated by saying that the reciprocal of 3 is 20, the reciprocal of 4 is 15, etc. The Babylonians borrowed the term they used to express the concept of the "reciprocal" from the Sumerians. (In Akkadian *igi* becomes *igu*, formally stated as *igi*.) In Sumerian *igi* signifies literally "eye," "look," and in the locative "in regard to," "in front of." Probably *igi*, "reciprocal," is a contraction of *igi-gal*, a compound that is given the sense of "reciprocal" and properly signifies "that which is in front of." It seems, therefore, that the reciprocal of a number *n* has been conceived as "the opposite of *n*," the "anti-*n*."

In Sumerian, 1/3 was expressed by *igi-3-gal*, 1/4 by *igi-4-gal*, etc. The Babylonians translate *igi-3-gal* by *salustu*, "the third (part)." "The third (part)" is what remains when we have taken away "the two parts" from the unity. But the Akkadian translation does not at all render the idea expressed by the Sumerian. *Igi-3-gal*, *igi-4-gal* seems to signify more "what is in front," "opposite to 3 and 4," consequently the "inverse of 3 and 4." Of course, this mode of expressing a fraction cannot be considered as a spontaneous creation of the language. Rather it is the result of an already learned reflection.[21]

Inherited from the Sumerians, the notion of the reciprocal occupies a very great place in Babylonian mathematics.

So that the reciprocal of a number may be expressed in a given system of numeration, it is necessary and sufficient that this number has no first factor other than that of the base number of the system. In this regard, the sexagesimal system is eminently privileged relative to the decimal system.

The operation that we call division offered to the Babylonian mathematician many occasions for using reciprocals. Let *n* be the divisor. If the reciprocal of *n* could be expressed in the sexagesimal system, if, following the Babylonian expression, "it could be untied," the division resolved itself into a multiplication of the dividend by the reciprocal of the divisor. It was done in two steps, of which the first was the conversion of $1/n$ into a sexagesimal expression. For this operation the scribes had different types of tables at their disposal.

The notion of the reciprocal was so familiar to the Babylonian mathematicians that it was easy for them to complicate a simple operation with a double inversion. Thus, in problems 35 and 38, the

---

[20] Thureau-Dangin, *TMB*, pp. ix–x.

[21] Cf. chapter 6, the discussion "Division" in the section "Fractions."

scribe, having to obtain the square of 12, *unties* the reciprocal of 12, that is 5'. The square thus obtained being 25″, he then *unties* "the reciprocal of 25″," which gives him 2'24, the square he was looking for.[22]

Each of these two reciprocals had a name. One was called in Sumerian *igi* (from which comes the Akkadian *igu*), the other was called in Sumerian *igi-bi*, "its reciprocal" (from which comes the Akkadian *igibu*).[23]

These two terms are applied, for example, in problems 29 to 34 of the tablets from the Old Babylonian Period, which consist of searching for the three sides—the flank, the front, and the depth—of a cave while knowing its volume and knowing that the side is equal to *igu* and the front to *igibu*. For example, if the *igi* has the value of 3/2 the *igibu* will have the value of 2/3. It is obvious by its very definition that the surface, which is the product of the *igu* multiplied by the *igibu*, will have the value 1. Therefore, the only unknown is the depth. As we have seen, the reciprocal of the number n can be transcribed as $1/n$, which is comparable to pharaonic enumeration.

If it were a question of the fraction m/n, the Babylonian mathematicians seem to have expressed it by means of the formula "m times the reciprocal of n," conforming apparently to a Sumerian tradition. . . .

The Babylonians, as we shall see, knew exactly how to calculate certain surfaces and certain volumes, particularly those of the pyramid and of the trunks of pyramids with square bases. The theorem attributed to Pythagoras was familiar to them.

They had no term to express the notion of angle. The inclination of a wall or of an embankment was never defined by the angle that this wall or embankment made with the horizontal plane. It was said the *ukullu* or "slope" is of so many cubits (of height).[24] The relation envisaged is exactly the inverse of what we express by saying that a slope is of so many centimeters by meters, or of a particular percent. The slope, if it is of an embankment, is 1 cubit to 1 cubit, which corresponds to an inclination of 45°. If it is a wall of unbaked bricks, it is 50″ (of *ninda*), or 5 digits per cubit. If it is a wall of baked bricks, it is 12″30‴ (of *ninda*), or $1\frac{1}{4}$ digits per cubit.

The Babylonians were satisfied with a rough approximation of the relation of the circumference to the diameter ($\pi = 3$). As Neugebauer and Waschow have shown, they knew the "Heronian" formula of approximating irrational square roots: $a + r/2a$ (see problems 158 and 232).

They conceived all planar figures to be on a vertical plane. Our terminology reflects an analogous way of seeing because we speak, for example, of the "base" and the "altitude" of a triangle or of a trapezoid. The Babylonians represented the triangle and the trapezoid in an inverted position from what we customarily use. This explains why the triangle is designated by the term "head of a nail" and the trapezoid by the expression "forehead of an ox.". . .

The Babylonians termed the perpendicular as "descending" and conceived of it only in the etymological sense of the term (direction of the plumb line).[25]

---

[22] The convention adopted by the author for transcribing the sexagesimal system into our mode of numeration uses degrees, minutes, and seconds to designate the unity, 60, and its fractions, and the sign ' for their multiples. Thus: unity = 60, transcribed as 1° or 1; 1/4 = 15, transcribed as 15'; 1/12 = 5, transcribed as 5'; 1/3600 = 1/60 of a minute is written 1″; 1/144 = 1/4 + 1/6 of a minute, thus 25″. The square of 12 equals 144 (or twice 60 = 120) + 24 = 2'24, etc.

[23] Thureau-Dangin, *TMB*, pp. x–xii.

[24] Cf. above, "Fundamentals of the Trigonometry."

[25] Thureau-Dangin, *TMB*, pp. xiii, xvii.

Concerning the Rhind Papyrus, let us note in this regard a discussion of the word designating the altitude of a triangle. The calculation of triangular surfaces "will be done correctly," but only one point remains obscure, the Egyptian word that defines the altitude, because the word *mryt* that should designate the altitude can be interpreted as "side" according to one of its meanings as the "banks" of a river (the Nile). In this case the multiplication of the half-base of a triangle by its "side" would apply only to the right triangle. But the drawing that accompanies problem 51 of the Rhind Papyrus clearly shows an isosceles triangle, which is called "the pointed."

In his presentation, Peet honestly leaves the choice open between height and side, but Erman and Ranke prefer to deny that the Egyptians had the capacity for calculating the surface of a triangle(!), and adopt "side" for the meaning of *mryt*.[26] A little reflection and knowledge of the pharaonic way of thinking will easily remove any doubt. This word has a direct link with *mry*, which signifies "to love," and "magnet," that which attracts. Now the banks of the river "attract" by reversal of the current. With this word, therefore, it is really a question of the meaning of "that which is attracted," as it is also with the plumb line, the vertical.

> Everything indicates that in geometry Babylonian science never went beyond everyday practice. It was in another direction that the Babylonians exercised their mathematical speculation. The incomparable instrument of calculation used by the Babylonian mathematicians was of a nature particularly conducive to a path that leads to the algebraic method. The expression of number in this scholarly system attained a degree of simplicity, homogeneity, and abstraction that has never been surpassed. With a system of numeration of such suppleness, the scribes of Sumer and Akkad were remarkably prepared in the art of solving numerical problems and for the "logistics" that led them to algebra.
>
> Before tackling the Babylonian algebraic problems, a preliminary remark is necessary. Babylonian mathematics ignores the use of symbols. So in order to state, for example, that such a size equals so much, the scribes made use of a nominal proposition: "such a size (is) so much," where, in accordance with the established custom of the Akkadian language, the copula is not expressed. . . .[27]
>
> The preceding is sufficient to show that the Babylonians did not have any way of writing what we would call a "formula."[28]

Thureau-Dangin did not emphasize the geometric origin of these calculations, and found instead an algebraic mentality, even without the use of symbols that would permit the "formula."

Now this statement proves that the geometric mentality had influenced their thought, but the scholarly form, which the sexagesimal system represents, invites "intellectualizing," which moves away from geometric representation (by considering 60 to be unity, this system is incomparably perfect because 60 is divisible by 1, 2, 3, 4, 5, 6, and 10). Our mathematicians see progress in this, but we see here the beginning of the descent toward our own intellectual mathematics, and a loss of the theological base that relates calculation to a cosmic conception.

The geometric origin connects Babylonian mathematics to pharaonic mathematics. It is no longer a question of looking for the origins of this knowledge in one people or the other; the geo-

---

[26] A. Erman and H. Ranke, *La Civilisation égyptienne* (Paris: Payot, 1952), p. 480.

[27] The same form of expression as in Egypt.

[28] Thureau-Dangin, *TMB*, pp. xvii–xix.

metric foundation connects both to the same theological source, which had been preserved in Egypt, whereas in Babylonia the mentality deviated.

This indisputable fact is perhaps at the root of the symbol of the Tower of Babel, which represents the moment when intellectual pride disturbed understanding by the use of a multiplicity of languages to express the unity of directive given by the mystical source. Opinions diverged since the rule of knowledge no longer existed. This is definitely confirmed by the dialectical mentality of the Eleatic Greeks.

———

Here, now, are some examples of problems, presented in the following three ways: (1) problems such as they are transcribed by Thureau-Dangin in degrees, minutes, and seconds in the sexagesimal system; (2) problems such as they would appear to our algebraists, that is, with their statement and their resolution expressed in our present form, summarized in formulas; (3) some examples of these problems retranscribed into whole numbers and fractions using our usual decimal system to render them more accessible, and with their geometric solution as suggested by the statement and the implied method.

We look in Babylonian mathematics for a demonstration of the knowledge applied, but not explained, in pharaonic mathematics, especially in the Rhind Papyrus. We transcribe it into geometry, which in itself is not a novelty, but the relationships that we make in doing so, plus the application of the principle of trigonometric notation by $1 : n$, allow us to approach the motive of the mentality of the Ancients, which is our essential goal.

The First Four Problems As Translated by Thureau-Dangin (Old Babylonian Period, tablet BM 13901)

Problem 1

"I have added the surface and the side of my square: 45′.

"You shall put 1, the unity. You shall divide into two, 1 : (30′). You shall cross (30′) and 30′ : 15′. You shall add 15′ to 45′ : 1. This is the square of 1. You shall subtract 30′, which you have crossed, from 1 : 30′, the side of the square."

Problem 2

"I have subtracted from the surface the side of my square: 14'30.

"You shall put 1, the unity. You shall divide into two, 1 : (30′). You shall cross 30′ and 30′ : 15′. You shall add to 14'30 : 14'30°15′. This is the square of 29°30′. You shall add 30′, which you have crossed, to 29°30′ : 30, the side of the square."

Problem 5

"I have added the surface and the side of my square and the third of the side of my square: 55′.

"You shall put 1, the unity. You shall add the third of 1, the unity, thus 20′ to 1 : 1°20′. You shall cross 40′, its half, and 40′ : 26′40″. You shall add to 55′ : 1°21′40″. This is the square of 1°10′. You will subtract 40′, which you have crossed, from 1°10′ : 30′, the side of the square."

Problem 7

"I have added seven times the side of my square and eleven times the surface: 6°15′.

"You shall write 7 and 11. You shall carry 11 to 6°15′: 1'8°45′. You shall divide into two, 7 : (3°30′). You shall cross 3°30′ and 3°30′ : 12°15′. You shall add to 1'8°45′ : 1'21. This is the square of 9. You shall subtract 3°30′, that you have crossed, from 9: you shall inscribe 5°30′. The reciprocal of 11 cannot be untied. What must I put to 11, which gives me 5°30′? 30′, its quotient. The side of the square is 30′."[29]

The Four Preceding Problems As They Appear to Our Algebraists

Tablet BM 13901 gives twenty-four problems among which the first seven correspond exactly to what we define today by an equation of the second degree of x, and which reduce to the general form, $ax^2 + bx = c$.

Here is a brief summary of the four problems as transcribed using the modern algebraic form:

Problem 1

"I have added the surface and the side of my square $= c$."

$$x^2 + x = c \quad \text{solution: } x = \sqrt{\left(\frac{1}{2}\right)^2 + c} - \frac{1}{2}.$$

Problem 2

"I have subtracted from the surface the side of my square $= c$."

$$x^2 - x = c \quad \text{solution: } x = \sqrt{\left(\frac{1}{2}\right)^2 + c} + \frac{1}{2}.$$

Problem 5

"I have added the surface to the side of my square and the third of the side of my square $= c$."

$$x^2 + bx = c \quad \text{solution: } x = \sqrt{\left(\frac{b}{2}\right)^2 + c} - \frac{b}{2}.$$

Problem 7

"I have added seven times the side of my square and eleven times the surface $= c$."

$$ax^2 + bx = c \quad \text{solution: } x = \frac{\sqrt{\left(\frac{b}{2}\right)^2 + ac} - \frac{b}{2}}{a}.$$

[29] Thureau-Dangin, *TMB*, pp. 1–3. In these problems, Thureau-Dangin uses the colon in place of our equals sign.

The Same Problems Retranscribed into Whole Numbers and Fractions with Their Geometric Solutions

Problem 1

"I have added the surface and the side of my square = 3/4.

You shall put 1, the unity.

You shall divide 1 into two = 1/2.

You shall cross 1/2 and 1/2 = 1/4.

You shall add 1/4 to 3/4 = 1.

This is the square of 1.

You shall subtract 1/2, which you have crossed, from 1 = 1/2, the side of the square."

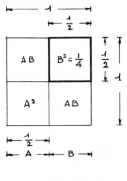

Fig. 68

The solution of this problem corresponds to our algebraic formula $(a + b)^2 = a^2 + 2ab + b^2$, in which a is the side of the square we are looking for, and b *always* has the value of half of the unity (and not of a), whatever may be the side of the square, because $2ab =$ one side. The given sum of "square plus its side" is therefore equal to $a^2 + 2ab$ and it is missing b^2, which the scribe adds, being $(1/2)^2 = 1/4$ in order to complete the square from which he extracts the root. Next he *subtracts* the 1/2 that "he has crossed" and finds side a of the square he is looking for.

Problem 2 is based on applying the inverse of the formula in the preceding problem, and consequently, it completes problem 1: $(a - b)^2 = a^2 - 2ab + b^2$.

The scribe begins by adding the square of 1/2, which is 1/4, and then takes the root of the square thus obtained and *adds* the 1/2 that "he has crossed" in order to obtain the side a of the square he seeks.

The statements and the solutions of these problems nevertheless suggest a different form of thought than ours: when the scribe writes at the beginning, "I have added the surface, and the side of my square = n," is he thinking of a linear side and a squared surface, which, added together, have a surface for their sum? For him n is a surface since he immediately completes it by adding the missing square b^2, finally obtaining the perfect square.

If the problem posed the addition of a surface, considered square, with its side a line, it would represent a mental and scholarly calculation that is not consistent with the spirit of the Ancients, because it would not correspond to their mentality, which remains technical. At least, this is the way these things present themselves to us.

Let us remember that the first fact of creation can only be space, which, increasing in density, becomes measurable in time and space, in other words, in volume. Now, the pharaonic mathematician, like the Babylonian, cannot, in these conditions, consider anything that is not volume, and it is in this way that we must understand the spirit of the problem: the side for him is not a line, that is, the side of a planar surface, but rather the side of a volume the surface of which is a section.

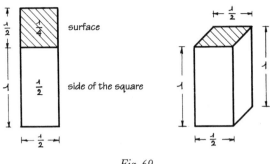

Fig. 69

For example, the height of the volume equals 1. Its horizontal section has 1/2 as its side and 1/4 as its surface. The "side of the square" is therefore represented by one of the vertical faces.

If we regard the problem posed as referring to a volume, and if we add to the given surface the side of this volume (accepting the value 1 for the height), we obtain in the plane half the gnomon that increases this surface, but it will always fall short of being a complete gnomon by a small square, that is, b^2 in the formula $a^2 + 2ab + b^2$ (fig. 70).

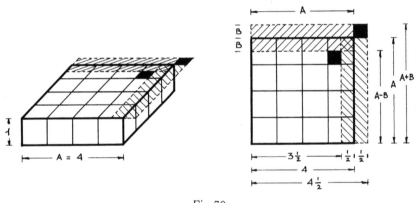

Fig. 70

For example, *the square plus its side* = 20, the given number.

$$\sqrt{20\frac{1}{4}} = 4\frac{1}{2}; \quad \text{thus the side } A = 4\frac{1}{2} - \frac{1}{2} = 4.$$

The square minus its side = 12, the given number.

$$\sqrt{12\frac{1}{4}} = 3\frac{1}{2}; \quad \text{thus the side } A = 3\frac{1}{2} + \frac{1}{2} = 4.$$

In order to clarify what we have just said and to help open the door to the mentality of the Ancients, let us take for an example the term *crossing* that is understood as a multiplication as well as, moreover, what is imposed when abstract numbers define a plane. We see that the "function" of crossing, as for example 5 × 5 represented by Γ, evokes the pharaonic sign Γ, which is used in the Berlin Papyrus to designate the "root of a square" and depicts the two sides (gnomon) that determine the square.

This crossing of the two elements of the gnomon[30] is always formed so that one square unit of the rectangle is always covered by another unit. Thus when drawing a square with a side of 7, we read in the plane a surface area of 49 that, in reality, carries two small square units through the b^2, and for the ancient mathematician this surface suggests 50.

Let us take a surface of side 7. If we suppose it to be a volume, thus an outside surface with side 7 and height 1, we can call this height "the side." It will be composed of seven unit squares, and the volume will be defined by "two sides," thus equaling $2 \times 7 = 14$. If, on the other hand, we wish to add one unit to the side with the value 7 of the square of 49, this will form a gnomon of *two sides* minus one unit, being two sides in which two units overlap each other, and we calculate not $2 \times 8 = 16$, but $(2 \times 7) + 1 = 15$, or $(2 \times 8) - 1 = 15$.

Thus, we have in the statement of the problem a possible play among the numbers 14, 15, and 16. The play of differences that we find in pharaonic as well as in Babylonian calculation is based on the ratios between these values. This implies a completely different mentality at the basis of the calculations founded on geometry, which we find in both the Rhind Papyrus and the Babylonian tablets.

To clarify further, when we speak of "crossing" and imply multiplication, we obtain, for example, $5 \times 5 = 25$, but "crossing" means "hiding" one of the units. So, when we cross in whole numbers, we define by the two rows at right angles to each other the square 25 (a surface that can also be represented by five rows with five square units each, thus by addition). But when we cross a fraction with another fraction, the hidden unit is the surface we are looking for, for example, $(1/3) \times (1/3) = 1/9$. The squared surface 1/9 will not represent any value in itself if it is not defined by its ratio with the unity represented by "the side of the square" of which we take 1/3, being the rectangle measured as $1/3 : 1$ (fig. 71).

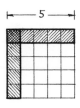 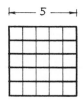 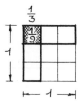

Fig. 71

Now, one of the characteristics of problems 48 to 55 of the Rhind Papyrus is that different units of linear and surface measure are used; the dimensions are given (when it is a question of areas) in measures of length, *khet,* then, during the calculation, we see that groups of square units of $1 : 1$ and of rectangular units of $1 : 10$ are used. Problem 48, for example, establishes the surface of a disk of diameter 9 inscribed in a square of side 9 and applies the classical formula: the surface of the square equals 81 and the surface of the disk equals 64. The problem has the following characteristics:

First, instead of multiplying eight units of length by 8, the scribe multiplies eight *square units* by 8. "To our modern feeling this is wrong. The 8 in question is, strictly speaking, one in units of long measure, viz. *khet,* and it is not until we multiply it by another unit of long measure, viz. 8 *khet,* that it can logically be expressed in square units."[31] But to the ancient way of feeling, it is surely 8 square units that are geometrically put eight times to obtain 64 square units, as a drawing can easily demonstrate. Moreover, Peet himself eventually arrived at this same conclusion.

---

[30] The gnomon is itself a surface made up of two rows of square units.

[31] Peet, *RMP,* p. 89.

Second, the result will not then be 64 square units but "6, and 4 square units." It is a matter of rows of 1 : 10 of which one takes 6 to make a rectangle with a surface of 60; it lacks 4 square units that one adds to this rectangle. It is a question therefore, of transforming a perfect square into a rectangle of the same surface.

Third, this way of seeing is confirmed in problem 50 of the Rhind Papyrus where, after having established the square of $8 \times 8 = 64$ in numbers, the scribe writes: "Its surface in area is 60 and 4 square units." He must have understood that the whole is calculated in square units.

In problem 51 the scribe operates on a triangle and, to obtain its surface, he says "to establish its rectangle," after having taken the half-base to multiply it by the height. He calculates in *khet* (units 100 cubits long), then in cubits, and finally transforms the obtained surface into rows of 1 : 10 *khet* to a side.

———∿∿∿———

Let us look at the following problems from the Babylonian tablets in this spirit.

Problem 5

"I have added the surface and the side of my square and the third of the side of my square $= 11/12$.[32]

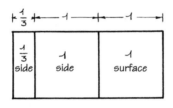 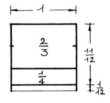

Fig. 72a

You shall put 1, the unity. You shall add the third of 1, the unity, being 1/3, to $1 = 1 + 1/3$. You shall cross 2/3, its half, and $2/3 = 4/9$.

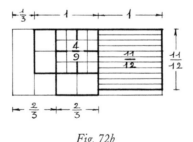

Fig. 72b

You shall add to $11/12 = 49/36$; this is the square of 7/6, or of $1 + 1/6$.

[32] Compare these fractional expressions with the sexagesimal Babylonian transcription by degrees, minutes, and seconds, above, p. 212, where, for example, 11/12 is written 55′.

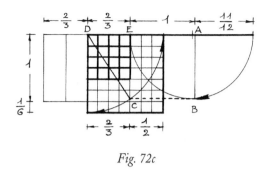

Fig. 72c

You shall subtract 2/3, which you have crossed, from 1 + 1/6 = 1/2, the side of the square."

Figure 72a represents the statement of the problem, namely, the surface, the side, and one-third of the side whose sum is equal to a rectangle composed either of 2/3 + 1/4, or of eleven rows, each with the value of 1/12.

In figure 72b we put 1, the unity, plus its third, and we divide it into two rows each having the height 1 for a width of 2/3. We "cross" them, and the covered (overlapped) surface is 4/9, their square. It is a question now of adding the square 4/9 to the rectangle 11/12. This is only possible if the rectangle 11/12 itself becomes a square, and one geometric gesture accomplishes this transformation, making all calculation unnecessary.

Figure 72c takes for a radius half of 1 + 11/12, which is 23/24, and draws a semicircle that takes 23/24 as its center on the straight line *EA*. The line *AB* is the geometric mean between 1 and 11/12, thus it is the side of the square having a surface value of 11/12. This height is carried over to *EC*. The triangle *DEC* has the roots of 4/9 and 11/12 for its sides. Its diagonal *DC* is therefore the root of the sum of their squares, that is,

$$\sqrt{\frac{4}{9} + \frac{11}{12}} = \sqrt{\frac{16+33}{36}} = \sqrt{\frac{49}{36}} = \frac{7}{6}, \text{ or } 1 + \frac{1}{6}.$$

The surface 11/12, or 33/36, has become the gnomon that is added to the square 16/36 to form the "false square" from which we can extract the root, and it only remains to eliminate the numbers that have served as intermediaries; the crossed 2/3 being subtracted leaves 1/2, the side of the sought-for square, which then has a surface value of 1/4 (fig. 73).

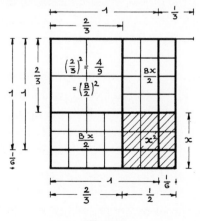

Fig. 73

Problem 7

"I have added seven times the side of my square and eleven times the surface $= 6\frac{1}{4}$.

You shall inscribe 7 and 11.

You shall carry 11 to $6\frac{1}{4} = 68\frac{3}{4}$.

You shall divide 7 into two $= 3\frac{1}{2}$.

You shall cross $3\frac{1}{2}$ and $3\frac{1}{2} = 12\frac{1}{4}$.

You shall add to $68\frac{3}{4} = 81$. This is the square of 9.

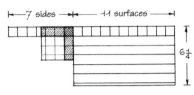

Fig. 74a

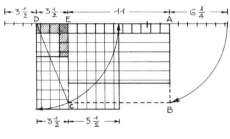

Fig. 74b

"You shall subtract $3\frac{1}{2}$, which you have crossed, from 9, you shall inscribe $5\frac{1}{2}$. The reciprocal of 11 cannot be untied. What must I put to 11 that will give me $5\frac{1}{2}$? It is 1/2 its quotient; the side of my square is 1/2."

In figure 74a, inscribe the seven sides and the eleven surfaces, giving each a surface value of 1. Carry 11 to $6\frac{1}{4}$, meaning multiplication, thus establishing the rectangle whose surface value is $68\frac{3}{4}$. Divide 7 into two and cross; this signifies the establishment of the square of $3\frac{1}{2}$, which is $12\frac{1}{4}$ in surface. Adding these two surfaces gives a square number whose side is 9, which is done in two steps.

In figure 74b, first transform the rectangle with a surface of $68\frac{3}{4}$ into a square that can be added to the square of $12\frac{1}{4}$. This square then becomes the gnomon. There is no need to look for the root of $68\frac{3}{4}$ by calculation; it is enough to draw the semicircle taking $(11 + 6\frac{1}{4})/2$ for the radius. The height AB will be the geometric mean between 11 and $6\frac{1}{4}$ and will give the side of the square with $68\frac{3}{4}$ for its surface.

Second, this height AB is carried over to form EC, which constitutes the triangle DEC. The diagonal DC of this triangle is necessarily the root of the sum of the two added squares, $68\frac{3}{4} + 12\frac{1}{4}$, or the root of 81, which equals 9.

The final calculation of the scribe eliminates the intermediaries that helped him to construct his square. Thus, he subtracts the "$3\frac{1}{2}$, which you have crossed," from 9. Then he divides the remainder, that is, $5\frac{1}{2}$, by 11 and the result is 1/2 or the side of the square he has been looking for.

The scribe does not give a proof because he is certain of his result. Indeed, if the side of the square he seeks is 1/2, then seven sides equals $3\frac{1}{2}$, eleven surfaces equals $2\frac{3}{4}$, and their sum equals $6\frac{1}{4}$.

———∾∾∾———

In tablet BM 13901 the first seven problems apply the theory of the gnomon, so they are conceived and resolved geometrically; the Ancients remained faithful throughout to this method that we have transposed into algebraic formulas, which has caused us to lose the original geometric vision. The following two problems, numbers 8 and 9, are based on the difference or sum of two unequal numbers, which are the unknowns.

These first eleven problems are most often grouped two by two, in this way giving a statement and its "inverse."

Problem 12 brings together all we have learned in the preceding problems and is therefore particularly interesting. It combines the theory of gnomons with the Pythagorean theorem and the possibilities of similar right triangles, determined by dropping a perpendicular onto the hypotenuse, which then becomes a diameter.[33]

Geometric Solution of the Problems, Transcribed into Our Present Form[34]

Problem 8

> "I have added the surface of my two squares: 1300.
> I have added the sides of my squares = 50.
> You shall divide 1300 into two, you shall inscribe 650.
> You shall divide 50 into two = 25. You shall cross 25 and 25 = 625.
> You shall subtract from 650 = 25. This is the square of 5.
> You shall add 5 to the first 25 = 30, the side of the first square.
> You shall subtract 5 from the second 25 = 20, the side of the second square."

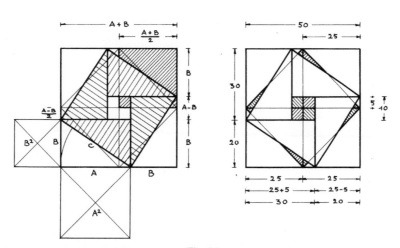

Fig. 75

1. By adding two squares together, the statement of the problem evokes the Pythagorean theorem, $A^2 + B^2 = C^2$, in which C is the hypotenuse of the triangle ABC; its square equals 1300.

2. The addition of sides A and B of the two squares A^2 and B^2 allows the larger square to be established with 50 for its side, which is $(A + B)^2$.

3. We divide the square C^2 in two. Now this square is formed of *two rectangles AB plus a small square with A − B for its side* (fig. 75). Its half has the value then of

$$\frac{C^2}{2} = AB + \frac{1}{2}(A - B)^2 = 650.$$

4. Divide the length $A + B$ in two and make the square. The square of $A + B$ is equal to *four*

---

[33] Cf. above, "Functional Development of the Law of Right Triangles."

[34] For the statement of problems 8, 9, 10, 11, and 12, cf. Thureau-Dangin, *TMB*, pp. 3–6.

rectangles AB plus the square of the difference between *A* and *B*. The fourth of this square, or $[(A+B)/2]^2$ is the value therefore of *rectangle AB plus one-fourth of the square of the difference*. We write this as:

$$\left(\frac{A+B}{2}\right)^2 = AB + \frac{1}{4}(A-B)^2 = 625.$$

5. Subtract the square thus obtained from $C^2/2$. The difference between the two products is exactly $\frac{1}{4}(A-B)^2$, which is the square of the half-difference. Also, we take the root, which is $\sqrt{650-625}$, or $\sqrt{25}$, which equals 5.

6. The side 5 is equal to the half-difference between *A* and *B*. Therefore, the scribe adds $(A+B)/2$ to it, or $25+5$, which equals 30, and deducts it from "the other 25," obtaining 20. These are the two sides, *A* and *B*.

Problem 9 is based on exactly the same principle, but in reverse. Problem 8 gives the sum and problem 9 the difference between *A* and *B*. The surface is the same, 1300. The difference between the sides is 10.

Problem 9

He scribe takes half of $1300 = 650$.

He takes half of 10 and makes the square $= 25$.

He subtracts 25 from 650 and finds 625, the square of 25.

He puts 25 two times, then he adds $5 = 30$, for the side of the first square. He subtracts 5 from the other $25 = 20$, which is the side of the second square.

The method used in these two problems is very important because it demonstrates the knowledge and application of "pivoting squares," one of the essential foundations for calculating angles that are notated $1:n$.[35]

Thus, the work executed in these two problems uniquely rests upon the difference and the sum of two unequal lengths, *A* and *B*. Recalling in this respect that the difference between a 45° angle, or $\widehat{1/1}$, and any other angle determined by a ratio $B:A$ will always be $\widehat{1/1} - \widehat{B/A} = (A-B)/(A+B)$, an angle directly readable in the "turning square" (fig. 75), being $\widehat{1/1} - \widehat{20/30} = (30-20)/(30+20) = \widehat{10/50}$, which is the angle of the diagonal of square *C* in relation to the horizontal of $A+B$.[36]

These problems therefore have the aim of teaching a method.

Problem 10

"I have added the surfaces of my two squares: $21\frac{1}{4}$.

The side of one is less than the side of the other by one-seventh.

"You shall inscribe 7 and 6. You shall cross 7 and $7 = 49$. You shall cross 6 and $6 = 36$. You shall add 36 and $49 = 85$. The reciprocal of 85 cannot be untied. What must I put to 85 that will give me $21\frac{1}{4}$? Answer, 1/4. This is the square of 1/2. You shall carry 1/2 to $7 = 3\frac{1}{2}$, the side of the first square. You shall carry 1/2 to $6 = 3$, the side of the second square."

---

[35] Cf. above, "Addition and Subtraction of Angles in Proportional Notation," and fig. 63.

[36] Cf. above, "Functional Development of the Law of Right Triangles."

The solution of this problem is simple and self-explanatory; it is based on the theorem $A^2 + B^2 = C^2$. If we state it $x^2 + y^2 = C$ and $y = 6/7$, the operations can be summarized as follows. First, the scribe considers 7, the denominator, equal to seven units (a procedure comparable to the method in problem 25 of the Rhind Papyrus), and consequently, 6/7 has the value of six units. Second, he finds the sum of their squares and divides this sum by the given sum C. The root of the resulting coefficient is the number by which it is necessary to divide 6 and 7 to find the sides.

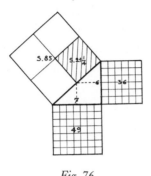

Fig. 76

Problem 11 is similar to the preceding problem but with a nuance. The value x is $y + y/7$, the ratio is thus 7 to 8. The scribe proceeds exactly as in the preceding problem.

Problem 12

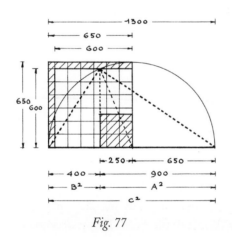

Fig. 77

"I have added the surface of my two squares = 1300.

I have crossed the sides of my two squares = 600. You shall divide into two 1300 = 650. You shall cross 650 and 650 = 422,500. You shall cross 600 and 600 = 360,000. You shall subtract 360,000 from 422,500 = 62,500. This is the square of 250. You shall add 250 to the first 650 = 900. This is the square of 30, the side of the first square is 30. You shall subtract 250 from the second 650 = 400, this is the square of 20. The side of the second square is 20."

1. The solution of this problem lies in the application of what has been called the functional law of right triangles.[37] If the perpendicular is dropped onto the hypotenuse, considered as a diameter, from the apex opposite this diameter, the height is the geometric mean between the two segments that are determined on this diameter; thus the square of this height plus the square of the difference between the half-diameter and each segment is equal to the square of the half-diameter.

The scribe operates with knowledge of this fact so that he draws a geometric diagram following these directions, and in this way demonstrates that the geometric function guides his thinking.

2. He finds the squares of numbers that are themselves already square and rectangular surfaces. This suggests that the hypotenuse is the sum of two squares, A^2 and B^2, and in this case the height is in fact the rectangular number AB.

---

[37] Cf. ibid.

3. The figure suggested by the scribe's singular method of working contains all the elements of the addition of two angles, notated as $1/n$ (fig. 77): the two sides being sought are 20 and 30; the square of 20 is 400 or B^2; the square of 30 is 900 or A^2; the sum of the two squares is 1300, the whole hypotenuse; the product of 20×30 is 600, the altitude of the triangle.

The angular ratio is defined by $600/900 = 400/600 = 20/30$, and the double of $\widehat{20/30}$ is equal to $\widehat{20/30} + \widehat{20/30} = (600 + 600)/(900 - 400) = 1200/500$ for the hypotenuse $900 + 400 = 1300$. This is the angle at the center defined by half of these numbers, 600 and 250, for the radius of 650.

The Diophantine triangle thus formed is a 5, 12, 13 triangle resulting from the duplication of 2/3. The square with the shorter side of 5 (or 250) is equal in surface to the gnomon determined by the difference between the radius or the hypotenuse 13 (or 650) and the altitude of the triangle 12 (or 600).

———～～～———

Tablet BM 34568, dating from the time of the Seleucids, gives a series of problems that relate to Diophantine triangles.[38]

Problem 118[39]

"The side is 4, the front 3. What is the diagonal?

"Considering that you do not know it, you shall add the half of your side to your front: this is the diagonal. You shall multiply 4, the side, by $30'[1/2] = 2$. You shall add 2 to $3 = 5$. The diagonal is 5. Or you may add the third of your front to your side; this is the diagonal. You shall multiply 3, the front, by $20'[1/3] = 1$. You shall add 1 to $4 = 5$. The diagonal is 5."

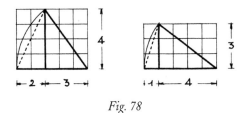

Fig. 78

The scribe operates in an irregular fashion, which requires that he know the principle of the angles referred to in $1 : n$. He takes half of 4, the side, and adds it to 3, the front. This process determines the angle $1 : 2$ (fig. 78). Indeed, if we add $\widehat{1/2} + \widehat{1/2} = (2 + 2)/(4 - 1)$ this equals $\widehat{4/3}$, and the diagonal equals $4 + 1$, which equals 5.

Or again, he takes the third of 3, the front, and adds it to 4, the side, which consists of adding the angles $\widehat{1/3} + \widehat{1/3} = (3 + 3)/(9 - 1) = \widehat{6/8}$, which is simplified to 3/4, or 3 divided by 4, and the diagonal is $(9 + 1)/2$, which equals 5.

[38] In the statement of this problem, we have put the fractional equivalent in brackets.

[39] This problem is the first of the tablet BM 34568. Cf. Thureau-Dangin, *TMB*, p. 57. Problems 119 and 120, which we treat next, are numbers 2 and 3 of this same tablet.

Problem 119[40]

> "The side is 4 and the diagonal 5. What is the front? Considering that you do not know, 4 times 4 : 16; 5 times 5 : 25. You shall subtract 16 from 25 : leaving 9. What by what must I multiply in order that there be 9? Three times 3 : 9. The front is 3."

Here the method is standard and we can recognize the application of the Pythagorean theorem. There is, therefore, an intention on the part of the scribe to oppose this method to that using the angles $1 : n$.

Problem 120[41]

> "I have added the diagonal and the side = 9. The front is 3. What are the side and the diagonal?
>
> "Considering that you do not know it, 9 times 9 = 81 and 3 times 3 = 9. You shall subtract 9 from 81, leaving 72. You shall multiply 72 by 1/2 = 36. By what must I multiply 9 to have 36? You shall multiply 9 by 4 = 36. The side is 4. You shall subtract 4 from 9, leaving 5. The diagonal is 5."

The statement of the problem—the addition of the diagonal to the side of a triangle—corresponds to the division of an angle into two.[42] In order to recover the original triangle, it is necessary to multiply this angle or this "ratio" by 2.[43]

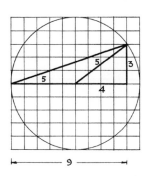
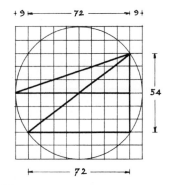

Fig. 79

The front is 3. The diagonal plus the side equals 9. We find the square of 3, which we subtract from the square of 9, which goes back to the operation described for the addition of two equal angles:

$$\frac{\hat{3}}{9}+\frac{\hat{3}}{9}=\frac{2(3\times 9)}{9^2-3^2}=\frac{\text{the known front}}{\text{the side to be found}}=\frac{54}{72}.$$

The series of operations is clear. The result, 72, must be divided by 2, then by 9, in order to find the side, as the number 54 must be in order to find 3, the front.

---

[40] This problem is as it appears in Thureau-Dangin, *TMB*, where the colon replaces the equals sign.

[41] For the original statement of this problem in the sexagesimal form see Thureau-Dangin, *TMB*, p. 582

[42] Later attributed to Hipparchus.

[43] Cf. above, "Addition and Subtraction of Angles in Proportional Notation," and fig. 62.

Tablet Dating from the Old Babylonian Period[44]

Problem 168

"Ten brothers, 1 mina, and 2/3 mina of silver.[45] One brother is raised above the other. What amount he is raised above I do not know. The eighth part is 6 shekels. How much is one brother raised above the other?

"In working it out you determine the reciprocal of 10, the number of men; that gives you 6'. You shall carry 6' to 1 mina and 2/3 mina of silver; this shall give you 10'. Double 10', this shall give you 20'. Double 6', the part of the eighth, this shall give you 12'. Subtract 12' from 20', this shall give you 8'. Let your head remember 8'. Adding 1 (above) and 1 (below),[46] this shall give you 2. Double 2, this shall give you 4. You shall add 1 to 4; this shall give you 5. Subtract 5 from 10, the men; this shall give you 5. Determine the reciprocal of 5, this shall give you 12'.[47] Carry 12' to 8'; this shall give you 1'36". It is this by which one brother is raised above the other."

This problem is presented as an arithmetic progression in which one is given the sum, the number of terms, and part of the eighth term, these being designated by naming the first brother as the largest term. The unknowns are then the rate and the first term. We can verify the simplicity of the Babylonian procedure by means of the following diagram.

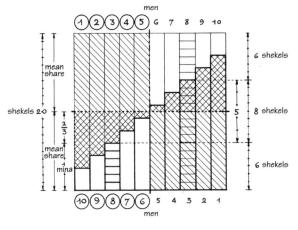

Fig. 80

The number of terms is 10 brothers.
The sum is $1\frac{2}{3}$ minae of silver, which is 100 shekels.
The mean share is 10 shekels.
The eighth part is 6 shekels.

[44] Thureau-Dangin, "Textes de l'Université de Strasbourg," *TMB*, p. 82. This is the first problem of Strasbourg tablet 362.

[45] One mina of silver equals sixty shekels.

[46] The scribe counts the intervals "below" the eighth brother, the share of which is known, and "above" the third, which is its symmetric part. See O. Neugebauer, and A. Sachs, eds. *Mathematical Cuneiform Texts* (New Haven: American Oriental Society, 1945). The "1 above" is the interval between the first and second brother, the "1 below," the interval between the ninth and tenth. Thureau-Dangin, *TMB*, p. 83, note 1.

[47] The reciprocal of 5 is 1/5 and, in the sexagesimal system, gives $60' \div 5 = 12'$.

We are able to understand the series of operations by following the diagram (fig. 80):

1. Establish the mean share, that is, divide 100 shekels of money by ten men, which equals 10 shekels.

2. Double this mean share knowing that double the mean share is the sum of the mean terms as well as of the extreme terms, which equals 20 shekels.

3. Double the known part of the eighth brother, this part being the complement of the part of the third brother, or $6 \times 2 = 12$ shekels.

4. Subtract double the part of the eighth brother from double the mean share, which is 20 shekels minus 12 shekels, which equals 8 shekels.

5. Count the intervals made between the eighth brother and his symmetrical counterpart, the third brother, which is five intervals. One interval will have the value of 1/5 of the 8 shekels, which will be 1′36″.

The "rate" or the "difference" is therefore 8/5 shekels. This is the answer to the question posed, because 8 shekels divided by 5 equals $1 + 3/5$.

There are several points to notice about the way this problem is stated and resolved. As in problems 40 and 64 of the Rhind Papyrus, the first brother is the largest term, and the progression is therefore considered as decreasing, which explains the use of the terms "above" and "below."[48]

The method for dividing a number by another always consists of multiplying the number by the reciprocal of the dividing number. For example, to divide 100 by 10, one "unties" the reciprocal of 10 and multiplies 100 by the reciprocal of 10 (1/10), a method frequently applied in the Rhind Papyrus.

The last operation, done in order to count the intervals between the eighth and the third brother, is understood more easily through the diagram than by the technique used by the Babylonian mathematicians. Instead of directly counting the intervals between the eighth brother and his counterpart, the third brother, they can be readily shown by the following arrangement:

$$
\text{Row of brothers} \begin{cases} 1 \quad . \quad 2 \quad . \quad 3 \quad . \quad 4 \quad . \quad 5 \quad \text{above} \\ 10 \quad . \quad 9 \quad . \quad 8 \quad . \quad 7 \quad . \quad 6 \quad \text{below} \end{cases}
$$

The calculator adds the intervals between the brothers 1 and 2 and between 10 and 9, which makes 2. Then he doubles that and *adds* 1, and finally subtracts the five intervals he has found from the number of terms (that is, from the ten brothers), knowing that there are in all arithmetic progressions as many intervals as there are terms, minus 1.

Conclusion

In transcribing the solutions of the problems from the Babylonian tablets into algebraic formulas, we lose sight of the geometric thinking that determines the way these problems are stated as well as their solutions. The Ancients were able to find the correct and simple solution without recourse to those elements characteristic of algebra: the unknown *x*, negative numbers and squares, the equality with zero, in other words, without the equation properly so called.

The statement of the problem and its solution are descriptions of a geometric gesture, as is the case in pharaonic mathematics. The latter prefers to give the *proof* of the results obtained, which is none other than the inverse of the calculation, while the Babylonian prefers reasoning directly with the inverted form.

[48] Cf. chapter 6, "The Rhind Papyrus," problems 40 and 64.

Among both peoples there was a similar geometric origin of their mathematics, but two different mentalities quickly arose. That of the Babylonians opened the door to a "scholastic" way of thinking in which the "supposition" slowly replaced the fact, the geometric technique.

The "problem" implies an awareness of the existence of an unknown. The method of finding it can only be by the substitution of an unknown value with a supposed value. The algebraic method does not give any quantity to x, but the Ancients affirm that the unknown has a value of One, therefore the elements of the problem can only be fractions. Fractions are "positive enumerations," not negative values. Adding is composing with elements, but multiplying creates growth, which is geometric. In subtraction, the quantities to be subtracted are not negative but "inversely positive."

This is the whole mathematical philosophy of the Ancients, and it is this that allows them easily and simply to solve problems that our methods only complicate. Now, simplicity demands clarity and clarity comes from mastery over the question, whereas the novice always tends to make things complicated.

What we have glimpsed of Babylonian mathematics shows a principal concern with the calculation itself, a quantitative solution of the problem. What we now know about pharaonic mathematics, on the contrary, shows us (through their fidelity to the principle of proportion) a special preoccupation with connecting everything to a unifying element through the law of harmony.

Our present preoccupation is opposed, in Ancient Egypt, by a universal preoccupation with the everlasting. This is confirmed by everything we know about the life of the Ancient Egyptians.

It is to Eratosthenes and to Theon of Smyrna as well as to Plato that we turn again for confirmation of this view.

> Eratosthenes says that the ratio is the principle that gives birth to the proportion, and it is also the primary cause of the creation of all things that are arranged in an orderly way. Every proportion is indeed composed of ratios, and the principle of ratio is equality. This is evident: for each species there is a certain element or principle that belongs to it, into which all other elements are resolved while it itself does not resolve into any of the others. Now this principle is necessarily not decomposable and indivisible, for anything that can be decomposed and divided is called a set, not an element.[49]
>
> The elements of the substance are therefore indivisible according to substance; those of quality are so according to quality; those of quantity are so according to quantity. And each thing is indivisible and whole according to whether it is an element of a composed or mixed thing. Thus, the element of quantity is the unit, *that of size is the point,* that of ratio and of proportion is equality. For unity cannot be divided into quantity, nor the point into size, nor equality into multiple ratios. Number is born from the unit, *the line from the point,* ratio and proportion from equality, but not all in the same manner because unity multiplied by itself does not engender as the other numbers do: one times one is one, whereas *by addition the result increases to infinity.*[50]

I have emphasized those passages in Theon's text (a comparatively recent work) that reveal a Euclidean deviation from the original pharaonic thinking by allocating to the point an original dimension, with the movement of this point forming the line. This makes of the world an addition

---

[49] Eratosthenes was a librarian in Alexandria, where he drew upon such a broad scientific background that he was called one of the greatest geometers of antiquity; but without doubt he was honest, for none of his texts give any indication that he attributed this knowledge to himself. It was because of ignorant but prolific compilers that he was given such exalted status. This displaces, but in no way diminishes, the greatness of this man who was so able to understand the thought of the Ancients.

[50] Theon of Smyrna, *Le Nombre de Platon,* part 2, §31, pp. 135–37.

of points, an erroneous concept deriving from the atomist principle. We have said, and seen, that at the origin pharaonic philosophy can only see a volume whose *analysis* manifests the surface, the line, and the point or vertex. The hypothetical point is then a real point, ternary within unity (the true atom), of three irreducible elements, recognized even in our day as neutron, proton, and electron, curiously identical, in their nature, with the Salt, Sulfur, and Mercury of ancient Hermeticism.

—⁓—

"Plato seems to believe that the mathematical link is singular and that it consists in proportion. 'Indeed,' he says in the *Epinomis,* 'it is necessary that every figure, every combination of numbers, every harmonic grouping, and every astronomical revolution manifest the unity of proportion to him who would learn according to the true method; now, this unity will be apparent to he who correctly understands what we teach; he will recognize that a single link naturally unites all things.'"[51]

Indeed, harmonic proportion contains within itself all possibilities. Is this not the function of this unity, of this link that naturally unites all things?

[51] Ibid., p. 137.

Chapter 8

THE *CANEVAS*
Living Architecture of Number

The decree is to grow. Now, all growth is made by the scission of elements. Thus, "to grow" means to proceed by duplication—1, 2, 4, 8—in other words, to divide.

THE ARCHITECTURAL GRID OF THE BUILDERS OF THE TEMPLE

Now that we have examined—in a still more or less Western mathematical spirit—the main problems of the mathematical papyri, we shall look at the bases for the resolutions of these same problems according to the pharaonic mentality, and we shall see the simplicity with which their solutions were envisioned. Now, the simple solution indicates mastery over a question.

We should recall and summarize here some of the principles about which we have already spoken. The mentality of the Ancients is, as we recall, geometric (functional), and, in Egypt, it always refuses the scholarly form that substitutes the mental concept for graphic means. It remains faithful to the fractional system, refusing a decimal system that necessarily moves away from geometry. The link between fractional calculation and geometry is made by the trigonometric notation of $1 : n$. This synthesizing notation allows us to place canon, architecture, and calculation on a sort of "backdrop" that we call the *canevas*,* the grid pattern of squares used by the *Bauhütte* [mason's guild] of the temple builders. We might be tempted to see ordinates and abscissas in the *canevas*, but this would not be "pharaonic."

Let us add another very important element offered by the mystical function ϕ that permits "the squaring of the circle" through the fact that $\pi = 1.2 \times \phi^2$. Moreover, this function ϕ is the essence of all mathematics since it naturally defines the proportion $a : b :: b : c$ (where c represents $a + b$) and the (logarithmic) coincidence of the additive series with the geometric.[1]

---

[1] The division of a straight line into two proportional segments allows, in the end, only two types of division, one of which is division into two equal parts, and the other into "extreme and mean ratio." Cf. Ghyka, *Esthétique des proportions,* chap. 2, "De la Proportion."

* Because of the special methods used by the Egyptians in developing their grid surfaces, we will continue to use the word *canevas* (plural, *canevas*) to describe its basis.

By recalling again the theological principle that puts One at the origin of creation, and the numerating development as a dividing function, we obtain the guiding principles of pharaonic mathematics.

—⁓—

Here again are some of the philosophical premises:

In the Unique as an absolutely homogeneous milieu, neither time nor path exists: each moment is equal to every other.

Genesis begins only with the scission of this homogeneous milieu and, because of that, endures until the reunification into an absolutely homogeneous milieu.

The cause of the scission is thus the "original evil," the heterogeneity to be overcome. Genesis is then the unifying activity of that which is disunited. This genetic possibility is necessarily contained in the nature of that which divides the homogeneous, and it constitutes time. The homogenizing activity is uniform but is relatively quick or slow: the genesis of the whole containing the genesis of the particular. The seed is the first stage of the return to homogeneity; but it still requires its complementary—and substantially nutritive—milieu until the annulling of the complementation.

This is the Hermetic biophilosophical thesis that has its theological form, and also its mathematical expression, in the geometric base delineated by the pharaonic *canevas* and by the sages of all times. (Cf., for example, the Mayan *canevas* in plate 57, and the *maṇḍala* or plan of the Hindu temple, fig. 197.)

There is a natural geometry and a mental geometry. The latter allows absolute circles and numbers, but natural geometry cannot allow these except by applying itself to what is fixed and dead. The impulse to all movement and to all form is given by ϕ, since it is the proportion that summarizes in itself the additive and the geometric, or logarithmic, series. Phi is the impulse for the whole number 5, but starting from 5, ϕ cannot be defined in rational numbers. It can only be defined *through the harmony that it engenders*. Through musical harmony, and therefore only through our sensation of music, and not by reasoning, can we know absolute ϕ. This fact indicates the way of the pharaonic mentality and of the true Pythagoreanism developed from it. We have five senses with which to judge living reality. The mental concept would have cadavers, numbers, and arrested forms. It "supposes" invariables for points of reference. But nothing in the universe is invariable. Our science obviously knows this, but it still believes that we must approach the knowledge of matter with mental mathematics, when the Ancients, more wisely than we, attained this knowledge through the metaphysical principles of their theology.[2]

—⁓—

The *canevas*, which presents itself as a ground plan on which—in a childlike manner—one can draw figures, is actually *a consequence*. It is the result of numerical functions, and only afterward does it present itself for the play of ratios and proportions.

The deeper purpose for the existence of the *canevas* is that we are only able to reason with whole numbers (n). Now, although a figuration (such as the ratio of the diameter to the circumference, or the diagonal of a square) offers a finite image, we are dealing in these cases with indeterminable, irrational ratios. Thus, the diagonal of the square 1 is an indefinable n but must figure in our reasoning as a whole, finite n. Moreover, we wish to remain symbolists.

[2] Cf. in this regard Daniel Berthelot, *La Physique et la métaphysique des théories d'Einstein* (Paris: Payot, 1922), a small, little-known work in which the author tries to show that Einstein's theory of relativity confirms a number of elements of traditional metaphysics.

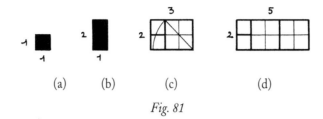

Fig. 81

Let us pose a square, and then add to it the same square again, forming the rectangle 1 : 2 (fig. 81a–b). If we then construct on side 2 of this rectangle a new square, it will have the value 2^2 or 4, and the new rectangle will have the value 2 : 3 (fig. 81c).

The diagonal of square 4 is read as 3 in whole numbers instead of as 2.828... , and if this larger square is given the value 1^2, the diagonal will have a value of $1\frac{1}{2}$ (1.5 instead of 1.41421...).

Continuing this construction, we add to 2^2 a new identical square that gives us a rectangle with the value 2 : 5 (fig. 81d), and the square constructed on its larger side will have the value 5^2 or 25. The diagonal of 25 + 25 equals $\sqrt{50}$, which is here 7 instead of 7.071... (fig. 82a). We come closer and closer to a more precise number.

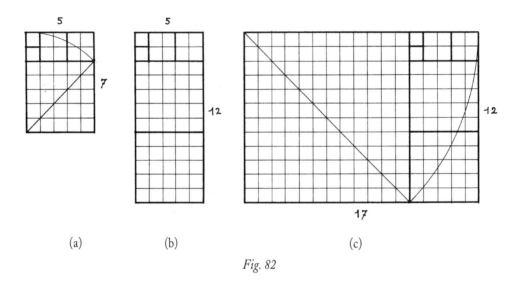

Fig. 82

If we consider the square 5^2 as having the value of 1, its diagonal in this case will be $1\frac{2}{5}$, which equals 1.4, a little smaller than the actual number. But in continuing to draw a new square on the side 5, we form the side of another new square 5 + 5 + 2, which equals 12 (fig. 82b–c), corresponding to the formula given by Theon: *Each new side is equal to the side of the preceding square plus its diagonal, and each new diagonal is equal to two sides of the preceding square plus its diagonal.* For example: side = 5, diagonal = 7; the new side = 5 + 7 = 12; the new diagonal = 5 + 5 + 7 = 17 (or 12 + 5); the exact value of the diagonal is $\sqrt{144 + 144}$, or $\sqrt{288}$, and $17^2 = 289$.

In summary, if $\sqrt{2} = 1.41421...$, then

$$a = \quad 3 : 2 \ = 1.5 \qquad \textit{by excess}$$
$$b = \quad 7 : 5 \ = 1.4 \qquad \textit{by deficiency}$$
$$c = 17 : 12 = 1.41666... \ \textit{by excess}, \text{ etc.}$$

We notice an alternating pattern where the squares of the diagonal numbers are at first larger and then smaller by one unit than twice the square of the side numbers.[3] Moreover, we can see this progression develop as a spiral.

This genesis of numbers brings us closer and closer to the true number that can only be reached in infinity, blending anew with the Origin, with the difference or scission becoming smaller and smaller. Now, this system *creates the canevas* and represents the *architecture of number,* while its spiral progression gives us its *function.*

This constitutes the geometric system that allows us to read irrational numbers in whole numbers, which become increasingly precise to within infinitesimal fractions.

The root of 5 through ϕ, the root of 2, and the root of 3 are framed on this simple principle, which will create the appearance—through the *canevas*—of the "harp of harmony" as a result of these fundamental functions.

THE THREE FUNCTIONS OF THE *CANEVAS*

The series of numerical ratios that approach closer and closer to the square roots of 2, 3, and 5 are based on three functions.

First, let us consider two origins, one for the numerators and the other for the denominators. The two origins are common to the three roots, but the development of the growth of the numbers varies for each.

One origin is $1 + 1$, giving the rectangle $1 : 2$.

The other origin is $1 + 2 = 3$, giving the rectangle $1 : 3$.

The $1 : 2$ rectangle will generate the *denominators* of the roots of 2 and 5 and the *numerators* of the root of 3.

From the $1 : 3$ rectangle, the *numerators* of the roots of 2 and 5 and the *denominators* of the root of 3 will be generated. This last therefore has the same origin as the two preceding, but inverted.

The numerators and the denominators of the fractions are to be considered here as ratios between whole numbers. The numerators for the root of 2 are what Theon calls diagonal numbers, whereas the denominators represent side numbers, since the root of 2 is the diagonal of a square.

Second, the genesis of these numbers will be made by adding successive squares. The rhythm of growth varies for each root and conforms to the formation of numbers by means of the medieties. A succession of rectangles will be obtained that obeys a constant ratio.

Third, if one is to construct an outer and an inner spiral from the successive rectangles thus determined, one must find the centers of the curves and of the spiral.[4] The figure thus determined by these centers is different for the three roots. For the roots of 5 and 2, both the outer and inner spirals are constructed, but for the root of 3 only the outer spiral is possible. The latter root does not contain an inner spiral.

---

[3] In effect,

Side	Double square	Diagonal	Its square	Difference
2	8	3	9	$9 - 1 = 8$
5	50	7	49	$49 + 1 = 50$
12	288	17	289	$289 - 1 = 288$

[4] The transition from the *canevas* to the spiral is the passage from mineral to plant, as the cubic development of the *canevas* is the passage from plant to animal.

The character of the inner and outer spirals of the two series of numbers that furnish the root of 5 is given in the ϕ series tending toward perfection. If the centers of the outer spiral are brought together, then a rectangular spiral is formed that will have for its successive sides the same numbers as those of the rectangles that generated it.

The two originating figures 1 : 2 and 1 : 3 have an identical function, but are not superimposable. Nevertheless, their spirals, when they attain their absolute perfection, should be rigorously parallel.

THE *CANEVAS* AND $\sqrt{5}$

There are two origins:

The 1 : 2 rectangle gives the series of denominators.
The 1 : 3 rectangle gives the series of numerators.

Origin 1 : 3	1	3	4	7	11	18	29	47	76	123
Origin 1 : 2	1	1	2	3	5	8	13	21	34	55
Inverses	$\frac{5}{1}$	$\frac{5}{3}$	$\frac{10}{4}$	$\frac{15}{7}$	$\frac{25}{11}$	$\frac{40}{18}$	$\frac{65}{29}$	$\frac{105}{47}$	$\frac{170}{76}$	$\frac{275}{123}$

The $\sqrt{5}$ has the simplest rhythm of growth. The originating 1 : 2 rectangle is already formed from 1 + 1; the length 2 becomes the side of a square that is added to the original rectangle, giving 3. This 3 becomes the side of a new square that is added to the preceding 3 : 2 rectangle and gives the new ratio 3 : 5 (fig. 83).

We rediscover in this progression the numbers of the series passed on by Fibonacci, which is generated by adding the two preceding numbers to obtain the next number: 1, 1, 2, 3, 5, 8, 13, 21, 34, 55, 89, 144, etc.

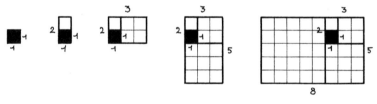

Fig. 83

The ratio between two successive numbers of this series tends to approximate ϕ. By taking three successive numbers of this series, the logarithmic function of ϕ allows one to find, for example, unity, ϕ, and ϕ^2 in them, since $1 + \phi = \phi^2$, as is the case with $8 + 13 = 21$, where the ratio 13 : 8 will be considered as an approximate value of ϕ, and 21 : 8 as the value of ϕ^2 for a unity of 8.

Proceeding in exactly the same way with the originating 1 : 3 rectangle, that is, by the addition of a square, the first square, which has a side of 3, is added to the original rectangle and gives the ratio 3 : 4.

The second square, which will have 4 for its side, when added to 3 equals 7 and gives the second ratio 4 : 7 (fig. 84). By continuing in this way we form the series of numbers: 1, 3, 4, 7, 11, 18, 29, 47, 76, 123, 199, etc. *This is another series of numbers, different from the one attributed to Fibonacci, in which the ratio between consecutive terms tends toward ϕ, and which is formed by the summation of the two preceding terms.*[5]

---

[5] I will designate the inverse of the Fibonacci series of ϕ, known as F, by the letter R.

We are able now to bring these two series together, each of which has ϕ for the ratio between each of their successive terms, and which between them define $\sqrt{5}$. Let us note that the initial denominators provide the ratios $1 : 2$, the octave, then $2 : 3$, the fifth, and that the first numerators give $1 : 3$, an octave and a fifth, then $3 : 4$, the fourth, and then they tend toward ϕ.

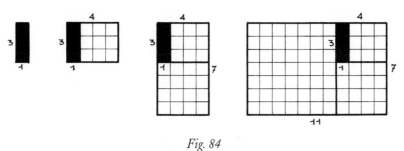

Fig. 84

The Number Five

The number Five is the quintessence that governs all without itself being apparent.

It is the hypotenuse of the sacred triangle.

In the chapter on the mystical number we said that the function ϕ is essential; it is part of the mystery of the primordial action of division. It cannot therefore be a result of the number Five; Five must be defined by the action of ϕ.

The preceding account shows this effect by means of the numbers whose ratios are the basis of musical harmony. We are then in absolute conformity here with the very ancient tradition related by Pythagoras.

The Fibonacci series is inscribed in this series. The series of additions and multiplications is natural, thus the Fibonacci series is imposed as a consequence that renders the function manifest.

The *canevas* makes the series that is complementary to the Fibonacci series known to us, which leads us to see the root of the number Five as a consequence of the function ϕ and not as the generator of this series.[6]

THE *CANEVAS* AND $\sqrt{2}$

There are two origins:

The $1 : 2$ rectangle gives the series of denominators.
The $1 : 3$ rectangle gives the series of numerators.

Origin $1:3$	1	3	7	17	41	99	diagonal numbers
Origin $1:2$	1	2	5	12	29	70	side numbers
Inverses	$\frac{2}{1}$	$\frac{4}{3}$	$\frac{10}{7}$	$\frac{24}{17}$	$\frac{58}{41}$	$\frac{140}{99}$	

The growth is made by the addition of two similar squares that have for a side the larger side of the preceding rectangle. Thus, to the originating $1 : 2$ rectangle we add two squares of side 2, for a total of $1 + 2 + 2$, or 5; then, to the $2 : 5$ rectangle we add two squares of side 5, which makes $2 + 5 + 5$, or 12, and so on.

[6] Cf. table 5, p. 245. We can obtain the R series by adding and subtracting the powers of ϕ and their inverses, therefore by means of irrational numbers. Cf. Michel, *De Pythagore à Euclide*, p. 612 et sqq. But, this procedure is diametrically opposed to that of the *canevas*, which uses only whole numbers to establish ratios that come nearer and nearer to the function ϕ.

To the originating $1:3$ rectangle we add two squares of side 3 making $1 + 3 + 3$, which equals 7; and to the latter is added two squares of side 7 making $3 + 7 + 7$, or 17, and so on (fig. 85).

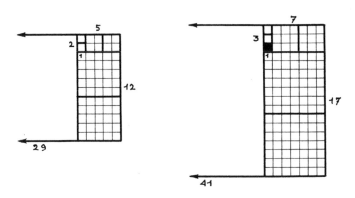

Fig. 85

The series 1, 2, 5, 12, 29, etc., represents the sides of the squares whose diagonals are, respectively, 1, 3, 7, 17, 41. These two series, moving away from the unity—as Theon put it, "unity containing in potentiality the side and the diagonal"—tend toward a closer approximation of $\sqrt{2}$.

Each number, being obtained by addition, represents a side plus the diagonal of the preceding square in such a way that the ratio of successive numbers to each other is $1 + \sqrt{2}$, and with its diagonal each determines a half-angle of $45°$, which is $22\frac{1}{2}°$, or half of the angle $1:1$.

Angles. The first two originating ratios, $1:2$ and $1:3$, which impose themselves in these constructions, are then the two "halves" of the angle $1:1$, as demonstrated by their addition:

$$\frac{\hat{1}}{3} + \frac{\hat{1}}{2} = \frac{2+3}{6-1} = \frac{5}{5} = \frac{\hat{1}}{1}.$$

The angular difference between the two "halves" will become smaller and smaller as our coefficients approach $1 + \sqrt{2}$, and the sum of two ratios taken from the same row, with one ratio from each of the two origins, will be absolutely complete, as:

$$\frac{\hat{3}}{7} + \frac{\hat{2}}{5} = \frac{15+14}{35-6} = \frac{\hat{29}}{29} = \frac{\hat{1}}{1}.$$

Harmony. In this case, it is the first two ratios of $\sqrt{2}$ thus formed that give the ratios of the fifth, 3/2, and its inverse, 4/3, the fourth, since their product is equal to 2/1, the octave. The first ratios possible between 1 and 2 are the first harmonious intervals between the initial tone and its octave. This is the passage from One to Two.

Germ. The germ, or $2 - \sqrt{2}$, is represented by a series in which we discover all our numbers, but in the ratio of numerator with the following denominator. Let us recall that $\sqrt{2} = 3/2$, 7/5, 17/12, etc.; the germ equals 3/5, 7/12, 17/29, etc.; and the germ multiplied by $1 + \sqrt{2} = \sqrt{2}$.

Generation. The generation by addition, always of two successive squares, allows us to conclude that in the final definition it is $\sqrt{5}$ that generates these figures.[7]

---

[7] N.B. Each *canevas* contains within itself the function of the root that it will generate.

THE *CANEVAS* AND $\sqrt{3}$: A SYNCOPATED SERIES

Origin 1 : 2	$\dfrac{1}{1}$	$\dfrac{2}{1}$	$\dfrac{5}{3}$	$\dfrac{7}{4}$	$\dfrac{19}{11}$	$\dfrac{26}{15}$	$\dfrac{71}{41}$	etc. or	$\dfrac{\sqrt{3}}{1}$
Origin 1 : 3									

Inverses	$\dfrac{3}{1}$	$\dfrac{3}{2}$	$\dfrac{9}{5}$	$\dfrac{12}{7}$	$\dfrac{33}{19}$	$\dfrac{45}{26}$	$\dfrac{123}{71}$	etc.

Starting from the origin 1 : 2 one adds two squares of side 2 to total $1 + 2 + 2 = 5$, then a single square of side 5 to make $2 + 5 = 7$, and so on, always continuing to follow this alternation of the addition of two, then of one, square. The original figure 1 : 3 is constructed in exactly the same way and provides the series of numbers listed above. The $\sqrt{2}$ and $\sqrt{5}$ generate the figure.

As in the roots studied previously, by superimposing the numerators and denominators we provide the ratios that constitute $\sqrt{3}$. Between them, the numbers found in this series have for a ratio the two coefficients $1 + \sqrt{3}$ and $(1 + \sqrt{3})/2$ in alternation. This alternation is in accordance with the generation of these numbers. We can observe that only every other time is the ratio even and divisible and in correspondence with the construction of the *canevas*.[8] The construction of the outer spiral, however, shows the character of "containing" for $\sqrt{3}$ only, a series of ratios all of which are as $1 : \sqrt{3}$.

VARYING THE ORIGINATING CENTER OR HEART OF THE CONSTRUCTION

Throughout the entire study of Ancient Egyptian architecture, and notably in the temple of Luxor, we find all these numbers, and at the same time, we very often find examples of "pivotings" that give a living character to the geometric whole.[9]

There must be a motive behind these pivotings. The operation that rejects irrationals in favor of the nearest rationals is now justified, seeing that, thanks to the constructions of the *canevas*, one is able to read the numbers that continue to approach the irrational functions, coming within infinitesimal quantities, which, as in the example of $\sqrt{2}$, vary from $+1$ and -1 of a fraction that in growing larger, diminishes more and more the value of the difference.

The basis of the pivotings is the play of the geometric transcription of functions such as $(a + b)^2 = a^2 + 2ab + b^2$; but also, as we shall see, $(a + b)^2 = 4ab + (b - a)^2$, if b is larger than a, a formula that plays on the *sum* and the *difference* of two unequal sizes and is the base of numerous applications of algebraic character from the Old Babylonian Period.

Let us admit these two unequal sizes posed at right angles to each other, and we discover there the angular ratio $1/n$, which was discussed in chapter 7. The formulas of addition and subtraction of angles described as $1/n$ demonstrate the following laws:

---

[8] The series of these numbers is formulated as follows:

$$\frac{a}{b} \times \frac{3b}{a} = 3, \quad \text{then} \quad \frac{a + 3b}{b + a} \times \frac{3(b + a)}{a + 3b} = 3, \text{ etc.}$$

For example, the first form is $(2/1) \times (3/2) = 3$; the second form will be $(3 + 2)/(1 + 2) = 5/3$, and its inverse $= 9/5$. Continuing in this way, $(5 + 9)/(3 + 5) = 14/8$, a ratio divisible by $2 = 7/4$, its inverse $= 12/7$; then $(7 + 12)/(4 + 7) = 19/11$, a ratio not divisible by 2, its inverse $= 33/19$; then $(19 + 33)/(11 + 19) = 52/30$, a ratio divisible by $2 = 26/15$, its inverse $= 45/26$, etc.

[9] Cf. chapter 13.

First, the difference between any angle and a 45° angle or $1\hat{/}1$ always follows the formula $1\hat{/}1 - A\hat{/}B = (B-A)/(B+A)$. For example, taking the first two possible ratios, 1/2 and 1/3, which are the center and origin of each figure of the *canevas*, we have seen that their sum is equal to 1/1 (fig. 86).

Fig. 86

Second, recall that the addition of two equal angles always produces a Diophantine triangle. Thus $1\hat{/}2 + 1\hat{/}2 = (2+2)/(4-1) = 4\hat{/}3$, and its diagonal is $4+1 = 5$. The sum of $1\hat{/}3 + 1\hat{/}3 = (3+3)/(9-1) = 6\hat{/}8$, and its diagonal is 10. We find then, with the two first ratios, the formation of the first 3, 4, 5 Diophantine triangle in the form 4/3 and 6/8, or 3/4.

This is the sacred triangle. The *canevas* demonstrates an actual architectural plan of numbers, and from the beginning we can observe in it the function ϕ, the harmonic proportions, and the 3, 4, 5 triangle given as a universal foundation.

Finally, the difference between $1\hat{/}1$ and $3\hat{/}4$ is the angle 1 : 7, in the same way that the difference between $1\hat{/}2$ and $1\hat{/}3$ is $1\hat{/}2 - 1\hat{/}3 = (3-2)/(6+1) = 1\hat{/}7$ (fig. 87). The combination of the duplication of $1\hat{/}2$ and $1\hat{/}3$ gives the length 9 (as 3×3) and the length 8 (as 2×4) for a base (fig. 87).

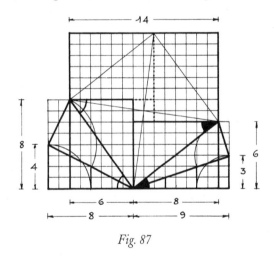

Fig. 87

These two lengths, 8 and 9, evident here, are related to musical harmony and are at the very heart of the "hieratical pavement" (figs. 94 and 95). This is the tone in music and also the ratio between the diameter of a disk and the side of a square of the same surface area.[10]

The sum of 8 and 9 is 17, the famous number of Jābir. It is associated with 28 and is the key number for the "balance" (*mizan*, measure of balance).*

---

[10] See problem 48 of the Rhind Papyrus.

* "The use of the balance in alchemy implies the existence of correct proportions of the qualities in metals. Each metal has two exterior and two interior qualities: for example, gold is inwardly cold and dry, outwardly hot and humid; silver is just the reverse—hot and humid inwardly, cold and dry outwardly. Each quality has four degrees and seven subdivisions, or altogether twenty-eight parts. According to Jābir, everything in this world exists by the number 17, divided into the series 1 : 3 : 5 : 8. He assigns each of the twenty-eight parts of the qualities to one of the letters of the Arabic alphabet, and bases the four-fold division upon the series 1 : 3 : 5 : 8. The opposing natures of the metals are in the ratio of either 1 : 3 or 5 : 8, or vice versa." S. H. Nasr, *Science and Civilization in Islam* (Cambridge: Harvard Univ. Press, 1968), p. 263.

The length remaining after the addition of the angles is 8 + 6, or 14, and 14 represents the number of digits in one-half of an Egyptian royal cubit. The ratio 8 to 9 is also the Ogdoad of eight primordial gods that give the Great Ennead. Thoth is said to be "master of the Eight," as Atum-Ra is the first of the Heliopolitan Ennead.

Let us recall here the importance of the sacred triangle and of the angle 1 : 7 that derives from it, which we will develop further in the chapter on cubits.

The Egyptian division of surfaces is made according to the Thotian principle by successive halvings, or dimidiations. In principle, it will be the large square of side 10 with a surface value of 100. Its half-surface is 50, and half of the half-surface is 25. The sides are then 10, $\sqrt{50}$, and 5, respectively. Now, the root of 50 is irrational and is not transcribable in whole numbers (fig. 88a).

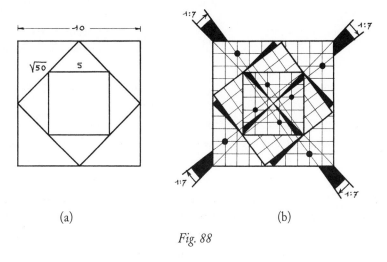

(a)   (b)

Fig. 88

In contrast, four 3 : 4 triangles, by their diagonals of 5, determine a square with a surface of 25 inscribed in a square of side 7 with a surface of 49. From this last there is one square unit lacking for it to be the half-surface of the large square with a surface of 100 (fig. 88b).[11]

The pivoting of the length 7 on an angle of 1 : 7 corrects this length, which becomes $\sqrt{50}$ or 7.071... (fig. 89).

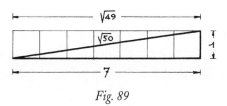

Fig. 89

This is then the quantity determined by the ratio of the angle 1 : 7, which, here, represents the missing unit and determines a center for the pivoting of the inscribed square in order to turn this rational quantity into an irrational value (fig. 87).[12]

This pivoting, represented by 1 : 7 (the angle of Amun), demonstrates a general principle of Nature and is the real cause of the *living* vibration that oscillates between the whole number and its irrationality, in other words, between a definite, arrested state and its continuity or revitalization.

---

[11] If 4 = *A* and 3 = *B*, the surface 49 = $(A + B)^2 = 4AB + (A - B)^2$. See the demonstration and explanation of the Babylonian problem 8 in chapter 7, appendix 2, and figure 75.

[12] See plate 64 for the application of these functions in the temple of Luxor and in the cubits. Cf. chapter 10.

Any phenomenon of an energetic order is made in this way from a composition of "seven factors" resulting from the contraction of "nine functions," as shown in the following scheme:

Red   Orange   Yellow
            Yellow   Green   Blue
                        Blue   Indigo   Violet

three triads of one nature that manifest seven aspects: the first triad is warmth, the second triad is coolness, and the third triad is intermediate in temperature.

—⁓—

The living cell, in order to multiply, divides itself following the Thotian division, as the number of vibrations of sound divides itself in 2, 4, 8, 16, 32, etc., 16 being considered musically as the lowest-pitched sound.

In addition to its nucleus, the first cell contains within itself the centrosome, which divides itself first and determines two poles that direct the movements of the chromosomes (always the same number for each species) and act as *attracting poles,* determining the scission of the nucleus.

The child's total height at birth is divided into two nearly equal parts by the place of attachment of its umbilical cord. Then, little by little, the lower part grows longer in relation to the upper part. The original ratio 1 : 1 becomes 1 : ϕ, passing through alternating phases of growth in such a way that the prepuberty phase can reach 1 : 1.7, while ϕ equals 1.618.... In human growth we again discover the Fibonacci series: 1/1, then 3/2, 5/3, 8/5, etc., tending toward a perfect ϕ.

These proportions in phases of growth are very carefully observed in pharaonic figurations, and it is this that allows us to determine the age of a royal figure. We recall the importance of the king as a solar representative, and this fact also enables us to situate the time of day, and likewise, the date of the year.

This alternating movement of growth, the two poles that the construction of numerical ratios demonstrates to us through the *canevas,* is evident throughout all of life in the created world.

—⁓—

In the figure at the heart of the *canevas,* the originating 1 : 2 rectangle pivots on its diagonal, which in turn becomes the axis between two poles *A* and *C*.[13] This pivoting cuts the large side *AB* of the rectangle into two segments, which are to each other as 3 and 5, one of the first ratios of ϕ.

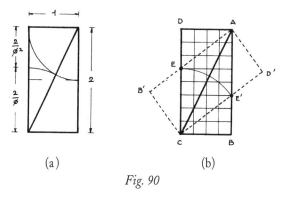

(a)   (b)

Fig. 90

[13] Let us recall here that this is the double square 1 : 2, the diagonal of which is $\sqrt{5}$, thus the origin of all the numerical ratios that serve, in principle, as the base for the nave in our Gothic cathedrals. The diagonal is the spirit of the form. The number Five belongs to the diagonal and creates all vegetation.

This rectangle then has the value of 4 to 8, and the first division into whole numbers is thus 3 : 5 : : 5 : 8, which evokes the function ϕ by oscillating around it (fig. 90b), the function being represented in its absolute form by the golden section (fig. 90a).

Segment *DE*, equal to 3, is the small side of the triangle *DEA* in which the large side is 4 and the diagonal 5. This diagonal *EA* is equal to the large segment *EC*. The angle of slope is then 4 : 3 and it is the sum of two angles 1 : 2 ($\widehat{BAC} + \widehat{CAB'}$). This is the sacred triangle.

In order to obtain, by the pivoting of the 1 : 2 rectangle on its diagonal, the division according to the golden section, one must choose, from among the whole numbers in the development of the *canevas* by the coefficient ϕ, the number 144 as the value ϕ^2 for the large side. The choice of this number is dictated by the different lengths in the temple of Luxor representing Man, with and without the crown of the skull, and varying between 144 and 140 fathoms. We indicate here the method for determining these numbers.

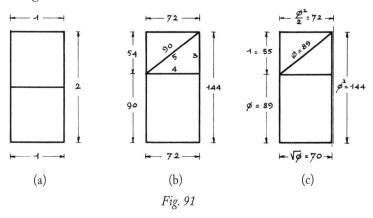

(a)   (b)   (c)

Fig. 91

a) The originating 1 : 2 rectangle.

b) The pivoting shown in the preceding figure divides the large side 144 into two lengths that are to each other as 54 and 90, for the diagonal, 90, and the large side of the triangle, 72.

c) The division of the length 144 into the golden section defines the lengths 55 and 89, and the shortened segment 89 becomes the diagonal of a triangle with 55 and 70 for its sides,[14] instead of 54 and 72. To have a better grasp of the narrowing of the original rectangle, we must draw a semicircle with the large side of the 1 : 2 rectangle as its diameter (fig. 92a). Divide this large side

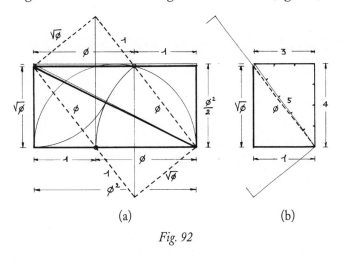

(a)   (b)

Fig. 92

[14] The triangle with sides 55 and 70 has 89 for its diagonal, thus:

$$55^2 = 3025 \quad \text{for } 1^2 = 1$$
$$70^2 = \underline{4900} \quad \text{for } \sqrt{\phi^2} = \frac{\phi}{\phi^2}$$
$$\text{Total} \quad 7925$$
$$89^2 = 7921 \quad \text{for } \phi^2$$

into two segments that are to each other as 1 is to ϕ and draw the perpendicular to this point. This height is shorter than the radius. Whereas the radius has a value $(1 + \phi)/2$, this height equals $\sqrt{\phi}$ and becomes the large side of a triangle with 1 for its base and ϕ for its diagonal.

It is now possible to draw the rectangle that, in pivoting on its diagonal, divides its length into two segments that are to each other as 1 is to ϕ. The angle of the slope is that of the Pyramid of Cheops (fig. 92b).

The measurements of this pyramid are in cubits: the altitude is 280 (or 4×70) for the half-base of 220 (or 4×55), numbers in which we rediscover the F series.

The primary triangle is that of the Pyramid of Chephren, that is, 3 : 4, with 5 for the diagonal (fig. 92b). Similarly, the 1 : 3 rectangle is constructed on this common diagonal by pivoting in one direction or the other, either by inverting its own diagonal or by a new pivoting.

From the combination of these different rectangles and their pivotings result the numbers and figures for which we have here given a synthesis (fig. 93), and that now make comprehensible and evident the double series 1, 2, 4, 8, and 1, 3, 9, 27, cited by Plato[15] as the architectural essence called the "Soul of the World," giving the development of surfaces, volumes, harmonic numbers, and the ratios of musical harmony.

The joining of the points 1 : 1 gives the initial note, then 1 : 2 produces the octave; the ratio 2 : 3 gives the fifth, and 3 : 4 provides the fourth, and thus are obtained the first two harmonious intervals occurring between 1 and 2. The joining of 4 to 9, being the square of 2 to the square of 3, gives two fifths, and finally, the ratio of 9 to 8 gives the value of a tone.[16] The bringing together of the cube of 2 and the cube of 3, that is 8 to 27, gives three fifths, which is an octave, a fifth, and a tone. This series, 1, 2, 3, 4, 9, 8, 27, which has been taken as an anomaly or an error, is thus justified and demonstrated by this arrangement, 2 and 3 being the lines, 4 and 9 the squares, and 8 and 27 the cubes.

The geometric series 1, 2, 4, 8 gives the values of one, then two, and then three octaves (logarithmic function). The geometric series 1, 3, 9, 27 gives an octave plus a fifth, then two octaves and two fifths, and finally three octaves and three fifths.

There is a harp of string lengths that must not be confused with the principle that gives the proportions defined by the angles obtained from the positions of the various points of these two geometric series.

The extension of the diagonal 8 to 27 (fig. 93) crosses the extension of the line joining points 4 and 9 at point B, which establishes a large right triangle with a base of 24 and a height of 36, in other words, the ratio 2 : 3.

Points 2 and 3 drawn to B define, in their turn, 24, the two musical ratios 3 : 4 and 4 : 5, on this common base. Points 1 and 1 drawn to B give the first ratios of ϕ, that is, 3 : 5 and 5 : 8, as we have already found in the pivoting of the 1 : 2 rectangle on its diagonal (fig. 92). Thus the harp of numbers (fig. 93) gives the same fundamental ratios as the pivoting of rectangle 1 : 2 on its own diagonal (fig. 92).

All is held in the very heart of things, which makes understandable the importance of these simple ratios that are at the basis of all the variations that spring forth from them. These fundamental numbers are at the origin of the series that move toward equilibrium through alternation, the numbers that most closely approach the absolute.

---

[15] Plato, *Timaeus*, in *The Dialogues of Plato*, trans. B. Jowett (Oxford: Clarendon Press, 1953), 35b and c; Theon of Smyrna, *Le Nombre de Platon*, part 2, §38. See appendix at the end of this chapter.

[16] Here it is a question of the ratios of the lengths of the vibrating string, except in the case of 9 to 8, which gives the tone.

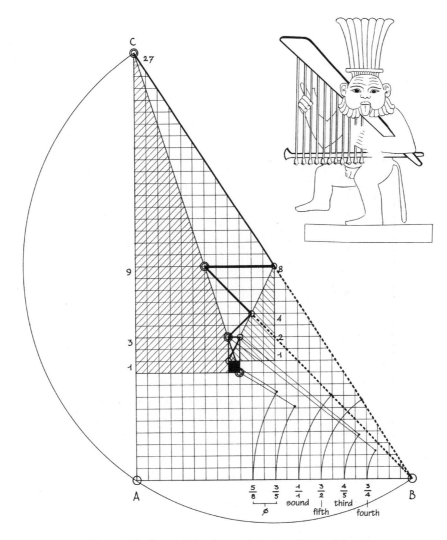

Fig. 93. The Harp of Numbers and the Bes of Philae (pl. 48)

The base of triangle *ABC* equals 24, the altitude 36, the numbers of time and of the cycle. In the large triangle *ABC,* there are two hachured triangles: *left,* the triangle 9 to 27, on the diagonal marked by the points of the numbers of the series of triples, 1, 3, 9, 27; *right,* the triangle 4 to 8, on the diagonal marked by the points of the numbers from the series of doubles, 1, 2, 4, 8. The junction of these points determines Plato's enumeration 1, 2, 3, 4, 9, 8, 27.

Phi is at the origin; it defines itself only by the harmony it engenders. The tone, that is, our experience of hearing the exactitude of the tone, is for us the absolute moment of ϕ, that which reason, that is, calculation, is unable to express. It is also for this reason that we can consider the intelligence of harmony as a supernatural state.[17]

These few explanations summarized here present the foundations of a vast development explaining the essential character of the *canevas* and shed a ray of light on the "secret" of the architectural "grid" that constitutes it.

[17] See introduction to part 1, "Elements."

We conclude this explanation with a drawing of the development of a square spiral in a grid with sixty-four units to each side (fig. 94) and the development of eight possibilities on this surface, which we call the "hieratic pavement," from the spiral with 1 : 2 for its origin.

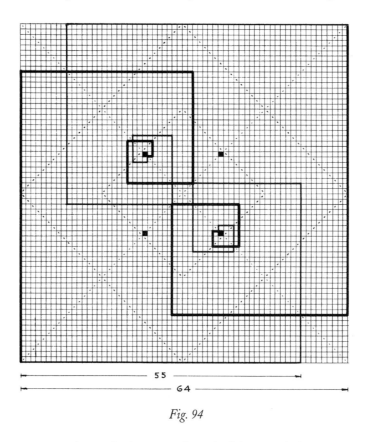

Fig. 94

Hieratic pavement with 1 : 2 for its origin, formed of four spirals "closing" at number 55 and determining the grid with a side of 64, the number of the *wedjat* eye of pharaonic volumes.

Then we add, in order to complete all the possibilities of numbers, the development of a square spiral with 1 : 3 for its origin, showing how the first center is incorporated in the second, which is placed on a grid of 88 for each side and indicates the *residual unity.* We see that the residual unity of the 1 : 2 development becomes the center and starting point for the development of 1 : 3 (fig. 95).

Let us note that the greatest length that "closes" the 1 : 3 square spiral is 76, or 19 × 4. To this length 12 is added, which gives a total of 88, or 22 × 4. Let us recall, in this regard, *the two typical Egyptian* canevas, *one of nineteen squares and the other of twenty-two squares.* Here the geometric development coincides, through the number 19, with astronomical movements, which leads us to see this way of proceeding with mathematical, figured thought as conforming to the bases of cosmic mechanics.

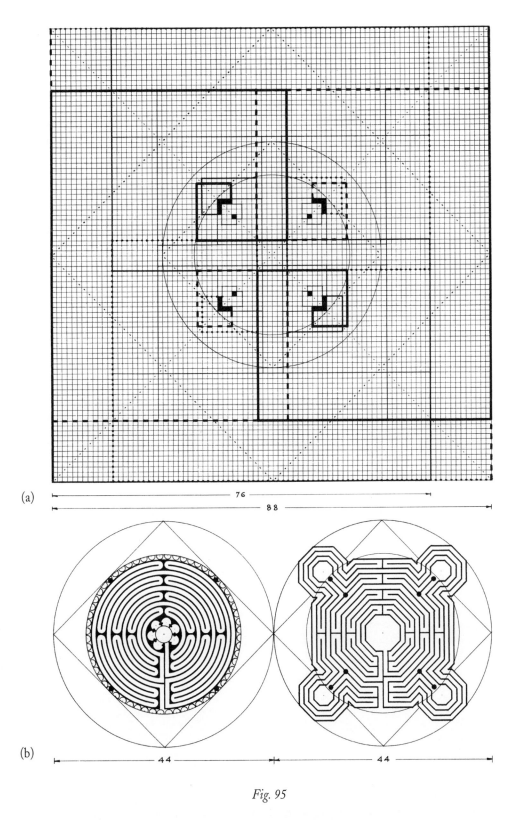

Fig. 95

(a) The hieratic pavement formed of two times eight spirals, determining eight centers. *(b)* The labyrinths of Chartres *(left)* and Reims. The labyrinth of Reims is constructed on the eight centers of the hieratic pavement. These figures can be superimposed on the grid of our hieratic pavement.

When the spiral reaches the number 55 (heavy line, fig. 94), it passes again exactly over the length 55 of the opposite spiral (fine line). The figure "closes" at number 55. The "ejected" square of side 9 gives the square a total of 64 for the side, the cube of 4, which is the side of the central square.[18]

In connecting the eight spirals (in fig. 95) the figure "closes itself" on the number 76, and the "ejected" square equals 12, which gives the length 88 to the whole square.

It is important to establish that the closing is made at the ninth spiral, counting the unity, or at the eighth if both opposing spirals start in the same place. Likewise, the first unity of the series 1, 1, 2, 3, etc., no longer appears in these spirals, which allows us to pose:

	Nun					1		
1	Atum					1		
2						2	3	
3					3		4	
4				5			7	
5			8			11		
6		13				18		
7	21					29		
8	34					47		
9	55					76		

Nun is the first One. Atum creates the Ogdoad, which with himself added constitutes the Ennead. The ratio $76 : 55 = 1.381966...$, or $1 + 1/\phi^2$,[19] or, again, $\sqrt{5}/\phi$.*

But in all there is only a total of $8 + 9$ numbers, that is, 17, the famous number of Jābir, the origin of which until now was unknown.

———✳———

Let us mention again that in order to draw our figures we are mentally and practically obliged to begin at the heart. In natural genesis, on the contrary, the function moves from the exterior toward the interior, as does spirit when it is made concrete in matter. We are concerned here with a spherical whirling whose volume is impossible to objectify or distinguish, but for the numbers imposed by reason.

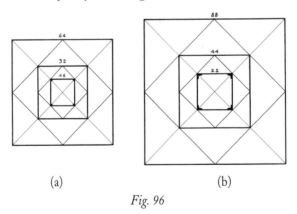

(a)   (b)

Fig. 96

The centers obtained by Thotian division: *(a)* origin 1 : 2; *(b)* origin 1 : 3.

---

[18] Cf. note 4 in this chapter, regarding the cubic (animal) development of the *canevas*.

[19] See the Pyramid of Snefru, fig. 66.

* See Lucie Lamy, *Egyptian Mysteries*, p. 9.

TABLE 5

The Root of 5 and the Fibonacci ϕ Series

The first possible ratio is $1 \times 5 = 5$

Its arithmetic mean is $\dfrac{5+1}{2} = 3$ or $\dfrac{3}{1}$

Its harmonic mean is $\dfrac{2(5 \times 1)}{5+1} = \dfrac{10}{6}$ or $\dfrac{5}{3}$

$\left.\right\}$ Musical proportion

In continuing to follow the above principles we are able to establish the following series, comparing it to the double series of F and R.

		Division by 2	F series	R series
$5 = \dfrac{1}{1} \times \dfrac{5}{1}$			1	1
Arithmetic mean Harmonic mean				
$5 = \dfrac{6}{2} \times \dfrac{10}{6}$		$\dfrac{3}{1} \times \dfrac{5}{3}$	1	3
$5 = \dfrac{8}{4} \times \dfrac{20}{8}$		$\dfrac{4}{2} \times \dfrac{10}{4}$	2	4
$5 = \dfrac{14}{6} \times \dfrac{30}{14}$		$\dfrac{7}{3} \times \dfrac{15}{7}$	3	7
$5 = \dfrac{22}{10} \times \dfrac{50}{22}$		$\dfrac{11}{5} \times \dfrac{25}{11}$	5	11
$5 = \dfrac{36}{16} \times \dfrac{80}{36}$		$\dfrac{18}{8} \times \dfrac{40}{18}$	8	18
$5 = \dfrac{58}{26} \times \dfrac{130}{58}$		$\dfrac{29}{13} \times \dfrac{65}{29}$	13	29
$5 = \dfrac{94}{42} \times \dfrac{210}{94}$		$\dfrac{47}{21} \times \dfrac{105}{47}$	21	47
$5 = \dfrac{152}{68} \times \dfrac{340}{152}$		$\dfrac{76}{34} \times \dfrac{170}{76}$	34	76
$5 = \dfrac{246}{110} \times \dfrac{550}{246}$		$\dfrac{123}{55} \times \dfrac{275}{123}$	55	123
$5 = \dfrac{398}{178} \times \dfrac{890}{398}$		$\dfrac{199}{89} \times \dfrac{445}{199}$	89	199
$5 = \dfrac{644}{288} \times \dfrac{1440}{644}$		$\dfrac{322}{144} \times \dfrac{720}{322}$	144	322
$5 = \dfrac{1042}{466} \times \dfrac{2330}{1042}$		$\dfrac{521}{233} \times \dfrac{1165}{521}$	233	521
			etc.	

Note: Let us compare here the words spoken by Thoth in the Theban temple of Amun and the geometric progression of ratio 2:

	1
I am 1 who becomes 2	2
I am 2 who becomes 4	4
I am 4 who becomes 8	8
I am 1 after this	15 = sum

Recall that the Great Ennead of Thebes comprises fifteen *neters,* and that Thoth, master of numbers, occupies the fifteenth digit on the royal cubit of 7 palms. If we consider that the fifteenth number in the F series ends a cycle, the sixteenth becomes a new unity:

the sixteenth + the seventh number of the F series = 1000 or unity

the seventeenth + the eighth number of the F series = 1618 or ϕ

the eighteenth + the ninth number of the F series = 2618 or ϕ^2, etc.

The F series gives ϕ through the ratio between each of the successive terms. The R series gives the series of powers of ϕ directly in whole numbers, which are already very close approximations beginning from the fifth power.[20]

Power of ϕ		R series
1	1.618034...	**1**
2	2.618034...	**3**
3	4.236068...	**4**
4	6.854102...	**7**

TABLE 6

The Root of 3

The first possible ratio is $1 \times 3 = 3$

Its arithmetic mean is $\dfrac{3+1}{2} = \dfrac{4}{2}$ or $\dfrac{2}{1}$

Its harmonic mean is $\dfrac{2(3 \times 1)}{3+1} = \dfrac{6}{4}$ or $\dfrac{3}{2}$

$\left.\right\}$ Musical proportion

	Arithmetic mean	Harmonic mean		Division by 2			
$3 =$	$\dfrac{1}{1}$	$\times \dfrac{3}{1}$					
$3 =$	$\dfrac{4}{2}$	$\times \dfrac{6}{4}$	$\dfrac{2}{1} \times \dfrac{3}{2}$	then	$\dfrac{2+3}{1+2} =$	$\dfrac{5}{3}$	
$3 =$	$\dfrac{5}{3}$	$\times \dfrac{9}{5}$		then	$\dfrac{5+9}{3+5} =$	$\dfrac{14}{8}$	
$3 =$	$\dfrac{14}{8}$	$\times \dfrac{24}{14}$	$\dfrac{7}{4} \times \dfrac{12}{7}$	then	$\dfrac{7+12}{4+7} =$	$\dfrac{19}{11}$	
$3 =$	$\dfrac{19}{11}$	$\times \dfrac{33}{19}$		then	$\dfrac{19+33}{11+19} =$	$\dfrac{52}{30}$	
$3 =$	$\dfrac{52}{30}$	$\times \dfrac{90}{52}$	$\dfrac{26}{15} \times \dfrac{45}{26}$	then	$\dfrac{26+45}{15+26} =$	$\dfrac{71}{41}$	
$3 =$	$\dfrac{71}{41}$	$\times \dfrac{123}{71}$		then	$\dfrac{71+123}{41+71} =$	$\dfrac{194}{112}$	
$3 =$	$\dfrac{194}{112}$	$\times \dfrac{336}{194}$	$\dfrac{97}{56} \times \dfrac{168}{97}$	then	$\dfrac{97+168}{56+97} =$	$\dfrac{265}{153}$	
$3 =$	$\dfrac{265}{153}$	$\times \dfrac{459}{265}$		then	$\dfrac{265+459}{153+265} =$	$\dfrac{724}{418}$	
$3 =$	$\dfrac{724}{418}$	$\times \dfrac{1254}{724}$	$\dfrac{362}{209} \times \dfrac{627}{362}$	then	$\dfrac{362+627}{209+362} =$	$\dfrac{989}{571}$	
$3 =$	$\dfrac{989}{571}$	$\times \dfrac{1713}{989}$		then	$\dfrac{989+1713}{571+989} =$	$\dfrac{2702}{1560}$	
$3 =$	$\dfrac{2702}{1560}$	$\times \dfrac{4680}{2702}$	$\dfrac{1351}{780} \times \dfrac{2340}{1351}$	then	etc.		

The division by 2 is made every other time in order to simplify the ratios.

Note: The two pairs 265/153 and 1351/780 are the ones that Archimedes used for the approximate ratios of the square root of 3 in his calculation of the ratio of the circumference to the diameter. Cf. Tannery, *Mémoires scientifiques,* 1:229.

[20] The value of ϕ is 1.61803398875..., so that the list of powers given above is slightly greater.

5	11.090170...	**11**
6	17.944272...	**18**
7	29.034442...	**29**
8	46.978714...	**47**
9	76.01315...	**76**
10	122.9918...	**123**
11	199.0050...	**199**
12	321.9968...	**322**

The R series in relation to the F series establishes the square root of 5. Now, in this series ϕ plays the role of a relationship, not of a number, because any number of this series can serve as unity for the following one. Once again, the assertion that ϕ is a function and not a number finds confirmation.

TABLE 7

The Root of 2

Diagonal and Side Numbers

The first possible ratio is $1 \times 2 = 2$

Its arithmetic mean is $\dfrac{2+1}{2} = \dfrac{3}{2}$

Its harmonic mean is $\dfrac{2(2 \times 1)}{2+1} = \dfrac{4}{3}$ } Musical proportion

		Arithmetic mean		Harmonic mean			
2	=	$\dfrac{1}{1}$	×	$\dfrac{2}{1}$			
2	=	$\dfrac{3}{2}$	×	$\dfrac{4}{3}$	$\dfrac{3+4}{2+3}$	=	$\dfrac{7}{5}$
2	=	$\dfrac{7}{5}$	×	$\dfrac{10}{7}$	$\dfrac{7+10}{5+7}$	=	$\dfrac{17}{12}$
2	=	$\dfrac{17}{12}$	×	$\dfrac{24}{17}$	$\dfrac{17+24}{12+17}$	=	$\dfrac{41}{29}$
2	=	$\dfrac{41}{29}$	×	$\dfrac{58}{41}$	$\dfrac{41+58}{29+41}$	=	$\dfrac{99}{70}$
2	=	$\dfrac{99}{70}$	×	$\dfrac{140}{99}$	$\dfrac{99+140}{70+99}$	=	$\dfrac{239}{169}$
2	=	$\dfrac{239}{169}$	×	$\dfrac{338}{239}$	$\dfrac{239+338}{169+239}$	=	$\dfrac{577}{408}$
2	=	$\dfrac{577}{408}$	×	$\dfrac{816}{577}$	$\dfrac{577+816}{408+577}$	=	$\dfrac{1393}{985}$
2	=	$\dfrac{1393}{985}$	×	$\dfrac{1970}{1393}$	$\dfrac{1393+1970}{985+1393}$	=	$\dfrac{3363}{2378}$
2	=	$\dfrac{3363}{2378}$	×	$\dfrac{4756}{3363}$	$\dfrac{3363+4756}{2378+3363}$	=	$\dfrac{8119}{5741}$
2	=	$\dfrac{8119}{5741}$	×	$\dfrac{11482}{8119}$	$\dfrac{8119+11482}{5741+8119}$	=	$\dfrac{19601}{13860}$
2	=	$\dfrac{19601}{13860}$	×	$\dfrac{27720}{19601}$	etc.		

These ratios cannot be simplified by division.

Appendix: Extracts from Plato

The World[21]

Summary. Such was the whole plan of the eternal God about the god that was to be; he made it smooth and even, having a surface in every direction equidistant from the center, a body entire and perfect, and formed out of perfect bodies.

The Soul of the World

It envelopes everything and forms the sky. And in the center he put the soul, which he diffused throughout the body, making it also to be the exterior environment of it, and he made the universe a circle moving in a circle, one and solitary, yet by reason of its excellence able to converse with itself, and needing no other friendship or acquaintance. Having these purposes in view he created the world a blessed god.

The Soul of the World precedes the body. Now God did not make the soul after the body, although we are speaking of them in this order, for when he put them together he would never have allowed that the elder should be ruled by the younger, but this is a random manner of speaking which we have, because somehow we ourselves too are very much under the dominion of chance. Whereas he made the soul in origin and excellence prior to and older than the body, to be the ruler and mistress, of whom the body was to be the subject.

Composition of the Soul of the World. And he made her out of the following elements and on this wise. From the being which is indivisible and unchangeable, and from that kind of being which is distributed among bodies, he compounded a third and intermediate kind of being. He did likewise with the same and the different, blending together the indivisible kind of each with that which is portioned out in bodies. Then, taking the three new elements, he mingled them all into one form, compressing by force the reluctant and unsociable nature of the different into the same. . . . [H]e . . . mingled them with the intermediate kind of being and out of three made one[.]

First divisions of the mingling. [Then] he again divided this whole into as many portions as was fitting, each portion being a compound of the same, the different, and being. And he proceeded to divide after this manner. First of all, he took away one part of the whole [1], and then he separated a second part which was double the first [2], and then he took away a third part which was half as much again as the second and three times as much as the first [3], and then he took a fourth part which was twice as much as the second [4], and a fifth part which was three times the third [9], and a sixth part which was eight times the first [8], and a seventh part which was twenty-seven times the first [27].

How the intervals of the series thus formed have been filled. After this he filled up the double intervals [that is, between 1, 2, 4, 8] and the triple [that is, between 1, 3, 9, 27], cutting off yet other portions from the mixture and placing them in the intervals, so that in each interval there were two kinds of means, the one exceeding and exceeded by equal parts of its extremes [as for example, 1, 4/3, 2, in which the mean 4/3 is one third of 1 more than 1, and one third of 2 less than 2], the other being that kind of mean which exceeds and is exceeded by an equal number. Where there were intervals of 3/2 and of 1/3 and of 9/8, made by the connecting terms in the former intervals, he filled up all the intervals of 4/3 with the interval of 9/8, leaving a fraction over, and the interval which this fraction expressed was in the ratio of 256 to 243. And thus the whole mixture out of which he cut these portions was all exhausted by him.

---

[21] From the *Timaeus*, pp. 1165–66. [Headings added by the author.]

The sky, the equator, and the ecliptic. This entire compound he divided lengthwise into two parts which he joined to one another at the center like the letter *X,* and bent them into a circular form, connecting them with themselves and each other at the point opposite to their original meeting point[.]

Their movements. [A]nd, comprehending them in a uniform revolution upon the same axis, he made the one the outer and the other the inner circle. Now the motion of the outer circle he called the motion of the same, and the motion of the inner circle the motion of the other or diverse. The motion of the same he carried round by the side to the right, and the motion of the diverse diagonally to the left. And he gave dominion to the motion of the same and like, for that he left single and undivided[.]

The planets.[22] [B]ut the inner motion he divided in six places and made seven unequal circles with their intervals in ratios of two and three, three of each, and bade the orbits proceed in a direction opposite to one another. And three [sun, Mercury, Venus] he made to move with equal swiftness, and the remaining four [moon, Saturn, Mars, Jupiter] to move with unequal swiftness to the three and to one another, but in due proportion.

Position of the body of earth within the soul. Now when the creator had framed the soul according to his will, he formed within her the corporeal universe, and brought the two together and united them center to center. The soul, interfused everywhere from the center to the circumference of heaven, of which also she is the external envelopment, herself turning in herself, began a divine beginning of never-ceasing and rational life enduring throughout all time. The body of heaven is visible, but the soul is invisible and partakes of reason and harmony, and, being made by the best of intellectual and everlasting natures, is the best of things created.[23]

[22] What Plato says (circle, planets, etc.) is only comprehensible as we see it now, through geometry—the evocative symbol for which no single theory can take account.

[23] This account of Plato's, which transcribes itself in numbers and geometric functions, just as the architecture of the *canevas* shows it, evidently has yet another meaning!

Chapter 9

THE COSMIC PRINCIPLE OF VOLUME

In the preceding pages I have often alluded to volume in explaining, among other things, the "intelligence of the heart" as a synthetic vision in volume, in maintaining that the first perceptible aspect of the Universe (the Creation) can only be spatial, and also in referring to volumes in connection with sound and harmony.

In contrast to how we arrive at volume (from the bottom up) by the supposed movement of point to line, line to plane, then plane to volume, the Ancients *begin* with volume, from which proceed their own definitions of surfaces (planes), edges (lines), and vertexes (points).

It is then essential that their *calculation* use volume as its starting point, their unity being this volume. This is difficult for us to gain access to through our mode of operating, for our scholarly method, with its imaginary elements, arises from a position opposite to that imposed by reality.

As a continuation of this study, we are going to indicate here the way to proceed in order to understand one of the profound meanings of the fractional system, and the importance of the fractions 2/3 and 1/3, so as to catch a glimpse of the simplicity of the means used for defining square and cube roots, all of which is founded on the principle of harmony. Since harmony is, by definition, the cosmic order, which, in breaking apart always and inevitably, through affinities, puts itself back in order once again, it was thus by obeying the laws of harmony that the pharaonic masters were able to establish a system that, while being particular, keeps its universal quality.

Now, the intelligence of musical harmony is humanity's most sensitive tool of verification. The ear, as a sensory instrument, and hearing, as a means of judging, form the only sense that allows us to verify directly the harmony of two aspects of a phenomenon, what we might call the Verb, the essence of things. For all other verification we require objective experience.

Hearing detects the subtle differences between sounds, the concord or the discord of tones, therefore of vibrations and wavelengths, and allows us to modify these sources of sound until a perfect harmony is reached. This gives a positive, experimentally reliable character to the sense of hearing that enables us to understand the importance that the Ancients attributed to musical harmony; it is this that imposes itself as the basis for investigating the laws governing Nature. Nothing can replace this natural and innate criterion because any other means of verification, being objective, is fallible.

THE PRINCIPLE OF THE SQUARE ROOTS OF THE LINEAGE OF 2 AND THE CUBE ROOTS OF THE LINEAGE OF 3

One of the first bases for a study of surfaces and volumes is to investigate the behavior, in a geometric progression, of squares and cubes. Let us take for an example the geometric progression with 2 for its ratio and its first term, and above that write down the series of natural numbers, or the arithmetic progression of rate 1, with unity for its first term. In order to begin, and to clarify the series, let us recall that in this double progression the arithmetic series corresponds to powers that act as logarithms for the numbers written directly below them. Thus, we read the power of the cube on the line above, 1 + 2, or 3, and the cube of 2 on the line below, 2 × 4, or 8. By thus adding any two terms of the upper row together, for example, 2 + 4, or 6, the product, in this case 4 × 16, or 64, is read on the lower row. *The arithmetic series plays the role of logarithm for the geometric series.*

We will designate the numbers that are squares by the letter *S*, and the cubes by the letter *C*.

A series:	1	2	3	4	5	6	7	8	9	10	11	12	...
G series:	2	4	8	16	32	64	128	256	512	1024	2048	4096	...
		S		S		S		S		S		S	
			C			C			C			C	

As indicated by Theon, we observe that square numbers are found under every other number and cubic numbers under every third number. The coincidence of a square number and a cubic number can only be made every 2 × 3, that is, every six numbers; thus, the first occurs at the power of 6, the second at the power of 12, and so on. It is apparent from this series that among the numbers of the geometric series of 2 presented here, only 64 and 4096 are simultaneously a square surface and a cubic volume.

The consequence of the rhythm established at the beginning of the arithmetic series 1, 2, 3, corresponding to the geometric series n^1, n^2, n^3, makes understandable the logarithmic principle by the aid of which one extracts square and cube roots. In order to find the square root of a number in the geometric series, one divides the corresponding number in the arithmetic series of powers by 2; in order to find the cube root, one divides the corresponding number in the series of powers by 3 and then reads the respective corresponding numbers in the geometric series.

If we take as the power of 1 the number for which we want to establish the geometric series of square and cube roots, we cannot use, to establish the series of its powers, the current form of notation that expresses roots by means of a radical sign surmounted by the number by which it is necessary to multiply this root to find the number *n*. Furthermore, these "indices" would by no means act in a logarithmic way for the geometric series, since it is impossible to subtract the index 2 from the index 1 to find the cube root of *n*; this leads nowhere. If, on the other hand, one simply applies the principle of division by 2 and by 3, as stated above with regard to the increasing series, it becomes evident that the series of powers of roots will be a fractional series.

Let us construct then a series of fractions that acts logarithmically for the geometric series of base numbers written in the lower row by giving, for example, the index 1 to the number 4096, and by taking the power 1/12 as the limit. Obeying the pharaonic conception, as in the case of cubits that are read in two directions,[1] we write the decreasing series from right to left because it proceeds in the direction opposite to the increasing series:

[1] Cf. chapter 10.

$\frac{1}{12}$	$\frac{1}{6}$	$\frac{1}{4}$	$\frac{1}{3}$	$\frac{5}{12}$	$\frac{1}{2}$	$\frac{7}{12}$	$\frac{2}{3}$	$\frac{3}{4}$	$\frac{5}{6}$	$\frac{11}{12}$	1
2	**4**	**8**	**16**	32	64	128	**256**	512	1024	2048	**4096**
$\sqrt[12]{n}$	$\sqrt[6]{n}$	$\sqrt[4]{n}$	$\sqrt[3]{n}$		$\sqrt[2]{n}$		$\sqrt[3]{n^2}$				n

In this table, established by reversing the preceding series, it is evident that only certain fractions actually act as "roots." Beginning with the power 1, these are the fractions 2/3, 1/2, 1/3, 1/4, 1/6, and 1/12. We recognize here the beginning of the two progressions used in the Rhind Papyrus for the multiplication of numbers by fractions: 1, 1/2, 1/4, ..., which is the inverse geometric progression of ratio 2, and curiously, that which begins with 2/3, namely, 1, 2/3, 1/3, 1/6, 1/12, ..., which is the geometric progression of ratio 2 with 2/3 for its origin.

Here we find the two fractional lineages that are those of the powers of the square and cube roots, and whose geometric function can be graphically demonstrated (see fig. 99). Geometrically, we say that "there is one mean geometric term between unity and a square number, and two mean geometric terms between unity and a cubic number."

Indeed, the square root multiplied by itself restates the number, as the addition of its power with itself restates the Unity (1/2 + 1/2 = 1). The cube root having 1/3 for its power will be multiplied two times by itself to recover the number in the same way that its power must be added two times: 1/3 + 1/3 = 2/3, and 2/3 + 1/3 = 1. This is why the series of powers of cube roots necessarily begins with 2/3, which corresponds to the power of the cube root of the square of the number *n*. Thus, the geometric demonstration places unity between the 1/3 power and the 2/3 power of the number, the latter being by definition the square of the former.[2]

The geometric demonstration (fig. 99) makes the series that is imposed by the successive dimidiations of fractional powers understandable, because the construction amounts to finding the square root of the preceding number, and corresponds then to the division by 2 of the preceding power. This construction applies as well to both the series of squares and of cubes, and provides the two series: 1, 1/2, 1/4, 1/8, ..., and 1, 2/3, 1/3, 1/6, ...

A conjunction is possible between the square and cube roots only up to the power of 1/6, as in the increasing series. In effect, 1/2 − 1/3 = 1/6 and 2/3 − 1/2 = 1/6.

These two geometric progressions are intertwined in such a way that they constitute a sort of chain in which each time four terms form a geometric progression, three of these successive terms are in arithmetic proportion and three are in harmonic proportion. The reduction of the fractions into whole numbers generates the numbers often encountered in the course of the problems in the Rhind Papyrus:

$\frac{1}{12}$	$\frac{1}{8}$	$\frac{1}{6}$	$\frac{1}{4}$	$\frac{1}{3}$	$\frac{1}{2}$	$\frac{2}{3}$	1
				2	3	4	6
		2	3	4	6	8	12
2	3	4	6	8	12	16	24

In this sequence the same numbers recur indefinitely; 2, 3, 4 are in arithmetic proportion and 3, 4, and 6 are in harmonic proportion; 2 × 6 equals 3 × 4 and constitutes the geometric proportion. Now, as we have seen, it is at the power 1/6 that there is a possible conjunction between square and cube roots. This is the stage at which we read in whole numbers, underneath 1/2, 2/3, 1, the series

---

[2] The standard formula of fractional notation of powers is $a^{m/n} = \sqrt[n]{a^m}$, thus $n^{2/3} = \sqrt[3]{n^2}$.

that will result in numbers characteristic of the cube: six surfaces, eight vertices, and twelve edges, numbers that form a harmonic proportion.[3]

MUSICAL HARMONY AND VOLUMES

A relationship obtains between musical harmony and the double logarithmic series of fractional powers. We observe here (in a different arrangement) the three fundamental proportions that make up musical proportion, and this causes us to look again at the ratios of the musical scale in order to see if we can find there (like the two ratios, 3/2 and 4/3, the fifth and the fourth, on either side of the square root of 2) approximate and compensating ratios, one of which is the surface for the other and whose product is exactly 2. We would then have the approximate cube root of 2 and its square, which allow for the reconstituting of the volume. The functional logarithmic series serves as the base, *the fractions are added like the musical intervals, the numbers or ratios of the roots are multiplied like the ratios of the vibrations.*

Thus, let us look for the cube root of 2 and of its square, 4. Between 1 and 2, the octave, there are six tones. One-third of 6 is two tones, the major third. Two-thirds of 6 is four tones, which is a fifth plus a half tone.[4]

Let us recall these essentials: one tone equals 9/8, three and one-half tones equals 3/2, the fifth, and a half tone equals 256/243. Following the method indicated,[5] and simplifying the results, we obtain:

$$\text{the major third = two tones} = \frac{81}{64}, \text{ or } 1.2656..., \text{ for } 2^{1/3} = 1.25992...$$

$$\text{the fifth + half tone = four tones} = \frac{128}{81}, \text{ or } 1.58024..., \text{ for } 2^{2/3} = 1.5874... \, .$$

The results obtained for the two cube roots of 2 and its square are only approximate compared to the cube roots expressed in decimal form, but they present the advantage of answering to the condition that one be exactly the "reciprocal" of the other,[6] and they allow for the integral reconstitution of the volume 2. In effect, 128 is the double of 64 and consequently the product of 81/64 and 128/81 is 2.

The ratios corresponding to the cube roots of the numbers of the geometric series of ratio 2, that is, 2, 4, 8, 16, 32, 64, are found by the same procedure: the cube root of 16 is double that of 2 and consequently has the value of 81/32; the cube root of 32 is double that of 4 and corresponds to 256/81. Now, the geometric series of ratio 2 is precisely the basis of the subdivision of the *hekat*, 1/2, 1/4, 1/8, 1/16, 1/32, 1/64, in which each fraction is represented by one of the parts of the *wedjat* eye.[7]

The bas-reliefs on monuments and tombs often depict the barrels used to measure grain. In certain cases they are represented as groups of different sizes and proportions; among others, one series of barrels arranged in increasing order of size testifies to the fact that there was a system of "volume development" established on the principle of proportional growth.

---

[3] By adopting the radical sign $\sqrt{}$ in place of the fractional notation of powers, our present mode of calculation breaks up the harmony of the system of fractional calculation that the Ancients wisely preserved.

[4] Cf. p. 198 on the principle of the division of volume of pharonic measure by 1/3 and 2/3, and chapter 5, tables 1 to 4.

[5] Two tones = $(9 \times 9)/(8 \times 8)$ = 81/64, and four tones = $(3 \times 256)/(2 \times 243)$.

[6] The product of a number and its simple reciprocal is always 1, for example, $(3/1) \times (1/3) = 1$. Thus we put the term *reciprocal* in quotation marks when we mean it in a multiple form, as for example, $(a/b) \times (3b/a) = 3$.

[7] Cf. chapter 5 and fig. 9.

For example, the ratios between the diameters of two successive barrels appear to be as 81 is to 64, or again as 9 to 8. The latter ratio seems to be preferred, because it serves equally well for the calculation of the surface of a disk, as the Rhind Papyrus teaches. In order to obtain the proportions of two cylinders one of which has double the capacity of the other, it suffices to give one of them 72 for the diameter and 81 for the height, and to give the other 81 for the diameter and 128 for the height; the volumes will be to one another exactly as 1 is to 2. This procedure, if it were verified by the figurations in the tombs, would open the door to all sorts of possible combinations.

The musical scale, on the other hand, does not allow one to find the cube root of 3, but nevertheless the *khar*, representing 2/3 of the cubic cubit, plays an important role in pharaonic measures of capacity. Thanks to the use of the numbers of harmony, the problem can be resolved without having to extract the cube root of 3; knowing that for calculations of volume the Ancients divided the volume by a surface, the only unknown is the depth, or height. Thus, it is only a question of establishing two surfaces that are between them in a proportion that allows the definition of this height in whole numbers.

In the Cairo Museum, for example, there is a basalt cylinder (therefore symbolic) with an interior section of diameter 4 to height 3, therefore with 5 as hypotenuse. Its volume is equal to the square of 8/9 of its diameter multiplied by its height, the calculation yielding 54 and 72, respectively, for height and diameter. If we ask what the proportions are that will give a barrel whose capacity is equal to one and one-half times that of the basalt cylinder, we could proceed in the following way: the cylinder with one and one-half times the capacity of the basalt one will have 9/8 of the preceding for its diameter, that is 81. The surface of its disk is equal to 72^2, and we simply divide this surface by the desired volume 3/2 to establish its height, which is 64.[8]

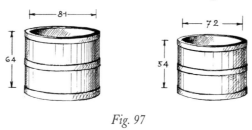

Fig. 97

The small barrel (in the Cairo Museum) has a height of 54 and a diameter of 72. Its volume is 2/3 of the large barrel, which has 64 for height and 81 for diameter, and whose volume is consequently 1.

The ratios derived from these proportions are as follows:

$$\frac{\text{diameter of large barrel}}{\text{diameter of small barrel}} = \frac{81}{72} = \frac{9}{8} = 1 \text{ tone}$$

$$\frac{\text{height of large barrel}}{\text{height of small barrel}} = \frac{64}{54} = \frac{32}{27} = 1\frac{1}{2} \text{ tones}$$

---

[8] The small barrel has a volume of $54 \times 64^2 = 221{,}184$, because 8/9 of 72 is 64. One and one-half $\times$ 221,184 = 331,776, the capacity of the large barrel. The ratio between the surfaces of the two disks is 81/64. It is sufficient to divide the volume 3/2 by this ratio to find the desired height: $\frac{3}{2} \div \frac{81}{64} = \frac{3 \times 64}{2 \times 81} = \frac{192}{162} = \frac{64}{54}$ = the ratio between the heights.

$$\frac{\text{surface of disk of large barrel}}{\text{surface of disk of small barrel}} = \frac{81}{64} = 2 \text{ tones}$$

$$\frac{\text{volume of large barrel}}{\text{volume of small barrel}} = \frac{81}{64} \times \frac{32}{27} = \frac{3}{2} = \text{the fifth} = 3\frac{1}{2} \text{ tones.}$$

Thus, by remaining only within the numbers of harmony, it is possible to establish cylindrical volumes that are in a rigorously exact ratio of capacity with respect to one another. The numbers used in these calculations are familiar; they are also met with in the papyri, on the monuments, and in the numbers of harmony.

Thus the barrels, *ip.t,* which serve to measure grain or to count, *ip,* allow us to approach the meaning of the term used in the first gloss of the Surgical Papyrus, where it specifies that "to examine a man is to count [*ip*] . . . the measure as one measures with a barrel [*ip.t*]. . . ." The gloss continues in such a way that "to measure" means in this case "to count—*ip*—the rhythm of the heart."[9]

The barrel is thus understood as a container *measuring a given number* of particulars, separated from one another, such as grains or the pulse. This is a beautiful image of symbolic relationships that, through their functions, connect a utilitarian object with a living function.[10]

———~~~———

Our familiarity with the method of ciphered, or enumerated, calculation causes us to forget easily the mode of proportional calculation that is characteristic of pharaonic mathematics. Now, the fact that we calculated with an imperfect coefficient for π—defined as the surface of a disk through the square of 8/9 of the diameter, but remaining consistent with this imperfect coefficient in the calculation of its sphere—in no way affects the proportionality that results from it. Thus, the volume of a sphere is equal to 2/3 of the volume of the cylinder that contains it. The ratio is then $1 : 1\frac{1}{2}$, or $10 : 15$. Now, the volume of the cube containing the same sphere will be, taking either 1 or 10 for its volume, 1.9098... or 19.098..., respectively. The sphere plays the role here of the invariable reference 10 in relation to its cylinder and its containing cube.[11] In this case, knowing one of the three terms, such as the sphere, is knowing the other two: the three indispensable elements for defining a given proportion are always bound together by an invariable reference term.

This can only apply to elements of a similar nature. For example, between $\sqrt{\phi}$ and $4/\pi$, the values of which are within 0.001 of each other, a reference value cannot exist because $\sqrt{\phi}$ is a function and $4/\pi$ is a surface divided by a coefficient belonging to the curve, even if we use $\pi = 1.2 \times \phi^2$. It is a question, in a numbered expression, of an absurdity that draws out the importance of the proportional method. This latter excludes any imaginary possibility. Thus it is possible to calculate with simple whole numbers provided that the number used to determine one of the terms be the same for the calculation of the other elements of the proportion.

This simple observation conforms with the vital principle and is applicable as much to the metaphysical philosophy of the origin as to all natural phenomena, including physiology. There is necessarily always a mean term between extremes (or complements) of the same nature, and this mean term plays the role of an invariable reference, being of the nature of both extremes. Thus, as is said in Hermetic theology, the soul is the mean term, invariable, between the spirit and the body.

---

[9] Cf. chapter 14.

[10] It is interesting to juxtapose our notion of sound as waves with the pharaonic approach, which considered sound as volume.

[11] Cf. chapter 11, "The Numbers 7 and 19."

In pharaonic Egypt, one would say that the white crown is what unites the black Nubian origin and the red crown of Lower Egypt.

THE PROBLEM OF THE DUPLICATION OF THE CUBE[12]

FINDING THE CUBE ROOT GEOMETRICALLY
BY THE DIMIDIATION OF THE POWERS 1/2 AND 2/3

The tradition teaches that it is necessary to insert one mean term between unity and the number whose square root one is trying to find, and two mean geometric terms between unity and the number whose cube root one is looking for.[13] In the latter case one of the terms is the square of the other. The geometric transcription of this proportion consists of crossing two geometric progressions of three terms perpendicularly. These are 1, $n^{1/3}$, $n^{2/3}$, and $n^{1/3}$, $n^{2/3}$, n (fig. 98).

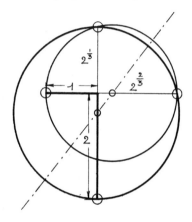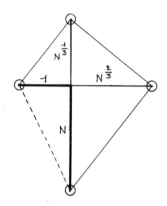

Fig. 98

This construction is only possible if one knows one of the two mean terms that allow us to define the other, however, we must assume that we do not know them and that it is necessary for us to find the geometric procedure through which we arrive at this drawing.

The two mean terms, the objects of our search, are the 2/3 and 1/3 powers of *n*, and we know that the power 2/3 is between *n* and its 1/2 power and that the power 1/3 of *n* is between its 1/2 power and unity, but we do not know in what proportion.

We know, on the other hand, that the "oscillating squares" generate a decreasing progression of powers, 1/2, 1/4, 1/8, etc., of *n*, and the intended purpose is to construct, in a similar way, a decreasing progression of powers (2/3, 1/3, 1/6, etc.) of *n* by means of "oscillating squares." The first construction must allow for the establishing of the second, and the same play of alternation and constant oscillation that discloses these constructions suggests two ways to proceed:

---

[12] Cf. Theon of Smyrna, *Le Nombre de Platon,* note 1, "The Problem of the Duplication of the Çube, Mechanical Solution of Plato," p. 333: "Plato first resolved the problem of the two proportional means. He used an instrument made of two parallel rulers one of which was fixed while the other slid between the grooves of two perpendicular uprights." The "mechanical" solution did not solve the problem.

[13] Regarding this, we refer back to the "dialectical" dispute, based on Democritus, of Plato's assertions concerning the geometric means of planes and volumes. These discussions lead nowhere. In their study of these problems, the Greeks forgot the principle of Unity, which is the very foundation of ancient thought, and which is recalled by Plato.

First, one can study the figure that provides two cube roots that compensate each other, one by excess and the other by deficiency, and two cube roots of the square of the number that also compensate each other. These four results allow us to draw the two unknown branches of the cross, each a little over or under the exact size, and the proof through the curves will give the perfect result.

Second, one can study the figure that gives the correct result directly and that generates the required succession of powers.

These two constructions necessarily have the only known term, that is, the progression of the powers 1/2, 1/4, 1/8, etc., as a point of departure. Let us take, for example, 2 and its square 4. The beginning point for generating oscillating squares is always to consider the sides of the initial square as the four hypotenuses of four inscribed triangles. These four hypotenuses are divided by the altitudes of four interior triangles into a ratio defined as 1 to n (fig. 99, square $ABCD$), and the semicircles drawn by taking the hypotenuses as diameters define the height of each triangle. This height, we recall, is the geometric mean between 1 and n and consequently has the value $n^{1/2}$.

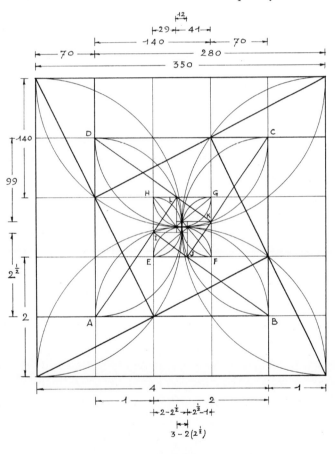

Fig. 99

The square $ABCD$ has $2 + 1 = 3$ for its side. Side AB is the hypotenuse of the triangle AIB, and the diameter of the semicircle with $\frac{1}{2}AB$ for its radius. The perpendicular raised from AB to I between 1 and 2 touches the semicircle defining the altitude of this inscribed triangle as $\sqrt{2}$.

The number 2 is the only number that allows the square $ABCD$ to be circumscribed by a square that corresponds to the formula $n^2 + 1$, because 4 is the only square in which the difference between it and its root is 2, with the result that the square $ABCD$ is both $n^2 - 1$ and $n + 1$.

This figure shows the functions expressed in relation to unity and their transcription in the form of whole numbers issuing from the "canevas" of $\sqrt{2}$.

The constant characteristics that we find in all "oscillating squares," designated as n, are the following:

By taking the square *ABCD* (fig. 99), each side of which has the value $n + 1$, as the starting point *the next square will have $n - 1$ for its side* and will be divided into two segments that are to each other as 1 is to $\sqrt{n}$. Their actual lengths are $\sqrt{n} - 1$ and $n - \sqrt{n}$. Here we rediscover the *germ*, but this germ is always a rectangular number, because it is the product of the *root minus* 1 and the *root*.[14]

The third square generated from the heart of the figure has as its side the difference between the germ (*EJ*) and the root (*JF*) minus 1. *This difference is always a square number, whatever the value of n, and this number is the square of the root minus 1.* Consequently, the difference between the germ and the root minus 1 is the fourth power of the root minus 1, so the heights that define it are to the 1/4 power of n.

Should one consider this square number, determined thus at the heart of the image, as a new germ? Let us look more closely at this construction and its play of alternation. In the large exterior square the unity is at the right; in the following square, *ABCD*, the unity is at the left; and finally in the third square, *EFGH*, the height that functions as the unity ($\sqrt{n} - 1$) is again at the right. Conversely, since it is a question of a play of proportions, we could also say for this small square that its sides are each cut into two segments that are to each other as 2 is to $\sqrt{2}$; in this case, the difference between 2 and its root would indeed be the *germ*.

In the *canevas,* if we take the series of numbers providing the ratios of the square root of 2 in order to transcribe the irrational functions demonstrated by figure 99 into whole numbers, it is not necessary to take any particular numbers. The crossings of eight whorls with 2 for their beginning point determines a central square with 35 for its side; it is the length 70 of the sixth element of each whorl that is divided exactly in two. The crossing of eight whorls with 3 for their beginning point defines a central square with 50 for a side; it is the length 99 of the sixth element of these whorls that is divided by 2 and is within one unit of being exact (being 49 instead of 50).[15]

The ratio 99 to 70 between these two lengths represents the square root of 2, and by adopting this ratio as the numerical base (fig. 99), unity will be represented by the number 70; and consequently, $5 \times 70 = 350$ will be the outer side, $70 \times 3 = 210$ the side of the square *ABCD*, and finally, 70 will be the side of the square *EFGH*. This unity is divided into two segments whose lengths are 41 and 29, in which we recognize the ratio of the root of 2 preceding that of 99 to 70.[16]

The difference between 41 and 29 is 12, which represents the side of the small central square at the heart of the figure, and 12 plays the role of the unity for the group 17/12, which immediately precedes the group 41/29. It becomes difficult to give the name "germ" to the side of this small central square that plays a role of the greatest importance. It appears finally as the nucleus. It is this nucleus that will divide itself into unequal parts and bring about the passage from the geometric series of powers 1/2, 1/4, 1/8, … to the series of powers 2/3, 1/3, 1/6, ….

Like the nucleus that gives life to the cell, this "nucleus" gives movement to our figure, since it is this "difference" that defines the angle of inclination of the square formed by the diagonals of the four interior triangles. Its dividing is going to determine a new angle that will govern the series of volumes.

---

[14] Here, as an exception, we keep the term $\sqrt{n}$ used in chapter 5, "The Root."

[15] Cf. chapter 8, "The *Canevas* and $\sqrt{2}$," and table 7.

[16] Ibid.

Even though we started from the exterior in order to construct the inverted geometric progression of the squared functions by taking unity and the number as the outer limit,[17] the development is going to be made from the center toward the exterior where we will obtain the final, geometrically proven result.

As primitive and approximate as it may be, the starting point will be the dividing of the central nucleus. Into how much? In order to find a ratio approaching the cube root of 2, what is it that must be added to one part and subtracted from the other at the middle of side *EF* (fig. 99) so that this side can be divided into two segments that will be to one another as 1 is to the cube root of 2? What fraction of the nucleus will allow us to establish this ratio? Based on our investigation, a single function, dictated by the first division of pharaonic volumes, will answer this question: 2/3 and 1/3.

Let us try with the first whole numbers drawn from the *canevas* in order to make the operation more understandable. The side of the small central square is 12; one-third of it is 4, and two-thirds of it is 8. We can also use its sixth, which is 2.

It is a matter of subtracting from one part and adding to the other one of these fractions of the nucleus to the half-side 35 of square *EFGH* in order to obtain the approximate ratios we are looking for:

$$\frac{2}{3}\begin{cases} 35+8 = \frac{43}{27} \\ 35-8 = \end{cases} = 1.592592... \quad \text{instead of } 1.5874... \text{ for } 2^{2/3}$$

$$\frac{1}{3}\begin{cases} 35+4 = \frac{39}{31} \\ 35-4 = \end{cases} = 1.25806... \quad \text{instead of } 1.259912... \text{ for } 2^{1/3}$$

$$\frac{1}{6}\begin{cases} 35+2 = \frac{37}{33} \\ 35-2 = \end{cases} = 1.21212... \quad \text{instead of } 1.2246... \text{ for } 2^{1/6}$$

The calculation allows quick verification that the cube root of 4 thus obtained is too large and the cube root of 2 is too small. It is also easy to see that the product of these two ratios does not give exactly 2; nevertheless, with these numbers, which are found directly through the *canevas*, one can form pairs of ratios in which the product will be exactly 2 and thus answer to the essential condition of the stated problem.[18]

We are going to prove, by means of geometry, the necessity of the division of the "nucleus" by 2/3 and 1/3 in order to pass from the powers 1/2 and 1/4 to the powers 2/3 and 1/3. In beginning from this initial given, it is necessary to refer to the angular play that allows the approximation of the correct coefficient to occur. It is a question of finding the pivot angle that allows this passage from one series to the other.

Let us take as a starting point the division of the central nucleus into three parts; one-third of the nucleus will define the angle we are looking for. The division of the nucleus into thirds gives us the choice between two angles, α and β, whose functional roles we distinguish and designate by their particular characters: α = the *generating angle* and β = the *pivot angle*.

[17] We recall here that only the number 2 allows for beginning the construction with the square of a number, since the square *ABCD* that then is in second position corresponds to both $n^2 - 1$ and $n + 1$.

[18] The above functions, established with the numbers from our tables, have these results: the cube root of 4 would equal 1.59324... and would therefore be too large; the cube root of 2 would equal 1.2583... and would therefore be too small; the 1/6 power of 2 would equal 1.12132... and would therefore be too small.

There are several methods for constructing ratios that are exactly self-compensating; the simplest method consists in dividing 2 by the original chosen ratio. Starting from these original ratios, there is also a formula with which we can come closer and closer to the irrational coefficients we are looking for.

The angle we are looking for is between these two angles (fig. 100).

Fig. 100

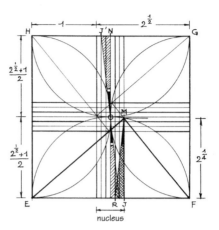

In the square *EFGH*, the two segments *JF* and *EJ* are proportionally to each other as 1 is to $2^{1/2}$. The nucleus therefore has the value of $EJ - JF = 2^{1/2} - 1$, and its division into thirds determines the width *RJ* $= J'N$. The *pivot angle* has $RJ = J'N$ for its perpendicular and *NO*, that is, the half-sum of *EJ* and *JF*, for its larger side. The *generating angle* has *RJ* for its perpendicular and *JM*, that is, the geometric mean between *EJ* and *JF*, for its larger side. The generating angle is larger than the pivot angle.[19]

We have already established how the "oscillating squares" generate from the exterior toward the interior the succession of fractional powers of a number by successive dimidiations. The halving of the angles must be noted as well: each pivot angle is half the preceding generating angle (fig. 101).

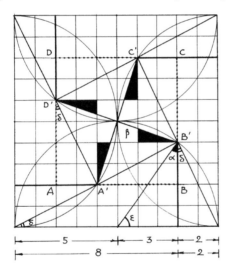

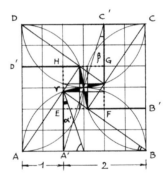

Fig. 101

Draw a figure similar to fig. 99, that is, a square with $4 + 1 = 5$ for its side, but subdivide each unit in two in order to read the angles in the form of whole-number notation.

Angle δ has a ratio of 1 to 2. Angle ε is its double and has a ratio of 4 to 3. Angle α, the generating angle, is the inverse of ε and thus has the value of 3 to 4. Angle β, the pivot angle of the square $A'B'C'D'$ is defined by the difference between 45° and δ and is consequently half of α. Its ratio is 1 to 3.

In the square *ABCD* the generating angle α' has a ratio of 1 to the square root of 2, and the pivot angle of the interior square *EFGH*, angle γ, is therefore half of angle α'.[20]

[19] We recall that $2^{1/2}$ is equal to $\sqrt{2}$. The length *NO* being the median of the square, the nucleus is divided into six. In this regard, let us recall that six is the side of the perfect cube, because the sum of the surfaces that surround it is equal to its volume, 216.

[20] In fact, the subtraction and addition of angles allows us to verify the geometric demonstration of fig. 101 by calculation.

The particular character of the two angles, α and β, can be summarized as follows:

Angle α is always double the pivot angle of the interior square generated by the figure. It is contracting (centripetal) and generative. Angle β is the pivot angle generated by the preceding figure. It has a dilating (centrifugal) character and causes growth.

The division of the nucleus into three determines two angles (fig. 100) that have exactly the same functional characteristics as angles α and β of the original figure (fig. 101).

With the generating angle α one is able to construct fig. 102, which provides the four coefficients that are required and generates a new pivot angle β that approaches the perfect angle we are looking for.

The construction established with the generating angle α is based on the proportion having the power 1/6 for its mean term, thus, $n : n^{5/6} : n^{2/3} = n^{2/3} : n^{1/2} : n^{1/3} = n^{1/3} : n^{1/6} : 1$, and corresponds exactly to the essential condition that was posed, which consists in finding *the approximate values for the cube roots of 2 and 4 so that they compensate each other absolutely.* Indeed, the products of $b \times c$ and of $a \times d$ allow the full recovery of the quantity 2 in all its integrity.

Moreover, in taking the means of lengths a, b, c, and d, it is possible to draw the two unknown branches of the cross (fig. 98) by proceeding in the following way:

$$\frac{a + 2b}{3} = 1.25992..., \text{ for the cube root of } 2 = 1.25992...$$

$$\frac{2c + d}{3} = 1.5874..., \text{ for the cube root of } 4 = 1.5874....$$

By virtue of these mean terms whose degree of precision is practically unverifiable, the establishment of the cross is possible, and drawing the two semicircumferences will give the irrational and absolute result. The problem of the duplication of the cube is thus solved in this way.

Our goal, however, is to find the function that allows the final cross to be generated by means of the oscillating squares, and this genesis can be made only by means of the perfect pivot angle obtained through successive oscillations. The pivot angle β, found by the simple division of the nucleus into thirds for the length NO (fig. 100), was too small by about $0°2'9''$. The second pivot angle β', determined by the generating angle α (fig. 102), is too large by about $0°1'3''$. The last construction establishes the mean between these two angles and provides the pivot angle β'', which is perfect and is verified by drawing the curves (fig. 103).

Thus, the principle 2/3 and 1/3 is shown to be the constant that controls all the operations we have conducted in order to find the perfect angle. This principle applies as well to the numbers 3 and 5, thanks to which the pharaonic system of measures, based on the geometric series of 2, then division by 2/3, and finally by 20 and 30, is resolvable and therefore explained.

Summary and Conclusion

It is necessary to begin with a simple element showing the function of two series, one of which starts with 1/2 and the other with 2/3. We just saw that in a square with n (the number) plus 1 for the side, one generates toward the interior a series of oscillating squares and a series of ratios through which we obtain the inverted progression of the powers of n, 1/2, 1/4, 1/8, etc.

The division into three of the "nucleus" obtained at the center of the figure determines the pivot angle that allows for the construction, by reduplication, of the generating angle, by virtue of which one then proceeds to the series of powers 2/3, 1/3, 1/6, etc. (fig. 102).

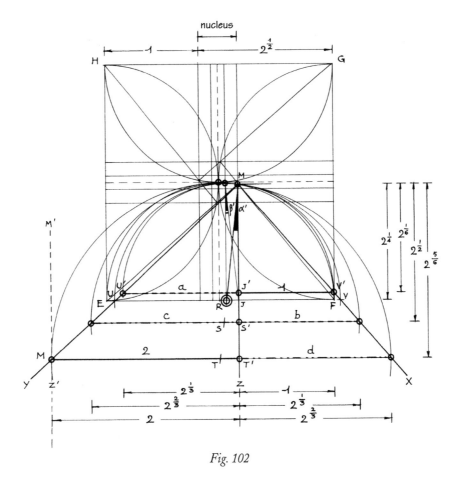

Fig. 102

In the square *EFGH*, one-third of the nucleus *RJ* determines with *JM* a triangle having for its hypotenuse *RM*, which is the radius, taking *R* as the center, for the semicircle with *UV* as the diameter. This straight line is cut into two segments, *VJ* and *JU*, which are to each other as 1 is to the approximate cube root of 2, for the height *JM* that passes proportionally from the power 1/4 to the power 1/6.

To restore these proportional lengths to their actual sizes in relation to the unity *JF*, draw two lines perpendicular to each other from the apex *M* that pass, respectively, through *V* and *U*, and continue to *X* and *Y*.

The crossing of the vertical *FG* with the line *MX* determines the point *V′*. The line parallel to *UV* drawn from *V′* to *U′* is divided into two segments: *V′J′*, equal to 1, and *J′U′*, segment *a*, which represents a value in excess of the cube root of 2.

Extend the vertical *MJ* to *Z*. Carry over onto this vertical the height *MS′*, which is equal to the square root of 2. The line parallel to *U′V′* drawn through the point *S′* determines the two segments *b* and *c*, which equal, respectively, the cube root of 2 by deficiency and the cube root of 4 by excess.

Draw the vertical *M′Z′* to a distance 2 on *MZ*. Where this vertical crosses *MY*, draw the parallel to *UV*, which crosses *MZ* at *T′* and is divided by this point into two segments, which equal, respectively, 2 and the cube root of 4 by excess, segment *d*.

The extension of the radius *MR* to *S* and to *T* allows us to draw semicircles with *MS* and *MT* for their radii. These semicircles should cut the lines *MY* and *MZ* at the points where they cross the horizontals established by extending *SS′* and *TT′*, respectively.

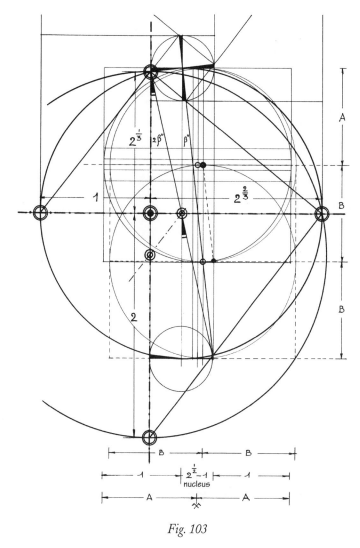

Fig. 103

The length A is equal to $(2^{1/2} + 1)/2$ and the length B is equal to the radius RM of fig. 102. If we take the total width of the nucleus as the shorter side and $2B + A$ as the base of a triangle for which the angle of the apex β'' is the pivot angle we are looking for, then $2\beta''$ becomes the generating angle of the final figure in which the proportional values $1, 2^{1/3}, 2^{2/3}$, and 2 provide the geometric progression.

This entire study is governed by the pharaonic division of unitary cubic volume (cubic cubit) into 2/3 (the *khar*) and the division of the *hekat* (1/30 of the cubic cubit) into 1/2, 1/4, 1/8, 1/16, 1/32, and 1/64. This system associates the division of the volume by 3 with the division by 2.

We can only understand the multiplication of a number by the fractional series 2/3, 1/3, 1/6, … *beginning* with 2/3—an anomaly that has always intrigued mathematicians—through the system of powers in fractional form that becomes evident in this exposition.

With the demonstration made and the principle known, it is sufficient to begin from the whole numbers at the base of the *canevas* to realize the angles and ratios in proportional notation, which the construction of the hieratic pavement based on 1 : 2 and 1 : 3 demonstrates.[21] The numbers we

[21] Cf. chapter 8

have indicated (fig. 99) are found in the construction of the hieratic pavement of the square root of 2 and allow the direct passage to the progression of the powers 2/3, 1/3, 1/6, etc.

The problem of the duplication of the cube that Plato had tried to solve "mechanically" appears to have been a traditional legacy from pharaonic Egypt,[22] whose geometric solution was no longer known in Plato's time.

This will be applied in the temple in order to establish the axes that thus play a universal, functional role in realizing the harmonic relationship between 2 and 3, which is the unification of the two elements at the base of the Universe, elements contradictory to each other in the way the poles of an axis, or oil and water, can be.

GNOMONIC GROWTH OF CUBES AND A PRACTICAL METHOD FOR EXTRACTING A CUBE ROOT

The growth of a cubic volume is made by the addition to the original volume of a gnomon composed of elements that are themselves volumes. The first cube is 1, followed by the cube of 2, that is 8. The difference is then 7, the first "gnomon" number. This gnomon is formed of seven small cubes, each with a value of 1. The third cube is 27; the difference between 8 and 27 is 19. Now 19 is composed of the following 7 elements (fig. 104): 3 times the surface A^2 of the enclosed cube, multiplied by the side 1 or B; 3 times the side A of the enclosed cube, multiplied by the surface 1 or B^2; 1 times the cube of 1, or B.

In numbers we have then,

$$3 \times 4 \times 1 = 12$$
$$3 \times 2 \times 1 = 6$$
$$1 \times 1 \times 1 = 1$$

Total 19.

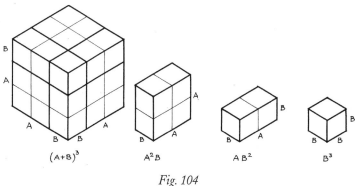

$$(A+B)^3 \qquad A^2B \qquad AB^2 \qquad B^3$$

Fig. 104

Let us recall the algebraic formula that corresponds to the decomposition of our cube $(a + b)^3$ into the enclosed cube and the seven elements of its gnomon: $(a + b)^3 = a^3 + 3a^2b + 3ab^2 + b^3$. If we want to apply this formula to extract a cube root of whatever number, we shall call x the length that is added to a to form the side of the given volume n. We subtract the volume whose side a is known from n, and the remainder should decompose into $3a^2x + 3x^2a + x^3$.

---

[22] Cf. chapter 13. Notice the angular differences between the axes of Amun, Mut, and Khonsu, which are as 2/3 and 1/3. Cf. also vol. 2, plate 44 and fig. 238, the hypostyle room built on the cube root of 4, the functional angle of which is given in relation to north.

Leaving aside the x^3, the remainder divided by 3 is then equal to $a^2x + ax^2$. If we replace our formula with a form of language that closely conforms to the ancient mind, we would say: "I have added a^2 times my side and a times my surface, which equals c."

Now, the solution of this problem is given in one of the Babylonian tablets,[23] and with it, it becomes child's play to extract any cube root with, let us say, an approximation to the first degree by excess, since we know that in leaving out the x^3, our result will be a little too large.

Let us look, for example, at the cube root of $234\frac{1}{2}$. The largest cube in this number is 216, whose cube root is 6. We take the remainder, $18\frac{1}{2}$, and divide it by 3, which is $6\frac{1}{6}$. Continuing from this stage, we only have to follow the model of the ancient problem while specifying one detail: the number of sides will always be the square of the number of surfaces. With this said, we operate as follows:

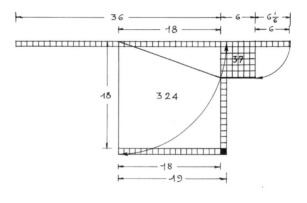

"I have added 36 times the side of my square and 6 times the surface = 6 + 1/6.

    You shall write 36 and 6.

    You shall carry 6 to $6\frac{1}{6}$ = 37.

    You shall divide 36 into two = 18.

    You shall cross 18 and 18 = 324.

    You shall add to it 37 = 361.

    This is the square of 19.

    You shall subtract 18, which you have crossed, from 19; you shall inscribe 1.

    The reciprocal of 6 is 1/6.

    Multiply 1 by 1/6 = 1/6. This is the side of my square."

Fig. 105

Thus, 1/6 represents the value of that which we call x; and the cube root of $234\frac{1}{2}$ is 6 + 1/6. The proof is that the square of 6 + 1/6 is 38 + 1/36. The cube of 6 + 1/6 is 234 + 1/2 + 1/216.

The reconstituted cube with the side found in this way is 1/216 in excess. Now, the chosen example eliminated the difficulty of extracting the square root (19 in this case). Knowing that the so-called Heronian formula was then generally used, this extraction is not an obstacle. Taking 256, for example, and by operating with the method described above, we can verify the margin of error by doing the following "proof": take the square of the found cube root and divide the number whose cube root one seeks by this square. The two roots obtained will be by excess and by deficiency. The cube root of 256 by excess is 6.35; $6.35^2 = 40.3225$, and $256 \div 40.3225 = 6.34881...$. Now, $(6.35 + 6.35 + 6.34881) \div 3 = 6.349603...$, which, when compared with the cube root of this number given in our current tables, is identical to the fourth decimal place.

—⁓—

Given the rapidity and remarkable simplicity of this method of extraction, it can be asked why it is not taught in our schools. The formula for the definition of the cube and its gnomon has certainly been known since the greatest antiquity. This is the formula that at present serves as the basis for extracting cube roots, but in its application to our decimal system the procedure of calculation becomes particularly long and complicated.

The method inspired by the Babylonian calculation is, on the contrary, extremely simple. Having at its disposal a table of cubes in whole numbers, one looks for the largest cube contained in the number whose cube root one must extract. The remainder is divided by 3 and corresponds to our algebraic formula $a^2x + ax^2$. Now the algebraic formula $ax^2 + bx$ is constantly used in second-degree equations. One need only substitute b with a^2 to discover the equation that can be used to find the cube root of any number.

The "proof" that leads to an almost perfect result is inspired by the ancient method of calculation that always looks for the "reciprocal" of a coefficient, and finally, for the established mean based on the fundamental law governing cubes, 1/3 and 2/3, which a new application in the "*canevas* of volumes" will clarify even further.

THE *CANEVAS* OF VOLUMES

There exists a *canevas* for cube roots as for square roots, although their formations are very different. In order to construct a *canevas* of cube roots, one must not lose sight of the laws governing the natural formation of geometric series. By allowing oneself to be guided by these laws, one is able to perceive a series leading gradually toward the cube root of a number, notably toward that of 2, the most irrational root and the most difficult to find, because 2 is the only number whose square is less than any cubic number, and consequently the only one that requires the finding of two unknowns.

All numbers above 2, as for example 3, have a square larger than the first cube, 8. Knowing that between 1 and 3 one must insert the cube root of 3 and its square, 9, it is possible to construct the first approximate geometric proportion of four terms by looking first for the cube root of 9; this is necessarily 2 plus a fractional amount, which will be put aside for the moment. Already, one can put between 1 and 3: 1 . x . 2 . 3. To find x, take the square of 2 and divide it by 3, making 4/3. One obtains the first possible approximation that can serve as a starting point: 1 . 4/3 . 2 . 3, which can be transcribed into whole numbers as 3 . 4 . 6 . 9. From this point on, the searcher can remain "caught" for a long time by a procedure that seems, at first glance, to be the geometric proof. This is done by means of a cross upon which the initial ratios are written by perpendicularly crossing the approximate geometric proportions, and the genesis series is easily conceived by adding together the opposite arms on the cross to generate the following: $3 + 6 = 9$ and $4 + 9 = 13$. The fourth arm is equal to 3×9, or 27. The only term left to find is the length of the third arm, which is $\sqrt{13 \times 27}$, or $\sqrt{351}$. Now, as in the present case, the happy circumstance in which the product of the extremes gives a square is only rarely encountered. Thus, the extraction of a square root by this method will always lead us to an irrational number that must be excluded from the procedure by means of the *canevas* (fig. 106). *In adding the two opposite terms that make up two of the arms of the new cross, the center of the cross shifts uniformly on the diagonal in the direction of growth of the two terms. The function is logical and unequivocal,* and it obeys, moreover, a function that we can transcribe by a formula that is perfectly correct and that constitutes a constant.

In this construction, each phase determines a rectangle that has a value in itself, but that also represents an arrested moment that does not engender a series. The true method is simple and its very simplicity is its beauty: it begins from the absurd and does not depend on any prior calculation. It is the number 2 and the mystical function ϕ that represent the perfect model.

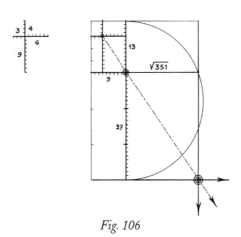

Fig. 106

Between 1 and 2 there is only the unity 1, and the first cross will have three equal arms 1, 1, 1, whereas the fourth will have the value of the double of 1, or 2. It is essential to add a fifth term, which is double the second, that is, 2, to this beginning.

Starting from here it is necessary to obey the fundamental law according to which *squares are governed by the number 2 and cubes by the number* 3, the law that is applied in the division of the "nucleus" into 1/3 and 2/3. Thus, *the original terms are added three by three* and constitute a new series of four terms to which it is necessary to add a fifth:

$$1 + 1 + 1 = 3$$
$$1 + 1 + 2 = 4$$
$$1 + 2 + 2 = 5$$
$$2 \times 3 = 6 \quad \text{and} \quad 2 \times 4 = 8.$$

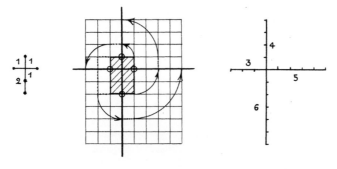

Fig. 107a

This first formation corresponds approximately *to within a unit* to the condition posed by two geometric proportions crossed perpendicularly: $3 \times 5 = 15$ and $4^2 = 16$; and $4 \times 6 = 24$ and $5^2 = 25$. The addition of the first origin numbers defines the numbers of the sacred triangle, which results as well from adding two 1 to 2 angular ratios by the harmonic proportion in which 3 and 6 are the extremes, 4 the harmonic mean, and 5 the mean term of the subcontrary to the harmonic.[24]

[24] Let us recall that the construction of the harmonic proportion between 1 and 2, or *b* and *a*, leads to numbers formed in the following way: the largest term = $a^2 + ab = 6$; the smallest term = $b^2 + ab = 3$; the harmonic mean = $2ab = 4$; the subcontrary mean = $a^2 + b^2 = 5$.

Finally, the sum of the cubes of 3, 4, and 5 is equal to the cube of 6. This first cross is then made up of numbers that have particularly remarkable properties.

The genesis series is made by addition as before:

$$3 + 4 + 5 = 12$$
$$4 + 5 + 6 = 15$$
$$5 + 6 + 8 = 19$$
$$2 \times 12 = 24 \quad \text{and} \quad 2 \times 15 = 30.$$

These four numbers already provide a good approximation for the cube root of 2. Their use is attested to in the Rhind Papyrus[25] when the scribe asks for the division of the quantity 2 by 19/12, and finds 24/19 as the result, expressed in the form of unit fractions. The operation returns to dividing 2 by the cube root of 4, and the result is the cube root of 2. These numbers also occur among those in the "human canon" and, finally, in a grid in the tomb of Ukhotep at Meir,[26] demonstrating the application in *canevas* form.

The construction resulting from the addition of the three terms is a logical function but with an inversion (figs. 107a and 107b). *The addition is made in the opposite direction of the growth of the terms,* that is, as a result of a retrograde movement.

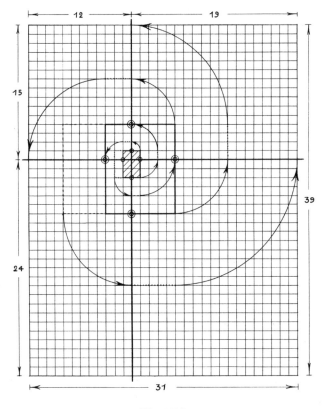

Fig. 107b

The numbers increase in a clockwise direction; they are read counterclockwise. The center does not move; the numbers are counted on the grid.

[25] Cf. problem 32 of the Rhind Papyrus.
[26] Cf. chapter 37, and fig. 247 (vol. 2).

The series of numbers obtained by the successive addition of three terms following the given model (figs. 107a and 107b) constitute the following groups:

$$46, \quad 58, \quad 73, \quad 92,$$
$$\text{then } 177, \quad 223, \quad 281, \quad 354,$$
$$\text{then } 681, \quad 858, \quad 1081, 1362, \text{ etc.}$$

This last group is still only the fourth addition starting from the sacred triangle, and already the coefficients transcribed into our decimal system are:

$$\left. \begin{array}{l} \dfrac{1362}{1081} = 1.2599444958... \\[2mm] \dfrac{1081}{858} = 1.2599067599... \\[2mm] \dfrac{858}{681} = 1.2599118942... \end{array} \right\} \quad \text{mean} = 1.2599210499....$$

The mean of the three coefficients obtained, 1.259921..., is comparable with the cube root given in our current tables, 1.2599, or, better yet, to that found as the mean in our logarithmic tables after interpolation: 1.259921....

The ratios given above always allow for the recovery of the quantity 2 because they are established by means of "reciprocals," something our decimal calculation never allows.

The numbers govern. Even in starting from the absurd, there are imperative laws through which one arrives at perfection, on the condition of obeying the numbers and not suppositions.

Example from the *Canevas* of the Cube Root of 3

The numbers beyond 2 all have squares larger than the first cube, which is 8. Thus 3 has 9 for its square and its cube root is equal to 2 plus a fraction.

The first numbers that are necessary for the *canevas* are 1 . 1 . 2 . 3, and the triple of 1 is 3. The series unfolds by successive addition following the model given for the number 2, thus,

$$\begin{array}{ll} 1 + 1 + 2 = \; 4, & \text{which is simplified to 2} \\ 1 + 2 + 3 = \; 6, & \text{which is simplified to 3} \\ 2 + 3 + 3 = \; 8, & \text{which is simplified to 4} \\ \multicolumn{2}{c}{3 \times 4 = 12 \;\text{ and }\; 3 \times 6 = 18, \text{ which is simplified to 6 and 9.}} \end{array}$$

It is remarkable that here again the four numbers resulting from the addition of the origin numbers are identical to those resulting from the establishment of the harmonic proportion of 1 to 3 in which the extremes are 4 and 12, and the harmonic mean term is 6. On the other hand, the subcontrary mean does not provide the third term; that case only occurs when looking for the cube roots of 2 and ϕ.

The second addition provides the following ratios:

$$\begin{array}{l} 2 + 3 + 4 = \; 9 \\ 3 + 4 + 6 = 13 \\ 4 + 6 + 9 = 19 \\ \quad 3 \times 9 = 27 \;\text{ and }\; 3 \times 13 = 39. \end{array}$$

The third addition determines the ratios:

$$9 + 13 + 19 = 41$$
$$13 + 19 + 27 = 59$$
$$19 + 27 + 39 = 85$$
$$3 \times 41 = 123 \quad \text{and} \quad 3 \times 59 = 177.$$

The original ratios already provide these coefficients:

$$\left.\begin{array}{l} \dfrac{123}{85} = 1.447058... \\[2.2em] \dfrac{85}{59} = 1.4406779... \\[2.2em] \dfrac{59}{41} = 1.4390243... \end{array}\right\} \quad \text{mean} = 1.4422534... \text{ for } \sqrt[3]{3} = 1.44225....$$

Example of the *Canevas* of the Cube Root of 5

The number 5 has 25 for its square, very near to the cube of 3, or 27. The third term intervening between 1 and 5 will be accepted as 3, and the second is obtained by taking the whole number nearest to $(3 \times 3)/5$, which is 2, to verify the proportion, whence the series of numbers that constitute the first possible ratios: 1, 2, 3, 5. The fifth term will be 2×5, or 10.[27]

The additions succeed one another as follows:

$$1 + 2 + 3 = 6, \qquad\qquad \text{which is simplified to } 3$$
$$2 + 3 + 5 = 10, \qquad\qquad \text{which is simplified to } 5$$
$$3 + 5 + 10 = 18, \qquad\qquad \text{which is simplified to } 9$$
$$5 \times 6 = 30 \quad \text{and} \quad 5 \times 10 = 50, \quad \text{which is simplified to 15 and 25}$$

It should be noted that here again the two extreme terms obtained by the first addition, 6 and 30, are identical to those formed by the harmonic proportion established for 1 to 5 in which the mean term is 10, as is the second term of the above series.

The reduction of the numbers found allows the successive additions that furnish the numbers 17, 29, 49, and 85, and also 145. The third addition determines the series 95, 163, 279, 475, and 815.

Stopping the additions at this point, the mean of the coefficients determined thus far gives the following numbers:

$$\left.\begin{array}{l} \dfrac{475}{279} = 1.7025089... \\[2.2em] \dfrac{279}{163} = 1.7116564... \\[2.2em] \dfrac{163}{95} = 1.7157894... \end{array}\right\} \quad \text{mean} = 1.7099849....$$

We can compare the mean of the three coefficients to the cube root of 5 in our tables, 1.7100, which is greater, or to that calculated from the tables of logarithms, 1.709975.... The fourth solution gives 1.7099767....

---

[27] Thus, $1 \times 3 = 2^2 - 1$, and $2 \times 5 = 3^2 + 1$.

Already the third addition, beginning from the original imperfect ratio, gives a result that to the fourth decimal place is as precise as that found logarithmically, so that when all is said and done, the *canevas* is in practice simpler and handier than any other method. By pushing the additions further, the verification is automatic and allows one to obtain the desired precision for the cube root of any number less than 8.[28]

CONCLUSION

We have not found any mention in the history of ancient mathematics of the practical, simple, and rapid method for extracting cube roots as described here by means of the gnomons. It was inspired by Babylonian mathematics but results from the totality of our studies of the ancient methods.

As for the method of extracting cube roots by the *canevas,* it is purely pharaonic and goes back to the very essence of the mathematical science of the Ancients: harmonic proportion and the other proportions that proceed from it.

It is thus the *numbers* of pharaonic Egypt that guide us by means of certain problems of the Rhind Papyrus, by the relationships of certain representations in the temples and the tombs, and, in general, by the numbers that govern the method of calculation and their applications in architecture.

We have mentioned the basalt cylinder (barrel) of Tuthmosis III in the Cairo Museum as an example of a symbolic object. When a cylinder whose median section is the 3 to 4 sacred triangle is sculpted in basalt, this "barrel" can only be a testimony because it is impossible to handle. We are dealing therefore with a symbol, not a measuring device intended for use.[29]

The study of pharaonic measures of capacity shows the use of subdivisions such as 2/3, 1/20, 1/30, and also 1/2, 1/4, 1/8, etc. This system corresponds completely to a very particular symbolic grouping that links together the numbers of time and musical harmony. It is difficult to admit that such a complex, cohesive system could have been developed by a people who were unable to extract the cube roots of the numbers that served as their foundation, that is, 2, 3, and 5.

We have been dealing with an orientation of thought that from the outset surpasses ours. These masters were able to establish a system in which the fundamental elements of time, length, and volume—therefore of space, path, and time—are linked together by the law of harmony that creates the cohesion of the Universe.

This allowed them to construct their mathematics on the simple foundation of whole numbers, *starting from premises that are philosophically correct and numerically false,* knowing that the *evolution* (the series) will arrive at the greatest precision that human conjecture can hope for.

Thus, the first rectangle formed in the interior of the *canevas* of the cube root of 2 is as 2 is to 3. The numbers resulting from the first addition are those of the sacred rectangle evoked by the section of the basalt barrel. The second rectangle thus formed is as 4 to 5. Finally, the resulting numbers of the second addition are 12, 15, 19, applied in the human canon to three positions of the body: kneeling, sitting, and standing. The rectangle thus formed is as 31 to 39, a ratio identical to that obtained from the geometric way of dividing the nucleus into three, starting from the numbers of the *canevas* of the square root of 2.

[28] For example, between 1 and 6, 2 and 4 will be placed. This is a bad start because if $2^2 = 1 \times 4$, $2 \times 6 = 12$, whereas $4^2 = 16$. Nevertheless, from the second addition we get 1.81728, compared with 1.8172... taken from our tables.
[29] Cf. above, fig. 97.

It appears more and more that the magical value of numbers has directed and unified the different systems of measure, of capacity, of the canon, and so on. Only the originating numbers have a real value, for it is only by virtue of knowing them that the series can be developed, quite naturally, through proportionality. Knowing the use of the group 3, 4, 5, 6 for the first possibility of the cube root of 2, and on the other hand the group 12, 15, 19, 24, it was impossible to discover the link that united them, and yet, their use is attested to in the Egyptian monuments.

We can see this link is given in a very simple way through the *canevas*, this architecture of number, by the addition of *three successive terms*. The numbers derived from it are real and, since they occur in certain cases in conjunction with the *canevas* established for the square roots, this opens the door to many possibilities.

Here we are far from the doubts and hesitations expressed about pharaonic mathematical knowledge.[30] This knowledge goes beyond a simple mathematics of quantity and relates the gesture of number to the gesture of life, as, for example, the numbers of volume to those of the human canon that conform to the laws of human growth.

I have said elsewhere that the earthworm is in some way the child of the sun; is not this eye of Ra for us the symbol of that which is vision for God?

The law of harmony governs affinities, and affinities govern the assemblage of all things, regulating the living equilibrium of the world.

This chapter on the study of volumes, though it presents difficulties to the reader, is nevertheless the one that most reveals the genuine orientation of the Ancients. If the extraction of cube roots drawn from Babylonian principles and based on the gnomonic composition of the cube remains accessible to our logic, the same cannot be said for the procedure of the pharaonic *canevas* of cubes. Here the mathematician finds himself before a difficulty that is no longer "mathematical"—which may be consolation to the nonspecialized reader. In pharaonic thought we are dealing with procedures that are directly contrary to our own.

Our thought and our science begin with facts, that is the effects, in order to seek out the causes. The pharaonic sage begins with the cause in order to arrive at the fact, the effect. It is absurd at the outset, exactly as the metaphysical and theological premise of the origin is absurd for our rational logic. We have already encountered a similar absurdity when Theon of Smyrna recalls the Pythagorean statement: "Since unity is the principle of all figures, according to the supreme generating reason, so also the ratio of the diagonal and the side is found within unity. . . . Let us suppose, for example, two unities, one of which is the diagonal and the other the side, because it is necessary that unity, which is the principle of all, be in potentiality both the side and the diagonal."[31]

Beginning from this fact, we observe that the diagonal *cannot* be equal to the side of the square. The sage said: at the beginning there is no possibility of distinction, the elements are equal to one another, in other words, at the beginning there is the Unity and a scission of the Unity into unities.

---

[30] In this regard, let us recall what Gillain wrote on an example of calculation for the trunk of a pyramid found in the Moscow Papyrus and corresponding to the formula $V = r(h/3)(a^2 + ab + b^2)$, a and b being the respective sides of each of the bases: "We are not unaware that its establishment results from relatively complicated considerations that seem to exclude all empirical thought. However, we shall observe its correct application in a problem from the Moscow Papyrus that was fortunately published by Professor Touraeff. . . . In the calculations of the papyri we have come across only the most simple squares and square roots; but we may expect anything from a people who knew how to arrive at the trinomial $(a^2 + ab + b^2)$ contained in one of the most algebraic of the formulas of three-dimensional geometry." *La Science égyptienne*, pp. 282–83.

[31] Theon of Smyrna, *Le Nombre de Platon*, part 1, §31, p. 71.

There is the same starting point for the establishment of the root of the first "space" given by *three unities* as the square is given by two: the original ternary principle from which comes the first ratio between *itself* and the *other* that results from it. The series is only addition, that is to say, "fractioning."

Now, the Universe, whether it is a question of an atom or the All, exists and persists by the grace of an internal equilibrium that we call harmony. Our senses, an effect of this equilibrium, disclose to us the elements of this harmony predominantly through the ear, which senses directly without being subjected to mental analysis.

These principles, expressed by simple numbers, are that which I call the "seed of the Temple," traces of which can be seen up until our great Middle Ages. The reasoning behind this kind of thought, which appears to us as nonsense, has also intrigued the exceptional scholar Paul Tannery. Certain irregularities of calculation, founded on principles belonging more to theology than to rational science, have led this researcher toward unexpected discoveries with regard to our Western thought. For example, when Tannery was studying the *Elements* of Eudoxus, he noticed a peculiar terminology, which he summarized as follows: "These numbers being multiplied, the ratios form a composite by addition; when the two terms of a ratio are elevated to the second or to the third power, the ratio is said to double, triple."[32] This anomalous language led Tannery to discover the important role that music plays in ancient mathematics. When Kepler called "sesquialter," that is, 3/2, the ratio between a cube and a square, he expressed a form of thought very close to that of the Ancients.

But Johannes Kepler was a genius. He was an inspired man when he wrote the *Mysterium cosmographicum*, the "Secret of the World," a work of youth that twenty years later he would not repudiate.

> Carrying on the ideas of Pythagoras, he wants to show how man imitates the Creator by a natural instinct, knowing how, in the notes of his voice, to make the same choice and observe the same proportion that God had wanted to put into the general harmony of celestial movement. In a closing chapter he specifies likewise the nature of planetary harmonies: Saturn and Jupiter make the bass, Mars the tenor, Venus the contralto, and Mercury the falsetto.
>
> Elsewhere he speaks of politics; he wants to prove that even the earth has a soul and knows the zodiac.
>
> From this milieu of chaos, this world of dreams, there bursts forth, in the last book, the third of the laws that bear his name, which he stated thus: "*The proportion between the mean distances of two planets is exactly sesquialter to the proportions of their periods of revolution.*" What he calls the sesquialter proportion is that in which the exponent terms are 3/2.
>
> Here, contrary to his habits, he does not make known the history of his ideas. We only know, and that from a famous passage, that he had looked for a long time, without doubt by similar means to those made known in his *Mysterium,* and that the light had come little by little. He had suspected the law by the eighth of March, 1618, but then was misled by an erroneous calculation and abandoned it. It returned on the fifteenth of May and then a very exact calculation convinced him of the truth of the law.
>
> "Eight months ago," he said, "I saw the first ray of light; three months ago I saw the day; finally, during the last few days I have seen the sun of the most admirable contemplation. I surrender myself to my enthusiasm; I wish to challenge the living with this naive confession that I have stolen the

---

[32] Tannery, *Mémoires scientifiques*, 3:70.

golden chalice of the Egyptians in order to form for my God a tabernacle far from the borders of Egypt. If you pardon me, I shall rejoice; if you reproach me, I will endure it. The way is cast, I write my book; it will be read by the present age or by posterity, it does not matter; it will be able to wait for its reader. Has God not waited six thousand years for a contemplator of his works?"

And he ends his book with a prayer: *Gratias ago tibi Creator Domine. . . .* In this way the third law that governs the planetary movements was established.[33]

What documents, still accessible in the seventeenth century, a time so rich in fervent seekers, had served Kepler? He did not care for the work of Eudoxus; instead, the "Platonic" regular volumes served as the starting point for his work, and the results are the three laws of planetary motion, the foundation of our astronomy.

Like the Ancients, Kepler was convinced that God, the Creator, could not have created a disordered world. This means that a "law of order" must be able to be extracted from observations of nature, and this law must necessarily obey numbers. If, in celestial mechanics, there is a gravitational force, it cannot act arbitrarily, and therefore it is subject to the same laws that govern numbers. And since the whole architecture of numbers yields to the pentagon and to the dodecahedron that is derived from it, that is, the forms resulting from ϕ, it is this number-principle Five that must govern all the others; in musical proportion this becomes the fifth, or 2/3 of the initial note in terms of string length (time), and 3/2 (sesquialter), in terms of vibrations (distance).

Kepler did not altogether follow this reasoning—it was too "dreamy," one would say—but it is this reality that finally inspired him. This reality is the nucleus divided into 1/3 and 2/3 that we discover everywhere in pharaonic Egypt.[34]

The fractional notation of powers that is required in pharaonic calculation allows for the simple, immediate expression of Kepler's third law, which is $T^{2/3} = R$,[35] where T is the time of revolution of a planet measured in days, hours, and so on, of the earth, while R is the radius, the mean distance of the planet from the sun. Thus, the relationships were established, fixing the proportional distances between all the planets of the solar system. It is enough to know one to know all the others.

> Through the reunion of the furthest opposing qualities, Kepler occupies a most exceptional place in the history of science. . . .
>
> Superb and audacious in his seeking, Kepler became as modest and simple as what he had found, and in the joy of his triumph, it was God alone he glorified. . . .
>
> The laws of Kepler are the solid and unshakable fundamentals of modern astronomy and regulate immutably and eternally the movements of the heavenly bodies in space. No other discovery could have better justified the utterance of the sage: "That which enhances science, enhances the work." No one else has given birth to such a large amount of work and as many great discoveries; but of the long and tedious way that he followed we know but little. None of the volumes written by Kepler are considered to be classic, these works are little read today; his glory alone will be immortal: it is written in the heavens. The progress of science is not able to diminish or obscure it, and the planets, by their ever constant succession and their regular movements, speak to this fact, century after century.[36]

---

[33] G. Bigourdan, *L'Astronomie* (Paris: Flammarion, 1917).

[34] Cf. also chapter 5, "Pharonic Volumes."

[35] This is translated as $\sqrt[3]{T^2} = R$.

[36] François Arago, *Oeuvres complètes* (Paris: Gide, 1865).

Kepler's Three Laws

1. The orbits of the planets are ellipses in which the sun occupies one of the foci.
2. Each planet moves in its orbit in such a way that the areas contained between the radius vectors are proportional to the time needed to travel the arcs contained between these radii.
3. The squares of the periods of revolution of any two planets are proportional to the cubes of their mean distances from the sun.

———

When Kepler stated his formula, he conceived it in notations with fractional indications; this notation necessarily implies a relationship with musical notation.

When he said that the proportion between the time and the radius is *sesquialter*, that is as 3 to 2, it should be understood that *the square of the time has the value of a cube*.

Here are the vestiges of a form of thinking that, very curiously, in starting from an entirely different base, we have happened to rediscover by the sole means of fractional notation.

Chapter 10

PHARAONIC CUBITS

MEASURES

Time, movement, and space are the three factors that allow for the determination of a measurement, whether in length or distance, in duration, or in volume. It is thus movement that is the essential factor, and movement requires a moving object. This moving object is mass.

We can further say that without mass there is no moving object, without a moving object no perceptible movement, without movement no measure in time or in distance or space. Volume is measured by length.

Thus, mass and distance in time are the bases of all measure, that is, of all mechanical measure, since it is a question of a movement of mass or quantity.[1] All these elements are relative because they mutually determine each other and make a "closed-circuit" equation. If any one of these elements were absolute—that is to say, vital and independent—the circuit would be broken.

Now, time is genesis, distance being a succession of phases; therefore mass represents the critical moment. Mass is a relationship between weight and volume.

Let us leave to mechanics the movement of the "mass" and its relative and resultant energy, which is no more "real" (perceptible) than nameless original energy whose contraction into volume forms matter. This matter is, in a certain sense, densified energy, and the only true activity, which measures all, is the contracting seed, *the contracting Verb* of virginal, cosmic energy.

Through this activity all that exists is "bound" in the real as well as in the figurative sense. This is the source of true weight. Heaviness specifies the degree of fixation of energy. We do not confuse density and weight. Thus, the seed is the greatest weight of the *species* that has generated it. But we relate movement with heaviness because movement is the reaction of weight, in the mechanical sense, as well as vitally in the radiation of energy.

---

[1] But this principle can be related to Adamic creation (Mosaic Genesis): Adam is made from earth, and the living soul is movement by the Spirit.

A body revolving at a constant velocity around a center will move farther away from this center in direct proportion to its weight. This *distance,* or radius, or measure of distance, is thus related to the weight and speed, the orbital distance covered in a certain time.

This is a universal law that is the basis of defining the measure of length established by the pharaonic sages. But this is not the place to speak of it in detail. The evidence for it does exist, and this makes the pharaonic system of measures extremely interesting because these measures are not arbitrary, and because they relate and unify all the physical principles of the Universe, while drawing their origin from the one mystical knowledge.

Defining the unit of measure as the sixth part of a circle, measured by a chord equal to its radius, unites measure, as a relationship of distance to time, to a general geometric function.*

Through the universal foundation of harmonic relationships, these general physical principles constitute a truly brilliant system of measure for volume, weight, distance, and time. Measures, in relation to the geometric construction for establishing the plan of the temple, are a basis impossible to ignore in the study of pharaonic teaching.

The synthesis that is this system of measures places them in obvious relation to the *neters* or functional principles of Nature. For example, in spite of the effort to unify measures with a system of centimeters, grams, and seconds, our Occidental world has kept specific measures in certain cases, such as the ounce for gold, the carat for precious stones, and the grain for pearls. Sailors count the displacement of the hull of a boat in tons, but these are tons of freshwater or tons of seawater, or the place occupied by the volume of a ton. The measure is adapted to the character as well as to the nature of the object.[2] This is governed solely by practical demands, such as the light-years used in astronomy. Other measures are purely relative, such as the "magnitude" of the stars, the albedo of the planets, or the force of the wind. In the mechanical field, it is always possible to systematize everything on the basis of a conventional system, but life, however, does not allow itself to be put into a "box" of an arbitrarily determined size.

The pharaonic system of measures addresses itself to life, the life whose essential functions are governed by triads of *neters.* Each triad controls a lineage made up of analogies from life, such as, for example, the traditional kinship of the planet Jupiter, the metal tin, and the sapphire (erroneous, incidentally, with regard to the sapphire, which is related to the moon; it is topaz that is linked to Jovian tin). There are Jovian plants, such as the grapevine and laurel, which are connected with gold and "iridescent" rubies. Burmese rubies are connected with Mars, as is the oak tree. What do these kinships that have been preserved by a tradition of "occult" and "occulted" science signify? That it is *actually* possible to *prove* experimentally the kinship between the stones, the metal, and the planet. There is unity in the Universe, and through numbers, colors, gestations, weights, and chemical natures one can read functions peculiar to these precise lineages. Everything obeys Heaven, in other words, cosmic harmony; it sets the tone and the mode of life, otherwise known as the "music of the spheres."

The survey that we offer here concerning the strange divisions of the measures of lengths and volumes[3] is sufficient to express the mystical and vital reasoning that guided the pharaonic sages in the organization of their science.

---

[2] Chinese acupuncture, now often used in Europe, has three measures (specific to each individual) for the three parts of the body—head, trunk, and limbs.

[3] Cf. this chapter, "Measures and Cubits," and chapter 5, "Pharaonic Volumes."

* The side of the hexagon equals the radius of the circle that circumscribes it.

From the moment that a measure lays claim to having a cosmic character, it must be based on a general function in order to be established, and on experimental, and therefore verifiable, data in order to be defined. We present here the exoteric elements of the question.

As we have already said, the Ancients considered the circle as a cycle. It signified a circuit of time, which requires a birth in order to pass from the first impulse (say, the seed) to its return (the putting forth of fruit as the new seed). The cycle is then a vital, circular movement each moment of which is nearly always the same distance from its center. Theoretically (as circle), this circuit closes; practically (in all of Nature), this circuit will diverge more or less widely between its beginning and its return. The coefficient π derived from ϕ, the impulse function, marks this divergence, no account of which will be taken (being a perfect circle) in the establishment of the principle.

Nonetheless, it is always a question of time, not of distance. Now, any original division of the circle must be sexagesimal because the circle's radius r is the length of the straight segment that can be placed six times on the circumference. The circle is divided in four parts by its axis poles (as in the celestial cycle of rising, culmination of the day, or zenith, setting, and nadir, that is, a horizontal and a vertical division), and the numbers 4 and 6, as factors of 24, give a complete division, with each part of the 24 corresponding in its turn to a divisibility by 6 or by 4. (Let us point out here that these are the numbers used to determine the relationship of time and distance.) This "system" that the geometry of the circle and the cycle imposes is then a first established fact for the function.

The second established fact is that of the geodesic, or shall we say, the variable meridian curve from the equator to the pole. It also results from a "geometric reasoning" that allows for the establishment of this curve *without taking any measurements on earth*. Slight variations can be derived from this that will affect measures of length from the equator as 0°, to the pole as 90° or, put in the pharaonic spirit, "two times one-eighth of the circle."

—⁓—

Since we are not entering here into the *esoteric* details of the question, we will limit our references to the facts that can be verified from the practical measurements that have been handed down to us from Ancient Egypt.

The cubits that have been found thus far in the temples and the tombs all measure from 52.3 centimeters, minimum, to 54 centimeters, maximum. The cubit measuring 52.3 centimeters to 52.5 centimeters being the most frequently found, it is best known as the royal cubit. We will now consider how it was established.

THE PRINCIPLE OF THE ROYAL CUBIT

The sun, Aten-Ra, creates the earth. The earth produces human beings, and human beings adapt themselves to the land. The succession of cause and effect implies a functional interdependence, which expresses itself in quality and quantity. Each phase of the becoming, through its form, is connected to the initial cause. In one way or another, the earthworm is the child of the sun and carries as its legacy a potential characteristic of its paternal, solar cause.

Present man thinks and can only think insomuch as he is child and heir of his heaven. He should seek the elements for his science within himself, whether it is a question of knowledge of the becoming of things, or of the objective world he perceives. Hermes said, "The Work is within you . . . ," and pharaonic Egypt would say with respect to measures, "Man measures the world."

At the entrance, to the right of the great corridor in the tomb of Ramesses IX in the Valley of the Kings at Thebes, the cycle of the Dwat[4] ends with a curious figure (fig. 108).[5] It is a royal mummy with arms raised, extending above the head the length of one cubit. This mummy is placed at an angle as the hypotenuse of a right triangle whose base and perpendicular are represented by a serpent.

In this figuration we are dealing first of all with the representation of a *principle*, then of a geometric figure.[6] Without any possible doubt, the triangle represents the sacred 3, 4, 5 triangle, and the length of the cubit of the arm is equal to 1.

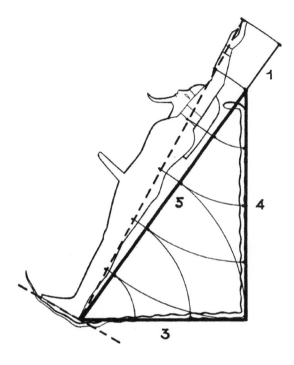

Fig. 108

We also know that man is given the value ϕ^2 with respect to his natural measurements defined by the navel.[7] As the hypotenuse, here he equals 5. Now, this figure must reveal a function that measures the cycle, being 5 plus 1, in cubits, or ϕ^2 plus its fifth, or $(2.618/5) \times 6 = 3.1416\ldots$. This is the value of the coefficient π, equal to $1.2 \times \phi^2$, or $12 \times \phi^2 = 31.416\ldots$. Thus, *twelve royal men measure the cycle of the heavens.*

The function ϕ, being in the impulse of the becoming at the origin, also provides, functionally, the *only real* value of the *cyclical* coefficient, being itself a cyclical number.

Our *rational* calculation of π is based on the mean of the inscribed and circumscribed polygons. Thus, one seeks to define a curve through straight lines, and this leads to the absurdity of infinity. This absurdity has been demonstrated by the *yin* and *yang* diagram of the Chinese (fig. 109).

---

[4] There are Heaven, Earth, and Dwat, which are the abodes of life, of what is visible, and of what is invisible.

[5] A figure whose geometric sense has never been understood.

[6] Cf. plates 62 and 63.

[7] See chapter 5, "The Mystical Number," and chapter 11.

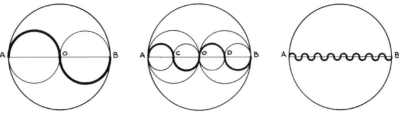

Fig. 109

The curves *AO* + *OB* = the semicircle *AB*. The curves *AC* + *CO* + *OD* + *DB* are also always equal to *AB*. By continuing to draw semicircles in this way, they become smaller and smaller and one arrives at an undulating line *AB* and, taken to infinity, to the *diameter*, *AB*, therefore: the diameter of a circle is equal to a half of it, and a circle is equal to two of its diameters. This *logic* is reasonable on the surface, but it is no more so than the way π is obtained in our present mathematics.

If we treat the *yin* and *yang* problem geometrically with triangles (fig. 110), and if we read it in reverse, we find there a parallel with the principle stated by Theon of Smyrna: "Unity contains in potential the side and the diagonal."

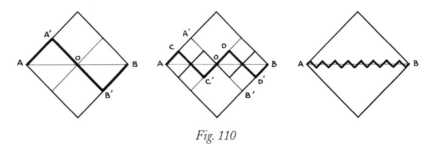

Fig. 110

No curve in the Universe is an absolute circle; it is always a question of *cycles*. The Egyptians accepted only the opening of the pupil of the eye as an absolute circle (and then only symbolically). All circles drawn to symbolize the sun are slightly flattened, and in carving the sun in relief, they gave it a rounded form representing a segment of a sphere, or a breast, often with a nipple in the middle (fig. 111); the sun is then considered to be the nourisher of the Universe.[8]

Fig. 111

The true coefficient π, which applies to astronomy and in general to all cycles, is a function of ϕ. Graphically, if the diameter has the value of 1 or 10, the one-sixth division of the circle

---

[8] This denies the childish supposition that the Ancients considered the sun to be a flat disk.

subtended by a chord *equal to the radius* 5 will be equal to $\pi/6$ [× 10], or 5.236..., which is $\sqrt{5}+3$. This is the value of the *royal cubit.*

If we accept the diameter to be equal to one of our meters, the royal cubit measures 0.5236... meter, an observed measure that also attests to knowledge of the meter.[9] It so happens that the Ancients knew the actual meter, which is only slightly different from our first international meter. They arrived at this by a special method. As for the equatorial circumference of the earth (which we accept today as 40 million meters), *they measured it by the fathom,* which we find to be the basis of the measurements for the temple of Luxor. The fathom is the *measure* of *circumference.* It has a numerical relationship with the cubit, which we shall discuss later on.

The royal cubit is the measure that reduces the curve of a circle into a straight line. The straight line corresponding to the royal cubit or to one of its fractions has a value of 5 in relation to 5.236..., or 1 in relation to 1.0472... (or $\pi/3$).

Now, if a person has the value of 1 in height, his arm span (fathom) will equal 1.0472.... The fathom is the measure of circumference and is the unit of measure for the earth's circumference (it "embraces").

Its practical variation being given, in its geodetic applications, by the latitude of the meridian, we will refer to what we still call today the fathom that is used by navigators. Along with its relationship to the average size of a person, the fathom is also the geometric result of the given theoretical fact of the royal cubit. To demonstrate this, we have no alternative but to speak of the mystical number ϕ, because its esoteric quality is the absolute guide to the great subtlety of pharaonic thought.

The royal cubit is the unit of measure of the cycle as a measure of time; it is the sixth part, in meters, of the coefficient π. Therefore, the theoretical cubit represents a straight linear measure that implies the measure of a curve. The cubit (as an instrument of measure) becomes then a table of all the relationships defining the applications of measure for curves, for volumes, and for geodetic and astronomical data.

THE PHARAONIC π

For the pharaonic mathematician the disk is a surface; therefore, it is the result of the multiplication of two whole-number values. It is not in his thinking to consider the circle, the boundary of the disk, as a geometric line. The circle is a path, a circuit. The absolute sphere does not exist in matter, it is a supposition. The circuit is not an absolute circle, or else it would be eternity in which any moment is the end that rejoins the beginning, the present moment.[10] Every circuit in Nature is a cycle that goes from the seed to its generated new seed, the new seed in which lies the past and at the same time the seed of a future, in other words, there is a difference in the impulsive seminal nature. The end, however similar it may be, is not identical to the beginning.

---

[9] "The Ancient Egyptians were perfectly well acquainted with this meter, as is frequently shown, but *they would not use it to measure a circuit.*" R. A. Schwaller de Lubicz, *The Temple in Man,* p. 60.

[10] The present moment is essentially bound to the magnitude time (which is genesis). Between the past and the future there is no comprehensible break because the present supposed rest, or stoppage, is still composed of past and future, and yet, the separation does exist; it becomes the *continuity* that escapes all measurement.

* *Brasse* in French. The *brasse* (*bras* in French means "arm" and *brasse* means "armful") is equivalent to the English measure of depth, the fathom. In Old English the word is *fæthm,* which means "arms outstretched."

It is therefore certainly not in the pharaonic mentality to calculate the circle by straight lines, as the Euclidean concept suggests in supposing the circle to be formed by the bases of triangles whose apexes are the center of the circle. The curve is a curve at every moment, that is, even the very smallest part tends to return to its beginning.

We have gone beyond the illusion of the atom as the smallest particle of matter and have recognized the moment where matter—the molecule—ceases to be matter and becomes an energetic complex. But we persist in believing that the smallest part of a circle (*infinitely* small?) will be a straight line, the side of a polygon. One may as well reason with *yin* and *yang* to prove that the circumference equals two of its diameters. Calculating endless decimal places of π lengthwise in centimeters, meters, and kilometers is mathematical acrobatics, but signifies nothing. It is evident that π can only be an irrational number.

One can object that π derived from $1 + 1/5$ of ϕ^2 is also irrational. This is true if one considers ϕ as $\sqrt{5} + 1/2$, *which is only an arithmetic definition of this function.*

With the refusal of pharaonic mathematicians to accept irrational roots and their replacement of these numbers by balancing them through inverses,[11] the coefficient ϕ could not be defined by the square root of 5, as we do. It can only be expressed geometrically. But whether it is transcribed arithmetically or geometrically, it always plays a cyclic and logarithmic role and only engenders values of similar function.[12] We have seen that the cycle has the value of twelve royal men, each being ϕ^2 or $\phi + 1$, so that the royal cubit equals $2(\phi + 1)$ for a radius with a value of 5. And $12(\phi + 1)$ divided by the diameter 10 has a value of 3.1416396..., accepting the arithmetic transcription of ϕ as equal to $\sqrt{5} + 1/2$.[13] This π is about 0.0005 larger than the present mathematical π.

The irreplaceable advantage of adopting the function ϕ as the basis for the coefficient π is that it allows for calculation with whole numbers.[14] In the regular sequence of the Fibonacci series of ϕ, any number can be chosen for unity and the following numbers will be ϕ and ϕ^2.

For example, in the series 5, 8, 13, 21, 34, 55, ..., if we take 34 for ϕ, 55 is, proportionally, ϕ^2, and the difference, 21, is equal to 1 because $\phi + 1 = \phi^2$; thus, $(55/5) \times 6 = 66$, which is equivalent to $(\phi^2/5) \times 6 = \pi$, and $21 = \text{diameter} = 1$, and $\pi = 66/21 = 3.1428...$, the same value for π as $22/7$, the π of Archimedes, used constantly, for that matter, in pharaonic architecture, being sufficiently accurate in practice.[15]

It suffices then to multiply the value of a diameter with the chosen unitary number in order to arrive at the π ratio without having to resort to an irrational number. For example, for the unity 21 and a diameter of 12 the circumference will be $(66/21) \times 12$, or, more exactly, in following the model given in the problems of the Rhind Papyrus, $21 : 66 :: 12 : 37 + 1/2 + 1/7 + 1/14$.

Thus, pharaonic mathematics remains faithful to its geometric mentality and to its philosophical directive.

---

[11] Cf. chapter 5, and chapter 6, the discussion of inverses in the section "Division," pp. 145–48.

[12] Cf. chapter 8.

[13] For the measurement of the royal cubit we accept here that verified with our present standard meters. Now in fact, there is a very slight difference with the absolute measure corresponding to Meudon's rectified international meter.

[14] This amounts to *representing* numbers through geometric drawings that let us perceive what can only be grasped through reason. Thus, we can draw a circle and its diameter one or the other of which is "reasonably" infinite.

[15] In choosing from the F series a larger number for ϕ^2, as, for example, in the progression 144, 233, 377, 610, ..., we have $(610/5) \times 6 = 732$ for π, and $610 - 377 = 233$ for unity. Then with this ratio, $\pi = 732/233 = 3.1416309...$. The ratio $22/7$ is used in problem 38 of the Rhind Papyrus.

MEASURES AND CUBITS

SOME GENERAL REMARKS ABOUT CUBITS

The cubit is a masterpiece because it creates a link between number and its function, and measure.[16] It is understandable that the cubits were often covered in gold. Much doubt has been cast on the scientific value of Egyptian measures because of the multiplicity of cubits and the so-called lack of precision among those found up to now.

One observes identical variants in the cubits, not only with regard to the half-meter-or-so length that represents a cubit, the variations in which are but a few millimeters, but also in the temples with regard to lengths of 5, 50, or 100 meters. This confirms the existence of several units of measure whose application is evidence of a great subtlety of thought, and it supports a valid argument in favor of the geodetic knowledge of the Ancients. The royal cubit implies a knowledge of the meter, and the fathom, which is a geodetic measure, implies knowledge of the circumference of the globe.

Now we find that the mean fathom of 1.85 meters is very clearly used in a number of monuments, and notably in the temple of Luxor. From where did the Ancients obtain this measure?

We know that a function exists *that allows one to draw precisely the meridian curve of the geoid.* We can therefore assert, without giving the proof here, that the functions of celestial mechanics were perfectly known to the sages of Egypt and that their knowledge of the geoid is *certain,* and, what is more, verifiable by very simple methods. The proof of our assertion is found in the application of these measures in the temple of Luxor.[17]

—∿∿—

Before we begin the study of the different cubits, it is essential to consider what each one was intended for in practice.

Each cubit is presented as a synthesis and summarizes in itself the elements necessary to solve problems affecting geometry, the measure of surfaces and volumes, and geodesy, among others.

It is certainly not without reason that the cubit had, carved on its faces, besides the subdivisions of measures, a list of the provinces of Egypt, as well as twenty-eight divine principles *(neters),* and sometimes also measures of volume or astronomical indications.

Hero of Alexandria informs us, "Geometry was first used for the measurements and divisions of land, which is why it is called surveying." Eustathius said that Sesostris made maps of the foreign countries he had traveled through and made a gift of them to the Egyptians. Clement of Alexandria, speaking of the knowledge of the priests, expressly mentions the geography and chorography of Egypt.[18]

Egypt was indeed divided into two distinct parts. The Land of the South and the Land of the North were always recalled during rituals by the symbol of the two crowns: the white crown of the Land of the South and the red crown of the Land of the North. Each of these two parts of the kingdom was in turn subdivided into a certain number of nomes (provinces). Lists of these nomes were carved in the temples and often about the precincts of the sanctuary of the sacred barque. One

---

[16] We are not referring to any study already made about cubits, but using only the documentation given to us by the monuments and our own verifications of cubits.

[17] Discussion of these questions must wait until proofs can be given in a future work devoted to the mystical geography of Egypt. [This work was never completed.]

[18] Cf. appendix, "Geographical Knowledge and Maps of the Egyptians."

list dating from Sesostris (Twelfth Dynasty) shows that there were twenty-two nomes in Upper Egypt, and eighteen nomes in Lower Egypt. At a later period the number of nomes in Lower Egypt increased to twenty.

These lists give the official name of the nome, symbolized by a grid pattern (the roads, one might say) surmounted by its emblem, for example, the hare for the fifteenth nome of Upper Egypt:

The lists also give the name of the capital determined by the hieroglyph symbolizing a city: a circle in which a cross was drawn (the crossing of two roads, one might say).

Now, can we not see in the emblem of the nome a sort of *"canevas"* of the country, and in certain crossings of this *canevas* the towns, figured by the circle enclosing a crossing? This would explain the measures handed down by certain classical authors that were established from a system of maps very similar to our own.[19]

For each nome the lists of the later eras mention the different names of the capital (which generally had a civil and a sacred name), the name of the principal *neter* of the place, the names of the sanctuaries, of the sacred barque, of its road, of its sacred tree, the names and titles of the high priest and high priestess, and so on. The lists also subdivided the nome itself into cultivated terrain, flooded terrain, and so forth, and finally, the part of the dismembered body of Osiris preserved there as a relic is mentioned.

The part of the body of Osiris, cut into pieces by Seth, designates a living function of the body of the Anthropocosmos, and by this fact gave the place that preserved it (symbolically) a cosmic location and characteristic appropriate to all the natural life of that place.

The myth thus effectively unified the geography, the chorography, and the form of worship in relation to the physiological regions of the human body.

—⁓—

With regard to the use of the fathom in the monuments, Herodotus left us the following text:

> Wonderful as is the Labyrinth, the work called the Lake of Moeris, which is close by the Labyrinth, is yet more astonishing. The measure of its circumference is sixty schœnes, or three thousand six hundred furlongs, which is equal to the entire length of Egypt along the sea-coast. The lake stretches in its longest direction from north to south, and in its deepest parts is of the depth of fifty fathoms. It is manifestly an artificial excavation, for nearly in the centre there stand two pyramids, rising to the height of fifty fathoms above the surface of the water, and extending as far beneath, crowned each of them with colossal statue sitting upon a throne.[20] Thus these pyramids are one hundred fathoms high, which is exactly a furlong (stadium) of six hundred feet: the fathom being six feet in length,

[19] Ibid.

[20] Might there be a reminder of this in the statue of the man seated "like Buddha" on the high seat (that of Isis) at Porto Raphtis, north of Athens, which is atop a rock that rises up at the entrance of the harbor, the home port of the sacred barque that every year on a certain date traveled to Delos, to the temple of Apollo? Cf. Plato's account of the death of Socrates in the *Timaeus*.

or four cubits, which is the same thing, since a cubit measures six, and a foot four, palms.[21]

Thus, the height of the pyramids of Lake Moeris is 100 fathoms, and 1 fathom = 4 cubits of 24 digits, or 6 palms; or 6 feet of 16 digits, or 4 palms.

READING CUBITS

Hero of Alexandria gives us two tables, in one of which, the "measures used in his time," he mentions a cubit of 32 digits. The other table is of "ancient measures," where he speaks of a cubit of 24 digits.

Now, among the cubits that have been found up to the present, the large majority are divided into 28 digits. There are only a few cases of cubits from the Late Period that are divided into 24 digits. There are the following different types:

- In wood or stone, in square or pentagonal sections and simply divided into four, five, six, and seven parts by engraved lines. All the specimens found are different.
- In wood or stone, divided into 7 palms, and each palm into 4 digits, giving the standard total of 28 digits. These cubits carry the name, written in hieroglyphs for each division, and the most complete carry a list of twenty-eight *neters,* one for each digit.
- Even more complex than the preceding, the last type carries additionally a list of the nomes of Egypt, that is to say, the twenty-two nomes of Upper Egypt plus six nomes of Lower Egypt on one of its sides; the remaining nomes are listed on the other faces. Often called "astronomical cubits," these last, of which only a few fragments survive, are covered with inscriptions that mention measures of volume, and so on.

As shown by the divisions of the types of cubits (fig. 112), the nomes and the *neters* are attributed to each digit.

Fig. 112

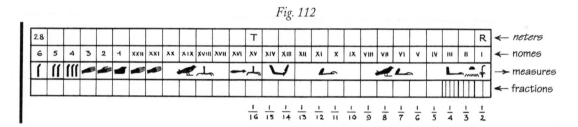

Unity   = 1 digit
1 palm   = 4 digits
1 hand   = 5 digits
1 fist   = 6 digits
2 palms   = 8 digits
3 palms   = 12 digits   = 1 small span
$3\frac{1}{2}$ palms   = 14 digits   = 1 large span
4 palms   = 16 digits   = 1 *djezer* cubit
5 palms   = 20 digits   = 1 *remen* cubit
6 palms   = 24 digits   = 1 small cubit
7 palms   = 28 digits   = 1 royal cubit

---

[21] *History,* trans. George Rawlinson (New York: Appleton, 1866), 2:149.

The enumeration of the digits is made from left to right, whereas the divinities and the nomes are read from right to left. In effect, the first *neter* marked above the twenty-eighth digit is always Ra, the first of the divine Ennead. Therefore, *the cubit must be read in both directions.* This statement is very important, and we should also keep it in mind for reading the measures.

The first fifteen *neters* are placed in the following order: Ra, the first of the Ennead, followed by Shu and Tefnut, Geb and Nut, Osiris and Isis, Seth and Nephthys; Ra is repeated with the tenth *neter*, Horus (tetraktys); after which come the four sons of Horus, and Thoth, who is placed at the fifteenth digit (when reading from right to left) and is thus the only divinity "in his nome," the fifteenth of Upper Egypt (reading in the same direction).

From right to left are read again the subdivisions of the digit, 1/2, 1/3, ..., up to 1/16. Now, it is interesting to put the increasing cubit at the end of the decreasing cubit, if one might say so:

$$\ldots \quad \frac{1}{10} \quad \frac{1}{9} \quad \frac{1}{8} \quad \frac{1}{7} \quad \frac{1}{6} \quad \frac{1}{5} \quad \frac{1}{4} \quad \frac{1}{3} \quad \frac{1}{2} \quad 1 \quad 2 \quad 3 \quad 4 \quad 5 \quad 6 \quad 7 \quad 8 \quad 9 \quad 10 \ldots$$

The idea of the inverse is expressed solely by the arrangement of the symbols, if we look at them in their natural direction. We can stress again the fact that according to the hieroglyphs there exist the following:

- A *djezer* cubit of 16 digits, "the sublime cubit," which would be half the cubit of 32 digits alluded to by Hero of Alexandria.
- A *remen* cubit of 20 digits, whose importance with regard to surface measures we shall see later on.
- A small cubit of 24 digits, which we will call the "human cubit" since the total height of a person is traditionally 4 cubits of 24 digits. This cubit totals 96 digits, the measure of the fathom or full span of the arms (without taking into account for the moment the difference between the actual height of the person and the arm span).
- Finally, the royal cubit of 28 digits, the "cycle cubit," the length that measures the arc of the circle of 60° for $r = 0.5$ meter.

Thoth, master of sciences and of writing, occupies the central place, whereas Ra, the sun, is both the first of the *neters* and the last in measure.

THE MEASURES

The First Fundamentally Important Base

The natural division of the cycle of time is indicated by the number of days required for the earth to complete its revolution around the sun. The pharaonic calendar counts 360 days plus the 5 epagomenal days consecrated to the birth of the *neters*. The value of the cycle is thus taken to be 360. Our division of the circle into 360 degrees (attributed to Hipparchus) most certainly comes from this ancient tradition.

Each of the 360 parts was subdivided into 60, dividing the circumference into a total of 21,600 units, each corresponding to 1′ of arc. Carrying over this subdivision to a large circle of terrestrial meridians, each minute of arc of the meridian represents 1000 human fathoms of length, a unit of measure preserved in our "nautical mile," which corresponds to 10 Greek stades or to 1000 fathoms, whose use by the Ancient Egyptians was related by Herodotus with regard to the pyramids of Lake Moeris.

One minute of arc at 45° latitude measures 1852 meters. But we note here that this actual, rational mean does not entirely conform with the pharaonic conception; for reasons concerning celestial mechanics and the principle we referred to earlier, the Ancients chose a fathom that could be confused with the equatorial fathom (although very slightly shorter), that is, 1.855 meters, a number precise enough to show the principle of the fathom and the cubits.

The fathom is itself subdivided by the numbers 4 and 6 of the division of time, which thus implies its traditional division into $24 \times 4 = 16 \times 6 = 96$ digits. This division provides two of the cubits engraved on the royal cubit: the fathom divided by 4 equals 24 fathom-digits, which is the length of the "human cubit" or the "small cubit" of 46.2 centimeters; and the fathom divided by 6 equals 16 fathom-digits, the length of the "sublime cubit" (*djezer* cubit) of 30.87 centimeters. We recall here that the present English foot is derived directly from the sublime cubit in that it is 1/6 fathom.

In the temple of Luxor, the fathom is frequently used as a unit of measure:

- The room of twelve columns, consecrated to the twelve hours of the day, measures 12 fathoms in length.
- The two sanctuaries V and VII, on either side of the central sanctuary, are 3 fathoms wide.
- The conception room (called "the room of the theogamy") is 6 fathoms long.
- The sanctuary of the barque of Amun (room VI) is 6 fathoms long. The width of the room is to its length as the chord of an arc of one-sixth of a circle is to this arc.

Thus in establishing a circle with 36 fathoms for circumference, as with the thirty-six decans in the cycle of time, each portion of 6 fathoms represents an arc of 60° having for a chord the proportional length of arc/chord = $\pi/3 = 22/21$ in whole numbers.

Recalling that the relationship between the height of a man and his arm span is as 1 to 1.0472 (on average)—that is, functionally, as 1 to $\pi/3$—room VI represents the proportions of a man with arms held out to form the shape of a cross; his height is equal to the radius. His arm span—or fathom—represents the arc of 60°. The man is outstretched east-west in the direction of the progression of the barque, and he measures the north-south arc with his arms (fig. 113).

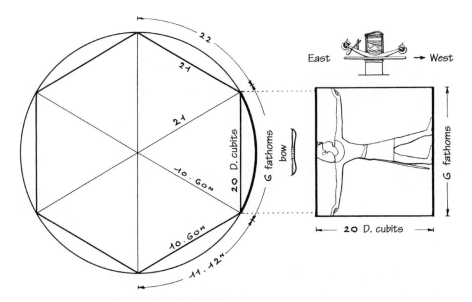

Fig. 113. Proportions of room VI of the temple of Luxor

The principal measures relating to the room of the barque of Amun—taking the mean fathom as the metrical unit and the ratio 22/21 for $\pi/3$—are the following:

$$\frac{6 \text{ mean fathoms at } 45° \times 21}{22} = \frac{11.1135 \text{ meters} \times 21}{22} = 10.6083... \text{ meters.}$$

Now, room VI actually measures 11.12 meters in length, which is 6 fathoms at 45° representing the arc of 60°, and 10.60 meters in width corresponds to the length of the chord subtending this arc.[22] The measure 10.60, which one finds for the length and width of room IV (in front of the sanctuary of the barque) is equal to 20 Dendera cubits, each one measuring 0.53 meters to 0.531 meters.[23]

Keeping with the teaching given by this sanctuary, the Dendera cubit plays the role of *radius* for the arc measured by the fathom. In fact, 12 Dendera cubits equal 6.365 meters, which can be compared to the value of the mean radius of the earth, 6,367,654 meters.

The use of this "radius cubit" is confirmed in the temple of Luxor by the base of the pylon measuring 63.65 meters, that is, 120 Dendera cubits (called "benediction cubits").[24]

Finally, the pylon that will be built by Ramesses II was already indicated in the construction of the east wall of the sanctuary of the barque at the time of Amenhotep III, which wall gives the slope and the basic measure of the future pylon on a scale ten times smaller. Its length at the base is in fact 6.365 meters.[25] Now, the pylon is the support for the bows.[26]

The principle is formal: *the length of 6 fathoms plays the role of the arc; this length multiplied by 3/π or 21/22 determines the chord of 60°, or the radius. The metrical value of this radius corresponds to 20 Dendera cubits.*

According to the teaching given by the sanctuary of the temple of Luxor, the circumference is accepted as 36 fathoms, each fathom corresponding thus to 10° of the circle. The relative *djezer* cubit is thus 10°/6, which equals 600'/6, or 100' of arc of this circle.

Recalling that it requires 1000 human fathoms to measure a minute of arc on the terrestrial circumference, in other words, that there are 21,600,000 fathoms for the entire circumference, the *djezer* cubit is contained 21,600,000 × 6 = 129,600,000 times in the circumference of the earth, or again 21.6(6×10^6). This is the origin of the Greek foot, the use of which spread throughout Europe.

[22] Measurements of room VI, east partition:

> length to the base = 11.085 m and 1° of arc to 30° = 110.855 m
> length to the register 3 = 11.12 m and 1° of arc to 45° = 111.135 m
> height of registers 1 and 2 = 1.852 m average.

Height of the figures in the front:

> registers 1 and 2 = 68 "Dendera" digits
> register 3 = 68 "fathom" digits

The use of digits on this partition wall derived from the Dendera cubit and from 1/96 fathom confirms the association of these two measures that we find applied in the plan of the room.

The use of 68 digits for the height at the front implies the use of the Fibonacci series since the ratio 68 : 42 = ϕ, by doubling the numbers of the series, with unity = 21 and ϕ = 34.

[23] Cubits numbered 50050 and 45933 in the Cairo Museum. Cf. plate 64. The blunted ends do not permit a precision greater than ±0.5 mm.

[24] Cf. plates 64 and 67.

[25] Cf. plate 100.

[26] Cf. plate 47. We can see here a play on words between the arc as a bow (weapon) and the arc of the curve. The same kinship exists in German. In the pharaonic language, even in mathematics, the circle has a particular name; however, the same term is used for the arc, the weapon, and the curve of the sky, as well as for the stretching of the cord in the ritual scenes of laying the foundation of the temple.

Notes on the *Symbolique*

Let us note that the two arms of the cross of the Man, that is, Cosmic Man, are not of absolutely equal length, as is the case traditionally with Christ on the Cross.

The four partitions of room VI are not strictly equal, two by two. We are dealing, in the measurements of this room, with the characteristic variations of life on the terrestrial globe, not only in the plan but equally, as we shall see, in the partitions and registers (see note 22 above).

The same is the case for room IV, and we recall in this regard the relationship of the number 4 with Hathor. The number 4 is marked in the temple of Dendera by the four-faced capitals (the four lunar phases) of the Hathorian columns. The four lunar phases are, temporally and vitally speaking, unequal, as are all the cycles and phases of cycles in time.

—◦◦◦—

For the record, let us note that room VI is the sanctuary—the altar—of the barque of Amun, which is to say the "house of Horus," "Hathor."

In *The Temple in Man*, I mentioned the kinship between the Amunian barque and the Christian Catholic monstrance in which the Eucharist is borne at the center of the rays of the sun, inside a silver crescent moon.

The Royal Cubit and Fathom

Room VI has given us the origin and the metrical value of the Dendera cubit of 53 centimeters, which is 1 *radius* cubit starting from 6 *fathoms* (arc). We should now look at the relationship between the fathom and the royal cubit of the ideal cycle.

The measure of the royal cubit, 0.5236 meter, represents the arc of a circle of 60° with a diameter of 1 meter. Now, the use of the meter is frequently attested to in pharaonic monuments.[27]

With regard to the meter taken as diameter, and its origin, I quote here a passage from *The Temple in Man*:

> Opposing a conventional, rational, CGS system, is a natural, vitally true philosophic system.
>
> What I've just said suffices to explain why the Ancient Egyptians' unit of measurement was always *variable*.
>
> We find the importance of the measurement called the "cubit" supported, however, by the exceptional nature of the "gift of the cubit" to very high dignitaries.
>
> We know, on the other hand, that a stable and unchanging basis exists, and that it results precisely from this natural philosophy, a knowledge to which the ceremony of the Royal Gift alludes. Thus, if the Ancients so carefully hid the secret of this knowledge from the uninitiated, it would be wise to look for the reason. Indeed, the fact of having in Nature, which is always moving, a fixed support (like that which Archimedes called for, "to take the world off its hinges"), would show that everything is connected by an unfailing logic; and this small fact would entail enormous consequences.[28]

—◦◦◦—

By a reversal of function, the fathom plays the role of the radius for the royal cubit that measures the cycle. The circumference of a perfect sphere the same size as the earth would theoretically be

---

[27] Cf. plates 79 and 80.

[28] *The Temple in Man*, pp. 61–62.

40,000,000 meters, representing 21,600,000 human fathoms. This equivalence allows us to establish the following relationships:

$$\text{A circumference of } 40,000,000 \text{ meters} = 21,600,000 \text{ fathoms}$$

$$\frac{1}{4} \text{ of this circumference or } 10,000,000 \text{ meters} = 5,400,000 \text{ fathoms}$$

$$\frac{1}{8} \text{ of this circumference or } 5,000,000 \text{ meters} = 2,700,000 \text{ fathoms.}$$

Therefore, 27 mean fathoms are equal to 50 meters. Consequently, 27/100 fathom is equal to 0.5 meter.

This metrical equality implies the division of the fathom by 100, representing a digit of about 1.852 centimeters, and 27 of these digits defines a measure of 50 centimeters, which serves as the chord equal to the radius of a circle with 6 royal cycle cubits as the circumference.

Having thus defined the value of the meter as 54 digits resulting from the subdivision of the mean fathom into 100, the royal cycle cubit is obtained by the function ϕ, as has been discussed with respect to the pharaonic π.

There exists a very curious functional coincidence that causes the intervention of the square root of 2 when one uses whole numbers derived from the series of the *canevas* instead of irrational coefficients. But first it is necessary to see how the cubit, by virtue of these subdivisions, allows resolution of the problems posed by the irrationals through extremely simple means.

The Second Base: The Cubit and Irrational Numbers

We have seen that the Ancients resolved the problem of irrationals through approximate coefficients and their "reciprocals," but when it is a question of combining two irrationals in relation to the circle, which is itself an irrational, this play of inverses is no longer applicable. Nevertheless, in order to allow for these calculations in practice, the Ancients retained simple numerical ratios by consequently modifying the measures. It is this ingenious system that upsets our considerations of their cubits.

For example, when it is necessary to establish a ratio between $\sqrt{2}$, $\sqrt{3}$, and π, or $1.2 \times \phi^2$, expressed in whole-number ratios, the function $\sqrt{2}$ and its inverse are equal to 7/5 and 10/7; the function $\sqrt{3}$ and its inverse are equal to 7/4 and 12/7; and if we take the approximation 22/7 for π, it equals 66/21.

These first approximations are still very unrefined; nevertheless, we should choose from among these the ratios that correspond to the subdivisions of the cubit and see how it is possible to combine them with each other, since it is impossible to use at the same time the inverses that would reestablish the equilibrium.

We chose 10/7 for the square root of 2, which becomes, in order to enter into relationship with π, $(3 \times 10)/(3 \times 7)$, which equals 30/21, or $\sqrt{2}$. For the root of 3 we take 12/7, which becomes $(12 \times 3)/(7 \times 3)$, or 36/21. With the unity 21 as the common denominator, we can combine these three functions according to a practical method that gives us whole numbers: $\pi = 66$, $\sqrt{2} = 30$, and $\sqrt{3} = 36$ in relation to the general unity of 21, which is implied but does not need to be expressed as the denominator. This unity 21 will be considered as radius, and its use as such is confirmed by the existence, on the votive—or benediction—cubit of Dendera,[29] of 1/21 and 1/42 of its total length, as in certain "*canevas*" established on this number.

---

[29] In German, *Weih-elle.*

The study of the cubits and their subdivisions, together with their application to the monuments, leads us to the following considerations:

$$\left.\begin{array}{l} \text{the square of } 1 = 21^2 = 441 \\ \text{the square of } \sqrt{2} = 30^2 = 900 \end{array}\right\} \; 441 \times 2 = 882; \text{ the difference} = 18.$$

The coefficient of $\sqrt{2}$ is too large, and if one uses it in order to double exactly a surface, the result will be visibly false. In the cubits, however, there are digits slightly longer or shorter than the standard digit representing 1/28 of their total length.

For example, if the cubit measures 52.36 centimeters long, its digit is equal to 1.87 centimeters, and we will see it modified geometrically so that 14 digits have a metrical value of 14.1421 digits, or $10\sqrt{2}$. Thus, 1.87 centimeters × 14.1421 = 26.445... centimeters, and its double provides a new cubit of 52.89 centimeters, a measure we do in fact come across among the cubits that have been examined.

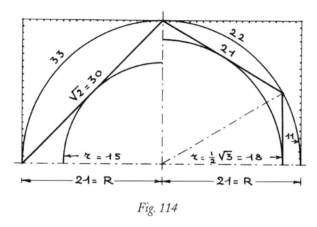

Fig. 114

For the quarter square on the *left:*

    $R = 21$ = radius of the circumscribed circle,

    $r = 15$ = radius of the inscribed circle = $\frac{1}{2}\sqrt{2}$,

    $c = 30$ = the side of the square = $\sqrt{2}$ for an arc = 33.

For the quarter hexagon on the *right:*

    $R = 21$ = radius of the circumscribed circle,

    $r = 18$ = radius of the inscribed circle = $\frac{1}{2}\sqrt{3}$,

    $c = 21$ = side of the hexagon, arc = 22.

The half-circumference has a π value of 22/7, or 66/21 for a radius of 21.

The *inverse* of this function will be the cubit that measures 52.36 centimeters divided by 28.2842..., or $20\sqrt{2}$, instead of exactly 28 digits, from which results a very short digit measuring 1.85... centimeters, equal to 1/100 mean fathom; and 28 of these shorter digits would make a cubit of 51.85 centimeters, which has not yet been found as a cubit of 28 digits, but one often comes across the *remen* cubit measuring 20 of these digits marked on the large royal cubit.[30]

In order to apply these whole numbers to the cubit of 28 digits by taking it as unity or radius (we know now that the Dendera cubit plays the role of radius for an arc measured in fathoms), it is necessary that we multiply by 28/21, or $1\frac{1}{3}$, and we will get, respectively,

---

[30] We encounter this measurement many times in the temple of Luxor as 5.18... m.

$$\text{Radius} = 21 \times 1\frac{1}{3} = 28 = 1 \text{ royal cubit,}$$

$$\sqrt{2} = 30 \times 1\frac{1}{3} = 40 = 2 \text{ } remen \text{ cubits,}$$

$$\sqrt{3} = 36 \times 1\frac{1}{3} = 48 = 2 \text{ small cubits (human cubits),}$$

$$\text{arc } 90° = 33 \times 1\frac{1}{3} = 44 = \frac{1}{4} \text{ of circumference with a value of 176.}$$

But the surfaces of the polygons calculated with these numbers will be erroneous. To obtain the double surface of a square with 28 standard digits, or what we call "royal digits" (1.87 cm) for its side, we will take 40 of the shorter digits, which we will call "remen digits" (1.8512 cm), each of which has a value of 1/100 fathom. These 40 digits represent 2 remen cubits. Now the study of the measures of the cubits demonstrates that *the larger part of each royal cubit includes the* remen *cubit composed of 20 shorter digits, allowing, with two of these* remen *cubits, for the establishment of a surface exactly double that of the cubit of 28 digits.*

In order to triple a surface with 21 royal digits to the side, for example, we take in this case the larger digit (1.8893 cm), and we obtain a perfect result here also, while keeping the round number of 36 digits for the side of the new square.[31] We thus see how modifying the length of the digit of the cubit cleverly allows us to obtain a correct result and at the same time avoid the irrational.

It remains to demonstrate how the modification of the metrical value of the digit does not depend on any calculation, but results from a very simple geometric function. If $\sqrt{2} = 7/5$ and unity is 5, its square is 25. The double of this square equals 50 and its side will be $\sqrt{50}$. Adopting 7 for the value of this side, its square will be only 49, so we have to enlarge the value of 7 by a small fraction in order to obtain $\sqrt{50}$.[32]

If we draw the triangle 1 : 7, its diagonal equals $\sqrt{49+1}$, or $\sqrt{50}$ (fig. 115).

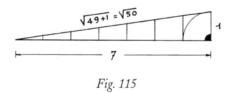

Fig. 115

By dividing the diagonal into seven equal parts, we obtain two different metrical units, one for the large side and one for the diagonal: *these are the two values of digits that we need.*

The transformation of the digit by the $\sqrt{3}$, always starting from the simple numbers we have adopted, is produced in an analogous fashion (we have said that $\sqrt{3} = 7/4$ or $1 + 1/2 + 1/4$, a coefficient we frequently find in the Rhind Papyrus): the unity is 4, its square is 16; triple this

---

[31] For example:

    21 royal digits = 39.27 cm, their square = 1542.133 cm²;

    30 *remen* units = 55.5361 cm, their square = 3084.258 cm²;

    the double surface of 21 royal units squared = 3084.266 cm²;

    36 larger units *(a)* = 68.003 cm, their square = 4624.408... cm², and *(b)* = 68.017 cm, their square = 4626.3... cm²;

    the triple surface of 21 royal units squared = 4626.3... cm².

  There is confusion between the larger digits for $\sqrt{2}$ or $\sqrt{3}$, because of the following numbers that are within 0.0002 of each other:

    a) $10\sqrt{2}/14 = 1.0101525...$ and 1.87 cm × 1.0101525 = 1.888985 cm

    b) $21\sqrt{3}/36 = 1.0103629...$ and 1.87 cm × 1.010363 = 1.889378 cm.

[32] We find this principle is again explained with regard to the *canevas*.

square is then 48. The square of 7 is 49 and is too large by one unit. We look for $\sqrt{48}$, that is $\sqrt{49-1}$, or $\sqrt{7^2-1^2}$. This time, if we make the diagonal equal to 7, the perpendicular equal to 1, the base of the triangle then will equal $\sqrt{48}$ (fig. 116).

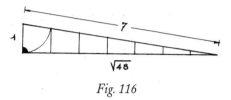

Fig. 116

Thus, we obtain the two values necessary to establish the surface 3, while preserving whole numbers but modifying the value of the digit. We have here (fig. 115) the angle 1 : 7, the angle of return of the axis of Amun, and this constitutes one of the essential geometric bases of the temple of Luxor.[33]

These principles are applied in two Dendera cubits (fig. 117) of different lengths, one of which (*A*) measures 53 centimeters, and bears, etched on its end, a small line that removes a portion of it so that the remainder measures 52.5 centimeters.

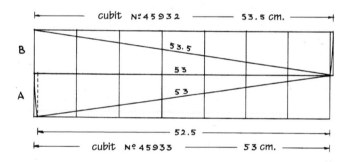

Fig. 117. Principle of increase and decrease in a cubit

The second cubit (*B*) measures 53.5 centimeters, and is therefore made up of 7 palms or 28 digits *larger* than those of the preceding example. In application they are the coefficient resulting from the geometric function of the angle 1 : 7:[34]

$$53 \text{ centimeters} \times 1.0101525 = 53.538 \text{ centimeters};$$
$$53 \text{ centimeters} \div 1.0101525 = 52.467 \text{ centimeters}.$$

The two cubits above form part of a group of three basalt cubits found in the temple of Dendera. These three cubits, which are square or rectangular in shape, have their total lengths divided into four, seven, five, and then six parts on their four surfaces.

The 28 digits of the royal cubit are divisible by 4 and 7, but the division by 5 and 6 of these Dendera cubits is unusual.

---

[33] Cf. plate 86; chapter 13, "The Axis of the Court of Ramesses"; chapter 15, "Numerical Study of the Terrestrial Skullcap" in the section "Diadem, I Assume Thee."

[34] See above, note 32.

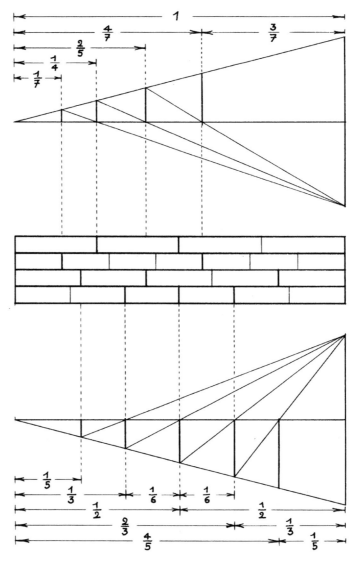

Fig. 118

The first division into the ratio 1 to 4 defines the ratios 1 to 7, then 2 to 5 and 4 to 7. By continuing this harmonic decomposition one obtains the numbers that are applied to the human canon (fig. 48).

The division into 6 proceeds from the original division into the ratio 1 to 2 and successively defines 1 to 3 and 2 to 3, and then 1 to 5, which thus links the two constructions. By continuing this decomposition, one obtains the number 17 of the "balance" of Jābir (fig. 46).

Now, once again we are going to refer to the "bolt" of pharaonic mathematics, and in doing so we shall observe that these subdivisions obey the genesis of harmonic division, which justifies the sacred character of the cubits. These numbers, handed down by the Temple, are the intangible foundations that serve as seeds. Their application in measure is rectified according to the geometric function that implies the natural division of the cubit itself.

Thus, through harmonic proportion, the pharaonic system links together all elements, measures, and proportions of growth.

Surface Measurements

Here is the application of these principles in measurements of surface area:

Surfaces		Side of square
setat	$= 1$ *arura* $= 10,000$ square cubits	1 *kht* $= 100$ cubits
remen	$= \dfrac{1}{2}$ *arura* $= 5000$ square cubits	$\sqrt{\dfrac{1}{2}} \times 100$ cubits
heseb	$= \dfrac{1}{4}$ *arura* $= 2500$ square cubits	$\dfrac{1}{2}$ *kht* $= 50$ cubits
sa	$= \dfrac{1}{8}$ *arura* $= 1250$ square cubits	$\sqrt{\dfrac{1}{8}} \times 100$ cubits, etc.

There is also the 1/16 *arura*, the side of which is 25 cubits, that is, 1/4 *kht*, and the 1/32, but here we are only studying the function that divides the surface with a value of 1 into two, and that then continues by successive dimidirations. Alternately, there is a rational side and an irrational side, multiple or submultiple of $\sqrt{2}$. In effect, the side of 1/2 *arura* equals $50\sqrt{2}$, counted in cubits, or $\sqrt{1/2}$, counted in *kht*, and the side of 1/8 *arura* equals $25\sqrt{2}$, and so on.[35]

We note that the word *remen* is used both to designate the *surface* with the value of 1/2 *arura* and as the name for the cubit of 20 digits that represents a length.

We want to point out as well that the word *heseb (hsb)* that is applied to one-fourth of the unitary surface is symbolized by a sign in the form of an ×. Why, if not to express the division of a square by its two diagonals? We generally admit that the sign × *(hsb)* recalls two crossed sticks and in standard translation the meaning "to break" is ascribed to it, but it can also mean "to calculate." Now, *hsb* designates 1/4 *arura* and it would have been very logical, had it been only a question of dividing the square (the *arura*) into four, to draw a vertical cross. Therefore *hsb* must indicate not a simple division but a function.

In dividing the square by its two diagonals, two of the triangles formed represent half the surface of the square, and resolve, geometrically, the problem of $\sqrt{1/2}$ or $\sqrt{5000}$, being *kht* and cubits, respectively.

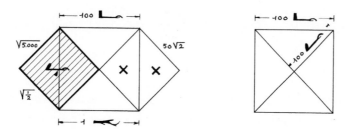

Fig. 119. Problem of the right triangle: the square of the royal cubit equals two squares of its remen

---

[35] It is worth noting that the sign *khet*, which means "wood," is used in place of the rope symbolized on the bas-reliefs. This wood signifies here the "cane" of the Bible, which is still used now, under the name of *qassab*, to measure the side of a *feddan*, a measure of land still in use in contemporary Egypt. The standard *qassab* is preserved at Giza in the large mosque, Gamā el-Kebir, and measures 3.85 m, that is, 200 digits of the "black cubit" (established exactly for 30° latitude), the cubit that measures the level of the Nile on the nilometer of Rhoda. (Cairo is located at 30° north latitude.)

Figure 119 is reminiscent of the "net for catching birds" while demonstrating as well the famous theorem of Pythagoras. The name of the practice of this bird hunt, "to take in one fell swoop," is written *skht,* the determinative of which has several variations (fig. 120).

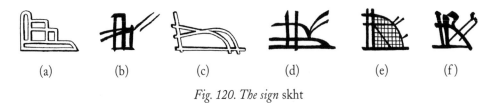

(a)   (b)   (c)   (d)   (e)   (f)

Fig. 120. The sign skht

(a) Hieroglyph, Twelfth Dynasty, tomb of Ukhotep; cf. plate 56; *(b)* hieratic sign, Rhind Papyrus, problem 64; *(c)* hieroglyph, Eighteenth Dynasty; *(d)* hieratic sign, Nineteenth Dynasty, from G. Möller, *Hieratische Palaeographie* (Leipzig, 1909), 2:464, Rollin Papyrus; *(e)* hieroglyph, Late Period; typographic sign, of the I.F.A.O.; *(f)* hieratic sign, Late Period, from Möller, 3:464, Papyrus 3030.

The sign *skht* is found at least once applied to "the royal apron," or more exactly, to the pleated loincloth that goes around the small of the back and crosses in front.[36] The sign *skht* is determinative of a crossing function that can be applied geometrically in all cases where the crossing will result in a form, such as in weaving, the casting of the first brick in the ritual foundation of a temple, or in the definition of a surface in geometry. The variations of the sign *skht* evoke the functions expressed by the geometric scheme reuniting the three fundamental proportions: arithmetic, harmonic, and geometric (fig. 121).

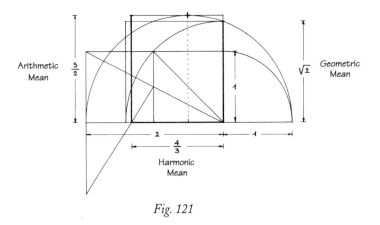

Fig. 121

The first form is the rectangle $1 \times 2 = 2$ squares. The second form is the rectangle $(3/2) \times (4/3) = 2$. The perfect square has the geometric mean $\sqrt{2}$ for its side.

Finally, a scene depicting "bird hunting" is always accompanied by a figure with arms extended holding a long scarf in order to "signal the hunters when the instant has arrived to close the net on the captured birds," as some would say. This is the case—either unique or rare—where a figure is represented with arms outstretched to form a cross, thus showing the arm span.[37]

---

[36] Cf. Gustave Jéquier, *Les Frises d'objets des sarcophages du moyen empire* (Cairo: I.F.A.O., 1921), p. 20, fig. 53.

[37] Cf. plates 56, 60, and 61.

In the bird-hunting scene in the temple of Karnak, it is the *neters* who pull the rope of the net, and it is Thoth who gives the signal with arms extended.[38] This alone would imply that this is not just a scene from ordinary life, but a teaching of the Temple.

Now, the Thoth of Karnak measures exactly 1.85 meters high, that is, 1 fathom. His abnormally large arm span gives the following proportions to the different parts of the arms: If the hand equals 3, the forearm equals 4, and the upper arm equals 5 (fig. 122).

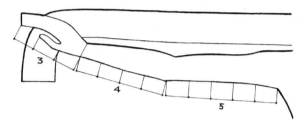

Fig. 122

Remen cubit = 5 palms = 20 digits

Royal cubit $\begin{cases} \text{forearm} = 4 \text{ palms} = 16 \text{ digits} \\ \text{hand} = \underline{3} \text{ palms} = \underline{12} \text{ digits} \\ \text{Total} \quad 7 \text{ palms} = 28 \text{ digits} \end{cases}$

Here again is the sacred triangle; it will control the measures and their relationships to one another, just as it governs certain human proportions. Let us note here that the proportions of the pelvic basin, our foundation, are established on this function and on the angle that derives from it, which moreover, indicates the angle of the dagger to the royal belt.

We have already thoroughly developed how the square of the *remen* cubit ($20^2 = 400$) will always be larger than half the square of the royal cubit ($28^2 = 784$, instead of 800), and how the value of the surface was rectified by using digits of different sizes, shorter or longer according to the use for which they were designated, and on what principle this correction was based.

It remains to demonstrate geometrically the way in which the sacred triangle is at the base of this play, and how it is very simple to rectify a length through it and because of it. This is the basis of the growth of the temple of Luxor and directs the rhythm of its axes (Amun and return). Measured in fathoms, its different stages give the numbers 40, 70, 100, 140, comparable to the numbers that govern the cubit, 8, 14, 20, 28, demonstrating that the fathom is considered as a fundamental unit of measure in this temple. We can then admit that for the whole of its length the temple has the value of *1 cubit,* composed of 28 digits, each of which represents 5 fathoms, which gives it an actual length of 140 fathoms for 0° latitude or 258 meters.

The square of the side 5 pivoting in the square of side 7 along the angle 3 to 4 summarizes the group of numerical functions and the metrical correction developed above; the square of 7, or 3 + 4, is formed of four rectangles plus the central square. This small central square is the pivot around which turns, in the angle of 1 to 7, the square of 5, whose side is the diagonal of the 3 to 4 rectangles (fig. 123).

[38] Cf. ibid., plates 60 and 61.

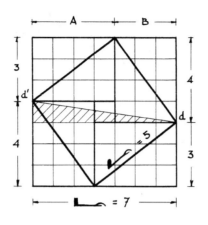

Fig. 123

The surface $(A+B)^2$ is always equal to $4AB+(A-B)^2$. The surface A^2+B^2 is always equal to $2AB+(A-B)^2$. The angle of pivot will always be equal to $(A-B)/(A+B)$, which, in this case, is 1 to 7. We rediscover our essential numbers: $4AB=48$, then $(A+B)^2=49$, and finally $A^2+B^2=25$, with the double of this square being that of the diagonal *dd'*, which represents $\sqrt{50}$.

This is the key to all the calculations that are also found at the base of the Babylonian problems of the Old Period.

Although this scheme, which must be regarded as functional, offers only approximate whole-number values, it indicates the way to follow for all the calculation of inverses that allow for resolution of the problems of irrationals, with an approximation to whatever precision desired, and this in a way that is more accurate and simple than with our decimal calculation.[39]

We have just shown here, in the form of the straight line and the square, and through the royal cubit, what is essentially the curve of the cycle that measures this cubit.

Summary of the Essential Data in the Study of Cubits

Governing Principles

Man measures the earth and furnishes all the units of measure.

The arc of meridian is variable according to the latitude. The cubits are adjusted for the specific locality to which they are related by the radius (the chord) of the moment of this arc.

---

1. A cubit must be read in both directions. The disposition of the digits, of the nomes, and of the divinities indicates this double reading, and the arithmetic progression of the digits, 1, 2, 3, 4, etc., moves in the opposite direction to the harmonic progression of the fractions, 1/2, 1/3, 1/4, etc., affirming the meaning of a number and its "reciprocal" and the perfect knowledge of the *reciprocal* role that any harmonic proportion plays in relation to an arithmetic proportion.

[39] The application of this principle is given in chapter 8.

2. As applied to the reading of measures, the "inequalities" of the divisions are found to be justified by the fact that they determine several different units of digits on one and the same cubit according to whether the larger subdivisions are read in one direction or the other.

3. A cubit can be divided into two unequal parts, each part thus belonging to a half-cubit of a different kind from the one that lets us suppose its total length.

4. There are two essential functions upon which the cubit depends: the ratios $7:5$ and $10:7$, which summarize one of the first possibilities of expressing the function of $\sqrt{2}$, and the ratio of the arc of 60° to its chord or radius, that is, $\pi/3$ to 1.

5. All units of measure are inevitably derived from one geodetic measure, the arc of meridian. The human fathom represents the thousandth part of 1′ of arc and serves as the initial measure; the cubits that derive from it vary according to the arc of meridian on which they are used.

6. The fathom is the unit of measure for the division of surfaces. Twenty fathoms to a square give a surface equal to half of 100 royal cubits squared, from which comes the division of the fathom by 100 that provides the digit of the *remen* cubit.

7. The fathom considered as the arc of 60° determines the cubit that serves as its radius. We see the application of this in room VI at Luxor: 6 fathoms ÷ $\pi/3 = 20$ benediction cubits of Dendera, which equals the radius of a circle with 36 fathoms as its circumference.

8. As a human measure, the fathom is divided into 4 cubits of 24 digits, thus into 96 digits. This is the human or small cubit. The cubit of 24 digits plus 1 palm has the value then of 28 digits and measures 0.5402 meter; this is the "black cubit" engraved on the pedestal of the black granite colossus that marks the knees of the Man of the temple of Luxor. We discover it again on the nilometer at Rhoda. This measure has been used continually for measuring the flooding of the Nile, and it was passed from the Copts to the Muslims.[40] It is frequently designated on the classical cubits of 0.525 meter with a length of 24 digits (small human cubit).

9. Twenty-seven mean fathoms equals 50 meters, from which it can be derived that 27/100 fathom is 0.5 meter. This length, considered as a radius or chord of an arc of 60°, determines the royal cubit, or the cycle cubit that measures 0.5236 meter (in true meters).

10. Each moment, each room of the temple, each cubit, develops a part of these fundamental ideas. There are many different *measures* according to the intention, but there is only one that links them all together: the fathom. Now, this fathom is as variable as the meridian curve of the earth, and it oscillates between 1.843... and 1.862... meters. From this derives all the "inequalities" one can encounter with respect to a single kind of cubit.

11. If one accepts that a degree of arc of the average meridian of the latitude of Egypt[41] can be divided into 21×10^4, we get a new cubit that we have not examined here, approximately 0.527 meter. This cubit is the standard for the nilometer of Elephantine. It is probably also the stade that was referred to by Eratosthenes; this stade is 300 cubits, which makes 700 stades to a degree, or 210,000 cubits.[42]

12. When it is a question of squares, the variation of lengths results from the function of the angle 1 to 7, which is the angle of the axis of return of Amun. When it is a question of curves, the variation obeys the geometric function defined by the angle that relates the axis of Amun to the northern axis.

[40] Eduardi Bernardi, in *De ponderibus et mensuris antiquorum,* p. 217, expressly states, from the testimony of several Eastern writers, that the *black cubit* was used to measure architectural works, precious merchandise, and the rising of the Nile.

[41] From 24° at Aswan to 30° at Giza.

[42] See the appendix, "The Nilometer of Elephantine," and "The Measurement of the Earth According to Eratosthenes."

APPENDIX

References for the Cubits Being Used in This Study

First, three basalt cubits of square cross section found at the temple of Dendera and preserved at the Cairo Museum as numbers 45931, 45932, and 45933.

No. 45931 is the benediction cubit seen in plate 64E, and no. 45933 is shown in plate 64D. These two cubits measure 0.53 meter to 0.531 meter. They take the place of the "radius cubits" subtending an arc of 0.3 fathom, as is demonstrated in room VI of the temple of Luxor (fig. 113).

No. 45932 is the cubit shown in fig. 117. With a length of 0.535 meter, it is the hypotenuse of the 1 : 7 triangle, having as its base one of the two preceding cubits measuring 0.53 meter, to both of which it serves as complement.

Second, five wooden cubits of a pentagonal section found in the tomb of Tutankhamun and kept in the Cairo Museum as numbers 61315 to 61320.

No. 61315 has a length of 0.524 meter. This cubit represents the length of the arc of 60° subtended by a chord of 0.50 meter. Thus, it is 1 cycle or royal cubit. It shows its *remen* of 20 digits, or 0.3715 meter. It is divided into two unequal parts, one of which is half the Dendera cubit, no. 45932.

No. 61320 has a length of 0.524 meter. This cubit, described in plate 64C, has the same characteristics as the preceding one.

Nos. 61317 and 61318 have a length of 0.525 meter. These two cubits are divided very regularly into 7 palms. The 2 palms of one of the ends are again subdivided into 8 digits. They show neither a division into two nor their particular *remen*. There is only one thing to point out: cubit no. 61317 has a small piece of ebony at each end that subtracts 7 millimeters so that the reading of this cubit measured from one of its ends to the ebony at the other end equals 0.518 meter, which represents 28/100 fathom, corresponding to 28 *remen* digits. This fact is very interesting on a cubit that specifically does not include its *remen* of 20 digits but indicates its value in another form.

No. 61316 has a length of 0.5285 meter to 0.529 meter. This cubit is shown in plate 64B. It is divided into two unequal parts and appears to be 1 radius cubit of 0.3 fathom at the mean latitude of Egypt (24° to 30°).[43]

——〰——

We have affirmed the existence of many different kinds of cubits:

1. The *royal cycle cubit* measuring 0.5236 meter to 0.525 meter, maximum, which represents the arc of one-sixth of a circle with 1 meter for its diameter. The cubits numbered 61315, 61320, 61317, and 61318, described above, are in this category.

2. The *radius cubits*, which can vary between 0.528 meter and 0.531 meter, represent the chord of the arc that is 0.3 fathom long. Their dimensions vary because the fathoms vary from 0° to 90° latitude. The relationship is 3 fathoms ÷ $\pi/3 = 10$ radius cubits. The two Dendera cubits numbered 45931 and 45933 belong to this category, as does the cubit no. 61316 of Tutankhamun.

3. The *black cubit* represents 28/96 fathom, and it varies for the same reason as the preceding ones. Its mean length is 0.54 meter. It is carved on the pedestal of the colossus of Ramesses (plate 46) and is the standard for the nilometer of Rhoda.

---

[43] In order to avoid any uncertainty about precision, only the cubits we have measured ourselves are studied here.

4. The *small* or *human cubit* represents 24/96 fathom. Its mean length is 0.463 meter. It is referred to on cubit no. 61315 of Tutankhamun.

5. The *remen cubit* is theoretically equivalent to 20/100 fathom. It is 0.3704 meter long. The measurements of the cubits demonstrate that it is related in actual usage to the cubit to which it belongs, as, for example, on cubits no. 61315 and no. 61320 of Tutankhamun.

The study of the dimensions of the different cubits presented above indeed allows us to encounter all of these elements again, but does there exist a cubit of 28 digits, each being 1/100 fathom? Given the fact that on several occasions we have found the lengths of 5.185 meters and of 51.85 meters in the monuments, and that cubit no. 61317 makes mention of the measure 0.518 meter by the subtraction of the small ebony tip, there is some reason to believe that it did exist, but no museum seems to possess an example. A very curious *double* cubit, however, coming from Gurob and preserved at University College, London,[44] is probably the only example of this cubit of 28/100 fathom.

This cubit is broken into two pieces, and by putting the two fragments together along the break, we can reconstitute the measure in the following manner:

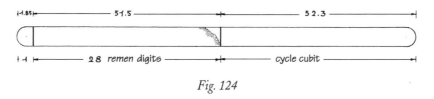

Fig. 124

According to the observation of the person who measured this cubit in 1955, it would be necessary to separate the pieces slightly, but the restoration cannot go beyond 0.52 meter for the portion to the left of the break. Now, 28 digits of 1/100 fathom at $0° = 0.516...$ meter; 28 digits of 1/100 fathom at $45° = 0.51863...$ meter; 28 digits of 1/100 fathom at $90° = 0.52126...$ meter. This last measurement is very improbable because it does not at all apply to the latitude of Egypt. On the other hand, the digit of 0.185 meter at the end allows us to suggest 0.5185 meter as the correct restoration, the more so since 0.518 meter + 0.185 meter = 0.537 meter, which is 28/96 fathom at $0°$. If we adopt the black cubit for the total measure of this cubit with one *remen* digit subtracted, we find 0.54 meter − 0.185 meter = 0.5215 meter.

Whatever it may be, since this restoration can only remain a conjecture from the point of view of the exact measure, it does confirm *the existence of the digit of 0.185 meter already found on other cubits, especially marked here, and from a cubit that is composed of twenty-eight of these digits, more probably being 0.5185 meter*, which fulfills the function of the *remen* for the cycle cubit, which is the cubit on the other side.

With these two cubits we could then directly measure the side of a square and its semidiagonal by taking 100 cubits of one kind for measuring the side and 70 cubits of the other kind for measuring the semidiagonal. For example, let us call cubit A the royal cycle cubit, measuring 0.5236 meter and cubit B the cubit of 0.51834, which would be its true value as a *remen*.[45] Thus 70 A cubits to the square = $(36.652 \text{ meters})^2 = 1343.3691 \text{ meters}^2$; 100 B cubits to the square = $(51.834 \text{ meters})^2 = 2686.7635 \text{ meters}^2$; the double of 70 A cubits to the square = 2686.7382 meters².

[44] Labeled no. 7 by Sir Flinders Petrie in *Ancient Weights and Measures Illustrated by the Egyptian Collection in University College* (London, 1926), and carefully remeasured in 1955.

[45] Applying the coefficient given on p. 292, note 31, the true value of this *remen* would be 0.5236... m/1.01015... m = 0.51834 m.

The Nilometer of Elephantine [46]

The nilometer of Elephantine Island could date back to the Ptolemies and was used until the time of Septimius Severus.*

This nilometer consists of a staircase constructed on the sides of a right angle, one side of which is parallel to the Nile and the other perpendicular to it.

On the wall of the staircase closest to the Nile, three vertical grooves 1 centimeter deep are carved.

The first groove has two large divisions, each of which is subdivided into fourteen parts. It bears the numbers 24 and 23 written in Greek and it is in front of a window 9.7 meters from landing three. The second is similarly divided and has the numbers 22 and 21 written on it. It is in front of a window 3 meters from the preceding one. The third has three large divisions numbered 20, 19, and 18, and corresponds to the opening of the door on the Nile.

The engineers Jollois, Devilliers, and Duchanoy, from the Department of Civil Engineering, and Descotils, Rozière, and Dupuis, from the Department of Mines, measured these divisions with very great care, as did the author (Girard).

It remained to determine the length of the large divisions, each of which undoubtedly represented the cubit used to measure the rising of the Nile. My traveling companions and I set out to achieve measurements of the greatest exactitude, with the following results:

First groove

24th cubit	536 millimeters	
23rd cubit	<u>518</u>	
Sum	1,054 millimeters	

The half-sum with the length reduced to cubits equals 527 millimeters.

Second groove

22nd cubit	527 millimeters	
21st cubit	<u>527</u>	
Sum	1,054 millimeters	

The half-sum with the length reduced to cubits equals 527 millimeters.

Third groove

20th cubit	543 millimeters	
19th cubit	529	
18th cubit	<u>509</u>	
Sum	1,581 millimeters	

One-third of the sum with the length reduced to cubits, equals 527 millimeters.

The author of this memoir then established the relationship between the sacred cubit of the Hebrews and the septenary cubit of the Egyptians found at Elephantine, and cites this passage from the Bible: "Ezekiel said he saw a man who held in his hand 'a cane or a measure length of six cubits; each of these cubits contained one cubit and one palm.' He said elsewhere, after indicating the dimensions of the altar of the holocausts: 'These measurements of the altar are expressed in a cubit that contains a cubit and a palm.'"

---

[46] From M. P. S. Girard, "Mémoire sur le nilomètre d'Eléphantine," in *Description de l'Egypte* (Paris, 1809–28), 1:6–16.

* Roman emperor, A.D. 193–211.

Finally the author explains the sacred character of the cubits that were preserved in the temples:

> A portable standard of this cubit of the nilometer was preserved in the temples of Serapis, a divinity to which the ancient Egyptians attributed the good fortune of the floods.[47] Whether because keeping this type of sacred cubit gave certain privileges to those who were in charge, or whether because the place where it was kept became by this alone an object of the greatest veneration in the eyes of the multitude, the emperor Constantine took the cubit from the temples of Serapis for the Christian churches.[48] The priests of the new cult came into possession of the "justice cubit" and continued to keep it as the authentic standard of original measurement. . . .

The Measurement of the Earth Attributed to Eratosthenes [49]

It would be a good idea to put an end to the legend that is taught in our schools attributing to Eratosthenes the mensuration of the arc of meridian between Elephantine and Alexandria, from which he would have deduced the size of the earth. This legend is established solely on the account given by Cleomedes—which had as its goal the demonstration that the earth was a sphere—and on a passage from Pliny, which says the following: "These are the facts that I consider worth recording in regard to the earth's length and breadth. Its total circumference was given by Eratosthenes (an expert in every refinement of learning, but on this point assuredly an outstanding authority—I notice that he is universally accepted) as 252,000 stades. . . .[50] Hipparchus, who in his refutation of Eratosthenes and also in all the rest of his researches is remarkable, adds a little less than 26,000 stades."[51]

Here now is the passage from Cleomedes[52] concerning Eratosthenes. It follows the account of Posidonius's demonstration of the size of the earth through geometric reasoning.

> Any one who has grasped these facts will have no difficulty in understanding the method of Eratosthenes, which is this. [1] Syene and Alexandria lie, he says, under the same meridian circle. [2] Since meridian circles are great circles in the universe, the circles of the earth which lie under them are necessarily also great circles. Thus, of whatever size this method shows the circle on the earth passing through Syene and Alexandria to be, this will be the size of the great circle of the earth. [3] Now Eratosthenes asserts, and it is the fact, that Syene lies under the summer tropic. Whenever, therefore, the sun, being in the Crab at the summer solstice, is exactly in the middle of the heaven, the gnomons (pointers) of sundials necessarily throw no shadows, the position of the sun above them being exactly vertical; and it is said that this is true throughout a space three hundred stades in diameter. [4] But in Alexandria, at the same hour, the pointers of sundials throw shadows, because

[47] "The terrestrial Serapis is depicted bearing a cubit and a modius on the head" (Jablonski).

[48] "The first Christians mutilated everything the temples contained, and covered up the sacred cubits in this general devastation. This was probably when the substitution occurred of the Roman for the ancient measures in Egypt, the use of which was outlawed . . . by ordinances of emperors who at this time wished to establish a uniform metrical system in all the parts of the empire. Nevertheless, right to measure and to announce the flooding of the Nile was maintained among the prerogatives of the Christian priests . . . subsequently, the sheiks of the Muhammadan religion replaced the priests in exercising this right" (Jablonski).

[49] Study made by Lucie Lamy.

[50] "De longitudine ac latitudine haec sunt quae digna memoratu putem. Universum autem circuitum Eratosthenes (in omnium quidem litterarum subtilitate set in hac utique praeter ceteros solers, quem cunctis probari video) duodentorum quinquaginta duorum milium stadorum prodidit. . . ."

[51] Pliny, *Natural History*, trans. H. Rackham, Loeb Classical Library (Cambridge: Harvard Univ. Press, 1938), 2.112–13.247, pp. 371–73.

[52] Greek astronomer who lived, according to some, in the fourth century, according to others, in the second century B.C.

Alexandria lies further to the north then Syene. The two cities lying under the same meridian great circle, if we draw an arc from the extremity of the shadow to the base of the pointer of the sundial in Alexandria, the arc will be a segment of a great circle in the (hemispherical) bowl of the sundial, since the bowl of the sundial lies under the great circle (of the meridian). [5] If now we conceive straight lines produced from each of the pointers through the earth, they will meet at the centre of the earth. Since then the sundial at Syene is vertically under the sun, if we conceive a straight line coming from the sun to the top of the pointer of the sundial, the line reaching from the sun to the centre of the earth will be one straight line. If now we conceive another straight line drawn upwards from the extremity of the shadow of the pointer of the sundial in Alexandria, through the top of the pointer to the sun, this straight line and the aforesaid straight line will be parallel, since they are straight lines coming through from different parts of the sun to different parts of the earth. On these straight lines, therefore, which are parallel, there falls the straight line drawn from the centre of the earth to the pointer at Alexandria, so that the alternate angles which it makes are equal. One of these angles is that formed at the centre of the earth, at the intersection of the straight lines which were drawn from the sundials to the centre of the earth; the other is at the point of intersection of the top of the pointer at Alexandria and the straight line drawn from the extremity of its shadow to the sun through the point (the top) where it meets the pointer. Now on this latter angle stands the arc carried round from the extremity of the shadow of the pointer to its base, while on the angle at the centre of the earth stands the arc reaching from Syene to Alexandria. But the arcs are similar, since they stand on equal angles. [6] Whatever ratio, therefore, the arc in the bowl of the sundial has to its proper circle, the arc reaching from Syene to Alexandria has that ratio to *its* proper circle. But the arc in the bowl is found to be one-fiftieth of its proper circle. Therefore the distance from Syrene to Alexandria must necessarily be one-fiftieth part of the great circle of the earth. [7] And the said distance is 5,000 stades; therefore the complete great circle measures 250,000 stades. Such is Eratosthenes' method. [8][53]

As it is easy to judge by the original text, Pliny speaks of the evaluation, or publication *(pro-didit),* of the size of the terrestrial circumference, and in the account given by Cleomedes we can extract the following points [as numbered in the above passage]:

1. We are dealing with a demonstration, not a measurement.

2. The point of departure for this demonstration is that Syene and Alexandria are on the same meridian. This is the first error: Syene is at 24°5′23″ north latitude and 32°54′ east longitude. Alexandria is at 31°13′5″ north latitude and 29°54′ east longitude.

The distance between parallels is 7°7′42″, whereas the estimation of Eratosthenes was 7°12′. This is an error of only about 4′, but there is a difference of 3° between the longitudes, and the arc of the circle that joins these two cities is consequently oblique, so that the distance between Alexandria and Syene that serves as the estimate of the measure of the globe must be computed *between parallels, not between zeniths.*

3. Cleomedes compares the celestial meridians with the terrestrial meridians and insists again on the fact that Alexandria and Syene are on the same meridian.

4. Eratosthenes, cited in addition by Strabo in his *Geography,* affirms that "the tropic passes necessarily through Syene since at noon on the solstice the gnomon gives no shadow." He adds that

[53] Cleomedes, *On the Orbits of the Heavenly Bodies,* 1.10, trans. T. L. Heath, in Morris R. Cohen and I. E. Drabkin, *A Source Book in Greek Science* (New York: McGraw-Hill, 1948), pp. 151–53.

this is true for a space with a radius of 150 stades, which represents, for determining a position on the globe, a value of 12′ to 13′.

Now, in the time of Eratosthenes, the tropic was at about 23°45′, and Syene was exactly under the tropic about 2700 years before our era, that is, at the time of the Old Kingdom.

5. The sundial that Cleomedes mentions is a half-sphere comparable to the Babylonian "polos" (fig. 125b).

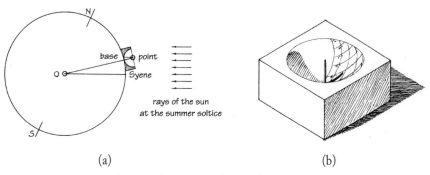

Fig. 125. The Babylonian polos

6. All this lengthy reasoning demonstrates only that the arc of the meridian between Alexandria and Syene is equal to what one reads on the sundial, since at Syene, the shadow is nonexistent at noon on the day of the solstice, and at Alexandria the angle that the shadow of the gnomon makes is equal to the angle that intercepts the arc between the two cities.

7. Consequently, since the arc read on the bowl is 1/50, the arc between Alexandria and Syene is 1/50.

8. No one says from what point Eratosthenes took the measure of 5000 stades that he gives for this arc and from which he deduces the dimension of the earth.

Among the opinions put forward concerning this distance of 5000 stades, there is one that supposes this to be a measurement taken between the two cities by walking. This is absurd from all points of view because these 5000 stades correspond to the distance between parallels, not between zeniths. On the other hand, the majority of scholars who have studied the subject think that since Eratosthenes was the director of the library at Alexandria, he was able to look at all sorts of documents and thus had used measurements established before him, in view of the perfection of the Egyptian cadastral survey.

A further question emerges: to which stade is Eratosthenes referring? The one commonly accepted as 700 to the degree, and which gives 252,000 stades to the terrestrial circumference, corresponds to 300 royal pharaonic cubits and not at all to the stades used by the Greeks.

All these considerations are very well summarized by the commentary of Laplace, which we cite here:

The measure of the earth attributed to Eratosthenes is the first attempt of this type that the history of astronomy offers us. It is very probable that long before this there were attempts to measure the earth, but of these attempts to find a similar value for the terrestrial circumference that conforms very closely to the results of modern calculations, nothing remains except some evaluations that were arrived at using calculations that were more inventive than certain. Considering that at Syene at the summer solstice the sun illuminated a well to its full depth, and comparing this observation to that of the meridian height of the sun at the same solstice at Alexandria, Eratosthenes found the celestial arc between the zeniths of these two cities to be equal to the fiftieth part of the circumference. As their distance apart was estimated at about five thousand stades, he gave two hundred and fifty-two thousand stades as the entire length of the terrestrial meridian. It is unlikely that for such an important investigation this astronomer would be satisfied with the gross observation of the solar illumination in a well. This consideration, along with the narration of Cleomedes, allows us to think that he used the observation of the meridian lengths of the gnomon at the solstices at Syene and at Alexandria. It is for this reason that the celestial arc he determined between the zeniths of these two cities varies a little from modern observations. Eratosthenes deceived himself in placing Syene and Alexandria on the same meridian. He deceived himself again in evaluating the distance between the two cities as only 5000 stades, if the stade he used contained three hundred times the cubit of the Elephantine nilometer, as there is some reason to think. Then the two errors of Eratosthenes would be almost completely compensated for, which would lead us to believe that this astronomer had only reproduced an ancient measure of the earth that had been executed with great skill and whose origin had been lost.[54]

Geographical Knowledge and Maps of the Egyptians
(from E. Jomard)

One should not be so surprised on seeing that a fact as important as the creation of maps, so honorable for the people who invented them, has remained obscure until the present day. But why is there today no authentic and impartial testimony to disperse these obscurities? Furthermore, is not the honor itself due to those who discovered maps, and is this not the cause of the silence of the Greeks concerning their true origin? Let us consider the Greeks in the era of Thales and Pythagoras, still plunged in an almost gross ignorance and suddenly proud to be in the possession of the sciences with which until then they had been unfamiliar. The Egyptians, on the contrary, a people isolated and ancient, worn by a long prosperity, communicating with reserve a small part of their knowledge to studious visitors, became indifferent to what use the visitors put their borrowings, and this knowledge was, moreover, lying unused on their ancient monuments. The petty thefts by the Greeks could not have been discovered in their own country; in Egypt these thefts were neither presumed nor prevented. How wonderfully Greek historians have concealed almost all the sources from which they had drawn!

The Greek writers of early times, and the Latin writers who copied them in recounting the history of the exact sciences, usually pass over Egypt—who is their mother—in silence. In order to discover the heritage of the Egyptians, one must come to a more recent time, a time when the vanity of the Greeks had ceased along with their political existence. It is to the Church Fathers that we owe the most instructive facts.

The reason for this contrast is easy to conceive. The early Christians valued the profane sciences very little; they had no interest in concealing the origins of the arts and letters. Born in Egypt, they knew the traditions of the country, and if they were strict with regard to the religion and morals of their ancestors, they did justice to their learning. The Greeks, on the contrary, greatly admired this wonderful knowledge, and it cost them nothing to appropriate it. It is true that they improved everything, and although we can reproach these disciples for being ungrateful, we cannot accuse them of having committed fruitless thefts.

---

[54] Pierre-Simon Laplace, *Exposition du système du monde*, vol. 6, *Oeuvres complètes* (Paris, 1884), bk. 5, chap. 2, pp. 411–12.

Saint Augustine said that the Egyptians were passionate about geometry. We cannot accuse Saint Clement of Alexandria of being too favorable to the Egyptians, so his account will not be suspect. Here is how he explains it in the sixth book of the *Stromates,* in an oft-cited passage where he described the functions of the priests of the colleges of Egypt:

"The *hierogrammate** is obliged to know the hieroglyphs, the cosmography and geography, the movements of the sun, the moon, and the five planets; the chorography of Egypt, the course of the Nile, the description of the temples and consecrated places, the measures and all things used in the temples."[55]

I will compare this well-known passage with passages from the Bible where we see evidence of Egyptian methods. Moses and Joshua have indeed borrowed from Egypt what they understood of the exact knowledge.

"Choose three men from each tribe for me to send up and down the country so that they can make a survey with a view to its apportioning, and then come back to me. . . . So the men left and went up and down the country, making a sevenfold list in the writing of all the towns . . ." (Joshua 18:4, 9).

Joseph narrates also, but in more detail, the same fact:

"So he sent men to measure their country, and sent with them some geometricians, who could not easily fail of knowing the truth, on account of their skill in that art. He also gave them a charge to estimate the measure of that part of the land that was most fruitful, and what was not so good."[56]

This measure of the country of Israel, ordered by Joshua in the same manner as the Hebrews had seen in Egypt, could pass for a true survey. It is the same work that had been done in the land of Egypt from a very distant age, and it is, in my opinion, the origin of topography and geography. To what exact and convenient use could one put these measures of each territory, the descriptions of the nomes, the knowledge of their limits and the subdivisions that Strabo described, if not by expressing all these proportions on the flat tables prepared for this work, such as those of which Apollonius of Rhodes speaks?

"It is said that a man left Egypt (Sesostris) to travel through Europe and all of Asia at the head of a strong and courageous army. He conquered a multitude of cities, some still inhabited today, and others abandoned because a great many years have elapsed since his time. The descendants of the men whom he established in Colchis still remain there and the colony is flourishing. They have preserved from their ancestors the engraved tables on which are drawn the borders of the earth and the sea, the routes and the roadways in a manner that serves as a guide for all travelers."[57]

We can ask ourselves by what procedure the Egyptians drew and traced their topographical maps. If there were no ancient monument to put our feet on the right path, such a question would at the very least be dubious. Fortunately, however, we possess a monument from the very hand of the Egyptians. I am referring to the reducing squares . . . used to make drawings of all types, in all kinds of scales, and to transfer them onto the place they were destined to be. One could enlarge or diminish the size by the same means generally used by the moderns. This procedure is based on a

[55] Clement of Alexandria, *Stromates,* 6.4.

[56] Josephus, *Antiquities of the Jews,* in *The Complete Works of Josephus,* trans. William Whiston (Grand Rapids, Mich.: Kregal Publications, 1981), 5.21, p. 108.

[57] Apollonius of Rhodes, *Argonautica,* 4.270–79.

* Sacred scribe.

consideration of the relationships of lines to one another, which is the basis of geometry. The Egyptian artists drew these squares over all the surfaces that they used for painting and for sculpture. The sides had the appropriate proportion to the plan that served as the model. The lines were drawn in red and at the time of execution these lines disappeared. But by good fortune, part of the sculpture that remained unfinished on the ceiling of Ombos, and in other places, have preserved this Egyptian method. Neither the lines of the figures nor the lines of the squares have been erased.

I have also found these reducing squares in the quarries the Egyptians used where they served as working plans for the builders. The most remarkable are those of Gebel Abufedah. I have seen there huge plane surfaces, hewn into designs, and squares drawn in red. In their midst are drawings of cornices or capitals of columns of various more or less complicated shapes. There were lines constructed on diverse angles, and curves cleverly drawn, composed of these kinds of designs. There is no doubt that these squares have been transferred from a smaller plan, prepared in advance and at the required size, onto these walls. This way they could lift the blocks and finish them outside the quarry.

There remain other monuments of the ancient topography of Egypt, and these monuments, although they are of a different type, are no less convincing or authentic: There are distances along routes that conform very closely to the latest observations, and the number of stades that the Egyptians reported to Herodotus, to Diodorus of Sicily, and to Strabo, when these travelers asked them about the distances to places, was very exact; there is a similar precision in the many measurements of Pliny taken in Egypt; and finally, those measurements of the ancient routes that the Romans adopted and translated without question and that we know today are accurate. I would ask how else these measurements, which are reported by Diodorus and Herodotus, could be as accurate as they are if the Egyptians had not possessed, as Clement of Alexandria reports, a detailed chorography, and if they did not have maps on which the distances were figured exactly. The distances one finds in these authors' works are not of the traveled routes; rather, they are straight-line measurements. They would have to have been measured from a bird's-eye view. How could the Egyptians have known these without the help of either maps or trigonometric observations? Moreover, the opinion I have put forward for the existence of geographic maps among the Egyptians has been accepted by several scholars, and the celebrated author of the *Exposition of the World System* has adopted it as well. Perhaps the preceding facts will add a high degree of probability to this view.[58]

E. Jomard drew up a "Table of Road Measures in Egypt." It compares the distances reported by the different authors in ancient measures with these same distances measured in meters on maps. We can discern the existence of several units of measure: the small stade of 100 meters (Herodotus, Diodorus, Strabo); the large stade of 100 fathoms (Diodorus, Strabo). Eratosthenes and Hipparchus used the stade representing 300 pharaonic cubits, which is commonly called the "stade of 700 to the degree." This confirms that the units of measure employed by the ancients and passed on by the Greeks correspond to an exact number of *meters,* of *fathoms,* and of *royal cubits.*

—⁓—

We have given here only brief extracts of this remarkable work, which is the report from the scholars of Bonaparte's expedition. These works are today relegated to the obscure corners of our

---

[58] E. Jomard, "Mémoire sur le système métrique des anciens Egyptiens," in *Description de l'Egypte* (Paris, 1809–28), 1:723–28.

libraries by the inventors of the "Greek miracle," who, however, are not the only guilty ones. Other interests are at stake.

After our study, particularly of the cubit and the *canevas,* we must recognize that without ever seeing a cubit, the scholars of Bonaparte's expedition were extraordinarily shrewd and precise in their studies. It would perhaps be fair and also useful for those who are not blinded by either scientific prejudice or misinterpreted faith to review and rehabilitate these authors.

Chapter 11

THE HUMAN CANON

THE *CANEVAS* GUIDE

Carefully observed theological prescriptions constitute the directive of pharaonic thought, as much in mathematics and geometry, as in architecture or sculpture. This fact reveals to us the meaning, unknown until the present, of the process of "putting into squares" that we call the *canevas*.

All architecture and all representations of figures or objects are constructed on a *canevas*-guide; this *canevas*, resulting from the theological directives of the Ancients, brings all proportions back to a basic idea. Now, these proportions are in no way arbitrary but correspond, for monuments, to astronomical principles, and for figures, to cosmic functions as they relate to human proportions.

The anthropocosmic philosophy bases all functions and all measures on the "crystallization" or "incarnation" of the Cosmos in man. Humanity *is the measure, the "atlas," on which living lands and their astronomical influences are read; it is the laboratory of all the miracles of the world.*

The choice of the *canevas* is of primary importance; through its number, it must summarize all the essential, "functional" proportions. The *canevas* serves as a stable foundation, formed of whole numbers belonging to the functional lineages that, by oscillation, tend toward the repose of the pendulum. This alternation is the characteristic of all growth and of the maintenance of life in its present form.

It is thus as a result of a specific science of the movements and times of revolution of the stars, and of growth on earth, that the choice of the numbers of the *canevas* could be made. Now that the importance of these lines is known, we can assert that the "forgetfulness" on the part of the artist that allowed them to survive is intentional. They first appear in the Fifth Dynasty (Saqqara). Lepsius was the first Egyptologist to take an interest in them, but some scholars later saw in them only a simple technique that facilitated drawing the figures. After that, the grid and the *canevas* have been made the objects of studies more or less successful, but enlivened by the conviction of the existence of a proportional canon.[1]

---

[1] For the history of this question, cf. Erik Iversen, *Canon and Proportions in Egyptian Art* (London: Sidgwick and Jackson, 1955).

Traces of the *canevas* have been found in tombs of all periods, in some temples, in the quarries, and on papyri. It can be seen from this evidence that certain basic numbers are applied to human proportions and to architecture.[2] There are two distinguishable kinds of figurations, those of the temples and those of the tombs.

The representations in the temples are all scenes of myth and ritual.[3] The king officiates as the royal priest in the presence of the *neters*. Purified and master of the two crowns, this king represents the royal principle, the incarnation of Cosmic Man, and his image was inscribed according to a canonic principle. Aside from the face bearing a certain resemblance to the reigning king, the essential proportions of the body remained invariably the same throughout millennia. Now, these figurations—which do not always correspond to our aesthetic concepts—emanate a sense of equilibrium and a serenity that make an impression on the observer. This alone is cause enough to seek out its reason.

The tombs of the nobles from all periods are those of the highest dignitaries. These are depicted in their human aspect, with their costumes, their attributes, and their particular characteristics. The scenes drawn from ordinary life unfolding in their presence are, for the most part, composed of figures much smaller in size than the master of the tomb, a variation that implies, apropos each scene, a "squared grid" of variable size.[4]

Now, whatever size the figures represented may be, whether in the temples or the tombs, their height from the soles of the feet to the top of the head (vertex) is divided by 19; this was the case from the first known lines until about the Twenty-sixth Dynasty. There is a single remarkable exception from the Eighteenth Dynasty in the tomb of Tuthmosis IV, where we find the only known case of twenty-one units from foot to vertex. Beginning with the Twenty-sixth Dynasty, the height to the vertex was twenty-two units and this remained the basis of the canon during the Late Period. It so happens that the number 19 is the source from which all that follows is derived; the use of nineteen, twenty-one, and twenty-two units corresponds to a philosophy, not to an arbitrary choice.

We pass too easily over this anomaly of the use of nineteen units for the height of a person whereas the royal cubit consists of 28 digits. Knowing that royal figures are measured by the cubit and must have very precise measurements corresponding to the symbolism and the teaching of the place, it is difficult to acknowledge an association, strange, to say the least, of two numbers having no apparent relation to each other: the 7 palms that govern the royal cubit, and the nineteen units of the height of a human being. This fact, which cannot be explained by any practical reason or by logic, inspires us to look for the deeper cause that dictated the use of these numbers.

Particularly since the Renaissance, and largely inspired by the masterpieces of Greek statuary, painters and sculptors have sought to establish a "human canon" that would serve as a foundation. Meanwhile, medical science had proceeded to note all the irregularities and deformities that can appear in the human body. Thus a human biometrics was created through which it is possible today to compare modern observations with the ancient canon. Now, establishing the ideal human canon around which oscillate the thousand nuances brought about by life has given rise to multiple studies and numerous systems.[5] Most of these systems are based on a common measure between one part of the body and its total size, such as the foot, for example, or the width of the hand, or the size of the head. For the establishment of these canons of principle, the height of a man is accepted as being equal to the arm span, as testified to in most of the drawings that have come down to us, in

[2] Cf. plates 52–67 and their legends.

[3] The exterior bas-reliefs are included even if they seem to be based on historical subject matter.

[4] Cf. plates 53 and 54.

[5] Cf. chapter 37.

contradiction, moreover, with the biometric principles that confirm the fact that the arm span of a man is *always larger* than his height.

By disregarding this nuance—however important—the Ancients would have been able, by making use of the subdivisons of their cubits, all of which are related to segments of the human body, to adopt a very simple *canevas* system: the small cubit is one-fourth of the arm span and measures 6 palms, and the *djezer* cubit corresponds both to the length of the foot and one-sixth of the arm span, and measures 4 palms; the common multiple of 4 and 6 is 24.

A *canevas* established on 24 would have made the link between the height of a person and the different cubits, and would have put the foot, the palm, and their digital subdivisons into consonance. And, if we accept that the height of the head is contained eight times in the total height, as in certain artistic canons, the consonance is perfect on all points. Indeed, this tempting solution was frequently adopted. Dr. H. V. Heller actually divides the total height of a human being into eight by taking the height of the head as the common measure.[6] A drawing by Hokusai (1760–1849) shows a division into sixteen for the *canevas*, which allows the navel to be placed at ten squares.[7] Finally, a drawing by Leonardo da Vinci inscribes a man with arms extended in a square (fig. 126). Leonardo thus takes the height of a man to be equal to his arm span. One rule of measure specifies that the height of a man is 4 cubits, each cubit divided into 6 palms and each palm into 4 digits.

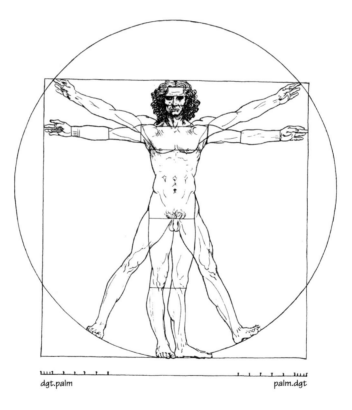

dgt.palm   palm.dgt

Fig. 126. Canon of proportions for the human body (from a study by Leonardo da Vinci)

The original has five lines of text written backward above the circle specifying that a man equals 4 cubits, 1 cubit equals 6 palms, and that 1 palm equals 4 digits. Under the measuring rule, the word *palm* and the abbreviation for *digit* were both also written in reverse.

---

[6] Cf. Ghyka, *Esthétique des proportions,* p. 276 and fig. 59.
[7] Cf. vol. 2, fig. 267.

Moreover, Leonardo, taking the navel as the center, draws a circle with $1/\phi$ for its radius in relation to its height of 1. This drawing reveals the most ancient traditions of dividing the height of man according to the golden section, and it shows the relationship that exists between man and the function of the pentagon.

The analysis of certain detailed squared grids from a tomb of the Twelfth Dynasty[8] demonstrates that the system presented above can be superimposed on the standard pharaonic canon, and thus, that it must have been envisioned in that way. This fact is again confirmed by the study of the figure of a naos on papyrus, which associates the two fundamental numbers, 16 and 19. Now, seeing that this simple solution had been recognized, and that it presented an inestimable advantage for bringing the cubits of measure into harmony with the figurations, why then did the Ancients prefer to adopt a number as impractical as 19 for the division of the human body? What can its relationship be with the number 7, which governs the royal cubits? Therein lies the mystery.

Its resolution confirms the care the Ancients took in rejecting the rational facility that characterizes us for the sake of the observance of the laws of vital functions that are sacred by virtue of their universality.

—∿∿—

Thoth, sculpted in human size in the the hypostyle room of Karnak, "gives the signal for the closing of the net" held by the king and two *neters*. Thoth, his arms extended, shows the development of the numbers adopted for the ancient *canevas,* including their values in measures. It must not be forgotten that the "net for capturing birds" must above all capture the spirit with the volatile, that is, fix the spirit.

THE NUMBERS 7 AND 19

With Thoth, Hermes, Mercury, we enter into the domain of life, that is, "that which comes and goes," the cyclic Osirian world, animated by Amun, lunar or solar, of which the lunar Amun is the Roman Jupiter-Amun.

Some of the titles given to Thoth, chosen from among his numerous names, make it easier to understand the nature of this *neter:* "thrice great," and also "twice great"; "master of truth" (justice, balance); "power that casts the deciding vote"; "judge of the two combatants";[9] *"neter* of the *neter-medu"* (sacred writing); "scribe of the Ennead of the *neters";* "Thoth-moon"; "master of the Eight"; "master of the city of Eight, in Hesert, at the heart of the temple of the net."[10]

Thoth is "master of . . ."; he is not the thing itself. He is not that which "comes and goes," but that which "causes to come and then to go back to its source." He is the creator of the cycles of that which renders apparent, but he is not writing, Seshat. Thoth is that which creates alternation, but he is not the weaving, Neith, who makes things tangible; Thoth can nevertheless become visible and perceptible—Thoth-mes—which is to say that he can be revealed: Her-mes, the secret (birth or incarnation of Hor).

Thoth is secret but numbers make him more accessible to us. The number of Thoth has a triangular essence. The seventh triangular number, the half-rectangle of 7×8, is 28, a perfect number.

---

[8] Cf. chapter 37.

[9] Or, "arbiter between the two adversaries" (Seth and Horus, Satan and Lucifer).

[10] Hermopolis Magna (el-Ashmunein), fifteenth nome of Upper Egypt.

```
        1                 1        1 1 1 1 1 1 1 1      7 × 8 = 56
       1 1                3        1 1 1 1 1 1 1 1      6 × 7 = 42
      1 1 1               6        1 1 1 1 1 1 1 1      5 × 6 = 30
     1 1 1 1             10        1 1 1 1 1 1 1 1      4 × 5 = 20
    1 1 1 1 1            15        1 1 1 1 1 1 1 1      3 × 4 = 12
   1 1 1 1 1 1           21        1 1 1 1 1 1 1 1      2 × 3 = 6
  1 1 1 1 1 1 1          28        1 1 1 1 1 1 1 1      1 × 2 = 2
```

28 = the sum of the first seven   2 = the origin rectangle
triangular numbers

Thoth, through the number 7, is linear because 7 is a prime number. He is triangular insomuch as he is 21 and 28, and hexagonal as a function of the number 7. As such, he becomes the source of the measures of cycles and of all that grows through the dividing action in ϕ.

The triangular series engenders all the others, and as Plutarch observes, the triangular numbers multiplied by 8 with the addition of 1 give the series of odd squares: $1 \times 8 + 1 = 9$; $3 \times 8 + 1 = 25$, etc.

Similarly, the triangular numbers multiplied by 6 with the addition of unity form the series of hexagonal numbers:

$$1$$
$$1 \times 6 + 1 = 7$$
$$3 \times 6 + 1 = 19$$
$$6 \times 6 + 1 = 37$$
$$10 \times 6 + 1 = 61, \text{ etc.}$$

All the hexagonal numbers are cubic gnomons: the number 7 is the gnomon for the cube of 1 to the cube of 2, and it engenders the number 19, the gnomon for the cube of 2 to the cube of 3, and so on; the first hexagonal number, 7, determines six points around a center; the second hexagonal number, 19, determines twelve points around the first hexagon, the twelve zones of the heavens (fig. 127).

Thinking in the Chinese fashion, we could say that 19, the square of which is 361, or 360 plus the central unit, is a circle as much as it is a hexagon. Now, the hexagon inscribed in the circle divides the cycle of time into 12, 24, 36, 360; it counts the twelve hours of night and the twelve hours of the day, the thirty-six decans, or the 360 days of the year (plus the 5 epagonemal days) of the pharaonic calendar.

The essential value of the number 19 (its primordial value) is justified by its functional relationship with ϕ. With the mystical function, we have seen that $1/\phi$ has a negative number, $1/\phi^2$ or 0.381966..., for its square. In the form of a positive value, the square of $10/\phi$ is equal to 38.1966..., which is two times 19.0983....

Twelve royal men measure the complete cycle, that of Heaven (which is visible to us) and that of the Dwat (the invisible heaven, that of transformations); the royal man has the value of ϕ^2, which is half of a royal cycle cubit. The royal cubit is divided into twenty-eight digits or (lunar) "days of Thoth." There are thus twelve times fourteen digits to a cycle, and each fourteen digits is equivalent in "time" to one royal man (the number 14 is traditionally called "the strong man" by sailors).

Now, the number 19.0983... is, in linear function (the relation), what the royal cubit is to the cycle and to time: *if the circle has the value of 120 (or ten times twelve royal men), its radius equals* 19.0983..., which also becomes the *side of the hexagon.*

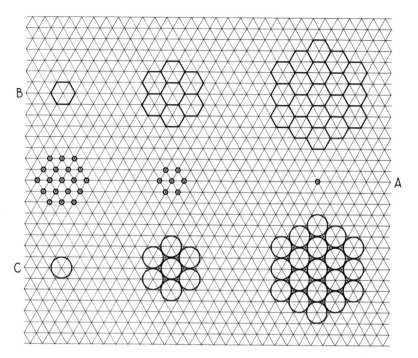

Fig. 127

A, growth by unit-points 1, 7, 19; *B*, growth by hexagonal surfaces 1, 7, 19; *C*, growth by disks 1, 7, 19.

The functional role of this number extends to volumes: the sphere inscribed in a cube has 0.5236 of this cube for its volume. The relation between the sphere and the cube is then 1/0.5236, which equals 1.90983..., so that, conversely, if the volume of the sphere is 10, the cube that circumscribes it would be 19.0983.... .

Another geometric function connects the number 19 to the function ϕ. The right triangle whose two sides are to each other as 1 is to ϕ has $\sqrt{3.1618...}$, or 1.902..., as its hypotenuse.[11] In this form, 19.02 is the diagonal of the *pentagon* when the diameter of the circumscribing circle is 20 (fig. 128).

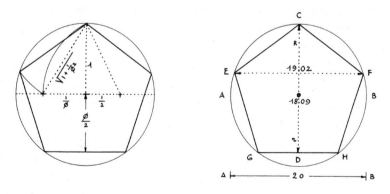

Fig. 128

The diameter *AB* = 20, the two radii *R* + *r* = 18.09 = *CD*. The diagonal *EF* = 19.02.

---

[11] The surface of the pedestal of colossus no. 3 in the court of Ramesses at the temple of Luxor applies this function and thus defines the height of the colossus. Cf. plate 21 and its legend, and figs. 205 and 206 (vol. 2).

The diagonal of the pentagon has the remarkable property of being the geometric mean between the diameter of the circumscribing circle and the height of the pentagon, as the numbers demonstrate:

$$\frac{\text{diameter}}{\text{diagonal}} = \frac{20}{19.0211} = \frac{\text{diagonal}}{\text{height}} = \frac{19.0211}{18.09017} = 1.05146\ldots.$$

These numbers can be compared to those of the pharaonic canon, 18 and 19 for the heights to the brow and to the top of the head. The kabbalistic tradition, which bases itself on the five limbs of the human body, including the head, inscribes Man in the pentagon in proportions in which we actually find the essential numbers that established the pharaonic canon.

Let us note here as well that this tradition sees a living soul in each star in the sky, and in Ancient Egypt we find these stars depicted with a quintuple radiation, which recalls the ideograms that in China, and elsewhere, represent Man (fig. 129).

(a)   (b)   (c)

Fig. 129

(a) The star (Egypt); *(b)* man, the principle (Chinese, Runes); *(c)* man, sexual (Chinese, Runes).

Cosmic Man is equivalent to 5. When he allows himself to be sexual, to be dual, he is chased out of Paradise, that is, he falls into the terrestrial world and its vicissitudes. Then he becomes 6.

The pentagonal function connects 19 to the regular polyhedrons. The icosahedron is enveloped by twenty triangular surfaces. Its twelve vertices each constitute a pyramid with a pentagonal base formed of five triangular surfaces. The six triangles that make up the hexagonal form and plane have become five in order to define the volume.[12] The radius of the circumscribing sphere to the icosahedron is 1.902… for an edge of 2.

Among its relations with the mystical function ϕ, the function that summarizes by itself alone all the possibilities of proportion, there is but one that connects the number 19 (in its capacity as an approximate number) to the generating "series" of the square root of 5 in whole numbers. This genesis associates the function with that defined by $1 + 1/\phi^2$ or 1.381966…. Recalling that the succession of terms corresponds to the form: $\sqrt{5}/1$, $(\phi\sqrt{5})/\phi$ and so on, *the relationship between each upper term and the following lower term is as* $\sqrt{5}/\phi$, or 1.381966….

This function, no doubt because of its generative character, seems to have played a very great role in pharaonic architecture. Indeed, it is itself the "seed" of two important numbers: the square of 1.381966 is 1.90983…, bringing us once again to this important number; and the square root of 1.381966… is equal to the side of the pentagon whose circumscribing circle has a radius of 1.

The median section of the ideal pyramid of Snefru is defined by the angle α of the base of the pyramid. The triangle *AEF* of the section has 1 to 1.381966… as its fundamental ratio. The point *D* (fig. 130a) on the diagonal determining the edge of the truncated pyramid confirms the function. Thus the ratio of the height *AC* of the truncated pyramid to the height *CF* of the ideal pyramid is 1 to 1.90983….

[12] Cf. vol. 2, fig. 286.

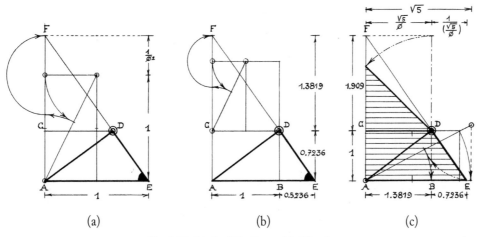

$$\text{(a)} \qquad\qquad \text{(b)} \qquad\qquad \text{(c)}$$

Fig. 130. Study of the Pyramid of Snefru

(a) For the base *AE* equal to 1, the height *AF* of $1 + 1/\phi^2 = 1.381966....$ The point *D* is obtained by drawing the perpendicular from *A* to *FE*. *(b)* For the plane surface *CD = AB*, equal to 1, the segment *BE* will be 0.5236. *(c)* For the height *AC* equal to 1, the height *CF* of the ideal pyramid will be 1.90983. The height *CF* of the ideal pyramid becomes the apothem of the upper pyramid of Snefru, forming what is called the Rhomboidal Pyramid.

Conversely, the ratio of the half-base of the upper pyramid *CD* to the segment *BE* of the base is 1 to 0.5236, that is, the definition of the functional value of the royal cubit. It is difficult to disclose more of these things through a single drawing.[13]

As a whole number, 19 is generated by 7 in the hexagonal series, as we have previously shown, but in that case it was a question of a genesis on a flat surface. The developed harmonic function makes the passage from 7 to 19 through successive divisions of the same initial length *PA* (synthesis 2, figs. 48 and 136).

The first stage gives the ratios 1/4 and 3/4. The second stage divides the length *PA* into 2/5 and 3/5, establishing the relationship of the fifth between the two segments. The third stage divides the length *PA* into 4/7 and 3/7, which determines the relationship of the fourth between the two segments. The fourth stage defines the numbers governing the pentagon, numbers identical with those forming the nucleus of the hieratic pavement.[14] The length *PA* is divided into 8/11 and 3/11. Now, 8 and 11 measure the directing rectangle of the pentagon that forms the foundation of the sacred naos.[15] Finally, the fifth stage divides the length of the "string" *PA* into two segments: 16/19 and 3/19.[16]

These are then the essential foundations of the royal canon: 3/19 represents the part of the body including the head and the neck. The sixteenth line is actually one of the constants of the canon and separates the spiritual and sensitive part from the physical-assimilative parts and limbs of the human body.

---

[13] Cf. figs. 66 and 67.

[14] Cf. chapter 13.

[15] Cf. plates 55 and 56, fig. 266 (vol. 2).

[16] It should be noted that in this succession of stages, the length *PB* increases following the geometric progression of doubling: 1, 2, 4, 8, 16, ... The difference *AB* is always 3, that is, it is a constant.

This application of the principle of harmony once more justifies the term *bolt* that we have given to it. It is already the key to all mathematical calculation, and we rediscover it here as being the model for the establishment of the human canon, just as later on we shall see that it determines the axes of the temple of Luxor, which will give birth in their turn to the other functions.

Thus do we see pure science and applied pharaonic science finding the unifying key in this law of order that creates the cohesion of the Universe. Harmonic proportion then provides justification for the numbers 7 and 19 and creates the link between the numbers of the royal cubit and those of the human canon.

The Number 19 in Astronomy

In Babylonia, the seventh, fourteenth, twenty-first, and twenty-eighth days, and the nineteenth day of the following month, that is, the forty-ninth day after the new moon of the preceding month, were considered "taboo." Nineteen was not named but counted as 20 minus 1.[17]

The legend attributes Meton with the discovery of the cycle of 19 years in which the cycles of the moon and sun coincide, a period that the Greeks, filled with enthusiasm, had inscribed in letters of gold on their public monuments. According to other testimonies the cycle of 19 years had been known before Meton. If we refer, however, to Aristophanes' celebrated satire *(The Clouds)* that ridicules the calendar of his time, it seems that it had not been in use.[18]

Be that as it may, the cycle of Meton claimed to establish the coincidence of 19 solar (therefore tropical) years with 235 lunation cycles, and it was quickly acknowledged that both these periods were too long. Callippus then proposed quadrupling the cycle of 19 years, but by taking 365.25 days for the solar year. At the end of two centuries this new cycle of 76 years, used especially by the Greek astronomers, was again recognized as being slightly too long. Hipparchus proposed to quadruple it again, which fixed the equivalence between 304 "Julian" years and 3760 lunations, with a difference of 1 whole day: 304 Julian years equals 111,036.0000 days; 3760 synodic revolutions of the moon equals 111,035.0184 days. The agreement is nearly perfect, but it is important to point out two essential facts.

First, the year adopted by Callippus and Hipparchus of 365.25 days corresponds neither to the tropical nor to the sidereal year, and undeniably originates from the pharaonic "fixed year" that was thought to be correctly identified as the "Sothic cycle."[19] It is interesting to note how Callippus and Hipparchus felt themselves obliged, in order to correct their calendar, to return necessarily to the pharaonic Sothic cycle, but with the small difference that they take it to be a solar year, not the proper Sothic cycle (Julian year).

Second, we just saw that it is the product of 16 × 19, or 304, Julian years (Sothic cycles) that coincides with a whole number of lunations. Now, these numbers originate from the harmonic function and are basic to the pharaonic human canon. Synthesis 2 (fig. 48) generates the numbers that we continually discover playing a part in the calendars.

The Babylonians, on the other hand, excelled in determining the periods of revolution of the moon and the planets. Establishing the periods of the planets was more complex than for the moon

[17] Cf. Bigourdan, *L'Astronomie,* p. 60, regarding the "taboo" character that can be related to the prescribed interdictions for the day of the Jewish Sabbath and the Christian Sunday.

[18] Cf. ibid., p. 69 et sqq.

[19] Cf. chapter 20, "The Pharaonic Calendar."

because of their stationary and retrograde movements, phenomena they accurately detected. They had several methods that took into account each of the variations of the synodic arcs. The goal was to establish as exactly as possible the relationship between the sidereal year of the earth and the sidereal revolution of a planet. For Jupiter they obtained remarkable results, comparable with those of modern astronomy.

After a long series of observations that took note of the dates of successive heliacal risings of Jupiter and its corresponding positions on the ecliptic, they defined the different variations of the synodic arc (of 28°15′30″ to 38°2′), which led them to adopt the mean value of the synodic arc as 33°8′45″, whereas Leverrier's tables give 33°8′37.54″ for the present era. The difference betweeen these two angular measurements is from a disturbance that happened before our era, so that the accuracy obtained is to 1/80,000 of the arc under consideration.[20]

The duration then given for the synodic revolution was 398.89 terrestrial days, compared to the present figure of 398.92 days. Finally, knowing that in 12 terrestrial years Jupiter accomplished about 11 synodic revolutions, the Babylonians established a correspondence that could provide a perpetual ephemeris for Jupiter of 83 terrestrial years for 76 (or 4×19) synodic revolutions of Jupiter.

Moreover, according to the modern tables, the sidereal revolution of Jupiter takes 11 Julian years plus 314.839 terrestrial days, so the "month" of Jupiter, the twelfth part of this year, is about 361 terrestrial days. Eleven Julian years plus 314.839 days equals 4332.589 days. Three hundred sixty-one terrestrial days times 12 equals 4332 days.

It is interesting to note the part that the number 19 plays in these cycles. The perimeter of the square with 19 for its side is equal to 76, the number of synodic revolutions of Jupiter in 83 terrestrial years.[21] The surface of the square of 19 is 361, the number of days that make up one-twelfth of Jupiter's cycle. Finally, the mean synodic arc of Jupiter, 33°8′, is only a little larger than the eleventh part of the circumference, approximately 32°44′. These two angles govern the southern part of the temple of Luxor, dedicated to Amun, the ram, the Jupiter-Amun of the Romans. The coincidence merits our attention.

—⁓—

The movements (duration and time) of the stars are not immutable: all is moving in the sky. But the law of harmony itself is invariable because it is proportional. If one of the elements varies, it will "harmonically" entail the adaptation of all the elements of the proportion.

Thus it is certain that an astronomical science founded on this law of order that creates the cohesion of the world will be more valid than our purely objective and rigid conception of the Universe. Our cold precision goes against life.

Now, through the agreement of the system of measures with mechanical and biological laws, through this same law of order, there appears to be a synthesis of the sciences. All this leads us to believe that we are approaching the divine, that is, universal, knowledge of the pharaonic empire.

This conviction will find disquieting confirmation in the remainder of this study, and will make clear the reason for the emphasis we have placed on the mathematical parts of this work.

[20] Cf. Bigourdan, *L'Astronomie*, pp. 222–23.

[21] The difference between 83 and 76 is 7.

THE TWO PHARAONIC METHODS OF USING THE GRID

The first method of using the grid, used from the earliest known *canevas* up to the Twenty-sixth Dynasty, divides the total height of a person into nineteen units so that eighteen units correspond to a line separating the forehead from the crown of the skull.

The second method, used from the Twenty-sixth Dynasty to the end of Greco-Roman rule, divides the total height of a person into about twenty-two and one-half squares, so that the line at twenty-one squares passes through the eyelid or the eyebrows.

The unique case mentioned above, where the total height is divided into twenty-one units, is found in the tomb of Tuthmosis IV. This division is related to the Thotian principle and the function of 3 times 7. This variation applies to a principle indicated by the meaning of the royal name, Thoth-mes, and proves that the choice of a canon of 19 or 22 has a philosophical significance and is not arbitrary.

Through their application in whole numbers, these two methods are connected to the two lineages of the additive series ϕ generating the root of 5, so that one implies and completes the other.

Certain very ancient *canevas*, as far back as the Fifth Dynasty, consist of only a few lines. Among these the eighteenth is always marked, whereas the nineteenth is omitted. This fact gives a valuable indication that allows us to formulate one of the fundamental tenets of the older canon: *The height* 18 *must be taken as the length that defines the location of the navel when divided by the golden section.* This eighteenth line will be the reference line. In the later *canevas*, established on twenty-two squares, it is the twenty-first line that is the reference line.

In comparing the two canons and the two cubits (as well as the subdivisions of the "Two Lands" of Upper and Lower Egypt), we can make the following distinctions. As the Anthropocosmos, Man summarizes and represents the essential functions of the Universe.

1. As number, he can be the multiple of 6, that is, 18, as in the standard canon, or the multiple of 7, that is, 21, as in the canon of the Late Period, and thus be connected to the two values of the two cubits of 6 and 7 palms (24 and 28 digits).

2. As the radius of the earth that he "embraces" *(hpt)*, he has the value of 19 for a circle valued 120 in the first canon, or 21 for a circle of 6×22 in the latter.

3. As *born* man divided at the navel by the golden section, he has the value of 18, and the fundamental proportion will be $18 : 11 = \phi$. The figure is then considered without the crown of the skull and divided in such a way that $18 : 11 : : 11 : 7 = \phi$ for the R series. In the second canon, he has the value of 21, and the fundamental relationship is $21 : 13 = \phi$, that is, $21 : 13 : : 13 : 8 = \phi$ for the F series. We rediscover here the two additive series of ϕ of the numerators and the denominators of the root of 5, that is, the two lineages of proportions.

4. As a summary of the two lineages of the effect of the golden section revealed by the *canevas*, he must also express the two essential functions of the proportions 1 : 2 and 1 : 3, the heart and origin of all proportions. The *kamutef* of Luxor will show us the passage from 18 to 21, numbers that are linked by 19.[22]

In the case of the *kamutef*, the joints of the stones determine a rectangle (4 : 10) in which the unity carried over nineteen times corresponds to the height of the *kamutef* from the soles of the feet to the forehead.

[22] Cf. plate 59.

Starting from this unit of the square, it is necessary to enlarge it to find the *canevas* of 18 to the forehead, or else to make it smaller to establish the *canevas* at 21 above the eye. Now, the triangles 1 : 2 and 1 : 3 will modify the original square and define the two units of the required square (fig. 131).

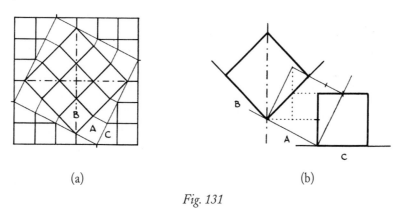

(a)   (b)

Fig. 131

(a) Side $A = 1$; side $B = 1\sqrt{10}/3$; side $C = 2/\sqrt{5}$. *(b)* The squares of sides B and C are found exactly at 45° (one-eighth of the cycle) because the sum of the angular relationships $\widehat{1 : 2}$ and $\widehat{1 : 3} = \widehat{1 : 1}$.

We should also recall that in the *canevas* generating the square root of 5, the two ϕ whorls cross each other and "close" in order to determine the "ejected" square whose side is added to the square formed by the whorls. The numbers resulting from these crossings are the following: $55 + 9 = 64$, defined by the original whorl 1 : 2; and $76 + 12 = 88$, defined by the original whorl 1 : 3.

Now, one-fourth of 76 is 19, the number of the standard *canevas,* and one-fourth of 88 is 22, the number of the *canevas* of the Late Period. The height of a person without the crown of the skull is thus 18 in the first case, and 21 in the second.

In the hypostyle room at Karnak, the scene of "hunting with the net" shows Thoth with arms extended,[23] and a *canevas,* established following the standard division of dividing his height *without the crown of the skull* by 18, gives him a total arm span of twenty-two squares between the ends of the fingers and twenty-one squares between the ends of the thumbs. *Thoth teaches the numbers governing the two canons, not human proportions.*

The two numbers chosen for the two canons, summarized by the lone figure of Thoth, represent the radius of the circles inscribed in, and circumscribing, the hexagon.

The man with 18 or 19 for his height becomes the radius of the circle inscribed in the hexagon, and the man with 21 or 22 for his height is the radius of the circumscribing circle.

We have here a geometric proof for universal relationships that clearly explains the reason for the choice of the two *canevas.* Thus, the numbers of the canon are not defined according to subjective principles but according to a basic universal doctrine.

It is well understood that here, as elsewhere, the pharaonic sages wished to record their thought on the invariable base of numbers, and for this purpose took the liberty of slightly modifying the mental scheme. In no case would the pharaonic expression be fixed in crystal; it was always vitally in keeping with the mobility of what is living.

[23] Cf. plate 60.

We can relate these two canons to the passage from the pharaonic to the Christian era: in the first, man is placed *under* the sky of the temple (the radius of the circle inscribed in the hexagon), and in the second, man is placed *on* the sky of the temple (radius of the circumscribing circle, fig. 132).

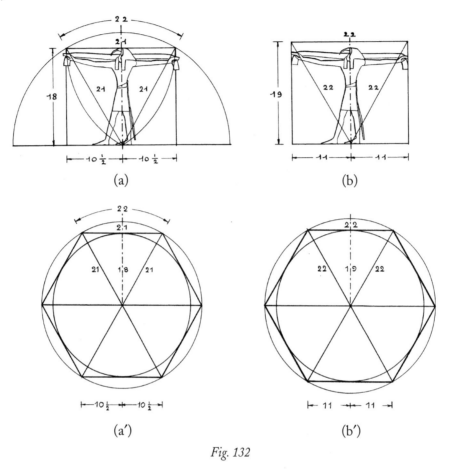

Fig. 132

(a and *a')* The number 18 takes the place of the inscribed radius; the length 21 between the thumbs becomes the radius of the circumscribing circle. The arc of each sixth of the circle is 22 for the value $\pi = 22/7$. The ratio for $\sqrt{3}$ is a multiple of 12/7. *(b* and *b')* The number 19 becomes the inscribed radius, the length of the arm span measured from the fingertips is 22, the radius of the circumscribing circle. The ratio for $\sqrt{3}$ is 19/11. The arc is irrational. The arc in *(a)* and *(a')* expressed as the number 22 is a straight line in *(b)* and *(b')*.

Finally, it is interesting to connect the two fundamental cubits of 6 and 7 palms, which are at the base of all pharaonic measures, with the circle of Willis,* which controls the arterial irrigation of the brain (fig. 133) and is composed of seven arteries on six sides: the hexagonal number 7, generator of the number 19.

* The hexagon of Willis" in French.

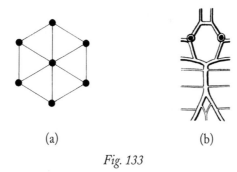

Fig. 133

(a) Hexagonal number; *(b)* circle of Willis.

HUMAN BIOMETRICS AND INVARIABLE PRINCIPLES

In order to understand thoroughly the value of a proportional canon of the human body, it is necessary to be personally involved in the study of the problem. The fundamental starting point is necessarily the skeleton, the infrastructure of our body. The dimensions of each bone and its proportions are, at the present time, carefully noted, but when it is a question of reassembling them to form a homogeneous and harmonious totality, we must consider the proportions of the living person, that is, human biometrics.[24]

There are certain points on the skeleton of the living body that are easy to locate and that determine some definite proportional elements. The articulations of the elbows and the knees are examples, as is the fact that the level of the iliac crest corresponds almost exactly with the level of the navel. The height of the chest is halfway between the crown of the head and the ischium. The sternal fork marks an essential point on the body: it is attached to the clavicles, which separate the head from the trunk, and it is the vertex of the anterior part of the thorax. But there is another very important point that has not been a serious concern in modern biometrics: the junction between the seventh cervical and the first thoracic vertebrae corresponds to the posterior vertex of the thorax and the end of the cervical spine. This point is one of the most important in the pharaonic canon because it is a vital node.

In order to grasp better the difference between the pharaonic canon and our current understanding of the issue, it is necessary to review quickly the invariable principles that are specific to modern biometrics and to provide, as an example, the best proportional canon established so far.

Dr. Richer, physician and professor at the Ecole des Beaux-Arts in Paris, has established a proportional canon that is not based on aesthetics, but rather on anthropometric givens. The comparison of this canon with a few other data that are also anthropometric will provide a brief sketch of the issue and some of the difficulties it contains.

---

[24] The following references, among others, can be consulted: F. Vandervael, *Biométrie humaine,* 2nd ed. (Paris: Masson); J. Decourt and J. M. Doumic, "Schéma anthropométrique appliqué à l'endocrinologie: Le Morphotype masculin," in *La Semaine des Hôpitaux de Paris* 10, no. 7 (July 1950); Dr. P. Busquet, *Traité d'anatomie clinique médicale topographique,* vol. 1 (Paris: Baillière, 1927); Ghyka, *Esthétique des proportions;* Proportions calculated by J. Denicker, and "Principaux caractères de l'homme moyen d'après Quetelet," in *Encyclopédie Française,* 4.56.6.; P. Richer, *Canon des proportions du corps humain* (Paris: Delagrave, 1933).

Richer takes the height of the head as a module, which he accepts as being contained seven and one-half times in the total height of the average person (fig. 134). The constant that is more generally accepted for this relationship is

$$\frac{\text{total height}}{\text{height of the head}} = \frac{100}{13} = 7.692....^{[25]}$$

The *height of the knees* (to the femorotibial line) corresponds to two heads, or 26.666, for a height of 100, compared to the extreme proportions resulting from other systems of measure:

$$\frac{\text{total height}}{\text{femorotibial line}} = \frac{100}{26.5} \text{ minimum to } \frac{100}{27.42} \text{ maximum.}^{[26]}$$

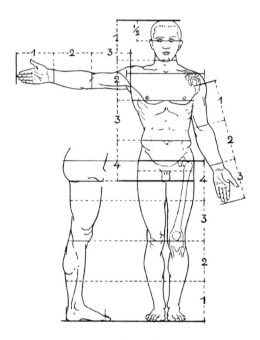

Fig. 134. Richer's canon

The *width of the shoulders* is equal to two heads, that is, to the height of the leg at the knee. We can also see the width of the shoulders as equal to one-fourth of the entire arm span. The *width of the hips*, or *bitrochanteric diameter*, is accepted as one and one-half heads by Richer, compared to 18.8 for a height of 100 according to Doumic. The *proportions of the pelvis* are very important. The average recognized by Hambidge, from measurements of a number of skeletons, established the ratio:

$$\frac{\text{hip width}}{\text{height of pelvis}} = \frac{1.309}{1}.$$

Its depth is defined by half its width.[27] The *diameter across the iliac crest* is 16.82 for a height of 100, according to Doumic.

[25] Following the convention most often used to establish a scheme for comparing proportions, here we accept 100 for the total height of a person.

[26] The maximum ratio given here is furnished by the measurements of one hundred young people aged seventeen and one-half years.

[27] Cf. Ghyka, *Esthétique des proportions*, p. 275. The accepted proportion for the female pelvis is 1.382..., according to Hambidge.

The *proportions of the rib cage* vary a great deal depending on the subject, and they are difficult to define because of the shape of this part of the skeleton. Its approximate maximum height corresponds to one-fifth of the height of a person. According to our authors its width (the transverse diameter of the thorax) varies, being between 16.28 and 17.2 for a height of 100. The average oscillates around one-sixth of the total height. Its greatest depth corresponds more or less to the height of the head, and varies between one-seventh and one-eighth of the total height.

The *height of the upper body* measured from the level of the top of the head to the ischium (gluteal crease) is practically equal to the height of the lower body measured from the soles of the feet to the greater trochanter. There is thus a very interesting overlap of these two measures.

To these two parts of the body Richer gives the size of four heads, which allows us to establish the following proportion:

$$\frac{\text{total height}}{\text{height of upper body}} = \frac{100}{53.333} = \frac{\text{total height}}{\text{height of lower body}}.$$

The various biometric averages furnished for this ratio are

$$\frac{\text{total height}}{\text{height of upper body}} = \frac{100}{52.16}, \frac{100}{52.57}, \frac{100}{52.4}.$$

Now, the average of these three ratios is exactly 100/52.37, practically the same as that of the ratio between the total height and the lower body.

This ratio is extremely important because in human proportions it reveals an essential function touched on with regard to the number 19—the relationship between the cube and the sphere. We can formulate this proportion in the following manner: *The height of the upper body is to the total height of a person as the volume of the sphere is to its circumscribing cube.* The relationship between these two volumes is evoked we recall, by the number 19, that is,

$$\frac{\text{volume of a cube}}{\text{volume of a sphere}} = \frac{1}{0.5236} = 1.90983....$$

The equality of the height of the upper body to that of the lower members is defined by the center of the area of superimposition of these two lengths, the midpoint of the height of the body, which Richer's canon expresses very well. Actually, the pubic symphysis (sex organs) exactly divides the height of the human body into two equal parts. This constant is important and all the canons agree on this point.

It thus appears that the height of the upper body of a man is to half of the total height as the arc of 60° is to its chord, because the proportion for the diameter is as 52.36... is to 50, given a height of 100. This constitutes a new, essential constant.

The navel, according to tradition, divides the height of man by the golden section. Anthropometrics specifies a nuance in the application of this fundamental proportion. The navel is normally a little higher in the female and a little lower in the male, and frames the absolute function of ϕ.[28] In fact, the height of the human being is divided by the navel into two segments that are to one another as 1 is to ϕ, *but on the condition that we cut off a small part of the crown of the skull.* The application of the golden section becomes relative then to a coefficient that we must define precisely.

---

[28] Cf. Ghyka, *Esthétique des proportions*, p. 58.

An average based on one hundred men nineteen to twenty-seven years of age (Doumic) provides the following coefficient:

$$\frac{\text{total height}}{\text{height of navel}} = \phi \times 1.03.$$

The measurements taken from thirty men between twenty-five and thirty years of age (Denicker) provides the coefficient 1.023, which is

$$\frac{\text{total height}}{\text{height of navel}} = \phi \times 1.023....$$

The measurements from one hundred subjects seventeen and one-half years old defined the coefficient as 1.036, or

$$\frac{\text{total height}}{\text{height of navel}} = \phi \times 1.036....$$

The mean between the two extremes is 1.03. This coefficient omits a small part from the top of the head, variable for each person, which constitutes the "particular coefficient" and corresponds to the crown of the skull.[29] The number 1.03 is interesting to keep in mind because it establishes the link between the first transciption of ϕ in whole numbers and its irrational value. The simplest ratio is $5/3 = 1.6666...$ and $1.6666 \div 1.03... = \phi$.

The *full arm span* (the fathom) is always larger than the height of a person. The ratios most frequently encountered fluctuate between 1.0303 (Quetelet), 1.044 (Denicker), 1.045 (Topinard), and 1.045 (Hambidge). Matila Ghyka is indeed accurate when he cites the ratio 1.045 between the fathom and the total height as among the constants of the human body.[30]

The function evoked by this number is, in its absolute form, 1.0472..., or $\pi/3$, and allows the establishment of the following equivalences by recalling the only true constants encountered in the course of this study:

$$\frac{\text{arm span}}{\text{total height}} = \frac{\text{height of the upper body}}{\text{height of the pubic symphysis}} = \frac{\pi}{3}.$$

In summary, *the height of the upper body corresponds to half of the arm span and to the height of the lower limbs. The width of the shoulders corresponds to one-fourth of the arm span, and the height at the knees is slightly larger than one-fourth of the arm span. The total height of a person is equal to the chord of an arc of 60° measured by the fathom. Thus, the human being can be considered as the radius.*

Recalling that the human arm span *measures* the earth's circumference, it appears that through essential proportions the human being summarizes the universal functions and measurements. Each individual has his particular rhythm that connects him very specifically to this or that numerical function and gives him his character. During this brief exposition, our concern has been with setting forth some of the fundamental proportional laws on which one is able to support a canon. These few laws are incontestably those that guided the choice of the basic numbers of the pharaonic canon.

---

[29] Cf. chapter 15, "The Crown of the Skull."

[30] Cf. Ghyka, *Esthétique des proportions*, p. 275. Two skeletons studied by Hambidge give the extreme coefficients of 1.0854 and 1.118 for the large spread.

APPLICATION OF THE STANDARD
PHARAONIC CANON

Definitions should only serve as a point of comparison. It is necessary to see the canon thus as a principle of proportions for constructing a figure. This allows one to take note of all the variations and symbolic deformations in the figure in order to understand the idea it was intended to express (the excessive height of the knees in the colossi of Ramesses at Luxor, for example, demonstrates the intent behind this play of inscription).[31]

There is the royal canon, but there is also the *neter* canon, that is, the canon modified following a natural principle or function proper to a *neter,* such as Thoth, Osiris, Anubis, Seth, Horus, Ptah, Mentu, and so on. The names of the nobles, who accented certain characteristics of the canon or *canevas* in their tombs, must also be noted.

For example, in the name Ukhotep, nomarch of Cusae,[32] *Ukh* is written with a double emblem knotted by a tie,[33] like the symbol of the city of Cusae whose name means "to tie," "to knot."[34] The spouse of Ukhotep was Thothotep, and their tomb strongly accents the tie, the knot, and develops a double numerical play throughout. Another example is Sen-nefer, whose name signifies "double perfection." This figure has two hearts on his breast, his tomb is double, and the scenes depicted therein express this dualism.[35]

The comparative study of the pharaonic canon with modern systems of biometrics allows us to make the following distinctions. The Ancients did not attempt to establish a "normotype" based on the most generalized human dimensions. The same scene in a tomb may show people whose proportions are exactly those of the average, normal person along with those of the master of the tomb drawn following certain anomalies characteristic of the royal canon: the shoulders may be larger and the knees higher than the biometric average. This distinction is intentional and is verified by the grids on which these figures are drawn.[36] There is the royal canon, which corresponds to Cosmic Man and summarizes essential functions, and there is the human canon. This latter corresponds to the average proportions of human beings, but emphasizes all the deformations relative to one or another trade or occupation and often to conditions surrounding the life.[37]

It does not appear that the ancients looked for a "common measure" governing their canon, which would have been quite contrary to their method. Let us recall that in acupuncture, the Chinese employ a different unit of measure for each part of the body, as for example, a certain phalanx of the finger for the limbs, the distance between the breasts for the trunk, and the distance between the eyes for the head. Comparatively, after a study of pharaonic figures, it is certain that neither the height of the head nor the length of the hand, for example, served as a "common measure" for the *whole* body. The pharaonic canon is much more supple and closer to life.

---

[31] Cf. plates 16–18, colossus no. 3.

[32] Cf. plates 52–56.

[33] Cf. vol. 2, fig. 249.

[34] Cf. vol. 2, fig. 251.

[35] Cf. I. Schwaller de Lubicz, *Her-Bak, Egyptian Initiate,* commentary 8, "The Teaching of Egyptian Tombs," pp. 373–87.

[36] Cf. plates 52–54.

[37] Cf. plates 55 and 56. Notice the adaptation of the appearances of the people to the activities in which they are involved, with papyrus gatherers in the marshes, net haulers, and cattle herders in front of and behind these. The last example shows that there is a symbolic meaning.

Among pharaonic figure sketches it is necessary to distinguish those that are completely "squared up" and those that only have a few reference lines. In those completely "squared up," a vertical line passes in front of the ear, in front of the back knee, and most often terminates at the line at the base of the one-third division of the back foot. Another important line, immediately in front of this one, passes through the area of the iris of the eye and terminates at the big toe of the back foot.

The line passing in front of the ear is on the static axis of a person both standing and walking. On this line are located the semicircular canals of the inner ear, which are the sense organs for direction and the perception of balance. When there is only one vertical line, it is this one that is drawn.

The axis of movement passes through the region of the eyes; the eyes are the luminaries, the eyes guide. One goes toward that which one sees, and in order to move forward one supports oneself with the big toe of the back foot.

One of the older figurations still preserving the reference lines is at Saqqara, in the tomb of Per-neb, a high dignitary of the Fifth Dynasty. The figures are not executed on a complete squared grid but only on one vertical line and six horizontal lines (fig. 135). A study of these figures shows that the canon of nineteen units to the top of the head is implied without being entirely drawn, which makes these few lines particularly interesting. The only vertical line indicated passes in front of the ear; it is the axis of stability for a standing figure. The six horizontal lines cut the body at precise points (fig. 135):

- The upper line passes through the demarcation of the hairline and corresponds to the eighteenth line of the *canevas* of nineteen squares.
- The line that passes through the base of the neck and the shoulders corresponds to the sixteenth line.
- A line that passes at the level of the crease of the armpit corresponds to fourteen and two-fifths squares.
- At the bottom of the rib cage a line coincides with the elbows and corresponds to the twelfth line of the *canevas* of nineteen squares.
- The gluteal crease is marked by the ninth line.
- The height of the knees, at the upper edge of the kneecap, corresponds to the sixth line.

The total height of the figures corresponds to 19/18 of their heights to the forehead, but *the nineteenth line is not drawn*. It is *the height* 18 that is here divided following the development of harmonic proportion having 1 to 2 (or 9 to 18) as a beginning point. The two upper lines, 16 and 18, establish the proportion 8 to 9, which defines the basic tone of the scale.

The other lines divide the height 18 into two and three. Here again the principles of musical harmony are adhered to through the canonical division by 1/2 (the octave), by 2/3 (the fifth), and by 8/9 (the tone), the height 18 being comparable to the vibrating string. The line at the level of $14\frac{2}{5}$ corresponds to the ratio 4/5 (the major third, two tones).[38] This line is determined by the harmonic decomposition in its geometric form, being the phase of development allowing the passage from the fifth to the tone, and producing perfect harmony (fig. 135). The fourth corresponds to the ratio 12/16, or 3/4.

[38] The ratio of 4/5 corresponds to an interval very slightly shorter than twice the first whole tone, 8/9. In effect, the two tones are equal in vibration to $9^2/8^2$, or 81/64, because the ratio of 5/4 (two tones) is almost the same as 80/64. This difference of 1/64 is correct, the octave actually includes two longer thirds and one shorter third. Cf. chapter 5, "Numbers and Ratios in Chinese Musical Pipes," appendix to the section "Pharaonic Volumes."

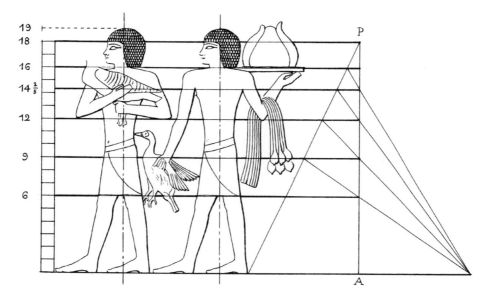

Fig. 135. Tomb of Per-neb (Saqqara, Fifth Dynasty)

On the essential lines of the canon that cross the figures, *left,* the intervals are drawn in a ratio of 18 to the forehead; *right,* a projection of the harmonic analysis corresponding to synthesis 1 (fig. 46).

This harmonic decomposition establishes the relationship between the human canon, musical harmony, and cosmic harmony,[39] and justifies the drawing of only these lines on the figures in the tomb of Per-neb, where one of the older known testimonies of the study of human proportions is found.

This tomb belonged to a nobleman. The crown of the skull, or the nineteenth part of the height of the figures, was not fixed by a line because it is variable. In effect, what distinguishes the human canon from the royal canon—the king being the perfected type—is precisely the value given to this part of the skull.

In the human canon (tombs of the nobility), the part exceeding the eighteenth line is variable, giving the figures a more or less flattened skull crown. In certain cases the height of the head is then diminished and can be contained up to eight times in the total height.

In the royal canon, whatever the age of the person and whatever his "particular coefficient," *the vertex will always coincide with the nineteenth line.* The coefficient determining the value of the crown of the skull is then indicated either by the line of the hair or by the diadem; it is this height that, divided according to the golden section, determines the location of the navel.[40] *The height of the head of an adult royal figure is always contained seven and one-half times in the height to the vertex.* This fact conforms to the proportions accepted by the anthropometric system.

Among the different "constants" encountered through anthropometric averages, it is necessary here to recall those that prove to be actually at the base of the pharaonic canon.

[39] Cf. the relationship of the essential lines of the canon to the nervous centers and circulatory system, upper part of fig. 136 and related text.

[40] Cf. biometric constants and personal coefficients in the preceding section, and the royal figures of rooms II and XX in the following.

- The constant relative to the division of the total height of a person into two equal parts by the pubic symphysis is strictly applied by the Ancients, and is verifiable in the bas-reliefs depicting nude figures.
- The ratio between the height of the upper body and the total height is

$$\frac{\text{height of the upper body}}{\text{total height}} = \frac{\text{volume of a sphere}}{\text{volume of cube}} = \frac{1}{1.90983...}.$$

This ratio is sufficient in itself to justify the choice of the number 19 as the value approaching this function: the total height of the standing figure is equal to 19; the height of the upper body of the seated person is 10. These numbers are the base, and a nuance in a drawing is sufficient to obtain the irrational function precisely.

- The full arm span corresponds to two times the height of the upper body and consequently equals 20, which approaches the real coefficient $20 \div 19.0983... = \pi/3$.
- These are some of the true "constants" that link the proportions of the human body harmoniously together, thus it is not surprising that the coefficient defining the height of the crown of the skull is precisely $\pi/3$; the location of the navel dividing the height, minus a small part of the head, is defined by ϕ, this apparently having indeed been one of the important directives of the canon. The measurements of numerous figures in the temple of Luxor confirm the meticulous use of the following formula:

$$\frac{\text{total height}}{\text{height of the navel}} = \phi \times 1.0472... .$$

The height of the navel multiplied by ϕ defines the lower edge of the diadem, and this fact emphasizes its importance.

Thus it appears that the older canon considers the total height of the king as the mean term of a geometric proportion that we can formulate as follows: *The height of a man without the skull crown is to the total height as the total height is to the complete arm span.* This principle of the "geometric mean term" directs the different body positions—kneeling, sitting, and standing[41]—and reveals the abiding concern of the Ancients to think in proportions, and not in fixed numbers.

Thus, the number 19 is found to be the whole number nearest to the irrational functions of human proportions. This number is generated by the developed harmonic proportion (synthesis 2, fig. 48) that begins with the ratio 1 : 3, or 1/4, which connects division by 7 to division by 19.

The comparison between a human skeleton[42] and a royal figure (fig. 136) shows that both obey the essential lines determined successively by this decomposition. In calling P the level of the top of the head and A the level of the bottom of the feet, the genesis is made in the following manner:

The first stage divides the height PA into 1/4 and 3/4, which defines the fourth on the vibrating string PA. This point is marked on the royal figure by the base of his necklace. On the skeleton it corresponds to the level of the seventh thoracic vertebra; its relation with the seventh rib, the last one attached directly to the sternum, is obvious. Functionally, the thoracic sympathetic ganglia 7, 8, and 9 start from the three roots of the large splanchnic nerve, the upper being the largest. This

---

[41] Cf. chapter 37.

[42] The skeleton is constructed according to anthropometric averages (cf. above, note 24); for the general proportions and for the details of each bone, see E. Olivier and A. Dufour, *Traité d'osteologie humaine* (Paris: Maloine, 1947).

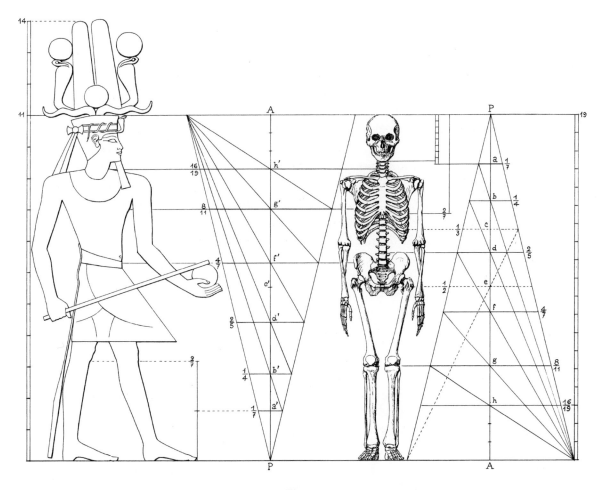

Fig. 136

Relationships between the harmonic analysis (synthesis 2), a human skeleton, and a royal
figure from the temple of Luxor (room XX, east wall, register 1, third tableau from north
to south).

very important nerve goes toward the semilunar ganglion of the solar plexus, which controls the
entire abdominal autonomic system. Also at the level of the seventh thoracic vertebra is a junction
of veins that is remarkable in that it receives all the parietal and visceral veins.[43]

The division of the total height by 4 also implies the division by 2 that defines the level of the
pubic symphysis. The harmonic division having 1 : 1 as its starting point in turn divides the height
PA into 1/3 and 2/3, the ratio of the fifth on the vibrating string. This point (at *c*) corresponds to the
base of the posterior part of the thorax, the junction of the twelfth thoracic vertebra with the first lumbar. The solar plexus is located at this level and its semilunar ganglion receives the large splanchnic
nerve. Thus, the two harmonic divisions complement each other, the more so in that the musical proportions are on the human body, indicated as much by the skeleton as by the vital centers.

[43] Cf. H. Merz, *Schéma d'anatomie topographique* (Paris: Doin, 1950), p. 45.

- The harmonic division with 1/4 for its ratio generates the ratio 1 to 7 (at *a*). The fraction 1/7 is in turn divided into eight. This gives the length of 2 cubits and 7 palms, or 56, to the length *PA*. The level of the chin is located between 1/7 and 1/8 of *PA*. The doubling of *Pa* is 2/7 from the top of the head and defines the level of the sternoxiphoid process, that is, the base of the rib cage corresponding to T9–T10 (Dr. Aubaret), the exit point of the small splanchnic nerve.

- The stage following this harmonic division divides *PA* into 2/5 and 3/5 (at *d*), the first ratio approaching the function $1/\phi$ in the F series. On the royal figure this level actually determines the upper edge of the navel. On the skeleton it corresponds to the upper level of the iliac bone, to the disk that separates the third lumbar vertebra from the fourth. It is actually here that the navel is located, oscillating slightly around this reference line. It is curious to note that the total height of a person is here divided into two segments that are to one another as 2 is to 3, while the five lumbar vertebrae are divided as 3 is to 2, that is, in the same relationship, only inverted.

  Recall again that according to the anthropometric averages the coefficient for defining the navel corresponds to

  $$\frac{\text{total height}}{\text{height of navel}} = \frac{5}{3} = \phi \times 1.03....$$

- The following stages divide the total height *PA* successively into 3/7 and 4/7, then into 3/11 and 8/11. The femorotibial line, the articulation of the knee, corresponds to this level.

- Finally, the last division leading to the canonical numbers is 3/19 and 16/19.

At this point, the pharaonic canon imposes an inversion of the harmonic division: *A* corresponds to the vertex and *P* to the soles of the feet. This inversion corresponds to an essential vital function. Are not the motor centers of the entire body inverted along the fissure of Rolando so that the motor center of the feet is found precisely at the vertex? Babinski's reflex, an indication of a rupture in the motor circuit, also confirms the relationship between the head and the feet. The divisions are then read from bottom to top (fig. 136, left).

- The doubling of 1/7, or 2/7, determines the femorotibial line of the royal figure, as the doubling of 3/19, or 6/19, determines the upper edge of the kneecap.

- The doubling of 1/4, 1/2, is designated by the crossing of the staff and the triangular loincloth.

- The ratio 2/5 coincides with the base of the *shendit* loincloth, which overlaps the preceding.

- The ratio 4/7 defines the lower line of the back of the belt and corresponds, on the skeleton, to the last lumbar vertebra at its junction with the sacrum, attached to the wings of the ilium—a very important vital zone.

- The line at 8/11 passes through the level of the breasts of the royal figure, which on the skeleton corresponds to the level of the fifth rib. (The human breast is located between the fourth and fifth rib, which is between lines 1/4 and 8/11.)

- Finally, the line at 16/19, one of the most important in the pharaonic canon, corresponds to the seventh cervical vertebra. This vital node is so important for the Ancients that it is here that the *neter* "gives life" to an individual when he offers the ankh from behind.

In fact it is from the lower cervical ganglion and the first thoracic ganglion, the stellate ganglion,[44] that the two roots of the lower cardiac plexus arise, which innervate the heart and establish a relation with the eyes. The sympathetic nerve contracts the heart and dilates the iris. (Its action is thus reversed from the heart to the eye.)[45] The entire area between the seventh cervical vertebra and the sternal fork is an essential arterial and venous intersection, defined on the figure by the height of his necklace, up to the level of the neck. This necklace, composed of several rows of pearls, often terminates at the back of the neck with two falcon heads that hold a crescent surmounted by a pearl (fig. 137). This arrangement strangely recalls the symbol of the upside-down crescent above an oval carved on the hieroglyph of the heart.

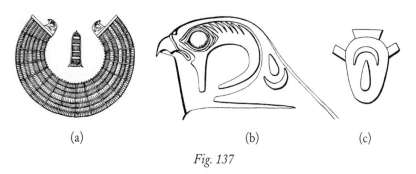

(a)   (b)   (c)

Fig. 137

(a) Necklace of Tutankhamun, from H. Carter, *The Tomb of Tut-ankh-Amen,* vol. 2 (London: Cassell, 1930), pl. 81. *(b)* Head of falcon, relief in granite, obelisk of Hatshepsut, Eighteenth Dynasty. *(c)* Sign of the heart, limestone relief, tomb of Hamose, Eighteenth Dynasty. The head of the falcon, symbol of the eye (eye of Horus), bears the symbol of the heart on its neck, the area of the stellate ganglion, which controls the oculocardiac reflex.

Between the sixteenth and nineteenth lines, the standard canon once more gives a particular importance to the eighteenth line, which marks the hairline, and corresponds to the superciliary arch on the skeleton.

The king represented here (fig. 136) wears a high crown composed of two plumes set above two ram's horns that support two uraei crowned by the solar disk. The height of the royal crown corresponds to a coefficient shown to be a constant by the measurements. Now, the harmonic decomposition justifies the the number used: the height of the crown is obtained by placing the 3/11 contained between the line 8/11 and the line 11/11 above the top of the head. The total height of the crowned king is thus equal to 14/11. This coefficient is extremely curious because it is framed

[44] The stellate [cervicothoracic] ganglion is extremely well developed in dogs, and the nape of the neck is an extremely sensitive center. A violent blow on this point can cause death. There is a connection here to the protective collar worn by Anubis and the pharaonic hunting dogs.

[45] "The sympathetic cervical nerves contain the dilating fibers of the iris. It is generally accepted that they come out of the medulla through the anterior roots of the eighth pair of cervical nerves and the first dorsal pair, and that they cross the ramification and go into the inferior cervical sympathetic ganglion.

François Franck estimates that these fibers come out of the medulla through the anterior roots of the last two cervical nerves and the first three thoracic nerves. They go back into the first thoracic ganglion, then on to the rings of Vieussens, back up to the sympathetic cervical nerve to arrive at the superior ganglion. They leave by the anastronomic ramification, which goes into the gasserian ganglion, crossing this ganglion and the ophthalmic branch of Willis, until it reaches the ophthalmic ganglion. It leaves there by the long ciliary nerves that go to the iris." Busquet, *Traité d'anatomie clinique,* 1:190.

by two functions derived from π and ϕ. We can demonstrate this in decimal form as follows: $\sqrt{\phi} = 1.272...$, $14 \div 11 = 1.2727...$, and $4 \div \pi = 1.2732...$.

Let us again recall that the plane of the ischium is defined in the pharaonic canon by the height of the upper body, which is equal to 10/19 of the total height, and that the total arm span is equal to about two times the height of the upper body, which gives the value 20. It follows then that the human cubit has a value of one-fourth of 20, or five squares, which is confirmed by the figures in which the cubit is drawn in five squares (fig. 140).

This developed harmonic decomposition undoubtedly determines the numbers of the royal canon, as is confirmed by the ratios 14/11 for the crowned king, then 10/19 and 16/19 for certain essential points. The fact of the enclosure of the kneecap between 2/7 and 6/19, and the doubling of these two fractional extremes, is also an important confirmation of this function.

The comparison of the different plans specified by the harmonic decomposition and its inversion with those of the human skeleton also shows that all these essential points are marked. If one wants to give a "volume" to this skeleton, one will find in the corresponding segments the units of measure one wants: both the width of the pelvis and the transverse diameter of the thorax oscillate around 1/6 of the total height.[46] This size corresponds to the segment *ce* between the lines 1/2 and 1/3. The depth of the pelvis, being approximately half its width, thus corresponds to 1/12.

The segment *g'h'* at the level of the shoulder corresponds to the length of an average hand[47] and to half of the biacromial diameter. The depth of the skull itself is very nearly equal to this. The width of the skull corresponds to 1/11 of the total height,[48] that is, half the distance between the vertex and the sternal fork, designated on the king by the top of the necklace.

The length of the cubitus (forearm) is equal to the segment *bd*, which is 3/20 of the total height and conforms to human measurements. Finally, the length of the humerus is very close to the bitrochanteric diameter (18.82 and 18.86, Doumic), and is nearly 3/16 of the total height.

In conclusion, *the two harmonic decompositions having 1 : 1 and 1 : 3 for their origins, and their inversions, furnish all the proportional sizes relative to the human being and serve as the foundation for the establishment of the pharaonic canon, at the same time they give evidence for the different numbers used by the Ancients.*

The temple of Luxor—the Temple of Man—strictly obeys these harmonic functions that make the link between the proportions of the temple, its deviations, and its orientations. The temple also follows the double rhythm of alternation and reversal required by harmonic proportion, which contains everything in essence, but always requires a reading and then another going in the opposite direction.

For example, the first ratio of 1/7, produced by 1/4, determines the dimensions of the different phases of the temple as it governs the principal subdivisions of the royal cubit of 28 digits. The temple successively measures, moving from *south to north*, 40, 70, 100, and 140 fathoms.[49] Conversely, the ratio 1 : 7 is the angle formed between the axes of the two repositories of Amun's sacred barque, and in returning from *north to south* there is a reversal.[50]

[46] To the preceding dimensions for the size of the pelvis, I add those of H. Merz, who gives 28 cm. The iliac diameter is 1/6 the height of an individual who is 1.68 m tall.

[47] The size of the hand varies greatly. In subjects of seventeen and one-half years, it is 10.5, as a minimum, and 11.5 (Denicker) to 12.2 as a maximum (Doumic). The size of *g'h'* corresponds to 11.48... for a height of 100.

[48] Cranial measurements taken in the Paris area give about 11.5 for the depth of the skull using a base of 100 for the height. The width corresponds to exactly 1/11 of the total height, the height at 13/100.

[49] Cf. plate 64.

[50] Cf. plate 86.

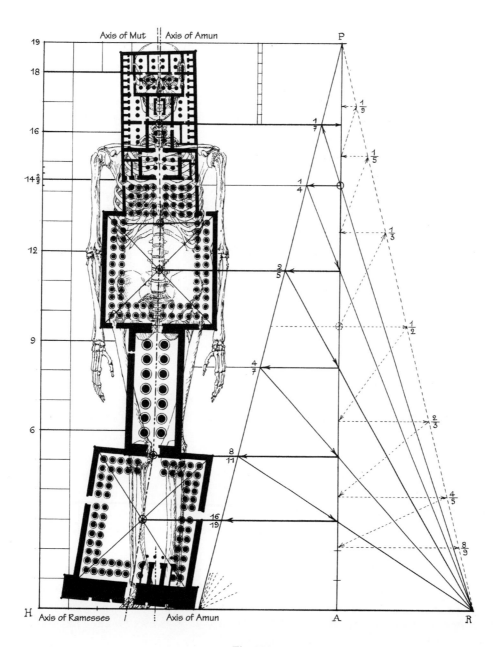

Fig. 138

The projection onto the temple and the skeleton of the three rhythms of Royal Man, *R*, and of the essential phases of human man, *H*. These harmonic moments specify the measurements of the architecture (skeleton and temple) as well as the location of the principal vital nodes of organic life and sources of energy. We point out here the seven occult centers: coccyx, solar plexus, cardiac plexus, stellate ganglion, fontanelle (vertex), and the "sanctuaries" of the nose and the thyroid.

The measures are given by the plan or the skeleton. The vital organic centers as well as the relationships and characteristic functions of organic life are depicted by images and texts on the walls and architraves.

But it is necessary to remember that the same harmonic law applies equally to the parts of the body, notably to the head. We have not mentioned the *inverse* of the harmonic proportion of the different rhythms in this summary exposition so as not to complicate the diagram.

On the plan of the temple, lines 2/5 and 16/19 correspond, respectively, to the point where the diagonals of the transept and the court of Ramesses cross (fig. 138).

The ratio 8/11 is both what defines the completion of the construction of Amenhotep III, which is at the pylon north of the nave, and the angular ratio that determines the orientation of this pylon with respect to north.[51] The reversal of the harmonic decomposition puts 8/11 in correspondence with the nourishing breast and makes certain "joints of correspondence" more evident than the numerical function would justify by itself.[52]

The twelfth line of the division by 19, mentioned in reference to the figures in the tomb of Perneb, coincides with the base of the rib cage. Now, the angular ratio 19/12 is precisely that which determines the orientation by its relation to the north part of the eastern wall of the hypostyle room, the *haty*.[53]

Finally, the deviation of the court of Ramesses with respect to the general axis of the temple (the axis of Amun) corresponds to 3/19, demonstrating that it was determined by harmonic proportion.

The skeleton was not made to correspond with the temple, the plan of the temple was established following the most exact measurements, and the study of human biometrics comes from doctors who are not at all concerned with the laws of proportion. *Now, the human body, its skeleton, the location of its vital centers, and all the essential points of the temple of Luxor correspond to the harmonic decomposition in such a way that man and the temple can be superimposed upon each other, which demonstrates the law of harmony as a universal law unifying all.*

Each part of the temple, each room, has its particular measure, and the figures portrayed on the walls are intimately related to the place where they are carved. For example, sanctuary I, located at the height of the royal headband, is measured in royal cubits,[54] and its proportions are, in plan, established on the relationship of 8 to 9, the tone. By contrast, room XII, with twelve columns upon which there are figures recounting the rising and setting of the sun—the cycle of the day—measures twelve fathoms. The relationship between the medulla oblongata and the soles of the feet (mentioned previously with reference to Babinski's reflex) was well known to the Ancients, as case 8 in the Edwin Smith Surgical Papyrus testifies. Thus, there is a metrical relation between room XII (the medulla) and the pylon of the court of Ramesses (the soles of the feet) in which the west wing measures 12 fathoms to its upper part, between the tori.

The temple teaches another very interesting relationship through an irregularity of construction confirmed by an idiosyncrasy of language: a very ancient anatomical term designates both "the two sides of the mandible" and the two posts of a door with its lintel.[55] The mandible opens and closes the mouth to receive food. Being double, like the two posts of a door, the mandible is a good example of a symbolism that evokes a function that connects a living process to something inert but functionally identical. Now, in the temple, the mandible corresponds to rooms II and VI, the mouth, while the entrance door to the temple is found between the two wings of the pylon, and the figures carved in room II are, through their dimensions, intimately related to those of the pylon itself, as the following example will more clearly show.

[51] Cf. chapters 13 and 28.

[52] Cf. plate 30, and related legend.

[53] Cf. plate 24, and chapter 33.

[54] Cf. chapter 15, "Diadem, I Assume Thee."

[55] Cf. chapter 14, "Some Anatomical Terms Used in the Papyrus."

PROJECTION OF THE *CANEVAS* ON TWO ROYAL FIGURES

THE KING OF THE ROOM OF ANIMATION

ASSOCIATING MEASURES AND THE FUNCTION φ THROUGH THE F SERIES

This king is located on the west wall of the "room of animation" (room II) of the temple of Luxor.[56] After receiving the two crowns from the hands of Seth and Horus, he is purified of life by Thoth and Horus and enters into the temple. The following scenes depict him accomplishing the "royal ascent" before entering the sanctuary where he will be "embraced by Amun."[57]

In this same partition, two stones that cross the entire thickness of the wall are characterized by the fact that the edge of one of their faces follows a very acute slope. These two stones are obviously blocks that belonged to an ancient pylon, and the angular measure of their batter is exactly what was adopted by Ramesses II for the building of his pylon. The relation between these two stones cut on a slant and the pylon of the temple is immediately obvious by this anomaly.[58] This relationship is confirmed by their locations: they are opposite each other and extend up to the line under the soles of the feet of the figures, thus defining a precise measure corresponding to the length of the base of the future pylon, reduced to one-tenth its size.

The projection of the pylon of Ramesses on this partition, when put in coincidence with the stones in question, places the king, purified of life, exactly in the doorway of the temple and between the two wings of the pylon. Religious ritual taught that only the priest-king, purifed and crowned, that is, the master of the two crowns, had the right to enter the sanctuary. The entire partition on which the pylon is projected precisely describes this part of the ritual.

—⁓—

The projection of a grid of nineteen squares to the top of the head of this royal figure and the equivalence of its dimensions in digits allows us to verify the measures and functions that it summarizes.

Height	in meters	in squares	in digits[59]
Top of head	1.377	19	72
Height of diadem	1.344	$18\frac{1}{2}$	70
Base of diadem	1.315		$68\frac{1}{2}$
Forehead	1.307	18	68
Shoulders	1.165	16	$60\frac{1}{2}$
Navel	0.8125	$11\frac{1}{5}$	$42\frac{1}{3}$

[56] For the location of the rooms, see vol. 2, figs. 198 and 226.

[57] According to standard Egyptology.

[58] Cf. plate 99.

[59] The digit used here is 1.92 cm, which corresponds to 1/96 fathom. The value of the square is obtained by dividing the height at the forehead, 1.307 m, by 18. The height at the vertex is very slightly less than these nineteen squares. The question here is the indication of a measure, the importance of which will be understood from the study of the five kings of the first sanctuary.

As in the majority of figures carved on the walls of the covered temple, the height to the forehead causes the measure of 68 digits and the height of eighteen squares to coincide.[60] The height of the diadem represents 70 digits and corresponds to eighteen and one-half squares. The vertex is then equal to 72 digits for nineteen squares.

The ratio of 72 to 70 confirms a ϕ function transcribable in whole numbers from the F series. This function plays an important role in the temple and is precisely indicated by the numbers of digits used (fig. 139).

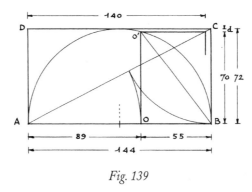

Fig. 139

The length *AB* is divided at *O* by the golden section. The difference between the perpendicular drawn at *OO'* and the length *AD* is equal to *d*. This difference carried over onto the diagonal *AC* proportionally shortens the length *DC*, as 72 : 70 = 144 : 140. The numbers inscribed on this figure are taken from the F series and represent $144 = \phi^2$, $89 = \phi$, $55 = 1$, and $70 = \sqrt{\phi}$. The coefficient is then $(1/2) \times \phi^2 \div \sqrt{\phi} = 1.0290....$

The definition of the part of the head that exceeds the upper limit of the headband relates to the general formula,

$$\frac{\text{height at the vertex}}{\text{upper edge of the headband}} = \frac{72}{70} = 1.0285... \text{ or } 1.029,$$

in its absolute form of ϕ. This coefficient is nearly identical with that of 1.03, which we encountered previously for $5/3 = \phi \times 1.03....$.

Theoretically, it is the height 18 to the forehead that is divided by the golden section to determine the location of the navel, as suggested by the ratio in digits of $68/42 = \phi$. The measurements taken on the actual site demonstrate that it is the height corresponding to the base of the headband that is strictly divided by ϕ, thus 1.315 meters $\div \phi = 0.8127$ meters, compared with 0.8125 meters measured at the site.

The height defining the lower line of the diadem determines, in turn, the height of the top of the head by the function $\pi/3$, thus 1.315 meters $\times 1.0472... = 1.377$ meters, which conforms to the measurement taken at the site. The coincidence is practically perfect using these irrational numbers. This is sufficient justification for the lack of absolute agreement between the whole numbers expressed in digits and in squares. *Here then is a typical case where the emphasis on measurement corrects the ratios in whole numbers from the general canevas to obtain the absolute function.* Furthermore, the measure indicated by the base of the royal headband is actually very important because it relates the king represented here (fig. 140) with the pylon, the projection of which is suggested by the two reused blocks.

---

[60] The measurments of the two kings given here make up part of a series of much more complete measurements taken on nearly one thousand figures in the bas-reliefs of the temple of Luxor.

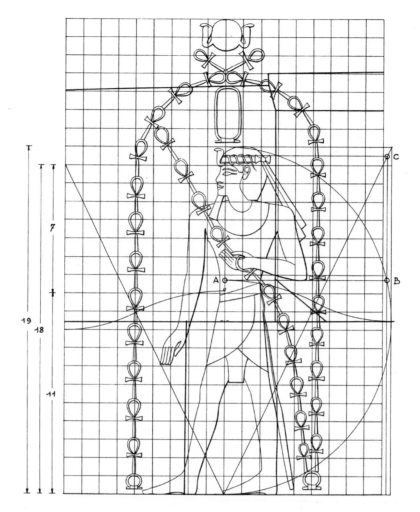

Fig. 140. The king depicted in room II, west wall, projected on a canevas of nineteen squares

Left, the division of the height 18 by the golden section comes to just above the eleventh square, and to the lower edge of the navel. *Right,* the projection of fig. 139 that defines the height of the diadem. The elbow rests on the line *AB* and not on the twelfth square.

Thus, 1.315 meters × 19 = 24.985 meters. Now, the height of the west wing of the pylon measured vertically from its base to the apex of its cornice at the northeast angle equals 25 meters (exactly 24.988 meters).[61] Similarly, 1.315 meters × 18 = 23.67 meters, a dimension comparable to the vertical height of the same pylon up to the upper limit of the torus terminating the cornice, 23.71 meters. This "coincidence" is not accidental; it confirms once again the analogy between architecture and Man. Thus, the total height of the pylon is considered to be 19 with the cornice and 18 without it, corresponding to one of the fundamental proportions of the human canon.

The total height of the king, as with numerous figures in the temple, also corresponds to one unit of a fundamental measure serving to measure the temple itself. This unit of measure is confirmed in sanctuary I with regard to the axes and orientations.[62]

---

[61] The measurement was taken with several triangulations, giving an accuracy of ±1 cm.

[62] Cf. chapters 13 and 40.

With regard to this figure in room II, we can again note the unique joining of the stones dividing its total height exactly in two. The division of the total height by the golden section determines line *AB* on which the left elbow rests. The right cubit, from the elbow to the end of the extended fingers, is inscribed in five squares, thus giving a theoretical arm span of 4 cubits or twenty squares. Finally, the number of ankhs that make up the vault around the king deserves our attention as well (fig. 141).

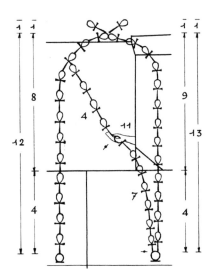

Fig. 141

Twenty-five ankhs make up the vault around the king, with eleven ankhs moving in a wave through the center. These are separated by the royal hand into 4 and 7. The whole figure consists of thirty-six ankhs, to which the two upper ankhs are added. This makes 38, or 2 times 19.

This king then, through his dimensions and his functions, links together the measurements of the temple, the pylon, and the royal man, crowned and "purified of life." Through the irrationality of the functions demonstrated by these measurements, he represents the superhuman Man.

THE KING WITH THE DIADEM FROM THE SANCTUARY OF THE BARQUE OF MUT (ROOM XX), ASSOCIATING THE MEASURES AND THE FUNCTION ϕ THROUGH THE R SERIES

Some measurements:

Height	in meters	in squares of 8.05 cm	in digits
Joint of stones	1.54		80
Top of head	1.53	19	
Height of headband	1.488	$18\frac{1}{2}$ approx.	
Base of headband	1.46		76
Forehead	1.45	18	
Joint of stones	0.905	$11\frac{1}{4}$	47

This king is carved on the west wall of the sanctuary of the barque of Mut (the mother), and it is his face that coincides exactly, through its proportions, with that of the pavement mosaic of the covered temple.[63]

[63] Cf. plate 36.

There are three horizontal joints: the upper joint, which at the back of the figure falls very slightly below the nineteenth line, forms an irregularity as it approaches the head, enabling it to pass one centimeter above the top of the king's head, showing that it is intended to indicate a height; the second joint cuts the figure at the level of the navel, the attachment to the mother; and the third joint cuts across the calf of the leg (fig. 142),[64] the place the queen touches to indicate the unit of measure when she is portrayed with the king in their colossal statues.[65]

As in the case of the king we just examined, the primary ratio of 18 : 11 for determining the navel is corrected here strictly following the function of the golden section: the joint of the stones at the navel is located a little above the eleventh square and corresponds to 47 digits, for a height of 76 digits to the lower edge of the headband. This is a use of the numbers from the R series giving the ratio of ϕ, and here again it is the height of the lower edge of the headband that is divided according to the golden number.[66]

The height up to the diadem multiplied by 1.0472... determines the height to the vertex to the nearest millimeter. The upper line of the royal headband is defined, for this figure, by the geometric function demonstrated by the ratio 72 : 70 expressed in digits by the majority of the figures of the temple.

The measurements of this figuration of a royal principle (fig. 142) from room XX are:

$$\frac{\text{total height to vertex}}{\text{height to the headband}} = \frac{1.53 \text{ centimeters}}{1.488 \text{ centimeters}} = 1.0282 \ldots = \frac{144}{140}.$$

This ratio confirms the two lengths of the temple that represent Man with and without the crown of the skull, that is, 140 and 144 fathoms.

The height of the face of this king represents the 190th part of the figure in the pavement, thus supplying confirmation of the measures and proportions of the mosaic of the covered temple.[67] This king wears a crown positioned above the top of his head. The total height measured there is 1.94 meters from the ground, which confirms the function that defines the height of the crown, which is 14/11 times the total height.

GENERAL SURVEY OF THE PHARAONIC CANON

The canon of proportions for the figuration of Royal Man, strictly obeying harmonic proportions—themselves issuing from the essential proportion of the function ϕ—is not an artificial construction. The numbers of these ratios are but the precise expression, framed by the biometric numbers of present man.

Living, modern man, in a state of genesis toward Cosmic Man, is, in his body, proportioned according to the law that governs the whole world. He serves as a provisional temple for the Being that animates the world, and as a model for the Temple erected by the sages.

The great organ of the Universe, if the artificial action of humanity does not temporarily interrupt it, can only produce the harmonious sound that creates the "music of the spheres" from the

---

[64] The joint of the upper stones, which adds a centimeter to the actual height of the figure, establishes the metrical correspondence between 47, 76, and 80 digits of a fathom valued at 1.92... cm each.

[65] Cf. vol. 2, fig. 206.

[66] We recall that the R series is the complement to the F series. Between them they establish the root of 5. It appears that when they are used, the R series is more feminine and the F series is more masculine.

[67] Cf. plates 35–37 and their legends.

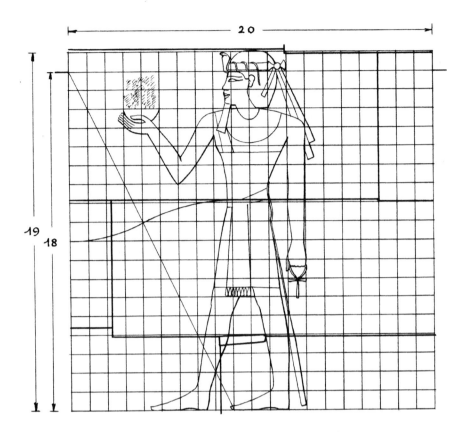

Fig. 142. The king with diadem from the sanctuary of the barque of Mut

worlds rolling in the Spirit, which we call the Void, but which is the "field of force" creating at every instant. It is the law of this music, source of all manifestation, that Pythagoras learned in pharaonic Egypt, as its applications prove to us today.

But if it were merely a question of bodily proportions and their applications in architectural work, this would remain only an aesthetic directive. Now, since Nature causes the human body to grow under the governance of the imperious harmonic proportion, this human being itself being the present final product of the general genesis, this same law presides equally over the formation of all beings that issue from it. Likewise it imposes itself on each organic part of the living organism, from the mineral to mankind. Indeed, the mineral being, which is essentially metallic, is the first entity to give bodily form to the original energy. "Nothing is nearer to God than that . . . ," says the philosopher. To our eyes, this kingdom is the first manifestation of harmony, but it requires knowing how to think in terms of "harmonies" and "discords" and not in atomic weights in order to find the organization there, because the entire scale of minerals is but a single body of multiple organs that we call metalloids and metals.

From these considerations springs the wonderful plan of the totality transcribed by the zodiac, and the natural elements and qualities grouped into families. But this is only a background on which it is necessary to project man in order to read it.

There is the Unity. The Unity divides itself, in the sense of the Heliopolitan Mystery, by the function ϕ, which we call the golden proportion because it has universal qualities. Phi is a function, not a number. Its geometric transcription is a symbolization and not a reality, since the geometric image is finite although formed from irrational values.

A number is the definition of a quantity, but a function is an activity. Thus the function ϕ always remains similar to itself, and if we want to transcribe it into numbers—always only approximate—these numbers will inevitably be a function of ϕ. This transcription of ϕ into numbers is a model but cannot be a numerated reality. The only correct understanding that we can have of this function is musical harmony, which is transcribed by what we call harmonic proportion.

The fractioning of the mystic Unity can be described as follows: an absolutely homogeneous and therefore uncompounded milieu divides itself into two parts, heterogeneous in relation to each other. This heterogeneity will be the first manifestation of Duality, as it would be for milk separated into butter and whey. It is the imperative *Fiat lux* that separates by an incomprehensible act, and this word is the musical scale, witness of the creative act, that is, of the manifestation of the occult Cause. The Kabbalah illustrates this by means of the "fall," in other words, the *dualization* of the angel summarizing Satan and Lucifer, who are Seth and Horus, the two brothers, enemies but inseparable, the true builders of the visible temple: the Universe animated by the breath of life, the divine breath that in the end will be the destroyer of the mortal. This "mortal" is the antinomy of the elements that have made the invisible Reality visible. Thus the principle of Duality, although it creates the Universe and its perpetuation, is also the gnawing principle of the corporeal aspiring toward immortality. This is the whole of the myth of Seth and Horus, and it is also the "bolt" of all science. Heterogeneity signifies not only opposition but also the separation of simultaneity into its complements, which, necessarily, create between themselves a proportionality that we call the function ϕ.

So there is Unity and Duality. Both are qualitative and not quantitative and together form the Ternary. This is not an enumeration but a qualification: the Unity, then the Unity divided by ϕ, will be 1 : ϕ. Numerated, this will be 1 : 2. This 2 represents a new *unity*, and since the relation, the *Fiat lux*, that exists between 1 and 2 is the musical scale, we say that 2 is the octave of 1.

Expressed in this numerated way, the Origin is the first relationship, 1 : 1, the causal, occult Unity; and the original Unity, at the same time qualitatively ternary, implies the second relationship, 1 : 2, as numbers. Functionally, the two parts are qualitatively unequal to each other, as $1/\phi$ and $1 - 1/\phi$, which creates our notion of *two*, the first *counted* number.

Schematically transcribed, this gives

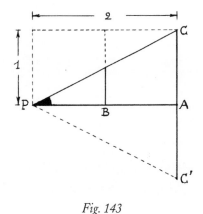

Fig. 143

In figure 143, CA can be any size, but AC' must be equal to it. Carried over to AP, the length CA will be equal to AB, or half of PA. The angles $\widehat{CPA}$ and $\widehat{APC'}$ are $1/2$, expressed in proportional notation. There are thus (1) a vertical 1 : 1; (2) a horizontal 1 : 1; (3) a first proportionality 1 : 2 ; and (4) the elements of the first surface 1 : 2, formed of two squares.

The first numbers of the scale between 1 and 2 result directly from this device, such as is shown in synthesis 1 (fig. 46), that is,

Proportion

$$\frac{PB}{PA}$$

that is, $PB : BA$

Synthesis 1

$$\frac{1}{17} \quad \frac{1}{9} \quad \frac{1}{5} \quad \frac{1}{3} \quad \frac{1}{2} \quad \frac{2}{3} \quad \frac{4}{5} \quad \frac{8}{9} \quad \frac{16}{17}$$

that is, 1 : 16   1 : 8   1 : 4   1 : 2   **1 : 1**   2 : 1   4 : 1   **8 : 1**   16 : 1

Synthesis 2

$$\frac{1}{49} \quad \frac{1}{25} \quad \frac{1}{13} \quad \frac{1}{7} \quad \frac{1}{4} \quad \frac{2}{5} \quad \frac{4}{7} \quad \frac{8}{11} \quad \frac{16}{19}$$

that is, 1 : 48   1 : 24   1 : 12   1 : 6   **1 : 3**   2 : 3   4 : 3   **8 : 3**   16 : 3

The first ratio 1 : 1 determines the original tone, the third, the fifth, and the octave. The octave is a renewal. With the number 8 the first unity, without body, has become the first volume; its proportion serves as a new beginning, 1 : 1.

The numerical development proceeds in one direction, from an origin to a phenomenon. The phenomenon, on the contrary, proceeds in the opposite direction because it is already an octave, that is, the first phenomenon that serves as a point of departure. This makes it difficult to understand the progress of this development; the metaphysical is superimposed in the opposite direction on the physical.

Theoretically (cerebrally), one is able to continue this series to infinity. The first proportion is an arithmetic progression at the rate of 2, and it develops according to a geometric progression of rate 2; but vitally the series is always complete the moment "One becomes Two and Two becomes Four and Four becomes Eight, that is, One," according to Thoth.

With the origin ratio of 1/8, that is, 1 : 7, all the possibilities are accomplished for the first time:

$$\frac{1}{57} \quad \frac{1}{29} \quad \frac{1}{15} \quad \frac{1}{8} \quad \frac{2}{9} \quad \frac{4}{11} \quad \frac{8}{15}$$

1 : 56   1 : 28   1 : 14   1 : 7   2 : 7   4 : 7   8 : 7

After the first volume, 8—also the first number of vibrations musically perceptible—considered as the first thing, come the numbers that apply to human proportion, the relationship between the size of the head and that of the body.

It is very easy with words to demolish an existing world in order to imagine, at will, a new one. But numbers never deceive us when one knows how to allow oneself to be led by them *naturally*, which our current mathematical knowledge no longer always does.

Pharaonic wisdom never confuses quality and quantity. The qualities are neither numbers nor measures; but numbers in relationship to each other are animated by qualities, that is, quality is the esotericism of number, Horus of the enumerator Seth.

The human body, from its conception to its birth and from its birth to its death, develops and degenerates in obedience to the law of harmony as does everything that exists, that is, becomes corporeal and disaggregates again. But each part of the human body, as each moment of the general genesis, has its particular mark, which, subject to the general law of harmonic development, creates a lineage proper to itself: the general lineages, the *neters*, the natural principles, each of which is a musical chord among all the possibilities immanent in harmonic numbers.

These are the powers emanating from the initial Verb of God, the archangels and the angels, the models, and by this fact, the protectors of each of the beings that momentarily have corporeal life.

And afterward, when all the *neters* will once again be intermingled in a synthesis, that is, in that actual harmony that the tone evokes into potential harmonics, this will be the realized Anthropocosmos, the Puruṣa, the Christ, Divine Man after his crucifixion on the cross that *measures* space.

This is the great lesson of the royal canon, modeled after the canon of human proportions, as much physical as spiritual.[68]

---

[68] This is sacred and must not be profaned by lifting out parts to make notes for the sake of curiosity. To speak of it, one must have studied and lived it. The author specifically forbade the reproduction of figs. 136 and 138 as well as the text concerning them without his special permission.

Chapter 12

THE ROYAL APRON

Today we possess only a few texts that discuss pharaonic mathematical knowledge. The Babylonians, on the other hand, wrote a great deal on the subject, and on clay tablets, a material most resistant to destructive influences (such as water and fire) and the passage of time.

The Ancient Egyptians wrote on papyrus, but they also did a good deal of sculpting, and this type of record could only survive with the monuments. We must look at what remains of those monuments for evidence of their knowledge.

We have shown the method of geometric notation of angles, and we are now going to pursue a demonstration of the trigonometric knowledge of these masters. Now, pharaonic riddles are remarkably intelligent and psychologically very astute. For the longest time the evidence, or what appears as such, has always been that which gets overlooked by the uninformed observer. This applies also to the trigonometric problems, set forth in a symbolism that is more important than the very mathematical meaning that had given rise to it. It is important to note, regarding trigonometric notation: *we are dealing with the curious apron worn by the royal symbol.* This is obvious to everyone, but we accept this peculiarity without seeing what it practically "throws" in the face of the observer.

We offer this new fact for investigators to contemplate. Having sketched seventy-two royal aprons (that is, nearly all those from the covered temple at Luxor) by tracing them directly, we then measured them with a protractor and by calculation, on both the tracing and on the sculpture itself, which allowed for a precision with the angles as exact as is practically possible to get. We present here some figures as appropriate examples. Now, the geometric functions of the rooms in which these aprons are depicted are related—as are the joints—to the geometric and vital function contained in these aprons and *guide the geometric construction of the panels and the surfaces of the walls.*

The angles and the aprons are constructed on the principle of proportional notation, that is, a base to a perpendicular, which produces the fraction $1/n$. The calculation of the angle of the slope of a pyramid confirms this notation.[1]

---

[1] See chapter 6, problem 56 of the Rhind Papyrus.

Perfect squares can only exist theoretically as the result of the multiplication of a number with itself. Their diagonals, however, will be irrational. Now, an angle is defined by the diagonal (hypotenuse) to a base and a perpendicular, but only the Diophantine triangles have diagonals that are whole numbers, and every angle $1\widehat{/}1$ will have an irrational diagonal, $\sqrt{2}$. This angle can only be defined by the ratio of the two sides of the right angle of a triangle, and the diagonal, as such, cannot define it. The diagonal will represent the "sighting" toward a point located on the perpendicular.

This is what the royal apron demonstrates by placing a sun or a lion's head on the angle. This is the point from which the rays or radii begin, making an angle with the base. The height of the perpendicular is always noted.

But certain aprons also present a second angle opposite to the first; in this case we are dealing with a notation of volumes (and no longer only of surfaces) indicated by the triangles; now, *these aprons are the pyramidal volumes.*

The Babylonian (or Sumerian) texts—as do the Egyptian—speak of the "diagonal" (a Greek concept) only as the "batter" or "slope," and designate this batter by a ratio $1 : n$ or $n : n'$.[2] It is this that forms the batter of a pylon, of a wall, of a post for a door, becoming, in architecture, the definition of a corner, that is, a mathematical hieroglyph. This leads us directly to the system of the *canevas*.

EXAMPLE OF A READING

C is the point from which the sighting is made. *AB* is the perpendicular. The sighting on *AB* defines the heights *a*, *a'*, *a"*, or *A* on the perpendicular. *CB* remains the large, invariable side. *Ba"*, *Ba'*, *Ba*, *BA*, are contained *n* number of times in *CB*. This number becomes the denominator of the fraction for which the height, read on the perpendicular, is the numerator.

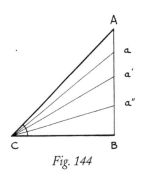

Fig. 144

PROBLEMS POSED BY THE ROYAL APRONS

In order to study these aprons, it is necessary to put together different elements that often seem incompatible to us at first.

1. We measure the angle in degrees. It is necessary to change the angle into a whole-number ratio.

2. When this angle determines a ratio of ϕ, it can most probably be transcribed by two numbers taken from the F series or the R series, giving a proportion of $n : n'$.

3. In order to demonstrate that this is an intentional play and not a coincidence, these angular ratios must have a meaning in relation to the location of the scene, that is, to the symbolic teaching of the particular place.

4. It is also necessary that the unit of measure of these aprons have a kinship with the wall and with the figure who wears it, that is, that it derives from the cubit used in this location. Having found this unit, one can establish a *canevas* in digits that should also be able to be inserted in the

---

[2] Cf. chapter 7, appendix, "Babylonian Mathematics."

large, general *canevas* of nineteen squares, or at least this unit will be a subdivision of each of these nineteen squares.[3]

5. Finally, it is necessary to note whether the base of the apron is horizontal or slanting with respect to the level of the tableau. If it is perfectly horizontal, it is inscribed so that it will not cause a problem in the general *canevas,* but if it is slanted, we must consider the angle formed by the apron itself, as well as the angle formed by its position in the general *canevas.* This obliquity can, for example, change a simple ratio, such as 3 : 4 into one that is functionally $1 : \sqrt{\phi}$.

READING THE APRONS

As an example of the reading of the royal aprons, we present here the ones depicted on the lintel above the east door that provides access to room XII, the room of twelve columns, the twelve hours of the day. At this entry, we see the royal ascent, the appearance of Ra, who is master of the day. This entire wall is consecrated to this principle. In all, six aprons are drawn here, all devoted to the "geometric keys."

The aprons on the lintel are given characteristic features in order to make tangible a symbolic significance, that is, a method of symbolic writing of a teaching in which the numbers merge with a vital aspect. The apron that has a phallic character through its location on the figure of the king is as "the seminal emission of the applied idea."

The apron that, in bas-relief, is depicted in plan is shown in volume in the statuary and has the aspect of a pyramid. (See in this regard the two "guardians" that were placed in front of the closing wall of the chamber of the sarcophagus of the king Tutankhamun. These pyramidal aprons are gilded.)

A detailed analysis of all the symbols connected with the figures on this one wall would require a whole volume. Our goal here is limited to indicating the way to follow for a reading of the aprons as numbers, and how their geometric functions relate to the indications given by the offerings and orientations.

At the third register of this east wall, the entrance of the sun is represented by the solar barque in which Ra-Horakhty is found. He is worshiped at his rising by twelve baboons (chapter 41, fig. 288).

The lintel above the east entrance of this room is a large stone measuring about 3.15 meters long, and on which are depicted: at the center, the king offering solid and liquid food to Amun; to the left, looking north, the king "venerating" the *neter* four times; to the right and going toward the south, the king offering the *shen* bread to Amun (fig. 145).

The royal figures are placed on this lintel so that the upper joint marks the places of the body corresponding to their vital significance. In figures B, looking north, and D, looking south, the joints separate the top of the body and the feet. The central figure C, however, is cut at the abdomen above the navel.

Recalling that north is the direction of inspiration, and south the direction of realization, the midpoint—the equator—is the synthesis. We will note that the fathom that is the basis for the measures of room XII and that determines the width of tableau C is the equatorial fathom (1.843... meters).

The aprons of the royal figures B and D, north and south, both have their rear angles giving the proportion ϕ, whereas the angle in front defines $\sqrt{\phi}$ in a rigorously precise way. The two aprons are opposed because the two kings are walking in opposite directions. Because he is venerating the

---

[3] Cf. chapter 11.

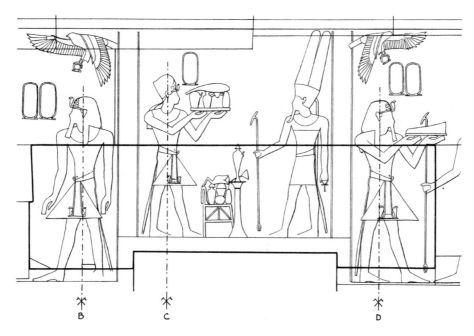

Fig. 145. Lintel of the east entrance of room XII (interior view)

neter, the northern one indicates the number principle. The king to the south, who offers the *shen* bread, the symbol of a ligature, indicates the geometric series of this number. The two together give the geometric laws and functions *that will develop those of the center;* this apron of the center of the lintel gives the form, as its joint cutting the abdomen specifies. For this latter, in fact, the front angle corresponds to the ratio 11 : 8, that is, 54°, determining the pentagon. The rear angle correponds to the ratio 11 : 7, which is $\pi/2$, determining the cycle, the curve.

These two ratios are the application of the possible plays that allow ϕ: the pentagon and the decagon, being the division of the circle into five and ten by the function ϕ, on the one hand, and the circle, being determined by $1.2 \times \phi^2$, or $1.2(\phi + 1)$ on the other (fig. 146).

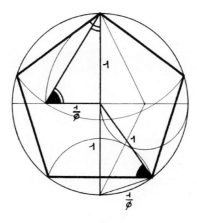

Fig. 146

The diagonal of the triangle with the radius 1 for height and $1/\phi$ for base determines the side of the regular pentagon. The side of the decagon has the value $1/\phi$ for the radius equal to 1.

In order to be able to transcribe into degrees, we will take the half-base of the apron as equal to 1 and its altitude as the tangent resulting from the geometric play adopted (fig. 147a). But if we reverse the matter and take the height as the fixed size, the notions are reversed; this height will be equal to 1, and the base will be divided into two unequal parts (fig. 147b) that will be equal to the unit divided by the coefficient of the tangent, that is, by its inverse. Thus, the apron whose height equals ϕ and whose base equals 1 will have 1 for its height and $1/\phi$ for its base.

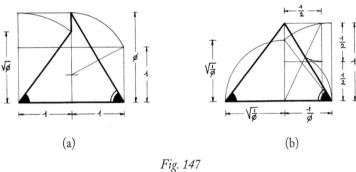

(a)   (b)

Fig. 147

(a) The half-base is 1; *right,* the construction of ϕ determines the proportion 1 to ϕ; *left,* the rabattement of ϕ, which becomes the diagonal and defines the height $\sqrt{\phi}$ for the base 1 of the triangle. *(b)* The total height is 1; the division of 1 by ϕ determines the width $1/\phi$ of the triangle on the right. The rabattement of 1 on the axis of the apron determines the value $\sqrt{1/\phi}$, which becomes the base of the triangle on the left.

This new interpretation allows us to ascertain that the diagonals thus cross at the height of the upper edge of the king's belt. And this way of seeing appears to be that of the Egyptians, as aprons drawn in the tomb of Ukhotep at Meir demonstrate.

Moreover, our transcription using the first system (the base divided into two equal parts) allows for a demonstration by means of the compass that corresponds exactly to our present way of seeing and facilitates our understanding, but it does not conform to the pharaonic mentality, for it always sees an aspect and its inverse, which implies both constructions.

Finally, the height of the figures is divisible, on the one hand, into eighteen squares to the forehead, and on the other, into a certain number of digits of the cubit used to measure them. It is a question of seeing how the following can be fashioned out of the geometric play of the apron:

- The division of the king into eighteen squares to the forehead and nineteen to the top of the head.
- The division of this same height into *n* digits measuring the apron and the figure.
- The possibility of finding a placement in the *canevas* for the apron, based either on the *canevas* of nineteen squares, on the digit that serves as the subdivision of these squares, or on allowing the proportions of ϕ to be established on the figure.

Now, in room XII, which is 12 fathoms long, we find the fathom that serves throughout as the unitary measure. The digits and cubits that derive from the fathom that will be used to measure the figures are on the east wall. Thus, in registers 2 and 3, the figures measure 68 digits from the soles of the feet to the forehead, each digit being 1/96 fathom. The number 68 is the double of 34. In the F series, if the unity is 13, the value of ϕ is 21, and ϕ^2 equals 34. This then gives the figure the value of ϕ^2 to the forehead. But there also exists the digit that serves as the *remen*[4] and that is 1/100 fathom. This digit is also used.

In one case we find the height to the forehead expressed by 18 × 4, or 72 units, which corresponds very conveniently on the one hand to one-fourth of the unit squares (18 × 4), and on the other to half the number 144, also taken from the F series, which allows for the transcriptions of ϕ into whole numbers.

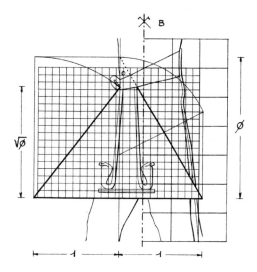

Fig. 148. Room XII, east wall, second register, north part, king B

The measurement for the width of the base of the apron is defined in relation to the general dimension of room XII, which is 24 digits, each with a value of 1/100 fathom. The height to the forehead of this figure is equal to 68 digits, each being 1/96 of this same fathom.

The angular function of the apron is rigorously correct. The division of its base into two equal parts allows the construction of the height ϕ in order to define the rear angle, and in the rabattement of ϕ it becomes the diagonal determining the height of $\sqrt{\phi}$, which forms the front angle of the apron.

This king, depicted at the north, gives the *principle*, that is, the functions and essential measures in their absolute aspect, which makes a strict coincidence with a practical subdivision of its general *canevas* difficult.

The royal apron (fig. 148) is nevertheless represented on the *canevas* established by taking the axis of equilibrium passing in front of the ear as the point of departure, and for the unit, the total height divided by 19. Each square is then subdivided into fourths, which gives a "grid" that serves as a guide for reading the angular ratios in whole numbers. It can be observed that the central axis of the apron passes through the middle of one of these subdivisions, which will cause us to divide each square into eight, not four parts.

The point where the two diagonals cross determines a height that corresponds then to thirty-four units for, at the rear, a base of twenty-one, a ratio in which we recognize two consecutive numbers from the F series that can be used to establish the ϕ angle; but the ratio determining the front angle would in this case be much less exact than that of the original, which is perfect (1 to $\sqrt{\phi}$).

Moreover, the subdivision of each square of the general *canevas* into fourths (or eighths) yields a unit slightly shorter than that which divides the length of the base of the apron into twenty-four (or

[4] Cf. chapter 10.

forty-eight). It necessitates a half-millimeter alteration for each square, hardly noticeable on some squares, but perfectly verifiable by calculating the different measures, and by studying the size of the apron.[5]

There would be, therefore, every reason to believe that in order to execute the apron, the carver would have used a compass—beginning with a formal measure—just as we would, and, without any concern for the general *canevas*, would have attained at the exact proportions that show the functions ϕ and $\sqrt{\phi}$ in all their purity while respecting the measures in all their integrity.

King D looks south, the direction of realization (fig. 149). He allows for the establishment of a *canevas* that precisely relates his dimensions to those of his apron, the angles of which are perfectly correct and can be read in whole numbers. The rear angle is ϕ and the front angle is $\sqrt{\phi}$. The *canevas* is established horizontally by dividing the height to the forehead by 18. The nineteenth line is at the vertex, under the serpent, the sixteenth at the shoulders, and the base of the apron comes to exactly six and one-half squares.

As for the width, using the axis of stability in front of the king's ear as the starting point, three squares to the left coincides with the line that marks the border of the tableau, and five squares to the right corresponds with the *was* scepter held by Amun.

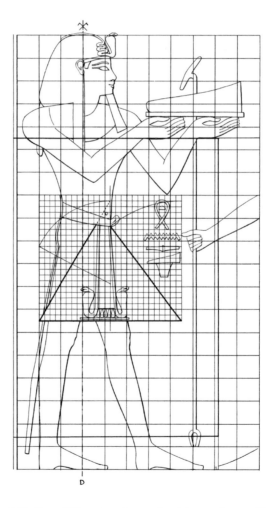

Fig. 149. Room XII, east wall, second register, south part, king D

[5] The thickness of the carver's mark itself comes to 1 mm. This, then, is the calculation that verifies that 24 digits of a fathom do not correspond to six squares of the general *canevas*.

The vertical axis starting from the half-base of the apron is within one-fourth of a square (of the *canevas* of 19) in front of the line passing through the eye. This axis coincides exactly with the front edge of the belt and implies the division of each of the large squares into fourths. This subdivision (in which each unit corresponds to one-thirtieth of a black cubit) gives twenty-six units as the base of the apron. Half of this is then 13; the geometric construction of ϕ, using 13 as unity, comes to the twenty-first small square and determines the rear angle. The rabattement of the value ϕ (or 21) onto the median axis falls very slightly above $16\frac{1}{2}$, which gives a very positive character to this group, and corresponds very well to the southern position of materialization for this figuration.

The diagonals cross at the upper edge of the belt at a height of 18 digits, with each of these digits having the value of 1/100 fathom, measured from the base of the apron, whereas the width of the apron of the king of the north measures 24 of these same digits.

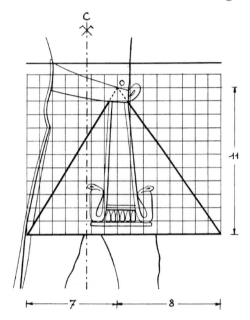

Fig. 150. Room XII, east wall, lintel over the door, king C

King C, located on the lintel of the east door of room XII, provides *synthesis* and *form* (fig. 150). The base of the royal apron is subdivided into fifteen units, and the diagonals cross at the height of eleven of these same units, dividing the base into two unequal segments of seven and eight units. The ratios that result are thus 11 : 8 for the front, which defines the angle of 54° of the regular pentagon,[6] and 11 : 7 for the rear, which represents $\pi/2$, for the standard π of 22/7.

Each small square represents $1\frac{1}{4}$ digits (valued at 1/100 fathom). If we place this grid on the general *canevas* of the figure, we would establish the following correspondence: each nineteenth of the total height is equal to two and two-thirds of these small squares, so three squares of the general *canevas* equal eight subdivisions of the apron.

We have just described the trigonometric method of reading the essential functions given by these aprons. This is still only a geometric play in which a deeper, vital meaning lies hidden. Later on we shall see, for example, a way of determining the geometric π corresponding to our presently known coefficient. We can say in passing that this secret is found implied in the apron of the central figure (the synthesis).

[6] The ratio 11 : 8 is used in the *canevas* of a naos drawn on a papyrus. Cf. plate 65 and figure 266 (vol. 2).

With regard to the aprons that have undergone the transformations and in which the angles are modified according to their inclination, they form part of a *symbolique* that should be discussed in relation to the entire wall.[7]

CONCLUSION

First, we note how the functional aspect of the human body serves as a basis for expressing a geometric key. We discover this same concern in the figures of the tomb of Ukhotep at Meir when speaking of the *angle* itself. All is in man, if we are willing to relinquish the mental concepts that satisfy the rational mind but remove us from Nature.

Now, the seed is a coagulant of spiritual (conceptual) nourishment carried by a passive feminine milieu. The principle of relationship, foundation of all mathematics (being $1/\phi$ or $\sqrt{2}$ and the numbers engendered by ϕ), is the seed that calls forth all the mathematical functions, engenders them, and this function ϕ *allows the transcription of numbers into geometry.*

The royal apron is a magnificent illustration that helps us to understand what our word *symbol,* so imperfect, wishes to express. This is not in any way related to the fantasies of certain symbolists in the West.

At this point I must leave the discovery of another important meaning of the royal apron to the sagacity of other investigators.

Second, the geometry of the royal apron (which is strangely reminiscent of the Freemason's apron) represents a living, moving geometry. Its shifting on the coordinates (the *canevas*) modifies, by illustrating them, the values of the numbers by connecting these different values to each other. The typical form is the transformation of the ratio 3 : 4 (hypotenuse 5) into 1 : $\sqrt{\phi}$ (hypotenuse ϕ).

---

[7] Cf. plates 68–74, and their legends.

Chapter 13

THE AXES

THE PRINCIPLE OF THE AXES

An axis is said to be imaginary because it represents, for a body revolving upon itself, an ideal line whose existence is not objectifiable but is nevertheless imposed by reason. A geometric axis is also an ideal line without breadth, an abstract moment that, necessarily, separates two parts, yet to which the mathematician must make reference.

We can better understand the importance of the notion of the axis with the example of a body revolving on itself. Let us "suppose" a point as close as possible to the pole of a planet, the pole that represents a place around which this body rotates. The tangential velocities change in accordance with the radial distances, but close to the pole this velocity is extremely slow, so that on the earth, for example, a person positioned on this pole would take a day of twenty-four hours to turn around once, whereas at the equator a point moves at more than 450 meters per second.

Theoretically, at the ideal point on the pole of the axis two tangential forces act in opposite directions on matter, causing its disaggregation. If this axis were to exist as a fixed point, it would necessarily be hollow, the empty center around which the wheel turns (Lao-tzu).

Now, for reasons of "material genesis," each body in the Universe, when it is not simply a fraction of matter projected by a "generating" body, turns around itself. The movement of physical rotation is the reaction of energy against its corporification by genesis (elsewhere I have described it as a revolt). This genesis is, in reality, a succession of states of a single substance, a series that we will call simple chemical bodies, minerals, plants, and animals, which represent vitally what the mechanical movement is physically, but in the opposite direction. Vitally, the axis is then the fixed point, the unalterable nucleus, the indestructible center, the Absolute, the present moment, ungraspable by the cerebral intelligence. Mechanically and graphically, the axis is nothing less than this inaccessible—that is, materially impossible—present moment. And the Nature that cannot endure this state, which nevertheless exists and represents its support, resolves this problem exactly as the pharaonic mathematicians resolved it: the axial pole moves unceasingly, constituting the "precessions," and any axis truly and *practically* an axis is so only on condition that it is in a state between the rational and irrational, between a plus and a minus, between an aspect and its complement, between a number and its inverse.

It cannot, however, be a question of a "plus" that is equal to a "minus." What essentially acts here is the division by the function ϕ, the golden section, creating the medieties, the arithmetic, geometric, and harmonic proportions.

In order to remain vitally in conformity with natural law, *the axes of the temple are always moving,* oscillating around the essential numbers of their origin so as to maintain a harmonic spatial growth. This can be understood by considering growth in general, whether plant or animal, when the linear growth, for example, of a bone, at the same time brings about a growth in volume and in all the elements involved, maintaining the harmony of the form in both part and whole by always remaining similar to itself.

Respiration, as alternation and oscillation, is the Verb of existence, the continuity or persistence of Being.

Wanting to oppose this natural reality with an imaginary fixity, wanting to find an invariable reference outside of the Unique, is to drown oneself in the turbid waters of a scholarly, purely mental science that blocks our understanding of life. When our concern is to see "the Temple in the image of Heaven," the temptation to erect a monument on these rigid precepts is like wanting to try to make a celestial globe turn round a fixed axis, which would be its annihilation.

In the temple of Luxor we can grasp the oscillation, the vital alternation, expressed in the architecture and verified by the numbers (measures and geometry), which represents an amazing accomplishment for the master builder, and fills us with admiration.[1]

—∿—

The vital axis of the temple of Luxor, the occult axis, is the axis of Amun. Its origin is drawn on the floor in room VI, the room of the Amunian barque, and from there it goes straight toward the Amunian altar of repose at the foot of the west wing of the pylon (figs. 151 and 152).[2]

THE AXES OF THE TEMPLE OF LUXOR

When drafting plans for an ordinary building, an architect draws a reference axis. For the architecture of the temple, whether it be, among others, pharaonic, Hellenic, or Hindu, or a Christian cathedral, the axis is the spinal column, filled with living marrow and carrying sheaths of nerves.

With man, who is a complete world, the head is placed toward the zenith, his north, the heaven of his inspiration, and the feet are to the south, the earth. The temple, as knowledge-bearing architecture, is oriented in relation to the celestial body, the earth. Its head is situated toward the North Pole, the place of inspiration, and its feet are to the south, the place of bodily realization. If its orientation is different from this, it is necessary to look there for a specific teaching or principle to explain this difference.

The Christian temple has the choir to the east,[3] side of the rising sun, the appearance of

---

[1] Cf. vol. 2, figs. 280 and 281.

[2] Cf. plates 85 and 86 and their legends.

[3] Exceptions must be made for certain early Christian churches founded on the principle of the saying, "Thou art the rock on which I build my church. . . ." Thus, the basilica of Saint Peter in Rome has retained the following orientation: the choir is to the west because Saint Peter is the principle of materialization (terrestrialization) of the Verb (not its humanization, which is Christ). From this fact comes his symbolic death on the inverted cross with his head toward the earth. This beginning takes place at sunrise, thus the entrance

puberty; the entrance of the faithful is to the west, side of the setting sun. Thus its teaching relates to what pharaonic Egypt calls the Dwat, the world of transformations, the side opposite to the day. The Christian birth takes place at midnight and corresponds to the sun, which then begins its reascension in order to be born into puberty with the day (twelve years). The sacrifice, the Passion, begins at night; the ascent toward the Cross begins with the birth of the day.

The Man of the temple of Luxor has his feet (the entrance) to the north and his head (the choir) to the south; this is the history of *incarnate* man. His *realization,* the formation, is made in the womb and begins with the centers of the head. His face looks east, toward the solar birth; created man enters terrestrial life, but born head downward, toward the south.

The sun passes from the southeast to the northeast in the course of half a year, and the east-west axis of the different parts of the temple (the ages of a human life) vary and indicate the times of the seasons.

The temple constructed on the human synthesis, which summarizes all the vital functions, fulfills three fundamental directives: the *trunk,* comprising the entire physical assimilative organism; the *head,* comprising the whole energetic assimilative organism; and the *sexual organism* of reproduction (procreation, that is, regeneration in the image of creation, but beginning from a typal specificity).

The limbs are the organs of exoteric action. If we draw a parallel between the three (or four) general centers of the body and the Elements, we get Earth for the trunk, passive and reactive; Water for the sexual organism, the milieu of all gestation; Air for the limbs, the milieu of action and movement that links Fire and Earth; and Fire for the head, the place of energy and influence.

Trunk-Earth, head-Fire, sex-Water—are indeed three axes that the creature necessarily obeys, and we must place these three axes, marked on the floor in the temple of Luxor, in relation to the three vital elements that together make up the living human creature (fig. 151).

The Gothic cathedral is conceived on the same principles.[4] One can, in principle, relate the axis of measures to the trunk, the geometric axis to the head, and the axis of Amun to gestation. But the profound meaning of these axes is subtler than such a "system," which is too rigid for the thought of the sages.

Life is *moving,* not in the sense of a mechanical motion, but in the sense of an alternation of becoming, a kind of *seasonal* alternation, an alternation of being and nonbeing. Thus, the work of the Temple is conceived *virtually,* beginning from Unity and proceeding to multiplicity, then *actually,* from the final form toward the final consequence of this form, a return to the Unique.

It is not at all simply a question of a conception of the complete plan of the temple and then of a successive construction of the building, beginning at the "apse" and proceeding to the pylons, but of a virtual realization, *as early as the covered temple,* of what the pylons would be. This is very important to note. We shall see that it is not a question of a supposition, because the proof is given by the figures drawn on the walls (plates 99–101).

This method of thinking through the "inverse," which we have rediscovered in Egyptian calculation, is important to point out because it governs the whole of pharaonic thinking. But calculating with the inverse is only the symbol of a vital function. For instance, it would be impossible to

---

is to the east. The principle of Peter is dominant in Rome and in the Lateran Basilica of Saint John for a similar, but not identical, reason. This church is *Ecclesia ecclesarium urbi et orbi.* Santa Maria Maggiore has its entrance oriented northeast (the summer period). Further, Roman and Byzantine churches are generally constructed on the geometric principle (as is the Hindu temple) of a combination of squares and circles (cycles). We must always study the orientation of the temples from "an epoch of knowledge" according to cosmic principles.

[4] In the first account, *The Temple in Man,* I noted the prototypical character of the temple of Luxor for later Gothic cathedrals. Cf. chapter 27.

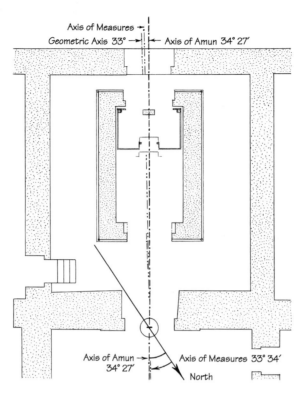

Fig. 151. Temple of Luxor, room VI, sanctuary of Amun's barque

Diagram of the axis of Amun and the axis of measures carved on the pavestones. In front of the threshold of the naos, a third line corresponds to the geometric axis. See chapter 40, plates 83 and 85 and their legends.

conceive of the becoming of the human body in one of its parts if the whole bodily organism were not virtually "conceived" or implied in the raison d'être of this part. Rationally, we add the parts in order to make the whole; vitally, the whole presides over the becoming of the part, as the general idea of a work to be realized presides over the study and the execution of what is to be made on this plan. This, however, is still only a gross image of what takes place in the realization of the temple, where "the general idea of the work to be accomplished" is absolutely moving in its realization as well as in the parts to be assembled.

Not for an instant can any part of a living body remain fixed (as required by our cerebral reasoning) without provoking sickness or death. This is also why the axes, which nevertheless appear to us as rigid, ideal lines, were conceived as the paths of celestial influences: they are but channels for influences that play their animating role in this living architecture, however firmly anchored to the ground they may be.

Let the faithful then come into this building; they will be subject to the effect of this occult influence, as vegetation is subject to the influences of telluric magnetism.

Is not Amun—who is the *amenti*, the setting sun, the *amen*, of all accomplishment, and the mysterious Fire (of Aries) of all vital impulses, the cause of vital movement? He will be both Amun-Jupiter, lunar, the sun of "mysterious spaces," then Amun-Ra, and then again Min-Amun, the ithyphallic Min. Does he not come, as Amun the Father, but typically lunar, to generate in Mut the dauphin Khonsu, this black Cadmus, who in the Thebes of Greece is symbolized by the swastika?

The axis of Amun starts in room VI, going from the altar of Amun's barque through the entire temple so as to make manifest, at the pylon, what is marked on the subfloor (occultly) at its beginning: the generating Fire of the generative power of Min (fig. 152). It passes through the entire body, animating each part with life, but in each part it will move toward the west in the direction of the celestial influences.[5]

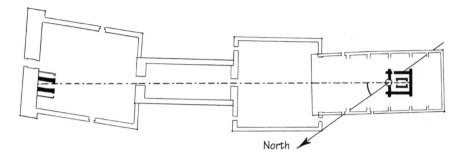

North

Fig. 152. The axis of Amun

The location in the temple of the room of Amun's barque (room VI), on the pavestones of which the three axes are drawn. The axis of Amun extends up to the altar of repose of Amun's barque in the south face of the pylon. This axis divides the foundation walls of these two sanctuaries exactly in two. See plates 86 and 87, the axis of Amun and its reflection, and plates 81 and 88, plans of the whole temple.

As we have said, the figured geometry is symbolic of a function, and through the numbers it will reveal to us the characteristic functions that would be impossible for us to explain in any other way without letting some doubts remain.

Geometry is gestation, it marks movement, growth, and alternation, as maternal femininity is gestating: Mut. It is the *geometric* axis (fig. 153) of gestation and of vegetation, the axis of Mut, that in the nave (the thigh, *men.t,* as well as at the base of the femur) will be Mut containing and carrying Hor, the Hathor (house of Hor) from which the prince, Khonsu, the dauphin, will be born. This dauphin, as Mer-n-ptah (Menephtah), is the base, the unity of measures, the "thing," the future king, *born,* the manifestation of Ra. Khonsu is the mystic axis of measures.[6]

Thus the three architectural axes of the temple of Luxor are, for the mystic Temple, the vital function represented by Amun-Mut under Amenhotep, and their fruit, Khonsu, under Ra-messes (Ramesses II).

The history of the monument seen as time-genesis is intermingled with the theological esotericism described by myth and given expression through the geometry (the cosmic measures) of numbers.

The geometric axis (Mut) starts from *A* (fig. 153) at the south wall of the covered temple, which it divides into two equal parts. It ends at *B* in the center of the northern limit of the platform of this part of the temple. Here it undergoes a deviation of 3° and crosses the peristyle court,

---

[5] The axis of Amun governs all the walls and east-west colonnades of the covered temple, and the peristyle court. Cf. vol. 2, fig. 280.

[6] The name changes mark the different states of the genesis. Thus we have the essential phases noted by Tum-Atum-Ptah-Min-Khonsu, whose original Sethian character comes from the eye of Ra, the sun, and evokes Aset (Isis), who becomes Mut-Sekhmet-Hathor through the lunar functions (Thoth). These are here mystic genealogies, not of successions, but of successive states of the same principle.

then it governs the constructions of the nave in order to reach the pylon that terminates the lunar work of Amenhotep III, at *C*. This axis forms, then, an angle of 36° with respect to north. Starting from point *C*, the axis of Mut again deviates by 7°27′ and becomes the longitudinal axis of the court of Ramesses, forming an angle of 43°27′ to north-south. At the threshold of the entry to the Ramesside pylon, at *D*, this geometric axis undergoes a final deviation, the extension of which coincides with the axis of the avenue of the sphinxes that proceeds toward the temple of Karnak. This last orientation of the axis of Mut is 45° from the north-south axis, that is, in the ratio of 1 : 1, defining the square and its diagonal with regard to the cross of the directions.

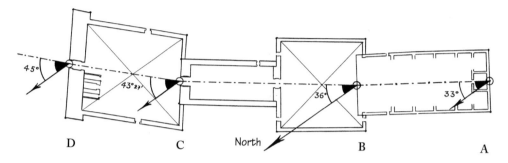

Fig. 153. Diagram of the (geometric) axis of Mut and its deviations

The moment of reference for the axes of the temple is in fact the invariable orientation of north to south, as the foundation ritual affirms by the sighting of the circumpolar stars in establishing the plan of the temple.[7]

It is in the nave, the thigh, that we find the statue of white limestone that portrays Amun and Mut seated,[8] near the door that marks the final stage of the work of Amenhotep III. It is thus in the femur—the determinative used to signify the inheritor[9]—that one finds, defined by the orientation of the general axis of the doors and walls, the angle that produces the pentagonal quintessence (36°), which is never drawn, but which is the soul of all vital movement.

We are here at the end of the work of Amenhotep III, the gestating work of Jupiter-Amun, which will bear fruit with Ramesses, Amun-Ra.

THE AXIS OF AMUN AND THE NAOS OF AMUN'S BARQUE

We call this axis the occult axis of the temple because, properly speaking, it does not have an architectural significance. It summarizes the governing, vital principles of the temple. It is directly connected with the principle of the pentagon, which, though it governs the entire hieratic geometry, is not formulated anywhere. The explication of its directive is given by the proportions of the naos in room VI, proportions we discover applied as well in the geometric particulars of a naos drawn on papyrus.[10] The base of this naos is formed by a rectangle in the ratio of 8 : 11 (or 16 : 22), in which the side 11 is the radius of the inscribed circle in a pentagon whose side is 16 (fig. 154).

[7] Cf. chapter 33.

[8] Cf. vol. 2, frontispiece.

[9] Cf. chapter 34, appendix, and fig. 242.

[10] Cf. plates 65 and 66.

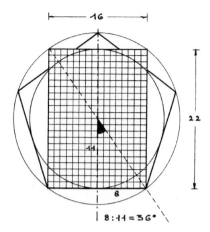

Fig. 154. The numerical ratio-principle of the pentagon

The angle determined by the ratio 8 : 11 is 36° and corresponds to the orientation of the axis of Mut in the nave, plus or minus 5′ of arc, while the axis of Amun—which, however, directs the naos of Amun's barque—is oriented at 34°27′ with respect to north. It is necessary, then, to investigate the relationship between these two angles, as well as the origin of the ratio 8 : 11 for the pentagon.

Now, the two axes of Amun and of Mut are bound together by the same function. This function has a pentagonal origin and the numbers that define the pentagon issue from the juxtaposition of the whorls of the hieratic pavement, with 1 : 3 and 1 : 2 for origin (male and female), crossing according to the function ϕ.

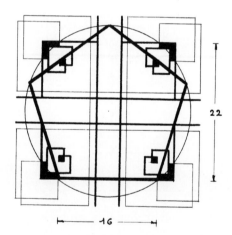

Fig. 155. Origin and growth of the hieratic pavement

Center of eight ϕ whorls with 1 : 2 for origin that determine, through their growth, the ejected square, which becomes the center of the whorls with 1 : 3 for origin. The distances between the centers, 16 and 22, determine the ratio of the side of the pentagon to its inscribed radius.

The essential numbers that are at the heart of the "hieratic pavement" (fig. 155) and that define the rectangle determining the pentagon are obtained as follows:

First, by growth (centrifugal) from the center toward the exterior, which determines the distances of sixteen squares between the hearts of the whorls of 1 : 2 and of twenty-two squares between the hearts of the whorls of 1 : 3. There are four centers for eight whorls, the unity being common to two whorls each time, and it is at the eighth number, without counting the unity, that the whorls "close" and superimpose themselves.

$$
\begin{array}{lcccccccc}
\text{Origin } 1:2 & 2 & 3 & 5 & 8 & 13 & 21 & 34 & \mathbf{55} \\
 & & 1 & & & & & & \\
\text{Origin } 1:3 & 3 & 4 & 7 & 11 & 18 & 29 & 47 & \mathbf{76}
\end{array}
$$

The "ejected" squares, with 9 and 12 for sides, are added, respectively, to the two numbers 55 and 76, and when they close, they determine two perfect squares whose sides are $55 + 9 = 64$, and $76 + 12 = 88$.[11]

Second, by division according to the Thotian principle, 1, 1/2, 1/4, starting from two times eight whorls (Thoth, master of the Eight) of which the two numbers 64 and 88 give a pentagon four times larger than the center pentagon of 16 and 22 (figs. 155 and 156).

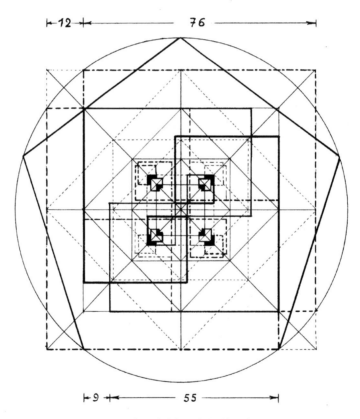

Fig. 156. Thotian division of the hieratic pavement

The whorls "close" at the eighth number without counting the unity, which is 55 for the 1 : 2 whorl (solid line) and 76 for the 1 : 3 whorl (broken line). The ejected squares with 9 and 12 for sides are added, respectively, to 55 and 76 and give the two squares having 64 and 88 for sides. The Thotian division determines from these squares the numbers 16 and 22 for defining the centers of the whorls and the central pentagon.

[11] Cf. figs. 94 and 95.

This is the resolution, according to the pharaonic mentality, of the determination of how the numbers that govern the pentagon (side, radius, and angle) are related to the axes of the temple.

As the hieratic pavement suggests, the two rectangles 16 and 22 are drawn perpendicular to each other. Being thus related to the general east-west orientation of the barque of this sanctuary, the directing rectangle of the pentagon, that is, of the naos, is placed so that it crosses at right angles to the first (fig. 157). In this position the axis of Amun, which cuts the first rectangle at its midpoint, divides the rectangle perpendicular to it into two equal rectangular parts, the diagonal of which is exactly the orientation in the ratio 11 : 16, being 34°27 ± 5′ with respect to true north (theoretical angle = 34°32′).

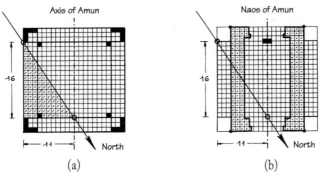

Fig. 157. Application of the hieratic pavement giving the axis of Amun

If this construction is oriented on true north-south, as the median axis, we determine the axis of the nave (thigh, *men.t*) in relation to the axis of Amun (fig. 158).

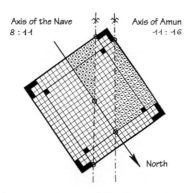

Fig. 158. Determination of the axis of the nave in relation to the axis of Amun

Now, it is this angle of 36° that the axis of the nave forms with north that, in its turn, makes understandable the "geometric reason" that governs the axis of Mut from the covered temple (head), oriented at 33° with respect to north (fig. 159). This angle corresponds to the ratio between the height of the pentagon and its side, in numbers for $R = 1$:

$$\cot 33°1′ = \frac{1.809...}{1.1755...} = 1.5389... \, .$$

Thus the proportions of the naos of Amun's sacred barque indeed give the geometric foundation permitting the definition of the axes drawn on the ground: the axis of Amun, that of Mut (head), and of its first deviation, the axis of Mut (nave). We still have to understand the third axis inscribed there, that of Khonsu.

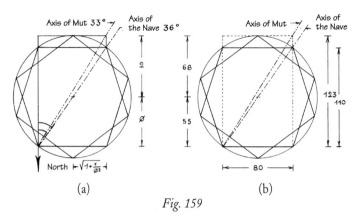

Fig. 159

The pentagonal function governing two of the angles that form the axis of Mut with north: that of the head, 33°, and that of the thigh (nave), 36°. *(a)* The irrational function of the pentagon; *(b)* the function transcribed into whole numbers. The ratio of 36°, 11 : 8, is equal to 110 : 80. The small radius equals 55; the large radius equals 68. The ratio of 33° corresponds to 123 : 80 ($55^2 + 40^2 = 4625$, and $68^2 = 4624$).

By completing each other, the proportions of room VI and those of the naos of the barque constructed in this room *specify the conjunction of the pentagon and the hexagon,*[12] *the two figures that govern all the axes of the temple.*

The axis of Khonsu, the axis of measures inscribed in the sanctuary, is the result of the superimposition of the hexagon and the pentagon, the function $\sqrt{3}$ that defines the first, and of the function ϕ that generates the second (fig. 160).

The angle 33°34′ that makes the axis of Khonsu with respect to north corresponds to the following coefficient ± 5′: cot 33°30′ = $\phi^2/\sqrt{3}$ = 1.5114... .

This extremely important ratio corresponds to the diameter of the sphere inscribed in the icosahedron with a value of 1 for its edge. That is, Khonsu brings about the regular Platonic volume that envelops the four others: *he creates the junction of the pentagon and the hexagon, that which determines volume.*

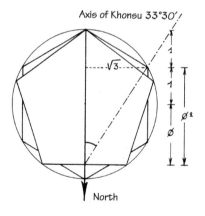

Fig. 160.

Superimposition of the pentagon and hexagon

The radius of the circumscribing circle is 2. The radius of the circle inscribed in the pentagon is ϕ. The radius of the circle inscribed in the hexagon is $\sqrt{3}$.

---

[12] Cf. fig. 113.

Let us summarize what has been said in the preceding pages about the character of the three axes of the temple:

The *axis of Amun* = sex-water = procreation = west, *amenti,* Amun.

The *axis of Mut,* the geometric axis = head-fire = gestating Hor in the nave (the thigh, *men.t*) under the name of Hathor (house of Hor).

The *axis of Khonsu,* axis of measures = trunk-earth, Khonsu, the mystic axis of measures, Mer-n-ptah (Menephtah), the dauphin.

The three architectual axes of the temple of Luxor are, for the mystic Temple, the vital function repre-sented by Amun-Mut and their fruit, Khonsu.

The determination of the three axes is confirmed in the covered temple by the particular orientation of the three rooms in which the three barques of Amun, Mut, and Khonsu are portrayed.[13] The sanctuary of Amun is entirely constructed on the axis of Amun, while the west walls of the chapels of Mut and Khonsu are oriented on the parallels of their respective axes.

The importance of the axes of Amun and of Mut (nave) is reaffirmed by the Romans who, when they built the colonnades and walls that surround the temple to the east and the west, placed them so that those of the east are parallel to the axis of Mut (nave) and those of the west *(amenti)* are parallel with the axis of Amun.[14]

THE AXIS OF THE COURT OF RAMESSES (NARTHEX)

We have explained how, with the nave terminating at the colossus of the knees, the work of lunar Amun is completed; but the axis of this Amun, beginning from the sanctuary of the barque (room VI), continues until it touches the south wall of the pylon that closes and opens the temple (fig. 152).

At this place in the Amunian chapel, all the symbolism of the sanctuary of the barque is found inverted (crossed), as if in a flat horizontal mirror: the top is crossed with the bottom, the right with the left, the north with the south, and the east with the west. This is the corporeal birth, the finishing touch. Here this axis is reflected in an angle that is exactly 1 : 7 (8°8′).[15]

Geometric explanation of this axis of reflection. The geometric origin of any hieratic construction in any age has always been the 1 : 2 rectangle because it allows for the demonstration of the function ϕ. When this rectangle pivots on its diagonal, it cuts its height into two segments that are to one another as 3 is to 5. The small segment 3 determines, along with the side 4 of the rectangle, the sacred 3, 4, 5 triangle (fig. 161a).

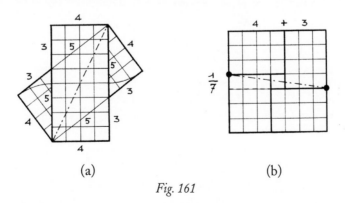

(a)   (b)

Fig. 161

[13] Cf. vol. 2, fig. 226, rooms VI, XX, and XIX.

[14] Cf. plate 88, and figs. 280 and 281.

[15] Cf. plates 64 and 86, and their legends.

The difference between the angle of 45° or 1̂/1 and the ratio 3 : 4 of the sacred triangle is 8°8′ or 1 : 7 (fig. 161b). It is evidently the east-west wall of the pylon that plays the role of reflector.

Axis of the narthex. We have seen, with Amun and the dynasty of Amenhotep in Amun (Aries), the domination of the pentagon, the quintessence, in all of the lunar becoming, which with the solar deity Amun-Ra finds its definitive accomplishment realized geometrically by the hexagon and illustrated by the hexagram, the complementation of two triangles, also called the Shield of David.

It is the hexagon, the diagram of the hexagonal numbers 7 and 19, that is now going to determine the axes of the narthex and the avenue of the sphinxes in relation to the axes of Amun and of Mut. Here are the angles (plus or minus 5′ of arc):

axis of Amun: 34°30′ = 11 : 16 measured 34°27′

axis of the nave: 36° = 8 : 11 measured 35°55′

axis of the narthex: 43°27′ = 18 : 19 measured 43°27′

axis of the avenue of sphinxes: 45° = 1 : 1 measured 44°56′.

The difference between the axis of the narthex and the axis of Amun equals 9°. The difference between the axis of the narthex and the axis of the nave equals 7°30′. The difference between the orientations of the axis of Ramesses (narthex) and the axes of Amun and of Mut (nave) imply the two lines of the pentagon and the hexagon by successive duplications: 4 × 9° = 36°, the angle of the pentagon; and 4 × 7°30′ = 30°, the angle of the hexagon.

Recalling what was said about trigonometry in proportional notation, it is always the angle 1 : 1 (45°) that serves as reference. The angle 9°, from the origin of the pentagon, is obtained directly through subtraction since it represents the difference between 45° and 36°, which in proportional notation (fig. 162) is as follows:

$$\frac{\hat{1}}{1} - \frac{\hat{8}}{11} = \frac{11-8}{11+8} = \frac{\hat{3}}{19}.$$

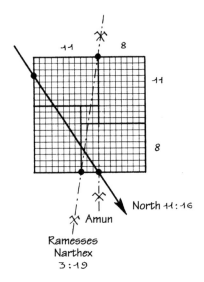

Fig. 162. Difference between the axis of Amun and the axis of the narthex

It is a question here of establishing the angle of 9° or $\widehat{3/19}$, which applies directly to the human canon; it is the difference between the axis of Amun and that of the narthex. In fact, with respect to north, the court of Ramesses is oriented not at 45°, but at about 43°30′. This is the ratio of a man with and without the crown of the skull, or 18 : 19.

It is only with the avenue of the sphinxes that we find the exact orientation of 45° in relation to north, that is, 1 : 1; it is also found in the ratio of 3 : 19 with the axis of the nave, or the axis of Mut.

The two angular differences 7°30′ and 9° link the pentagonal and hexagonal functions, the same ones that combine in the dodecahedron and the icosahedron. The axis of Khonsu, drawn in the sanctuary of Amun's barque, confirms this function through its angular ratio.

For confirming again the passage from the pentagon to the hexagon in the court of Ramesses, we must find in the temple itself an orientation that gives the difference of 7°30′ in relation to 45°, which exists between the axes of the nave and the narthex. This indication is indeed given by the north facade of the nave, namely, in the surface of the ancient pylon that marks the final stage of work under Amenhotep III and forms a transverse axis.

The orientation of this facade in relation to the north-south grid established on the temple is actually 37°30′ (fig. 163). Its angular difference from the avenue of the sphinxes oriented at 45° is then 7°30′, which confirms the indication of the angular function of the hexagon in the final constructions of Amenhotep III.[16]

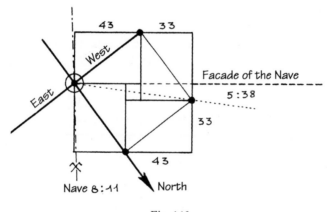

Fig. 163

The orientation of the facade of the nave, read on the north-south grid and placed on the corresponding plans in whole numbers in the ratio of 33 : 43. Operating according to the subtraction of angles notated as a/b, we deduct from it the value approaching 7°30′, as

$$\frac{\widehat{1}}{1} - \frac{\widehat{33}}{43} = \frac{43-33}{43+33} + \frac{\widehat{10}}{76} \quad \text{or} \quad \frac{\widehat{5}}{38} = 7°29′45″.$$

It is through a constant alternation between Amun and Mut that an interpenetration (one could say a "coitus") is defined between the mystic pentagon and the defined hexagon, the result of which is Ra-Amun in the form of Khonsu, the dauphin.

[16] Through certain intentional anomalies in the numbers of the temple of Luxor, which are indicated in this work, we can demonstrate π, its quadrature, and its cube. Consequently, we can be sure that the Ancients knew of it as well.

This complex analysis of the angular play of the axes has been necessary to make the living construction of the Temple perceptible. This is, however, not the way in which the master builder proceeded. We have rediscovered here the line of conduct of pharaonic thinking based on the principle of harmony, from which results, for those who possess it, a natural coordination of the different vital moments transcribed by this marvelous architecture.

The axis of reflection of Amun and its relationship to the sacred triangle, the axis of Mut defined by the pentagon and generating in its turn the other axes, and even the avenue of the sphinxes making mention of the angle of reference 1/1, are all united by a single original function: the "bolt." As we have already mentioned with regard to the Rhind Papyrus, to the angular additions and subtractions in proportional notation, to the numbers ruling the cubits, and finally to those that direct the pharaonic canon, the bolt generates harmonically the succession of fundamental numbers that govern the principal axes of the temple.

The bolt (fig. 138), constructed on the developed harmonic proportion, has the ratio $1 : 7$, the angle of reflection of the axis of Amun, for its beginning point. This ratio generates, among others: the ratio $3 : 4$ of the sacred triangle, the fourth; then $8 : 11$, the pair of numbers identical to that resulting from the hieratic pavement; and the angle of the pentagon, the axis of Mut of the nave. Finally, it establishes the ratio $3 : 19$, the angular deviation between the axes of Amun and of Ramesses (narthex). With this genesis, which has $1 : 7$ for its origin and which concludes at 19, a cycle is ended. This cycle opens, inverted on *AP* (fig. 136), the genesis of the proportions of man and therefore of the temple. Thus the bolt naturally gives all the proportions of the Temple-Man, as well as the numbers of the principal axes that regulate it.

The harmonic functions expressed through the architecture of the temple—its movements, deviations, and growth—are located between the two hexagonal origin numbers, 7 and 19. The same function links the Temple of Man and the figures represented on its walls. The same measures will be applied to all of them, with the same nuances and the same variations, which result not from arbitrary fantasy, but from the application of a living function. *The pentagon symbolizes the quintessence that governs all perfection.*

THE TEACHING OF THE FIVE KINGS OF THE SANCTUARY OF AMUN

All the principles and movements we have just described in their geometric aspect with regard to the orientation of the temple are anticipated and represented in the Holy of Holies by a series of five royal figurations.

On the first register of the west wall of the sanctuary that contained the golden statue of Amun with the ram's head (room I) there are five royal principles that are alternately face-to-face with Amun and Min-Amun, the Amun of fertility.[17] These five figures each measure 72 digits from the soles of the feet to the vertex and 68 digits to the level of the forehead,[18] but their measurements specify that there are different digit values for each one. Labeled A, B, C, D, and E from north to south, the direction in which they are pictured walking, the first king (A) measures 72 of the smallest digits, and the last king (E) measures 72 of the largest digits for their heights.

[17] Cf. plate 79.

[18] Cf. chapter 11, "Projection of the *Canevas* on Two Royal Figures," study of the king of room II.

This observation is extremely important because this use of slightly different measures according to the character of the figure is frequently encountered in the temple and entails the proportional modification of each part of the subject that conforms to the value of the digit used. Now, the sanctuary presents here the extreme values of these variations in a single group, variations that are made by a kind of growth from the north (A) toward the south (E), and confirmed by a similar increase in the height of the register on which the five kings are drawn.

Measured between the line of the base and the lower line of the sky that defines the upper portion of the tableau, the height of this register corresponds to 100 digits identical to those used for the figures, that is, there are 100 smaller digits to the north and 100 larger ones to the south. The extreme values of these digits correspond to 1/96 fathom measuring the arcs of meridian at 0° (south) and at 90° (north). Recall that the measurements of the meridian arcs vary according to the latitude and that each place on our globe thus has its particular measurement because of the flattening of the earth. The knowledge of this fact is confirmed by the west wing of the pylon of the temple, whose length under the torus is exactly 12 fathoms at 90° to the north and twelve fathoms at 0° to the south.[19]

It is very important to note in this sanctuary that the southern king is measured by the northern fathom and the northern king is measured by the southern fathom. Here again is another application of the inversion, already mentioned, that occurs along the fissure of Rolando, in which the motor centers are indeed inverted. Now, the sanctuary of Amun occupies precisely this part of the head in the Man of the Temple.

This fact suggests that we investigate the pylon itself for the solution of this metrical variation conforming to the measurements of the earth. Now, the axis of Amun is reflected against this pylon in the angle of 1 : 7, and it is a great marvel that it provides a remarkable approximation for the solution of this problem, which was only recently solved thanks to a considerable amount of geodetic work. According to the present data, 1′ of meridian arc at 0° equals 1842.9 meters, and 1′ of meridian arc at 90° equals 1861.66 meters.

Now, if one takes the fathom at 0° for the base of a triangle with 1 : 7 *as its angular ratio, its hypotenuse will be equal to the fathom at 90° to the nearest* 0.0005: 1842.9 meters × 1.0101528... = 1861.61 meters. This indication is provided by the variation of the height of the register of the sanctuary[20] and is explained in detail by the dimensions of the five kings that are represented there. Now, in the same way that the reflection angle of Amun establishes the link between the extreme measures of the meridian arcs (therefore, the different fathoms), the different axes of the temple establish the link between the measurements of these kings and the measurements of the temple itself.

Knowing the extreme values of the arc of the terrestrial meridian, we can deduce the mean value. Twenty-seven mean fathoms equal, we recall, 50 true meters. The meter is the reference measure for the royal cubit that represents $2 \times \phi^2 \div 10$ in meters, and its use for the temple is confirmed by the measurement of 10 meters for the width of the door of the Ramesses pylon.

The reference to the meter as a measure and to true north as the orientation allows us to establish a north-south grid in which each square has 10 meters to the side.[21] In proportional notation we can read these different orientations of each part of the temple with the help of this grid.

---

[19] Cf. plate 67. The western wing of the pylon recapitulates the essential units of measure encountered throughout the temple: the fathom, the meter, and the royal cubit.

[20] The register measures 192 cm to the north and 194 cm to the south. The variation of the digits in a fathom from 0° to 90° latitude is 1.91983... cm and 1.9395... cm, respectively.

[21] Cf. plates 81–83, plans of the temple on a grid oriented north-south, for which each square has a side of 10 m.

Each room of the temple has its own measure, just as each part of the body has its own measure, and just as each place between the equator and the pole of our globe has its own measure. It is by means of the fathom and the royal cubit that these measures are unified.

By their height, the five kings indicate five different measures: *king A* is related to the royal cubit; *king B* is measured by the digit that corresponds to 1/96 fathom at 0° latitude; *king C* has the digit of the fathom at 45° latitude as its base-measure; *king E* is measured by the digit of a fathom at 90° latitude; finally, *king D,* coming between them, is measured by the digit that corresponds to the fathom at about 30°, that is, the mean latitude of Egypt. Thus, kings B to E mark four essential moments of the measure of the fathom by degrees. This is confirmed by the height of the register on which they are carved.

The particular size of king A relates him to the size of the temple. The length of the Man of the Temple equals 19×10 times the total height of king A.

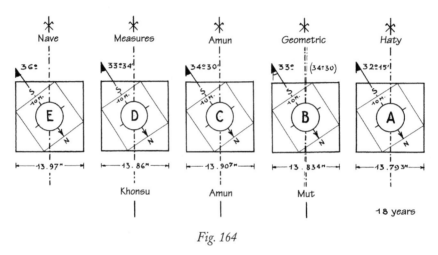

Fig. 164

Squares of 10 meters to the side, oriented north-south, are inscribed in the squares whose sides measure, respectively, ten times the height of kings A, B, C, D, and E. These exterior squares pivot on the interior squares until their sides become tangential to the angles of the latter. With respect to north-south, the exterior squares form the angles that correspond to the principal axes of the temple of Amenhotep III. *A,* axis of the *haty,* east wall of the hypostyle room. *B,* geometric axis (Mut); king B has a double rhythm through his two dimensions and is also connected to the axis of Amun. *C,* axis of Amun. *D,* axis of measures (Khonsu); the height of king D is measured by 72 digits of a fathom of the mean latitude of Egypt (24° to 30° north latitude). *E,* axis of the nave (Mut).

It is written on one of the architraves of the peristyle court, "Here is the place of the birth of the king, where he passed his infancy and from where he left crowned."[22] Now the Man of the Temple is only adult and crowned after the work of Ramesses, as is evidenced by the growth of the temple and by its proportions. The numbers of the harmonic development (synthesis 2, figs. 48 and 138) begin from the ratio of 1 : 7 and conclude with 19.

Using the measure ten times the height of king A as unity, a grid of nineteen squares is drawn

---

[22] This text is inscribed on the architraves of the east colonnade of the peristyle court. Its location corresponds to the position of the navel on the Man of the Temple.

on the temple. This gives a total length of 500 royal cubits[23] to the Man of the Temple. Using the measure of ten times the height of king E as unity (the largest), and multiplied again by 19, we obtain 144 fathoms at 0° latitude as its measure.

Now 500 royal cubits and 144 fathoms are the two fundamental measures of the temple and fix two moments of the gestation of the Royal Man. These will be made specific with regard to the growth of the temple and the study of the mosaic in the pavement.[24]

We can then use ten times the height of each king for the side of a square in which we inscribe a small square of 10 meters to a side, oriented to true north. The large squares will oscillate around the small ones and the angles of their movements will correspond to the principal angles of the temple (fig. 164).

Summary of the Synopsis of the Five Kings of Sanctuary I
Elements

Harmonic development gives the fundamental musical ratios. This establishes the proportions, in the form of whole numbers, which correspond to the principle axes of the temple and which develop, in their turn, by oscillation.

The heights of the five kings of sanctuary I are measured in digits of meridian fathoms going from 0° (equator) to 90° (North Pole). By their relationship to the unit (meter) oriented toward the north, these heights exactly determine the angles of the principal axes of the temple.[25] This cannot be a fortuitous coincidence, as our measurements at the temple itself were rigorously verified, which proves again the geodetic knowledge of the Ancients.

It is the angle provided by the reflection of the axis of Amun that is the principal indication of this group of ratios: it serves as the initial proportion ending with 19 for the harmonic development that governs the proportions of the temple, thus for the canon of the Royal Man, as well as for the orientations of the edifice on the geometric axis of Mut, the gestating mother, helmeted with a vulture headdress.

Fig. 165. Mut

The five kings are precisely situated in the sanctuary of Amun on the west wall, which is "transparent" with sanctuary VII (pineal gland), where the pituitary body is located in the head. This is the area that controls, among other things, the growth and sexual life of human beings.

[23] Cf. plates 88–90, plans of the temple on a grid that divides the length of 500 royal cubits by 19. Plate 15 shows a projection onto the temple plan of a skeleton established on this dimension.

[24] Cf. chapters 28 and 31.

[25] These axes also play a "correspondence" role in relation to the buildings, rooms, walls, and columns of the different parts of the temple that are related to the "Mut effect" described by the myth, a correspondence similar to that of the joints. Cf. chapter 17.

As with all the other walls, this part of the principal sanctuary is a work of teaching. The figures were sculpted in bas-relief and painted in colors; they are at the same time a teaching and a work of art. Our sensibilities are troubled and even shocked by this contradiction: if something is a scientific document, it cannot speak to our feelings for beauty. We would prefer to have feelings without lessons, or to accept lessons without the need for aesthetic scrutiny. We tend to remain ignorant of one aspect in order to understand the other, but here, the teaching and the work of art both testify to an exceptional mastery.

We must attempt to see and to live these two aspects simultaneously because that is the nature of the Temple: the conjunction of thought with the heart, of knowing with faith, of reason with feeling.

Remaining sensitive to beauty while renouncing sensual pleasure is an obvious absurdity and a surpassing of earthbound human capacity.

Part 4

The Architecture of the Temple

THEMES

Because you have seen me, Thomas, you have believed.
Blessed are those who have not seen, and yet believe.

John 20:29

Chapter 14

THE EDWIN SMITH
SURGICAL PAPYRUS

INTRODUCTION

Each passing hour in the twilight of our world raises a little further the veil hiding the light of the wisdom that illuminates, among other things, the glorious empire of the two pharaonic crowns. Neither the bloody cruelty of conquerors—those whom we make the heroes of history—nor the jealous fear of those who have given a new name to the eternal God on account of seeing their faith contradicted, nothing of any of this has been able to destroy all the proofs of the knowledge possessed by those great, privileged few of antiquity.

Here, some stones from a monument, there, some finely worked objects, here and there, a written document, come along to overturn the long-held opinion concerning the intellectual culture and science of humanity's ancestors. As one of the greatest philologists of Egyptology said in 1952:

> What I have just seen, after twenty-five years of absence from Egypt, shows me that there was a metaphysics and a high civilization as far back as 6000 years ago, a time that we had thought to be a primary stage of human development in the Nile Valley. . . .
>
> Today we have, thanks to the Edwin Smith Papyrus, an indisputable testimony of this scientific spirit, which very wrongly we had thought the Egyptians lacked. This splendid manuscript reproduces the beginning of a treatise on external pathology and bone surgery that methodically studied the injuries, dislocations, and interesting fractures of the entire body from head to foot.[1]

J. H. Breasted, the famous American Egyptologist, said,

> The current conclusion regarding the mind of the ancient Egyptian, a conclusion in which I myself heretofore shared, has been that he was interested in scientific principles, if at all, solely because of the unavoidable necessity of applying them in practical life. . . . In the field of Egyptian mathematics Professor Karpinski of the University of Michigan has long insisted that the surviving mathematical papyri clearly demonstrate the Egyptians' scientific interest in pure mathematics for its own

[1] Gustave Lefebvre, *Essai sur la médecine égyptienne de l'époque pharaonique* (Paris: Presses Universitaires, 1956), p. 6.

sake. I have now no doubt that Professor Karpinski is right, for the evidence of interest in pure science, as such, is perfectly conclusive in the Edwin Smith Surgical Papyrus.[2]

Before Breasted translated this papyrus, which is the oldest known treatise on surgery, the opinion of Egyptologists concerning the knowledge possessed by the pharaonic people was generally to regard it as being empirical, denying to the Ancients the scientific spirit, or rather, the spirit of pure science. Even now, there are still doubts, with some believing they see in certain passages the careful study and observation of a pure and reasoned science, while others deny this and see in the various cases treated only a purely empirical knowledge.

It is not my role to judge in this instance, the main reason being that I consider the problem badly posed because it was formulated with a narrow view of the possibilities.

At the origin of human history, or at least in the remote period that the most ancient Egypt inherited, I see a humanity very much closer to nature, that is, less artificial, than our "cerebralized" humanity. This primitive state—which is not animal-human but human endowed with a controlled consciousness—presents the typical quality of what our philosophy tries to express by "intuition," "a direct contact of spirit with spirit," which I see as a direct contact of functional consciousness with the characteristic function of an object.

With civilization, that is, with the comfortable adaptation of nature to the daily life of humanity, this sense is more and more blunted until, finally, we reach this tragic moment in which we find ourselves, where one lives for the most part in illusions and cerebral constructions, and lacks contact with natural life.

The best among us who have a sense of the loss of the "Kingdom" (of God or of knowledge?) or simply an awareness that they can no longer find responses to the fundamental questions raised by moral suffering, attempt, through religious meditation or the advice of yogis, to rediscover this commingling of spirit with spirit, *which characterized our remote ancestors.*

Today, through a great effort on our part, we must seek that which was, I am convinced, the possession of a widespread elite at the dawn of our humanity.

It is not a problem of choosing between science and empiricism; the only choice possible is between knowledge and know-how.

Know-how belongs to our era, and in the case of medicine and surgery, it involves information about the smallest fibers and circuits of the human body. With knowledge, however, comes the *functional* vision of organic groups, of physiological regions, and of harmonic resonances between moments of the living organism and nature in general: the direct *intuition.*

The fact of admitting to a "knowing" humanity prior to our mental-cerebral evolution is opposed to a rationally seductive evolutionary concept that searches for an apelike man as the link between the animal and the human. We easily consign to "time" these so-called transitional phenomena, which, if they were real, should yet today be verifiable. Now, we observe many cases of degeneration, but no example of an ascent of the animal toward the human in the sense specified by the evolutionary theory of our anthropologists. On the contrary, the more we know about "primitive" tribes, the more we discover that at the origin of their mores and customs there is a metaphysics based on essential principles curiously similar to those we observe everywhere. It is obvious that a similar thesis, which admits some sort of spontaneous appearance of the human phenomenon, can only be supported by concepts very different from those offered up by our materialistic rationalism.

[2] J. H. Breasted, *The Edwin Smith Surgical Papyrus* (Chicago: Univ. of Chicago Press, 1930), introduction, p. 15.

But to return to our surgical papyrus, when this treatise advises the practitioner to examine maladies by auscultation ("to count" it says), it does not recommend that he *observe* for the purpose of relating his observations to an immense accumulation of learning (as is the case in present-day medical practice), but rather for him to determine the "symbols" that evoke a vital, energetic, medical state of being in need of being reharmonized. This is why the language remains full of imagery and invokes analogies that serve as guides for intuition.

History

Edwin Smith acquired the papyrus that bears his name at Luxor in 1862. Even though he was able to read hieroglyphs, he considered himself incapable of publishing a translation of it. It was only after his death in 1906 that the papyrus was presented by his daughter to the New York Historical Society.

In 1920, J. H. Breasted was given charge of the translation. Hesitant at first before this heavy responsibility, he was so attracted by the "splendid handwritten columns of the magnificent papyrus" that he felt incapable of refusing. During this enormous translation work, and in spite of the great difficulties he had to overcome, Professor Breasted certainly experienced some exhilarating moments. The elements put at his disposal by Egyptology were not sufficient for him to penetrate the meaning of certain terms particular to this papyrus and otherwise totally unknown. For this reason, Breasted had to make use of all existing documents, especially the most ancient. By successive cross-checking, but also through analogies and sometimes through symbols, he reached a clarification of the scribe's intention.

In this papyrus we find many cases of figurative expressions, that is, symbolic terms that, if summarized in a word, no longer correspond to the intention of the wise author of this old treatise. As we continue, we will point out where there might be an "esoteric" meaning.

"After interpreting the document as best I could with my limited knowledge of the human body, I handed the manuscript to my medical colleague, Dr. Arno B. Luckhardt, who very kindly undertook the burdensome task of looking it through and appending his suggestions."[3] Among other things, this surgical treatise proves that the Ancients had sure knowledge of the organs of the head and their actions and reactions on parts of the head not directly affected by the injury; the circulation of the blood and the internal nerves of the brain; and the effects of head injuries that are transmitted by the nervous system to particular parts of the body.

This Surgical Papyrus, recopied under Sesostris (around 1800 B.C.), is a copy of a much older work written by an unknown author, probably at the time of the Pyramids. For the era of its transcription, the original text, which we believe could date back to Imhotep (period of Zoser, Third Dynasty, approximately 3500 B.C.), was in such an archaic style that the scribe was forced to add commentary to the cases cited in order to explain the numerous medical terms that were already out of date. Without these precious commentaries, the terms would be totally incomprehensible to us.[4]

The recto of the papyrus consists of seventeen columns of text (377 lines) written in black ink, with all the titles and some passages in red. It presents the study of forty-eight cases of injuries, beginning with the head, continuing through the face, then to the spinal column and the thorax. We could bemoan the fact that we do not have a similar treatise concerning the entire body, but it is the head that controls all the vital functions.

It is impossible to know if the original treatise contained and developed the cases of all the injuries in this way because the scribe, at the bottom of a column,

---

[3] Ibid., foreword, p. xix.

[4] Are we dealing here with words whose usages were lost, or with distinctive features of words (nonprofane meanings) that the commentator believed necessary to specify?

pausing in the middle of a line, in the middle of a sentence, in the middle of a word, . . . raised his pen, and ceased writing. After a pause, of which we cannot divine the cause, but during which his well-filled reed pen nearly dried, he again applied it to the papyrus. He made two more very faint strokes with the almost exhausted pen, which he thereupon dipped deep into his ink pot. After heavily retracing the two pale strokes, but so carelessly that the original faint lines are still visible, he laid down his pen and pushed aside forever the great surgical treatise he had been copying, leaving $15\frac{1}{2}$ inches (39 cm) bare and unwritten at the end of his roll.[5]

On the verso of the papyrus, after an empty space of 39 centimeters, three and one-half columns of text are written (sixty-five lines) consisting mainly of incantations against the pestilence. Then there is a column (twenty-seven lines) written by another hand, and devoted almost entirely to a prescription for "transforming an old man into a youth." According to Breasted, these incantations and prescriptions on the verso were added later and have no relationship with the recto.[6]

—∿∿—

The Smith Papyrus presents forty-eight cases classed by regions: the first eight are concerned with the vault of the cranium and the two following with the frontal bone and the eyebrows; then come four cases related to lesions of the nose and three concerning the zygomatic region (the cheeks); next come five cases of wounds to the temporal region (cases 18–22), then to the ear, the mandible, and the chin (cases 23–27). The section on injuries to the head, properly speaking, concludes here.

Case 28, immediately following, discusses a perforation of the throat and windpipe, then five extremely interesting cases, 29 to 33, relate to an injury, a sprain, a dislocation, a displacement, and a crushing of a cervical vertebra, respectively. Finally, the remaining fourteen cases take up different traumas in the region of the clavicles, the shoulder, and the top of the chest. Number 48, left incomplete, is entitled "Sprain of a vertebra of the back."

The treatise discusses very serious lesions, many of which leave no hope of recovery according to the diagnosis of the surgeon. Therefore, it contains more than one method of cure for any given injury. Owing to its concise style, we must weigh each word and investigate all the implied meanings, as the first commentary on the first case already testifies. Without this it would be difficult to understand what the surgeon intends when he says, at the beginning of each examination, "If you examine a man. . . ."

SOME ANATOMICAL TERMS USED IN THE PAPYRUS[7]

HEAD AND SENSE ORGANS

1. The hieroglyph for the *head*, including the whole skull and the face, is often written without phonetic elements and with the single determinative showing a face in profile. This offers two possible readings.

---

[5] Breasted, *Smith Papyrus*, foreword, p. xvi.

[6] Ibid., introduction, p. 6.

[7] Summary based on Lefebvre, *Parties du corps humain* and *Médecine égyptienne,* and Breasted, *Smith Papyrus*. The numbers and letters in each section are related to figs. 166, 167, and 168. For the pronunciation of pharaonic words, the convention followed here is to insert a short *e* between the consonants or groups of consonants. For example, *tbn* is read *teben, mtw* is read *metew.* Among the double letters that represent a single hieroglyph, we can mention *ou,* which we have transcribed by *w; dj* or *sh,* which are pronounced like *ch* in *chaise;* and *kh,* which is pronounced like *ch* in *achtung.*

The first is the word *tp*, whose meaning extends to any upper extremity. As we would say, for example, the "head of the femur," the Egyptians would say "the head of the eyebrows." The word *head* is also applied to numerous terms designating the chief or leader, "the *capitaine,*" "that which is at the head of."

The word *djadja* is used for the entire head and is written with the same determinative of a face in profile. It refers, among other things, to a "council of ministers." This term implies an idea of direction, but also of reflection, of discernment. It is used, for example, in the expression, "the seven orifices of the *djadja*" (fig. 166, no. 1) in regard to the eyes, the ears, the nostrils, and the mouth. Each of these seven "openings of the head" is designated by one or several particular words, of which here we will retain only the most frequently used.

a) The ears are called *ankwy,* "the living," in the religious texts, but more commonly *msdjryw* in the medical texts. The Ancients distinguished the right ear, that of the west, from the left ear, that of the east. In this regard, a text from the Ebers Papyrus says, "Two passages [*m.tw*] go to the right ear, through which enters the breath of life. Two passages go to the left ear, through which enters the breath of death."[8]

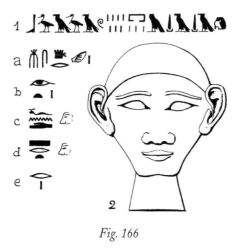

Fig. 166

(1) *babaw 7 m djadja (dj a),* "the seven orifices of the head": *(a) msdjr (m s dj r),* ear; *(b) irt,* eye; *(c) fnd,* nose; *(d) shrt (sh r t),* nostril; *(e) r,* mouth. (2) *hr,* the face

b) There are many words that refer to the eye, the iris, the pupil, the sclera (the white part) of the eye, but most of them are related more or less to mythology. The eye of Horus, playing a constant role in mythology, requires a very specific study, too complex to be gone into here. The most frequently used term to designate the eye in general is *irt,* represented by an eye.

c) The nose also has an equally rich vocabulary for its different parts, through which it appears that the Ancients accorded it considerable importance. Is it not thanks to respiration that we live? In fact the Ebers Papyrus (855a) says, "With regard to the air that enters the nose, it penetrates the *haty* through the lungs, and it is they who distribute it throughout the body."

---

[8] Why this distinction? Did the Ancients know that the arterial branches that irrigate the cortex all proceed from the circle of Willis, and are made up of the two vertebral and the two *internal* carotid arteries? Now, "of the two carotid arteries, only the left one receives the blood flow directly and in the same direction as the aortic current. Following this, it is easy to understand why blood clots proceeding from the left side of the heart usually return to the left side of the brain rather than to the right, and consequently why hemoplegia, or blood clotting, is nearly always a right hemoplegia. . . . Now the internal artery is in intimate contact with the eustachian tube and the anterior wall of the case of the eardrum." L. Testut and O. Jacob, *Traité d'anatomie topographique* (Paris: Doin, 1914), 1:143, 352.

The nose itself is called *fnd*. It is this term that is employed, for example, when in the temple of Luxor, the *neter* presents the ankh before the face of the king, while saying "To give life to his nose [*fnd*]."

d) Another term, *shrt*, when it is used in the singular, can be understood as "nose." When it is employed in the dual sense it can refer particularly to the nostrils: *shrty*, "the two nostrils." A passage from the tomb of Rekhemire makes the following distinction between these two terms: "The sweet north breeze for thy nose [*fnd k*], the wind for thy nostril [*shrt k*]."[9]*

This example proves that there is a distinction between *shrty*, which breathes the air (breathing as a function), and *fnd*, which animates through respiration. Indeed, dead air, like the stagnant air in caves and caverns, brings no life to the body.

2. The face is called *hr*, the forehead. We may note that in certain hieroglyphs of the Middle Kingdom (Twelfth Dynasty) there is a particular emphasis given to the crown of the skull in the form of the lunar crescent (fig. 166). The accent is placed on "the seven orifices of the face" by exaggerating the ears, which are depicted in front view, and also by enlarging and flattening the nostrils. The distinction between the left and right is accentuated by the lack of symmetry governing this face. The asymmetry we encounter in this small hieroglyph is also found in sculptural details and in the architecture and plan of a temple.

BONE STRUCTURE OF THE CRANIUM

The study of the vocabulary relating to the human skeleton presents a difficulty because the terms that are related to it most often concern not only a certain bone, but the area above and below it as well. Frequently there are several words that designate the same part, and only a systematic study of their use in all the cases where they are encountered allows us to know exactly what they mean. Such a study is at present nearly impossible because of the considerable number of words specific to certain writings that have not yet been found in any other papyrus. We mention here only the words whose meanings are now "relatively" clear, most particularly those used in the Edwin Smith Surgical Papyrus.

3. The cranium proper is called *djnnt* (fig. 167). This word is constantly used during the examination of head injuries, and it is noted each time whether the injury penetrates "up to the bone of the cranium" *(djnnt)* or not. We can be certain that we are dealing with the braincase when it is said, for example, in case 3, "perforating his cranium."

4. Another word, *hn*, has several meanings according to its use and its determinative. Literally, "coffer," we find it in the expression "your heart is in its coffer,"[10] in which it is determined by the symbol of a sanctuary of Lower Egypt (north). It is found again in "the coffer of the belly" determined this time by the symbol of a sanctuary of Upper Egypt (south).

In the Smith Papyrus, *hn* is employed in a particular sense, which becomes the object of a gloss by the scribe, "With regard to the *hn* of his head, it is at the heart of his vertex, the closest to his brain, this is the image of the *hn*."

This gloss is part of case 7, which discusses a perforation of the sutures of the cranium. The gloss of the scribe and the determinative of the word, which no longer represents a coffer but its lid, allows us to give *hn n tp* the broad meaning of "cranial vault," at least provisionally.[11]

---

[9] Cf. Lefebvre, *Parties du corps humain,* p. 18; Breasted, *Smith Papyrus,* p. 253.

[10] Cf. Lefebvre, *Parties du corps humain,* p. 24.

[11] When in case 7 it is a question of the "odor" of *hn,* this casts doubt on its translation as "bony vault." Is it a question of the dura mater that contains the longitudinal sinus in a fold? This would explain the end of the commentary, "the closest to his brain."

* Unless noted otherwise, translations from the Smith Papyrus are the author's own.

5. The top of the cranium, or vertex, plays an important role in pharaonic drawings: it supports the crowns, the symbols surmounting the heads of the *neters* and the kings. Its name, *wpt,* also used for "to open," "to discern," "to judge," is written with ox horns. The double character is significant and is found again in most crowns. The royal diadem bears the erect uraeus at the forehead, whose serpentine body curves from front to back dividing the skull longitudinally in the image of the sickle-shaped folds of the brain;[12] the separating character of the serpent is clearly indicated. It recalls, as the word *wpt* itself, the duality of the cerebral hemispheres that allow judgment, the grip of cerebral consciousness.

6. Let us recall that the braincase consists of eight bones: four individual bones, the sphenoid, the ethmoid, the frontal, and the occipital, and four that are paired, the parietal and temporal bones. In Egyptian, the bones are called *ks,* written with a sign that we meet also in the word for "annals," *gnwt,* which is to be understood as the "annals" that register the principal dates and thus constitute, so to speak, the skeleton of a science. The same hieroglyph serves also to designate the sculptor, particularly the stone sculptor, which creates a curious analogy when we see that indeed it is the skeleton that "gives and sustains form."

7. The different bony pieces that make up the braincase are designated by a special word, *pakt,* literally signifying "potsherd" or "shell," exactly as we speak today of the "temporal shell," for example. These bony pieces are united by the sutures, which also have names.

8. The sutures are of two types: "Whereas the frontal, the parietals, and the occipital bones are united by serrated edges that join one another, these same bones are joined to the temporal shell and to the large wing of the sphenoid bone by beveled edges. They are positioned so that the sphenoidal or temporal edge overlays the other edges entirely. It is because of this that, no matter what point of the vault suffers a trauma, any opening or closing of the bones is nearly impossible."[13]

Regarding the sutures, we still have to mention that after the closure of the fontanelles, "there remains, between the two bones, a slim fibrous bed, the sutural membrane, thanks to which the bones continue to grow in surface. This sutural membrane is to the bones of the skull as the joint cartilage is to the long bones of the limbs. When ossification encroaches (synostosis), the skull can no longer increase its capacity. It is toward forty-five years of age that this synostosis begins."[14]

The pharaonic term for the sutures is *tpaw,* explained in a gloss: "the sutures [*tpaw*] of his skull, it means that which is between one shell and another shell of his skull; the sutures are made of hide [or skin, *dhr*]."[15]

9. The word *dhr,* which then designates the sutural membranes, is actually determined by the sign for hide or skin. It also refers sometimes to the fontanelles.

10. Among the membranous spaces existing before the complete ossification of the child's skull, the large fontanelle (or bregma) is described in the papyrus in the following manner: "the weak place [*whnn*] in a child's crown before it becomes whole," or "before it becomes altogether stiff."[16]

11. Several terms are applied to the temporal region. We meet one of them again in the religious texts. It seems to designate most particularly the place on the skull covered by the royal princes' braid of hair. A second word is also used for the braid itself, and, in the Ebers Papyrus, in the expression: "Four *mtw* are in the interior of his temples [*gmhty*]."[17]

[12] Cf. plate 42; fig. 178; also chapter 39.

[13] Testut and Jacob, *Traité d'anatomie,* 1:19.

[14] Ibid., p. 18.

[15] Cf. Breasted, *Smith Papyrus,* case 7, gloss A [p. 436].

[16] Cf. ibid., case 6, examination [p. 166].

[17] Cf. Ebers Papyrus, 99, 7, and Lefebvre, *Parties du corps humain,* p. 14.

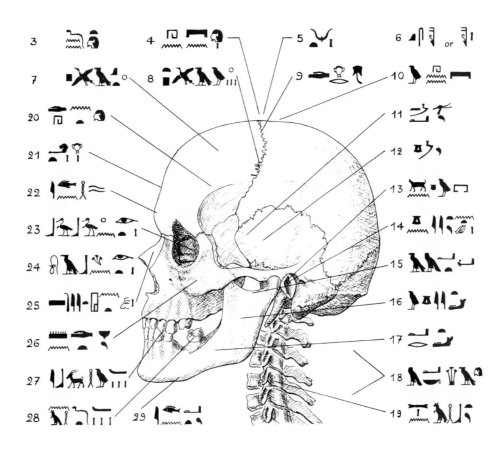

Fig. 167. Some anatomical terms of the skull and spinal column

3. *djnnt (dj n n t)*, cranium or skull

4. *hn n tp*, cranial vault

5. *wpt*, vertex

6. *ks*, bone in general

7. *pakt*, cranial shell

8. *tpaw*, sutures

9. *dhr*, sutural membranes

10. *whnn*, bregmatic fontanelle

11. *maā*, temporal region

12. *gma*, temporal shell

13. *khnw (kh n w)*, auditory passage or inner ear

14. *gnyt nt msdjr*, external auditory passage

15. *amāt*, sigmoid notch

16. *wgyt*, mandible

17. *ārt*, ramus of the mandible

18. *māk ha*, nape of neck, occipital region

19. *ths n nhbt*, vertebrae of the nape of the neck

20. *dhnt*, forehead

21. *hat hr*, forehead

22. *ihn*, eyebrow, ridges of brow

23. *baba n irt*, orbit of the eye

24. *wab n irt*, root of the eye

25. *shtyt nt fnd (sh t y t)*, sanctuary of the nose (the nose bones themselves)

26. *mndt*, cheek

27. *ibhw*, teeth

28. *nhdjt*, molars (?)

29. *ināt*, chin

In the Ebers Papyrus, yet another word, *maā*, is used several times. Written as Maāt, Justice, but with the sign for flesh and the head of a heron as determinatives, it seems to be related more particularly to the cortical centers under the temporal region. When it is a question of the buzzings produced *on* the *maā* that cause deafness, we can only be dealing with the cortex. When, on the other hand, in order to say "listen" the Ancient Egyptian says "give the *maā*," as we would say "lend an ear," he does not speak of the receiving organ of sound, but of the part of the brain that has the intelligence of sound perception. Finally, when the surgeon, in the case of injuries to the temporal region, takes particular note of the faculties of audition and elocution of his patient, he demonstrates the perfect awareness that the *maā* is the seat of the centers of association of audition and language. For this reason the temporal bone itself is always designated by another word.

12. The anatomical term specially employed to designate the temple and the temporal bone in the Smith Papyrus is *gma*, a word considered archaic. The scribe explains: "As for his *gma*, it is that which is located between the corner of his eye and the orifice [*gnyt*] of his ear, at the posterior extremity of his mandible."[18] According to this localization, the *gma* therefore contains the temporal shell, as well as the large wing of the sphenoid.

13. The term *khnw (n msdjr)*, literally "interior (of the ear)," designates the auditory passage of the inner ear. In the Smith Papyrus this term is used once with regard to the fragments of bone that the surgeon must extract after a fracture of the petrosal bone.[19]

14. The word *gnyt*, employed by the scribe in the gloss cited above as one of the points on the edge of the temple, is a new and unknown anatomical term not found in any other document. Only the commentary in question authorizes us to give it the meaning of "external auditory passage," as it is at the posterior extremity of the mandible.

15. Two interesting commentaries of the scribe describe the attachment of the mandible with the temporal bone in figurative language. In case 22 the surgeon is asked to put his finger on the posterior extremity of his *amāt* during the examination. The explanation of this new word, totally unknown outside of the Smith Papyrus, is as follows: "As for the posterior extremity of his *amāt*, it is the posterior extremity of his mandible [*amāt*], the extremity that is in his temple just as the talon of the *amā* bird seizes an object."[20]

The *amā* bird is not identified, but the image is vivid, and allows us to translate *amāt* as "sigmoid notch," and the posterior extremity of the *amāt* that penetrates into the temple as the "condyle" of the maxilla.

16. The mandible itself is designated by several terms. In one of the explanatory commentaries the scribe calls it *wgyt*. This word is found several times in the Smith Papyrus, and Breasted considers it more standard and less archaic than another term also designating the mandible and often used in the dual sense.

17. Here is Breasted:

A very rare and ancient word, *ārty* has a curious architectural and anatomical application, much like our words *buttocks* and *buttress*, both of which are covered by the single Egyptian word *ārty*. In an extended form it meant "one side," that is, the doorpost and half of the lintel, of a doorway.

Written . . . with the entire gateway as determinative it occurs in the Pyramid Texts (1740 b). Designating the whole gateway it was probably at first a dual, "two sides of the door." In this

[18] Cf. case 18, gloss B [Breasted, *Smith Papyrus*, p. 445].

[19] Cf. case 22, examination [ibid., p. 290].

[20] Cf. case 22, gloss A and Breasted, *Smith Papyrus*, commentary, p. 294 [and p. 448].

connection it passed over, perhaps in a derived form, to designate the council that sat in the city gate. Anatomically it appears already as early as the Pyramid Texts. . . . In our treatise it is employed twelve times to designate the mandible, and characteristically appears six times in the *dual*. This dual does not mean the upper and lower jaw; but refers to the *two sides* of the mandible. . . .[21]

In this correspondence noticed by Breasted, the Ancients' way of thinking symbolically appears in the parallel between the half and the whole of the mandible and the half and the whole of a doorway, which are designated by the same word and differentiated only by the determinative.

Let us keep in mind from now on that the blocks and sculptures of the wall separating rooms II and VI, which correspond to the jaw of the Man of the Temple, establish the relationship with the main entrance to the temple located between the two wings of the pylon.[22]

18. The occipital region corresponds to the term *mk ha* or *māk ha*. This word is employed in the Smith Papyrus to designate one of the points of the body where the physician places his hands and his fingers in the course of observing the rhythm of the heart; it is said that two vessels *(mtw)* converge there. It is often translated by "nape of the neck," but as another term is also applied to this region of the neck, it would be interesting to be able to make the distinction between them.

19. The nape of the neck proper, that is, the back part of the neck located between the occipital shell and the seventh cervical vertebra, is called *nhbt*. There is no possible doubt as to the meaning of this word. In cases of lesion of a cervical vertebra, the scribe specifies "a vertebra of the nape of the neck [*ths n nhbt*]." It appears by this expression that the Ancients distinguished, as we do, the seven cervical vertebrae from the thoracic vertebrae, the latter being called "vertebrae of the back."[23] Moreover, it is always the part of the neck called *nhbt* that is affected by rigidity in injuries that cause meningeal disease.[24]

20. The forehead is designated by several words. A very old word, *khnt* (already found in the mathematical papyrus, especially in the table of division by two: "*nis 2 khnt 3*," "call 2 in front of 3"[25]), signifies the anterior part of the head.[26]

Another term, *dhnt*, is employed in the Ebers Papyrus in the treatise on the heart, where it is said that two vessels converge there. Apparently, this word could instead designate the temporal crests, that is, the two sides of the forehead, although it does not appear to be written in the dual number; on the contrary, it is determined by the face in profile.

21. The word *hat*, or *hat hr*, "that which is in front" designates particularly the place of the uraeus on the forehead of the king. The same hieroglyphic group, derived from the arm, *hat.ā*, is used to designate the vizier, the nomarch, "he who is in front," but also the one who directs others, the one who holds all in his hands.

[21]Cf. Breasted, *Smith Papyrus,* case 7, commentary, pp. 187–88.

[22] Cf. plates 99 and 100 and commentaries.

[23] Cf. cases 29–33 concerning lesions of the cervical vertebrae, and case 48, lesion of a vertebra of the back.

[24] Cf. case 4, meningeal syndrome.

[25] Cf. chapter 6, "Table of Fractions with the Numerator 2," p. 171.

[26] The frontal bone, appearing only in adulthood, passes through curious transformations before the fourth month of life in the womb. This bone consists of six distinct pieces knitted together three by three. At birth the frontal bone is formed of two pieces separated by the mediofrontal or metopic suture. (The knitting of the suture begins only at about two years of age and is completed at around eight years of age.) There are cases, however, in which the metopic suture is definitively present in the *adult*. (This is found particularly among the Merovingians.) Cases also exist in which it is present, but incompletely so. There is, therefore, in the use of the word *khnt* for the forehead and for division, an intent to relate the original division of the frontal bone to "that which is in front of."

The use of this word *hat* to denote the part of the skull protected by the uraeus suggests the relationship of this region with our faculty of discernment, and therefore with our sense of judgment.[27]

22. The word *ihn*, the eyebrows, designates the bony region of the eyebrow ridge, and according to its use in the Smith Papyrus, it also applies to an injury in the "head of the eyebrows," penetrating as far as the bone.[28] This wound is not serious and can be repaired by several stitches, but a fracture that penetrates the frontal sinus is always a genuine cause for alarm. This danger was well known to the Ancients, as we will have occasion to see later on.

23. The orbital cavity is called *baba n irt,* "cavity of the eye" (generally written in the dual). The word *baba,* known from the Pyramid Texts, denotes a cavity or a hole punctured in the earth. It is employed in the ritual of the founding of a temple when the king, pickax in hand, breaks the ground to lay out the first furrow delimiting the boundaries of the temple.

24. Another term that is considered to be related to the orbs is *wab n irt,* literally, "root of the eye" (the root that branches out). We note that *wab,* "root," is determined by a plant and not by a small circle as is *baba.* We meet *wab n irt* in the following passage of the Ebers Papyrus (854e): "As for what deafens the ears, there are two *mtw* leading to the root of the eye that produce this."[29]

What are these two *mtw* and why do they cause deafness? Knowing that *mtw* can refer to any sort of channel or passage, such as those of blood or nerves, one of these could be an allusion to the optic nerve. Now it is known that in its intracranial passage, the optic nerve passes through the ganglionic optic center, the anterior quadrigeminal body. From their side, the auditory fibers go to the inferior quadrigeminal body. These two important centers are in intimate contact and are actually linked together so that afflictions to one can react upon the other.[30] It is therefore true that certain *mtw* leading to the "root of the eye" are profoundly related with those that lead to the ear.

"Root of the eye" cannot signify the orbital cavity, but truly has the sense of "root," which is specified by the small plant that determines it. Now the root brings nourishment to the plant. It is therefore certain that the text, in speaking of *root,* refers to nerve and blood channels.[31] If the channel leading to the eye is afflicted, there can very well be repercussions on hearing, as the ancient text states. This also proves, by the way, that the authors of these old papyri knew the internal anatomy of the skull very well.

[27] Cf. case 9.

[28] Cf. case 10.

[29] Cf. Lefebvre, *Médecine égyptienne,* p. 32.

[30] "The ganglionic optic center, consisting of the anterior quadrigeminal body, is related to the ganglionic centers of the motor nerves of the eye and of the iris, and also with the acoustic core, by unifying fibers. The anterior quadrigeminal body thus becomes the ganglionic center of the optical passage and of the passage of the auditory reflex. It is thanks to this center that the iris is able to contract without the intervention of the will, in cases where a too intense light impresses itself on the retina. . . . It is also because of this same center that when a noise strikes the ear, our eyes are directed toward the point in space from which this noise emanated. . . . According to Collet, in half the cases tumors of the quadrigeminal bodies are associated with auditory troubles. But then the inferior quadrigeminal body is always affected. In these cases, deafness is ordinarily bilateral and accompanied by ophthalmoplegia and ataxia. . . ." Testut and Jacob, *Traité d'anatomie,* 1:482. ("Ataxia": inability to coordinate movements.) Cf. J. Déjérine, *Sémiologie des affections du système nerveux* (Paris: Masson, 1926), p. 1120.

"The relations of the vestibular apparatus of the ear with the oculogyral nodes on the one hand, and the cephalogyral nodes on the other, explain the deviations of the ocular globes in nystagmus, as well as the positions of the head and neck in lesions of the vestibular apparatus. . . . Nystagmus can also be determined by auricular lesions, whether of the eardrum or of the labyrinth. Frequently, nystagmus gives way to mechanical irritations bearing on the deep parts of the ear." Déjérine, *Sémiologie des affections,* pp. 431, 1153. See also, ibid., "Les voies oculogyres et leurs relations avec les voies auditives," p. 428.

[31] There is a specific detail about the optic nerve to remember here. Approximately a centimeter before its entry into the posterior side of the eye, the optic nerve contains the nourishing artery of the retina, a branch of the internal carotid artery. This nourishing artery continues into the nerve itself.

25. The nose bone proper, *shtyt nt fnd,* literally "chamber of the nose" or better yet, "sanctuary of the nose," must be understood not only as the bones in question but also as the "sanctuary" that they protect and that determines this word. This part of the nose has an immense importance because it communicates with all the sinuses of the adjacent bones, and consequently with the base of the cranium.[32]

26. The area of the malar bone, of the zygomatic arch, and of the maxilla are all together called *mndt,* cheek. It is a curious word (most often written in the dual number) because it designates the breast as well, which determines it, and probably the lower eyelid.[33] Cases 15, 16, and 17 of the Smith Papyrus are concerned with this part of the face. The study of case 17 demonstrates the knowledge of serious repercussions that a blow to the maxilla can have: a fracture with a depression *(sd)* can cause a hemorrhage of the nostril and of the ear "that are on the same side as this fracture." More-over, the injured person suffers a contraction of the jaw (trismus), and a certain crepitation perceived on examination of the injury by touch determines a fatal diagnosis. If we are aware that a depression of the maxillary sinus (the antrum of Highmore) can cause an indirect fracture at the base of the skull, and be transmitted as well to the cribriform plate of the ethmoid,[34] we understand the seri-ousness of the case better. The maxillary sinus emerges in the "sanctuary of the nose," which explains the nasal hemorrhage. Finally, the crepitation noted by the ancient surgeons is an important clinical sign.

27–28. The teeth have many names. We will retain here only *ibhw,* which seems fairly general, and *nhdjt,* which is used in case 7 of the Smith Papyrus with regard to a contraction of the back and of the teeth caused by an injury to the skull. We can compare this word to the word for the tusks of an elephant according to Lefebvre, who suggests that it refers more particularly to the molars.[35]

29. Finally the chin, *inā* or *ināt,* designates, as always, not only the fleshy part of the face but also the bony region underlying it. This word is found in case 22 of the Smith Papyrus in which the surgeon is asked to place his thumb on the "chin" and a finger on the condyle in order to cause the fragments of bone caused by a fracture of the petrosal bone to come out. This gesture is inter-esting to note because it recalls the fact that a violent shock on the chin can transmit the trauma to the base of the skull, specifically, through the maxillary condyle.[36]

THE INTERIOR OF THE THROAT AND HEAD

There is a large number of terms relating to the throat, but their exact meaning has not yet been clar-ified.[37] In the Smith Papyrus some of them are used with regard to a case of dislocation of the clav-icles. "If thou examinest a man having a dislocation in his two collar-bones, shouldst thou find his two shoulders turned over, (and) the head(s) of his two collar-bones turned toward his face, . . ."[38] the surgeon first prescribes the reduction of the dislocated bones to their sockets, together with the proper adjustment of pads and bandages in order to hold them in place, and soothing applications.[39]

---

[32] Cf. below, fig. 168, no. 43, and commentaries.

[33] Cf. Lefebvre, *Parties du corps humain,* p. 17.

[34] Cf. D. Petit-Dutaillis and G. Guiot, "Fractures du crâne," *Encyclopédie médico-chirurgicale,* 15954, p. 3.

[35] Lefebvre, *Parties du corps humain,* p. 20.

[36] It is worth noting that Petit-Dutaillis and Guiot ("Fractures du crâne") only mention three possibilities for *indirect* fractures of the base of the skull: either from a blow to the chin or the maxilla, or from a vertical fall on the ischia.

[37] For references to words cited in this section, cf. Lefebvre, *Parties du corps humain.*

[38] Breasted, *Smith Papyrus,* case 34, p. 343.

[39] Ibid., p. 342.

The oddity of this case is that two apparently successive examinations are presented that in fact are two cases of different dislocations: "In this case we have two examinations, the first of which discloses only a dislocation without other injury; the second an injury of the overlying soft tissue, an injury which penetrates to the interior. . . . [The] first examination of Case 34, is discussed by itself as a complete case. . . ." [Here Breasted quotes Dr. Luckhardt:] "In the second case it is plain that the surgeon is discussing a backward dislocation [of the clavicle]. . . . In a so-called backward dislocation of the collar-bone the head of the bone lies behind the upper end of the sternum. This head presses on the trachea, esophagus, and larger vessels of the neck, causing difficulty in breathing and swallowing. Because of such pressure a semicomatose condition may supervene. In modern surgery the head of the bone is excised if ordinary methods of reduction fail."[40]

The gloss that follows this case would be of great interest if each word, rather than being translated generally as "throat," "gullet," "bosom," were given its precise meaning: "As for: 'a dislocation of his two clavicles [*bbwy*],' this means a displacement of his sickle-shaped bones. Their heads, attached [normally] to the superior bone of his sternum, extend toward his *htt* above which is the 'body' of his *bbyt*. It is the body that is above his *shashat*, two *mtw* are below it, one on the right, one on the left of his *htt* and of his *shashat*. They do not distribute to the lung."*

31. Here the clavicles are called *bbwy* (fig. 168), a new word that Breasted reconnects to another term, also very rare, *bb*, determined by a necklace similar to what covers part of the shoulders and the upper part of the thorax of the figures in the bas-reliefs. The scribe explains *bbwy* by "sickle bones" or "sickle-shaped bones," which is a very striking expression of the double S-formed curve of the clavicles. He also describes their attachment to the upper part of the sternum, that is, to the manubrium. Other cases in the papyrus demonstrate that each bone of the scapular belt has a suitable word: the bones in the shape of a razor for the shoulder blades; the upper sides, which are formally distinguished from the others; and so forth.

32. The word *bbyt* can be compared to the two preceding terms designating the necklace and the collar bones. On the other hand, *bbt* has the general sense of "cavern," "deep," "circular," "what encircles," "a collar or necklace," which leads us to see *bbyt* as what is called the "supraclavicular region" comprising the "supraclavicular chamber," protected by the large *usekh* necklace.

33. *Shashat* is also related to a necklace formed from a single row of pearls between which the *wedjat* eye is sometimes put, or else a scarab, forming amulets. These objects play a protective role for the organs they symbolize.[41]

34. In the expression "the body of his *bbyt*" it is possible to recognize the thyroid body.[42]

35. Another name for the throat is *khām*, including the anterior part of the neck as it is used in case 28, wherein still another, badly defined word, *shbb*, is found.

36. *Shbb* corresponds to the intersection of the trachea and the esophagus; we can then agree with Breasted's "windpipe." But the hieroglyph that determines this word (the head of an animal with a very long neck) shows that *shbb* can also signify the esophagus. This text can thus be understood: "A man with a gaping wound in his throat [*khām*] piercing his windpipe [*shbb*], if he drinks water he will choke; it goes out through the opening of the wound, which is very enflamed. He develops fever on account of this. . . ."

---

[40] Ibid.

[41] Oculocardiac reflex: modifications produced on the circulatory apparatus by the compression of the ocular globes. Cf. chapter 11, fig. 137.

[42] According to Ebbell; cf. Lefebvre, *Parties du corps humain*, p. 23.

*Cf. Breasted, *Smith Papyrus*, case 34, gloss A, p. 455.

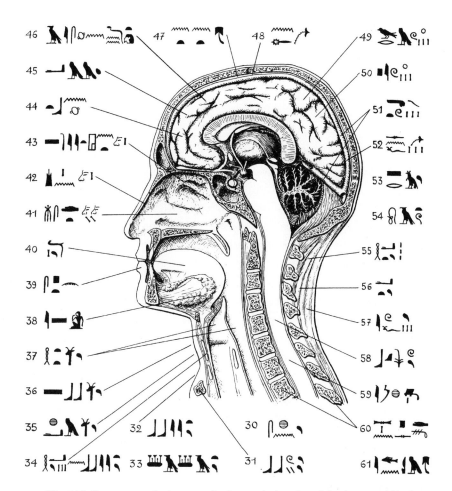

Fig. 168. Some anatomical terms referring to the interior of the throat and head

30. *skhn (s kh n)*, thymus
31. *bbwy*, clavicles
32. *bbyt*, supraclavicular region
33. *shashat (sh a t)*, larynx
34. *hāw n bbyt*, thyroid body
35. *khām*, throat
36. *shbb*, windpipe, esophagus (?)
37. *htt*, pharynx, trachea
38. *ish*, saliva
39. *spt*, lip
40. *ns*, tongue
41. *msdty*, nasal fossae
42. *iwn n fnd*, cartilage of the nose
43. *shtyt nt fnd*, the nose bones them-
    selves and the superior concha[1]
44. *tbn*, brain, crown of skull with
    the convolutions of the brain
45. *āmm*, brain

46. *aïs n djnnt*, cerebrospinal organs
47. *ntnt*, meninges
48. *nkh*, cerebrospinal fluid
49. *wrmw*, folds, convolutions of the brain
50. *piw*, wrinkles, convolutions of the brain
51. *mtw*, channels; longitudinal and
    lateral sinus
52. *snf*, blood
53. *shrtyw (sh r tyw)*, blood plexus
54. *wat*, muscle (masseter and temporal)
55. *hāwt*, body
56. *āt*, muscle, part, member
57. *iwf*, flesh
58. *bksw*, spinal cord
59. *imakh*, spinal cord
60. *ts n psd*, dorsal vertebrae
61. *inm*, skin

[1] See fig. 167, no. 25, which specifies that this term *shtyt* relates to both the nose bones themselves and to the "chamber" that they encircle.

37. On the other hand, *htt* is often related to respiration. Now *htt* is also determined by a head extended on a long neck, which in this case is related to the respiratory canal, the trachea.

With regard to the word *shashat*, which signifies the throat and also a necklace composed of several pearls (see above, no. 33), it could conceivably be translated as "larynx" because the larynx consists of five cartilages of a strange form, which can be compared to two rings with their setting (the cartilage), to a shield (the thyroid), and to two ewers (the arytenoids).[43]

If, finally, the "body of the *bbyt*" signifies the thyroid, we can now clarify the gloss on case 34 in the following way: ". . . the 'body,' which is above the supraclavicular region, is the body that is on his larynx. Two channels [*mtw*] are under it, one on the right, and one on the left of the trachea and of his larynx."

The lone examples of the *mtw* mentioned correspond then to the two "neurovascular bundles of the neck" containing the carotid artery, the jugular vein, and the pneumogastric (vagus) nerve united in a single casing, which must be opened to reach any one of them. The mention of these two *mtw* precisely in this place on the neck denotes true awareness of an anatomical curiosity.[44]

38. The lists contain a term that is applied to the buccal cavity. There is also a general term designating the saliva and signifying the "secretion of the mouth."[45] However, it is another word, *ish*, that is used in the Smith Papyrus in the course of the examination in case 7. "His saliva [*ish*] does not fall to the ground," and consequently indicates the spittle.

Ish is an ancient word encountered in the Pyramid Texts, and which Breasted connects with *ishsh*, "to spit," *ishw*, "to salivate," "to secrete." It is important to retain its meaning because it is with the root *ish* that the medical term *ishw* is formed. It refers to a swelling, tumor, or puffiness following an injury of the skull, and it is therefore necessary to include the sense of exudation, or oozing, whether of water or of blood, or even of "weeping."[46]

39. *Spt*, lip, is often written in the dual, *spty*, "the two lips." Also, "upper lip" and "lower lip" are distinguished. The connection of this word with the idea of enumeration has already been made with regard to pharaonic mathematics.[47]

40. The tongue is called *ns*.

41. Several terms exist designating the end of the nose, the flaps of the nose, the nostrils, and so forth. The nasal fossae are called *msdty* in the Ebers Papyrus, and the Smith Papyrus allows us to specify this term as referring to the inferior and middle conchae, according to the commentary on case 11, which locates them on the same level as the cartilage of the nose.

42. The cartilages of the nose are denoted by *iwn n fnd*, or "column of the nose." Case 11 discusses an injury in the "column of the nose," which disfigures the patient and causes a nasal hemorrhage. Gloss A locates this column as follows: "As for: 'the column of his nose,' it is the protruding part of his nose, up to its side, on top of the nose, and the inside of his nasal fossae [*msdty*]." Gloss B completes the information: "As for: 'his two nasal fossae [*msdty fy*]' [this means] the two sides of his nose, extending from his cheeks to the posterior extremity of his nose. The top of his nose is loosened."

---

[43] Cf. A. Erman and H. Grapow, *Wörterbuch der ägyptischen Sprache* (Berlin: Akademie-Verlag, 1926–55): *shashat* means throat (larynx), throat at the level of the Adam's apple, in "cut the enemy's throat." It relates to the necklace of the same name, of gold, of lapis lazuli, or of clay determined by a single row of pearls.

[44] To see the importance of this "neurovascular bundle" of the neck in detail, cf. Testut and Jacob, *Traité d'anatomie*, 1:746 et sqq. Animal sacrifice is made through bloodletting after cutting the throat and therefore evidently shows the section of this "bundle" or *mtw*, the *mtw* designating any channel, whether blood, nerve, etc. (see no. 51).

[45] Cf. Lefebvre, *Parties du corps humain*, p. 19.

[46] Cf. Breasted, *Smith Papyrus*, case 4, pp. 144–45.

[47] Cf. chapter 6, "Fractions."

Although initially a bit obscure, these commentaries leave no doubt as to the designation of the two words.

43. Case 12 gives "Instructions concerning an injury in the sanctuary of his nose [*shtyt nt fnd*]." The patient has a bent nose, a disfigured face, and considerable swelling. Gloss A of this case allows us to locate this very particular expression, *shtyt*, which is normally translated as "the nose bones themselves": "As for: 'a break in the sanctuary of his nose,' this means that which is in the heart of his nose up to the back part[48] extending between his two eyebrows."

According to this same commentary, which includes the posterior part contained between the two eyebrows, it is most certainly a question of the area protected by the nose bones themselves, that is, the third and fourth conchae. Now the use of *shtyt* to designate the nose bones proper and the area they protect gives Breasted the opportunity to make an interesting comment:

> Throughout the literature of ancient Egypt, *shtyt* is a religious word, and its appearance in our case is certainly its only medical or surgical use, if not its sole occurrence in a secular document. It is commonly employed to designate any sacred chamber. Hence we find it applied to the tomb . . . or even to the world of the dead, as in the Book of the Gates; but it was especially a general term for any sacred room, chamber, or building. Thus the room for the mourning women at Dendera and at Edfu is called *shtyt*. Likewise the crypts in the temple of Dendera are so called, and similarly an outlying chapel of the temple of Ombos. It is incessantly applied to the dwellings of the gods, especially to that of Sokar, or of the mortuary gods like Osiris and Anubis, but also of Ptah.[49]

According to the spelling established in the Nineteenth and Twentieth Dynasties, Breasted relates this word to a homonym that means "to be secret," "inaccessible." "Our surgeon writes the word in every case with the determinative of a house, and must be comparing the upper bony portion of the nose with a building, just as he designated the rest of it as a 'column.' . . . The less accessible portion of the external nose, the remotest from the entrance to the nares, suggests to the surgeon the barred and less accessible chamber of a sanctuary or temple. The term 'chamber' at once raises the question whether the surgeon was not thinking of the frontal sinus, especially in view of the extension of the *shtyt* to 'the region between his eyebrows.' "[50]

Actually, the very particular character of "inaccessible," "secret," "sacred," given to this part of the nose suggests that we investigate the reason. The frontal sinus, a hollow in the thick part of the frontal shell "between the two eyebrows," opens at the level of the superior concha of the nose. On the other hand, the maxillary sinus, the sphenoidal sinuses, and the ethmoidal cells also open into this "sanctuary" that is consequently in contact with the base of the skull itself and, because of this fact, is an extremely important and dangerous intersection. The structure of the nasal vault and its relations with the base of the skull are indeed very complex, as one is able to judge by a single modern description.

> The anterior portion of the nasal vault . . . corresponds to the nasal bones proper. . . . They hide the most narrow and dangerous part of the nasal fossae from the surgeon; also, their resection is legitimately considered as the "key" to all open operations carried out on the raised part of the nasal fossae. . . .
>
> At the level of the cribriform plate the nasal cavity is only separated from the cranial cavity by a slender bony wall, all the more fragile as it is pierced by numerous holes to allow the olfactory

[48] Literally, "posterior portion."
[49] Breasted, *Smith Papyrus*, p. 248.
[50] Ibid.

threads to pass. . . . The cribriform plate is easily broken in trauma of the anterior part of the skull. From there comes the profuse epistaxis and the discharge of cerebrospinal fluid through the nose, which is observed in fractures of the anterior portion of the skull. These are serious fractures, if we imagine that they are opened into a milieu so rich in microbes as are the nasal fossae.[51]

Without going into all the details of the connections of the different sinuses with the nasal vault, and the consequences that can arise from an injury to one or the other of them, it is enough to remember that the sphenoidal sinus, for example, is under the sella turcica where the pituitary body is lodged; its stalk descends into the middle ventricle.

The great importance that the Ancients give to the internal regions of the nose relates to the secret tradition concerning what the pharaonic sages called the "sanctuary," the sixth Hindu *cakra* referred to as the *ājñā cakra* or cavernous plexus.

It is this complex relation between certain vibrations of the inner ear—produced particularly by intoning the letter *m* (in Au*m*, Muha*mm*ad)—with the sympathetic and the vagus that helps to produce the states sought for in mantras and in the Muslim *zhikr*.

What did the Ancients know of the interior of the head? It has often been alleged that they could have known nothing of the constitution of the brain because from the time of making mummies, the brain was extracted through the nostrils. This fact demonstrates that mummification did not give them the occasion to make an anatomical diagram of the brain. On the contrary, the choice of the nostrils for drawing out the brain demonstrates a complete knowledge of the constitution of the skull. This is indeed the *only path for accessing the brain* through a natural opening (the nostrils). By this route one passes through the "sanctuary" and fractures the cribriform plate, thin and fragile as we have just seen. As soon as that is broken, the embalmer can gain access to the organs of the head, which have several names:

44. *Tbn*, which means "superior and rounded part of the head," "which covers," and also "circuit," "convolutions," which corresponds exactly to the crown of the skull containing the two cerebral hemispheres. The word *tbn* is found in an incantation for coryza (head cold), ". . . which breaks the bones, which shatters the skull, which plagues the brain [*tbn*], which makes the seven orifices of the head sick."[52] This is incontestably a matter of sinusitis, whose repercussions across the "sanctuary" of the nose toward the brain (*tbn*) and the different parts of the face are evoked here.

45. The word *āmm* is another name for the brain. It is used with regard to certain animals (fish, birds, and reptiles, and so on), but also for the human brain;[53] *āmm* relates above all to the cerebral function, whereas *aïs* signifies the cerebral viscera.[54]

46. Finally, case 6 of the Smith Papyrus, as Breasted said, is of extraordinary interest because it contains the first known description of the brain, going back at least to the time of the Pyramids. It is concerned with "a man who has a gaping wound in the head, penetrating to the bone, fracturing [*sd*] his skull, denuding [or tearing open] the viscera [*aïs*] of his skull." The word *aïs* designates the whole group of cerebral and spinal organs contained in the skull. The examination proceeds as follows: ". . . you palpate his wound; if you find that fracture which is in his skull like those corrugations that form on molten copper, and something there that throbs and flutters under your fingers like the weak place on an infant's crown before it becomes knit together . . ."

---

[51] Cf. Testut and Jacob, *Traité d'anatomie*, 1:506.

[52] Cf. Lefebvre, *Médecine égyptienne*, p. 54; *Parties du corps humain*, p. 13; Ebers Papyrus 90.16–18.

[53] Cf. Lefebvre, *Parties du corps humain*, p. 13.

[54] Cf. I. Schwaller de Lubicz, *Her-Bak, Egyptian Initiate*, p. 106.

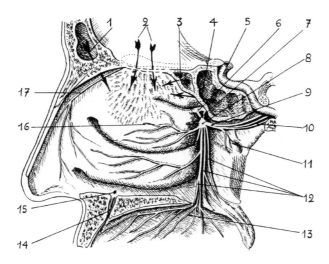

Fig. 169. External wall of the nasal fossae

1. Frontal sinus
2. Passage of the olfactory neurons
3. Ethmoidal cell
4. Sphenoidal sinus (the arrows indicate communication between the nasal vault and the sinus, 1, 3, 4, and the brain, 2, through the cribriform plate)
5. Internal carotid to its exit from the cavernous plexus
6. Maxillary nerve, upper, second branch of the trigeminal nerve
7. Nasopalatine nerve, rejoined by the internal surface of the nasal fossae, the nasopalatine canal, 14
8. Meckel's ganglion receives a sensory branch of the upper maxillary, 6, of the parasympathetic fibers that come through the vidian nerve, 9, and of the sympathetic fibers coming from the internal carotid through a branch of the vidian nerve, 10
11. Eustachian tube and its innervation
12. The three branches of the palatine nerve
13. The soft palate and its innervation
14. Nasopalatine canal where the nerve of the same name passes, 7
15. Location of Jacobson's organ.
16. Sensory branches of the nasal fossae accompanied by sympathetic and parasympathetic threads that come from Meckel's ganglion
17. Ethmoidal thread

The *sd* fracture corresponds to a depression of the vault, and the surgeon judges his patient's condition to be fatal. Therefore, it is a question here, not of a treatment, but of a study for its own sake, that is, it is a case of purely scientific interest. In the course of a gloss the scribe explains the first phrase of the statement of the case. "As for: 'fracturing his skull, tearing open the viscera of his skull,' [this means] the fracture is large, opening toward the interior of the skull. The membrane [*ntnt*] enveloping his brain [is] fractured [and] spills its fluid into the interior of the head."

47. The pharaonic word *ntnt*, "membrane," formed by the duplication of the same syllable, evokes the dual appearance of the meningeal group; however, its determinative, skin (or hide), can only designate the dura mater, which owes its name to its lack of elasticity, and consequently, can detach or break even though the bone structure of the skull remains intact (see case 8).

If *ntnt* "contains" the cerebrospinal fluid, however, then it alludes also to the soft meninges that contains the liquid, and *ntnt* would signify the two meninges that indeed envelop the whole group of cephalic organs. Now, although the meninges may be three in number, they present themselves in fact as two thin sheets, the meninges dura, or dura mater, lining the interior of the skull, and the soft meninges, whose fiber is suffused with the cerebrospinal fluid.[55]

48. The continuation of this gloss specifies that when this "membrane" is broken, the liquid *nkh* (cerebrospinal fluid) escapes and spills into the interior of the skull. The allusion is sufficiently clear to understand that this liquid is normally contained by this double membrane before it breaks. This word *nkh*, outside of its use in the Surgical Papyrus, is only encountered in the Pyramid Texts where it has the sense of "secretion,"[56] which confirms its determinative, the spitting mouth.

49. Gloss B of case 6, which attempts to explain the appearance of an exposed brain, uses some expressions that are very unusual to us:

> As for: "those corrugations [wrmw] *that form on molten copper,*" this is copper that the coppersmith rejects before forcing into the mold because of something foreign upon it, like wrinkles [piw]. *It says, "It is like ripples of pus."*[57]

According to Breasted, the word *wrmw*, translated as "corrugations," relates to the convolutions of the brain. This word is used in architecture to signify the crenels on the top of a wall, or again to designate the ribs of a tent, which produce an undulation along the length of its roof.

50. To explain *wrmw*, the scribe uses another word, *piw*, translated here by "wrinkles," although it is totally unknown outside of this text.

51. The word *mtw* plays an important role in ancient papyri, denoting equally all vessels, whether they be blood, nerve, or even ligaments. If instead of translating *mtw* by "vessels," we say "channels," then it would signify not only the channels of blood, lymph, and nerves but also the "energetic" channels in the sense of the "meridians" of Chinese acupuncture and the flows such as *iḍā* and *piṇgalā* around the vertebral column, as well as the mysterious and dangerous *kuṇḍalinī*, of the Hindu teaching.[58]

52. Certain *mtw* conduct blood, *snf*, such as, for example, the important longitudinal sinus veins that traverse the endocranial surface from front to back (fig. 168), which was certainly known to the Ancients; this will be easy to establish through study of the Smith Papyrus.

53. In addition to the word *mtw* in the Ebers Papyrus, we meet a particular term, *shrtyw* (or also *shtyw*), denoting a blood plexus in a very ancient text dating back to the First Dynasty.[59] This word signifies a sort of node that can denote a plexus, whether of blood or nerves.

54. The Smith Papyrus also gives us the opportunity to make the acquaintance of a term, *wat*, that refers to the temporal and masseter muscles attaching the rami of the mandibles to the temporal bones. Gloss B of case 7 figuratively describes this attachment with regard to lockjaw after a serious injury to the skull.[60] Gloss C explains in turn the word *wat*, but the difficulty of translating it gives rise to this reflection by Breasted: "The entire gloss is an illustration of how limited our

---

[55] Cf. Testut and Jacob, *Traité d'anatomie,* 1:86.

[56] Cf. Kurt Sethe, *Die altägyptischen Pyramidentexte* (Leipzig: Hinrich, 1908–22), 1961–65.

[57] Cf. Breasted, *Smith Papyrus,* p. 435; cf. pp. 167–73.

[58] The most recent histological studies have demonstrated that the walls of the viscera and the vessels contain cells and fibers of diverse natures, sympathetic and parasympathetic, sensory and autonomic. The arteries, for example, are externally surrounded by a superficial trellis of nerve fibers and are internally lined with a very dense nerve plexus. This arrangement demonstrates the existence of a vegetative system belonging to each vessel. Cf. G. Tardieu and C. Tardieu, *Le Système nerveux végétatif* (Paris: Masson, 1948), chap. 8, "Etude histologique du système nerveux contenu dans les parois des viscères et des vaisseaux."

[59] Ebers Papyrus, 856a, c, d.

[60] Cf. below, clinical study of case 7.

knowledge of Egyptian is, whenever we are called upon to deal with highly specialized terms; and even when the ancient commentator has furnished us with a definition we are often unable to understand the terms he uses in explanation."[61]

Thus it is with regret that Breasted gives the following translation: "As for: 'the cord {wat} of his mandible,' it means the ligaments {mtw} which bind the end of his jaw, as one says, 'the cord' of a thing in (or as) a splint."

The word translated here as "splint" is the homonym of the word that designates a certain apparatus prepared by the surgeon himself and applied externally to hold the pieces of a broken bone together after the reduction of a fracture (cases 35, 36, 37). Splints have been found dating from the Old Kingdom, one of wood, another of bark wrapped in linen, but since the surgeon of the papyrus speaks of a splint of linen, Breasted wonders if it is not a plaster splint.[62]

Whatever it may be, the comparison of the masseter with a splint is close enough, and if we add that these splints are always used in pairs, the allusion to the two essential muscles that cause the movement of the mandible is sufficiently clear.

On the other hand, the word *wat*, translated as "cord," is an archaic word encountered only in the Pyramid Texts. Extremely rare, Breasted relates it to the word *wawat*, "cord," which occurs only in the foundation ceremonies of the temple during the operation called "stretching the cord."[63]

The hieroglyphic symbol of *wa* is a cord that, although knotted, can be unwound, which in the case of *wat* would explain the ligaments that allow stretching or extension, but limit this extension by their "ligature." Its essential significance is "harnessing," "holding together," "binding."

55. The word *hāw, hāwt,* is used by the Ancients for the human body as a whole and, in general, a totality of a similar kind. Thus, *hāw* can be taken in the same sense as in our language: the Ancients speak of the "body of a fleet" as we say "the army corps," or of "the body of an edifice" as we say "the wing of a building." *Hāw* can then relate to an essential part, as we would say "the principal body," referring to a particular thing. For example, modern medical language uses this term to distinguish the body of a vertebra from its apophyses.

In the Surgical Papyrus, *hāw* denotes the entire body in the two phrases, "his body released from fever," and "that which his body breeds," with regard to a tumor or an endocrinal hematoma following a skull injury. It names a certain definite part, as the "thyroid body" (fig. 168, no. 34), or "the body of the ear," comprising the meatus and the auricle of the external ear. Finally, its use with regard to the scalp, or further concerning "an enormous injury to the shoulder that plowed the *hāw*" has caused *hāw* to be translated as "flesh" in numerous cases as, for example, in the gloss on case 31 relative to a dislocation of a cervical vertebra (see later on). We are dealing here then not with the flesh alone, but with the whole complex of muscles, ligaments, vessels, and so on, that is, with tissues.

In its exact meaning, *hāw* signifies an organic body or a part of the body with a vital, functional role (either an organic function, such as the body of the ear, and so forth, or a vital function, such as flesh animated by blood).

56. In a general way, *āt* designates a limb of the human body, and *āwt* the limbs. In the Surgical Papyrus, however, when the issue concerns the four limbs, it is specified as "the two arms and the

[61] Breasted, *Smith Papyrus*, pp. 189–91.

[62] Cf. ibid., p. 190. Cf. Hippocrates, "In the Surgery," particularly the description of compresses, bandages, leading strings, and splints used in fractures; precautions taken at the time of application of a splint; splint cradles, positions and postures given to the patient. *Hippocrates*, trans. E. T. Withington (New York: Putnam's, 1927) 3:59–81.

[63] Cf. Breasted, *Smith Papyrus*, pp. 188–89.

two legs." On the other hand, *āt* denotes any limb or part of the body that is given vitality by the *mtw*. In its exact sense, *āt* means a part of the body with the capacity for voluntary mobility (members and muscles). Thus, in several cases, the dual *āty* seems to relate to certain active parts of the body, such as the muscles or ligaments[64] as, for example, in the gloss on case 30 that explains what a wrench or a sprain is: "As for: 'a sprain [*nrwt*],' he is speaking of a tearing of two muscles [or ligaments, *āty*] although each remained in its place."[65]

"The sprain . . . is defined by the essentially ligamental character of the injuries: ruptures, elongations, and distentions without the surface articulations presenting anywhere a noticeable modification of their normal relationships."[66]

The scribe's gloss summarizes the character of the sprain through the essential words "tearing without displacement," and distinguishes it from another dislocation, the subject of the following case (31), where we will have the occasion to learn the word for spinal marrow, *bksw*.

57. The flesh, in the strict sense of the term, is designated by a specific word, *iwf*, when it refers to human flesh, and above all to animal meat.

58. The word *bksw* would be better translated as "spinal cord." The spinal marrow is indeed made up of several cords of white nervous fiber, conductors, surrounding the central gray matter.

Case 31

> *If you examine a man having a dislocation* [wnkh] *of a vertebra of his neck, should you find him unconscious of his two arms [and] his two legs on account of this, his penis in an erection on account of this, urine falls from his phallus without his being conscious of it, his flesh* [iwf] *received the air, his two eyes are* shsm ty.[67] *It is a dislocation of a vertebra of his neck extending to his spinal cord* [bksw] *which causes him to be unconscious of his two arms [and] his two legs. If it is the vertebra of the middle of his neck that is dislocated, it is a* mn sa [spermatorrhea] *which befalls his phallus.*
>
> *Then you should say concerning him: "One having a dislocation in a vertebra of his neck, he is unconscious of his two legs and his two arms, he [has] an incontinence of urine. An ailment that cannot be treated."*

Dr. Luckhardt assumes that the case presented by the ancient surgeon must be below the fourth cervical vertebra since the patient is still breathing. In cases of traumatic injuries of the lower five cervical vertebrae, it is presently noted that "the neurological signs can assume the well-known appearance of full quadriplegia. Schematically, this paralysis expresses the pattern of the inferior cervical marrow syndrome, which characterizes the absence of bulbar signs and extends to the four limbs. The prognosis of this quadriplegia is very serious. Its typical progression is toward death in a few days in a hyperthermic syndrome."[68]

---

[64] In the Ebers Papyrus, 51, 20, for example, *āty* designates two neck muscles.

[65] Lefebvre, *Médecine égyptienne*, p. 187, proposes the literal translation: "In what concerns *nerout*, he [the author] speaks of the tear produced between two members, whereas [however] each remains in place." For "he is speaking," see explanation, case 3.

[66] Cf. Y. J. Longuet, "Lésions traumatiques fermées du rachis cervical," in *Encyclopédie médico-chirurgicale*, 15825, p. 1.

[67] See the discussion of this word in case 20, p. 419.

[68] Cf. Y. J. Longuet, "Lésions et fractures des cinq dernières vertèbres cervicales," in *Encyclopédie médico-chirurgicale*, 15826, p. 3.

In case 31, the surgeon does not prescribe any treatment, but the scribe explains some of the details of the examination in three glosses:

> Gloss A. *As for: "a dislocation* [wnkh] *in a vertebra of his neck," he is speaking of a separation of one vertebra from another; the "body"* [hāw][69] *that is above is intact. It is as when one speaks of a dislocation* [wnkh] *concerning things that had been united and of which one has been disjoined from the other.*

The description corresponds to what we today call a complete dislocation (see fig. 170).

> Gloss B. *As for: "it is a* mn sa *[spermatorrhea] which befalls his phallus," [this means] his phallus has an erection, and there is a seminal emission from the extremity of his phallus. He is saying, "it remains stationary, it cannot fall downward, it cannot lift upward."*

This clinical detail concerning injuries of the marrow, particularly at the level of the fourth cervical vertebra, is very interesting and demonstrates an extensive knowledge of the connections among the principal vital centers.[70]

> Gloss C. *As for: "incontinence of urine," this means that the urine dribbles from his phallus [continually] without his being able to retain it."*[71]

Here is a modern account:

> *Permanent flaccid paraplegia* always results from a complete break in the cord, and is hardly ever observed except in cases of the marrow being crushed following a fracture, a dislocation of the vertebral column, or excessive compression. It is characterized by a total and absolute loss of the movements of the lower limbs, by the removal of muscular tone, and by the paralysis of the rectum and the bladder.
>
> Even though every trace of mobility may disappear, the muscles and nerves still hold all their electric, galvanic, and faradic excitability for a more or less long period of time.
>
> The limb thus seized gives the impression of an organ without life. . . . The urine flows continually. . . . The skin of the lower members is altered; it thickens and infiltrates. . . .[72]

By comparison, the ancient surgeon's expression designating quadriplegia is literally, "He ignores his two arms, his two legs." The literal translation of the commentary concerning the incontinence of urine, "the urine dribbles . . . continually" is parallel to Déjérine's description. Finally, the expression "his flesh [*iwf*] received the air" seems to express the infiltration and thickening of the flesh noted by Déjérine.

---

[69] Breasted translates this as "the flesh [*hāw*] which is over it being uninjured."

[70] Cf. chapter 17, discussion of room IV.

[71] The translation of the expression *nny mwyt* by "incontinence of urine" is inspired by the use of the word *nny* for the slowness of flood waters, or the fatigue or laziness of a sick organ or half-paralyzed limb. Cf. Breasted, *Smith Papyrus*, p. 332.

[72] Cf. Déjérine, *Sémiologie des affections*, pp. 265–66.

Case 31, which we have just given here in its totality, is one of a series of five related cases concerning different injuries to cervical vertebrae, which we will now quickly summarize.

Case 29 is a gaping wound penetrating to the bone, perforating *(thm)* a vertebra of the nape of the neck. The patient suffers from violent tremors and rigidity of the neck. The surgeon declares his ability to combat the ailment but does not pronounce any definite verdict.

Case 30 regards a sprain *(nrwt)*. It is painful for the injured person to turn his head. The doctor declares himself able to treat it.

Case 31, described above, is a complete dislocation *(wnkh)* with a fatal prognosis.

Case 32 concerns *nswt* in a cervical vertebra. The patient has a fixed head, being incapable of turning his neck. The surgeon declares himself able to treat it and explains the word *nswt* in a gloss. "As for: '*nswt* in a cervical vertebra,' he is speaking of a sinking of a vertebra of his neck toward the interior of his neck, as a foot sinks into cultivated ground. It is a penetration downward." It seems possible to compare *nswt* with an incomplete dislocation, or subluxation (fig. 170).

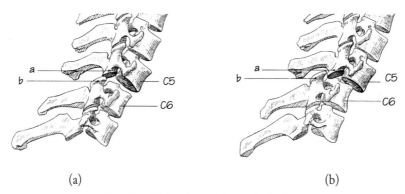

(a)   (b)

Fig. 170. Dislocations of the cervical column
(from Y. J. Longuet, "Lésions et fractures," Encyclopédie médico-chirurgicale, *15826, p. 3, fig. 2)*

(a) Incomplete dislocation; the body of C5 has slipped in front of the body of C6; however, the two articular facets *a* and *b* remain in contact in a small area. *(b)* Complete dislocation; the articular facets *a* and *b* have completely lost contact. The lower articular apophysis has jumped completely in front of the apophysis subjacent to it. The catching of these articular apophyses is feared, causing formidable difficulties for reduction.

This case is classified among the "mild forms," that is, those that present few or no neurological signs: "Their frequency is great. Nearly ignored before radiography, they are well known since the report of J. and A. Boeckel (1911). . . . *Nothing is easier than to fail to recognize a fracture or a dislocation of the cervical column.* . . . The practice of systematic radiography must here be an absolute rule. . . ."[73]

Finally, the last case of this series is concerned with a fracture of a cervical vertebra from an impact. The simplicity and conciseness of the exposition merits notice.

[73] Longuet, "Lésions et fractures," pp. 3 and 4 and related figures.

Case 33

> *If you examine a man having a crushing* [shm] *in a vertebra in his neck; if you find him*
> *[with] one vertebra fallen into the next one, while he is* dgmy[74] *and can no longer speak.*
> *It is his head falling downward that has provoked the crushing of one vertebra into the next*
> *one. When you find that he is unconscious of his two arms and of his two legs on account of*
> *this, then you should say concerning him: ". . . An ailment that cannot be treated."*

This case can be compared to the "fracture from a head-first fall," whose progression, depending on the violence of the impact, can cause rapid death with paralysis of the four limbs.[75] Two of the scribe's glosses indeed specify the nature of the injury and its cause: "As for: 'a crushing [*shm*] in a vertebra in his neck,' he is speaking of the fall of one cervical vertebra into the lower one; one has entered into the other, and can 'neither seize nor move.'"[76]

The second gloss specifies that the accident has taken place through a fall on the head, whose violence provoked a crushing of the vertebra.

It is important now to recall that today all injuries of the cervical column are extremely difficult to diagnose without the help of radiological examination, and diagnosis is subject to verification by examination. If the complete dislocation and crushing presented here are part of the "forms of evident symptomology," this is not the case for the sprain and the subluxation, which have the same exterior symptoms. One asks oneself how the ancient surgeon was able to distinguish, with so much certainty, a sprain from a dislocation, a displacement (subluxation), or a crushing, having only palpation and clinical and neurological signs for guides.

59. Another word designating the spinal marrow is *imakh*, met with in certain texts.[77]

60. Finally, the last case of the Smith Papyrus treats a sprain of a thoracic vertebra, *ts n psd* (vertebra of the back). The surgeon orders the patient to extend his legs, and then carefully and precisely notes their immediate contracture caused by the pain from the sprain of the thoracic vertebra. This is the last case of the papyrus, left unfinished by the copyist scribe.

Between the last case that concerns the crushing of a cervical vertebra and the case relating to the sprain of a thoracic vertebra, the scribe discussed different injuries to the pectoral girdle, clavicles, shoulders, manubrium, and so on (cases 34 to 47). This is the region above and below the clavicles, the vital importance of which is emphasized on the figures of the bas-reliefs by the *usekh* necklace (fig. 137). This is indeed the level at which the cross of the aorta distributes the blood to all the large vessels leading toward the head and arms. It is also at the level of C7–T1 that the stellate ganglion is found, the great importance of which is well known. Now the name of the counterweight that always accompanies the *usekh* necklace and that hangs down along the vertebral column of the figure is sufficient to emphasize its vital interest: it is *mānkh*, which literally means "in order to live," or "for life." In addition, the most ancient example of this word is found in the

[74] See the explanation of this word in case 22 below.

[75] Cf. Longuet, "Lésions et fractures," pp. 3 and 4 and related figures.

[76] Breasted translated this by "there being no movement to and fro," but in this case the literal meaning, "neither seize nor move," can better help determine the nature of the fracture from compression, and perhaps the associated dislocation. [Breasted, *Smith Papyrus*, pp. 339–40.]

[77] Cf. Lefebvre, *Parties du corps humain*, p. 30.

Pyramid Texts (Sethe 815a) where Horus is qualified as "master of his counterweight of truth."[78]

We are obviously dealing here with the desire to emphasize an essential vital center which, furthermore, is related to one of the "secret" plexuses or *cakras*.[79]

VARIOUS SKULL INJURIES

The first twenty-seven cases of the Surgical Papyrus are concerned with the head and are presented following a fairly specific order. Cases 1 to 8 treat different traumas of the skull without giving precise localizations. Cases 9 and 10 discuss injuries of the forehead and the ridge of the brow. Then, after presenting different injuries of the nose and cheek, the surgeon considers five fractures of the temporal region. Because these last cases, like the others of the papyrus, are localized, we could reproach the author of this treatise for omitting to tell us the exact point of the fractures of the skull. However, we can already deduce that since the forehead and the temple are treated separately, the first eight cases are particularly concerned with the upper and back parts of the cranium, that is, the vault.

Now there is a valid reason for not localizing an injury to the vault. Some ancient skulls preserve traces of fractures of all kinds; one of them shows a fissure traversing the whole vault from front to back; others show one or several fissures starting from the point of impact and spreading toward the base of the skull in such a way that the clinical signs are more important to note than the point of the trauma itself.

In each case, the ancient surgeon notes only the anomalies he has observed, and only the study of the case as a whole allows us to conclude that each of the injured people first underwent a general examination. Then the doctor examines the injury with his hands and notices the presence of swelling or hematomas. Finally, he proceeds to observe the mobility and the neurological signs.

The ancient surgeon has a great advantage over his reader because only through manual examination are the trajectories of the fissures on the skull disclosed to him. Thus, in order to compensate for the absence of this description (which he never gives) we have considered it useful to summarize here, as briefly as possible, the essential characteristics concerning the architecture of the skull and the consequences that this or that trauma can have.

The whole of the cranium appears as a large, flattened egg, entirely closed on all sides, with the exception of the occipital foramen that allows the passage of the spinal cord and two vertebral arteries, which, after being joined to form the basilar artery, converge at the circle of Willis. Moreover, two small orifices[80] located on either side of the sella turcica allow the passage of the two internal carotids, which, after bifurcating at the circle of Willis, irrigate a part of the interior of the brain and cortex. Finally, certain nerves also make their way through the sinuses from the bones at the base of the skull in such a way that a trauma to the vault, as it spreads to the base, can injure either the nerves or the vessels. This enables us to understand the importance that the ancient surgeon gave to nasal hemorrhages or hemorrhages of the ear and to the side where they were produced.

Now the lines of fracture do not spread out in an arbitrary way. It is understood today that the

---

[78] Cf. Jéquier, *Frises d'objets,* p. 66 and n. 7.

[79] Cf. fig. 136, on the harmonic decomposition and the human canon.

[80] Clinoid-carotid foramen.

skull is extremely resistant and elastic because it is made up of shells joined by sutural membranes. By contrast, each shell is formed of two superimposed plates, and it has been discovered that the internal plate, because of its shorter radius of curvature, can sometimes be fractured while the external plate remains undamaged. Finally, the dura mater has no elasticity and can also tear even though there is no damage to the external framework. The ancient knowledge of this particular fact perhaps explains an anomaly in the writing in case 8 concerning an injury to the bones of the skull with no superficial wound.[81]

On the other hand, knowing that all the shells of the skull are far from having the same thickness everywhere, it follows that the weaker parts offer less resistance to shock and will be the route taken by any cracks. It is important to know then the arrangement of the strong and weak parts that make up a veritable architecture of the skull.

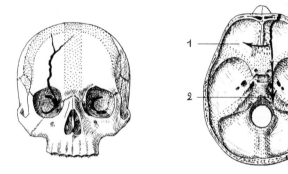

Fig. 171. Trauma to the frontal region

(1) Radiation to the other half of the anterior portion passing through the cribriform plate of the ethmoid; (2) the line of fracture, after passing through the ceiling of the orbit and the optic canal, can reach the petrosal bone. The stippled areas indicate the reinforced parts or "flying buttresses."

When compared to the keel of a boat, we can take the reinforced parts of the skull as being the hull, the deck, and the cross-timbers. The hull corresponds to the bottom part between the occipital foramen and the sella turcica, and the deck to the sinciput. The cross-timbers or "flying buttresses" are the six thick zones starting from the base of the skull and radiating out to rejoin the sinciput (figs. 171 and 172). This leads us to divide the surface of the vault into three strata to which certain lines of fracture will correspond.

Trauma to the frontal region (anterior stratum). Following the violence of the shock, the line of fracture can descend toward the orbit, traverse it, and then traverse the cribriform plate of the

[81] In all the other cases concerning a perforation, a fracture, or an accident with an external wound, the scribe writes *pakt* for shell; in this single case the shell is called *pawt*. "The skull is double along the middle of the head, and the hardest and most dense part of it is disposed both uppermost where the smooth surface of the skull comes under the scalp, and lowest where the smooth surface below is towards the membrane [dura mater]. Passing from the uppermost and lowest layers, the hardest and most dense parts, the bone is softer, less dense and more cavernous right into the diploe. The diploe is very cavernous and soft and particularly porous. In fact, the whole bone of the head except a very little of the uppermost and lowest is like sponge, and the bone contains numerous moist fleshy particles like one another and one can get blood out of them by rubbing them with the fingers." *Hippocrates*, 3:9. It seems that *pakt* can be understood as the ensemble of the two plates that Hippocrates calls "layers" that constitute the structure of the skull; while *pawt* seems to relate to the "primitive" part of these plates.

ethmoid, and after crossing the optic canal, reach the petrosal bone. In this way an injury to the forehead can have repercussions on the eyes, the nose, or the ears.

Trauma to the middle stratum (temple and parietals). Following the violence of the shock, the fissure can reach the petrosal bone and cause several types of fractures there, or else spread out from the other side of the base of the skull, after having passed over the sella turcica. It is important to have this well in mind so as not to speak too hastily of the scribe's errors with regard to certain hemorrhages caused by an injury to the temple (cases 18 to 22).

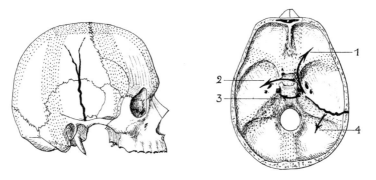

Fig. 172. Fracture in the temporal region

(1) Fracture parallel to the petrosal bone; (2) radiation through the sella turcica; (3) radiation passing through the occipitobasilar suture; (4) perpendicular fracture of the petrosal bone, opening the cavities of the middle ear. The stippled areas indicate the reinforced part or "flying buttresses."

Trauma to the posterior stratum. The line of fracture can follow the contour of the occipital foramen, or move toward the petrosal bone and break it, or again it may reach the cribriform plate of the ethmoid.

> We are going to note, in terminating this study of the workings of cranial fractures, that the exposures and lines of fractures that spread toward the base considerably aggravate the prognosis. Indeed, as we have already said, and as we are going to see again in the following, the base of the cranium is related to the cavities of the face (nasal fossae, ears, and so on). The result is that the fissures that spread to the base of the cranium allow the main location of the fracture to communicate with the nasal fossae or the middle ear, that is, with regions accessible to germs. Consequently, they expose the patient to all the infectious complications, and in particular to meningeal encephalitis, an affliction known to be extremely serious.[82]

Did the Ancients know of this arrangement of the skull? The medical papyri, like the mathematical papyrus, do not explain the ways their authors followed and the means they used to arrive at the brief expositions that have been handed down to us.

Recalling here that the arrangement of the numbers in the table of *2/n* as well as the proportions of the registers on which they were inscribed contain in themselves a teaching that we must read there, it is certain that the order in which the cases of the surgical papyrus are presented

---

[82] Cf. Testut and Jacob, *Traité d'anatomie,* p. 24

contains in itself an analogous teaching that must be discovered. Knowing now that an injury at any point on the vault can reverberate toward the base of the skull, we understand better that in the view of the ancient surgeon, the place of the trauma has a secondary importance. By contrast, clinical signs reveal the importance of internal damage and demand the greatest attention.

On the other hand, the fact that fractures of the nose and the maxilla were interposed between those of the vault and the forehead (cases 1 to 10) and the injuries to the temporal bone (cases 18 to 22) suggests that we seek out the reason. Fractures of the base of the skull can be caused by a trauma either to the root of the nose (cases 11 and 12) or to the orbital ridge (case 10). Indirect fractures of the base of the cranium are spread mainly by transfer, for example, through a shock on the maxilla that is transmitted in turn to the cribriform plate[83] (cases 15 to 17).

Only knowledge of these facts justifies the curious arrangement of the cases, which are concerned first of all with the vault, then with different points of access, direct or indirect, from the base of the skull, and finally with the temple, which protects the most important intellectual centers.

Case 1

[a] *Instructions concerning a wound* [wbnw] *in his head extending to the bone of his skull.*

[b] *If you examine a man having a wound in his head extending to the bone of his skull, without there being a cut* [kft], *you should palpate his wound, you should place your hand upon it. If you find that his skull is uninjured, that there exists neither perforation nor split nor fracture in it, then you should say concerning him: "One having a wound in his head while this wound does not have two lips . . . nor any cut even though it extends to the bone of his head. An ailment that I will treat."*

The title *(a)* invariably begins with "Instructions concerning. . . ." We encounter the word *wbnw*,[84] 142 times in the papyrus and it carries the broad meaning that we give to "wound." Written often with the sun from which rays emerge and determined by a mouth that spits, *wbnw* particularly designates all flesh wounds. It is used, however, in all the titles concerning superficial or deep wounds, and the exact nature of the trauma is specified in what follows the title, which says, for example in case 1, that this wound penetrates *(ār)*[85] to the bone.

The examination *(b)* contains several sections. The first sentence, which begins all the examinations of all the cases, is explained in gloss A, and implies, as we shall see later on, the general examination of the patient. The second sentence concerns the examination of the wound and the condition of the skull, any injury to the scalp being cause for fear that it might reach the bone. This examination is made by palpating *and* by the hand. The hieroglyphic group translated "to palpate," *djār*,[86] is determined by the finger and two small legs that are walking and expresses very well the passage made by the fingers on the skull in search of a possible bone injury. The surgeon ascertains that there is no fracture and declares himself able to care for this patient. However, his insistence

[83] Cf. Petit-Dutaillis and Guiot, "Fractures du crâne."
[84] *wbnw* means "lesion," "wound," "trauma," fig. 176, no. 1.
[85] *ār* means "to extend itself," determined by a route, it expresses the idea of "taking a path," of "traversing," fig. 176, no. 2.
[86] *djār*, "to palpate," fig. 176, no. 3.

and the repeated statement of the sentence that this injury does not have a cut *(kft)*,[87] that it does not have two lips although it penetrates to the bone, calls attention to itself and is the object of two glosses, unfortunately partly destroyed.

It would appear that the ancient surgeon definitely considered two kinds of wounds, those that have *kft* and those that do not. We can compare this distinction to the one made today, and draw an analogy between the modern definition and the scribe's gloss.[88] "As for: 'a wound that does not have *kft* [gash], although it extends to the bone,' this means a wound penetrating straight toward the bone, but it does not produce a gash [*kft*] in it. It says: 'a narrow wound that does not have two lips.' "

Nowadays, we make the following distinctions: first, simple wounds, in which "the scalp is only incompletely severed and the lips of the wound are not set apart"; and second, wounds with separation of the lips in which "the entire thickness of the scalp up to and sometimes including the periosteum is divided."[89] This second type of wound is precisely the subject of the second case of injuries to the skull, those in which there is a "wound with separation," *wbnw n kft*.[90]

At the end of the preceding gloss, when the scribe uses the expression "It says," he is alluding to the Book Pertaining to Injuries mentioned on a similar occasion in the gloss for case 5. This reference to a particular book about wounds supports our conviction that this papyrus is but a small part of an extensive body of knowledge of which we have here only a glimpse, and which requires us to weigh each word carefully.

The first gloss of the first case indeed teaches us all the implications that can be understood from a single brief phrase such as "If you examine a man . . ."

> Gloss A. *As for: "if you examine a man," this is counting someone*[91] *. . . like counting something with a barrel. Examining [or measuring]*[92] *as one counts a determined quantity with a barrel. Counting with his fingers in order to know . . . it is examining [or measuring] things with a barrel.*
>
> *To count a certain ailment is similar to the examination of a sick man in order to know the pace of his* haty.[93] *The vessels [mtw] which are in it [go] toward all the limbs. As for these, each doctor, priest of Sekhmet, will place his two hands, his fingers, on the head, on the nape of the neck, on the hands, on the "seat of the heart,"*[94] *on the two legs [or feet] in the course of his examination of the* haty, *because its vessels are in the neck, in the seat of the heart, because it speaks at the front of each vessel of each limb.*
>
> *He says: "examine" for his wound, on the vessels of his head, of his neck, of his two legs . . . of his* haty[95] *to know the instructions concerning what has occurred there. Speaking of examining a man to know the changes occurring in him.*

---

[87] *kft,* "cut," "gash," fig. 176, no. 4, can be compared to what Hippocrates calls a *hedra,* which he says signifies "cut" or "cleft." *Hippocrates,* 3:13–21, 25.

[88] We give here the gloss to case 18, that of case 1 being similar but partially destroyed.

[89] Cf. Y. J. Longuet, "Lésions traumatiques du cuir chevelu," in *Encyclopédie médico-chirurgicale,* 15953.

[90] *wbnw n kft,* fig. 176, no. 5, "wound with separation" or "injury with cut," where the wound is gaping.

[91] *ir khaï k s ip mn pw,* fig. 176, no. 6. Sentence written in red.

[92] *kha.t,* fig. 176, no. 7, "to examine," "to observe," synonym of "to measure."

[93] *haty,* fig. 176, no. 8.

[94] Seat of the heart, *st ib,* fig. 176, no. 9.

[95] Cf. fig. 176, no. 8b.

This gloss is very important because it not only specifies the implied meaning of "examining" ("measuring"), which begins each examination, but it also uses mathematical terms. The first sentence, written in red, is already a complete curriculum: "As for: 'if you examine a man,' this is counting [*ip*] someone. . . ." The word *ip* is used in mathematics in the sense of enumerating. Very curiously, it is also used in the sacred ritual in the course of which the final offering is the eye of Horus destroyed by Seth, which the officiating priest must find and restore, that is, "count" *(ip)* to Horus. This is the *wedjat* eye, the "healthy eye" (unharmed, whole), whose reassembled pieces form the standard *hekat* used to measure grains. The second sentence of the gloss indeed establishes the comparison, "examining [*kha.t*] as one counts a determined quantity with a barrel [*ipt*]." The word "examining" *(kha.t)* is actually synonymous with "measuring" *(kha.t)*. Now, we have said with regard to harmony that the system of measures of pharaonic volumes was based on the numbers of musical harmony and on the ratios of vibrations. All in the Universe is interconnected, and the measure of volume is a sacred symbol of the cosmic harmony, as man's heart beats the rhythm of time. It is in this way that a man is *examined,* or *measured,* as a specific quantity of grain is with a barrel.

The gloss insists on several repetitions of the comparison between the examination of a patient and the count of the illness that is in him "in order to know the pace of his *haty.*" It is clearly a matter of a general examination of the ill person, which calls for, among other things, what we call "taking the pulse." The insistence on the word "counting" leaves no doubt that the doctor must count the pulsations of the injured person to deduce the state of his heart, but also allows us to understand that the rate of respiration is not neglected and is part of the measure of the *haty.* The doctor is not content to take only one pulse. The commentator, after saying that the vessels "in the *haty*" are directed toward each limb, indicates several places on the body where the priest of Sekhmet, the doctor, will have to place his two hands and his fingers: on the head, the neck, the two hands, the two feet, and "the seat of the heart" *(st ib),* because it (the heart) "speaks at the front" of each limb. In order to know what to do concerning the changes happening in the *haty* and in the illness, the scribe insists, at the end of this gloss on the general examination of an injury to the skull, on then establishing a comparison of the heart rhythm directly with any possible arrhythmias in the limbs. The word *khpr,* translated by "changes," also means "to become." It would also be correct to translate it in a more modern form: "to know the progression of the illness due to the injury." Now, this demonstrates the knowledge of the repercussions that an injury of the brain can have on organic manifestations such as the rhythm of the heart, for example.[96]

Moreover, taking the pulses at different points on the body is apparently comparable to the exacting study of the pulses of different parts of the limbs practiced in Chinese acupuncture. It is known that for the physician trained in it, this practice gives a reflection of the energetic equilibrium of each organ.

At present, a particular circulation is acknowledged for the brain that justifies the instruction given to the ancient surgeon. "The conditions of the circulatory hydraulic system in the inextensible space of the braincase imposes some special conditions on the encephalic circulation. This fact explains that there is a response to each systolic wave of a thrust of cerebrospinal fluid toward the spinal openings, and a reflux of jugular blood (cerebrospinal pulse, jugular pulse, and cerebral pulse). At rest, the cerebral pulsation is tricuspal and behind the cardiac pulse by one-ninth of a

[96] For the study of this question, Cf. J. Delmas and G. Laux, "Centres sympathiques de l'écorce cérébrale," and "Centres autonomes diencéphaliques," *Système nerveux sympathique* (Paris: Masson, 1952), pp. 59, 49 et sqq.

second."[97] In addition, clinical data have demonstrated that the cerebral circulation can be completely different from the peripheral circulation (for example, a cerebral vasodilation contrasted with a peripheral vasoconstriction), and in conclusion, "everything proceeds as if in large part the brain could itself regulate its circulation."[98]

—∿—

What is the *haty*? This word is currently translated as "heart," but the group of texts relating to it offer the possibility of a larger meaning. The heart itself is called *ib*, a synonym of "dancer,"[99] an image expressing very well the rhythmic movements of this organ. *Haty* would instead be synonymous with "lord," "regent," "director"[100] and can be understood as the distributing center of the blood system. But as the texts formally say, "the vessels that are in it . . . toward the limbs," there is reason to understand the heart itself as the vessels that go out of it and return to it (pericardium?), in other words, the cardiac region.

This interpretation would be nearer to ancient thought, which is functional and allows the same word to be taken in its general sense in one context and in a more restricted sense in another. To take an example, case 18 concerns an injury to the temple *(gma)* and certifies, after an identical examination to that of case 1 cited above, that the temporal bone has not been perforated, cracked, or fractured. The first use of the word *gma* is concerned with the temporal region and the second with the temporal bone. When applied to *haty*, this way of seeing allows us to understand, looking at the entire text, the heart complex and vessels at one place, and at another place the heart itself. For example, there is this passage of the Ebers Papyrus: "[a] As for: 'his *haty* is at its place,' [b] this signifies that the 'fatty mass' [*ād*] of the *haty* is in his left side, it cannot rise upward, it cannot descend downward, being given that it is fixed in its place."[101]

In statement *(a)* the word *haty* signifies "heart," while in the commentary *(b)* *haty* cannot signify the cardiac muscle, translated here by "fatty mass," since it clearly appears that the *haty* contains this cardiac muscle *ād* in its left side. The assertion that the heart can neither rise nor descend alludes to the fibrous ligaments that maintain the pericardium in place, enveloping the heart and the large vessels that access it.

As for the accepted translation of the word *ād*[102] as "fatty mass" in place of its more particular meaning as the cardiac muscle, the symbolism of the hieroglyphic sign designating it is what will teach us its true significance. This word *ād* is written with the shuttle of the loom. How better to evoke the regular movement of coming and going than by the rhythmic sound of the shuttle that ceaselessly goes back and forth between the warps, opened and closed by the heddle? The translation of *ād* by a true correspondence with this image certainly conforms more closely to, and is nearer to, "cardiac muscle" than to "fatty mass."

Moreover, the heart cannot be functionally dissociated from the lungs. The lungs renew the blood that the heart sends to them, which the heart then redistributes to the entire body. *Haty*, in

---

[97] Cf. P. Cossa, "Vascularisation cérébrale et syndromes vasculaires," *Physiopathologie du système nerveux* (Paris: Masson, 1950), chap. 26, p. 721.

[98] Cf. ibid., pp. 722–23.

[99] Cf. I. Schwaller de Lubicz, *Her-Bak, Egyptian Initiate,* p. 94.

[100] A nomarch calls himself *"haty-a."*

[101] Ebers Papyrus, 101, 18.

[102] *ād,* fig. 176, no. 10.

its widest sense, refers to all the organs of animation, but *haty* is also the heart symbolizing these functions. In speaking of the object "heart," it is called *ib* and the cardiac muscle, *ād*.

—–∿∿–—

Case 3

> [a] *Instructions concerning a gaping wound* [wbnw n kft] *in his head, penetrating to the bone, perforating* [thm] *his skull. . . .*
>
> [b] *If you examine a man having a gaping wound in his head, penetrating to the bone, perforating his skull, you should palpate his wound; if you find him incapable of looking at his two shoulders and at his breast,*[103] *he suffers from stiffness in his neck. . . .*
>
> [c] *Then you should say concerning him: "One who has a gaping wound*[104] *in his head, penetrating to the bone, perforating his skull, he suffers from stiffness in his neck. An ailment that I will treat."*

Case 1 presents an injury without an opening, and case 2 presents an injury with an opening; both threaten the bone but do not reach it. The third case treats an injury that perforates the bone and this is specified in the title *(a)*. It is further confirmed in the course of the examination *(b)* and in the final diagnosis *(c)*.

After the general examination of the patient, implied by the first sentence, and the palpation of the wound, there is added here an examination of mobility. Because the bone has been perforated, there is reason to fear an internal injury to the skull, the significance of which can only be revealed through certain clinical signs. In the final diagnosis, the surgeon repeats all or part of the observed symptoms[105] and, depending on the case, there will be three prognoses: (1) "an ailment that I will treat," that is, he considers himself able to cure it, as in the present case; (2) "an ailment against which I will contend," that is, the result is uncertain but not hopeless; (3) "an ailment against which I can do nothing."

The treatment of case 3 consists of making some stitches, then applying fresh meat the first day without bandaging the patient, who must be tied to "his mooring stakes until the period of his *ih* passes."[106]

The following four glosses define certain expressions:

> Gloss A. *As for: "perforating* [thm][107] *his skull," this means . . . a small fracture that he has incurred, a fracture similar to a puncture in a piece of pottery. . . .*[108]

---

[103] Literally, "he cannot look at his two shoulders and at his breast," or perhaps, "his glance cannot find . . ."

[104] Literally, "one who is under his injury."

[105] The repetitions in the case, such as: "Then you should say concerning him: 'One who . . .'" are for the purpose of stressing the most important symptoms revealed for each case.

[106] *ih*, fig. 176 no. 24, is a word whose meaning can only be dictated by its medical usage. It is met with five times in the Smith Papyrus in the phrase, "until the period of his *ih* passes," and seven times regarding the consequences of an injury (see later on), where it is translated by "suffering" and by "lesion."

[107] *thm*, fig. 176, no. 11.

[108] Gloss partially destroyed. The comparison with a piece of pottery recalls MacEwen's note: "the sound of a cracked pot that one is able to hear listening from one side, the sound produced by the percussion of the skull from the other side." Cf. Petit-Dutaillis and Guiot, "Fractures du crâne."

The word *thm* is sometimes determined by the hieroglyph of a leg alone, and at other times by the leg and a small circle. It has the ordinary meaning of "to traverse," "to pierce through," which verifies the meaning of "perforating" by which it is translated here. The small circle that sometimes determines it suggests an injury made by a pointed object, such as an arrow or a lance.

Following the violence or impact of the blow, the perforation can, however, be more or less deep, as also witnessed by seven examples presented in the papyrus. Only two of them are hopeless, one is doubtful, and four can be cured. The next gloss (B) specifies the meaning of the first observed symptom:

> *As for: "[he is] incapable of looking at his two shoulders and at his breast," this means, it is painful for him to look at his two shoulders, it is painful for him to look at his breast" [literally, "at his sternum"].*[109]

Gloss C defines the second observed symptom:

> *As for: "he suffers from stiffness in his neck," this means the rigidity [caused] by this* ih *which he had had [and] which has shifted to his neck. His neck suffers on account of this.*

Do we need to see two distinct signs in the two commentaries? Does the first relate to the mobility of the look and the second to the mobility of the neck? Or, to summarize the two as Dr. Luckhardt has done: "The physical findings of inability to look at shoulders and breast and particularly the stiffness of the neck are quite characteristic of a meningitis or meningeal involvement. The stiffness of the neck really makes it difficult and painful for the patient to look at the shoulders or bend the head enough to look at the chest. . . . I think the rendering 'stiffness' ('rigidity') is very good. It is so used daily in medical practice to-day. It is due to reflex spasm of the musculature of the neck."[110]

Gloss D explains the strange expression used for part of the treatment:

> *As for: "mooring him to his mooring stakes," this means to put him on an appropriate diet, without making any medication [prescription] for him.*[111]

This commentary is to be understood in the sense of letting the patient rest—implied by the "mooring"—and of putting him on an appropriate diet until the time when his *ih* has passed. The fact of considering the patient, above all, as being "in shock" already appears here. This will be confirmed in the following cases.

—⁓—

Case 4

> *Instructions concerning a gaping wound in his head, penetrating to the bone, and splitting* [pshn] *his skull.*

---

[109] Literally, "it is not pleasant," from which "difficult or "painful" is derived.

[110] Breasted, *Smith Papyrus*, p. 130.

[111] Among the variants for the expression "mooring him to his mooring stakes" is one that might be translated "putting," or "setting," him "at his mooring stakes."

> *If you examine a man having a gaping wound in his head penetrating to the bone, splitting his skull, you should palpate his wound. If you find something disturbing* [nha][112] *there under your fingers, while he shivers greatly,[113] a prominent swelling* [ishw.w tkhb][114] *above. He bleeds from both his nostrils, from both his ears, he suffers from stiffness in his neck, he is incapable of looking at his two shoulders and at his breast.*
>
> *Then you should say concerning him: "One 'who is under' a gaping wound in his head, penetrating to the bone, splitting his skull. He bleeds from both his nostrils, from both his ears, he suffers from stiffness in his neck. An ailment with which I shall contend."*

The surgeon does not commit himself to curing it, but he affirms that he is able to contend with it and immediately prescribes a treatment:

> *As soon as you have found that this man has his skull split, you should not dress it; moor him to his mooring stakes until the period of his ih passes. His treatment is to sit. Make for him two supports of bricks until you know that he has reached a decisive point. You should apply an ointment on his head, [you] should soften his neck, also his shoulders therewith. You should do likewise to every man whom you find having a split skull.[115]*

Gloss A of the scribe explains the nature of the *pshn* injury:[116]

> *As for: "splitting* [pshn] *his skull," this means separating one shell from another shell, while the fragments are stuck in the tissue* [haw] *of his head and do not fall to the ground.*

Breasted correctly observes that the patient shudders and trembles when the wound is touched, during which time the surgeon observes the existence of the prominent swelling *(ishw.w tkhb)*, a new phrase whose meaning is explained in the following gloss:

> *As for: "ishw.w tkhb[117] which is above [the fracture]," it is a large swelling[118] [or tumor] that is over this split, which rises upward.*

Finally, the third gloss specifies the meaning of the verdict:

> *As for: "[until] you know he has reached a decisive point," it means [until] you know whether he will die or he will live. . . .*

---

[112] *nha*, "dangerous," "worrying," "perturbing"; fig. 176, no. 13.

[113] *anry*, "to terrify," "to tremble," "to shudder excessively."

[114] *ishw.w tkhb*, provisionally translated as "prominent swelling," will be discussed later.

[115] "A lesion in the head should not be moistened with anything, not even wine, much less anything else, nor should the treatment include plasters or plugging, nor ought one to bandage a lesion in the head. . . ." *Hippocrates*, 3:29.

[116] *pshn*, fig. 176, no. 12.

[117] *ishw.w*, fig. 176, no. 14; *tkhb*, no. 15.

[118] *wr*, "large," fig. 176, no. 16; *shfw.t*, "swelling," no. 17.

This kind of *pshn* wound is the subject of four cases in the papyrus,[119] and for each the surgeon declares either that he will treat it, or that he is going to combat the illness, but does not give a fatal diagnosis.

The whole of the examination and the glosses makes clear the importance that the ancient surgeon gave to the state of shock, of which shivering is a part. He was conscious of the need to tend to the immediate phenomena before intervening, and for this he sat his patient down, a curious position given that the modern tendency would be to lay him down.

It is important to emphasize here the notion of what is today called the "state of shock" that follows all trauma to the skull. A concussion or state of shock is undoubtedly suitable for the translation of the word *ih* in the sentence ". . . until the time of his *ih* [concussion] passes." This suggestion, confirmed by gloss C, demonstrates the awareness of the period that modern medicine calls "the free interval," that is, a time more or less long in which the concussion symptoms may either diminish or increase and which the ancient surgeon expressed by "until you know whether he will die or he will live."

Finally, the expression *ishw.w tkhb* is formed of two words, the first of which is connected with the idea of "weeping," "excreting," or "overflowing,"[120] and the second word also relates to humidity, or irrigation.[121] The corresponding modern term for the overflow of a more or less voluminous quantity of blood, according to the seriousness of the injury, is *hematoma*, also *edema*, or *ecchymosis*. The scribe explains these two technical words by "large swelling" or a tumor "which rises upward."

The word *shfw.t*, "tumor" or "swelling," merits a slight digression. The root of *shfw.t* is *shf*, which is part of the word *shf.t*, designating the head of a ram. A shepherd, asked about the characteristics of the ram, revealed to us a special quality of this animal that certainly explains the relationship between the words *shfw.t* (swelling) and *shf.t* (ram's head).[122] Between his horns the ram has a protuberance "like a ball of nerves," very sensitive to the touch. The uncastrated male likes his head to be caressed, particularly at the place of this bump, but the shepherd must beware because the animal, worked up and overexcited by the rubbing, can become mean and react violently. We are no doubt dealing with a point strongly innervated and flooded with sexual reactivity, and in any case "protruding." Remember also that at rutting time rams confront each other, and their struggle consists of brutally bumping each other's foreheads near the horns. This characteristic gesture is certainly related to the "bump" in question.

Thus, *sfhw.t* (swelling, tumor) would signify a bump that is particularly sensitive to the touch and that results from vascularization. This allows us to come nearer to the exact meaning of *ishw.w tkhb*.

---

[119] *pshn* wound in the zygomatic bone, case 16; in the temple, case 21; and in the humerus, case 38.

[120] *ishw.w* has the same root as *ish*, saliva (fig. 168, no. 38) or dribble. Used here in a verbal form *ishw.w* expresses the action of this secretion.

[121] Compare with the text of Hippocrates: ". . . and it is from the surrounding parts that lesions wherever they may be get inflamed and swollen by an afflux of blood." *Hippocrates* 3:31. Later on he calls inflammation "phlegmasia." An analogous idea must certainly govern the translation of *ishw.w tkhb*.

[122] Fig. 176, no. 18.

Case 5

Instructions concerning a gaping wound in the head, fracturing [sd] his skull.

If you examine a man having a gaping wound in his head penetrating to the bone, fracturing [sd] his skull, you should palpate his wound. If you find that this fracture [sd] which is in his skull sinks deeply under your fingers, [with] a voluminous swelling above it, he discharges blood from both his nostrils [and] both his ears, he suffers with stiffness in his neck, he is unable to look at his two shoulders and at his breast, then you should say concerning him: "One having a gaping wound in his head, penetrating to the bone, fracturing [sd] his skull, he suffers from stiffness in his neck. An ailment that cannot be treated."

Two points distinguish this case from the preceeding one: the nature of the injury *(sd)*,[123] provisionally translated by "fracture" and explained in a gloss, and the fact that this fracture sinks deeply under the fingers of the examiner.

The other symptoms are identical in the two cases, except for the shivering mentioned in case 4; and whereas in the first case the surgeon preserves a hope of saving his patient, in the present case the verdict is fatal, as elsewhere in the majority of fractures of this type designated by the word *sd*, which is commented upon as follows:

As for: "fracturing [sd] his skull," this means a fracture of his skull. The bones formed by this fracture penetrate [slide] into the interior of his skull. The Book Pertaining to Injuries says that this means a fracture of his skull into numerous fragments that penetrate [slide] into the interior of his skull.

Through this gloss it appears that the word *sd* can indeed be translated in the wide sense of "fracture," but also that a particular meaning can be given to it that corresponds to this description.

In the preceding case of *pshn*, the pieces of the bone remain fixed in the scalp. In the present case of *sd*, the numerous fragments penetrate into the skull. The hemorrhage through the two ears and the nose, and the meningeal symptom, lead us to conclude that there has been a rupture of the large vessels of the brain, and probably a fracture of the two petrosal bones. The damage seems serious enough for the ancient surgeon to lose all hope of saving his patient. This case is also beyond the capabilities of the modern surgeon.

Fig. 173. Fracture of the skull with embrasure

A splintering of the internal plate has torn the dura mater and caused a cortical contusion.[124]

[123] *sd,* fig. 176, no. 19.

[124] Cf. Petit-Dutaillis and Guiot, "Fractures du crâne," p. 2, fig. 1.

Case 7

> *Instructions concerning a gaping wound in his head penetrating to the bone, perforating* [thm] *the sutures of his skull.*
>
> *. . . You should palpate his wound. He shivers greatly. You should cause him to raise his face; it is painful for him to open his mouth, [that] his heart is tired for speaking, if you observe that his saliva falls from his lips without falling to earth, he discharges blood from both his nostrils and both his ears, he suffers with stiffness in his neck, he is unable to look at his two shoulders and at his breast . . .*

This examination is immediately followed by a first diagnosis:

> *Then you should say concerning him: "One who has a gaping wound in his head, penetrating to the bone, perforating the sutures of the skull. The cord of his mandible*[125] *is contracted. He bleeds from both his nostrils and from both his ears; he suffers from stiffness in his neck. An ailment with which I will contend."*

The practitioner, in spite of this group of symptoms, judges the case as serious but not hopeless. He prescribes the first treatment:

> *As soon as you have found this man [with] the cord of his mandible, his jaw, contracted, you should make for him something hot, until he be relieved and his mouth opens. You should dress it with an ointment of honey and shredded linen*[126] *until you know that he has reached a decisive point.*

The first examination is followed by several others after a certain amount of time in the observation of the injured person. Gloss A specifies the meaning of "sutures,"[127] and gloss B explains the contracture of the jaw and allows us to relate this symptom to what we today call lockjaw:

> Gloss B. *As for: "the cords of his mandible are contracted," this means a stiffening of the ligaments* [mtw], *which at the posterior extremity of the "clamp"*[128] *fasten it to his temporal bone. It is the posterior extremity of his jaw that cannot move to and fro;*[129] *it is not easy for him to open his mouth because of his* ih.

Taken together, the symptoms suggest the following. First, the stiffness of the neck suggests meningeal difficulties. Second, the "saliva" that does not fall to the ground is spittle or froth. Third, the description of painful lockjaw poses a problem about its origin; the association of the double otorrhea and epistaxis with the lockjaw leads us to imagine a fracture at the base [of the skull]

---

[125] The "cord of the mandible" is a special term designating the masseter muscle, *wat,* explained in fig. 168, no. 54.

[126] Or a "tampon" or "compress."

[127] Gloss given with explanation of figure 167, no. 8.

[128] "Clamp" or sigmoid notch, fig. 167, no. 15.

[129] Literally "can neither seize nor move," already encountered in case 33 concerning a crushing of a cervical vertebra. See fig. 168, no. 54, and gloss C, specifying the meaning of "the cord of his mandible."

involving the auditory passage. Finally, the patient shivers and his heart beats weakly. These signs attest to the state of shock so frequently found in serious trauma to the skull. Those so injured often have a central hyperthermia that is the opposite of that brought on by circulatory troubles with chilling of the extremities. These symptoms translate as "a stroke of the centers of psychic coordination and of the vital centers. . . ."

"Before attributing a fatal diagnosis to these observations, it is appropriate to apply heat to these wounds, to elevate the arterial blood pressure with cardiac tonics."[130] The ancient surgeon's first treatment indeed consists of preparing something hot for his patient. Two examinations will follow the first exposition. The diagnosis of the second examination will be fatal, whereas the third examination carries no diagnosis but will be followed by a new treatment. Instead of seeing two successive examinations, can they not be seen as two possible outcomes following a certain amount of time for progress? Both begin with the same expression, *ir swt:* "Being that [*ir swt*] you find . . . ," the outcome is fatal; "Being that [*ir swt*] you find . . . ," there is some chance of saving the patient.

This gives the practitioner another chance to solve the problem, but we are tempted to adopt this hypothesis because it corresponds to the observation of the patient implied in the last sentence of the first treatment: ". . . until you know that he has reached a decisive point." It is therefore logical to assume that we are now going to learn what this decisive point might be: either aggravation of the first symptoms or the appearance of new ones, revealing complications, in which case the practitioner deems his patient lost, or, on the contrary, symptoms might decrease without aggravation, and in this case the surgeon has some hope.

> Examination 2. *Being that you find that the body of this man has been released from fever under [the effect of] this wound that is in the sutures of his skull, while this man manifested convulsions* [tia][131] *under [the effect of] this wound, you should place your hand upon him. If you find his forehead moist with sweat, the ligaments of his neck tense, his face cyanotic* [tms], *his teeth and his back . . . the odor from the vault of his head is similar to the* bkn *of sheep, his mouth locked, his two eyebrows distorted, while his face is as if he wept.*
>
> *Then you should say concerning him:* "One who is under [the effect of] a gaping wound in his head, penetrating to the bone, perforating the sutures of his skull, he manifests convulsions [tia], his mouth is locked, he suffers from stiffness in his neck. An ailment that cannot be treated."

This examination reveals new symptoms that become very important by their appearance after a "free interval"; convulsions *(tia),* fever, perspiration, cyanosis of the face, facial paralysis (the face appears as if he were weeping), attest to the extent of the injury by revealing a cerebromeningeal trauma and vasomotor troubles, whose seriousness when they appear secondarily is now known. The clinical signs of the second examination suggest the idea of a hematoma of the internal capsule and the compression of the medulla. A modern surgeon would, given a similar case, arrive at a prognosis as dark as that of the ancient surgeon.

The scribe's glosses determine the meanings of several symptoms:

---

[130] Cf. D. Petit-Dutaillis, "Traumatismes cérébraux," *Encyclopédie médico-chirurgicale*, 15957, p. 2.

[131] Or "manifests *tia*"; cf. fig. 176, no. 20.

Gloss D. As for: "his forehead is moist with sweat," this means that his head perspires a little, like something sticky [moist].

Gloss E. As for: "the ligaments of his neck tense," this means that the ligaments of his neck are tense, stiff on account of his ih.

Gloss F. As for: "his face [is] cyanotic" [tms], this means that his face is red, mottled [irtyw], like the spotted seeds [irtyw] of the tms.t tree.[132]

Gloss G. As for: "the odor from the vault [hn][133] *of his head is similar to the bkn of sheep," this means that the odor of his crown is similar to the urine of sheep.*

Gloss I. As for: "his mouth locked, his two eyebrows distorted, . . . his face as if he wept," this means that he no longer opens his mouth [even to] speak. Both his eyebrows are deviated, one drawing upward, the other drooping downward like one who screws up his eyes while his face weeps.

The third examination, which comes immediately after the fatal diagnosis of the preceding one, is very short and summarizes the two observations. It is then immediately followed by a treatment:

Being that you find that this man has paled and shows signs of exhaustion, you should have made for him a wedge of wood, wrapped in linen and put into his mouth. You should have made for him a potion of carob bean. His treatment is to be seated, placed between two brick supports, until you know that he has reached a decisive point.

If we refer back to the entire first examination, this treatment would theoretically have to follow after a more or less long, but not specific, period of observation. We can observe that the contractions of the jaw have not diminished but that, in this second possibility resulting from the injury, there has been no modification other than paleness and exhaustion.

Gloss J further comments on these latter symptoms and provides the opportunity to show a typical form of expression of the ancient language:

As for: "he has become pale and has already shown exhaustion," this means, he has paled because he is "one [with whom] you should charge yourself, do not abandon [him]," given his exhaustion.

—∿—

One word remains troubling and that is *tia,* which is translated as "convulsion," by Dr. Luckhardt, who leaves a question as to whether it is "convulsion" or "delirium." This word, in its medical use, occurs only in case 7 of the papyrus, so Breasted asked pathologists to make a suggestion. Its use in

---

[132] Cf. Breasted, *Smith Papyrus,* pp. 194–96, the long commentary on the word *irtyw,* which can be translated by "color," or is more particularly related to the suggestion of spotted, marbled, or mottled, and in certain cases, blue.

[133] Cf. fig. 167, no. 4, the quotation from gloss H with regard to *hn.*

the Ebers Papyrus relates it sometimes to a plant, at other times to a grain, but this brings no clarification because its meaning remains unknown.[134]

This time we owe to myth the ability to suggest the meaning implied by *tia*, based on the symbolic sense that governs the thought of the Ancients. "Gardiner," says Breasted, "calls my attention to a passage in a magical text among the unpublished Ramesseum papyri which refers to the birth of Set and then proceeds: "before he comes forth (from the womb) to the world, *tia*."[135] Since Breasted proposes to investigate the meaning of this word *tia* in myth and Gardiner finds it used in the "mystery" of the origin, I will be more precise and say that in the Heliopolitan myth we are dealing with a styptic effect that divides the primordial waters and causes the earth to appear. It is, furthermore, the earth that serves as the determinative of this word *tia* in its form as "piece of earth."[136] It is essentially a question, then, of a "contracting action."

Case 8

> *Instruction concerning a fracture [sd] in his skull, under the skin of the head.*
>
> *If you examine a man having a fracture [sd] of his skull under the skin of his head [while] there is nothing at all above it, you should palpate his wound. If you find a voluminous swelling on the back of this fracture which is in his skull; his eye is crossed*[137] *because of this on the side which is under this contusion [skr]*[138] *which is in his skull; he walks by dragging [stumbling] the sole of his foot on the side under the bruise in his head.*
>
> *You should classify it as a blow from something entering from the exterior,*[139] *one who cannot release the head of the "fork" of his shoulder, one whose fingernails fall in the middle of his palm.*[140] *He discharges blood through his two nostrils, through his two ears, he suffers from stiffness in his neck. An ailment that cannot be treated.*

In spite of his diagnosis that the case is hopeless, the surgeon puts the injured under observation: "His treatment is to be seated until [he regains] his color, until you know that he has reached a decisive point."

Five glosses explain the essential symptoms:

> Gloss A. *As for: "a fracture [sd] in his skull under the skin of his head [while] there is nothing at all [no wound] above it," this means a fracture of the* pawt *[shells] of his skull, the "body" of his* djadja *being still intact [whole].*[141]

---

[134] It must be a case of a plant that causes convulsions, such as black henbane.

[135] Breasted, *Smith Papyrus*, pp. 181–82.

[136] Fig. 176, no. 20.

[137] *gwsh.t,* "across," "turned to the side," "divergent."

[138] *skr,* fig. 176, no. 21, determined by a man striking with a stick, has the common meaning "strike," "blow," "shock." But it can also be translated by "contusion," that is, "injury produced by a shock, with extravasation of blood."

[139] The introduction to this diagnosis is as unusual as the case it describes. It can be understood "you should distinguish it as a particular case, a strike by an exterior shock." This sentence, like the symptoms described, comes near to the old word "apoplexy," whose original sense was "to knock down," "to strike."

[140] Translation commented upon at length by Breasted, pp. 214–16.

[141] Breasted translates this by "smash of the shell of his skull, the flesh of his head being uninjured."

It is a question of a depression, without exterior wound, but it is difficult to specify exactly the nature of the bone lesion.[142]

> Gloss B. *As for: "he walks by dragging [stumbling] the sole of his foot," he is saying about his lazy walk [with] the sole of his foot on which it is not easy to walk because it is weakened and turns on itself. The ends of his toes are contracted towards the "belly" of the sole of his foot, they walk in grasping for [looking for] the ground. It says of him, "he shuffles."* [143]

This description is typical for the hemiplegic, and Dr. Luckhardt makes this remark:

> The surgeon sees this patient some time after the injury. I base this statement on the stated fact that the patient "walks shuffling with his sole." Immediately after an injury to the brain involving the motor cortex (or internal capsule) the opposite side of the body would be paralysed (hemiplegia) and walking would be impossible. However, the hemiplegic recovers the power of walking even if, after a few months, the affected arm may at that time still remain powerless. At this time the arm is particularly affected by what is termed "contracture." The upper arm is adducted (at the shoulder). This the scribe characterizes as "one who does not release the head of his shoulder-fork." The lower arm is bent at a right or acute angle with a pronated and slightly flexed hand and with the *proximal phalanges*, and *particularly the terminal ones, quite flexed. . . .*[144]

Déjérine calls this last symptom the "sign of the mechanical claw,"[145] an expression that can be compared with the scribe's "[his] fingernails fall in the middle of his palm."

The third gloss insists on the external cause of the symptoms manifested by the patient in spite of the absence of a superficial wound. The unusual introduction to the diagnosis immediately draws attention to the fact that this case is an anomaly.

> Gloss C. *As for: "struck by something entering from the exterior, in his side which is under this* ih," *this means the pressure which enters from the exterior in his side which is under this* ih.

> Gloss D. *As for: "to enter from the exterior," this means the breath of an exterior neter or death by the introduction of that which his body engenders [or "by the penetration of that which his flesh engenders"].*

These two glosses complete each other and can be transcribed into language a little more modern. This case is classified among those internal traumas caused by an exterior blow. Pressure is exerted on the side that has undergone the blow, which can cause death by penetration of "that which his body engenders" unless the *breath of the neter* comes to his aid.

---

[142] The fifth type of fracture described by Hippocrates is perhaps related to an analogous case: "The skull is wounded in a part of the head other than that in which the patient has the lesion and the bone is denuded of flesh. . . . When this accident occurs, you can do nothing to help; for if the man has suffered this injury, there is no possible way of examining him to make sure that he has suffered it, or whereabouts in the head it is." *Hippocrates* 3:19.

[143] The modern medical term for "a stumbling walk" is "steppage." Each time the scribe writes "It says . . . ," he is referring either to the surgeon or to the Book Pertaining to Injuries mentioned in case 5.

[144] Breasted, *Smith Papyrus*, p. 216.

[145] Déjérine, *Sémiologie des affections*, p. 216.

"That which his body engenders" is clearly an allusion either to a hematoma or to an abscess that exerts pressure on the cerebral mass. The anomaly of this case consists in the fact that the paralysis is produced on the *same side as the injury*, which implies a fracture by repercussion.[146]

Déjérine points out the rarity of cases of *homolateral hemiplegia*, or hemiplegia on the same side of the body as the lesion:

> Today it is still a very obscure question. . . . There are very rare, but authentic cases, in which homo-lateral hemiplegia results from an absence of decussation of the pyramidal tracts.
>
> But it is again met outside of these cases, and it is a question in these remaining cases, which are extremely rare, of the existence of homolateral hemiplegia even though the pyramidal tract decussation is normal. The thing has been observed to follow cranial trauma in certain hematomas of the dura mater, following meningeal hemorrhage, cerebral abscess, or tumors of the meninges. It is possible that the tumor or bloody discharge acts then only by forcing back the brain en masse and by compressing the outer tissue of the opposite side against the cranial wall (Babinksi and Clunet 1908, Claude, Vincent, and Levy-Valensi 1910).[147]

In summary: the ancient surgeon describes a depression of the skull with no external lesion; however, there is a major swelling of the scalp. This lesion is accompanied by a paralysis of the ocular motor nerve and a homolateral hemiplegia. The steppage gait is perfectly described, as is the hand contracted into a claw shape and the contracture of the upper limb. The hemorrhage through the two nostrils and the two ears, the stiffness of the neck, and the paleness of the patient complete this account.

The glosses specify that we are dealing with a case of compression resulting from a cortical contusion. The observation specifies that the paralysis of the limbs manifests on the same side as the lesion, demonstrating their knowledge of the crossed effect of the brain on the limbs and emphasizing the particularity of this case caused by a "cross-blow."

Still, in spite of the first unfavorable diagnosis, it appears that the practitioner took the decision to intervene surgically. He makes no mention of the act of operating, without which it would have been impossible to examine the interior of the skull in the course of the second examination, but there was evidently a trephination, as is evident in the following text:

> Examination 2. *As soon as you find that fracture* [sd] *which is in his skull like those corrugations that form on molten copper, [and] something there that throbs and flutters under your fingers like the weak place on an infant's crown before it becomes knitted together . . .*
>
> *When it happens that there is neither throbbing nor fluttering there under your fingers since the viscera of his skull is torn open, he bleeds through his two nostrils and his two ears, he suffers from stiffness in his neck . . . An ailment that cannot be treated.*

The first part of this second examination is identical to that of case 6 in which a fracture of the skull with an external wound had exposed the brain. The second part of this examination, identical to that of case 6, presents a problem for translation and interpretation. After describing the throbbing of the head, it is difficult to understand why the scribe would allude to the eventual

[146] Cf. Petit-Dutaillis, "Traumatismes cérébraux," 15956, fig. 4, focus point of contusion by repercussion.

[147] Cf. Déjérine, *Sémiologie des affections*, p. 230.

absence of those throbbings, but there is a pathological sign that makes it possible to understand the implied meaning in the second sentence:

> The meningeal dura, or dura mater, is a fibrous membrane, very resistant, of a bluish white color. It is on the inside of the bony skull and has very little elasticity, which explains why it is able to be detached and even torn open in certain traumas of the head, whereas the bone structure, elastic owing to the presence of sutures, can be depressed without fracturing. When one first discovers it on a living subject, it presents throbbings which are impressed on it by the brain. These throbbings, isochronic to those of the pulse, ordinarily disappear when an abscess exists underlying the brain (Braun's sign).[148]

Here, moreover, is an observation made on a subject having a fractured skull as the result of a fall from a motorcycle, and who had dizzy spells twenty days after the accident: ". . . two trephination holes attest to a dura mater that is not throbbing. The third hole confirms the absence of throbbing. *The decision to perform the trephination is made because of this symptom.* A large, standard opening is made and reveals a gray dura mater that is not throbbing. It is very much distended. A careful excision allows a clear serous liquid of meningitis serosa to spring up. A larger opening brings to light the causal focus, a small parietofrontal hematoma in front of the fissures."[149]

Thus, when the scribe notes the possibility of the cessation of the throbbing of the dura mater, he demonstrates indisputable clinical knowledge.

—∿∿—

Hippocrates developed at length the cases where it is necessary to perform a trephination,[150] but up to now there has been no proof of a trephination dating from the pharaonic period. Now, on the one hand case 8 testifies to this practice, and on the other hand, Breasted notes the existence of a skull of the Twelfth Dynasty that had undergone trephination:

> The statement . . . that no Egyptian bodies thus far exhumed show any traces of the practice of trepanning must now be modified. Dr. Aleš Hrdlička of the United States National Museum, in a letter dated May 22nd, 1929, has kindly reported to me the discovery of a trepanned skull taken from one of the "deep pits at Lisht." He further states that it "belonged undoubtedly to one of the nobler families of the XIIth Dynasty." I am greatly indebted to the kindness of Dr. Hrdlička for a photograph of this unique specimen. It would seem, therefore, that trepanning was known to the ancient Egyptians, but was apparently very rarely practised, if we may judge by the rarity of surviving examples.[151]

THE TEMPORAL REGION

What did the Ancients know of the cortical centers? The absence of any anatomical description of the brain has generated the long-standing belief that they were totally ignorant of this subject. But there is also no anatomical description of the human body and we have nonetheless recognized, in several cases of the Smith Papyrus, a rich vocabulary concerning the essential parts of the skull, the shoulders, and so on.

[148] Testut and Jacob, *Traité d'anatomie,* p. 88.
[149] Extract from a report by Dr. J. Lamy, 1956.
[150] *Hippocrates,* 3:47–51.
[151] Breasted, *Smith Papyrus,* addenda, p. 596.

In addition, it is only by means of the medical texts—however enigmatic they may be in their extreme terseness—that we can, by gathering together all of the given elements, gradually arrive at a more exact idea of the *minimum* of ancient knowledge in their accounts of the fundamental vital centers. Now, certain assertions pose problems, only one of which we will mention here.

Why does an old treatise, dating back to the First Dynasty, after speaking of the heart, affirm that deafness is caused by "that which is on the temples [*maā-wy*] of a man," and this is what provokes the humming sounds, the sharp pains, and "seizes" his air? This enigma can only be resolved by virtue of the knowledge of our physiologists, who show that in fact there is a relationship between the eustachian tube, the internal carotid, and the middle ear. It is recognized that arterial troubles can cause unbearable humming sounds and a badly functioning eustachian tube, which actually deprives the eardrum of air and can lead to deafness. But what, then, is the relation between the middle ear and the temple? What does this allusion of the old doctor mean?

We know today that the entire cortical region of the temple is irrigated to a large extent by the Sylvian aqueduct, a branch of the internal carotid. It is also known that an excitation of the cortex at the level of the temporal lobe (especially T1) produces "in the person the sensation of humming, of tick-tack, or rumbling."[152] Moreover, we know that the centers of auditory perception are located in this area of the cortex. So how should we explain the effects of "that which is on the temples," noted by the scribe and comparable to our modern observations, other than by the Sylvian aqueduct and the cortical region that it irrigates? Lesions of this artery indeed cause extremely serious problems.

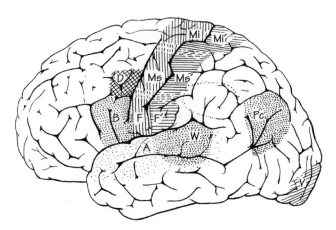

Fig. 174. Left profile of the brain
(from J. Déjérine, Sémiologie des affections du système nerveux*)*

In front of the fissure of Rolando, motor phenomena; behind, sensory phenomena: *Mi* and *Mi'*, the lower limbs; *Ms* and *Ms'*, the upper limbs; *F* and *F'*, the face, tongue, larynx, and so on; *D*, center of deviation controls for the head and eyes.

Language centers in the left brain only: *B*, Broca's area, center of motor images of articulation (injury here is followed by motor aphasia); *W*, Wernicke's area, center of auditory images of words (injury here causes alteration of interior language); *Pc*, curved fold, center of visual images of words; *A*, situated on the first temporal area, corresponds to the center of auditory perception; *V*, center of vision.

---

[152] Cossa, *Physiopathologie*, p. 258.

Moreover, the Ancients frequently asserted a connection between afflictions of the eyes and ears, to such an extent that to cure blindness they recommended a remedy to inject in the ear. Finally, other texts blame certain *mtw* of the occipital regions for causing visual troubles when they are afflicted. In this case, it is not the eyes but the nape of the neck that receives the treatment.

Let us recall that the Smith Papyrus has already instructed us that a lesion of the vault of the skull could cause hemiplegia, and we can also specify that an injury of the cortex in the region of the vault causes paralysis of the upper and lower limbs; a congestion or a lesion in the temporal region at the level of the Sylvian aqueduct affects the hearing; visual troubles are related to the occipital regions; and certain *mtw* establish a connection between the eyes and the ears.

Nothing is left for us but to compare this data with what is recognized as standard today, which gives rise to the following question: If the Ancients had already located, even in a general way, the centers mentioned above, would they have had the notion that the cortical zone corresponds to the faculty of language?

Cases 19 to 22, concerning lesions of the temporal zone, will answer this question.

—◦◦◦—

Case 19

Instructions concerning a perforation in his temple.

If you examine a man [having] a perforation [in] his temple, a wound [wbnw] above; while you observe his wound, say to him: "Look at your two shoulders." If his eye is painful when he turns his neck [only] a little,[153] *his eye is "shsm ty" in his side which is under this contusion [skr]. Then you should say concerning him: "One who is under [the effect of] a perforation in his temple . . ."*[154] *he suffers from stiffness in his neck. An ailment that I will treat.*

Several irregularities are seen in this short exposition. First, contrary to the parallel examination in case 3 concerning a perforation of the vault, it is not specified here whether the injury has perforated the temporal shell; neither does it ask for an examination by palpation of the wound. This palpation seems to be replaced by a visual examination.[155]

Second, this is the first time that the surgeon speaks to his patient and orders him to turn his head. In all the other cases he is satisfied to take note of the stiffness of the neck. What could the reasons be for these irregularities, if not that the trauma described is limited to a bruise? But the surgeon knows very well that the temporal shell is extremely thin and that a disturbance, even without a bone injury, can cause more or less extensive internal disorders.

The fact that the patient tried to turn his head demonstrates that he had perfectly understood the order he was given, and that his hearing is undamaged. On the contrary, the rigidity of his neck reveals an impairment from the meninges, and the *shsm ty* ailment of the eye holds our attention.

[153] Breasted translated this by "Should his doing so be painful (even though) his neck turns around (only) a little for him." However, the word *irt*, "to do," is written here exactly like the eye *(irt)*, which suggests that the translation given above is perhaps more admissible because the eye is afflicted.

[154] Lacuna in the text.

[155] Hippocrates describes the visual examination as preceding any palpation by the hands. *Hippocrates* 3:21.

Gloss A. *As for: "his two eyes are* shsm ty*," this means his eyes are marbled with red, like the veins of the* shas *flowers.*[156] *The Book Concerning Embalmings says about this: His two eyes are red, attacked [or injured,* djaw*] like the eye [whose] posterior face is sick [or weakened,* ahd*].*[157]

A passage from the Ebers Papyrus carries a definition of the *shsm ty* ailment, for the treatment given in this circumstance is destined to allow the patient to reopen his eyes.[158] Are we dealing with a ptosis, or with some other form of paralysis of the eyelid? This can result from various forms of meningitis and can as well be associated with a contracture, more or less transitory, of the eye muscles (*ophthalmoplegia,* from the Greek, "eye twitch").[159]

In spite of the dubious translation of the terms *djaw* and *ahd,* it is extremely important to determine this clinical sign regarding an injury of the temporal region. In the following case, where the perforation of the temporal shell is specified, both eyes will be *shsm ty,* but this word will no longer be explained by the scribe. It belongs to the specialists to suggest its precise translation with the help of case 20, in which the group of symptoms is more complete.

Case 20

Instructions concerning a wound in his temple, penetrating to the bone, perforating the temporal bone.

*If you examine a man having a wound in his temple, penetrating to the bone, perforating this temporal bone, his two eyes are "*shsm ty*," he bleeds through his two nostrils, very little, descending continually. If you place your fingers on the opening of this wound, he shudders greatly. If you ask him about his malady, he does not speak to you. Great tears descend from his eyes; he brings[160] his arm to his face very often, he wipes his eyes with the back of his hand as would an infant without knowing what he is doing.*

Then you should say concerning him: "One who is under [the effect of] a wound in his temple penetrating to the bone, perforating his temporal bone, he bleeds through both his nostrils, he suffers from stiffness in his neck, he is dgmy. *An ailment that cannot be treated."*

This examination is the most vivid and the most full of images in the whole papyrus. In spite of its brevity, it clarifies several points concerning the ancient surgeon's general method of investigation.

---

[156] For translation by "marbling" [ruddy] or "color" cf. Breasted, *Smith Papyrus,* pp. 195–96.

[157] *djaw* fig. 176, no. 26, can be translated by "afflicted," "attacked," "injured," or perhaps, "curved," "hooked," "cracked" (as opposed to something straight); cf. Breasted, *Smith Papyrus,* p. 282; *ahd,* fig. 176, no. 28, has an ordinary sense of "weak," "debilitated," "injured," "infirm," "faltering," perhaps "paralyzed"?

[158] Ebers Papyrus, 38, 18.

[159] For "ptosis" (or blepharotosis), cf. Déjérine, *Sémiologie des affections,* p. 1138 et sqq. For "external ophthalmoplegia" with fallen eyelids, cf. ibid., p. 1145, and for other cases pp. 1145–50 et sqq. The mechanism of the narrowing of the palpebral fissure (ptosis) is now under much discussion. Some think that it is due not to a paralysis but to a sympathetic irritation. Cf. Tardieu and Tardieu, *Le Système nerveux végétatif,* p. 274. Moreover, the fact that the eyes are "marbled" or of "red color" reveals a strong conjunctivitis that can be enough to cause occlusion of the eyelids.

[160] A translation that may be closer to what the scribe wanted to express may be "he 'grabs' with his arm toward his face very many [times]."

After observing the perforation of the temporal bone, the *shsm ty* state of the two eyes is noted. The eyelids are blinking (ptosis?) and the eyes are bloodshot, as in fractures of the front part of the skull. The aspect of epistaxis is very exactly described: it is light but continuous. This ptosis (or drooping of the eyelids) by paralysis of the common ocular motor nerve, the watering of the eyes through the impairment of the parasympathetic or the facial nerves, the shudders provoked by lightly touching the wound, the bilaterality of the signs, all evoke the possibility of the impairment of the intracranial venous sinus, or, at the very least, an impairment at their centers by this perforation or its extension.

For the first time in the cases of skull fractures, the questioning of the patient is mentioned. This interrogation is implied in all the cases,[161] so the fact of mentioning it regarding an injury of the temple demonstrates the particular interest that the practitioner gives to verifying the ability to listen and respond. The injured person, however, is incapable of responding. Is it because he cannot hear? Or because he is unable to speak? The text formally says "he speaks not," therefore alluding to a form of aphasia.

The unconscious gesture of wiping his tears and its very frequent repetition resembles what is called *apraxia*. The fact that the patient moves his arms proves that there is no hemiplegia. Finally, the stiffness of the neck is from a subarachnoid hemorrhage or from an impairment to the cerebral trunk, and explains the hopeless verdict regarding this patient: "he is *dgmy*," and "an ailment that cannot be treated."

Case 21

Instructions concerning a split [pshn] *in his temple.*

If you examine a man having a split in his temple, if you find a protruding swelling on the back of the split, while he bleeds from his nostril, and from his ear under this split, it is painful for him to hear speech on account of this.

Then you should say concerning him: "One who is under a split in his temple, he bleeds by his nostril, by his ear, under this contusion [skr]. *An ailment against which I will contend."*

Knowing that a fracture of the temporal bone can radiate toward the base and reach the petrosal bone, it is fitting to emphasize that the ancient surgeon notes only the epistaxis, the homolateral otorrhea, and the pain in hearing, but not complete deafness.

Case 22

Instructions concerning a fracture [sd] *in his temple.*

If you examine a man having a fracture [sd] *in his temple, you should place your thumb upon his chin, your finger upon the back end of his sigmoid notch* [amāt f], *while the blood descends through his two nostrils and from the interior of his two ears under [the effect of] that fracture* [sd].

---

[161] Hippocrates describes at length the questioning of the injured person about circumstances and the weapon that caused the injury. *Hippocrates* 3:21–22.

Cleanse it for him with a linen-covered twig until you see the splinters in the auditory channel of his ears.

If you called him, he is [remained] dgmy, he spoke not.

Then you should say concerning him: "One who has a fracture [sd] in his temple; he bleeds through his two nostrils, through his two ears, he is dgmy, he suffers from stiffness in his neck. An ailment that I cannot treat."

We are dealing here with a fracture, *sd,* therefore with a depression. The commentary relating to case 5 makes it clear that the pieces are driven into the interior of the skull. Furthermore, the splinters that come out of the auditory passages help us to understand that there is a fracture of the petrosal bone—on only one side if, as Breasted thinks, the dual number is a mistake—or on both sides by repercussion.

The brain damage is considerable enough to determine the epistaxis and the bilateral otorrhea, the contracture of the neck, and the injury to the language (and auditory?) centers. An unknown word, *dgmy*[162] is explained by one of the scribe's glosses:

As for: "he is dgmy," this means that he remains silent, in a state of enfeeblement [gmw, prostration], without speaking, like someone who is under [the effect of] inhibition [dgy][163] by that which enters from the exterior.

According to this gloss, the aphasia is certain, but given the extreme brevity of all the texts of this papyrus, each word of it demands to be carefully weighed. Now it seems that *dgmy,* explained by three symptoms, represents a syndrome. First, the patient is silent *(gr),*[164] in a mute state, perhaps mentally dulled. Second, he is *gmw,*[165] an extremely rare term meaning "affliction" or "enfeeblement," and determined by a prostrate figure. The word *gmw* could signify the state of extreme prostration in which this man is found after a trauma as serious as a depression in the temporal region. Finally, he speaks not *(nn mdt),*[166] that is, he can neither articulate nor pronounce his words.

The scribe's last sentence "like someone who is under [the effect of] inhibition by that which enters from the exterior," leads us to understand that this state of aphasia and prostration is from a discharge causing pressure on the temporal cortex. Furthermore, if we recall that there is necessarily a fracture of the petrosal bone, as is evidenced by the splinters coming out of the ear and internal hemorrhage revealed by the epistaxis, the meaning of the word *dgmy* summarizing all of them appears as a more or less comatose state caused by the extreme seriousness of the fracture.

Now this part of the cortex is traditionally called the Sylvian territory, where the principal areas of audition and language are located, as well as the motor centers of the face and the larynx. The

[162] *dgmy,* fig. 176, no. 29.

[163] *dgy,* fig. 176, no. 32, "weakness" (or paralysis?). It is said of a Libyan king taking flight that "his two feet are *dgy*"; this suggests translating it by "shocking" that is, "struck with stupor," or, what would be medically more correct, "inhibition," that is, "arresting or suppressing the function of a part of the organism."

[164] *gr,* fig. 176, no. 30. The root *gr* is thus part of the word *gr.h,* which means the night, which can imply an idea of obscurity by *gr.*

[165] *gmw,* fig. 176, no. 31, is met with in the stele of the seven-year famine with the meaning of "to cry," "to lament," "to be under affliction," "failing."

[166] *mdt,* fig. 176, no. 33. This word is formed from the same root as *mdw* (the hieroglyphic sign), "the word," "sacred speech," and is related therefore to the fact of pronouncing, of saying the word. Cf. I. Schwaller de Lubicz, *Her-Bak, Egyptian Initiate,* chap. 4, "The Divine Word."

totality of this examination formally demonstrates the knowledge on the part of the ancient surgeon of the locations of these centers. The two locutions that he uses to express aphasia are, very curiously, close to the distinction made in our day between the two forms of impaired language: (a) an alteration of the interior language (Wernicke), in which the patient hears words but no longer understands them, as if they were strange to him; and (b) motor aphasia, in which the intelligence remains more or less intact but there is a rupture between the principal centers of language, and the patient is incapable of finding words and of articulating them (Broca). Also, it is recognized that in spite of these distinctions, one of the centers is rarely injured by itself. In what might be the seat of the injury, "all the modalities of language are ordinarily affected."[167]

Finally, although its context allows it to be given, among others, the meaning of aphasia in its widest sense, every time the word *dgmy* is used in regard to fractures of the temporal bone, it is determined by an eye, whereas words that express the use of language are generally determined by a man holding his hand to his mouth. Knowing that the Ancients frequently saw relationships between the eyes and the ears, it follows that *dgmy* requires a special study that considers all the cases where it is encountered.

In order to facilitate this investigation, here is a summary of the five cases in which this word is used:

Case 13. Fracture, *sd,* (with depression) on the side of the nose. Epistaxis and otorrhea of the same side; lockjaw; crepitation under the fingers during palpation; the patient is *dgmy,* determined by a prostrate figure;[168] verdict fatal.

Case 17. Fracture, *sd,* (with depression) of the maxilla and the zygoma. Epistaxis and otorrhea of the same side; bleeding through the mouth; crepitation under the fingers during palpation; lockjaw; the patient is *dgmy,* determined by a prostrate figure; verdict fatal.

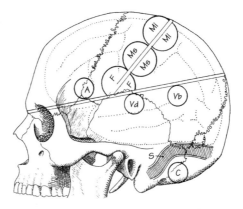

Fig. 175. Projection of the principal cortical centers on the cranial skeleton
(from Testut and Jacob, Traité d'anatomie topographique*)*

A, Verbal aphasia, Broca's center; *Vd,* verbal deafness, Wernicke's center; *Vb,* verbal blindness, curved fold; *C,* cerebellum; *S,* lateral sinus *(hachured); F,* motor and sensory centers of the face; *Ms,* motor and sensory centers of the upper limbs; *Mi,* motor and sensory centers of the lower limbs.

---

[167] It is interesting to recall the German opinion of an injury to both temporal lobes, which can be translated by what they call "deafness of the soul." The patient retains hearing but no longer has consciousness of the sounds that impress the ear. Finally, let us recall in this regard the pharaonic expression "to lend the temple" for the sense of listening, while today we would say "to lend an ear."
[168] Fig. 176, no. 34.

Fig. 176. Some medical terms from the Smith Papyrus

1. *wbnw*, wound (case 1)
2. *ār*, to travel along, or through, continue
3. *djār*, to palpate
4. *kft*, cut, gash
5. *wbnw n kft*, gaping wound, open injury
6. *ir khaï k s ip mn pw*, "As for: if you examine a man this is counting someone."
7. *kha.t*, to examine or observe; synonym of to measure
8. *haty*
8b. *haty*, heart and its vessels
9. *st ib*, "seat of the heart"
10. *ād*, cardiac muscle (written with the weaving shuttle)
11. *thm*, to perforate (case 3)
12. *pshn*, to split (case 4)
13. *nha*, dangerous, anxious, perturbed
14. *ishw.w*, from the root *ish*, to spit, exude, ooze
15. *tkhb*, relates to irrigation, dampness
16. *wr*, large, big
17. *shfw.t*, swelling, edema, tumor
18. *shf.t*, ram's head
19. *sd*, fracture, fracture with depression, spike hole (case 5)
20. *tia*, convulsions? (case 7)
21. *skr*, strike, gives a blow, from which contusion results (case 8)
22. *si*, (to walk), stumbling, tripping
23. *rwty*, exterior, periphery
24. *ih*, "concussional state," shock?
25. *mdjd*, pressure (case 8, gloss C)
26. *djaw*, afflicted, attacked, injured? (case 19)
27. *hr pwy*, "face which is to the back" resulting from posterior face (case 19, gloss A)
28. *ahd*, weak, debilitated, impotent, infirm
29. *dgmy*, a syndrome that can be translated as "coma"? (case 22)
30. *gr*, to be still, to be silent
31. *gmw*, to be afflicted, feebleness, prostration?
32. *dgy*, weakness? "sideration"? inhibition?
33. *mdt*, to speak
34. *dgmy*, same word as no. 29, but determined by a prostrate figure; coma?
35. *nrwt*, sprain (case 30)
36. *wnkh*, dislocation (case 31)
37. *nswt*, displacement or subluxation (case 32)
38. *shm*, crushing (case 33)

Case 20. Perforation of the temporal bone. The two eyes are *shsm ty* and bloodshot; double epistaxis, slow and continuous; shivers when the wound is touched; the patient does not speak when questioned; he weeps profusely, making a constant, repeated, unconscious gesture with his arm to wipe his tears; neck stiff and painful; the patient is *dgmy*, determined by an eye with a raised eyebrow; verdict fatal.

Case 22. Fracture, *sd,* (with depression) in the temporal bone. Fracture of the petrosal bone; double epistaxis and otorrhea; the injured person is silent, he does not speak when he is called, his neck is stiff and painful; he is *dgmy*, determined by one eye; the gloss allows us to understand that there is discharge from the Sylvian aqueduct; verdict fatal.

Case 33. Depression of one cervical vertebra onto another following a fall on the head. The injured person is affected with quadriplegia; he cannot speak, he is *dgmy*, determined by the eye drawn twice; verdict fatal.

It is possible that *dgmy* corresponds to the state that we call a "coma." This can be complete or partial (the patient seems to be awake). By definition, a coma is the rupture of the contact that a being has with the exterior through his senses. Thus, "like someone who is under [the effect of] an inhibition by that which enters from the exterior" suggests the idea of a hematoma, a cerebral edema, or an intracranial hypertension syndrome, which would cause this coma.

MAGICAL INCANTATIONS

To end this brief exposition of some cases from the Surgical Papyrus, we include here a single passage from this treatise that presents an incantation to be spoken, as a spell, for the advised remedy:

Case 9

> *Instructions concerning wound in his forehead* [hat hr] *fracturing* [sd] *the shell of his skull.*
>
> *If you examine a man having a wound in his forehead, fracturing the shell of his* djadja, *you should make for him: an ostrich egg triturated with fat and placed in the mouth of his wound. Then after this you should make for him: triturated ostrich egg made as a poultice [in order to] dry this wound.*
>
> *You should place him under a covering for the use of the doctor. You should remove it the third day [when] you will find it bound to the shell [and] in color as that of the ostrich egg.*
>
> *The following incantation is a spell for this remedy:*
>> *Repelled is the enemy who is in the wound,*
>> *Cast back, the evil that is in the blood,*
>> *The adversary of Horus [of each] side of the mouth of the Luminous One* [akh t].
>> *This temple* [maā] *will not founder.*
>> *Within it there are no enemies of the channels* [mtw].
>> *I am under the protection of the Splendid One;*
>> *My deliverance is the son of Osiris.*
>
> *Then after this you should cool it [with] a compress of figs, fat, and honey, cooked, cooled [and] applied to it [the wound].*

A single gloss follows this case:

> *As for: "a covering for the use of the doctor," this is a band* sshd *which is "under the hand" of the embalmer, which he applies on this remedy that is on this wound, which is in his forehead.*[169]

The statement specifies the nature and the place of the injury: a *sd* fracture, or a depression of the skull, in the frontal region *(hat hr)*, that is, probably about in the place generally occupied by the royal uraeus. Given that each case of *sd* fracture cited in the papyrus is fatal, the completely abnormal exposition of this case is surprising at first view. After treating the injury with a preparation of triturated ostrich egg, it is proposed—and it is the only case in the papyrus—to pronounce the incantation, the translation of which we have given above. Contrary to his habit, the ancient surgeon mentions no examinations and makes no diagnosis. Two cases of probably analogous skull fractures, however, can shed light on this peculiarity. One of them shows a fatal injury, the other a lesion that was not followed by immediate death. In the first, the skull of a soldier from the Eleventh Dynasty shows a circular fracture several centimeters in diameter in the forehead above the eye. Several fissures lead from this fracture toward the base of the skull and reach the orbit. There is an understandable danger to the eye in such a case. In the second, the skull of a high priest of Amun at Thebes shows an injury made by a blow from a mace to the frontal bone. There are indications that death did not follow immediately, although, as in the preceding case, this fracture consists of a round hole of several centimeters.[170]

Experiments have proved that the ablation of one or both frontal lobes does not affect life directly or, properly speaking, the intelligence. It does have repercussions, however, on the depth of the personality, "the subject becomes superficial, indifferent, puerile, incapable of intellectual concentration, adapts with difficulty."[171] For these reasons, we can understand that the surgeon does not make a judgment, but immediately treats the patient so that "in accordance with the ambient conditions," he takes the chance of curing him.

It is obvious that this incantation, intended as a spell for a formula, is meant to evoke the characteristic effects of the remedy. Two applications are spoken of, one of which is necessary to heal the wound, and the other to disinfect the blood and to close the wound.

Now, the egg contains two substances; one is the white that coagulates, the other is the yoke—yellow and sulfurous—that is a coagulant. Therefore, one part must help to close the wound, the other resists fermentation and infection. From this the allusion to "the enemy who is in the wound" and to "the evil that is in the blood" is derived. The eye is in danger; we can understand the allusion to the adversary of Horus who is on either side of the Luminous One—one of the names of the eye and also of Isis—then to Osiris and to his son Horus, who both appear thanks to Isis, the Splendid One, who is the substance of life.

Reading symbolically with the help of the hieroglyphs, it is necessary to understand *maā*, temple, as "hearing," so that the phrase "this hearing will not founder" has meaning when we know

---

[169] According to Breasted, the "covering for the use of the doctor" ["covering for physician's *hn*"] should be a kind of bandage especially prepared for doctors by the embalmer. The commentary explains it by the word *sshd,* designating the linen strips wrapped around mummies. The Egyptians were masters in the art of bandages, and the coverings of the mummies were veritable masterpieces, bearing witness to an extraordinary skill and an unfailing precision. Breasted, *Smith Papyrus,* pp. 222–24, and plate 3.

[170] Cf. ibid., plate 7, figs. 13 and 14.

[171] Cf. Cossa, *Physiopathologie,* pp. 938–39.

the danger he is in. With regard to the enemies of the *mtw*, this enemy is always determined by a crocodile, related to Apophis, the serpent-dragon, enemy of Ra, just as the crocodile is one of the forms of Seth, the contracting power, the enemy of Horus. From this we can understand that there is no contraction of the *mtw*. Inasmuch as it is a *magical incantation*, it is necessary to see here the use of *living* substances that can prevent the deterioration of the tissues.

Professor Breasted was surprised to see a surgical treatise suddenly include a magical formula or incantation after having witnessed an exact science of practices based on long and precise experiments. It is obviously in a rather pejorative sense that the incantations and magical procedures often found in papyri are cited. The disdain that these questions inspire is motivated by an erroneous interpretation of the meanings of the words and a misunderstanding of the pharaonic mentality. The memory of sorcery, which was popular in past ages, also intervenes, a memory still very close to us who have only recently entered the scientific era. Although we have become reasonable, positive, and rational, we are still young on this path, which in our vanity, incites us to view with scorn these beliefs in the supernatural, in beneficent (but most often malefic) powers in the service of those who possess the secrets of incantation or the projection of spells.

Above all, it is necessary to distinguish magic from sorcery. Magic appeals through harmony to natural cosmic energy; sorcery is addressed to an influence of the psychic atmosphere, therefore to an energy emanating from a complex of human life.

Each of these actions has a double character. Magic may be abstract or "technical." The technical form requires the insemination of a milieu, leaving to nature the generation of the fruit. The abstract form requires knowledge of the rhythms of cosmic harmony, *playing the role of the abstract seed* to which one can only offer the milieu in order to generate the fruit: the sought-for effect. The rhythms are conditioned by the astronomical order and astral emanations. These are those moments, *classified and defined,* that are called *neters*.

Now, the reason behind the anthropomorphization of these principles is not the childish one given by historicism. It is known that a *neter* is attributed to each part of the human body. The *neter* is but an aspect of the harmony of natural forces. These forces are understood in their energetic quality, but also in their forms as living beings. Thus the human body, given over to the symbols of the *neters,* represents the totality of the work of nature that the specific symbol, from an aspect of the meeting of forces, momentarily colors. To appeal to a *neter* means, then, to investigate the favorable moment for the desired effect, but ignorance of the nature of the *neter* can produce a contrary or unfavorable effect.

The action of the *neters,* thus understood, will always be produced in a disordered milieu, such as in fermentation or in organic—or inorganic—disequilibrium, constituting the *conceptive* milieu. The formula of incantation, that is, the appeal to the sought-for activity in a given milieu, is nothing other than a specification of the effect that one desires.

It is a question here of a perfectly practical and even rational science, using a metaphysical power that nevertheless is situated in the same way that an irrational number is in mathematics.

This is by no means a chimera.

The practicing pathologist knows perfectly well that within a defined area certain illnesses or certain accidents, such as hemorrhagic phenomena, are often produced in a series. He also knows that certain illnesses can be aggravated or cured without our being able to say why. Obviously, to know these things, he would have to be a magician in the true and good sense; this means that it would be necessary for him to consider the phenomena of life in relation to the entirety of the rhythms of Nature and not—as we do—as isolated phenomena.

As for the appeal to psychical-emotional forces, this makes use of analogies. It will either be good, as is the prayer addressed to helpful entities above man, or bad, if we try to act upon our fellow creatures for a selfish goal, which is wrongly summarized by the term *sorcery*. There cannot be any confusion between magic and sorcery.

The *neters* are not what our universities think they are. They are real powers that act when one knows how to invite them to, not by formulas of "black magic" or other forms of sorcery, but by knowing cosmic laws. The same experiment in the same physical conditions can produce very different, even opposite, effects because of ambient conditions. This concerns everything that is of an organic nature, susceptible to fermentation and germination. The place, moreover, can also play a role, and thus no one has ever, for example, been able to match the quality of Munich's beer anywhere outside of Munich, or make a true camembert other than in Normandy.

An anecdote will make my meaning more explicit. A friend one day introduced me to a pomade or ointment composed of fats and resins, having the consistency of wax polish. The secret of its composition had been kept in his family, who had received it from a soldier of Bonaparte's army in Egypt. Cut in very thin layers and placed on a wound, abscess, or deep burn, this pomade is left on the spot for several days until it comes loose by itself, after which, a fine, new skin is formed on the wound. The cure, which I observed myself, suppressed all pain and left no scar. The formula for the composition of this ointment requires, besides the ingredients, a strict observance of the ambient conditions.

The stock of this precious product having been exhausted, my friend himself promised to make some more for me, but being rather skeptical, he did not take into account the required conditions concerning the "ambiance." One day, having to treat an abscess, I applied this new ointment. The abscess became carbuncular, so much so that in continuing to treat it with the ointment, it produced a serious gangrenous condition.

Having inherited the formula for this product, I have been able to experiment and learn some "magical formulas," that is, the ambient conditions and their influences. My friend, now deceased, unfortunately never knew how to "evoke the *neters*" who do not refuse to help the poor world when it knows to "pray" to them properly.

The "magical" formulas of the Surgical Papyrus are related to these procedures. The many oils, ointments, and pomades of the Temple have nothing in common with their counterparts in our pharmacopoeia.

—∿—

There is another question. It is often said, in connection with a diagnosis, that the practitioner should place a hand on the wound, then palpate with the fingers. I know, from seeing it done with such assurance by those who are so gifted, that it is possible to locate an ailment by passing the hands slightly above the body, even though that part of the body is not entirely exposed. The monitoring of the general condition of the body happens next with the same procedures on the phrenological centers of the head. The doctor, with his ordinary means, has only to confirm it. This is said without taking into account the "magnetic" effect of the hand that helps in the cure by reabsorbing the fever and, when one knows how to "invoke the *neter*," the sickness as well.

In closing this chapter I affirm the integral truth of what has been said, a truth rigorously tested and verified, if only to put an end to absurd interpretations, skeptical or fantastic, which misrepresent the "holy reality of the *neters*."

But as the sage said, *Cape, si capere potes.*

CONCLUSION

In comparing the methods of investigation, we note the total absence of instruments in the work of the ancient surgeon. We know, however, of at least one case of trephination, which implies the use of tools and, moreover, at Kom Ombo, there is a bas-relief that depicts all sorts of surgical instruments. There is, then, an effort to reconcile the chief concern with clinical symptoms.

Although they serve the practitioner, the great quantity of observations that presently comprises the richness of our medicine also presents the anguishing problem of choosing between a number of possibilities to make a diagnosis. It is his observation of the remarkable clinical sense of the Ancients that caused the admiration that Professor Leriche expressed to us during a visit to Luxor.

—⁓—

The few examples from the Surgical Papyrus cited here, some of which are related to the themes of the Temple discussed in this work, prove that certain diagnoses are impossible without the actual knowledge of the internal organs and the vital resonances that exist between them.

The fact of verifying symptoms, such as the paralyses, aphasias, aphonias, and so on, following localized injuries, clearly shows the existence of command centers for the organs through their location in the brain. The sensory and motor phenomena are presently known; but what still escapes us is the localization of the centers of intelligence and their correlations. Just yesterday it was still believed possible to locate exactly the chain of connections, and today we have attained the healthier notion that there are probably extended zones, as if certain parts of the cerebral matter constitute a kind of inclusive organ commanding very complex functions such as, for example, auditory intelligence.

When the "mechanism" of a sense organ has been damaged or destroyed, it naturally modifies its receptivity. Today, however, the problem in neurophysiology is to find the *intellective* centers that might in the end lead to the possible localization of the faculties for the perception of phenomena.

The research procedures of our scientists in this regard can only turn out to be negative; they cut out certain parts of the brain and observe the result. This is pure empiricism. Now it seems that in these experiments two essential facts are neglected that distort the outcomes that we believe could be deduced. First, the medical excision is "clean" in comparison to the wound, that is, care has been taken to avoid discharges of blood, which leaves the nerves in a healthy state. But at the time of the injuries or hematomas or abscesses, the organ is sick. The *mtw*, (or channels) are disturbed and repercussions occur in other parts of the cerebral organism. Second, it is certain that the removal of one part of a set of two, such as one of the cerebral hemispheres (a rare operation, but successful in serious cases), necessarily causes a revitalization, at least momentarily, of the remaining healthy part. The new observed state cannot, therefore, be absolutely conclusive in revealing the functional nature of the remaining part.

These are two objections (purely philosophical on my part since I do not have the competence to discuss the case with specialists), but they do indicate a possibility of error in the conclusions that can be drawn from these experiments. Moreover, it was logical for our electronic-atomic era to think of the electromagnetic effects that connect the various cerebral centers and eventually to note their functional characteristics by their wavelengths. This has as yet yielded nothing, although I consider that this is an approach to the problem, but on the condition that the mechanistic character of "electromagnetism" is renounced as well as the illusion of the "wave" in the way that it is considered today.

In the anthropocosmic conception of the Ancients, there is certainly a relationship between the "substantial" nature of the various areas of the brain and identical states of cosmic "substance" in the astronomical positions of the sky, the Universe being absolute Man. This way of seeing joins together the fact that the sense organs responsive to the relationships between human beings and their surroundings are not created to observe the surrounding phenomena, but rather *result from the energetic action* of these phenomena. I have already suggested this image: the banks of the river are not made to carry it; it is the river that forms and modifies the banks. As for intelligence, or consciousness, that is, the complex organizer of received impressions, it can only be the effect of an identity, that which, by definition, is supernatural, which is to say, beyond bodily forms.

The medical papyri as well as the Pyramid Texts assign a *neter* to each part of the human body.[172] One is inclined to see a gesture in this, which, if not childish, is at least of an imaginative character, motivated by theological reasons.

I think it is necessary to see in this anthropomorphizing of vital functions, corporified in humanity, a reason dictated by wisdom. It is not a part of the living human body that one attributes to the *neter*, but the characteristic function of the *neter* that is embodied in the human being. The *neter* is the functional principle of an aspect of Nature. Together they constitute the totality of the knowledge of the genetic work of the Universe, knowledge that is an exceptional power, rarely given and carefully protected under the superior guidance of the Temple.

Now, all science, all research, not guided by this Ariadne's thread is individual science and research, isolating parts from each other that can then no longer be reunited, which creates a state of uncertainty, and finally, a disaggregation of human society! Each speaks its own language, understanding is impossible.

But in transferring to life, corporified in all the kingdoms and supremely in the human body, the synthesis-*neter* of an essential functional type, the study of any part through the myth (the historical, theogonic form), attaches itself to the whole without this whole being necessarily actually known by the isolated individual in its complete and applied sense. By virtue of this fact, each will speak the same language as the others while studying a single part of nature.

Let us take an example to illustrate this proposition. The animal "form" that most particularly represents the visual sense is the bird, the brain of which is almost entirely retinal. It is then to the bird in general that one should address oneself in order to study this organism.

Among birds, the falcon summarizes, through its life, habits, and constitution, a collection of conditions most particularly appropriate to demonstrate the functional relationship of the visual sense with its cerebral surroundings.[173] The falcon serves as symbol, and Horus is its *neter*. Through Horus the "eye principle" enters into myth, that is, it unites with the natural genesis.

Horus is the son of Isis, the Luminous One, spirit in its feminine aspect, lunar, and thus of a white character, lymphatic, the coagulable feminine albuminoid and reflector in the cathodic lunar sense.

Isis conceived Horus by the Osirian phallus that was isolated from the dismembered body of Osiris, whose limbs were scattered about. In other words, Osiris is the principle of regeneration, of

---

[172] For example, in the Pyramid Texts (1304–15): The face is Upuat (the jackal who opens the ways); the two eyes are "the great" (Isis) before the souls of Heliopolis; the toes are "the souls of Heliopolis." The nose is Thoth; the tongue is assimilated to *maāi*, the trustworthy, and related to the barque of *maāt*. The two soles of the feet are the two barques. One vertebra, placed between the jaw and the shoulders, is assimilated to the bull *sma* (who severs), etc.

[173] The eye shows the optic nerve whose axis is formed by a nourishing artery with an empty center, a kind of magnetic axis surrounded by a rich network of fibers opening out into the retina, of a character that we can, comparatively, call electronegative.

the constant renewal of nature, by virtue of bringing the annual flux and reflux of energy. He is the *principle* of renewal insomuch as he is the channel of this cosmic energy, and this is why only his phallus or *mtw*, the *conduit*, serves as the indeterminate impregnator in place of a determined seed.

Now, the eye offers us the unique occasion to study in its constitution the culmination of a nerve in its living state. The only channel, *mtw*, of the human body that it is possible for us to know in a living state is the phallus, and this is why, moreover, it serves as the symbol for the word *mtw*.[174]

The study of the eye as the *neter* Horus brings us through myth to the link that leads us throughout nature: the eye is no longer an isolated organ, but the result of a group of functions, both in its evolution—as son of Osiris and Isis—and in its activity and effects in connection with the functional whole of man (as, for example, with the cardiac plexus).[175]

This is but a very simplified example of the meaning of the myth in relation to man's organism and life, because the whole "history" of the myth of Horus, Isis, and Osiris and all that unfolds from it has yet to be analyzed and studied.

Thus, thanks to myth, which is none other than the anthropomorphized symbolization of the general and essential functions of universal life, one is able to devote oneself to a particular study without abandoning the story of the whole, that is, without specialization intervening and distorting the synthesis without which all effort leads to disorder.

Thus the position of the Ancients with respect to the secrets of human life is absolutely different from our own. Through the knowledge of the essential, primordial phenomenon, source of a philosophy (or rather of an intuitive logic), the investigation of natural phenomena, in the case of surgery that occupies us here, is no longer required. There is no need for an anatomy, a vivisectionist butchery, as practiced by our science, which, among other things, searches for the secrets of the human brain in the animal brain, especially that of the monkey, even though the cerebral phenomenon of man is infinitely more subtle than it is in an animal such as the chimpanzee, for which impressions are direct, primitive, and relatively unsynthesized.

This explains why the papyrus never speaks to us of surgical interventions that, nevertheless, were surely used, as proved in case 8, which necessarily implies a trephination, as does the trepanned skull of Lisht. That which was possible for responsible men linked to the Temple was probably carefully kept secret from the people. It is not only a matter of surgical practices, although respect for life and the human body might motivate a particular discretion, but one never finds elsewhere any explanations of the technical or mechanical procedures that were obviously used to cut certain stones, to erect monolithic obelisks, or to lift the immense blocks of stone in constructions, for example.

It certainly seems as though a veil was voluntarily thrown over these aspects of technique. This might be to keep certain abnormal methods used in material work secret, or to leave the knowledge of more mechanical procedures only in responsible hands, which if passed into the hands of the people, might risk engendering an unfortunate modification in social order and "evolution."

The Temple seems to have been apprehensive about putting that which could possibly cause people to deviate from their life close to nature into the irresponsible hands of the masses. These learned men, in the pure sense, certainly possessed it; all the works testify to a superior guidance.

---

[174] The phallus contains a channel whose walls are highly irrigated and rich in nerve sensitivity. Ejaculation through this channel is due to this "undulating" innervation, alternately contracting and dilating, a role that today is beginning to be recognized also in veins and arteries. Alternation always, alternation of polarity of one and the same energy.

[175] Cf. fig. 137.

But what seems to have been feared above all was the "scholastic" way of thinking, which removes us from nature.

Why?

Let us suppose for a moment that our world, discovering that energy is imprisoned in matter, and for stupidly selfish reasons, brings about the catastrophe that leaves our earth desolate. Let us suppose again, which is less probable today, that an elite is able to survive and begins again to construct a new era of humanity with the healthy human elements that remain. Would this elite not have the wisdom to guide the people in such a way that they do not make the same mistakes again in the future?

This reasoning is still in the manner of our current thinking. In Ancient Egypt, it was not a matter of a thinking elite, in the fashion of our learned and scientific men, but, on the contrary, of an elite "initiated" into the true secrets of nature and not to the mechanical and rational secrets.

The principle of this reasoning is acceptable, but the elements are imaginary because our humanity has arrived at an ending, whereas the sages who founded the pharaonic empire were still close to an intuitive consciousness, inspired by the *neters*, the natural powers.

—∿—

Now we are going to move on to the architecture of the Temple. This involves nothing more than the application of everything we have just seen, with the addition of the specifications given by the texts, the figures, and the numbers. Through the principle of harmony, the Temple represents a synthesis of all the aspects we have noted with regard to the *canevas*, mathematical thought, and the characteristic directives made available through this presentation of the surgical papyrus.

Chapter 15

THE DIADEM

THE CROWN OF THE SKULL

A person kneeling is deprived of the limbs necessary for locomotion, he can no longer move. If this person then joins his hands, he also takes away the limbs necessary for action, he can no longer act. These actual gestures are also symbolic: they create a state of passivity, and represent the voluntary abdication of personal independence, the acceptance of a superior authority. The "tying" of the legs in the Buddhist "lotus" posture does this even more completely. We come across this posture in Egypt as well. This gesture of abdication of the personality is in itself a prayer, more genuinely so than the mental wording of a request or an act of adoration.

We understand the language of gestures. Thus, a sitting figure, with hands separated and palms opposed, represents the *dialectic* in the sculpted figures on our cathedrals. In the case of Buddha, this same gesture is one of *teaching*, which is a more valid interpretation, since teaching is opposing a knowledge to an ignorance, and it also expresses metaphysical reality (the role of the left hand) within physical appearance (the action of the right hand).

The living gesture speaks and says what can never be transcribed into words in an equally vital way. This is the true symbol.

Joining arms and legs for prayer is the immediate gesture, but the true prayer, that is, the merging with the *neter*, demands, on the one hand, the life of the person, and on the other, the abstraction of his ego, the selfish being of cerebral or mental reflection.

This alone is the victory over the mortal personality: Nicodemus, the second birth in the Gospel. This is why the *still symbolic* statuary of the cathedrals depicts this saint with the crown of his skull held in his hands.[1] This is also why saints in Byzantine art—the principal figurations of the established Orthodox Church—are portrayed with flat heads, without the crown of the skull.

The physiological significance of the suppression of the cortex is summarized at the end of this chapter. The gesture and its consequences, removing the part of the brain that governs all personal

---

[1] Cf. plate 43.

reactions and decisions, is symbolized by the lotus posture and by prayer, signifying no more than the act of making a human being drowned in intellectual complications "simple."[2] It marks another state, the state of pure intuition, which is to say that it allows the innate knowledge of the *neter* (cosmic function), the Anthropocosmos in man, to speak.

It is at the same time Adamic Man (not chased out of terrestrial paradise) and the man who has been subjected to the trials of corporeal incarnation.

So, what is this cerebral mass that enables the organized being to become aware of itself, thus creating what we call our psychological consciousness? It is the mirror of Heaven; but the mirror is facing the earth and has not yet turned over to face Heaven. It is the *substance* of that which is only *image* turned around by the mirror, but a flat horizontal mirror that reverses up and down, right and left. It is man outside the Temple.

Let us recall, in this regard, the conversion of Saint Paul, who was going out to fight Christian teaching and who was thrown face down against the earth by the heavenly fire, and who then rose into the vision of truth,[3] which, in relation to what we said about the crown of the skull, justifies the *extra muros* church in Rome, consecrated to Saint Paul and built in the form of the *tau* (T).*

In Pharaonic Egypt the marking of the crown of the skull, separated by a headband or a joint, is both the key to the mystical objective and the key to all thought based on the inverses.

—∿∿—

Egyptian figurations carefully indicate—with a headband, crown, diadem, or joint—a demarcation line for the top of the cranium, thus separating the crown of the skull.[4]

The ϕ proportion of the human body, measured from the soles of the feet to the navel and from the navel to the top of the head, varies with age. The Greeks counted as unity the distance from the top of the head down to the navel, thus falsifying the proportion, which is only correct for the unity of navel to headband, which cuts off the crown of the skull. It is thus possible for us to determine the age of the figure in question, which takes on its full meaning once we know that the king is the sun who is young and pubescent in the morning, fully mature at noon, and an old man in the evening.

The head is considered to be the "covered temple," the sanctuary of the human body where all the control centers are gathered. The head is represented in the pavestones of the covered temple at Luxor, which at the same time provides the proportional unit for Man as represented by this temple.[5] The physiological and organic study of the head is extremely complex. Let us point out the most immediately interesting facts.

Within the organs of the encephalon the following must be distinguished:

1. The medulla oblongata and the pons, the terminal point at the top of the spinal column.
2. The cerebellum, the center for the coordination of stimuli coming from the periphery or the cerebrum, and the regulator of all the movements required for standing or moving (equilibrium).
3. The cerebrum, with its two hemispheres, the control center for activity and the inscription of ideas.

---

[2] This is also the implied meaning of *demos,* "the people" or "the simple," "that which is subordinate," in *Nicodemus.*

[3] Acts 9:1–9.

[4] Cf. plate 39.

[5] Cf. plates 34–38.

* St. Paul's Outside the Walls.

4. The triple complex of the olfactory glands, the pituitary gland, and the pineal gland, which form the true "holy of holies," since all faculties of intelligence and sexual activity rely particularly on them.

Twelve pairs of cranial nerves leave the medulla oblongata and the pons and control the whole life of the head, except for two: the pneumogastric nerve, which innervates and relates the head to all the other vegetative functions of the body, and the spinal nerve, which connects the head and the neck.

The two hemispheres of the cerebrum are made up of the outer layer (cortex or mantle), composed of gray matter, and a white mass underlying the nervous fibers.

From the cortex, with the two lobes of the cerebrum, stem all the orders for every action of the body; it is from the frontal ascending convolution, along the fissure of Rolando (as well as along its extension on the inner surface of the cerebrum, the paracentral lobe), that all the motor impulses stem.

This is the location of what is medically called the "upside-down man" [or homunculus], because from top to bottom, all the body's commands leave in an inverted pattern: the highest point of the fissure of Rolando controls the feet, whereas the bottom of the fissure is where the controls for the head are located.

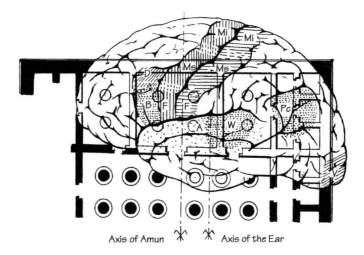

Axis of Amun   Axis of the Ear

Fig. 177. Projection of the left profile of the brain onto the southern part of the covered temple

In front of the fissure of Rolando are the motor fibers, behind it, the sensory fibers: *Mi* and *Mi,* the lower limbs; *Ms* and *Ms,* the upper limbs; *F* and *F,* the face, tongue, larynx, etc.; *A* (first temporal), the sensory center of audition; *V,* sensory center of vision (reflecting center).

Centers of language, in the left brain only: *B,* center of articulated language (the weaving of the Verb); *W,* center of the auditory images of words (the intelligence of the image by hearing); *Pc,* center of the visual images of words.

Let us point out that this double part of the cerebrum is precisely that part that regulates the life of relation, determining what I call the center of *cerebral intelligence,* the part that requires comparison, as opposed to the Ancient Egyptians' "intelligence of the heart," which gives the direct concept without the necessity of comparison by opposition.[6]

---

[6] Generally speaking, the brain, the center of all coordination of notions, is therefore the seat of all *personal reactions.* With all ancient peoples, the "simple-minded" were considered to be inspired, or *susceptible of being directly inspired,* acting in the absence of all personal, reasoned will.

Let us also note that the two hemispheric lobes of the brain are separated by a lamina (an extension of the dura mater) that ossifies with age and is shaped like a scythe (fig. 178). This lamina acts as separator, not only in fact, but also symbolically, by dividing the cortical part of the brain in which ideas and the faculty of reasoning intelligence are registered into two halves. It is not simply a question of separating a single organ into two parts, but separating a function into the two aspects that form psychological consciousness and "cerebral" intelligence. Any "notion" is the consciousness of a definition through the oppostion of two possibilities, one affirmative, the other negative. The observed fact is the affirmative pole, and, taken to an extreme, *its negation makes it comprehensible* and creates the faculty of reasoning. Through this organ we are able to understand only by means of successive eliminations and then a final selective choice, which for man is ordinarily the only possibility of augmenting his knowledge.

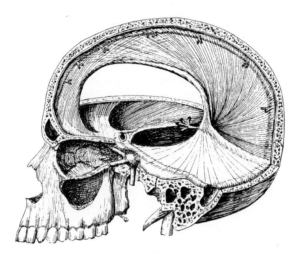

Fig. 178. The falx cerebri formed by an extension of the dura mater

At its upper and lower parts, the longitudinal sinuses run to the lateral sinus. Behind the orbit, the gasserian ganglion or trigeminal nerve divides into three main branches: (1) the ophthalmic nerve, which innervates the ocular and nasal mucous membranes and the ophthalmic ganglion; (2) the maxillary nerve, which innervates the orbit, Meckel's ganglion, the opening of the eustachian tube, the pharynx, and the nasal fossae (fig. 169); and (3) the mandibular nerve, which innervates the temples, the masseter muscle, the mouth, the tympanic cavity, the malleus muscle, the teeth of the mandible, and the otic ganglion.

These three ganglions receive their sympathetic nerve fibers from the plexus of the internal carotid artery and some parasympathetic nerve fibers from various sources. The sympathetic fibers have their interaxial centers located in the spine between C6 and T2.

In the pharaonic human canon, the gasserian ganglion is situated on the eighteenth line and C7 on the sixteenth line; the ratio is that of the tone, 8 to 9.

Thus the falx cerebri (the scythe of Maāt) actually separates the organs of cerebral intellection by creating psychological consciousness, thanks to the scission of consciousness into affirmation and negation. It is by this fact the symbol of Maāt, justice, in other words, of judgment. The two lobes of the brain are the seat of the affirmative and negative inscriptions, making it the instrument for the transcription (psychological consciousness) of the direct and unique, intuitive intelligence of "Adamic Man."

The description of this "direct and unique intellect" escapes us, as do all notions of unity, which, nevertheless, reason forces us to accept.

If, in the figuration of man, we symbolically separate the crown of the skull, we allow only Divine Man, Adamic Man (Kadmon) before his fall into nature, to remain, because after the fall he will find himself in constant opposition (male Adam and female Eve), and must, therefore, be born and die; he will no longer be able to understand anything by merging (identifying) with the creative Unity, but only by the comparison of complementaries (psychological consciousness).

In the Greek style, it is natural man—man here below—who is depicted with this crown of the skull, as it shows the golden section.

In their temples the ancient Egyptians speak only of the principles of the World and of Cosmic Man or Anthropocosmos. Now, by removing the skullcap when the intent requires it, they separate out the organ that is the symbol of the fall from direct and divine intelligence into transitory Nature; and this double brain (right and left) becomes the principle of the sexualization and of the intelligence of the Created World. This is one of the aspects that particularly interests us in the *symbolique* of the temple of Luxor.

The results of various experiments show that the ablation of the two hemispheres of the brain allows man to continue living, but with no discernment whatsoever, therefore with no personal judgment.[7] This part of the encephalon's organs thus plays a very important role in the evolution of consciousness. The two hemispheric lobes of the brain are the instrument of memory and decision, therefore of choice.

The figuration of "prenatural" man, without this part of the brain, therefore represents the divine principle of the *neter*, capable of living and acting, but only as the executant of an impulse received from elsewhere; thus, he plays the part of intermediary between the hyperphysical (outside Nature) impulsion and its execution within Nature, without personal choice. In this regard, he is an entity with a primitive, "prenatural" (antephysical) character.

Natural man, on the other hand, uses his cerebral instrument as a means for "suffering Nature" ("suffering" understood as profound experience brought about by the conflict of consciousness, not as sorrow). He will use it as a tool of his knowledge and his freely determined actions; these actions will then be in agreement or at variance with natural harmony. When, for example, through his experience, he will have developed his consciousness to utmost perfection, he will no longer need this cerebral instrument for its acquisition, but solely in order to *act* in this incarnation. This is the aim of yoga.

The life of this "superman"—in pure contemplation and ecstasy (ex-stasis)—will again be that of "divine" man, but in consciousness, that is, no longer as a blind *neter*, but as a being carrying within himself all knowledge, the sum of all possible experiences.

Thus Man without the crown of the skull symbolizes both prenatural Adamic Man and Man having "surpassed" Nature. Terrestrial man, undergoing birth and death, is placed between the two.

It is interesting to find this organ contained in an external bony framework, such as an insect's carapace. This characteristic, as well as the sutures of the skull and the entire shape thus formed by the crown of the skull, can be compared to the image of the scarab,[8] the theme of which was of special interest in Egypt during the transition period from the Eighteenth to the Nineteenth Dynasties, also the period in which the temple of Luxor was built and consecrated to the spiritual conception and birth of Royal Man.

---

[7] See the experiments relating to this in the appendix, note 2.

[8] Cf. plate 40.

The profile of the man's head that serves as the symbolic basis for this temple is depicted without the crown of the skull, as we are going to show later on, when we shall see what the state of the man is who corresponds to this representation.[9]

—∿∿—

Ancient Egypt, having a "vitalist mentality" in every form of expression, borrows human limbs, gestures, and organs in order to symbolize the esoteric functions of Universal Man.[10] It is therefore equally logical to choose the most characteristic types of animate creatures to represent these organs and functions. In this anthropocosmic doctrine, each plant and animal species represents a stage in the evolution of consciousness, and, so to speak, the "living organ-type" of that phase of evolution.

The anthropocosmic principle is only valid if the human principle is All. In man there exists he who *knows,* and he who, after the separation of the ego—the expulsion from terrestrial paradise—comes into contact with his environment. This latter renounces Unity; he is himself and the other. The other, which is the world described to us by the senses, is a reflected projection of our innate knowledge. This image is only relatively real, as is our own image reflected in a mirror, which we ascribe to ourselves.

The principle of *innate knowledge* belongs to transcendental philosophy. The senses seem to establish a relationship between the object and knowledge that we have of it, innate in us. These objects are therefore only objects insofar as we ourselves already share, functionally speaking, that which specifies them.

Who is it then that distinguishes the object for us, as being outside of ourselves? *Vitally,* there is no separation: that which specifies the object makes it knowable to us by the fact that the specification is innate in us and has formed us, such as we are; the "form" and the nature of the object are within us. In this case there is no problem of identification since there is no division with regard to quality.

Consciousness of the separation only begins with comparison. This comparison is only possible if a neutral, indifferent state creates the effect of reflecting by splitting the form in two: on the one hand, there is the *reality* that is its unique and general specificity; on the other, there is the image reflected in a direction that is no longer general but determined, which gives rise to the "outside of ourselves" illusion, making the form corporeal.

During the deep sleep that eliminates the mirror, or rather the reflecting cerebrality, the illusion no longer exists except for a brief persistence of the mnesic image.

Reflection, in a determined direction, creates the senses. There is therefore the *center of intelligence,* the place of concentration of the qualitative character of what is functionally innate; then there is the sensory tool that is the instrument of projection of the cerebral reflection.

It would seem that the senses inform us of the existence of an object, but in fact they are what *make the object* corporeal to the psychological consciousness.

The feeling of objective reality does not simply arise from cerebral action toward the outside, but, by means of the senses, from a crossed function of a reflection toward the intellect. The white cerebral matter is then "lunar" in the sense that it has the character of a neutral, indifferent environment, a *reflector* of impressions. This reflection is oriented toward the five aspects—light,

---

[9] Cf. plates 34–38.

[10] The *puruṣa* of the Vedas (cf. Upaniṣads).

odor, sound, taste, touch—corresponding to the five principal elements that constitute the senses (touch should be considered as a general sensitivity represented by any state toward an identical state).

The brain, by itself, is not an "evil" in the spiritual sense; it is, *outside Man,* the ultimate sublimation of his physical substance—white, silvery, neutral—the *satellite* of the organized *body.* It is the substance that registers impressions, and if the five channels (the senses) did not project the reflection of these impressions toward the outside, the illusion of the objectively real would not exist; only the knowledge gained through the identity of our being with Universal Being would remain.

In the pharaonic temple, the lunar cerebral mass, the satellite of the human body, is separated from the secret sanctuaries. Outside the wall of the temple *(extra muros),* this satellite forms an entire architectural group devoted particularly to the Thotian character (Thoth-mes), which can still be verified at Karnak.[11] This part of the temple of Luxor, with the skullcap bearing the crown, is at present destroyed and buried under a roadway and block of houses, but hunks of stone embedded in the earth are still visible in the garden of the Luxor Hotel.

DIADEM, I ASSUME THEE

The crown of the skull comprises the parts of the brain that permit judgment and cerebral discernment. It can be removed without the vital centers being affected. Natural man with his "innate" consciousness would survive, but all intervention of the psychological consciousness would be removed; he would obey cosmic thought without his own thought being able to disrupt it.

This is the symbolic significance of the removal of the skullcap, depicted in Egypt, as we have said, by the crown, the headbands, and often by the joints of the stones in the mural sculpture[12] or by other means. We come across the same intention in India and in primitive Byzantine iconography in figures with very flattened skulls. The removal of the crown of the skull is intentional.

The imposition of the "royal headband," a rite transmitted to the West, and in similar forms customary with all peoples, finds its true significance in pharaonic Egypt.

The first question is, if the separation of the crown of the skull aims at separating the part of the brain that judges against the divine will, where is this boundary located? The boundary obviously varies according to each individual. Now, the natural cubit of man, from the elbow to the extremity of the ring (solar) finger, is the small human cubit that measures 24 digits. For a man of correct proportions this measure is exact, but *it is considered to be* 24 *digits* (6 *palms*) *in all men regardless of the fact that their heights vary.* Therefore, the *relative royal cubit* will be 7 palms or 28 digits, and this length, closing itself into a circle, designates the place on the skull of the scission. The royal headband is thus *symbol* and *measure* at the same time.[13]

The symbol of this pharaonic royal headband (known as a *diadem,* from the Latin) is explicitly defined by the diadem found in the tomb of Tutankhamun. The circle is divided, from front to back, by the undulation of the serpent, which represents the separation of the cranial hemisphere into two parts.[14] On his forehead the king wears the Egyptian raised cobra and the vulture's head,

---

[11] From excavations and studies undertaken on this subject by Alexandre Varille.

[12] Cf. plate 39.

[13] *meh* refers to "cubit of measurement"; *mh* refers to "diadem," "crown"; Erman and Grapow, *Wörterbuch.*

[14] Cf. plate 42; fig. 178.

animal symbols of the two principal functions, organically characterized by the pituitary body and the pineal gland (the third eye represented in Buddhism by a ruby or a diamond).[15] These two primordial and essential glands are independent of the dualizing encephalon and therefore free from psychological judgment. Their importance is underlined by these symbols, and their activity is accentuated through the de-emphasis of personal judgment.

The king, girded with the diadem, is enthroned as a superhuman being, the guide of his people, instituted by the grace of God—and not as a man. It is regrettable for this king if, as head of state, he obeys his personal judgments, and it is unfortunate for the people who accept such a man.[16]

The royal principle is sacred provided not only that the imposition of the diadem be a symbolic gesture, but that this king be naturally gifted, or educated to acquire this gift of "abstraction" or "mastery of the ego."

The diadem, having become a crown, which in turn *replaces the personal skullcap,* signifies this king's state of consciousness, his place in the superhuman genesis. We can go deeper into the subject by studying the meaning of the various pharaonic crowns.

Christian kings wore for their "crown of the skull" the crown with Christian emblems: the Christic spirit thus replaces personal judgment.

In the Luxor temple the phases of the ritual take place in each room through which the officiant must pass. The officiant is always represented *as king,* and can only enter the secret sanctuaries as a crowned king, in other words, in his capacity as a superhuman being. This same principle is observed in Brahmanic Hindu temples.

The *diadem as measure* gives this measure its royal character by the line separating the human from the divine. This "cubit-measure" is directly related to the fathom, which is *the human measure of the earth.* Anthropocosmic man, the ultimate product of the earth, carries within him all the given facts of this earth, including the elements that measure it. Marine tradition has preserved the fathom as one-thousandth of the average nautical mile, which equals 1′ of meridian arc at 45° latitude. This arc varies from the equator to the pole, that is, from 0° to 90°, because of the flattening of the terrestrial globe. Further on, we shall come across the elements that demonstrate the Ancient Egyptian knowledge of this geoid (the terrestrial globe flattened at the North Pole), and we have already spoken at greater length of "measures." This relationship between the fathom and the royal cubit in regard to the diadem is again confirmed by the "North Pole skullcap" of our globe. In chapter 11 we spoke of the subtle squared-grid system based on 19 for the human canon. Now, man is the *reference* for all pharaonic knowledge to such a degree that the sages conceived the earth itself according to the human canon. The polar radius, or half-axis of the earth, is considered to be

---

[15] A. Erman, *La Religion des Egyptiens* (Paris: Payot, 1937), p. 91: "As we have seen and will again have the opportunity to see, the solar eye is endowed with its own force. It appears in a story of which, unfortunately, we can understand only half. We read there that Ra had once sent forth his eye (no doubt to fight some enemy or other), but that it had not returned. Then Ra dispatched Shu and Tefnut to bring it back. The eye became angry because of this and from its tears men were born, yet another play on the words *remyt,* 'tear,' and *romet,* 'man.' But the eye *was incensed when it returned and found that another had grown in its stead.* The god then took the eye, if we understand correctly, and placed it in the shape of a serpent on his forehead. Henceforth, the solar eye *governs the whole world,* for this serpent worn by Ra on his forehead is the symbol of his power. From this moment onward, Shu was called Onuris [Anhur], which means *he-who-has-brought-back-the-faraway.*"

[16] Concerning the sacred character of the royal coronation, we can recall that the kings of France in particular were anointed by the oil of the Holy Phial that conferred on them the supernatural power of healing scrofulous evils by touch *at the end* of the ceremony. We should mention again the statue of Nicodemus, Saint Nicasius (see plate 43), in the portico of the cathedral of Notre Dame at Reims, the church of the royal coronation. This cathedral, begun in the twelfth century, was built on the foundation of the former cathedral built by Saint Nicasius around the year 400.

a man standing on the plateau cut by the equator (fig. 179).[17] This division into nineteen units or squares places the cap between 73° and 74° north latitude, outlining at the pole a cap surrounded by the fringe of the continents, which at that place collapse into the abyss of the Arctic Ocean.[18]

In the cone-shaped space formed by two meridians joined at the pole, the equatorial arc between these two meridians is the *same in number of fathoms* as the parallel arc at 73°34′ of latitude is *in number of royal cubits*. This polar cap is the cap of Man-Earth and thus locates the terrestrial diadem that surrounds the "fontanelle" of the terrestrial head. As in the fontanelle of the newborn,[19] the terrestrial North Pole is the magnetic place of absorption of cosmic energy, the Archaeus that gives life, but it also becomes the place where bodies, the corporeal part of life, come to die. Several old traditions can be linked to this fact, such as the gesture of benediction by laying the hands on the head.

As we can see, the diadem as the separating line of the crown of the skull is the symbol of an important reality.

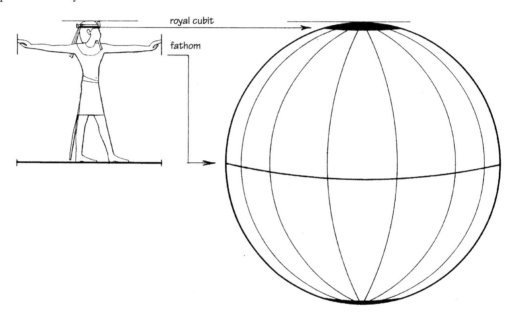

royal cubit

fathom

Fig. 179. Man standing on the equatorial plateau

Numerical Study of the Terrestrial Skullcap

We are concerned with the following principle: the actual measurements of the earth flattened at the pole modify the results established below by a few minutes of arc for a perfect sphere having 40,000,000 true meters of equatorial circumference.

---

[17] This reminds us of the fissure of Rolando in the cerebral mass; the scythe plays the part of the equator for the hemispheres.

[18] This can be related to the legend of the Maelstrom. What is called the "polar cap" is the ice cap or floe that stretches from the pole to about 73°–74° north or south latitude. But we need to mention that the principle of the human and terrestrial cap only applies to the North Pole (*mh* means "cubit," *mht* means "north," *mhn* means "diadem"), whereas the South Pole is the place of birth of the continents, and therefore of the beginning of the earth. In pharaonic times, the south was called *res;* its symbol is *sout,* the scirpus rush, which is, moreover, the first vegetation to appear from silt. The temple of Luxor, which is the place of the gestation and youth of the king, is called Apet of the South.

[19] The Edwin Smith Surgical Papyrus defines the fontanelle of the newborn as "the weak place in the child's crown before it is joined together." Cf. fig. 167, no. 10, and commentary.

$$\text{Equatorial circumference} = 21{,}600{,}000 \text{ fathoms} = 40{,}000{,}000 \text{ meters}$$

$$\text{Radius of the sphere} = \frac{21{,}600{,}000 \text{ fathoms}}{2\pi} = 6{,}366{,}182 \text{ meters}$$

$$\text{Cap circumference} = 21{,}600{,}000 \text{ royal cubits} = 11{,}309{,}900 \text{ meters}$$

$$\text{Radius of the cap disk} = \frac{21{,}600{,}000 \text{ royal cubits}}{2\pi} = 1{,}800{,}000 \text{ meters}$$

The radius of the disk cut out by the cap is the sine of a triangle whose hypotenuse is the radius of the sphere. Man is supposed to be standing on the equatorial plane whose circumference is measured in fathoms; his royal headband coincides with the earth's cap, which is measured in royal cubits (fig. 179).

For a sphere measuring 21,600,000 fathoms in circumference at the equator, the disk measuring 21,600,000 royal cubits in circumference is at latitude 73°34′30″.

Now, the ice floe that forms the polar cap is located on the globe between 73° and 74°, thus framing the theoretical angle determined by calculations for a perfect sphere, that is, one that does not take into account the flattening of the earth, which slightly modifies the sphere.

The search for the closest ratios in whole numbers that define the angle of approximately 16°26′ leads to two solutions that are directly linked to the essential functions governing the variations of the cubits.[20] First, the angle with base 7 and side 1 has $\sqrt{50}$ as hypotenuse, and its value in degrees is 8°8′. Its doubling determines the Diophantine triangle 7, 24, 25, whose angular value is therefore 16°16′. Second, the angle with hypotenuse 7 and side 1 has $\sqrt{48}$ for base, and its value in degrees is 8°12′43″. Its doubling determines the triangle that has a side of $2\sqrt{48}$, with a base of 47 and a hypotenuse of 49. Its angular value is, consequently, approximately 16°26′, in other words, within a few seconds of the theoretical angle we are looking for.

As the pharaonic cubits show, the two suggested angles govern the latter's principal metrical deviations. The angle 1 to 7 is the angle of reflection of Amun, but it is also the angle that governs the variants of the different arcs of the terrestrial meridian. Now, there is a relation between these angular values and those in the temple of Luxor with regard to north. The south wall corresponds to the royal headband of the Man of the Temple; it is perpendicular to one of the walls of room V, the place where the uraeus of the royal headband is located and whose orientation is at about 32°30′ from true north,[21] that is, at an angle four times the value of the angle of reflection of Amun.

The south wall of the covered temple must then represent the length of a royal cubit measuring the circumference of the crown of the skull of the Man of the Temple, in relation to a fathom that should be represented by the base on which he stands (the courtyard of Nectanebo), in the image of man placing his feet on the equator (fig. 179).

Indeed, the ratio between the theoretical fathom and the royal cubit, 1 mean fathom ÷ 1 royal cubit = 3.5367..., is as the ratio that exists between the two lengths of the temple mentioned above:

$$\frac{\text{the length of south wall, courtyard of Nectanebo}}{\text{length of south wall, covered temple}} = \frac{130.9 \text{ meters}}{37.0 \text{ meters}}, = 3.537\ldots$$

a coefficient that represents $2.5\sqrt{2}$ or 3.53552... in its irrational form.

In fact, the fathom and the royal cubit are thus linked by the root of 2, but, in the temple, the

---

[20] Cf. figs. 115 and 116.

[21] Plus or minus 5′. Cf. chapter 39, appendix.

south wall of the covered temple measures 20 fathoms and the courtyard of Nectanebo 250 royal cubits.

Here, fathoms and cubits are inverted because a child is born head down, therefore toward the south. At that moment it finds itself in the same position as the "upside-down man" on the fissure of Rolando. Once he is born, he will stand with his feet downward, toward the south, on the equator.

Appendix
Note 1

On the subject of the zones of the brain, we must point out the "auditory zone," located under the temporal bone. This explains the Egyptian expression "to give the temple [*maā*],"[22] which means "to pay attention." Therefore the meaning of "opening one's intelligence to speech" is what is implied in this locution. This proves that the Ancients attributed more value to the vital function than to the organ of perception; nowadays, we would say "lend an ear." It also confirms the ancient knowledge of the centers of life and intelligence demonstrated in the Edwin Smith Surgical Papyrus.

Note 2

Here is the result of the experiments quoted by E. Gley in his "Effects of the Eradication or Destruction of the Brain and Particularly of the Cerebral Hemispheres" (*Physiologie*, 2:945):

> In the case of the dog, the eradication of the cerebral hemispheres was carried out successfully by Goltz (1889–91), who even succeeded in keeping an animal alive for eighteen months, and also by Rothman (of Berlin) who kept one alive for over three years (1909–12).
>
> Goltz's "brainless dog" had lost all spontaneity and was insensitive to all psychical stimuli, calls, petting, the sight of a cat, etc. Nevertheless, it could walk, albeit clumsily, when it was pushed; when pinched, it would start to growl or bark or try to bite; it could hear loud noises; its pupils contracted in the light, but its gaze always remained fixed, as though lost; placed on a sloping surface, it managed to hold itself so as not to slide; it ate with difficulty, and moreover, it did not go after its food, and left on its own, it would have died.
>
> Rothman's dog was deaf and blind, and it also lacked the sense of smell, whence the abolition of all sexual life; it could maintain its balance and walk; it paid no attention to other dogs or to people; it experienced hunger and satiety.
>
> In summary, debrained animals retain, besides the organic functions, the functions of the coordination of movements and of equilibration; they also retain emotional expression. Otherwise, they behave like automatons. What is removed with the cerebral cortex is the organ of the higher psychic functions, of memory, of the association of perceptions and ideas, of reflection on sensations and representations; in short, the organ of intelligence, or, rather, of the intelligences—that is, the syntheses of various psychic processes and the adaptations of all these to the manifold conditions of life.

Note 3

One must not confuse the crown of the skull, which contains the physical organ of the brain, with the coronal circle that surrounds—underlines—this skullcap, but with which we cannot concern ourselves here because it corresponds to the channels of energy flux that belong to a more subtle

---

[22] Cf. fig. 167, no. 11.

aspect of the human body. On the other hand, I cannot remain completely silent on this subject, for to ignore it would be to translate badly the symbols in Egypt that refer to it, for example, the royal diadem. This diadem symbolizes the crowning of wisdom, that is to say, the continual animation of the centers of higher life in the head. Its circuit ends at the central point in the forehead, symbolized in Egypt by the frontal uraeus. When the Egyptians speak of channels in the human body, they are referring not only to physical channels (nerves and vessels) but also to circuits of energy.

Fluxes of energy are as much nutritive fluxes as "magnets" of the universal force. They are not necessarily carried by physical vessels. They could, for example, be considered fluxes of induction that emanate from specific centers precisely located and following definite pathways enveloping physical matter. The true meaning of the "meridians" in Chinese acupuncture is linked to this knowledge.

Chapter 16

THE JOINTS:
GUIDES FOR READING

We always start from the following proposition: The motive for everything in the architecture of the pharaonic temple is supplied by a symbolic reason, which becomes didactic through the strict observation of an esoteric canon.

Just as everything in the Universe is bound by the same breath of life, within the architecture of the temple it would be a mistake to consider a part without relating it to the whole. Thus, we cannot dissociate one element of the construction from the others, since they are all used to express the same thought. It is therefore a matter of investigating the link that unifies the elements of this construction with the numbers, inscriptions, and figurations of the myth, thereby creating the magic of the anthropocosmic temple.

These reasons lead us to seek out the significance of the lines where the stones join, cutting the figured inscriptions and hieroglyphic signs in a manner that, at first sight, may seem disconcerting. While simplicity and strength of construction should have caused the builders to use regularly carved blocks of stone, we observe instead major dissimilarities in the sizes of the blocks (which vary in weight from 100 or 200 kilograms to over a ton), some of which, in addition, have their lateral sides cut on a bias or nicked with "setbacks" that greatly complicate the construction work. These irregularities have been interpreted as the intent to give these walls, which are some eight or more meters in height, a greater resistance to telluric vibrations. If such is the case, it is difficult to understand why the stone often chosen as the foundation for these masses of sandstone was calcareous stone, which crumbles much more easily. In addition to this, rows of sandstone blocks have been observed to have been carved against the grain, which weakens the resistance to vertical thrust. Moreover, the whole construction of the temple of Luxor (as with many other monuments) gives us the impression that the builders cared very little about the weight of the masses of stones to be manipulated, which enables us to affirm that since this problem was not an obstacle, nothing prevented the architect from building his walls with blocks of sufficient surface area to allow for the sculpting of panels without disrupting the figuration with unattractive joints.

The joints, apparent in the assembly of the walls, from the beginning could only mean three things: (1) they separate as a cut would; (2) conversely, they can be used to join two separate elements indicated by the figurations; and (3) they emphasize, whether it be a geometric construction governing the inscriptions by way of numbers *(canevas)*, or a function.

The study of these joints demonstrates yet another intention: to guide the reading throughout the temple, and in the case of the temple of Luxor, this is of great importance *on the condition that this architecture actually represents the body of man.* This fact being demonstrated, as we shall see, *the temple of Luxor becomes the revelation of the vital meaning of the texts that we find inscribed in other temples and steles,* they being consecrated to only parts of the anthropocosmic whole.

Since the joints visibly form a part of the transcription of pharaonic thought, we need to study how their usage was systematized. For the Ancients, "system" did not mean a rational and invariable order as it does for us, but rather an adaptation to the vital meaning, a symbolic inscription. For example, it is certain that a doorway always means an entrance or exit, but it can also mean an entry authorized "on condition," if not a stopping point. It may be a single or a double door. The "functional" meaning attached to a figuration or a gesture guides the use of a symbol.

Now, we, who in some way have the privilege of visiting this monument in its state of ruin, should not forget that in the time the temple was alive, these joints were invisible, covered with colors and often with silver plating or gold repoussé.

The joints and pieces thus take on, among other meanings we shall make clear, the character of magical symbolism, necessarily creating, in a spiritual sense, an atmosphere of cosmic reality strangely disconcerting to the visitor.

The joint between two stones links as much as it separates, and it always emphasizes. It has various aspects that we will analyze.

One of its meanings depends upon its location in relation to the image and the conscious intent of the builder. The temple of Luxor confirms that the stone joints have a specific purpose, which proves that, first, the joints play a very important hieroglyphic part in indicating the esoteric meaning of the inscriptions, and, second, the temple of Luxor is truly devoted to the Anthropocosmos, and *through its architecture it truly represents man,* as the coinciding superimposition of the skeleton on the plan of the temple demonstrates.[1]

The overall survey of the entire temple, followed by the study (made possible through precise scale drawings of the bas-reliefs) of the stone joints that cross the sculptures, and finally, a complete epigraphic survey, allow us today to classify the horizontal joints into three types: (1) *correspondence joints,* which physiologically relate the parts of the human body;[2] (2) *location joints,* which indicate in each figure the correspondence between a particular part of the body and a particular part of the temple (which represents the human body);[3] (3) *conducting joints,* which guide the reading of certain ritual formulas, thus casting light on their intent.[4]

—◦◦◦—

There is growth of the Man of the Temple and thus a *growth* of the squares, *if a squared grid is applied to each phase in the same manner as to the whole.* This is certainly not the case here, but there is a geometric growth translated into a *number value* by the movement (pivoting) of the original square.[5]

[1] Cf. plate 15.

[2] Cf. plates 26 and 27.

[3] Cf. plate 28.

[4] Cf. plates 29 and 30.

[5] Cf. fig. 164, and vol. 2, figs. 202 and 203.

We must never forget that if the technique requires that successive moments be fixed, it must be done in stages that show the vital movement. The temple speaks of life, and does not describe apparent forms.

We must choose between the construction and the teaching that is inscribed in it. The figurations that will be carved onto the walls are like the names we bestow upon each part and organ of the body. The structure that, in this temple, marks the proportions and—by measures—the stages of human growth is the living body. This will again be completed by multiple movements, that is, through the variations in the orientations and heights of the walls, because we need to remember that we are dealing with a body, and therefore with a volume.

These particulars are outlined on the floor and the walls by geometry (therefore by numbers) and by all the symbols that reveal, with the name, the function of each area of the living body.

The essential relationship between the *canevas* of a wall and the joint that relates to human physiology can only become clear through the geometry unique to a specific location. This geometry develops a defined proportion, and it is therefore only a question of establishing the smallest unit for the side of the square used, governed by the proportion. This will be the unit of the *canevas*.

The point of departure for such a construction, the continuation of which should inevitably be correct, is necessarily supplied by a characteristic module, as we know in the case of the crown of the skull providing the specific module for the proportions of the human body.

It is in sanctuary I, Amun's sanctuary, that we should look for this basic proportion that will establish all the proportional relationships of the temple. This is similar to the relationship between the size and the form of the Nectanebo courtyard and the base of the colossus.[6]

There is a determinism that results from an original, given condition in the human embryo that fixes the length of the life, the size, and the growth of the person it will be. But this virtuality (typal impulse), as for itself, will be free of all rational determinism.

The joint and the location of the key do not vary, but the symbol (figures, attributes, hieroglyphs) can undergo modifications with the *age* of Man.

The age in question, while it is related to Royal Man, conceived and brought into the world, then having grown in "this place" that is the temple of Luxor, also refers to Man represented by the evolution of the whole of pharaonic Egypt. This empire is conceived like a human fetus that during the nine decans of three precessional months* is gestated to be born into the world as the redeeming, Horian Verb.

Thus the dates of the age of the empire of the Two Lands will be found in precise places in the temple, the body of Cosmic Man. This justifies certain effacements and alterations to the figurations.

These joints between the stones in the construction of the walls of the rooms, used to site the location of the figures so as to establish living, functional correspondences with the human body, and to guide the reading of the liturgical texts (as our plates show, along with their accompanying legends), are already disconcerting to us because of the difficulty such a construction represents with regard to the bas-reliefs and texts that these walls will receive.

Now, this is complicated even more by the fact that the outlines of these joints, with the movement of certain representations and then again of the inscription of numbers and measures, will constitute a "speaking" mosaic.

There is only one way of considering such a work, and that is to look at the wall as if at a tableau, a surface united by a carefully calculated size, width, and height.

---

[6] Cf. vol. 2, figs. 209–11.

* See chapter 20, note 3.

drawn as the *symbolique* requires: the exact sequence, the size of the figures in relation to their importance, gestures, attributes, and symbolic colors. *Horizontal lines are drawn on the finished tableau* corresponding to the location and to all the aims we have just pointed out, in addition to the vertical lines that correspond to two further ends: the isolation of the limbs, attributes, and hieroglyphs from other parts of the body, thus pointing out the symbolic "functions"; and the cuts fixing numbers and measure, of which we will speak later on.

These lines on the tableaux divide them into sections and *give form to the blocks to be carved and assembled. It is the figured inscription that makes the wall; the joints merely replace the plan of the under-linings* appearing on the general tableau, guiding the construction with blocks cut precisely according to a preset size.

The Idea presides; knowledge, which is transcribed by *symbolique*, compels; the carving of the stone makes it real—in such a way that the entire temple can be executed in an image developed according to a plan; moreover, even without the imaged *symbolique,* the temple will be totally expressed by the ensemble of blocks of stone cut according to predetermined sizes.

For the reading we can therefore set aside the monument's technique, forget that we are dealing with joints between stones and see only a design and the underlinings on a tableau. Thus, moreover, it is for the reading of the symbolic significance that our surveys of the walls are presented, along with our files of measurements—*without which any survey would be unusable.*

Chapter 17

THE COVERED TEMPLE: THE HEAD

If the intention of the Egyptians were truly to outline a human head in the pavement,[1] the door-ways and openings should then correspond to the internal and external channels of the head. Now, in studying the figure of a sagittal section of the head that shows the location of the central organs,[2] we can see that all the openings can be found in the plan of the pavement, if we take into account that this plan shows superimposed sections and must include not only sections of the different planes of the volume of the head but also what is projected by a frontal view.

We thus have the synthesis of a human head in the structure.

Under these conditions, the rooms and openings take on an extraordinary meaning. We will only note here a few important general facts, since a complete study of the relation of the myth with the physiology of the human head—its glands, organs, and circulation of the blood and humors—would require a lengthy work.

The crown of the skull does not appear in the image of the head in the covered temple, which stops at the normal height of the pharaonic headband with the facade of the south wall. We are therefore dealing with Adamic Man, with divine intelligence, prior to the fall (birth) into Nature, in other words, with the Idea of Man.

The figure of man serving as symbol-base for the temple of Luxor is prenatural *neter*-man, for the nasopharyngeal opening remains closed and will only be opened at the end of the pharaonic per-iod. This would be the period of his natural animation or terrestrial incarnation, corresponding to the moment when the child breathes in air as it is born into this world. Until this date, this *neter*-man does not breathe the outer air and only lives through his inner ear, symbol of his direct inspiration.

[1] Cf. plates 34–37.
[2] Cf. plate 38.

The respiratory tract is indicated, on the axis of the temple, from the hypostyle room (lungs) to room XII (rear nasal fossae), by an uninterrupted series of long paving stones that pass through all the doorways and under the wall—still closed under Amenhotep III—that separates rooms VI and XII. It is here, at the site of the nasopharyngeal orifice, that we find, on the side of room VI, a niche in the exact spot where, at the end of the pharaonic period, an opening was to be made. Moreover, from the architecture we can see that the idea of a passage was expressed from the beginning by the large pavestones passing under the still-closed wall, and by the first course of stones that, in this place only, links room VI to room XII.

In support of this thesis, we present here a physiological description of the action of swallowing, which will provide us with an opportunity to introduce a brief example of interpreting the correspondences between a physiological function, the architecture, and the figurations.

During the act of swallowing we do not breathe into the lungs; now, if at this moment one closes one's nostrils, the hearing of external sounds is altered. Understanding is thus opened. This is not mere supposition, but the secret of the occult effect of pronouncing certain words (mantras). The reason for this is that the eustachian tube, which admits air to the tympanic cavity (middle ear), is usually closed and opens only at each swallowing movement by the following mechanism: the rear nasal fossae normally communicate with the buccal part of the pharynx via the nasopharyngeal passage (part of the wall between rooms VI and XII, opened in the Late Period). This passage is blocked by the action of the muscles of the staphylopharyngeal pillars, which contract and join during swallowing. At that moment, the orifice of the eustachian tube opens under the pressure of the soft palate (south wall of room II, representing the coronation).

Now, for swallowing to occur there must be a liquid medium; the production of saliva is thus of great importance. The salivary secretion of the submandibular and sublingual glands (north of room II, representing the swamp)[3] is instigated by the "tympanic cord," a nerve so named because it passes through the tympanum. The nerve that innervates these glands is called the tympanolingual nerve, but experiments have shown that it is only the tympanic cord that gives these glands their secretory fibers.

It is possible to relate this phenomenon of "the call to the inner ear" with the gesture of "swallowing one's saliva" that occurs in moments of extreme concentration, when one finds oneself hard pressed for an answer.

The organs of the true intellect (not intelligence), in particular the pituitary gland (hypophysis) and the pineal eye (epiphysis), are located in the southern secret sanctuaries.

The pituitary gland, corresponding to the entrance to sanctuary I (the central secret sanctuary), is thus considered a doorway, in other words, a passage.[4]

Room I contains what physiology defines as, and I quote, the "trigonum or four-pillared vault that joins the two horns of Ammon." There could be no better description of the architectural aspect of this sanctuary.[5]

[3] Let us quote Hippocrates on this subject: "In this way, too, the glands profiting from the surplus present in the rest of the body, the nourishment of the body is also their nourishment. Thus in any parts where there is fluid, there are also glands. Here is proof: where there is a gland, there too are hairs, for nature makes glands and hairs, and they both fulfil the same office, the one (i.e., glands) with regard to what flows to them, as was described above, while the hairs, taking advantage of what is provided from the glands, grow and increase by collecting the excess that is cast out to the surface. Where the body is dry, there is neither gland nor hair. . . ." *Hippocrates*, 8:111.
[4] Cf. plates 36–38, and fig. 226.
[5] Cf. plate 38 and fig. 226.

The beginnings of the cornices of the naos subfoundation form a body with the southern columns.

In this same room the "choroid plexuses" are located, in which a mysterious transformation takes place: medicine holds that the blood entering the choroid plexuses comes out (supposedly by dialysis)[6] in the form of a crystalline liquid, colorless like springwater, the cerebrospinal fluid. The figurations in this room also seem to indicate an elaboration—at least partial—in these plexuses of a red ferment of the blood, aided by the cerebrospinal fluid that comes from the medulla.[7]

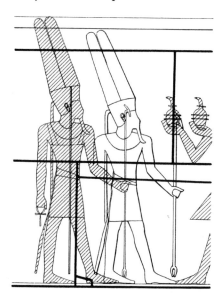

Fig. 180. The wall separating room I, the west wall (in white), *from room VII* (hachured)

In room I, Amun is holding the *was* scepter that is projected, on the opposite side of the wall, into the milk urn offered by the king represented in room VII. Behind Amun, a line defining the tableau falls on the axis of equilibrium in the representation of Amun drawn in room VII.

The *was* scepter held by the Amun of room VII falls exactly on the axis of equilibrium of the Amun of room I (semicircular canals of the inner ear).

The three southern sanctuaries are separated by walls. This separation does not exist in the human head, but internal exchanges, still unexplained today, take place in these areas of the brain, and the walls here provide typical instances of "transposition."[8] The reading of a wall (image and text) remains absolutely incomplete without its complement given on the opposite side of the same wall. An example is the *was* scepter of Amun on the wall of room VII that constitutes the axis of equilibrium of Amun as represented in room I (fig. 180). We can affirm that through their walls these three rooms are completely linked by transposition. There is even another similar transposition between room V and room I (fig. 181).

---

[6] As if the dialysis of the blood would be sufficient to provide all the particular characteristics to the cerebrospinal fluid, which cannot be confused with the blood serum.

[7] Let us recall here the nature of the fruit from the tree with which one can write indelibly in red, described in appendix 1 of chapter 30 and plate 26. As for the Ancients' knowledge of the cerebrospinal fluid, this is proven by the description of the brain in case 6 of the Edwin Smith Surgical Papyrus (chapter 14, pp. 390–92).

[8] Cf. chapter 43.

It is of course understood that we are only dealing here with the transposition of the scepters, but everything must be interpreted: the type of crown, the joints, the bifurcation of the forearm, gestures, offerings, the small stone pieces embedded in the king's thigh in room V that allude to the phallus, and so on.[9]

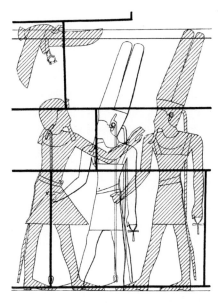

Fig. 181. Wall separating room I, east wall (in white), *from room V* (hachured)

In room I, Amun is holding the *was* scepter whose lower part coincides with the vertical joint of the stones, and whose visible part is projected into the king's axis of vertical stability represented in room V. The king, slightly inclining, is stretching his arms out to Amun, who stands before him. His only arm, represented in profile, divides into two forearms. His axis of vertical stability, which normally passes through the ear (the semicircular canals of the inner ear providing equilibrium), here passes through the cerebellum, the motor center for equilibrium.[10]

The scepter held by the Amun in room V projects to the nape (cerebellum) of the Amun appearing in room I, and the hook of this scepter touches the other Amun's ear, thus linking the two centers of balance—the inner ear and the cerebellum.

Further on we shall show a similar instance, but of "transparency," on the sides of the wall separating rooms XII and V. This wall represents the "cribriform plate of the ethmoid" through which the olfactory branches pass, and represented on the walls we find, on the side of room XII, the cloths (weavings), and on the side of room V what Egyptologists call the "boxes for cloths."[11]

These figurations exactly coincide through transparency, so the cloths—or what they symbolize, that is, the weaving of the Verb[12]—pass through, and we once again pick up these cloths on the

[9] Cf. plate 76, room V, west wall.

[10] Cf. plates 67–69. The figure transformed in room VI is inclined so that the ear of the new figure corresponds to the cerebellum of the old.

[11] Cf. chapter 18; cf. chapter 43 and plates 97 and 98.

[12] See particularly the tradition of the Dogon. Cf. M. Griaule, *Dieu d'eau, entretiens avec Ogotommeli* (Paris: Editions du Chêne, 1948).

east side of the wall separating rooms V and I, and in the final offering of the "choicest oil" feeding the cerebral matter.[13]

Let us point out that cloth is formed of a warp and a weft that create a tangible surface with two complementary elements, as we can see throughout all of nature, with male and female—positive and negative—producing tangible phenomena by complementation. Cloth, which we find mentioned as an image of creation by the "Word" in many ancient traditions, is thus a perfect symbol for expressing this abstract function.

—–ₘₘ–—

The eye is located in the east part of room XII, marked on the ground by the pavestones. In this room the theme of the twelve hours of the day is developed. The young king (the sun) enters at the east and reaches puberty. The measures confirm this, and it is possible to follow the ages of the king with their help.

In this same room is seen the solar barque bearing the naos containing the falcon crowned with the solar disk (fig. 288). Here, accent is placed on the eye by the reference to Horus. We know that the brain of a bird is *retinal,* that is, it contains more specially developed cerebral organs of vision. Thus one should principally seek in Horus the symbolization of the eye, and its relation to the center of visual consciousness.

The medulla oblongata, from which stem the twelve pairs of cranial nerves, ends in room XII on the west side. From the medulla the marrow continues into the spinal column, and from the marrow stem all the sensory and motor spinal nerves. Now if there is a central interruption of the nervous motor tract, excitation of the surface of the soles of the feet will show that there is a break in the motor arc.[14]

It is therefore interesting to point out that the theme of the "nine bows" located under the king's feet[15] is indicated in the temple by the group of archers portrayed on the north side of the east wing of the pylon, which corresponds to the foot placed in front, the active one. In addition, the west wing, representing the supporting back foot, is linked to room XII by having the same measure of length, 12 fathoms.[16]

The correspondence between the medulla oblongata and the pylon is made exact by a "transparency" in the north wall of room XII at the point on the sagittal section corresponding to the passage of the marrow. A stone carved on a bias following the same slope as that of the pylon passes through the wall and, by the nature of its size, evokes this pylon (fig. 182). In addition, in the pavement below, a short path made of white limestone pavestones completes the idea of passage.

The sanctuary of the altar of Amun's barque (room VI) brings together, appropriately enough, several functions. It is located precisely at the back of the mouth (pharynx), where the food and air

---

[13] In plate 28, the two figures numbered 1 and 9 frame the naos of Amun, and the joint emphasizes their skullcaps.

[14] Normally, stimulation of the soles of the feet causes a flexion of the toes toward the sole, and when the big toe dissociates itself from the other toes—in other words, remains extended while the small toes are bent—this is a sign of central interruption of the nervous motor tract (Babinski's reflex). In case 8 of the Edwin Smith Surgical Papyrus we find the description of a skull lesion with the result—among others—of a reaction that is analogous to what today we call Babinski's reflex, recognized only since the beginning of this century (cf. chapter 14).

[15] Cf. plate 47C.

[16] Cf. plate 67; the west wing of the pylon measures 12 fathoms between tori, under the cornice.

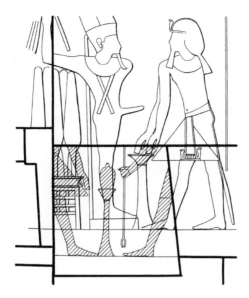

Fig. 182. Wall separating room XII (in white) *and room III* (hachured). *View of room XII.*

The stone that passes through the wall has the same slope as the pylon. Among other characteristics, the vertical joints in room XII define the king's right foot and the leg of the ithyphallic Amun, onto which the table of offerings is projected in transparency. It is carved on the other side of the stone, in room III, where the vertical joints cut the right leg of the king and the left leg of the *neter*.

that support life are admitted and where the voice, *the speech that creates,* is amplified.[17] The barque is located at the site of the uvula and controls the opening and closing of this junction. The barque goes, as the symbolism requires, from east to west;[18] the naos opens on the north side.

It is on one of the pavestones, in front of the step of the sanctuary of the barque, that the front profile of an ithyphallic Min is carved.[19] In the threshold between rooms IV and VI the key is embedded at the place where the axis of Amun and the axis of measures cross.

Room VI deserves particular attention (in a cathedral, this is where the altar is located), since it shows us, among other things, the state of this sanctuary under Amenhotep III, before the present naos was erected under Alexander the Great.

The fittings still exist for the socle of the barque, for the wooden naos, for the entry step, and for the twelve posts that supported a veil surrounding the naos and the four columns of Amenhotep III. The same is true for the two low ramps leading up to the sacred barque.

[17] On the subject of this speech that creates, it is said that Ra, the creator, created the *neters* by his speech, and men with his tears. In these texts there are always cabalistic plays on words. Now, in room VI, on the west wall, the "fifteen" *neters* of the Theban Ennead are represented, and on the north and south walls, groups of seated *neters*. Notice as well that in room II, the mouth, we see the "*neter* coming from the north,*" thus from Heliopolis and Memphis.

[18] At Karnak in the corresponding sanctuary, the barque is not found crossing the door of the naos, but is positioned in the same direction as this door, the sanctuary being oriented east-west.

[19] A large fragment of pink granite with the name of Tuthmosis III and portraying an ithyphallic Min was reused on the top of the roof of the sanctuary of Philip Arrhidaeus at Karnak, with the sex organ placed in the direction of the east-west axis of the temple. Cf. J. de Rouge, "Etude des monuments du massif de Karnak," in *Mélanges archéologie égyptienne et assyrienne* 1 (1873): 68; G. Legrain, *Le Logement et le transfert des barques sacrées,* Bulletin de l'I.F.A.O. 13 (Cairo, 1917): 18.

It was at the site of the old columns of Amenhotep III that Alexander's naos was built. Let us take note of a tendency to reveal, from this time on, what had hitherto been kept secret. This naos is a masterpiece for the study of numbers. The Ptolemaic era, marking the end of the Egyptian mission, had as its goal "opening the doorways" to the teachings of the past times, which motivated the actual construction of the symbolic doorways that characterize this time.[20]

Above and beside the door opening from room VI to room II there are two scenes of breast feeding, and on one of them, the joint of stones underlines the mouth of the prince and the maternal breast. In room II, near this very same door, another scene of breast feeding is located.

—⁓—

In room IV, the sanctuary devoted to the four elements, we find ourselves in the throat, in the conduits for air and for solid and liquid foods.

This is a "passage," as is shown by the figurations on the walls. Processions bringing chests and vases are portrayed to the west, and to the east are the carriers of ointments and perfumes, as well as the journey of the three sacred barques of Amun, Mut, and Khonsu.[21]

At the third register (from bottom to top) on the west wall, a single joint cuts the figures at the level of the sex organs, and the pavestone that marks the trachea is "broken" at the place of the Adam's apple.[22] It is a well-known fact that at puberty the voice breaks, which establishes a relationship between the throat and the sex organs, and this correspondence is mentioned in the Edwin Smith Surgical Papyrus.

"A man . . . if it is the vertebra of the middle of his neck that is dislocated, it is a . . . [spermatorrhea] which befalls his phallus."[23] The seminal emission is a phenomenon observed today in the case of a break in the vertebrae of the neck due to hanging.

Now, the west wall of room IV corresponds exactly to the cervical vertebrae, and through a joint on this wall we find the confirmation for the following important relationship: the two generating Amuns portrayed on this register have the *phallus* cut longitudinally by the horizontal joint, a dislocation of which passes under the chin of the king's *ka*, corresponding to the *middle cervical vertebra.*

On the east wall, at the first and third registers, the single joint cuts the thighs of the royal figures. This joint refers to the nave (the thigh of the Man of the Temple) where we see the procession of the barques of Amun, Mut, and Khonsu portrayed on the second register of that wall.[24]

Mut's barque is in the center and it so happens that the scale drawings of the stones and the breach in the wall separating rooms IV and IX have allowed us to verify a strange instance of transparency in this place.[25]

Beneath Mut's barque in room IV a stone on which the Mut bird (the gestating Nekhebet) is engraved passes through the wall. On the room IX side there is an inscription located between Bes (sexual power) and the node of Apet (the gestating belly). This text exalts the queen and her capacity to vivify and bring into the world . . . fire *(tka)*.[26]

---

[20] In the Ptolemaic era, many doors from the constructions of Amenhotep III at Luxor were altered.

[21] Cf. plate 31, east wall, room IV.

[22] Cf. plate 34, plan of the paving of the covered temple.

[23] Cf. chapter 14, case 31, p. 394.

[24] Cf. plate 31.

[25] Cf. vol. 2, fig. 233.

[26] The text at this place is very damaged, but the same text can be found at Deir el-Bahri.

Above this stone in room IX, there is a scene of giving birth: the queen is seated on a cubic throne, her two arms supported by two female *neters,* while opposite her stand two feminine principles, the one awaiting the child about to be born, and the other carrying the *ka* of the future child on her arm.

A horizontal joint passes at the upper level of the throne, thus detaching the upper body and thighs from the lower legs; this is the symbolic birth. The queen is called "Mut in the barque," and her projection in transposition on the other side of the wall (room IV) seats her in the front of Mut's barque, whereas the *ka* is at the back, the symbol of a connection through the barque between body and soul as separate entities. This is an example of an indirect transparency since the *only* stone to truly cross is the stone on which the text concerning birth is inscribed.

It is a question here of the principle, not of the actual birth of the king. This is what the central picture of the lower register known as the "scene of the theogamy" confirms: here, yet another horizontal joint coincides with the level of the seat on which Amun and the queen are sitting; now, this seat is a sky supported by Neith and Selkit, the two female *neters* who preside over parturition (fig. 298). In truth, the scene represents an apparition.

At the third register, the scene of breast feeding bears the same characteristics. The horizontal joint underlines the seat on which the queen rests, her two fists joined, while the royal child and its *ka* are fed by two female *neters.* Beneath this seat the two children suck the milk of the celestial cow directly.

On the lower register, Khnum of Elephantine models the two children on his potter's wheel: the king and his *ka*[27] in the form of two small *adult* men (fig. 201). Opposite Khnum, Hathor holds up the key of life. (At Deir el-Bahri, it is the frog, symbol of the renewal of life, Christmas, who holds this position.)

From a physiological point of view, it is interesting to point out that the scene of the theogamy is located exactly at the level of the thyroid body, which the Egyptians called "the body"[28] and which was therefore well known to them.

Portrayed on the south wall of room IX is the purification by water, poured from two vases held by Mentu and Tum, whose streams cross above the young prince—small but with adult proportions. The remainder of this wall is devoted to the giving of the name (baptism) in the presence of Thoth and of Seshat (*neter* of the signature) and of the *neters* bearing the red and white crowns of the North and South.

On the north wall, the king is adult. Now, this wall corresponds to the clavicle, where the first and last points of ossification are formed. Let us point out, with regard to the characteristics of the joints, the picture on the left, located at the first register of this wall, in which the king sacrifices the oryx by cutting his carotid. The blade of his knife is blurred by the joint that thus cuts the throat of the animal, and this joint continues toward the phallus of the king who holds the horn of the oryx with his left hand.[29]

Finally, on the east wall corresponding to the beard of the Man of the Temple, the *sed* festival or jubilee, the renewal (regeneration), is represented.

---

[27] For an explanation of what the Ancients call the *ka* cf. I. Schwaller de Lubicz, *Her-Bak, Egyptian Initiate,* part 2.

[28] Cf. Lefebvre, *Parties du corps humain.*

[29] Let us recall that the oryx is a Sethian animal and it is Horus who, in the mythical and symbolic legend, tore off the testicles of Seth who, in turn, had torn out the eyes of Horus.

We must also point out that in room IV (located at the level of the throat) all the beards of the royal figures are reworked. These beards, which were on the figures when they were first carved, were removed, then *replastered* and recarved, probably at the time of the reworking of this room under Alexander the Great.

Conclusion

As these pages have demonstrated, the thought of the Ancients is expressed by an entire complex of elements that are based on myth and that must be studied in their synthetic sense at the site, not merely from some writings read in a study.

We do not see with the same eyes as the pharaonic sages. They observe an object, but without regarding it as such. They focus on its functional character, forgetting the objective aspect.[30]

———

It has been said that the master builders of the cathedrals expressed themselves in stone. But in the study of Egyptian monuments, who has thought to pay as much attention to the measurements, in order to find in them the meaning of the numbers, as to the figurations based on pharaonic myth? Who, in this same spirit, has attempted the true reading of the hieroglyphic signs?

This implies the study of the intentional meaning of each piece of evidence. Thus, having noted the separation of the crown of the skull, one should try to find out what it means, since this point was emphasized. One should not conclude, on the basis of an apparently simple text, that the Ancients meant to say something that we understand; rather, one should try to find out why they expressed themselves thus.

The Ancients never "popularized" anything; to the uninitiated they provided only the minimal *useful* teaching. The explanation, the philosophy, the secret connection between the myth and the sciences, were the prerogative of a handful of specially instructed men. Did not Pythagoras wait thirteen years before being admitted into the temple? Did he not, in his own teaching, impose silence on pain of death? Therefore this teaching was not put in writing and did not represent a mere learning, but gave power to the initiate who had to guarantee that it would never be abused.

Herodotus often mentions the obligation he was under to remain silent concerning "sacred" subjects. These instructions, therefore, had not been written down. Druidic teachings, as well, were the privilege of a priestly class, guardians of the most secret, oral traditions of the people.

People cling obstinately to the "classical" prejudice and, in order to defend this thesis, prefer to consider the Ancient Egyptians as simplistic primitives. By denying the high knowledge of Ancient Egypt, they will end up even diminishing the value of the Greeks. Did not the Ancient Greeks go to educate themselves in the sanctuaries of Lower Egypt, as close to the source as possible? They had fewer prejudices than their modern champions! When Professor Grapow, mistaken by the tricky interpretation of the word *mtw,* denies the Ancients a knowledge of the nerves, of the circulation of the blood, and so on, we can remind him that the Hippocratic texts, as Iversen has recently confirmed, borrowed extensively from pharaonic documents, and did so around 450 B.C. Now these texts deal with the nerves, the circulation of the blood, and the glands.

Some will claim that Greece was able to understand, and elucidate rationally, what the Ancients had "dimly suspected" or known empirically, when in fact the documents of the Greeks that have reached us intact are rare, whereas pharaonic texts and monuments provide inviolate evidence of

---

[30] For example, *mtw,* which is used to designate all the "conduits," vessels, channels, etc. Cf. Edwin Smith Surgical Papyrus.

their concepts and modes of expression. What has been transmitted to us through the indirect channel is that "analytical" mentality that is in direct opposition to the approach of the Ancient Egyptians, and was certainly excluded from the Greek Mysteries. This rational, "mechanistic" mentality is guilty of having led us to the disaster of which even the most blind today have some foreboding, because mere convenience does not represent progress of consciousness, and the spirit of collectivity imposed by mechanization represents a stultification of the individual.

In conclusion, the pharaonic teaching shows us Man composed of three beings: the corporeal being, the sexual being, and the spiritual being. Each has its body and its organs. These three beings are interdependent through the flow of fluids and the nervous influx; the spinal marrow is the column of "fire" that connects the whole and effects the transformation of the corporeal into energy and spirit.

The being properly called "corporeal" is the body: the chest and abdomen, where the organs for the assimilation of solids, liquids, and air are located. The head is the container of the spiritual being, where the blood, elaborated throughout the body, is *spiritualized* in order to nourish the nervous flux and prepare the "ferments" of the blood and the "seed."

This is a very condensed account of an aspect of the Anthropocosmos.

In the head, the entire encephalon could be thought of as a fetus in gestation: it is bathed and penetrated by the cerebrospinal fluid, of a typically Amunian (amniotic) character,[31] and the choroid plexuses (chorion) bring to this point the nourishing blood, which *itself will be spiritualized.*

Contemporary medicine gives all the centers and organs very detailed, descriptive names, drawn from Greek or Latin. No vital link coordinates this purely encyclopedic science. One would search in vain in Ancient Egypt for this sort of science, and for a vocabulary that would not be symbolic.

The myth is a whole, the synthesis of all science, since it transcribes the fundamental knowledge of the laws of genesis that apply to everything. Thus the *neters* have their significance, in medicine as well as in astronomy or theology, which is the metaphysic of the Becoming and the Return.

Their meaning must be sought in this spirit, just as we find the whole Christic teaching of the Gospels explained through the Passion.

---

[31] Let us further note that in the embryo, insofar as the neuropores are not sealed off, the cerebrospinal fluid *is* the amniotic liquid.

Chapter 18

SANCTUARY V

THE ESSENTIAL SECRET SANCTUARIES

The formation of the organized being begins with the head. The head is the place of ideal determination of the body's organic functions, and thus one must look there to see the governing principles.

Among the three vital centers to which the three secret sanctuaries of the temple of Luxor are devoted, two are consecrated to endocrine glands—the pituitary body (hypophysis, room I) and the pineal body (epiphysis, room VII). In front of the latter on the side of the forehead (to the east), room V is devoted to the olfactory bulb, the olfactory brain.

The three sanctuaries of the encephalon each have only one entrance into the room of the eye and the twelve hours of the sun. These three sanctuaries are devoted to the triple Verb, which is at the basis of all becoming, and which during the Amunian period will provide a body for the animating spirit. This incarnation, which the temple of Luxor recounts, is translated in room IX, called the "room of the theogamy." This indeed concerns an "incarnation of the Verb," or of a spiritual concept, which is verified by the fact that the seed is called the "odor of the god," and this seed, or promise, is received, not by an ordinary woman, but by a woman designated as "Mut in the barque,"[1] in order to bring into this world a perfect being, identified with Amenhotep, the mystical name for the king Nebmaātre. The name Amenhotep means (as translated) "the peace of Amun," which would be more correctly expressed by "equilibrium in Amun," because the word *hotep (htp)* is the reverse of Ptah *(pth)*, the fire fallen to earth. It is a question of the original Fire, reversed, or turning back toward the heavens within an Amunian milieu, which causes a burning fire to be vivifying.

With the three secret sanctuaries not only do we have a description of the three aspects of a single Verb, in numbers as well as in physiological functions, but also, in the case of this temple, we

---

[1] Here paternity is attributed to Amun acting in the name of Tuthmosis, and "Mut in the barque" represents the queen.

have the position of the vital centers for the "catching hold" of life, those points of fixation from which the entire body will form and develop.

The entrance doors of the three sanctuaries are each proportioned according to the function of the number that governs these centers. They are controlled by the functions of the square, the pentagon, and the hexagon, but for each of these sanctuaries, the functions are developed according to the governing principle. Thus, in room I, the sanctuary of Amun, we find the inscription of *principles;* in room V, the sanctuary of the primitive olfactory sense, the *determination;* and in room VII, the center of the pineal body, the mathematical *reason.*

The door of room V determines, by the function ϕ, the ratios of the square, the pentagon, and the hexagon, and the room itself is proportioned on the principle of the root of 2. At the side of this door is the transparency of the cloths and the boxes for cloths that we note further on, while this transparency also contains a reversal of the function ϕ into the function $\sqrt{2}$.

The doorway to room I, Amun and the pituitary body, describes the triple function, a principle expressed by the hexagon and governed by the pentagon, which is the written form of the spirit (fig. 183).

Next, the doorway to room VII, the room of the epiphysis, the gland of the ancient pineal eye, develops these functions in reference to the 3, 4, 5 triangle. These are certainties acquired not by a vague schematic drawing, but from extremely precise measurements taken on the spot.

Throughout the whole of pharaonic Egypt we find this interpenetrating play of pentagon and hexagon, which preside over the formation of the human body, and particularly over the formation of the skull. This allows for a functional determination, and not just a description, of racial evolution, such as in the extreme types designated as brachycephalic and dolicocephalic.* The general form is the consequence of the relationships of location and interaction of the vital glands that separate from each other at the origin and move away from one another with the expanding development of psychological consciousness.

THE SIGNIFICANCE OF SANCTUARY V

An Example of Transparency

The three centers of the encephalon that are depicted in the secret sanctuaries all necessarily influence sexual life, but the olfactory center, in addition to this action—its internal activity—plays the role of a sense with an external, informing activity. At their biogenetic origin, the three centers play an informing role, but in the development of the being the pituitary and the pineal bodies surrender this role to specific senses.

In the present view, the relationship of the pituitary with the exterior requires the intermediary of the visual centers, and the pineal gland has as its intermediary the center of the intelligence of sound,[2] in spite of its originally being the "cyclopean" eye.

The centers of vision and hearing have no *direct* action on the sexual functions. For it to be understood, vision passes through the cerebral filter; hearing passes directly to the pineal gland, which then transmits to the emotional center (the sympathetic system). From the "vital-sexual"

---

[2] Cf. this chapter, appendix 1, note 1.

* Brachycephalic: short-headed or broad-headed, the breadth of the skull being at least four-fifths its length; dolicocephalic: long-headed, the breadth is less than four-fifths its length.

top of the ceiling • room XII

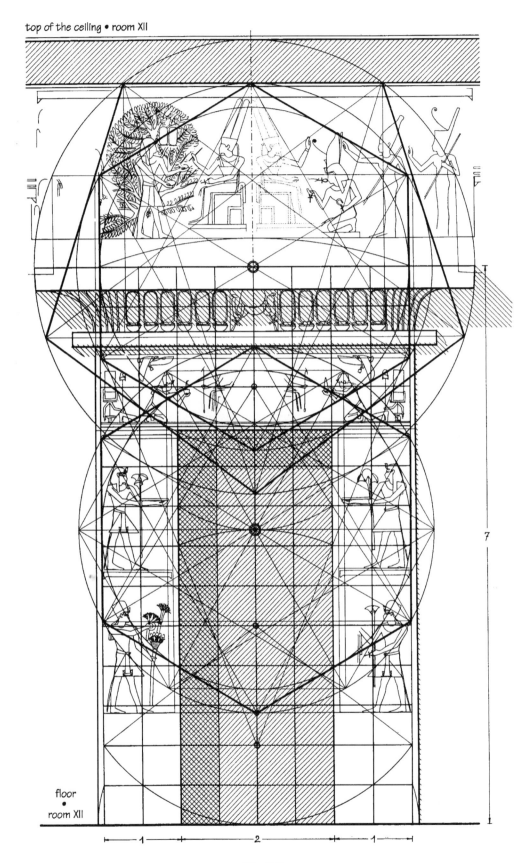

floor
•
room XII

Fig. 183

point of view, the pituitary gland, by analogy, plays a "sympathetic" part, and the pineal gland has a pneumogastric function (acting as a brake).[3]

We now know that hieratic symbolism chooses from nature the most typical mineral, plant, and animal beings for functional expression.

Among terrestrial vertebrates the olfactory brain, which is the most primitive, has its animal form in the serpent, for which the naja (the cobra) of Egypt is the typical representative, the symbol.[4]

If a sagittal section of the head is placed on the plan, we can see that the olfactory bulb is in room V and the olfactory zone in room XII. The wall separating these two rooms corresponds to the cribriform plate of the ethmoid, through which the olfactory ramifications pass, and room V is exactly at the same height that the uraeus should occupy on the forehead and coincides with the convolutions of the serpent's coiled body.[5]

The center of the olfactory bulb is the original, cerebral "informant" in a living organism with a central nervous system. It is, moreover, worth noting that it has a direct relation to the selective, intestinal function of the trunk[6]—the joints lead us to this—and, esoterically, to the seminal "Fire."

The "perfumes" and "perfumed ointments," the "resins," represented in this room on its forehead side,[7] play a very important part in the hieratic *symbolique*. They are not to be generally interpreted, but should be studied in all their specific nuances. The oils and ointments are often called the "secretion of the *neter*."[8] The symbol always evokes the function, not the object.

[3] Schematically, the sympathetic system has a contracting and accelerating action. The action of the pneumogastric function is to dilate and is opposed to that of the sympathetic. Thus, if the pituitary contracts muscular fibers, the pineal dilates them, halts the activity of the sympathetic, and plays the role, among others, of a cardiac brake.

This must serve only as a comparison for the action and reaction of the pituitary and the pineal glands, although, in fact, the activity of the sympathetic and the pneumogastric systems cannot be dissociated as two antagonistic systems would be. There is interchange of activity between them according to the environment and the conditions in which they act, as in the two endocrine glands.

[4] Cf. appendix 2.

[5] Cf. plate 38 and fig. 226 (vol. 2).

[6] From the residue of the first forms of primitive cells there remains in human beings a relationship between the digestive tract and the olfactory cells. In addition we recall that there is a correspondence between intestinal and brain disorders.

[7] See plate 77 and commentary.

[8] It is not the chemist but life we must ask to recognize the nature and meaning of oil, resin, certain mineral fats, and their kinship with the nails and hair.

Fig. 183. Central door of the south wall of room XII

The width of the door frame equals half the total width contained within the two lines that determine the outside edge of the tableaux carved on the doorposts. This enables the width of the door to be divided by 8.

The height from the bottom of the torus and the soles of the feet of the figures on the lower register equals the diameter of a circle circumscribing a hexagon the width of which, 8, defines the inscribed circle. The diameter that circumscribes the hexagon thus determined becomes the diameter of the circle inscribed within a regular pentagon. The diameter of its circumscribing circle equals the total width of the cornice of the door, as well as the width of the upper tableau. This pentagon, drawn by using the middle of the width of the cornice on its upper edge as center, determines the room's ceiling.

The total height of the door represents fourteen units compared with the eight units that determine its width without the border.

It is the selective function, discerning, or rather dividing into two, that is represented by the olfactory center as a living, secret sanctuary of this temple, whose *essential and abstract aspect* is noted by number. Its geometric function is used to express it (fig. 184).

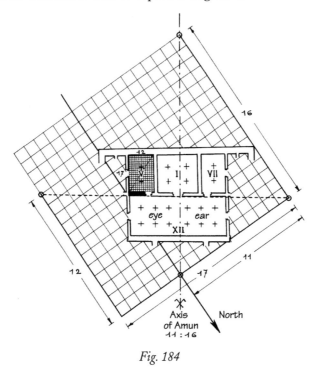

Fig. 184

Room V, olfactory center, cobra-uraeus; room I, the sanctuary of Amun, pituitary body; room VII, pineal body, the young king at age twelve.

The part of the covered temple that contains the three sanctuaries, I, V, and VII, as well as room XII, is laid out by taking the axis of Amun as a starting point, which is in the ratio of 11 : 16 with respect to north. The north wall of room XII is exactly perpendicular to it. The south wall of room XII, in the part that separates it from sanctuary V, undergoes an important deviation, and its orientation corresponds to the ratio 12 : 17.

The proportion for the plan of room V is established on 12 small cubits by width and 17 small cubits by length; now, the ratio 17 : 12 corresponds to the approximation (in excess) of the root of 2, the complementary ratio (in deficiency) being 24 : 17. The *canevas* is established on the north-south orientation.

The proportion for the plan of room V is established on the function of the root of 2, expressed by a ratio of whole numbers of small cubits, and the orientation of its north wall corresponds to the same coefficient. So, through the stone joints of the bas-reliefs depicted on this wall[9] we can refer back to this function in the peristyle court (the stomach), whose north wall is the only one in the entire temple to be rigorously parallel to the north wall of room V. The function of the irregular quadrangle of the peristyle court is the development of the square root of 2, or the division in two of the surfaces. The idea of the original function of the scission, or division into two, which makes the number Two from One, is therefore clearly noted geometrically.

[9] Cf. plates 97 and 98.

Using an example of "transparency" in the hieroglyphic architecture, we touched on the "dual" character of the olfactory center in *The Temple in Man.** Here are the reasons for that assertion, recalling the text of that passage: In the transparency, if the wall were of glass, we would be able to see, for example, a sign or a figure drawn on the back side that would fill in a blank space left on the front side. A naos or a barque can remain empty and be merely a container whose content can be found on the other side of the wall in a room where its theme is specially treated. In the case of transparency the stone *passes through the wall* and marks the link between the two images (and the two ideas).

An example of transparency exists in the wall separating room XII from room V. On the side of room XII, the bas-relief carved on this wall depicts the king offering the symbols of the cloths, while in room V, on the opposite wall, are found the "boxes for cloths."[10]

This inscription of the "cloths" and of the "box for cloths," placed here in transparency, deserves special attention in order to confirm—along with the proof of the Ancients' knowledge of the most secret functions of the human organism—their method of teaching and the way we should seek to decipher it, because here is one of the secrets of the true reading of the texts, which requires an analysis of the synthesis that the Temple represents.

Thus in room V, at the place where the hieroglyph for the "box for cloths" is to be found, the olfactory bulb is located at the level of the forehead where the cobra rises, and where the king receives the sacred unction of the "ointments" represented in the same room.[11]

We should remind ourselves again that the serpent represents the primitive being whose first developed, informing center is the olfactory one, which marks the beginning of the cerebral day, as the sun, when it rises in the east, marks the visible day.

The characteristic of transparency of the wall, placing as it does the hieroglyph for the cloths of room XII into the symbol of the "box for cloths" depicted in room V—this wall corresponding to the "cribriform plate"—would be enough to establish a relation between the symbol for cloths and the olfactory bulb. To this is added the characteristic of what *weaving* represents as a symbol, that is, the intertwining of threads, just as nerves are interlaced so as to make sensible (tangible, like the perspective vision of the eye) the contacts of the individual with the environment.

The olfactory bulb, with its tract [*bandalette*] dividing in two, constitutes an organ whose image becomes intermingled in the pharaonic symbol for cloth (fig. 185). Since we are dealing with a primitive organ, which is extremely important for all organized, primitive (sexual) life, it merits using as a model. Thus do we see the symbol of the cloth offered by the king whose single arm divides in two portrayed in room V.[12]

---

[10] The term "box for cloths" is used to designate the figure called *mr.t;* it is the chest or container that can be pulled (a sleigh) and that is surrounded by four cloths, white, green, red, and the *adma* cloth, which covers the soul of the dead. The *adma* strip of cloth is mentioned at the end of the text of the female divinity in room XII. In chapter 53 of the ritual, it is said that ". . . Amun takes his headband [*sed*] with the *adma* strip of cloth. . . ." The headband that girds the forehead is precisely located at the level of the three secret sanctuaries. Cf. plates 97 and 98.

[11] Cf. plate 87.

[12] In plate 76, room V, west wall, and plate 38 we can follow the olfactory fibers, some of which pass into the "white commissure," where they intertwine. Then the olfactory fibers move toward the four centers. This remark will be of interest for a future study of the texts of the ritual.

*See pp. 103–4.

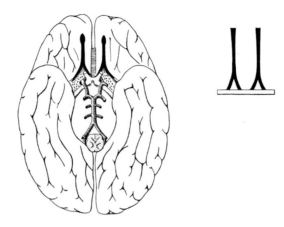

Fig. 185. The brain viewed from the bottom

From top to bottom, that is, from the front to the back: the two olfactory bulbs continue through the two olfactory tracts, which each divide into two "roots" that frame the anterior perforated space. The two optic nerves cross (optic chiasm) and take the name of optic tracts. Behind the optic chiasm is the pituitary stalk. Here, the circle of Willis is outlined, made up of the two vertebral arteries that enter at the base of the skull through the occipital foramen. They come together under the name of the basilar artery and divide once again to constitute this strange hexagon that surrounds the pituitary stalk.

In the temple, the circle of Willis corresponds to the level of the door of sanctuary I, going into room XII. See the geometric study of this door, fig. 183, and the circle of Willis, fig.133.

It is quite obvious that exoterically the symbol for cloth comes from the action of weaving, wherein the heddle spreads the threads of the warp to allow the shuttle to pass with the thread of weft; but the image of the olfactory bulb corresponds so perfectly, and the choice of the site in the temple where it is inscribed is too significant, for it not to suggest a desire to emphasize an esoteric intention. This is what we wish to point out here.

The principle of the function of weaving is represented in myth by the feminine Neith (the Greek Athena) crowned with the red crown. She is symbolized by a sign that is often transcribed by a crossing of two curves (fig. 186b), but which represents two bows, opposed in their sheath, able to shoot the two arrows that cross each other, as do the warp and weft (fig.186a).

This is also related to the creative Word, which is called "weaving" among the Dogon.[13]

The issue of weaving and of the olfactory center in relation to the serpent is so important that we deem it necessary here to summarize a few essential notes concerning Neith, Tayt, Buto, and the serpent. It is indeed difficult for our mentality to understand that the principle of weaving can at the same time be the cloth and that the one who offers the cloth is himself the cloth. It is not a question of confusion but of the very essence of magic, or rather, of the phenomenon resulting from a functional identity.

The uraeus, the cobra, is assimilated to Wadjet, the royal goddess of the North, the serpent divinity of Buto. Wadjet, in the form of a uraeus, is attached to the royal crown as a protector inseparable from the head of the king. In her capacity as sovereign of Lower Egypt, she borrows the red crown *(nt)* from Neith, which thus becomes the definitive emblem of the royalty of the Delta.

---

[13] Cf. Griaule, *Dieu d'eau.*

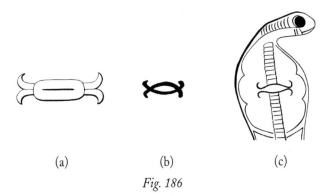

(a)   (b)   (c)

Fig. 186

(a) Sign crowning the head of the female *neter* Neith, tomb of Tutankhamun, stone sarcophagus; *(b)* hieratic sign (Möller, *Palaeographie,* 542b); *(c)* sign engraved on the cobra's chest, on the east side of the throne of the seated colossus of Ramesses II, court of Ramesses at Luxor, west colossus.

Buto, the capital of the North, is double. Two districts can be distinguished: Dep, the sacred city of the goddess Wadjet, where her temple stood, and Pe, "the place" par excellence, the royal town of Horus where the king of Lower Egypt had two residences mentioned in the Pyramid Texts, the Neser Palace and the Nu Palace.

The sacred name of Buto, the capital of the nineteenth nome of Lower Egypt, is Per-Wadjet, its profane name being Ammt, "the town of the eyebrows."[14] The eyebrows of Osiris are preserved at Buto.

The invention of weaving is attributed to Tayt, who represents simultaneously the town of weaving, the weaving, the cloth, and who is the *neter* of weaving. Her name is written with the determinative of a serpent. The name of Tayt was also given to the town of Buto.

Tayt is the cloth, that is, she represents the effect of weaving, of what, in general, takes on form by crossing.

"The strip of cloth [*bandelette*] is assimilated, as usual, to a divinity, Tayt, the goddess of the strip of cloth; in this capacity she has a divine body with which she can embrace the body of the God as she envelops it."[15] "The strips of cloth are the two hands of Tayt in her capacity as the regent who throws out the fluid of life."[16] ". . . You were given, the night [of embalmment], the oils and the strips of cloth from the two hands of Tayt."[17]

Neith, venerated at Sais (fifth nome of Lower Egypt) is also considered to have invented weaving. The name of the Serapeum of this nome is the "house of fabrics" *(ha-menkh),* famous for its production of cloth. The ear of Osiris was preserved there as a relic. The Book of the Dead and the

---

[14] The name is thus given exoterically by the sign, here of the eyebrow, and its place in the human body. Its esoteric function is designated by the character of the *neter.*

[15] Alexandre Moret, *Le Rituel du culte divin journalier en Egypte,* Annales du Musée Guimet 14 (Paris: Leroux, 1901), p. 189; also this chapter, appendix 1, note 2.

[16] The tomb of Rekhemire. Cf. ibid., p. 190.

[17] The tale of Sinuhit. Cf. ibid. Here are the different translations given of this text: "You were assigned the nights among the oils of embalmment and the strips of cloth (coming) from the hands of Tayt." G. Maspero, *Les Contes populaires de l'Egypt ancienne* (Paris: E. Guilmoto, 1911), p. 91. ". . . the night will (then) be assigned to you with oils (of embalmment) and strips of cloth (coming) from the hands of Tayt." Gustave Lefebvre, *Romans et contes égyptiens de l'époque pharaonique* (Paris: A. Maisonneuve, 1949), p. 17.

As long as we do not know the deeper meaning of the problem, it will always be impossible to translate correctly the secret of allegorical inscriptions. For example, the night mentioned here is related, in Hermeticism, to the Cimmerian shadows.

litanies of Osiris tell us that Sais was also divided into two quarters: Upper Sais and Lower Sais. The symbol of this nome is two crossed arrows.[18]

The reason for the choice of the serpent as the symbol for the principle of duality may seem strange, but everything in this animal is double, or dual, including its forked tongue and its sexual organs. It has a double penis, and the female has a double vagina; the testicles and the double ovaries of the higher animals are their vestiges.[19] These are the extraordinary characteristics of this reptile that justify its choice as a symbol in this case, as well as its symbolic role as *division,* as *opposition,* signified by the Tree of Good and Evil in the Mosaic Genesis.

The olfactory center, linked to the principle of dividing in the serpent, and recalling the original scission, makes room V into a synthesis as well as the place where the faculty of discernment and the moral sense are located.

The interpretation of the teachings of the pharaonic temple should therefore not be confined to a writing translated into language, but more essentially become a symbolic interpretation containing the architectural writing within it. The transparencies here are extremely important because the division of the plan into distinct rooms is exclusively motivated by the location of the functions of the vital centers. The paragraphs of the ritual distributed in these "vital places" thus take on a definite meaning by the "physiological topography," extended to a generalized significance as principles of the creative Work, demonstrated in its reality.

Logical Conclusion

First, the strange physiology of the serpent and the extreme importance of the olfactory sense for its life (although it does not have, strictly speaking, an external nasal organ) directs us toward the deeper meaning of its choice as a symbol. The choice expresses the Ancient Egyptians' vast knowledge of the natural sciences; much of what our science has only recently observed, the Ancients obviously knew. We can even assert that they knew "at least that much" because the theme of the olfactory center, described here in room V, is far from being exhausted by what we have just demonstrated.

Second, the location of the olfactory center in the room of the cobra-uraeus, sanctuary V, leaves no room for doubt and is, moreover, confirmed by the words of the ritual inscribed on the wall on the side of room XII, which we have included in plate 97 for this reason.

With the sign of Neith being placed on the cobra's "chest," across its trachea (fig. 187), there is an indication of a relationship between the function of weaving to make corporeal and the fixation of the spirit by respiration. The "weaving" of what animates (air) and what is animated (blood) is carried out by respiration.

Let us recall the characteristic respiratory function of the cobra, which draws itself up and puffs out its entire body by compressing the pocket (or hood) that forms its chest. Here are some observations.

When the cobra draws itself up into a defensive position, its breathing can be heard, and at the same time, it puffs out and releases its trachea and its entire body right down to the anus. There are two phases: the inhalation, in which the trachea becomes hollow, while the lateral parts widen as they curve, and the whole body can be seen filling and puffing out; and the exhalation, in which the body empties slowly while the trachea is puffed out to its maximum, as is the submaxillary area (it seems as if the air is retained only to filter out slowly).

The duration of one complete inhalation and exhalation is twelve to sixteen seconds. The

---

[18] It is obvious that this listing of a historical character for the common people has a functional esoteric meaning.

[19] For the zoological study concerning the olfactory sense and the physiological characteristics of the serpent, cf. appendix 2.

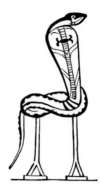

*Fig. 187. The coiled and raised cobra on the symbol for cloth
and bearing the sign of Neith on its chest, tomb of Amenhotep II*

mouth is always closed, except occasionally when the cobra rapidly waves its forked tongue. The respiration of the cobra is related to the solar respiration of the day.

Third, the function of dividing in two, characterized by the entire nature of the serpent (he who, with his tongue, also has "forked" speech), is also rendered by number in the function of dividing expressed by the root of 2, which explains the abstract meaning of the represented symbol.

This is but one example from a general study of one room; the care taken to express universal thought is found in the same way again and again in all parts of the temple.

Conclusion of the Teaching

First, the olfactory intelligence plays the part of *discernment* in the animal organism. It is the sense that separates or polarizes, doing so sensorially with the sense of smell, and deeply through internal action on the primitive, intellectual faculties (other than the sensorial olfactory sense).

It is this frontal area that encloses the psychological (moral) tendencies, the separative nature of which can go so far as to cause one to commit a crime.

Second, the faculty of discernment, located in the olfactory bulb, is the seat of judgment in man but also the seat of the vital *distribution* to the two endocrine glands of the vital source, reunited in the secret sanctuaries. Because it divides, it also reveals the secret of the reunification of that which, being Amunian (the pituitary group), is the *milieu,* with that which *acts* in this milieu (the pineal group).

The Fire that separates (Seth) also contains the Fire that unifies (Horus)—Satan and Lucifer.

The substance, or milieu, and the Fire that acts in this milieu are symbolized on the royal forehead by the head of the vulture (Nekhebet), which secretes the mucilaginous liquid of digestion through the nasal openings, and the head of the cobra with the venom (the Fire) that coagulates this substance.

These are basic elements of the teaching of sanctuary V, concerning the tangible and occult activity of the formed organ.

Appendix 1

Note 1

It is impossible for me to *prove* my conviction concerning the relationship between the pineal gland and the cerebral center for the intelligence of sound (or more precisely of tone). I can only recall the "legends" and what Hippocrates and Granet say about the customs concerning the relation of the ear to sexual prowess, and therefore essentially to the pineal gland, which, perhaps, allows us to make a comparison.

"Those who have undergone incisions beside the ears copulate, it is true, and they ejaculate, but their ejaculation is not very abundant, and is inactive and not fecund; for the greater part of the sperm comes down from the head, *along the ears,* to the spinal cord, but this tract is closed by the scar following the incision . . ."[20]

And, "The ears . . . are cut off of prisoners of war, whose virile force they want to diminish. . . . When one gives force to an oath by using the blood of a victim, the blood is taken near the ear . . . and it must be drawn from the left ear, for it is the left ear that is cut in prisoners of war before their sacrifice as they are held tied by the left hand."[21]

The pineal gland. Galen (A.D. 131) called it the *scolecoid* and, at that time, he indicated that it was already called the *epiphysis.* Certain authors then assumed that it was meant to serve as a sluice for the amount of spirit necessary for the maintenance of physical equilibrium. Descartes considered it to be the seat of the soul.

> The epiphysis was for a long time considered to be a regressive organ, devoid of clearly established functions. Histology demonstrates its secretory function of hemocrinia and neurocrinia, and physiology and clinical work show its action on growth (an antagonistic action to that of the hypophysis) on puberty, on the development of the external genital organs, and mainly its antigonadotropic action. Both histology and physiology have given full value to the knowledge of these nervous connections. Like the hypophysis, it possesses afferent and efferent fibers. However, these fibers are less known than those of the hypophysis. It is known that some of them come from the thalamus, the hypothalamus, the ganglions of the habenula and the cortex by the *taenia thalami,* from the mamillary bodies by the anterior pillar of the trigonum, and from the retina by a retinoepithalamic sheath. Finally, there are connecting fibers between the hypothalamus and the epithalamus.[22]

In room VII, the king is a young boy between seven and twelve years of age, and this is the only place in the entire temple where he is accompanied by his mother. The age of seven is the beginning of intellectual awakening.

Note 2

Shabaka, the Ethiopian king, characterized in the figuration by a double uraeus worn on his forehead, had the external facade of the south wall recarved at the place where the uraeus should be located, that is, the outside part of the south wall of room V.

Note 3

On the subject of the double character of room V, see plates 75 to 78 as well as their commentaries, in chapter 39.

On the east wall, at the level of the forehead, the listing of the oils and perfumes that are applied "to the forehead" of the king is depicted twice. On the west wall, the strips of cloth, or cloth pieces, are offered by the king whose one and only arm is divided into two. On the south wall, the lower register, Amun is represented twice. One of the figurations is painted in red, the other in blue, and the head and the features of both Amuns are carved on two reused columns. The red Amun receives the two streams of water in a double pool. On the north wall, the transparency of the boxes for cloths refers to a text written on the opposite wall in room XII, on which are mentioned the "two goddesses" (uraeus-vulture) determined by the two serpents.

[20] Hippocrates, *Oeuvres complètes,* trans. Littré (Paris: Baillière, 1851), 7:473.
[21] Granet, *La Pensée chinoise,* pp. 383, 364–65.
[22] Cf. Delmas and Laux, *Système nerveux sympathique,* p. 58.

Note 4

On the relationship between dualization and olfaction, one must note the use of the root *sn* in the words designating the number two, the action of smelling,[23] and incense for burning (fig. 188).

The word *snsn* can be found in room XII above the offering of cloth, in transparency with the boxes for cloths in room V.

Fig. 188

(1) *sn*, root; (2) *snw*, meaning two, or double; (3) *sn* (determined by the nose) to smell; (4) *snsn*, meaning, "smell," "sniff," "scent"; (5) *sntr*, the name of the incense in the form of resin for burning.

Note 5

In the court of Ramesses at the temple of Luxor, on the inside partition of the east wall, behind colossus no. 3, we find the litanies of Amun. We can read in line 101, "All the cloths of Tayt [are] of Amun who did the weaving" (fig. 189).

Fig. 189. Line 101 of the litany of Amun

In this litany, Tayt, meaning simultaneously the material, the weaving, and the *neter* of weaving, is determined by a serpent. It is obvious that the entire dualized and reunified Universe comes from Amun and belongs to him.

APPENDIX 2

To confirm the dual character of the serpent, we present here the result of studies carried out on the strange dualization of its sexual organs by F. Angel.[24]

> *The genital organs.* The ovaries and testicles are in front of the kidneys. The oviducts develop from the lower part of the ovary as far as the vaginal pocket, a communal space located below the rectum and opening onto the cloaca. Its vaginal part can be more or less *bilobate* or *divided into two parts.* Before the period of reproduction, the oviducts are reduced to small ligaments, but once fertilization has taken place, their extension becomes considerable. Usually there are more ova in the right oviduct than in the left. . . .
>
> The hemipenises form *two* erectile *appendages,* one on each side of the anal crease. They are activated by a retracting muscle that is related to one of the caudal vertebrae. They offer many differences in aspect, in conformation, and in the development of their respective parts, according to family or type. . . .
>
> The hemipenis has a dorsal side and a ventral side; the latter always carries a furrow or *sulcus* that courses through it obliquely over its entire length and *bifurcates* when the apex is divided. It consists of three principal parts: the peduncle, the body, and the apex.

[23] Cf. I. Schwaller de Lubicz, *Her-Bak, Egyptian Initiate*, chapter 8.

[24] F. Angel, *Vie et moeurs des serpents* (Paris: Payot, 1950).

The peduncle, forming the base of the organ, presents no particular characteristics. The same cannot properly be said of the body itself. Sometimes simple, short and wide, sometimes extremely elongated, it can be more or less *divided into two symmetrical parts* and can have (except in the Boidae where it is smooth) either isolated back bones, or else very numerous ones that vary a good deal in distribution according to the species.[25]

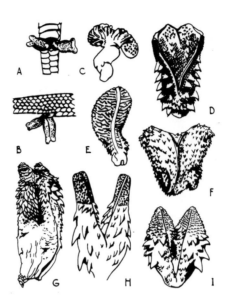

Fig. 190. A few types of conformation of ophidian hemipenises
(from Angel, Vie et moeurs des serpents, fig. 107, p. 243).

A, Ventral view of the hemipenises (measuring 13 mm in length) of a young *Natrix nuchalis* male shortly after its birth; *B*, the same viewed laterally; *C*, hemipenis of a constrictor; *D*, hemipenis of *Xenodon güntheri*, ventral view; *E*, hemipenis of a *Drymobius bifossatus*, ventral view; *F*, hemipenis of a *Micrurus marcgravii*, ventral view; *G*, hemipenis of a *Lachesis muta*, dorsal view; *H*, hemipenis of a *Bothrops castelnaudi*, ventral view; *I*, hemipenis of a *Bothrops neuwiedi meridionalis*, ventral view (figures from *C* to *I* from F. Villard).

As for the importance of the olfactory sense in this animal, a sense long denied to it, here are the experiments related by the same author:

Sensations. In general one can admit that (1) the sense of smell, for them [snakes] is more important than sight; (2) the sense of hearing, of touch, and of taste are far from playing as vital a part in the behavior of individuals as that of the first two.

Smell. The organs of smell are not very developed. The very short tract of the nostrils goes onto the front of the palate in an olfactory chamber of small dimension, walled by an epidermis devoid of glands or olfactory elements. . . .

An accessory apparatus, "Jacobson's organ," born from the mucous membrane of the nasal cavity, consists of a pair of cylindrical tubes situated between the nasal sacs and the buccal arch. . . . Jacobson's organ is densely invested with nerves and its olfactogustatory role seems assured when the serpent holds its prey in its mouth before swallowing it.

---

[25] Ibid., pp. 241–42.

The ancient authors did not grant much value to the role of the olfactory organ in serpents. . . . Modern research has refuted the opinions expressed by the authors of the *Erpétologie générale*. They show, on the contrary, that in spite of its weak development, the olfactory apparatus plays one of the most important parts in the lives of serpents: it intervenes when these animals look for each other to reproduce, hibernate, or gather in "balls" to hunt prey.

The movements used for the recognition among themselves of the subjects or of the sexes of the same species are guided by odors emitted through the integuments and not by those elaborated by the cloacal glands. Sight only intervenes in a secondary manner. The experiments of Noble and Clausen (1936), following those of other biologists, have demonstrated that serpents whose eyes had been carefully covered followed "by smell" a trail traced by the experimenters on sand or on stones. The experimenters rubbed these surfaces with the body of a serpent (while avoiding touching them with the anal region). On the other hand, a trail made by rubbing with the cloacal region was not only not used or followed by the animals, but avoided. They did not even cross it during their movements.

These observations show that, first, a "blinded" serpent is capable of finding its species members (male or female) by following, through scent, the trace of their passing through a given area; and second, the attraction is not from the odorous substances coming from the cloacal glands, but indeed from those emitted through the skin of other parts of the body.

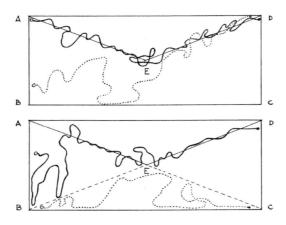

Fig. 191. (from Angel, Serpents, *fig. 110, p. 249)*

Above: the paths taken by two male *Storeria dekayi* starting from two different points on *AB*. The *AED* rectilinear line was made by the rubbing of the integuments from the body of another serpent. The first male follows the trail, the second searches for it, and, having found it, ends at D with the other. *Below:* the *AED* trail is obtained by rubbing the body; the *BEC* trail (dotted line) is obtained with the secretion of the cloacal glands. The first male searches for the *AED* line and having found it, follows it; the second avoids the *BEC* trail (from Noble and Clausen).

It has also been noted that there is no sexual attraction outside the mating period, since a male is equally able to follow the trail of another male or that of a female. This is what takes place in the winter gatherings, or in the formation of "balls of serpents." The same cannot be said of the mating season when the male recognizes more quickly the trail of a female, which he would not do in any other season. Similarly, during that time, the male does not follow the trail of another male. There is therefore reason to believe that during the mating period, the female emits through her skin a (still undetermined) substance capable of attracting the male, which allows him to distinguish the sex that emitted it.

Let us look into the role of olfaction in the search of prey. If, during experiments, we draw on a flat stone of 70 cm × 160 cm with water into which a few mud worms have been squashed, and if we place a serpent at one of the ends of the trail, the reaction is obvious: the animal follows the trail that has been created.[26] However, the time used to cover the path varies according to the species used for the experiments (9.5 minutes for a *Storeria dekayi*, and 16 minutes for a *Thamnophis sirtalis*).

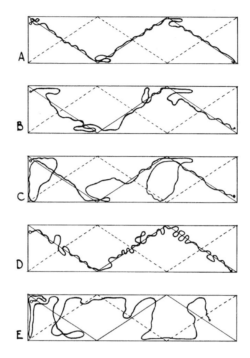

Fig. 192. Results of experiments on the search, by smell, of food by serpents (from Angel, Serpents, *fig. 165, p. 137. We have added to this a summary of the principal characteristics of figures A, B, C, D, and E).*

The sinuous lines indicate the path taken by the animal. The diagonal lines show the trail laid out by the experimenters by rubbing food (squashed mud worms) onto the plate. The dotted diagonal lines show the line made with distilled water (see the text for the detailed explanation of the figures). (From Noble and Clausen.) *A,* Distance covered in 9.5 minutes by a *Storeria dekayi; B,* distance covered in 16 minutes by a *Thamnophis sirtalis; C,* course completed in 36 minutes by a *Storeria dekayi,* one of whose nostrils had been blocked; *D,* course completed in 19 minutes by a *Storeria dekayi,* the functioning of whose Jacobson's organ had been destroyed by cauterization; *E,* course completed by a snake whose nostrils and Jacobson's organ were rendered incapable of action; the movements become dull and even do not take place.

The same result, a positive one, is obtained with snakes, the tip of whose tongue has been sectioned and their eyes covered; therefore these organs do not seem to intervene efficiently. If we use individuals in which the nostrils have been blocked (see fig. 192C), the time taken to cover the

[26] See fig. 192, A and B.

course of the trail is considerably prolonged (36 minutes for the *Storeria dekayi*). Moreover, by anni-hilating the function of Jacobson's organ through cauterizing, the time will be further prolonged (19 minutes for the *Storeria dekayi*), although still less than in the preceding one whose nostrils had been blocked (fig. 192D). Finally, if the nostrils and Jacobson's organ are rendered incapable of action, the snake shows no reaction in the presence of the odor trail created by food; its movements become dull or even do not take place (fig. 192E).

In conclusion, we can admit, along with the American authors, that neither the eye, the tongue, nor Jacobson's organ is absolutely necessary to the snake in its search for food, or to follow the trail left by an odorous prey. These acts are solicited by the olfactory organ whose role is reinforced in certain special cases . . . by special structures known under the name of "labial cavities or facial cav-ities." Until recent times, their function was unknown.[27]

Here now are a few extracts concerning the role of olfaction during the mating period:

Glands situated in the anal area omit a liquid with a violent and characteristic odor that seems to act as a means of defense rather than a means of recognition between the two sexes searching for each other at the mating period. Even at a distance, the males are guided by smelling odors emit-ted by the integuments of the females' bodies. We pointed this out in the chapter on sensations. To the trails drawn by us, we could add here the result obtained by G. K. Noble in his experiments on the intervention of chemical senses in mating. They show that the odors emitted by the bodies of the females of one given species attract the male of that species and that those arising from the secretion of the cloacal glands leave them indifferent, or even repulse them, contrary to the old, gen-erally accepted ideas. The figures [below] demonstrate this.

The figure [193B] (white surface) represents the trail followed by a *Thamnophis sirtalis* male in search of a partner during the mating period. On a glass or a mirror previously rubbed with the skin of the flanks of a female ready to mate the journey of the male represents a long arabesque. But if the mirror is rubbed with the secretion of the cloacal glands [fig. 193A], the same male will avoid its contact; he will move along the edge of the prepared surface.

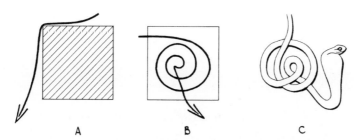

Fig. 193 (from Angel, Serpents, *figs. 109A and 109B, p. 247)*

A, Pane of glass rubbed with the secretion of the cloacal glands; *B,* pane of glass rubbed with the skin of the flanks of a female ready to mate; *C,* frontal pharaonic uraeus, as it is drawn on the *khepesh* headdress.

---

[27] We have not given here the passages concerning the "labial cavities and facial cavities," sensory plates located between the nostril and the eye, and whose role is still not well defined. The question here is of a sense able to detect vibrations to which our senses no longer react. It has not been determined whether it is thermal, luminous, sonorous, or electromagnetic action that is at work. Angel, *Serpents,* pp. 134–38.

In the following experiments, another male is made to intervene, with these results: just as the trail formed by the secretion of the female cloacal glands is avoided by the male suitor, so also the trail obtained by rubbing the integuments of another male on the same pane of glass so as to cross the trail left by the female's skin will hinder the progress of the male beginning to follow the latter. This is what figure 194A shows in which a *Thamnophis butleri* male, after following the female's trail, abandons it at the approach of the trail made by the other male.

In figure B, where the attempt is carried out with a *Thamnophis sirtalis* male, the meeting of the second parallel line obtained by using another male also causes the suitor to abandon the female's trail.

From these various experiments, it is only the odors emitted by the integuments of females ready to mate that allow males to follow their trails and to find them for mating.[28]

It is interesting to point out that the angle of the path drawn by the experimenter influences the snake, as if its "sense of smell" preceded it, to continue in the same direction. This obliges the snake to turn in a new direction instead of immediately following it.

Figure 194 shows that when the animal smells the presence of a male on the trail of a female he is following, he leaves his path believing that it is no longer useful to follow her. He therefore does not look for combat.[29]

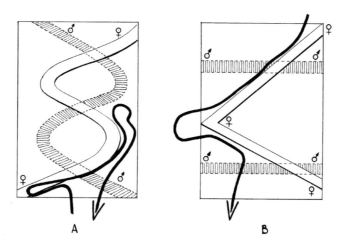

Fig. 194 (from Angel, Serpents, *fig. 111A and 111B, p. 249)*

Notes on Jacobson's Organ

Terminal nerve; vomeronasal organ. Besides the olfactory fibers, the anterior brain receives a *terminal nerve,* proof of a true Jacobson's organ or vomeronasal organ in reptiles.

This organ is a special development of the olfactory area. Although it is absent in fish in its capacity as a special organ, it is present in amphibians in which it forms a part of the rhinal cavity. More differentiated in reptiles, it forms a special part of the rhinal cavity, located, in the *Sphenodon,* near the choana, and, in tortoises, near the nasal septum. In snakes and in lizards, there is no communication with the rhinal cavity, but it opens into the buccal cavity.

[28] Angel, *Serpents,* pp. 246–48.

[29] This refusal to fight can be related to the traditional characteristic attributed to Saturn (lead), who is called "he who does not wish to fight."

Rudimentary in crocodiles, and absent in birds, it can be found in Monotremata, Marsupalia, Ungulata, and in rodents, in which it communicates with the mouth as well as with the nose by means of the nasopalatine duct (Stensen's duct).

It functions as an olfactory organ of the mouth in snails and lizards; it is accentuated by the forked form of the tongue that enables the animal to carry odorific substances against its buccal openings.

Jacobson's organ has a double innervation, olfactory and sensory. Its sensory fibers are derived from the trigeminal and the terminal nerves.[30]

---

[30] C. U. Ariens Kappers, G. C. Huber, and E. C. Crosby, *The Comparative Anatomy of the Nervous System of Vertebrates, Including Man* (New York: Macmillan, 1936), chapter 9.

Chapter 19

CROSSING

Elsewhere, I attempted to indicate the nature of "crossing" with physical examples, like the nervous reaction that is inverse to an external influence, as in the case of light on the optic nerve creating the complementary effect.[1] These are basic images for awakening the mind to a characteristic mentality, such as we observe in Ancient Egypt, or again in China, and which is typically found in the expression of wisdom addressing itself to its disciples. The Cross is α and ω, and the "bronze serpent" on the Cross gives life. . . .

Man crucified in space is the Anthropocosmos.

The cross is the equatorial plane of a body in revolution around itself. It is the four directions that define the abstract center.

The cross is the symbol of life because for us life is simply the ability "to react."

We see the mechanical reaction, but do we understand the vital reaction? Is it not the latter that, intimately, causes the gross external mechanical reaction, that is, of the body toward another body? When the organic body reacts to an external influence we are tempted to call it "a vital reaction," but it is still only a subtle mechanical reaction of an energetic nervous system, provoked by the external influence.

The true meaning of "vital reaction" is to be sought in the *intensity* of the reaction, then in the consciousness that responds to the call, that is to say, the constitutive, defining, specifying power of the "object."

The electricity of "force fields" is a crossing; electromagnetic induction is a crossing; nervous sensitivity is a crossing; the endocrine effect is a crossing; intelligence is a crossing—in short, all phenomena are crossings, that is, they are symbolized by the ungraspable point *situated* by the four cardinal points.

Every cause is to be considered as an activity that is relatively positive or negative. The phenomenal consequence of the cause is always "cathodic" because the reabsorption of the causal

---

[1] *The Temple in Man*, chapter 7.

476

activity without resistance would only be a nullification, and because resistance necessarily provokes a reaction.

The phenomenon of electrical influence and of its inductive effect is a perfect image to make understood the vital principle whose physical aspect is merely an analogy. Here are the correspondences:

$$\begin{aligned}
\text{quantity of energy} &= \text{influence} = \text{first force field;}\\
\text{rupture} &= \text{alternation} = \text{rhythm} = \text{enumerated number;}\\
\text{induction} &= \text{first crossing} = \text{reaction} = \text{intensity} = \text{tangible phenomenon;}\\
\text{Tesla effect} &= \text{second crossing} = \text{vitalizing effect.}
\end{aligned}$$

The physiological effect of the first induction on the nervous system is an intense excitement produced by the synchronization of the vibrations, which can go so far as to cause death. The physiological effect of the Tesla effect is an animation, which becomes manifest by the heating of the blood and fluids, and an excitation of the nervous sensitivity (Arsonval effect).

All this is still mechanical and seems childish when compared with the analogous effects having a vital character. Through induction, a small *quantity* is transformed into a great *intensity* (quality). This is quite probably the mystery of the endocrine glands whose effect, by induction relays, is magnified into vital intensity. All tangible observation is the effect of a crossing (induction) of the nervous flux, which, itself, is already the effect of a first crossing in the assimilation of food.

The human body contains and is surrounded by fluxes of energy, the true channels of life, the vital arteries, *mtw,* of which the Ancients speak and which our physiologists confuse with the blood vessels.

It is essential to take note of this fact in order to interpret the correspondences and orientations that the representation of the pharaonic Temple suggests to us by the joints of the stones. The universal principle of the crossing (the cross) is applied throughout pharaonic thought. It is the vital key to all that appears in the Universe.

The principle of reactivity is applied by means of an esoteric *symbolique.* It is imposed by the fact that an intellectual (unsituated) definition is impossible. This definition must therefore *be evoked* by reaction, but one cannot describe it without situating it in time and space, without therefore "fixing" it.

Through its static and concrete nature, the symbol, as synthesis, evokes the functional and qualitative whole from which it results, that is, it vitally evokes its "insituable" definition.

This way of thinking is the key to the pharaonic mentality.[2] This mentality, incidentally, is similar to that found in China.[3]

It is in this spirit that we must look at the architectural writing of the temple, such as the "transparencies," as well as the "medieties" in calculation, and the "musical" phenomenon of harmonious ratios. These ratios are vitally analogous to the crossing of "the head with the body" and of the organs of the head with the organs of the body, such as the ovaries with the eyes, the vital centers of the encephalon with the limbs, and so forth.

The crossing that is figuratively transcribed by an X, or by the "reflection" in a mirror, or by the crossing of the scepters of the mummified pharaoh is, in reality, a "spiritual" function analogous to

---

[2] See chapter 2.

[3] Cf. Granet, *La Pensée chinoise.* This idea can also be related to the principle of the "homeopathic" therapeutic method.

the neutralization of an acid by a base, which forms a salt. It is the *essence* of the phenomenon, the cosmic law that must serve as a guide to thought in every case.

Alternation appears as a compensation: the alternation of growth in length and volume, in anterior and posterior limbs, the alternation of tides and of waves, the alternation of life and death—all existence expresses itself in terms of alternation. This is the phenomenal appearance that in reality is *crossing,* and crossing is for alternation what musical harmony is for sound. The true meaning of the crossing is the alternation of the visible with the invisible, of the abstract with the concrete, of the actual with the potential. We see the one, observe it with our senses, but we do not perceive its complement. It is this relationship that is α and ω, the All.[4]

All the images and analogies that we can imagine have the sole aim of *evoking* the unformulated or unformulable consciousness of the real meaning of the crossing. The tangible evokes the intangible by negation: *this strange affirmation of an unformulated certainty that is the negation.*

It is this mysterious mirror that, vertically, reverses right and left, then, horizontally, reverses top and bottom, that pharaonic Egypt, in a state of superior consciousness, manipulates in all its works, making them so difficult for us to describe; it is a mentality that we must never forget to acknowledge if we wish to receive the teaching of the Ancients.

The crossing is a function that the cross symbolizes through the crossing of two lines, that is, of two paths or two double orientations. In any event, the effect of the crossing is the determination of a neutral center point. This neutral center is the esoteric purpose of the *gesture* of the crossing. As such, this neutral center point is neither a plane nor a mathematical point without physical reality; it can only be the center of a volume whose importance varies with the intensity of the crossed lines or paths. This volume is, however, not material; it is the contractive, or centripetal, functional center.

The neutral center may be compared to a neutron of the atom, a *magnetic* center that holds the entire structure in equilibrium.

This is the law that the whole of pharaonic thought obeys: that which is below (seed) must rise (new seed principle) in order to be turned downward again (new active seed).

The affirmation that *Earth is in the image of Heaven* is not only an inversion but also a crossing.

Pharaonic thought is based on this principle of the crossing, in mathematics as much as in medicine, in architecture as much as in the significance of the myth.

---

[4] This alternation is today called vibration, the physicists' wavelength, which only leads to a deviation from the vital meaning of the physical phenomenon.

Chapter 20

THE ZODIAC

THE GENESIS OF THE EMPIRE

Our history over the last two thousand years has been one of dispersal, of scattering, into the Greek, Roman, Byzantine, Islamic, Moorish, and Vandal eras, the Holy Roman Empire, the Gothic influences, then the struggles for independence of the Christianized regions into national constitutions, whether French, Nordic, Austrian, Spanish, or other. It is with the arrival of the precessional Age of Pisces—the Tower of Babel that lacks the triangular foundation stone—that the Temple ceased to be alive.

Now, the Temple is knowledge, that is, the science of genesis and cosmic harmony. Our history is made up of struggles, of individual egoisms, and of expediencies that lack the discipline of a conscious aspiration leading beyond mortal man. With the Christian period, humanity left the Temple and climbed up *onto* the Temple, as Greece and Rome show by their no longer placing their statues under the heavens (as in Egypt) but upon columns and roofs.[1]

Indeed, with the Christic revelation, the natural and logical consequence of Ancient Egypt, the Osirian cycle—thus the doctrine of the cycle of terrestrial reincarnations—ends. The dogma of the Redemption renders man independent of the obligations of this reincarnation.

It is a promise that each must realize individually; therefore, it is a breaking up of the human grouping, for the Church can only give general instructions: it can no longer guide man collectively except by means of general, moral directives, seeing that this man must realize Christ within himself through his own effort, an effort that the principle of cyclic reincarnation *does not concentrate into a single lifetime.*

---

[1] Cf. plate 25. In this plan of Luxor in the Roman period, notice the two crossroads to the east and the west where two groups of four columns are attributed to the first and second tetrarchies. In each case, two of these tetrarchs "are Jovians, that is, they claim to be descendents of Jupiter, who in Egypt is Amun." Pierre Lacau, *Inscriptions latines du temple de Louqsor,* Annales du Service des Antiquités de l'Egypte 34 (Cairo, I.F.A.O.), p. 44.

This phenomenon is demonstrated in Brahmanic India, which was able to remain coherent through millennia under the tutelage of the principles of reincarnation and the caste system. It was able to push away, toward Tibet, Buddhist individualism, which, in order to uphold itself, became concentrated and isolated in that country inaccessible to the foreigner. There the Temple could be created, yet leave people free to follow their own ways. Thus, the Temple is able to select individuals and to cultivate knowledge, thereby becoming a radiant and at the same time attracting sun. After the Crusades, the Christian attempt by the Knights Templar to reconstitute this center failed in the West; the *dissolving influence* of the precessional period of Pisces *did not allow* this rebirth, and likewise, it brought about the demise of the Brahmanic and Buddhist Temples. And yet the *vital necessity* of unification or centralization, characteristic of the Temple, today urges humanity to call upon collective social principles that have an economic and proletarian basis, with a materialistic philosophy as the "cornerstone." It is a human temple built on quicksand, not on rock.

Our mentality, formed by our history, makes us skeptical of the assertion that an empire could have been founded on knowledge while situating its beginning according to given astrological facts, that is, that it could have been organized according to given cosmic facts, as, in a very small way, all farmers and gardeners must do in order to harvest their crops.

Only an originally theocratic government could establish such an order: a king reigning over social affairs, counseled and guided by a sage, or a college of sages, guardians of the knowledge.[2] Now, the whole of the known history of pharaonic Egypt confirms this formula, based, in anticipation of the future, on the successive incarnation of three principles, pillars of wisdom, through Imhotep, son of Ptah (Fire), then Amenhotep, son of Hapu (Water), and finally Petosiris, taken together, the solar, lunar, and terrestrial lineages. A parallel can be made with the analogous Hermetic principles symbolized by Sulfur, Mercury, and Salt. These three principles constitute the Unity of the Verb, and although they are theoretically qualitatively distinct and mutually define each other, there is an interaction between them that manifests the four elementary qualities. This schematic accord of the three principles with four elements plays a constant part in pharaonic Egypt, like an embryonic human genesis that becomes the image and guide of this empire's evolution. This gestation takes place over a period of nine months, that is, the nine decans of three precessional months: Gemini, Taurus, and Aries.[3]

In the fourth month, the human fetus manifests its existence by moving; it becomes viable in the seventh month, then, during the eighth month undergoes a renewal that enables it to be born in the ninth month.

In the history of pharaonic Egypt, the beginning of the fourth month of gestation corresponds approximately to the year 4300 B.C., which is the date of the unification of the empire and the beginning of the Dynastic Period. It is the first historic dynasty and begins with Menes (a name related to *men*, foundation, and also to *men.t*, the thigh, and to Mentu).

This pushes the conception of the empire back to approximately 2160 years before Menes. This period, comprising three months of gestation, constitutes the Predynastic Period ruled by the sign of Gemini, which has a double character. All the evidence dating from the Predynastic Period shows a duality: the kingdom of the North (red crown) and the kingdom of the South (white

---

[2] The Holy Roman Empire, the barrier between the Roman and Byzantine Christian churches, was an Occidental attempt at a similar theocratic empire.

[3] One precessional month is approximately 2160 years. One decan represents ten days of a month, therefore 720 years, which in turn represents one month of gestation. Cf. chapter 36.

crown) were still separated and would only be reunited under one scepter with Menes, the sole king of the North and the South.

These three decans of predynastic history—the three months of gestation before the manifest life of the fetus[4]—constitute the period of "polarization." This is the embryonic phase during which the poles and the complements define themselves, the innermost glands as much as the nervous centers, and the distinction is made between the male and the female. For Egypt, it is the time when two double towns, Pe and Dep in the North and Nekheb and Nekhen in the South, were built, the towns of coronation for the kings of Lower and Upper Egypt. The two thousand years before Menes are thus devoted to the duality of Gemini (Shu and Tefnut).

With the accession of Menes to the throne, the vernal point entered the sign of Taurus, the Bull, whose cult became official from approximately 4300 B.C. to 2100 B.C. The cult of the bull Apis is the oldest evidence of animate symbolization in historical Egypt. In the First Dynasty, periodic festivals attached to the royal festivals took place in his honor, and his name, Hap, is included with several royal names from that time. Toward the end of the cycle, large temples were built and consecrated to Mentu-Ra, the stellar divinity who enjoyed total supremacy during this period and whose sacred animal was the bull.[5] The last kings of this cycle still associated Mentu to their name (Mentuhotep, Eleventh Dynasty).

The detailed history of the kings from the first dynasties to the Mentuhoteps, in other words, during the complete Taurus cycle,[6] is not well known; however, as tradition asserts, it was the time of the greatest purity in morals and of the greatest wisdom in government. The papyri and the texts date the establishment of all sciences back to this period, and declare them of divine origin, that is, *prescribed and revealed through celestial harmony.*

From approximately 2100 B.C., the official cult, beginning with Amenemhet (Twelfth Dynasty), is that of Aries—Amun—who was to reach his apogee at the second decan of the sign in 1500 B.C. with the dynasty of the Amenhoteps (Eighteenth Dynasty). Thus Amun, who is one of the "primordial Eight," only had total supremacy over the other *neters* while the precessional sign of Aries dominated.[7]

The definitive end of the empire came in about 60 B.C. with Cleopatra. This corresponds to the beginning of the precessional sign of Pisces.

This basis for a gestation through nine decans of three zodiacal signs is, in my opinion, unquestionable, because it is absolutely confirmed by the cult of the ram, and it ends with this sign, preceded by the cult of the bull. One can point out in this regard that in the human figures in the Cheops (Khufu) period, in the tombs of the nobles at the foot of the Great Pyramid, there is emphasis placed on the strength of the neck, astrologically governed by Taurus. It is obvious that one sign does not erase another, and in the gestation the influence of the bull continues, submitting to the influence of a new cosmic period without the exclusion of the effects of past influence: today contains yesterday. The solar genesis contains the terrestrial genesis in one of its periods, and the terrestrial genesis, in one of its periods, contains the genesis of the empire, just as the empire contains in one of its periods the entire human genesis.

---

[4] The tombs of this period show burial in the fetal position.

[5] Cf. chapter 36 for details on the sacred bulls.

[6] It is also the period of the cult of the Minotaur in Crete, of which very little is known.

[7] We understand by the word *sign* here the signature of time, when, in reality, it is a question, astronomically, of the influence of the constellation.

Esoterically, it is the law of genesis in itself that must be considered, not its particular application to individuals. The mayfly lives a complete cycle in a day. This is comparable, for example and in the opposite direction, to the tangential speed of the earth in rotation, which, at the equator, is about 464 meters per second, whereas at the theoretical pole a snail would walk at an excessive speed in the same amount of time. It is nevertheless the same sphere.

THE ZODIAC IN EGYPT

Since its origin, Egypt has certainly known the zodiac, and it is Egypt that left us the signs used to designate the "zones of the sky."[8]

> Trismegistus speaks of the "zodiacal band" and of the "twelve figures of animals." According to Lucian, the Egyptians "imagined twelve divisions in the fixed sphere and attributed to each the representation of familiar figures." Some of these represent aquatic animals, others represent men, others, beasts, birds, and others represent different animals.
>
> Arago points out that there is general agreement that in the zodiacal constellations we can see the emblems of the twelve Egyptian divinities that presided over the twelve months of the year. Thus Aries was consecrated to Jupiter Amun; Taurus was used to represent the god or the bull Apis, and so on.
>
> For Macrobius, "the twelve signs of the zodiac are related to the nature of the sun" in the mind of the Egyptians.
>
> It is generally thought that the Egyptian zodiacal figures were borrowed from the Chaldean and Greek zodiac. This is not what is demonstrated.[9]

The Ancient Egyptians' knowledge of the twelve zones, subdivided into thirty-six decans on the zodiacal band, is neither questioned nor questionable. The only argument concerns the Ancients' use of the figures represented at Dendera on the circular and rectangular zodiacs sculpted in the Late Period. Two examples, however, are enough to show how the ancient sages understood these signs and figures.

On a demotic table, in the tomb of Ramesses VI, the sign of Capricorn is expressed by the ankh (key of life), and the sign of Leo by a knife (see table 8).

The beginning of the reascent of the sun during the sign of Capricorn (festivals of Khoïak, Christmas) is the astronomical rebirth of the year, of the new, annual Osirian life. The transfer of this seasonal fact onto the sign of Capricorn in general, and therefore also onto the precessional month, is evident.[10]

As for the "knife," which is not there in place of the Lion, but in order to express its function more clearly, one must remember that the period dominated by the sign of Leo is the period that

---

[8] In 1856, Brugsch, relying on Letronne, Biot, and so on, suggested again that the zodiacal figures were of Greek or Chaldean origin [see table 8, note a].

[9] E. M. Antoniadi, *L'Astronomie égyptienne* (Paris: Gauthiers-Villars, 1934), pp. 65–66. Antoniadi was an astronomer at the Observatory of Meudon. He very sincerely took upon himself the task of looking exclusively in the Greek texts for any mention of pharaonic astronomical knowledge transmitted to the Greeks. But he was completely unaware of the hieroglyphs and the pharaonic symbols.

[10] Cf. chapter 36, in which we show that the functional image of Capricorn in the temple of Luxor is symbolized by an aquatic tadpole but with its hind legs resting on the earth. It is associated with the sign *chen*, the circle of time.

TABLE 8

	A	B	C	D		A	B	C	D
I					VII				
II					VIII				
III					IX				
IV					X				
V					XI				
VI					XII				

A, Signs from the zodiac of Dendera; *B*, hieroglyphic origin of the demotic signs;[a] *C*, demotic signs found on the eight sides of four tablets giving the month and the day of each planet's entry into each zodiacal sign during a period of twenty-eight years;[b] *D*, present conventional signs.

I   Cancer is replaced by a scarab in the tomb of Ramesses VI.
II   Leo is replaced by a knife in the tomb of Ramesses VI.
III   For Virgo, the demotic sign reads *rpa*, which Brugsch translates by "the young," "the virgin."
IV   For Libra, the scales that frame the sun rising between the mountains are simplified by this single symbol in the demotic.
V   Scorpio is symbolized by a serpent in the tomb of Ramesses VI.
VI   Sagittarius is symbolized by an arrow in the tomb of Ramesses VI.
VII   Capricorn is symbolized by an ankh in the tomb of Ramesses VI.
VIII   Aquarius is symbolized by water in the tomb of Ramesses VI.
IX   Pisces is symbolized by a fish in the tomb of Ramesses VI.
X   For Aries, the demotic sign signifies the skin, determining all species of mammals.
XI   For Taurus, the demotic sign reads *ka*, name of the bull.
XII   Gemini—Shu and Tefnut—is symbolized by the two plant shoots in the demotic and in the tomb of Ramesses VI.

[a] Cf. H. Brugsch, *Nouvelles recherches sur la divison de l'année des anciens Egyptiens* (Berlin, 1856). The astronomical indications contained in these tablets correspond to the period of Trajan.
[b] According to Brugsch, *Nouvelles recherches*, pp. 53–61. In addition, the existence of certain signs of column B, in the tomb of Ramesses VI, is noted by Antoniadi, *Astronomie égyptienne*, pp. 65–70.

separates the two spheres of influence, spring-summer from autumn-winter for us,[11] and the beginning of the inundation for the Ancients.[12] In the zodiac, Leo is opposite Aquarius. For this separative reason the symbol of Leo is used to represent the bolt. It is the break between opened and closed, before and after, and Leo has always played this part in pharaonic Egypt. That it would have been depicted thereafter in the zodiac of Dendera is natural, and the Greeks had no reason to introduce into Egypt the figure of a lion, an animal unknown in their homeland.[13]

I stress: it is the function that mattered to the sages, not the object. He who does not understand the significance implied in the word *function* will never penetrate the teaching of wisdom, whether it be pharaonic or of another time or place. But, as far as it is possible to judge, I believe that never has this teaching been spoken more clearly than in Egypt.

The signs of the zodiac form a part of the instruction of the Temple in that they are *functional symbols;* but the zones of the sky at that time were always indicated just as they really are, by groups of stars and not by symbols. Nowadays, these figurations are clung to in order to seek the astronomical knowledge of the Ancients, which is a mistake. The zodiacal zones are constellations; the symbols are to be read for their esoteric meaning and not in transcription.

The figuration of the phases of the zodiac constitutes functional hieroglyphics; they form a part of the innermost teaching of the Temple.

The choice of these figures—animals, humans, or composites—corresponds to the active, "influential" character of the zones in the sky, grouping together the fixed stars, but this general "tincture" allows the individual action of the principal stars in the stellar groups to survive. This is why the Ancients represented the zodiacal band unrolled like a papyrus. It was necessary for the empire to be in its last phase of life before the Temple could leave to the Ptolemaic prattlers the task of drawing the circular stone zodiac at Dendera. Now, the figuration that we see sculpted there are pharaonic, although of Ptolemaic construction.

The circular representation addresses itself to general influences, or *combinations* of influences, specified by the figurations (which are hieroglyphic) and naming each type of *animation* precisely, whence came the name *zoe-diac,* or circle of life. The Dendera zodiac confirms this in a striking way, since the signs absolutely do not follow each other in a regular, schematic manner, but are spirally interwoven.[14]

All rational attempts at finding the intent behind this interweaving and these groupings of figures have failed. And with reason! Who in present times can believe or believes in the astro-animalic influence of the starry sky? The farmer? The gardener? They observe; they are neither philosophers nor "savants." As for our science, it is satisfied with recognizing caloric effects and all sorts of radiations coming from the sun. This, it seems, is sufficient in our time.

Certainly, the eye of Ra is the great visible and tangible power, but for the Ancients, this does not answer all the demands imposed by observation.

The interpretation of the meaning of the *stellar groupings* on the zodiacal band, which intrigues Egyptologists, is only possible owing to the system of the *canevas,* the principles of which we have

---

[11] The end of August is the period of molting for the Galliformes, among others.

[12] "When they want to represent the floods of the Nile, called Nun in Egyptian, which means "new," they draw a lion . . . because when it is in conjunction with Leo, the sun renders the floods of the Nile more abundant. This is so much the case that when the sun remains in this constellation, the new water often reaches double its usual flow. This is why the Ancients who worked on the building of the temples made the canals and conduits of the sacred fountains in the shape of lions" (Horapollo, *Hieroglyphica,* 21).

[13] Imported from Babylonia?

[14] Cf. fig. 195b.

already shown, and through symbols chosen from among the parts of the human body, such as the eyes, the arms, the legs, the elbows, the knees, and so on.[15]

In each grouping there are vitally important stars (not always the brightest) that dominate by their influence. The traditional knowledge of these stars has come down to us through Islam in the Arabic names that our astronomy preserved before having them "poeticized" by designating them as α, β, and so forth.[16]

Moreover, this tradition that stresses certain *powerful* stars has been preserved in the figurations of the zodiac *that were later drawn on the groupings of stars.*

The sun passes annually through each of the theoretical twelve zodiacal regions and their figurations. Thus the sun is at a different place every day in the figure for the month, but its influence varies depending on the conjunction it makes with the stars, in Taurus for example, of the eye, of the nape of the neck, of the sex organs, or of the thigh. This is yet another reason for projecting an imagined figure on an area of the starry sky.

Having recognized that a group of stars influenced certain vital dispositions, its hieroglyph was sought, as was done in the case of writing in choosing the animal type or, generally, the gesture that incarnates or symbolizes that characteristic activity. Thus, for example, the bull is the hieroglyph that summarizes and symbolizes the whole of the characters of a stellar grouping. This does not mean that the hieroglyph is figuratively traced on this area of the sky. The issue in that case is of a rather naive concept for a popular transmission of the science. Thus, through the Ptolemies, the Temple allowed for the perpetuation of a tradition.

The stars in the sky are for us the living cells of the body of Cosmic Man, and their groupings situate the different centers (vitally organic) of this body.

> Celsus reports that, "according to the Egyptians, the human body is occupied by thirty-six genies or etheric gods who have divided it up into so many parts." And "they know the names of these genies in their indigenous language . . . and, by invoking them, they heal various illnesses." Hermes speaks of the "thirty-six decans located in the center of the circle of the universe and of the zodiacal circle." Firmicus Maternus explains "that each zodiacal sign is divided into three . . . decans," and "each decan concerns only one star." The question of decans can be summarized by saying that the twelve zodiacal constellations were each subdivided into three parts characterized by one brilliant star. This forms thirty-six divisions called decans and corresponds to the same amount of ten-day periods in the regular year of 360 days. Sothis was its queen. The heliacal rising of each decan took place at the beginning of each ten-day period.[17]

When, by the movement of the earth—or of the sun, it does not matter which—the sun as seen from the earth is in one of these vital areas of Cosmic Man, it activates the emanation of this center. This emanation is neither physical nor "vibratory" as we would illusorily like to call it; it is simply energetic (the Archaeus), and all that lives and grows by seed or fermentation fixes this energy, whose "nature" and "tincture" we later find in the product. This therefore influences the behavior of living beings in every way.

---

[15] We see that the elbows and the knees are used to designate angles. We find the notion of this kinship also expressed by the Greeks in the words γόν, "angle" and γῶν, "knee." Cf. chapter 7.

[16] Such as Aldebaran, Altair, etc.

[17] Antoniadi, *Astronomie égyptienne*, pp. 77–78.

Pharaonic medicine takes the astronomical periods into exact account:

Six paragraphs of the Treatise of the Eyes mention the periods in the year when it is recommended to take a particular remedy, appropriate for strengthening the sight: "Another remedy for strengthening the sight. It must be done from the first month of winter until the second month of winter. . . ."

Another formula tells us a treatment that is recommended "from the third month of winter until the fourth month of winter." Yet another mentions at the same time, the summer, the winter, and the inundation, that is, the three times of the Egyptian year, without distinction.[18]

From this, astrology was born, whose significance is much deeper than a mere "-mancy," a divinatory science.

At any rate, it is essential to keep in mind the place where the sun is to be found—not in degrees, but vitally—according to the intent of the image. For example, the sun in Gemini can be in one or the other of the twins Castor and Pollux (or Shu and Tefnut), or in the hand that links the two. The shining eye of Taurus is burning desire; the nape of his neck is power, but blind power (the bull takes hold of his adversary with its horns, and, because of the strength of his neck, throws him into the air); his sexual prowess is fiery but fugitive and unreliable; his thigh is the only stability found in him.

The choice of figures (hieroglyphs) is certainly one of the most grandiose expressions of knowledge, and the sublime testimony of the wisdom of the Ancients.

THE ZODIAC AND THE PRECESSION
OF THE EQUINOXES

The observatories in Egypt pointed out the movement of the stars every year and drew up annual tables of their risings and their settings, of which some scattered remains have reached us. By the report of Achilles Tatius, it was said that the Egyptians "had measured and were the first to do so, the sky and the earth, and that they inscribed the knowledge they acquired in this way on columns for future generations." Proclus Diadochus even attributes to them the discovery of the precession of the equinoxes: "May those who believe in the observations that have the stars moving around the poles of the zodiac toward the east by one degree every hundred years, as Ptolemy and Hipparchus before him, know . . . that the Egyptians had already taught Plato the movement of the fixed stars. For they used previous observations, which the Chaldeans had undertaken a long time beforehand with the same result, having been taught by the Gods prior to the observations. And they did not only speak once, but many times . . . of the advance of the fixed stars."

It is possible that the Egyptians, being extremely precise observers and scrutinizing the sky over many long centuries, recognized the general advance of all stars toward the east. But we have no proof of this and they did not mention any of this to the Greeks.[19]

Thus Antoniadi raises an objection to Proclus Diadochus's affirmation of the knowledge of precession on the part of the Egyptians and Babylonians and concludes by attributing this discovery to Hipparchus. The fact of the cults and their duration, the characteristics of the Dendera zodiac, and the pharaonic calendar conflict with this conclusion.[20]

[18] Lefebvre, *Médecine égyptienne,* pp. 87–88.

[19] Cf. Antoniadi, *Astronomie égyptienne,* p. 78.

[20] Cf. below, "The Pharaonic Calendar."

The predominance given to the bull and then to the ram in the cults whose durations and dates conform to the durations and dates of the precession leaves no room for doubt as to the conscious nature of the gesture. Adding to this is the duality of everything we know about the predynastic period, the era of Gemini, the Twins, confirmed by the discovery of the oldest cultural center of the time at Medamud.[21]

I invite philological Egyptologists to accept without prejudice this thesis as a hypothesis. They will then certainly come across many proofs of its reality.

The temple at Dendera was built in the Ptolemaic period (ca. 100 B.C.) on the site of a very ancient temple also consecrated to Hathor, or "House of Hor," the House of Life.[22] The inscriptions in one of the crypts of Dendera reveal that this temple was built according to plans provided by Imhotep, son of Ptah (Third Dynasty, or about 3500 B.C.), and the zodiac itself not only confirms the knowledge of the precession of equinoxes held by the pharaonic sages but also proves by certain anomalies that it is only a copy of a similar, much older representation. We will see that the date of this copy is indicated by the zodiac itself, as well as the date of the foundation of the historical empire.

But for this it is necessary to remind the reader as succinctly as possible what we mean by the precession of the equinoxes, which forms the basis of the pharaonic calendar.

First, the axis of the terrestrial globe, in its daily rotation, is inclined at approximately 23°30′ to the plane of the annual circuit of the sun, or ecliptic.

Second, after seventy-two annual circuits or years, the pole itself moves by about 1° of arc in the opposite direction from the daily rotation. The terrestrial pole therefore makes a complete circular path around the pole of the ecliptic in roughly 26,000 years. This circuit has a radius equivalent to 23°30′.[23] Thus, in 13,000 years our Pole Star (a projection into the sky of our North Pole) will be on the opposite side of the precessional circuit, and the star nearest to this celestial North Pole will be Vega, the beautiful and bright star of the Lyre.

Third, the inclination of the terrestrial axis on the plane of the ecliptic is what creates our seasons, as the sun apparently "swings" in summer by 23°30′ above the equator, and in winter to 23°30′ below it. It thus passes twice a year exactly over the equator; these are the equinoxes. Therefore, at the spring equinox, the sun as it rises on the horizon at six o'clock in the morning marks in the sky the position of our equator which at that moment cuts the ecliptic line. This is the vernal point, which moves by 1° every 72 years and passes successively through the twelve constellations of the zodiac in the direction of Gemini, Taurus, Aries, and so forth.

Last, it is obvious that it is the vernal point of 21–22 March that points to the beginning of spring, whatever its position in the zodiac, but because of the precession, the constellations in the nocturnal sky change for the same season. Thus today, Orion and Sirius dominate our winter nights, but in approximately 13,000 years they will be in the summer sky, beneath the horizon and invisible to us.

To summarize:

a) The terrestrial pole follows a cyclical path called the *precessional cycle*. This cycle moves the vernal point in the opposite direction of the apparent annual circuit of the sun through the zodiacal constellations.

---

[21] Cf. plate 50 and its legend.

[22] It has been thought possible to identify Hathor with Venus, which is a mistake. The pharaonic Venus is Sekhmet, the wife of Ptah (Hephaestus-Vulcan).

[23] The tilt of the axis of the earth remaining, of course, approximately the same.

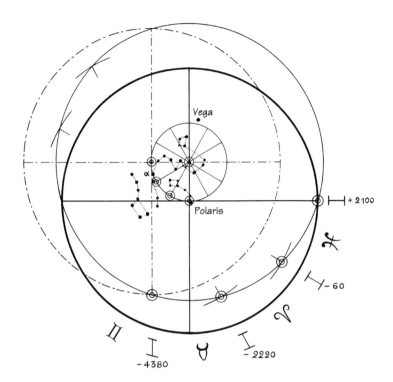

Fig. 195a. Diagram of precessional movement

Light lines, the small circle described by the pole of the earth around the ecliptic pole, and the large circle of the zodiacal constellations. *Dark line,* the equatorial circle of the earth in the year A.D. 2100, at the end of the influence of Pisces. This circle, crossing the ecliptic circle, determines the vernal point for its time. *Dotted line,* the equatorial circle of the earth in the year 4380 B.C., at the end of the influence of Gemini and at the beginning of Taurus. This circle, crossing the ecliptic circle, determines the vernal point for its time. Between these two extreme dates come the passage of Taurus to Aries in the year 2220 B.C., and the passage from Aries to Pisces in the year 60 B.C.

N.B. We have drawn the ecliptic here as a circle, but in fact it is slightly elliptical.

b) The movement of the vernal point constantly modifies the influence of the constellations for a same season.

c) During the precessional cycle of approximately 26,000 years (known as the Platonic Year), the inclination of the terrestrial axis, which is always 23°30′, changes orientation, having for a same season the North Pole inclined toward the sun; then, after 13,000 years, it is the South Pole that will be inclined toward the sun.[24]

---

[24] In this succinct explanation there are many "approximately's" because the mechanism of the celestial body is in no way mechanically rigid. Everything moves and these complex movements produce constant variations in time and in position. Thus, around the year 50, the precessional month was exactly 2160 years, but today it is no more than about 2148. A reduction in the duration of approximately 12 years of precession since the year 50 of our era until 1942 has been confirmed. Is this reduction final or will it be followed by a new acceleration? The alternating character of all that lives leads us to believe the latter. Otherwise, from now on the precessional cycle would be 24,433 years starting from 1942, and the end of life on our globe would obviously be accelerated more and more. But, meanwhile, the 6000-year calendar of the duration of pharaonic Egypt can be considered to be stable.

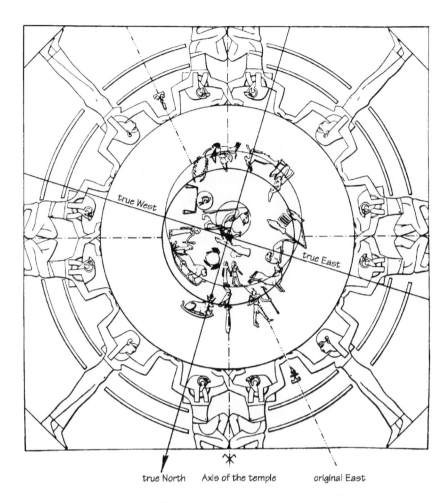

true North   Axis of the temple   original East

Fig. 195b. The zodiac of Dendera

Seen from underneath, which reverses the east-west orientation, this figure shows only: the circumpolar constellations of the Dragon (Apet), the Great Bear (the thigh), the Small Bear (Anubis); the twelve figures of the zodiac; Orion (figure wearing the white crown), Sirius (in the form of a cow in the barque), and the falcon on the papyrus marking the axis of the temple.

Dark lines, the true north-south and east-west lines; the equatorial circle has the pole of the earth as center, which corresponds to the center of the zodiacal disk; *light line,* the circle described by the pole of the earth around the ecliptic pole (in the breast of Apet), and the ecliptic circle of the signs of the zodiac; *dotted lines,* the axis of the temple and its perpendicular line; *three-dotted line,* the east-west line defined by the hieroglyphs *iabtt* (east) and *imntt* (west).

Figure 195a shows the crossing of the equatorial circles with the ecliptic circle, with these crossings determining the location of the vernal point in the zodiac following the movement of the terrestrial pole.

Now, the zodiac of Dendera is a circle drawn in a square (fig. 195b). This square is oriented according to the general axis of the temple. On the other hand, the temple is oriented at about seventeen degrees east from true north.

The disposition of the zodiacal signs determines the location of the ecliptic pole within the breast of the female hippopotamus, Apet (corresponding to the constellation of the dragon), whereas the center of the great circle of the figure defines the terrestrial pole.

The perpendicular to the true north-south axis passes through the terrestrial pole (thus, tangentially to the small circle described by the pole of the earth in 26,000 years). This east-west perpendicular defines the vernal point on the crossing of the ecliptic circle with the equatorial circle of the earth. The vernal point indicated by true east-west corresponds to the middle of Aries and dates this zodiac at about the year 1200 B.C. (Ramesside era).

Moreover, the sculptures have an east-west line marked in hieroglyphics, which is an anomaly because it is related neither to the axis of the monument, nor to the true orientation. There are thus three dates indicated by this zodiac: *(a)* the perpendicular to the axis of the monument, defining the end of Aries and the beginning of Pisces on the circle of the ecliptic, *the date of construction of the building and the sculpting of the zodiac; (b)* the true east-west line situating the vernal point in Aries, *the date of the apogee of the Amun-Aries cult under the Amenhoteps and the Ramesses; (c)* the "false" east-west line determining the end of Gemini and the beginning of Taurus on the ecliptic circle, *the date of the foundation of the empire with Menes and of the installation of the cult of the sacred bull, Apis.*

The mere fact of having been unaware of the east-west orientation, whose origin was marked by the sculpture itself, was the cause of the ignorance until now of the true meaning of the zodiac: it is a monument to pharaonic chronology and further proof of the organization of this empire "in the image of Heaven."[25]

THE PHARAONIC CALENDAR

The calendar, or the system of measuring time, is essentially based on the annual circuit of the earth around the sun, determining the seasons by the inclination of the terrestrial axis. Now everything in the Universe moves, and harmonizing all the movements of the earth, moon, sun, and so forth, is the headache of astronomers.

Our present calendar is purely conventional because it bases the year 1 on the birthdate of the Lord Christ. This in no way situates the date astronomically and will not allow a future humanity to specify an important date from our years in the universe. We are content to rectify the duration of the annual circuit of $365\frac{1}{4}$ days more or less every four years, every century, every four centuries, in an endless round. We lack an element of reference more stable than our ecliptical promenade that would situate the Anno Domini *n* in case an accidental interruption caused the year 1 to be forgotten.

One of the most remarkable institutions of Ancient Egypt is certainly that of the calendar.

[25] Fig. 195b was drawn from a photograph of the zodiac that is at present in the Louvre. It was not established according to astronomical calculation but from evidence imposed by the axes and orientations: the true north-south and east-west axes are drawn according to the indications given by the plates in the *Description de l'Egypte* (Paris, 1809–28), which indicate the position of the temple in relation to magnetic north (vol. 4, plate 8) and the declination of magnetic north in relation to the true north of the time (ibid., plate 2).

The original east is indicated by hieroglyphic symbols for east and west carved on the planisphere itself. These axes and the center of the picture are defined by the figure itself and the orientation of the temple to north. The pole of the ecliptic was calculated in July 1822 by J. B. Biot, who made a drawing of both the ecliptic and equatorial circles on this planisphere, basing his work only on astronomical and mathematical data. He put the pole of the ecliptic within the breast of Apet. Biot was not able to consider the original east-west symbols because at the time of his work, the meanings of the hieroglyphs were not yet known.

After the study of all the documents, it is now perfectly understood that this calendar could only have been established, at the latest, in the year 4240 B.C. Moreover, by exactly determining "New Year's Day" (First of Thoth), we have been able to determine that this calendar was established at Heliopolis.

Now, it is impossible to establish a calendar that would allow the two essential cycles imposed by nature, the lunar month and the solar year, to coincide. The pharaonic sages considered the lunar cycle and the solar cycle separately, and joined these to the cycle of Sirius, or Sothis, the star of Isis. The result was a rather complex calendar consisting of three kinds of years: the fixed or Sirian year, the vague or conventional year, and the tropical year, the true solar year on which all agricultural work was regulated.

The quarter moon, the hieroglyph of the month, provides information on the origin of this division in time. But this same symbol is used to designate two kinds of months, the lunar and the conventional.

First, each day of the lunar month was named according to the phases of the moon. The festivals of the full moon and of the new moon had always been observed since the most ancient times. An account dating from Sesostris III (Middle Kingdom) shows that the payment in kind of the scribes of the temple was calculated from lunar months of 29 and 30 days in turn.

Second, the conventional months of 30 days were used for civil acts and for calendar dates.[26] Twelve of these months were necessary for a complete cycle of 360 days, which corresponded to the division of the celestial cycle into thirty-six decans, each containing 10 days. The Pyramid Texts reveal that even in the most ancient times there were added the "five days that are found throughout the year, during which the gods were born" (the 5 epagomenal days).

According to the religious tradition, this is then the origin of the vague year of 365 days upon which all civil acts were dated, and which the Pyramid Texts date back to the time of the birth of the gods. But this 365-day year is too short by about a quarter of a day, and it happens, as the old texts say, that "the *perit* season comes during the *shemu* season, that the months are displaced . . . ," which would have encouraged them at some time or other to correct this vague year as we have done today. Quite to the contrary, according to a text dating from the first century A.D., the kings at the time of their coronations gave sermons in the temple of Isis "without inserting a month or a day, without modifying one festival day, but continuing to measure the 365 days that had been established by the Ancients."[27] This fact underlines the extreme importance attributed to the maintenance of the vague year, and our chronologists today understand the reason for this, for the slightest disruption in the calendar would have destroyed forever the possibility of reconstituting the history of Egypt.

Indeed, next to this vague year, there was a very special cycle, the fixed year, called the "year of God" by Horapollo, that corresponds exactly to our Julian year of 365.25 days. The vague year moved within this fixed year, and they coincided every 1460 years.[28] The first day of this fixed year, its New Year's Day, was the heliacal rising of Sirius. A short while ahead of time, the Egyptian temples received the order from Heliopolis to celebrate the New Year on such and such a date of the vague year, making for what we call today double dates. Now, three of these double dates have

[26] Originally the months were not named. The year was divided into three seasons of four months each, and the months were called first month of the season of inundation, second month of the season of *shemu*, etc. An important religious festival belonged to each month, which gave birth to the later naming of months, still preserved today through the Copts.

[27] Raymond Weill, *Chronologie égyptienne* (Paris: Geuthner, 1926), p. 58.

[28] 1460 fixed years equal 1461 vague years.

reached us and enable us to fix precisely (to a four-year approximation) the dates of the reigns of Tuthmosis III, Amenhotep I, and Senusret III. The establishment of the date of the foundation of the historical empire, however, lacking double dates, offers as many variations as there are Egyptologists who have studied this question.[29]

But to what does this fixed or Sirian year correspond exactly, adopted as it was by the Ancients as a stable basis for their calendar? It is neither the tropical year of 365.24219879... days (the time contained between two consecutive returns of the earth to the spring equinox), nor the sidereal year of 365.256361 days (the time that elapses between two successive conjunctions of the earth with the same star). The tropical year is shorter and the sidereal year is longer than the Sirian year.

We have just said that every 1460 years the vague year coincided with the Sirian year; however, since the tropical year is a little shorter, at the end of the cycle the sun (and its seasons) is slightly ahead by a little over $11\frac{1}{3}$ days. "But, because of the precession of the equinoxes on one hand, and the movement of Sirius on the other, the position of the sun in relation to Sirius is displaced in the same direction and almost exactly by the same amount."[30]

The calculations established by astronomers indeed show that the length of the Sirian year was as follows:

> in the year 4231 B.C., 365.2498352 days;
> in the year 3231 B.C., 365.2500000 days = Julian year;
> in the year 2231 B.C., 365.2502291 days;
> and so on.

We can see from these figures that during the Old Kingdom, the Sirian year was identical to the Julian year, and we can only admire the high science that had discovered such a coincidence, for Sirius is the only star among the fixed stars that allows this cycle. We can thus suppose that Sirius plays the part of the center of the circuit of our entire solar system.[31]

Sirius, which was called Sothis by the Greeks and *spd.t* by the Egyptians and referred to as the Great Provider, is continually evoked in the Pyramid Texts. For example, "Isis comes to thyself [Osiris], glad of thy love; Thy seed rises within her, penetrating [*spd.t*] as Sirius [*spd.t*]. Horus penetrating [*spd*] comes out of thee in his name, Horus who is within Sirius" (1635–36).[32]

Osiris is the principle of renewal, hence the cycles, and it is considered that in these texts Horus is issued from Isis-Sothis, begat by Osiris, the cyclic renewal. Thus, there is an identification of the Horian Light, the very essence of life, with the emanation that creates the "Eye of Ra," our sun, and with the Osirian myth in general.

We must think with the Ancients.

Contrary to what we might think in seeing how deeply religious they were, the pharaonic sages did not encumber themselves with prejudice. For them there exists no opposition between a spiritual state and a material-corporeal state, nor any abstraction opposed to the concrete. These are the

---

[29] Cf. appendix, "The Foundation Date of the Pharaonic Empire."

[30] Cf. Eduard Meyer, *Chronologie égyptienne*, trans.: A. Moret, Annales du Musée Guimet 24 (Paris: Leroux, 1912), 2nd fasc., p. 15.

[31] Antoniadi, *Astronomie égyptienne*, p. 29. Among the ideas that the Greeks owe to the Egyptians is the idea that "Sirius is a sun."

[32] There is a play on words between *spd.t*, "penetrate," "penetrating," written with the pointed triangle (in the various meanings that we can attribute to the English word) and *spd.t*, "Sirius," also written with the same pointed triangle but determined with a star. In this sentence *spd.t*, "penetrate," must mean an emanation of the "provider" star *spd.t*, Sirius.

mental illusions of a mind that is the child of dualization, and that can only operate in duality and through the enmity or the marriage of complements.

For the sages there were only states of consciousness. What for us is transcendence was for them a graspable state through a widened state of consciousness, not a power *ex machina*.

All is One and everything is within this absolute One.

What for our physicists is wavelength and vibration was for the sages in no way limited to corporeal matter, but was the definition of all that is perceptible to our five physical senses and comprehensible to our intelligence, limited to the cerebral functions. All in the Universe is made up of alternations and inversions, which are the manifestation of life, and life is continuous creation: the original scission of the ungraspable Unity.

But the alternation and inversion of what?

It is the alternation of "density" in general, and essentially, of one and the same energy. Density means the reduction into volume of space, that is, of energy. The inverse is the inevitable, compensating complementation of each element of alternation.

Thus, the whole Universe is *living* and all of life's phenomena contain a concrete element of alternation and an energetic element of the same nature as this concretization. The concrete aspect can be grasped through cerebral conception, the energetic aspect is graspable through the other state of consciousness that is the intelligence of the heart, the source of intuition.

Esotericism is the knowledge of this internal state that brings about alternation and that rational thought cannot grasp, whence the conclusion that what is rational is not—and cannot be—real.

Now, the rational is based on syllogism and syllogism is fundamentally and purely empirical, descriptive of what is perceptible to the cerebral mentality. Symmetry and syllogism, as we understand them, remain foreign to the pharaonic thinker. For him there exists only a vital logic. He is, in a certain way, scientifically opportunist, that is, for him a phenomenon is situated in an environment and a moment. If all the conditions were recreated to obtain the same phenomenon, this phenomenon could be similar, but it will never be identical because the moment would have changed. Time is genesis, and genesis is, naturally, irreversible.

The mental need for simplification that is predominant in us does not correspond to the pharaonic mentality, and even less would it do so at the time the calendar was established, which necessarily relies on the complexity of astronomical movements. The Ancients obviously adapted the influences and cycles of the stars to the corresponding demands of particular activities, such as the lunar calendar to agriculture, the solar calendar to the seasons, the temple calendar to the numbers, and the dynastic calendar to the great cycles. Thus, there is a variety as apparently complex as the variety of cubits, and with the whole certainly coordinated as simply as in the case of cubits.

I am not sufficiently competent to analyze and study the astronomical questions. This is work for an astronomer, aided by an Egyptologist-philologist, but one who would also be gifted with a philosophical sense, a curiosity to seek out causes; but it is absolutely impossible to understand the true meaning of the pharaonic calendars without the symbolic reading, which reveals an esoteric significance whose existence I affirm.

———

Function is universal. Thus the light seen by my eye is a phenomenon that defines objects in a certain manner and renders them "objectively" perceptible to me. But there is also a mental light, a spiritual light, a *Fiat lux;* in short, I must, analogously, call light all that will outline a form to render it capable of being grasped by one of the states of consciousness.

Now, it is the method of our mentality to extract the function from a phenomenon in parts. Thus when studying light, for example, from a purely physical point of view, by speaking of photons, wave mechanics, or electromagnetic reaction, we know—or believe we know—the "light" phenomenon.

The character of pharaonic thought is to speak of light in such a way that its definition embraces all aspects in all fields at once, by considering the universality of the function without decomposing it into its particular appearances. This is the spirit of myth, and for these sages all explanation is a myth of the spirit of a function.

This seems strange to us because our "mental decadence" prevents us from suspecting even the possibility of an intelligence of the heart, which is also an intelligence of the world, looking from the heart of reality toward an appearance, and not—as would seem normal to us—from isolated objects in order thus to reach the heart at the center, the sun that creates the objects.

We must admit that for him who has consciousness of this synthesis, through his particular sensitivity that prompts him to *understand* more directly one of its many aspects, the nature and even the mechanism of the other aspects of this function must become mentally available to him.

We have discussed harmony in its relation to pharaonic mathematics, we have also related it to consciousness through affinity. But, more universally, there is the harmony that constitutes genesis, because a "vital logic" tells us that without this harmony no seed would bear healthy fruit.

Between the precession of the poles of the terrestrial axis and that of the solar axial poles, between the inclination of the ecliptic with respect to the sun and the inclination of the terrestrial axis, between the earth's annual circuit around the sun and its own rotation, and the circuit of the sun around its *Sothic nucleus,*[33] finally, among all these movements of the celestial bodies, there also exists a relation whose laws are part of the same harmony that creates music.

I believe there is a science that liberates us from the need to embark upon thousands and thousands of calculations for the sake of an astronomy that reveals to us nothing of the essence of things.

APPENDIX

The Foundation Date of the Pharaonic Empire

The principal documents at our disposal for establishing the Egyptian chronology are the following:

1. A diorite plaque, carved on both sides, lists the names of all the kings from the beginning to the Fifth Dynasty. Beneath the name of each king, the height of the Nile floods is noted year by year as well as the essential events of the reign. If this stone had been found in its entirety, it would have been a precious document for the reconstitution of the history of the Old Kingdom. Unfortunately, only a few small fragments remain, one of which is preserved at Palermo,[34] and the others at the Cairo Museum. The most serious study of the Palermo Stone seems to be that of Borchardt.[35]

2. The Royal Papyrus preserved in Turin, written under Ramesses II, provides a list of all the sovereigns of Egypt since the beginning. It begins, like the Palermo Stone, by listing the "reigns of the gods" *(neters),* then the "companions of Horus" *(shemsu-hor),* and has the historical period begin

---

[33] Sirius is a double star. The central star has a density of 0.9 (in relation to water = 1), whereas its companion, much smaller, has a density of 50,000. This double star therefore bears a great resemblance to what we know of the atom's nucleus. It can be called the nucleus of the world in which the entire solar system would play the role of a planet or electron.

[34] Which has earned it the name of "Palermo Stone."

[35] L. Borchardt, *Die Annalen und die zeitliche Feststellung des Alten Reichs der ägyptischen Geschichte* (Berlin, 1917).

with Menes, the first king of Upper and Lower Egypt. This precious document notes the number of years of each reign, and, here and there, main historical divisions are given a total number of years. Found intact, the papyrus was torn to pieces during transport and only a small part of the fragments are readable. A thorough study of this document was undertaken by Meyer.[36]

3. According to tradition, Manetho wrote a *History of Egypt,* but it was lost and only pieces of it were transmitted by later authors. The comparison of the dates given in the Turin Papyrus with the "Manetho lists" casts serious doubt on the authenticity of the latter, and has permitted diverse chronologists to "interpret" them according to various methods.

We can judge the uncertainties of the dates attributed to the foundation of the empire by Menes from the following list.[37]

	Date of estimating	Date of estimate
Steindorf	1900	2500 B.C.
Newberry Garstang	1904	3000 B.C.
Erman	1929	3000 B.C.
Ed. Meyer	1904	3315 B.C.
Sethe	1905	3360 B.C.
Bunsen	1845	3623 B.C.
Lepsius	1857	3892 B.C.
Lielblen	1863	3893 B.C.
Von Bissing	1904	4000 B.C.
Lauth	1865	4157 B.C.
Borchardt	1917	4240 B.C.
Brugsch	1877	4455 B.C.
Maspero	1910	5000 B.C.
Flinders Petrie	1911	5546 B.C.
Unger	1867	5613 B.C.
Both	1845	5702 B.C.

Borchardt cites the methods of Sethe, Brugsch, and Flinders Petrie as being serious, although they were led into error by data that are not included here. The date found by Borchardt corresponds to the date of the foundation of the calendar (4240) and coincides, very closely, to the date established on the basis of the precession, which I place around the year 4300 B.C.

The Two Pole Towns of the Myth

Heliopolis and Elephantine are the two pole towns of the myth. At Heliopolis, according to tradition, the sun shone for the first time on the sacred *benben* stone. It is also in this place that priests taught the myth of Atum-Ra. "When Atum emerged from the Nun, the primordial waters, before the birth of the earth and the sky, and before a worm or a reptile had been created, he found no

---

[36] Meyer, *Chronologie égyptienne.*

[37] Given by Borchardt, *Annalen,* pp. 48–50.

place where he could stand. So he climbed up a hill and raised himself up on the *benben* stone at Heliopolis. Then he found that he was alone and he thought of creating companions for himself. He begat himself. . . ."[38]

But it is at Elephantine (and at Biggeh) that one finds the cult of Seth-Isis and of the abyss of the beginning. It is for this reason that myth locates the two sources of the Nile, that of the sky and that of the earth, at this site.

Ptah, to whom the modeling of the world is attributed, is venerated at Memphis, and it is at Elephantine that we find Khnum, who fashioned what is created on his potter's wheel.

Now, the location of these two towns on our globe is not haphazard. Heliopolis, which is believed to have occupied the site of the present village of Matariyah, would be at 30°7′ north latitude. Memphis would have been at 29°51′, and the pyramids (Giza, Abu-Roash) are built on the left bank of the Nile between the two latitudes, in other words, at about 30°. Elephantine is at 24°5′ latitude north, and Biggeh a little further south, opposite Philae.

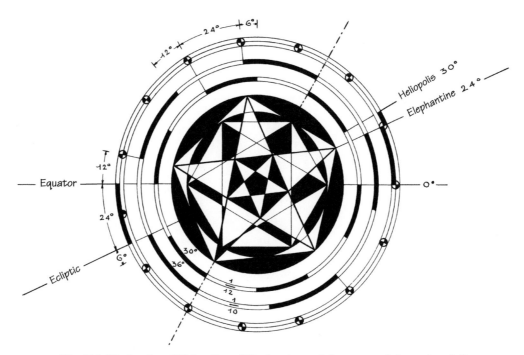

Fig. 196. The location of Heliopolis and Elephantine and the passage of the tropic at 24°
(without taking minutes into account)

Tradition suggests that on the one hand, Elephantine is under the tropic, whereas on the other, the tropic is at 24° latitude. Now, the inclination of the ecliptic diminishes with time by 47.6″ per century. In 1950 it was 23°26′44″, so consequently it would have been 24′ in about the year 2500 B.C., that is, in the Old Kingdom. The locations of Elephantine and of Biggeh, between 24° and 24°5′, therefore justifies the tradition, since between the years 2500 B.C. and 3000 B.C., it was indeed under the tropic.

The 6° that separates the two towns situated by the two poles of the myth represent the difference that exists between one-tenth of a circle defined by the pentagon, and one-twelfth of a

[38] Erman, *Religion des Egyptiens,* p. 116.

circle defined by the hexagon. This geometrical definition makes the original placement of these two geographically extreme places of the cult comprehensible, and it is thus necessarily between these two extremes that the measure between parallels must have been taken of a terrestrial meridian arc of 6°, that is, one-sixtieth of a circle, or one-fifteenth of a quarter of a circle. This number is the number of the relation between time and the path of the sun's course.

Chapter 21

THE HINDU TEMPLE

It seemed to me interesting to include here a few extracts from the work of Stella Kramrisch on the traditional laws of sacred architecture in India according to Vedic precepts.[1] We find in this work descriptions of the same rites as those shown in the bas-reliefs of pharaonic Egypt, but the interesting thing about the Hindu tradition is that its rites are still observed today, confirming what we have said about the same practices in Ancient Egypt.

> Although this ritual diagram is neither the ground-plan of the temple nor necessarily the plan of the site, it regulates them. It may be coterminous with the site of the sacred precinct, or with the extent of the main temple building (prāsāda) only; or it may be drawn on an altar, and of standardised size. It is drawn on the ground prior to the building of the temple and on it the temple stands either in fact or symbolically. In principle it is always square and is the record of an architectural rite. The knowledge of its correct execution forms the first part of the science of architecture. . . . The square is divided into compartments and the diagonals are drawn. The name of the square is Vāstupuruṣamaṇḍala. Puruṣa is the universal Essence, the Principle of all things, the Prime Person whence all originates. Vāstu is the site; in it Vāstu, bodily existence, abides and from it Vāstu derives its name. In bodily existence, Puruṣa, the Essence, becomes the Form. The temple building is the substantial, and the "plan" (maṇḍala) is the ritual, diagrammatic form of the Puruṣa. Puruṣa himself has no substance. [6–7][2]

The square symbolizes the sky in the sense of the essence of the four elements. We are therefore dealing with the Verb. The cycle belongs to an existence that undergoes renewals the aim of

---

[1] Kramrisch, *The Hindu Temple*. This is an extremely instructive work that the author, with much patience and certainly not without difficulty, published almost at the same time as *The Temple in Man,* a coincidence that delights me. [Page references to *The Hindu Temple* are in brackets.]

[2] The Upaniṣads present Puruṣa as Cosmic Man, which I call Anthropocosmos.

which is to attain the "reliberation" of the Verb following its reincarnations [*avatars*] in various existences for the sake of recognizing the original consciousness.

Puruṣa is the Anthropocosmos, that is, the perfect, noncorporeal cosmic being, but in whose image the corporeal human being is formed and into which it transforms itself. The square character of this "Sky of the Elements" is represented in Egypt by a straight line with angular extremities, and it is said that the sky is carried by four pillars. The curve belongs to Osiris, the principle of renewals.

> . . . [T]he ground from which the temple is to rise is regarded as being, throughout on an equal intellectual plane. It is at the same time terrestrial and extra-territorial. It is the place for the meeting and marriage of heaven and earth, where the whole world is present in terms of measure, and is accessible to man. . . .
>
> Man here is the patron or Yajamāna (lit. the sacrificer) on whose behalf the temple is built by the architect who is guided by the priest in the principles of his work. In the diagram of the Vāstupuruṣa a communication is established between man (puruṣa) as the patron of the work and the Puruṣa, the Essence of all things. At the definite time and place where the temple is to be set up, all times and all places congregate in the symbolic diagram of Vāstupuruṣa. . . . [t]he architect, who builds the temple, works in conformity with the knowledge of the priest. . . .
>
> A treatise on architecture . . . says: "He, who begins to work as an architect (sthapati) without knowing the science of architecture (vāstuśāstra) and proud with false knowledge must be put to death by the king as one who ruins the kingdom (rājahiṃsaka); dead before his time, his ghost will wander on this wide earth. He, who though well versed in the traditional science is not skilled in the work will faint at the time of action like a timid man on the battle-field. He, who is expert only in his workmanship, but unable to understand the meaning of the traditional science, will like a blind man be misled by anyone." . . . [7–8]
>
> Then follows the description of the four classes of craftsmen (śilpin).* . . .
>
> ". . . Vāstujñāna (the knowledge of Vāstu), architecture, will be explained by me for the pleasure of the astronomers and astrologers, as it has been transmitted from Brahmā to our days through an unbroken series of sages. Building is begun under favourable stars. They are consulted when the ground is taken possession of and when the rite of depositing the Germ of the temple is performed. The regents of the planets and the stars have their allocation in the diagram of the temple and their images are carved on its walls. By them are regulated the measurement of the whole building and its parts; the life of the donor (yajamāna), and the age of the temple too. The temple is built in the likeness of the universe and is its reduced image. The architect of this world image, the temple, is looked upon as descended from, and in his sphere alike to, Viśvakarman, who made all that exists in the universe. The architect in charge of the building is therefore generally called Sthapati. The name means "master of what stands or abides." [10–11]
>
> . . . [A]ll extraneous matter (śalya, "thorns") has to be removed from the soil, so that it does not stand in the way of the divinities who henceforward will be assigned their places; its presence also forebodes evil to the builder and is felt as an uneasiness and local irritation in various parts of his body. Magic is active and divinatory science establishes the correspondence between the soil to be built on and the body of the builder. Either has to be made pure by the respective rites, ready for setting up the temple, beginning each work on an auspicious day, and under a favourable star. The purification of the soil is complete when the ground has been ploughed repeatedly, . . . watered, sown

---

*Kramrisch is quoting from the *Samāraṅgaṇasūtradhāra*.

and planted with all kinds of grain and when these have flowered and ripened. Then it should be ploughed again. Then the earth is clean. . . .

The ploughing and the sowing of the sacrificial ground with all kinds of grain preceded the piling of the Fire altar (agni-cayana). After the introductory libation (prāyaṇīya) of the Soma sacrifice, the altar site was ploughed by twelve oxen, twelve furrows were made and then the seeds were sown. . . . "Even as this broad Earth received the germ of all things that be" is the Germ (garbha) of the temple deposited in her. . . . [U]nder auspicious stars new life is entrusted to the soil and another cycle of production begins, an assurance that the rhythm of life has not been interfered with. . . . [T]he chief architect should graze the cows with bulls and calves on the land till it is stamped down. . . . That the cattle stay on the land ensures its further purification. The whole process of ploughing, sowing and reaping, of grazing the cattle on the site of the future temple should be repeated after one year. [14–16]

These words require no further explanation; what is said here could have been said exactly about the pharaonic temple.

THE PLAN

. . . The form of the Vāstupuruṣamaṇḍala is a square. This is its essential form. It can be converted into a triangle, a hexagon, octagon and circle of equal area and retain its symbolism. . . .

The relation of the Vāstupuruṣamaṇḍala to the site-plan, ground-plan and vertical section of any building is similar to that of the tonic and any musical composition. [21–22]

Square and Circle: Vedic Origins

"The shape of the Vāstu for the gods and Brāhmaṇas is prescribed as square." . . .

Square and circle are co-ordinated in the architecture of India. . . . In the sacrificial shed (prācīna-vaṃśa-śālā) are three altars, two of them on the east-west line . . . and one to the south of the line. Of the two altars on the east-west line, the one at its eastern end is square, the other at its western end is circular. . . . [22–23]

The square Āhavanīya hearth at the eastern end of the sacrificial shed is in the middle of an area, one fathom (vyāma) square.

This length of a fathom is also the height of a man, from the soles to the root of the hair on the forehead, and remains throughout Indian art and symbolism the perfect proportion. . . . [23, n. 7]

We find here the same care taken to use the human fathom as a measure, thus creating, as in pharaonic Egypt, a link between Man and the Universe through measure.

The Square Maṇḍala of the Earth and of the Ecliptic

. . . All the cyclical numbers in Hindu cosmology are essentially based on the period of the precession of the equinoxes. They are exact fractions of the number 25,920. . . . [36–37]

Death, destruction and varied ills result from a wrong orientation. If the building were to obstruct the course and order of the cosmos it would provoke disorder in the kingdom, and in the body of the builder. [38–39]

The knowledge, in the wisdom of the Ancients, concerning the precessional cycles is thus also proved by the Hindu texts.

When I asserted, for the first time in 1942, that the dynastic architecture (the chronology) of Ancient Egypt was based on precessional times, also controlling the symbols of worship, it was received with skepticism. I was then unaware of this Vedic teaching. A single wisdom governed the world in the past.

The Two Main Types of the Vāstu Diagram
The Maṇḍala of 64 Squares

. . . [T]he Vāstu of 64 squares is meant for the construction of shrines and for worship by Brāhmaṇas and the Vāstu of 81 squares is for the construction of other buildings and for worship on behalf of kings. [46]

The Organism of the Plan

The square of the Vāstupuruṣamaṇḍala is divided into small squares and in diagonals . . . Their points of intersection are the vital parts and tender spots (marma) of the site. These must not be hurt or interfered with by setting up pillars, doors, or walls on them.

The identification of this body built of Breath which is coterminous with the Vāstumaṇḍala, with that of the builder who is the Yajamāna and patron, and with the plot, is no abstract theory. It is felt in the living tissue of the body of the donor who is the builder (kāraka) of the temple. . . . Were the organism of the ordered plot brought out of order and disturbed in its interknit functioning as plan and symbol, the builder would suffer in the corresponding parts of his body and earthly life; death will befall him should he obstruct by building on them, the main vital parts of the plan, its head, heart and so on; and minor evils will be his if he disregards the lesser junctions and lines. Builder and building are one; the building is a test of the health and probity of the builder, his "alter ego," his second body; if the building be a sacred one, a temple, this second body is his sacrificial body born from a second birth, the conscious sowing of seed, into a prepared soil and the depositing of the Seed of the building to be which is the germ of the Puruṣa, the Essence that dwells in the body of the temple. This new birth and transubstantiation has for its level the surface within the limits of the maṇḍala. [52]

. . . [T]he sacrificial victim, man and his successive substitutes, horse, bull, ram, and the goat, mingled in the mortar, their heads originally having been placed in the first layer of the altar[3] . . . the sacrificer, as victim, is his transformed self in the symbol of the golden man immured in the altar. . . .

The sacrificer puts down the golden man, laying him on his back (uttāna). He lays him down with his head towards the East, for (with the head) towards the East this Agni (the Fire altar) is built up. [69] . . .

In the net of this plan the figure of Man is caught, not by its likeness, but by its proportion and symmetry in its parts. . . .

The reference to the "figure of man" as a place of co-ordinated function, is made factually and repeatedly in Brāhmanism and Buddhism, in sacred texts and works of art. [71]

Our brief study of the *canevas*, the "grid of the master builder," expresses the importance of the numbers quoted here in relation to the numbers of harmony. We also see the play of the numbers of the musical tone, 8 and 9, in the Vedic *maṇḍala*.

Here, only the magic of numbers is at stake. It is also at play in the pharaonic temple, as in the temple of Luxor, which, moreover, indeed represents Man, the Puruṣa or Anthropocosmos, in its architecture.

The Man of the temple of Luxor also looks to the east, to the rising of Ra, the celestial Fire, Agni.

---

[3] In a foundation deposit made in an oval shallow basin under an Ethiopian colonnade at Karnak, there has been found a "herbivore head with a sectioned skullcap, the muzzle turned toward the east, and at the south of the head, a paw of the same animal, shoulder blade to the west and the bones folded at right angles to each other." C. Robichon, P. Barguet, and J. Leclant, *Karnak-Nord IV,* Bulletin de l'I.F.A.O. 25 (Cairo, 1954), fasc. 1, p. 38.

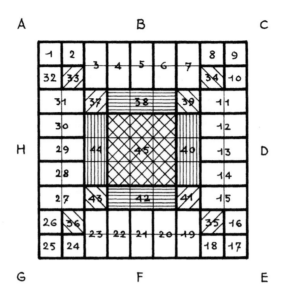

Fig. 197. Diagram of the Hindu temple conceived on the square of 9.
[Adapted from The Hindu Temple, *p. 32]*

The Descent of the Vāstupuruṣa

. . . [I]t has its parallel in the falling to earth of the severed limbs of the dead Satī. All over India, wherever a part of her dismembered body fell, Pīthas come into existence. All of them together represent the wholeness of India as a sacred land. In a map of the sacred geography of India each Pītha would have to be marked by one of the letters of the alphabet, of which there are 51 in the Sanskrit alphabet, symbols of lettered sound and of the Word. The Vāstupuruṣa in his fall, defeated, yet whole, on coming to earth, acquires the shape of his yantra to which are assigned 16 letters of the alphabet. [73]

A study of mystical geography of pharaonic Egypt, which we will endeavor to publish, will also confirm what is said here on the *pīṭhas* principle of India. It is the dispersed limbs of Osiris's body that indicate the vital parts of the country, the country being the body of the natural renewal of the supernatural Anthropocosmos. "Before the work is begun, the axe, the line, the hammers, and all the other instruments are worshipped with incense, flowers and unhusked rice. This makes them fit to accomplish the task in the hands of the competent craftsmen ready for the inspired moment of action." [120] (Today, pneumatic drills and other instruments are blessed with petrol, the oil of stone from the depths of the earth and of the destructive fire, which is able to call these works back to itself.)

Symbol of the Entrance and the Exit: The Door and the Statues

The rivers have their source and origin in heaven. Thence they descend to earth. On the entrance of the early temples their images are carved to either side of the lintel ("patanga"; "ūrdhvapaṭṭikā"). On its middle the image of the main divinity of the temple, and to either side of it those of other great Gods are carved. This then is the celestial region whence the rivers have descended. . . . [315]

The celestial region is also indicated on the lintel by a frieze of the Navagrahas, the nine planets. . . . [315, n. 40]

It is said that the Nile comes from the sky and that it has two sources: one from the sky and the other from the earth. They are strange to look at, these Niles, who are male but with the attributes of a pregnant woman.

The Temple as Puruṣa

As in the beginning, so also on the completion of the building, the rite of auspicious germination . . . is enacted and oblations are given at night. Then at dawn, of another day, the Sthapati, the master architect, and the Sthāpaka, the priest architect, ascend the Vimāna and with a golden needle, perform the rite of opening the eyes (netra mokṣa) of the Prāsāda in front of the cupola (Śikhara) of its High Temple (Harmya).

The Sthāpaka then instals the Prāsāda, in its concrete shape (prāsādamūrti) on its altar or pedestal (dhiṣṇyamūrti) and places in it the Seed (bīja) of the Temple. [359] . . .

The continuity and perfection of the work are assured according to the particular tradition in which it was started. The science of architecture having its origin in Brahma and being transmitted by an unbroken series of sages preserves its integrity in the planning and building of every temple . . .

When the building is completed and consecrated, its effigy in the shape of a golden man, the Prāsāda-puruṣa, is installed in the Golden jar, above the Garbhagṛha. . . . The effigy is invested with all the Forms and Principles of manifestation. While the Vāstupuruṣa "Existence" lies at the base of the temple and is its support the Golden Puruṣa of the Prāsāda, its indwelling Essence, sum total of all the Forms and Principles (tattva) of manifestation and their reintegration lies in the superluminous darkness of the Golden jar on top of the temple. . . . The ascension of the Golden Puruṣa cancels the descent of the Vāstupuruṣa. [360] . . .

Within these two movements the Hindu temple has its being; its central pillar is erected from the heart of the Vāstupuruṣa in the Brahmasthāna, from the centre and heart of Existence on earth, and supports the Prāsāda Puruṣa in the Golden jar in the splendour of the Empyrean. [361]

What does our time with its materialistic mentality, its skepticism without anxiety for the Truth, empty of soul, have to say about these rites, this magic, these temples? They have been built but have fallen into ruin, as does everything made by mortal man. These builders—in passing—were born and died like others. What is there of the *sacred*, of the eternal in that? What does Puruṣa, the Anthropocosmos, matter, that abstraction that is used as a model for the future of the still mortal man, who one day is supposed to attain immortality?

Ecclesiastes is always present.

The stupifying egoism of it is the seed that will always resuscitate again, for men view an immortal existence in the image of what they are today.

The temples of the sages are not the imaginations of idealistic dreamers, they are books that teach the science that provides proof of knowledge. The choice of the place where the temple will be erected, the observation of germination from the sown seed—the animation of this earth—is the first serious lesson. To see only symbolic gestures in the ritual, that is to say, as one generally understands the symbol in its theatrical aspect, is to understand nothing of its aim and of the real symbol: these gestures are the action indispensable for realizing the experiment that proves the sacred science. This experiment gives proof of the reality of the continuation of Being, its recurring birth through substance and its successive forms, the reality of immortality.

While waiting to know what is asserted by the sages, we must believe. Not believing makes the search for knowledge impossible. But believing or not believing will do nothing to change the fact that, in the end, everyone must undergo experience.

Chapter 22

THE MYSTIC TEMPLE:
A MEDITATION

THE PARVIS

This is the domain of the search for the right path in the midst of a chaos of possibilities. Three ways are open to us: faith in a traditional belief, philosophy and its many approaches, and science with its halting progress.

The means available to us are inspiration and intuition, rational thought, and experimentation. Inspiration and intuition are personal; rational thought requires confirmation through experience; and experimentation shows isolated facts with no vital link between them.

What are we seeking? We need to know the meaning of the Universe, its source and aim, in order wholesomely to conduct our existence and the development of our faculties. Then we would like to know where we come from and where we are going.

Traditional belief tells us of a *creation:* man is here because he was created to be here, issued from a Will in the image of that Will. He is Man-Universe because it is Man who looks and questions.

Philosophy analyzes the problem, forgetting that the means it uses can reveal only those means; thinking cannot explain thinking, otherwise it would be a creation.

Science experiments with facts and can only subtract and decompose finite data. It is an analysis of composites. In the end, it comes upon an energy that, for science, can still only be a *thing*. This is not an answer.

Thus, here is man placed by his thinking *in front of* the facade of the Temple that is the Universe, this man who, but for his thinking, is *in* this Temple.

It is thinking, cerebral activity, that drives us from the Temple and expels us from Paradise.

And it is faith that calls us back.

But thought exists; it shows us the object of faith. If it did not show us the object, faith would not be faith, it would be an identity of ourselves with the Whole and of the Whole with ourselves. As long as there is belief, there is thought: this is man outside the Universe who believes in the Universe.

The circle that forever closes upon itself, this unbroken circuit, is damnation, Sisyphus and Tantalus.

On my knees in the center of the parvis, I would like to break this circle of damnation, to believe no longer, to think no longer. To be only in Being. Why kneeling? To eliminate from my body that which makes me walk, to eliminate this symbol of movement, the ceaseless running of Ashaverus.

This closed circuit is the evil. It is this evil that caused the coming of the inspired "messengers," the Prophets, and the Apostles. It is this evil that has tormented all the thinkers and lovers of wisdom, who through reason, have sought the break in the circle, and it is this again that brings anxiety and despair to the hearts of scientists.

This evil creates a delirium that inspires men to the most audacious, most heroic deeds, in a need for escape that makes their blood boil by inciting them to appeal to all manner of oblivion, to all the "firewaters," and even to all fires. To flee, even to travel among the stars.

And why not annihilation to escape from this madness?

There is already a hope in recognizing the existence of this evil and in what it consists. This is even essential. Does not evil consist in the fact that man wishes to find something other than man?

Is this not quite simply the meaning of the motto in the temples of all times: "Man, know thyself"? Or even better: Man, recognize thyself in everything. Man, thou wilt never find other in the Whole than thyself. What couldst thou find with thy means that would not be thyself? Canst thou be outside the Whole? Can the world for a mouse be anything other than mouse?

The endless circuit, I have imagined it, I invented it; it does not exist, I do not have to break it. The Vedas show us Puruṣa, Cosmic Man. The Gospel shows us man without sin, He who never invented an endless circuit, He whom thinking never expelled from Paradise. Pharaonic Egypt shows us Horus in his role as Redeemer . . . in fact, they *show* us nothing at all. They all say to us: You are that! If you do not believe that you are that, you will be nothing but a poor, damned soul, condemned to the endless torments of a circuit that always brings you back to the same problem. And it is true.

The only way, the only true way, is that of the human sphinx, this sphinx who poses the question to the blind Oedipus, the ridiculous question that only one blind of spirit finds serious because he believes himself able to see by thinking.

And the proud will say, "So then I am the world?" He has not understood yet how thinking itself is evil. If *you* are the world, then what am I? Am I *also* the world? Two worlds, a number of worlds? Man is all humankind, one sole Truth, one sole Man, one sole World, one Whole.

I am not a world, the world is not I, I am not "in front of" the world, there is no separation, if there is, I will fall back into evil.

The sun rises young in the east, it grows, becomes old, and dies senile in the west. Thus the cardinal directions are situated. I look at these things because I am these things. I am born at midnight; I arrive at puberty, grow up, grow old, die—I situate the cardinal directions. I am not "in front of" what I observe; I observe because I am that.

There is evil within me, it is this that suffers; but the man I am was stone with the stone, he is the man of today, he will be the man of tomorrow, and he will be the end of this appearance, an appearance for the evil in me that is just as illusory as the appearance.

We must not make concessions to thinking, which is the evil. We must not say: "that which I was before coming into being," because we have never ceased being what we were; otherwise it is the Other, the illusory that visits us. Mephistopheles appears before Faust as soon as Faust *poses the questions to himself,* as soon as he places himself in front of the Temple's facade. We have all asked questions of philosophy and the sciences, and we have all been deluded by dialectics, and this is where the error lies. We have not been deceived; it was the evil within that was deceived. We can question forever and receive no reply, this has no importance; if the "question" is absurd, how could the answer be valid? How can we question in the face of what we are? The only valid questioning is to get inside of this or that, we will then *live* this or that, and that will be the true answer.

If I am not stone with the stone, I do not *know* it. If I am not tree with the tree, I do not *know* it. If I am not he who is before me, I do not *know* him because *I myself* pose him as another "me" in front of me.

And the power of identification is within man because the world is Man and can only be Man. The consciousness of this is the Temple in Man.

THE DOOR

Here history begins, the analysis of the world. I am Fire, the fire that is the marriage between Heaven and Earth. It partakes of what is below through its root, and it partakes of what is above through its source.

Fire is twofold but not double; it is the number Two, the Unity that multiplies itself. It is the "consciousness" of every seed, the foundation of all that is self-maintained; Ptah within ithyphallic Min. This third of the first Verb is born of the function Two. It is the Verb, but neither word, nor speech; it is the acting action.

This arcane Fire is at the origin and at the end and in all. It is this fire that links together all diversities. One can never speak of these things without falling back into error, except by showing the kinships between activities by means of symbols.

The point of the pyramidion "that is in heaven" attracts the Fire of the world, as do thorns and the sharp needles of the agave on which, in the evening, the dragonfly comes to drink of this fire, brought by a very subtle dew. Like an eager womb, the furrow of the earth calls out for *ta-meri*, this Fire-bearing dew, two aspects of the one Fire: one the Fire of Water, and the other the Water of Fire. Two forms of calling, two forms of reply.

The very first form of the Verb is number. One in itself is indemonstrable. Two demonstrates One through the action of movement; Four is planar orientation; Eight is the first *thing*, volume. Thus "with the utterance of Thoth," all is said, and the first "thing" is Eight.

The Universe is nothing but number, because number is, in its neutrality, the definition of the function of activity.

When the indemonstrable, indivisible, unimaginable, and universal One becomes Two, there is the tangible, the decomposable, the demonstration of One. If it is then said that the third, which is this demonstration, is Fire, Man-Universe names that which he knows to be at the beginning and at the end of all things, a Fire that is in all things, in flint, in iron, in anything composite, and in the atom, as well as in the heat of blood and in the pungency of pepper. It is always the number Three to the two natures of which it is the firstborn son, the marriage of Heaven with Earth.

When Thoth, who from One became Two, says that from Two he becomes Four, Man-Universe situates the "directions" onto the One and Two axis that lights and maintains the central Fire. These are the four directions, and as strange as it may seem for the "erring human," these orientations are fixed and not relative. Midnight is in equilibrium with midday as morning is with evening. Midnight is the mysterious, incomprehensible birth; the east is the pubescent advent of Fire; midday is bright maturity; and the west is the death of the senile body, the wedding of the visible with the invisible, the conception. Morning, the east of the Fire, is Two and Three, Five; midday is the equilibrium of the two Fires, Six; evening, the west, is the copulation of Three and Four, Seven. Thus, the axis with the equator make the Eight that is One in the *thing*, any tangible thing, the Man-Universe volume, through which exist all volumes.

Three colossi of the morning Fire watch over Nature's conflict. Three colossi of the afternoon Fire stand guard over the repose of what has been realized. Thus is framed the power of the central door of midday equilibrium, Cosmic Man, the completed idea in the living cycle of its form.

The "erring human"—he who sees with the senses and not with the spirit in functional identification with what the a priori of numbers represents—sees matter in the "statistics" of these functions. The atom is the battlefield of these forces, or powers, that make up space. There are many of these atoms in the "statistics" that appear as matter, but there is only one with regard to the consciousness of the function.

Thus, number is the purest and most perfect expression of the esotericism of knowledge. Three is the essence, activity, the immortal impulsion in all things. Five is the soul of all shape and form, and at the heart of forms is Eight. Four and Five create the body, upon which the appearance, which is Seven, rests. But in Six, which is light, the living forces are in equilibrium and cancel out one another, becoming container and contained.

Number is function and it governs. Three can only be adapted into volume through the triangle. Four can only fit itself into volume through the square . . . thus, each one can only fit into volume by the nature, the *neter*, that it symbolizes. Now, volume is the north-south axis and the four directions, three measures, and six poles whose symbol is the cube of the *neter* Four.

The door is the key to all measure, it is the place where the imponderable falls into the ponderable, the indeterminate into the determined, through the two Fires, one multiplied by two, three times.

THE NARTHEX

In the conception of the temple, this place appears last. In the initiation into the temple, it comes first. Here are initially taught those who have known how to knock at the door in the name of Hor-thma-ā, the God Sabaoth of Israel.

Here the unmoving begins to move, and the waters of confusion separate the disciple from the one rejected, but both are on the threshold of the Temple. Skepticism helps faith; from both the Light will be born. It is the opposition between facts, the projection of rational thought, that will open hearts through the awareness of the unfitness of this deceptive path. The new seers, the princes of future royalty, are gathered together, whereas those who avoided the pitfall of this test are led directly through the exterior path of the walls, some to the peristyle, some to the hypostyle, of the covered temple, where they will greet the new seers after their trials.

The talker rejoices in and is content with words. The disciple must be silent and act. His work, whether it be intellectual or practical, will show his understanding on the one hand, and his knowledge on the other.

What is understood by the intelligence of the heart is set aside and always guarded. What is comprehended only by cerebral intelligence requires another struggle through the antinomies.

The activity of emotion is what fixes intelligence and memory. Some people are moved only by the form of thought, others only by the forms revealed through one of the five senses. The sage is moved by all forms at once.

Emotion has its active source in the Fire of Ra and thus manifests, through the organic sun, the Fire which, originally, fell to earth through Ptah, on the threshold of the door, the light in the darkness.

That which is fixed, containing in its blackness the secret jewel, Min-Ptah, is the center that must link the germ above to the root below, a black colossus meditating on the throne of this ligature. This is the mine of metals. It is also the concept that speaks as much to the heart as it does to the brain. Then, for the reprobate, begins the trial of water. Will he know how to draw from within the heart's expansion the vivifying air charged with spirit? Will he know how to grow as a living plant?

THE NAVE: THE VESSEL

This is the place of the prayer that is a call, the support for the ponderous, and the way of the seven double stages of the Passion: to believe and to doubt, to climb and to descend, light of the intellect and shadow of comprehension, joy of liberation and sadness of the bodily prison, hope of mystical marriage and despair of mortal love. As the black man observes in the fresco by Nicolas Flamel, "The procession is very pleasing to God when it is made in devotion." The barque of Amun carries away, like the Ark on the waters of Nun, all that lives, and, in the deluge, rejects what is dead in order to salvage that which would be mortal by remaining within the constraint of the body.

Seven times Amun floats on the water in the barque, carrying the breath of life in the eternal tabernacle, the divine naos. He goes down and up the Hapi, the Nile of the celestial waters and the earth's depths, seven colors, seven sounds, seven heavens, seven perspectives of thought, seven columns of light, seven columns of shadow.

It is only at the seventh trial that the triumphant disciple is admitted to communion, that the house is opened to receive its master, that virginity can conceive without sin that which was in it from all eternity, and that now comes to it. The announcement of the first ecstasy, the new door, which is the third, and thus manifests the meaning of the first two. There is the door through which one enters the house and the door through which one goes out. And the house is the container that gives form, as a vase gives form to water. The house captures, holds, constrains. Sanctity lies in being able to leave it, free of all constraint, but rich with the knowledge of forms.

THE PERISTYLE: TRANSEPT AND WOMB

What has been conceived must gestate. The peritoneum envelops the places of gestation, the new death and the new but glorious birth. This is the last purifying death, the eighth month that prepares the new birth that will no longer be head downward, but upward toward the heights. And highest is the tendency toward the source, toward that which is simultaneously container and contained, the spiritual air.

The disciple who has already glimpsed the light must now endure the wilderness of this light, it is his last but terrible prison and the great fast, because he must feed himself from within. Light without shadow, light that consumes everything. He must know that the damned is the one who knows best how to pray. He has *wanted* the light and recognizes that he has lost that which, within himself, wanted it. He must now be the light or else he will fall irretrievably and finally into what is, in the face of what is not; into what is heavy in the face of what is light; into him who only perceives, into him who still prays.

But having passed this test and having learned to *be* instead of thinking, he will receive the baptism of the Fire in the *haty,* the heart, which being itself Fire, fire can no longer harm.

THE COVERED TEMPLE, ENTRANCE TO THE CHOIR

Entrance—birth to immortality in the covered temple, the place of renewal without death, of nourishment by the nectar of the dew and the ambrosia of air, Hathor. The lion of the heart that opens, closes, and governs the world's blood flow, and the eagle who in the lungs captures the solar fire.

The baptism of Fire is given with "the oil found in the house of the sage," say the proverbs, the unction that makes of the ordinary man the king of men, he who alone has the right to enter the Temple, covered by the roof of heaven.

First, the senses in-formed the interior (vegetating nature); then memory retained what the senses said (animal nature); then the brain denied (human nature); now the knowledge of the heart speaks to what is external, it separates out that which conforms to it, and is therefore pure, from that which is impure. The innumerable variety of a world in gestation is reduced in this place to the dualism of the original Fire, but, being joined, these "two" are henceforth a single Fire.

Adam and Eve, male and female, *yang* and *yin,* are no longer opposed; they return to the paradisaical unity, and this unification will take place in the sanctuaries of the Temple of the unifying body: the head.

The Verb became flesh and now the flesh proclaims the Verb.

What has mysteriously been realized up to this moment in the rains and droughts, in the caves of the earth, in the winds, in the air, in the clouds, in the innumerable conflicts of Nature, all this goes into these sanctuaries to be reduced to its most simple and subtle spiritual forms, through the revelation of the Amunian altar, through the corridors hidden from profane eyes that do not know how to see, through the numbers that profane ears do not know how to hear. Here is accomplished that which was said by Hermes: *the visible becomes invisible* in these "endocrinal" rooms that receive the afflux and only give energy in return; *the invisible becomes visible* through the will that orders that, through action, the spirit become manifest.

Man has received the unction. He is king, *Man-symbol* of universal and immortal Man, who served as his model. The divine Temple animates this king who is then freed from the human temple, his gestating egg, to have dominion over all perishable works.

THE SANCTUARY

The sword broken into duality at the time of its conflict against the sovereign Unity has been brought back to the primordial Unity to be victorious against Seth and all his monsters. The human being has undergone all the trials, awakening the divine breath that is Immortal Man and that has always been his life. The human was the image of Man living in the indivisible Spirit within the sanctuary, an image that the human can but parody.

The sacrificial altar is the place of the conjunction of Amun's spiritual water with the active odor of God, the formulation of the Verb. By the five angles of the perfect face (the Hathorian pentagon) the five verbs go out and come in, thus giving rise to the five intelligences. Acting and reacting in itself is the creative work.

This is the mystery of the reaction, which, in the sanctuary, the head of the Universe, formulates the Verb, manifests the world, creates intelligence. Here is revealed the secret of the Door through the doorways of the senses. It knocks to come in and receives the answer. Ashaverus does not reply, hence his condemnation to turn forever in the closed circle. The light knocks, enters, and comes out *seeing*. The voice receives its own echo from inside; among the Batrachia, the internal middle ear (from the pharynx) forms and is the first response to its own voice. Life is the consciousness that awaits the call to which it responds. In Innu of the North, the Heliopolis of above, Tum in Nun, by masturbating, creates himself: in action, which would not be action otherwise, resistance is immanent.

The sun is only sun through its vassals, the planets, issued from its being and reflecting its verb as moons. Immutable reality hidden behind the illusion of appearances. If we look at he who knocks at the door without entering or leaving, if we look at the object and not at its function, we are deceived and lost. This is the secret meaning of the door: the reversal of the "light," from the head to the heart, from form to function, from the appearance through the senses into the reaction that is life.

Through the functions that make up Man there is a commingling with the Universe, which is Man.

The sanctuary sublimates the numbers into principles that penetrate all things like incense smoke.

Above all other Principles reign the Three, in their sanctuaries. One is the principle of the odor that coagulates; it gives everything from metal to blood its fixity. It orients, it attaches. It is the salt of knowledge, but it can also be the support of evil. It is this that speaks in Adam saying, "I have not found what is flesh of my flesh." In it resides the desire for the *invariant* that haunts scholarship. It is the archangel who, at the eastern door, guards Paradise Lost with the sword of Fire.

The second, the one of midday, is the humor that sublimates. It separates and conjoins, the door of coming in and going out. It renders volatile the most fixed and seizes the most subtle; it is the moving Spirit that is moved. It is the soul of femininity, the milk of the celestial cow, Mut, then Hathor, indifferent to good as to bad, the silvery spirit, from the metal to the white humors and the ovaries, the crystalline, lunar Amun and the spermatic Amun-Ra, the secret of the hidden Amun.

The third principle is the color of the west, visible but intangible. It is the seat of the intellect, the force of Min and the paternity that causes death and rebirth. Causing movement without being moved, it is the light of consciousness, the serpent's venom, the universal antidote. It makes the child pubescent when, through it, Mut becomes Hathor (Ra in Amun), when, at the hour of the death of day, that which will make the glorious resurrection of midnight is conceived.

Each of these three principles, cosmic *neters,* is a separate entity, but they are a unity in the cycle of day and night of genesis, when at the crossroads of the cosmic pharynx, the verb of the Ogdoad linked them. The Ogdoad forms space from the breath of the four, each of which is male and female, humid and cold, dry and cold, hot and humid, dry and hot.

This is the number Two, principle of multiplication.

The head of Cosmic Man is the holy place where the *neters*—the principles—reign, as likewise, the forms of thought reign in the human head.

Here corporeal needs and the heart's desires become will, the imperative of the *neters*. And the most saintly of wills is the one that denies the illusory in favor of the cosmic reality of the desires of the *neter*.

THE APSE, EXTRA MUROS

The separation of the crown of the skull that belongs to humanity outside of the Temple.

The vertex of the human . . . Saint Paul, Heaven, fallen face downward on the ground, crowned with thorns: *Ecce homo* (with a helmet of iron), who will be raised up, turned over to face Heaven, illumined. But this is also the temple of fiction, the reflecting mirror guarding the words made in the image of the Verb, until such time as the crown of realities and divine inspiration might be lifted up to it. The fontanelle of the entrance of life and of its departure at the death of the body.

Would that this life be captured in the aureole of the red crown in the white, or the white in the red, the *aura* of Man, consciousness freed from the prison of forms. This is the place of supreme sublimation, the end of temporary forms, where spirit is body after all its tribulations. But was not the skeptic told, "Happy is he who without touching has yet believed"?

THE TEMPLE OF MAN

THE TEMPLE OF MAN

APET OF THE SOUTH AT LUXOR

≈

R. A. Schwaller de Lubicz

Translated from the French by
Deborah Lawlor and Robert Lawlor

Illustrations by Lucie Lamy

Inner Traditions
Rochester, Vermont

Inner Traditions International
One Park Street
Rochester, Vermont 05767
www.InnerTraditions.com

First English language edition published by Inner Traditions International, Ltd. 1998
Originally published in French under the title *Le Temple de l'homme*
Copyright © 1957, 1993, 1998 by Éditions Dervy
Translation copyright © 1998 by Inner Traditions International

Library of Congress Cataloging-in-Publication Data
Schwaller de Lubicz, R. A.
[Temple de l'homme.   English]
The temple of man : Apet of the South at Luxor / R. A. Schwaller de Lubicz ;
translated from the French by Deborah Lawlor and Robert Lawlor.
p.   cm.
Includes bibliographical references and index.
ISBN 978-0-89281-570-8 (alk. paper)
1. Occultism—Egypt.   2. Temple of Luxor (Luxor, Egypt)—Miscellanea.   I. Title.
BF1434.E3S3613   1998   97-21877
001.9—dc21   CIP

Volume 2 of two-volume slipcased edition
Printed in China

10 9 8 7 6

Text design by Virginia L. Scott and Peri Champine. Layout by Peri Champine.
This book was typeset in Adobe Caslon with Centaur as the display typeface.

Jacket and slipcase cover image: statue of Ramesses II, builder of the Ramesside court at Luxor.
Photograph by Georges and Valentine de Miré.
Hieroglyphs on jacket flaps, front cover stamp, and title pages
are the Egyptian words for *The Temple of Man.*
Endpapers are based on royal cartouches from the Eighteenth Dynasty.

THE
TEMPLE
OF MAN

VOLUME 2

Statue of Amun and Mut

Here we draw near to secret Egypt, the aspect that will reveal to us the pharaonic mentality, the mode of thought of the masters of this empire.

(Chapter 4)

Part 5

THE PHARAONIC TEMPLE

Chapter 23

THE ARCHITECTONICS OF THE PHARAONIC TEMPLE

The master builder said to the disciple:

"You come from the earth, it has nourished you, and you will return to the earth. This element holds and keeps the other elements.

"Know that everything that, of itself, diffuses outward without form needs a receptacle. Thus, Air retains the Fire of the Universe, and Water retains Air, as Earth is the vase that holds Water and gives it form. Thus, Earth is the container of All. I speak to you of the earth upon which you tread, the gross image of the spermatic Earth of which you are made.

"Always see, in the lower things that your senses reveal to you, the image of things that your spirit alone can conceive when your senses are closed to the world of transitory appearances.

"I will speak to you of architecture, not of building technique.

"The man of the earth lives in his houses of earth. The *neter* comes from heaven and creates earth; the house is but emptiness enclosed. The forms of the world, in which are inscribed the laws of the Becoming and the Return, frame this emptiness. It is necessary to learn to read these signs in order to reach the sanctuary through the labyrinth of 'possibilities.' Learn how the doors are bolted by the secret of Nature, or else you will never attain the goal.

"But the emptiness is defined only through the law of numbers. Numbers impose the form of the limits. This is the foundation. And through this Idea the formless spirit becomes, grows, and vegetates into formed matter, since everything is sustained by the process of vegetation.

"There is growth from the earth skyward; there is formation in going from one horizon to the other. Then there is what is inside and what is outside. From the inside comes the ripened sap that gives the seed; from the outside comes the nourishment that the sky brings to earth. This is the Idea of the Temple, the House of God.

"Listen. The man who lives in his house imprints it with his thought, the rhythm of his being. The house where a *neter* dwells is impregnated by its Idea and the nature of its being. It is *its* house and not another's; do not search for what will not be there. But the Whole converges to define this *neter* because it is He and yet inseparable from the Whole.

"When you know the orientation of the God for which you wish to construct a dwelling place, you know the Idea that will take form, that is, the basis of the plan. On this basis draw the number, or "geometry" of this *neter*. This element of the origin will necessarily guide you toward all the forms that can result from it, but it will only be a guide and not an image.

"Know the secret of number because it engenders. It is a seed that carries a fruit of its species within it. Mark the plan of this 'inevitability' on the floor of the temple for those who will come after you, so when the time arrives to remake this dwelling, they may construct a new one on this base. Any new form is made from the death of the preceding one. The heavens are a sphere that rolls the Becoming; the *neter* is of the heavens; come to live on earth, it must take form there in accord with the heavens, like a plant.

"Next, arrange the enclosures according to number as they are found to be in the living organism of this *neter*, in keeping with its 'becoming.' Thus you will make the geometry live. Time is growth and becoming; it is your only true measure. Each *neter* has its time, as does each seed that gives fruit. And know that, for man, the soul is fixed in forty days: Maāt; and it stirs in the fourth month. It can live at the seventh lunar month: Osiris; or else at the ninth solar month: Horus.

"Transcribe these numbers into cubits, digits, and thumbs, and into diameters, through the secret of measures; then set the boundaries of your houses in the house of the *neter*.

"Thus, the indestructible idea will take form in transitory matter. It will grow in its plane, and from this plane it will grow like a plant toward the heavens. Open and close the corollas of the columns according to the nature of the months of gestation of the *neter*, from the entrance to the naos, and choose the stones in this spirit. Know that the work of your hands, if it conforms to the Idea, will be creative and harmonious; thus the temple will be made indestructible. What difference if the stone and earth crumble; the Idea is of the nature of the *neter* and will be merged in God.

"All this is archi-texture.

"In order to understand numbers, know that Unity is triple in nature like the Verb of God. All number is founded on this trinity of point and on the triangle of surface; but the ternary volume is constructed on the four columns of the Elements or essential qualities of things. Only the Creator can proceed from a point toward volume, and from nothing, create All.

"But you, as creature, must look for the point by proceeding from volume; because every perceptible thing is volume, is space or Spirit enclosed.

"The logic of your brain has no power over number. Number is the Verb of God and governs intelligence. Leave the numerals that count things to the intelligence of the head; search for number in the intelligence of your heart.

"Look at your hand. On its inside surface, which is active, the destiny of your incarnate soul is drawn. Do not confuse it with the back of this hand where the law that presides over Becoming is inscribed. On this side the three phalanges of the fingers give the proportion of the sacred number, the section of all harmony. Never prostitute this number, under pain of disgrace; however, its secret is well protected from the profane.

"Your hand has four fingers, the elements of Osiris; it has twelve phalanges, the zones of the sky. The fifth finger governs the others, as spirit does form. It is the fifth essence of things. The inside of your hand is active, but I will also tell you this: The second inside phalanx belongs to Min-Amun, the procreative milieu. Now you will be able to make hands speak.

"The first surface is the triangle and its root is the incomprehensible Unity. When this Unity-surface—the triangle—divides in two, there is male and female, a couple procreating through the four Elements: this is the square cut by its diagonal.

"The four Elements are the square of heaven. Understand that the side of a square is the foundation of every right triangle. Draw the diagonals in the square; they form four triangles that are equal to one another and thus manifest the essential law that rules right triangles, the law of the whole applied science of numbers. Now you know only its function. Look for its nature and on this basis draw the *canevas* for the architecture of the world.

"The first number is Three, the second is Four, the third is Five. These are the primary values of the sides of the sacred right triangle, whose application has innumerable consequences.

"Every surface is curved, because the world is a Becoming and a Return; all within it is cyclic. Calculate as if a surface were a plane, but with numbers that rectify this plane into a curve; otherwise you will be a surveyor and not a geometer of the Temple. Only draw the curve for the sky and for what relates to Osiris: the Becoming and the Return. Our numbers are universal and our measures are established to rectify the straight line into the curve, planes into volumes, length into time, heaven into man, genesis into life. God is the model because he is the Master of all in All.

"Watch a man grow when he is detached from his mother, because the living soul in him tends to shape this body toward a perfect proportion.

"Man is made in the image of heaven; look at the imperfections of the body to know the faults he has yet to pay for, but know that he *is the Universe;* this is why you should take him as your model, as the reflection of the creator God. The whole work of creation is in man; put man in his place in the Temple. He is born and he will die; between these extremes he lives.

"This life is the expression of consciousness.

"The heart beats the rhythm of time; the lungs breathe and link intangible substance to living matter; the organism digests, separating the pure from the impure.

"His face is his life's utterance; his mouth expresses his thought; his eyes reveal his consciousness. His voice can render all the sounds of Nature, any words that are expressed. Each gesture of man speaks. He is the complete incarnation of the intangible and inaudible Verb that through this form makes itself known. Make the statue live by causing the truth of the *neter* to be expressed in it.

"If you represent a human body on the wall, show only one of its sides if the other is identical; show it facing forward if there is an inequality in the two parts, because human beings are a duality in their fallen nature, but Unity in their origin.

"In man, the east side receives, the west side gives. Evil is in his brain, which always separates; good is in his heart, *ib hati,* which—always—unites.

"Thus, you will make the image of man speak.

"Watch the animals of the air, the water, and the earth. Each expresses one of the aspects of which the whole is Man-King. Each one expresses one of the words of the divine language that is the Universe. Make the animals, plants, and colors speak; make them say what they in truth are. Guard yourself from making them spokesmen of what you yourself think. Elevate what is light; lower what is heavy; learn to know what causes the heavy to rise and what makes the light fall and gives weight to it. Spirit is that which is most light, and the "odor of the *neter*" is that which is most heavy, as the seed incarnates spirit and reduces it into body.

"In this way make the temple speak; and then draw the encircling wall around it, the collar of Fire, in order to drive away the enemy of life, this life that desires eternity. Plant flagpoles at the entrance, magnets of heaven, that their flame may be nourished by the spirit of the four winds.

"I have given you here the rudiments of a great science, so that you might learn to distinguish the builders of human dwellings from the master builder of the temple. May this guide you in what you must learn."

—⁓—

The disciple, remaining alone, saw the companion of the master builder coming toward him.

"My brother, I have been directed to lead you through the science of architecture, to show you particularly the sites at which you can observe what will subsequently be hidden from your eyes in the finished work. But I would be ungrateful if I were to attribute to myself the high science that was taught to me. So I will explain these things to you in the same way the answers to my questions were given to me.

"First of all, is not water the beginning of everything? Thus, we use the mean level of the highest groundwater to establish the horizontal and the foundation mark of our monuments.

"The fathers of our fathers observed long ago the time it takes for the earth to increase through the depositing of silt and for the heavens to cause the level of the waters to rise. Thus, we know in advance the time of the collapse of our works, gnawed away in their foundations like a root that dies after giving its fruit, and which then reinseminates the earth; and we calculate its life by the rhythm of the cycles of the sky so that the growth of our temples might conform with the changing of the great seasons of the Universe.

"Let us now consider the principal directives of applied architecture.

"*Without philosophy there is no architecture,* only building technique.

"The temple must be read like a book. If it had nothing to teach, it would be but a house for people instead of the house of God. If the *neter* that it shelters is beautiful, the house will be beautiful; if the *neter* is displeasing, the house will also be so because it is the description of the *neter*.

"If it were only a matter of describing a myth, one would be able to write on the walls as one does on a papyrus; this would not be THE TEMPLE. To build the house of a *neter* is to create the Idea of this *neter* in every sense, with the material as with the measurements and the texts on the stones. The Idea, thus materialized, is inscribed forever in the substance of the Universe; but there must be no error.

"The secret is in understanding the meaning represented by the *neter*. Now, every *neter* is but one aspect of the Whole that is Unity; it can only be considered when integrated into one or the other of the great lineages, the one to which it belongs.

"The teaching as a whole is that of the genesis of the world. To situate only a phase of it would make no more sense than to describe one part of the human body without connecting it to the entire body through a general function. This is the first directive.

"What good would this teaching be if it were not the key to a science that we could usefully apply in our lives, and still more so in the afterlife? We are not concerned with a play of thought, but with a sacred reality. If fantasy embellished a *neter* with attributes for an aesthetic purpose, it would be an unpardonable error, even though done in ignorance, because its image must be true, without a trace of falsehood. This is the reason for a rigid canon that cannot be changed except by the sage who has the knowledge of the time and the secret of the writing.

"The teaching is given for those who live on earth, who come and come again to search there for the way that leads toward the Immortal. This is our world of duality, of birth and death, and of rebirth in bodies. Everything here is double, and one of the two defines the other; everything here is crossed, the weak defines the strong, the low measures the high, and aversion calls forth sympathy. Here reigns the fallen Sethian prince, who in making good created evil, and in making evil called forth good. This determines the succession in the architecture of the temple, and it is the second directive.

"Those who already know how to renounce the body for the life of the soul alone no longer need walls to delimit the emptiness and fix it into mortal forms. For them the time has come in which God alone is the Temple; for them there is no longer a temple on earth. Know what you search for; but when you look at the temple, know that you do not look at the unique Creator, but at the teaching of this world, born of the Unique; therefore let your work conform to the goal that this imposes.

"Do not be concerned with the material duration of your work. Place sandstone, which represents Earth, upon limestone, representing Air, if the Idea requires it. What does it matter if the limestone crumbles, or if the construction of clay and silt, representing Water, risks caving in. Choose granite for Fire because that is where it comes from.

"Know also that all life is the fruit of the black destruction of death, that this blackness is the root, the origin of what will be white or red, like the veins that sometimes run through our black stones.

"Cut the stones in the quarry itself; choose them judiciously. Give them the measurements foreseen on the plan, because the joints must measure the images; they can separate the head from a figure, or cut out a part of the body. Choose the stone stratum that conforms to the principle to be expressed.

"Let each room—each chapter of your book—be conceived as an entity, even if it means building walls that will one day fall; but place a link through joining walls only if the idea 'traverses' from one room to the other. Embed your key-stones in the wall and the ground at the exact places of the measures and numbers that establish the plan. Make the Idea rise from the ground to the architraves, from the earth to heaven, where the laws are inscribed. Make the gods rise toward God, as the sun attracts to itself the flower of the plant.

"This is the third directive.

"The number of scenes represented is limited by the general canon, but each scene is the foundation on which, through measures and attributes, a thousand nuances of thought are inscribed.

"Know that the door expresses the key of the idea that is transcribed in the place into which it leads. Make this door a precise study, because the temple will only be consecrated if no error is committed. As for the obelisks, they will search the sky for the generative Fire of the temple; the master will inscribe on them the laws that cause the worlds to revolve.

"And now come, touch with your hands and see with your eyes the transcription of what I have said to you, because you must observe how we work. You will see that we carefully 'turn under' the previous temple in order that it be the seed and the bed of life from which will come forth the new temple conforming to a new time. You shall count the number of stone layers in the foundations, and you shall learn their significance. You shall observe the choice of inscriptions: they will be guides for those who know how to read them. You shall look for the teaching in the foundation deposits and the cornerstones. You shall see with what love of truth our masters founded the empire of knowledge and of great prayer."

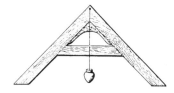

Chapter 24

PREFACE TO THE PRESENTATION OF THE ARCHITECTURE OF THE TEMPLE OF LUXOR

As archaeology and philology, standard Egyptology is addressed to specialists; but the teaching, which the knowledge implied in the established facts allows one to gather, is addressed to a public that is interested in the "causes" of life. It is correct to acknowledge that the guiding thought behind the establishment of the pharaonic empire, which in its writing, its myth—in short, in all its essential elements—persisted over millennia, must have been of a solidity such that it could not grow old. In its reality and because of this fact, pharaonic Egypt should still be at least as relevant as our most recent discoveries in microphysics.

There has been the desire to view this myth and its symbolism as a syncretism of various beliefs and tribal totemisms; but the uncovering of the tombs of the first dynasties shows that, from the time of its historical origin, the writing, myth, and symbolism were complete and constitute a solidly established base.

Moreover, we search in vain in pharaonic Egypt for explanatory written documents, or for "theories" in the sense accepted in the West since the time of Greek influence. Theory belongs to the era of research and no longer has any meaning when the problems are resolved.

The historical era of this empire presents itself as a period of political and religious application of a certain knowledge and a proven science; it no longer shows any interest in demonstrations and experiments, but simply applies the preserved tradition.

It is understandable then that this received science became altered more and more as it was passed on. It is psychologically sound to see a teaching become more and more complicated, a teaching that, at the time of the first dynasties, was still very pure and, accordingly, was transcribed by simple and essential methods—that is, in a synthetic spirit—as numbers, geometry, and biological symbioses.

This "progress" into complexity through the extension of the *symbolique* became clearly manifest after the Middle Kingdom, and reached its climax with the Ptolemaic conclusion of the pharaonic empire's political existence.

There is *knowledge* in Egypt; it has been there since the most remote times and has nourished humanity for millennia. In the end, its routine application was able to induce the invaders—particularly the argumentative Greeks—to look for the "reasons" that demonstrate such and such an axiom or tradition, which previously was transmitted and retransmitted as an article of faith with no curiosity about investigating the causes and the knowledge that led to it.

But there is a fundamental difference between an investigation of the grounds of knowledge through a posteriori reasoning and this same investigation through intuition, illumination, and spiritual experience with its experimental *demonstration*, in a word, through the esotericism of Nature.

The first leads to a necessarily mechanistic rationalism because it is based on quantitative data and their interactions; the second leads to spiritual sources, accessible only to the privileged few of the "Temple."

Ancient Egypt never explains the reasons for its behavior; the papyri give practical applications in mathematics and medicine that imply knowledge that was never revealed to the practitioners. The general conclusions of experiments and the theory of laws, indispensable in the phases of research that belong to our era, have no reason to exist in pharaonic Egypt, where, nonetheless, we meet an extraordinary civilizing work of exceptional duration.

It is the architectural monument, consecrated to worship based on the *symbolique* of the myth, which supports the evidence of this certitude, demonstrating a science whose applications radiate in all directions. Until now the pharaonic temple was never studied in its significance as a work that *speaks* to us because it kept mute before the questions put to it by a rational and analytical mentality.

Knowledge can only be synthetic; because of this it can only be intelligibly transcribed by the architectural monument, that is, by a *simultaneity of plane and volume*, accomplished in Egypt through the *symbolique* of the writing, the image, and the statuary. To this is added a complete architectural *grammar*, represented by the shape of the stone blocks: their joints, overlappings, and "transparencies" and "transpositions" in the walls comprise a subtle grammar in which the finish of a carving or its rough aspect, the absence of essential parts—such as the eye or the navel—the reversal of right and left, and so forth, play the role of accents, declensions, conjugations, and conjunctions.

Being consecrated to a definite principle, an Egyptian temple becomes what might be called a "library," summarizing, in an exhaustive manner, all that can be known about that subject.

This is the result of our study of the temple of Luxor, which we are trying to prove by the facts presented in this book, which is a development, and a continuation, of *The Temple in Man*.

It is, however, impossible for us to reduce to a "plane" description, that is, a rational one with logical connections, that which is a simultaneity of planes and volumes and a simultaneity of complementaries. This is the only descriptive form possible for esoteric teaching, unless one has recourse to literary parable, which would only add another enigma to that of the architecture.

The link between the various given elements must be made *intuitively*, especially in this work where long parentheses (necessary for precision of thought) might appear to separate us from the subject.

For an architectural reading it is necessary to take into account all the impressions that one experiences upon entering the building. The first thing that stands out is the form of the room, that is, the plan. We are never indifferent to this form, whose quadrangle satisfies us through its equilibrium, but also seems to imprison us. The impression given by a square is very different from that given by an elongated rectangle, and, for example, if we enter into the round room of a tower, we are at a loss to know where to begin. As for volume, a low ceiling "crushes" us, whereas we "breathe" in a room with a ceiling of harmonious height. The high vault raises our vision in spite of ourselves.

Thus, the simple plan combined with the volume "speaks" to us, and it is this combination that initially can serve to express something to us without the intervention of reason. It addresses itself to the feeling that results from our living relationship to the milieu, alive through its form.

This is art, in its pure sense, which expresses itself in a verb that we cannot transcribe into words. In the same way, for example, the palm reader or the graphologist tries vainly to formulate systems that would make his practice more scientific, a practice that is and will remain a "-mancy" because the esoteric—that is, the inner meaning, the sense of volume, the sense of life (or vitalistic sense)—cannot be rationally transcribed on the surface plane.

In geometry, we know that it is impossible to cover the surface plane with pentagons in a continuous fashion; but pentagons do fit together in space to form a dodecahedron. Esotericism addresses itself to a sense of volume that we are unable to comprehend cerebrally without cutting it into planar slices, or without supposing it to be composed of planes in movement. *Rationalism is planar.* Only volume, and therefore architecture in general, is able to express the esotericism of a teaching for which an irrational moment is *prime mover.*

Through an assemblage of words we can describe the chronology of the creation, according to the tradition, by speaking of a ternary unity from which the passive-active duality results, which in turn forms the quaternary of the Elements. We can also symbolize this by the doors, the towers, and the levels of the facade of a cathedral but without, for all of that, being any more advanced in knowledge. These are empty words, empty of vital meaning, because the facade of this building is still only a plane.

But when this plane becomes a vertical facade elevated on a geometric plan based, for example, on the golden number, then the symbolic significance becomes complicated by a *function of growth* on the one hand, and by spatial location on the other, since this facade evokes the complementary walls that are going to make up the volume of the building.

Then the ternary of the doors comes alive, explaining the rite that, in words and gestures, expresses what the written word is unable to formulate. The central door consecrates the edifice, the faithful enter by the north door, as the living fluid enters at the North Pole of our terrestrial globe, and the south door becomes the holy door of "regenerations" (to be compared with the pharaonic *sed* festival).

We could thus analyze the esoteric meaning of the duality of the towers (or the double pylon with its obelisks) and the squaring of the cycle of the Elements—that which alone permits location in space, that is, volume.

To complete this example, let us note a *fourth dimension* in architecture, that of time, given by the *orientation.*

When we try to describe the teaching of a sacred architecture, we must necessarily proceed by piecemeal descriptions, and the connections must be made by the reader (because no one else can do it for him or her), after we have facilitated this understanding by specifying precise situations. But is this not the case for understanding anything of a living, moving character, in any sort of study? Is it not necessary to see a synthesis, indescribable in its simultaneity of place, volume, and time? For what purpose, we might ask? But is it not already a valid purpose to awaken a sense of superior intellection?

Current scientific research is leading slowly but surely toward the evidence of this logically inexpressible simultaneity. Mathematics is still a subterfuge obscuring our way back to the architectural methods that were so useful to the Ancients, who, as mathematicians, had recognized the impossibility of bequeathing the knowledge to future times in the form of theoretical mathematics alone, unless it become geometry in space.

Now, all this will appear strange and remain incomprehensible for those who never occupy themselves with the mystery of this phenomenon called "life," and with the problems inseparably connected with the reason for being and the goal of life.

During the last century it was believed that life was a mechanical complex that could be rationally understood; only the vegetable and animal kingdoms were considered living. The mineral kingdom—inorganic—was made part of a vitally inert state of Nature.

For the Ancients, on the contrary, life began with Spirit, that is, with the active—but still abstract—emanation of the One God, the indefinable source. In our day, with the advances in atomic theory, we begin to see this so-called inert mineral world peopled with strangely active atoms, with each molecule becoming a universe in itself, swarming with star-atoms in which forces play that no longer belong to the old physics of gravitation, but instead to powers of affinities and repulsions, of transformations of energy into light, and this occurring under the "supervision" of an extraordinary concentration of energy. And this energy, of which we know nothing (an ignorance that we mask under the name of "velocity"), again appears as the end of everything. In spite of their repugnance, the most conformist of our scientists begin to suspect the existence of a metaphysical world; perhaps one day they may also suspect transcendental powers, that is, powers both inside of and beyond matter, which appear as matter.

Life begins with the atom, a word that is inappropriate, by the way, when we consider that this atom is still a composite and still allows a scission, precisely into those energetic elements that manifest life. Now with the atom we are still far from organic life, but it is probable that we will eventually discover that organs are only "crystallizations" or materializations of these qualities, that is, of these potentialities characterizing the primitive, energetic functions of the atom; natural transmutations, indisputably demonstrated today, are but a symbolic form of that vital action, fundamental for all life, which is assimilation.

For the moment, we have only begun to approach this frontier where the attempt will be made to translate the function, in physics, into *vital function*, where, as with "alchemy," it is thought possible to justify the so-called dream of the Ancients through scientifically verified facts. Following this, as one might suppose, will come the phase in which we will find the *synthetic expression* for all domains of life, including the energetic, kinetic life of the atom, in the psychospiritual and metaphysical affirmations of the old tradition.

I appear to be prophesying and to believe in a sort of return to the past. This is incorrect. From pharaonic Egypt to our day, there has been an acquisition for humanity—an acquisition belonging to a domain for which there is no accounting—that thought does not know how to define, and which, it seems, is the only aspect of the phenomenon of life that constantly evolves: consciousness.

Our philosophers declare that consciousness is indefinable because it is indissociable from thought. This is true for the cerebral or psychological consciousness. But the self has no need to be *aware* of itself for there to be consciousness. From the sole fact that anything whatsoever *is*, it is its "me," in other words, it is qualified; it is itself defined in time and space, and in its own functions. The chemical affinity of a molecule is a selective function, therefore a first form of consciousness, and this will evolve until it becomes, in the organized being, psychological consciousness. Now, the chemical consciousness of a molecule is but the manifestation of a functional, global consciousness of the potential powers of the energetic grouping of the atom. Then, even closer to the reality, we observe that this atom is formed of a "Sirian" nucleus (from Sirius, the Sothis of the Ancient Egyptians, which they called the Great Provider), that is, of a sun with a double nucleus, one positive and the other neutral, surrounded by seven stages (from K to Q), actual or potential, of negative particles, each with its own rotation, and turning at enormous speeds around the nucleus in various elliptical orbits, undergoing precessions that incline the planes of the orbits in all directions, creating magnetic fields . . . ultimately, this atom is a universe that our mathematics is no longer sufficient to calculate.

From the moment there is an identity of nature with function, largeness or smallness becomes irrelevant. If we need a telescope to observe one and a microscope to observe the other, it appears that we also need the vision of the spirit, because the senses are no longer able to observe the reality of the facts in their complex simultaneity.

Finally, the atom of the mechanists, of the mathematicians and engineers, leads us straight toward the Anthropocosmos, and this means that we will find in the constituent forces of matter potential arrangements analogous to those which are manifest in the final goal of this Universe, the goal that for us is man.

Life appears first in the atom; then, passing through present man, life wants to become Man Accomplished: cosmic consciousness.

It is in the possibility—acquired by a large part of humanity—of being able to observe and understand the existence of this reality that *our progress* consists, in comparison to a very small minority of privileged beings admitted to the "Mysteries" of the ancient Temples.

The "Temple in Man" has expanded.

I prefer to envision existence as being caused by a scission or separation within itself of an incomprehensible Unity, then . . . how the Tum of the pharaonic sages, being of the same nature as the chaotic waters, Nun, coagulates these waters to cause the appearance of Atum (the original Adam) under the form of the "Ogdoad," the four elements doubled into male and female. Thus, the Heliopolitan Mystery symbolizes the creative function of this "Fire," which at Memphis will fall to earth to be the Luciferian Ptah, both the generating and the destroying fire: Sethian and Horian.

If the *raison d'être* of life is to become conscious of itself, then *the goal of life* is cosmic consciousness, the consciousness of the Whole, beyond all transient, mortal contingencies.

To admit this and to try to deepen our experience of it, which is the teaching of all revelatory religions, is worth the pain of living. We are now going to look at how, through the remains of a great temple, the pharaonic masters passed on the foundations of knowledge.

Chapter 25

THE TEMPLE OF LUXOR

The conception of the pharaonic temple differs completely from our own. Each temple is consecrated to a divine principle, and it is also entirely adapted to the *symbolique* of this principle, while
being inseparable from the whole.

In order to illustrate these differences in architectural conception, we can compare the temples of
Luxor or Karnak with the temple of Edfu. The latter is conceived as a nesting of seven naoi, one inside
the other, whereas the temple of Luxor is conceived in its length as a sequence of phases of growth.

Taken together, pharaonic temples, throughout the whole of this empire extending the length
of the Nile, represent an overall teaching; each temple can be seen as a particularly developed theme
or chapter. This will be verified in a study of the geographical division—what I call the "mystical
geography"—of pharaonic Egypt,[1] but even a general glance affirms that no pharaonic temple is the
exact replica of another. Therefore, there is a question with each one as to whether it is an arbitrary
conception or a systematic instruction.

Architecture is a living language. When the printing press dethroned architectural teaching, it
eliminated the Spirit as well, leaving the empty letter.

Any building, no matter how simple, has a soul because it is a volume. Volume is necessarily indefinable Spirit-substance arrested in space. It is living, it is specified, it is number, and therefore music.

The more consciousness presides at its realization, the more clearly this volume-edifice explains
the teaching that it contains. The African village hut serves as a symbol of the metaphysics of a
tribal tradition, as does the Hindu temple, the Christian cathedral, and—supremely—the pharaonic
temple.

And the building can speak in all ways, through the material, the foundation, the plan, the elevation, the covering, the lighting, the orientation—not to mention the site. The building speaks the
language that only spirit can understand; it is sacred writing. Above all, it is to the monuments that
the archaeologist looks in order to draw nearer to the soul of the history of a past time. But, do we
still know how to read the architectural message?

---

[1] Work in preparation [never completed].

It is as much to relearn this way of reading as it is to rediscover the Ancient Egyptian teaching it transmits to us that we have gone more deeply into the study of the temple of Luxor, the pharaonic "Apet of the South." It is located on the right bank of the Nile, from which it is now separated by a road that goes to Karnak. Today, the sandstone blocks on the banks of the river still show the location of the ancient loading dock.

The real orientation of the temple is given by the axis of Amun, an occult axis in the sense that it is not practically useful as a reference for the architecture. Moreover, the median construction axis is broken at precisely marked places and veers toward the east. This deviation is warranted by the intended figuration of the temple.

The geodetic location is 25°43′ north latitude and 32°39′ east longitude relative to Greenwich.[2] With respect to a "real" longitude that uses 0° passing through the Pyramid of Cheops, the temple of Luxor is then at about 1°30′ east longitude.[3]

We do not have sufficiently precise *astronomical* data relative to the axes of the temple to be able to note them here. Generally, we can affirm that these axes relate to Jupiter and the Moon for all of the temple up to the court of Ramesses (the narthex), where the sun intervenes in the strong deviation marked at this point.

Precise calculations should be made by an astronomer with a sufficiently open mind to devote to this research, and with, for that matter, a fundamental interest in the study.

Let us recall here our previous allusion to the habitual confusion concerning the orientations. We say "north-south" and "east-west"; this is vitally (esoterically) false. North-south is the axis of the rotation of the terrestrial globe. The north attracts, absorbs; the south repels, rejects. This is the magnetic axis of the world.

The orientations depend upon the *cycle* and include east for rising, midday for maturity, west for retiring and conception, then midnight for the mystic birth.

The temple of Luxor has its entrance at the north, that is, toward midnight of the cycle, and the essential sanctuaries, as well as the apse, are located toward the south, at midday, the formal realization.

Christian initiatic cathedrals generally have the entrance at the west (the evening, conception), and their apse is at the east, the rising, the advent. The Divine Passion begins with night, the ascent of Golgotha with morning, and the highest moment of the cosmic crucifixion is at midday. The redemptive death takes place in the afternoon, and the placement in the tomb is in the west, at evening. The Resurrection takes place on the *third day*, not after three days. It takes place in the morning—the east—two days later.

Thus, the orientations in the temple speak in accordance with the cycles of time. The north-south axis creates the seasons, it is an alternation. The diurnal cycle is a continuous succession of birth, maturity, death, and renewal.

Alternation produces existence, the maintenance of the species by the seed. The cycles of renewal make evolution, the march toward the Beyond; it is the same being that, by and in itself, is renewed.

With the temple of Luxor we begin with night, toward midnight, and have realization toward midday, symbolized by the south. The infant is born headfirst, oriented *downward* (the south). Here, north and south are combined with midnight and midday. This is not a metaphysical birth and passion, but a cosmic-human realization.

[2] H. Engelbach, *Introduction to Egyptian Archaeology* (Cairo: I.F.A.O., 1946), p. 77.
[3] In pharaonic Egypt we have good reasons to adopt a meridian system based on this spot.

The construction of this temple was made in four stages, and each stage left an architectural "anchor point" for the following, from which one can conclude that a plan of the whole existed from the beginning. These stages correspond to human measurements at birth, and to the essential phases of growth, according to the most recent biometric data.

The materials utilized consist principally of rose sandstone and white limestone, according to the symbolic directive. Black, rose, and gray granite are reserved for statues.

The apparent disorder of the pavestones in the covered temple revealed to us the existence of a mosaic that depicts a head, the precise model for which exists in room XX in bas-relief. The size of this mosaic face serves as a reference for the proportions of the human figure, if the temple represents the height of a man.

The figure we call king B on the west wall of sanctuary I gives us the exact measurements of the size of the temple. The king's head, resculpted, but in a manner that does not obliterate the first proportion, indicates the two important phases of his growth, that of twelve years and eighteen years, which relate to the human genesis of this temple.

Because it was the first one of its type ever observed in Egypt, the reality of the pavestone mosaic[4] was at first doubted. But since then similar pavestone mosaics have been discovered at the temple of Mentu at Karnak, during the I.F.A.O. excavations by Robichon, Leclant, and Barguet.[5]

The existence of the head depicted in the pavestones, the coincidence of the phases of human growth with the phases of construction of the temple (the newborn being the size of the covered temple), and the coincidence of the divisions (head-neck, chest, belly, thighs, legs, and feet) of a skeleton constructed according to biometric data with the architecture, already constitute a body of evidence proving that the temple of Luxor actually represents the human body. We were satisfied in 1949 to present these arguments. We agree, however, that a doubt might have nevertheless remained. This doubt disappears with the reading of the joints of the stones as we present them here.

It was important to develop these proofs, which probably make the temple of Luxor a unique monument in the world, although all initiatic temples have had the projection of the Universe in Man as their object. Here, however, the form and the proportion of the architecture superimpose themselves on the complete body of man, which gives to the inscriptions (ritual hieroglyphics, bas-reliefs, transparencies, transpositions, connections given through the joints, and geometric keys) the value of biological revelation, according to their location on the human body, which, thus, plays the role of an atlas for *vital functions*.

The pharaonic ritual, well known to Egyptologists, reveals here all its vital, mystical significance. This not only concerns the living, organic, divine manifestation in the Universe, but also the law of genesis in general, encompassing the astronomical and mineral worlds.

Man as issue of Original Creation is Universe. On his body, senses, organs, assimilative functions, and vital nervous centers—both physical and those of cosmic, energetic coincidence—all knowledge is inscribed.

Through the geometry and proportions of the plane, numbers, the stages of consciousness from the abstract to the physically concrete, symbolized by the registers of the walls and the principles inscribed on the architraves, allow for everything to be said in volume.

[4] *The Temple in Man,* chapter 6.

[5] Cf. Jean Leclant, "Fouilles et travaux en Egypte," *Orientalia* 19 (1950), p. 368 and fig. 25; Robichon, Barguet, and Leclant, *Karnak-Nord IV,* fasc. 1, p. 20, and figs. 40, 41, and 42a.

That we might know how to read all this is, for the time being, less important than knowing that all has been said there; thus, we can learn how to approach the thought of these masters who were able, and who dared, to raise such a monument. This temple is still in good enough condition for us to be able to learn a great deal from it, except for, of course, what was deliberately effaced by sages who saw no reason to put within reach of the unworthy what is reserved for those who recognize only the Unique as the sole value worthy of being investigated.

Part 6

PLATES, LEGENDS, AND COMMENTARIES

. . . the use of images as signs for the expression of thought leaves the meaning of this writing . . . as clear and accessible as it was the day it was chiseled in stone; for a seat, a falcon, a vulture, a piece of cloth, a placenta, a leg, or a human posture will never change so long as there are people on earth. This [is] . . . sacred writing.

(Chapter 2)

Let us look at each thing in its natural name. This name is written—it is the Symbol—but it cannot be uttered; it speaks for itself.

 To explain the Symbol is to kill it, it is to take it only for its appearance, it is to avoid listening to it.

(Introduction)

PLATE 1

Stele of Suti-Hor

Chapter 26

AMUN AND SUTI-HOR

AMUN, SOURCE OF BIRTHS,
CREATOR OF THE *NETERS*

Amun, creative Verb, ternary Unity, Amun, the unknowable,
He makes Eternity by closing the ring of Becoming and Return,
He makes Existence, He who is the Being, the Being who animates, Father of the Neters.
He is in the nourishing Water of things,
He is that which in things receives nourishment.
All that exists is from Amun, all is offered to Him.
He appears in Horakhty who opens the doors of Knowledge,
The colors Black and Green and White and Red are of Amun, Master of the Four Winds.
Amun is the Life of the ocean waters of the world, Nun.
He, the imponderable, contracts himself into that which is weight,
Amun, the unknowable, is seed and matrix of all things.

Amen.

(Inspired by the litanies to Amun carved on the east wall of the court of Ramesses in the temple of Luxor.)

FRONTISPIECE • STATUE OF AMUN AND MUT

This statue, in white limestone, is located at the entry to the nave (the knees), on the west side, facing toward the sunrise.

SUTI-HOR:
THE ORIGINAL BUILDERS

Plate 1 • Stele of Suti-Hor

Standard Egyptology provides a historical context for the brothers Suti and Hor, who are said to have played a preeminent role as architects in the reign of Amenhotep III and directed the works of Amun in Luxor, as the stele specifies.

On this granite stele, presently in the British Museum (no. 838), it is impossible to see the figures of Suti and Hor, which were effaced during ancient times. Suti and Hor parallel Seth and Horus, the two aspects of the archangel fallen to earth.[1] We discover them again in the preestablished plan of the pylon drawn on the east and west faces of the wall separating room VI, the room of Amun's barque, from room II, the room of purifications and crowning.

—∿∿—

As an homage to the memory of our friend and collaborator, Alexandre Varille, we give here his translation, done in 1942, of the "Hymn to the Sun" from the stele of Suti-Hor. If he were still with us, he would know how to evaluate the living meaning hidden in this text under the historical form.

Hymn to the Sun

Salute to Amun when he rises as Horus of the eastern horizon by Amun's master of the works Suti, and by master of the works Hor. They say:

"Homage to you who is the perfect Ra of each day, who rises each morning without respite, and who is the Khepri burdened with work. We have your rays in our eyes and are not able to perceive them. The most pure gold is not comparable to your splendor. Carver whom you carved yourself, you have cast your own body, O sculptor who has never been sculpted. You who are alone in your species, you who travel over the heights of eternity, and under whose Image are the ways of millions, such is your splendor, such is the splendor of the firmament; your colors are more brilliant than its colors.

"When in navigating you traverse the heavens, all men contemplate you; you continue (under the earth as well) hidden to their eyes. You present yourself in the morning as a daily task. The navigation of your barque is impeccable, under Your Majesty. In a short day you devour a space of millions of hundreds of thousands of miles. Each day is for you but a moment, and after traveling through it, you retire. In the same way you accomplish the hours of the night. You carry out this course without respite from your efforts.

"All eyes see by your grace; and they cease to see when Your Majesty is retired. You put beings in movement in order to emerge. Your rays create the morning; they open the eyes that awaken. You lie down in the regions of Manu, and at the same instant they sleep as if they were dead.

"Homage to you, Disk [Aten] of the day, who has created humans and who has given them life. Grand falcon of speckled plumage who has come in order to raise himself up by his own means, appearing of his own accord without being put in the world, Horus the elder who is in the middle of the celestial Nut, for whom gestures of joy are made at the rising as at the setting.

---

[1] Suti and Hor speak sometimes in the plural and other times in the singular, as if they were a single person, the fallen archangel.

"Founder of what produces the ground, Khnum, Amun of humans, who carries along with him the inhabitants of the Two Lands, from the greatest to the smallest. Beneficent mother of the Gods and of men, patient and untiring worker when he makes them in incalculable number. Valiant herdsman who leads his beasts; their shelter, he who gives them life.

"He who hurries, he who runs, he who accomplishes his revolutions, Khepri of the illustrious birth, raising his perfection in the belly of celestial Nut; giving light to the Two Lands from his Disk [Aten], the primordial of the Two Lands, who created himself and who saw himself while he was creating himself.

"Unique master, who reaches the extremity of the earths each day, viewed by those who circle on them, emerging as a figure who contemplates from on high what passes during the day. He composes the seasons with months, sets the atmosphere ablaze to his liking, makes the freshness of the air to his liking. He causes the human body to extend or to retract. The whole earth gesticulates like the monkeys who awaken at his rising each day to salute him."

The master of works, Suti, [or] the master of works, Hor, he says:

"I am master in your Apit and director of works in your official sanctuary, which your son has made whom you love, the master of the Two Lands, Nebmaātre,[2] gifted with life. My master has confided in me the direction of your monuments, knowing my vigilance. I have been an energetic master, in what concerns your monuments, having done things in conformity with your desires, because I know that you take pleasure in the observances of Maāt. You make great he who practices it on earth; and, as I have practiced it, you have made me great. You have accorded me favors on earth in Karnak, because I take part in your retinue when you show yourself in public. I am an equitable man who has a horror of injustices. There is no man who prides himself on the words of a liar, and in particular my brother, my double, with whom I share opinions, because he came out of the belly (at the same time as me) on this blessed day."

The director of Amun's works in Luxor, Suti [or] Hor [he says:] "Whereas I am the master in the west, he is master in the east [and vice versa]. We are to direct great monuments in Apit, to the south of Thebes, city of Amun. Allow me to grow old in your city, to act by ruling myself according to your perfection, to be at the west place of the heart's peace. That I may be united with the favorites, continuing my way in peace. Give me a soft wind at the time of boarding, and may I receive the headbands on the day of the *wag* festival."[3]

---

[2] Neb-maāt-re is one of the names of Amenhotep III.

[3] Alexandre Varille, *Hymne au Soleil des architects d'Amenophis III, Suti et Hor,* Bulletin de l'I.F.A.O. (Cairo, 1942).

Chapter 27

GENERAL VIEWS OF THE TEMPLE OF LUXOR

—∿—

Plates 2–11

The whole universe is held in a single gesture.
Here, consecrating a temple is identical to giving
life to the terrestrial body and, generally speaking,
animating in the sense of the highest science.

(Chapter 30)

PLATE 2

Aerial View of the Temple of Luxor

. . . the temple of Luxor is conceived in its length
as a sequence of phases of growth.

Taken together, pharaonic temples, throughout
the whole of this empire extending the length of
the Nile, represent an overall teaching; each temple
can be seen as a particularly developed theme or
chapter.

(Chapter 25)

PLATE 3

Aerial View of the Temple from the North

*The history of the monument seen as time-genesis
is intermingled with the theological esotericism
described by myth and given expression through
the geometry (the cosmic measures) of numbers.*

(Chapter 13)

PLATE 4

The Temple Seen from the Northeast

Pharaonic Egypt is essentially practical.
It deals with Nature and works with
natural means, in which it sees the symbols of
spiritual states, knowable only intuitively.

(Chapter 2)

PLATE 5

Part of the Colonnade of the Hypostyle Room

Through the geometry and proportions of the plane, numbers, the stages of consciousness from the abstract to the physically concrete, symbolized by the registers of the walls and the principles inscribed on the architraves, allow for everything to be said in volume.

(Chapter 25)

. . . hieratic symbolism chooses from nature the most typical minerals, plants, and animals for functional expression.

(Chapter 18)

PLATE 6

Part of the West Colonnade of the Transept (Peristyle Court)

Knowledge can only be synthetic; because of this
it can only be intelligibly transcribed by the archi-
tectural monument, that is, by a simultaneity
of plane and volume, *accomplished in Egypt*
through the symbolique *of the writing, the image,*
and the statuary.

(Chapter 24)

PLATE 7

The Colonnade of Amun and the Southwest Corner of the Court of Ramesses

Whether it was a question of spirit, life, cosmogony, theology, or geometry . . . in general, the pharaonic sages did not conceive of any separation in principle among these domains.

(Chapter 5)

PLATE 8

Two Colossi from the South Portico of the Court of Ramesses

*. . . the empire of the pharaonic sages is so mar-
velously instructive, for it recounts the cosmic genesis and all the revelations of the spirit through its
forms, names, and works—the* symbolique *of its
existence.*

(Elements)

PLATE 9

North Facade of the West Wing of the Pylon

This empire is a book that speaks of the slightest nuances of thought, just as the ancient temples and our cathedrals are books that speak through their architecture and figurations.

(Elements)

PLATE 10

Pylon and Eastern Obelisk

Being consecrated to a definite principle, an
Egyptian temple becomes what might be called
a "library," summarizing, in an exhaustive
manner, all that can be known about that subject.

(Chapter 24)

PLATE 11A

Avenue of Sphinxes, View from the East

PLATE 11B

Avenue of Sphinxes, View from the North

Chapter 27

GENERAL VIEWS
OF THE
TEMPLE OF LUXOR

The architectural or pictorial inscription of the pharaohs has no more an immediate, didactic goal than does the apple tree, the fruit of which is an apple and not a peach. The inscription is the description of the phases of knowledge, that is, of the cosmic genesis, expressed in radiant forms, speaking simultaneously of all aspects, from the physical to the spiritual.

—⁓—

At first glance, the architecture of the temple of Luxor is disconcerting. From the south sanctuary to the north pylon the axis continually deviates. Nearly every enclosure on the plan is irregular; what seems to be square has a rhomboidal form; the space between columns sometimes enlarges in the direction of the sanctuary, thus modifying the effect of perspective. Furthermore, the entire construction is executed in several phases. We could call the temple of Luxor a parthenon on the basis of its kinship in principle with the Parthenon of Athens. Its preferred designation is "theogamic" temple; but it is actually, in the profound sense of its consecration, the true Parthenon, that is, the temple dedicated to the spiritual conception of Man.[1]

Even though they never acquiesced to aesthetic considerations, but only to the reality of the symbol, the pharaonic builders always achieved masterpieces of harmony, even in the intentional deformities and distortions required to create symbolic and geometrical precision.

For them nothing was sensual, and this shocks our Western aesthetic sense. All becomes didactic, of an esoteric character, through the correct *symbolique;* it is a teaching for the understanding, for the pure intellect, which no explicit word can describe.

---

[1] Parthenogenesis is taken here in the sense of "creation," not in the "zoological" meaning of being male and female at the same time, as is the case with androgynous mollusks.

We have a great many proofs that nothing in their work was the result of negligence, chance, or personal fantasy, enough to cause us to look for the hidden meaning under apparent disorder. To avoid this research would be to miss the point of archaeology, which is to learn what the past has to teach us, not to impose our own concepts on the Ancients.

The temple of Luxor can be compared with a Gothic cathedral. But in Christian architecture one must not confuse the basilica with the cathedral taken in the sense of the "high place of teaching." Karnak is the royal temple of synthesis; *Luxor is the cathedral of high teaching.*

The general plan of the cathedral corresponds to a precise canon: two towers, a narthex, a nave triple in principle with seven windows, and on the walls of which would later be drawn the Stations of the Cross. Then comes the transept and the entrance proper to the sanctuary.

The choir, separated from the transept by the rood screen, is itself divided according to the importance of the worship, with the altar being the table of daily sacrifice, and the repository carrying the Sacred Host in its silver, moon-shaped barque. In churches with the privilege to celebrate the papal mass, the bishop has his throne behind the altar, hidden from the public. It is there that he celebrates the sacrifice, as in the Holy of Holies (as is the case in Orthodox worship).

The arrangement of the temple of Luxor is identical to that found in the canon of the Gothic cathedral.[2] A double pylon here replaces the two towers; the court of Ramesses is the narthex; and the two rows of seven high columns with opened corollas together with the two side aisles, the walls of which are decorated with bas-reliefs depicting the procession of the barques, form the nave. After the nave with the two rows of seven columns comes the peristyle, jutting out to the east and west, forming a cross (the transept);[3] then comes the covered temple and its striking parallel with the choir of the cathedral.

The high altar, here represented by the naos that contains the sacred barque (symbolizing the lunar crossing) is found in the choir proper, room VI, with rooms IV and VIII taking the place of the front choir. Originally, the room for the naos did not connect to the rooms to the south.[4]

The side chambers, linked by room XII, recall the ambulatory around the choir; the twenty-seven small chapels opening onto the chambers indicated above would correspond to the "radiating chapels." Finally, the central sanctuary, room I, where the statue of Amun is found, is located in the place of the apsidal chapel.

The old tradition required the choir to be separated from the transept by a rood screen, and the ambulatory itself could be closed by decorative works such as wrought-iron grills, tombs, and so on. At Luxor there is no connection except for the central door opening into room VI, between what we call the "choir" and the rest of the temple; the chapels destined to receive the barques of Khonsu, Mut, and the king are only connected with the great hypostyle hall. It is thus these last chambers, along with room VIII and the two small adjoining chambers, that would constitute the rood screen of the cathedral.

[2] Cf. plate 2, aerial photograph of the temple and its surrounding walls, and fig. 198, plan of the temple giving the names of its different parts and the numbers of the rooms; also fig. 283.

[3] Customarily, a more learned etymological meaning for *trans-saeptum* is "beyond the enclosure." One forgets that the nave is septuple in length.

[4] This is noted by Pierre Lacau in *Le Plan du temple de Louqsor,* Mémoires de l'Académie des Inscriptions et Belles Lettres 18, no. 2 (1941).

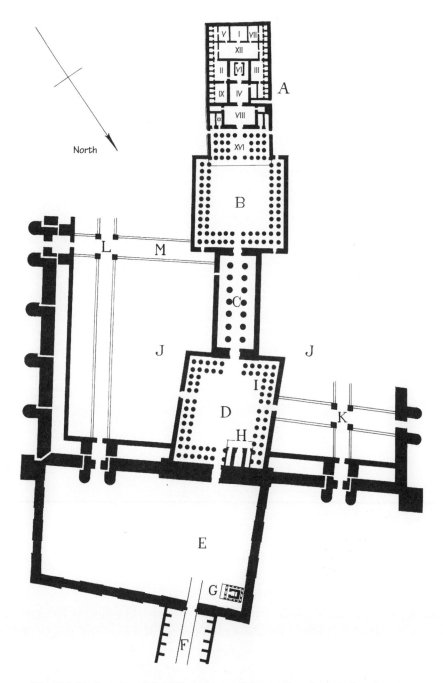

Fig. 198. Designation of the different parts of the temple and numbering of rooms

A, covered temple; *B*, peristyle (transept); *C*, great colonnade (nave); *D*, court of Ramesses, (narthex); *E*, courtyard of Nectanebo (parvis); *F*, avenue of the human-headed sphinxes; *G*, domus of Isis; *H*, repository of the barques, chapel of the reflection of Amun; *I*, bas-reliefs of the royal princes' ascent to the temple; *J*, Roman fortress; *K*, crossroads of Aquarius; *L*, crossroads of Scorpio; *M*, *via vitae*.

Rooms: V, I, VII, the three sacred sanctuaries; XII, room of the solar journey; II, room of animation and of the crowning; VI, sanctuary of the barque; III, room of the descent into the Dwat, partly destroyed; IX, room of the royal conception (theogamy); IV, room of offerings (the four elements); VIII, room of transformations, of solar character; XVI, hypostyle room (the *haty*); XX, chamber of Mut.

This rood screen includes stairways to the right and left. In the temple of Luxor a stairway remains to the west and some indications show that in the original construction there may have been another stairway to the east.

—⁓—

In the following pages we will describe the bas-reliefs as they appear to the uninitiated and in the way that they are still seen in our day by most Egyptologists, but we should not forget that we are dealing with gestures in the symbolic sense that must be interpreted according to their vital intent.

Plate 2 • Aerial View of the Temple of Luxor

This aerial view was taken on September 18, 1945, by the Egyptian Army Air Force.[5] The court-yard of Nectanebo and the avenue of sphinxes are not shown, as these were only excavated in 1949–50.

This photograph allows us to see the location of the eastern part of the Roman wall with its towers, today concealed under a garden. We can also notice the four pillars at the crossings of the roadways executed by the Romans to the east and west of the temple (fig. 198, *K* and *L*).

In 1881 the temple of Luxor was not yet excavated; only the southern part was visible. In 1885, G. Maspero, director of the Service of Antiquities, undertook the work of excavation. This work was continued periodically until 1945 by Grébaut, de Morgan, Legrain, Daressy, Baraize, Ahmed Fakhry, and Labib Habachi. In 1949–50, Zakaria Goneim uncovered the courtyard of Nectanebo north of the pylon and the beginning of the avenue of sphinxes going toward Karnak.

Plate 3 • Aerial View of the Temple from the North

This photograph shows the Roman wall east of the temple, with its towers, the door, and the crossing roadways.

To the west the Roman door can be seen, giving access to the north-south lane that, bordered by columns, crosses the east-west lane leading from the loading dock to the narthex. A few blocks from this dock are visible at the edge of the Nile.

Exterior Bas-reliefs

Doubtlessly, none of the exterior walls of the temple had any bas-reliefs under Amenhotep III. It was during the Ramesses period that the east and west faces of the covered temple were decorated, leaving the exterior walls east of the nave and transept in their unfinished state.

Ramesses II constructed the narthex as well as the pylon, the exterior walls of which are covered with bas-reliefs relating (according to the official version) tales of his battles against "foreign countries," particularly the battle of Kadesh, a city that has been located in the valley of the Orontes in northern Syria.

Figure 199 shows the location of the bas-reliefs in the temple of Luxor cited in this work (circled numbers) and the numbers of the corresponding plates.

[5] This and the following photograph were taken at our request through the intermediary of Alexandre Varille.

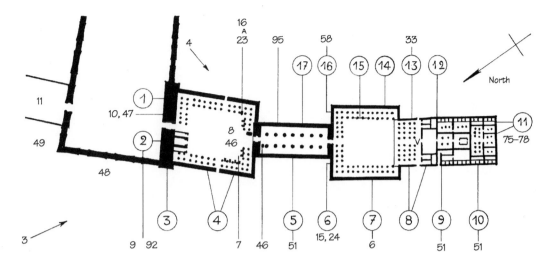

Fig. 199. Location of the bas-reliefs and corresponding plates

1. On the east wing of the pylon, a depiction of the battle of Kadesh in the valley of the Orontes. Near the door between the two wings of the pylon, eight archers in nine chariots, each harnessed to a pair of horses, can be related to the theme of the "nine bows" on which the king rests his feet (plates 10 and 47B).
2. On the west wing of the pylon, a depiction of the Egyptian camp south of the city of Kadesh. This scene has been modified while allowing the lines of the preceding bas-relief to remain (plates 9 and 92).
3. Bas-reliefs removed from the west face of the pylon.
4. Ramesside bas-reliefs.
5. A figure on a horse, riding sidesaddle, preceding a line of chariots. This is a very rare representation whose appearance at this point of the temple has a symbolic meaning in relationship with the projection of the Man of the Temple (plate 51B).
6. Bas-relief depicting the foreign prisoners whose hands have been severed. The location of this scene of "severed hands" in this particular place coincides with the height of the wrist of the man projected on the temple (plates 15 and 24).
7. Representation of thirteen pairs of horses harnessed to thirteen chariots (plate 6).
8. Part of the base of the covered temple, left unfinished.
9. Beginning of the dedication of Amenhotep III, carved on the exterior periphery of the subfoundation of the covered temple (plate 51B).
10. A passage in the text of the dedication that mentions a gold statue of Amun with a ram's head, found in sanctuary I (plate 51B).
11. Bas-relief entirely remade by an Ethiopian king of the Twenty-fifth Dynasty. The kings of this dynasty are characterized by the fact that they wear a double uraeus, and it is noteworthy that the bas-reliefs recarved by one of them are located in the temple at the level of room V, related to the royal uraeus (plates 75 to 78).
12. End of the dedication on the base of the platform.
13. Exterior wall of the hypostyle room upon which bas-reliefs of all sizes are carved in no particular order. Some "pieces" of stone are embedded in them as proof of more ancient monuments underlying the various parts of the bodies of the figures (plate 33).

14. The exterior wall of the peristyle court remained in unhewn stone under Amenhotep III and was never finished.

15. Text inscribed on the architrave of the east colonnade of the peristyle court, relating that the temple is the place of the birth of the king, where he was reared as a child and from where he would leave, crowned.

16. Representation of the *kamutef* carved during an undetermined period (plate 58).

17. Exterior east wall of the nave, remaining unfinished from the time of Amenhotep III (plate 95).

Figure 199 also indicates the position in the temple of Luxor of the following plates: 3, aerial view from the north; 4, the temple seen from the northeast; 5, part of the colonnade of the hypostyle room; 7, southeast corner of the court of Ramesses; 8, colossus no. 4; 11, avenue of the human-headed sphinxes; 16 to 23, colossus no. 3; 46, seated black colossus and statue of Amun and Mut; 48 and 49, courtyard of Nectanebo.

PLATE 4 • THE TEMPLE SEEN FROM THE NORTHEAST

In this photograph, one notices that the exterior east walls of the transept and the nave have remained unfinished.

To the left, one can see the four bases that supported the columns topped by statues of emperors and erected during the Roman era (fig. 213).

On the right, in the foreground, can be seen the tomb of Abu el-Haggag, the Muslim sheikh about whom legends and the tradition of certain rites, perpetuated to our day, go back to the pharaonic era. Thus, in the court of this mosque, between the capitals of the Ramesses columns that had been used to support them, some barques can still be found. These are modern replicas of the three sacred barques that were kept in ancient times in the three chapels set against the west wing of the pylon in the interior of the court of Ramesses.

Every year on the feast day of Abu el-Haggag, these barques, filled with children, promenade around the city. This recalls the procession of the sacred barques coming from Karnak to Luxor on certain days of the year.

This procession is depicted on the interior walls of the nave. The journey from Karnak to Luxor is depicted along the west wall (right thigh), and the return to Karnak is drawn on the east wall (left thigh).

At the departure from Karnak, the three barques of Amun, Mut, and Khonsu, accompanied by the king's barque, are carried on the shoulders of the priests; they are then deposited in four large boats. The boats are drawn along the waterway by means of oars or a towline from the bank, where a large retinue accompanies them. At the head of the procession, a priest chants a hymn in honor of Amun. Then come the "functions," symbolized by soldiers, standard-bearers, guitar players, players of boomerang-shaped clappers, and so on. In the midst of those hauling the boat, some men drop to their knees when the sacred barques pass.

On the occasion of this grand ceremony, horned cattle are sacrificed and certain choice cuts are presented as offerings, just as it appears that they are still offered in our day to the sheikh of the mosque.

On their arrival at Luxor, the sacred barques enter the temple and are placed in the three repositories of the court of Ramesses. In the covered temple, the barques of Amun, Mut, and Khonsu are represented in room IV, carried by priests in windblown robes with no other officiant than the king, who perfumes them with incense (plate 31).

PLATE 5 • PART OF THE COLONNADE OF THE HYPOSTYLE ROOM (SEEN FROM THE SOUTH)

The roof of the hypostyle room is open at the north and is supported by thirty-two papyriform columns arranged in two groups of sixteen. The shafts of these columns are composed of eight stems united at the upper part by five ties. The capital is formed by the extension of these eight stems. This form of column is also found in the covered temple and in the transept constructed by Amenhotep III.

The text of "Giving the House to Its Master" is located on the second register of the east wall in this room (plate 30). Under the dedicatory frieze encircling this hypostyle room, the enumeration of the nomes of Upper and Lower Egypt is carved, fragments of which remain on the east, south, and west walls.

Here, we are in the *haty,* the chest, which contains the heart and the lungs: respiration. The binding of the two Lands, Upper and Lower Egypt[6] is made around the sign *sma.* Now the binding *(sma)* is made around the trachea, which culminates in a symbol that represents the lungs *(sma).* It is through respiration that the fixation of the spirit and the reanimation of the blood is made.[7]

PLATE 6 • PART OF THE WEST COLONNADE OF THE TRANSEPT (PERISTYLE COURT)

The wall that borders the transept on the west side is located at the place of the spinal column.[8] Depicted on this wall are thirteen pairs of harnessed horses, extending to the height of the thirteenth, or first lumbar, vertebra.[9] The marrow that runs through the twelve thoracic vertebrae penetrates the first lumbar vertebra, from which comes the bundle of lumbar and sacral nerves that terminate it. In anatomy, this place is called the "horse's tail."

Here we see the vertebrae and their marrow symbolized by the wheel of a chariot drawn by moving horses, one of whose front legs (either left or right) is poised and abnormally rigid on the point of the hoof, while the other foot penetrates forward into the wheel of the next chariot.

On the basis of this *symbolique,* we have concluded that each time we encounter a series of chariots harnessed in this way, we can relate them to the marrow or to an influence on the central nervous system.[10] Thus, we recall the direct relationship between the central nervous system and the sole of the foot, that is, the north face of the pylon, where a vertical series of harnessed horses

---

[6] Cf. plate 46 and fig. 295, the representation of the two sides of the throne of the seated colossus, of the union of the Two Lands around the sign *sma.*

[7] *sma-wi:* "to renew."

[8] Cf. plates 15, 24, 28, and chapter 40, "The Three Axes."

[9] That is, twelve thoracic and one lumbar vertebrae.

[10] Let us recall here that the horse, the essential symbol of the Poseidonian initiation (cf. the front of the Parthenon at Athens), represents the living Amunian water, here the cerebrospinal fluid that bathes the marrow. The foal is born in the amniotic sac, which the mare shreds with her teeth after the birth, and the foal comes out streaming with water.

is carved. This fact caused me to state in *The Temple in Man* that the Ancients were aware of the nervous reaction called Babinski's reflex, the reaction that discloses an interruption in the central nervous system.

Now, with the Edwin Smith Surgical Papyrus, translated with commentary by Breasted, we have proof that the Ancients had this knowledge, which has only been classified by our scientists since Babinski's time.[11]

PLATE 7 • THE COLONNADE OF AMUN AND THE SOUTHWEST CORNER OF THE COURT OF RAMESSES

In each intercolumnar space of the porticos of this court there is a standing colossus with its left leg forward. Two seated colossi in black granite are placed framing the entrance of the nave at the knees of the Man of the Temple.

In the nave there is a double row of seven bell-shaped columns supporting the roof. These columns, from Amenhotep III, are composed of a single stem of papyrus, and the capitals are flowers in full bloom. Three fine ribs run the length of the cylindrical shafts, recalling the characteristics of this Cyperaceae.

On the right, toward the Nile, are vestiges of Christian buildings.

On the left, in the lower part of the photograph, is the edge of the roof of the Abu el-Haggag mosque.[12]

PLATE 8 • TWO COLOSSI FROM THE SOUTH PORTICO OF THE COURT OF RAMESSES

The monolithic colossus[13] on the the right, bearing cartouches of Ramesses II on its loincloth, its shoulders, and its belt buckle, is cut out of a block of rose granite that rests directly on the ground, and today is slightly buried. The total height of the block is about 8.64 meters, that is, $4\frac{2}{3}$ fathoms or 28 *djezer* cubits of the black cubit.[14]

All the dimensions of this colossus are derived from the fathom. Its essential measure is the height measured from the soles of the feet to the forehead, corresponding to the upper edge of the ears of the colossus and at the level of the eighteenth square of a figuration on a *canevas*. This height is 5.55 meters, or 3 mean fathoms.

The line that determines the forehead (presently visible near the right ear) marks the base of the white crown that fits tightly around the king's head. Now the height of three fathoms is the unit of measure that determines, on one hand, the height of the crowned king, and on the other, his division at the navel according to the golden section:

$$\frac{\text{height of the crowned king}}{\text{height of the king to the forehead}} = \frac{7.06 \text{ meters}}{5.55 \text{ meters}} = \sqrt{\phi}$$

$$\frac{\text{height of the king to the forehead}}{\text{height of the navel}} = \frac{5.55 \text{ meters}}{3.43 \text{ meters}} = \phi.$$

[11] See case 8 of the Surgical Papyrus, chapter 14.

[12] Cf. plate 4 and legend.

[13] The colossi are numbered starting from the northeast corner of the court of Ramesses. This one is no. 5.

[14] On the one hand, the pedestal is covered with saltpeter, and on the other, its very acute slope does not allow greater precision than several centimeters in its measurement. The dimensions given here are established according to the average level taken on the cleared places of the stone at the level of the front foot.

The left colossus (no. 4), the head of which is destroyed, is characterized by very sharp sculpting that gives it very precise dimensions. The pleated loincloth and the beveled edge of the dorsal stele, for example, are remarkable for their distinctness and are astonishing to find in a hard white, red, and black granite that is very rich in large, white crystals. A black vein in the granite makes a bracelet around the king's left wrist.

Quite probably from Tuthmosis, this colossus today carries cartouches of Ramesses II, who had altered the pedestal as well as the dorsal stele and carved a figure of the queen in bas-relief on the backing under the left leg. The king rests his feet on nine bows, five under the back (right) foot and four under the front.[15] The tail, *sed,* between his legs, is sculpted in fine waves and still shows traces of red and yellow paint.

Ramesses II recarved his cartouche in sunk relief at the place of the old cartouche on the belt. A necklace of five rows of pearls encircles the shoulders of the colossus. His breasts are widely aureoled.

The bottom of the nipples is exactly 4 meters from the soles of the feet.

The fastener of the left fist, measured in front, close to the thigh, is 2.22 meters from the pedestal, which is 1.2 mean fathoms. The bottom of the navel is 3.33... meters from the soles of the feet, which is 1.8 mean fathoms.

The height of the queen confirms the fact that the fathom is the unit of measure that governs this colossus. From the soles of the feet to the vertex she measures 1.84 meters, which is exactly 1 fathom at 0°. From under her sandals to the vertex, her height is 1.85 meters, which is 1 mean fathom.

Her height to the top of the plumes of her crown is 2.50 meters. As with the king, the meter and the fathom are associated, which is understandable if we remember that 27 mean fathoms equal 50 meters.

PLATE 9 • NORTH FACADE OF THE WEST WING OF THE PYLON

On the left we can see the right post of the doorway, the lintel of which is now broken, but the ledge of whose cornice is still visible. Below, two vertical grooves held the two flagpoles resting on granite pedestals. These flagpoles reached above the pylon and flew cloth streamers from their tops.[16] They were held in place by heavy wooden beams going across the thickness of the pylon in openings above the grooves. These flagpoles, which must have been more than a meter in diameter, were made by assembling pieces of wood covered with a thickness of bronze plating. They were intended "to receive the four winds."[17]

The north facade of the west wing of the pylon is covered with scenes and inscriptions, distributed in the following way: Under the torus, two horizontal lines of text frame the uraeus frieze, alternating with cartouches of Ramesses II.

Under the openings reserved for holding the flagpoles, there is an immense tableau, bounded above by the sky and below by a band of water, and occupying the entire width of this wing. This scene essentially represents the royal camp established in the Orontes Valley, in northern Syria, a little to the south of Kadesh, just as Ramesses II prepares to engage the Hittites in battle.[18]

Starting from the horizontal band that depicts the water as far as the bottom of the pylon, the entire facade is divided into vertical columns of text that recount the events of this battle.

---

[15] Cf. plate 47.

[16] Cf. fig. 268.

[17] It may be interesting to note here the Chinese saying, "The flag floats in the wind. Who moves it?" The response is, "It is neither the flag nor the wind; it is the spirit."

[18] Cf. fig. 291.

The Egyptian army, commanded in person by the king, contained four divisions: the division of Amun, that of Ra, and those of Ptah and Seth. The king established his camp and left for reconnaissance. He then met two Bedouins who came to him and said that they were envoys of the tribal chiefs subjugated by the prince of Khatti whom he was preparing to fight. These Bedouins indicated the exact position of the prince of Khatti, and affirmed that the chiefs of the tribes, their brothers, desired to submit to the authority of the pharaoh and abandon their former master.

Now these two Bedouins were spies in the service of the prince of Khatti, delegated by him to give false information and to indicate to him the exact position of Ramesses II's encampment. In truth, the enemy army was hiding in ambush near Kadesh, as a spy in Ramesses' service hastened to inform him, revealing the true character of the two Bedouin spies. They were thrashed until they finally confessed that the prince of Khatti was allied with numerous neighboring countries and that his armies were admirably equipped with foot soldiers, archers, and assault chariots, "numerous as the sands."

While the king was hearing of this treachery, the greater part of his army, not knowing of all this, was attacked by surprise and retreated toward the position occupied by His Majesty.

> It was in this way that the army of the prince of Khatti enveloped the people in His Majesty's escort, who were close to him. But when His Majesty became aware of them, he entered into a rage against them, like his father Month, the master of Thebes. He seized his war attire and he put on his armor; he resembled Baal in his wrath. Then he mounted his chariot, and drove it at great speed, all alone. He plunged into the army of the prince of Khatti and all his numerous allied peoples. His Majesty was similar to Seth, the powerful, as he battled and massacred them. After cutting them to pieces, His Majesty threw them one on top of another into the tides of the Orontes.[19]

The large tableau on the left indeed shows the king, seated on a throne, debating with his subjects while the two spies are given a flogging. To the right, behind the king, we see the camp formed by a surrounding wall of raised shields, in the middle of which rises the royal tent. The whole camp is filled with unharnessed horses and resting soldiers, while a line of chariots enters through the east door representing the attack of the Hittites. The battle of the Orontes is represented on the east wing of the pylon.

The representations conform with the story, so it is troubling to observe that this north wall of the west wing has undergone a major alteration by Ramesses himself. Originally, at the place in which the two essential scenes—the king seated on his throne, and his camp—are presently located could be found, respectively, Ramesses II seated, but facing the opposite direction, and the king standing in his chariot, drawing his bow. Traces of the older sculpture are still very visible and mark the intention to allow the two superimposed scenes to remain.[20]

PLATE 10 • PYLON AND EASTERN OBELISK

To the left, we find one of the two obelisks that, generally speaking, frame the entrance to the temple. This obelisk is still partially buried, which prohibits us from knowing its dimensions. Its western counterpart is in Paris, at Place de la Concorde.[21] It rested on a rose-granite pedestal, the north and south

[19] Erman and Ranke, *La Civilisation égyptienne*, p. 713.

[20] Cf. chapter 41, the descriptions of the transformations of the bas-reliefs, plate 92, and fig. 291.

[21] The dimensions of the west obelisk given by Lebas are as follows: height of the shaft without the pyramidion, 20.90 m, that is, about 40 cycle cubits (20.94 m); total height with the pyramidion, 22.84 m, a measure related to 44 cubits of 28 *remen* digits, each being 1/100 fathom. We find this measure again in the length between tori of the east wing of the pylon under the cornice (cf. plate 67).

faces of which are ornmentated with four baboons with hands raised in sculpted relief. This granite pedestal is itself placed on a trapezoidal base.

One can see, in the right part of the photograph, the double crown of the seated colossus in black granite east of the door. This colossus is set against a stele, whereas the western one is supported on a small obelisk. The western colossus is sculpted in a block of black granite, chosen in the quarry so that the red crown is carved out of a red vein running through the block.

On the north face of the east wing of the pylon, to the left of the doorpost, we can see nine pairs of horses harnessed to eight chariots, each of which are occupied by a driver and an archer. This symbolizes the nine bows on which the king rests his feet, the pylon coinciding with the sole of the foot of the Man of the Temple. (Cf. plate 47 and fig. 244.)

Plates 11A and 11B • Avenue of Sphinxes (Dromos)

We enter the temple of Luxor by way of the long avenue of sphinxes that begins at Karnak and ends at the esplanade (the parvis) located in front of the pylon. We pass through the door between the two towers of the pylon, against which are supported the colossi, incarnating the *neter*, the spirit within things.

During the excavations of 1949–50, the courtyard added by Nectanebo and the first sphinxes of the avenue leading from Luxor to Karnak were uncovered.[22]

In 1893, Daressy had already noted that in the area occupied by the Luxor city police, a building from the Saitic period was found among some debris, and that the avenue of ram-headed sphinxes, which starts from Karnak and leads to Luxor, at this point undergoes a transformation: the ram's heads were replaced by human-headed sphinxes whose pedestals bear the royal legend of Nectanebo II.

It is the point where this avenue arrives at Luxor that had then been recently discovered. The sphinxes indeed have human heads, which is notable because this avenue belongs to the Temple of Man, whereas the sphinxes on the avenue near its origin at Karnak—the basilica consecrated to Amun, the zodiacal Ram—are bordered by ram-headed sphinxes.

The total width of the dromos is 27 meters, which is 50 black cubits. It contains a roadway in the center, paved in sandstone, whose total width is 6.28 meters, or 12 royal cycle cubits.

Two rows of sphinxes with human heads and the cartouches of Nectanebo II line the dromos. These sphinxes are set against two unfired brick walls, 92 centimeters thick (1/2 fathom) covered with a whitewash that is still visible. These walls closed off public access to this paved road, which continues into the courtyard of Nectanebo.

The entryway to this courtyard is in sandstone, while the walls, about 5 meters thick, are of unfired brick and placed in curved layers so that they form bows both in plan and in cross-section (plates 48 and 49). At the bottom of plate 11B, we can see the pylon, the two seated colossi, and the eastern obelisk.

[22] Cf. plate 2.

Chapter 28

THE GROWTH
OF THE TEMPLE

⟶∿⟵

Plates 12–15

This temple represents what I have called a "prototype" of our great cathedrals. There is a double pylon; a nave of two times seven columns recalling, with the procession of the sacred barque, the fourteen Stations of the Cross; a transept; a choir; and an altar with its barque; then the apse with the secret sanctuaries.

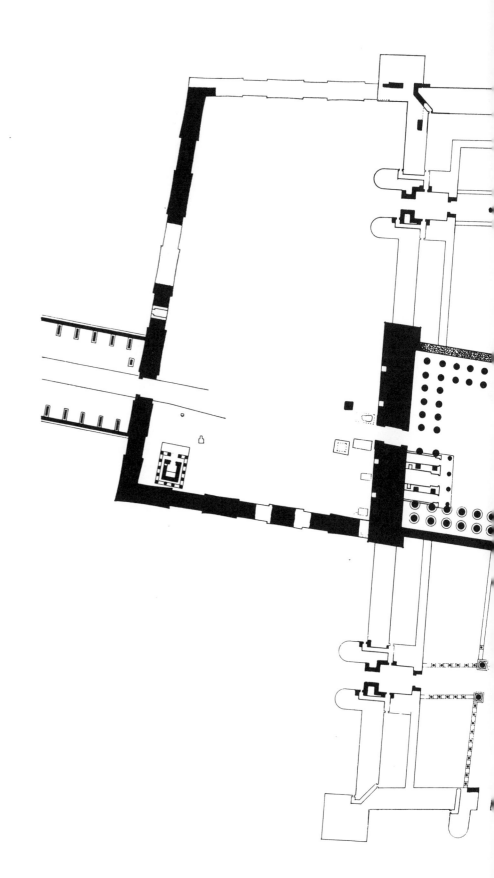

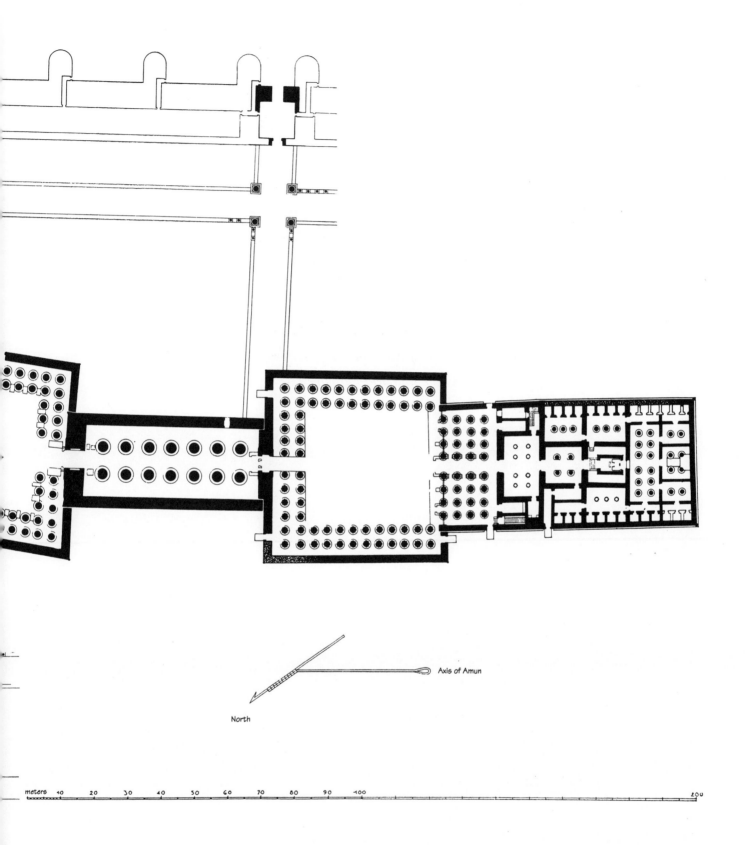

Axis of Amun

North

meters 10   20   30   40   50   60   70   80   90   100   200

PLATE 12

Plan of the Temple in Its Present Condition

Pharaonic thought refuses to build on such an invariable base because life is moving and progressing. Destruction and death are likewise moments of life; *they are transitions, and "tomorrow" contains the past.*

(Chapter 6)

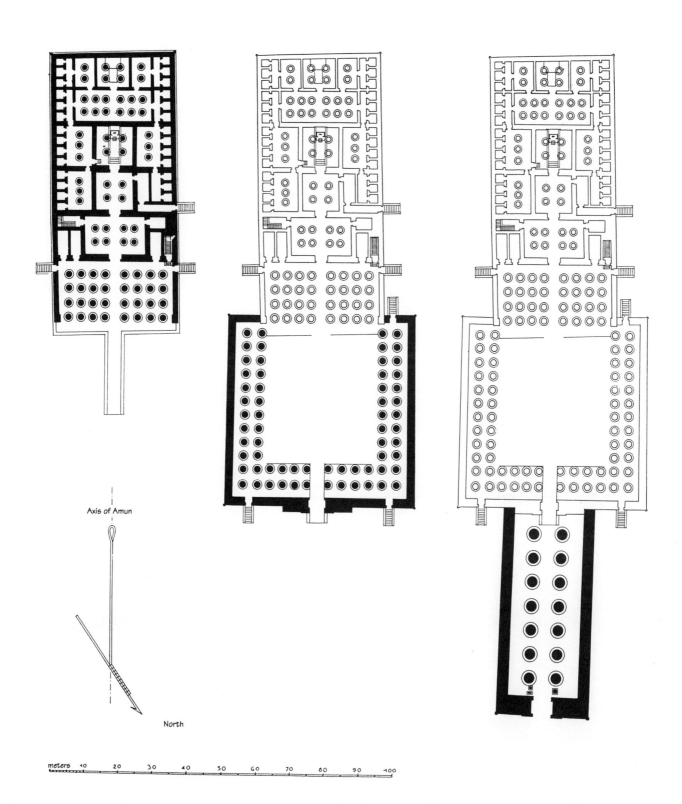

Axis of Amun

North

meters 10   20   30   40   50   60   70   80   90   100

PLATE 13

Plan of the Three Successive Constructions of Amenhotep III

. . . today contains yesterday. The solar genesis contains the terrestrial genesis in one of its periods, and the terrestrial genesis, in one of its periods, contains the genesis of the empire, just as the empire contains in one of its periods the entire human genesis.

(Chapter 20)

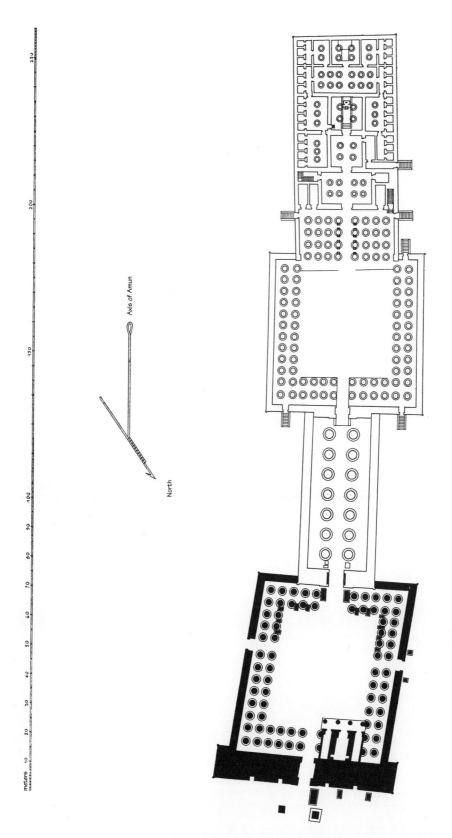

PLATE 14

Plan of the Temple in the Ramesside Period

*Man conceived by the
Creator is Universe.
On his body, senses, organs,
assimilative functions,
and vital nervous centers,
both physical and occult,
all knowledge is inscribed.*
                    (Cf. Chapter 25)

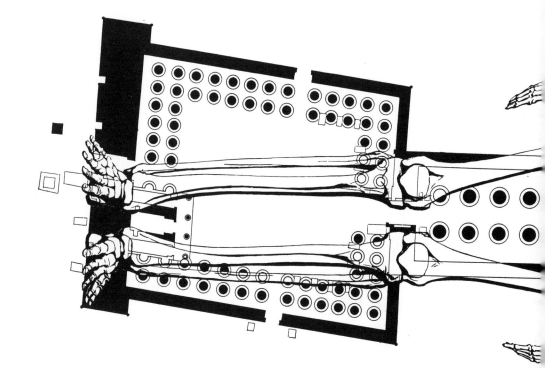

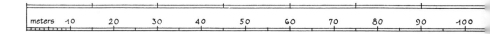

meters 10   20   30   40   50   60   70   80   90   100

Axis of Amun

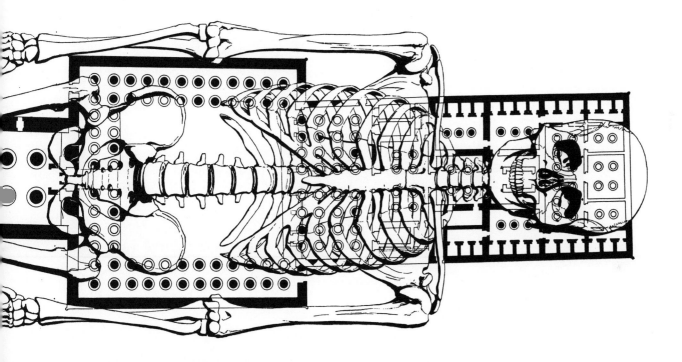

1 meter

Skeleton

200

Temple

PLATE 15

The Temple and the Proportions of Man

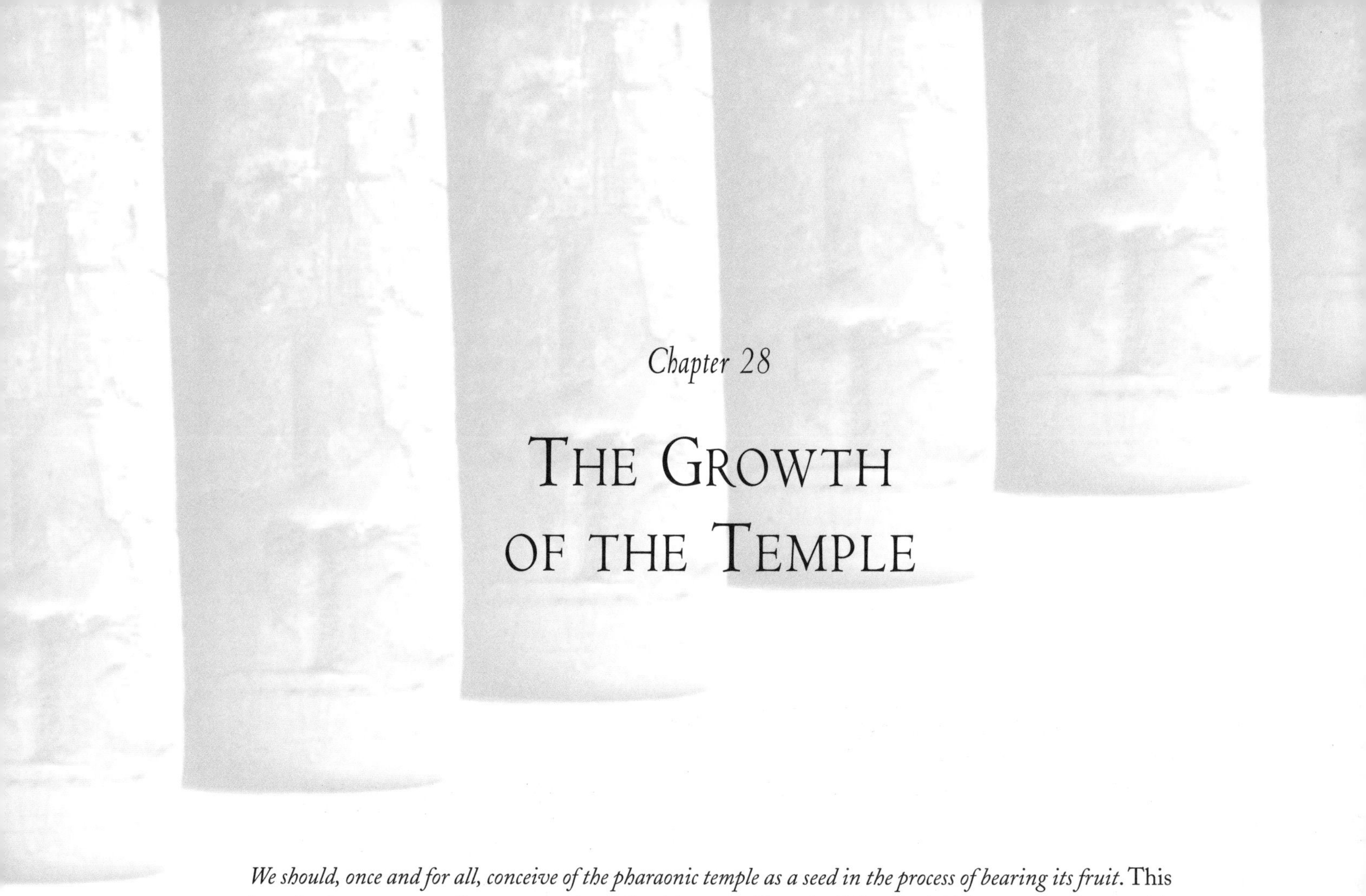

Chapter 28

THE GROWTH
OF THE TEMPLE

We should, once and for all, conceive of the pharaonic temple as a seed in the process of bearing its fruit. This is truly the most grandiose conception of architecture. But a building is rigid by nature. One could, if need be, produce figurations that would bring to mind this gestation, but that would be rational, not vital, as was the spirit of the Ancient Egyptians. For them, every part of a building must be alive. This characteristic of gestation may have been what prompted Herbert Ricke[1] to consider pharaonic architecture as "vegetal." This is correct, since all gestation comprises both growth and vegetation; but this strict framing into a formula, corresponding to the Western mentality, is devoid of life. Growth unfolds in three dimensions; and gestation is a constant transformation until it reaches the perfection of the new seed.

"Man, knowest thou thyself and thou shalt know the Universe and the gods," says the wisdom. In this spirit, it is appropriate also to cite John (2:25): ". . . he could tell what a man had in him."

For his part, did not Moses—who grew up in Egypt—also affirm that "Man is made in the image of God"? Man is then considered as the summation of the Universe. The temple of Luxor was built in order to explain these things.

PLATE 12 • PLAN OF THE TEMPLE IN ITS PRESENT CONDITION

Plate 12 is a precise survey of the temple of Luxor and its surroundings in 1952 and shows the condition of the various structures at the time of their discovery. These include the temple of Amenhotep III, its enlargement with the court of Ramesses and the exterior plyon, the courtyard of Nectanebo, in which we find the chapel of Isis located on the extension of the axis of Amun,

---

[1] Herbert Ricke, *Bemerkungen zur ägyptischen Baukunst des Alten Reichs,* vol. 1 (Zurich: Borchardt Institut, 1944).

578

and, finally, the Roman constructions, the surrounding east wall of which, visible in the aerial photographs, is now under the city garden.[2]

PLATE 13 • PLAN OF THE THREE SUCCESSIVE CONSTRUCTIONS OF AMENHOTEP III

First Phase

On the "tank"-shaped foundation filled with stones from previous buildings, and where the definitive "growth" of the seed thrown into this place will be realized, the platform of the base is established.[3]

On this platform, in accordance with the idea of the temple, the "geometric functions" defining the measures and the principal axes governing the construction will be traced. The unit of measure that provides the geometric foundation will also be used for the face laid out in the pavestone mosaic,[4] and on the outlines etched in this pavement will be raised the walls and columns that rest on the mosaic with no other foundation.

The whole of the covered temple is divided into two unequal parts, the longer of which, toward the south, contains the sanctuaries; the shorter opens toward the north with the hypostyle room, the roofing of which is supported by two times sixteen columns.

Second Phase

Amenhotep III added a square peristyle court to the covered temple, wider than the original structure, and surrounded on the interior east, west, and north faces by a portico of sixty-four columns arranged in double rows.[5] At the time of this construction Amenhotep III removed the dedication on the north face of the platform of the covered temple as well as the long ramp that gave access to it; incidentally, this ramp, envisioned from the beginning, began at the height of the navel of the adult man and gave access to the covered temple representing the infant at birth.

Third Phase

Next, added to the peristyle court—this time constructed lengthwise—was the great colonnade of Amun, the nave, containing a double row of seven columns; this ended the work of Amenhotep III.

PLATE 14 • PLAN OF THE TEMPLE IN THE RAMESSIDE PERIOD

The temple of Amenhotep III was continued widthwise by Ramesses II with the strongly offset court (the narthex), bordered on its four sides by a double row containing seventy-four columns plus four square pillars built into the thickness of the east and west walls of the chapel of Amun's barque, two on the right and two on the left of the axis of Amun and its return.[6] The repositories of the barques of Mut and Khonsu are each side of this chapel.

Today the Abu el-Haggag mosque conceals the bases of the columns of the northeast corner of the court. To the north, this court is bordered by the pylon.

---

[2] Cf. plates 2 and 3.

[3] Cf. plate 94, the various foundations.

[4] Cf. plates 34–37, the pavestone mosaic.

[5] The colonnade of the peristyle court is bordered on the south by the hypostyle room, forming with it a total of ninety-six columns.

[6] Cf. plates 85 and 86.

General Laws of Human Growth

For a long time it has been recognized that the essential characteristic of the phenomena of growth is its discontinuity. On envisioning the whole of an organism or one or another of its parts, one is struck by the fact that development does not progress in a regular and continuous manner, but proceeds, on the contrary, by alternate phases of rest and sudden bursts. The rhythm of these alternations is, moreover, quite irregular and affects a physiognomy in a particular way according to the type of tissue and organ considered. . . .

It is especially with regard to the skeleton that the great *law of alternation* is verified. The long bones thicken for six months and elongate during the following six months. These two phases alternate between the two segments of the same extremity of whatever kind. For example, the bones of the forearm thicken while the humerus elongates, and vice versa. . . .

After birth, there are three periods where growth is particularly rapid. The first occurs during the first year and continues during the second year. The height, which was about 50 centimeters at birth, lengthens by 20 centimeters the first year and by 10 centimeters during the second. At two years, the height is about 80 centimeters. This is three-fifths more than it was at birth and nearly half the size it will attain in adulthood. The second period of lengthening occurs at six or seven years. A last phase of rapid growth occurs around twelve or thirteen years, that is, the time of the first manifestations of puberty. . . .

In the intervals between the periods of lengthening, growth continues at a very decelerated rate. On the other hand, the largest weight gains occur during these times.[7]

This is the alternation of lengthening and thickening, an alternation that we can observe in the successive stages of growth of the temple, one time in length, the next in width.

The first stage of the temple represents the size of the infant at birth. The newborn is characterized by the considerable development of its skull, the volume of which is equal to half of what it will be in adulthood; further, the circumference of the head is 2 to 3 centimeters larger than the thoracic perimeter; and finally, the height of the head of the newborn is contained four times in the total length of the body.

In the temple, the head of the child-king will include the south sanctuaries and room XII, thus all the vital centers[8] whose placement will remain unchanged during the development of the man. These centers do not move during growth, and *it is as if the central organs of life and of the intellect, located in the sanctuaries, were the fixed point that governs the whole growth of the body.*

The height of the infant at birth is divided into two equal parts by the navel. Now, at the halfway point of the length of the covered temple, in room IX, the representations of the "theogamy" and of the childbirth are found.[9] The sex organs, which divide the adult into two equal parts, divide the height of the newborn in the proportion of 3 to 5 (the first F series ratio of ϕ).

The Westcar Papyrus, a prophetic text attributed to the Fourth Dynasty concerning the child-king who would be the head of the lineage of the Fifth Dynasty, gives a cubit for the length of the newborn; now, the royal cubit of 28 digits represents "a cubit plus a palm," which is 7/24 fathom.

The height of the royal infant at birth, according to the ancient tradition, allows one to know his future arm span, thanks to which it is possible to determine his height both to the vertex and without the crown of the skull as an adult, if one knows his personal coefficient.[10]

---

[7] Vandervael, *Biométrie humaine*, pp. 78–82.

[8] Cf. plate 38.

[9] Cf. fig. 223.

[10] Cf. chapter 11.

Numbers and the Growth of the Man of the Temple

We call "seed" the synthesis of all the characteristics that are still potential that this seed is going to gener-
ate. The same is true for the infant child, who is born with all the characteristics, definitively arrested, of
that which it will physically become. Consequently, we must consider the sizes indicated at birth. We will
find there a general law of human growth that vitally summarizes all the fundamental data we have seen
applied in the cubits, the human canon, the axes of the Temple of Man, and so on.

The first proportion that stands out in the newborn is the length of the head to the total height, which is 1 : 4. The second proportion that stands out is the division in half of the total length by the position of the navel. These are the first two lineages of the harmonic decomposition.

On the basis of the initial division by 4, the developed harmonic decomposition gives the proportional moments that are applicable to the adult human body.[11] Its projection onto the covered temple (fig. 200) determines the placement of all the essential east-west walls (with the exception of the one that separates room XII from the secret sanctuaries), and, because of this, what is drawn on these walls relates back to the same proportional points of this harmonic decomposition on the adult body. Thus, through the law of harmony we can follow the becoming, which is also human growth from birth to the adult state. This is a stable and undeniable basis.

All this is confirmed in the room of the birth (room IX) through the fact that Khnum, the potter who fashions the human body, gives the newborn the proportions he will have as an adult (fig. 201).

The harmonic proportion with 1 to 4 for origin generates, toward P, the fraction 1/7 of the total length PA. Each seventh is 4 digits of the royal cubit. The length of the covered temple representing the newborn is thus one royal cubit of 28 digits, confirming the tradition, and the entire temple representing the human adult has a length equal to the royal cubit in which each digit is represented by 1/2 fathom.[12]

The distance between the exterior facade of the southern wall of the covered temple, P, and the northern facade of the door of sanctuary I is contained seven and one-half times in the total length of the covered temple, PA, which corresponds to the proportion of the human head in relation to the height of the adult man.[13] This also confirms our suggestion of seeing in the three secret glands the fixed point of attachment with regard to the entire development and growth of the human body; the pituitary, the central gland, controls the others.

Harmonic proportion determines the location of the vital centers in the body (plexuses, *cakras*), while it is the function ϕ and its corresponding arithmetic form, the root of 2, that governs growth.

The harmonic decomposition starting with 1/4 leads in one direction (toward P) to the numbers of the royal cubit, and in the other (toward A) to the number 19 of the human canon. This might lead us to establish a *canevas* of nineteen units for each of the four phases of growth, A, B, C, D (figs. 202, 203, and 204). Now, if we were to represent growth as a juxtaposition of squares of a *canevas*, the sizes of which correspond each time to arrested numbers, we would be reasoning in a schematic fashion. This then would only be an addition of what we call corpses. In reality, growth indicates a becoming. We should therefore envision a geometric growth where, figuratively speaking, one phase engenders the following one: size A must pass to size B through the function ϕ, with size A giving the original value. *The child carries potentially in itself the elements of its particular growth.*

---

[11] Cf. vol. 1, figs. 136 and 138.

[12] Cf. plate 64, the cubits and the plan of the temple measured in fathoms.

[13] The length between the southern facade of the covered temple and the northern facade of the door of room I (without cornice) is 10.70 m, and the length PA (without cornices) is 79.75 m. The exact ratio is then 1 to 7.454.

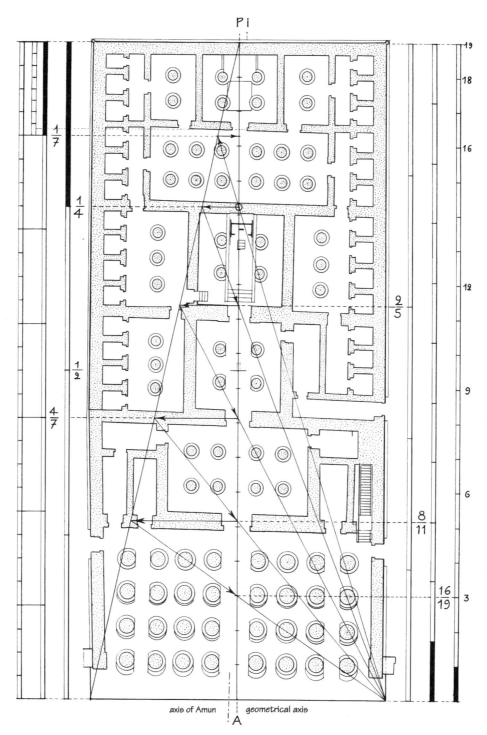

Fig. 200. Projection on the covered temple of the
harmonic decomposition starting from 1/4 of the total length PA

The decreasing development toward *P* determines 1/7 and the 28 digits of the royal cubit (at left). The increasing development toward *A* successively determines the ratios 2/5, 4/7, 8/11, 16/19. The ratio 8 to 11 governs the orientation of the nave with respect to north. The ratio 16 to 19 determines the division by 19 of the human canon. The crossing of the axes on the threshhold of rooms IV and VI corresponds to the division of *PA* into two segments, which are to each other as 8 to 11.

Fig. 201. Khnum modeling the child-king and his ka *(double) on his potter's wheel*

Hathor gives them life with her left hand. Her right arm bears a left hand and Khnum has two right hands. Luxor, room IX, west wall, first register, first scene toward the south (restored).

The length *OA* of the covered temple represents unity [see fig. 204].

The *second stage of the temple* adds the "court of the belly" and marks the end of infancy, that is, about two to two and one-half years. This is the age called "the age of the belly"[14] during which the thorax remains relatively small relative to the abdomen.

At this age the child attains half of its future height, and it is therefore at this stage of the construction that we can know, on this basis, the length of the adult Man of the Temple: in relation to the unit defined as *OA*, the second stage of the temple, *OB*, represents ϕ, and the total length *OD* is consequently 2ϕ.

The *third stage of the temple* of Amenhotep III is comprised of the nave, in which the seven times two columns have capitals of blossoming corollas. This period of growth is called "the age of respiration"[15] and is not without relation to the development of the thyroid (the weight of which has doubled since birth), which affects growth in length.[16] This is the period of the sudden growth spurt of the lower limbs. It is a vegetative phase.

[14] A. Thooris, *La Médecine morphologique* (Paris: Doin, 1937), p. 211.

[15] Ibid.

[16] Here, we can compare the processional barques of the nave with the barques of the east wall of room IV that corresponds to the location of the thyroid, which we also saw in the sanctuary of Amun (pituitary gland). Cf. plate 31 and fig. 223, and plate 38.

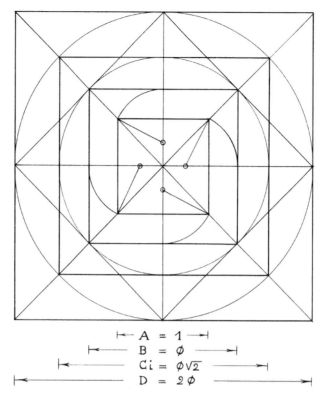

$$\vdash\!-\; A \;=\; 1 \;-\!\dashv$$
$$\vdash\!-\!-\!-\; B \;=\; \phi \;-\!-\!-\!-\!\dashv$$
$$\vdash\!-\!-\!-\!-\; Ci \;=\; \phi\sqrt{2} \;-\!-\!-\!-\!-\!-\!\dashv$$
$$\vdash\!-\!-\!-\!-\!-\; D \;=\; 2\phi \;-\!-\!-\!-\!-\!-\!-\!-\!\dashv$$

Fig. 202. Diagram of growth by ϕ and by $\sqrt{2}$

A represents the unity corresponding to the length *OA* [fig. 204] of the covered temple;
B = ϕ and corresponds to the length *OB*; *Ci* = $\phi\sqrt{2}$ and is obtained by pivoting the preceding square on its diagonal; *D* = 2ϕ, total length of the temple *OD*.

Growth occurs based on the root of 2, taking *OB* as the new starting unit. In other words, the
diagonal of a square of side *OB* determines the length *OCi*, culminating at the southern face of the
pylon of Amenhotep III. The length *OCi* in its turn becomes a new unit or side of a square in which
the diagonal leads to *D* (figs. 202 and 204).

Now, the architecture of Amenhotep III ends with his pylon at *Ce* and not at *Ci*. There is thus
a reason for the fact that the construction surpasses the limit *Ci*. First the measures, then the harmonic decomposition, and finally the axes of Amun and Mut impose on us the numbers and proportions that are derived from the pentagonal function (fig. 203).

This imposed pentagonal function has its reason for being insofar as it is a function of vegetation, but in its turn, it obliges us to consider the initial length 1 of the newborn as having the value
ϕ. In this way, the second stage *OB* will be ϕ^2; the third stage will be $2\sqrt{3.618...}$, that is, 2×1.902,
and the final length *OD* will be $2 \times \phi^2$, the two royal men who functionally represent the royal
cubit.[17]

The intermediate phase of rapid growth that occurs in the child at about twelve or thirteen
years of age is indicated by the western door of the Ramesside court, at which the avenue coming
from the loading dock ends. In the axis determined by the southern doorposts of the eastern and

[17] Cf. chapter 10.

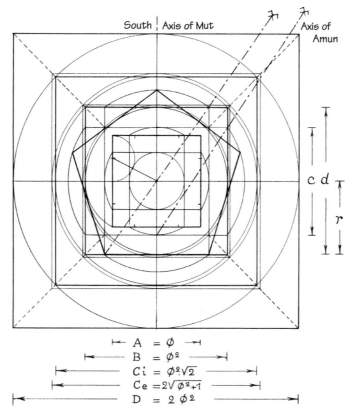

South ⋮ Axis of Mut   Axis of Amun

c d
r

$$\vdash\!\!-\; A \;=\; \phi \;-\!\!\dashv$$
$$\vdash\!\!-\!\!-\!\!-\; B \;=\; \phi^2 \;-\!\!-\!\!-\!\!\rightarrow$$
$$\vdash\!\!-\!\!-\!\!-\!\!-\; C_i \;=\; \phi^2\sqrt{2} \;-\!\!-\!\!-\!\!-\!\!\rightarrow$$
$$\vdash\!\!-\!\!-\!\!-\; C_e \;=\; 2\sqrt{\phi^2+1} \;-\!\!-\!\!-\!\!\rightarrow$$
$$\vdash\!\!-\!\!-\!\!-\!\!-\; D \;=\; 2\,\phi^2 \;-\!\!-\!\!-\!\!-\!\!\rightarrow$$

Fig. 203. Diagram of the development of the pentagonal function
combined with the functions ϕ and $\sqrt{2}$

The side of the initial square, *A*, equals ϕ. Its division by ϕ determines the square at the center with 1 for its side. The diagonal of the rectangle 1 to ϕ is equal to $\sqrt{1+\phi^2}$ or $\sqrt{3.618} = 1.902... = c$. This diagonal is the side of a pentagon that is the diameter of the inscribed circle of the square with side *B* or *d*.

$$\frac{d}{c} = \frac{2.618...}{1.902...} = 1.376, \text{ and determines the angle of } 36° \text{ or } \frac{\widehat{11}}{8}$$

$$\frac{c}{r} = \frac{1.902...}{1.309...} = 1.453..., \text{ and determines the angle of } 34°30' \text{ or} \frac{\widehat{16}}{11}.$$

These ratios are those of the orientations of Mut (nave) and of Amun with respect to the north-south axis.

western doorways of the court of Ramesses, a variation in level and a stone piece embedded in the pavestone mark the point where the axis of the nave (axis of Mut) culminates.[18] The princes, coming from the Nile (Hapi), enter into the temple through the western door of the Ramesside court.

Now, if the covered temple represents unity, the length *OE* is ϕ^2, and if the length *OA* is ϕ, this length *OE* becomes ϕ^3.

[18] In *The Temple in Man* we noted the importance of this point, which a subsequent excavation showed us to be especially marked by the Ancients with this key.

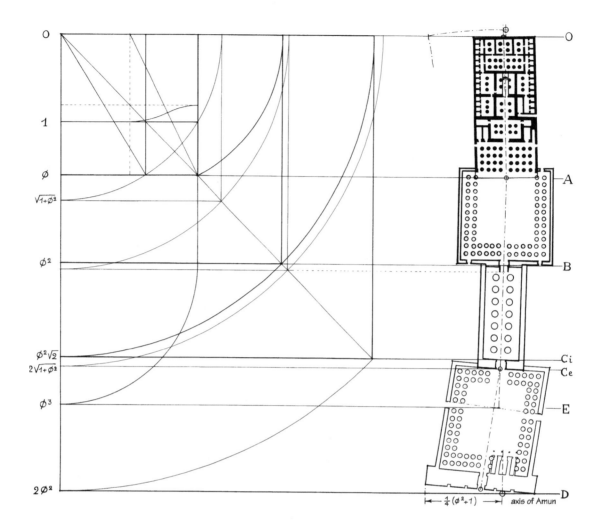

Fig. 204. Growth of the temple

	Measure : ± 10 cm	Function	Calculated
OA = covered temple	79.75 m	ϕ	= 79.82 m
OB = north transept wall	129.15 m	ϕ^2	= 129.15 m
OCi = south nave wall	182.60 m	$\phi^2\sqrt{2}$	= 182.64 m
OCe = north nave facade	187.75 m	$2\sqrt{\phi^2+1}$	= 187.67 m
OD = northwest corner of pylon	258.35 m	$2(\phi^2)$	= 258.30 m
OE = princes' entrance	209.15 m	ϕ^3	= 209.00 m

The total length of the temple not including the cornice and socle is 258 meters, or 140 fathoms at 0°, measured on the axis of Amun and its perpendicular. With the foundation of the base of the pylon of Ramesses the total length comes to 258.35 meters, and with the south cornice of the covered temple, the total length comes to 258.65 meters, corresponding to 140 fathoms of 1.8475 meters. (One hundred of these fathoms measure the arc of meridian at 30° north latitude, the location of the Pyramid of Cheops.)

The complete series, ϕ, ϕ^2, $2\sqrt{3.618\ldots}$, ϕ^3, and $2\phi^2$ summarizes the numerical functions of the growth of the Man of the Temple (fig. 204).

The first stage of the temple, OA, considered as a unit with the value of ϕ, gives the half-length OB of the entire temple OD ending with the pylon of Ramesses II when it is multiplied by ϕ.

Now, the half-length of the temple coincides with the exterior facade of the north wall enclosing the transept (measured from its northwest corner on the perpendicular to the axis of Amun), and Amenhotep added a rabbet to this length at the north, to the right and left of which would be fitted the walls of the nave.

The total length of the covered temple and of the transept, counting this rabbet, represents 250 royal cycle cubits, which gives the formal indication that the temple conforms to the functions and essential measures governing the cubits:

On one hand, the monument measures 140 fathoms (258 m) and functionally is $2\phi^2$ in comparison to the length of the covered temple, which is ϕ. On the other hand, the Man of the Temple measures ϕ^2 in meters, that is, 500 royal cycle cubits, or 261.80 meters. The difference between the 500 royal cubits and the 140 fathoms represents the crown of the skull cut by the south wall of the covered temple.[19]

PLATE 15 • THE TEMPLE AND THE PROPORTIONS OF MAN
(PROJECTION OF A SKELETON ONTO THE TEMPLE)

The skeleton represented in plate 15 is shown facing front. It has been drawn according to the averages established by modern biologists for the proportional sizes of each bone and the general proportions of the human body.[20] The most general constants are, first, the division of the height of the human body by the navel according to the golden section: the two parts are to each other as 1 is to ϕ with the elimination of the crown of the skull. Now, the numbers for the growth of the temple give it the function ϕ^2 for length. This length, measured from the pylon to the south wall of the covered temple, is 140 fathoms and corresponds to the Man of the Temple without the crown of the skull.

The Man of the Temple, summarizing functions and measurements in one monument, is actually valued as ϕ^2 in meters when the skullcap, cut off by the south wall, or the difference between 258 meters and 261.80 meters, or 500 royal cycle cubits, is added to him. Moreover, on the west wall of sanctuary I, which gives all the measurements and essential functions of this temple, king A furnishes—by his height to the vertex—the unity that when multiplied by 19×10, corresponds to 500 royal cubits, thus confirming the height of the Man of the Temple.[21]

The second constant is the division of the height into two equal parts by the pubic symphysis: the total measure is given by the length from the north face of the Ramesses pylon and the wall that separates the nave from the transept and corresponds on the skeleton to the pubic symphysis. Taking the 130.90 meters on the monument, we must double this length to obtain the height of a person with the crown of the skull, which will be 261.80 meters, or 500 royal cubits, that is, in meters, $100 \times \phi^2$, corresponding to 10×19 times the height of king A in sanctuary I.

---

[19] The diagonal of the rectangle having a length of $2\phi^2$, or $5.236\ldots$, and a base of 1/4 ($\phi^2 + 1$), or $0.9045\ldots$, is $5.31364\ldots$. The ratio between the length and the diagonal of this rectangle is $1.01481\ldots$, the coefficient by which 140 fathoms at 0° must be multiplied to obtain 500 royal cubits (fig. 204). This coefficient is identical to the one that serves as a link between the two measures of the kings A and E of sanctuary I.

[20] Cf. chapter 11, "Human Biometrics and Invariable Principles."

[21] Cf. chapter 13, "The Teaching of the Five Kings of the Sanctuary of Amun," and plate 80.

The skeleton is projected onto the temple so that the pubic symphysis coincides with the wall that represents it; the remainder must allow us to verify whether or not the general proportions of the other parts of the body correspond with the architecture. The scale is as follows: 1 meter of the skeleton equals 150 meters of the temple, which is therefore 150 times larger than man.

This man would measure 1.7454 meters, a dimension that is 18/19 fathom at 0°. This 18/19 plays an important role in the *canevas* and in the orientation, as we shall see later on. Let us note now that the axis of the court of Ramesses in relationship to north is at an angle of 18/19 in *a/n* notation.

Let us now look at the projection.

By placing the soles of the feet at the level of the pylon, the knees coincide with the thick wall that separates the narthex from the nave. The iliac crest, which corresponds to the level of the navel, would locate the navel at the center of the "court of the belly" (transept). The inscription on the architrave of the east colonnade mentions at this point that "here is the place of the birth of the king, where he will spend his infancy and from which he will go out crowned."

The xiphoid process (the point of the sternum) is at the last row of columns of the hypostyle room, the *haty*. The clavicles are superimposed on the thick wall that separates the first two hypostyle rooms (XVI and VIII) of the "closed temple," properly speaking. Room IV is at the level of the seventh cervical (and first thoracic) vertebra, an important vital node corresponding to the stellate ganglion. It is at this point that the *neters*, in certain cases, give life (ankh).

Rooms IV and IX correspond to the level of the throat, above the clavicles. We should remember here that the first and last points of ossification are formed in the clavicles and that, also, room IX, the north wall—therefore on the clavicle—represents the adult king in the room in which his spiritual conception, his birth, his future evolution, and his second birth (*sed* festival) are described.

The head takes up all the sanctuaries. The room of the barque (VI) is the place of the mouth, the creative Verb, according to tradition. Indeed, we find there the figures of the great Theban "Ennead"[22] on the west wall, and the representations of the *neters* on the north and south walls.

The eyes are in room XII, the room of the solar cycle, the twelve hours of the day and the twelve hours of night. The sun enters at the east in its morning barque, and goes to rest in the west, in its evening barque. Now, the sun is called the "eye of Ra," symbolized by the falcon.

The part of the brain containing the three vital centers is located in the "secret sanctuaries," I, V, and VII.

In sanctuary I we find, on the west wall, the five kings that give us the units of measure of the temple, units that vary from the first king to the last and that confirm the play of growth in the monument (cf. plates 80 and 81).

The arms do not figure in the temple, but nevertheless we find at the height of the left wrist of the skeleton, on the exterior north wall of the transept, bas-reliefs showing severed hands (cf. fig. 199, no. 6). Notice that the representation of the *kamutef*, "the androgynous Adam," is sculpted exactly at the level of the pubic symphysis (cf. fig. 199, no. 16).[23]

—⁓—

[22] "Ennead" *(sic)* of fifteen *neters.*

[23] We regret not having been able to excavate at the location of the top of the humerus.

Plate 15 has but one goal: to show that a human skeleton marks the correspondence of the principal points of the edifice in accordance with the human form. The proofs that this was actually the intention of the master builder of the temple are given further on.

—◁∿▷—

One might be surprised at the specific measures we give, with an uncertainty of only ±10 centimeters, on a monument so in ruins. Nevertheless, we affirm after checking many times and with much difficulty, that we have specified nothing that is not absolutely correct. It is this conscientious study alone that has allowed us to draw the conclusions given in this book.

Our plans of the different phases of the temple were drawn to a scale of 1/100, the pavement, to a scale of 1/25, and the walls, to a scale of 1/20.

CONCLUSION

The geometry and numbers demonstrating the coincidence of the architecture of the temple of Luxor with the phases and proportions of human growth, the principal instances of which we have just noted, are undeniable.

This demonstrates a real knowledge of the phenomena of life on the part of the Ancients, and leaves us astonished before the strength of their faith, which could synthesize this knowledge in a monument with such skill. Faced with these facts, readers who are less critical than myself might pose the following questions:

We judge these problems on the basis of data presently known on growth, and then rediscover that data in this architecture. How, then, did this work of stone teach these things without the benefit of our present knowledge?

To this I respond: If we had not discovered these numbers and proportions in this monument, *which we knew to represent man,* we would not have deemed it necessary to compare them with those of our science in order to identify here the science of the Ancients for a public unaware of these matters.

This first objection that could be posed is therefore not viable.

Let us admit then that the master builder wanted to represent the proportions as well as the phases of gestation of the growth of the human being through the monument; does this communicate something more than our present science can explain in words, and thus without using a monument?

My initial response is no, if we are content to regard the problem in a superficial way and according to our analytic way of thinking. But . . . when we see these ratios and numbers inscribed in the monument related to those of the pharaonic calendars, or to the division of time according to the double influence of the lunar and solar periods, and, then, to the lunisolar periods of nineteen years, as well as to the *double rhythm* of the vague year in the Sothic cycle that serves as a reference throughout the great periods of the precessional months, then we begin to glimpse, by means of these coincidences, the *causes* of the variations in time of organic growth and of the alternations between the elongations and widenings of the bones and muscles, as well as the nature of the periods that affect the development of the head, of the *haty,* of the abdomen, and of the legs.

These facts allow us to glimpse the existence of a functional identification of the particular with cosmic causes.

When we observe that these same numbers, which determine the grid on which the plans of the various ages of man are traced, are the numbers that derive from harmony and determine the five regular (Platonic) polyhedrons, as well as their relationships to one another—those polyhedrons that Kepler used to calculate and establish his famous formula, $R = \sqrt{t^2}$, in order to determine the distances of the planets[24]—then we see in these numbers more than a simple phenomenon interesting only as human biometrics, because they correspond to cosmic mechanics.

I therefore conclude: through these few basic elements concerning human growth that we have given here, established in this astonishing monument that is the temple of Luxor, is revealed to us the existence of a synthetic vision that unifies all vital phenomena under one unique law.[25]

"Man, know thyself."

[24] Cf. chapter 9.

[25] Let us note here that just as, with regard to the axes, the axis of Amun is occult and governs, for planes, the pentagon is occult and governs, and for volumes, the dodecahedron is occult and governs.

Chapter 29

A COLOSSUS
OF THE TEMPLE

—*᭯᭯᭯*—

Plates 16–25

Man, or the human principle considered as an incarnation of cosmic functions, that is, Anthropocosmos, is the universal symbol to which everything relates.

(Chapter 4)

PLATE 16

Colossus No. 3 of Ramesses II, Three-Quarter View

The form-idea cannot be described; it must be felt and lived.

True poetry is magic, and magic is identification with form, body with body, Spirit with Spirit. The All in One, Ecce homo, *is the symbol above all symbols; and man is not an image, a condensation of the Universe; man is the Universe.*

(Introduction)

In Ancient Egypt, as in China, the king embodies the Cosmos for his people and represents the incarnation of the present state *of humanity's achievement. . . .*

(Chapter 3)

PLATE 17

Colossus No. 3 of Ramesses II, View from the Front

. . . the pharaonic teaching shows us Man composed of three beings: the corporeal being, the sexual being, and the spiritual being. Each has its body and its organs. These three beings are interdependent through the flow of fluids and the nervous influx; the spinal marrow is the column of "fire" that connects the whole and effects the transformation of the corporeal into energy and spirit.

(Chapter 17)

PLATE 18

Colossus No. 3 of Ramesses II, View from the Back

Everything lives and therefore assimilates, grows,
and reproduces, a fact that extends to monuments
and statues, conceived and executed on multiple
axes simultaneously.

(Chapter 4)

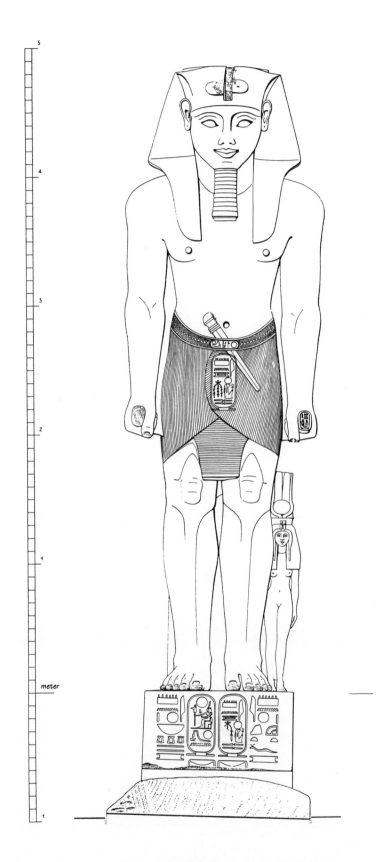

PLATE 19

Scale Drawing of Colossus No. 3 of Ramesses II, Front (West)

. . . the only indisputable doctrine is the doctrine that synthesizes all possible points of view around the basic "forms." This simultaneity of vision is the essential quality to be developed, the only quality valid for the "spirit of the problems" of knowledge. A describable solution to a problem is only possible if none of its elements is fixed *as an invariable form; the solution must adapt to all possibilities.*

(Elements)

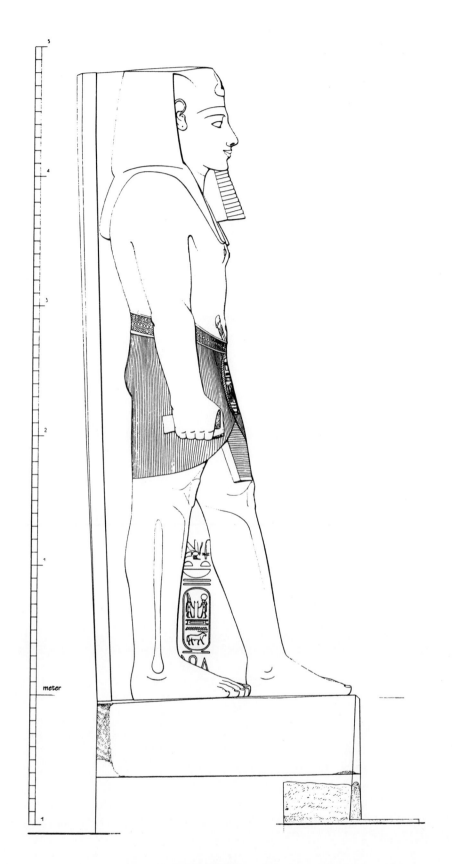

PLATE 20

Scale Drawing of Colossus No. 3 of Ramesses II, Right Profile (North)

All architecture and all representations of figures or objects are constructed on a canevas-*guide; this* canevas, *resulting from the theological directives of the Ancients, brings all proportions back to a basic idea. Now, these proportions are in no way arbitrary but correspond, for monuments, to astronomical principles, and for figures, to cosmic functions as they relate to human proportions.*

(Chapter 11)

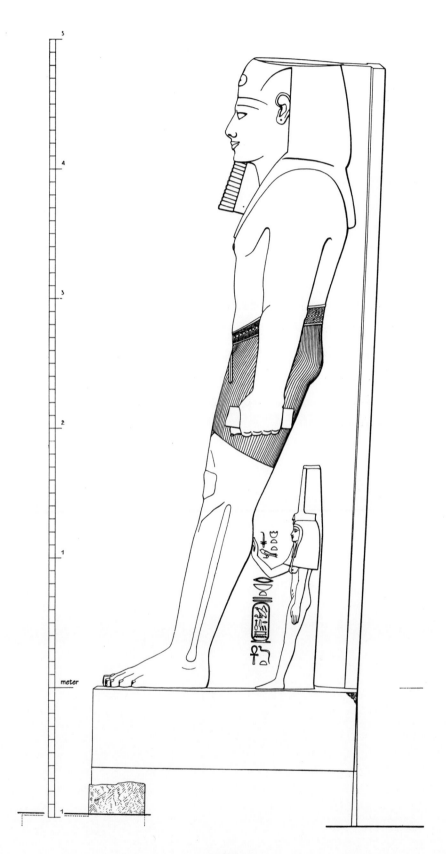

PLATE 21

Scale Drawing of Colossus No. 3 of Ramesses II, Left Profile (South)

. . . man, being the last creature, is a unity, an image of the Unique. And the violet of the field is equally a unity in the image of the Unique, who, Himself, is indefinable, save by all the unities (finite images) of all the possible types of the creation.

(Chapter 6)

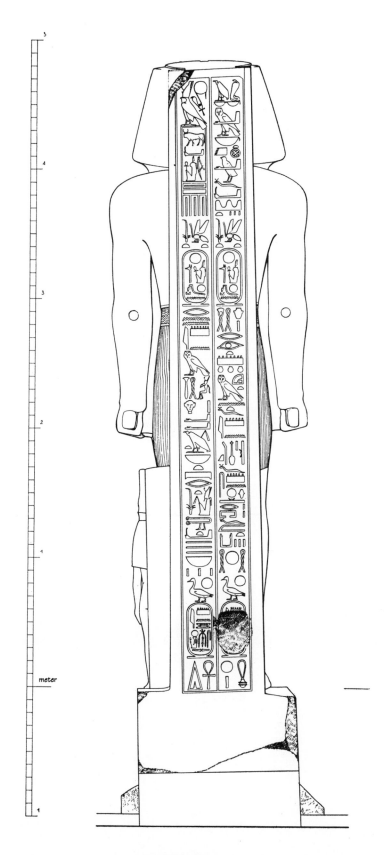

PLATE 22

Scale Drawing of Colossus No. 3 of Ramesses II, Dorsal Stele (East)

To live is to grow and to keep growing in all directions at the same time. Evocation belongs to the sense of space; it is the vision and experience of volume with and within volumes.

(Introduction)

To demonstrate the esoteric sense we have only the symbol that, through architecture, speaks to us in volume.

(Chapter 5)

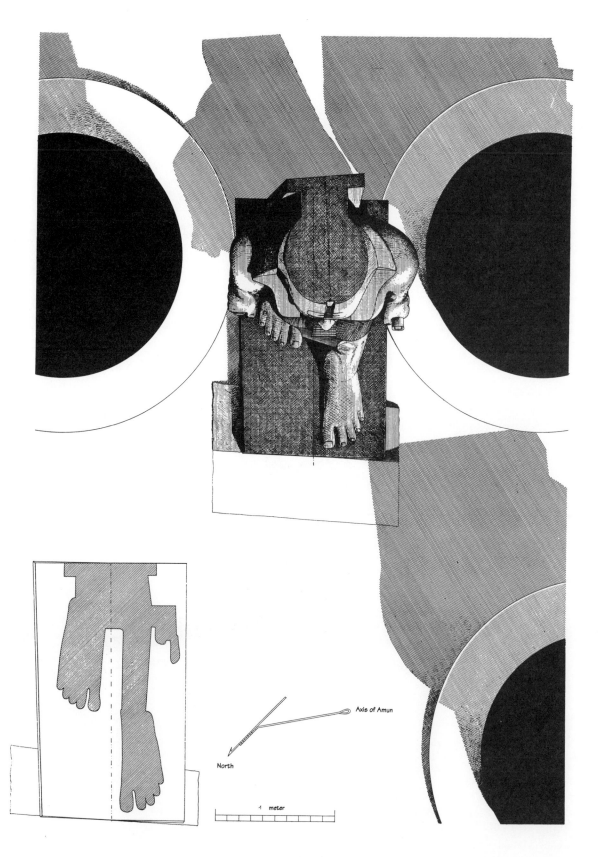

North

Axis of Amun

1 meter

PLATE 23

Colossus No. 3 of Ramesses II, View from Above

The anthropocosmic philos-
ophy bases all functions and
all measures on the "crystal-
lization" or "incarnation" of
the Cosmos in man.

(Chapter 11)

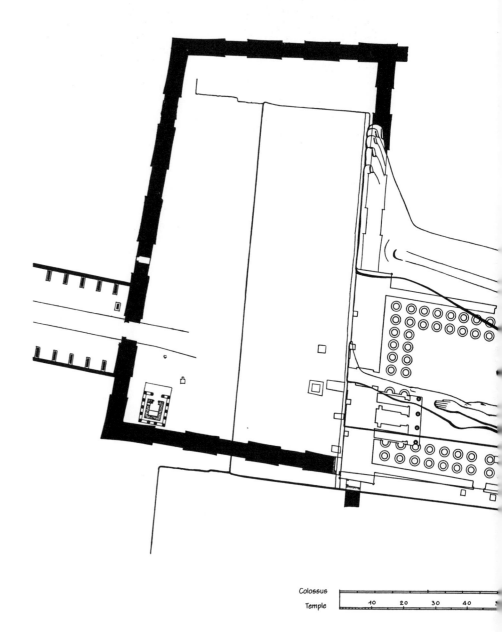

Colossus

Temple

10   20   30   40

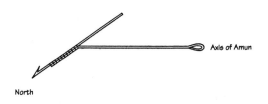

Axis of Amun

North

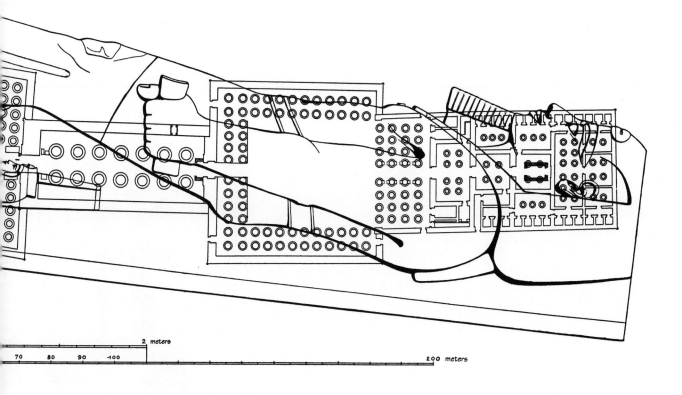

2 meters

70 80 90 100

200 meters

PLATE 24

Projection of Colossus No. 3 onto the Temple of Luxor

With the Christic revela-
tion, the natural and
logical consequence of
Ancient Egypt, the
Osirian cycle—the cycle
of terrestrial renewals—
ends. The dogma of the
Redemption renders man
independent of the obliga-
tions of reincarnation.

It is a promise
that each must realize
individually.

(Cf. chapter 20)

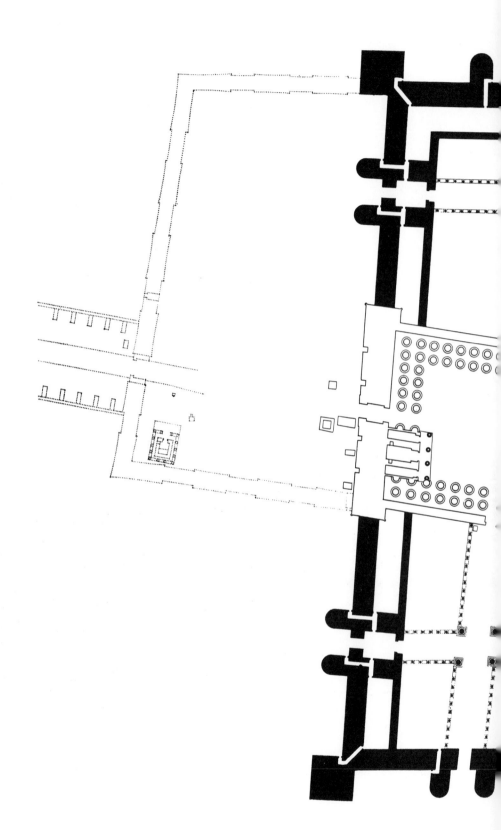

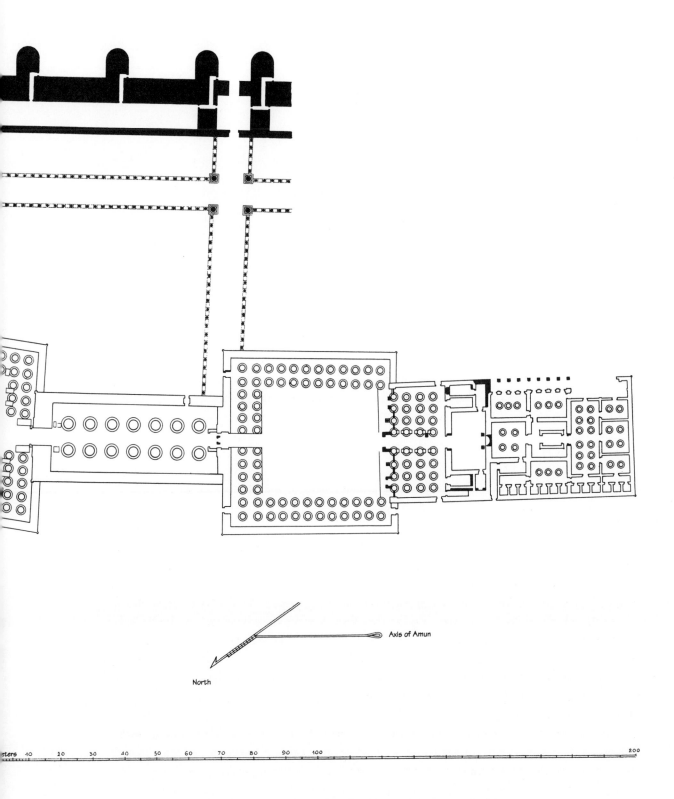

North

Axis of Amun

meters 10 20 30 40 50 60 70 80 90 100 200

PLATE 25

The Temple in the Greco-Roman Period

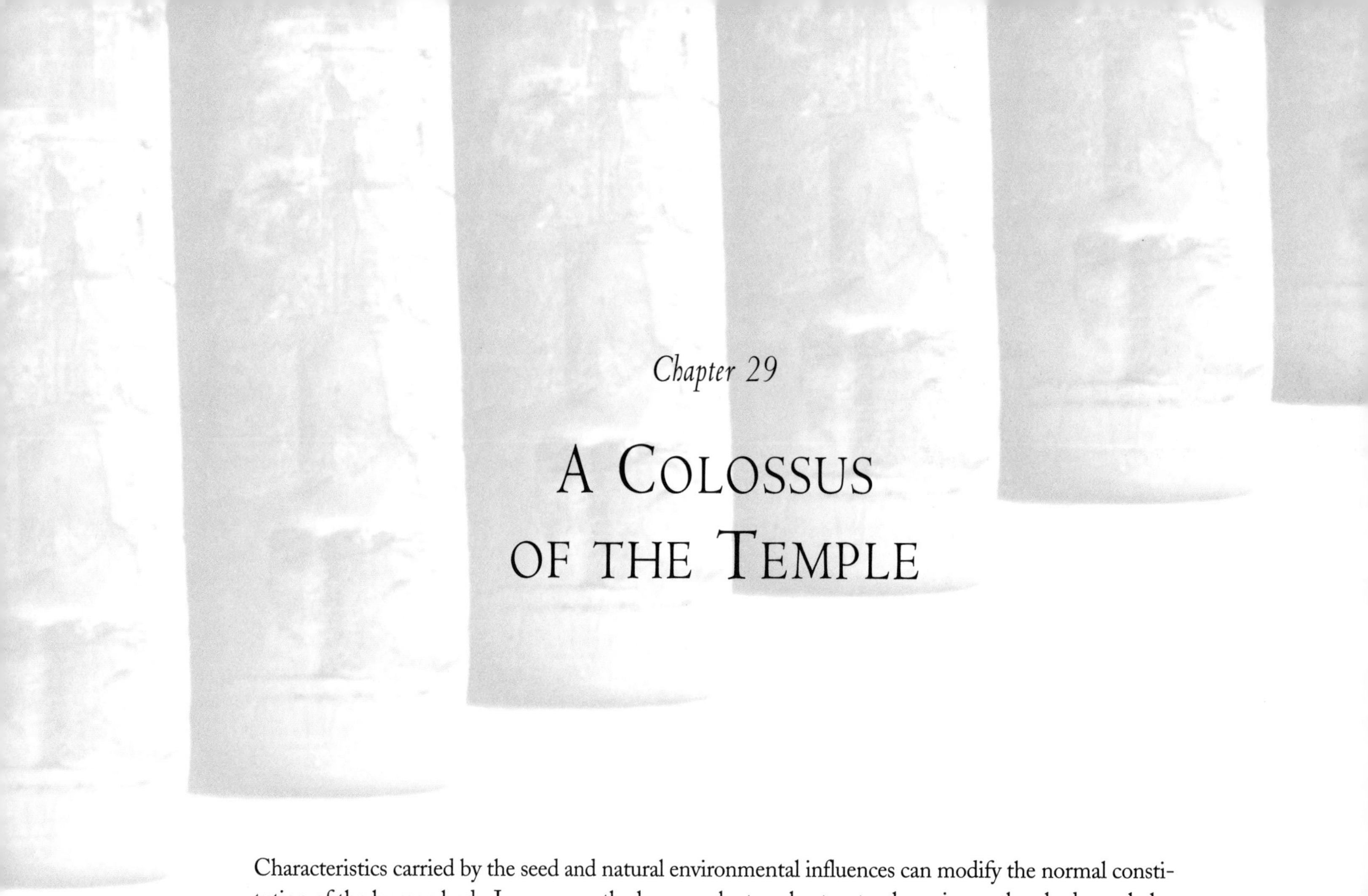

Chapter 29

A COLOSSUS
OF THE TEMPLE

Characteristics carried by the seed and natural environmental influences can modify the normal constitution of the human body. In one case, the legs may be too short or too long; in another, hydrocephalus may deform the head, or the hands can have six fingers—these are easily observed phenomena.

On the statues in the sanctuaries we often find represented intentional modifications of the norm for the body. It is no longer a matter of simply observing these peculiarities, but on the contrary, we are moved to investigate the natural (cosmic) causes that could produce these anomalies.

When the *hotep* [peace] of lunar Amun (Amenhotep) is realized and Ra (the sun) must appear, or be born *(mes)*, with Ra-mes-s (Ramesses), it is necessary to establish this power on the earth. So the bas-reliefs and hieroglyphs, until then only lightly incised, will be deeply cut into the stone.

Ramesses finished the temple of Luxor with the court of the narthex and the pylon. The important statues then give the measure of man, but they have lower legs that are abnormally reinforced and too large with respect to the femur.

We want to point out the importance given to the lower legs specifically in this court, which in relation to the temple represents the lower leg; on the outsides of the calves one can see the strongly accented marking outlining the peroneal muscles, characteristic of great walkers.

Ramesses is the solid terrestrial seat, the entrance into matter of what is spiritualized by the Amenhoteps and the Tuthmoses. At the same time it is the passage from the eighth month of the embryo and the entry into the maturity of human birth.

This is a strange teaching.

To illustrate one of the obvious aspects of the importance of these colossi of Ramesses, we show here, thanks to very precise measurements, the relationship that exists between one of these colossi and the measurements of the temple, or more exactly, the functions that govern them.

PLATES 16–18 • COLOSSUS NO. 3 OF RAMESSES II

This colossus is located between the columns of the eastern portico of the court of Ramesses (narthex). It is the third starting from the north, and faces northwest.[1]

---

[1] Cf. fig. 199.

The statue and its pedestal, which have been neither altered nor recut from an older group, are sculpted out of a single block of rose granite. Although perfectly finished, the cutting of the edges has less of a living quality than that of colossus no. 4, described in plate 8.

The double crown is missing. It was cut from another block and was placed on the upper part of the *nemes* headdress, the surface of which is flattened to receive it. The uraeus on the forehead has also been taken away; above the headband that encircles the forehead the body of the coiled serpent can be seen, as well as the notch made in the granite to receive the projecting part of the chest and head of the raised cobra.

This colossus carries the cartouches of Ramesses II on the facade of its pedestal, on its loin-cloth, on its belt, and on the stele against which it leans. He holds the royal seal in his two closed fists, and the left one, intact, has his name carved on it.

A dagger passes through his belt, below the navel. Behind his left leg, the queen, sculpted in the round, places her right hand on the king's calf. There is a vertical inscription under the queen's elbow that gives her name: "The great wife of the king, mistress of the Two Lands, Nefertari, beloved[2] of Mut."

Opposite the buttress bearing this text, on the north face, an inscription can be found in the name of Merneptah,[3] son of Ramesses II.

The stele that supports the king carries (east face) two columns of text. The text of the south column (at left) reads: "The solar Horus, vigorous bull, beloved of Maāt, the king of the South and of the North, Usermaātre, chosen of Ra, whom Amun has raised [nourished] as a child in the arms of Mut, mistress of heaven, that he could become the king stirring all the lands. The son of Ra, Ramesses beloved of Amun, gifted with life."

The text of the north column (at right) reads: "The two mistresses vulture [and] cobra, the protector of Egypt Kemi [black earth], the one who subjugates the foreign mountains, the king of the South and of the North, Usermaātre, chosen of Ra, inspired of heart to create a foundation in the *apet* of his father Amun who created his perfection [realization]; the one who solidly established his temple in eternal work, the son of Ra, Ramesses, beloved of Amun, as Ra."[4]

Let us note that in the inscription in the south column of the stele, the passage, "whom Amun has raised as a child," is found at the same level as the one on the north column, "in order to create a foundation in the *apet*," so that we can read from left to right "the child in the *apet*."[5] The decoration of the columns that frame this colossus includes a tableau surmounted by the "sky," which is found at the level of the king's breasts.[6]

---

[2] We adopt for *mer* and *meri* their true sense, *aimant* ["loving," "beloved," but also "magnet"] as the magnet attracts iron, as the earth attracts the dew.

[3] *Menephtah*, inexact transliteration of the Egyptian name *Merneptah*.

[4] French translation by Alexandre Varille, 1942.

[5] Cf. plate 22, drawing of the dorsal stele.

[6] This fact is verified by measurement. Here then are some characteristic measurements of these columns (within 1 or 2 cm, given their deterioration), and their variations:

    width of the abacus = small diameter of the capital = 1.40 m to 1.42 m
    diameter of the base of the shaft = 1.74 m to 1.76 m
    maximum diameter of the shaft = 1.98 m to 2.00 m
    height from the pedestal to the base of the capital = 7 m
    height from the pedestal to the base of the abacus = 9 m
    height from the ground to the base of the abacus = 9.43 m or 18 royal cubits
    height from the ground to the base of the architrave = 10.32 m or 20 cubits of 28 *remen* digits, each being 1/100 of a fathom
    height from the ground to the top of the architrave = 11.58 m or 22 royal cubits.

  It is notable here that the cut of the column at the level of the base of the abacus is principally square, and that the diameter of

Plates 19–22 • Scale Drawings of
Colossus No. 3 of Ramesses II

Cut out of a single block, the colossus with its pedestal does not rest directly on the ground, but is lifted up and supported on a group of sandstone blocks to the height of the bases of the neighboring columns. Of this subfoundation, a single stone is still visible; the others, coated with saltpeter on the surface, are in large part presently covered by cement. This stone on which the granite pedestal is supported is of a piece with the pavestones of the court, but projects above its neighboring stones. In a circular arc to its upper part, it formerly extended past the granite pedestal to the north, the west, and the south. As is shown by markings, the west face has been recut, certainly at the time of the placing of the colossus, in order to make it fit the surface of the pedestal (plate 23).

Today, the entire statue is slightly inclined toward the south. Our plans show it in its present position, but through a detailed study we have been able to discover the position it must have had when it was put in place during the Ramesside era.

Presumed Position of the Colossus in the Ramesside Period

The median line of the dorsal inscription of the name of Ramesses II, along with the axis of the west face of the pedestal, between the two cartouches of the king, determines a vertical front-to-back plane.

The two columns of text to the right and left of the buttress of the king's left leg are not parallel (cf. plates 20 and 21); that of the name of Mut Nefertari (plate 21) inclines toward the back, and the other, the name of Merneptah (plate 20), inclines toward the front. The colossus can be considered in its vertical position when the right-left plane coincides with the bisecting line of the axis of the Mut Nefertari and Merneptah texts, and when the front-back plane, determined by the median line of the dorsal stele, is rectified vertically toward the north. When the statue is in this position, the lower part of its granite pedestal is horizontal and the principal characteristics are as follows:

Front view (plate 19)
- The cartouche on the king's loincloth is vertical.
- The ground of the pedestal between the two feet of the king is horizontal.
- The south, lateral edge of the pedestal is vertical.
- The queen's axis is inclined toward the south and is parallel with the north edge of the pedestal.

North profile (plate 20)
- The top of the left foot is horizontal.
- The top of the right foot is perpendicular to the Nefertari text (in transparency with that of Merneptah).
- The east, lateral edge of the pedestal is parallel to the axis of the Merneptah inscription.

South profile (plate 21)
- The upper edge of the pedestal behind Queen Nefertari is perpendicular to the queen's text.

---

the capital at this level is *a circle inscribed* in the square, while the maximum diameter of the shaft is that of the *circumscribing circle* of this square. On the other hand, the interval between the axes of these columns oscillates between 3.95 m and 4 m, the rectangle formed by the ground. The base of the architrave and this interval are in the proportion of 1 to ϕ^2.

- The upper edge of the pedestal between the queen's left foot and the king's left foot is perpendicular to the Merneptah text (in transparency with that of the queen).
- The upper edge of the pedestal under the king's left foot is perpendicular to the bisecting line of the angle formed by these two inscriptions, and which we consider to be the real vertical axis of the colossus.
- The west lateral edge is vertical and forms a right angle with the upper edge of the pedestal.
- The east lateral edge is parallel to the queen's text and forms a right angle with the upper edge of the pedestal corresponding to it.

General Proportions and Measurements of the King

Further on, we give a table of the principal measures of the king's height adjusted to a mean level taken between his feet. Here are his essential measurements:

1. The pubic symphysis, necessarily invisible, is marked by the location of the solar Ra engraved on the cartouche on the loincloth. It divides the total height into two equal parts.

2. The navel divides the height between the soles of the feet and the base of the ureaus into two parts that are to each other as 1 is to ϕ.

3. It is interesting to note another characteristic function of this colossus: the height from the soles of the feet to the height of the breasts, multiplied by $\sqrt{2}$, determines the total height of the king to the vertex.

Measurements and General Proportions of the Queen

First, the navel divides the height between the soles of the feet and the forehead, under the uraeus, into two parts that are to each other as 1 is to ϕ. Second, the height from the soles of the feet to the nipples, multiplied by $\sqrt{2}$, determines the total height to the vertex.

In the two tables, we give all the measurements that allow us to verify these proportions. We indicate the dimensions in meters and give their equivalence in cubits or in digits. Finally, we give the number of squares of the appropriate *canevas* to this statue, with the height of the king considered to be 19 to the upper corners of his headdress (fig. 206).

THE NORTH AS THE SIDE OF INSPIRATION OR PRINCIPLE (PLATE 20)

The total height of the king represents ϕ^2 for the unit of 1 fathom. The use of this unit of measure is confirmed on the dorsal stele by the indication of the 2 fathoms between the baseline of the stele and the base of the section containing the Horus name of the king (fig. 205).

This stele also refers to the height "ϕ fathoms" through the base of the royal cartouches that correspond on the colossus to the upper limit of the belt at the back as well as to the left elbow (thus the north).

The total height of the king to the vertex again represents $\sqrt{2}$ in relation to the height of his nipples; this proportion is indicated on the dorsal stele by the upper curves of the two royal cartouches.

The total height of the king corresponds finally to $10/\phi^2$ or 3.81966... in relation to the back width of his pedestal taken as unity. The total height of the pedestal is then $\phi/2$, and its width on the north face is ϕ; the pedestal, which represents the seat, also confirms the function ϕ governing this colossus.[7]

[7] Cf. chapter 5, "The Mystical Number."

The King's Measurements from the Pedestal at the Level of the Left Heel

Heights	Meters	Cubits; functions	Squares
Top of *nemes* headdress	4.85	9 black cubits	19.2
Corner of headdress	4.80		19
Bottom of uraeus	4.63	10 human cubits	$18\frac{1}{4}$
Top of ears	4.60		
Forehead	4.55		18
Chin	4.06		16
Shoulders	4.02		
Breasts, top of nipples	3.43	4.85 meters $\div \sqrt{2}$	$13\frac{1}{2}$
Left elbow	2.91		$11\frac{1}{2}$
Center of navel	2.845	4.60 meters $\div \phi$	$11\frac{1}{4}$
Top of cartouche	2.62	5 royal cubits	
Center of solar Ra	2.415	half-height	$9\frac{1}{2}$
Right fist, attached	2.00	2 meters	
Left fist, bottom of royal seal	2.025		8
Bottom of loincloth	1.67		$6\frac{2}{3}$
Knee under kneecap	1.455		$5\frac{3}{4}$
LENGTHS			
Left foot	0.82		
Right foot	0.92	$1/2$ fathom $= \dfrac{4.82 \text{ meters}}{5.236}$	
UPPER PLANE OF PEDESTAL			
Length of north edge	2.06	110 R digits	
Length of south edge	2.10	4 royal cubits	
Width of east face	1.27	68 R digits	
Width of west face	1.19	64 R digits	

The Queen's Mean Measurements from the Pedestal

Heights	Meters	Functions; digits	Squares
Top of plumes	$\left\{\begin{array}{c}1.735\\[4pt]1.71\end{array}\right\}$	92 R digits[a]	
Crown	1.365	72 D digits	
Uraeus	1.345	72 R digits	$5\frac{1}{3}$
Vertex	1.31	$2\frac{1}{2}$ royal cubits	
Queen's headband	1.275	68 R digits[b]	
Bottom of uraeus	1.265		
Forehead	1.255		5
Chin (broken), approx.	1.145	61 R digits	
Breasts	0.925	$\frac{1}{2}$ fathom	$3\frac{2}{3}$
Navel[c]	0.79		$3\frac{1}{8}$

Note: There is a difference of 1 cm between the measurements taken in front and on the side of the foot. It is thus necessary to add or subtract 0.5 cm to the mean measures given here according to whether they are read from the front or in profile.

[a] The R digit is 1/28 of the royal cubit of 52.36 cm or about 52.5; cf. plate 64, cubit C. The D digit is 1/28 of the basalt cubit, found at Dendera, of 53 cm; cf. plate 64, cubits D and E.

[b] Sixty-eight R digits = 1.2716 m, instead of 1.275 m measured on the queen and 1.27 m measured on the east face of the pedestal of the colossus.

[c] Height of the navel, from the soles of the feet, multiplied by ϕ is 0.79 m × 1.618 = 1.2782 m = height of the queen's headband. The height of the breasts multiplied by $\sqrt{2}$ is 0.925 × 1.4142 m, which equals the height of the vertex of the queen. Exactly $2\frac{1}{2}$ royal cubits = 1.309 m, the royal cubit being the fundamental measure that governs the Man of the Temple.

Originally the statue wore the white crown encased in the red, and the classic proportion given by the figures in the bas-reliefs of the temple of Luxor for the determination of the height of the crowned king presents two possibilities. First, *for the crown encasing the forehead,* the height between the soles of the feet and the forehead, multiplied by $\sqrt{\phi}$, determines the total height of the king with his crown, a proportion we find applied to colossus no. 5.[8]

Second, *for the crown placed on the headdress* and thus added to the total height for the vertex; in this case, the total height of the king, multiplied by $\sqrt{\phi}$, determines the height of the crowned king, a proportion we find applied to colossus no. 3.

If we take as our base the crown presently lying on the ground, belonging to colossus no. 2 and of the same dimensions as no. 3, we can verify what the total height of the latter would be with the double crown: 4.85 meters × $\sqrt{\phi}$ = 6.17 meters to the top of the red crown, the measurement to the knob of the white crown being somewhat greater. Now, 6.17 meters represents 20 *djezer* (or sublime) cubits for each 16 digits of a mean fathom, that is, a geodetic measurement.

[8] Cf. plate 8 and its legend.

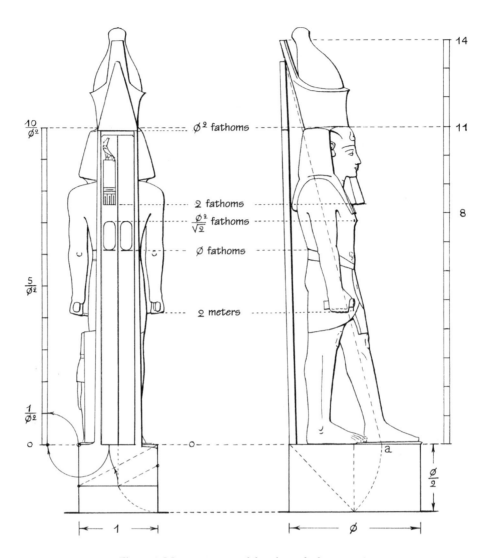

Fig. 205. Measurements and functions of colossus no. 3

Width of back of pedestal	= 1.27 meters = unity.
Length of north surface of pedestal	= 2.06 meters = ϕ.
Height of the back surface of pedestal	= 1.03 meters = $\phi/2$.
King's height to vertex	= 4.85 meters = $10/\phi^2$.

Total height of the colossus is ϕ^2 fathoms at $45° = 1.852\ldots$ meters $\times\ \phi^2 = 4.849\ldots$ meters.

Height of dorsal stele is ϕ^2 fathoms at $0° = 1.843\ldots$ meters $\times\ \phi^2 = 4.825\ldots$ meters.

Measurements of 2 fathoms and of ϕ fathoms indicated on the stele are related to the fathom at $0°$.

The north face of the pedestal is inscribed in a 1 to 2 rectangle, not counting the surface irregularities. This surface then represents a double square. The rabattement of the diagonal of one of them from the upper edge of the pedestal determines point *a*. The line leading from this point to the top of the red crown corresponds to the angle of the crown and to the movement of the king's left leg. At the right, the ratio 14 : 11 defines the height of the red crown.

Moreover, the study of the pharaonic canon has revealed, based on harmonic decomposition, the essential numbers for determining the height of the crowned king.[9] The genesis of this decomposition leads to 8/11, and the quantity carried over from the difference 3/11 defines the ratio 14/11. This ratio is framed by two irrational functions and offers the possibility of two interpretations: $\sqrt{\phi} = 1.2720...$; $14/11 = 1.2727...$; $4/\pi = 1.2732...$.

In arrested numbers, the crowned king has the value of 14/11 of his height to the vertex, but, functionally, he can be considered as either $\sqrt{\phi}$ or as $4/\pi$.

These two coefficients are from the numbers of growth functions: ϕ or $\sqrt{\phi}$ is the number of the Horian or solar function of growth, which is continuous; π and the function of π is the function of cyclic growth, which is Osirian or lunar.

The South As the Side of Realization (Plate 21)

The functions that relate the measures and proportions of the king, the queen, and the pedestal are as follows:

- Height of the queen to the headband equals the width of the back of the pedestal.[10]
- Height of the queen to the headband times ϕ equals the north length of the pedestal.
- Height of the queen to the headband times 1.902 equals the diagonal of the pedestal.
- Half-height of the colossus equals the diagonal of the pedestal.[11]

The diagonal of the pedestal carried over two times determines the height of the king, so that if the queen has the value of 5 to the headband, the king will then be 18 to the forehead and 19 to the vertex as marked by the angles of his headdress. Nineteen being the normal division of human height for this canon, the queen is thus 5 if the king is 19.[12]

The functional number of the king is 19. This number, however, can result from two distinct functions, each of which is as essential as the other: the diagonal of the 1 to ϕ rectangle $= \sqrt{\phi^2 + 1} = 1.902$, and half the square of $6.18034 = 60/\pi = 19.0983...$.

It is a question here of nuances between the two functions that are indicated by the two possible heights of the king to the vertex, that is, 4.80 meters to the corners of his headdress and 4.85 meters to the top of his headdress. The two heights theoretically equal 19. On the pharaonic *canevas*, the height to the forehead is 18; it is therefore this measurement that must be the basis for establishing the unit of length of the *canevas* (fig. 206).

The unit of measure corresponds exactly to the fifth part of the height of the queen to under the base of the uraeus, which is 1.264/5 meters, and the correspondence between the *canevas* projected in fig. 206 and the measurements taken on the colossus itself can be metrically verified on the table of measures.

If now we were to take one-fifth of the exact width of the pedestal (1.27 m) for the unit of the square, we would have 0.254 meter as the unit of the square. Now, 19.0983 of these squares determine the maximum height of the *nemes* headdress, which is 4.85 meters.

---

[9] Cf. fig. 136.

[10] We should note here that the width of the back of the pedestal represents 68 digits for its north length of 110 digits, 1.27 m and 2.06 m, respectively. In these numbers of digits we recognize the ratio 55/34 in the F series.

[11] Cf. tables of the king's and queen's measures and the note relating to the latter.

[12] The division of the queen's height by 5 recalls the function of 5 and the pentagram of Hathor. [Hathor's face conventionally describes a pentagon.]

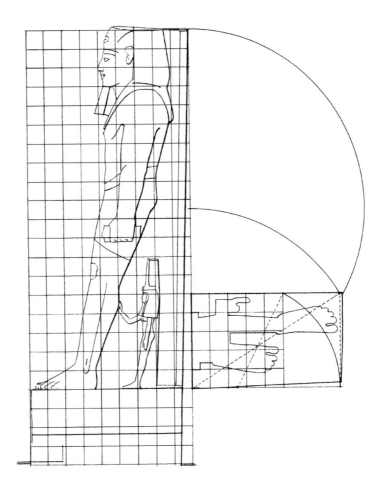

Fig. 206. Projection of the standard canevas on colossus no. 3

$$\frac{\text{Height of the king to the forehead}}{18} = \frac{4.55 \text{ meters}}{18} = 0.25278... \text{ meters}$$

for the side of the square that is the unit for drawing the *canevas*.

The slight differences between the two measures that we observe here (for example, 4.80 and 4.85) correspond to the two moments of the walking colossus,[13] since the hips necessarily are somewhat swayed by the forward position of the left leg, which otherwise would be longer than the right leg.

Here, as in the whole temple, one notes living movement while remaining faithful to the exact relationships among the numbers. This is the reason that the surface of the pedestal is not absolutely flat, but takes account of movement, which slightly differentiates the height measurements when they are taken, for example, from under the right foot or the left foot of the king, and for the queen, whether from in front or in profile.

--

[13] Walking, movement in the vital sense, is, as we affirm elsewhere, the vital function of growth. Cf. above, legend accompanying plate 20 with regard to the two functions ϕ and π.

Essay:

The Colossus with Respect to the Geographic Position of Luxor

The tilt of the earth's axis with respect to the ecliptic was assumed by the Ancients to be 24° (fig. 207, angle *A*).[14]

The position of Luxor on the globe is 25°43′ north latitude (±1′) (fig. 207, angle *B*). With respect to the vertical at the summer solstice at Luxor, the solar rays at midday make an angle of 25°43′; this less 24° equals 1°43′ (fig. 207, angle *C*). With respect to the vertical, and at the winter solstice at Luxor, the solar rays at midday make an angle of 25°43′; this plus 24° equals 49°43′ (fig. 207, angle *D*).

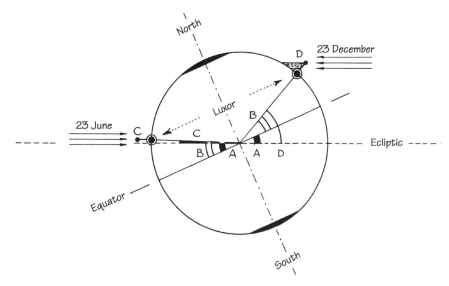

Fig. 207. Position of Luxor on the globe

In figure 207, angle *A*, the position of the equator in relation to the ecliptic (24°), is determined by the right triangle formed by the vertical height of the stele from its upper, inner edge dropped to the plane of the pedestal and forming a right angle with it (see fig. 208). The diagonal runs from the front edge of the pedestal to the interior, upper edge of the stele.

Angle *C*, or the angle of the shadow of a gnomon at the summer solstice, is equal to the slope formed by the south side of the dorsal stele upon which the king leans in relation to the vertical, so that if we were to place the colossus facing north, his stele would incline in oblique light at 1°43′ at noon, on 23 June. This is the place where the name of Horus is carved on the spinal column "of fire," which the stele represents.

Angle *D* is that of the shadow that would place the forehead of the queen on the front of the pedestal on 23 December; an opposition of lunar *(yin)* feminine to the solar *(yang)* masculine, that is, the culminations of the two solstices.

―⁓―

We must note that each colossus has its own characteristics as to its measurements, its proportions, and its angular plays.

---

[14] In the Ramesside era, the tropic of Cancer passed several minutes south of 24°, but tradition seems to have preserved the angle of 24° for the obliquity of the ecliptic, probably because of its function linking the hexagon and the pentagon.

Fig. 208. Definition of the angles of the colossus

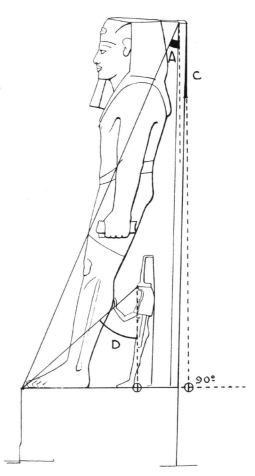

Sloping height of the stele = 4.825 meters.
Length of the south face of pedestal = 2.10 meters.
Thickness of stele at top = 0.10 meter.

Angle *C* is the angle of the tilt of the stele with respect to the vertical. It is 1°43′, or about $\widehat{3/100}$ in whole numbers. The vertical height becomes 4.822... meters, and the distance between the vertical and the stele is 0.1445 meter.

Angle *A* is defined by the vertical height from the interior edge of the stele through its perpendicular dropped to the level of the pedestal. The angular relationship is 4.822/2.1445 = 2.2489 = cot 23°58′20″, or about $\widehat{4/9}$ in whole numbers.

Angle *D* is defined by the triangle with its vertical height equal to the height of the queen to the vertex, and for the base, the distance is contained between the end of the pedestal and the vertical tangent to the queen's forehead.

PLATE 23 • COLOSSUS NO. 3 OF RAMESSES II, VIEW FROM ABOVE
Relationships of the Pedestal of the Colossus to the Courtyard of Nectanebo, the Parvis

The plan of the pedestal and the different horizontal sections of the colossus allow us to perceive the twisting movement impressed on the dorsal stele so that the king, looking west, slightly turns his head toward the south, *carrying along with his gaze the inscription drawn on the stele.* The axis of the flattened surface of the headdress is perpendicular to the oblique line made by the upper edge of the stele in relationship to its base. The stele thus undergoes a helicoidal torsion.

We have seen that the pedestal of the colossus is the seat upon which are inscribed the geometric functions whose development determines the measures and proportions of the king and also those of the queen. Similarly, the Nectanebo courtyard, the parvis, is the *foundation* of the Man represented by the Temple, figured as "colossus."[15]

The surveys of the base of the colossus on the one hand, and the Nectanebo courtyard on the other, were made with the greatest precision and with no preconceived ideas, which allows us to summarize their measurements and to establish their metrical and functional ratios.

[15] Cf. plate 24.

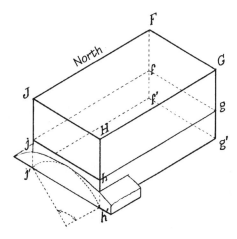

Fig. 209. Measurements of the pedestal of the colossus

The granite pedestal forms the irregular parallelepipeds *FGHJ* and *fghj*. The extension of its vertical sides to the ground determines the lower plane *f′g′h′j′*.

	Upper plane	Lower plane (± 5 mm)
Lengths	*GH* = 2.10 meters	*g′h′* = 2.10 meters
	FJ = 2.06 meters	*f′j′* = 2.095 meters
Widths	*GF* = 1.27 meters	*g′f′* = 1.29 meters
	JH = 1.19 meters	*j′h′* = 1.21 meters

Mean height to the front on the axis of the cartouches equals 0.975 meter. Mean height to the back from the baseline of the stele to the ground is equal to the height *Gg′*, which is 1.03 meters.

Verified on the scale drawings and calculated taking the slope and the two single right angles *FGH* and *Gg′f′* into account, the essential diagonals are as follows:

diagonal of the surface of the base *f′h′* = 2.465 meters
diagonal of the back side f′G   = 1.65 meters
diagonal of the volume *Gj′*   = 2.618 meters.

Henceforth, let us note that the length of the temple, with the addition of the crown of the skull, is equal to fifty times the axial diagonal of the colossus.[16] Taking this reference into account, it is possible to compare the Nectanebo courtyard, which is an irregular quadrilateral shape, with the pedestal of colossus no. 3, characterized by inequalities in all its dimensions.

The pedestal of the colossus breaks down into two parts: the granite pedestal, which is part of the same stone as the statue, and the sandstone base that connects this pedestal to the pavement of the courtyard (fig. 209).

[16] This diagonal is measured from the upper edge of the front of the pedestal to the upper edge of the back of the stele. Cf. fig. 212 and plate 24.

On the western side of the sandstone base there is a stone that extends past the pedestal to the north and to the south, and that has an arched upper edge. This stone has been cut at a right angle on its western side and is of a piece with the face of the granite pedestal to the level of the pavement into which it is fitted.

The height of the granite pedestal and of its base is not the same on its eastern and western sides, which allows us to postulate a small walkway between the courtyard itself and the portico. The measurements taken show us that the pavement in front of the portico is higher by a few centimeters than what it is in back of the colossus under the colonnade. (fig. 209).

The Nectanebo courtyard is surrounded by a wall of unbaked bricks. The construction of the walls in both plan and elevation is bow-shaped,[17] and the pylon is set into this surrounding wall such that its own exterior contour is also slightly bowed. Only the northwest corner (*C*, fig. 210) is presently visible, characterized by its stone construction resembling the shape of the prow of a ship, resting on the corner of raw bricks.[18] The northeast corner (*D*, fig. 210) is determined by its interior corner, found intact in the excavations; its exterior reconstruction is based on that corner and the average thickness of the walls, which is about 5 meters. The southeast corner (*A*, fig. 210) has been demolished since the construction of the surrounding wall by the Romans, but vestiges of its interior corner (*a*, fig. 210) have been found in the foundation. The west and north walls of this courtyard have been found almost whole, so that with these elements it is possible to arrive at a close approximation of the measurements and orientations of this courtyard.[19]

The *axis of the south wall* is parallel to the north facade of the pylon and corresponds to its median longitudinal axis. The *axis of the west wall* is parallel to the northern part of the west wall of the Ramesses court, and forms a deviation of 10°, or about $\widehat{3/17}$, with the axis of Mut (geometric axis of the head).

The *northwest corner* is determined by the crossing of the west wall of the Nectanebo courtyard with the axis of Mut (geometric axis of the head). The *axis of the north wall* together with the axis of Amun forms a right angle less 10°, with the result that the ratio between the west and north walls of the courts is, perpendicularly, the same as that between the axes of Amun and Mut (head).

The *axis of the east wall* with that of the north wall forms a right angle when increased by the angle 1 to 7 (angle of reflection of Amun).

Now that we have determined the orientations of the enclosing walls of the Nectanebo courtyard, we only have to consider their respective lengths.

The south wall corresponds to the place where the colossus places his feet. Let us recall in this regard that man is considered to be the radius of the earth, placed on the plane of the equator.[20] The earth measured at its "polar skullcap" has the same number of royal cubits that the circumference contains in fathoms, just as the "colossus" of the temple measured at the diadem (south wall of the covered temple) has the same number of royal cubits as the plan of the foundation measured in fathoms. We find here the rigorous application of this function, but with a reversal of notions: the royal headband measures 20 fathoms, and the south wall of the parvis is 250 royal cubits long,

[17] Cf. plates 47–49.

[18] Ibid.

[19] Cf. plan in plate 12.

[20] Cf. fig. 179.

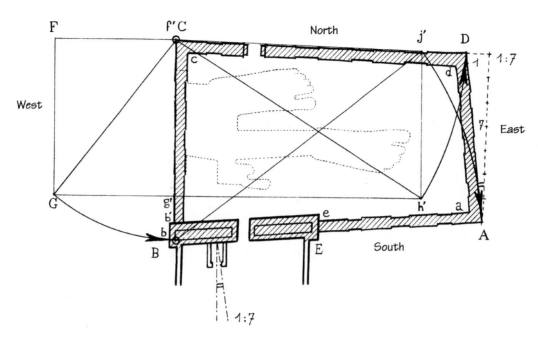

*Fig. 210. Projection of the inverted pedestal of the colossus,
enlarged fifty times, onto the Nectanebo courtyard*

Comparison of the dimensions of the courtyard with those of the diagonals of the pedestal.

South wall	north face	{ thickness of surrounding wall		5.00 meters
		interior length *ae*		63.80 meters
		length of pylon *eb'*		62.20 meters
		total length		**131.00 meters**
	south face	{ exterior length *AE*		69.20 meters
		exterior length *EB*		63.60 meters
		total length AB		**132.80 meters**
North wall		{ interior length *cd*		113.50 meters
		exterior length *CD*		123.50 meters
West wall		{ exterior length *Cb'*		75.60 meters
		exterior length *Cb*		82.50 meters
East wall		{ interior length *ad*		60.20 meters
		exterior length *AD*		70.20 meters

Diagonal *f'h'* of the surface of pedestal $2.465 \times 50 = 123.25$ meters
     comaparable to length of north wall   123.50 meters
Diagonal *f'G* of back side of pedestal $1.65 \times 50 = 82.50$ meters
     comparable to length *Cb* of west wall   82.50 meters
Diagonal of the volume *Gj'* or *bj'* of pedestal $2.618 \times 50 = 130.90$ meters
     comparable to length of south wall, north face   131.00 meters

which, functionally, by a double crossing of the measures and the intervention of the square root of 2, comes to[21]

$$\begin{aligned} \text{royal headband} &= \text{south wall of covered temple} &&= 70.71 \text{ royal cubits} \\ \text{equator} &= \text{south wall of parvis} &&= 70.71 \text{ mean fathoms.} \end{aligned}$$

The length of the south wall of the parvis, measuring 250 royal cubits or 70.71 mean fathoms, represents half the height of the Man of the Temple.[22]

As we have seen previously, the length of the west wall is defined by the crossing of the two essential axes. This length, added to the total length of the temple, that is, from the south wall of the covered temple to the northwest corner of the Nectanebo courtyard, gives a total length of 180 fathoms.[23] We still have to determine the lengths of the east and north walls of the parvis.

The projection of the inverted pedestal of the colossus onto the Nectanebo courtyard, enlarged fifty times and with its face turned toward the east, puts the corner f' of the pedestal into coincidence with the northwest corner C of the courtyard, which allows us to observe that the rabattement of the three essential diagonals defining the volume of the pedestal of the colossus determines the sizes of the four irregular sides of this courtyard (fig. 210). The back edge $f'g'$ of the pedestal is oriented following the axis of the west wall of the courtyard. The edge $f'j'$ of the pedestal will thus be perpendicular to the avenue of the sphinxes.

The diagonal of the lower surface of the pedestal determines the length of the north wall of the courtyard. The diagonal of the east back side of the pedestal defines the length between the northwest corner of the courtyard and the point of crossing of the extension of the south wall in b (fig. 210).

Finally, the diagonal of the volume defines and confirms the length already found for the south wall, which is 250 royal cubits.

—〜〜—

As a plane surface, the Nectanebo courtyard is constructed on the diagonals of the volume of the pedestal of the colossus. By bringing this surface of the Nectanebo courtyard over into the volume of the pedestal, one obtains figure 211 in which $h'j'$ is the chord of an arc the length of which is AD, the east wall of the courtyard.

In conclusion, the trapezoidal shape of the enclosing walls of the Nectanebo courtyard represents the matrix form that contains all the elements for determining the pedestal of colossus no. 3 and its height above the ground. This is said only for the sake of demonstration, because it is the pedestal of this colossus that is the container giving the elements of the Nectanebo walls.

PLATE 24 • PROJECTION OF COLOSSUS NO. 3
ONTO THE TEMPLE OF LUXOR

The study of the measures and proportions of the colossus of Ramesses has allowed us to observe that the position of his navel divides his height by the golden section,[24] thus determining his adult age. Now in order to correspond to this age, the proportion of the height of the head in relationship to the total height of the figure ought to be as 1 is to 7.5, which we can verify by the following dimensions:

---

[21] Cf. chapter 10.

[22] Cf. chapter 28 and plate 15.

[23] The total length of the temple with the parvis is 258 m plus 75.60 m, which equals 333.60 m, or 180 fathoms of 1.853 m or 181 fathoms at 0°.

[24] Cf. above, table of the king's measurements.

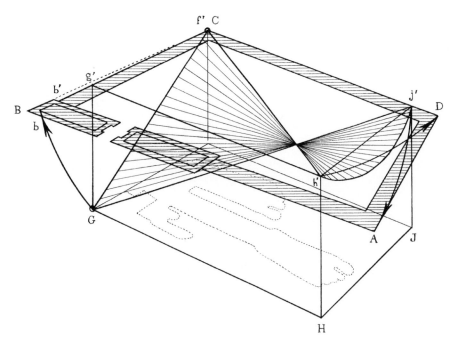

*Fig. 211. Projection of the plan of the courtyard of Nectanebo onto
the inverted pedestal of the colossus enlarged fifty times.*

The measurement from the level of the chin to that of the edges of the headdress is 0.74 meter, and the height of the colossus to this point is 4.80 meters. The ratio is thus

$$\frac{\text{total height}}{\text{height of head}} = \frac{4.80 \text{ meters}}{0.74} = 6.48...,$$

and not 7.5 as the canon would require. We observe this same proportion between the face represented by the pavestone mosaic[25] and the total length of the reconstituted Man of the Temple with the crown of his skull established on the proportions of this face.

Moreover, the study of the Nectanebo courtyard in relation to the pedestal of the colossus has confirmed the essential relationship that also exists between the colossus and the temple: *the diagonals of the pedestal times fifty determine the dimensions of the parvis, as the axial diagonal of the colossus times fifty defines the length of the Man of the Temple.*

The hypotenuse of the triangle determined by the vertical height of the stele lowered onto the plane of the pedestal on its central axis is the fiftieth part of the length of the Man of the Temple.

This hypotenuse measures 5.308 meters, or 2.88 fathoms at 0°, so that the length of the temple is 144 fathoms at 0°, or 265.392 meters.

Now, while the height of the head was contained about 6.5 times in the vertical height of the colossus, the hypotenuse represents 7.17 times the height of the king's head, which corrects the indicated proportion by giving the statue, as seen from a certain distance and by means of perspective, the correct proportion between the head and the height corresponding to the age of eighteen to nineteen years. Now, since this colossus gives this double proportion by its vertical height and by its diagonal, it is possible, by virtue of the indicated angle, to find how far away the observer must be in order to reestablish the correct proportion through perspective.

---

[25] Cf. plates 35–37 and their commentaries.

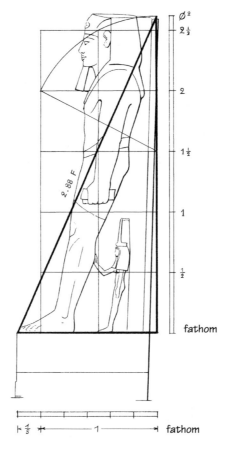

Fig. 212. Axial diagonal of the colossus

The length of the axial diagonal of the colossus measured on the scale drawings at 1 to 10 is 0.53 meter, which is 5.30 meters on the monument. The following calculations verify this dimension.

The stele being twisted, its angle at its median part is about 1°28′. The distance between the vertical and the pedestal is 0.123 meter, and is added to the base of the pedestal, which on the median axis is about 2.09 meters. The base of the triangle then measures 2.21 meters for the vertical height of 4.825 meters. These dimensions correspond in fathoms to:

$$
\begin{aligned}
\text{base} &= 2.211 \text{ meters} = 1.2 \text{ fathoms at } 0° \\
\text{height} &= 4.825 \text{ meters} = 2.618 \text{ fathoms at } 0° \\
\text{hypotenuse} &= 5.308 \text{ meters} = 2.88 \text{ fathoms at } 0°.
\end{aligned}
$$

Numerical function: $\sqrt{(1.2)^2 + \phi^4} = \sqrt{8.2941}$ in absolute value, comparable with $\sqrt{8.2944} = 2.88$.

Three important points result from this construction:

$$
\begin{aligned}
1\tfrac{1}{2} \text{ fathoms} &= 2.765 \text{ meters} = \text{bottom edge of belt, front left} \\
2 \text{ fathoms} &= 3.686 \text{ meters} = \text{bottom of the king's beard} \\
2\tfrac{1}{2} \text{ fathoms} &= 4.607 \text{ meters} = \text{bottom of the ureaus} = \text{height of ears.}
\end{aligned}
$$

It is evident that this hypotenuse will always be the same, whatever the angle of the stele.

—⁓—

In conclusion, the colossus carries in itself the "two rhythms" that are everywhere affirmed in the course of our observations. This double rhythm is connected as much to the problem of growth as to the different cubits found in Egypt.

The double rhythm indicates the following two lineages of measure: 500 royal cycle cubits[26] and 144 fathoms at 0°.[27]

—⁓—

The projection of the scale drawing of colossus no. 3 on the plan of the temple gives all the numbers and measurements we have just indicated. This is again justified by the fact that the hand of the queen on the king's calf is exactly at the spot where this colossus is located in the court of Ramesses.

Summary of the Changes to the Temple During the Pharaonic Period between the Eighteenth and Thirtieth Dynasties

Each temple can be related to a historical moment. This fact becomes important when the mystical names of the kings of that era are taken into account.

The construction executed under Amenhotep III[28] (1411–1375 B.C.), son of Tuthmosis IV, contains, in the thickness of its walls as well as in its "tank"-shaped foundation, numerous blocks from a previous temple.[29]

A probe into sanctuary I has shown that the "tank" contained—like the one of Mentu at Karnak—column drums and smoothed pavestones, together with a block of limestone bearing the inscription "the house of the *neter*."[30]

The pavement of the covered temple contains numerous cube-shaped blocks that very likely were the foundations, in squared sections, of the pillars. In one case, the disjunction of the stones revealed the cartouche of Tuthmosis.

The numerous sixteen-sided column drums, characteristic of certain buildings of the Tuthmoses at Karnak, were reused in the southeast and west walls of the covered temple.[31]

Most of the embrasures have blocks at their bases, one surface of which is cut on a bias that corresponds to the slope of the pylons. The walls themselves sometimes contain one or two of these blocks, which always represent something of symbolic interest.[32]

Only the lower courses of the west wall of the nave currently remain, permitting one to observe that numerous drums of large cylindrical columns were used in the construction of this wall, which is entirely "filled," in contrast with the east wall of the nave, which is "hollow."[33]

Looking at all these facts together, we are certain of the existence of a previous temple. In addition, four monolithic columns in red granite—of admirable cut and curve—are presently

[26] Plate 15, projection of the skeleton onto the temple.

[27] Plate 24, projection of the colossus onto the temple.

[28] The Greek form of this name is Amenophis.

[29] Cf. plate 94C, tank-shaped foundation.

[30] This fragment of limestone did not have a cartouche that allowed it to be dated and was respectfully put back in its place (fig. 293).

[31] Cf. plate 78.

[32] Cf. plates 99 and 100 and their commentaries.

[33] Cf. plate 95.

structural elements in the portico that comes before the three chapels of the barques erected by Ramesses II in the narthex. Their architraves still carry the remains of an inscription of Tuthmosis III on their upper surfaces. Ramesses thus turned these architraves over to reuse them, as was quite probably the case with the four columns that support them.[34]

The character of the reused stones and columns in places that correspond to the same symbolism in the building of Amenhotep shows a kinship between the two succeeding temples.

———～～～———

Until now we have only developed the essential phases of the growth of the temple.[35] It is necessary to point out some important modifications that took place during this growth, especially concerning the bas-reliefs. Amenhotep III covered all the rooms of the covered temple with bas-reliefs, with the exception of the small chamber opening onto the hypostyle room and located to the east of the room of the barque of Mut.[36] The facade of the doorway of this "unfinished" chamber[37] has a representation of Khonsu on the lintel. The west wall has no bas-reliefs, and on the east partition only the first register has been begun and left unfinished by Amenhotep III. Now, it is worth mentioning that *this bas-relief was never reworked by any of the kings who succeeded him, because Khonsu is still a primitive stage of what the king will become.* We observe this primitive character, heavy and somber, in the temple of Khonsu at Karnak, which is, moreover, joined to the temple of Apet that contains the tomb of Osiris reborn. There are two aspects of Khonsu, one of the Osirian, lunar phase, and the other of the Horian, solar phase.

The few fragments remaining of the interior partitions of the peristyle court (transept) are from Amenhotep III.

In the nave, the two doorposts of the southern doorway opening onto the transept bear the ritual scene of "Giving the House to Its Master," above which five lines of dedication describe this pinewood door, worked with copper, bronze, and fine gold, and designate this scene by its name, which speaks of the power and the majesty of Amun of the origin.

The exterior facade of the northern doorway of the nave marks the end of the constructions of Amenhotep III, and on the doorposts the ritual scene of the consecration of the temple is represented, similar to the preceding one (that of the southern doorway).[38] The texts on the architraves of the great colonnade of the nave, inscribed from north to south, were drawn by Amenhotep III, but as we shall see later on, they were hammered out and reworked by Seti I.

As for the two interior partitions of the nave, it is difficult to know if Amenhotep restricted himself to the single decoration of the southern doorway described above, or if he began the bas-reliefs that now bear the cartouches of his successors.

———～～～———

[34] Cf. plate 87. We limit ourselves here to the most characteristic examples.

[35] Cf. chapter 28.

[36] Cf. fig. 198; room XX is the chamber of Mut.

[37] Egyptologists want to see this as the chamber of the king's barque in spite of the bas-reliefs representing Khonsu. It is true that Khonsu is at the genetic origin of the king.

[38] Cf. plates 29 and 30, and figs. 217, 218, and 219. These two representations are now the only ones that bear the cartouche of Amenhotep III on the bas-reliefs of the "third stage" of the temple.

At Luxor as everywhere else, Akhenaten (Amenhotep IV, 1375–1358) effaced, by means of systematic hammering out, all figures of Amun and all the *neters,* as well as their legends, with the exception of Tum of Heliopolis. This was a considerable task, for none of the architraves—the lowest of which was nearly 8.4 meters high, and the highest was 20 meters—were spared.

This pharaoh constructed an edifice consecrated to Aten (the solar disk) at Karnak. This monument was subsequently entirely razed. Ramesses II reused a large number of blocks with the name of Akhenaten on them in his pylon at Luxor. We should recall that with Akhenaten begins the material, concrete phase of the sun; this phase would be continued by the Ramesses, who will implement the *reversal* of its domination.

Amenhotep IV took the name Akh-n-aten, "advent of the solar disk," and not "advent" or "birth of Ra," the solar principle that Ra-mes-s, or Ramesses, would come to represent.

—⁓—

From the historical point of view, the Eighteenth Dynasty ends in great confusion, and it is therefore difficult to put the royal names in their chronological order. At the temple of Luxor we meet the name of Ay (Kheper-Kheperu-Ra, "transformation of the sun's transformations") in the dedication on the doorposts of the southern doorway of room VIII and under the bas-reliefs of Amenhotep III. This point corresponds to the clavicle of the Man of the Temple.[39] Also, the bas-reliefs of the exterior facade of the north pylon of the nave[40] (that is, at the knee) are attributed to Ay.

The cartouche of Tutankhamun is visible in the nave under the capitals of certain columns, and there is considerable uncertainty about the decoration elements of the nave that can be attributed to him.

Finally, Horemheb ("Horus in a state of renewal"), according to current opinion, altered the cartouches of the previously mentioned kings. Also, today, we find his name on all the interior partitions of the nave as well as on the facade of the pylon of Amenhotep III. In one of his texts, Horemheb, incidentally, attributes to himself only the renovation of the temple constructed by Amenhotep III.

—⁓—

With Ramesses II ("birth of the sun," 1298–1232), the Nineteenth Dynasty brings the important addition of the narthex. His predecessor, Seti I (1318–1298), restored the Amunian bas-reliefs hammered out by Akhenaten in the constructions of Amenhotep III. Everywhere the stone was resurfaced and recarved, and sometimes replastered, and Seti I left his cartouche in numerous places, along with a dedication attesting to the fact that he had "renewed" the temple; all his work is in shallow relief.

Ramesses II covered with bas-reliefs the exterior and interior sides of his pylon, as well as the exterior and interior facades of the narthex. The construction of the south portico of the narthex entailed the reworking of the bas-reliefs on the facade of the Amenhotep III pylon, the lower part of which has been demolished, while the upper part is still visible above the roofing.[41] Ramesses

---

[39] Cf. plate 28, no. 12. The two signatures of Ay are found on the right and left doorposts under figure no. 12 and its opposite.

[40] Cf. plate 27 and its legend.

[41] Cf. note 39.

made major modifications to his own carvings, as, for example, the "reversal" of certain tableaux;[42] he also covered the exterior west partition of the nave with bas-reliefs.[43] The bas-reliefs executed by Ramesses are in sunk relief.

The son of Ramesses, Merneptah ("beloved of Ptah") inscribed his name on the buttress supporting the front leg of the colossus in the narthex, on the king's right. His cartouche is also found at several important points in this court, notably at the entrance to the repository of Amun's barque on the two doorposts,[44] and in the southwest corner of the narthex under the representation of the "ascent of the princes" toward the pylon depicted at this point.[45]

Finally, Seti II, the last pharaoh of the Nineteenth Dynasty (which ended in 1200 B.C.), filled in the sloping steps of the northern doorway of the nave, covered with bas-reliefs by Ramesses II, and thus removed the double door that was there and that had an architectural and symbolic importance. He then covered his "padding" of bas-reliefs with his name.[46] These carvings are in sunk relief, and his cartouche is again seen in the nave and in the transept.

This removal of the door that had connected the two knees now allows them to separate, since with Ramesses, the Man had grown from seven to twelve and then to eighteen years (maturity), giving him, with his mobility, his independence. At least one could thus interpret the gesture of removing this door between the two *future* knees, since with Amenhotep this pylon was the resting place of the feet of the Man, still a child of seven or eight years. Now, it is evident that this child also had knees, and the growth of the legs was not made by simply adding on to the soles of the feet. Since, on the other hand, all the proportions of the human body accord with the measures and proportions of the finished temple, *in which the phases of growth are marked,* we should see the different gestures (such as the opening or the closing of a door, a double swinging door becoming a single door, and so on) as functional symbols and not as concrete facts.

In the course of the Twentieth Dynasty (1200–1085), Ramesses III covered the exterior walls of the covered temple with bas-reliefs and left a stele describing his works. He also carved his cartouches in the hypostyle room under the dedication of Seti II and altered the dedication carved by Merneptah in the narthex under the "ascent of the princes."[47]

Ramesses IV deeply carved the dedications that we presently see at the base of the east and west partitions of the nave. Below these he added his cartouches, which he also carved at the bases of the partitions of the hypostyle room (the *haty*) as well as at the bases of the shafts of the columns of this room.[48] Ramesses VI altered the cartouches of Ramesses IV at the bases of these columns.

---

[42] Cf. plates 9 and 92.

[43] Cf. fig. 199, the description of all the exterior bas-reliefs.

[44] Cf. plate 87, the repository of Amun's barque.

[45] Cf. fig. 268.

[46] Cf. plate 28, fig. 7, located at the knee of the Man of the Temple.

[47] Cf. fig. 268.

[48] At Karnak, Ramesses IV inscribed his cartouches beside those of Ramesses II on the columns of the hypostyle room; they are to be found on the capitals as well as on the bases of the shafts.

During the Twenty-first Dynasty (1085–950) a votive inscription by the priest Pinedjem, and another by his son Ramenkheper, let it be known that they made repairs in the temple.[49]

—⁓—

In the Twenty-fifth Dynasty (751–656), the last decan of the gestation (entering into the ninth month),[50] the black Ethiopian kings governed Egypt. The first of these kings, Shabaka, covered the interior doorposts at the entrance of the pylon of Ramesses with bas-reliefs, as well as the interior east face of the recess of this door, which had only a single swinging panel, placed on the west side, where the hinge socket is. A single swinging door panel about 5 meters long can only have had a symbolic meaning, as would narrower double doors; a double door necessarily means an entrance through a separation.[51]

Shabaka presumably also constructed a pathway paved in granite on either side, a colonnade constituting a portico to the north of the pylon of Ramesses II. The drums of these columns, carved in relief and bearing the cartouche of this pharaoh, are presently serving as pavestones in room VIII of the covered temple and testify to the existence of this colonnade. Moreover, at the north of this pylon of Ramesses II, the excavations of 1950–52 revealed a paved pathway formed from large blocks of red granite, of which only the west part could be cleared. The first block presently visible is at a distance of around 23 meters and the last about 40 meters from the north face of the pylon. Some of these blocks of granite had also been reused as paving in the east and west parts of room VIII, most probably by the Romans when they elevated the level of this room. These elements allow us to suppose that Shabaka had erected on the parvis at Luxor a colonnade similar to the one whose complete elements can still be seen at Karnak, executed by Taharka, some distance in front of the second pylon.[52]

Shebitku, the successor of Shabaka, demolished a bas-relief of Ramesses III on the exterior south wall of the covered temple at the level of room V and replaced it with two scenes bearing his cartouche. Now, these Ethiopian kings were characterized by the wearing of a double uraeus, of which one was systematically scraped off by the following.[53] The period of the black kings corresponds to the time from the eighth month of fetal gestation to the ninth month of completion, after which comes the birth: the Greco-Roman period.

—⁓—

The Thirtieth Dynasty (378–341) brings to a close the history of pharaonic Egypt with Nectanebo (the last king before the conquest by Alexander), who constructed important buildings throughout the entire empire.

---

[49] The inscription of Pinedjem is found on the north face of the pylon of Amenhotep III, behind the seated black granite colossus, to the east, that is, at the knee. That of his son is found at the door of the hypostyle room, that is, at the *haty*.

[50] Cf. chapter 20.

[51] The dimension of this door is exactly 5.17 m and represents 10 cubits of 20 *remen* digits. Cf. chapter 10.

[52] Jean Leclant, "Fouilles et travaux en Egypte 1950–51," *Orientalia* 20, no. 4 (1951), notes the existence at Karnak of a granite pavement in the great colonnade of Taharka in front of the second pylon, another granite pavement in the Ethiopian colonnade to the east, and finally a similar pavement in the temple of Mentu, dating from the same period.

[53] Cf. plates 75–78, sanctuary V and its relation with the serpent, the uraeus, olfaction, and dualization. See fig. 199 for the location of this bas-relief.

At Luxor, there is a stele in quartzite in front of the left doorpost of the entrance to the parvis, relating to this door and bearing the cartouche of Nectanebo II, attributing to him the construction of the door in question and the enclosing wall of unbaked bricks outlining the parvis. The dromos is lined by sphinxes with human heads in his name, and Nectanebo thus concludes the history of the genesis of the Man of the Temple.

—⁓—

The fact that the dimensions of the parvis are defined by the diagonals of the pedestal of the colossus inverted in the ground and turned around so that it faces toward the east, whereas in the court of Ramesses it looked west, corresponds to the following symbolism: *(a)* the colossus goes out of the temple; *(b)* he is upside down in the gound; *(c)* his orientation is turned around, with east becoming west, but since he is upside down as in a vertical mirror, the south corresponds to the south.

The reversal of orientation is related to the reversal of the Ramesside bas-reliefs of the west pylon.[54] The inversion in the earth evokes, in its association with the thematic group of the bow, the black earth, and so forth, the constructions executed "under the feet" of the Man of the Temple by the Ethiopian kings, Shabaka and Shebitku. This relationship comes through in the addition by Shabaka of a portico with red granite pavement and the red granite pedestal that serves as the base of the colossus projected onto the temple, and the fact that this pavement is the only part that still remains of this portico.

It is necessary to insist on the fact that through the inversion, what was high is now low and vice versa. Now, the two inscriptions carved in the temple by the Ethiopian kings are found "high up" in the temple on the royal headband, and "low" in the temple at the feet.[55] Thus these kings, wearing the *double* uraeus, carved their inscriptions at the *double* part of the brain, the part in which man is "upside down,"[56] and at its opposite end, the feet,[57] the physiological importance of which we have seen through their reactions' revealing the condition of the central nervous system.

In this study of the inscriptions of the royal cartouches, it is essential to observe the correspondence of the mystical name of the king with the physiological part of Man, revealed to us by the temple of Luxor.

The points where the successors of Amenhotep III carved their cartouches are principally the clavicle, the knee, the thigh (the nave) during the Eighteenth Dynasty, then in the *haty*, the knee, the thigh, and the calf during the Nineteenth Dynasty.

It is again necessary to observe the particular character of these so-called usurpations; thus Tutankhamun carved his cartouches high up on the columns of the nave, while Ramesses VI carved them on the bottom of the shafts of the columns of the hypostyle room, and Ramesses IV carved them on the bottom of the lateral partitions of the nave, for example.

PLATE 25 • THE TEMPLE IN THE GRECO-ROMAN PERIOD

We can clearly distinguish two periods: the Ptolemaic period (332–30 B.C.), and Roman rule (30 B.C. to A.D. 395).

---

[54] Cf. plates 9 and 92.

[55] The south wall of the covered temple.

[56] The pylon, the two wings of which are separated by a door.

[57] Cf. chapter 15, "The Crown of the Skull," and fig. 154.

From the Ptolemaic period, graffiti in the name of Kap-ha-amen, located on the north face of the north wall of the transept, mentions the repair in acacia wood of the naos, which had fallen into ruins.[58]

Graffiti of Ankh-pa-khrod, priest of Amun, royal scribe, and chief of works of the temple, mentions the execution of repairs at Luxor. The restorations began in the third year of Alexander, lasted thirty-nine months, and were taken up again under Philip Arrhidaeus.[59]

The most important modification effected under the reign of Alexander the Great was that of room VI. Alexander removed the four columns of Amenhotep III that were supporting the roof and constructed the sandstone naos that bears his name. At the base, he left the pedestals of the old columns visible.[60] He raised the floor about 30 centimeters and reworked most of the bas-reliefs in this room, as he did those of room IV. Prior to Alexander, the entire north partition of room VI had to have undergone serious damage, because he entirely rebuilt the northern entrance with small blocks of stone that allow us to define very exactly the parts restored by him, which he signed in this room by replacing the cartouches of Amenhotep III with his own.

In addition to these restorations, for which the cartouches designate the period, there are numerous modifications in the bas-reliefs thoughout the covered temple, especially on the door-posts, which are discernible only by some particularities of style. Very often these doorways have had the edges of their posts trimmed, and the ankh that marks their central axis on the lintel remade or moved, which leaves us to suppose that the leaning of the walls toward the west, presently observed in the whole western part of the temple on the side of the Nile, was already beginning to threaten the monument at the time of Alexander, through the infiltration of river water.[61]

Philip Arrhidaeus constructed an outer door in his name in front of the northern door of the nave between the two seated colossi of black granite.[62] Another outer door was constructed at an undetermined period, north of the southern door of the nave.

With regard to the Roman priod, during the excavations of 1950–51, a small peripheral building was uncovered in the northwest corner of the Nectanebo courtyard. A small sanctuary open toward the east, surrounded by a portico of fourteen columns, it was set on a platform of baked and unbaked bricks. The sanctuary itself is built with unbaked bricks, with the exception of some parts emphasized in baked bricks. The columns are also made from unbaked bricks coated with stucco.

Only the two columns that frame the eastern entry of the portico were resting on sandstone foundations. One can still see the two sandstone doorposts at the entry of the sanctuary, and at the ground level of the sanctuary, two column drums reused as pavestones and etched with an axis line.

A sandstone lintel, 2.10 meters wide and 0.47 meter high carries a Greek dedication from A.D. 127: "For the emperor Caesar Trajan Adrian Augustus and to all his family; to Zeus Helios, the Great Serapis, Gaius Julius Antoninus, the honorable uncrowned, at his own cost, who having restored the sanctuary, consecrated the statue, by reason of his vows and his piety, under the prefect of Egypt [name hammered out]. He was also neocorus of the Great Serapis himself, and he consecrated the other statues. Year 10 of the Emperor Caesar Trajan Adrian Augustus, 29 of the month of Tybi."[63]

[58] Cf. Georges Daressy, *Le Temple du Louqsor* (Cairo: Imprimerie Nationale, 1893), p. 52.

[59] Cf. ibid.

[60] Cf. plates 83 and 90, plans of room VI.

[61] We approach then the end (birth of man) of pharaonic times, the period of the precessional passage from Aries to Pisces.

[62] Cf. plates 24 and 25.

[63] Cf. Leclant, "Fouilles et travaux en Egypte 1950–51," p. 456.

The interior walls of the sanctuary had at first been covered with a coating of blue stucco, and a second time with a coating that imitated marble plaques. Among the statues discovered in the interior, an Osiris-Canopus was found on the ground, and a limestone statue of Isis was found in the edge of the sanctuary, probably in place. Two bulls, one in limestone, the other in granite, were later discovered during the excavations.

On the exterior partitions of the sanctuary, a semicircular niche at the south was emphasized by a row of baked bricks 1.85 meters (1 fathom) long. A rectangular niche on the exterior west partition was also underlined with a row of baked bricks and also measured 1 fathom in length.

After the construction of this monument, the area between its west face and the wall surrounding the Nectanebo courtyard was filled in by a buttress of unbaked bricks that enveloped the western columns of the edifice. This restoration probably dates from the same era as the baked brick channels traversing the north wall of the Nectanebo courtyard and culminating in the avenue of sphinxes, to the right and left of the dromos.

The Serapeum that we just described was consequently buried at the same time as the Nectanebo courtyard, quite probably at the time the temple of Luxor was transformed into a fortified camp. Let us note that this small sanctuary is exactly on the extension of the axis of Amun.

—⁓—

The city of Antinoe is in another part of Egypt, in the fifteenth nome—the nome of the hare—not far from Khemenu, the sanctuary of Thoth, "master of the Eight." This city was founded by Hadrian in A.D. 130.

The legend recounts that Antinoüs, a Bithynian slave of great beauty and a favorite of Hadrian, sacrificed his life by throwing himself in the Nile to avert an oracle that predicted a painful loss to the emperor. To honor his memory, Hadrian built the city of Antinoe on the eastern bank of the Nile where Antinoüs drowned, as well as a temple consecrated to Antinoüs divinized. He had numerous statues erected in his image, the beauty of which were famous.

Let us put legend and fact together concerning the emperor Hadrian.

According to the legend, the most beautiful of men sacrificed himself for the good of the emperor. In fact, Hadrian built the city and the temple to the glory of Divinized Man.

During the same period, there was an inscription carved in Greek on the lintel of the entrance door of the Serapeum at Luxor and, nearly a century and a half later, after uncovering the construction of Nectanebo *representing* the pedestal of the Man of the Temple, the Romans put up a double wall around the temple of Luxor, transforming it into a fortress. This enclosing wall in baked bricks is characterized by semicircular towers that rise up at regular distances with square towers at the corners.[64] Four doors pass through this wall; two are at the north and one is at the west that opens onto the roadway leading to the loading dock. The one to the east is at the level of the midpoint of the temple. Starting from each of these doors and within the wall, four pathways bordered with columns cross each other, two by two. There are two on the east and two on the west in the image of the city of Antineopolis (Antinoe). At each of these crossings, the Romans erected four columns on four square-based pedestals, with human statues on top (fig. 213). These four pedestals are still intact and allow us to read the inscriptions that give the exact date of their construction.

---

[64] Cf. plate 25. The changes attributed to the Romans are in black. The surrounding wall and its towers are visible in the aerial photographs (plates 2 and 3). It can be noted that the northern door of the west part shows traces of grooves, which makes us think of a portcullis-like gateway. The raising up of the paved floor of room VIII must coincide with the closing of the southern door of this room and its transformation into a semicircular niche in order to accomodate a statue.

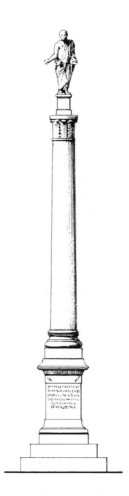

Fig. 213. Roman column reconstituted according to elements found at Luxor

To the west, these four bases were dedicated to the emperors of the first tetrarchy, two Augustuses, Diocletian and Maximian, and two Caesars, Constantius Chlorus and Galerius (A.D. 300), by Aurelius Reginus. These four inscriptions are opposite the east-west pathway, the axis leading from the river to the temple. The name of the dedicator is inscribed on a carved line that straddles a joint between two blocks.

To the east, the four pedestals are dedicated to the emperors of the second tetrarchy, two Augustuses, Licinius and Galerius, and two Caesars, Constantine and Maximinus Daia (A.D. 308–309), by Aurelius Maximus. "Under the first tetrarchy Diocletian and Galerius, and under the second Galerius and Maximinus Daia, who have been the two Augustuses and the two Caesars of the east, are *Jovians,* that is, they claim to be the descendants of Jupiter, who in Egypt is Amun."[65]

The four inscriptions of the pedestals are opposite to the north-south pathway, the principal directions of the crossing. One epigraphic characteristic of these dedications is that the names of the emperors on all four of them are painted in yellow whereas the rest are painted in red.[66] "These

[65] Cf. Lacau, *Inscriptions latines du temple de Louqsor,* p. 20.
[66] Ibid.

two groups of four columns are of the same type as the four columns that also marked the *crossing* of the two main streets in the city of Antinoe. The four columns of Antinoe carry a dedication to Alexander Severus."[67]

This comparison between the city of Antineopolis, dedicated to the *divinization of a man,* and the modifications brought to the temple of Luxor *after* the turning over of the colossus in the earth is compelling. In the legend of Antinoüs and Hadrian we are invited to see a meaning that is less human and more profound than simple personal history.

Throughout historical Egypt, the common people lived in the Osirian faith, which is a teaching of renewal and evolution through reincarnation of the living soul; man then lived under the sky, under the ordinances of the heavens. The Horian cult, that of deliverance and redemption, was reserved for the initiates of the temples, for those who knew how to renounce joyously the appearances of the world for the sake of the Divine Verb that animates them.

With the end of the pharaonic mission, preparing the advent of Christianity, which is the word of deliverance for all, man begins to raise himself up and symbolically places himself in the Heaven of the Temple, a symbol that is maintained to our day in Roman churches, after having appeared in Greece and, in the Greco-Roman era, in Egypt at the very end of the sign of Aries-Amun.

[67] Ibid, p. 44.

Chapter 30

JOINTS AND PIECES

—⁓—

Plates 26–33

The myth is a whole, the synthesis of all
science, *since it transcribes the fundamental
knowledge of the laws of genesis that apply
to everything. Thus the* neters *have their
significance, in medicine as well as in astronomy
or theology, which is the metaphysic of the
Becoming and the Return.*

(Chapter 17)

PLATE 26

The Young King Standing in the Persea Tree

Every natural type is a revelation of one of the natures and abstract functions that rule the world, a verb of the divine language, that is, of the entities or fully realized principles (neters). *They are fully realized in the sense that they are types or definite stages in the cosmic embryology of humanity.*

(Chapter 2)

PLATE 27

The Adult King Kneeling in the Persea Tree

The joint between two stones
links as much as it separates,
and it always emphasizes.

(Chapter 16)

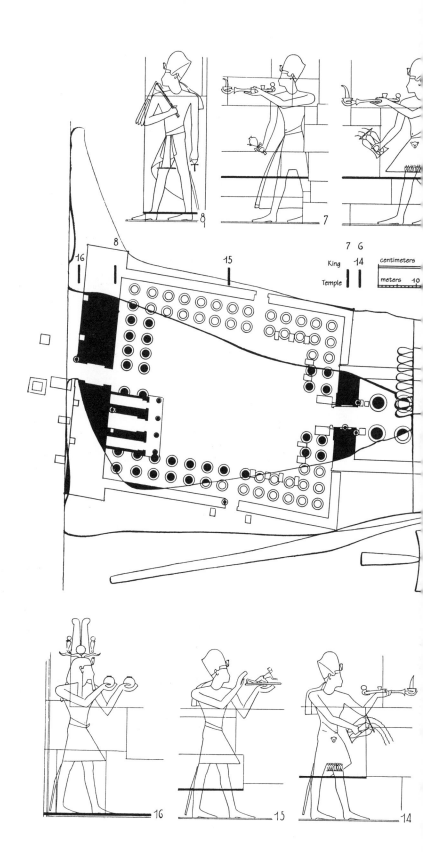

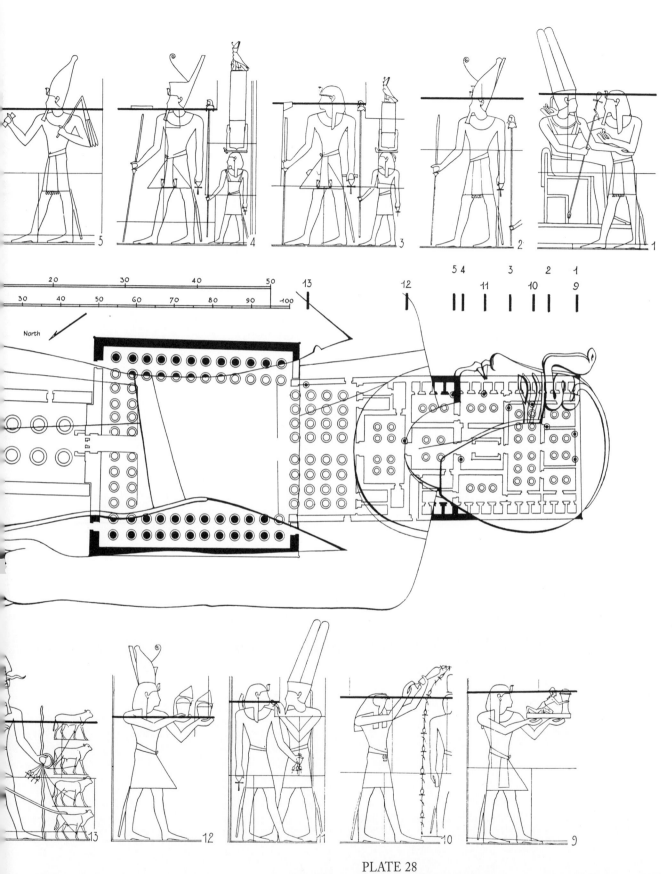

PLATE 28

Some "Location" Joints on the Man of the Temple

"Giving the House to Its Master."
Who is the true master if not life?
Its true terrestrial house is the human body.

(Chapter 30)

A

PLATE 29

Bas-Reliefs of the Consecration of the Temple

B

. . . the joints play a very important hieroglyphic part in indicating the esoteric meaning of the inscriptions . . .

(Chapter 16)

PLATE 30

Text of the Consecration of the Temple

*. . . these sages believed in
indestructible life; they
lived and drew their
knowledge and their
science, and therefore also
their symbolism, from the
manifestations of life. . . .*

(Chapter 7)

meters 1 2 3

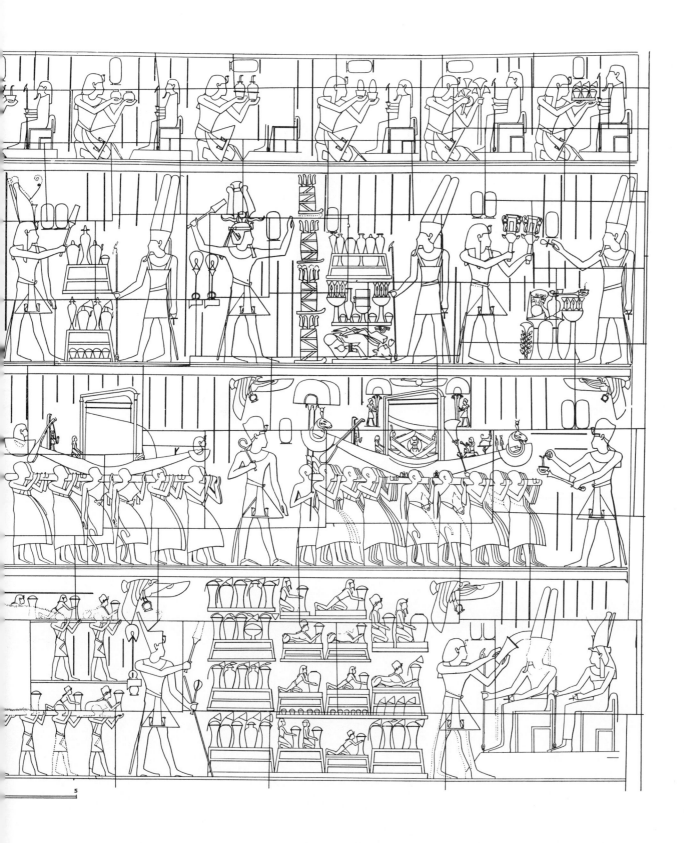

PLATE 31

East Partition of the Offering Room (Room IV)

*The joints and pieces . . .
take on . . . the character
of magical symbolism,
necessarily creating, in
a spiritual sense, an
atmosphere of cosmic reality
strangely disconcerting to
the visitor.*

(Chapter 16)

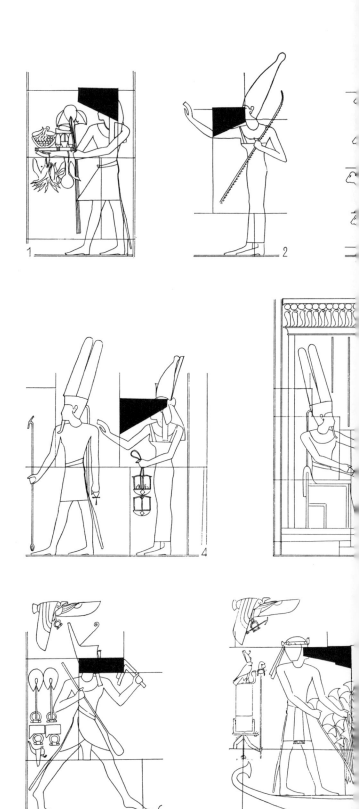

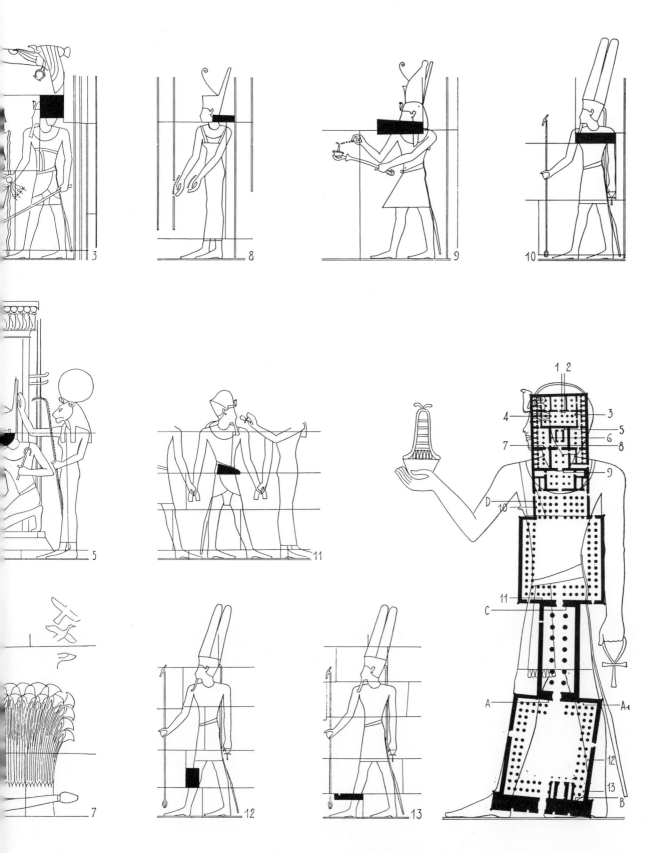

PLATE 32

The "Location Pieces" in Relation to the Bas-Reliefs

Form is what animates and characterizes, but form cannot be described when the thing is a Symbol.

By definition, the Symbol is magic; it evokes the form bound in the spell of matter. To evoke is not to imagine, it is to live; it is to live the form.

(Introduction)

In order to know the true secrets of life, it is necessary to abandon the quite alluring but misleading arguments of science and learn how to look upon that which, by dint of our seeing, we no longer notice.

(Chapter 2)

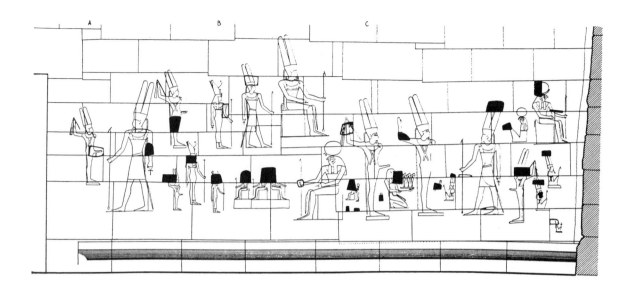

A   B   C

PLATE 33

The Seed Pieces

Chapter 30

JOINTS AND PIECES

We maintain that each stone in the walls of the Luxor temple was cut according to preestablished measurements; likewise, the layer of stone was chosen with an exact knowledge of the tableau to be drawn on it, with the joints being located in such a way that they intentionally cut the head, feet, hands, attributes, and so forth, of the figures. All of this makes up part of the hieroglyphic writing. Epigraphy alone will never reveal the secret teaching of the sages. It is necessary to learn to *read the images.*

The plans and figures given here show, better than any explanation, the reality of this figuration of Man as the basis of the architecture of the temple. This representation—verifiable by the indicated proportions—is only an image, however. The intention of the master builder goes far beyond a simple figuration. Since we are dealing with Man, and since the architecture takes into account his vital centers and passageways, the meaning of the sculpted and bas-relief figuration refers to these as well.

It is a magnificent lesson for all to be able to study, across time, the knowledge—then already thousands of years old—that was passed on to these builders of true temples. Each vital center is marked. The glands and vital relationships between the organs, represented in the tableaux, show their correspondences with the *neters* who control them; this sheds a great deal of light on one of the true meanings of the pharaonic pantheon, and on pantheism in general.

To read them requires that we observe the following:

1. The *placement of the scenes,* taking into account whether two, three, or four registers are used, and the character of the controlling, as well as the reacting, organ.

2. The *cross-references* establishing the physiological relation between the organs emphasized by the joints and their *vital functions:* thus the relationship of blood and lymph flow, that is, irrigation and nutrition; then the metabolism to which the different centers contribute, complemented by the indication of acupuncture points. We must no longer overlook the occult centers, the *cakras.* One same anthropocosmic knowledge links all the traditions.

3. The *conducting joints* that teach us how to read the meanings of the ritual formulas.

PLATES 26 AND 27 • CORRESPONDENCE JOINTS

Plates 26 and 27 show a very important case in which the pituitary is referred to a point located on the knee.[1] It is tempting to say—as has been said with regard to certain assertions in *The Temple in Man*—"What did the Ancient Egyptians know about the endrocrine glands?" After sufficiently observing the matter in the study of the temple, we believe that pharaonic science was certainly further advanced than our present science, but by a different path than that of our mechanistic and analytical mentality.

Let us take the example of the bas-relief located on the north face of the south wall of room XII, above the lintel of the door leading to the secret sanctuary of Amun, room I.[2] This bas-relief represents a royal figure standing in a tree of leaves and fruits. He seems to play the role of the trunk of the tree from which the branches spread out, marking exact places on the body. This royal figure offers two fruits, one in each hand. Amun is seated on a throne before him, holding the ankh (key of life) in his left hand, while in his right hand he holds a stylus in order to write the king's name on the fruit.

According to his proportions, the royal figure is between seven and eight years old, which is demonstrated by the fact that the height of his head is contained 6.7 times in the height of his body, and by the ratio of his total height to the height of his navel.

The tree depicted is the persea of the classical authors.[3] The fruit of the persea has a noteworthy characteristic: if one places a piece of white linen on the seed and draws letters or figures on it, the lines will appear blood red and are indelible. We can thus assume that Amun draws the name of the king on and with the fruits.

To summarize, the eight-year-old royal child receives his indelible name from the principle, or *neter*, Amun. The child is put in a tree, and the branches mark places on his body as if they were growing out of them. Two cartouches are placed above his left shoulder; above them are the symbols "son of Ra" and *neter-nefer*.

A horizontal joint passes through the eyes of Amun and those of the royal child. Another horizontal joint, after cutting the calf of Amun, is diverted so that it passes under the patella of the royal child's knee. A third, vertical joint cuts the nose of this figure, the left shoulder and the right arm, and meets the one that passes under the patella of his left knee, clearly isolating it.

We can now analyze this symbol, *but only on the condition that it might have a significance in relation to the general meaning of the temple*, which represents a new approach to the scholarly study of the thought of the Ancients.

According to the figure outlined on the pavestones on the floor of the covered temple, and according to the study of the proportions of the general figure of the man represented by the architecture of the temple, the bas-relief sculpted above this door is located at the place of the pituitary stem, extending toward the south into the Amunian sanctuary room I, and toward the north into room XII, consecrated to the twelve hours of daylight, and located at the height of the eyes.[4]

[1] The importance of the knees in relation to the pituitary action will be clarified in the appendix (p. 664), but we must note here that the point known in acupuncture as *san-li*, whose action on the pituitary is very important, although generally unknown, is located precisely at the indicated spot. [*San-li*, "three-mile point," is St 36.]

[2] Cf. chapter 18, "The Essential Secret Sanctuaries," and fig. 183.

[3] Cf. appendix note on the identification of the ancient persea tree, p. 662.

[4] Cf. appendix note concerning the relation between the pituitary gland and sight, p. 666. Also, see plate 38 and chapter 17.

If, then, the temple of Luxor actually represents man, the joint of the knees, and particularly the left knee, invites us to search in the architecture for the place where this knee might be found.

Now, on the wall of the second pylon, in front of which are found the seated black colossi—representing the knees—we find this same figuration of the persea reproduced, with the royal figure pictured no longer as standing, but kneeling. Nowhere else in the temple is this living tree represented.

This bas-relief was carved by Ramesses on the north face of the pylon that marked the end of the construction of Amenhotep III (fig. 214).

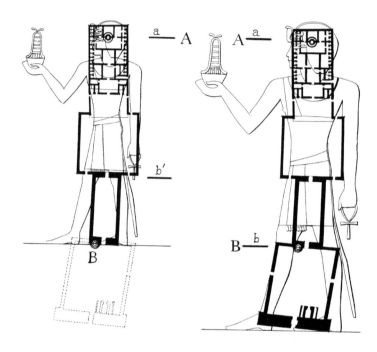

Fig. 214. Two stages of the construction of the temple

Left, the temple at the end of the reign of Amenhotep III; *right,* under Ramesses II. King B, depicted on the west partition of sanctuary I, is projected on the temple in two phases corresponding to his growth (prepuberty and adolescence). The bas-relief of plate 26 is located at point *A.* The bas-relief of plate 27 is located at point *B.*

The position in the temple of the two bas-reliefs in plates 26 and 27 thus corresponds to the two places in the body emphasized by the horizontal joints cutting the royal figure depicted in room XII (fig. 215): at point *A* the young king is pictured standing in the persea (plate 26); at point *B* the adult king is pictured kneeling in the persea (plate 27).

The *upper joint (a)* passes through the eye and is therefore at the level of the representation of the tableau at point *A.* On the figure of the adult king, the *lower joint (b)* passes under the patella at the level of the representation of point *B* carved by Ramesses, which did away with the older bas-reliefs carved by Ay on the pylon of Amenhotep III.

The *lower joint (b′)* on the figure of the young king coincides with the level of the sex organs of the adult king and evokes the vital relationship eye–pituitary–sex organs–knee (fig. 214 *left,* and fig. 215).

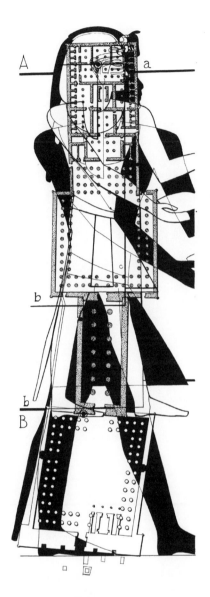

Fig. 215

Superimposition of the royal principle depicted in room XII in *A* onto the temple at the two stages of its construction (third stage of Amenhotep III and Ramesses II) and at the two corresponding ages of his growth.

The bas-relief illustrated in plate 27 is found on the second register of the interior partition of the south wall of the Ramesses court, under the roof of the portico added by this pharaoh.

Still visible above this roof, on the facade of the pylon of Amenhotep III, are the crown, the headband, and the top of the head of the large figure of Horemheb, which was probably carved under Ay.

During the construction of the narthex under Ramesses II, the upper edge of the roof tiles of the south portico were laid to coincide with the base of the king's headband carved by Ay, whereas the upper part of this roof corresponds to the level of the eye of this figure. These coincidences refer back, in the temple, to the eye and to the line of the forehead, that is, to the representation of point *A* in room XII.

Plate 27 shows the transformation brought about by Ramesses to the bas-relief of Ay. We can see that Thoth, carved behind the kneeling king in the persea, inscribes on the palm frond the number of years at the height of the knees of the older figure effaced by Ramesses.

These two figures of the king in the persea teach us the significance of the correspondence joints and furnish us with a new proof that the architecture of the temple indeed symbolizes Man. The significance of such a play of inscriptions is that it makes the vital relationships between the physiological centers tangible, as in an anatomical drawing, but in an imaged form that alone can express synthetic thought. The branches that issue from the man's body mark the places affected by the influence of the pituitary. The inscription in red (blood red) occurs only on the figure in the room of the eye with the standing king. For the same representation (the king then being on his knees) at the place of the knee, Thoth marks the age on the palm frond: this is related to growth. Amun, seated in front of the royal figure, holds the key of life in one hand and presents the palm of years, thus the duration of life, in the other.

The location of the tableau above the door connecting the room of the eyes with the secret sanctuary consecrated to Amun, and its relation to the knees, reveals to us that the Ancients knew about the vital relationships between the controlling centers of the head and all the parts of the body. In the following appendix[5] there is information as to what we presently know about the pituitary functions related to the eyes and the effects of light—thus related to room XII, consecrated to the eyes—as well as to their influence on genital evolution and growth. We can compare our present knowledge to what the Ancient Egyptians teach us.

The obligation to say everything, not only in plan but also in volume through the architecture of the temple, naturally requires a method. It is very difficult to explain in words the abundance of teachings that only the monumental symbol can transcribe, but the essential point is here demonstrated by the proofs that bear witness to the temple of Luxor as consecrated to anthropocosmic Man, represented in architecture, sculptures, texts, and statuary.

APPENDIX

Notes on the Persea

Determining the species of the tree represented in plate 26 raises a complex problem. Based on the image, Dr. L. Keimer designates this tree as being the persea of the Ancients; but since naturalists do not agree about the identity of the persea of the classical authors, we will present here the different views that have been advanced.

1. Keimer and Schweinfurt both suggest that the persea of the classical authors is quite probably the *Mimusops schimperi* Hochst. of the Sapodilla family.[6] The fruit of this tree is a berry of one or several locules, and as large as a nut.

2. The majority of naturalists identify the Egyptian tree described by Theophrastus under the name of persea as the avocado or *Persea gratissima* Gaertn. The leaves are alternately oval and elliptical, and become narrow at the base. They are somewhat leathery, smooth and green on top, being fuzzy and bluish green underneath. The fruit has the form and the size of an average pear, about 10 centimeters long; the flesh is thick and succulent, the flavor recalling somewhat that of butter or certain squashes.

"The lines drawn with the pit on a white wall become blood red after a time and can only be effaced by repainting the wall, and then with some difficulty."[7]

---

[5] See the sections on the pituitary gland and the sexual mechanisms of birds.

[6] Cf. Ludwig Keimer, *Die Gartenpflanzen im alten Ägypten* (Hamburg: Hoffmann und Campe, 1924), 1:31–37, 94–99, 144–46, 176–77.

[7] G. Nicholson, *Dictionnaire pratique d'horticulture* (1892–93), 4:27, 28.

3. Rafeneau-Delille thinks that the persea of the Ancients described by Theophrastus was not the avocado at all, as had long been believed, but rather a balanites. The balanites cannot be related to any family, but seems to be a relative of the Olacaceae. The balanites of Egypt, which Linne called *Xymenia aegyptica,* is quite a rare tree today, native to Egypt, Nubia, and Abyssinia. Its fruit is a unilocular and monospermous ovoid drupe, with a pentagonal, lined pit.

Here are the passages from Theophrastus concerning the persea:

> Thus in Egypt there are a number of trees which are peculiar to that country—the sycamore, the tree called persea, the balanos, the acacia, and some others. . . .
>
> [T]he persea, which in appearance is large and fair . . . most resembles the pear in leaves, flowers, branches, and general form, but it is evergreen, while the other [carob] is deciduous. It bears abundant fruit and at every season, for the new fruit always overtakes that of last year. It ripens its fruit at the season of the etesian winds;[8] the other fruit they gather somewhat unripe and store it. In size it is as large as a pear, but in shape it is oblong, almond-shaped, and its colour is grass-green. It has inside a stone like the plum, but much smaller and softer; the flesh is sweet and luscious and easily digested; for it does no hurt if one eats it in quantity. The tree has good roots as to length, thickness, and number. Moreover, its wood is strong and fair in appearance, black like the nettle-tree; out of it men make their images, beds, tables, and other such things.[9]

Let us review the three identifications proposed for this tree:

1. *Mimusops schimperi* has a fruit the size of a nut, which is a berry. Therefore it does not have a pit. It is difficult to see how this could be the persea described by Theophrastus, whose fruit is "as large as a pear, but in shape it is oblong, almond-shaped, and its colour is grass-green, [and] inside a stone like the plum. . . ."

2. Given that Theophrastus cites both the balanos (balanites) and the persea, he therefore distinguishes these two trees, and it still seems there is no way that they could be thought of as a single tree.

3. The fruit of the *Persea gratissima,* or avocado, in the hand of a child (fig. 216), is indeed the size of a pear, has the oblong shape of an almond, is green in color, and contains a pit as large as a

Fig. 216

Photograph of an avocado in the hand of a child of ten years instead of a child of eight years. The proportions are those of the bas-relief described here.

---

[8] The summer winds, according to Pliny (*Natural History,* 18.68) correspond to the month of July. In 13.17, Pliny repeats nearly verbatim the passage of Theophrastus, but in a slightly confused manner.

[9] Theophrastus, *Enquiry into Plants,* trans. Sir Arthur Hort, Loeb Classical Library (New York: Putnam's, 1916), 1:291, 295–97.

plum in its interior. It also ripens during the season of the "etesian winds," that is, in July. Finally, the leaves of the avocado are evergreen. All these characteristics lead us to favor the avocado as conforming to the description of the "persea of the classical writers."

We have ourselves made the experiment of drawing with a steel stylus on a piece of linen placed over the pit of a fresh avocado fruit. It is certain that any fruit with a more or less tannic pit would give a brown or black, more or less indelible line, but we have obtained a truly indelible, blood red line from this pit.

Notes on the Pituitary Gland

The pituitary gland is lodged in the sella turcica, and located behind the optic chiasm. It is connected to the brain (third ventricle) by a small gray column, the pituitary stem (which crosses the door between room XII and sanctuary I; fig. 226).

The pituitary gland consists of two lobes, the anterior lobe, a reddish, ovoid mass, which results from an invagination of the primitive pharynx, and the posterior lobe, a smaller, gray-colored mass, which derives from the brain and depends on the middle (or third) ventricle. There is a synergy of the pituitary gland, the infundibular region—that is, the entire area of implantation—and the middle ventricle located between the two optic tracts.

The anterior lobe of the pituitary gland controls the development of the skeleton, the growth of the body, the development of the genital organs, and governs the menstrual rhythm of the ovaries.

The posterior lobe exercises a cardiovascular hypertensive action and facilitates the contraction of the smooth muscles of the organism. It is the regulating center of the metabolism of water (Amun) in the body and probably has an action on urinary secretion.

Growth and Prepuberty

The secretions of the anterior lobe have a direct action on growth, and in particular on the connecting cartilage of the lower limbs—the femur, the tibia, the side of the knee—and on the nails.

The removal of the anterior lobe stops growth. Conversely, the injection of an extract of this lobe provokes gigantism to such an extent that the connecting cartilages of the growing bones are not able to knit. Gigantism is due to hyperfunction of the pituitary gland.

At puberty, growth occurs in the lower limbs, often to the extent that there is an actual pelvic gigantism (which helps us to understand the connection of the pituitary gland to the knee). The tree on the lintel of the door of room XII leading toward room I is to the left, that is, on the side of the anterior lobe of the pituitary gland. (It is understood that the entire figuration of this lintel can be studied in the same fashion.)

Hormones

The anterior lobe produces, among others, two genital hormones, one of which activates the secretion of folliberin each month, and the other then provokes secretion by the corpus luteum. The removal of this lobe causes atrophy of the adrenal glands, the thyroid, the parathyroid, and the genital glands.

The posterior lobe secretes a hormone called vasopressin, which governs the tone of the vessels, and also secretes a hormone called oxytocin, which provokes the contraction of the smooth fibers of the organs.

Among the most recent studies on the sympathetic nervous system are the following extracts from the work of J. Delmas and G. Laux:

> It is thus that the neuroendocrine diencephalon governs the various forms of metabolism, anabolic through the parasympathetic and catabolic through the sympathetic. It rules the metabolism of glu-

cosides, lipids, and proteins; it maintains the constant chemistry of the blood environment; it acts on the secretion of hormones, of diastasis (enzymes). It is a hydro- and thermo-regulator; it controls the equilibrium of blood tension and governs the alternations of the waking and sleeping states. By its morphogenetic action it triggers the increase in weight and height of the individual and the harmonious development of the genital area. It governs the entire lisso-motor system, all the glands, external and internal. Finally, it is the essential factor of the instinctive, emotive, and feeling life, without which psychic life would only be pure and cold ideation. Harvey Cushing, cited by Delay, writes, "There, in this small, middle, and archaic zone at the base of the brain, which could be hidden in the tip of one's thumb, is concealed the essential resiliency of the instinctive and emotional life that man tries his best to cover with a coat, a skin, an inhibiting cortex."

After this long enumeration, we should include the idea of individual tempermant, or better, of the "terrain" with its reactions specific to each individual. This notion summarizes the visceral, somatic, and psychic behavior of each human being, and gives us, henceforth, a solid, scientific base through the diencephalic functions.[10]

Therefore, the same conclusions are reached as those that are evident with regard to the human canon.[11]

The pituitary gland is the endocrine gland that holds all the other endocrine glands under its dependence by means of hormones. The importance of the endocrine glands for the correct operation of the organic functions is so great that we can see that the pituitary-hypothalamus coupling is truly the great center of organic regulation (P. Chauchard).[12]

To summarize a very complex study concerning the diencephalic, autonomic centers of the sympathetic system from which we have taken the above two quotations, here is the conclusion of Delmas and Laux:

In conclusion, we can isolate three fundamental regions in the middle diencephalon that are certainly connected with each other, but their afferent and efferent channels allow us to imagine that they are *functionally specific.* These are the regions of the hypothalamus or the infundibulum framed by the optic tracts and *systematically centered on the optic canals and on the pituitary body;* the tubero-mamillo-trigonal region that appears as the autonomic center of the olfactory passages; finally, the *epithalamic region centered on the pineal gland.*[13]

Here, then, demonstrated by the science of today, are the reasons for the existence of the three secret sanctuaries, the mooring posts of life, as we maintained in *The Temple in Man* in 1949.

Notes on the Seasonal Sexual Mechanisms of Birds

In order to emphasize the intimate relation between the eye, the visual centers, the pituitary gland, and the sexual cycle, here is a summary of some experiments and observations concerning the seasonal sexual cycle of birds:[14]

[10] Delmas and Laux, "Centres autonomes diencéphaliques," *Système nerveux sympathique,* p. 50.

[11] Cf. chapter 37, "The Problem of Establishing a Human Canon."

[12] Delmas and Laux, *Système nerveux sympathique,* pp. 57–58.

[13] Ibid., p. 58, our emphasis.

[14] Summarized from Jacques Benoit, "Reproduction, caractères sexuels" and "Hormones, determinisme du cycle sexuel saisonnier," *Traité de zoologie,* vol. 15, *Oiseaux* (Paris: Masson, 1950), p. 462 et sqq.

A. External Factors

1. The influence of muscular exercise reveals itself to be weak or nil on the seasonal sexual cycle of birds.

2. The alimentary factor has no noticeable action; however, wheat exposed for 250 hours to light rich in ultraviolet rays strongly stimulated genital activity.

3. Heat, which stimulates the sexual activity of fish, amphibians, arthropods, coelenterates, and so on, does not influence the sexual activity of birds.

4. Light is certainly the most active factor; artificial light was able to advance the period of reproduction by several months, including the seasonal development of the testicles, the period of singing, and so forth, and even increased the latter up to three times per year. Conversely, a sudden reduction of light caused a reduction of growth, or a regression of the sexual organs.

The specific nature of the action of light is confirmed by experiments on ducks who were given a diet reduced by one-fourth or even one-third, and at the same time exposed to artificial light. In three weeks they showed strong testicular growth. In short, artificial light brings with it a precocious puberty in a few days.

Similar experiments made with females give the same results, only less rapid. It seems, moreover, that being around males is necessary in order to make them capable of ovulation.

B. Role of Internal Factors

The pituitary (to which certain encephalic nervous centers, particularly the hypothalamus, must be associated) is at the origin of the sexual cycle. . . .

Pituitary activity varies cyclically during the year, in synchronization with the activity of the gonads, which it controls. Increasing progressively in winter, this pituitary activity reaches its maximum in spring, accentuating the sexual cycle in birds, which thereafter diminishes, toward the end of spring, and in summer comes again to a state of rest, which lasts several months.

There exists therefore a seasonal cyclic activity of the pituitary. It persists in the absence of genital glands in the case of castrated male ducks.[15]

C. Action of Light on the Pituitary Gland

In spite of a certain autonomy of cyclic activity, the pituitary can be "influenced by light, which controls it and assures in most cases its synchronization with the meteorological cycle of light. . . ." Various experiments, which we will summarize briefly, further show to what degree and by what means light acts in domestic ducks to stimulate the pituitary gland and the gonads.

The removal of the anterior lobe of the pituitary in male ducks previously stimulated by light is followed by a rapid regression of the testicles, which withdraw to a state of total rest, including their tubes and their interstitial elements, in spite of the continuation of the artificial light. If we implant the pituitaries of ducks that have been stimulated by light into prepubescent female mice, the cytological examination of these pituitaries supplementarily and incontestably proves the *real activation of the pituitary by light,* which thus plays the role of a *strictly indispensible intermediary between the rays of light and the gonads.*

But how is light able to excite the pituitary? Various experiments where light was focused on different parts of the body and the head show that the rays are only active at the level of the orbital region. Light localized on the retina releases the gonadostimulating mechanism by an oculopituitary

[15] Ibid., p. 465.

reflex. But light also acts in a powerful way by other means. It actually stimulates the gonads when the optic nerves are cut and also when the eyes are surgically removed. In this case light acts as a stimulant of the nerve centers linked to the pituitary and located in the hypothalamus[16] (particularly to the supraoptic nucleus) and even in the rhinencephalon. Indeed, if we direct light to these different regions and to the pituitary itself by means of a thin quartz rod appropriately directed, the pituitary and the testicles are strongly stimulated. In addition, sectioning the pituitary stem, in other words, separating the pituitary gland from the brain, prevents the pituitary from being stimulated by light. This leads us to suppose that light rays can stimulate the anterior pituitary by means of nerve channels, either by lighting the retina and thus releasing an *optico-hypophysio-sexual reflex,* or by directly stimulating the deeper nerve centers situated and localized in the encephalon (hypothalamus, rhinencephalon) *(encephalo-hypophysio-sexual reflexes).* In fact, these various pathways intertwine. Indeed, the experiment shows that rays of light, at least visible rays of long wavelength, penetrate very easily and deeply into the tissues, going through skin, bone, muscle, and vessels to strike the anterior and interior periphery of the brain as far as the hypothalamic region.[17]

Discussion

The seasonal sexual cycle of birds therefore reveals two essential causes that combine their effects: an internal physiological rhythm of pituitary activity, which has a certain autonomy, and an external rhythm, mostly but not exclusively determined by the seasonal variations of solar light. It is presently impossible to say how the parts are related to the internal and external factors in the seasonal sexual cycles in different bird species. These parts are different for different species and their precise determination requires long and patient experiments. In all cases, whether or not they are due to internal factors (autonomous pituitary rhythm), we must recognize that solar light plays an important role in the regulation of this rhythm and in the fulfillment of the sexual cycle. It acts first of all to synchronize the pituitary cycle with that of the seasons. We must understand that in normal cases such a synchronization (which obviously varies according to the species) is always found. In some cases, it also acts to give a supplementary action to the spontaneous pituitary function. Sometimes even these two combined factors are insufficient to draw out complete sexual activity, for example, ovulation in sparrows or starlings. In these species, as with the pigeon and others, a psychic factor of the proximity of other birds, and essentially of males, becomes necessary to bring sexual activity to its maximum realization.[18]

Let us recall that room XII is the room of the diurnal solar cycle consecrated to the eye of Ra, symbolized by the falcon.

PLATE 28 • LOCATION JOINTS

We should here reproduce all the walls of the temple, because everywhere the joints are located at places related to the human body: the eyes, room XII; the mouth, room II; the chin, room IV; the breasts in the hypostyle in the columns with lunar bases; the knees at the north door of the nave; the calves at the west entry to the court of Ramesses, and so on. In plate 28 we present a series of figures that show the systematic use of the joints in this spirit.

It is necessary, however, not to forget that the method of "cross-reference" and the "conducting joints" of which we have already spoken are everywhere and are combined with the "location

---

[16] The projection of the sagittal section onto the temple (plate 38) shows that room I indeed corresponds to this zone.

[17] Benoit, "Reproduction," p. 467.

[18] Ibid., pp. 468–69.

joints." Further, location joints are found in the high registers for certain regulating organs in the head, and in the lower registers for organs of action. Thus the jaw will be marked on the "physical," that is, the lower register, and the eyes or the glands of the head will be in the upper registers.[19]

The system for conducting the reader through the Man of the Temple consists of looking at the first royal figure on the first register to the right or the left of the *entrance* to the room, which *always has a horizontal joint corresponding to the place where this figure is located on the human body that the temple as a whole represents.* The joint designating this location is not necessarily the only one cutting that particular figure, but it is the principal indication of the location, and—since it is actually a question of the Anthropocosmos symbolized by the royal figure—the other joint becomes a vital *correspondence joint* on the body. It guides us toward the part of the temple that, physiologically and vitally, corresponds with the place on the body indicated by the location joint.

In plate 28 we project onto the plan of the temple the human figure that summarizes the measures and proportions of its double play, that is, king B (cf. plates 79 and 80). The plate will also take us through some of the rooms of the temple, as we observe only the joints and horizontal stones in order to verify their correspondence with the location of the room in the human body.

All of the figures represented here, with the exception of Horus, are *the first figures located next to the entrance or on the first tableau of a wall on the lower register.*

Nos. 1 and 9 frame the support of the "chest" or naos that formerly must have contained the statue of Amun. They are carved on the south partition of room I, and the upper joints cut the crowns of their skulls in the same way that this wall removes the skull of the Man of the Temple.

No. 2 is in room V, west partition. The upper joint underlines the forehead, in the same way that the wall to the corner on which it is carved cuts the forehead of the king in the projection onto the plan. On this same wall the joints cut the foreheads of the five kings who are represented on the first register, rising from the forehead to the height of the headband (cf. plate 76).

No. 10 is in room XII, east partition, which is consecrated to the entrance of the sun, Ra, the falcon. Also, it is particularly the eye of the falcon Horus that is emphasized by the upper joint. We recall in this regard the importance of the eye for birds, and especially falcons.[20]

No. 3 is located at the east corner of the north partition of room XII. We see on the projection that we are concerned here with the area of the nose; thus, the upper joint cuts the figure at this point.

No. 11 is in room II. This is the opening of the mouth, the entrance, to which, moreover, all the symbolism of this room also corresponds. A break in the joints of the stones cuts the king's mouth but not that of Amun, who "gives him life" through the mouth and the nose.

Nos. 4 and 5 are located, one in room VI, north partition, to the right of the entrance, and the other in room IX, east partition. These two figures are on opposite sides of the thick wall that corresponds to the chin. It is actually in the thickness of this wall, encrusted in a threshold tile of the door that connects rooms IV and VI, that the "piece" that allows us to define the exact length of the face in the pavestones is found (plate 37).

No. 12 is on the left post of the doorway leading from room VIII to room IV, that is, on the north face of the wall separating the sanctuaries from the hypostyle rooms, and corresponding to the clavicles.

No. 13 belongs to the first scene represented on the east wall of the hypostyle room: the king leads the four calves (the thymus), and a joint crosses his chest exactly at the place that it occupies in the temple.

---

[19] See the detailed explanation of plate 28 below.

[20] Recalling what we said previously, we will find the joints emphasizing the eye of the royal figure in the upper registers of this partition.

Nos. 6 and 14, carved by Horemheb, frame the doorway going from the nave to the narthex. Here we are here at the knees, thus the lower joint crossing these figures passes through this point.

No. 7 is located in the thickness of this same doorway and was carved by Ramesses; a joint here also emphasizes the knees.

No. 15 is at the interior of the west side entry to the court of Ramesses. The lower joint cuts the calf of the figure.

We note that on the interior partition of the west wall of this court, from the west side entry to the Ramesses pylon, the lower part of the calves of a series of figures is systematically emphasized by a joint that, through successive interruptions, descends progressively from midcalf to the ankle.

No. 8, located in the small east chapel of the repository of Amun's barque on the south face of the west wing of the pylon, has the heel cut by a joint.

Finally, no. 16 is placed on the doorpost of the entrance to the temple. It is on the north face of the pylon that represents the soles of the feet. It is also accentuated by the joint of the stones.[21]

Plates 29 and 30 • Conducting Joints

Plates 29 and 30 provide an example of the reading of the correspondences for the very important liturgical formula "Giving the House to Its Master."

As the joints will prove, it is not solely a question of a simple formula of inauguration, or of consecration of the temple. The whole Universe is held in a single gesture. Here, consecrating a temple is identical to animating the terrestrial body and, generally speaking, animating in the sense of the highest science.

Up to now, this formula, as with many others commonly found, only signified in Egyptology a banal phrase that affirms the consecration ritual of a temple to a *neter*, its "patron."

Thanks to this exceptional temple, which becomes a general key by depicting *man represented through architecture,* we are able to give to the ritual formula a meaning in vital relationship to the human cosmos. In plates 29 and 30 and in figures 217 to 221 we present the four tableaux (A, B, C, D) in which the formula of "Giving the House to Its Master" is inscribed; they are located at points 1, 2, 3, and 4 of the temple, with the joint-guides that oblige us to follow the steps of the reading and to see their connections to the human body.

These drawings and photographs are intentionally placed here out of their reading order. The text of "Giving the House to Its Master" refers to a vital function; in this spirit there is thus a subsequent logic that we are going to investigate, allowing ourselves to be guided by the position of the joints.

Tableau A (fig. 218), carved by Amenhotep III on the eastern post of the north door of the nave, is located at point 3 on the plan. *A single horizontal joint cuts the two figures at the height of the sex organs, that is, at point 2 of the plan.*[22]

Tableau B (fig. 219 and plate 29A), carved by Ramesses II on the interior face of the west wing of the pylon, is located at point 4 of the plan. Before the text of "Giving the House to Its Master," and facing Min-Amun, the king holds the *mākes* staff as well as the white *hedj* club in his left hand. *Four horizontal joints emphasize four points on the bodies of the two figures.*

The king, in the white crown, is placed slightly lower than the lines of the joints that on the ithyphallic Amun are correctly located at points 1, 2, 3, and 4 and that intentionally mark the phallus, which, on him, is at the level corresponding to the height of the king's navel, and recalls the *kamutef* and the androgyny of the origin.

---

[21] The door of the pylon being partly buried, it has been impossible to see the lower register; this figure is carved on another register.

[22] This scene, placed behind the pedestal of the seated black granite colossus, and located at the knee, cannot be photographed because it is too close to the statue.

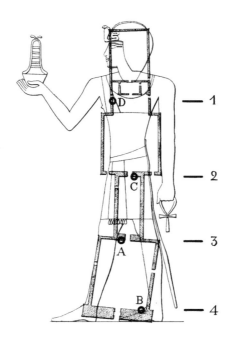

Fig. 217. Placement in the temple of Luxor of the scenes of "Giving the House to Its Master"

Location of tableaux A, B, C, and D at points 1, 2, 3, and 4, and their relation to the human body represented by the projection of king B of sanctuary I.

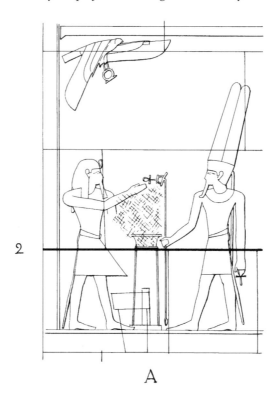

Fig. 218. North facade of the pylon of Amenhotep III

Tableau A, located at point 3 of the plan. The one horizontal joint cuts the two figures at the height of the sex organs, corresponding to point 2 of the plan.

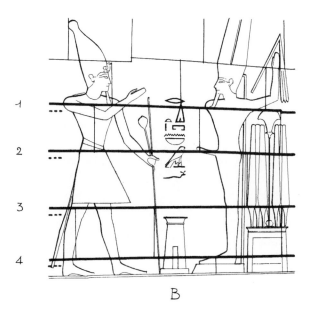

Fig. 219. Interior facade of the west wing of the pylon of Ramesses II

Tableau B, located at point 4 of the plan. The four horizontal joints mark the figures in
four places on the body that correspond to points 1, 2, 3, and 4 of the plan.

If we raise the king to the height of the pedestal underneath Amun's feet, the joints will be
located exactly at 1, 2, 3, and 4; the androgynous phallus will become the male phallus, a fact we
must emphasize to understand this development.

Tableau C (fig. 220 and plate 29B), carved by Amenhotep III on the western post of the north
face of the door that separates the nave from the transept, is located at point 2 of the plan.

The king, wearing the red crown, holds the *mākes* staff in his left hand and the ankh in his right
(the hands are reversed). Amun, facing the king, holds the *was* scepter in his left hand, from the
end of which the *chen, djed,* and ankh are arranged horizontally so as to form, with the two scepters
(that of the king and that of Amun), an elongated rectangle in which the "Giving the House to Its
Master" formula is inscribed, above a symbolic representation of the facade of the sanctuary.

A single horizontal joint marks these two figures at the level of the chest, and corresponds to point 1.
This joint also crosses the hieroglyph *per,* signifying "house."

Tableau D (fig. 221 and plate 30) is located on the interior partition of the east wall of the
hypostyle room or *haty* and corresponds to point 1 on the plan. Between the king holding the
mākes staff and the white *hedj* club, and Amun holding the *was* scepter, there are fifteen columns
of text that descend to the line of the ground and, above, end at the level of the upper joint of the
tableau.[23]

Two horizontal joints mark the two figures: the upper joint corresponds to the location of bas-
relief D in the temple at point 1; the lower joint cuts the knees of Amun, and passes under the king's
loincloth, stopping in front of his left knee. It corresponds to point 3.

[23] Cf. fig. 237 for proportions and measurements of this text, and fig. 238, which shows its location and orientation.

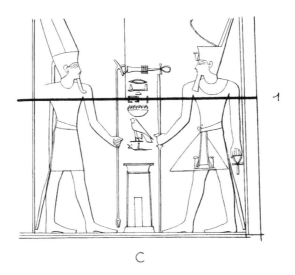

C

Fig. 220. North facade of the door of the transept

Tableau C, located at point 2 on the plan. The single horizontal joint cuts the figures at the level of the chest and corresponds to point 1 on the plan.

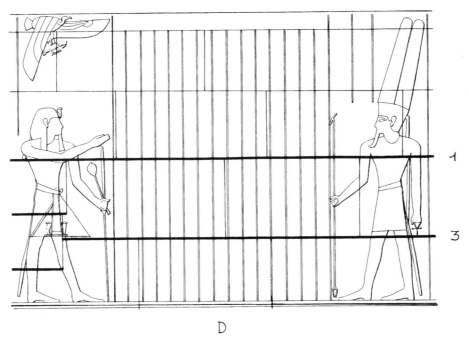

D

Fig. 221. Hypostyle room, east wall, register 2, location of the columns of the text of "Giving the House to Its Master"

Tableau D, located at point 1 of the plan. Two horizontal joints cut Amun at the level of the chest and of the knee, corresponding to points 1 and 3 of the plan.

The joint that crosses the back calf of the king is related to the entrance of the princes, that is, to their presentation at the temple;[24] the other joint cuts the top of the thigh[25] where, on the west and east walls in the nave, the procession coming from Karnak toward Luxor and returning to Karnak is depicted.

Let us now see how we must learn to read the teaching given by these different joints.

If we begin from the front door marking the end of the constructions in the era of Amenhotep III, that is, at point 3 where bas-relief A is located (fig. 218), we have *a single reference* that points, by means of the horizontal joint at the level of the sex organs, to point 2 where scene C is found (fig. 220).

From this point, the single horizontal joint passes through the chest and leads us to the hypostyle room at point 1, where we find scene D (fig. 221) and the large text concerning the ritual scene of "Giving the House to Its Master." From here we are sent back again to point 3 from which we began, since the upper joint 1 is the location joint of this scene, and no joint has led us to point 4, to scene B on the pylon.

So, proceeding in another way, if we begin from point 2 (the sex organs), the only horizontal joint leads us to point 1 (the chest), where we find the large text of this ritual scene. From there, the lower joint passing through Amun's knee leads us again to point 3, corresponding to tableau A, that is, we are obliged to recommence the same cycle in which scene B is excluded because it is a synthesis.

Conclusion

The first animation occurs through conception (the sex organs) at point 2, scene C. *Who is the true master if not life? Its true terrestrial house is the human body.*

The second animation is made by the "breath," respiration at actual birth, at point 1, scene D.

The third animation occurs at the beginning of the awakening of intellectuality, at the age of seven to eight years, the age of the transformation of the pineal gland, which marks intellectual awakening. This moment corresponds to point 3, scene A, at the knee.

Finally, the last animation occurs at maturity and corresponds to the crowned king going out of the temple, at eighteen to nineteen years of age, indicated by tableau B, at point 4, which at the same time refers to all the points in which this scene is portrayed. It marks the sexualization of the king crowned with the white crown.[26]

PLATE 31 • EAST PARTITION OF THE OFFERING ROOM (ROOM IV)

We shall note on this partition only the essential correspondence joints. There are four registers, counting from bottom to top:

Register 1. The consecration by the king of the offerings, comprised of vases and ungents, in the presence of Amun and Mut. The only joint cuts the thighs of all the royal figures, and consequently refers to the nave (thigh), on the interior partitions of which are represented scenes from the procession of the sacred barques also found on the second register of room IV.

---

[24] Cf. fig. 268, the presentation at the temple, or the ascent of the royal princes toward the Ramesses pylon represented at the level of point 3 (fig. 217).

[25] Compare with fig. 136, vol. 1.

[26] Cf. chapter 15, "Diadem, I Assume Thee." The photographs in plates 29 and 30 imperfectly render the bas-reliefs because of lighting difficulties, and in the case of plate 29A, because of the damage done by the local people who inhabited these ruins for a time and dug out holes to secure wooden support beams.

Register 2. The three barques of Amun, Mut, and Khonsu are carried by priests whose robes have the form of sails filled by the wind. The lower horizontal joints cut the thighs, then the calves, then again the thighs of the carriers of the barques, tracing a curve that accentuates the curve of the barques (mosaic).[27]

Register 3. Six scenes of the ritual are depicted here. The king, in the five scenes at the left, is cut by a single horizontal joint at the level of the thigh, consequently referring to the sacred barques represented in the nave.

Register 4. Nine kneeling royal symbols presenting offerings to nine *neters.*

In this section concerning the correspondence joints, we must be content to note the most characteristic examples, since it would be impossible in this limited space to make a detailed study of the teaching contained in all the joints.

—⁓—

The complexity of the joints and the difficulty of assembling the blocks, particularly in the second register, clearly shows that there is an intention there and that the joint plays an integral role in reading the tableau.

Each partition is a complete book, the meaning of which is vitally connected to the teaching of another partition,[28] even if the latter is located in another monument in Egypt. Man is the Universe in all its complexity.

PLATE 32 • THE "LOCATION PIECES" IN RELATION TO THE BAS-RELIEFS

In *The Temple in Man* we noted that there were always "keys" on the walls and on the ground of the pharaonic temple that are guides for measures.[29] It is too easy to attribute the "small pieces of stone" embedded in certain blocks to being the repairs of errors on the part of the sculptors. But the error lies in interpreting this fact in this way. *Each stone has a value and a significance.* We have found a great number of these "keys" that had to have been placed at the time of construction; certain keys are of such a particular size that they could not have been put in position at any other time.

—⁓—

Just as we have seen the joints of the stones marking, on the figures in the bas-reliefs, certain points of the body, indicating either their position on the Man of the Temple or their physiological relationship to other points, so we will also see that the pieces mark a "sector" of influence.[30] These pieces are to be read by taking into account the place in the temple where the bas-relief in which they are embedded is located, the vertical and horizontal lines that cut the figure, its attributes, crown, and gestures, and sometimes also the transparencies.

---

[27] Cf. fig. 223, the barque of Mut.

[28] Cf. chapter 17, where we discuss the systematic removal of all the royal beards on this partition as well as all the other partitions of this room. The beards were scraped down, replastered, then recarved, thus marking two successive transformations of the initial bas-relief in room IV that is located on the projection of the Man at the level of the throat and consequently the beard. Cf. figs. 136 and 138 (vol. 1), location of the seventh *cakra.*

[29] Cf. chapter 31, the "pieces" of the pavement marking the outline of the chin, the angle of the mouth, etc., and chapter 40, the "piece" where the axes of the covered temple cross, incised in the sanctuary of the barque, etc.

[30] The diagram of locations in plate 32 shows both the positions of the various pieces numbered from 1 to 13 and the position of the four scenes, A, B, C, and D of "Giving the House to Its Master" and A₁, the ascent of the princes, fig. 268.

Let us note, for example, the piece in the form of a half-disk in figure no. 5, in which the king's profile is carved. This piece had to have been intentionally cut in this form, which corresponds to the symbolism of the place.

The pieces in figures 1 and 2 located in room XII include a part of the head and face. It is possible to understand their importance in the light of relationships established in the Surgical Papyrus among ritual, architecture, and the human being. Each piece presented here would require a long explanation. But it may be sufficient to observe by means of the plan that all of them correspond, on each figure, to the location the bas-relief occupies in the Man of the Temple. We only describe one example in detail to give a glimpse of the method of reading.

Figure no. 3 is located on the second register of the west partition of the room (room XII) of the sun—the setting sun. The royal figure holds four coiled-up ropes in his right hand, which terminate with four keys of life, and which restrain four calves by their front left legs. The calves are speckled, white, red, and black. A stick with a phallic quality, which the king holds in his left hand, designates and isolates the black calf.

The royal figure wears a blue headdress with a uraeus, and this headdress conceals the ear. The piece that characterizes this figure, passing in front of the ear, marks out the whole back part of the skull, thus including the cerebellum. Now, the projection of the sagittal section[31] specifies that this figure is located at the level (in the temple) of this organ, which is the center of coordination of perceived sensations (sight, hearing, touch) and controls the movements necessary for balancing, while the semicircular canals of the inner ear indicate the direction of movement in space. The vertical joint passing in front of the ear (center of balance) links the temple to the navel. From this point a horizontal joint serves as a baseline for the white calf.

A joint cuts the feet of the king at the height of the ankle, and the hoofs of the black calf. Now, the calves symbolize nourishment through the taking of milk. Mut, hovering above the king's head, carries the *chen,* that is, the "binding" through the lymphatic vessel.

This phase of gestation of a white "fixity" evidently cannot be separated from all the subsequent instruction described on the rest of this partition. We find at the beginning of the second register that the king wears a warrior's blue helmet, holds the key of life in his left hand, and pours water from three vases in his right hand onto a calf turned on its back in the position of a mummified gazelle.

This is the place of the sensory center of vision, that is, the lunar reflector of light that creates the center for the intelligence of vision. This zone, cut out by the piece, also contains the medulla and the pons. The only other joint cuts the two feet and therefore relates this part of the brain to the innervation of the feet.[32]

Plate 33 • The Seed Pieces

The upper part of plate 33 represents the exterior side of the east wall of the hypostyle room. This group of bas-reliefs is on the side opposite the one on which the scene of "Giving the House to Its Master" is carved.[33]

[31] Cf. plate 37 and fig. 226.

[32] Cf. chapter 14, case 8.

[33] Cf. plate 30 and fig. 221.

Each figure represented has a related piece. Certain of these pieces are still in place, and others are missing (in black on the drawing of the whole group).

The details of the three figures, *A*, *B*, and *C*, show three pieces still existing in the hollowed-out cavities that were made to hold them. These pieces clearly show that they were made as part of the bas-reliefs of other monuments, but they all relate to the part of the body in which they are inserted.

A, Min, or Amun the Generator. The piece comprises both the new bas-relief and an older one. Indeed, we can observe the line of a text that belongs to an earlier scene under the phallus of Min. The sculpture of the phallus in the piece is much deeper than that of the bas-relief in which it is embedded.

B, Mut. Here again the piece preserves the lines of an older representation. This piece cuts the arm, but the arm of the earlier figure was in relief and was not at the same angle. Note that a very small figure (graffito) has been carved in Mut's belly.

C, Min-Amun. The piece in the raised hand and the *nekhakha* scepter form an angle above the hand. The scepter of the earlier Min was also not at the same angle.

The *kamutef* represented in plate 58 carries a piece that also came from another bas-relief. A flower from an older decoration is carved on this piece, which suggests the stem of this flower and the naos on which it was set, elements now missing on the representation of this *kamutef*.

One can also note that this piece bears traces of an earlier dorsal pillar engraved in relief and larger than that of the *kamutef* to which the piece has been added. These elements, in combination, show that these pieces are not for the purpose of repair, but are symbolic gestures for reading the whole.

Chapter 31

THE MOSAIC FIGURE IN THE FOUNDATION OF THE TEMPLE

—◌—

Plates 34–38

*For an architectural reading it is necessary to
take into account all the impressions that one
experiences upon entering the building. The first
thing that stands out is the form of the room, that
is, the plan. . . . [T]he . . . plan combined with the
volume "speaks" to us, and it is this combination
that . . . addresses itself to the feeling that results
from our living relationship to the milieu, alive
through its form.*

*This is art, in its pure sense, which expresses
itself in a verb that we cannot transcribe into
words.*

(Chapter 24)

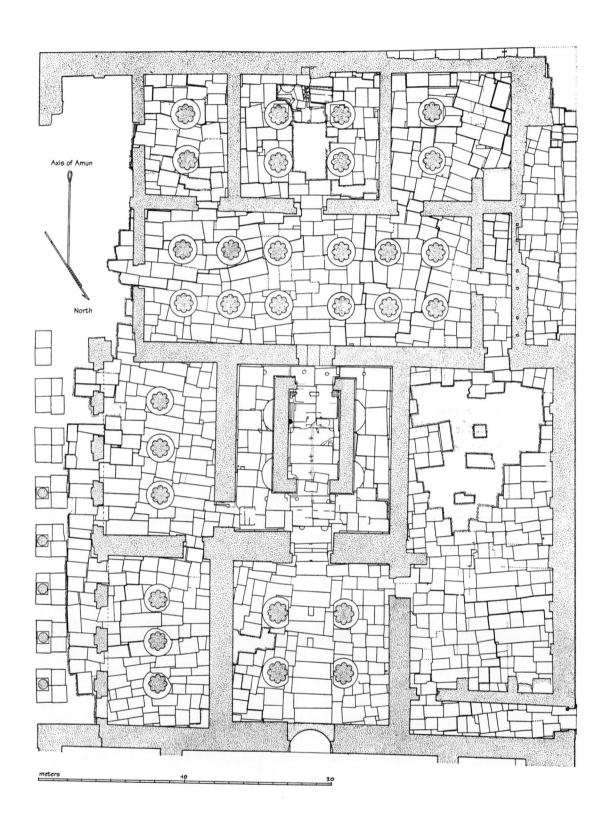

Axis of Amun

North

meters 10 20

PLATE 34

Plan of the South Part of the Pavestone Mosaic of the Platform

Let us recall, in the Gospel of Luke, the arrival of the child Jesus in Jerusalem with his parents when he was twelve, and how, getting lost in the temple, he astonished the doctors with his intelligence and knowledge.

PLATE 35

The "King with the Diadem" of the Sanctuary of the Barque of Mut

Humanity is the measure, the "atlas" on which living lands and their astronomical influences are read; it is the laboratory of all the miracles of the world.

(Chapter 11)

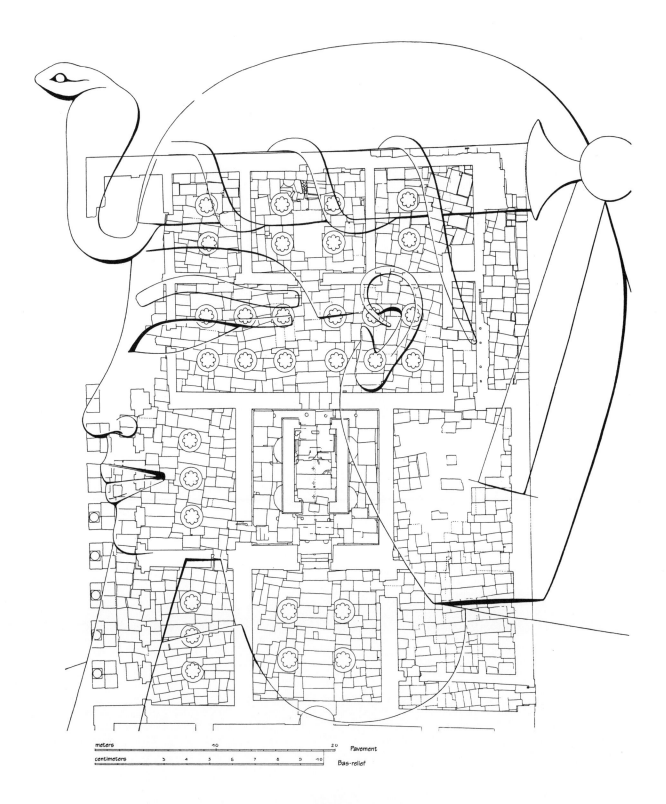

meters ⟨scale⟩ 10 20   Pavement

centimeters ⟨scale⟩ 3 4 5 6 7 8 9 10   Bas-relief

PLATE 36

The Profile of the King on the Mosaic

The head is . . . the "covered temple," the sanctuary of the human body where all the control centers are gathered.

(Chapter 15)

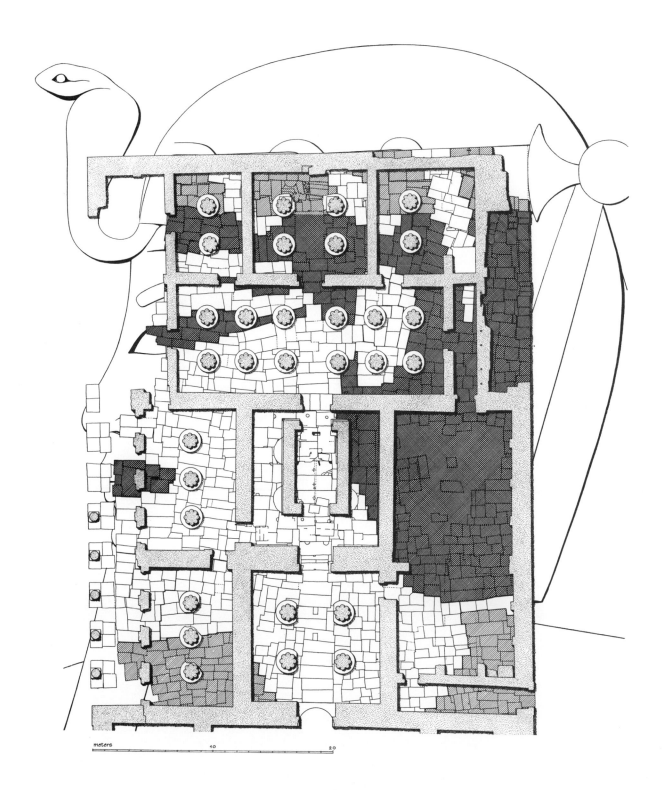

PLATE 37

The Covered Temple on the Mosaic

The formation of the organized being begins with the head. The head is the place of ideal determination of the body's organic functions, and thus one must look there to see the governing principles.

(Chapter 18)

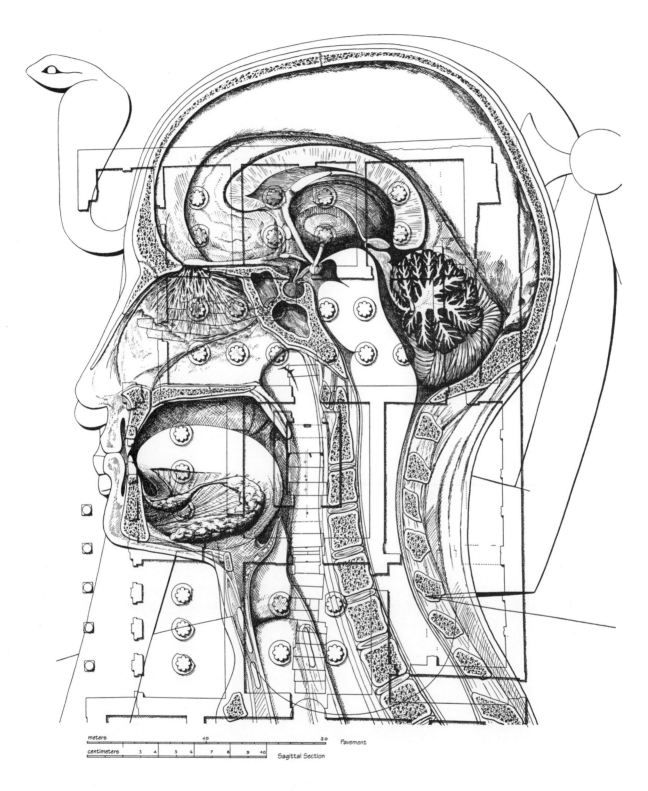

PLATE 38

The Controlling Centers of the Head in the Covered Temple

Chapter 31

THE MOSAIC
FIGURE IN THE FOUNDATION
OF THE TEMPLE

The covered temple at Luxor does not rest directly on the ground, but on a rectangular foundation crowned by a grooved cornice. This construction, upon which the pavestones that constitute its cover are placed, is in the form of a tank, or cistern.[1] Probes made at several points suggest a similarity between the foundation "tank" of the temple of Luxor and the one for the temple of Mentu, of which we show a sectional view in plate 94.

The bottom of the tank seems to be composed of new stones, and the tank itself is filled with a jumble of various stones, some of which are inscribed and reused from an earlier monument. All of this is mixed with earth.

The platform covering the tank at the Karnak temple of Mentu is at the upper level of the cornice, whereas at Luxor the pavement is set at the level of the torus of the cornice. The walls and the columns do not have their own foundations but rest directly on this stone platform (fig. 222).

The pavement of the platform of the temple of Luxor is conceived as a mosaic. It is made of very disparate pieces, which is surprising in itself, knowing with what care the rest of the building is constructed. This arrangement motivated us to investigate the reason. In our plan (plate 34), there is nothing "reconstituted;" we have only carefully sketched each stone.

The different elements of a face in profile are sufficiently visible to permit making a complete drawing of it giving the proportions of the face of the Man of the Temple, but without the crown of the skull. The walls of the temple are placed on this pavement (plate 37), situating the different parts of the head on it, as the sagittal section shows (plate 38).

The cornice crowning the stylobate is above the level of the pavestone mosaic (fig. 222). As a cornice, it plays the same role for the stylobate as does the cornice of a pylon, a naos, and so on.

---

[1] Cf. plate 94 and its legend.

688

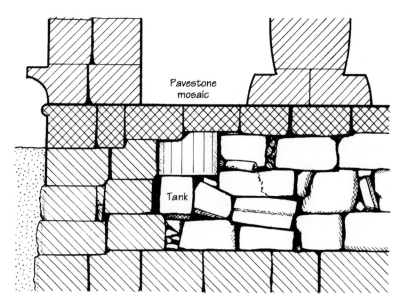

*Fig. 222. Diagram of the vertical section of the tank-shaped foundation
of the covered temple of Luxor*

The pavestones are laid at the upper level of the torus. The first course above the pavestones constitutes the cornice upon which rest the exterior walls.

The exterior walls of the covered temple rest on the upper part of the cornice and with it create
a crown;[2] and the whole temple placed on the pavestones thus represents the place for the recording of the teaching. It is necessary to accept this as a general image, the analysis of which is
extremely complex.

PLATE 34 • PLAN OF THE SOUTH PART OF
THE PAVESTONE MOSAIC OF THE PLATFORM

One is struck by the apparent incoherence of the arrangement of the stones that make up this pavement. The first three or four rows near the south wall are parallel and perpendicular to this wall up
to a point toward the west, room VII,[3] where all the blocks suddenly are placed at a very pronounced
angle, which necessitated a skillful assembly between the two "movements" thus indicated. In room
XII, on the east side, the stones were adjusted to evoke the curves of the eye, while on the west side
the stones arranged on the angles imposed by the contour lines of the ear again become parallel and
perpendicular to the walls toward the center.

Starting from the north in room IV, the central pathway, which then passes through the door
leading toward the sanctuary of the barque, is marked by a succession of large stones that continue
in room VI under the limestone paving and actually constitute a "path" that stops at room XII at
the second stone from the north wall of this room.

In room II, in front of the central pillar of the east partition, a group of three stones creates an
empty space in which there is a small block of granite that served as a door socket and contains a

[2] Cf. chapter 15, "Diadem, I Assume Thee."

[3] For the location of these rooms, cf. fig. 226.

cavity in its central part. A key-point is marked here and determines the location of the mouth. Now, on the bas-reliefs, the corners of the lips are always indicated by circular hollows.

In the embrasure of the door leading from room IV to room VI, a large reused roof stone has a hollow down the center of its entire length; this straight cavity was filled with sand and various ritual materials, then covered by a long flat stone (today broken in two pieces). On the north and south sides of this large roofing stone, there are two small cavities, the north one of which contains a key-piece, the point of the crossing of the three axes of the temple, incised on the floor of room VI.[4]

In order to define the measurements of the pavestone mosaic, we must consider the essential points thus marked, such as the large stone tangent to the first column in the southeast corner of room XII, which determines the upper edge of the eye, and also another large pavestone north of the central column of the western group of columns in room XII coinciding with the base of the ear. The position of the chin becomes obvious in the thickness of the wall separating rooms IV and VI, just as the top of the headband can only be the south wall, and the headband itself is consti-tuted by this wall and the rows of stones from the mosaic that are parallel to it. In the northwest entrance corridor, the line of pavestones includes a double curve that subsequently merges with the wall that marks the place of the clavicles.

We thus have all the essential points determining the measures and allowing us to seek out what face is represented by these pavestones (cf. plate 37, in which certain stones are indicated in a darker color to make the image of the face appear). The elements of the mosaic allow us to dis-cover the bas-relief of the figure whose head will exactly superimpose itself on the face marked by the joints (plate 36).

Let us recall that on the architrave of the peristyle (transept), on the east side and at the height of the navel, we find inscribed the assertion that *the temple is the birthplace of the king*. This leads us to look in the room of the theogamy (room IX) for the birth of this king. There we find Queen Mutemwia (Mut in the barque) in the state of parturition. Now, the barque does not appear on this partition, but is located in "transposition" exactly at the same level in room IV (fig. 223).[5]

On the second register of the east partition of room IV, the barque of Mut is framed by the barques of Amun and Khonsu accompanied by royal figures, none of whom, out of discretion, look at the barque of Mut in which the divine birth is proceeding. It is therefore in the room of the barque of Mut (room XX) that we will look for the figure who is the human figuration serving as the model for the mosaic of the covered temple.

PLATE 35 • THE "KING WITH THE DIADEM"
OF THE SANCTUARY OF THE BARQUE OF MUT

The room of Mut's barque (room XX) is in the form of an elongated rectangle. On the north side it opens onto the hypostyle room through a large door that takes up the whole wall, anticipating the passage of the barque and its bearers. The east, south, and west partitions only have two regis-ters, each topped by a frieze of a uraeus coiled on a basket[6] alternating with the royal cartouches. These uraei, with the royal disk above them, are oriented from north to south, where they meet on the south wall and frame the two cartouches containing the mystical names of the king,

---

[4] Cf. chapter 40 and plate 84.

[5] Cf. plate 31 and chapter 17.

[6] What is referred to as a "basket" recalls the basket that was carried in Greece in processions during the Bacchic mysteries, and that was forbidden to be opened on pain of death. This symbol is represented by a half-disk, sometimes carved in lines forming a braid.

*Fig. 223. The barque of Mut in transposition between rooms IV and IX;
room IV, east partition, second register, room IX, west partition, second register*

Shaded, Queen Mutemwia, awaiting the royal infant, seated on a cubic seat, projected on the front of the barque. The infant's *ka* is projected on the rudder. The stone that traverses the wall shows, in room IV, the vulture (gestating Mut) upon which rests, in transparency in room IX, the sign "the node of Apet, who gestates," next to which is carved the text relating to the birth.

Amenhotep and Nebmaātre,[7] which constitute the axis of this room. From north to south, all the tableaux are sculpted on east or west partitions and are reflected on the opposite partition as if in a mirror. They meet on the south partition to the right and left of the axis of the room.

In the upper register the king, seated, then kneeling, makes the ritual offering in the presence of Mut's barque, placed on an altar in the image of the one that was kept in this place in earlier times.

In the lower register four tableaux show the king in the presence of Mut, in her different aspects, and in the course of four ritual scenes, similar from east to west but different in their details, as we shall see later on.

It is the fourth king from the entrace who serves as the model for the pavestone mosaic and who will henceforth be designated as the "king with the diadem."

[7] All the names of Amenhotep are on the east part of this frieze, and "Neb-maāt-re" is on the west. There is thus a formal indication of *two* aspects. It is notable that in the entire area of the covered temple south of this room, the royal cartouche is never carved on the upper frieze, which carries only images of the uraeus or the *khakeru*.

At the end of the chapel, on the east and west partitions, there are two similar figures both crowned with the double plume and offering to Mut the symbol of the clepsydra,[8] hammered out in the two scenes (fig. 224). This symbol of the clepsydra, here in Mut's chamber, certainly relates to the time of gestation, confirmed by the palm branch of years held in the hand of the Mut to the west. Now, the figuration of these two kings is an actual image of the mosaic of the temple; under their feet is a second line, emphasizing them, and these two figures are the only ones in the sanctuary with their feet placed on a double line.

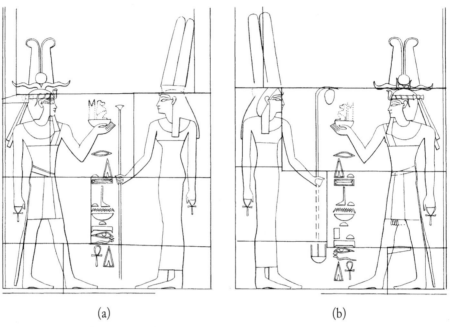

(a)   (b)

Fig. 224. The king offering the symbol of the clepsydra to Mut,
room XX (room of Mut's barque), first register

(a) East partition, fourth scene *(b)* west partition, fourth scene.

Various nuances distinguish the figurations on these two partitions. On the east partition, Mut holds the *wadj* scepter of the opened flower, while on the west partition she holds the branch of the years and the symbol of the *sed* festival.

On the east, the upper joint cuts the skullcap of the king and coincides with the upper edge of the headband, while on the west, the upper joint passes just above his vertex.

On the east, a vertical joint passes through the axis of the king's eye and connects the two horizontal joints, one cutting the skullcap and the other passing under the belt. The navel, which should be located in front of this joint, has not been carved, whereas on the west, the middle horizontal joint passes exactly at the level of the figure's navel.

On the east, the breasts are not drawn, and the belt, as well as certain details of the crown, is left unfinished, whereas on the west, all the details are complete.

---

[8] The baboon is seated before the clepsydra and both are in a basket. The clepsydra is a cylindrical or conic vase, pierced at the bottom, in the interior of which there is a graduated spiral line. This vase was filled with water that emptied out drop by drop to mark time. Sometimes found at the opening of the hole was a baboon, symbol of time because of its behavior at the rising and setting of the sun and thus at the two equinoxes.

Finally, these two kings, who face each other, are presented as if they were reflections of each other at two different moments: the eastern king has two right hands, and the western king has two left hands. The eastern king is an apparition, still unfinished, with neither navel nor skullcap, while the western king is represented in extreme bodily detail, with the joint emphasizing the navel and the skullcap marked by the diadem; but both figures are standing on the double line indicating the earth.

The omission of the breast of the king to the east, which is perfectly drawn on the figure to the west, accents the nourishing, white, milky quality that is specific to this place in the temple, at the top of the lungs (thymus);[9] this quality is also emphasized by the joints between the stones of this room that seem to allow the plaster to flow freely through their gaps.[10]

These two figures will determine the essential proportions that govern the face in the pavestone mosaic of the covered temple, through the relationship between the height from the soles of the feet to the upper edge of the headband (carved on one, and emphasized by the joint on the other) and their total heights to the vertex:

$$\text{eastern king:} \quad \frac{\text{total height to vertex}}{\text{height to stone joint}} = \frac{1.54 \text{ meters}}{1.495 \text{ meters}} = 1.03...$$

$$\text{western king:} \quad \frac{\text{total height to vertex}}{\text{height to headband}} = \frac{1.53 \text{ meters}}{1.488 \text{ meters}} = 1.0282....$$

The upper edge of the royal headband is compared with the south wall of the temple, and this relationship determines the size of the crown of the skull, which is added to the length of the temple (140 fathoms) from the north face of the pylon to the south wall. Now, with 140 fathoms representing the height of the Man of the Temple *without* the crown of the skull, it is sufficient to multiply this length by the coefficient indicated by the two "kings with diadems" in order to arrive at his total height, thus:

$$140 \text{ fathoms} \times 1.03.. \quad = 144.2 \text{ fathoms at } 0° = 265.76 \text{ meters}$$
$$140 \text{ fathoms} \times 1.02857... = 144 \text{ fathoms at } 0° \quad = 265.40 \text{ meters.}$$

The two indicated variants, 1.03 and 1.02857, are indistinguishable in practice. We have already met them in the study of the general proportions of the human canon; these two coefficients are always derived from the function ϕ.[11]

Furthermore, from the study of the proportions of the different parts of the face of the western king in the room of Mut's barque, we learn that if we give the value 1 to the height between the chin and the upper eyelid, the height between the upper eyelid and the top of the headband equals $1/\phi$, so that the crown of the skull equals $1/\phi^2$, and the total value is 2 (fig. 225).

In the covered temple, the key-stones cited above determine precise points in the pavement and allow us to define the measurements of the face in the mosaic. The distance between the long stone embedded in the threshold of the door between rooms IV and VI determines the level of the chin.

---

[9] The thymus reaches its maximum development in the child around two years of age, the end of breast feeding, then progressively declines.

[10] This characteristic of construction is peculiar to this room, where the joints of the stones for the most part have a centimeter of exposed plaster. This would suggest an enlargement of the chapel by a resurfacing of the walls. The proof that the exposed plaster is intentional is given by the fact that one of the *wadj* scepters of the uraeus frieze is *sculpted in relief* on a vertical joint *in this plaster,* projecting out from this joint. In this regard, remember also the use of exposed plaster in the *mammisi* (room of birth and breast feeding) of Dendera.

[11] Cf. chapter 11, "Application of the Standard Pharaonic Canon," "Projection of the *Canevas* onto Two Royal Figures," and figs. 139, 140, and 142.

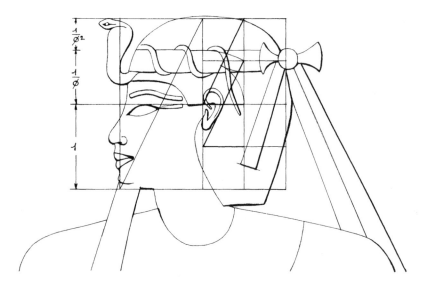

Fig. 225. Study of the proportions of the head of the "king with the diadem." Room XX,
west partition, first register, fourth scene from the north

This level is 33.17 meters from the exterior facade of the south wall that determines the upper edge of the headband. The upper eyelid is marked in room XII by a large pavestone 20.50 meters from the key that indicates the chin. This fact allows us to compare the face in the mosaic to the proportions of the "king with the diadem" as follows:

$$
\begin{aligned}
\text{chin to upper eyelid} &\quad= 1 = 20.50 \text{ meters} \\
\text{chin to headband height} &= \phi = 33.17 \text{ meters} = 18 \text{ fathoms at } 0° \\
\text{chin to vertex} &\quad= 2 = 41.00 \text{ meters.}
\end{aligned}
$$

The height of the missing skullcap is thus $1/\phi^2$, exactly 7.83 meters, which we must add to the length of the temple in order to have a representation of the complete Man, being 258 meters plus 7.83 meters, or 265.83 meters. We can compare this last result with the two previous results, 265.76 meters and 265.40 meters. The latter represents 144 fathoms at 0°.

This study of the facial proportions of the king with the diadem thus only confirms the measurements found previously, those defined by colossus no. 3, by king E in sanctuary I, and by the size of the covered temple,[12] all of which converge toward this final measurement of 144 fathoms, determined here by the pavestone mosaic, for the total size of the Man of the Temple.

PLATE 36 • THE PROFILE OF THE KING ON THE MOSAIC

In order to project the profile of the king with the diadem, which we have just studied, onto the pavement of the covered temple, we must know the relationship between the dimensions of this

[12] In the study of growth, we have seen that the covered temple, measuring 79.82 m, represents the size of the newborn, and that traditionally one royal cubit equals the size of the newborn, or 7/24 of the adult armspan. Knowing the armspan and the height of the Man of the Temple *without the skullcap* (258 m), it is easy to calculate the height of this man to the vertex, knowing that it is the geometric mean between the two known heights. The result of this calculation gives 265.71 m for the height to the vertex for the Man of the Temple.

face and those of the temple. The height measured vertically on the king's face from the line that separates the jaw from the beard to the upper line of the headband is 0.174 meter.

As we have seen, the distance between the measurement key that marks the plane of the chin on the mosiac of the covered temple and the south wall considered as the upper edge of the royal headband is 33.17 meters, or 18 fathoms at 0°.

The ratio between these two measurements is then as follows:

$$\frac{\text{chin to headband height on pavement}}{\text{chin to headband height of king}} = \frac{33.17 \text{ meters}}{0.174 \text{ meter}} = 190.63.... \ .$$

Here we discover approximately ten times the coefficient 19.0983.... We have already observed this coefficient in the relationship between the half-height of colossus no. 3 and the back width of his pedestal.

The diadem of the bas-relief is perpendicular to the vertical axis of the figure. The south wall of the covered temple in its entirety is perpendicular to the axis of Mut, which governs the three sacred sanctuaries, while all the other east-west walls of the covered temple are perpendicular to the axis of Amun.

The position of the face projected so that the upper edge of the headband of the king with the diadem coincides with the south wall of the covered temple brings the vertical axis of the figure into parallel with the axis of Mut. It is this deviation that causes the king to lean slightly forward relative to the axis of Amun, which governs the temple, and displaces his eye, which could be superimposed on that of the pavement if the vertical of the figure were parallel to the axis of Amun.

Looking at the east wall of room V, we find that it corresponds to the point where the uraeus is on the human figure. On this east wall the bas-reliefs show the gift of the "perfumes of the festival," by virtue of whose unction the king is consecrated.[13]

PLATE 37 • THE COVERED TEMPLE ON THE MOSAIC

Plate 37 shows the south part of the covered temple with the walls *placed* onto the pavestone mosaic of the platform.

PLATE 38 • THE CONTROLLING CENTERS OF THE HEAD
IN THE COVERED TEMPLE

This sagittal section has been made according to present medical data and projected onto the temple. The profile of the king with the diadem is also indicated. The reference for these two figures is given by the height from the chin to the vertex.

We can observe a difference between the proportions of the pharaonic face and the profile of an actual person: the pharaonic profile shows a longer midsection for the face (the nose, emotive character), whereas the present profile reinforces the lower part of the face (the more material character).

We see three "stages" on the sagittal section projected onto the plan. First, the upper stage comprises the entire cranium, containing the brain, which corresponds to the three southern sanctuaries, V, I, and VII. Next, in the front, on the east part, the ethmoid and sphenoid bones support the "viscera of the head," and separate the brain from the front and back nasal fossae,[14] which

---

[13] Cf. chapter 39, the description of the partitions of room V.

[14] Cf. chapter 14, "The Interior of the Throat and Head" in the section "Some Anatomical Terms Used in the Papyrus," and fig. 168, no. 43 and related text, and fig. 169 and related text.

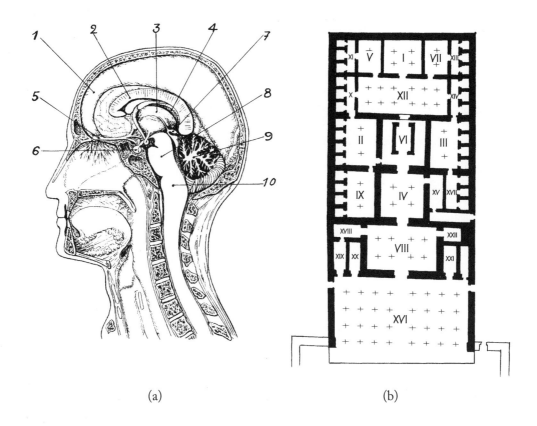

(a)   (b)

Fig. 226. (a) Sagittal section; (b) numbering of the rooms of covered temple

(a) 1, falx cerebri; 2, corpus callosum; 3, third ventricle; 4, choroid plexus; 5, olfactory bulb; 6, pituitary gland; 7, pineal gland; 8, pons; 9, cerebellum; 10, medulla oblongata.

(b) Rooms: I, secret sanctuary of the statue of Amun;

II, room of animation and crowning;

III, room of the descent into the Dwat;

IV, offering room (the four elements);

V, room of duality, offering of cloth and unguents;

VI, sanctuary of Amun's barque

VII, room of the presentation of the prince by his mother;

VIII, room of transformations, of solar character;

IX, room of the royal conception;

X, room of the dawn;

XI, room of the unction;

XII, room of the solar journey;

XIII, XIV, XV, XVII, XVIII, XXII, all destroyed;

XVI, hypostyle room, the *haty;*

XIX, room of Khonsu's barque

XX, room of Mut's barque

XXI, room of the king's barque (?), destroyed.

correspond, in superimposed sections, to the orbital cavities. This stage corresponds to room XII. The wall that separates room XII from room V represents the cribriform plate of the ethmoid, located under the olfactory bulb (fig. 226, no. 5). The soft palate coincides with the wall that separates room XII from rooms II and VI, containing the mouth.

In the back, west part, starting from room XII, the medulla continues into the marrow of the spinal column, represented by the west partitions of rooms VI and IV.[15] Below the chin, room IX is located in the space between the beard and the neck; room IV corresponds to the throat.[16] The upper part of the falx cerebri (fig. 226, no. 1) is outside the temple.

The three southern sanctuaries are united by the corpus callosum (fig. 226, no. 2), which connects the two hemispheres. Likewise, the walls separating these three rooms link them again by "transposition."

Sanctuary I corresponds to the third or middle ventricle (fig. 226, no. 3), located between the optic tracts and communicating with the lateral ventricles found in each hemisphere. These ventricles each have three extensions called horns. The lower extension in the temporal lobe is called "Ammon's horn."

The thalamus is a large ovoid ganglion that defines the third ventricle with its inner surface. Its commissural fibers fan out into the different cerebral lobes.

The choroid plexus, or four-pillared vault (fig. 226, no. 4), is located under the corpus callosum and, like it, is a commissure. The posterior pillars of the choroid plexus come back into the lateral ventricles, the horns of Ammon. The anterior pillars send out a bundle of fibers that enter the olfactory tract, thus uniting rooms I and V. Now, the wall separating these two rooms has on it the representation of the ritual scenes that depict the offering of cloths.[17]

The olfactory bulb (fig. 226, no. 5) corresponds to sanctuary V, the olfactory tract, which then divides and goes toward the four centers. In this sanctuary, the ritual requires the offering of four cloths of different color.[18] The pineal gland is located in room VII (fig. 226, no. 7). It is here, at the age of the awakening of intelligence, that the royal child is presented to Amun and Mut, accompanied by his mother.

In room XII, to the east, the eye and nasal fossae are projected, including the zone of olfactory sensitivity. At the center, the pituitary gland (fig. 226, no. 6) rests on the sella turcica, the stem of which pentrates into sanctuary I, relating it to the thalamus.[19] Finally, to the west, there is the pons and the medulla oblongata (fig. 226, nos. 8 and 10) out of which come twelve pairs of cranial nerves. We can again note that the circle of Willis is located at the level of room XII[20] (under the brain), assuring arterial circulation.

When we penetrate into the skull through the occipital foramen, it is quite remarkable that the two vertebral arteries are united into a single "basilar artery," in order to divide again in encircling

[15] Cf. chapter 17.

[16] Ibid.

[17] Cf. chapter 18.

[18] Cf. chapter 39.

[19] Cf. chapter 30, legends of plates 26 and 27, and the appendix on the physiological relationship between the pituitary gland and the optic tracts.

[20] Cf. vol. 1, fig. 133.

the pituitary stem. It is even probable that it is here that we must investigate the cause of the actions and reactions of the sympathetic and parasympathetic systems through the phenomenon of hysteresis (induction) of the nervous flux. Concerning this, we must remember the hexagonal construction that governs the door of sanctuary I.[21]

The cerebellum is at the extreme west of room XII (fig. 226, no. 9). This unconscious motor center controls the movements necessary for balancing by reflex, and is also capable of obeying the will.

[21] Cf. vol. 1, fig. 183.

Chapter 32

THE CROWN
OF THE SKULL

———ᨀ———

Plates 39–43

The royal principle is sacred provided not only that the imposition of the diadem be a symbolic gesture but that this king be naturally gifted, or educated to acquire this gift of "abstraction" or "mastery of the ego."

(Chapter 15)

PLATE 39

The Crowned King in the Sanctuary of Mut's Barque

*The pharaonic people, whose sole concern was
the afterlife and who sacrificed everything to the
life of the soul, which represents the immortal
principle, were also extremely practical and
very "down to earth" in all their expressions.
Everything was for them a symbol of a* function
*participating in the genesis of tangible Nature,
an image of the genesis of immortality.*

(Chapter 4)

A

B

C

PLATE 40

The Scarab and the Crown of the Skull

The Light of the World needs a substance to carry it in order for it to become visible; in this way the symbol carries the invisible, which it evokes and to which it gives life.

PLATE 41

Crypt of Dendera, the Appearance of Ra

The diadem as measure *gives this measure its
royal character by the line separating the human
from the divine.*

(*Chapter 15*)

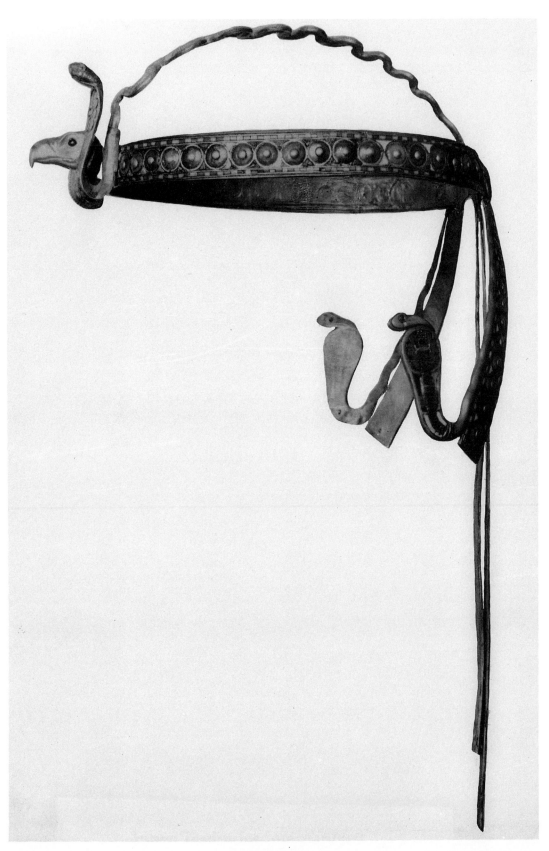

PLATE 42

The Diadem of Tutankhamun

. . . the true prayer, that is, the merging with the
neter, *demands, on the one hand, the life of the*
person, and on the other, the abstraction of his ego,
the selfish being of cerebral or mental reflection.

This alone is the victory over the mortal
personality: Nicodemus, the second birth in the
Gospel. This is why the still symbolic *statuary*
of the cathedrals depicts this saint with the crown
of his skull held in his hands.

(Chapter 15)

PLATE 43

Saint Nicasius Carrying the Crown of His Skull

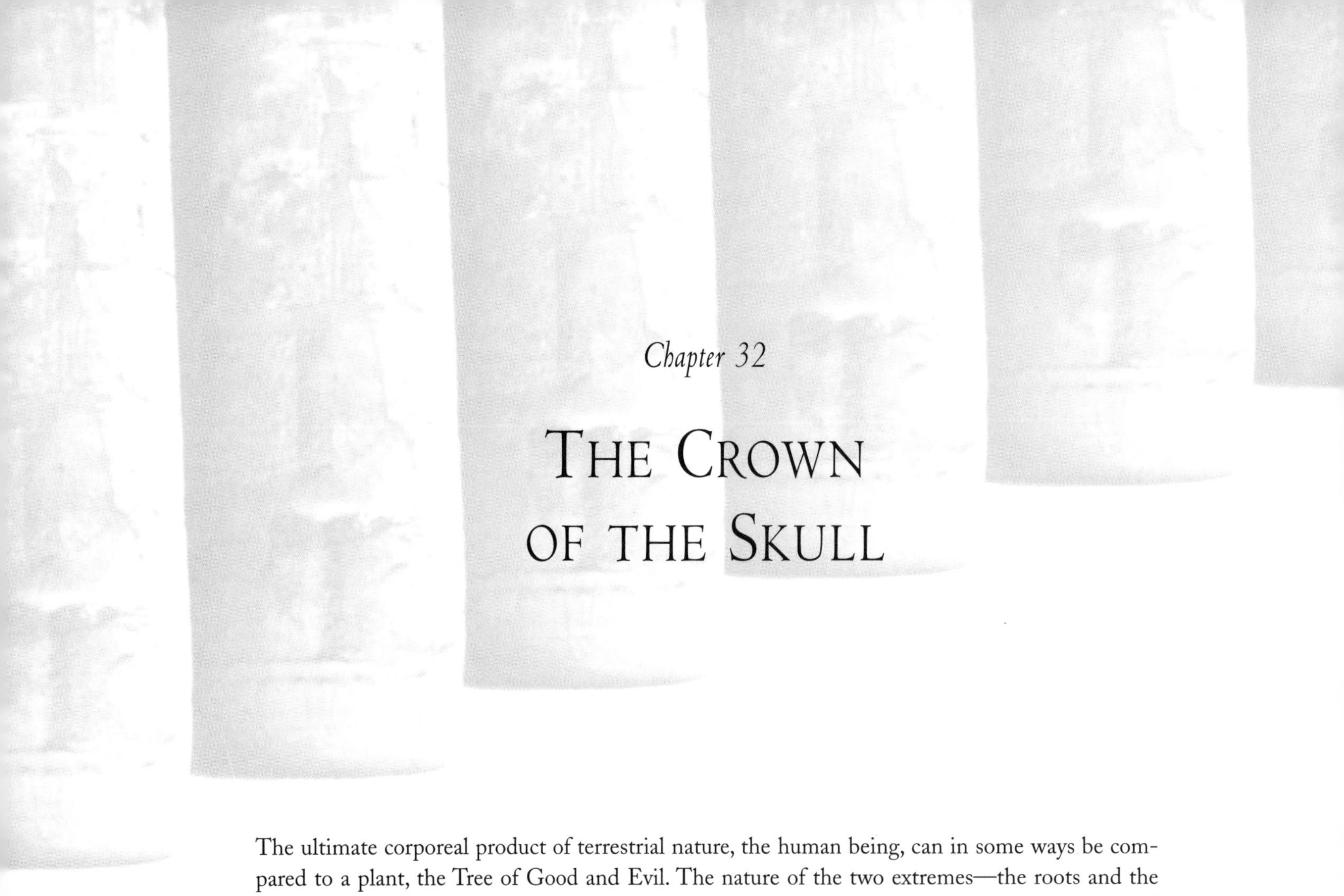

Chapter 32

THE CROWN
OF THE SKULL

The ultimate corporeal product of terrestrial nature, the human being, can in some ways be compared to a plant, the Tree of Good and Evil. The nature of the two extremes—the roots and the flowers, or intestinal organs and cerebral matter—show them to be connected by the same original spirit. In the intestinal convolutions, the nourishing substance undergoes a "co-ruption" that separates the pure from the impure, two aspects of the same fire from which the original chaos is made.

Thus, the biblical Kabbalah speaks to us of the fallen archangel who takes away with him the memory of the divine light, the chaos composed of Seth, the mephitic Satan, and of Horus-Lucifer, who carries the light and causes it to reappear. It speaks of the same history that the pharaonic cabala describes through the struggle between Seth and Hor—the builders of the temple that is Man. Finally, it is Hat-Hor, the house, the container of Horus, which, in the folds and recesses of its cerebral matter, gathers the pure, like the flower bearing the most subtle and sublime substance that will serve thought as well as form the seed of reproduction.

These are Hermetic utterances, of universal meaning, that link physiology to theology. Thus the lunar substance, which builds the "house of Horus," *captures* the most subtle spirit of organic elaboration, holds it, and reduces it to earthly embodiment, dualizing what by nature is one. This lunar reflection of the original light is but a reaction: here the creation becomes procreation; the animating Breath becomes speech; the virtuality-synthesis becomes memory; love, or natural affinity, becomes desire; the ineluctable consequence of the Cause becomes intention; and the Cause becomes Mystery. This laboratory of imitation constitutes the problem, so important, of the crown of the skull.[1]

PLATE 39 • THE CROWNED KING IN THE SANCTUARY OF MUT'S BARQUE (ROOM XX)

The royal figure represented in this plate is located on the first register of the west partition of the sanctuary of Mut's barque. We have seen that the four scenes on the lower register of this partition

[1] Cf. chapter 15.

710

each had their counterparts on the east partition, and that the scenes proceed from north to south.

In the first tableau, near the entrance, the king offers a vase topped with a flame and gives the incense. In the second tableau, the king presents to Mut two vases containing the *mm* grains,[2] drawn in detail on the west side, but summarized on the east side by a simple horizontal stripe.

The third tableau is a rather rare representation that we only find at Luxor on the east and west partitions of this sanctuary, and on the second register of the north wall (consecrated to Mut) in the room of the birth (room IX): the king "striking the ball." In these three representations the king's headdress consists of a headband and a crown composed of two plumes placed behind the solar disk (fig. 227). In room XX, however, the king's crown has, in addition, the two horizontal horns of Khnum and two uraei that frame the two plumes.[3]

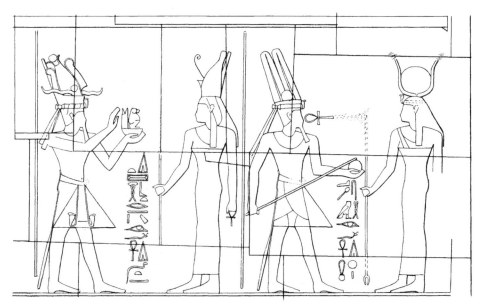

Fig. 227. The king offering the clepsydra, and the king striking the ball. Room IX,
north partition, register 2.

Whereas in the chamber of Mut this figure is immediately behind the king with the diadem presenting the clepsydra, in the room of the birth he precedes him, but in the two rooms these two scenes are side by side.

The north wall of the birth room is located at the level of the clavicles, the first and last point of ossification of the skeleton; thus, the king here is represented as an adult. A stone "piece" cuts the right shoulder of the king offering the clepsydra, thus the right clavicle is emphasized by a horizontal joint, which is therefore the "location joint." By an irregularity in the figure's axis, this joint next passes at the upper level of the king's chest, under his necklace and under the necklace of the king who strikes the ball. It then plays the role of a correspondence joint and refers us precisely to the room of Mut's barque where we discover these same two ritual scenes, with variations only in the headdresses.

[2] We are not dealing with simple grains, but a substance that "causes the milk to rise."

[3] The head of the king who strikes the ball on the west partition is given in plate 39. Cf. vol. 1, fig. 136, the king striking the ball on the east partition.

The face of the king with the diadem in the fourth tableau (room XX) is the image of the mosaic in the pavement of the covered temple. But whereas the upper joint passes above the vertex, in the third tableau the joint passes above the head of the king striking the ball, marking out a very characteristic piece relating this joint to the upper part of the headband (plate 39). This piece replaces the crown of the skull and in the king's headdress cuts off a section that in height is proportionally equal to that of the skullcap of the Man of the Temple, which is missing on the pavestone face.

Above the headdress that encloses the king's head are two horizontal horns, similar to those of Khnum (the potter *neter* who fashions the body), supporting two plumes with a solar disk at their base and flanked by two uraei surmounted by disks. The horizontal joint cuts these horns. This figure of the king wearing his heavy crown, rich in symbolic meanings, is admirable for the simplicity of the drawing and the finish of the execution (of the ear, for example). The relief is so faint that it is the shadows that actually, and very skillfully, give the outlines and details of the face—the eye, the nose, the mouth—and the heads of the cobras. This level of mastery can only be the legacy of a long line of artists and artisans.

PLATE 40 • THE SCARAB AND THE CROWN OF THE SKULL

The design formed by the sutures on the upper surface of a skull is strangely similar to the dorsal surface of the scarab. It is also interesting to compare the braincase that holds the organs of the encephalon with the shell of this insect.[4]

There is a stylized scarab (plates 40A and 40C) currently located at the northwest corner of the sacred lake of the temple of Karnak. Sculpted in high relief, placed on a granite pedestal, and found broken at the edge of the lake, this scarab has been restored by archaeologists. The front surface of the cylindrical pedestal is flattened to form a stele completely carved in sunk relief and in the name of Amenhotep III. The kneeling king makes an offering of two *nw* vases to Tum of Heliopolis. The solar disk, alone in relief and in between the two extended wings crowning the text, forms part of the name Nebmaātre inscribed in the vertical axis of this stele. This disk, symbol of Ra, is the only element in relief in this intaglio group.

Because it is near the sacred lake, and because of the figures on it, this monolith is a synthesis of the Heliopolitan myth that teaches the birth of Ra who comes out of *nw*, the primordial waters. The winged disk Ra, the scarab *kheperr*, and Tum of Heliopolis symbolize the ternary of the creation that serves as a symbol for the path of the sun.

The choice of the scarab to symbolize the creation, thus also the diurnal appearance of the sun, is worthy of meditation. One chooses an insect, and from among this animal-form, chooses the one that, in its becoming, obeys what thought can grasp of a mysterious function that is becoming without comprehensible cause. In the evolutionary chain of living beings, the insect is not biologically situable. Indeed, it is the *subterranean* form of life, which develops through the characteristic metamorphoses of worm and of pupa before it can live in the sun.

And among these beings of the hidden world—animals with external skeletons (shells) and not yet any internal bony structure or framework—the sacred scarab is typified by its manner of living, its way of feeding, and above all its mode of reproduction.

The scarab fashions a perfect ball with dung, which it rolls underground for nourishment and which it excretes as quickly as it eats. When it is time to reproduce, it fashions another perfectly round ball, but only from sheep's dung. Then begins a task from which the ancients borrowed all the symbols with which the myth of the mystery of creation was written.

---

[4] Cf. chapter 15, "The Crown of the Skull."

*Fig. 228. The sacred scarab rolling its ball; compare with the scarab from the tomb of Ramesses IX,
plate 42. Based on a photograph from J.-H. Fabre,* Souvenirs entomologiques,
1st series (Paris: Delagrave, 1922), pp. 24–25.

The *kheperr* scarab[5] is the only animal known on earth that makes the gesture of "rolling" a perfect sphere fashioned by itself, a gesture that can be compared to the diurnal movement of the solar sphere, which apparently moves across the sky from sunrise to sunset. The scarab is the only one to bury a ball in the ground and to give birth to its eggs there. The transformations are then made in total darkness, because this ball remains under the earth for several lunations, the birth finally occurring in a humid environment, which summarizes very well the Heliopolitan myth, recalled by certain phrases in the hymns to the sun: "Homage to you who is the perfect Ra of each day, who rises each morning without respite and who is the Khepri burdened with work. . . . Carver whom you carved yourself, you have cast your own body, O sculptor who has never sculpted. . . . You who travel over the heights of eternity . . . you continue (under the earth as well). . . . He who hurries, he who runs, he who accomplishes his revolutions, Khepri of the illustrious birth . . ."[6]

The very particular form of the *nw* vases, and their offering on the stele of the scarab at the sacred lake of Karnak, leads us to compare them to the sacred scarab's ball during the hatching of the eggs. When the female has fashioned the ball in total darkness, she clambers up and begins the work of preparing the nest that will receive her egg. "The pill, at first exactly spherical, now has a strong pad that encloses a kind of crater that is not very deep. . . . The plastic ball, encircled on one side, becomes hollowed into a groove, beginning from the neck; it is then drawn into an obtuse projection. At the center of this projection, pressure is put that causes the material to flow to the edges, producing the crater with its deformed lips."[7]

The profound meaning of this *nw* vase that is used many ways in hieroglyphic writing can only be revealed by the totality of the myth, symbol, and all the observed facts. One understands that the meaning of the *nw* vase containing, this time in the form of water, the three primordial principles might serve as the basis for a temple whose theme is that of the aquatic aspect of the origin.

Other themes will be based on the primordial Earth, or on the original Fire, or even on Air, that is, on one or another of the four Elements, which by their qualities are necessarily at the origin of things, but are also potentially contained in the *Fiat lux*. These variations have been the subject of multiple disputes among the Greek philosophers and also among the "alchemists" of the Middle Ages.

[5] *Kheperr* is the name of the scarab; *kheper* is also the verb "to become," "to transform." Khepri is the name of the sun at its rising or at its setting, whereas Ra is more particularly the name of the sun at its culmination at noon. Tum, the third name of the rising or setting sun, is connected to the Heliopolitan myth of "He who does not yet exist."

[6] Cf. chapter 26, "Hymn to the Sun."

[7] Cf. Jean-Henri Fabre, *Souvenirs entomologiques,* 5th series (Paris: Delagrave, 1922), pp. 54–55.

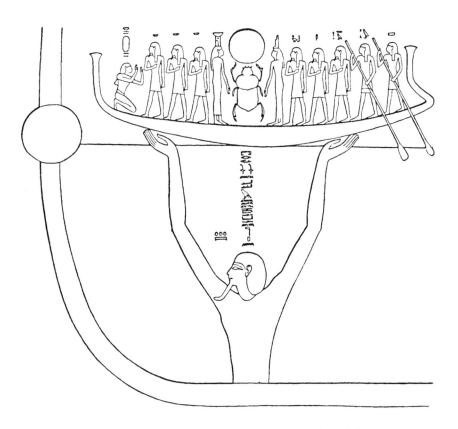

Fig. 229. The birth of the sun, Khepri, carried by the primordial waters,
nww, *after having created himself in Nun*

Let us note the river Nun and the dualizing action indicated by the two arms. This explains
the direct symbolism: Ra issued from the river Nun.

For example, at the temple of Mentu at North Karnak detailed excavations have brought to
light a passageway to the main temple and to its entry door.[8] Now, at the level of the upper paving
four immense circular blocks of white limestone, contrasting with the double paving of red granite
that preceded them on the ramp leading to the temple, attracted the attention of the excavators.

Fig. 230. The female scarab preparing her ball for hatching.
Based on a photograph from J.-H. Fabre, Souvenirs entomologiques, *plate 4, p. 128.*

---

[8] Cf. Robichon, Barguet, and Leclant, *Karnak-Nord IV,* fasc. 1, pp. 32, 34.

Buried in the ground just at the threshhold to the entrance, these four cylindrical limestone blocks were found to be the bases of old columns. They had been turned upside down and recut to form *nw* vases. In the axis and in front of these blocks was a fragment of a broken statue, in green stone—a hand holding a *nw* vase (fig. 231).

Fig. 231. The nw *offering vase*

In the same foundations of the door and behind the "four bases," a kneeling statue was found holding a *nw* vase in each hand, its hands resting on its knees. Is this not a perfect example of the observance of the symbol that we find in all of the objects or monuments that the Ancients have left us, thus sanctifying all their works? Knowing that *mnw* signifies "foundation" and associates the root *mn*, "basis," with that which is symbolized by the *nw* vase shows us the relationship between the metaphysical, primal waters and the notion of the basis or foundation.

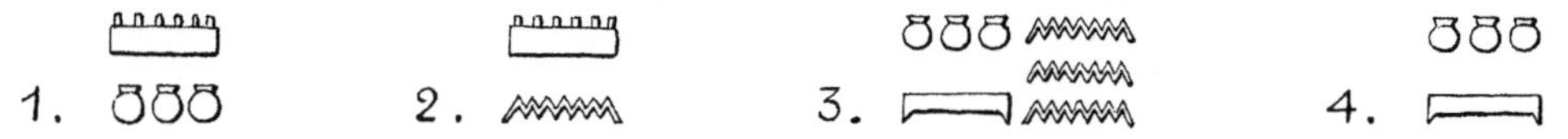

Fig. 232

1, *mnw*, "foundation" in the sense of that which persists. But the *nw* vases suggest also the idea of "to make appear" in the sense of "to create." 2, *mn*, "established," "fixed," "the foundation" (same root as *mn.t*, "the thigh"). 3, *mw.w? nwnw? nnw*, "the primordial waters" (*Wörterbuch*, 2.14). 4, *nw.w*, name of the principle of the division of the primal waters (fig. 229).

The Legend of the Scarab Related by Horapollo

The choice of the scarab as the symbol of the sun and of becoming is explained by Horapollo in the following way.

> Wishing to signify what is born alone, or the becoming, or the father, or the world, or a man (the male), the Egyptians depicted a scarab.
>
> It is born alone because this animal proliferates itself without being carried by a female, because it is the only one who is created in the following way. When the male wants to procreate his young, he takes cattle dung and fabricates a ball of it with a form similar to that of the world. He rolls this with his hind legs from dawn to dusk facing toward the rising sun to reproduce the image of the world. Indeed, this ball is carried from the east toward the west as the course of the stars is directed from the west toward the east. Then, having hollowed a hole, he buries himself in his ball for twenty-eight days, that is, the number of days it takes the moon to go through the twelve signs of the zodiac.

During the time that they live under the earth, the young of the scarab takes on a living form. The scarab uncovers the ball on the twenty-ninth day and throws it in water because, it is believed, this is the day of the conjunction of the moon and the sun, as well as the birth of the world. When the ball opens in the water, the animals, that is, the scarabs, leave it.[9]

It is obvious that the description of the birth of the scarab by Horapollo has a symbolic goal. The tradition concerning the scarab as a symbol of transformations, of the becoming, the appearance, and the coming out of the waters, could have justified the apparent "errors" of Horapollo, who, in his story, gives true facts mixed with legend.

1. It is the female scarab, not the male, who fashions the ball especially destined to receive the single egg.[10]

2. Horapollo reverses the movements of the stars, which is true if, by the stars of which he speaks we understand the earth, which actually turns from west to east and creates the appearance that the Great World turns from east to west.

3. The scarab does in fact bury its ball in a hole hollowed out of the ground, but Horapollo omits one important detail: After she has dismantled her ball and carefully sorted out any large particles, the female scarab reconstitutes it and prepares it to receive the single egg, which, walled up in this exactly sculpted nest, will have to hatch completely alone and undergo the successive transformations into a worm and then a pupa before appearing in the light of day.

4. Horapollo speaks of only one lunation for the gestation of the scarab, whereas the real time that elapses between the burial of the ball and the appearance of the new generation is four lunar months, that is, one pharaonic season, not one lunar month. The first month is given to the brooding and hatching of the egg. The second month corresponds to the phase during which the worm grows and is nourished from the contents of the ball. During the third month—in a striking similarity to the royal mummy wrapped in his bandages—the pupa prepares for rebirth. Finally, when the scarab takes its completed form, "the head and the thorax are dark red except for the teeth, which are toned down with brown. The abdomen is an opaque white, the wing cases are a transluscent white, very slightly tinted with yellow. . . . This costume darkens by degrees to form a uniform ebony black. Approximately one month is necessary for the horn armor to acquire a firm consistency and definite color."[11]

Now, according to Fabre, twenty-eight days represents the pupal phase. In his studies, this duration was an object of special attention; the time varies, but within the narrow limits of twenty-one to thirty-three days, with the average from about twenty observations being actually twenty-eight days, so that in fact Horapollo spoke accurately, and he found a way to mention in this regard the knowledge of the *twelve signs of the zodiac.*

5. It is not the scarab, as Horapollo says, that on the twenty-ninth day uncovers its ball and throws it in the water; but since the female forms it around the first fortnight of May in *dry* earth, this earth must necessarily be wet at the time of maturity in August and September to allow hatching. When Horapollo speaks of the birth of the scarab leaving the ball thrown in water, he alludes to the

[9] *Hieroglyphica,* 1.10.

[10] Cf. B. van de Walle and J. Vergote, "Traduction des Hieroglyphes d'Horapollon," *Extrait de la Chronique d'Egypte,* no. 35 (January 1943): 49:

　　a) "That which is born alone," translated here from the word μονογένης, which can signify, according to the Church Fathers and the gnostic writers: 1) only son, or daughter; 2) αὐτογενης.

　　b) The scarab, *khprr,* thus represents the verb *khpr,* "to become."

　　c) "The father" is perhaps to be compared with *skhpr,* "to cause to become," "to procreate."

[11] Fabre, *Souvenirs entomologiques,* pp. 84–85.

birth of the world, that is, to what is related in the Heliopolitan Mystery, according to which Ra, as Tum, is born from the primordial waters. Bringing the myth close to reality, we observe that August-September, the period of the appearance of the new scarabs—which can only occur in Europe thanks to the autumn rains—is the time of the high waters of the Nile (the inundation) in Egypt.

Plate 41 • Crypt of Dendera, the Appearance of Ra

This plate shows a part of an extremely curious tableau above the entrance door (east) in a crypt of the temple of Hathor at Dendera (fig. 233). The entire scene shows Ra, then Tefnut and Shu, Nut, Hu, the cow Ahat, and again Ra, who is thus represented at each extremity but in two different forms. To the left he is standing with his thighs spread, but his legs are replaced by two forearms, with the hands making the gesture of picking up something. To the right he is represented by a human head, seen from the front but intentionally deformed, suggesting the image of the scarab. The crown of the skull has a scalloped sign above it similar to the one that crowns the hieroglyph signifying the appearance (fig. 234), and that is the stylized reproduction of the head of the scarab, whose eyes are recalled by the small buttons to the right and the left of the base of the crown. The name of Ra is written above in an unusual way.

Fig. 233. Appearance of Ra

To the left of this curious figure, the celestial cow, Ahat, bears the face of Hathor carved at the top of its left thigh. Its belly is identified as the starry sky on which the solar barque navigates, the "sun that Nut [the sky] swallows each evening and puts into the world each morning. . . ."[12]

Fig. 234. Ptolemaic hieroglyph symbolizing the appearance of the sun

According to the classical translation this is "a hill from which springs forth the sun in the morning" (phonetic *kha*), whence the expression "appearing gloriously" *(khai)* is derived, which is applied to the king.

---

[12] The symbol of the cow, as important in Ancient Egypt as in India, is related to Hermetic doctrine through its double digestion and its effect, the nourishing milk, as well as through its lunar nature.

Thus, each morning after its nocturnal course the sun Ra reappears, leaving the primordial waters *nw*. The caricatured face that symbolizes it is a cryptogram uniting the scarab *(kheperr)*, the face *(hr)*, and the appearance *(kha)* in a single image, alluding to cerebral substance insofar as it is a product of a Hathorian effect. Under this tableau is the text that relates the mythic origin of the plan of this temple.[13]

PLATE 42 • THE DIADEM OF TUTANKHAMUN

Here is the description of Tutankhamun's diadem given by Howard Carter, who discovered Tutankhamun's tomb:[14]

> . . . a magnificent diadem . . . completely encircling the king's head—an object of extreme beauty and of simple fillet type. In design it comprises a richly ornamented gold ribbon of contiguous circles of carnelian,[15] having minute gold bosses affixed to their centres, and . . . bordered with a lapis lazuli and torquoise coloured glass pattern . . . with, at the back, a floral and disk-shaped bow . . . inlaid with malachite and sardonyx[16] . . . from which hang two ribbon-like gold appendages similarly decorated. On both sides of the fillet are appendages of a like but broader kind, and having a massive pendant uraeus attached to their front margins [which encircle the ears]. The back pendant ribbons, and the side appendages . . . are hinged to the fillet, and were thus adaptable to the wig over which the diadem was worn.
>
> The insignia of northern and southern sovereignty of this diadem . . . were found lower down, separate, and on the right and left thighs respectively,[17] and as the king lay within the sarcophagus, east and west—his head towards the west—the uraeus of Buto being on the left side [therefore to the north] and the vulture of Nekhebet to the right [at the south], the insignia took their correct geographical position, as did also those emblems on the coffins. Both of these golden emblems of royalty have grooved fastenings on the back, into which fit corresponding T-shaped tongues upon the diadem. They are thus movable and could be fitted on to whatever crown the king might have worn.
>
> The golden Nekhebet, with obsidian eyes[18] . . . is a remarkable example of fine metal-work. The shape of the head [and its particularities] make it quite clear that the bird, representing the Upper Egyptian goddess, was the *Vultur auricularis*.[19] . . .
>
> This diadem must have had a very early origin, inasmuch as it seems to have derived its name *Seshnen*[20] and form from the circlet-ribbon worn on the head by men and women of all classes, as

---

[13] Text that we cite in chapter 33.

[14] Howard Carter, *The Tomb of Tut-ankh-Amen* (London: Cassell, 1930), 2:110–11, 256.

[15] The carnelian is assigned to the sign of Scorpio, the dwelling place of Mars, and has a feminine character. [Author's note.]

[16] The sardonyx [sard] is a quartz of a fawn-orange color, finer than the carnelian with which it has some similarity. [Author's note.]

[17] Let us note that the name of Tutankhamun is inscribed on the capitals of some columns in the nave at Luxor (the femur). On the other hand, the figures in the tomb of Tutankhamun also place a characterizing accent on the force of the thigh, but the proportions imposed by the size of the head give the royal figure different ages of transformation. [Author's note.]

[18] Obsidian is a stone of the nature of feldspar, of volcanic origin, vitreous in nature and dark green or black in color according to where it is found. Obsidian, according to Pliny, had been discovered in Ethiopia by Obsius, fourteen centuries after Tutankhamun. "This stone is very dark in colour and sometimes translucent, but has a cloudier appearance than glass, so that when it is used for mirrors attached to walls, it reflects shadows rather than images. Gems are frequently made of it. . . ." Pliny, *Natural History*, 36.67. [Author's note.]

[19] Or "sociable vulture" of Shelley and Nicoll, corresponding to *Torgos tracheliotus nubicus* in Colonel R. Meinertzhagen, *Nicoll's Birds of Egypt* (London: H. Rees, 1930), 2:428, and to *Autogyps auricularis* or *Autogyps auricou* in A. E. Brehm, *La Vie des animaux* (Paris: Baillière, 1878–85) 3:476. [Author's note.]

[20] The name *seshnen* is only one of the names of the diadem. [Author's note.]

far back as the Old Kingdom, some 1500 years before the New Empire. Moreover, there is evidence enough to show that we may consider it to be among ancient Egyptian funerary appurtenances, since it is to be found mentioned among the coffin texts of the Middle Kingdom, and diadems of this kind are known to have been found thrice in connexion with royal burials: once analagous but not identical, at Lahun, among the jewellery discovered by Professor Sir William Flinders Petrie of a Princess Sat-hathor-iunut of the Middle Kingdom; and twice in the royal Theban pyramid-tombs of the Seventeenth Dynasty—one upon a burial of an Antef, the other mentioned in connexion with the Ancient Egyptian plunderers of the burial of Sebek-em-saf.

It is again appropriate to observe that the uraeus carries the sign of Neith on its chest, and by its undulations the serpent divides the brain and continues to play its dualizing role.

PLATE 43 • SAINT NICASIUS CARRYING THE CROWN OF HIS SKULL

This statue of Saint Nicasius dates from the end of the fourteenth century.[21] There is another representation of this saint on the north portal of the facade of Reims cathedral, to the right of the "smiling angel." Saint Nicasius, the second bishop of Reims, was murdered by the Vandals in 407. He is represented there also without the skullcap. His two hands are broken, but on his stomach the attachments of the skullcap that he carried in his hands remain. The costumes of these two figures are similar.

Now, Reims is the place of the consecration and the coronation of the kings of France. Here the holy chrism is preserved, which miraculously descended from the sky according to the legend that attributes this gift from heaven to Saint Remy.

The life of Saint Remy has been written by Hincmar, archbishop of Reims.

The birth of this glorious doctor and confessor of the faith had been prophesied by a hermit in the following circumstances. At the moment when the persecution by the Vandals desolated all of France, a saintly, blind hermit prayed ardently for peace for the church of the Gauls. Now, an angel appeared and said to him: "Know that the woman who is called Ciline will bring into the world a son by the name of Remy who will deliver his people from the attacks of the wicked." Thus the hermit, as soon as he awoke, made his way to the house of Ciline and told her of his vision. And as the woman refused to believe it because she was already old and had given up hope of bearing a child, the hermit said to her, "Know that when your child has taken the breast, you only have to rub my eyes with the milk that I might immediately recover my sight!" And indeed all came to pass in this fashion.[22]

From his youth, Remy avoided the world and entered into a monastary. But at twenty-two years of age, his renown, which grew unceasingly, caused him to be chosen by the people to be archbishop of Reims. And he was a man of such sweetness that when he ate, the sparrows came to his table and he fed them from the palm of his hand. One day, he visited the house of a woman, and saw that there was no more wine there. Saint Remy entered into the cellar, and made the sign of the cross on the wine barrel; suddenly the wine sprang forth in such abundance that the entire cellar was flooded.

Clovis, the king of France, was then pagan, and his pious wife was not able to lead him to conversion. But one day, seeing himself threatened by the immense German army, he made a vow to the

[21] The statue belongs to Mme. Hein, antiques dealer, 48 rue de Lille, Paris. Cf. chapter 15, "Diadem, I Assume Thee."
[22] Cf. the legend of the eye of Horus being cured by Hathor with the milk of a gazelle, chapter 44, p. 1016.

God his wife worshiped. He would convert if God would grant him victory over his enemies. And God gave him the victory, so the king conveyed himself into the presence of Saint Remy and asked to be baptized. But arriving at the baptisimal font, the bishop and the king found that the holy chrism was missing. But there was a dove hovering in the air carrying an ampule full of holy chrism its beak, with which the prelate anointed the king. This ampule is preserved in the church at Reims, where it still serves today at the coronation of the kings of France.[23]

Reims cathedral, begun in 1211 on the plan of Jean d'Orbais, replaced the church where Clovis was baptized. That church had been constructed by Saint Nicasius about 400 and was destroyed in 1210 by a fire.

"In the pavement of the nave, spanning the distance beneath the third and fourth ribs, there was formerly a labyrinth, in the center of which the four architects who can be considered as the authors of the monument were represented. It was removed in 1778, but ancient manuscripts have preserved the text of the inscriptions that accompanied these figures."[24] We have already seen the importance of this labyrinth based on the essential functions of the *canevas*.[25] In the image of this labyrinth, the two towers of the facade of the cathedral have an octagonal plan flanked by four turrets that rise up above the gallery of the kings.

"At Notre Dame of Reims, the balustrade above the promenade of the chevet and of the radiating chapels is unusually high and is proportionately out of scale, and causes the apse to wear a double crown. Now, the apse most often forms a semicircle, and "the apsidal sanctuary is the mystic 'pillow' of Our Lord, and the altar represents the head."[26]

In a gothic cathedral the choir is always elevated by several steps. Now, at Reims a high walkway surrounds the whole choir and forms a curve a *segment of whose arc is cut* at the upper part of the choir. This recalls the front surface of the pedestal on which the scarab of Karnak rests; there a segment of the circle is also cut. These two removed sections of the curve symbolize the removal of the crown of the skull, both on the pedestal of Karnak and in the cathedral of Reims, where, during the royal sacramental ceremonies, personal thought is symbolically replaced by the crown.

[23] *La Légende dorée du Bienheureux Jacques de Voragine,* trans. Teodor de Wyzewa (Paris: Perrin, 1910), pp. 76–77.

[24] R. de Lasteyrie, *L'Architecture religieuse en France à l'époque gothique* (1926), 1:69.

[25] Cf. vol. 1, fig. 95b.

[26] L. C. Dezobry and T. Bachelet, *Dictionnaire général de biographie et d'histoire de mythologie, de géographie ancienne et moderne comparé* (Paris: Delagrave, 1889).

Chapter 33

THE MOON
IN THE HATY

⁓

Plates 44 and 45

There is no function in the Universe that in its humanly energetic, psychological, psychic, and mental form cannot be observed and recognized by the human being. But the key is reason. This is why the pharaonic sages . . . have attributed a neter, *a cosmic principle, to each part of the human body, its organs and vital functions.*

(Chapter 3)

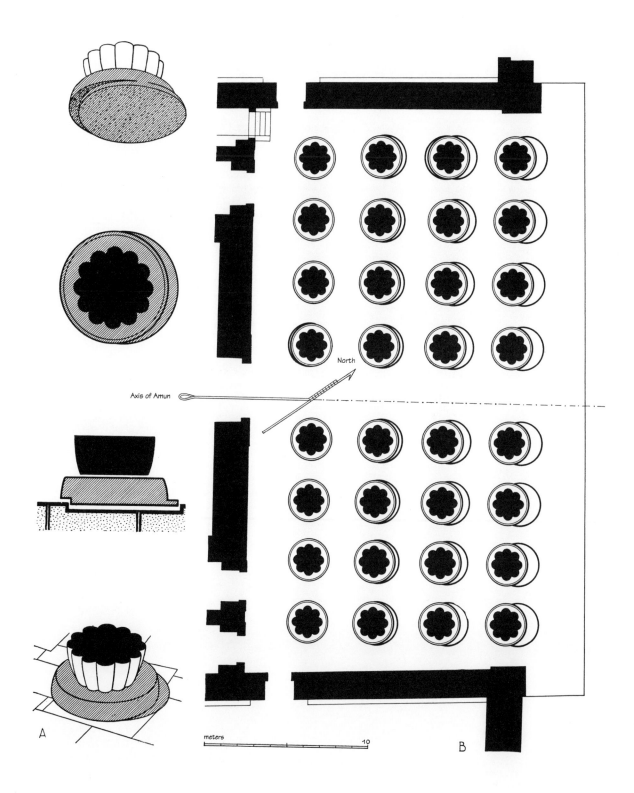

North

Axis of Amun

meters   10

A   B

PLATE 44

The Lunar Crescents in the Hypostyle Room of the Covered Temple

Whether it is a natural or a compound image,
or a conventional sign, the property of the
symbol is to be a summarizing representation,
which is commonly called a synthesis.

(Chapter 2)

PLATE 45

The Lunar Crescent and Femininity

Chapter 33

THE MOON
IN THE HATY

Here in the *haty* we are at the place where, through respiration, the joining of spirit with body is accomplished. It is the place of the second animation through the breath, birth into this world; it is here and here alone that we find the great inscription of which there is but one other known example, that of the temple of Tuthmosis III at Medinet Habu (west bank, *amenti,* of Thebes).

> The two texts are identical and graphic variations are practically nonexistent. . . .
>
> As will be seen, we have more here than a text of "Giving the House to Its Master";[1] it is also more than a text for "consecration of the temple" *(Hausweihe,* according to Sethe); it is a ritual foundation of the temple in a very concise form, a kind of summary, beginning with the scene of "stretching the cord" and concluding with the consecration of the divine dwelling through the sacrificial ritual.
>
> This extremely concise, archaic ritual leaves no apparent link that relates the sentences to one another. . . .[2]

In order to understand better how a single word of this inscription can summarize a whole group of ritual gestures, and the reason why it is carved precisely in this place in the temple, we believe it is necessary to give here a summary description of the foundation ritual as the bas-reliefs show it in some temples of the Late Period. These bas-reliefs transcribe in imaged form facts either observed during the course of certain recent excavations or recounted in various ancient texts.

The dedication that encircles the "tank" on which the covered temple of Luxor rests informs us about the author of this monument:

> Long live Horus, victorious bull, appearing in truth [Kha-m-maāt], who maintains the laws, who pacifies the Two Lands, golden Horus, of the victorious arms that crush the Asiatics [Setiu[3]], *neter*

---

[1] The traditional formula is found again at the top of our text: "How beautiful this dwelling is! There is no dwelling equal to it."

[2] P. Barguet, "Le Rituel archaïque de fondation des temples de Médinet Habou et de Louqsor," *Revue d'Égyptologie* 9 (1952): 2–3.

[3] Setiu, or Sethians, implies "who crushes the wicked" (the burning fire).

nefer . . . eldest son . . . inestimable egg [*ikr*] of Amun, reared[4] in the castle . . . master of the Two Lands, master of the rites, Nebmaātre, son of Ra from his belly, his "beloved" master of appearances, Amenhotep, prince of Thebes, he has made in foundation [monument, *mnw*] for his father Amun . . . the sublime Apet, his great place of the first time, in perfect works of eternity . . .[5]

Thus it is the king, the master of the two crowns and of the laws and rites, to whom the building of this temple whose name is Apet of the South is attributed. We only have to read his titles to know that as the "son of Ra," the God-chosen, this king has the right to build. Now, all the texts relating to the building of a temple represent the king as the active power, acting in the name of his father, "Universal Master." When the king is spoken of in these sacred texts, it is well understood that the royal person is only a symbol of the True King, the universal son of Ra, because the limited power of terrestrial kings is only a pale reflection of the omnipotence of the True King.

Myth says that when the *neters* (the gods) reigned, a "book of foundation for the temples of the *neters* of the first Ennead" was drafted by Imhotep, son of Ptah. This book was carried away to the heavens by the *neters*, but Imhotep "let it drop to the north of Memphis." The temple at Edfu was erected in the Late Period following the prescriptions of this book, which was used to establish its "great plan."[6]

In one of the crypts of the temple of Dendera, a text attests to the divine origin of the plan of this temple, executed "following a general plan written in ancient script on the skin of a goat at the time of the servants of Horus."[7]

Thus the divine origin of the prescriptions according to which the plans of the temple were drawn is attested to in monuments of the Late Period and confirmed by the more ancient texts. Now, it is the king, consecrated and crowned, the inspired one, having set aside his "personal thought," who transmits the divine will to man throughout the phases of the empire. A manuscript on leather from the Twelfth Dynasty relates the remodeling of the temple of Ra at Heliopolis following the prescriptions from a "divine book." This manuscript describes the great council held by the king for this occasion and the ritual words pronounced; then, crowned with the royal headband, the king leaves the temple and completes the foundation ritual, whose most often represented essential gesture is of "stretching the cord" and planting a stake in the earth.

The two hypostyle rooms of the temple of Edfu show several operations that we must give here in no specific order, as some of them are found there several times in various sequences:

- The departure of the king preceded by the instructions and by Iunmutef.
- The king and Seshat, mistress of the divine books, each with a mallet with which they strike a stake into the earth. This scene is called "stretching the cord between two stakes."
- The king hollows a furrow with a pickax.
- The king pours out the contents of a barrel.
- The king grinds up a brick.
- The king offers a row of small bricks on a platter.
- The king encircles the temple with grains of incense.
- The king "gives the house to its master."

---

[4] Literally, "nourished at the breast."

[5] From an unpublished translation by Alexandre Varille.

[6] From Alexandre Moret, *Du Caractère religieux de la royauté pharaonique,* Annales du Musée Guimet 15 (Paris: Leroux 1902), pp. 130–31.

[7] Ibid., p. 131. The servants of Horus relate to the mythic, prehistoric period.

Fig. 235. King "Scorpion"

Fragment from the head of a limestone club. Cf. J. E. Quibell, *Hierakonpolis* (London: Egyptian Research Account, 1900), part 1, plate 26c.

To this is added certain purifications and ablutions as well as the "ritual run." At Soleb (Nubia), in a temple of Amenhotep III, the king knocks on the door of the sanctuary twelve times, then brings a fire into the temple and purifies the naos "by illuminating it four times with a lamp lit by the sacred fire."[8]

The oldest representation of an inauguration scene, which goes back to the Predynastic Period, has been found at Hierakonpolis. King "Scorpion,"[9] wearing a white crown, holds the plow in his two hands, while a smaller figure in front of him holds a kind of basket (fig. 235). Beyond them, another figure holds a bundle of wheat stalks. The ground upon which the king's feet are placed shows undulations, signifying that it is flooded soil.

By itself this simple scene summarizes one of the essential phases of the foundation ceremony that the latest excavations at North Karnak have allowed us to observe.[10] The foundations were made by cutting trenches over the entire ground. In the lower part of these trenches, traces of a hoe have been observed, which suggests the image of Ra "digging with a hoe" and confirms the texts. On an architrave of the Ramesses court in the temple of Luxor can be read: "a great foundation trench [*mdwt*] has been hollowed by Seshat, lady of the master builders."[11] Moreover, at Edfu it is specified that the king digs with a hoe down to the water level for the perfect temple.[12]

[8] Ibid., p. 139.

[9] It is conceivable that by means of King Scorpion a date of the year was specified, the month ruled by Scorpio, October 21–November 21, the eighth month after spring. It is also the eighth month of human gestation, the time of renewal in preparation for birth at nine months, November 21–December 21, Christmas, and the Khoïak festivals in Egypt.

[10] Cf. Robichon, Barguet, and Leclant, *Karnak-Nord IV,* fasc. 1, p. 9 et sqq., concerning the excavation of a Ptolemaic portico containing four rows of columns resting on four bases whose foundations have been carefully studied, measured, and drawn.

[11] Legrain, *Le Logement et le transfert des barques sacrées*, p. 60.

[12] This scene is located on the exterior of the surrounding wall, and in the two hypostyle rooms. Cf. Emile Chassinat, *Le Temple d'Edfou*, 15 vols. (Cairo: I.F.A.O., 1897–1985), 2:60; 3:106, 166; 7:45.

The last assertion specifies that the trench must reach the level of the underground water; now, in this instance it can only be the infiltration water corresponding to the high-water level of the Nile. The excavation mentioned above actually proved that the foundation trenches had contained a small quantity of water.

> The footprints of those who walked in this mud have been noted and plaster molds taken. They are particularly clear in foundation A, where several people, one of whom was a child, were moving about, some with bare feet, some in sandals. One of them bent down and his pleated loincloth impressed its mark in the ground. The presence of people wearing sandals seems to indicate that some of those present were more important than simple workers. A block from the red chapel of Queen Hatshepsut, for that matter, shows priests proceeding with their feet sunk below ground level, which is marked by an incised straight line.
>
> All around the partitions of the trenches, about 40 centimeters above the bottom and parallel to the water level contained in the various foundation basins, lines have been drawn that are by definition perfectly level. . . .[13]

Above these lines, some reference points painted in red were also found. Thus the water served as the reference level for the construction of the temple. This explains the surprising levelness of certain monuments, as, for example, the base of the first pylon at Karnak, which through its length of about 112 meters is rigorously horizontal. It is not off by even a centimeter (a fact that can be verified only with the help of our modern instruments).

After this first operation, represented on the monuments by the king holding the pickax or hoe in his hand, the bottom of the trench was re-covered with sand. The excavation at North Karnak even allows us to determine that this sand must have been poured starting from a particular place. The bed of sand is about 30 centimeters thick, and contained various small bricks, the arrangement of which was different for each of the foundations: "In one there are three small bricks of white material covered in gold leaf. These bricks determine the three apexes of a large right triangle. There is also a fourth brick of green material. . . ."[14]

On the depictions we indeed see the king grinding a brick or bringing some small bricks of earth or metal[15] "to establish the four corners of the temple." The earthen bricks symbolize the union of earth and water; the small bricks covered in gold and those of the green material found at North Karnak symbolize accomplishment and plant growth.

Excavations made in the buildings from all periods reveal that foundation deposits were a standard rite, but that each deposit was in accordance with the symbolism of its particular place. Thus, we can see that the temple of Mentu at Medamud, dedicated to the bull at the period corresponding to the sign of Taurus, contained, among other foundation deposits, four long-horned cattle heads.[16] In other places one observes the presence of such things as charcoal, fragments of stones, various sacrifices, and so on. For example, at Karnak, at the temple of Mentu, a deposit with the

---

[13] Cf. Robichon, Barguet, and Leclant, *Karnak-Nord IV*, fasc. 1, p. 11. After more than twenty centuries, it is extremely moving to be able to relive this foundation scene through the imprints left in muddy earth, thanks to the minute care brought to the excavation by Clément Robichon, to whom belongs the credit for uncovering an entire temple of unbaked bricks, in the same earth used to form the bricks. It is a unique work of excavation in the annals of archaeology and a fine example to follow.

[14] Ibid., p. 12.

[15] Also at North Karnak a foundation deposit has been found that contains, along with a gold brick, gold in all forms, fashioned into wires, plates, strips, etc.

[16] Cf. legends of plates 50 and 51.

name of Taharka (from the period that corresponds to the last decan of Aries) contained, among other objects, "a head of a herbivore (length 0.25 m, width 0.10 m, approximately) with the crown of the skull cut off, the muzzle turned toward the east, and south of the head a leg of the same animal, a shoulder blade to the west, and bones folded up in a right angle with respect to each other."[17]

Finally, one of the essential operations, summarized under the title of "stretching the cord," consisted of determining the orientation of the temple. At Edfu, the king speaks thus in the presence of Seshat: "I have taken the stake and the mallet by the handle, I have grasped the (measuring) rope with the goddess Sefekht; my gaze has followed the course of the stars; my eye has turned toward the Great Bear; I have measured time and counted (the hour) with the clepsydra, then I established the four corners that define the temple."[18]

The precision of this text is very important because it specifies that the king looks at the movement of the stars and the Great Bear, an allusion to the circumpolar stars that the Ancients called "the Indestructibles." By taking a sighting on one star of the Great Bear at a determined hour of a determined day, one specifies this day of the year, because the circumpolar stars make a complete turn around the Pole Star in a year. The further the star is from the center, the easier it is to specify the date. The seven-starred constellation of the Great Bear is an obvious choice for a sighting star.

Fig. 236. Seshat and the king stretching the cord between two stakes

[17] Robichon, Barguet, and Leclant, *Karnak-Nord IV,* fasc. 1, p. 38. It is undoubtedly a bovine head.
[18] From Brugsch, cited by Moret, *Du Caractère religieux,* p. 132.

At the temple of Seti at Abydos, Seshat expresses herself thus:

I have grounded it with Sokaris; I have stretched the cord for the placement of the walls; while my mouth recited the great incantations, Thoth was there with his books . . . to establish the enclosure of its walls, Ptah-Tatanen measured the ground and Tum was there. . . .

The mallet in my hand was of gold; with it I struck the stake, and thou, thou wast with me in the form of Hunu, thy two arms held the hoe. Thus the four corners were established as solidly as the four pillars of the sky. It was Neith who pronounced the charms [*sa*] and the protective formulas for the temple, and Selkit placed her hand on these works made for eternity.[19]

The text inscribed on the second register of the east wall of the hypostyle room of Luxor is far from being very explicit, because only the first sentences are directly related to the ritual scenes that we have just described.

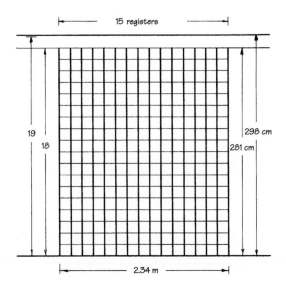

Fig. 237. Proportions of the surface bearing the text of "Giving the House to Its Master," second register of the east partition of the hypostyle room of the temple of Luxor.

This text is written on fifteen columns. Each has an average width that can be taken eighteen times in the height of the inscription. The text is bounded on its upper edge by a joint of horizontal stones. The bottom of the sky defining the tableau is 19.1 units from the baseline.

$$\text{Width of one column:} \frac{2.34 \text{ meters}}{15} = 15.6 \text{ centimeters}$$

$$\text{height of text: } 15.6 \text{ centimeters} \times 18 = 280.8 \text{ centimeters}$$

$$\text{height of sky: } 15.6 \text{ centimeters} \times 19.1 = 298.0 \text{ centimeters.}$$

Here, the function evoked is: $\frac{298 \text{ centimeters}}{234 \text{ centimeters}} = 1.2735...$, comparable to the coefficient of $4/\pi = 1.2732...$.

---

[19] Ibid., pp. 132–33. In the first place, the ritual of the cord includes the *mystical definition of the enclosure* on which the temple will be built, thus that which will keep this place at the center of the Two Lands. This process recalls the magic circle drawn to make an area taboo.

After having asked for the keeping of silence before Buto, then for listening and holding still, it is prescribed that King Nebmaātre pronounce the eulogy to the dwelling without equal four times for his father Amun. Then the word is given to the *neters* themselves: " 'Read thy formula!' say the gods of the marshes and of the papyrus thickets. 'That thy string bends the two stakes!' says Seshat, mistress of incantations, who has carried the two lords."[20]

As previously said, there is an allusion here to the "scene of the cord," in the course of which, by the sighting of the stars of the Great Bear, the orientation of the temple is determined. This gives true north as the reference. Now, the fact that the temple of Luxor represents Man justifies the inscription in the part corresponding to the *haty*—that is, the lungs and the heart—of this very rare Hermetic text that is replicated in the Eighteenth Dynasty temple at Medinet Habu. According to the Theban tradition, it is related to the primordial gods buried in this place.

Moreover, the concise phrase "read thy formula" is to be understood as the formulas recited by Thoth or Sia at the time of the construction of a temple.[21] Thoth, *neter* of the Moon, Thoth, who is found "in his nome" on the royal cubits, the master of all measures, Thoth, the lunar principle (Mercurial), cannot be absent from this work. He brings measure, that is to say, the "materiality" that determines or makes the abstract gifts of the evoked *neters* tangible.

—⁓⁓—

At the height of the Man of the Temple's breasts, the columns in the hypostyle room in the covered temple of Luxor have socles for bases that, through a very particular characteristic in the cut of the stone, allow the understone to form a crescent-shaped border (plate 44). The bases of these columns, like the rest of the superstructure, rest directly on the pavestones of the platform, while the crescents are embedded in it. The lower disks were not very thick and neither was the ledge very large. The bases at Luxor, which unfortunately have been cemented over in the modern era, no longer allow the ledges to show. We can see only the crescent-shaped cavities roughly outlined in the pavement; they are about 7 centimeters high.[22]

The detail of a base of a similar column found intact at the temple of Mentu at North Karnak allows us to affirm that these crescents were intentional and therefore have a symbolic purpose. The cylindrical socle shows an offset flat disk at its lower base, *cut out of a single block of stone* along with the socle proper (plate 44A, the socle of the columns at Mentu seen from different angles).

The sizes of the crescents of the four rows of columns increase going from south to north. Related to this intentional use of the lunar qualities of the nourishing breast—that is, lymphatic, white, Thotian—we notice the folds marked under the breasts on the statue of the queen that touches the calf of the south colossus in the funeral temple of Amenhotep III (colossus of Memnon, Thebes, plate 45). The bases of the columns in the hypostyle room at Luxor represent the occultation of one disk by another.

---

[20] Cf. Barguet, "Le Rituel archaïque de fondation," p. 8 and note 3: "We understand that the cord bends the two stakes in the manner of a bow; the classical formula is 'to stretch the cord between the two stakes' " (Chassinat, *Edfou*, 2:31). The word translated here by "the two stakes" is written in the texts of both Luxor and Medinet Habu with the sign of a necklace, which can also signify gold. The two lords are Seth and Horus.

[21] Ibid., note 1, suggests the kinship between the word here translated by "formula" and the word that begins all the cases of the Surgical Papyrus: "Instructions concerning. . . ." A word formed from the same root "is used in speaking of the formulas recited by Thoth, or Sia, at the time of the construction of the temple."

[22] This had led to the belief that these columns had moved.

There is evidently a relationship between the nourishing breast and milk and the celestial, nourishing cow. Now, "to nourish" means to cause growth and corporification.

The *haty* is the place of respiration and of the heartbeat, the diastolic and systolic movements that symbolize volume. This movement of the chest of the *haty*, which nourishes with air and blood and is associated with maternal nourishment and with the Thotian symbol of celestial nourishment, perfectly accounts for the choice of this place for the text of "Giving the House to Its Master." Furthermore, the room in which this text is inscribed has a geometrical relationship to the function of the growth of volumes,[23] becoming thus a true masterpiece of symbolism.

The text of the consecration of the temple of which we have just spoken is carved on the second register of the east partition of this room. The orientation of this wall with respect to north is about 32°12′, an orientation very particular to this partition, which is not parallel to any of the three axes inscribed in the floor. If we consider the hypostyle room as a rectangle whose sides are parallel and perpendicular to this wall in their orientation, the width of the resulting rectangle is the distance between the north face of the platform and the threshold of room VIII; the length is the distance between the two interior ledges of the east and west walls.

This rectangle is characterized by the fact that one of its diagonals is oriented exactly east-west. Thus, in dropping a north-south perpendicular from one of its corners, we obtain a cross with four unequal arms that are in a proportional relationship and that grow from 1 to 4, the values of its extremes. Interposed between 1 and 4 are two geometric means that by definition are its 1/3 and 2/3 powers (fig. 238).

The centers of the two circumferences, necessary to prove this growth of volume, are found on the axis of the room, perpendicular to the text of the consecration of the temple. Starting from this text, the extension of this axis crosses the Nile and passes through the temple of Medinet Habu located on the west bank, where the only example of an identical text is found. Now, the text of Luxor is retrograde and in some way plays the role of a reflection, as if each column of the text were turned around.[24]

The synthesis of the numbers, measurements, and texts gathered in this place, the *haty*, evoke the phrase of the Surgical Papyrus: "To measure [to examine, *kha*] . . . as one counts [*ip*] with a barrel [*ipt*] . . . as one measures [*kha*] a sick man in order to know the pace of his *haty*."

Since the text of the consecration of the temple is carved on the east partition of the hypostyle room of Luxor, and leads us to Medinet Habu by the perpendicular of its orientation, it is interesting to note that at Medinet Habu, in the sanctuary of the temple of Tuthmosis III in which the same text is carved, there is a curious irregularity through the arrangement of the tiles of its roof. Instead of being placed all in the same direction and held up by architraves as everywhere else, these tiles are *perpendicular to each partition*. Through this turning movement we are reminded of the oscillating squares.[25]

---

[23] Cf. chapter 9. Notice that the number of columns in the hypostyle rooms increases according to the geometric progression of 2. There are four columns in the offering room, eight in the second hypostyle room, two groups of sixteen, or thirty-two, in the *haty*, and finally 64 columns in the peristyle court (the number of the subdivision of the *hekat*).

[24] There are two examples on this wall of "right hands holding the *sekhem* scepter," which are shown in plate 93, 6 and 7.

[25] Cf. chapter 9.

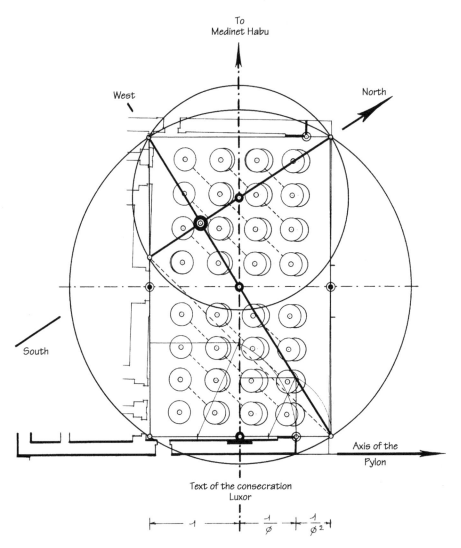

Fig. 238. Plan of the hypostyle room of the temple of Luxor.

The extension of the east wall toward the south ends at the level of the wall marking the clavicles; its extension toward the north ends at the axis of the pylon.

The rectangle defined by the parallel and perpendicular lines to this wall is as 1 to 1.5874, or the cube root of 4. The diagonal of this rectangle is oriented east-west. The north-south perpendicular defines the cross whose branches are to each other as $1 : \sqrt[3]{4} : \sqrt[3]{16} : 4$. The columns are parallel to the hypotenuse of the 1 to 4 triangle *(dashes)*.

This arrangement determines toward each corner, by changing the direction of the tiles, four points that are common to three tiles, and without support. Four columns dating from the period of Achoris were made of older column drums, many of which are in the name of Tuthmosis III. These possibly replace columns of an earlier period and prop up the ceiling under these four points (fig. 239a).

Finally, notice that the orientation of the axis of the *haty* following the west bank of the Nile is also the one that leads to the temple of Amenhotep, son of Hapu—the wise master builder of Amenhotep III—because the axis of this temple is parallel to it, that is, it has the same angular relationship to north.

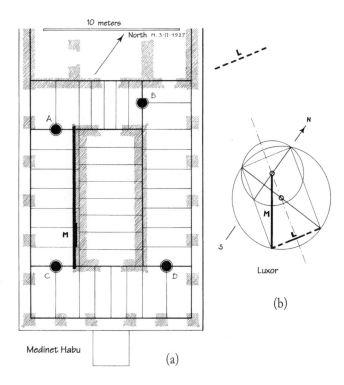

Fig. 239. (a) Diagram of the roofing of the temple of Tuthmosis III at Medinet Habu; (b) diagram of the directional rectangle of the hypostyle room of Luxor.

The semidiagonal of this rectangle serves as the radius of the circumscribing circle. Half of the (N-S) perpendicular to this diagonal is the radius of the small circle.

L is the position of the consecration text at Luxor; M is the orientation of this same text at Medinet Habu.

The right triangle formed by the hypotenuse M and the half-base L is 2.5448... on its perpendicular, when the base is 1.

It is curious how close this number is to the two functions of ϕ and π. If we call this new relationship a:

$$\sqrt{\phi} = 1.272... \text{ and } 2\sqrt{\phi} = 2.544...$$

$$\frac{1}{2}a = 1.2724... \text{ and } a = 2.5448...$$

$$\frac{4}{\pi} = 1.2732... \text{ and } \frac{8}{\pi} = 2.5464...$$

The geometry that we have just presented for the room of the *haty* at Luxor provides the key that allows us to draw the value of the volumes directly on a surface.

By being extended several kilometers, the axis of the room of the *haty* gives the axis of the temples on the other bank of the river, demonstrating that it is not a question of a geometry pertaining to one monument or to one detail of a partition, but a geometry that radiates throughout the whole country, linking together the essential points of the sanctuaries.[26]

---

[26] We will discuss this again in a future work on "mystical geography." [Never completed.]

Chapter 34

THE KNEES

---⚮---

Plate 46

. . . all initiatory temples are founded on the principle of Anthropocosmos, that is, "man as Universe," the anthropomorphization of divine thought, whether in its totality or in one of the cosmic functions innate in man, the ultimate product of Nature.

(Chapter 3)

PLATE 46A

East Seated Colossus, Court of Ramesses

From the moment that a measure lays claim to having a cosmic character, it must be based on a general function in order to be established, and on experimental, and therefore verifiable, data in order to be defined. We present here the exoteric elements of the question.

(Chapter 10)

PLATE 46B

Statue of Amun and Mut

PLATE 46C

Facade of the Pedestal of the East Seated Colossus, Court of Ramesses

Chapter 34

THE KNEES

The pharaonic *symbolique* shows a particular interest in the knees, and this is confirmed by the Temple of Man at Luxor. The doctrine of the Anthropocosmos, seeing in man a complex, final being of the terrestrial genesis, prompts us to study the character, life, and gestures of each part of the body: if the elbow, for example, is stopped in its backward flexion by the shape of the heads of the bones of the forearm and the humerus,[1] the knee is stopped in its forward flexion by a free patella bathed in synovial fluid. Rationally, following our reasoned way of thinking, the same system would be able mechanically—in a robot, for instance—to serve the same purpose for both the elbows and the knees. Creative Nature therefore has vital reasons for acting differently in the two cases.

In the tomb of Ukhotep at Meir, consecrated to the binding of the spirit expressed in numbers, the bent arms and knees serve to bring a mental trigonometry back to a vital trigonometry. This intention is indicated by the figure of a man, nearly skeletal, resembling a plant with leaves growing from his bones (fig. 250). This is a beautiful example of hieroglyphic symbolism. Elbows and knees are represented as moments in which genesis, by dualizing, has created a new orientation whose relationship is precisely what we conceive of mentally as an angle. In the forearm, the humerus divides into radius and ulna; the femur divides into the tibia and fibula, both requiring an articulation that becomes what in music and arithmetic we can call the mean term between One and Two.

In all of nature the function of vegetal growth is an effect of dividing in two, provoking a narrowing in the original cell that will create the separation. The relationship between the first cell and the two new cells thus generated is that which we perceive as harmony and as the "geometric and harmonic mean terms," that is, between the first unity and the multiple that results from it. This is the universal function that the human body reveals to us through the elbows and the knees, the

---

[1] The humeroulnar joint is characterized by the olecranon of the ulna, which blocks the inferior part of the humerus like a pair of pliers.

742

cause and the nature, and this through the vital relation between the parts of the body and the essential vital centers. We need to pay attention to what the Ancients urge us to observe in their figurative language.

A kneeling statue holding two *nw* vases in its hands, which are placed on its strengthened knees,[2] is to be considered as an example of esoteric writing. We need to contemplate the relation between the *nw* vase—symbolizing the primordial water, substance without form, the waters of the origin without specification—and the force of the knees. In biblical Genesis, as in the Heliopolitan Mystery, is this not the environment where the *black* earth separates from the spirit that floats on the waters? In this symbol, it is the containing vase that symbolizes the earth, therefore the knee is placed here.

———

At the temple of Luxor, the pylon terminating the monument under Amenhotep III marks the age of the royal child who is seven or eight years old,[3] and therefore corresponds to the place of the soles of the feet of this child. At the end of the construction by Ramesses, this same pylon will be the place where the knees of the adult king are found. Thus it appears that there is a connection between the soles of the feet and the knees.[4]

On the north side of this pylon of Amenhotep III, the *black* colossi—fixed because they are seated—mark the knees (plate 46A). On the south side, corresponding to the location of the patella, is found the seated group of lunar Amun and Mut in white limestone (plate 46B).[5] The articulation is then located in the door in the middle of the pylon, thus splitting it in two.[6]

The group in white (Amunian) limestone relates the part played by the "waters above" of Genesis to the other aspect of the *nw* waters found in the Amunian waters (the cerebrospinal fluid) of the head. The *nw* waters are the milieu of the primordial scission. It is necessary then to read in them the principle of the scission at the same time as its effect. This effect relates the cerebrospinal fluid to the soles of the feet and to the articulating part of the knee, the fixed corporeal power.[7]

The "waters" are evoked on the lateral surfaces of the throne of the colossus by the two Niles that form the joining of the waters from above and below (the two crowns) through the breath that is symbolized by the ligatures on the trachea that terminate with the *haty* (heart and lungs). As always, these two Niles are androgynous, with two natures—male and female, fixed and volatile.

The black granite colossus is composed of three blocks out of which are cut, respectively, the pedestal, the seated colossus on his throne, and the double crown that now lies on the ground. These three blocks define two horizontal joints, one of which passes under the feet of the king and the other at his vertex. No other joint could have traversed the carved figures on the throne yet there is one cut in the stone marking the two Niles at the level of the knees. There, a prism-shaped stone was inserted in the throne to insist on the importance of the knees at their location in the temple (fig. 240). Thus there is the desire to relate this point to the feet and vertex.

[2] Cf. Robichon, Barguet, and Leclant, *Karnak-Nord IV,* fasc. 1, pp. 32, 34.

[3] Cf. fig. 214.

[4] We direct our attention to the word designating the knee, which at the same time can designate the bow, or more particularly in cabala, the tension of the bowstring. Now, the bows are engraved under the feet.

[5] Presently, in front of this group, there are two other limestone statues, one of which is double.

[6] Cf. plate 15.

[7] Cf. below, appendix.

*Fig. 240. West facade of the throne of the east seated colossus located
in front of the east post of the north door of the nave*

The separation of the colossus and its pedestal under the soles of the feet plays the role of a joint. The prism-shaped piece inserted in the monolith constitutes a joint of stones cutting the knees of the two Niles.

It is obviously surprising to see the black colossi of the knees accented and related to the waters of the Nile, and the kneeling statue related to the waters of the spherical *nw* vase. It is no less surprising to see this articulation thus surrounded with synovial fluid.[8] There is a vital connection between the knees, the soles of the feet, and the meninges. Let us recall in this regard that in cases of head injury that have caused a hematoma or edema with pressure on the meninges, there are, among other observable symptoms, the nervous reactions of the soles of the feet (Babinski's reflex), the Achilles tendons, and the knees (Kernig's sign), and the reaction to the shock.

The Black Cubit of the Colossus (Plate 46C)

On the front of the pedestal of the colossus, two figures wearing the dauphin's braid and clothed in the panther's skin relating to the inheritor are face to face, framing a representation of the *sma* sign. This sign, uniting the plants of the North and the South, is surmounted by a horizontal band in sunk relief that measures 54 centimeters. This length corresponds to a cubit of 28 digits, a little larger than those used for the royal cubits discovered in the temples and tombs. We are dealing here with the "black cubit," the ancient measure probably handed down through the Copts to the Arabs, who used it as the unit of measure for the demarcations of the nilometer at Rodah. Its origin, until now considered to be fabled, is undeniably pharaonic. This cubit is only found on black stones or those that correspond to their symbol, such as the black silt brought by the inundation that is the reason for the name of Egypt—Kemit, "the black"—from which comes the designation of the science of "al-Kemit."

---

[8] "All the articulations of the body allow for a fluid sac. The characteristic of the knee is to have a patella surrounded by synovial bursae, of which several could develop abnormally through frequent kneeling." Cf. Testut and Jacob, *Traité d'anatomie,* 2:976–83.

Fig. 241. Cube statue from the Twenty-sixth Dynasty (Louvre)

The cubical statue gives the five essential measures of the canon: the height of the head
and the leg, and the length of the arm, cubit, and foot.

This black cubit is carved on the pedestal of the colossus so that it is located at the height of the
knees of the figures that frame it, again emphasizing this point and attracting attention to its location
at precisely this spot.

Let us recall that the natural human cubit is 24 digits, that is, one-fourth of the arm span or
fathom of 96 digits. The cubit of 54 centimeters bears proof of the existence of a hieratic measure
of 28/96 fathom.[9] The temple is measured in fathoms.

Moreover, the cubit that measures 28 digits of a fathom is the length of the circumference of
a man's diadem. This black cubit shown at the knee gives us, therefore, two principles of measure:
the hieratic measure relative to the fathom that is applied to the temple and to the royal cosmic
principle, and the principle of the specific measure of man.

APPENDIX

With regard to the femur and what I said about it[10] concerning the fixed part of the physical
human being that serves as the element of personal reincarnation, I will cite here what Professor
G. Lefebvre has said, in order to emphasize the differences of interpretation among Egyptologists
of a single word when the esoteric meaning is unknown, which is, however, very understandable.

A word that deeply puzzles the curiosity of Egyptologists, and rightfully so, is *iwā*. It is used in
speaking of people, and especially of animals. Concerning the latter, it is not inconceivable that the
word might, as Loret supposed, refer to the flesh surrounding the femur, prepared by a butcher for

[9] A mean fathom at 45° measures 1.852 m. One digit of a fathom is equal to 1.852 m divided by 96, which equals 1.9293 cm. The
length of the black cubit corresponds to 28 of these digits determined in this way, which equals 54.0204 cm.

[10] "In man the absolute fixed salt of his being is formed in the femur, the foundation and support of the physical body (the Egyptian
men.t)." Cf. vol. 1, p. 35.

placement in a tomb at the disposal of the dead. This definition obviously cannot be applied as such to the human *iwā*. Is it then a word that designates the femur, the human thigh? In truth, we have too few examples of its use to be able to decide. One rare, valuable text is drawn from the funerary papyrus of Nebseni (BD 172). After citing and describing the shoulders, the arms, the heart of the dead, and before referring to his stomach and his navel, this papyrus (1, 24) mentions the word *iwā*, which Naville, the first publisher of the papyrus, translates and comments upon as follows: "The lower portion of the body or trunk, to which, as in French, the word *entrailles* is applied; *iwā* also refers to posterity and descendents." Moret, improving on this idea, suggests for *iwā* the translation "generative organ." Lacau did the same in a recent publication, thinking that "*iwā*, femur, must have designated the sexual organs as a euphemism, from which comes the name of inheritor."

Nothing, however, proves that *iwā*, "inheritor," is derived from the anatomical *iwā*. The two words may be homophonic and nothing more, the sign [of flesh encircling the femur] being in the case of the femur an ideogram preceded by the reading elements; in the other case it is an improper determinative. In addition, I repeat that it does not seem the Egyptians ever used euphemisms of this sort, as did the Hebrews. They always used the word itself, the technical word, without concern for modesty. We all agree that the word "thigh" as such is used in expressions in paragraphs 54, 60, and 61 with no euphemistic intent. It describes bluntly rather than veils how a child is taken from the maternal breast.

It would not be difficult for me to agree with the opinion of Möller concerning the meaning of *iwā*. In his edition of the Rhind Papyrus, 1.10.4 (p. 45), he translates *iwā* as *Muskeln* and the word *awa* of the parallel demotic text as *Glieder.** We could therefore definitely place it in the category of general terms, along with *haw, iwf, mt,* in which case its ideogram would allude not to the bone but to the flesh and muscle surrounding the bone.[11]

Fig. 242. Group hieroglyph iwā *designating the inheritor, determined by the femur*

In conclusion, the analysis of Lacau, whose idea is to see not only the designation of the femur in this word but also the sexual organs of generation, would seem justified, in that it is actually supported by the use of this word in texts, giving it the character of *inheritor.*

Because of the teaching given in the traditional knowledge of the fixation of the indestructible nucleus in the bone of the femur, it is obvious that the idea expressed by the "bone of the femur" necessarily includes that of inheritor and regeneration. This is to be understood in the sense of a "personal reincarnation," carrying over the acquisition of a particular existence. We are not dealing here with children conceived during the lifetime of the deceased through his seed.

[11] Lefebvre, *Parties du corps humain*, pp. 56–57.

Muskeln, "muscles"; *Glieder,* "limbs," "joints."

Chapter 35

THE BOWS

—⁓—

Plates 47–49

. . . the importance of considering the vital cause of enumeration in the Universe . . . consists in revealing the knowledge of the powers that create the genesis. Numbers are then no longer merely notations that designate quantities, but the expression of living functions.

(Chapter 5)

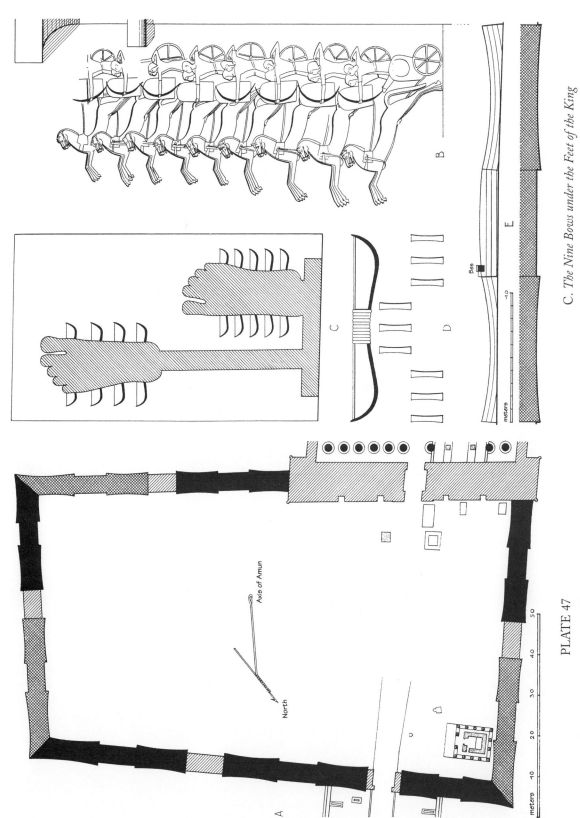

PLATE 47

A. *Plan of the Courtyard of Nectanebo at Luxor*

B. *The Nine Archers of the East Wing of the Pylon at Luxor*

C. *The Nine Bows under the Feet of the King*

D. *The Nine Bows*

E. *The Arch of Nectanebo at Philae, Land of the Arch*

*It is not without reason that the Ancients placed
the harmonic relation at the origin of their mathematics. But rather than seeing a . . . proportion as
a foundation for calculating, we must see instead
the . . . expression of a vital function.*

(Chapter 5)

PLATE 48A

The Arch of Nectanebo at Philae, Land of the Arch

PLATE 48B

The Arches of Nectanebo at Luxor

PLATE 48C

Bes Playing the Harp (Arch at Philae)

. . . the Egyptian technique and their symbolique
attest to a realistic sensibility and to faculties of
reasoning, contradicting the view held of an age
that is "primitive and mystical."

(Chapter 2)

PLATE 49

End of One of the Arches at Luxor

Chapter 35

THE BOWS

The presentation of a fact always includes at least two principal aspects: the positive fact as it strikes our mental observation, and its symbolic significance. The latter has two aspects: one is knowledge, that is, that which relates to magical science or genesis; the other is what teaches the universal spiritual meaning of the expansion of consciousness. Expansion of consciousness always signifies a movement toward identifying specified being with cosmic Being.

Above all, the facts revealed by the figurations, by the architecture and numbers, and then by their *symbolique* of knowledge are what we have to look at here. We can, however, with regard to the bows and the test of the "drawing of the bow," evoke their psychospiritual objective in Egypt through what is said about them in China.

If a function is designated by a particular word, as in European languages, the connection between the instances in which this function occurs—that is, its universal character—is no longer directly expressible in words. But if the function is designated by an image that encapsulates it, we can introduce this glyph into all the descriptions in which the specificity of this function occurs, thus creating a vital link for the reader between apparently diverse facts. Thus we observe the scenes of the "drawing of the bow" by the king; nine bows are traced on the soles of the royal ceremonial sandals, on the pedestal bearing the statue (plate 47C), and on the footstools. We find these nine bows again on the pylon in the form of archers carried in horse-drawn chariots.[1] Moreover, we have seen these harnessed chariots, without archers, designating the thoracic vertebrae,[2] which indicates a relationship between the vertebrae, the marrow, and the soles of the feet. Now, in addition to this relationship, the Man of the Temple evokes a principle of knowledge by means of the nine bows and the submission of the vanquished: the bearded, yellow-skinned people of the east, the red-skinned people of the west crowned in feathers, and the black-skinned people of the south, prostrate.

[1] Cf. plates 10, 47B, and fig. 244.

[2] Cf. plate 6 and chapter 27.

756

The king, in the traditional Kabbalah, has always implied a particle of eternity hidden in the black earth[3] at the heart of the seed. This is the invincible power in the seed that projects germ and root and draws the animating spirit of all things toward the earth. But it is the Spirit that must conquer the power, still Sethian, that creates what is "below"; and this will be the victory of the king, of the king of nature, of the king in us, the turning of Seth into Horus, the two brothers or two aspects of a single unity, enemies fighting each other, antithetical symbols of noble combat. In Kemit, copper is the symbol of that which is impure and heavy and which falls to the bottom, but which is colored like the sun, red like gold, the imitation of perfection. The arrows of the victorious king must penetrate a "brick" of copper, cut through it in order to make the heavy earth light, to create out of the impure and leprous the purity that cures the leper (fig. 243).

These are not meaningless words. They designate a positive fact; they are also symbolic and have a mystical meaning. The trial of the drawing of the bow is found in Japan, in the doctrine of Zen, as well as in China.

> During the long winter nights, a royal festival is indeed celebrated. On this occasion the chief undergoes a great test. He demonstrates that he has been chosen by Heaven to be in command.
>
> To become the Son of Heaven, Yao, this sovereign who "appeared as the sun" must fire arrows at the sun. He thus succeeds in overcoming his celestial counterpart. As soon as he conquered the emblem of the sun, he was worthy to reign (*Hui-neng tzu*, 13). The drawing of the bow is an inaugural ceremony in which one's virtue can shine forth. But the test will turn against an unworthy chief. By a reflex action that punishes the incapable magician, the arrows drawn toward the sky fall back to earth in the form of lightning. The drawer of the bow will be mortally struck down because, without possessing the required qualifications, he has attempted to awaken and capture the energies of the Fire. . . .
>
> Huang-ti was Thunderbolt. Under the name of Ti-hong, he was also identified with a celestial waterskin. The waterskin Ti-hong is a bird and at the same time a leather sack and drum. There is also an owl (his name is drum of night) who is a sack and upon whom thunderbolt and arrows rebound. There is, finally, a drum that is an owl, producing the wind from his breath; all red with fixed eyes, he represents a forge and its bellows. He is also red as a molten mineral and as high as the Mountain of the Sky, rich in copper; the Celestial Waterskin has a name: Chaos (Huen-tuen). The chaos dies when the lightning pierces it seven times. But this death is a second birth. It is an initiation. . . .[4]
>
> The great test of nobility . . . is the game of the drawing of the bow. . . . It is a musical ceremony, regal as a ballet. . . . All the movements must be made in cadence, and the arrow not sent precisely on the right note can never touch the goal (or at least does not count) (*Li-chi* 100.2.699). The archers, while advancing and withdrawing, while turning and re-turning, must *touch the heart* of the ritual rules. A correct attitude of soul within, a right attitude of body without, this is what is necessary to hold the bows and arrows firmly, carefully. Bows and arrows held firmly and carefully, this is what allows us to say that we have touched the center of the target. And it is thus that virtue is made known. . . .[5]

---

[3] Kemit, one of the names of pharaonic Egypt signifying the "black" land of Havilah (Mosaic Genesis).

[4] Marcel Granet, *La Civilisation chinoise* (Paris: Renaissance du Livre, 1929), pp. 234–35.

[5] Ibid., pp. 339-40.

At the archery contests, one is able to demonstrate his skillfulness or his honesty . . . and the quality of his will in letting fly his arrows in a skilled rhythm . . . and straight to the goal. When one lets them fly with force, one proves one's vitality and one's valor, the power of one's genius. Thus does one construct bows, by considering the will and the vitality of the one they are destined for. To evaluate the dignity that this person merits, it is sufficient, through examination, to estimate the *power* of his bow. The strongest bows bend the least. In order to make a perfect circle, it is necessary then to use nine bows, but only if they are the king's bows, but one can make a perfect circle with seven lord's bows, with five grand officer's bows, or with three official's bows (*Chu-li*, 7.2, p. 596).[6]

The chief is a rising sun and victorious. He is also an archer. Each chariot is occupied by a trio of warriors. The place of the driver is in the center, that of the lancer is to the right . . . the archer is then to the left. The left is the place of the chief. *The left is the honorable side and the east is also.*

Holding his bow *in his left hand, his left arm uncovered,* the archer, wherever he goes, carries himself *at the left hand,* the side of the rising and victorious sun (*I-li*, 100, pp. 123, 125, 144).[7]

In the mystical sense, the archer who still dualizes by sighting the target and has not himself become the arrow, does not attain unity, is not yet conscious, but remains only mortally and mentally aware.

The scenes depicting the king drawing the bow are numerous in Egypt. Some describe the king "appearing on his harnessed chariot as Mentu in his power," and most of them specify that the king accomplishes his performances in "the presence of his army . . . in front of the entire earth."

On a block of red granite in the temple of Karnak, Tuthmosis III is shown standing on a chariot (of which only a single wheel can be seen); the reins of the two galloping horses harnessed to the chariot pass behind the small of his back. The king holds the bow with his left hand, his wrist protected by a special brassard that archers wear.[8] He stretches his bow with his right hand and prepares to shoot a new arrow. The wooden target, vertically placed in front of him, is already pierced with seventeen arrows. Three others, after going all the way through it, have fallen behind it.

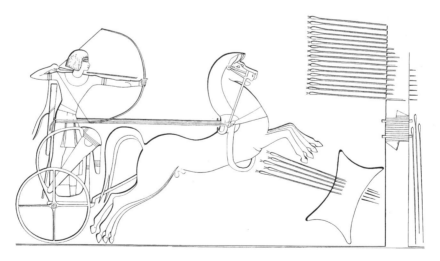

Fig. 243. The king drawing his bow

[6] Granet, *La Pensée chinoise*, pp. 296–97. Let us note that the total number of bows for "perfecting the circumference" is twenty-four, that is, 9, 7, 5, 3, the first odd numbers except 1, which is the center.

[7] Ibid., pp. 367–68.

[8] These brassards, several examples of which have been found in royal tombs of the Eighteenth Dynasty, are of leather. Cf. Jéquier, *Frises d'objets*, p. 217.

According to texts that accompany similar scenes, the upright wooden pole represents the first test in the drawing of the bow. This test, which consists of "splitting all the wooden targets as if they were of papyrus . . ." is then followed by His Majesty attempting the test of piercing with his arrow the copper target placed on the ground.

The text from Karnak makes it clear: "a large target of raw copper[9] on which His Majesty has drawn. Even though three digits thick, the very strong could penetrate it with numerous arrows. They went through to the other side to a distance of three palms from the target." This is the "king's blow."

—⁓—

The king is said to be "master of the Two Lands," and in affirming his power over "foreign countries" the ritual texts put the "nine bows under his sandals." The royal, seated statues are indeed often represented with the soles of the feet resting on nine bows. In the particular case of the colossus in a walking position, the king places his left, front foot on four bows, while the right foot is supported by five bows inscribed on the pedestal (plate 47C).

The courtyard of Nectanebo (plate 47A) is the pedestal of the royal colossus, giving the elements of the volume of the pedestal by its plan (plate 24 and figs. 210, 211). Now, the encircling wall of this court that forms the parvis of the temple of Luxor is entirely constructed in raw bricks in such a way that both in plan and in appearance the design of concave curves alternating with straight or slightly convex sections is clearly visible (plates 47A and 48B). The concave arches are formed of beds of unbaked bricks placed in curves; at the end of each curve the bricks have been recut to give the vertical. If we observe that one arch contains two curves connected by a straight section, and if we thus analyze the enclosing wall of the court, it becomes obvious that the parvis is enclosed by nine arches [bows].

In order to mark the intention of making the arched shape, the northwest corner was constructed with blocks of sandstone cut in curves on three sides, forming a sort of prow that gives movement and form to the arches. For this purpose there was no hesitation in combining blocks of stone with unbaked bricks (plate 49).

At Philae, called the "land of the arch," the substructure and beginning of an enclosing brick wall of Nectanebo's is an arch in dressed stone. The beds, similar to those at Luxor, are curved and served as a foundation for the brick wall that has now disappeared, having been washed away by the waters of the Aswan dam (plates 47E and 48A). At the junction of one of the two concave curves with the convex curve that connects them, a Bes playing the harp is sculpted in bas-relief. We have spoken of this in regard to the "harp of numbers" (plate 48C).[10]

The theme of the nine bows located under the king's feet is indicated at Luxor by a group of archers carved on the north face of the east wing of the pylon, near the entrance door, and consequently at the level of the soles of the feet of the Man of the Temple (plate 10).

At this point there are nine pairs of horses harnessed to eight chariots, each, except for the first chariot represented with only half a wheel. For the missing chariot, the eighth one from the bottom, the half-wheel is symbolized by the torus of the door. These eight chariots for nine harnessed horses carry eight archers drawing their bows (plate 47B). The ninth bow, evoked by the

[9] Raw copper, that is, as it comes from the mine without planishing or alloying.
[10] Cf. chapter 11, "The *Canevas* Guide," and fig. 93 (vol. 1).

ninth horse-drawn chariot, is symbolically replaced by the curve of the cornice, which is not only an allusion to the principle of the eight-ninths of a string that gives the fundamental tone in music, but also a figuration of this principle (fig. 244).

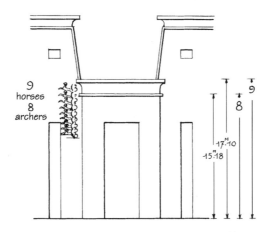

Fig. 244. Door of the pylon of Ramesses II

This ratio of 8 to 9 is confirmed by the door itself. The height from the ground to the torus is eight-ninths of the total height. The Bes playing the harp carved on the arch at Philae calls attention to the relationship between music (harmony) and the arches.

At Luxor, the totality of the architecture (the Man of the Temple) and the bas-reliefs develops a synthesis in which harmony links the vital functions together.[11]

The bow is the symbol of the "power" that in every case manifests as *tension*. It is this tension in sap that causes germination in the springtime, and in general the thrust toward life. This growth, this renewal, is always made harmoniously under the impulse of the first scission that governs proportion, ϕ.

---

[11] The association of the drawing of the bow with the harnessed chariots, which symbolize the vertebrae, is an image by analogy of form. The vertebra is a wheel, its hub is the marrow, and the "Poseidonian" horses—the symbol-key of Mediterranean initiation (see the Parthenon at Athens)—are related to the cerebrospinal fluid.

Chapter 36

THE ZODIAC

—✺—

Plates 50 and 51

. . . the Temple is knowledge, that is, the science of genesis and cosmic harmony.

(Chapter 20)

It is with the arrival of the precessional Age of Pisces—the tower of Babel that lacks the triangular foundation stone—that the Temple ceased to be alive.

(Chapter 20)

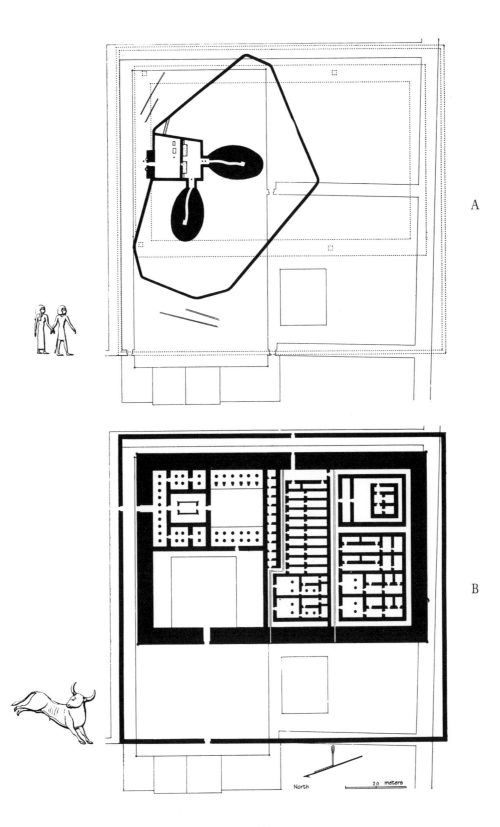

A

B

PLATE 50

The Successive Sanctuaries of Medamud

A. *The First Temple*   B. *The Temple of Sesostris III*

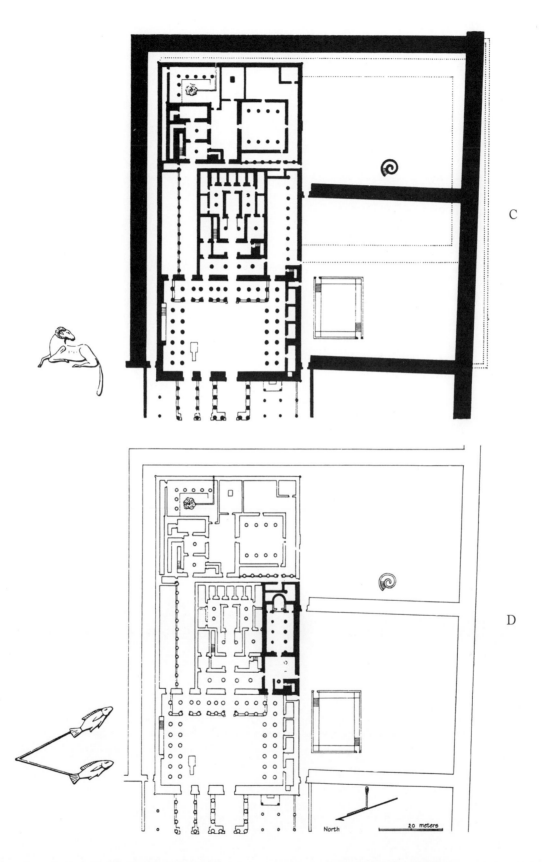

C

D

C. *The Ptolemaic Temple*   D. *The Christian Church*

North   20 meters

The signs of the zodiac form a part of the instruction of the Temple in that they are functional symbols. . . .

(Chapter 20)

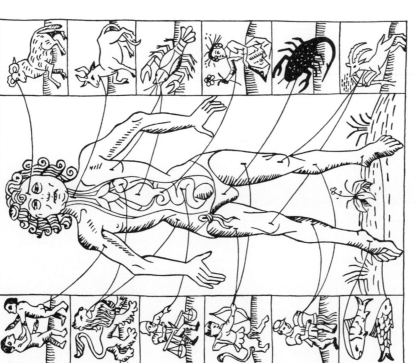

PLATE 51

The Zodiac

A. *Man and the Zodiac in the Middle Ages*

B. *The Temple of Luxor and the Zodiac*

A

B

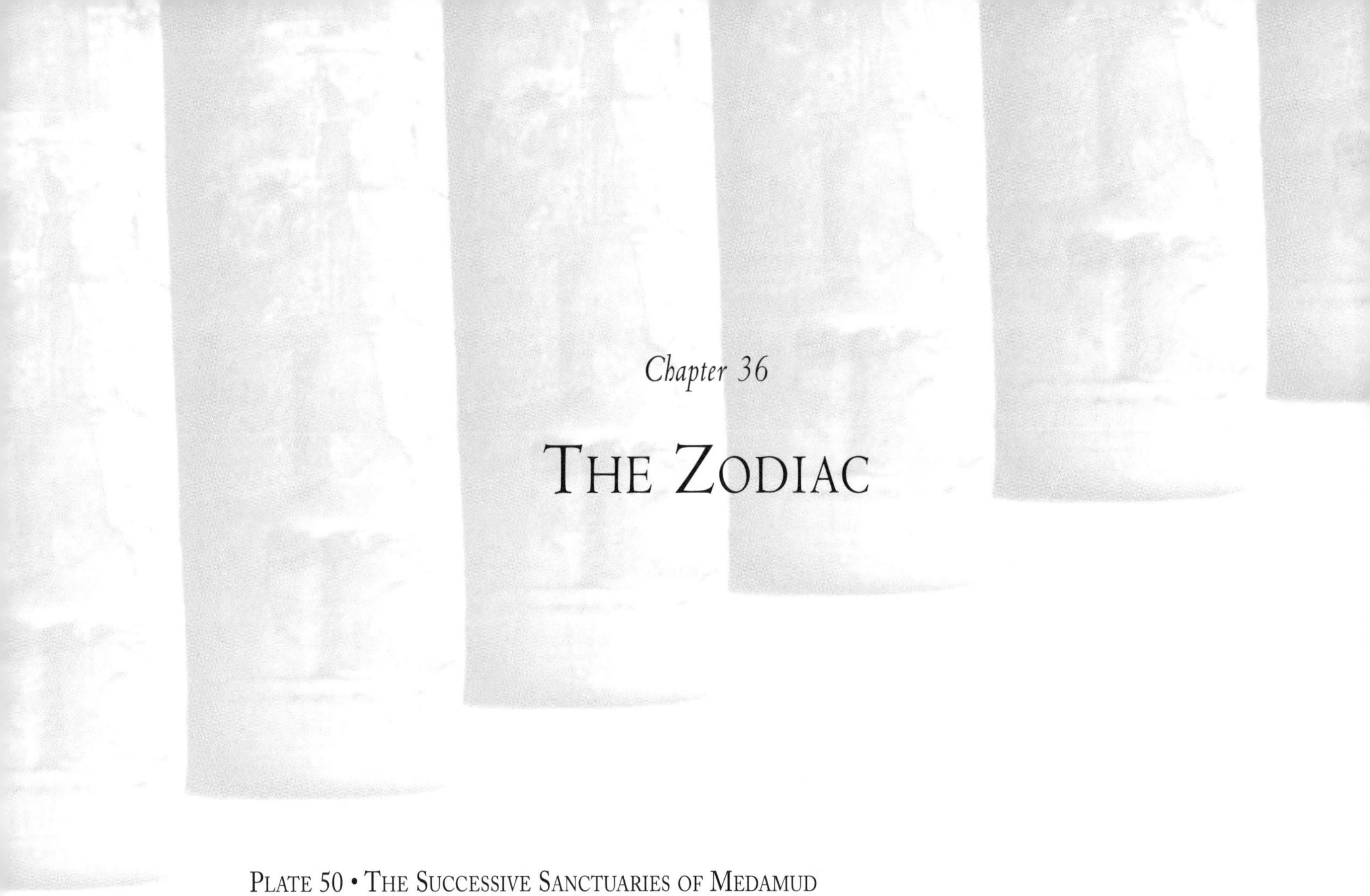

Chapter 36

THE ZODIAC

PLATE 50 • THE SUCCESSIVE SANCTUARIES OF MEDAMUD

Medamud is the only excavated site in Egypt in which monuments were built on top of one another from prehistoric times to the Christian era. There are four sanctuaries, and they bear witness to four successive cults: *(a)* the earliest temple, from the Predynastic Period; *(b)* the temple of the Middle Kingdom consecrated to Mentu and his sacred bull; *(c)* the temple of the Ptolemaic period consecrated to Amun, the ram; *(d)* the Christian church.

To grasp better the exceptional importance of this site, we must understand the spirit of the myth.

The Spirit of the Myth Related to Medamud

"A plurality of names does not make a plurality of things," is an old adage of Hermetic philosophy. This means that a single original thing evolves toward its predestined end, and its name changes progressively with the phases through which it passes.

We must distinguish two phases in the philosophy of causes. The transcendent cause produces the natural cause. The first *is* and *is not,* which is to say that relative to nature, it is nonexistent, while nevertheless still being the totality as universal cause. In pharaonic Egypt, this transcendental cause is Tum.

Natural cause consequently will then be this same Tum, "fallen to earth," that is, the first thing, Ptah.[1] This already necessarily contains in itself two natures, still joined as twins, which can consequently become either complements or opposites. As definitions of inert natural states they are complementary, but become opposites if there is a separative action through generation.[2] For example, homogenized milk, left to itself at a moderate temperature, will enter into an acidic fermentation that forms coagulated milk (curd) and watery milk (whey). From this moment on, these

---

[1] The Greek Hephaestus or Roman Vulcan.

[2] See the myth of Seth and Horus.

twin brothers, water and fat, will be irreconcilable. Grain placed in a humid and temperate environment will be separated, by fermenting, into germ and root, twin brothers that once separated are irreconcilable, although of the same nature and indispensable to one another. These are the principles, universal in their function, described by myth and constituting the cosmological history that is applied in all cases, which, in spite of their variety, are reunited in those anthropomorphized principles that are the *neters*. This, however, is but an overall view. Pharaonic myth goes into detail of such complexity that without the Ariadne's thread of the general thought, it is impossible to rediscover therein the universal principles that comprise the knowledge.

The principal phases are clearly marked by what are called the cults: of Tum at Heliopolis (Innu of the North); of Ptah, the Fire fallen to earth, that is, solidified and fixed, at Memphis; of Thoth at Hermopolis (the Hermetic transition); then at Thebes, the realization of the reuniting of what had been separated. These are definitely not opposed cults or political struggles of a theological character, as Egyptology has supposed, but an expression of the phases of genesis, therefore also of the genesis of the empire of the pharaohs.

Now, all that is natural, that is, that belongs to the created Universe, is maintained in existence by virtue of two poles, the two complements that make up the appearance, the phenomenon. This duality was always respected by the sages. It is thus that Tum of Heliopolis, the Innu of the North, finds his complement in Mentu at Armant, the Innu of the South. This complementation is not only an equilibration of principle, but is, above all, an analysis of the character of Tum. That which makes up the (solar) force of Tum, the self-created power, then becomes the fixed point of all that exists in the Universe, the indestructible being issued from the Unity, thanks to which a reunification of opposites can be accomplished. This is the final goal, without which the genesis would have no meaning. This moment of fixation, occurring below, is Mentu, the bull; it is of the nature of the *ka* and gives to Innu (Armant) the bull Buchis, which is white with a black head. This is the fixed point—this "salt of the earth" of the Gospels, this corporeal solidity that attracts, repulses, or retains the Spirit, this foundation, this heart of the metal, this salt in the femur in man and in the left front hoof of the four-footed animal, this black bull, origin of the white bull, Mentu, represented as a human figure with the head of a falcon, crowned by the sun and surmounted by two feathers, issued from the original twins contained in Tum—it is this fixed point that must be understood in order to glimpse the profound meaning that the four superimposed sanctuaries of Medamud reveal to us.

The successive building of three pharaonic temples confirms for us the conscious gesture of aligning the cults with the cosmic dates of the precession of the equinoxes. On the other hand, the sequence of the cults—Gemini, Taurus, and Aries (Shu-Tefnut, Mentu, Amun)—teaches us the true meaning of the zodiacal "representation," its "esoteric" reading (which will gladden some hearts) that, beginning with the solar Lion in the direction of precession, allows us to read the exact progression of the genesis of a cosmic work.

The twin tendencies will split into the terrestrial Mentu (the black bull) and the aquatic, spiritual fire, Amun. It is Mentu that retains the solar fire (Ra) through the fixed salt.

When one reads this strange history through the names and activities of the *neters*, it is difficult to see clearly the actual meaning contained there, that is, as long as one regards these *neters* only in a literary fashion, as allegorical symbols, and does not give them an objective reality.

The study of Alexandre Varille concerning the origin and meaning of the earliest temple at Medamud,[3] formed of two mounds, forced him to put forward hypotheses that he found unsatisfactory until the time I was able to demonstrate to him the coincidence of these cults with the

---

[3] C. Robichon and A. Varille, *Description sommaire du temple primitif de Médamoud*, Recherches d'archéologie, de philologie et d'histoire 11 (Cairo: I.F.A.O., 1940).

characteristics of the phases of the zodiac read in the "backward," precessional direction. The sense of dualism insisted on in the texts then became evident to him. This was the point of departure for a reconsideration of the pharaonic chronology, and a new justification for understanding the variations and geographical locations of the cults, a perspective that has nothing in common with theories of politico-theological disputes.

Mentu is affirmed through four eras,[4] which accounts for the four places consecrated to the bull of Mentu: Innu of the South (Armant), Djerty (Tod), Madu (Medamud), and Uast (Karnak). But at the Serapeum of Memphis (Saqqara) the sarcophagi of the twenty-four bulls of the day are found, Saqqara being the place where the Fire of heaven fell to earth, where Tum took form.

Historical Survey

Mentu is depicted in the form of a man with the head of a falcon whose headdress consists of the solar disk with two tall plumes coming out of it. This is Mentu-Ra. In the Late Period the falcon's head is sometimes replaced by a bull's head. In the temple of Luxor, after the purifications and the placing of the crowns, the king, flanked by Tum and Mentu, who take him by the hands, accomplishes the "royal ascent" toward the sanctuary of Amun.[5] Tum follows him; Mentu precedes him but with his head turned toward him.

The relation between these two *neters* is obvious from the names of the essential places of their cults. At Innu of the North (Heliopolis), Tum is venerated as the *neter* of the origin; at Innu of the South (Hermonthis), Mentu was the supreme divinity at the end of the Middle Kingdom. But while Tum always remains the intangible abstraction,[6] the Unique, the cult of Mentu undergoes, in the course of time, variations that only the astronomical periods can justify.

Tum, through his name, symbolizes at the same time All and Nothing, both the totality of possibilities and perfections, and the Nothingness, the negation. He is the Divine Verb "emitted," the self-polarizing energy, "he who existed before being himself created," the creator of all the *neters*. He is known by only one figural representation: in human form, wearing the two crowns, and, at Luxor, always without a navel.

Tum becomes Ptah at Memphis, where he is represented in the triad of Ptah-Sekhmet-Nefertum. Ptah is called Ptah-Tatanen, creator of the earth, to whom one day would be assimilated the sacred bull of Heliopolis of the South, the bull Buchis of Armant.

The cult of the sacred bull goes back to the most ancient dynasties. At Heliopolis the black bull Mnevis was venerated, whose whole body must have been covered with tufts. One of his names, "the herald of Ra [of the sun], he who causes the truth to ascend to Atum,"[7] intimately connects him to the cult of Atum-Ra, master of Heliopolis of the North. At Memphis, the bull Apis was venerated, the black bull that has certain characteristic markings: a white triangle on his forehead, a white spot in the form of a crescent on his flank, and an eagle on his neck. His title was "living Apis, herald of Ptah, he who causes the truth to ascend to the god with the beautiful face."[8]

In the South, the white bull of Min was venerated as well as the four bulls of Mentu. The characteristic signs of these are little known today except for the bull of Heliopolis of the South

---

[4] The first four months of embryonic gestation, the forty days of the biblical Exodus, Jesus' forty days in the desert, the forty traditional days of natural philosophy . . .

[5] Cf. plate 99.

[6] The depictions and legends of Tum were never effaced in the bas-reliefs at Luxor.

[7] From J. Vandier, *La Religion égyptienne* (Paris: Presses Universitaires, 1949), p. 236.

[8] Ibid., p. 235.

(Armant), which was white with a black head and was called Buchis. These four bulls were attached to the four temples built at Karnak, Medamud, Tod, and Armant, and dedicated to Mentu-Ra. Of these four sanctuaries, Medamud (Madu) is the only one that at the present time offers the complete history of the monument and brings an important confirmation of the relationship of astronomical epochs to the myth.

It is customarily acknowledged that in the Eleventh Dynasty (2200 B.C.) the kings named Mentuhotep chose Mentu for the supreme god of the Theban nome, and that the Twelfth Dynasty is marked by the ascension of Amun to the highest rank with the reign of Amenemhet, founder of the Twelfth Dynasty (2000 B.C.).[9] Now, it was in about 2200 B.C. that the precessional signs changed: the vernal point left Taurus and entered Aries.

At Medamud we see the signature of the end-times of the cycles, except for the Christian church, which marks the beginning of Pisces.

Plate 50A • The First Temple

The first temple, built on a natural hillock, has undergone a transformation since the time of its origin. In its first state it was composed of a polygonal, enclosing wall of unbaked bricks covered with a white coating that surrounded a sacred wood in which the so-called cult edifice itself was found; a court preceded by a pylon gives access to two winding corridors that penetrate into two earthen mounds sheltering two sanctuaries (fig. 245).

Fig. 245. Mounds of the original temple at Medamud

One of the corridors is oriented north-south. It has a double meander and two altars at the entrance. The other is oriented east-west, and has only one meander and a single altar. If we judge by the height of the enclosing wall, which was terminated by a hogbacked crown at 1.75 meters, the height of the corridors could not have been over 1.50 meters. These galleries did not have doors and their winding character made it impossible to see into the sanctuaries from the exterior. The floors of the corridors were covered with fine sand. At the entrance of the south gallery two cylindrical, earthen pillars were able to support an offering plate or a brazier; a single pillar of the same type was found at the entrance to the east gallery.

There was no construction under this edifice, but only a thin bed of black earth in which two prehistoric objects were found.[10]

> The original temple of Medamud underwent several important modifications. A second court was added to it preceded by a pylon with masts. The circular pedestal of one of these masts, carefully cut in a block of sandstone, has been found in place to the right of the entrance door.
>
> The axis of the new pylon is not the same as the first. At the time of this change, the structure had to be modified and the entrance to the original pylon displaced.
>
> The connection of the new pylon with the enclosing wall and the wall of the court produced a sort of triangular alcove with a soft surface that was used as a storage place for cult objects.
>
> On the right side of this new court there are two rectangular, brick benches covered in ash. They were used to heat the crucibles found in the surrounding area.[11]
>
> Intact or in ruins, it is this enlarged building that Sesostris III found at Medamud when he wanted to construct his great fortified temple. He completely razed the walls and mounds of the monument and burned the trees of the sacred grove to assure a solid foundation on cinders for his buildings, which were established exactly on the place of the original temple.[12]

The later constructions would respect the orientations of the two original mounds and would always retain the double character, the opposition at right angles, north-south and east-west.

Plate 50B • The Temple of Sesostris III (Middle Kingdom)

The temple of Sesostris III appears as a great enclosing wall that surrounds two distinctly separate groups of monuments, separated by an east-west wall without any opening. The buildings to the south have their principal entrances toward the east. The north part is divided in two by a north-south wall, established exactly on the axis of the original mound with the double meander and the two altars. The sanctuary itself, consecrated to Mentu and his sacred bull, is thus located in the northeast corner of the enclosing wall.

This sanctuary is oriented north-south and has a double entryway. The north entry crosses a long room with a single longitudinal colonnade before penetrating the sanctuary; the west entry crosses the court, then the wall built on the ancient mound, and heads toward a court lined with double porticos that have Osirian columns, before entering into the covered sanctuary to the south. The monument as a whole appears as a fortress, and its principle door is named "Sesostris drives off the evil from the lord of the Theban nome who resides at the heart of Medamud."

Sesostris III made six foundation deposits in cubic form. Four are arranged in a square to the northeast and northwest corners of the enclosing wall and on all sides of the corridor that divides the southern structures. The two others are located at each end of the original north-south mound. The four exterior deposits contained three bull's heads and a cow's head. The two interior deposits contained no bones and marked the axis of orientation of the west enclosing wall of the sanctuary.

---

[10] Cf. plate 94A, the original temple founded on virgin ground.

[11] Hundreds of elongated crucibles have been found in the interior of the enclosing wall.

[12] Robichon and Varille, *Description sommaire du temple primitif de Médamoud*, pp. 1–4.

Sesostris III left the court located in the northwest corner of the yard empty, under which was found the second original mound. In this court, above the east-west mound, Tuthmosis III later established a square foundation platform that provides the exact demarcation and the orientation axis of the constructions of the future Ptolemaic sanctuary dedicated to Amun, the ram. The center of this square (the crossing of the diagonals) would become the exact center of the naos of the barque of Amun. Thus, twelve centuries later, the plan defined by Tuthmosis was realized. This pharaoh placed nine foundation deposits around the platform in cylindrical holes. Now, in the temple of the Bull, oriented north-south, the holes containing the foundation deposits were square (north-south is axial) and in the temple of the Ram, which would be oriented east-west, the holes are round (east-west is cyclic). Among other objects, one of these round holes contained an offering cup in the form of a spherical skullcap on the edge of which six bulls alternate with six shallow, gold cups. This confirms the emphasis on the cyclic character of these deposits.

Plate 50C • The Ptolemaic Temple

The present temple of Medamud was built in the Greco-Roman Period by Ptolemy VI on the site of the previous temples. This great temple, surrounded by an enclosing wall of bricks constructed by Tiberius, has before it a sphinx-lined road leading to a loading dock. The entrance in the surrounding wall goes through a monumental sandstone gate, also erected by Tiberius.

The temple itself has the form of a long rectangle oriented east-west. It faces west and has the appearance of a sort of pylon in front of which three curious kiosks are placed, one at the center and the other two toward the north, each in front of a door.

The temple as a whole is divided into three parts: First, the large peristyle court, which is lined on three sides by a portico with a double colonnade. Second, the temple of Amun itself, which is oriented east-west with two doors that open to the west and that are on the axis of the central kiosk and its neighboring kiosk to the side. Third, the temple consecrated to Mentu, which is oriented north-south and is totally separate from the temple of Amun. It can be accessed in two ways: through a door on the west located on the axis of the third side kiosk, or through a door on the south that one approaches after encircling the entire temple on the outside.

The naos of the barque of Amun, constructed on the place of the original mound with the single meander, is encircled by several rooms that occupy the platform built by Tuthmosis III.

Built on the preceding sanctuary constructed by Sesostris III, the temple consecrated to Mentu is surrounded on three sides by an enclosing wall on which the Niles bringing their offerings are depicted. These figures are facing toward a tableau, carved on the southern exterior facade of the temple of Mentu and in its axis, that depicts a Roman emperor before the bull of Medamud. Thus, it is the north-south mound, the one with the double meander, that is and remains connected to the bull-Mentu principle. It is the east-west mound with a single meander that would return to Amun.[13]

In the central kiosk, fragments of bas-reliefs and inscriptions describe a local festival that goes back to the Thirteenth Dynasty. "One of these inscriptions is particularly interesting because it brings us face to face with one of these *saltatores mimici*, according to Lucian. In Egypt, these people expressed in their dances the most mysterious elements of religion. . . . These are dancers 'of words,' that is, mimes."[14]

---

[13] At Luxor the east-west walls of the covered temple are governed by the axis of Amun.

[14] Etienne Drioton, "Médamoud, les inscriptions," *Rapports sur les fouilles de Médamoud 1925–*, Fouilles de l'I.F.A.O., rapports préliminaires, vol. 4 (Cairo, 1927), fasc. 2, pp. 14–15.

The miming gestures are the expression of the feeling conveyed in music, as Hickmann has well understood through his investigations of the sacred traditional songs of the Copts.[15]

The dances and gestures that accompany music and song are found in all the initiatic temples of antiquity.

Gesture animates the word; without it, the word is a purely cerebral communication, conventional and "cold."

The word without gesture is particular; it is addressed only to those who are instructed in its significance, who know its language.

The gesture speaks to everyone; it is thought in action, it is hieroglyph.

A feeling requires the gesture in order to be communicated in kind. Gesture is the speech of emotion, of the most profound sentiments.

The mime and the dancer address themselves to the most immediate and most subtle aspects of human intellection.

Thus, sacred dance is a part of the Temple, a commentary on the music and a realization of the rhythm. But sacred dance is even more than that: it knows the functional, cosmic meaning of each part of the human body. The gestures of each part—fingers, hands, arms, legs, feet, stomach, chest, spinal column, head, eyes, and so forth—are the active script that puts the human being in a living, emotional communication with the Universe. This same intention must be seen in the depictions of often eccentric dances found in the figurations in pharaonic tombs, for example.

In the tombs of the Fifth Dynasty, Professor Montet notes several dancing scenes,[16] and the texts that accompany them, which cannot be transcribed into common language, show an incontestable symbolic meaning.

—〜〜—

The northern kiosk that gives access to the door leading to the temple of Mentu also preserves fragments of texts among which there is a hymn that lets us know the qualities and powers attributed to him:

> Spirit of sperms, as many as there are in the whole world! . . .
>
> It is he who has placed Ptah as chief of the artists to create all the works of his heart.
>
> It is he to whom we call in the hour of sickness: he arrives immediately near to him who calls his name.
>
> Speaking with his mouth, acting with his hands; there is no one to oppose what he has undertaken. . . .
>
> Hearts are his bread, and blood is his water; he is pleased with their smell. . . .
>
> Valiant bull whose horns are of iron to kill all who approach . . .
>
> His venom instantly shines; he cuts with the sword; his commandment destroys the flesh.
>
> There is no antidote against him in recorded texts; there is no conjuration against him in the hieroglyphs.[17]

---

[15] Hans Hickmann, *Observations sur les survivances de la chironomie égyptienne dans le chant liturgique copte*, Annales du Service des Antiquités de l'Egypte 49 (Cairo: I.F.A.O., 1949), fasc. 2, p. 418 et sqq.

[16] Pierre Montet, *Les Scènes de la vie privée dans les tombeaux égyptiens de l'Ancien Empire* (Strasbourg: Imprimerie Alsacienne, 1925), p. 367.

[17] Drioton, "Médamoud, les inscriptions," pp. 38–40.

A fragment of text on the inside of the door of this kiosk mentions the ancient origins: "Those who are under the belly of Nut, those who are on the back of Geb . . . ,"[18] that is, Shu and Tefnut, Gemini.

Plate 50D • The Christian Church

The first Christian church was established on the south side of the Amunian temple. Its east-west axis is parallel to the direction of this temple. The apse of the church was supported on the old stable of the ram of Amun, and its entrance is to the west.

—⁓—

This succession of constructions coincides chronologically with the *end* of the phases of the zodiacal precessional months, from Gemini to the beginning of Pisces. The cult of Aries ceases with the beginning of Pisces, the Christian symbol, around the year 60 B.C., just as approximately 2200 B.C. was the end of the cult of Taurus, which had begun around 4300 B.C., at the end of the cult of Gemini. These dates correspond to known dates in pharaonic chronology.

Let us note that Sesostris III (Senusret) founded the temple of the Bull at the end of the precessional passage through this sign. This fact is symbolized by the existence of several statues of this pharaoh at Medamud that represent him with the characteristics of an old man.

PLATE 51 • THE ZODIAC

Plate 51A • Man and the Zodiac in the Middle Ages
Plate 51B • The Temple of Luxor and the Zodiac

The doctrine of the Anthropocosmos has in all times related the human body to the starry sky through zodiacal symbols. It was therefore necessary to look for the existence of these figurations in the temple; some zodiacal signs are indicated there through their symbols or by their characteristic functions.

Aries is assigned to the head and Taurus to the nape of the neck. The dedication carved on the periphery of the pedestal of the covered temple begins uncharacteristically at the height of the nape (fig. 199, no. 9) with the formula "Long live the golden Horus, powerful bull . . . ," leaving the whole part of the socle north of this point marked by its lack of an inscription.

This same dedication continues toward the south to the point corresponding to the west door of room XII (fig. 199, no. 10), and mentions the "statue of Amun in gold, with the head of a ram . . . ," which should be found in the central sanctuary I. Finally, graffiti above this same west door of room XII shows a ram's head placed on a pedestal. The accent placed on the ram at this point in the temple, corresponding to the head, incontestably alludes to the astrological rulership of this sign over this part of the human body.

Leo is depicted at the level of the chest (the *haty*, fig. 246a) in room VIII, on the eastern part of the north wall, where the king is seated on a throne with a lion (the sun and heart) sculpted on it.

In room XVI, the bases of the columns draw lunar crescents by hiding part of one disk with another (plate 44), symbolizing Cancer (the moon, breasts, stomach). We find here an example of the frequent transposing of Leo and Cancer, which is also found in the zodiac of Dendera. This can be compared to the transposition of Leo and Cancer in the two groups of signs of the zodiac sculpted at the base of the central porch of Notre Dame in Paris.

[18] Ibid., p. 33.

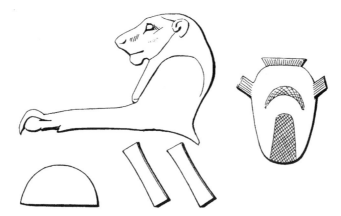

Fig. 246a. Haty *is written with a lion protome followed by the determinative for the heart*

The sign of Virgo rules the belly at the level of the navel. We find the inscription that confirms the meaning of the temple as "gestating the Royal Man" at this level on the west face of the architraves of the east colonnade of the peristyle court (fig. 199, no. 15). This gestation is made in the "androgynous" or Adamic body, as indicated in the *kamutef* mentioned in this same text.[19]

The importance of the role played by the zodiacal sign of Scorpio regarding sex is known through the Metternich Papyrus where Isis struggles with a scorpion in front of her and another one behind, both of which want to sting her son Horus to death.[20]

Sagittarius rules the thighs. In the temple, the thighs correspond to the great colonnade of the nave, on the inside east and west walls of which is depicted the procession of the barques on the water, the flux that emerges from the calves and ends at the top of the femur. (Here we hit upon an important problem about which we will speak in another work regarding "mystical geography.")*

On the exterior face of the west wall of the nave we find in the center (Sagittarius) a very rare figuration of a warrior seated sidesaddle and brandishing a bow.

In front of the door of the nave, at the knees, the mythic Capricorn is replaced on the dorsal stele of the seated colossi by the tadpole, who is shown with his aquatic tail and his back feet bent, holding a fixed point on land. This tadpole signifies duration. One could object that it is always found on these same colossi, but that would be forgetting that the temple of Luxor specifically reveals to us that the seated black colossus signifies what the knees are for man: the principle of the angle,[21] of strength and foundation, related to the pituitary gland, connected with seminal power, and therefore with continuity.[22]

[19] In the zodiac of Dendera, beneath the sign of the Virgin holding a wheat stalk, there is another figure of the Virgin holding a child.

[20] This part of the temple of Luxor corresponding to the lower belly is badly ruined and no longer allows us to investigate the symbols that relate to Libra and Scorpio.

[21] Cf. chapter 7, "Fundamentals of the Trigonometry."

[22] The influence of the knees and the femur on the production of seed is almost unknown in present medicine. This relates to the formation of a "fixed point" that inscribes innate consciousness and transmits the heredity of this acquisition, and is concerned with reincarnation. Cf. chapter 34, appendix.

Let us recall with regard to the thigh (femur) the Greek myth of Dionysus, conceived by Jupiter with Semele. Jupiter keeps the infant conceived with the dying Semele in his thigh. Now, this is Amun, who would be called Jupiter-Amun by the Romans.

*Never completed.

Aquarius, often symbolized by libations, corresponds to the calf, and it is at this place in the court of Ramesses, at the height of the "door of the princes," where the avenue lined with columns leading to the Nile converges, that the end of the axis of the nave is marked by a key-piece (fig. 281), from which a small canal leads in the direction of the river.

Now, a myth relates that in the island of Biggeh, a little south of Aswan, there was a tomb of Osiris whose reputation surpassed that of all the others. The left leg of Osiris was buried there and the priests thought that this leg was the seat of one of the two sources of the Nile, and they showed how the water came out of it in jets. From this source sprang the fertilizing water of the Nile, and in this place Osiris was identified with the Nile. "It was the great Nile that created wheat with the water that is in it, and that caused the trees and flowers to shoot up," said the priests. "And it is reborn in its season and its limbs renew themselves each year."[23]

This tomb of Osiris was called the Abaton. The bas-reliefs represent it as a cavern in which Osiris, in the form of a "Nile," holds a vase in each hand from which a jet of water springs: this is the symbol of Aquarius.

The Origin of the Symbol of Capricorn

Capricorn, like Sagittarius, is one of the composite figures of the zodiac. It governs the winter solstice at the moment when the sun, at the festivals of Khoïak (Christmas), begins its reascent from the depths of the setting "waters," that is, the night. The west is the sunset, with the autumnal equinox in Libra, for the complete *day* that the year represents. The sun reappears on about the twenty-first of March with Aries, rising in the east.

This is the reason why Capricorn is aquatic in the hindquarters and terrestrial in the front. As such, its horns do not have a direct meaning, but they take on significance if we understand this figure as an inheritance of the symbol placed, in Egypt, at the knees, ruled by Capricorn.

The tadpole first develops its back feet, which it puts on land as if they were front feet, while its aquatic tail still exists. Placed on its head is the double palm, which counts the years, because the palm is the natural symbol of the measure of the lunar months of the year: the phoenix palm gives forth a palm leaf plus a fraction of the next one every month so that at the end of a year there are twelve palm leaves and a fraction.[24] Thus, there are as many palm leaves as there are lunar months in the solar year of $365\frac{1}{4}$ days.

Under the sign of the tadpole (the future Capricorn) is placed the *chen* (fig. 246b, *b*), which signifies the event determined on the string of continuity. When two tadpoles are each carrying a palm and placed in opposition, the moment of past time separated from the time that is beginning is indicated, that is, a continuous duration.

Faultfinders will object that this sign is also found elsewhere than at the knees of the Man of the Temple of Luxor, but the lion, the moon, the ram, and so on, are also found elsewhere. *The determination of the meaning of a symbol is one of the great discoveries that the temple of Luxor brings, for this as well as for the ritual and other signs,* which is precisely what allows us to decipher their significance when they are used in other places.

[23] Cf. Erman, *Religion des Egyptiens,* pp. 431–35.

[24] This symbol of the measured time of the year is common in pharaonic Egypt. It signifies duration, which is why it is used as a traditional symbol in the Gospels and for Palm Sunday, etc.

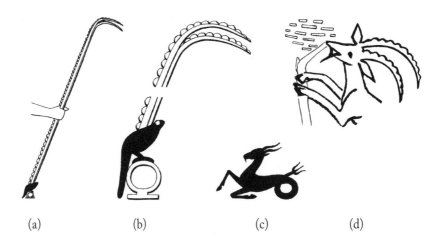

(a)   (b)   (c)   (d)

Fig. 246b. (a, b) Pharaonic signs; (c, d) signs from the Middle Ages

(a, b) The double palm placed on the back of the tadpole, the back feet of which rest on the *chen* sign; *(c)* the sign of Capricorn with a fish tail ending with a trident, after forming a loop; *(d)* detail of the sign of Capricorn showing his two scalloped horns (cf. plate 51).

The sign of the tadpole-Capricorn surmounted by a palm is found in several places in the temple of Luxor, among others: to the right and left of the doors of the repository of Amun's barque, and at the east and west entrances of the court of Ramesses; on the dorsal steles of the seated black colossi, located at the knees, before the door leading from the narthex to the nave; under the Osirian curve of the naos of Alexander; and, held by two female *neters,* both at the east entrance of room XII, where the king is born at midnight (Christmas) in order to be introduced, pubescent, to the rising of the sun (six o'clock in the morning), corresponding to the spring equinox,[25] and in the room of the birth, on the west partition, at the time of the presentation of the newborn child to Amun (the royal birth).

In other words, we find this sign at the entrances of the temple and at the entry into life. This is an example of a play of correspondences through symbols, just as with the joints of the stones.[26]

[25] The title of this scene is "Royal Ascent toward the Sanctuary." In transparency the king has the red crown and offers incense in the vase of fire.

[26] Cf. plates 26–28 and chapter 30.

Chapter 37

THE MASTER BUILDERS' GRID

Plates 52–67

*Scrupulously observed theological prescriptions
explain the character of pharaonic thought,
as much in mathematics for calculation as in
geometry and for trigonometric notation, and
this reveals to us the meaning, unknown until the
present, of the process of "putting into squares"
that we call the* canevas.

(Cf. chapter 11)

PLATE 52

Tomb of Ukhotep (Meir), West Partition, North Part

The canevas *serves as a stable foundation, formed of whole numbers belonging to the functional lineages that, by oscillation, tend toward the repose of the pendulum. This alternation is the characteristic of all growth and of the maintenance of life in its present form.*

(Chapter 11)

PLATE 53

Tomb of Ukhotep (Meir), West Partition, North Part

10 cm

*. . . the dividing into two,
the scission, is not made
into two equal parts, and
the articulation is the function of the scission. This is
the philosophy of the mystical function* ϕ *viewed in
its trigonometric aspect,
as it may be in all aspects
of Nature.*

(Chapter 7)

eter

PLATE 54

Tomb of Ukhotep (Meir), North Partition, West Part

Through musical harmony, and therefore only through our sensation of music, and not by reasoning, can we know absolute φ. This fact indicates the way of the pharaonic mentality and of the true Pythagoreanism developed from it.

(Chapter 8)

PLATE 55

Tomb of Ukhotep (Meir), North Partition, Center

. . . there is a kinship between the cause of branching out in the plant . . . and the articulation of the elbow and knee in the human being. There will be an inequality between the two lines thus engendered. One is "Heaven" and the other is "Earth." One is unitary, the other divisible. . . .

(Chapter 7)

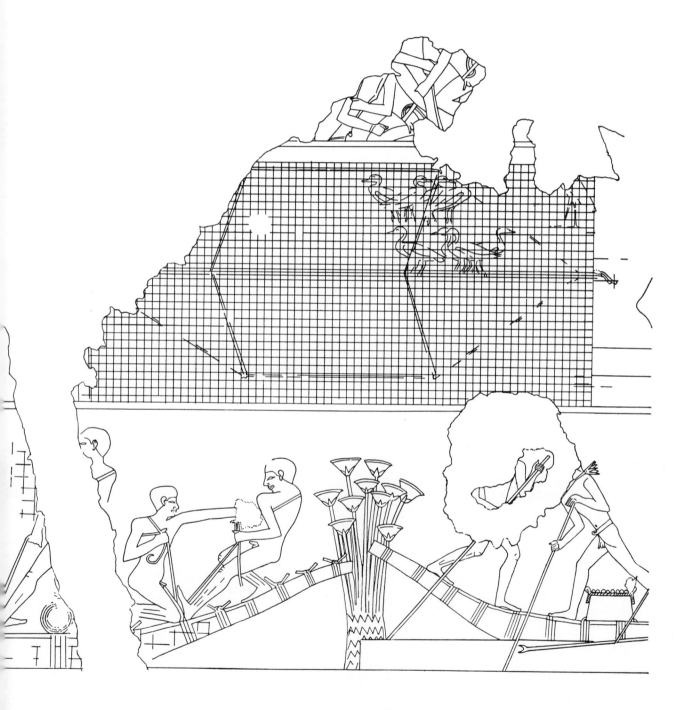

50 cm

PLATE 56

Tomb of Ukhotep (Meir), North Partition, East Part

If I prefer Ancient Egypt to the Maya, to India, China, Babylonia, or Greece, it is because . . . its entire "culture" is founded on a symbolic form of writing. This attests to an unsurpassable wisdom, which dared found an empire on the purely symbolic expression of its writing. Any writing formed from an arbitrary, conventionally alphabetical system may in time be lost and become incomprehensible.

(Chapter 2)

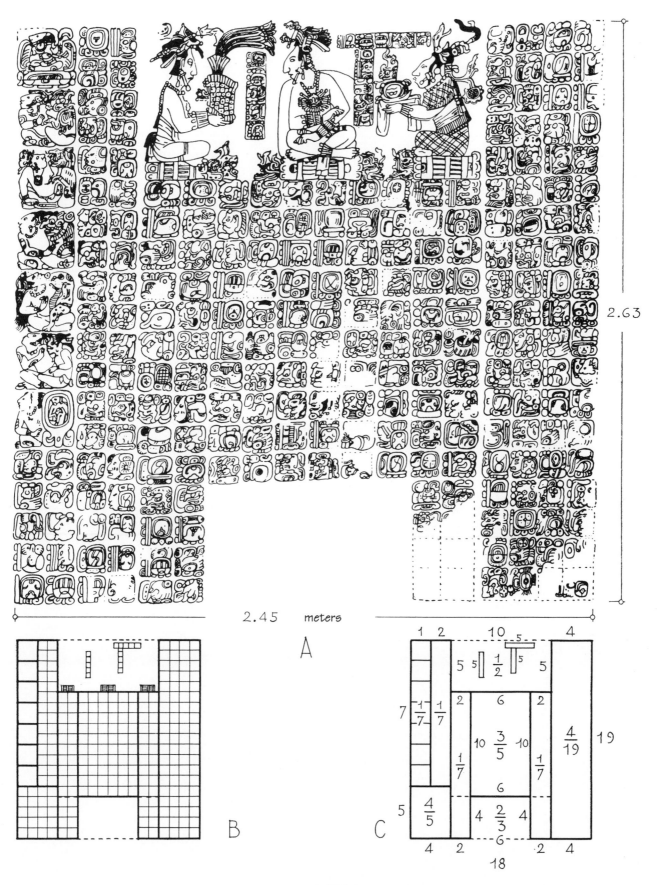

PLATE 57

A Mayan Grid

It is thus that the golden number . . . is to be regarded as a creative or separating power; it is the power that provokes *the scission, and consequently is not derived arithmetically from the root of 5, because the* power five *is not a cause but a result of this function* φ.

(Chapter 5)

PLATE 58

The Kamutef *of the Northeast Corner of the Transept*

Any figuration is a "mental" transposition of a function, a symbol. In the same way a numeral is a mental transposition of a number, that is, of the definition of a function.

(Chapter 5)

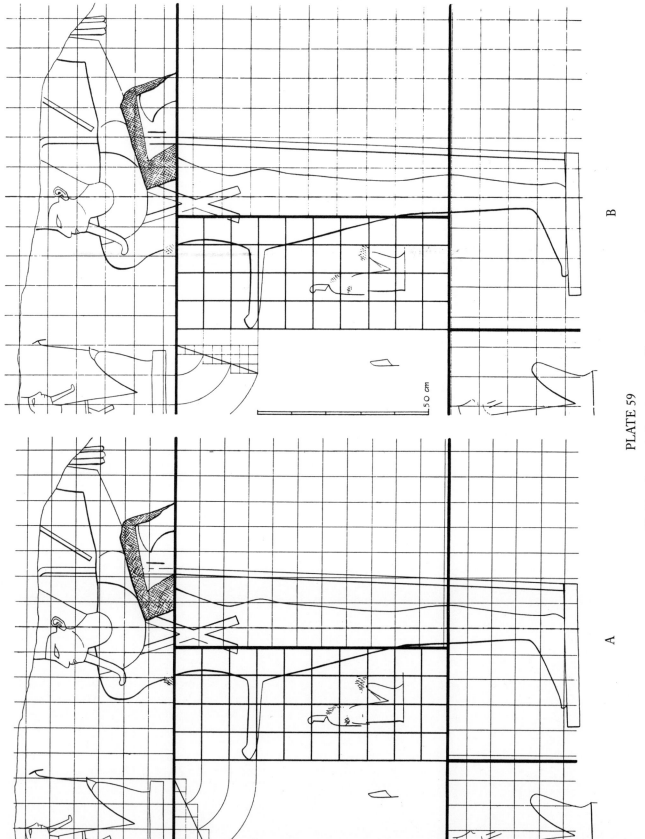

B

A

50 cm

PLATE 59

The Two Geometric Functions of the Kamutef

. . . to penetrate the thought of the Ancients, we rely on the architecture and the geometry that guides it, rather than on descriptive texts.

It is the gesture that speaks and unveils.

(Elements)

PLATE 60

Thoth, Master of the Net, Karnak

Thoth is "master of . . ."; he is not the thing itself.
He is not that which "comes and goes," but that
which "causes to come and then to go back to its
source." He is the creator of the cycles of that
which renders apparent, but he is not writing,
Seshat. Thoth is that which creates alternation,
but he is not the weaving, Neith, who makes
things tangible; Thoth can nevertheless become
visible and percepible—Thoth-mes—which is to
say that he can be revealed: Her-mes, the secret . . .

(Chapter 11)

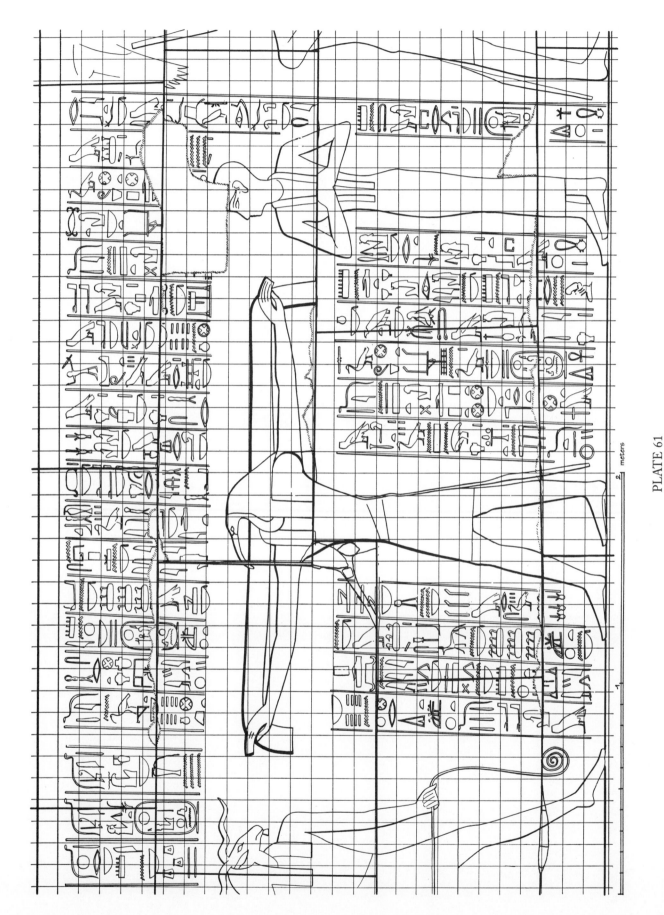

PLATE 61

Thoth, Master of Numbers, Karnak

Present man thinks and can only think insomuch as he is child and inheritor of his heaven. He should seek the elements for his science within himself, whether it is a question of knowledge of the becoming of things, or of the objective world he perceives. Hermes said: "The Work is within you . . . ," and pharaonic Egypt would say with respect to measures: "Man measures the world."

(Chapter 10)

PLATE 62

Tomb of Ramesses IX, the Measure of the Cycle

No curve in the Universe is an absolute circle; it is always a question of cycles.

(Chapter 10)

PLATE 63

Tomb of Ramesses IX, Study of Measures

1 meter

The pharaonic system of measures addresses itself to life, the life whose essential functions are governed by triads of neters.

(Chapter 10)

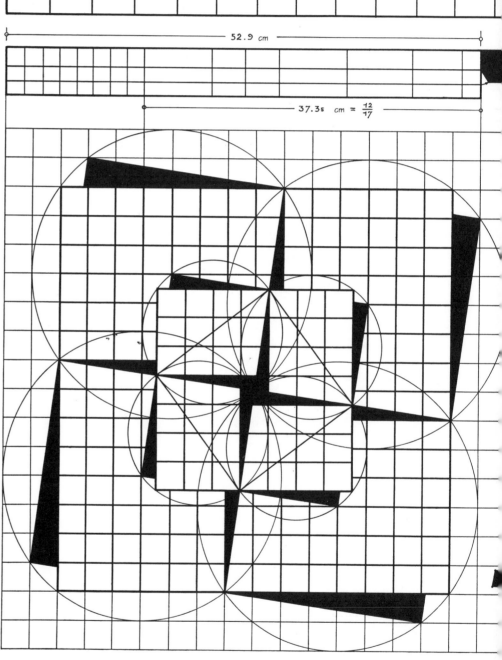

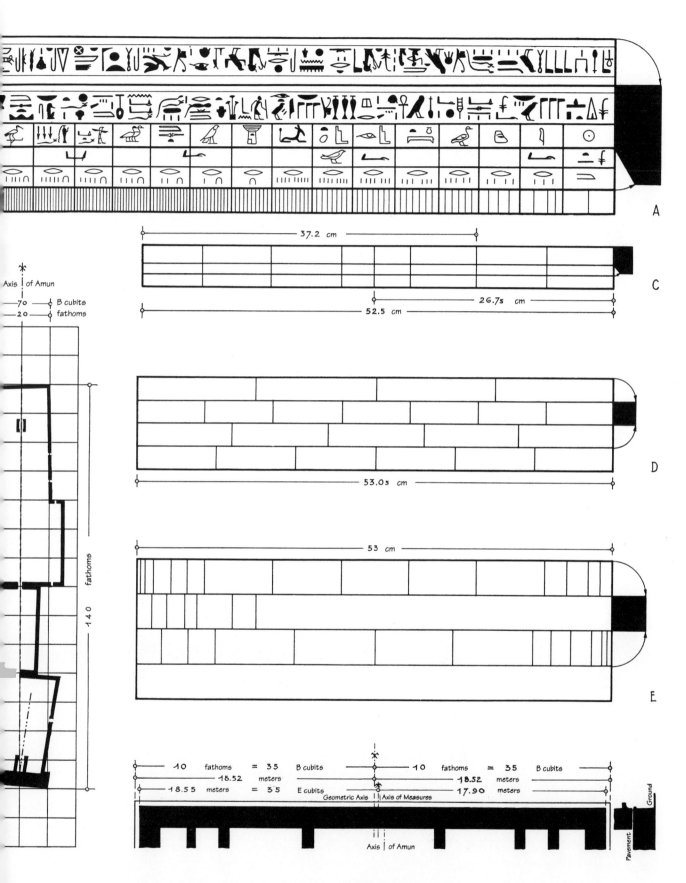

A

Axis | of Amun

—70— B cubits
—20— fathoms

140 fathoms

C

37.2 cm

26.7₅ cm

52.5 cm

D

53.0₅ cm

E

53 cm

10 fathoms = 35 B cubits   ✳   10 fathoms = 35 B cubits
18.52 meters   18.52 meters
18.55 meters = 35 E cubits Geometric Axis | Axis of Measures   17.90 meters

Axis | of Amun

Pavement
Ground

PLATE 64

The Cubits and the Temple

Any building, no matter how simple, has a soul because it is a volume. Volume is necessarily indefinable spirit-substance arrested in space. It is living, it is specified, it is number, and therefore music.

(Chapter 25)

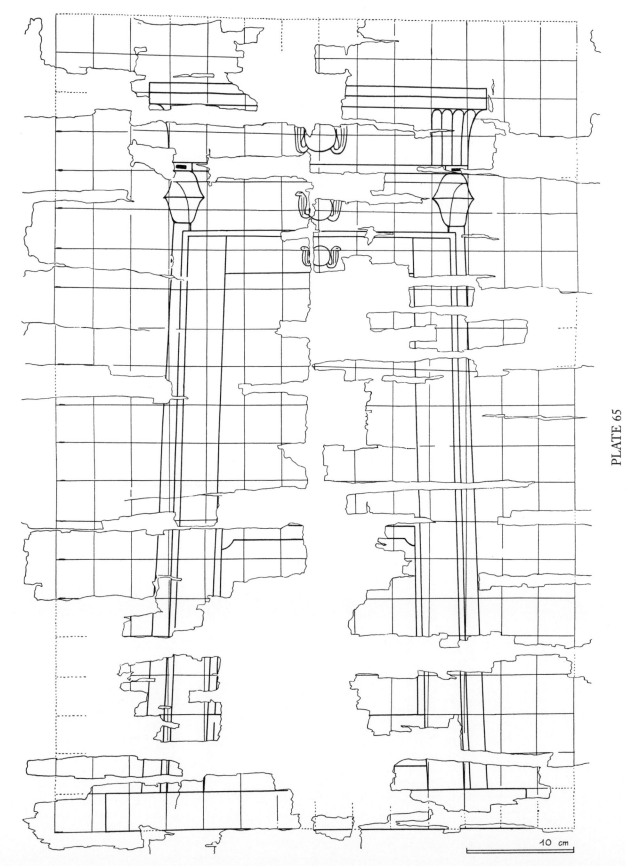

PLATE 65

A Naos in a Grid Drawn on Papyrus (Front View)

10 cm

The impulse to all movement and to all form is given by ɸ. . . . Phi is the impulse for the whole number 5, but . . . ɸ cannot be defined in rational numbers. It can only be defined through the harmony that it engenders.

(Chapter 8)

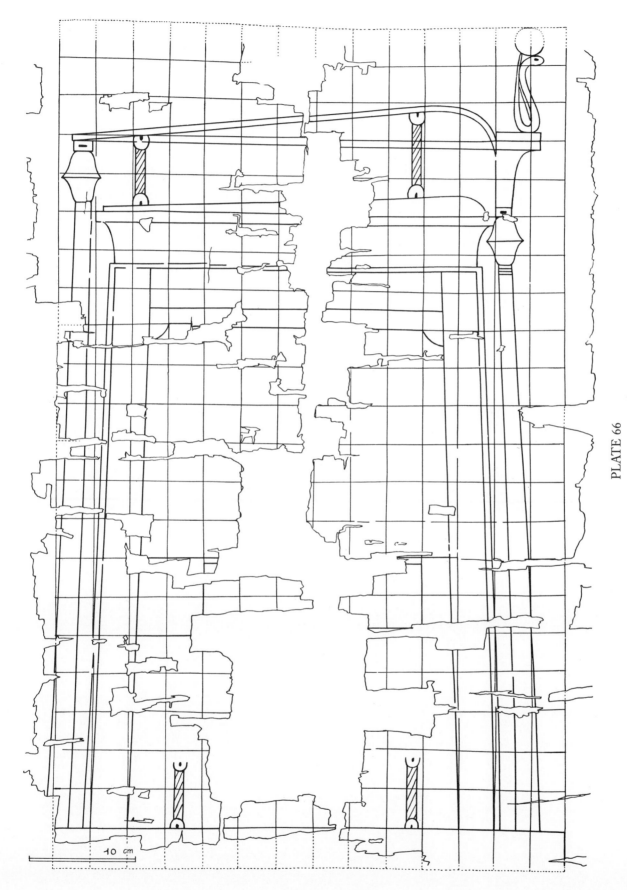

10 cm

PLATE 66

A Naos in a Grid Drawn on Papyrus (Side View)

The cubit is a masterpiece because it creates a link between number and its function, and measure.

(Chapter 10)

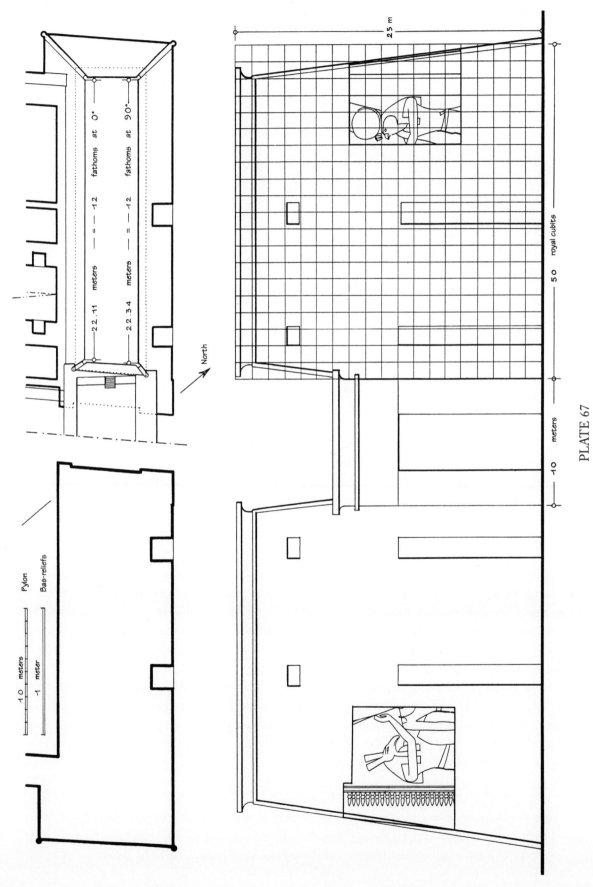

North

— 22.11 meters = 12 fathoms at 0°
— 22.34 meters = 12 fathoms at 90°

Pylon
Bas-reliefs

1 0 meters
1 meter

25 m

5 0 royal cubits

1 0 meters

PLATE 67

The Grid and the Measurements of the Pylon of Luxor

Chapter 37

THE MASTER
BUILDERS' GRID

THE PROBLEM OF ESTABLISHING A
HUMAN CANON

Research into what constitutes the normal proportions of the human body has been a preoccupation of artists and physicians of all times, the former for aesthetic, the latter for medical reasons.

From the Renaissance until the last century, artists were especially preoccupied with establishing a canon that answered to the sense of the beautiful in the human body. No general canon was agreed upon, however, because the criteria were subjective and conditioned by the many abstract elements that result from racial variations and from personal predispositions in the understanding of harmony.

This kind of incoherence in the different definitions of human beauty, perfectly justified by environmental conditions such as climate, country, and the evolution of consciousness, has prompted our scientists, since the last century, to try to find common ground on which to establish a frame of reference. Anthropologists have given a scientific character to this study, which has aroused numerous controversies between two opposing camps: One side proposes the definition of the ideal human type, whereas the other looks for a system of classification that allows the various morphologies to be arranged into several essential groups.

Anthropometrics is the method of investigation common to the two opposite camps. Both sides have accumulated very important material that would allow the study of human proportions to begin, if agreement were possible about the system to be employed.

It will be interesting to summarize briefly here the position of present researchers so we can compare it with the pharaonic point of view.

The Ideal Human Type

Quetelet, basing his position on the fact that the variations in anthropometric characteristics obey Gauss's law, has called the "average man" (1835) the type that would be obtained by taking the average value of the dimension of each segment of the body on a great number of individuals. . . .

812

The doctrine of the average man has had considerable influence on anthropologists and statisticians. It is particularly on this idea that Viola, from 1903 to 1905, based the Italian constitutionist method. . . .

Although it is accepted by most modern authors, the "average man" has aroused objections. One of the most well known of these comes from the French mathematician Cournot. "Let us suppose," he says, "a triangle, the sides of which are related to each other in a determined proportion. Let us now make a random variation in the length of each side a certain number of times and then calculate the three arithmetic means of these variations. These three averages will no longer correspond to the lengths of the sides of the original triangle, and it would be impossible to reconstitute this triangle. In the same way, the ideal proportions of man being given, if we make a random variation in the dimensions of each characteristic, the calculation of the average values of these characteristics will not give the original proportions. A doctrine that attempts to find ideal proportions using these methods is therefore false."

Viola refuted this objection in 1905. "It rests," he said, "on an equivocation." Cournot supposes a "free" or accidental variation for the three sides of the triangle, one that would be independent of all law, as would be the case, for example, with the height of the houses of a city. But this is not the case for the average human because the different characteristics vary according to the Gauss curve and not freely as is supposed by Cournot.[1]

The Classification of Actual Types

Everyday experience teaches us that a very great diversity of forms and proportions exists among adult subjects. Apart from the differences in height, which are the most striking, a great number of other differences are found, in particular regarding the length and volume of the various body segments, and as a result, we never meet two people who are absolutely the same.

For a long time people have attempted to bring order to this diversity and to group the infinite variety of individual types into clusters with a more or less large number of points in common.

This concern became particularly interesting when it was perceived that the subjects who could be grouped under the same type of body structure often present striking resemblances with one another in other areas as well. Among these we can mention physiological behavior, psychology, tastes, aptitudes, and morbid tendencies. The observation of such relationships suggests extremely old notions of "constitution" and "temperament," which today are again respected by the followers of neo-Hippocratic medicine.[2]

—◊◊◊—

The objection of the mathematician Cournot regarding the average person is basically true, though excessive in its expression. For example, if we measure 100 hands, 100 forearms, and 100 arms from 100 individuals, and then establish an average for each of these segments, it would be impossible to discover the particular rhythm that links each of these parts in order to reconstitute the whole arm of any particular individual. At the very most, we would be able to approach an average proportion, but with the feeling that we would brush past a function without ever being able to reach it. A comparative study of several skeletons, on the contrary, permits us to observe several coefficients that

[1] Vandervael, *Biométrie humaine*, pp. 101–2.
[2] Ibid., p. 104.

govern all individuals. It is in this way, moreover, that Hambidge proceeded, which allowed him to discover that

> in each skeleton measured from the front and in profile, there is a harmonic rhythm of rectangles that is always akin to those of the module $\sqrt{5}$ and ϕ. But with the exception of certain nearly unalterable proportions, normal human skeletons do not fluctuate and deviate around an ideal or average type as we would suppose. Rather there is a characteristic, dynamic "symphony" based on a very rigorous (to 1/10 mm) pattern for each individual, the patterns for different individuals, moreover, being quite varied. . . .[3]
>
> As we can see, this "symphonic" conception of human proportions is very different from the theory of the "ideal canon" generally accepted as furnishing a unique scale (or at least one for each sex). However, the two concepts are not absolutely contradictory. First, nothing prevents us from selecting one out of a great number of dynamic themes and adopting it as the common type or ideal subtype. This is probably what the Greek sculptors did (canon of Polyclitus). Second, in operating on a number of normal (healthy) skeletons of the same sex, and as much as possible from the same race, we nevertheless find certain stable averages. . . .[4]

The golden section is not a product of mathematical imagination, but the natural principle of the laws of equilibrium.

Since all generation calls for a growth in volume, and since all growth can only be made in a harmonious rhythm, that is, a rhythm proportional to a particular coefficient, and since this rhythm is undeniably governed by ϕ, it is enough to know the module (coefficient) particular to the species or to an individual of that species, or of the *neter* principle, in order to create a living, harmonious, magically correct form, developing an architecture or an image on this module with ϕ.

The pharaonic sages envisioned the problem of a canon of proportions taken from the human body from a different point of view than our present anthropologists, and this point of view demonstrates the true orientation of their thinking.

Humanity regarded as Anthropocosmos, or human cosmos, carries in itself all the elements of the measures of the world and of harmony, expressed organically and through numbers. There is therefore a perfect man who is the king; in other words, the sacred royal type is the representative of Cosmic Man. In his figuration, he summarizes all the fundamental proportions, each part of the body corresponding respectively to one of the essential functions of the genetic work of the Universe. The relation of all these parts constitutes harmony, which represents perfected Man.

In this schema, true because it corresponds to all the possibilities expressed in a living being, the characteristic variants of terrestrial man are projected, thus offering the possibility of knowing—at the same time as the types and deformations—their causes, their source, as well as their relationships with cosmic influences (zodiacal dates), local influences (dryness, humidity, and so on), racial and geological influences, and the nature of occupational deformations.

[3] Ghyka, *Esthétique des proportions*, p. 260.
[4] Ibid., p. 274.

Astrology explains the humors, temperaments, and characters . . . , which is only possible by referring to the royal type, invariable because it is free from all influence. We are speaking here of the hieratic king of the bas-reliefs, not of the reigning kings who themselves represent the perfect type for the astrological time and the genetic phase of the empire: the guide (Manu) bearing the symbolic marks of these dates.

It must never be forgotten that if in pharaonic Egypt writing is made of images, then the figurations are in their turn a form of writing, and the human body—applied, for example, to the *neters*—becomes the support of a thinking that speaks in a universal sense of causes, precisely because the human body represents all functional possibilities.

STUDY OF AN APPLIED *CANEVAS*: THE TOMB OF UKHOTEP AT MEIR

The cross-ruled bas-reliefs in plates 52 to 56 come to us from the tomb of Ukhotep, nomarch of Cusae (Kas), capital of the fourteenth nome of Upper Egypt, located slightly south of the nome of Thoth (fifteenth nome). Ukhotep, son of Senbi, had a son named Senbi and a wife, Thothotep. As the grand vizier under Sesostris I,[5] he had the highest titles that can be accorded to a dignitary—unique (confidential) friend, treasurer, great chief of the priests of Hathor (mistress of Cusae), scribe of the divine books, master of all the scepters and costumes, "unique of his kind and without rival," "he who dominates the secrets that one sees alone. . . ."[6]

The entrance to the tomb, hollowed out of the rock, is to the east, and the scenes covering the north and south partitions are directed toward the west, where a niche containing a statue of the nomarch is hollowed out of the center of the west partition. Thus, it divides the bas-reliefs into two groups: those of the south, which are entirely sculpted and do not contain any trace of a grid pattern apart from one exception, located in the southwest corner (fig. 247); and those of the north that preserve, in numerous places, the lines of a grid.

In their totality, these partitions are divided into three registers occupied by small figures turned toward the nomarch, who is represented as much taller, and by himself takes up several registers.

The entire north part of the tomb is particularly interesting for our study, not only because of the lines of the grids but also because of the different positions of the figures and their unequal dimensions, which necessitated in the various *canevas* that each square unit vary according to the scene represented, following a definite system. Therefore, we will successively study, first, the different *positions;* second, the detail of the *proportions* analyzed by the subdivision of the initial square; and third, the functions that determine the *relationships* of the squares to one another.

The Different Positions

The theoretical canon establishes the total height of the standing man as equal to nineteen squares. The two essential and invariable lines are then 18 and 16, marking the forehead and the beginning of the shoulders. This interval of two squares is the only characteristic common to three positions, standing, seated, and kneeling (plates 52 and 53), and in the three cases, the number of squares counted from the ground is, respectively,

---

[5] Twelfth Dynasty, 2000–1788 B.C.

[6] Cf. A. M. Blackman, *The Rock Tombs of Meir,* 6 vols. (London: Egypt Exploration Society, 1914–53), 2:3, and plate 15.

standing: 16 to the shoulders, 18 to the forehead, 19 to the vertex;
seated: 12 to the shoulders, 14 to the forehead, 15 to the vertex;
kneeling: 9 to the shoulders, 11 to the forehead, 12 to the vertex.

These three positions provide three groups of numbers that are worthy of notice.

The three heights to the shoulders are to one another as 9, 12, and 16. They constitute a perfect geometric proportion in which the mean term, 12, is the square root of the product of the extremes.

The three heights to the forehead, 11, 14, and 18, constitute a near geometric proportion established with the numbers of the *canevas*. The perfect geometric proportion is 1 to $\sqrt{\phi}$ to ϕ. The ratio 18 to 11 is as ϕ to 1, and the ratio 14 to 11 is as $\sqrt{\phi}$ to 1.[7]

The three heights to the vertex, 12, 15, and 19, are very near the function that rules the growth of volumes. These three numbers also form an imperfect geometric proportion, which is completed and corrected through a second proportion 15, 19, and 24. The number 12 plays here the role of the unit for the number 24, which equals 2. The perfect proportion interposes between 1 and 2 the two geometric mean terms that are the cube roots of 2 and of 4, represented here by 15 and 19. The proof of the use of these numbers as an elementary base for the duplication of the cube is given in the southern corner of the west partition in the second register through the only background grid pattern drawn in this part of the tomb. This grid pattern is composed of a rectangle nineteen squares high and twenty-four squares long, and has no drawing on it. This rectangle is set up in such a way that the perpendicular drawn to its diagonal gives the geometric proof that we are clearly dealing with the irrational ratio of the cube root of 2.

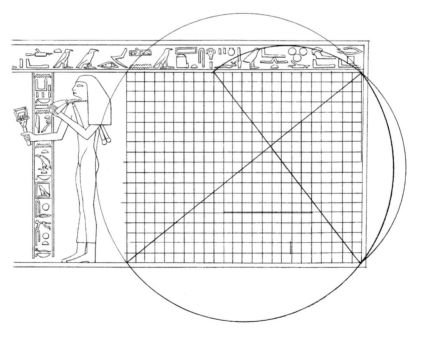

Fig. 247. Tomb of Ukhotep, grid pattern for the west partition, south corner, register 2

[7] The product of $11 \times 18 = 198$, whereas $14^2 = 196$.

It is above this rectangle demonstrating the function of the growth of volume and giving the whole numbers that enable the drawing of it[8] that the text is found that qualifies the nomarch as "noble chief without equal, ruling the secrets . . ." (fig. 247). The sistrum and *menat* players that follow this rectangle, as well as the harpist sculpted in the third register, confirm the relationship between the growth of volume and musical harmony.

In conclusion, the choice of the numbers governing the canon reveals a true teaching, and the inequalities of the squares are explained by the correction that is imposed by an irrational geometric function transcribed into whole numbers. Finally, in the three groups of numbers studied, *the seated man is the geometric mean term between the kneeling man and the standing man.*

Some Proportional Details Analyzed by Means of Subdividing the Initial Square (Plate 53)

Seated on a chair, Ukhotep is located on the third register at the north corner of the west wall. Through his location he should provide the functional "principles." He is drawn in black on a red grid. The rectangle in which he is inscribed is eleven large squares wide and fifteen high. These squares are subdivided vertically and horizontally into five, except for those that constitute the stool, of which 4×5 remain white and 3×5 are subdivided only vertically. Without taking into account their actual measurements, we will call the value of each small division "1 digit." The essential proportions indicated are:

- the height of the stool equals five squares, or 25 digits
- the height of the upper body equals ten squares, theoretically 50 digits, but actually 2 digits are subtracted, leaving 48 digits
- the forearm and the extended hand equals 24 digits, which equals a small cubit
- the forearm and the closed fist equals 20 digits, which equals a *remen* cubit
- the femorotibial connecting point equals 28 digits, which equals a royal cubit
- height of lower leg and knee equals 30 digits.

In numbers of digits, this figure gives the three values inscribed on the pharaonic measuring cubits,[9] and by comparing these indications with present-day biometric data, we observe the following proportional constants:

Taking the general average, the ratio between the height of a standing man and his upper body (head, neck, trunk) when seated is 100 to 52.36. Now, knowing that the ratio between the height of a person and his arm span is 100 to 104.72...,[10] it follows that the height of the upper body is half of the arm span. In choosing for the "canon" the ratio of 19/10, which equals the standing height to the height of the upper body, the Ancients evoked with a simple method the "ideal"

---

[8] The product of $12 \times 19 = 228$, whereas $15^2 = 225$. The product of $15 \times 24 = 360$, whereas $19^2 = 361$. Cf. the genesis of these numbers in chapter 9, figs. 107a and 107b. Cf. problem 32 of the Rhind Papyrus in which the requirement is to divide 2 by 19/12. The answer is 24/19 expressed in the form of unit fractions. The canon gives the second term of the proportion interposed between 12 and 19, that is, 15.

[9] Cf. chapter 10.

[10] The ratio between the fathom and the height of a man most often encountered is 1.045.... For the study of the proportions of the human body, besides the works already cited, we must mention the excellent tables of Decourt and Doumic, "Le Morphotype masculin" [see chapter 11, note 24].

function that gives the upper body the value of half the arm span. This is considered as $\pi/3$ for the height of a person with the value of 1. This comes to the following. If

$$\frac{\text{total height}}{\text{upper body height}} = \frac{100}{52.36} = 1.9098...,$$

then

$$\frac{\text{upper body height}}{\text{total height}} = \frac{10}{19.098} = 0.5236...,$$

which is the principle of the royal cycle cubit. It can also relate to the connection between the volume of the sphere equal to 10 and the cube in which it is inscribed, which is 19.0983..., starting from the function ϕ^2 for π.

Moreover, anthropometrics confirms the principle whereby the "human cubit" is contained four times in the length of the arm span. The figuration of the seated Ukhotep teaches, thanks to its small subdivisions, its relationship with the pharaonic measuring cubits and the number of digits adopted for them: the small cubit has 24 digits and corresponds in number to that of the vizier, and consequently, the arm span must be 4 small cubits of 24 digits, or 96 digits. The height of the upper body being, as we have seen, half the arm span, it must be 48 digits and not 50, as is specified by the vertex of the figure coming 2 digits short of the top of the fifteenth square (plate 53).

Subdivided in this way in accordance with the *canevas* principle, the superimposition of this figure thus summarizes the ratios that rigorously conform to anthropometric data and in no way contradicts the functional principle of the canon on which the figure is inscribed, but rather confirms it.

In the chapter on the cubits, we have shown the geometric function from which the numbers applied here to the human canon are derived. These numbers confirm that the cubit of 24 digits, marked on the royal cubits as the "small cubit," is actually the human cubit. *Thus man, as the Anthropocosmos, summarizes the measures of his Universe.*

The only divergence between the actual human canon and the canon of the *canevas* drawn here is the height of the femorotibial line. In the normal person, this is about one human cubit and consequently ought to measure 24 digits and not 28, here the value of the royal cubit. We are thus dealing with something we have noticed with regard to the royal canon. The proportions of the body of Ukhotep absolutely conform to the canon, except for the height of the lower leg. This measures a royal cubit instead of a small cubit. The accent is thus placed on the part of the leg governed by the zodiacal sign of Aquarius, the essential character of everything described in this tomb.

The Relationships of the Different Squares to One Another
(Plates 52 and 53)

Two small figures, a superintendent and the "bearer of the sandal bag," stand behind the seated Ukhotep (plate 53). In front of the nomarch, on the other side of a table of offerings, is the embalmer Henu, the young son of Ikeru, pouring pure water. He is followed by his son Ankh, who presents the vase of fire and offers incense (plate 52). The two kneeling figures make the *hotep* gesture and are followed by a figure named Khnum. This group has necessitated three grids with different dimensions, the largest of which is that of the vizier.

The superintendent and the bearer of the sandal bag are drawn on a square base for which *nineteen squares read in height coincide with eleven of Ukhotep's squares read in width* (fig. 248). The rabattement of the nineteen small squares onto the eleven large ones establishes a ratio between them of 19 to 11, which is part of the series of numbers generating the square root of 3 by successive additions of a ratio and its inverse.[11] The chair provides the base numbers that are the point of departure through the squares that remain white and those ruled vertically. The first denominators after unity are 3, 4, and 11, and the first numerators after 1 and 2 are 5 and 7.

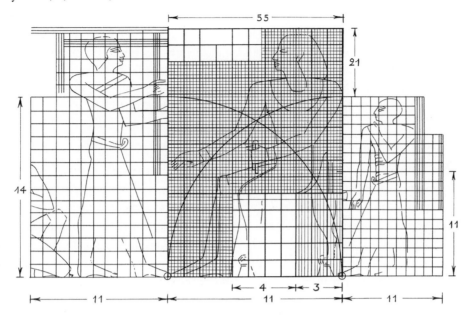

Fig. 248. Synoptic table of the different squares and the functions that connect them, west partition, north corner, register 2

Center, Ukhotep, seated; *right*, the sandal bearer (plate 53); *left*, Ankh, son of Henu, approaching the seated nomarch (omitting the offering table and the figure of Henu from plate 52).

The rectangle in which Ukhotep is drawn is proportioned according to the genetic function of this series of ratios, expressed by 15 : 11. One of the primary ratios, 7 to 4, is stated by the fact that the fourteen squares of the sandal bearer coincide with eight squares, read in height, of the vizier.

The eleventh line of the sandal bearer is the only one that extends into the large grid pattern (read vertically). This number is the chosen unity here, which confirms the width of the tableau that has eleven squares.

In summary, the large grid pattern of Ukhotep is to that of the sandal bearer as the square root of 3 is to 1, and it teaches us the numbers by means of which the *canevas* oscillates around the irrational.

The two embalmers, Henu and his son Ankh, are drawn on a grid whose nineteen squares should correspond to fifteen squares of the vizier, but this ratio is modified by a deviation of the upper border so that *fourteen squares of Henu, read in height, correspond to eleven squares of the nomarch, read in width*. In this ratio of 14 to 11 we recognize 4 : π, derived from $\pi = 1.2 \times \phi^2$ of the F series.[12]

Two questions arise: First, what is the connection between the square root of 3 and π, the functions that frame the vizier? Second, why, in the subdivision of the large squares of the vizier, are fifty-five small squares in width equal to fifty-four in height?

---

[11] Cf. chapter 8, "The *Canevas* and $\sqrt{3}$: A Syncopated Series" in the section "The Three Functions of the *Canevas*." See the list of these ratios and their genetic function.

[12] Cf. ibid., "The *Canevas* and $\sqrt{5}$," and the Fibonacci series.

This anomaly can be explained by a brief calculation. The total height of the rectangle that frames the nomarch is 5×15, which equals 75. After subtracting 54 from 75, 21 remains, which determines, at the level of the nomarch's head, the rectangle that has a ratio of 21 to 55. If we give 21 the value of unity, the number 55 corresponds to ϕ^2 and consequently $1.2 \times \phi^2 = 66$, or π.

In conclusion, Ukhotep, through his proportions transcribed into digits, provides the relationship between the measuring cubits and man; through the ratios between the three *canevas* he gives the functions of the hexagon and the circle; and through his irregularities, he draws attention to the base numbers. Finally, he is the connection between the straight line and the curve through the function ϕ^2.

PLATES 54–56 • TOMB OF UKHOTEP, NORTH PARTITION

The principles are expressed at the north: Ukhotep and his wife, Thothotep, are portrayed at the western end and contain in potentiality the totality of the themes and functions developed in their presence. These are the largest figures in the tomb and consequently they contain all the others. Furthermore, the irregularities of how they are drawn reveal their functional character and their "particular coefficient": the tableau in which they are drawn provides all the movements, angles, and deviations of the rest of the partition, corresponding to the two natures, male and female, because duality is emphasized in all the figurations in this tomb. That which is first raised is then lowered, that which is fluid becomes fixed; that which is spiritual is corporified.

The whole of the wall is divided into three registers in which the direction of the scenes is from east to west, toward the standing vizier and his wife, and the themes should therefore be read from right to left, the direction in which the small figures are moving.

The uninterrupted lower register contains scenes of boats in the papyrus thickets of the swamps (plate 56). By observing the positions of the figures one can determine the angular play indicated by the position of the poles and by the articulations of the knees and the arms, which are the hinges of the human body and are here related to what vegetates and grows. Now, the triangle, determined by the angle, is growth through the seminal power.[13] *The angle is the ligature point of two principles;* the figures bind the reeds in bunches, and by making a boat out of them, these reeds will float. The rushes, the original plant of the marshlands, are tied together in order to float, and the raftsmen are standing on the ground. It is necessary to read these things as animated drawings. We next notice the age of these raftsmen, or a sign of their aging given by the old man who supports himself on a cane by the end of the boat. He indicates that the goal of the operation is attained, which is confirmed by the fact that the bunches of tied rushes are carried by several men on whom these burdens become heavier and heavier, until they are put down again on the ground (plate 55). The winged creatures are placed upside down and carried as an offering along with a calf's head, some bones surrounded by flesh, a *khepesh* thigh, and squashes, which are a fruit rich in water (plate 54). All these scenes lead to our two great figures, who are principles because they are not pictured with navels. These principles are designated by their names, one of which is the feminine of the other, but both are *hotep (htp)*, that is, the reverse of the name Ptah *(pth)*, the Fire fallen to earth. One gets the impression here of reading a text by a Hermetic master from the Middle Ages.

The middle and upper registers are interrupted by a seated Ukhotep (plate 55) accompanied by his wife, who is sitting on her heels and is much smaller than he. The greater part of the middle

---

[13] In this regard, see the hieroglyph designating the number 3 written in the middle of the phallus. Note also the exposure of the genitals on this partition.

register is occupied by the scene of "hunting birds with the net," drawn on a grid (plate 56). This net contains some winged creatures and is fixed by a knot at each end: the one on the right to a stake that is not drawn; the one on the left to a rope pulled by the men. This rope is in turn fixed to the ground by a stake, and it can be seen that in spite of the tension the four men exert on it toward the left (which ought to release the end attached to the stake), the rope remains taut. Immediately following the net, the three musicians—singer, harpist, and flutist—teach that the laws of harmony revealed by the numbers of the net and the laws of musical harmony are one and the same. As for the singer, he holds one hand in front of himself and the other beneath his ear, as is still done today by the singers of *zhikr* in order to make the sounds of certain letters vibrate, in a way similar to the magical effect of the Hindu *Aum*.

On the upper register, the bulls, after being tied with great effort, are caught in a lasso, then walk very docilely, preceded by a skeletal man and followed by a heavyset man, who direct the bulls toward the seated nomarch. Clearly, the nomarch plays the role of a divider, separating the images of the upper and middle registers, and allowing the lower register to continue uninterrupted. This separating role is clearly indicated by the fact that the scenes behind the nomarch are nothing more than functional in relation to the idea described in front of him: that which the horned cattle represented is now explained by the wrestling men as being only a reversal; as for the middle register, the scenes of the net and the musicians are transformed behind the nomarch into offerings, some of which are held up and others lowered.

Fig. 249

Taken together, we see everywhere in these figurations the idea of linking, of knotting. The knot is the juncture, the fixation, but it should be noted that in every case both ends of the tie can be seen. The actual symbol of the *ukh* is a strap encircling the *wadj* scepter surmounted by two feathers: vegetal growth, knotting, aeration (fig. 249).

What is it in nature that binds? Or rather, through what means does nature bind? Through air. The most subtle must necessarily be bound in order to become the most material.[14] Each detail of the tomb analyzes this theme, and we see, for example, on the south (realization) wall, among the scenes of the hunt in the desert, a man who leads three bulls tied by three ropes that he holds in his hand. This man is *a tree*, his arms are branches, his hair and his face are leaves, and the stick on which he supports himself marks the appearance of a bud at each place of its branching (fig. 250). The three ropes by which he holds the bulls subsequently become only *two*.

---

[14] Air is the subtle nourishment essential to life.

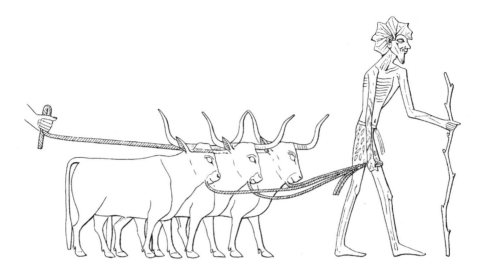

Fig. 250. Detail of the south partition

Figure leading three bulls by three ropes that unite in his hand, and of which only two ends are seen when they leave his hand, which evokes the relationship 2 to 3.

The three bulls have their horns tied by a single rope whose end is folded to form the *s* sign in the hand of a figure who guides and restrains the bulls from behind. This same sign is held in the right hand of the seated Ukhotep, plate 55.

Now, Ukhotep is master of Cusae (Kas), whose symbol is the joining of two long-necked felines (fig. 251). This strange figure has already been related to the sign *sma-ta,* the joining of the Two Lands around the trachea. Finally, the name Kas can be related to the word signifying "to bind," "to attach," "to knot," and it has been interpreted as "meaning that the enemies of Osiris have been tied up at this place by his son Horus."

Fig. 251. Symbol of the city of Cusae (Kas),
capital of the fourteenth nome of Upper Egypt

This symbol recalls the Narmer Palette, which I take to represent the ancestor of the Emerald Tablet.

Brief Analysis of the Geometric Functions of the North Partition

If we use the axis of equilibrium of Ukhotep as the vertical, the *canevas* on which the standing nomarch and his wife are drawn (plate 54) shows certain irregularities.

- All the verticals of the large *canevas* are parallel to the axis of equilibrium of the vizier.
- The horizontals are exactly perpendicular only at the shin level of the nomarch, five squares high to four wide. The horizontal lines stop when they touch the back leg of Thothotep; the second and third lines include two strokes, one above the other, one of which stays horizontal while the other is slightly angled.
- Between the axis of equilibrium of Thothotep and the stick on which Ukhotep is supported there is a complete break in the horizontal lines. They begin again on a slightly higher level.
- Still another sloping line can be noticed that crosses the vertical tangent to the bent knee of the vizier. This line, drawn in several sections, is perpendicular to the deviations in the upper border of the tableau and to the registers of the small figures, and thus indicates their movement.
- A slight slope makes the tableau somewhat wider at its upper edge than at its base.

These two heights and these two widths impose a double proportion. The ratio between the maximum height and the smaller width determines the angle γ (fig. 252), which defines the function of the pentagon. The ratio between the largest width and the smallest height is 3 to 4 and defines the sacred triangle. The junction of these two proportions determines the slope of the upper and left side borders.

Ukhotep is standing in the 3 to 4 triangle, and his personal coefficient as well as the angle of his stick corresponds to the geometric functions derived from the sacred triangle.

His height to the vertex is $18\frac{3}{4}$ instead of 19, and by taking the fraction that extends beyond the line of the forehead as 1, it can be placed twenty-four times in his height to the forehead and twenty-five times in his height to the vertex. The angle thus determined has a ratio of 7 to 24, double the angle 1 to 7, defined by the angle of his stick. The inverse, 24 to 7, is double 3 to 4, the generating angle of the preceding two.[15]

The axis of equilibrium of Thothotep gives the vertical and becomes the large side of the right triangle 1 to 7 for which the vizier's stick is the hypotenuse. Thus, it is this that specifies her particular coefficient. Conversely, it is he who, through the 1 to 7 triangle, will give the metric nuances between the units of their squares, some larger and some smaller, causing the breaks and certain slight slopes in their *canevas*. All of this is the principle of the passage from the square root of 49 to the square root of 50, which governs the *remen* and royal cubits that we see evoked here.[16]

Thothotep comes out of the governing triangle of the pentagon, and her personal coefficient is the function ϕ. She holds the *wadj* scepter in her hand; the height of the scepter is 17 with respect to the height of 19 of the *canevas*, and corresponds to $\sqrt{5}/2$ (plate 54). The crown of her skull is slightly higher than her husband's, and it is contained twenty-two times in her total height and twenty-one times in her height to the forehead. Here the function of the cycle $\pi/3$ that governs the royal cubit is evoked.

[15] Cf. chapter 7, "Addition and Subtraction of Angles in Proportional Notation."
[16] Cf. chapter 10; chapter 15, "Diadem, I Assume Thee."

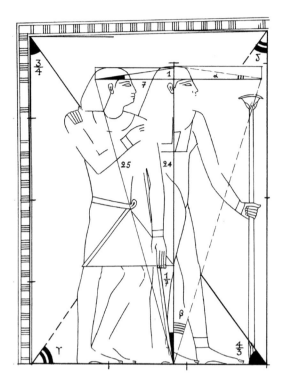

Fig. 252. North partition, west corner

Relation between the particular coefficient of Ukhotep, the angle of his stick, and the 3 to 4 triangle in which he is inscribed. The triangle that governs the functions of Thothotep is related to ϕ and to the functions of the pentagon.

In conclusion, the geometric functions expressed in the figure of Ukhotep are those of the sacred triangle, and connect to the passage from surface 1 to surface 2 by means of the angle 1 to 7. The functions governing Thothotep are irrational; they are connected to the pentagon and rule the ratio π.

The gesture of the embrace of the male principle, Ukhotep, by the female principle, Thothotep, demonstrates a ligature that is manifested geometrically by the association of the two functions governing the cubits. The slopes, angles, and other irregularities are the methods employed to coordinate them.

It is particularly important for us to see the confirmation here of what we have observed elsewhere. The sacred triangle (Ramesses IX) or the hexagon (Thoth of Karnak) is attributed to the male and solar character, whereas the feminine aspect is connected to the functions of the vegetative pentagon (Seshat and Thothotep). We will continue to find a similar distinction between the axis of Amun with its return (the angle 1 to 7) and the axis of Mut that defines the pentagon in the Temple of Man at Luxor.[17]

---

[17] Cf. chapter 20; commentaries on plates 80–90.

The "Net for Capturing Birds" in the Tomb of Ukhotep,
North Partition, East Part (Plate 56)

The very great importance given to the net, which is revealed upon a close study of it, prompts us to provide here, in detail, its principal elements. As always, the Ancients have chosen from among practical tools, whose functions are invariable, the image that best represented the intimate meaning of the thought they wanted to express. The "hunting of birds" with the net signifies the capture of the spirit or of the abstraction, in other words, that which is not otherwise graspable save through the means that the net symbolizes.

With the image of the net, allusion is made to a primordial action—that of making spirit concrete (giving form). This is confirmed by the play of the numbers in the tomb of Ukhotep and by the intervention of the *neters*, particularly of Thoth (Hermes) at Karnak.[18]

—ᴡᴡ—

The capturing of wild birds by means of a net is frequently represented in the tombs of dignitaries. The most complete description known is in the tomb of Ti at Saqqara (Fifth Dynasty), in three tableaux that describe three distinct operations: (1) the placing of the net; (2) the net remaining open while the birds come to rest on the pond, with the men silently waiting for the signal to close the snare; (3) the closing of the trap and the capture of the birds.

In all scenes of this type these three operations are summarized in one or two images at most, and in every case the interpretation is rather difficult for anyone who has never seen traps of this sort, because the bas-reliefs are drawn according to a synthesis-scheme that represents the open net, the net in the process of being closed, and the closed net all at the same time. But even allowing for the portrayal of three moments in one, in all the cases some irregularities persist that have especially held our attention, and that the net at Meir helps to clarify, thanks to the *canevas* on which it is drawn.

The functional principle of these bird traps—which are still used in central and southern France—is the following: two rectangular nets are arranged on both sides of a pond, each fixed by two stakes at the corners of the pond (*a, b, c, d* fig. 253). These two rectangles are made rigid by mooring stakes from one side to the four corners of the pond and from the other to the four exterior corners of the net (*e, f, g, h*). Ropes are fixed to these four corners and the corners are tied two by two, from one side to a stake driven into the ground (*A*), and from the other to the single rope pulled by the men (*P'*). The two rectangular nets are supposed to lie on the ground awaiting the arrival of the birds. During the wait, silence is recommended to the hunters, who are hidden in the reeds and who keep themselves ready to act on the signal of the head of the team. When the number of birds resting on the pond is sufficient, the leader unfurls a long scarf. At this signal the men suddenly pull on the rope, causing the two flaps to rise upright and then close down on the pond.[19]

This is the practical explanation suggested by the use of a similar device by poachers in our day. But the drawings of the bas-reliefs do not conform to this description. The two rectangles on each side of the pond are never drawn. In the first stage, the image ought to represent a hexagon, and the length of the ropes should be *hAf* and *eP'g* (fig. 253).

Now, all the depictions of snares, open or closed, show the hexagonal form of *dLbaKc*. From this we can assume that the flaps of the net are held up vertically on each side of the pond.

[18] Cf. plate 60.
[19] From Montet, *Scènes de la vie privée,* pp. 47–48.

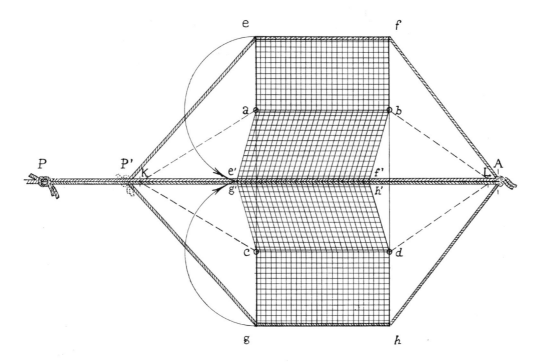

Fig. 253. Superposition of the open and closed net, suggested by its practical use, upon the pharaonic design

Open net: *hAfeP'g*. Closed net: the tightened rope from *P* to *A* and the square *abcd*. The pharaonic design: *dkbaKc*.

When the net is closed shut, the image should no longer show the pond covered by two rectangles held at the center by the double rope, and it should no longer be drawn as a hexagon, which, however, is how it is represented. Further, the ropes from the side of stake *A* should be loosened, whereas they are still taut, at least if there are only two ropes attached to stake *A* and sliding in the eyes of the knots on the outer sides *ef* and *gh* of the nets. An experiment demonstrates that by pulling on the rope tied to the two preceding at *P'*, the flaps would close and the knot would arrive at *P*; the ropes would form only a double line from *A* to *P*. But in the drawing of the image, which should show its practical application, the lengths of the ropes before and after the closing of the trap do not correspond to the reality. Thus, the net was used as a symbol, and the grid pattern leads us to see in this figure the intention of exhibiting the geometric functions and numbers that we can read on the *canevas* (fig. 254).

The pond is a square of 26, half of which is 13 and corresponds to *QB*. All the action unfolds between the two knots, *P* and *A*. The distance measured between these knots (taking the average of the other squares for the unsquared part) corresponds to eighty-nine divisions. The distance *QA* between the edge of the pond *bd* and the stake *A* driven into the ground that marks the end of the *canevas* is twenty-one squares (figs. 254, 255). The half-width of the pond is 13, so the distance *AB* is equal to 21 + 13, or 34; this measurement is also the height of the register with the upper border. We recognize here a series of numbers that constitute the additive series 13, 21, 34, ..., 89, completed by the number 55, which corresponds to the distance between knot *P* and the center *B* of the pond. This is the F series in which each term is to the following one as 1 is to *φ*. These numbers result from the harmonic decomposition of the total *PA*, or 89 (fig. 255).

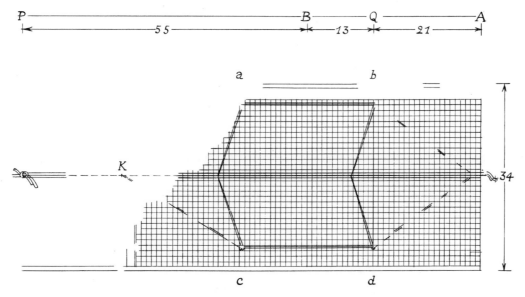

Fig. 254. Design of the net on the north partition of the tomb of Ukhotep with the principal numbers that it reveals

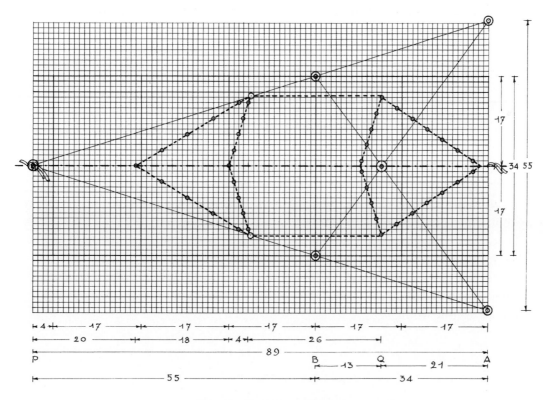

Fig. 255. Harmonic decomposition

The width 55 is equal to the length *hf* of the open net of figure 253.

To make this construction, it is necessary to draw a perpendicular line from the center rope to point *A* and then complete the grid by taking the breadth of the pond plus the two open flaps placed on the ground at each side for the width (figs. 253–255). This gives a complete grid and will allow us to understand the numbers indicated by the representation of the net in the tomb of Ukhotep. These numbers make clear that it is unnecessary to add the actual lengths of the ropes before and after the closing of the net.

The presence of musicians near this net, the harmonic division of which reveals the numerical series of the golden section, is a great and deep teaching, which demonstrates through an image the origin of the Pythagorean assertions according to which the mathematical link is unique and consists in proportion. "Every figure, every harmonic grouping, every astronomical revolution, manifests the unity of proportion to him who would learn according to the true method; now, this unity will be apparent to he who correctly understands what we teach; he will recognize that a single link naturally unites all things."[20]

This is the teaching of this tomb: one cannot dissociate musical harmony from the geometrical functions of the golden section that govern growth and vegetation. Also, the grid patterns of the net and of the men who are pulling it are in the relationship of the fifth. Growth and vegetation cannot be dissociated from the cycles of time that govern them; also, the ratios between the *canevas* of the pullers of the net and those of the bearers of offerings are to each other as 3 is to π,[21] the function governing the cycle cubit already indicated by the "particular coefficient" of Thothotep. (Keep in mind that Thoth is master of time and rules lunar time.)

Harmonic proportion is this "link that naturally unites all things," and it is in this also that we must look for the function that connects all the very diverse *canevas* of this wall of the tomb of Ukhotep, whose name is written with the symbol of the *link* (fig. 249). Thus the gestures of the scenes, the "particular coefficients," the numbers of the *canevas*, the proportions of the tableaux, are all harmoniously connected by one and the same function and all the possibilities that it implies.

———————

The person who is conscious of his being, by saying "*I* live, *I* die, *I* move, *I* walk . . . ," knows how to distinguish the continuous Being (the *I*) from the provisional, terrestrial form that this *I* animates; there is also an intimate, "esoteric," functional sense that animates the perceptible thing. It is therefore appropriate that this person should inscribe on his "eternal dwelling"—which we call a tomb—the intimate, living, immortal meaning of the knowledge acquired in the field of his earthly activity, in conformity with the gifts that belong to his being that survives.

Thus, these small "eternal dwellings" open an infinitely large domain to the spirit and become the "lodges of initiation" for the intelligence of the heart.

This is only possible if the speaking symbol (the hieroglyph) is given a root that designates the functional notion animating the various applications that can be given to the figured object, creating thus a cabalistic writing.

———————

[20] Cf. Theon of Smyrna, *Le Nombre de Platon*, part 2, §31, p. 137.

[21] See the numerical demonstration in fig. 256.

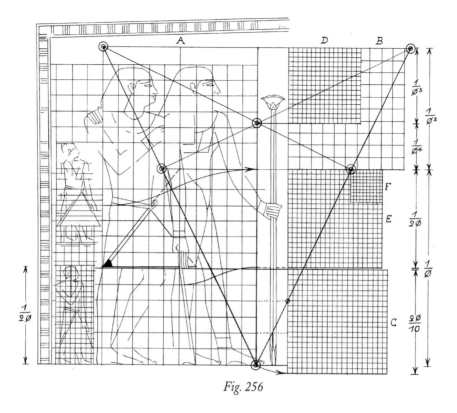

Fig. 256

A synoptic table of the functions that govern all the *canevas* of the north wall, on the basis of harmonic decomposition. This decomposition, established on twenty squares, determines the height from the base of the apron to $1/(2\phi)$ with the back angle of this loincloth in the relationship of 1 to $2/\phi$.

$$A = \text{square of the standing nomarch} = \text{unity} = 1$$

$$B = \text{square of the seated nomarch} = \frac{2}{\phi^2}$$

$$C = \text{square of the offering bearers} = \frac{2\phi}{10}$$

$$D = \text{square of the wrestlers (third register)} = \frac{1.25}{\phi^3}$$

$$E = \text{square of the pullers of the net} = \frac{1}{2\phi}$$

$$F = \text{square of the net} = \frac{1}{3\phi}$$

The offering bearers and the pullers of the net are in the same register, so that twenty-one C squares are equal to twenty-two E squares in height; and twenty-three D squares are equal to twenty-two E squares, numbers approximating irrational functions:

$$\frac{C}{E} = \frac{2\phi}{10} : \frac{1}{2\phi} = \frac{4\phi^2}{10} = \frac{\pi}{3} \quad \text{and} \quad \frac{E}{D} = \frac{1}{2\phi} : \frac{1.25}{\phi^3} = \frac{\phi^3}{2.5\phi} = \frac{\pi}{3}.$$

This study was made after the publication of the tracings at one-sixth scale that were done very carefully by Blackman [*The Rock Tombs of Meir*], who has kindly allowed us to use his plates. We have reconfirmed the precision of his work. The accuracy of these scale drawings is confirmed by the fact that certain irregularities cannot be accidental because they correspond exactly to the complexity of the functions that are also found at Luxor.

The word *skht*,[22] used in the tomb of Ukhotep at Meir to designate the "the bird hunt" and the "marshy terrain," has numerous uses, the general sense of which seems to be "to seize" with the added meaning of "to stop" or "to give form."

The phrase written above the men pulling the net in the tomb at Meir provides two of the essential uses of this word:

- "Placing the snare [*skht*], taking the birds into the snare [*skht* plate 56] by the best men of the marshlands [*skht*, plate 55]." The latter word, determined by a straight horizontal band topped by three bundles of rushes, designates the wetland, which, after the retreat of the floodwaters, is ready to be seeded.
- A feminine *neter* named Sekhet was the divinity of the land left wet after the withdrawal of the waters. Determined by a female figure holding a duck in one hand and a fish in the other, her son was Heb, the "net" *neter*, and she was the protective divinity of all those who took birds and fish with nets in the flooded lands.[23]
- Thoth, master of the city of the Eight, is also "master of *skht*" in the sense of weaving and of the bird hunt, as we will see later on (plates 60 and 61).
- *Skht* also signifies "to weave" and designates the land, the district, and the place of weaving.
- In mathematics, regarding a decreasing arithmetic progression: ". . . until taking into the net [*skht*] he who is under the last."[24]
- In medicine, regarding an incantation, the eighth incantation against a sickness or an epidemic: ". . . the tension [?] [*skht*] of thy net avoid me . . . I am one of thy escaped birds."[25]
- In the ritual of the foundation of the temple: "Grinding, to form [*skht*] the first brick . . ." in the sense of "uniting water to earth," that is, "earth seizing the water."
- A case in which the royal loincloth that encircles the small of the back is called *skht wat* (*wat* means "one," or "unique," or "particular") and is translated by "loincloth with a tail."

Thus, this word *sekht* is the cabala at the heart of the reading.

———

We can now see how the tableaux in the tomb of Ukhotep are an example of the application, through the human canon, of the living functions of the "master builder's grid."

Fig. 257. Expressive emblem: the symbol
of the fourteenth nome of Upper Egypt, the "nome of the tree"

[22] The *kh* is pronounced as the German *ch* in *nacht*. One can read it as *sekht;* not writing the vowel is conventional.

[23] Cf. Montet, *Scènes de la vie privée*, pp. 4–7.

[24] Cf. chapter 6, problem no. 64. For the symbol *skht*, see chapter 10, fig. 120 (vol. 1).

[25] Cf. Breasted, *Smith Papyrus*, "Eighth Magical Incantation," 1.8.20.10.

This relationship between the names of the nomarch, the nome, and the city (to which are connected the functions of the bearer of this name, along with the play of numbers and the vital symbolism expressed in the genetic meaning revealed in this succinct analysis of a single wall of the tomb of Ukhotep at Meir) should put Egyptologists on their guard against a too simplistic, so-called historical explanation.

An extraordinary refinement of thought and an uncommon science are expressed here in a writing that our rationalistic training no longer understands at first glance, but that allows us to glimpse a mode of thinking that must lead toward knowledge of a vital character that is lacking in our time.

THE USE OF A GRID BY THE MAYA

PLATE 57 • A MAYAN GRID

This hieroglyphic panel comes from the temple of El Palacio, located at the center of the Palenque site.[26] It is

a hieroglyphic panel 2.45m wide and 2.63m long. It is remarkably well preserved and of a still unequaled execution with 262 signs, of which only 7 are illegible.

The most remarkable idiosyncrasy of this ensemble is that the initial series of seven glyphs, which correspond to the year 672, is represented not by simplified signs, but by figurations of complete gods or animals.[27]

For the study of their writing, Mayan monuments include painted or engraved inscriptions that decorate the walls or steles of their religious buildings, as well as carved inscriptions that are more numerous and the best preserved.

It is upon this group of documents that the wisdom of a remarkable group of researchers has been exercised. Their study has led them to decipher the hieroglyphs and the Mayan signs and, by this path, to the knowledge of their mathematical and astronomical science.

To write numbers, the Maya utilized points and horizontal bars. The point was equivalent to one unit, the bar to five units. For example, three superimposed bars surmounted by four aligned points represented the number 19.

Their system of numbering was vigesimal,[28] whereas ours is decimal. . . .

The Maya knew the zero as we do, which they represented by a stylized conch shell. . . .

Besides the system of transcribing numbers by bars and points, the Maya represented the numbers from 0 to 19 by glyphs, all of which include a head.

Their writing counted, moreover, 20 glyphs to designate each of the days of their religious calendar, 19 glyphs to designate each of the months and the supplementary period of 5 days of the solar calendar, and 9 glyphs to designate each of the periods of time: *kin, uinal, tun, katun, baktun, piktun, kalabtun, kinchiltun, alautun.* There is one glyph for the moon, one for the planet Venus, four glyphs for the cardinal points and their corresponding colors, and nine glyphs for the divinities of the lower world. The principle gods of the Mayan pantheon also had their glyphs. At the present time, 150 hieroglyphs have been deciphered, being close to one-third of the signs catalogued until now. The task of archaeologists is further complicated by the fact that each glyph has several variants.

[26] Cf. P. Rivet, *Cités Maya* (Paris: Albert Guillot, 1954), fig. 71.
[27] Ibid., p. 92.
[28] The Celtic system of calculation.

Mayan writing was undoubtedly essentially ideographic, but it seems that it allowed for certain syllabic elements. Its use was only completely abandoned at the beginning of the eighteenth century after the destruction by the Spanish of the last independent Mayan city, Tayacal, in 1697. We can be absolutely sure that the Mayan hieroglyphic system had nothing in common with the Egyptian hieroglyphic system.[29]

Beneath the reproduction in plate 57 of the hieroglyphic panel and to the left, in *B,* we give a diagram with only the squares; in *C* the numbers of the squares are included to facilitate the reading. They have been classified in this way to allow reading of the glyph numbers in lengths, surfaces, and ratios at a single glance.

Note that the numbers that generate this figure are found constantly in Egypt:

The seven large squares to the left. The neighboring column gives the same relationship, 1 to 7, but each unit is divided into four and provides the number 28. This fact recalls the number of digits on the royal pharaonic cubit.

The general height of this tableau is nineteen glyphs, for a width of 18, the identical ratio to that of the pharaonic human canon.

The eighteen squares at the bottom are divided into three groups of six each.

The rectangle in which three figures are inscribed that are ten glyphs wide and five high evokes the 1 to 2 rectangle and gives fifty squares as the surface. These three figures, which represent the three celestial principles of the origin, are seated on three straw mats recalling the sign *pe,* which is taken to mean a mat but is identical with the "barrel" that is used for measuring grains and that is part of the word *pt,* the sky.

The tableau measures 2.63 meters in height, which corresponds within a centimeter to 5 pharaonic royal cubits.

We discover here the fundamental relationship of 1 to 7 by means of which passage is made from the surface 49 to the surface 50, in which are inscribed the three figures on a square with a surface of 100, therefore the double.

Very certainly there is a kinship in the expression of the knowledge of the old traditions among the Maya with the same pharaonic tradition, but presented in an ideogrammatic fashion that is more difficult to decipher than the always pure hieroglyphic writing.

INVESTIGATION OF THE *CANEVAS* IMPOSED BY THE REPRESENTATIONS AND PROPORTIONS OF THE FIGURES

PLATES 58 AND 59 • THE *KAMUTEF* OF THE NORTHEAST CORNER OF THE TRANSEPT: A STUDY OF ITS GEOMETRIC FUNCTIONS

The bas-relief in plate 58 is sculpted on the outer face of the north wall of the "court of the belly," or transept, of the temple of Luxor (fig. 199, no. 16), and its placement therefore corresponds to the level of the sex organs of the Man of the Temple. Let us recall that the whole exterior east facade of the transept, as well as the northeast corner, is of rough-hewn stone. Extending out from the mass of unhewn blocks, the north facade is smooth, but no bas-reliefs were carved there under the reign of Amenhotep III. Only some graffiti from a later era—of which this *kamutef* is a part— are found, in no apparent order, on this wall.

---

[29] Rivet, *Cités Maya,* pp. 51–54.

We are dealing with a *kamutef* (the literal meaning of which is "bull-his-mother") that signifies the primordial seed acting in itself, or self-conception, that is, the "Adamic creation" (Adam Kadmon).[30] In the myth, *kamutef* is actually associated with the origin of the creation as well as with the Hermopolitan revelation.

The first lands surged up from the primordial waters, "the marvelous hill of primordial times." On this hill the first manifestations of life appeared, the frogs and serpents that formed the first four divine couples. From this comes the name "the city of the Eight," which designates Hermopolis, capital of the nome of Thoth. These eight primordials had names that mean the primordial waters, the obscurity, the secret, the eternal.[31]

But before the creation of these first four divine couples, there was "He whose name is hidden" (Amun). He appeared first in the form of a serpent Kamutef, and then became Irta, that which is made into earth.

—∿—

In the *kamutef* represented here, the chest and the calf are traversed by two horizontal joints linked by a vertical joint that separates out the whole front part of the figure. A second vertical joint under the joint cutting the calf defines a measurement that allows us to draw a rectangle with the proportion 4 to 10 between these first three joints (fig. 258).

Nineteen times the height of each unit thus defined by the joints is the height between the soles of the feet and the line that separates the forehead from the figure's headdress. The study of the different pharaonic canons teaches us that there are only two possible *canevas*: eighteen squares to the forehead for nineteen to the vertex in the earlier era, and twenty-one to the forehead for twenty-two and a fraction to the vertex in the Late Period. It is therefore necessary to modify the unit indicated by the joints. It should either be a little larger to obtain the unit of the older *canevas*, or a little smaller to obtain the unit of the *canevas* of the Late Period, and this research leads to a curious result:

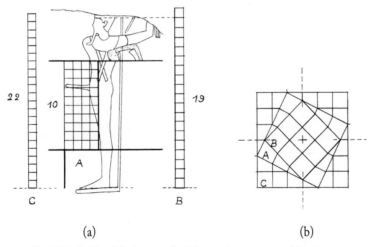

(a)   (b)

Fig. 258. Study of the kamutef *of the northeast corner of the transept*

(a) The rectangle in the proportion 4 to 10 is defined by the joints of the stones and the extension of the interior joint, and defines side *A* of four squares. *(b)* Side *A* is the hypotenuse of a triangle with a base of 4 and a side of 2. Each unit *C* is $2/\sqrt{5} = 0.8944....$ Side *B* is the hypotenuse of a triangle with a base of 3 and a side of 1. Each unit *B* is $\sqrt{10}/3 = 1.0541....$

[30] Already noted in *The Temple in Man*.
[31] Cf. I. Schwaller de Lubicz, *Her-Bak, Egyptian Initiate*, p. 135.

Let us call *A* the unit square of the small side of the rectangle defined by the joints of the stones. First, four *A* units make up the *hypotenuse* of a triangle in the proportion 1 to 2, the base and perpendicular of which are measured in the smaller *C* units, which allows us to establish the *canevas* of the Late Period, twenty-two squares and a fraction to the vertex.

Second, three *A* units serve as the *base* of a triangle in the proportion of 1 to 3. The subdivision of its diagonal into three defines the value of side *B*, which allows us to divide the height of the *kamutef* to the forehead by 18 and 19 to the vertex, following the older canon.

The sum of the angular ratios 1 to 2 and 1 to 3 equals 1 to 1 so that square *B* is at 45° in square *C* (fig. 258b).

Here the joints have led us to establish an originating grid that in turn is in some way the mathematical "androgyne" for the two canons.

Plate 59A shows, moreover, the application of the ϕ dividing formula for the *kamutef*: the phallus, instead of being at the halfway point of the height of the body, is at the navel. The *canevas* of twenty-two squares demonstrates this by the relationship between the numbers 13, from the soles of the feet to the phallus, and 21, to the forehead between the eye and the headdress, where the twenty-first square occurs in the Late Period, the time in which the demonstration we have just made enables us to place this bas-relief.

Also, we should note that in the *canevas* of nineteen squares, the sixteenth line always crosses the base of the neck, a proportion that is not precisely applied in this figure (plate 59B). On the contrary, the level of the shoulders corresponds to the nineteenth line of the canon of the Late Period and conforms with it. This allows us to date this figuration to after the Twenty-sixth Dynasty.

This image of the *kamutef* thus becomes the description of the passage from one canon to another by starting from the original functions 1 to 2 and 1 to 3. This is a very beautiful numerical illustration of the mysterious Heliopolitan principle of the self-creation of Tum manifested at Heliopolis. Heliopolis, Memphis, and Hermopolis[32] are the places consecrated to the three principles in the creative Unity.

MYTH AND SYMBOLISM

The fortress built on the shifting sands of rational materialism is now in the process of collapsing. Rational evolutionary theory is no longer a sturdy railing for the biologist, but a thread that threatens to snap at any time. The opinions forged in this time of great pride remain standard principles, and as for religious themes and the origins of the great systems of religious metaphysics, there is the conviction that they are superstitions born of human egoism and the fears of primitive peoples when faced with the forces of nature.

And thus, even today, it is assumed that pharaonic religion began in this way, in spite of the certainty we now have of the existence, since the First Dynasty, of a sound metaphysics, a complete writing, and a symbolism that serves as the basis of the whole history spread out over four thousand years.

The incoherence of meaning in the texts on stone and papyrus is attributed to the need for ambiguity when speaking of the "gods" and their activities in order to impress the people and to leave them to fill in the gaps with their imaginations and superstitions. The clergy is seen as a band of profiteers preying on the fears of an uncultivated people, with politico-religious struggles for the supremacy of various bogus "gods" attributed to them.

---

[32] Hermopolis became el-Ashmunein in Arabic times, the Jewish Aeschmain, the mercurial spirit of the Hermeticists.

So certain Egyptologists believed they could fill the gaps in the "logical meaning" they desired by an imaginary "historicism." This is understandable, in a pinch; what is inexcusable is when these authors do not distinguish an authentic text from their own fabrications.

A mythic legend, or anthropomorphization of metaphysical principles, is already a "historical" form put at the disposal of the people so they will be able to remember and spread this teaching; it is not a ruse to deceive them. Certain children's tales and many customs still have the goal of the *preservation,* in our time, of certain teachings of a Hermetic character.

How can we make people understand that it is one and the same principle, the names of which change according to the phases of genesis, unless we represent these phases by different figurations? Symbolism distinguishes Isis from Maāt, Hathor from Mut. There is only a single femininity, but it acts differently in different environments. When a *primordial serpent* is shown that becomes Kamutef, then Irta, the principle of dividing in half, of androgyny is evoked, and through this a realization of the tangible with earth for its image, the process of birth. Then these phases are synthesized in Amun. And this Amun is both lunar and solar, the two essential lineages in the Universe, which symbolize the two crowns of the Two Lands of the kingdom (the Cosmos). Certainly, the ultimate stage of perfection will be the *reuniting* of these two crowns, the complements, the antagonisms, the powers that order the transitory, mortal aspects of the Universe.

When these things are written with images and not with letters or conventional signs, it is in the *functional* meaning of that which the image represents that one must look for the significance that a *grammatically incoherent* (but vitally logical) composition will impart.[33]

When one uses the letter *n*, represented by an undulating line, a wave in general, which can signify what we call "energy," in order to speak of the primordial milieu, and therefore of the energetic but not yet polarized milieu, then one will write *Nun,* the primordial *ocean,* with two *n*'s, the waves separated by a space, as Moses said: the waters above and the waters below. The *waters above* appear in *darkness,* in *night,* in *shadows,* as long as they are not thrown down to become the *mound* of earth, the coagulation of spirit, also the prison of the fire Ptah, the Sethian aspect that has been, like Prometheus, chained to a rock for stealing fire from heaven. It is therefore a question of the principle of scission, primordial but also universal, and at the origin of all life. All this happens simultaneously. In order to explain it (because we are the slaves of time and space), we must split that which is a singular phenomenon, what we will call karyokinesis, conception, and so on, and in general, the *Fiat lux.*

How can one speak of the disputes of idiotic clergymen who are hungry for power when the issue concerns the organization of an empire of wisdom, the knowledge of whose secrets alone gives the human being all the power that he or she can receive in this life? We are dealing with the sacred aspect of Hermeticism. This has nothing to do with the transmutation of the atom through mathematical formulas and cyclotrons. Saint John the Evangelist cannot be confused with some "catch as catch can"* wrestler.

When one wishes to indicate the phase that follows the emergence from the primal ocean of the land, the separating of earth from water, one writes *nw, nu,* symbolized by undulating lines accompanied by three vases and the sky; this is the Water, the contained energy, now having form. There

---

[33] R. Abellio, in his work *La Bible, document chiffré, essai sur la restitution des clefs de la science numerale secrète* (Paris: Gallimard, 1950), believed himself able to rediscover this secret meaning based on the fact that the Hebraic letters have a numerical meaning. Now, this transcription into numbers is a new enigma. Nevertheless, this attempt is in honor of the spirit of this author who presented the esoteric significance that, evidently, the Prophet wished to transmit under the pretext of a story that was not to be taken literally.

*In English in the original.

are then the two elementary oppositional principles: Fire and Water. Would you prefer our medieval symbols $\triangle$ and ∇? The Egyptian image speaks more explicitly than our conventional symbols, since the three vases are also a trinity, and Ptah, wrapped as a mummy, then represented as ithyphallic Min, is a seminal fire and causes the mounting flux symbolized by the *nekhakha*, the stick from which a triple stream comes out in droplets,[34] held above the right arm of this Min.

Frogs—living amphibious beings—symbolize, along with serpents, the passage from aquatic life to terrestrial life, to living on air. We should look in the organic constitution and in the metabolisms of these animals for the vital transformations that allow them to live either in the air or in the water. The functions of life could certainly never be better symbolized than by means of an animal whose organism is specified for a particular environment.

Moreover, every function has its active aspect and its complementary passivity. A principle-element, such as Fire, Air, Water, or Earth, has a masculine, active character or a feminine, passive character, passivity being shown by the addition of the letter *t* at the end of a name. The symbol of this letter is the crown of the skull that represents the lunar nature, passive and reflective. Thus, the four elements become the principial Ogdoad.

Through the symbolism of objects and imaged gestures, one can, without long phrases, establish a writing that links all living functions together and thus expresses an essential metaphysics through the tangible manifestations of life.

———ᴡᴡ———

Here is what has been transcribed by A. Erman regarding the definition of Thoth (Djehuty, also signifying lead):[35]

> One day, while Ra was in the sky, he said: "Have Thoth come to me." And he was led to him at once. The majesty of this god said to Thoth, "Be in the sky in my place, while I shine for the blessed in the lower regions. . . . Thou art in my place, my replacement, and thou shalt be thus named, Thoth, the replacer of Ra." Then all sorts of things came into view because of Ra's play with words. He said to Thoth *"I shall cause thee to embrace* [inh] *the two heavens by the beauty of thy rays"—then the moon* [iah] *was born.* Further on, alluding to the fact that Thoth as the replacer of Ra occupies a level only slightly subordinate to him, *"I shall cause that thou sendest* [hab] *greater than thee"—then the Ibis* [hb] *was born,* the bird of Thoth.[36]

This certainly parallels the fourth day of biblical Genesis, which is concerned with the creation of the luminaries of the day and the night. The moon is presented as a *replacement,* shining in the night as a reflector, but also at certain times communicating with the sun, the day.

The translation of the last phrase: *"I shall cause that thou sendest* [hab] *greater than thee"* is certainly not correct, because the lunar effect will be attributed to Mercury, Hermes, in the form of water, which is not "greater than Thoth," but the manifestation of his power containing the Elements, the Ogdoad. Furthermore, his living representative will be symbolized by the ibis *(hb),* the white bird of the swamps, who searches in them with his beak for the worms (a primitive form of life) that constitute his food.

---

[34] Cf. vol 1, fig. 1.

[35] Lead is here understood as the original mercurial metal.

[36] Erman, *Religion des Egyptiens*, pp. 90–91. This author honestly distinguishes the authentic texts from his personal reflections.

Another curiosity to be noted here is the fact of the appearance of "all sorts of things . . . because of Ra's play on words." "And God led Adam through the Garden of Eden in order to name all the things living there. . . ."[37]

To learn the true name of a thing is to know it. Certainly, it is not just a matter of words, but of the vital location of a thing in "Eden." This Verb is a "weaving" that creates the thing (Neith, the weaving; Seshat, the signature, the name).

PLATES 60 AND 61 • THOTH, MASTER OF THE NET, KARNAK

This bas-relief is located on the third register of the west part of the south wall of the hypostyle room at Karnak and makes up part of the scene called "the bird hunt." Thoth and Seshat, as with all the figures on this wall, were first sculpted in relief by Seti I, then recarved in sunk relief under Ramesses II. A line remains around the figure, giving the contour of the original reliefs. On the upper part of Thoth's head and under the soles of his feet, the old line merges with the edge of the new carving.[38]

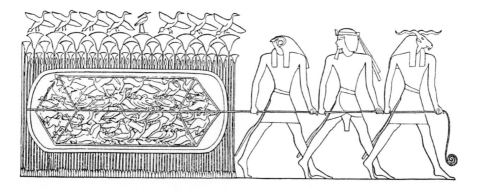

Fig. 259. Scene of hunting with the net (Karnak, temple of Amun)

The net is pulled by Horus, the king, and Khnum.

The entire scene includes, on the left, a net filled with winged creatures (caught in the net) sculpted in relief in a pond with rounded edges, located in the middle of a papyrus thicket surmounted by seven birds in full flight. These birds, three on one side and four on the other, who have "escaped from fixation by the net," are divided by the *benu* bird, the phoenix. The rope that longitudinally crosses the net is pulled by the falcon-headed Horus and by the king, who both look toward the net, and by the ram-headed Khnum, who holds the end of the rope that is unrolling in a spiral and who looks at Thoth (figs. 259, 260).

Thoth faces them, his arms extended in front of a long scarf with curved-down ends. Notice that he does not hold this band of cloth in his hands; his hands are pressed against it. Through this gesture Thoth evokes the measure of the arm span, or fathom.

---

[37] Genesis 2:19–20.

[38] Relief, what stands out; intaglio or sunk relief, what is carved in, penetrating. Here, as elsewhere in this period, an alternation between the two is noted.

Seshat, at the right, holds in her two closed, opposed hands a band of cloth that passes behind her neck and marks the significance of Thoth. Thoth is named "master of the city of the Eight" and of the "temple of the net."

Plate 61 • Thoth, Master of Numbers

Without preoccupying ourselves with the thousand metrical nuances that occur in any pharaonic use of the grid, correcting the approximate ratios read in whole numbers into absolute functions by means of the irregular squares, we draw a *canevas* on this bas-relief, based on the height of Thoth. This *neter* does not have a skullcap, so consequently, his height must be divided by 18.

All the registers are carved on a very pronounced slope; thus in order to establish a regular grid pattern, we take the lines of the earth and sky as horizontals and their perpendiculars for verticals. The vertical axis that serves as the point of departure is the one passing through the edge of Thoth's headdress, the point corresponding to the axis of equilibrium passing in front of the ear on the human-headed figures.

Measured between the interior edges of the bas-relief, from the soles of the feet to the top of the head, Thoth is 1 mean fathom in height (1.85 m). The unit that results from the division of 1 fathom by 18 represents the side of a one-unit square.

It is enough to count the number of squares that mark the essential points:

- The full arm span of Thoth is twenty-two squares, that is, eleven squares on each side of his axis of equilibrium.
- The height of the edge of the register above Thoth's head is nineteen squares and thus corresponds to the height of a man with the crown of the skull.
- The distance between Thoth's axis of equilibrium and Seshat's is fifteen squares.
- The distance between Thoth's axis of equilibrium and the line that marks the end of the vertical text inscribed behind Seshat is nineteen squares.
- The total height of the register under the sky is twenty-six squares, and twenty-seven squares with the sky.

We find here some fundamental numbers and ratios: Thoth is inscribed in a double rectangle in the proportion of 19 to 11, that is, one of the approximate ratios for the square root of 3. This function is confirmed by the rectangle determined by the distance 15 between the axis of Thoth and Seshat and the total height, 26, under the sky. These two ratios come one after the other in the *canevas*.[39] Now, the square root of 3 defines the hexagon.

Seshat is inscribed in a rectangle of 8 to 19. The diagonal of the square with 19 for its side that starts from the axis of equilibrium of Thoth crosses the vertical at a height of 11, and in the rectangle of Seshat, determines the 8 to 11 rectangle. This coefficient is that of the regular pentagon, which is found in the plan of the naos drawn on papyrus (plates 65 and 66 and fig. 266) and which governs the naos of Luxor (fig. 284).

Thoth, master of numbers and measures, organizer of the cycle of time, located at the heart of the measuring cubits, patron of scribes and of all writers, by his height gives the fundamental measure, the fathom. He teaches the essential numbers through his proportions, relative to the

[39] Cf. chapter 8. Each ratio requires its "reciprocal" to form the following one. The growth of 11 to 15, as well as that of 19 to 26, results from the generating function already encountered in the tomb of Ukhotep at Meir, fig. 248.

hexagon and the division of the cycle into six. But it is Seshat who gives form and makes possible the passage from the straight line to the curve, through the function evoked by her "particular coefficient," which is the same as that of Thothotep in the tomb at Meir. From the ground to her forehead, Seshat measures 1.84 meters, and from the ground to her vertex, she measures 1.93 meters. By taking the exact dimension of a fathom at 0° for her height to the forehead, her height to the vertex will be defined as 1.843 meters × 1.0472 = 1.93 meters.

Moreover, the extended arms of Thoth represent the arm span, or fathom. Let us not forget that "fathom" in hieroglyphic language also means "to embrace," that is, "to surround," and that the arm span is thus inevitably a curve, here transcribed into a straight line, like the royal cubit.[40] Thus, Thoth and Seshat give the functional principles that govern the cubits and allow the transformation of the curved line into the straight line (and vice versa), which is further verified by the measurements found on the monument itself.

Fig. 260. Geometric study of a scene from hunting with the net

> Thoth, master of the city of the Eight, indicates the numbers relating to the hexagon, and Seshat, those relating to the pentagon.

One might have been tempted to see these representations of "capturing with a snare" in the tombs of the nobles as "scenes from private life," particularly as the master of the tomb is shown hunting the birds himself with a boomerang, fishing with a harpoon, and so on. But when this figuration is found *in a temple* with the king flanked by two *neters* as actors, themselves pulling the net under the orders of Thoth, accompanied by Seshat, we can no longer see this as a simple scene from ordinary life, and it is obvious that this image has a symbolic purpose and is related to myth.

The texts accompanying Thoth designate him as "master of the city of the Eight who presides

---

[40] The entire arm span measures twenty-two squares; the interval between the thumbs of the *neter* measures twenty-one, coinciding with the cross formed by the scarf. This allows us to consider the arm span as an arc of 60° for the length of the rope indicated by the thumbs. Cf. vol. 1, fig. 132.

[*hesert*] in the heart of the 'temple of the net.'" The reference here is to the sanctuary of Hermopolis, capital of the fifteenth nome, consecrated to Thoth. It is thought that the name of this temple should be attributed to the legend according to which Seth had been taken into the net by Horus at this place.[41]

Here Thoth directs the operation of "capturing with a snare" by giving the signal to close the net. It is said that he extends his arms like a bow in order to release the scarf. He has crossed the swamp full of birds and fixed the snare so that these waterbirds, destined to serve as an offering to the *neters,* particularly to Amun, master of Karnak, could be captured. Behind him is Seshat, characterized by an absence of attributes—neither crown, nor scepter, nor jewelry—only the strip of cloth around her neck, the two ends of which she holds in her fists, which oppose each other.

Seshat is here assimilated to Neith, mistress of the fifth nome in Lower Egypt, regent of Dep, mistress of Sais (double cities). The Saitic nome was placed under the protection of Neith, to whom the invention of weaving and cloth was attributed. Her city was famous for the manufacture of cloth, and its Serapeum bore the name of "house of fabrics"; preserved there as a relic was the ear of Osiris.[42] Normally determined by two crossed arrows, the emblem of the region, or nome, attributed to Neith is written here with two fingers (?).[43] Seshat is then described as that which conceives and nourishes the royal infant from her breast, the infant who will appear on the throne of Horus, as Ra. . . .

This very complete depiction of Thoth, accompanied by Seshat, confirms that the theme of the net constitutes a cabala that in fact signifies the capturing of what is abstract.

With this clarification of the significance of the "bird hunt," it is obvious that we must study each net in this spirit. The net serves as an image that adapts itself to various possibilities.

PLATES 62 AND 63 • TOMB OF RAMESSES IX

This painted bas-relief is on the south wall of the third part of the access corridor to the tomb of Ramesses IX. The whole of this wall is divided into two clearly distinct parts, the left one containing three registers and the right one (plate 62) allowing for only a single register divided vertically into two tableaux.

The tableau on the right shows the king wearing the *atef* crown surmounted by a ram's head and including, with the uraeus, four solar disks, all placed on the horizontal horns of Khnum. The king offers a small Maāt seated on a basket to Ptah—in one of the aspects of Osiris—and to Maāt, both of whom stand on a wedge-shaped pedestal, a symbol of Maāt. This mummified Osiris holds two *was* scepters in his hands, which are opposed to each other. Maāt, *neter* of justice and of the scales, who separates the pure from the impure, here brings about the passage of the whole number (the line) into the cycle through the function ϕ.[44]

The tableau at the left shows the king in the form of the ithyphallic and mummified Osiris, one arm raised above his head, resting on an inclined plane on a mountain and forming the hypotenuse of a triangle, the side and base of which are represented by an undulating serpent. In

[41] Cf. H. Gauthier, *Dictionnaire des noms géographiques contenus dans les textes hiéroglyphiques,* 5 vols. (Cairo: I.F.A.O., 1925), 1:66, 4:48. The name of this sanctuary is *h.t ibty,* "temple of the net" (?).

[42] The ear, being "to hear," "to understand," the "weaving of the Verb," etc.

[43] Cf. Gauthier, *Dictionnaire des noms géographiques,* 1:158. This emblem is read *āq*? or *djebauy*?

[44] Cf. below, fig. 262.

front of the mummified king, above the cartouches of the name of Ramesses IX, the scarab rolls his solar ball out of the mountain with his hind legs.

This scene is rare, as only two other examples of it are known, both on papyri. One, in the name of Her-uben, songstress of Amun-Ra, king of the gods, has the dedicatory inscription, "Book of What Is in the Dwat."[45] This papyrus has only three scenes, the last of which is similar to that of Ramesses IX: the dead person is in front of the door leading to the tomb of Osiris, and behind this door, guarded by a lion-headed figure holding a whip in his hand, is a long serpent holding four upright mummified sons of Horus in its coils. The body of the serpent extends under the mountain and forms the base and perpendicular of a triangle of which Osiris, with his arm raised above his head, forms the hypotenuse.[46] The text accompanying this Osiris is translated as follows: "Osiris, he who awakens in health, he who is at the head of the west, great *neter*, residing in the Dwat, this sacred earth, this mound of Khepri"[47] (the mound of Khepri, that is, the hill of transformations). In the tomb of Ramesses IX, the text inscribed to the left of the scarab rolling its ball with its hind legs is quite enigmatic:

> This *neter* is thus: his two arms are in the gesture of exultation above him, his two legs are in the place of the destruction, the living scarab, birth of this great *neter*, is in the *qerert*[48] of this *neter*. He calls Osiris and Osiris calls him. This *neter* is in the Dwat (plunged) in thick shadows, the serpent Nehep is his guardian, it encircles his form at the moment of the birth of Ra. May Horus, who appears at Thebes, be with thee and protect thee![49]

—⁓—

It was during my first visit to the Valley of the Kings at Luxor in 1937, at a time when I was already interested in pharaonic measures, that I was struck by this curious figure in the tomb of Ramesses IX.

Without then having the time to take the measurements, I took note of the drawing, because the fact of depicting a mummified royal figure forming the hypotenuse of a triangle that appeared to me to have sides of 3 to 4, and raising its arm to 1 cubit above its head, would suggest seeing there a relationship of 5 + 1, with the king, as the hypotenuse of the sacred triangle, having the value of 5, plus the raised arm.[50]

Since the height of a man represents ϕ^2 through his proportions, the intention could be to indicate six-fifths of his height, which gives the value 3.1416... for π.

In order to establish the meaning of this figuration it was necessary to do a precise study correlating it with other known facts. It is a question here of much more than the simple revelation of a number. It must be justified by, and must result from, a philosophy related to theological principles, and, in the customary mode of pharaonic thinking, it must necessarily have a universal character.

---

[45] The second papyrus is also in the name of a chanteuse of Amun. Cf. Alexandre Piankoff, *Les Deux Papyrus "mythologiques" de Her-Ouben au Musée du Caire*, Annales du Service des Antiquités de l'Egypte 49 (Cairo: I.F.A.O., 1949), fasc. 2, pp. 7–10.

[46] In this papyrus, the hypotenuse is generated by the mummy with its arm raised, in contrast to the figure in the Ramesses IX tomb in which the arm is above the serpent's head.

[47] Piankoff, *Les Deux Papyrus "mythologiques" de Her-Ouben*, p. 10.

[48] *qerert* = "cavern."

[49] Piankoff, *Les Deux Papyrus "mythologiques" de Her-Ouben*, p. 11. In these two citations we have replaced the word *god* with *neter*.

[50] Cf. vol. 1, fig. 108.

The mummy, as the chrysalis that is about to hatch, is drawn within the mountain from which the scarab, rolling his ball, the symbol of the solar emergence, is leaving. This is the end of the genesis in the Dwat (the world of the night of terrestrial life, the time of the migration of the soul), which will cause the appearance of the visible solar cycle. This is the reason for the measurements in *meters* of the frame surrounding the figuration, the meter being exclusively reserved for diameters and the radii of circles, because cycles are always measured in cubits for time and in fathoms for distance. Thus the measures reveal the vital conditions, that is, the phases in life; at the same time the teaching of this tomb is that of the passage from the straight line to the curve, the abstract distance from one point to another, which governs the apparent movement of a cyclic genesis. That which separates one thing from another is vitally not a distance but a duration, a difference in phases of becoming.

Some essential measures, nearly all of which are exact, enable us to analyze the principal functions of this figuration in the form of numbers and proportions.

Certain very particular points of reference found on this bas-relief consist of black lines and red lines painted on the stucco *after* the sculpture was made—therefore useless for the execution of this work—that emphasize the essential units of measure governing the geometry of the whole bas-relief: red lines give the measurement in meters, black lines indicate the "movements" of the figure.

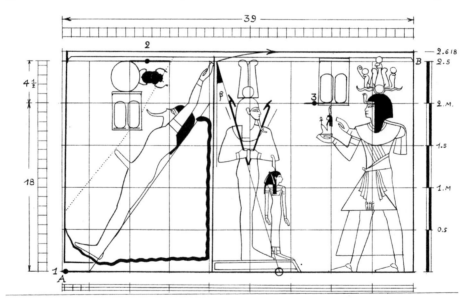

Fig. 261. Tomb of Ramesses IX, Valley of the Kings (Thebes)

Relation of the meter to π and the royal cubit

At point 1, a horizontal red line is painted *over* the black baseline that constitutes the horizontal of the tableau.

At point 2, a red line is drawn tangent to the upper part of the solar disk; it is 2.50 meters from the baseline, that is, from the extension of the red line at point 1.

At point 3, a red horizontal line coincides with the base of the royal cartouches and is 2 meters from the baseline.

These three red lines define the half-meter as unity, which is recalled in several other places in the design.

The height of 2 meters, divided by 18, determines the square unit used to measure the totality of the two scenes (plate 63). The standing king actually measures nineteen of these squares to the vertex, sixteen to the shoulders, and eighteen to above the eyebrows, that is, to the lower line of the band of the headdress.

If we use the half-meter for unity, being the distance between the horizontals at points 2 and 3, a grid demonstrates that the mummified king inclined on the mountain is actually the hypotenuse of a 3 to 4 triangle suggested by the serpent (fig. 261). If the base of the triangle is 3, or 1.50 meters, its height is 4, or 2 meters, and its hypotenuse is 5, or 2.50 meters.

The vertical axis of Osiris-Ptah standing on the pedestal is exactly 2 meters from the vertical border on the right; the small Maāt presented as an offering is 1 meter from it. This Osiris-Ptah holds two *was* scepters in his hands that form, with respect to the vertical, two different angles. The scepter in the left hand determines the relationship of 1 to ϕ^2 (angle γ in fig. 262) that gives the *function* of what the right hand specifies. The scepter in the right hand determines the angle β with the vertical, which allows the transformation of the length of the chord of the angle of 60° into the length of its arc. The extension of this *was* down to the baseline and up to the height of 2.5 meters represents the diagonal that measures 2.618 meters, that is, 5 royal cycle cubits, and its rabattement onto the line of the vertical coincides with the upper line of the sky (fig. 261).

The angle β found here is demonstrated in the sanctuary of the barque of the temple of Luxor.[51]

The subdivision of 2 meters into eighteen squares gives the value of 6 digits for the side of each square. Each digit represents 1/100 mean fathom. The height of 2.50 meters is twenty-two and one-half squares, and the total length of the two scenes is thirty-nine squares (fig. 261). The result of these numbers is the proportion 78 to 45, whose reciprocal is 45 to 26, in which we can recognize a ratio coming from the *canevas* for the square root of 3. The measurements confirm the precision of this function. The length 4.33 meters is measured between the lines of the vertical borders. Divided by the height between points 1 and 2, it gives the correct proportion, or

$$\frac{4.33 \text{ meters}}{2.50 \text{ meters}} = 1.732 = \sqrt{3}.$$

Thus the rectangle that frames this double scene is the controlling rectangle of the hexagon that governs the division of time. Its large diagonal *AB* (fig. 261) is 5 meters and enables us to draw a circumscribing circle with a radius of 2.50 meters, of which each arc of 60° measures 5 royal cubits, or 2.618 meters, indicated by the height of the tableau with the sky.

—⁓—

We have thus functionally, metrically, and geometrically verified that the meter measures the diameter and that the royal cycle cubit measures the arc of 60°.

In conclusion, the figure of the royal mummy as the hypotenuse, with his arm raised, actually evokes the functions made precise in the whole of the tableau. As the hypotenuse, the king has the numerical value of 5; this fact leads to the principal function of $6/5 \times \phi^2$, defining the coefficient π.

[51] Cf. fig. 284.

This bas-relief once again applies the transformation of the straight line, or radius, into the cycle curve, or royal cubit. As for the precise value of π, this is given by the scepter held in the right hand of the standing Osiris-Ptah.

The mathematical key of this tableau, in which the mummified king in his mountain is only a functional symbol, is given by the central figure that establishes a relationship between the heights of Maāt and of Ptah; these heights are to each other as the radius of a circle (Maāt) and the height of the pentagon (Ptah) inscribed in the circle (fig. 262).

The side of the pentagon is the width of a rectangle whose length is two times the radius of the inscribed circle (in dotted lines, fig. 262). This rectangle being crossed at a right angle (as in the sanctuary of the barque of Amun at Luxor)[52] determines the displacement angle of a second pentagon superposed on the first, and through which are given all the angles and all the geometry of this figure and its consequences: the vertical axis of Ptah coincides with the height of the first pentagon; the vertical axis of Maāt coincides with the diagonal of the second pentagon.

By means of this geometric play (fig. 262) we see that shifting the rectangle formed from the elements of a pentagon at a right angle determines a new pentagon that pivots 18° on the first, and this play allows the geometric determination of a perfect π, and thus the mathematically precise squaring of the circle.[53]

This whole scene, including the two tableaux, is inscribed in a rectangle that on a circumscribing circle cuts out the hexagon, which applies the functions defined by the pentagon. Here

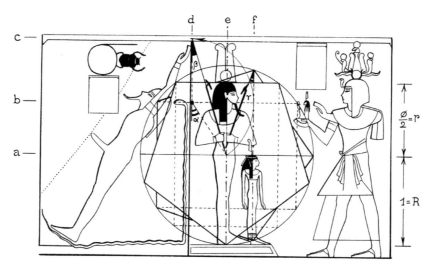

Fig. 262. Definition of the pentagon by the height of Maāt and Osiris-Ptah

The rectangle with half (*ab*) of the side of the pentagon for its length, and half (*de*) of the radius *r* of the inscribed circle for its width, is cut by its diagonal. The acute angle measures 34°32′. Half of this angle is obtained by adding the height *ab* to the diagonal, which gives the length *ac*. The triangle formed by *de* and *ac* has a hypotenuse with a length of 3.14159... for the length *ac* considered as 3.

---

[52] Cf. ibid. and vol. 1, fig. 157b.

[53] Cf. chapter 40, "Discussion Concerning a Perfect π" and fig. 284.

once again we find this pentagon-hexagon relationship that is at the foundation of the vital functions described through Apet of the South.

Maāt is a principle and not some thing; she is what we can translate as justice, the scales, and in this scene, it is she who makes the scission of Ptah from which comes the quintessence that is translated by the pentagon.

CUBITS AND TEMPLE

Plate 64 • The Cubits and the Temple

Plate 64A

This cubit represents the typical standard cubit.[54] Carved of wood, it is divided into 28 digits, and on its sloping face there is an enumeration of the different divisions: digits, palms, hand, fist, small span, large span, *djezer* cubit, *remen* cubit, small cubit, and royal cubit, reading from left to right.

On the top face, twenty-eight *neters* can be seen, each attributed to a digit. Ra, the first of the Ennead, corresponds to the last digit; the *neters* are therefore enumerated from right to left. Also from right to left, the fractions of the digit can be read on the vertical face; the values are written above.

The dedication occupies the back face and half of the top. This cubit was published by R. Lepsius in *Alte Ägyptische Elle* as number 1, from a rubbing of the original, which is preserved at the Turin Museum. It was placed in a case in 1939 during the war and has remained there ever since, for which reason we have not been able to get either a photograph of it or any other verification of its measurements. Lepsius gives it a total length of 52.5 centimeters. This would make it the cycle cubit, which is one-sixth of a circle with a radius of 0.5 meter.

Plate 64B (No. 61316, Cairo Museum)

This cubit, found in the tomb of Tutankhamun, is made of wood and has the cartouche of the king on its back face. Its total length is 52.9 centimeters ±0.5 millimeter, maximum. It is divided into 7 palms, the first two of which on the left are subdivided into 8 digits and the last on the right makes reference to 1 digit. It is further divided into two half-cubits. The following characteristics can be noted with regard to these measures:

1. The total length, 52.9 centimeters, is close to the radius cubit at Dendera (plate 64, D and E). This measurement derives from the function applied in the sanctuary of the barque in the temple of Luxor,[55] which establishes the relationship between 6 mean fathoms measuring the arc of 60° for which 20 radius cubits serve as the chord.

2. It is divided into two unequal parts that represent, on the left, a half-cubit of 53.5 centimeters,[56] and on the right, a half-cubit of 52.3 centimeters or 1 cycle cubit.

3. Read on the 5 palms to the right, it contains a *remen* cubit of 20 digits. This cubit corresponds to the division of the length of the entire cubit by the square root of 2.

---

[54] Cf. vol. 1, fig. 112.

[55] Cf. ibid., fig. 113.

[56] Cf. ibid., fig. 117, cubit no. 45932.

In contrast, the *remen* cubit, read on the 5 palms on the left, measures exactly 20 digits of the division by 28 of this cubit, which is 37.8 centimeters.

Plate 64C (No. 61320, Cairo Museum)

This cubit, like the preceding one, was found in the tomb of Tutankhamun and bears his cartouche. It is made of wood and is covered with blue paint. Its total length of 52.5 centimeters classifies it among the cycle cubits. It is divided into 7 palms. The central palm, divided in two, divides the cubit into two unequal parts.

1. The part on the right measures 26.75 centimeters, that is, half of 53.5 centimeters, the half-cubit already encountered on cubit B and noted in the same way.

2. This cubit has two different values for the *remen* cubit according to whether it is read in one direction or the other:

3. The 5 palms on the right measure 38.2 centimeters, that is, 20 digits of a cubit of 53.5 centimeters and therefore the same value as the half-cubit that it refers to on the same side.

4. The 5 palms on the left measure 37.2 centimeters, that is, 20 shorter digits that result from the division of the total length of this cubit by the square root of 2. These 5 palms constitute therefore its particular *remen*.

The intention of indicating two different measures for the *remen* is made clear by the two ways of reading, in one direction or the other, and since we are dealing here with a centimeter of difference, this cannot be regarded as the result of negligence. In practice, the small *remen* can be the side of a square, the diagonal of which is equal to the entire cubit.

Plate 64D (No. 45933, Cairo Museum)

This is a basalt cubit, square in cross section, found in the temple of Hathor at Dendera. Its length varies from 53.05 centimeters to 53.1 centimeters. It is a radius cubit of the same nature as the previously studied cubit B, and it obeys the same functions. Its cross section is equal to 1/21 of its length. One surface is divided into four parts, the next one into seven, and the two remaining into five and six successively.[57]

The subdivisions of the cubit into fourths, sevenths, fifths, and sixths impose their common multiples on two consecutive faces and define the subdivision of the total length into 28 digits, then into 35 digits and 30 digits, and finally into 24 digits. Now, these units of measure are actually found both on the cubits themselves and on the monuments. For example, certain "shorter" digits correspond to 1/30 cubit, whereas on certain cubits the first digit, noticeably longer than the others, corresponds to 1/24 cubit.

We should note the arrangement of these divisions because in its development, the division into fourths and fifths frames the division by 7, which evokes the fundamental relationships for the square roots of 3 and of 2. These are the original ratios that are recalled here, since in order to balance the measurements it is necessary to make use of "reciprocals."

Plate 64E (No. 45931, Cairo Museum)

This cubit, also found at Dendera, is of basalt and is square in cross section. It is also called the "benediction cubit" because of the dedication carved on one of its faces. Dedicated to Hathor at Dendera by the strategist Panas,[58] this cubit is thus dated about 200 B.C. Its length of 53

---

[57] Cf. ibid., fig. 118. From this we can understand the reason why these subdivisions are marked on the cubits of the temple and the sacred character that was accorded to the cubits.

[58] Translators of this dedication have not been able to agree on the exact meaning of the whole text.

centimeters classifies it among the radius cubits. It is used in the temple of Luxor to measure the width of the sanctuary of the barque and the room of offerings.[59]

The subdivision of its sides is similar to that of the preceding cubit, although it presents a variation. We shall call the four sides *a*, *b*, *c*, and *d* so that, as read from top to bottom in plate 64, we can see the details as follows:

(a) Division into 7 palms. The first palm on the left is in turn divided by 2, 4, 8, and 16. The first palm on the right is successively divided by 3 and by 6.

(b) The next side is divided into 4 and 5 and their multiples, and carries the dedication.

(c) The third side is divided into 6. The first division on the left is again subdivided by 3, and the first on the right by 2, 4, 8, and 16.

(d) The fourth side is bare.

It should be noted that the law of crossing and inversion was observed here: the division of the palms by 3 is on the right, whereas the division of the sixths by 3 is on the left.

The essential characteristic of this cubit is not only that of bringing together on two sides the relationships 7 to 4 and 7 to 5 relative to the square roots of 3 (hexagonal function) and of 2 (function of the square), but also of giving the measurement correcting these original relationships through the unequal divisions on the side divided into palms.

First, on the left, two smaller palms allow the construction of a square whose half-diagonal exactly corresponds to one-fifth of the total length of the cubit (fig. 263, sides *a* and *b*).

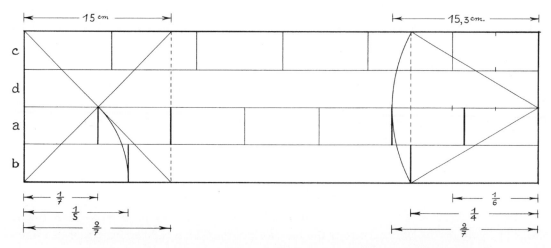

Fig. 263. Diagram of the development of the benediction cubit of the temple of Dendera

Each side is 2 digits in height, or 1 half-palm, so that developed, the cubit measures 2 palms in width for 7 in length. *Left*, on side *a*, two shorter palms at 7.5 centimeters each. Thus 7.5 centimeters × √2 = 10.60 centimeters, which is 1/5 of 53 centimeters noted in *b*. *Right*, on side *a*, there are two larger palms that measure 15.3 centimeters. Thus 15.3 centimeters × √3/2 = 13.25 centimeters, exactly 1/4 of the total length marked on surface *b*. Side *c* is divided in sixths, each of which, multiplied by √3, corresponds to two larger palms, 8.833... centimeters × √3 = 15.3 centimeters.

[59] Cf. vol. 1, fig. 113.

Second, on the right, two larger palms allow a similar play for the square root of 3. If we multiply the length of these two palms by half of the square root of 3, we get exactly one-fourth of the total cubit (fig. 263, *a* and *b*).

Third, the three central palms give the average division of the cubit into exactly seven.

Finally, let us recall that the benediction cubit E and cubit D measure 53 centimeters and 53.1 centimeters, respectively, and they are two of a group of three cubits found at the temple of Hathor at Dendera. The third cubit measures 53.5 centimeters.

If cubits E or D are the base of a 1 to 7 right triangle, the third cubit of 53.5 centimeters will be its hypotenuse, exactly as the larger palm of cubit E is the hypotenuse of this same triangle with the mean palm as base, which becomes in its turn the hypotenuse for the shortest palm.[60]

These inequalities observed on the full lengths of the cubits and in their subdivisions confirm the conscious use of *shorter* and *longer* measures that justify their irrational geometric ratios, while at the same time preserving the simple ratios of the natural divisions imposed by the harmonic division following the genesis starting with 1 to 1 and 1 to 3.[61]

The South Wall of the Temple of Luxor

The total length of the south wall of the temple with the cornices is 37.05 meters, or 20 fathoms of 1.852... meters at 45°. The south wall is located at the level of the royal headband, which measures a cubit of 28 digits on a man. It therefore evokes multiples of 7 as a "royal cubit," and, moreover, it can be divided into two equal or unequal parts in the likeness of the cubits. Now, the temple summarizes the entire group of these functions: the *geometric axis* divides the length of the south wall with the cornice into two equal parts, each measuring 10 mean fathoms and coinciding with thirty-five B cubits from plate 64.[62] Next, the *axis of measures* divides the length of the south wall without the cornice into two unequal parts: 18.55 meters to the east, which is thirty-five E cubits, and 17.9 meters to the west, which is 100/30 of the black cubit carved on the pedestal of the black colossus located at the knees.

The *ankh* sculpted on the dedication of the stylobate of the covered temple divides the length of the south wall *inversely* by giving the greatest width to the west side, 18.75 meters or thirty-five royal cubits (C in plate 64).

The Temple of Luxor

The side of each square of the grid pattern on which the plan of the temple is projected is 10 fathoms. The figure on the left summarizes the functions of the 3, 4, 5 right triangle that determines the pivot on the angle 1 to 7, thus geometrically correcting the square root of 49 into the square root of 50.[63]

The growth of the temple in length represents, for the different phases and considering only the exterior mass of the building, the values, in fathoms, of 40, 70, 100, and 140, numbers that recall the function-bases of the cubits relative to the approximate values and their inverses for the square roots of 3 and 2.

---

[60] Cf. ibid., fig. 117.

[61] Cf. ibid., fig. 118.

[62] A coincidence, if we recall that cubit B is itself derived from the fathom. It must be exactly 10.026 fathoms to equal the corresponding cubits.

[63] Cf. vol. 1, fig. 115.

The total length of the temple of Luxor is 258 meters, or 140 fathoms at 0° latitude. If we consider this length as representing a cubit of 28 digits, the temple summarizes the functions we have just studied in the cubits themselves. This comparison is not an assumption on our part because the measurements of the temple prove it. Moreover, the standing colossus in front of the west wing of the pylon is 9.215 meters in height from the soles of the feet to the top of the white crown, that is, his height is contained twenty-eight times in the length of the temple, for which he plays the digit in relation to the temple as the cubit. Now the length of 9.215 meters actually represents 5 fathoms at 0°, which becomes the unit of measure of the temple.

Just like the developed harmonic decomposition with the starting point of 1 to 3, the temple summarizes the following essential functions: the division by 7 that connects the royal cubit to geodetic functions, and the division by 19, which links it to the human canon.[64]

Technical Demonstration of the Table of 2/n by Means of the Cubit

The D and E cubits immediately suggest the relationship between the different divisions of two consecutive sides. Let us recall that the divisions of 4 and 7 define 1/28. This is quite obviously the principle of the vernier. Now, in applying a vernier of this type, it is easy to determine the reduction of 2/n into fractions with a numerator of 1.

For example, to transform 2/3 into its unit fractions, we look for the arithmetic mean term between 1 and 3, which provides the first denominator of 2. Let us slide the digit divided in half under that divided in thirds by taking two cubits carved inversely to each other: 2/3 is then 1/2 plus a fraction that is equal to $1/(2 \times 3)$, or 1/6.

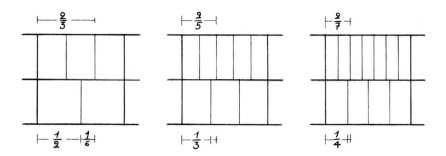

Fig 264. Principle of the vernier applied to the cubits

To find 2/5 we use $(5 + 1)/2$ as the denominator, that is, 3, and by sliding the digit divided into 3 under the one divided into 5, we can read directly that

$$\frac{2}{5} = \frac{1}{3} + \frac{1}{3 \times 5} = \frac{1}{3} + \frac{1}{15}.$$

Finally, to find 2/7 we proceed in exactly the same way; the denominator is 4 and the result is

$$\frac{2}{7} = \frac{1}{4} + \frac{1}{4 \times 7} = \frac{1}{4} + \frac{1}{28}.$$

With these three models, we can then decompose all the multiples of 3, 5, and 7.

[64] Cf. plate 88.

Furthermore, in reading the smallest divisions marked on the digits, all denominators can obviously be obtained up to $1/(15 \times 16)$, or $1/240$ of a digit, that is, $1/6720$ of the total cubit, which defines hundredths of millimeters. We get a glimpse here of a disconcertingly simple and practical knowledge that can be applied not only to calculation but also to all techniques.

THE GRID AND ARCHITECTURE

PLATES 65 AND 66 • A NAOS (TABERNACLE) IN A GRID DRAWN ON PAPYRUS

These plates reproduce a drawing executed on papyrus, probably in the Eighteenth Dynasty. According to the description of F. Petrie, who acquired it,[65] this papyrus was found at Gurob, rolled up and torn in the middle. Putting the pieces together allows us to reconstruct it almost to the original dimensions, which he estimates to be approximately 60 English inches long (1.524 m) and 21.7 inches wide (0.55118 m).

This papyrus is divided into squares by red lines; the drawing of the plan itself is in black. It depicts the facade and the profile of a wooden naos "suspended in a canopy." It should be noted that the cornice of the naos seen from the front should be hidden by the capitals of the columns of the canopy that are in front and that, nevertheless, this cornice is drawn in very fine black lines over the drawing in heavy black lines of the columns. There is formal intent here to mark all the essential points of the naos without omitting anything. The naos is placed on a pedestal that measures one square in height. Above the door of the facade of this naos is a disk flanked by two uraei that marks the median axis. Similar disks are found on the cornice of the naos and on that of the canopy. The extreme right side of this cornice is subdivided into four parts, one of which is smaller than the others, by the four palm leaves that generally ornament this architectural part of the monument.

In the drawing of the side view, one can clearly distinguish the naos with its cornice above and its roof curved to the front, encircled by the canopy, the roof of which also curves down, its forward extremity supported by the cornice and two small columns. These small columns have papyrus flowers for capitals topped by the shape of the space defined between two of these flowers (fig. 265).

These complementary shapes are significant in pharaonic thinking, which intentionally affirms by means of negation in the same way that it evokes abstraction (spirit) through tangible forms.

A uraeus rises up the cornice of the canopy, surmounted by the solar disk. The form of the naos of Tutankhamun can be found in this drawing.[66] Four braided ropes are presumed to have held the naos in its canopy. Here are the numbers of squares that can be read on the *canevas* that associates the front and the side.

Interior naos:
height without base, with cornices	= 16 squares
width of facade at base	= 8 squares
width of facade at level of the torus	= 7 squares
length of the naos at the base, side view	= 11 squares
length of naos between tori under the cornice	= 10 squares.

---

[65] Cf. Sir Flinders Petrie, *Ancient Egypt* (London: Macmillan, 1932), p. 24.

[66] Cf. Carter, *The Tomb of Tut-ankh-Amen*, vol. 1, plates 68 and 39.

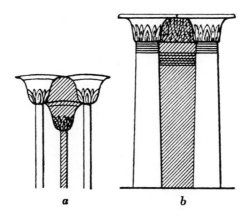

Fig. 265. Shapes defined by empty space

(a) Small columns of the naos; *(b) sed* festival column from the room of Tuthmosis III at Karnak, defined by the two columns with capitals in front of a blooming papyrus, given here as an example.

This group of numbers allows us to verify that the facade of the naos is inscribed in a rectangle of 8 to 16, or 1 to 2.

The projection in plan of the proportions at the base and indicated by the number of squares constitutes a rectangle eleven squares long and eight wide (fig. 266). The 8 to 11 rectangle defines the pentagon; 8 is the side of the pentagon and 11 is the diameter of the inscribed circle. The circumscribing circle defines the position of the small columns of the canopy that do not correspond, in the side view, to an exact number of squares, but to thirteen squares plus a fraction on each side.

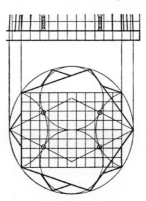

Fig. 266. Plan of the naos drawn on papyrus

Projection in plan of the length of eleven squares and the width of eight squares of the interior naos, which defines the governing rectangle of the pentagon.

The ratio of the side view is 11 to 16, in which we find another essential function of the pentagon.[67] The interior naos summarizes the proportions of the initial 1 to 2 rectangle, as well as the ϕ and pentagonal functions.

[67] Cf. vol. 1, figs. 154 to 157.

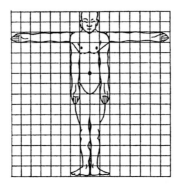

Fig. 267. Human canon by Hokusai

Drawing taken from one of Hokusai's sketchbooks

The construction of the pentagon is governed by the function ϕ evoked here by the relationship 10 to 16. This original ratio for the value of ϕ is found in a drawing of Hokusai (fig. 267) in which the height of man "without skullcap" is equal to sixteen squares and is divided by ϕ by the position of the navel at the tenth square.

Canopy:

height without base, with cornice	= 18 squares
height with curved roof	= 19 squares
height under the head of the uraeus	= 20 squares
height of the solar disk	= 21 squares
total height with pedestal and disk	= 22 squares
width of facade at the level of the abaci	= 8 squares
width of facade at the upper level of the cornice	= 9 squares.

The principal proportions evoked by these numbers are the following: the facade of the canopy is inscribed in the 9 to 18 (or 1 to 2) rectangle, and if the curvature of the roof is considered as equivalent to the human skullcap, we again find here the eighteenth line defining the fixed line of the upper part of the cornice. The nineteenth line is the upper limit of the curvature, as we have observed in the human *canevas*.

Let us recall finally that in China, the Royal Man has the value of 8 or 9. Here we find an analogous evocation through the two unequal columns that mark the two heights of the two nesting naoi, 16 and 18, corresponding in the human canon to the two fixed lines, those of the shoulders and the forehead. This naos appears to have been conceived on the human canon because it summarizes the essential harmonic functions and numbers of the *canevas*.

The function ϕ is confirmed by several details of the drawing. The width of the sky is eight squares, its height thirteen in profile, and the height of the disk is twenty-one, giving the sequence 8, 13, 21 of the F series. The complementary R series, 7, 11, 18, ... is found here as well, as it is in the human canon.

It is again necessary to note that the total width of the drawn squares is 14 and the height is 22; thus, each drawing is inscribed in a rectangle with the proportion of 22 to 14. The two drawings being originally put end to end, the papyrus must have been forty-four squares long, so that the overall proportion of the grid pattern was 44 to 14, in which we see 22 to 7, or π derived from the F series.[68]

—✺—

A word must be added with regard to the dimensions of this papyrus, which justly intrigued Flinders Petrie, because they can only be explained by means of the fathom and the *remen* digit.

As the drawing shows, the papyrus is badly damaged, and to establish the dimensions of the square unit it was necessary to choose from among the best pieces. According to Petrie, the dimension that results from the average of the best squares is 1.3614 English inches, with certain squares reaching 1.373 inches maximum.[69] Actually, this metrical unit does not derive from the commonly known royal cubit, but from 30 *remen* digits divided by 16, or in other words, the width of the papyrus (0.555 meter) is equal to 30/100 fathom and represents the value of sixteen average squares.

The height of the interior naos is sixteen squares and thus gives the metric unit of 30 *remen* digits. The accepted length of the papyrus of forty-four squares, each equaling 3.4687 centimeters, is 152.6 centimeters, conforming to the restoration indicated and to the value of the square unit established on the basis of the *remen* digit.

AN APPLICATION OF THE *CANEVAS* TO THE ARCHITECTURE OF THE TEMPLE OF LUXOR

PLATE 67 • THE GRID AND THE MEASUREMENTS OF THE PYLON OF LUXOR

The whole pylon consists of two towers (or wings) separated by a door. An interior staircase gave access to the upper platform; it started from the east side of the east wing and ascended to the level of the lintel of the central door, the ceiling of which formed a landing. From there, a second staircase crossed the west wing and ended at its upper part. Except for the blocks that connect one side of the exterior walls of the pylon to the other at this double staircase, the two wings are hollow, which poses a very interesting technical problem.

In its present state, the west wing is completely exposed and still has a large part of its crown, which has allowed us, thanks to the numerous triangulations and measurements verified on each accessible part, to be sure of the precision of the dimensions (allowing for the movements caused by water infiltration). The east wing is partly buried in the ground, and its middle part has been severely dislocated, which makes it difficult to give the exact slope and dimensions. Nevertheless, by extending the measured and triangulated slope on its east face, it is possible to restore the total length of the monument with an estimated error of about 10 centimeters in either direction.[70] The essential dimensions resulting from this are as follows:

---

[68] Cf. chapter 8.

[69] 1.3614 English inches = 3.458 cm and 1.373 English inches = 3.4874 cm.

[70] Length between restored tori under cornice   = 22.94 m
   batter calculated on east face   = 3.35 m
   distance between door and vertical corner of west torus = 0.87 m
                    Total   = 27.16 m.
  With an excess of 10 cm, there remains 27.06 m.

- The length of the mass of the west wing of the pylon equals 26.60 meters.
- The width of the door with its posts equals 10 meters.
- The restored length of the east wing at its base equals 27.06 meters, ±10 centimeters.
- The total length of the pylon equals 63.66 meters, ±10 centimeters.
- The length of the west wing at its base from the doorpost up to, but not including, the torus is 26.20 meters, or 50 royal cubits.
- The length of the west wing between the tori at its upper part, under the torus of the cornice, is 22.34 meters, or 12 northern fathoms on the north facade, and 22.11 meters or 12 southern fathoms on its south side.[71] The average length thus represents 12 meridian fathoms at 45°.
- The height of the west wing from the base to the top of the cornice is exactly 25 meters at the northeast corner and corresponds to 13.5 mean fathoms at 45°.

In these few measurements the pylon summarizes the fathom, the meter (which derives from it and is confirmed by the width of 10 meters for the central door), and the royal cubit. Finally, the total length of the two wings and the door is 63.66 meters, corresponding to 120 radius cubits (cubit of 0.5305 meter), which we have already seen, along with the fathoms they define, in the room of Amun's barque.[72]

This pylon is the base, the foundation of the Man of the Temple, as its measurements verify. Through its 12 fathoms between tori under the cornice it is connected to room XII (the eye), and through the ratio between the fathoms and the radius cubits, the function of $\pi/3$, it is connected to the room of Amun's barque (the mouth, the Verb). Finally, it proves the application of the different cubits to various lengths so that the nuances we have read on the cubits are no longer questionable.

If the height of the cornice of the pylon's west wing is taken as representing one unit, the height of the pylon without the cornice is equal to eighteen, and its total height equals nineteen. Thus, the cornice is comparable to the crown of the skull of Man, which is confirmed by the representation of the pylon on the south partition of the court of Ramesses; the ascent of the princes toward the temple is carved in such a way that the cornice of the pylon corresponds to the crown of the skull of the royal princes (fig. 268).

The dimensions, in numbers of squares, are thus: a total height of nineteen for a height without the cornice of eighteen, and a length at the base without torus equal to twenty, for an upper length between the tori equal to seventeen.[73] These are the fundamental numbers of the "human canon," applied to the monument. The metrical relation between the height of 25 meters and the length at the base of 26.18 meters (or 50 royal cycle cubits) imposes the functional correction for the approximating ratio of 19 to 20, which must be 19.0983 to 20. Thus, the height represents a radius measured in meters, and the length represents the arc of 60° defined by this radius and measured in royal cycle cubits.

---

[71] We call a "northern fathom" the fathom that measures the arc of meridian at 90° of latitude, and a "southern fathom" that which measures the arc of meridian at 0°, the latitude of the equator.

[72] The radius of the earth, for a sphere with the same meridian, is 6,367,654 m, compared with 63.66 m (±10 cm) for the length of the base of the pylon.

[73] The ratio between the fathom and seventeen squares suggests the ratio 17/12 found in the *canevas* for the root of 2.

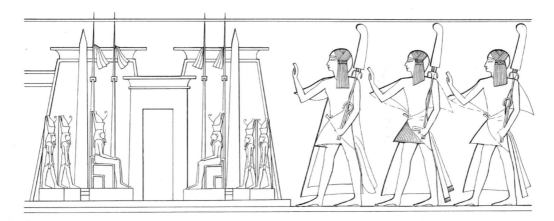

Fig. 268. Ascent of the princes toward the temple Luxor, court of Ramesses

We have omitted the joints of the stones in this illustration.

———

While taking the dimensions of each stone of the covered temple of Luxor, our attention was attracted by certain blocks inserted into the walls. These blocks were perfectly polished and cut according to a certain characteristic slope that immediately recalled the batter of the pylon. The side cut at an angle was set into the thickness of the wall, but in following the joint we were able to measure the angle with respect to the true horizontal with the aid of a level. Moreover, with vertical strings stretched on the walls we were able to verify the angular reading by measuring and calculating the batter.

Now, many of these sloped stones were used elsewhere before being used in the covered temple of Luxor, particularly in the doors or in certain partitions on which the idea of "passage" is evoked.

Their most characteristic use is found in the wall that separates the room of Amun's barque from the room of the "coronation" (rooms VI and II). This whole wall has only three blocks "in transparency," that is, blocks that traverse the full thickness of the wall and thus connect the two rooms. Two of these blocks are cut following a carefully measured angle and are found at a distance that was also very precisely measured; finally, by extending the angled joints far enough we could simply and directly verify the angles and the measurements defined by these stones.

It was then that we undertook the task of determining the dimensions and the batter of the pylon of Luxor in order to compare them with those of the reused stones. Different batters were taken on each side at different places, taking into account the play of the blocks at certain points that have more or less settled because of the construction of the "hollow" pylon.

As the plan (plate 67) makes clear, the west face of the west wing is necessarily "veiled," because the edge of its lower plane is not parallel to the edge of its upper plane. The extreme sizes of the angles at the junction of the vertical edges of the north and south faces are perceived to be equal to the batters of these facades.

The north facade has an average batter of 83°17′ to 83°20′ (cot 2/17); the posts of the north door are at a batter of 83°33′; the south facade has an average batter of 81°52′ (cot 1/7).

The angular measurements indicated by the slanted stones traversing the wall that separates rooms II and VI are as follows:

Southern block:
  surface of room II 83°33′ to 83°40′
  surface of room VI 83°33′ to 83°43′
Northern block:
  surface of room II 83°15′ ⎫
  surface of room VI 83°16′ ⎬ ±5′

Comparatively, the reused blocks indeed give the two essential batters of the north face of the pylon, the mass of the west wing, and the slope of the door. The batter of the south side of the pylon corresponds to the ratio of 1 to 7, which places it in relation to the angle of return of Amun that is "reflected" beginning at this wall.[74]

The angular analogy between the two reused stones and the pylon gives a basis for assuming that these stones belonged to an analogous pylon, before Amenhotep III, and their placement in the walls facing each other at a definite distance apart suggests extending the line of their batters. In room II the extension of the batter indicated by these two blocks up to the baseline that passes under the soles of the feet of the figures in the first register defines a length that is, on a one-to-ten scale, that of the Ramesside pylon. We can therefore see, on the wall of room II, the projection on the scale of one to ten of the pylon constructed much later by Ramesses. Its base is at the level of the soles of the feet of the figures, since the pylon itself is located at the soles of the feet of the Man represented by the temple.

It is in fact in room II that the purified, crowned king performed the "royal ascent toward the temple" by passing through the door that leads to the sanctuary.[75]

Seth is carved on the northern sloped stone, and Seth is "master of the South." On the southern sloped stone we find the falcon crowned with the solar disk,[76] Horus, "master of the North." Their positions are reversed on this wall on which the *neters*, who are said "to come from the North," are coming from the South. If we project these two stones onto the pylon of Ramesses, considering the orientation indicated in this place by the crowns of the figures represented on the central door, then Seth, master of the white crown of the South, will take his place at the east, and Horus, master of the red crown of the North, will take his place at the west, which arrangement is correct with regard to their respective significance.

The stone cut on a slope, corresponding to the west side of the pylon—Horus—gives the exact angle of the batter of the north and the west faces that are joined at this place by the torus.

The stone on the left side—Seth—corresponding to the eastern end of the pylon, has a slope that indeed corresponds to the north facade, but is not exactly that of the east facade. Nevertheless, by extending these indicated slopes to the horizontal at ground level and then measuring on the wall of room II, we find the exact length of the pylon in the proportion of one to ten.

Thus we are dealing once more with this typically pharaonic method of simultaneously presenting the various aspects of an object with a single image, as we have seen in the figure of the gestating Mut, the vulture, one of whose wings is shown from the inside and the other from the outside, the body being in profile and the tail being seen in plan.

---

[74] Cf. plate 86. The repository of Amun's barque leans against the south facade of the west wing of the pylon.

[75] The word for door is *art*, and *arty* signifies "jaw." These rooms II and VI are at the place of the jaw, *arty*. Cf. plate 38 and chapter 31, fig. 226, and chapter 14, fig. 167, no. 17.

[76] The two feathers that define him as Mentu are removed from the reused block.

In transparency, the north stone links Seth in room II with the animals of the desert represented in room VI that are being offered in sacrifice by the king who is crowned with the white crown and holds the white club in his hand. Now, is not Seth, in the ritual, assimilated to the animals of the desert? The southern stone, through its upper joint, removes the plumes of Mentu and shows only Horus and his solar disk. In transparency the disk is projected into the naos of the sacred barque represented in room VI (fig. 269).

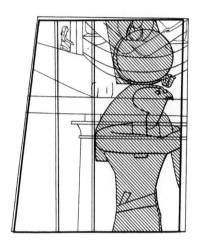 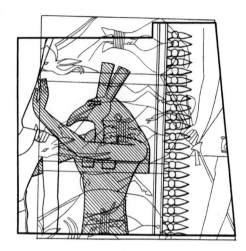

Fig. 269. The two reused stones that link room II (hachured) *and VI* (in white)

On the pylon of Ramesses, the projection of these two stones from room II, enlarged ten times, reveals the metrical relationship between the *canevas* drawn on the pylon and that of the figures in room II. The unit square of the west wing of the pylon on its north face corresponds to 25 meters divided by 19, or 1.315 meters, the measurement equal to the height under the headband of the figures in room II.[77] The projection of the pylon onto the wall of room II places the double baptism with the ankh exactly in the door.[78]

The pylon includes the principal door that leads to the interior of the temple. Through the measures, the master builder inscribed the proportions of the human body there; he adapted the measurements and the batters of the walls to the directions of the orientations; meters, cubits, and fathoms are inscribed there, and through the figures on the walls of rooms II and VI, he related the front door of the temple to the gesture of purification, the preparation required in order to have access to the Holy of Holies.

———

It is the character of pharaonic thinking always to summarize in a single, symbolic image all the aspects of an entire subject. North creates south. South creates north. East creates west. West creates east.

Thus we understand nature, but we forget that it is not a question of a simple complementation or polarization of notions, but of an activity: a thing actually creates its own opposite, so it is the white crown that creates the red crown and vice versa. In this, there is a lesson for how to read natural functions that our scholarly thought, our mentalized thinking, no longer respects.

[77] Cf. vol. 1, fig. 140, and analysis of the measurements.
[78] Cf. plate 99.

The spirit of synthesis predominates in every case. This is what makes our task so difficult and often so thankless, for in describing these things we must of necessity repeat the same instructions, the same numbers, the same gestures, which are actually repeated but with variations that we must learn how to read.

CONCLUSION

The importance of the *canevas*, which I call the "master builder's grid," is only understood through a technical and geometric way of thinking. Scholarly thinking, that is, working with abstract and imaginary elements, must be distinguished from this directive that is offered by the *canevas*. The *canevas* is a true architecture of number that allows us to read numbers in both planes and volumes. We look at this grid as a plane, but the Ancients conceived it in space as well, which they demonstrate through the principle of the *s'km* in which a length is conceived simultaneously as a band and as a series of prisms, square in section. Indeed, if it is a question of a surface, this length is itself a band-surface, and if it is a matter of a volume, it must also be a volume. The unit of reference of this measure always has the value of a square unit for the surface, or a cubic unit for a volume.

If we remember that for the pharaonic sage nothing in the created universe is absolute, we can understand that all of his logic is based on alternation, the constant balancing of the poles of every phenomenon. In mathematics this always leads to a search for the closest possible degree of precision located between a plus and a minus. Rather than starting from an extreme balancing, which results in an absurd consequence, this thinker knows that by reducing the amplitude little by little he can attain all the precision desired; he also knows that the absolute is not the middle between the two extremes, that it cannot be situated between them. Its name is the *"Neter* of *neters,"* what we call the One God.

This principle brings an extreme suppleness into the rigid application of the canon-base. One needn't bother making a grid of rectangular units in place of square units. One obeys the numbers, not the form. In order to clarify these things we have presented the tomb of Ukhotep at Meir, a tomb exceptionally rich in applications of the *canevas*, or more accurately, consecrated to the use of the *canevas*. We find there the data of the human canon in the three positions of standing, seated, and kneeling, where the seated man is the "geometric mean term" between the extremes.

We also see there the net for the "bird hunt" giving a harmonic decomposition according to the golden number, and next to it the musicians and singers that express in music the law of harmony already expressed by numbers.

This tomb shows us also the suppleness of the applied symbolism when we look for the exaggerations that accent a gesture or a vital state, reaching the point of a characterizing deformation but never becoming grotesque. Thus, the skeletal man who leads the bulls, and who is followed by a heavyset man, expresses the mineral character (the bones) and at the same time the "residual part," which, after death, will be the magnet for reincarnation. The gesture of the bent knee of Ukhotep entails a shift in the grid, which is then adapted to its feminine principle, Thothotep. The genesis from one state to another is shown in "animated image," a representation that can be either simultaneous or kinetic. To read this symbolism requires close attention because a vast knowledge is developed in very few images, the particular fact evoking a universal function.

The principle of the grid is not exclusively pharaonic; it is found in the Mayan civilization as well as in China and Japan, that is, in each epoch in which a wiser humanity has refused to allow itself to be dragged toward an intellectualized way of thinking—something Babylon, for example, was not able to resist. Our West, distant inheritor of this deviation, intentionally treats as primitive (in a pejorative sense) peoples who have not followed this "scholarly" path. We cannot judge otherwise because our mentality, formed by this directive, has separated us from nature by replacing its teaching with the imagination to the extent that today we must conceive of adapting the human organism to the requirements of machines. But Nature is and remains the stronger power; it is she that in the end will dominate. Were a single cog in the wheels of our civilization to miss, the whole thing would collapse.

The power that dominates in nature is, in Apet of the South, symbolized by the *kamutef*. It is said, "From nothing God created the world." "God," an abstraction, "nothing," a negation; this is making much out of *absences* in order to create the world. We purposefully content ourselves with abstract words and this tempts us to attribute to them a concrete meaning. The Ancients are symbolists and draw upon natural and living facts in order to evoke the function of the inexpressible. The *kamutef* is an example of this. The phallus is placed at the location of the navel, the maternal attachment. A natural birth is denied, but receptive femininity is replaced by active, seminal masculinity. This is the Adamic hermaphrodite, the first living being who must necessarily contain in itself two natures: yes and no, good and bad, high and low. . . . The archangel in falling brings a ray of the Light, of the fire, of the divine—that is, supernatural—power. Now, our *kamutef* is represented as Min. Min is the effect of Ptah, the celestial power fallen, that is, coagulated, in earth. This Ptah (Vulcan or Hephaestus) is fixed in earth. He can no longer move by himself (this is symbolized by his bound legs), but he becomes the bow that launches the arrows, this activating force that provokes the separation of the waters of the earth from the waters above, different from the waters below; and this *separative action* will be called *the expanse,* which has a double nature, Shu-Tefnut. With what appears to be above his raised left arm, improperly called the "whip," the *kamutef* becomes this space, this separative force, still necessarily androgynous; the *nekhakha* scepter, which floats above his hand held up toward the sky, is the staff; and I mean precisely *the staff,* as in the wand of Wotan, the rod of Moses, the staff of the pilgrim, and the royal scepters. From the end of this staff flows a triple stream, in the form of droplets, which constitutes the waters above, now having a triple nature in two. We shall speak later of this third principle. Each new activity of the genesis assumes a new name in myth along with a new figurative gesture, which has been wrongly interpreted as a new person whose significance is not understood. It is necessary to incorporate into a real order each principle of the unique fact that is the genesis.

It is in the disproportions of the *kamutef,* as in those of Thoth at Karnak, that the meaning of these figures, explained by the numbers, is revealed. It is never necessary to look for an aesthetic significance in pharaonic figures: they are a writing. The above-mentioned tableau from the tomb of Ramesses IX is another example; it teaches the evolution of the straight line (the meter) into a curve that defines the royal cubit, it is the passage from the square to the disk, that is, the internal function that provokes the curved path of movement. This teaching is connected with that of the *kamutef;* it is the going forth of Ra from the terrestrial mountain toward the light, it is the Horian reappearance of Osiris that creates vital and cyclic movement.

It is always by virtue of the *canevas* that these numbers become tangible and speak.

Now, all these demonstrations—Ukhotep at Meir, the Maya, Thoth of Karnak, the tomb of Ramesses IX—are again applied in Apet of the South, the temple of Luxor. The naos of the papyrus confirms the geometric play of the naos of Luxor. The Temple is a synthesis of everything these *canevas* can teach us through the principle of unequal division, through the selection of different cubits and their adaptation to the orientations, and, finally, through the projection of the pylon onto the wall of the sanctuary of the barque. The two profiles of Seth and Horus, in complementing each other at the rising and at the setting, evoke one another: the white *(hdj)* through the red *(dshr),* the nocturnal moon through the diurnal sun. Their meaning is identical to the teaching of the tomb at Meir.

If on the one hand, it is life that links all functions to each other, on the other, it is the grid of the master builder that links the geometric and numerical expressions, and it is Man who is the mean term between numbers and life through his measurement of the world transcribed by the cubits.

Chapter 38

TRANSFORMATIONS AND MUTATIONS

Plates 68–74

Movement is the symbol that carries the gesture,
but since movement (the mechanical movement of
the arm, for example) can only affect the corporeal,
and the question here concerns a "vital movement,"
the Ancients could only evoke a "genesis" by the
symbol of movement. This genesis is considered,
then, as a movement of becoming . . .

(Chapter 4)

PLATE 68

Movement

*Our objective, rational, Euclidean thought holds
that two straight lines meeting at a point make an
angle. But what intrigues the Ancient Egyptian is
the point of intersection and the two straight lines.
He sees an* articulation, *therefore a* cause *of the
dividing into two.*

(Chapter 7)

PLATE 69

Dividing in Two

The living gesture speaks and says what can never be transcribed into words in an equally vital way.

(Chapter 15)

PLATE 70

Transformation of the Elements

It is necessary to see the canon thus as a principle of proportions for constructing a figure. This allows one to take note of all the variations and symbolic deformations in the figure in order to understand the idea it was intended to express.

(Chapter 11)

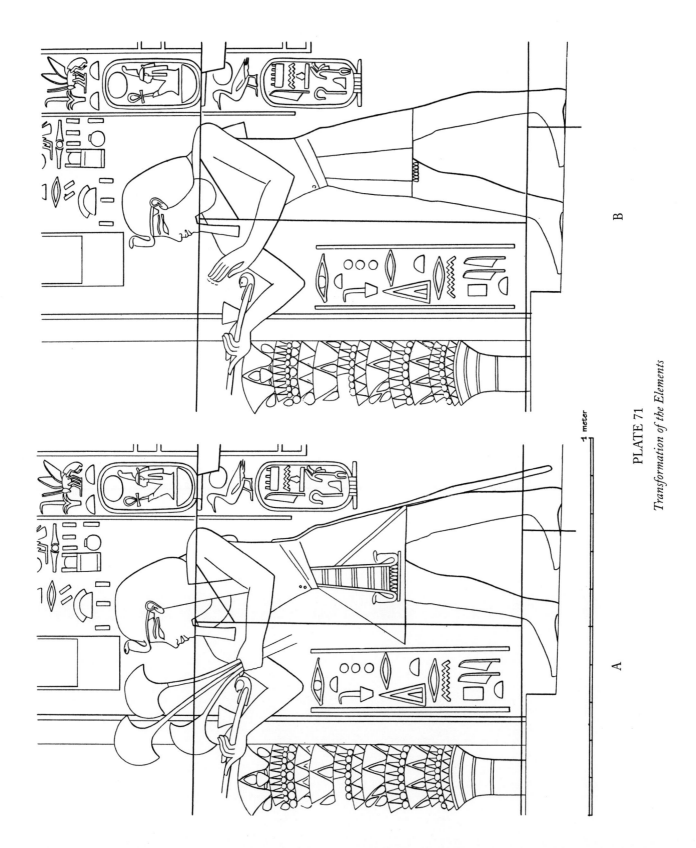

PLATE 71

Transformation of the Elements

1 meter

A

B

The royal apron is a magnificent illustration that helps us to understand what our word symbol, *so imperfect, wishes to express. This is not in any way related to the fantasies of certain symbolists in the West.*

(Chapter 12)

PLATE 72

Movement of the Kingdoms

. . . the geometry of the royal apron . . . represents a living, moving geometry. Its shifting on the coordinates modifies . . . the values of the numbers by connecting these different values to each other.

(Chapter 12)

PLATE 73

Movement of the Kingdoms

. . . here, as elsewhere, the pharaonic sages wished to record their thought on the invariable base of numbers, and for this purpose took the liberty of slightly modifying the mental scheme. In no case would the pharaonic expression be fixed in crystal; it was always vitally in keeping with the mobility of what is living.

(Chapter 11)

1 meter

PLATE 74

Movement of the Kingdoms

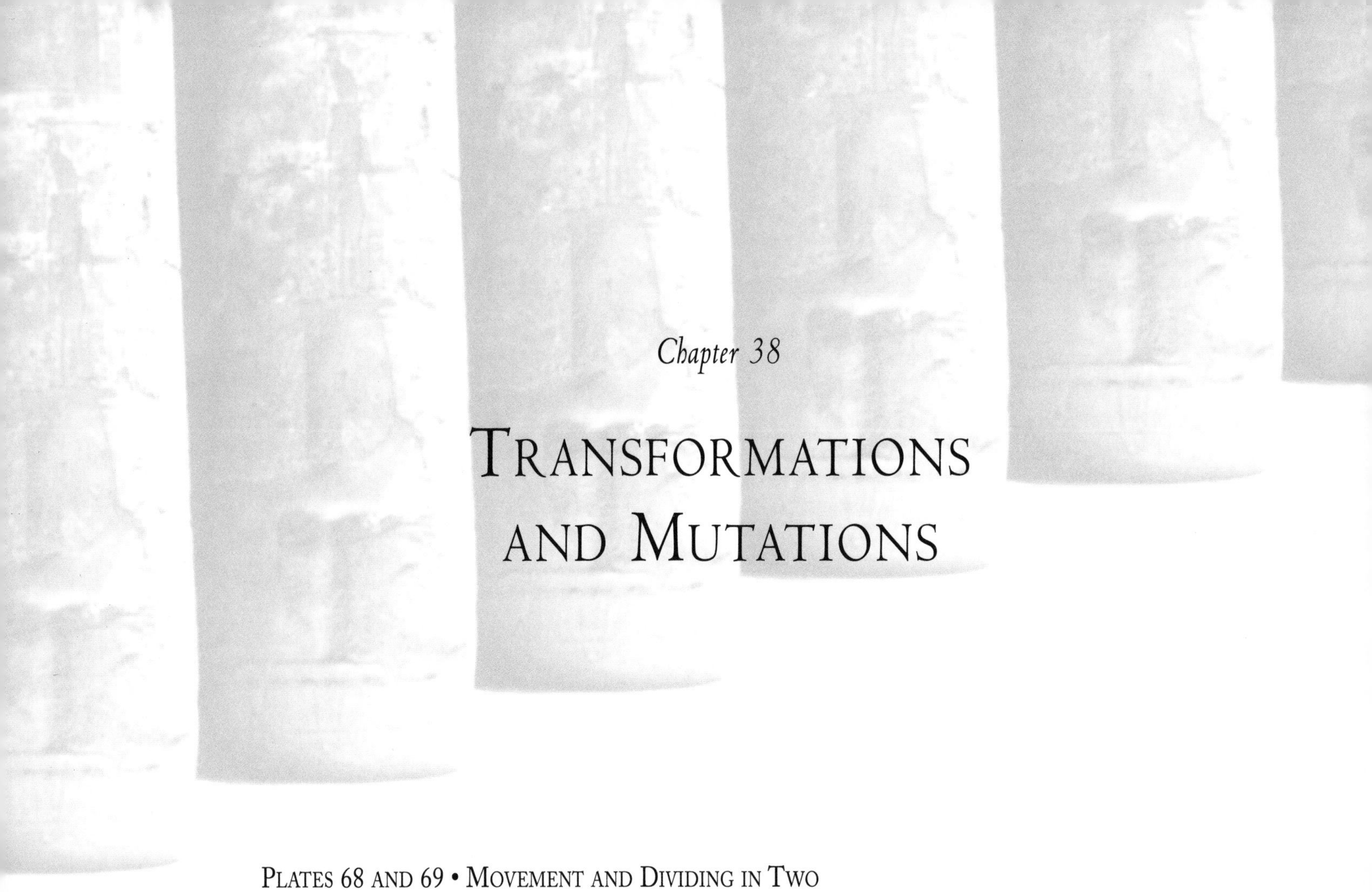

Chapter 38

TRANSFORMATIONS AND MUTATIONS

PLATES 68 AND 69 • MOVEMENT AND DIVIDING IN TWO

The bas-relief pictured in these plates is found in room VI on the first register of the east partition (plate 100), in front of the representation of the barque of Amun in its naos.

Between the king and this naos, on a table of offerings, the four red *desher* vases are placed, and above them are four white *nem wt* vases placed on a shelf with no support. The royal figure is in motion and pours water from the white vase he holds in his two *right* hands. It is said that he must make this purification four times, once toward each of the four cardinal points.

Movement is marked in this figure by modifications in the sculpture that indicate two stages, but the king does not change attributes, costume, gesture, or offerings in passing from the first to the second stage. The essential transformation is in the shift of the center of equilibrium. The *sense* of the perception of equilibrium located in the ear becomes superimposed on the motor center for balancing located in the cerebellum.

The joint of the vertical stones goes from the left ankle to the middle of the neck at the level of the shoulders (sixteenth line of the canon) and cuts the necklace in two. This joint isolates the shoulder and the left arm, the right forearm, and the front corner of the apron, as well as the cardiac region. Its extension would pass through the ear, thus indicating the axis of stability of the figure as he straightens up again.

In the first stage, this vertical line was directed toward the back part of the head (cerebellum) without, however, ending there. We can thus definitely discover in the intent of the text a relationship between the cerebellum and the intelligence of equilibrium in its vital expression. This figure clearly represents a separating movement indicated by the nature and the symbol of the vases.

We have often commented on the importance the Ancients gave to this axis of equilibrium. One representation, which goes back to the Old Kingdom (fig. 270),[1] shows a royal figure holding

---

[1] Cf. Jéquier, *Frises d'objets*, fig. 211, from Auguste Mariette, *Les Mastabas de l'Ancien Empire* (Paris: F. Vieweg, 1884).

Fig. 270. Royal figure holding the āba *scepter in his hand, crossing over the staff (Old Kingdom)*

his staff exactly on the equilibrium axis passing in front of his ear and dividing the body in two. This symbol is completed by the crossing of a double baldric of pearls, and, in the guise of a breast-plate, the symbol of Hathor (here the symbol of harmony) on the stomach. The vertical staff is held in the left hand, while the *āba* scepter in the right hand[2] is crossed horizontally over the staff.

One could read this as "to cross on the axis of equilibrium," that is, to stabilize the equilibrium.

PLATES 70 AND 71 • TRANSFORMATION OF THE ELEMENTS

This figuration, also altered, is found on the west wall of room VI in front of the moving figure who offers the four vases to the sacred barque, east wall (plates 68 and 69).[3]

The sanctuary of the barque of Amun originally included four columns framing a ramp that rose toward a wooden naos (tabernacle) containing the sacred barque. This barque is depicted on both the east and west walls of room VI, the two representations facing each other as if reflected. Only the symbols that accompany the two figures change, adapting themselves to the eastern and western orientations. Twelve holes remain in the white limestone pavement that were for placing the stakes supporting the veil that surrounded this sacred place.

At the time of Alexander (300 B.C.), a sandstone naos was constructed on the site of the ancient columns; these were not lifted out, but cut above the ground in such a way that their pedestals and a small part of the columns themselves remained. A part of the pedestal of the ancient column is embedded in the pedestal of the new naos, and the remaining fraction of the column has been included in the construction.

Now, at the time of the first sanctuary, the axes were already drawn on the ground on the sandstone pavement and covered by the limestone pavement. The key for the crossing of the axes on the threshold of the door of this room also existed at that time. Through this we can see that all the geometric and trigonometric elements were noted; it is, however, only with the construction of the naos of Alexander that the key pentagonal function was explained by the proportions of this naos (plate 83 and fig. 284). Before this date, the essential elements of the pentagon were inscribed in the king's apron in its first stage (fig. 271).

[2] Cf. plate 93, *āba* scepter, nos. 1, 2, 6, and 7, and fig. 292.

[3] Because of the lack of space and very bad lighting, the photograph makes the outline of the first stage difficult to see.

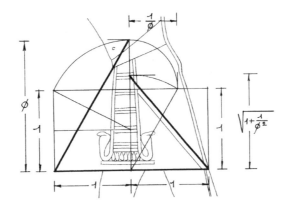

Fig. 271. Geometric study of a royal apron, room VI, west wall

The front angle determines the relationship 1 to ϕ. The rear angle determines the relationship 1 to $\sqrt{1 + 1/\phi^2}$, which defines the side of the pentagon for which the radius of the circumscribing circle is 1. The rear angle gives the application, through the pentagon, of the function ϕ indicated by the front angle.

This bas-relief offers us an example of a numerical alteration with regard to changes in the offering, the headdress, the loincloth, and the gesture. Only the presentation of the offering of the "cubit with incense," separated from the rest of the figure by a vertical joint, does not vary.

In the first stage the king wore the *nemes* headdress and held the cubit with incense in his right hand[4] and three blooming papyrus flowers in his left hand; he was also wearing the triangular apron with a tail. He is said to be offering incense and the gift of the first vegetation of the season (plate 71A).

In the second stage, he wears the close-fitting headdress and is belted with a simple loincloth *without tail,* which is very rare. This removal of the triangular apron and of the tail coincides with the changing of the ritual gesture and of the offering: the left hand is now open and becomes a right hand, thus active; it *has given* the first fruits, the plant kingdom has played the passive role. This king is now separated from the plant kingdom, and yet the reference to this kingdom has not been removed in the column of text. As the extension of the spinal column, the ritual tail is the symbol of animation by the terrestrial fire, which is the cause of vegetation. In the second stage this figure no longer has this relationship with the terrestrial fire and no longer has the plants to offer; but the presence of two navels indicates a second birth. Thus a change is made to coincide with a vital function, geometrically expressed.

Thus, in the first stage, the king offered plants and wore the triangular loincloth indicating, through its angles, the ϕ and pentagonal functions that rule vegetation.

Moreover, already under Amenhotep III the intercolumnar spaces of this sanctuary were in the proportion, with respect to each other, of the radii of the circles that inscribe and circumscribe the pentagon, and the orientation of the principal axes of the temple also applied this function.

There would, therefore, be good reason to think that this figure was changed at the time of the construction of the naos applying these functions, an assumption that is acceptable if we recall that

---

[4] The cubit with incense is a wooden shaft with a hand carrying the vase of fire at one end and a falcon's head at the other, in front of which is the jar containing the incense.

Alexander completely altered the upper part of the north wall of this room, as well as its door, and replaced the cartouches of Amenhotep III that were there with his own.

PLATES 72–74 • MOVEMENT OF THE KINGDOMS

This bas-relief is found on the first register of the west wall of the room of the barque of Amun (room VI). It is separated from the king of the preceding plate by the tableau of forty offerings. In the photograph of plate 72 one can verify lines from the first stage on the royal figure as well as on the offerings. The two stages are reconstituted in plates 73 and 74, except for the destroyed parts that have not been restored.

The first stage (plate 73) includes animal offerings buried under a pile of grain, with three papyrus flowers set up in front of the table of offerings. The second stage (plate 74) removes the grain as well as the papyrus, and the animal offering is augmented by a *khepesh* thigh, three ribs, and four hearts. In both cases the king makes the same gesture of offering the fire with his left hand while he holds three gold or silver vases in his right hand pouring three streams of purifying water. This transformation or "animalization" is expressed by the modifications in the proportions of the apron.

In this case there are two possible readings for the angles of the same apron at each stage: first, with respect to the horizontal of the base of the apron, which does not coincide with the horizontal of the *canevas* of the figure; second, with respect to the line of the base of the apron's front panel, which is parallel to the horizontal of the general *canevas* and thus shows two possible readings.

We are therefore going to study the geometric functions of this royal apron in its first stage (fig. 272) and its second stage (fig. 273).

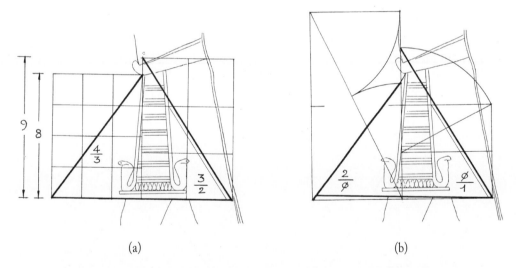

(a)   (b)

Fig. 272. Geometric study of a royal apron, first stage, room VI, west partition

The angles of the apron read *(a)* with respect to the base of the apron; *(b)* with respect to the horizontal of the tableau.

In the first stage of the bas-relief, figure 272a shows that the angles of the apron with respect to its own base define the two mean terms, arithmetic and harmonic, between 1 and 2, constituting musical proportion: at the rear is the fifth and at the front, the fourth; the difference between them determines the tone, and their product equals 2, the octave. In figure 272b, the apron, in relation to the general *canevas* of the figure, thus with respect to the true horizontal, expresses the double function of ϕ through growth and through scission. At the rear, the half-base of the apron represents the unit that grows in order to define the height ϕ; it is the act of growth. In the front, the half-base of the apron is also unity, and the height of the triangle becomes $2/\phi$ by scission. It is a question here of the function ϕ and its inversion.

The two readings have the same outcome:

$$a)\ \frac{3}{2} \times \frac{4}{3} = 2$$
$$b)\ \frac{\phi}{1} \times \frac{2}{\phi} = 2.$$

The same result is obtained with whole numbers and the irrational function ϕ.

In these two readings, the angles at the base are modified, whereas the sum of the two angles at the apex remains virtually identical. It is indeed remarkable that the transformation of the triangle formed of whole numbers into another triangle formed of irrational values gives an apex angle of the same value to within the practically imperceptible difference of $0°7'$.

Through this demonstration, in which the product in the two cases equals 2, and in spite of the changes in the ratios, musical harmony (whole numbers) is brought into relationship with the principle of harmony based on the function ϕ. Now, these numbers and ratios correspond to the first stage of the figuration comprising the plants (papyrus) and the vegetal character of the offerings.

———

The second stage of the drawing of the apron (figs. 273a and 273b) leaves the rear angle unchanged, with the two preceding angular readings still there. By contrast, the front angle is modified. The play of the inverse and the mean terms between 1 and 2 are removed as well as the dividing function 2 : ϕ. The reading on the general *canevas*, that is, with respect to the horizontal of the tableau *(b)*, or with respect to the base of the apron *(a)*, presents an inversion of the functions.

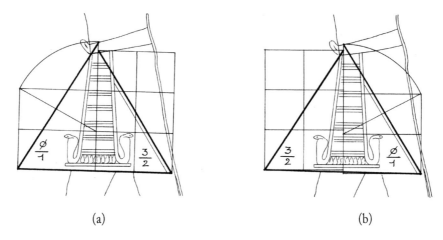

(a)   (b)

Fig. 273. Geometric study of a royal apron, second stage; room VI, west partition

Angles of the apron read *(a)* with respect to the base of the apron; *(b)* with respect to the horizontal of the tableau.

The second stage establishes an oscillating equilibrium between rational harmony and its irrational cause ϕ. There is a cessation of growth by division, that is, fixation.

At this moment, the change from the plant offering into the animal organism animated by the hearts is shown. This puts cold trigonometry into a vital relationship with life, symbolized by the offerings, and is yet another magnificent demonstration of the pharaonic mentality.

Harmony commands, reason demonstrates, and it is a superior synthesizing intelligence proper to man that makes the link.

This justifies our use of the term "magical science" to describe the science of the Ancients, founded on the intelligence of the heart, which is what conveys the feeling and vision at the heart of the object.[5]

The trigonometric character of the loincloths is always indicated by radial lines that start from the front angle and very often extend to the sloping back line, passing under the front, designed panel. Because the front and rear angles are different in most cases, one can wonder why only one set of radial lines is drawn for the two indicated angles.

The loincloth studied here gives the ratios that belong to musical harmony. This suggests that we draw the harmonic decomposition evoked by this apron (fig. 274a).

The development of the harmonic decomposition, starting from this first base, defines a series of ratios through the drawing of radial lines that begin at the front angle and actually end at the sloping back line. The horizontals in this layout, moreover, define the location of the groups of horizontal lines on the front panel of the apron. In the present case, the distance between each group of horizontal lines corresponds to 1/9 of the total height (fig. 274a).

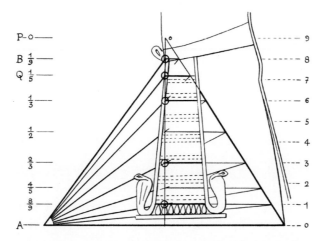

Fig. 274a. Drawing of the harmonic decomposition evoked by the numerical functions of the apron

The height PA, perpendicular to the base of the loincloth, is 9, the segment PB is 1. The mean term PQ resulting from the harmonic division is $\frac{1}{5}PA$, and the mathematical formula that allows the mean term to be established is intimately linked to the function connected to the subtraction of angular relationships notated by $1/n$, thus:

$$\frac{\hat{1}}{1} - \frac{\hat{1}}{9} = \frac{9-1}{9+1} = \frac{\hat{8}}{10} = \frac{\hat{4}}{5} = AQ, \text{ or } PA - PQ.$$

[5] Let us recall that the aprons are pyramids.

This discovery recalls that the aprons, having a trigonometric rationale, are connected with harmony, the function evoked here by the horizontal lines of the apron's front panel.

Always and everywhere, at the base of pharaonic geometric and mathematical expressions, we find the harmonic law. The apron described here is to be considered a revelation of these functions, and we should regard it as a symbol, because all aprons do not demonstrate the link that unites trigonometry to harmony so explicitly.

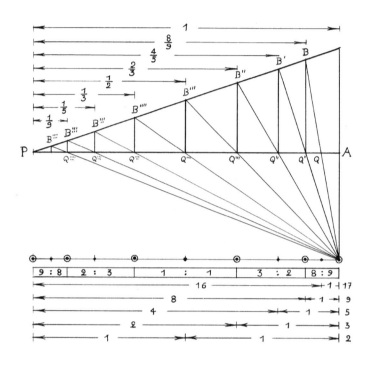

Fig. 274b. Synthesis 1

Fig. 46 from vol. 1, chapter 6; compare with fig. 274a.

APPENDIX: THE PHARAONIC PROCEDURE FOR MODIFYING THE ANGLES OF THE APRON BY INCLINING THE BASE

The problem is to diminish the height of the triangle from ϕ to $1\frac{1}{2}$. We would proceed by diminishing this height. The Ancients, by modifying the slope of the base of the triangle, reduced its height as well, but without touching the apex. This is easily accomplished through the proportional notation of angles, and conforms to pharaonic thought, which is the opposite of our methods.

We draw a grid on the apron parallel to the horizontal of the tableau, the unity of which is equal to half of the digit that measures the figure. We then extend the two hypotenuses to the point where they meet, which gives a total height of 34 common to the two triangles; the width of the right side of the base of the apron is 21, which makes one of the ϕ to 1 ratios taken from the F series. For the front triangle, the height remains the same and equals 1. By extending the hypotenuse to the true horizontal, the proportion 34 to $22\frac{2}{3}$ is obtained, that is, 1 to 2/3.

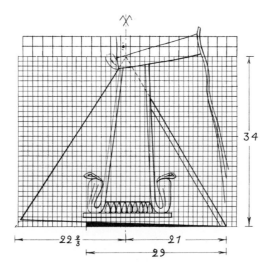

Fig. 275. Study of a royal apron; room VI, west wall

Modification of the angles of the apron through the slope of the base

With respect to the horizontal of the tableau, the rear angle defines ϕ *and the front angle defines the ratio of the fifth.* To invert these functions, it is necessary to subtract the front angle from the rear angle through the procedure of proportional notation:

$$\frac{\widehat{34}}{21} - \frac{\widehat{3}}{2} = \frac{68-63}{42+102} = \frac{\widehat{5}}{144} = \frac{1}{28.8}.$$

The difference obtained, reduced to $1/n$, is very close to 1 : 29, and is actually the simplest and most perfect angle for establishing the sought-for difference. Here is the proof:

$$\frac{\widehat{3}}{2} + \frac{\widehat{1}}{29} = \frac{87+2}{58-3} = \frac{\widehat{89}}{55}.$$

The angle 1 to 29 is the difference between the ratio 3 : 2 and the pair from the F series that follows the ratio 34 : 21, read in digits on the *canevas*.

It is necessary then to raise the base of the apron one band, with 1 for height and 29 for length (by taking the half-digit for the unit). This is the simplest method for showing in practical terms the modification of these angles.

———

As proof of refinement of thought and harmony in expression, let us look at the ratio between the measures of the place in which this figuration is found and its own proportions.

The east and west walls of room VI where this figure is carved measure 6 fathoms. The north and south measure 6 fathoms $\div$ $\pi/3$ = 20 radius cubits.[6] Each of the 28 digits of this radius cubit is 1.895 centimeters. Now the height of this king to the forehead is exactly 128.9 centimeters, measured on the spot, which corresponds to 68 digits of the radius cubit, 68 digits being equal to 128.86... centimeters obtained by calculation. These are exactly the same digits that served for drawing the grid placed on the apron studied in fig. 275.

[6] Cf. vol. 1, fig. 113.

Chapter 39

A Secret Sanctuary

⟨⟨⟨⟩⟩⟩

Plates 75–78

It should never be forgotten
that the theological directive is always piously
respected, and that, above
all, the play of thought
that has no geometric
confirmation is excluded.
Nevertheless, it is not to
this directive only that
mathematical thought is
confined. There is another
mental disposition that is
very difficult for us to
understand today; it con-
sists of a kind of alliance
between a very practical,
realistic sense, and the
"feeling" I call "spatial
vision."

(Chapter 6)

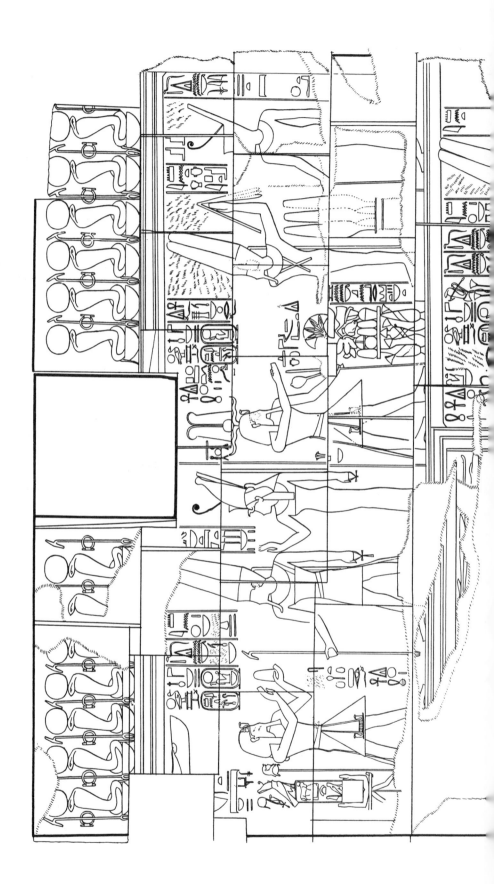

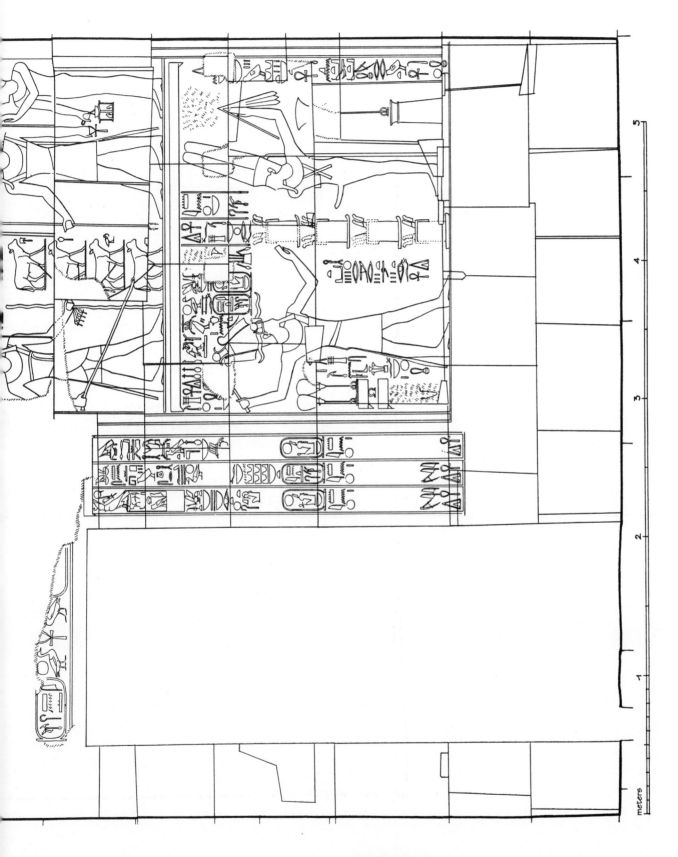

PLATE 75

Sanctuary V, North Partition

It is the selective function, discerning, or rather dividing in two, that is represented by the olfactory center as a living, secret sanctuary of this temple, whose essential and abstract aspect is noted by number.

(Chapter 18)

meters 1 2

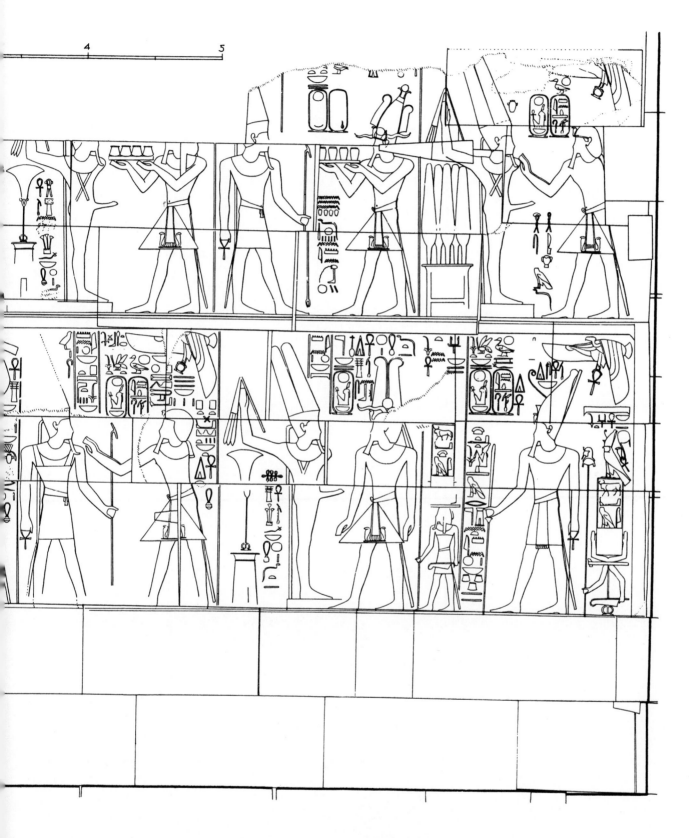

PLATE 76

Sanctuary V, West Partition

*It is . . . upon the knowledge
of functional identity—
the philosophy of the Unity—
that the magic of religious
rituals, the liturgy, and
the perfect architecture of
the temples are established.*

(Chapter 1)

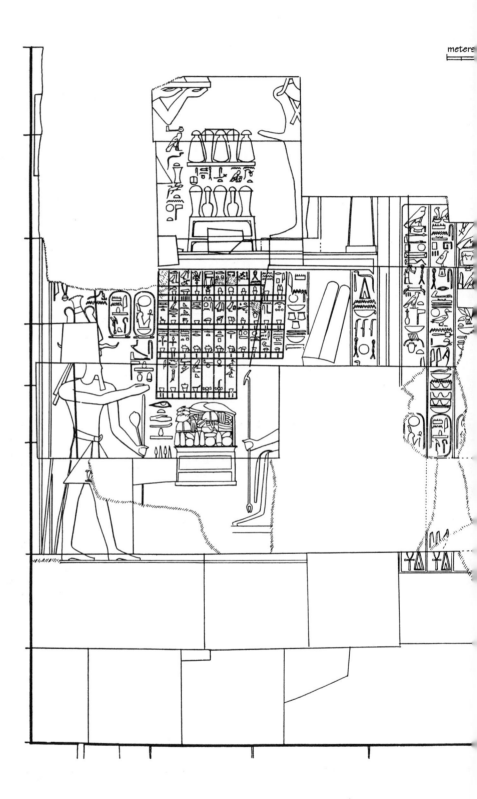

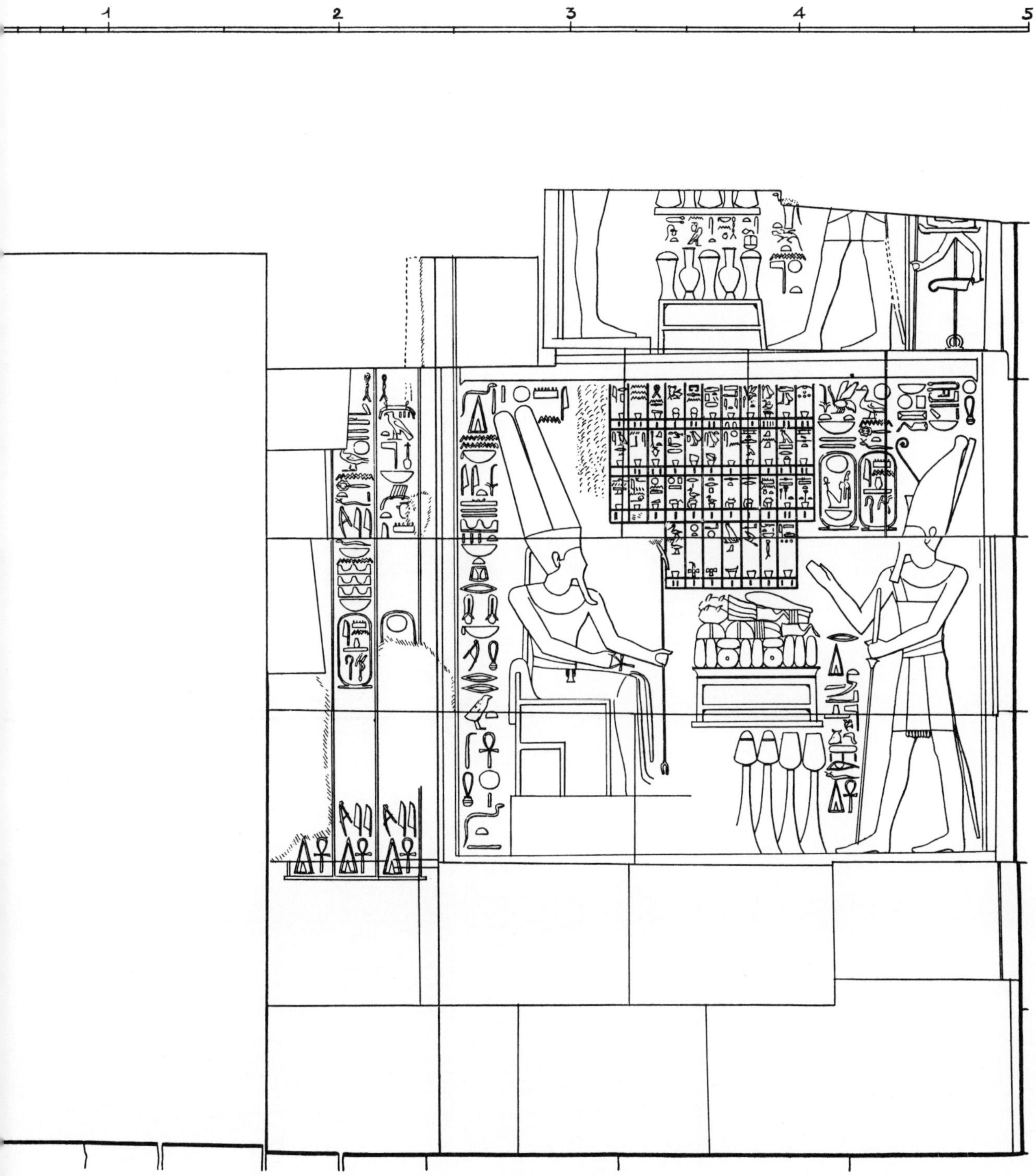

PLATE 77

Sanctuary V, East Partition

Number is the definition
of the functions, and it is
in this sense only that the
Universe is number.

(Chapter 5)

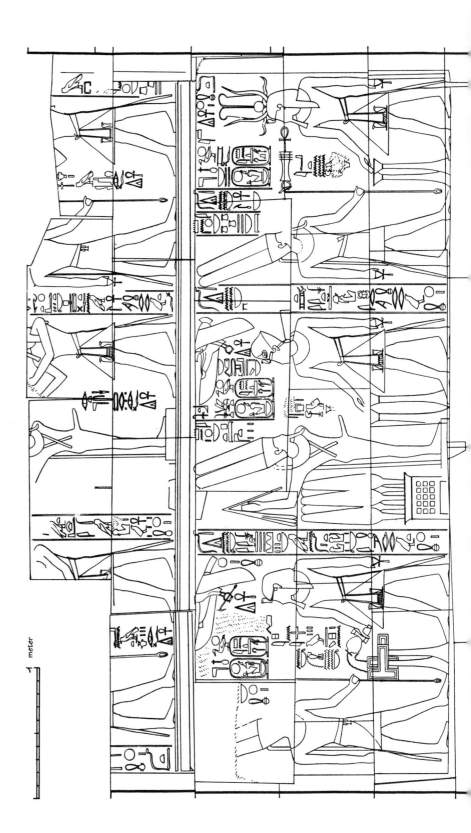

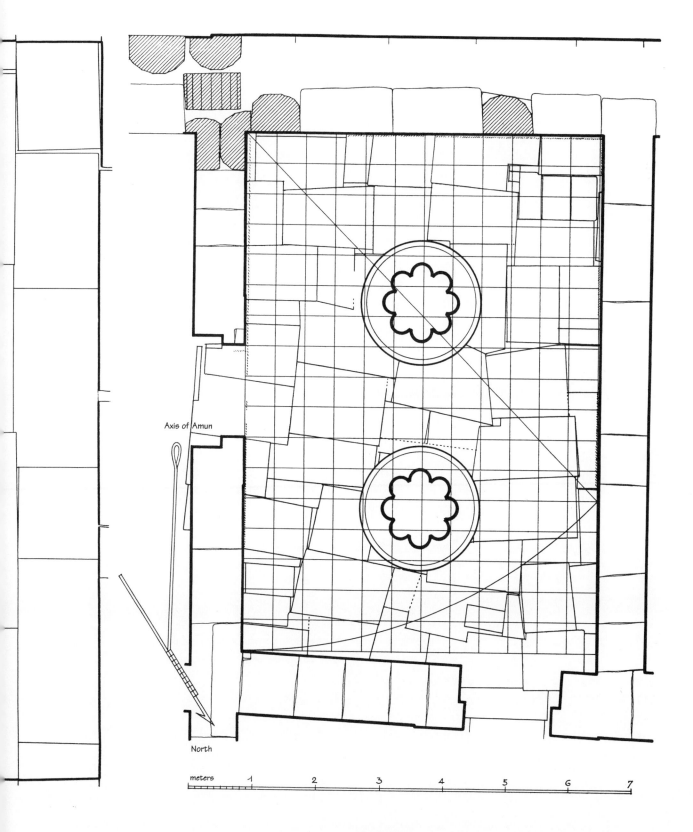

Axis of Amun

North

meters   1   2   3   4   5   6   7

PLATE 78

Sanctuary V, South Partition and Plan

Chapter 39

A SECRET SANCTUARY

The three secret sanctuaries of the covered temple are located at the base of the headband encircling the head of the Man of the Temple; sanctuary V is the eastern one. It opens to the north on the room of twelve columns and presents a typical case of transparency, which I noted in *The Temple in Man*,[1] and which was truly a revelation of how to read architectural writing.[2] I noted then the choice of this place—consecrated to the uraeus, the serpent on the forehead—is related to the olfactory sense and its "dualizing" significance. A thorough study of this sanctuary shows that it is entirely dedicated to the *dualizing* principle of understanding, which itself creates the moral intelligence through the oppositions of good and evil, and the oppositions of affirmation and negation that form the faculty of reasoning, psychological consciousness, and discernment. This fact is marked by the principles of the dualization of number, that is, the root of 2, and through the serpent, a typically dual being, as well as by the representations in this room that have a dual quality.

PLATE 75 • NORTH PARTITION

The north partition—the only intact one in this room—allows us to get a general idea of the arrangement of the tableaux that covered the walls of the sanctuaries: above a base without any decoration, the tableaux are drawn on three registers, each with a double underline representing the earth and topped by a long band symbolizing the sky. The entire group of tableaux is for the most part framed by a border resembling the one that surrounds the cubic thrones,[3] which, in general, is made of a wide band of gold inlaid with semiprecious stones (lapis lazuli, turquoise, and carnelian) or red, green, or blue glass paste. The whole is crowned by a frieze of uraei in woven baskets.

---

[1] Cf. *The Temple in Man*, pp. 102–5.

[2] Since that time, young archaeologists have often wisely taken into account the possibilities of transparency, but are still afraid to acknowledge it.

[3] Cf. fig. 295.

894

Each tableau represents the king performing certain gestures or ritual offerings in the presence of the *neter* of the place. The several columns of texts above these scenes, however, repeat untiringly, throughout the temple, the same benediction formulas that have no apparent connection with the subject depicted. Only one short inscription in front of the king specifies the nature of the particular scene. These laconic texts are indeed only the title of one of the phases of ritual of the daily worship, including not only the gestures represented, but also the "words to speak" while executing them.

These words are known thanks to certain papyri. The Berlin Papyrus[4] gives sixty-six chapters that each contain a title and a more or less long text. The comparison of the manuscript with the figurations in the temples led to the discovery in the temple at Abydos that twenty-nine of the Berlin Papyrus chapters were written in the seven chapels of that temple, whose reliefs specify the ritual gestures relating to each text.

The number of chapters and their order varies in the different sanctuaries,[5] whereas the ritual of the Berlin Papyrus is arranged in a logical sequence of ceremonies only some of which are developed in a particular part of the temple.

According to the texts, the formulas were spoken and the ritual gestures executed by the "priest on duty that day"; however, it was always the king, or royal principle, who was represented as performing the divine worship. Depicted in room II of the temple of Luxor[6] are particular scenes showing the purifications of the king and his "royal ascent" toward the sanctuary before performing the divine rites, after his having received power over the Two Lands and their two crowns from the hands of Seth and Horus.

From there, one can follow the progress of the king toward room XII, which serves as a sort of hypostyle for the three sacred sanctuaries (rooms V, I, and VII).[7] First, he passes through the narrow corridor (room X) where he performs the purification with incense, then, on the exterior doorposts of the eastern doorway of room XII, in the lower register, the king "goes toward the sanctuary, purified," wearing at the south (on the left) the white crown and at the north (on the right) the red crown, according to the correct orientation of each crown.[8]

In the interior of room XII, starting from the east entrance (sunrise), the procession of the king goes in two opposite directions: one toward the west, passing by the north and returning toward the south in order to enter sanctuary VII, then sanctuary I; the other goes directly toward the south in order to enter sanctuary V, then sanctuary I.

Sanctuary I thus receives the king under two aspects, the one of day (through the east and south), and the other of night (by the north and west), which are united here, whereas sanctuary V receives only the king of the day, and sanctuary VII only the king of the night.[9]

The ritual is addressed to the statue of the *neter* contained in the gilded wooden or stone naos. The doors to it were closed each night at the setting of Ra, the sun, by a bolt whose bond was

---

[4] Cf. Moret, *Rituel du culte divin journalier.*

[5] At Abydos, the sanctuary of Isis includes thirty-six tableaux, that of Harmachis thirty-five, that of Amun thirty-four, that of Ptah twenty-six, and the sanctuary of Osiris nineteen. At Luxor there are twenty-four tableaux remaining in room V, and there must have been around thirty-six of them originally.

[6] Cf. plate 100.

[7] See the location of these rooms in fig. 226b.

[8] The title "Going in toward the Sanctuary" is found in chapters 22 and 24 of the ritual.

[9] For the orientation of the crowns and the procession of the king, cf. fig. 287.

sealed. These words of the ritual allow us to understand that each night the *neter* undergoes the Osirian "passion" by recalling the myth in which the body of Osiris is dismembered by Seth. The largest part of the ritual consists of reuniting scattered pieces of the divine body thrown in the waters, of repulsing the enemies, and of recovering and restoring—"counting"—to the *neter* the eye of Horus, through which he is united with his soul.

On the north wall of room XII, one of the scenes refers to the part of the ritual in the course of which the priest-king, at daybreak, breaks the bond, snaps the sigillated earthen seal, slides open the bolt, and opens the two doors of the naos, which are compared to the doors of the sky and the earth.

To the south, the officiant, taking in hand the white club and the *mākes* staff, "appears as king," preceded by Upuat, the "opener of the way"; he is then purified again by Thoth and Horus, who pour two crossed streams of the ankh of life over his head. On the south partition of room XII in the lower register, the king offers the "four cloths."[10] In the upper register he performs the purifications four times with four red vases and four white vases (fig. 276 below).

Next to the scene of the presentation of cloth is the entryway that leads from room XII to room V. On the *left* doorpost, the royal officiant wears the white crown of the South, whereas on the lintel, it is the king making the "great stride" and located on the *right* who wears the white crown;[11] there is a crossing here, characteristic of the principle of weaving that makes manifest what is invisible.

Let us recall that here we are in the *shtyt*,[12] the "sanctuary," of the sixth *cakra* (secret center), and the wall that separates room XII from room V is situated at the level of the "cribriform plate of the ethmoid" of the Man of the Temple; olfactory sensation is perceived in the upper part of the nose by the olfactory filaments that traverse the cribriform plate and transmit it to the olfactory bulb. From there the olfactory bundles divide in two and lead toward four centers.

Now, the wall separating room XII from room V, most of whose stones extend the full thickness of the wall to its opposite side, presents one of the typical cases of scenes and texts begun on one side and completed on the other side of the partition. It is on this wall, in transparency, that the offering of the "four cloths" is found on the side of room XII, and on the same wall in room V, the four "boxes" destined to contain the cloths.[13]

In room 12, the king presents the four strips of cloth, followed by a female *neter* who holds two strips of cloth.[14] The text concerning this offering is written above the female divinity, who is quite probably Renenutet. Her name, partly defaced, has only the *ut.t* remaining and the determinative of the serpent placed on a basket. Now at the time of the Pyramids, Renenutet, serpent-divinity and protectress of the harvests, was assimilated to the divinity of weaving and of cloth itself. This "divine cloth" was the eye of Horus that is in Tayt,[15] as is Renenutet herself.

---

[10] Cf. plate 97.

[11] Cf. fig. 290.

[12] Cf. fig. 168, no. 43.

[13] Cf. plate 75, north partition of room V, and chapter 43.

[14] Cf. plate 97, south partition of room XII, offering of the four cloths.

[15] Cf. Pyramid Texts, 1755–94, partially cited in chapter 43.

The text of room XII is very difficult to transcribe. The sentences contain repetitions, transformations of the same word, homonyms untranslatable into our language, and a sonority that must have had an amazing effect when they were pronounced with a full knowledge of their significance. In order to bring back this magic it would be necessary to have a Kara, like the musician-poet I knew in Athens, who succeeded, using his monotone song alone, in making the frogs gather on Lake Marathon during a presentation of dances, and who made an eagle descend onto the chained Prometheus (who was rather frightened!) during a performance of the *Prometheus* of Aeschylus at Delphi.

Thus the text of the offering of the cloths, which can be seen in parallel with chapter 49 of the ritual in the Berlin Papyrus, mentions the offering of cloth *(mār)*, of the strip of cloth *(mnkht)*, of the eye of Horus coming from Nekhebet, through which it is perfect *(mnkh)*, through which it appears *(akh)* in this its own name for the four strips of cloth *(mnkht)* that are united *(dmi)* to him in this his own name for cloth *(idmi)*. . . .[16]

It is a question here, in a single tableau, of the offering of four cloths: the white, the green, the red, and the *idmi* cloth. The ritual further includes a fifth chapter entitled "Offering the Strip of Cloth."[17]

In transparency on the opposite side of this wall, in the first register of the north partition of room V, are the four "boxes for cloths" consecrated by the king, and in the second register, the four calves—black, red, white, and spotted.[18] Through their colors these recall the four herds of bulls of the sun, "of the colors white, black, red, and spotted" that state a problem of undetermined analysis that Archimedes, in a letter to Eratosthenes, would have proposed to the Alexandrian geometers, a problem considered unsolvable.[19]

The third register of the north wall of room V (plate 75) includes two tableaux. In the left one, the king offers white bread to Amun followed by Mut, regent of the sky, who makes the gesture of influx with her left hand toward the nape of the neck of this *neter*. In the tableau to the right the king makes the gift of divine offerings, consisting of various kinds of food surmounted by lotus flowers, in the presence of ithyphallic Amun followed by Amunet, the feminine (passive) aspect of Amun.

On the other side of the wall in room XII and at the same level are the two tableaux that show the quadruple purification by the king with the red and white vases. Each of these libations is made four times "by turning around the *neter*," and by pronouncing the incantation that affirms that his eye, his head, his bones, are reunited, healed, and purified (of all impurity) by Thoth.[20]

[16] See chapter 43 for the current translation of this passage of the ritual. We are certainly dealing in these texts with a poetic form and a litany-like character, which Moret, struck by the phonetic cabala, had already foreseen.

[17] Cf. the ritual in the Berlin Papyrus, chapters 48 to 53, which follow the two chapters 46 and 47 on the four white and four red vases.

[18] In relation to the four calves, here is a passage concerning the vision of Zechariah (6:1–5): "Again I raised my eyes, and this is what I saw: four chariots coming out between the two mountains, and the mountains were mountains of bronze. The first chariot had red horses, the second chariot had black horses, the third chariot had white horses and the fourth chariot had (vigorous) piebald horses. I asked the angel who was talking to me, I said, 'What is the meaning of these, my lord?' The angel answered, 'These are going out to the four winds of heaven after standing before the Lord of the whole world.'"

[19] Cf. Tannery, *Mémoires scientifiques,* 1:118, on the problem of the bulls of Archimedes. The conclusion of the author is that a volume of 744 pages of 2500 numbers each would be necessary to print the numbers asked for by the epigram.

[20] Cf. chapters 46 and 47 of the ritual.

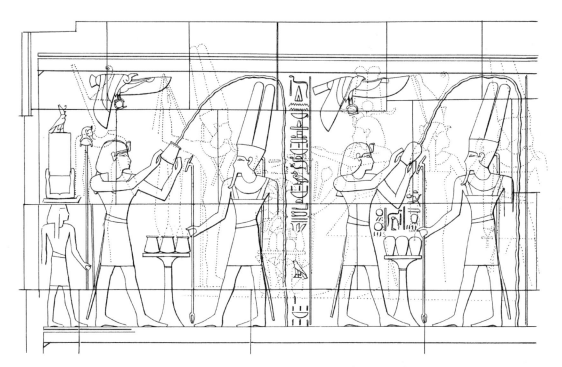

Fig. 276. Transposition between room XII (solid lines)
and room V (dotted lines)

Now, the symbolism of these scenes represented in room XII is completed in transposition by the scenes depicted in room V (fig. 276).

On the left, the king pouring the libation over Amun with the red vase is in transparency with Amunet wearing the red crown (fig. 276). On the right, the king pouring the libation over Amun with the white vase is also in transparency with Mut, who wears the white crown hiding the red. The gesture of influx of Mut's left hand is in transparency with the ear of Amun in room XII.

At the center, the column of text inscribed in room XII mentions the offerings of "food" that are not shown on this wall but are in transparency on the other side in room V where the title "divine offerings," *maā*, can be seen above the table of offerings and crosses in transparency with the vertical text of room XII, which mentions them.

The king offering the white vase is projected in transparency onto the king walking in the opposite direction, crowned with the two feathers of Shu supported by the horns of Khnum; he is ready to consecrate the offerings and holds the *mākes* staff and the white club in his left hand.

This is an example of transposition completing a teaching. This teaching will only be understood if one gives to each figure and each of the gestures the significance of the substances evoked and the functions symbolized.

Let us finally point out here that again there is a crossing. The Mut bird, generally Nekhebet the white, oversees the tableau of the ablution with the red vase, while the ablution with the white vase is supervised by the Horus bird. The two birds hold the *chen,* symbol of a ligature.

Plate 76 • West Partition

The west partition of room V includes three registers, only two of which are still there. We see the king five times on this wall; each time his single arm divides into two forearms, and the legend specifies that he offers the cloths four times: the *nemes* veil three times and the *mnkht* strip of cloth once. Here are five chapters of the ritual relating to the offering of four strips of cloth and to the covering of the *neter* with the *nemes* veil, associated in the Book of Funerals with the white crown of the South originating from el-Kab (temple of the white vulture, Nekhebet), when this *nemes* veil covers the head of the *neter*.[21]

On this partition the four white vases and the four red vases are again offered, as well as incense. Finally, the *medjet* oil is joined once to the offering of the *nemes* cloth. This aromatic oil is used each day for the ritual unction of the forehead. The detail concerning these "holy oils" or fats is given on the east wall of this room.

—⁓—

Plate 77 • East Partition

The east partition of room V is divided in two by the door opening on three chapels preceded by a straight corridor (room XI). In the first register two tableaux face each other and frame the door. The one on the right (south) shows the king making the forty offerings. The one on the left (north) shows the king as he prepares to consecrate them.

In the second register five unguents or perfumes are presented. The ritual speaks of the royal unction transferred to the *neter* of the place that daily receives this homage with the liturgical variation of the day. Nine oils are used: a canonical oil—the *medjet* unguent—used daily, and, depending on the festival days, eight other oils.

Room V gives only the names of the five sacred unguents with which it is specifically concerned; these holy oils (the chrism) were used to anoint the forehead of the *neter* (as with the king) in order to burn away all malefic influences that are obedient to Seth and to give the *neter* all power and all royalty (the crown). On the other hand, the ritual associates these "oils" with the eye of Horus, or considers them as "what comes out of" the eye of Horus.

—⁓—

Plate 78 • South Partition

Like the other walls, the south partition of room V had three registers (of which only two are still intact), each containing three tableaux.

In the middle register the king, walking from west to east, first offers the white *nemst* vase, then waves incense with the *snter* resin, and finally offers the *ānti* resin,[22] in liquid form since the word is determined by a vase.

---

[21] Cf. Moret, *Rituel du culte divin journalier,* p. 238. Recall the Gospel of St. John (20:7): ". . . and also the cloth that had been over his head; this was not with the linen cloths but rolled up in a place by itself."

[22] According to Lieblein, the word *ānti* designated "incense" and not myrrh, and according to Loret, the word *snter* designated a resin taken from turpentine, both cited in Jéquier, *Frises d'objets,* p. 319. We cite the names of the resins as they are presently translated by Egyptologists, but it is obvious that incense, mastic, bitumen of Judea, myrrh, etc., are only symbols for substances that have their equivalents in physiological substances. Let us note that there is a simple and natural method to make liquid myrrh without any addition . . .

On the lower register, walking from west to east, the king washes the double support of the vases in the presence of a blue Amun; in the center he makes the same gesture before an ithyphallic Amun. To the east the king pours water out of a vase in the shape of an ankh, which falls in a double stream into a double basin and in front of Amun, whose body is red (which is very rare).

The head and the crown of the red Amun to the east and of the blue Amun to the west are sculpted on two column drums of Tuthmosis that are reused in this wall.[23] The accent is placed here on duality, the double aspect that sums up the theme of this room.

In the southeast corner of this sanctuary two other column drums of Tuthmosis are reused, and the double crown of the king is carved here (east wall).

On the exterior side of the south wall are again two drums of this same type of column put into the thickness of the wall. Exactly below these two reused blocks, the dedication text carved on the socle mentions the "columns" in the form of *columns* of the temple. Now, these reused column drums were invisible before the wall was damaged. We mention this fact because there is a direct relation between the Thotian (Mercurial and Amunian) character of Tuthmosis and the brain.

The south wall corresponds to the band that encircles the head. Let us recall that in the head the entire brain can be considered as a gestating fetus: it is enveloped by the cerebrospinal fluid,[24] of a typically Amunian character (amnion), and the choroid plexus (chorion) brings the nourishing blood, which itself will be spiritualized.

—*w*—

In speaking of the waters above,[25] symbolized by the triple stream of the *nekhakha* scepter, I mentioned the *third* state that is joined to the *two* natures. Here we are dealing with what is called the "eye of Horus." The fact of speaking of an eye shows that it is a question of an appearance, and the fact of attributing all power to it gives it the aspect of a Fire (or active energy).

The "evolutionary" theories of our philosophers, paleontologists, anthropologists, and biologists give the impression of a sort of very learned childishness: to wish to judge the history of life by the light of terrestrial life alone is impossible. Our earth is part of the sun, and life begins at the extreme limit of the solar sphere of which we see only the dense center, from animating warmth to burning heat, luminous to our eyes. Heat is thus from light, still too subtle to be perceived by our optic nerve, but perceptible to our pineal eye, of which only the pineal gland remains. The conditions of life on other planets are different from ours, but it is absurd to infer the possibility or the impossibility of life there in our same human form. It is well known that anaerobic and microbial as well as other forms of life exist in an environment of carbonic gas. Ants and other insects are not averse to swimming in sulfuric acid but die in a more or less corrosive alkaline environment. There are all kinds of adaptations.

The appearance of human being occurs at the extreme limit of the solar sphere (the solar system), and this being divides itself into all the other forms of life. In its purgatorial passage on earth it is the cerebral, mental phase that develops. Meanwhile the human heart continues to beat the seconds of its life through its innate consciousness, without cerebral consciousness.

Forms are transitory, and to wish to construct a schematized science on present forms is per-

[23] Cf. plate 78B, the ground plan of room V.

[24] Cf. case 6 of the Surgical Papyrus in which the brain, its membranes, and the liquid they contain are mentioned.

[25] Cf. chapter 37, conclusion.

haps useful, but presents nothing certain or stable. This is why the sacred teaching is based only on realities that do not vary with time and the phases of gestation. The knowledge is the knowledge of the essence-phenomenon that is the reference for all accidental phenomena. "Man is created in God's image," says the biblical text, and procreation is "in the image" of the creation. In the image, but not in identity.

It is said that men are born from the tears of the eye of Ra, that is, from the salty waters of Nun, the primordial chaos. The Heliopolitan Mystery shows us Tum who, creating himself, comes out of these waters as the first earth, the *kamutef* of the temple, and in him is the fixed point that contains all, but in terrestrial form. This fixed point is nourished by Spirit, that is, by the single substance still without form. This substance will take form thanks to the fixed terrestrial point that will "weave" spirit into tangible substance. These waters then bring with them that which animates the first earth in that they are ejected *(htp)* by the burning fire called Ptah, the fire fallen to earth. This ejection, or ejaculatory function, is called Min, and through its aquatic and spiritual character, Min-Amun. Carrying thus in the waters above that which universally animates or specifies the first earth, these waters make perceptible and, above all, visible, that which was invisible, "the odor" of earth. Now, the specificity by itself—which is soul—has neither body nor appearance before nourishment has rendered it material, and it is this first appearance *(her)* that will be called the "eye of Ra." In order then to be corporified and become the All-Powerful, it must itself be that which is fixed and gives itself body—the royal body in the white crown—which can only become such when the spirit (Thoth) rules over the first fixity, having itself become fixed: Thot-mes (Tuthmosis). Then the eye of Ra will animate this perfect body and appear, Her-mes, the rebirth of the face, *her*.

As for specificity, that is, the coloring or animating particularity, when it is carried in the waters above, it is called Hat-hor, the house of Hor or Her (Horus), and its appearance is that of the eye of Ra (the visible sun). It is an unguent, triple in nature, issued from the fourth that remains below. This aspect is represented by the "boxes for cloths" and the "four calves," those who suckle milk, the first of which is black, the second white, the third red, and the fourth spotted. These are the four "elements" as well as the four phases, because the elements of this philosophy are in reality phases of the becoming.

It is thus in the sanctuary of olfaction that we must find the story of the odor or soul, as well as its separation (or division outside of the chaos), then the nature of the unguents that will animate the forehead of the crowned king. This is a great and mysterious story that, under the royal symbol, is applied to all of nature, in the image of the reality. This story is no more metaphysical than the "creation of Adam," since it is actually a matter of the cosmic becoming.

Appendix:
Technical Procedure for
Surveying the Walls and Ground Plans

The walls of the temple of Luxor have been surveyed using the following method:

1. On all the walls of the covered temple and on the columns, a horizontal line was marked as a reference level for all measurements of height.

2. Strings were tightly stretched on each wall, at regular distances to mark the verticals.

3. The dimensions of each wall were established with regard to the horizontal and vertical reference lines.

These measurements thus taken include, with respect to the horizontal, the line of the ground, the different heights of the registers, the line of the ceiling, if existing (the tiles of the ceiling were measured as well, when possible), and all the heights of the foundation stones taken at each corner of each block; and with respect to the verticals, the height to each stone joint and to the base of all the vertical lines separating the different tableaux and the registers containing hieroglyphs, and all the essential points of the figures, thus allowing them to be drawn afterward in outline.

4. All the vertical dimensions for each figure (knees, belt, navel, shoulder, neck, mouth, nose, eyes, headband, and so on) and of the tableau on which it is represented have been recorded on specially printed cards, and the essential points of supplementary measurements—such as certain details of the hands, of the headdress, or the offerings—have been noted on location sketches.

5. Partial verifications of the spaces between the joints of each stone have been made that take into account the redressing of certain of them by Akhenaten's effacings and the subsequent restorations that have exposed the plaster contained in the interior of the walls. All the blocks not dressed were cut as dry joints and leave no space between their joints. All the rejointed blocks contained plaster, so it was necessary to calculate the distance between the plaster and the joint of the neighboring stone in order to determine the possible play of the blocks.

6. Other partial verifications have also been made, thanks to the vertical lines of the registers and the tableaux; certain blocks being disjoint so that these lines were no longer in alignment, the measurements then of each disjunction allowed the reestablishment of the original positions of these blocks. The partial verifications of the spaces and the joints have enabled the length of each wall at each foundation to be determined.

7. In order to be able to see the whole of the walls—which average nearly 11 meters long and 8 meters to 9 meters high—plates were drawn to the scale of 1/20 for each of them. On each plate, a first drawing of the blocks and the tableaux was made, and only according to the data taken with regard to the vertical and horizontal lines.

Next we drew the figures and the tableaux according to the measurements recorded on the cards, any error being immediately verifiable since the essential measurements had been taken twice, once with respect to the lines of reference and again with respect to the tableau. The drawings have been executed in accordance with the *current state* of the walls.

Finally, the hieroglyphs were drawn on the plates after having been measured one by one in relation to the essential lines of the tableau and those of the joints of the stones, which has, in drawing them, allowed for a third verification.

There are considerable advantages to this method of surveying. Because of the general line indicating the level plane, it is possible not only to know the different pavement levels but also to know all the damage caused by movement of the ground, and finally to be able to see the absolute coincidence between the two partitions of the same wall. The drawings of the blocks of stone enable us to see which ones are identical to one part or another of this wall. In certain cases, probing the thickness of the wall itself allowed us to verify which blocks "traverse" it and which do not, and to note dovetails when they exist in the joints.

Because there is rarely enough space to stand a sufficient distance from a tableau, the average height of which is 2 meters, with the distance in front of it generally only 2 meters because of the columns, photographs are extremely difficult to make geometrically perfect in a temple such as that of Luxor, even when using a wide-angle lens, which inevitably deforms the image. All the photographs taken in these conditions, however, can be adjusted or rectified by being projected onto a *canevas* established for each tableau.

———

The plans of the pavement of the covered temple have been made by surveying the stones one at a time, following a principle similar to that applied to the walls, that is, by drawing a general grid pattern established on a single reference axis for the entire length of the temple and extended into the court of Ramesses and the courtyard of Nectanebo. We could therefore easily calculate each deviation of a wall. The only difficulty was in the considerable play of certain parts of the pavement in the covered temple, play caused by infiltrating water that has sometimes caused bulges in this pavement and consequently disjoined certain walls whose present orientation is no longer what it was originally. The restoration of each wall has allowed the verification of the plans and the reestablishment of the dimensions and true orientation of the walls.

There has not been any shifting in the heart of the monument; rooms IV and VI have hardly even budged and their measurements are exact. The dividing walls between rooms IX, II, and III are also exact. In room XII, however, it was necessary to make all sorts of cross-checks to establish its precise dimensions and only have barely a centimeter of hesitation over a length of about 22.20 meters; this precision could be attained thanks to surveying and measuring the architraves on both sides, which confirmed the measurements used in this place. Room I, the central sanctuary, has shifted slightly, but the walls of the two sanctuaries, V and VII, have shifted considerably and their measurements are difficult to make exactly. Nevertheless, it is possible to indicate here the dimensions within 1 or 2 centimeters and the orientations within ±0°5′ for each partition of room V.

> North partition: 5.56–5.57 meters
> South partition: 5.59–5.61 meters
> East partition: 7.87–7.89 meters
> West partition: 8.14–8.16 meters

The lengths of the east and west partitions are very different (27 cm) because of the orientations of the south and north walls, each of which follow a particular angular relationship. The lengths of the south and north walls are more or less equal to within several centimeters; the difference is also due to nuances in the orientation.

The south wall is at 32°30′ of east-west orientation, ±0°5′, and the east wall is practically perpendicular to it. On the pavement, the line on the ground for the plan of the east wall does not exactly coincide with this wall. The line is based on the geometric axis, which proves that the deviation of approximately 0°30′ from the east wall is intentional.

The north wall is at 35°18′, ±5′, and is thus parallel and perpendicular to the east and north walls of the hypostyle court, the angular ratios of which can be transcribed into whole numbers, by 12 : 17 and 17 : 24 (35°13′ and 35°18′40″, respectively).

These two ratios are $\sqrt{2}/1$ and its reciprocal, $2/\sqrt{2}$, and correspond to the function of the plan of room V. This duality evoked in the north through the orientation is symbolically marked in the south by the dual character of the figurations. The proportions of the plan are as follows:

$$\frac{\text{length of the east partition}}{\text{length of the north wall}} = \frac{4.25 \text{ fathoms}}{3 \text{ fathoms}} = \frac{7.8766... \text{ meters}}{5.56 \text{ meters}} = 1.41666... = \frac{17}{12}.$$

The west partition, the particular orientation of which is 32°40′ ±5′ with respect to north, suggests a coefficient related to the "skullcap" of the earth,[26] and accentuates, through the joints of the stones, the skullcaps of the figures depicted in its first register. Starting from the north, the upper joint passes through the level of the forehead of the king entering the sanctuary, that is, at the level

---

[26] Cf. chapter 15, "Diadem, I Assume Thee." The east and west walls give the two functional angles for the polar cap (skullcap) of the earth.

of the eighteenth square, then "rises" a little at each figure in order to cut, on the last king located at the south, only the part that would be covered by the royal headband (plate 76).

Finally, let us recall that the west wall of room V is in transposition with the east wall of room I. In room V, the joint of the stones that passes at the level of the eighteenth square passes in room I above the crown of the skull of the figures in transposition, establishing the fundamental ratio of 19 : 18 between the two partitions (fig. 277).

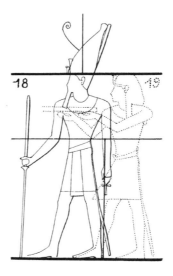

Fig. 277. Transposition between room V, west partition (solid lines)
and room I, east partition (dotted lines)

Chapter 40

THE AXES
OF THE TEMPLE

—⁓—

Plates 79–90

*The head is the container of
the spiritual being, where
the blood, elaborated
throughout the body, is
spiritualized in order to
nourish the nervous flux
and prepare the "ferments"
of the blood and the "seed."*

(Chapter 17)

E   D

C   B   A

PLATE 79

The Holy of Holies, West Wall

The "Holy of Holies" expresses the function-keys *from which the living phenomenon results. This is said in "numbers" at the places on the human body where the glands of the encephalon, the centers of life, are located.*

(Chapter 5)

PLATE 80

The Holy of Holies, West Wall, Two Ages of the Temple

The orientations depend upon the cycle *and include east for rising, midday for maturity, west for retiring and conception, then mid-night for the mystic birth.*

The temple of Luxor has its entrance at the north, that is, toward midnight of the cycle, and the essential sanctuaries, as well as the apse, are located toward the south, at midday, the formal realization.

(Chapter 25)

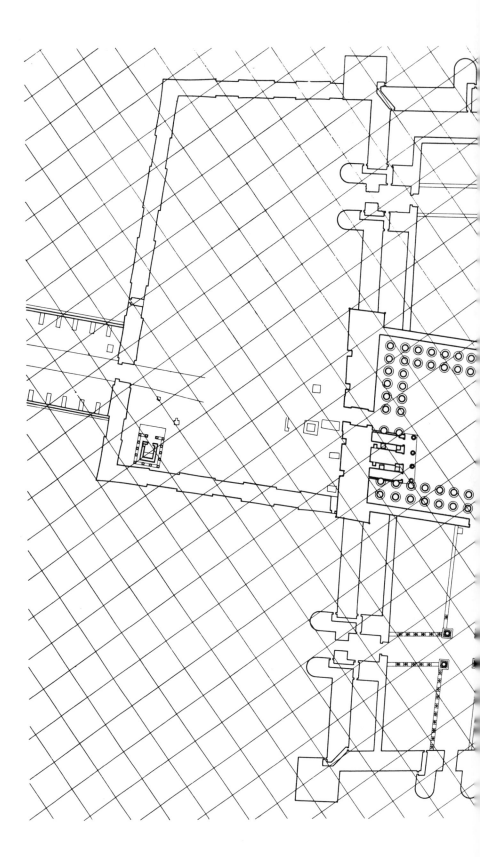

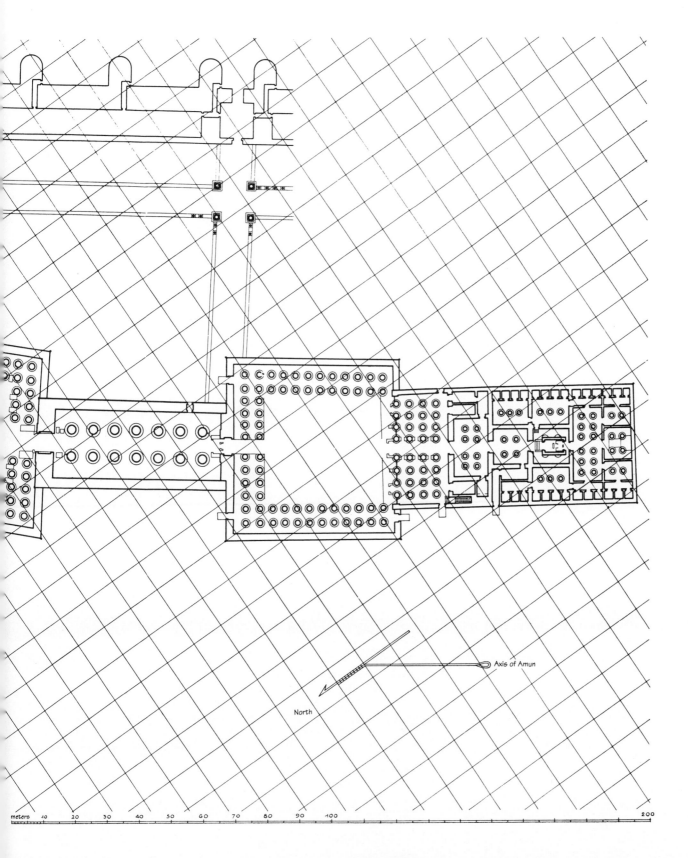

meters 10   20   30   40   50   60   70   80   90   100   200

North

Axis of Amun

PLATE 81

The Temple of Luxor on the Orientation Grid, General Plan

Man crucified in space is
the Anthropocosmos.

*The cross is the equatorial
plane of a body in revolution
around itself. It is the four
directions that define the
abstract center.*

*The cross is the symbol
of life because for us life is
simply the ability "to react."*

(Chapter 19)

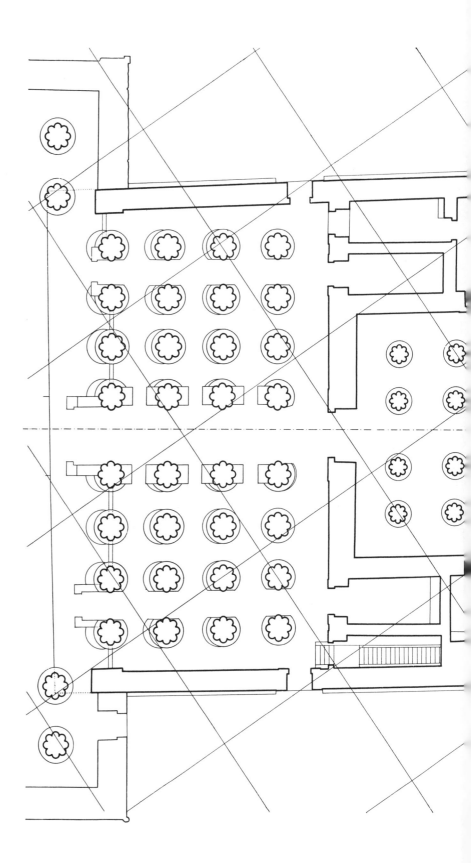

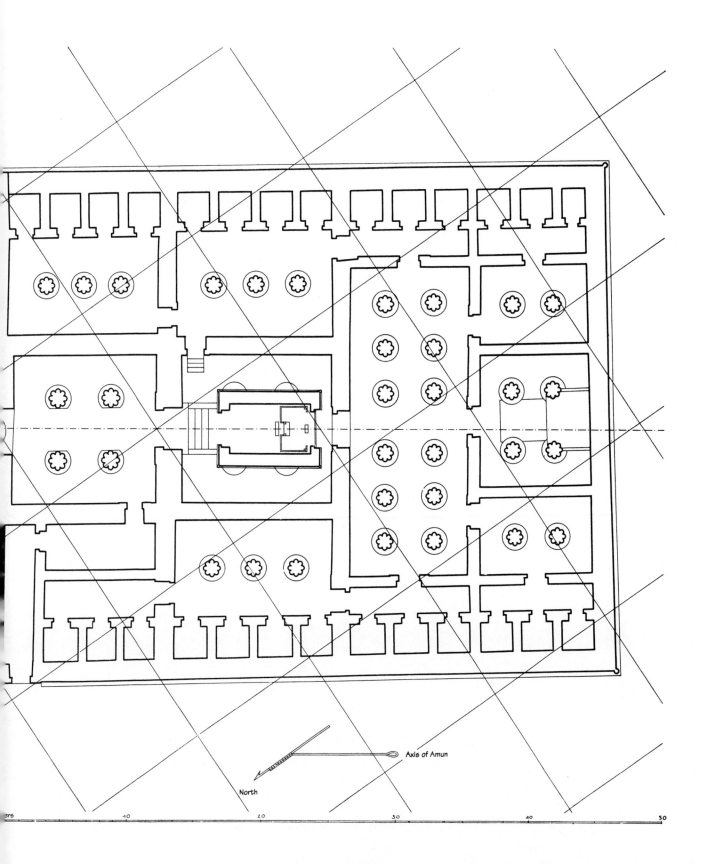

Axis of Amun

North

PLATE 82

The Covered Temple on the Orientation Grid

In order to remain in vital conformity with natural law, the axes of the temple are always moving, *oscillating around the essential numbers of their origin so as to maintain harmonic spatial growth.*

(Chapter 13)

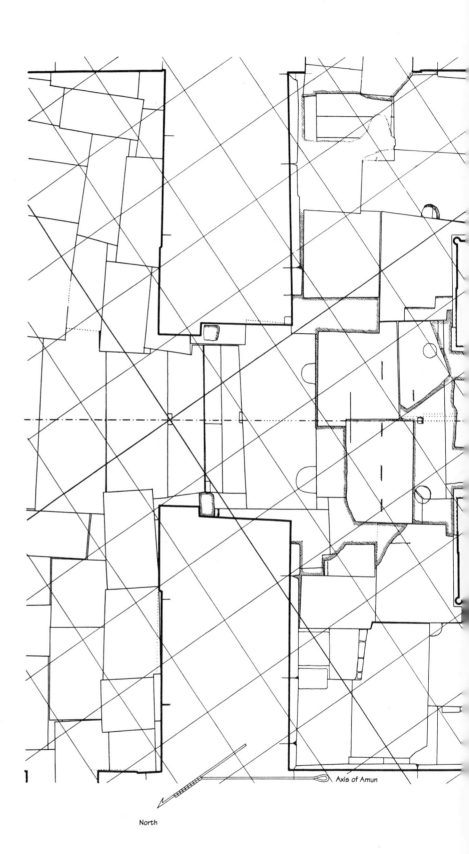

Axis of Amun

North

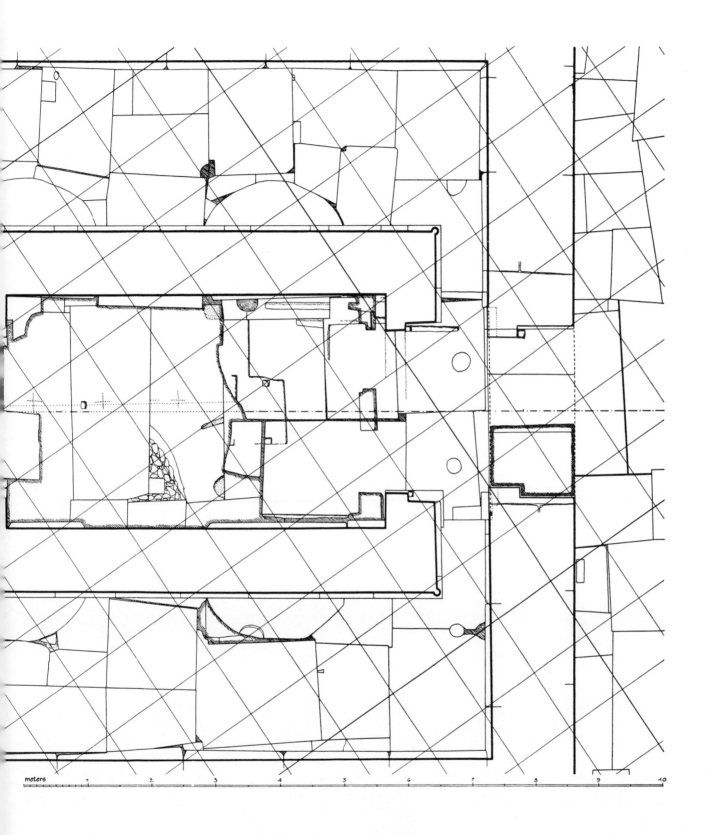

meters 　1　　　2　　　3　　　4　　　5　　　6　　　7　　　8　　　9　　　10

PLATE 83

The Sanctuary of the Altar of Amun's Barque on the Orientation Grid

It is in the secret sanctuary, in the subfloor, that the irrational median axis is marked, the present moment between past and future, between before and after.

PLATE 84

The Secret Sanctuary of Amun

Indication in the subfloor of the geometric axis of Mut *(left)* and termination of the axis of
Khonsu (axis of measures) *(right)* on the wall, marked by a key-piece.

When our concern is to see "the Temple in the image of Heaven," the temptation to erect a monument on these rigid precepts is like wanting to try to make a celestial globe turn round a fixed axis, which would be its annihilation.

(Chapter 13)

PLATE 85

The Axes of the Temple Inscribed in the Sanctuary of the Altar of Amun's Barque (View from the South)

*It is this mysterious mirror
that, vertically, reverses
right and left, then, horizontally, reverses top and
bottom, that pharaonic
Egypt, in a state of superior
consciousness, manipulates
in all its works, making
them so difficult for us to
describe.*

(Chapter 19)

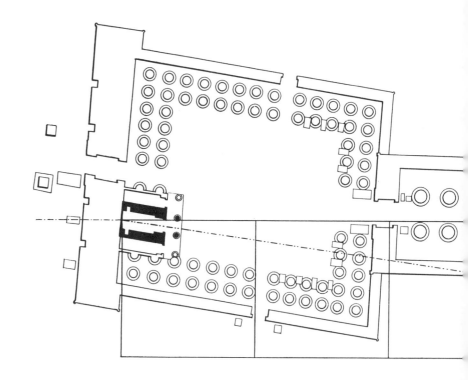

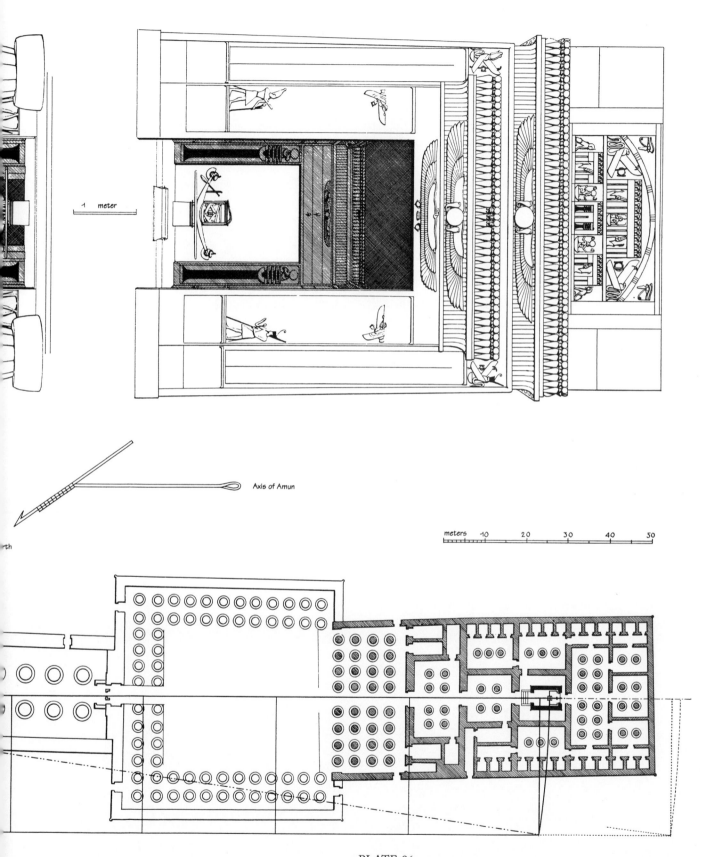

1 meter

Axis of Amun

North

meters   10   20   30   40   50

PLATE 86

The Axis of Amun and Its Reflection

Reaction is the reversal of the direction of the action, provoked by the resistance immanent in the nature of the activity, or "action in function."

(Chapter 4)

PLATE 87

The Mirror of the Axis of Amun

For the architecture of the temple, whether it be, among others, pharaonic, Hellenic, or Hindu, or a Christian cathedral, the axis is the spinal column, filled with living marrow and carrying sheaths of nerves.

(Chapter 13)

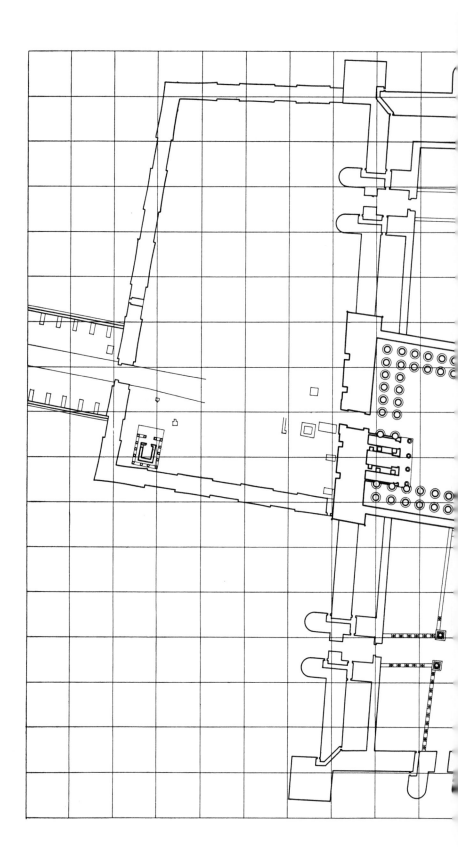

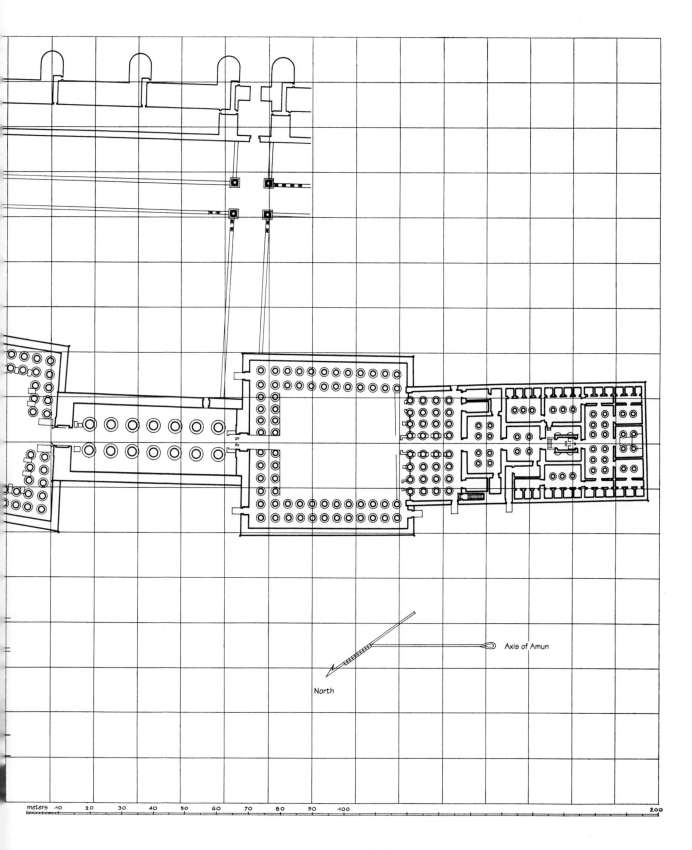

meters 10 20 30 40 50 60 70 80 90 100 200

Axis of Amun

North

PLATE 88

The Temple of Luxor on the Grid of Amun

Vitally, the axis is then the fixed point, the unalterable nucleus, the indestructible center, the Absolute, the present moment, ungraspable by the cerebral intelligence.

(Chapter 13)

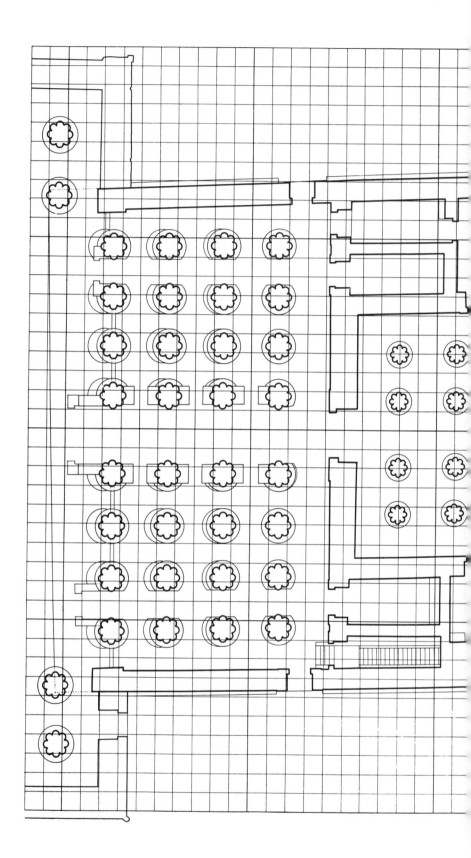

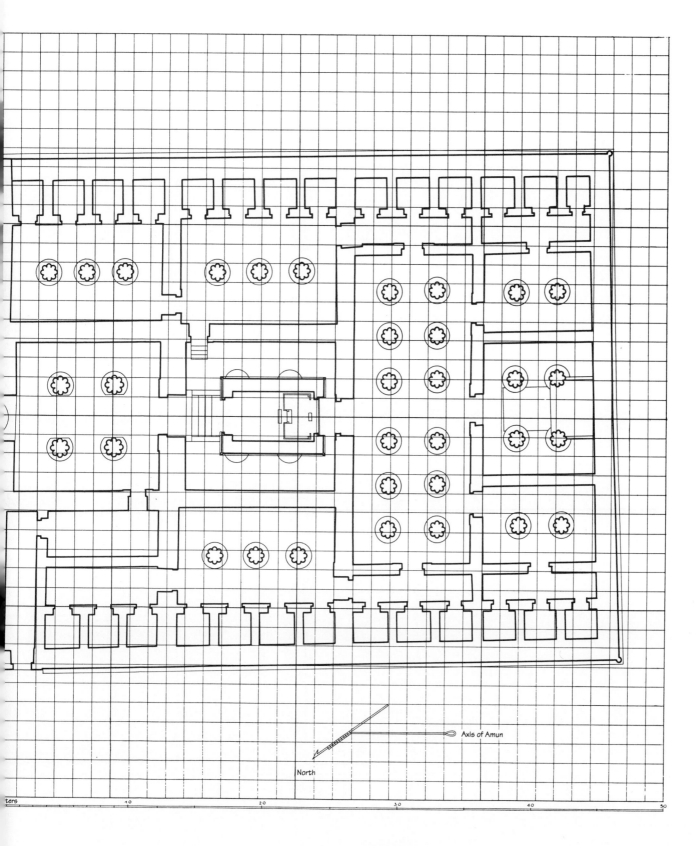

Axis of Amun

North

PLATE 89

The Covered Temple on the Grid of Amun

The axes . . . are but channels for influences that play their animating role in this living architecture, however firmly anchored to the ground they may be.

Let the faithful then come into this building; they will be subject to the effect of this occult influence, as vegetation is subject to the influences of telluric magnetism.

(Chapter 13)

Axis of Amun

North

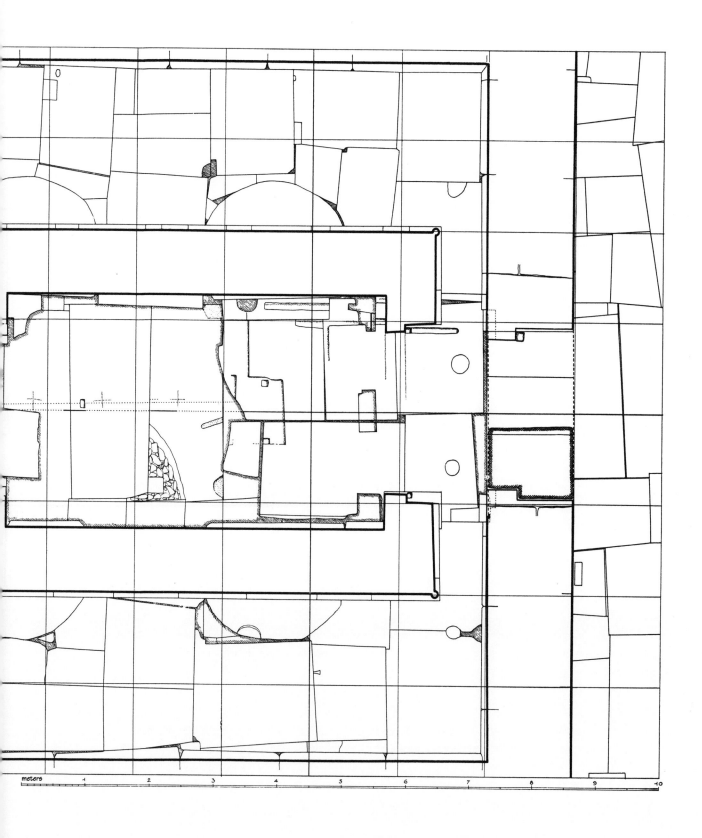

meters   1   2   3   4   5   6   7   8   9   10

PLATE 90

The Sanctuary of the Altar of Amun's Barque on the Grid of Amun

Chapter 40

THE AXES
OF THE TEMPLE

It is the axes of the temple of Luxor that cast the greatest light on the architectural principle of the pharaonic temple. They are marked on the floor, and this fact can be verified.[1]

The temple is constructed on three essential axes: (1) *the axis of Amun,* cut into the sandstone pavement of the sanctuary of the barque, and which we have called the occult axis of the temple; (2) *the axis of Mut,* or geometric axis, which plays the role of the median axis and undergoes several essential deviations in the course of the different stages of evolution of the temple; and (3) *the axis of Khonsu,* or axis of measures, also inscribed on the floor under the naos of the barque.

We are dealing with a living temple, and nothing in it could or should have a cadaverous rigidity. The axes are, because of this fact, precise as to orientation on the terrestrial globe with respect to their aspects with the heavens, but they also always have a complement that fixes an oscillation, in the same way that the walls follow the axes while maintaining, through nuances, their own numbers.

These are not to be seen as inaccuracies, because all movement, all vibration, is justified, as we see in room V.[2]

It is this construction on three axes that gives movement to the entire architecture, thus creating this "living state" of which we have spoken. Each of these axes has, in addition to its mystical significance, a concrete significance related to it.

Each wall of the covered temple is constructed on one or another of the three axes. Thus, each wall and its inscription must be studied according to the axis that governs it.

There is neither defect nor incoherence in the architecture of the temple, as the rooms at acute and obtuse angles or the colonnades that are not quite parallel would lead one to believe. And even if one does not want to believe the reasons given here for those who wish to understand them, the concrete fact nevertheless remains that in the temple of Luxor the walls obey a law proper to each of the three easily verifiable axes inscribed in the platform.

---

[1] Cf. vol. 1, figs. 151, 152, and 153.

[2] Cf. chapter 39, appendix, on the surveying of room V. At its base the east wall preserves the line on the ground established on the geometric axis, and it is constructed forming an angle of about 0°30′ with this drawing.

THE HOLY OF HOLIES

PLATES 79 AND 80 • THE WEST WALL

The Holy of Holies, which can be accessed through room XII, is a room whose roof was supported by four columns. The dedication carved around the subfoundation of the covered temple says that this sanctuary contained a gold statue of Amun with a ram's head. This statue was located in a tabernacle that rested on the cornice of a ledge made partly in the south wall and partly in the drums of the southern columns. The south face of these columns also has a ledge for the attachment points of this naos, the outline of which is drawn on the south wall against which it leaned. Thus the monument still preserves sufficient vestiges to make this reconstruction (plate 84).

The whole central part of this room no longer has its pavestones, and a sounding has allowed us to observe the nature of the contents of the foundation tank.[3] Exactly under the naos containing the statue of Amun, a small block of reused limestone bears the inscription "the house of the *neter*"[4] and by its presence confirms the consecration of this place.

The Holy of Holies measures 18 royal cubits wide by 16 cubits long by 16 cubits high. Its plan is thus established on the simple ratio of 8 to 9, the musical tone, which also recalls the numbers used for the approximate calculation of the surface of the disk in relation to the square.[5] The same proportion is used for the frieze of uraei above the registers, the height of which equals one-ninth of the total height of the north partition. This wall, the only one that remains completely intact in this sanctuary of Amun, is its entrance wall. It contains a base and three registers of equal height. The height of each register is ϕ with respect to the foundation, whose value is 1.[6] Thus the three registers plus the base represent $3\phi + 1$, and their total height is seven-eighths of the total partition, that is, 14 royal cubits. Between the last line of the upper register and the frieze of uraei there is an interval corresponding to the difference between one-eighth and one-ninth, or one seventy-second occupied by the standard border that constitutes the frame of the tableaux.[7] This arrangement is particular to this room;[8] the north wall makes the principles clear, and the remains of the other walls confirm the uniform use of the ratio of 1 to ϕ between the base and the height of the register, with very small nuances that are closely dictated by metrical variations.

From the north entrance, the registers rise slightly in the direction of the king's walk toward the altar of Amun. This ascent, visible on the right and left sides of the door, continues on the east and west walls, causing the metrical variations to which we have just referred.

This movement of broadening toward the sanctuary is a characteristic one that is applied not only in the registers but to the whole architecture of the temple; thus, certain colonnades widen slightly in the direction of the holy place.[9] This movement imparted by the architecture is

---

[3] Cf. fig. 222.

[4] Cf. fig. 293.

[5] Cf. chapter 5, "Pharaonic Volumes."

[6] This arrangement recalls the division of the Rhind Papyrus into six bands, the first of which is 1 for the five others each equaling ϕ.

[7] It is said that Thoth gained one seventy-second of each day of the year, in order to constitute the five extra days of the year that are the days of the birth of the principal *neters*. Seventy-two is the mean number of heartbeats per minute of the healthy man. It is also related to the numbers of time.

[8] The height of the uraeus frieze varies in each room. The relationship to the geometric theme developed in each of them must be sought in it.

[9] For example, the widening of the nave and of the colonnade of room XII from east to west following the progression of the solar barque (cf. figs. 282 and 287).

comparable to certain irregularities found in the walls that frame, for example, an entryway. The most striking example is the wall separating rooms VI and IV. When seen in plan, the two sides of the door that provides access to the sanctuary give the impression of opening and closing;[10] there is a double movement, as there actually is in this place with the entrance and exit of the sacred barque (plates 83 and 90).

These nuances, more or less perceptible throughout the whole of the temple, impart a sort of vibration that is imperceptible to the eye, but which the faithful inevitably experience when they enter into it. On the west wall of sanctuary I (plate 79), the accent on the movement of ascent is given by the joint of the stones that, in the north, passes under the line of the register, accentuating it somewhat, before crossing and uniting with it in order to extend beyond it to the south under king E. This first register of the west partition gives some important measurements:

- The height of the register from the baseline to the lower boundary of the sky is 100 fathom digits. The figures carved below it measure 72 of these same digits.
- The height of the register that represents the sky is 2 meters plus or minus the difference caused by the variation in growth.
- The height of the register with the line of its upper edge is 2.025 meters to 2.045 meters, that is, plus or minus this same variation.

The division by ϕ of the largest height of the register determines the height of the base, and the division of 2 meters by ϕ fixes the height of the joints of the stones under king A. There is here the indication of a double play confirmed by the enlargement of the kings toward the south, an enlargement that corresponds, between kings B and E, to the two extreme values of the digits of the fathom at 0° and at 90°. As we have already said, this variation corresponds to the difference between the large side and the diagonal of the angle of 1 to 7, the angle of the reflection of Amun; it is a variation already observed in the pharaonic cubits and justifying their variants.

Having established that the mean between the two extreme values of the fathom enables us to define the meter, and that the meter is related to the royal cubit through the function ϕ, the Holy of Holies does indeed summarize the essential measures governing the temple and the cubits and the law that unites them.

The meter is imposed as a reference measure, and reference to it in different essential points of the temple confirms its use:

- The height of 2 meters for the register on which the five kings of the west partition are carved is not an exception, it is the constant height of all the registers in this room, the first including the sky but not the baseline, the two others with the sky and the baseline. Taking into account this nuance of application, the height of 2 meters is the dimension most often encountered throughout the covered temple for the height of a register.[11]

---

[10] In this regard we should point out that in many tombs, in the same door, the entrance and the exit are marked, respectively, by intaglio sculpture and relief sculpture (surveys made by A. Stoppelaere).

[11] In room V, north wall, for the first register, the height between the baseline and the lower line of the sky is 2 m. This measurement applies also to the other walls of this same room, with the width of the uraeus frieze diminished.

- The interior length of the west partition of the peristyle court is 50 meters, which is 27 mean fathoms.
- The vertical height of the west wing of the pylon is 25 meters measured from the ground to the summit of the cornice at the northeast corner (±1 cm).
- The east wall of the *haty* that supports the ritual foundation text of the temple would have an exact length of 200 meters if extended to its crossing with the axis of the door of the pylon of Ramesses II on the south side. The foundation texts specify the sighting of a star in the Great Bear in order to establish an hour for a day of the year, but also in order to locate true north by two sightings made an equal amount of time before and after midnight. This is a further reason for taking the meter as the basic measure and true north as the reference orientation.
- Finally, the door of this pylon with its doorposts is 10 meters wide. Thus the "orientation grid," following a number of directives given by the temple, is established on a north-south grid pattern, each square of which has a side of 10 meters. The point of departure of this *canevas* is given by the key placed at the crossing of the axes of Amun and Khonsu at the door of the sanctuary of the barque of Amun (plates 81, 82, and 83).

Through this "*canevas*-guide" it is possible to read the orientations of each wall of the temple in the form of whole-number ratios.

———

The five kings of the west wall give five very slightly different measurements by their respective heights. The two extreme measurements can be related to the double rhythm observed in the course of the study of the pavestone mosaic[12] corresponding to the principle phases of growth: that of about twelve years of age, which is the beginning of puberty, and that of eighteen to nineteen years, which is the final term of growth for the Man of the Temple. Recalling that the proportion of the height of the head to the total height varies with the age of the figure, if one wishes to indicate a particular age, one should take this nuance into account.

Thus, the first king (A) to the north is the smallest, and his head is contained 7.1 times in his total height measured from the soles of the feet to the vertex (1.379 m). He therefore marks the age of eighteen to nineteen years, and his height, multiplied by 10 and carried over 19 times, corresponds to the size of the adult Man of the Temple, which is 261.80 meters or 500 royal cubits.[13]

The last king (E) to the south is the largest, but his head is only contained 6.5 times in his total height (1.397 m). He thus marks the age of twelve years, and his height multiplied by 19×10 determines the largest measure of the Man of the Temple, which is 265.40 meters or 144 fathoms at 0° of latitude.[14]

The three other kings are located between these two extreme measurements.

King B has two very clearly marked height measurements: one is from the ground to the vertex, and the other is from the ground to the head of the uraeus. Traces can also be seen of two superimposed faces: the first has been corrected in such a way that the old profile remains as a testimony and point of comparison with the new profile (fig. 278a).

---

[12] Cf. plates 34–37 and chapter 31.

[13] Cf. plate 15.

[14] Cf. plate 24.

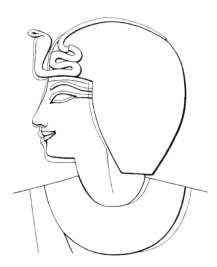

Fig. 278a. The profile of king B

Note the double line of the necklace, the lower part of the face, the eye, the upper forehead
and the uraeus, and the break in the serpent's body, which give the king a double face.

Indeed, if one wants to change the age of a figure on a bas-relief, one need only modify the size
of the head, not that of the limbs, which are limited by the baseline. This is exactly the problem of
the proportional modification of the head in the course of growth that we find applied to king B.

The first profile gives the head a size of two-thirteenths of the total height, thereby indicating
the proportion of a child of twelve years. The corrected profile reduces the height of the head,
which is then contained 7.1 times in the height specified by the uraeus, and the proportion
becomes that of an adult at eighteen to nineteen years. This rectified face also indicates two ages
of the temple. Now, this bas-relief is found at the place that physiologically corresponds to the profound transformations at the age of puberty. The east wall of room I is indeed in transposition with
room VII, (corresponding to the pineal gland), the only place in the whole temple where the child
king is shown being presented (offered) by his mother.

King B in the Holy of Holies has no navel and is thus an Adamic creation and not a procreation through woman, which makes him a principle, like the *kamutef*.

The only joint that crosses horizontally passes at the base of his chest, dividing him in such a
way that the part between the height of his head and this joint corresponds to the height at birth
(covered temple) with respect to the total height (entire temple).

—⁓—

Man breathes and his heart beats. These movements are the manifestations of his life; their cessation is death. Now, the temple is conceived in the image of living man. A "common measure"
applied to each part of the temple could correspond only to a mental scheme, too systematic to be
true. Thus, the projection on the temple of a *canevas* with ten times the height of king A for a unit
(plates 88, 89, and 90) represents but one aspect of the temple, a "moment" in its genesis. The five
kings formally teach that there are five different measurement values, each relating to a particular
place in the whole of the monument. The *canevas* observed in the tomb of Ukhotep at Meir
demonstrates that the Ancients did not hesitate to employ two slightly different values for squares

in the same scene, a fact confirmed by the break and the resumption of the lines in the grid pattern.[15] The variation applied at Meir is also that given by the base and the hypotenuse of the angle 1 to 7, the same difference obtaining between kings B and E of the sanctuary. It would be possible to conceive of the true *canevas* governing the building of the temple as composed of squares of varying sizes whose placement is already indicated by their relation to the principal axes.[16]

Thus, the five kings of the sanctuary of Amun show the Man of the Temple as conceived with the nuances that give him life. Each essential point is animated by the ritual placements of incense and certain other materials; the walls open and close as in inhaling and exhaling; the right differs from the left as west from east. The harmonic play of numbers, proportions, measures, and orientations are the secret of its life. In this regard, the dedication carved on the pedestal is not just the expression of human vanity when it declares that this monument is a "monument of eternity."

THE LINES ON THE FLOOR

PLATES 83, 85, AND 90

Excavations of the temple of Mentu at Karnak have demonstrated that certain lines marked on the stones of the temple facade correspond to the lines of the axis marked in the subfoundations of the monument.

The examination at Karnak of a pylon on the so-called incomplete facade, the stones of which were left unfinished, has shown that each cornerstone of each course bears the line of the angle of the monument and the axis of the torus on its upper face; on their lateral surfaces the line of the batter was also carved.

At Luxor, the tank upon which the covered temple rests (plate 94C) is itself a construction, and the lines that can be seen on the pavement and that govern the superstructure are in all likelihood replicated in the understructure, as is shown by certain filling stones that are aligned according to one of the essential axes (plate 84).

The three axes of Amun, Mut, and Khonsu are carved in the sanctuary of Amun's barque on the sandstone pavement of the platform. This sandstone pavement was again covered by a limestone pavement that preserved these axis lines and has kept them intact since the time of Amenhotep III (plate 85).

In surveying the pavement of the covered temple, it was observed that some of the limestone pavestones were missing and had been replaced by earth. The removal of this earth revealed the sandstone pavement, and the three inscribed axes were discovered.

On the large sandstone pavestones, two lines, still visible (plate 85), separate slightly from each other while generally going from north to south. If one stands at the south end of the sanctuary and looks toward room IV to the north, one can distinguish the axis of Amun, oriented at 34°27′ with respect to the true north-south, at the left. The hammered-out axis of Khonsu (axis of measures) oriented at 33°34′ is on the right. In front of the threshold of the naos, a third line, the axis of Mut (geometric axis), is oriented at 33°±5′.

The extensions of the axes of Amun and Khonsu toward room IV cross at the small key-piece embedded in the sandstone pavement on the threshold of the door between rooms IV and VI.

[15] Cf. plate 54.
[16] Cf. vol. 1, fig. 164.

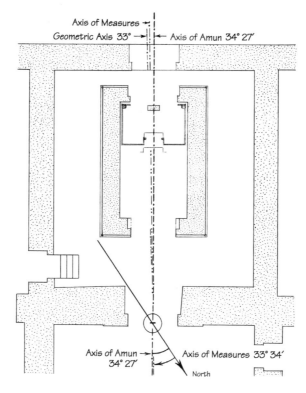

Fig. 278b (vol. 1, fig. 151)

Diagram of the three axes inscribed in the sanctuary of Amun's barque and their point of crossing on the threshold of the door from room IV to room VI (cf. plates 83 and 90, and the description of the key-piece, p. 690).

The axis of Mut governs the construction of the south part of the covered temple. Its extension into sanctuary I coincides with the edge of one of the filling stones of the tank (plate 84), which determines the median axis of the south part of the temple, of sanctuary I, and of the naos that contained the golden statue of Amun. In the south wall, the edge of a characteristic rectangular key-piece corresponds exactly to the extension of the axis of Khonsu.

At the base of each wall of the covered temple there remain (when the pavestones are in good condition) lines laying out the plan of the monument, including the doors. We have been able to reconstruct some of the destroyed walls on our plans thanks to these lines on the floor that preserve the original plan. All these lines in the covered temple are parallel or perpendicular to one of the three axes incised in the sanctuary floor. This fact allows us to affirm whether they are related to Amun, Mut, or Khonsu, their son.

For example, in room XII the north wall is rigorously parallel to its line on the floor, which is exactly perpendicular to the axis of Amun. The east wall makes an angle of 0°30′ to its line on the floor. The line is parallel to the geometric axis (Mut), and the wall follows the axis of Khonsu (fig. 279). This is the wall on which the barque of the rising sun is depicted (fig. 288).

Still visible on the floor is the axis line of the center of the column, and from the side of the east wall, three lines define the center and the diameter of this column. These indications at the beginning of the north colonnade, and the colonnade itself, exactly follow the axis of Amun.

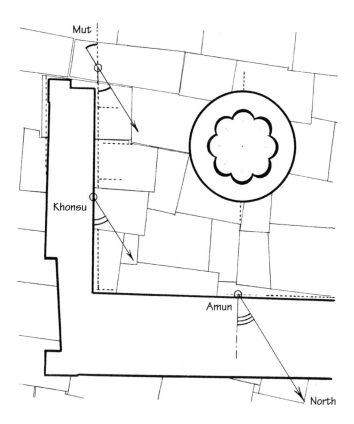

Fig. 279. Northeast corner of room XII, showing the lines on the floor and the intentional deviations of the construction of the wall with respect to these lines

THE THREE AXES

PLATES 81–90

The Axis of Amun

The axis of Amun governs the construction of the room of Amun's barque (room VI) as well as that of the naos of Alexander. The walls and the east-west colonnades of the covered temple are raised perpendicular to this axis in obedience to its "pulsation," indicated by certain lines on the ground that make an angle with it of about 0°20′. In room XII, for example, the wall and the row of six columns to the north are constructed on a line exactly perpendicular to the axis of Amun (fig. 280a). Between certain columns the south colonnade preserves vestiges of a line that deviates approximately 0°20′ with respect to the axis of Amun, in such a way that the double colonnade in the east-west direction broadens toward the west. It follows the direction of the path of the sun indicated on the east and west walls by the barques of the rising and setting sun.

The hypostyle room contains four rows of east-west columns: the two northern rows follow the axis of Amun, and the two southern rows follow the same slight deviation carried over from room XII. The columns of the central north-south corridor of the hypostyle room are also parallel to this axis (fig. 280a).

In the transept, the double colonnade on the north side is placed exactly like that of room XII. The double colonnade of the west side is parallel to the west wall and exactly perpendicular to the

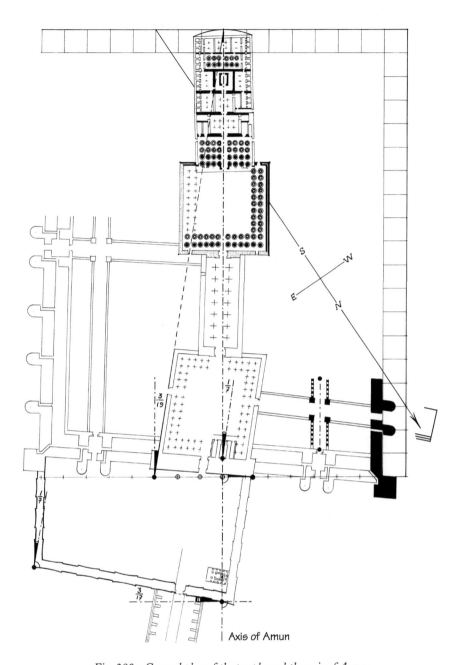

Fig. 280a. General plan of the temple and the axis of Amun

In black, the walls and columns governed by the axis of Amun; *crossed lines,* the walls and columns constructed on the deviation of the axis of Amun.

south colonnade of room XII. There is a similarity of orientation here that relates the colonnades and the walls of room XII to the west and north colonnades of the peristyle. As with the joints, it is a question of a system of correspondences, but here governed by the axes.[17]

[17] The complete plan of the temple with the Roman constructions constitutes a rectangle of 16 to 19, corresponding to the harmonic proportions of the temple. This is shown in fig. 138 (vol. 1). The governing function is harmonic proportion.

The similarity of orientation leads us from room XII—in which the medulla oblongata and the pons are found, the beginning of the spinal cord—to the coccyx, where the spinal column terminates at the level of the sex organs. Thus, the axis of Amun, starting from the pituitary center, ends its role as an axis when it gets to the sex organs and connects these two vital centers. The axis continues and culminates at the foot of the Man of the Temple, from which it again reflects toward the medulla oblongata.

All this would be only a geometric exercise indicative of a mathematical turn of mind if one did not take into account the vital—and esoteric—meaning that the principles joined in this ternary of Amun (male), Mut (female), and Khonsu (the product) represent.

This ternary, male or odd, female or even, and neuter or rectangular, is found throughout nature, which survives only through procreation by means of the complements (dualization) that characterize it. But following the stages of life these principles take on a different aspect and their *names* change. Those who are originally Ptah, Sekhmet, and Nefertum become Amun, Mut, and Khonsu in the human genesis. That which would have been Ptah, a pure fire, will be with Amun a water of lunar or solar fire; that which would have been with Sekhmet a Venusian water will be with Mut a lunar water, the one warm, the other cold. That which would have been with Nefertum a heavy and red earth will be with Khonsu a subtilized and black earth that will be characterized by the bringing together of all the scepters, except the flowering *wadj*.

It is necessary then to see in Amun a coagulating liquid substance like male sperm, and in Mut a substance that is also liquid, but susceptible of being coagulated by Amun, and everything that is said in the temple, from the locations in the body of the man through the symbols and texts, is to be studied in the context of a vital consideration of these characters.

The axis of Amun, to which, starting from the peristyle, no wall or colonnade any longer conforms, nevertheless secretly continues toward the north: its extension to the pylon culminates at the center of the north wall of the repository of Amun's barque built by Ramesses II, and ends at the south face of the west wing of the pylon. The same symbols that frame this axis at its beginning in the sanctuary of the barque (room VI), where it is drawn on the floor, are found, identically, in the repository where it ends (plates 86 and 87).

In room VI two ram-headed *djed* pillars frame the open door of the south interior facade of the naos; an Osirian curve surmounts the exterior north facade of the naos, and two *djed* pillars frame its median axis; to the right and left of the door of the naos, the king wears the red crown of the North at the west, and the white crown of the South at the east;[18] the barques drawn on the east and west walls of room VI are directed toward the north, which confirms the equality indicated in this place by the two crowns: north is equivalent to west.

At the pylon two ram-headed *djed* pillars frame the *closed* door carved on the interior north facade of the repository. Another Osirian curve, here located on the north interior facade, crowns the door drawn between the two *djed* pillars; the two kings represented on the doorposts of the entryway and on the lintel now wear the red crown in the east and the white crown in the west—there has been a crossing of the orientations, as testified by the crowns. The barque represented on the west wall of this chapel is directed toward the south. Here, contrary to the indication given in room VI, south is equivalent to west.[19]

---

[18] Cf. fig. 287.

[19] Let us remember that north is inspiration and south is realization, therefore causing east and west, successively, to play the same roles.

On the architrave of the portico preceding the door of the repository of Ramesses II, the axis is marked by two vertical cartouches with the name of this king. On either side of these cartouches, two Amuns seated back-to-back each present the ankh to the falcon who makes up part of the standard titulary of Ramesses II (plate 87).

These two Amuns rarely meet each other in the titulary. We know of only two other examples in the area of Thebes: one is at the temple of Seti I at Gurnah, and the other, carrying an identical theme, is on an architrave, reused but upside-down, in the ceiling of the naos of Alexander.

Two facts are to be noted in this reemployment: first, the anomaly of the figuration of Amun in the title of Ramesses II and its reuse precisely in the sanctuary of the barque of Amun. Second, the *inversion* of the architrave at the extremities of the axis of Amun.

In spite of the reversal of the orientations given by the crowns, the sacred barque preserves the east-west direction in the two sanctuaries, there being simply a reflection as in a vertical mirror: right becomes left, but without changing the orientation. The two barques are distinguished, however, by their design; the naos of the barque of the sanctuary of Amenhotep III is surrounded by a veil, whereas the repository of Ramesses II leaves Amun and Ra visible.[20]

The axis of Amun goes from south to north when governing the constructions of the sanctuary of Amenhotep III up to the north wall of the peristyle, and it returns from north to south when governing the building of Ramesses II. It is then "reflected" on an angle of 1 to 7 (8°8′) by the north wall of the repository of Ramesses, which forms an angle of half of 1 to 7 with this axis.[21]

The measured distance between the end of the repository of Ramesses II and the central cross carved on the sandstone pavement of Amenhotep III is 420 royal cubits (7 × 60), in a straight line on the axis of Amun. The hypotenuse of the 1 to 7 triangle determines the length of 120 mean fathoms, and its rabattement coincides with the "procession of the odor" that preceded the wooden naos containing the sacred barque. Under this walk can still be seen the hammered-out lines of an ithyphallic Min (plate 85) who *will be made manifest* by Ramesses II in his repository, where Min is depicted on the east partition in front of the barque.

The ideal extension of the axis of Amun into the courtyard of Nectanebo passes through the sanctuary of Isis at the point where the statue of Isis was found during the excavations of 1950–51.[22] This axis defines the orientation of the north wall of this parvis through its perpendicular lessened by 10° (the angle 3 to 17). The east wall of the parvis is oriented according to the perpendicular of the north wall plus the reflection angle of Amun, 8°8′ (the angle 1 to 7, fig. 280a).

In the last Roman constructions the west enclosing wall of the fortress and the north-south pathway bordered with columns were both constructed parallel to the axis of Amun, which crosses the path leading toward the Nile, thus affirming the continuity of observance of the laws of the Temple in the Roman era. There was no religious conflict.

The angle of the axis of Amun with respect to north corresponds to an orientation of the temple at a certain determined hour (through the sighting of a star of the Great Bear, the "thigh" of the heavens). It is useful in this regard to consult the list of "solar hours" of the temple of Edfu.

---

[20] Cf. plate 101 and fig. 300.

[21] The north wall of the repository of Amun leans against the pylon and is not exactly parallel with it; it forms an angle of 38°36′ with the east-west line, which is 34°32′ + 4°4′.

[22] Cf. Leclant, "Fouilles et travaux en Egypte 1950–51."

Amun governs the number Seven, the number of nature, that is to say, the "constituting elements" of the phenomena of our world. We encounter this number in music in the seven notes of the scale that resonate harmoniously for our ear, in the seven spectral colors of white light, in the physiological cycle of the ages seven, fourteen, twenty-one, and 6 × 7, or forty-two years, characteristic of certain changes, and in the up to seven electron shells in the atom.

At the specific stage of human consciousness of our earth (as a planetary globe in the solar system), nature is septuple.[23] In reality, this sevenfold structure is the result of nine stages, because the third and the sixth of the seven appearances are divided in two. Thus, in the colors of the spectrum there are two yellows and two blues; the yellow and the blue are both the end and beginning of a series:

Red	Orange	Yellow (warm)		
		Yellow	Green	Blue (cool)
			Blue	Indigo	Violet (moderate)

The Axis of Mut

The axis of Mut, indicated by the third line of sanctuary VI, is called "geometric" because it is the median, longitudinal axis of each of the successive parts of the temple; it governs materially (fig. 281). It begins at point *A*, at the end of sanctuary I (plate 84), where it divides the tabernacle, the sanctuary, and the south wall of the covered temple into two equal parts. It culminates at *B*, where it divides the south face of the platform into two equal parts. In the covered temple this axis governs all the lines on the floor for the north-south walls of the three secret sanctuaries, as well as the south and west walls and the north edge of the platform. It also governs the west wall of the chamber of Mut's barque (room XX) and the two north-south walls of room VIII (in black in fig. 281).

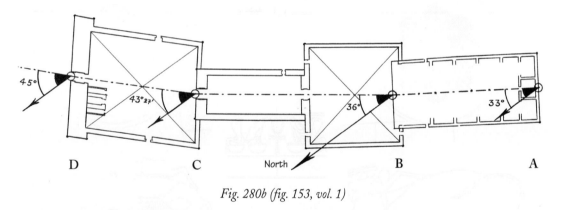

Fig. 280b (fig. 153, vol. 1)

The axis of Mut (covered temple) is oriented at 33°±5′ with respect to north-south for its whole length, *AB*.[24] From point *B* this axis deviates by 3° and through its orientation (36° in relation to north-south) determines the pentagonal function. It crosses the peristyle court (the belly) and governs the construction of the nave by passing through the center of its doors. It culminates

[23] It appears that the number 7 has a specifically terrestrial nature. This characteristic opens the door to an eventual study that would harmonize the various globes of the planetary system.

[24] Cf. vol. 1, fig. 159.

at point *C*, but a piece embedded in the pavement of the Ramesses court, emphasized by a difference in height, marks its extension to *C'*. Between *B* and *C*, the geometric axis governs the east colonnade of the transept, the nave, and also the enclosing wall and the east colonnades of the Roman constructions (in black in fig. 281).

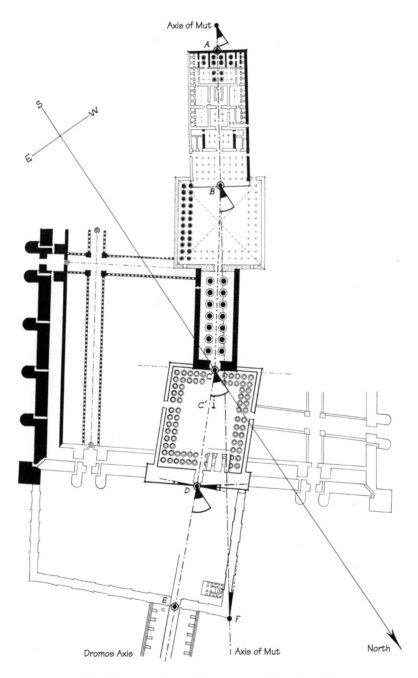

Fig. 281. General plan of the temple and the axis of Mut

The axis of Mut, the geometric axis, undergoes three deviations: *AB* governs the walls and columns of the covered temple *(in black); BC* governs the wall and colonnades of the transept, the nave, and the eastern part of the Roman enclosing wall (also *in black*); *CD* governs the narthex; *DE* governs the dromos.

The geometric axis of the nave, *BC*, makes an angle of 3° (about 1 to 19) with the geometric axis of the covered temple, *AB*. The north facade of the nave makes an angle that is one-half of 3° to the perpendicular of *BC*. This facade is therefore oriented at 37°30′ with respect to the east-west line (45° less 7°30′). The Roman colonnade that goes from the crossroads on the east to the *kamutef* is parallel to it (fig 281).

From point *C* the geometric axis, in a new orientation, governs the Ramesses court and ends at *D* at the north facade of the pylon (fig. 281). The angular difference between sections *BC* and *CD* is 7°30′, which corresponds to the hexagonal function, or more exactly, to the division of the cycle into 4 × 6, which corresponds to the twenty-four hours of the day.

From point *D* the geometric axis conforms to an angle of 45° (1 to 1) with respect to true north. It crosses the Nectanebo courtyard (the pedestal) at *DE* and continues north, dividing the avenue of the sphinxes into two equal parts, which leads in a straight line to Karnak, where it ends at the ninth pylon. The axis of the dromos, *DE*, corresponds to the orientation *CD* of the court of Ramesses plus 1°30′. This difference, ±0°5′, recalls the difference between the axis of Amun and the geometric axis of Mut in the covered temple.

Finally, the axis of Mut in the covered temple (*AB*) seems to play an analogous role to that of the axis of Amun. Its extension northward culminates, against the pylon, in the repository for Mut's barque constructed by Ramesses II. The mass of the pylon forms an angle of 6° with the perpendicular to the axis of Mut, *DE*, and an identical angle with the perpendicular to the axis of Mut, *AB*. Thus, the "reflection" of the axis of Mut forms an angle of 12°. This angle results from the division of the cycle by 30, and this construction is one consequence of the combination of the pentagon and the hexagon that divides the circle into 5 and 6. Thus 33°, the axis of Mut, *AB*, of the covered temple, increased by 12°, equals the ratio of 1 to 1 or 45°. This is the axis of the dromos toward Karnak, the final (or original?) orientation, because north-south is the reference, and the angle 1 to 1 is the first possible ratio.

Just like the extension of the axis of Amun in the parvis, which determined the north and east walls, the extension of the axis of Mut, *AB*, in the courtyard of Nectanebo, culminates at the northwest corner in the shape of the prow of a boat, at *F* (fig. 281).[25] The west wall of this courtyard is oriented following this axis increased by 10° with respect to north.

In summary, the successive deviations of the geometric axis alternate the functions of the pentagon and the hexagon. It is thus that Amun-Mut give *form* and *measure* to the narthex as their offspring, Khonsu.

—∿—

Just as we can observe an oscillation in the axis of Amun in room XII, in the hypostyle room, and in the north portico of the transept, there is a pulsation around the axis of Mut (nave): the rows of columns on the east side of the nave and the east portico of the transept are parallel to the west wall of the nave, and conversely, the rows of columns on the west side are parallel to the east wall (fig. 282). It follows that these two colonnades would open out toward the south, while the walls of the nave widen toward the north.[26] There are two directions, as indicated by the bas-reliefs: on the west wall the procession of the barques is coming from Karnak toward the temple of Luxor,

[25] Cf. plate 49. The cornerstone shaped like a prow is an example of a *pierre croche* (curved stone), known to ancient "journeymen" ["*compasnions*"].

[26] Interior width of the north nave = 20.55 m, ±5 cm; south nave = 20.17 m, ±5 cm.

and on the east wall the return to Karnak is carved. The small piece marked in the pavement of the court of Ramesses (*C'*) as the end of the median axis of the nave corresponds to the place in which the sacred barques branch off in order to head toward the Nile, to the loading dock.

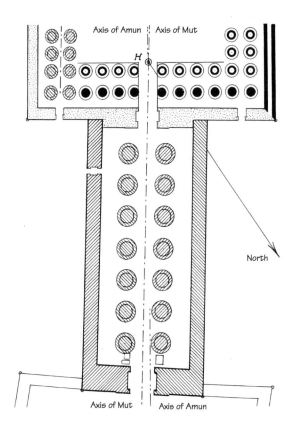

Fig. 282. Detail of the oscillation of the construction around the axis of the nave

Hachured (both directions), the east and west walls of the nave and its colonnade. The same orientation exists for the east colonnade of the transept. The direction of the hachures indicates the movement of widening. *Solid black circles*, north colonnade of the transept, constructed perpendicular to the axis of Amun. *Black-and-white circles*, the west wall, west colonnade and south row of the north colonnade of the transept, which conform to the deviation of the axis of Amun. The axes of Mut and Amun cross each other in the transept at point *H*.

The Axis of Khonsu

The axis of Khonsu, or axis of measures (33°34'), carved in the sanctuary of the barque and then hammered out, crosses the axis of Amun at the key-piece, already mentioned, on the threshold of room VI. This axis divides the north and south facades of the covered temple into two unequal parts in the same way the "votive" cubits are divided. This inequality relates not only to time but, above all, to the principle of the variation of the solar influence before and after noon. It would indeed be an error to want to apply the formula of the "Temple in the image of Heaven" in a purely schematic relationship.[27]

---

[27] The hour between noon and one o'clock is the hour consecrated to Khonsu.

In the covered temple, the axis of measures governs part of the north-south walls (in rooms XII and IV), as well as the facades of small side chapels that still exist. The east exterior wall is parallel to it in the part between the south facade and the large wall corresponding to the clavicles. Beginning from this point, the east wall makes a major deviation and is oriented at 32°15' with respect to north-south. The chapel of the barque of Khonsu,[28] located to the east of the room of the barque of Mut, has its west wall oriented according to the axis of Khonsu (33°34') and the east wall oriented according to the deviation mentioned above.

The axis of Khonsu passes between the axes of Amun and Mut and divides the angle they make into two parts, one of which is one-third and the other two-thirds. It therefore plays the role of the dividing element of the "nucleus" that presides over the transition of the progression from the powers of 1/2 to the powers of 1/3, these latter governing the development of volumes (the product).[29]

Apart from the few north-south walls that it governs in the covered temple, the axis of Khonsu—which, moreover, is effaced—no longer plays an architectural role, the axes of Amun and Mut having already defined the essential orientations of the entire temple including the parvis. There is only one orientation that they do not rule: the axis that passes through the east-west doors of the court of Ramesses, extended by the Romans with a colonnade that goes to the western entryway of the surrounding wall leading toward the Nile. This "axis of the east-west doors," marked in the court of Ramesses by a change of height in the pavement and by the piece that indicates the end of the axis of the nave at *C'*, is, however, important enough for us to investigate the cause of its particular orientation. It is through the door on the side of the Nile that the royal princes, the dauphins (Khonsu), enter. The orientation of this east-west axis is 41°44' ±5' in relation to north. The axis of Khonsu being 33°34', their difference is 8°10', and here we find again the angle 1 to 7 (8°8') equal to the reflection angle of the axis of Amun, but perpendicular to it.

—∿—

Of course, no direct link exists between the master builders of the cathedral in Paris and the master builder of the temple of Luxor. It is therefore interesting to note the coincidence of the proportional sizes and the *overall* variations of the axes of these two sanctuaries, a coincidence that could not be fortuitous, but must correspond to a common, living, geometric directive.

The superposition of the plans of the two monuments (fig. 283) excludes the court of Ramesses—replaced by the narthex under the towers of the cathedral—that Luxor develops with its significance. The crown of the skull, corresponding to that of the Man of the Temple, cut off at Luxor, is added to the cathedral.

Notre Dame in Paris is characterized by its calm equilibrium and its sobriety. In its facade and in its plan we find the same observances and nuances of a living movement as those of the temple of Luxor: the vertical central axis does not divide the facade into two equal parts; and the right is not identical to the left.

Each of the three doors obeys a different geometric function in establishing the ogives; the center door gives the general law.

[28] This chapel, the unfinished bas-reliefs of which depict Khonsu, is generally considered as that of the royal barque; however, the lintel of its door formally portrays Khonsu.
[29] Cf. chapter 9.

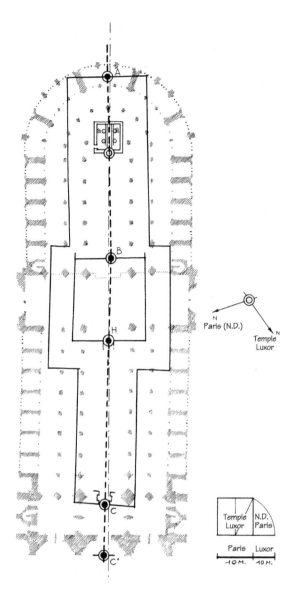

Fig. 283. Superposition of the plan of the temple of Amenhotep III at Luxor and the outline of the plan of Notre Dame in Paris

Comparison of the two scales and the two orientations. The letters *A*, *B*, *C*, *C'*, and *H* correspond to the letters on figures 281 and 282.

In the whole of the facade, the left side (north, inspiration) tends toward the romanesque curve and the right side (south, accomplishment) is clearly pointed (gothic). This corresponds to the same indications of orientation as those in the pylon and in room XII of the temple of Luxor, where north is assimilated to east and south to west (romanesque and gothic). This asymmetry is found again in the inequality of the width of the two towers of Notre Dame. The row of twenty-eight kings above the three doors, through the inequality of their distribution (seven, nine, and eight), give the essential numbers that govern their geometry and allude to the two essential numbers of the cubit, 24 and 28, through the four kings projecting out on the four pillars.

As in Egypt in its great period, we find in Notre Dame in Paris a very beautiful example of harmony created from an asymmetry that at first glance appears to be "perfectly symmetrical."

THE NAOS OF ALEXANDER
AND THE GEOMETRIC π

In our study of the tomb of Ramesses IX (figs. 261 and 262), we noted the angle β. We found this same angle in the study of the proportions of the "particular coefficient" of Thothotep at Meir (fig. 252). While noting this angle β on these occasions, we promised to speak of it again. This angle is of the utmost importance, which is emphasized by the fact that it is defined and applied in the sanctuary of Amun's barque at Luxor.

The proportions of the plan of the naos of Alexander are established on the governing rectangle of the pentagon so that the small side of the naos corresponds to the side of the pentagon, the length to the diameter of the inscribed circle, and the diagonal to the diameter of the circumscribed circle. In perpendicularly crossing the rectangle of the plan of the naos, the diagonal *AB*, carried over to the axis of Amun toward the south at *C*, defines the length *AC* (fig. 284).

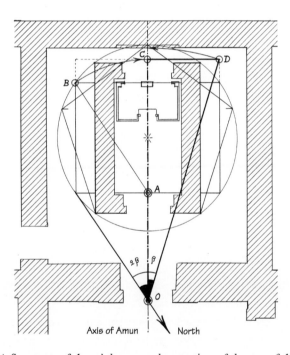

Fig. 284. Sanctuary of Amun's barque and proportions of the naos of Alexander

The axis of Amun, *OC*, forms an angle with true north that is double the angle formed by the axis of Amun and the hypotenuse *OD*. This angle *COD* is equal to the angle β, which we noted in the angle of the scepter of Osiris-Ptah in the tomb of Ramesses IX. This determines the triangle *COD* of which *CD* is an irrational length with respect to *OC* when given the value of 3. Then *OD* is, in relation to 3, an already very perfect π of 3.141595, compared with π as it is presently calculated, 3.1415927.... .

We thus have a method of drawing an almost exact π in a straight line, which makes a geometric squaring of the circle possible.

The proportions of the room containing this naos apply this function: the length of the east-west walls is equal to 3 for the length of the north-south walls equal to π.[30]

The arrangement of the four columns originally built by Amenhotep III in the place of the present naos of Alexander determine, by the distance between their axes, the proportion 1 to 1.236..., which corresponds to the ratio of the radii of the inscribed and circumscribing circles of the pentagon. These four columns therefore imply the function of the pentagon, the governing rectangle of which was only realized by Alexander.

In establishing the human canon on 18 and 19 for the height of man to the forehead and to the vertex, respectively, the Ancients chose the nearest whole numbers to the ratio between the height and the diagonal of the pentagon.[31] Traditionally, the pentagon has been associated with the representation of man. Now, the pentagon allows us to establish geometrically the values of the square and cube roots of π.

The pharaonic people were great geometers.

DISCUSSION CONCERNING A PERFECT π

The figure of Ramesses IX, like the sanctuary of the barque of the temple of Luxor, accentuates the relation between the 3, 4, 5 triangle, the pentagon, and the hexagon.

It seems that the Ancients did not have to draw the pentagon to establish this geometric understanding, the pentagon being for them a sacred figure, implied and respected. The crossing of the two 8 to 11 rectangles was sufficient to obtain the same "practical" demonstrations of the functions instanced, as much in the case of the figuration of Ramesses IX as in the sanctuary of the barque at the temple of Luxor.

The knowledge of the ϕ functions by pharaonic geometers simply cannot be doubted, but one could reasonably object: with regard to the definition of the coefficient π that results from this geometric play, how were they able to draw the conclusion that they were dealing there with the value of π, and particularly with a more precise π than that obtained by $1.2 \times \phi^2$?

Our present knowledge of a π calculated by polygons allows us to observe and to judge, but the Ancients did not have this criterion at their disposal. So is it not a fantasized pretension on our part to conclude that it was a conscious geometric activity on the part of the Ancients, especially their knowledge of the fact that this angle β is that of a triangle that establishes a relation of 3 to π between the large side and the hypotenuse?

We can observe these disconcerting coincidences:

1. The angle made by the axis of Amun with north represents double the angle β (fig. 284).

2. The rectangle formed by room VI of the barque of Amun is established on the proportion of 1 to $\pi/3$, but this can be related to a π that equals $1.2 \times \phi^2$.

3. The beautiful monument of the naos of Alexander, constructed in room VI, has a plan established on the governing rectangle of the pentagon.

4. The columns of Amenhotep III, on the bases of which the naos of Alexander is constructed, form a rectangle of 1 to 1.236... (from center to center of the columns), which is the relationship between the radii of the inscribed and circumscribing circles of the pentagon ($\sqrt{5} - 1$).

[30] Cf. vol. 1, fig. 113, the proportions of room VI. We note that all the measurements given were taken on the spot with the greatest care, and the geometric lines were studied on large-scale plans with measurements always checked.

[31] Cf. vol. 1, fig. 132.

5. The tomb at Meir, the *canevas* of which we have analyzed, shows us that the the 3, 4, 5 triangle is intentionally displaced in order to obtain the proportion of the governing rectangle of the pentagon, 1 to 1.376.... The registers indicate, by the number of squares, the ratio 22 to 21, or approximately $\pi/3$ (in whole numbers).

6. The tableau of Thoth at Karnak gives the numbers of the hexagon to Thoth and those of the pentagon to Seshat.

7. The drawing of the naos on papyrus has the proportion 1 to 2 in elevation and the rectangle of the pentagon in plan, which also evokes the ratio 22 to 21, therefore the function $\pi/3$.

8. The ratio of the length of the royal cubit, 0.5236 meter, to the radius of the circle is the function of π, which implies the knowledge of the meter with regard to π equaling $1.2 \times \phi^2$.

Above all, it is evident that the coefficient π is used intentionally. Now, it was as obvious to the Ancients as it is to us that the elements for establishing the value of this coefficient—like $1.2 \times \phi^2$—are irrational; they could not therefore have doubted the relativity of their π with respect to a more precise coefficient.

The search for a more precise number (in proportional notation and not as we write here in figures and decimals) must have necessarily oriented them toward the pentagon, which is entirely irrational through its construction based on ϕ. But this still does not explain the knowledge of a more perfect π through the angle β, which corresponds to 3.14159.... .

Nevertheless, in order to establish the royal cubit, the coefficient π must already have been known. The knowledge of an approximate π through 22 : 21 appears in the constructions, then, functionally, through $12 \times \phi^2 = 10\pi$, the π of the cycle of time, fully adequate to establish the π of the royal cubit, as a practical measure, at 3.14164.... .

It is also easy to establish the coefficient π empirically by measuring the relationship between the diameter and the circumference of a circle of any dimension. Moreover, the ratio of the areas of the disk and the square used in the Rhind Papyrus, $8^2 : 9^2$, implies an already excellent π of 3.16049....

There is therefore a reference for finding a more precise number than that imposed by logic. Now, the certainty of approaching a more perfect π can only be given by a function that, originally, gives an approximate π. This function must then be a ratio that develops naturally, revealing a number that becomes more exact, as the ratios of the F and R series do for the value ϕ. Rationally, this condition is offered by the inscribed and circumscribed polygons, but this is not "pharaonic."

The tableau of Ramesses IX can be instructive in resolving this problem. Indeed, everything here is oriented, first, toward the meter, that is, the diameter or radius of the circle; second, toward the law of the right triangle through the sacred 3, 4, 5 triangle; third, toward the pentagon and the construction of the angle β that results from it, this angle being half of the original angle given in the temple of Luxor by the angle made by the axis of Amun with respect to north; and fourth, toward the coefficient π in general.

If we apply the indicated geometric construction that comes from the pentagon to the 3, 4, 5 triangle we have, first, the triangle 3 to $(4 + 5)$, which is proportionally 3 : 9, and second, the new hypotenuse will be $\sqrt{90}$, which equals 9.4868..., and its ratio to 9 will be 1.0541..., or $\pi/3$ for a π that equals 3.1623..., which gives to π the value of $\sqrt{10}$, very close to the ratio 256 : 81, or 3.16049..., observed in the Rhind Papyrus with regard to volumes.

It then becomes evident that this procedure, applied to the irrational values of the pentagon, and thus to the values derived from ϕ, will give a more perfect result. We only have to find the *transition function* between 3, 4, 5, or, the right triangle in general, and the relationship between the small radius, the side of the pentagon, and their hypotenuse.

Now, the curve of the circle or cycle is the effect of movement, and the movement defines the limits of a surface cutting and measuring the volume. The regular volumes show us the origin and what results from movement: the octahedron defines the tetrahedron by pivoting, the tetrahedron gives the cube and the cube gives the dodecahedron formed from twelve pentagonal surfaces.

The projection of the icosahedron, engendered by the dodecahedron, produces a hexagon and a pentagon, and the dodecahedron is a *construction* starting from a planar surface formed of hexagons that cannot constitute the surface of a volume *without contracting from six to five sides.*

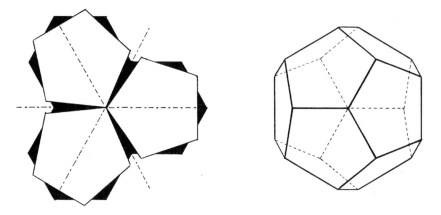

Fig. 285. Contraction of hexagons that fill the plane into pentagons,
which join to form the dodecahedron

Starting from the dodecahedron, only the icosahedron, formed of twenty equilateral triangles, can result from its movement. The next volume, but then only semiregular, that can be formed on the icosahedron is the triacontagon composed of twelve pentagonal faces and twenty equilateral triangles. But the idea of wanting to create a curved surface by multiplying flat surfaces will always be contrary to the pharaonic mentality.

The contraction from six to five through the ratio of the hexagon to the pentagon is constantly evoked where the pharaonic tradition speaks of π. We find it in the tableau of Thoth at Karnak, in the tomb of Ramesses IX, in the sanctuary of the barque of the temple of Luxor, and then in the passage from the work of Amenhotep III to that of Ramesses II in the *growth* of the temple.

The figuration of Ramesses IX is oriented toward *function* by relating Maāt and Ptah (fig. 262). Now, Ptah is the contracting, earth-forming fire of the Heliopolitan Mystery, the Tum become corporeal, and Maāt is the milieu having a separating function (the pure from the impure, the high from the low); it is the balance from which comes the principle of justice and the first manifestation of consciousness and conscience.

The metaphysical theme is thus: a contracting, styptic force coagulating an undifferentiated milieu into a form that can only be a "formless" sphere containing all forms. In other words, the regular solids result from the sphere and end in the octahedron and not the other way around, as logic might suggest. The passage is from the curved surface to a surface composed of equilateral triangles, and from these, which are the elements of the hexagonal planar area, to the pentagons forming surfaces of volume.

There is a contraction toward rational elements from an irrational given that cannot be separated into isolated elements. This progress toward the Becoming is clearly marked by the geometry of the figuration of Ramesses IX, which calls for *the principle of harmonic division* (fig. 286), just as it prescribes, moreover, the philosophy of the Becoming.

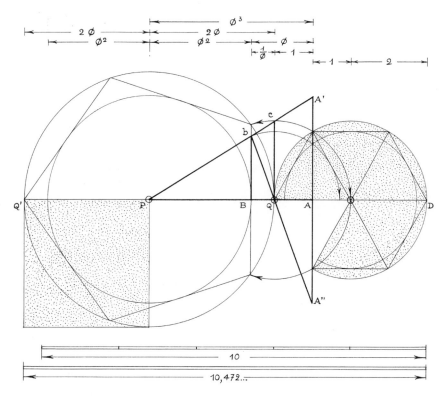

Fig. 286. Demonstration of the hexagon-pentagon relationship and the contraction of six triangles into five

If $\dfrac{PA}{PB} = \dfrac{a}{b} = \dfrac{\phi}{1}$ and if $AA' = AA'' = PB$,

$PA = a^2 + \text{ab} = \phi^2 + \phi = \phi^3$,

$PB = b^2 + ab = 1 + \phi = \phi^2$,

$PQ = 2ab = 2\phi$.

The ratio between PQ and PB is as 2ϕ is to ϕ^2, which is 2 to ϕ and corresponds to the ratio between the radius of the circumscribed circle and the radius of the inscribed circle of the pentagon. The height Bb is equal to ϕ and Qc equals 2. The diagonal Qb is then $\sqrt{3}$, so that Qc and Qb are to each other as the radii of the circumscribed and inscribed circles of the hexagon for which each side equals $2QA$.

The total length $Q'D$ is equal to $4 \times \phi^2$ or 10.472.... This length is equal to five-sixths of the curve that circumscribes the hexagon with a radius of 2. In surface, $4 \times \phi^2$ or 10.472 represents the square of the radius of the circumscribing circle of the pentagon, and this surface equals five-sixths of the surface of the disk formed by the circle circumscribing the hexagon. Because of the harmonic proportion applied to the geometry of the hexagon and the pentagon, we are dealing here with the inversion of the ratio $(\phi^2/5) \times 6$.

—◇—

One can calculate by various procedures a sufficient mathematical π that will always be only an approximation between a straight line and curve, whether with right triangles, by cutting into bands (the Chinese and Japanese procedure), or by using polygons. By these paths π will necessarily be an indefinable number.

If one were able to give a numerical value to the circle through the different curved elements—therefore through movement—and not through straight lines, we would arrive at an absolute π, but it would be untranslatable into numbers. Therefore the true and absolute π must be considered as a *function,* and not a number, and this function is a *contraction* by a center—presumably acting equally in all directions—on a "spatial substance."

This *fact* exists, geometry can demonstrate it, but cerebral intelligence cannot grasp it. In principle, it is a question of the gravitational phenomenon conditioned by an energetic "density," but of a nonpolarized energy and not a kinetic energy. This is the obstacle to the definition of the gravitational force starting from the circuit-formula, $E = mc^2$, because first it is necessary that *energy* become *mass.*

We always come back to the Heliopolitan Mystery, experimentally demonstrable, but which no reasoning can explain.

Demonstrating geometrically the relationship and the passage from the pentagon to the hexagon is typically pharaonic.

It is the generative function that matters in their mentality and not the element of a mechanical ratio like π as a coefficient in the calculation of cosmic mechanics. In this case the function ϕ, which is the original power of the scission, would be more valid in their eyes than a π translated adequately into numbers precise enough for technical work.

We always have a tendency to investigate the invariable—what I call the cadaverous—in the study of phenomena, without taking movement into account, the alternation that is the character of every living thing, of everything that makes up our universe. We seek the value of the great circle of the earth to within a few minutes of arc when in fact we know that the earth breathes, expanding and contracting; we want to know the circuit of the planets and other astronomical movements to within meters when we know and observe that these paths and durations are constantly varying.

These are seductive supporting points to conclude that there are laws, but for the Ancients there is only one law, that of genesis; it is philosophical, but its principles apply to everything in practice. It is a "functional science," whereas our science is concerned with momentary finalities.

Conclusion: Movement, Symbol of Life

Through their orientations and their slight oscillations, the axes of the temple relate the building to certain areas of the sky and to the characteristics of the planetary movements relative to the movement of the earth as it travels in space. I do not have the competence necessary to provide precise details of these relationships; this would be work for an astronomer. After having noted the principle incidences of these orientations and oscillations with the lines of the walls and of the rows of columns, all that remains to speak of is the impression one receives when one has had the privilege of passing hours in meditation in the midst of what remains of this temple.

Only with difficulty does the eye notice variations in the construction; while what remains is only an impression of equilibrium and serenity, all is vibrating as a sound would that resonates and continues to vibrate within us when the ear can no longer hear it. In this state then everything seems possible. But when, in the return to our agitated world, vibrating for nothing, drowned in its singular utilitarian preoccupations, and unfortunately growing more and more amoral, one considers improbable all the subtleties displayed in this sacred architecture. And we have had to measure and check completely to prove that these things are true and not imagined. We can only prove that these movements have a logical sense, and by doing so bring life to a rigid, cadaverous notion, whereas the goal of the Temple is to raise our being toward the Being that animates all.

Ancient visitors to Egypt could say that these people were the most religious in the world, which must be true when we ourselves, today, in the midst of these ruins (of that which is perishable) are still deeply moved by the atmosphere that reigns there. The walls and columns, however, are without the glowing colors that illuminated them, devoid of the strips of silver and gold repoussé that ornamented certain bas-reliefs; the ground of the sanctuary of the barque is bare of the virgin silver plating that covered it, the doorways no longer carry the swinging doors of rare wood encased in bronze, gold, and silver and the precious stones that decorated them; the sanctuary of Amun is missing its statue of "new gold," the space is devoid of the perfume of secret resins that expand the heart. . . .

But beyond the ear, in those who know how to listen, the mantric litanies whose magic has impregnated the stones still vibrate, and will remain there until their decomposition into dust. And we can no longer believe that this once was real. . . .

Thus Asclepiades, the pseudo-Apuleius, long ago prophesied,

A time will come when it will appear that it was in vain that the Egyptians have served the divinity with piety and zeal . . . because the divinity will return from the earth to heaven and Egypt will be delivered to abandonment; the country that was the seat of religion will no longer be the abode of the gods. . . . O Egypt, Egypt, only fables will remain of your beliefs, which will seem incredible to future generations, and only words on stones will remain to recount your acts of piety![32]

---

[32] Erman, in *Religion des Egyptiens,* cites this quote to close his book, a book so precious and precise that we can both deplore its derisive attitude toward ancient Egypt and be surprised at the choice of the prophesy of Asclepiades to conclude it. Asclepiades lived between the fourth and fifth centuries A.D.

Chapter 41

RECEIVING AND GIVING

Plates 91–93

The true meaning of the crossing is the alternation of the visible with the invisible, of the abstract with the concrete, of the actual with the potential. We see the one, observe it with our senses, but we do not perceive its complement. It is this relationship that is α and ω, the All.

(Chapter 19)

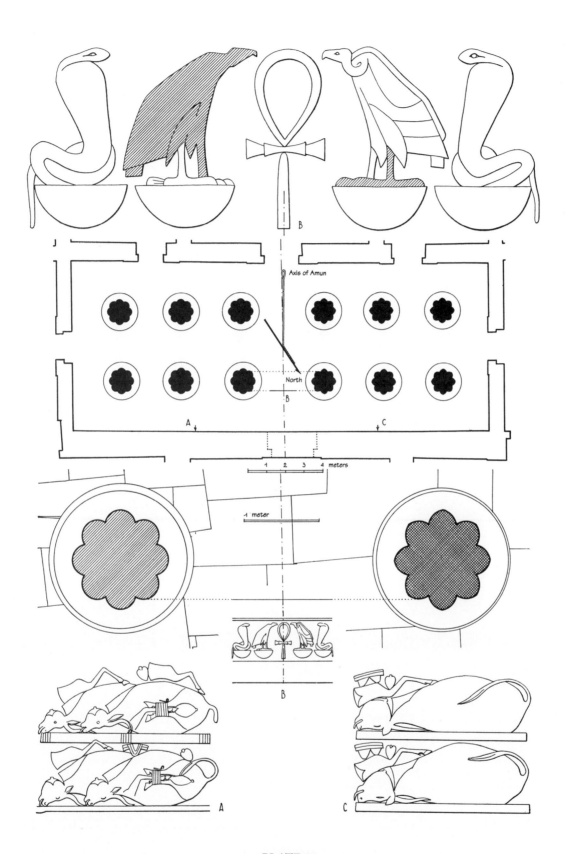

PLATE 91

Orient and Occident

In the Symbol, that which evokes is the soul that animates the thing, its life.

(Introduction)

Cultivating simplicity of being and seeing in oneself is the first task of anyone wishing to approach the sacred symbolique *of Ancient Egypt. This is difficult because the obvious blinds us.*

(Chapter 2)

PLATE 92

Sunrise and Sunset; the Luxor Pylon

The universal principle of the crossing (the cross)
is applied throughout pharaonic thought. It is the
vital key to all that appears in the Universe.

(Chapter 19)

PLATE 93

Right and Left

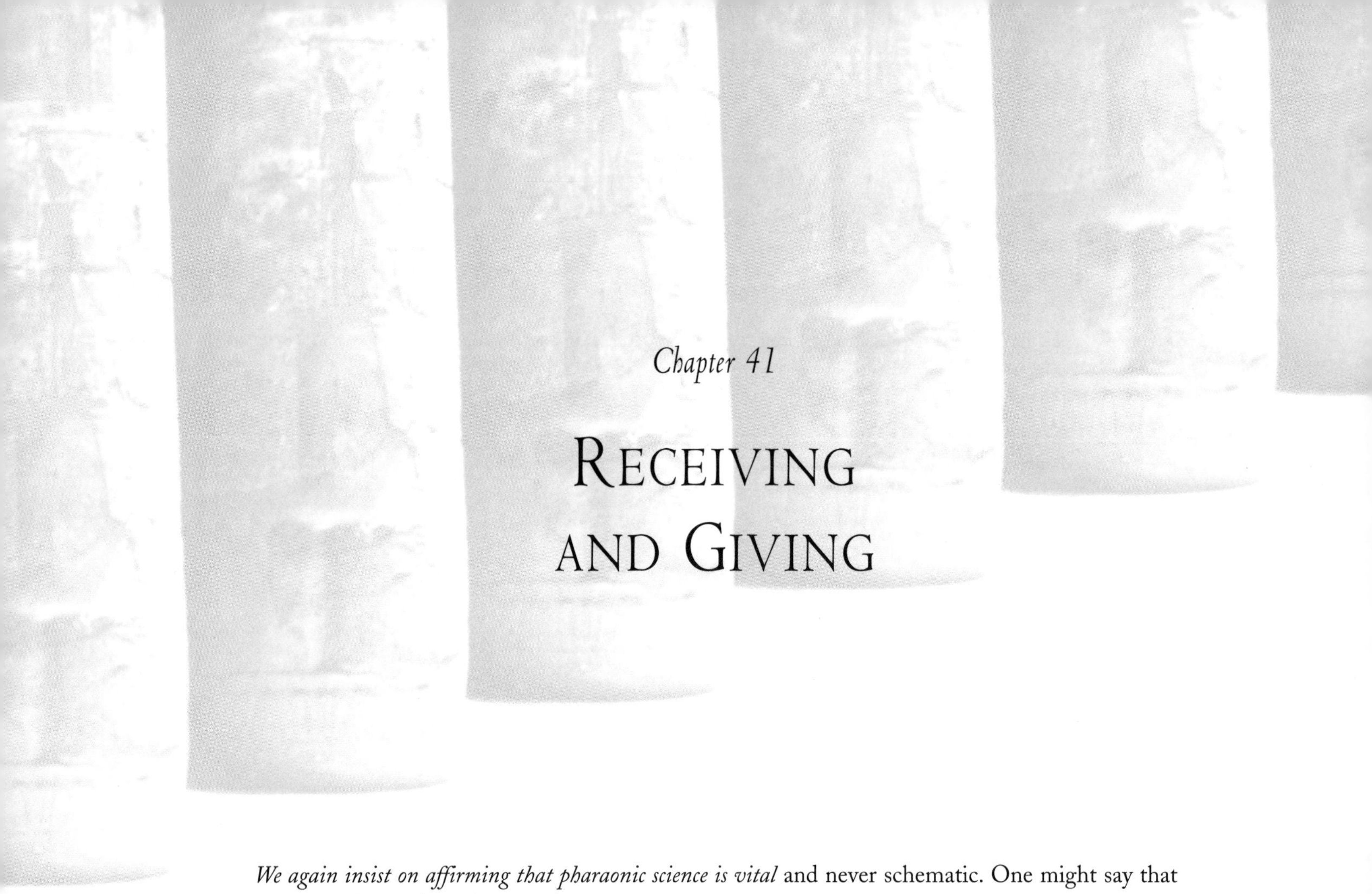

Chapter 41

RECEIVING
AND GIVING

We again insist on affirming that pharaonic science is vital and never schematic. One might say that pharaonic Egypt has a horror of symmetry.

The culminating point of the sun at noon does not divide its course into two equal parts. There are variations in the durations, from sunrise to midday and from midday to sunset; but the most important thing to note is that the sun before noon is vitally not the same as the sun of the afternoon, as any experienced nurseryman knows perfectly well. It is not a matter of an accumulation of heat throughout the day, but of a different radiation that affects all of life, as an emission of ultraviolet or infrared rays might do.

A variation in growth and ripening in every living thing results from this; the numbers and measures applied to these two states are consequently not identical. Let us acknowledge, in terms of the myth, a Sethian and a Horian significance to these relationships; indeed, in the composition of the statues and figurations, the numbers and measures that correspond to the characteristic mythic lineage are used.

PLATE 91 • ORIENT AND OCCIDENT

In its totality, the plan of room XII presents two rectangles added together end to end, each having 1 for its width and 1.272... or 1.2732..., that is, $\sqrt{\phi}$ or $4/\pi$, for its length.

The embrasures of the east and west doors indicate the direction of entrance and exit, from east to west. This fact is verified by the orientation of the movement of the figurations there and by the widening of the colonnade as it follows this direction. From this widening movement it follows that the north wall and colonnade are exactly perpendicular to the axis of Amun, while the south wall and colonnade undergo a deviation with respect to this axis.

The plan of the colonnade teaches yet another nuance through the direction of the movement of the officiant: the three groups of columns located in front of the doors of the three sanctuaries open out toward the south; from the north side, the interval between the centers of these columns measures 6 royal cubits (3.14 m), and from the south side this intercolumnar space is 6 black cubits (3.24 m) for the east and west groups leading to sanctuaries V and VII.

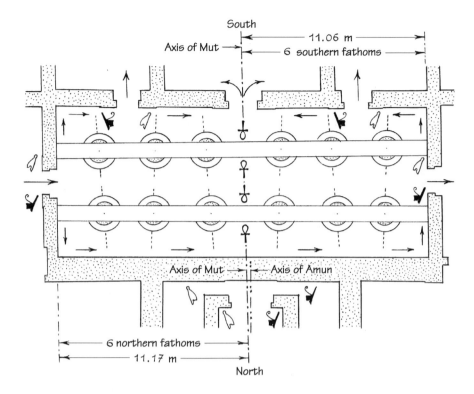

Fig. 287. Diagram of the plan of room XII with architraves

Division of the room into two unequal lengths by the axis of Mut, indicated by the ankhs engraved on the architraves, and the movement of the opening of the columns toward the three sanctuaries from east to west. The arrows indicate the direction of the king's movement in the scenes on the partitions; note the crossing of the orientation of the crowns at the doors of sanctuaries V and VII.

The median axis of the central intercolumnar space conforms to the axis of Mut (or geometric axis), which crosses the perpendicular of the axis of Amun. The whole room is divided into two parts by the axis of Mut, which is confirmed on the two faces of the architraves by the ankhs from which the inscriptions lead out in opposite directions. These ankhs coincide with the median axis of the intercolumniation and, consequently, with the axis of Mut.

The axis of Mut, however, divides the room so that the two east-west lengths are clearly unequal. The east is 6 northern fathoms (at 90°) and the west is 6 southern fathoms (at 0°), which determines the total length of 12 mean fathoms. Room XII, consecrated to the progress of the sun, particularly takes account of the difference between the morning and the afternoon, between the east and the west (sunrise and sunset), in all its architecture and figurations.

On the east partition in the center of the third register the morning barque is depicted in which Horakhty (Horus of the double horizon) appears in his naos (fig. 288). The texts that frame it specify that Ra is "adored in the morning" by the king and that the subjects, his creatures, acclaim him when they see Ra, in the quality of Khepri, go forth (from the horizon) in his infant form.

Under the sky, supporting the sacred barque of the sun, two groups of six baboons raise their hands in a gesture of adoration before Ra, and it is not insignificant to note that the proportions of the tableau in which the solar barque is carved are as 1 to ϕ^2, the function directing the establishment of the cycle cubit that measures it (fig. 289).

Fig. 288. Appearance of the sun; solar barque of the morning, room XII, east wall,

register 3. Tableau restored from the elements that survived effacing and damage to the joints.

The barque, the naos, Ra-Horakhty, and the small Harpocrates located at the front of the barque have remained intact since the time of Amenhotep III. The nine figures on the barque have been hammered out and then recarved, probably by Seti I. The arms of the first female figure located in the bow are presently damaged by a joint, as are the tops of the heads of all the figures.

Of the twelve hammered-out baboons, there remain on the left only six pairs of feet to define their exact location, and the two arms of the first baboon in the gesture of adoration. On the right, a nearly complete baboon has enabled us to reconstruct the others, for which only the upper curves of the heads are still visible. This restoration, done in order to complete our drawing, has a symmetry and a regularity that certainly do not correspond to the original sculpture, but we could not allow ourselves to represent variations according to our judgment.

The naos is framed at the right and left by two times seven uraei and is crowned by five plus four uraei.

On the west partition there are vestiges that, although badly damaged, allow us to observe that men and no longer baboons are worshiping the sacred barque at its setting. In a long hymn of adoration of the sun, the hieroglyph Ra is represented as descending in each column of text, thus showing the progress of the sun setting toward the horizon.

The north partition, in which the figurations all face in the same direction, from east to west, can also be divided by the dimensions of the first register into two distinct parts, in the image of the plan of the room. All the figures on the eastern half are larger than those on the western half, although the register on which they are represented is uniformly 120 digits of 1/100 fathom (2.22 m) for the whole length of the room, that is, exactly one-tenth of the total length of the room (22.20 m).

The average height of the figures of the eastern half is 3 black cubits to the vertex, while those of the western half measure 3 royal cycle cubits.[1]

---

[1] The vertexes of most of the figures in the western part coincide with a joint of stones. Their average dimensions are established by taking the height from the soles of their feet to their shoulders as a base and taking into account that this height represents 16/19 of the height to the vertex and 16/18 of the height to the forehead.

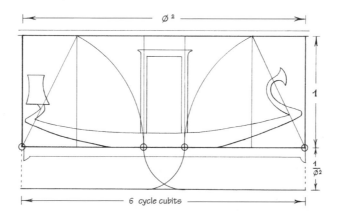

Fig. 289. Proportions and measurements of tableau of Ra's barque

Length between the vertical lines of the edge of the tableau: 3.15 meters = 6 royal cycle cubits = ϕ^2 for the height of 1.205 meters between the two skies under and on which the barque navigates. The height of the frieze of baboons, including the lower sky, represents $1/\phi^2$, the function that determines the position of the naos and its width to the middle of its two vertical posts.

The metrical nuances existing between the figures of the east and the west relate them to the measurements of the colonnades: the largest figures, measured in *black cubits*, are to the east and are related to the widest spread of the columns on the south side, whereas the smallest figures, measured in *royal cubits*, are to the west and are related to the intervals of the columns on the north side. The relationships between the orientations correspond to those of the crowns before their crossing, which takes place only at the door of the three sanctuaries (fig. 287).

The offerings also obey the distinction between east and west governing this location. At the places marked *A* and *C* (plate 91) on the north wall one sees on the morning side two pairs of desert animals presented as a sacrifice, and shown belly side up; on the evening side, there are only two animals, which are shown from the back.[2]

The detail of the hieroglyphs on the architraves further confirms the intention of attributing renewal to the sunrise and realization to the sunset, as we have already observed in the chamber of Mut, which particularly expresses this difference: on the east side many details of the figurations are unfinished, whereas on the west side they are completely finished.

In room XII, on the architrave of the north colonnade (plate 91 at *B*), on both sides of the geometric axis marked by the ankh, the dedication reads toward the right and toward the left. On the side of the sunrise, the sculpture of the Mut bird (the vulture) remains in a rough state, except for the right leg and claw, which are perfectly finished; now, it is the claw that takes and fixes. The proof that this figure is intentionally unfinished is that the curve of the lower part of the neck has been cut, which prohibits the figure from being finished. On the side of the sunset, the design and the sculpting of the Mut bird are completely finished except for the left leg and claw; they are no longer part of the body of the winged creature, which represents the embodiment of the volatile. The drawing of the uraei is complete, but the two serpents are not absolutely identical.

---

[2] We know of only a single exception to this presentation of animal sacrifices in the whole covered temple where the front is presented in the east and the back is presented in the west. This exception is found on the south wall of room III, that is, on the back of the north wall of room XII, west side. This anomaly indicates that a "crossing" exists in this place. Physiologically, this place is at the base of the medulla where there is a decussation (crossing) of the pyramid fibers.

In room XII, the group of six columns to the east does not have the same character as that of the six columns to the west: the cross section of the eight lobes of the columns of the rising sun are semicircular arches; and the cross section of the eight lobes of the setting sun show them as pointed arches.

Thus, the regular, romanesque curve (based on one center) belongs to the Orient, and the ogive, gothic, or double curve (based on two centers) belongs to the Occident. We find the same treatment of east and west through rounded and pointed curves in the great monuments of the Middle Ages, when such knowledge still existed.[3]

In room XII there is always a play of crossing: the columns with foils that have one center are to the east, where two animal sacrifices are offered two times. The columns with two centers are to the west, where a single animal sacrifice is presented two times.

This crossing is again characterized by the orientations of the crowns in this place: the king wearing the white crown, who was found on the left and on the exterior of the entrance doors of the covered temple, as well as on the exterior of the east entrance of this room, is now on the right on the lintels of the doors that lead to sanctuaries V and VII (fig. 290).

At the entrance of the central sanctuary of Amun, the two kings depicted on the lintel wear the blue helmet, but the one on the right offers the white bread while the one on the left presents the vase of fire.[4] In this case the red crown and the white crown are symbolized by the offerings. The whole *symbolique*, including certain blocks of white limestone and red granite that were reused in the pavement, confirms this intention of indicating the two lineages, one white, the other red, and their crossing in this place.

Fig. 290. Scene of the "long stride," room XII, south wall, lintel of the door leading to room V

Left, the king wearing the red crown holds the *hpt* oar (?) in one hand and the *hpt* rudder (?) in the other; behind the king, under the half-sky, is the sign of the scorpion. *Right*, the king wearing the white crown holds two *hs* vases in his hands; behind him, under the half-sky, is the sign of the *ka*.

Notice on the left the table of offerings on the pedestal of the throne of Amun; on the right the table appears to rest on nothing. On the left, the line that frames the scene touches the lower point of the sky; on the right a similar line passes outside the end of the sky. On the left, the loincloth is crossed toward the front; and on the right it crosses toward the back.

---

[3] Cf. chapter. 40, "The Three Axes," remarks regarding Notre Dame in Paris.
[4] Cf. vol. 1, fig. 183.

In the part of the brain corresponding to this place all perceptions cross, a fact thus very explicitly affirmed by the figurations (the reversal of the flows of nature and of consciousness). This reversal is an essential function of nature, which we also find indicated in the zodiacal medallions of the central portal of Notre Dame de Paris.

Plate 92 • Sunrise and Sunset; the Luxor Pylon

An entire tableau representing one of the phases of the battle of Kadesh, located on the west wing of the pylon, was first carved by Ramesses II and then underwent some important alterations. The lines of the first bas-reliefs are still visible under its present form.[5]

The first design included two principal scenes: on the left, the king was seated on his throne, and on the right the king was standing in his chariot, drawing his bow toward the west. Both figures were looking west (fig. 291).

The alteration of the bas-reliefs shows the following two essential facts: First, the king drawing the bow has been effaced and replaced by the camp of the Egyptians, outlined by the shields raised upright next to one another and forming a fortress wall in a great rectangle, in the middle of which the royal tent is erected. Thus what was mobile, the camp, is fixed. Second, the seated king, turned west, is replaced by the king who is now seen seated on a throne, said to be of gold, looking east, while under his feet two spies receive a flogging (plate 92).

The king is looking at his two cartouches. One bears his mystic name, Amun-Ra-mes-s (birth, or realization of Ra), the other, User-Maāt-Ra stp-n-Ra (appearance of the energy of Ra).

The character of crossing, more exactly, of meeting and inversion, is typical of the whole bas-relief. Over the sky above the king, in the frieze of horses drawing war chariots, each with an archer and a driver, the horses can be seen crossing just above the king's head. Behind the king, servants cross their flabella. Above the head of the king drawing the bow, we observe from the first stage of the bas-reliefs an analogous crossing. From the east door of the camp, a file of six horse-drawn chariots cross the camp at an angle and rise toward the upper register where they encounter the horses coming from the west (fig. 291).

Under the palisade of shields outlining the camp along its length, the harnessed chariots galloping from west to east meet a stopped chariot whose drivers, on foot, hold the horses back while bending toward the opposite side in front of an empty chariot whose driver, standing next to it, also leans toward the back. This chariot is sheltered by a parasol, the only one represented, which leads us to suppose that this is the royal chariot.

The character of the crossing, typical in the bas-reliefs of this west wing, is remarkable if we remember that it is from the south side, at the end of the chapel of Amun's barque, that the axis of Amun is reflected, the extension of which, going through the pylon, would end at the king seated on his throne.

The reversal of the orientation is in direct relation to "the axis of the return of Amun," which is reflected at an angle of 1 to 7 and lets us assume that the chapel where this axis ends was constructed at the same time that the modifications to the bas-reliefs were made.[6]

On the north face of the east wing of the pylon, representing the great battle of Kadesh near the Orontes, there is no inversion, which confirms the intention of a crossing for the west wing only.

[5] Cf. plate 9 and commentary.
[6] Cf. plates 86 and 87.

This magnificent and colossal tableau sculpted on the western part of the pylon of the temple of Luxor, through the perfection of its composition and finish, once again compels us to reject any thought of unskillfulness or bad workmanship on the part of the pharaonic artists. Consequently, we must honestly accept the idea that any deformation or so-called unskillfulness has a reason behind it whose meaning we must investigate. I hope this fact has been sufficiently demonstrated in this book through the different meanings—geometric, functional, physiological, and, in general, vital—that have been brought to light.

With the pylon we are at the exterior of the temple. More exactly, with this north face, we are before what is *under the feet* of the Man of the Temple, but also before the first act of the drama of the creation. The *symbolique* of this imposing composition will prove this fact.

Figure 291 is the central part of the tableau that faces the sunrise, which we have reproduced here stripped of the tangle of innumerable lines intentionally left from the preceding tableau showing the action, the battle, oriented toward the sunset.[7]

The figuration of the combat was as perfectly composed and finished as that of the royal camp oriented toward the rising of Ra. Now, these two sculptures are Ramesside. There was no hesitation to destroy such a work of art and carve a second bas-relief on the first, some parts of which are preserved, and these already demonstrate a symbolic reason motivating this work, since nothing would have prevented the complete effacing of the first composition.

To this symbolic reason are joined many others, such as, first of all, the titulary of the . . . king? Is not this king the symbol, as Anthropocosmos, of the eye of Ra, the luminous golden center, animator of our world? First, he is called "birth of Ra," next, "appearance of the energy of Ra": the historical foundation of the legend serves to symbolize the esoteric gesture of the myth.

The ensemble represented here is called the "battle of Kadesh" (Qdch).[8] Now, the geographical as well as the historical location of this battle is the subject of considerable uncertainty. There is general agreement that it occurred at the time of Ramesses II in the country of the Hittites, present-day Syria, northeast of Egypt, which is, for Egypt, the place of the sunrise between spring and summer.

In the first tableau, the figurations look toward the sunset; in the second tableau, which shows the camp, the battle being "finished," they await the rising of the sun.[9] Therefore, the entire action took place in the darkness of night, the sun being under or in the earth. This fact is typical of all of the Ramesses, whose bas-reliefs are characterized by intaglio carving, in contrast to those of the Amenhoteps, which are etched more superficially, another symbol. This sunk-relief carving is accentuated with the first four Ramesses and, starting at a depth of 2 digits, reaches 8 and 10 digits—real caverns—with Ramesses IV. What are called arbitrary styles in the bas-reliefs are in fact functional symbols that correlate with phases of the genesis, the Becoming of the cosmic work.

This battle of Kadesh is that of light against darkness, but it is also the *fixation* (in the form of earth) of this light. It represents the first great victory of knowledge over ignorance, the Becoming of Tum of the Heliopolitan Mystery. Without it there is no possible entry into the Temple. Tum, or Atum (Adam), is the product of this battle, which is described by the tableaux on the pylon.

---

[7] When the second theme of this tableau was sculpted, certain parts of the first were effaced, others covered over in thin layers of plaster, and the deepest sculptures filled with stucco, except, of course, for the royal figures. Today, long after, the plaster has fallen off, allowing the older sculptures to appear.

[8] Cf. Gauthier, *Dictionnaire des noms géographiques*, 5:182.

[9] The east wing of the pylon shows, on the north face, the whole entanglement of the battle itself and the victory of the king—looking east—near the Orontes (the subterranean Nile). In the second depiction of the west wing, in which everything is reversed, both the beginning and the end of this combat are shown.

Fig. 291. Pylon of Ramesses, west wing, north face, central part

This figure shows only the two royal figures of the first stage, and the camp and the royal figure of the second stage, as well as the essential gestures revealed by the movements of the horses and chariots.

The story of the battle[10] is symbolic as well, in relating how Ramesses, the sun-king, all alone hunted and vanquished with one gesture all the veils of night.

The battle scenes and those of the camp, with the great king seated on his golden throne, are framed above and below by the armies on horseback and on foot that meet but do not interpenetrate.

The Poseidonian quality is clearly marked here by the fact that the horses in the lower frieze are galloping on the water. There are the waters above (the heavens) and the waters below (the water of the earth). The question here is of the living waters symbolized by the animal and man.

But the march and countermarch of these movements is incomprehensible if the principle of this symbol remains unknown. To get our bearings in this imbroglio, we will call the pharaonic people the "Occidentals" or Amunians, and the enemies the "Orientals" or Sethians. Now, the text as well as the titulary of the king presents him as Ra, the solar principle.

The (solar) attack is made by the Amunians, the pharaonic people, coming from the sunset against the Sethians, the people of the sunrise. There is thus a reversal of the natural path of the sun, exactly what happens during the night, where apparently, from a particular perspective, the sun, which has set in the west, travels under the earth from west to east. It is therefore *followed* and preceded by the night.

This is clearly a nocturnal war. First the Sethians seem victorious over the Amunians at sunset. Then, the sun-king finally defeats the dark Orientals at dawn, the phase that is symbolized by the Oriental army on the left of the lower frieze in which everyone is looking east and no longer

---

[10] Cf. chapter 27, commentary on plate 9, the story of the battle of Kadesh according to standard texts.

cares about the arrival of the Occidental army on the right. The chariot with an umbrella signals the Oriental chariot; its guard is obsessed by the announced arrival of the rising sun.

It is above the great king looking east that the encounter of the two armies is represented. This is therefore truly the dawn, because the solar king, who is still under the earth, looks east where he will soon appear.[11]

The first tableau represents the attack of the sun, the evening and the night, against the eastern shadows that come now from the west. The file of six rising chariots cuts this night into two sections at midnight. Everything is reversed in the frieze at the bottom: the Sethian troops that, above, came from the east now, below, go toward the east.

The camp represents the night and, at the center, the royal encampment is closed, without doors, in the middle of the night. The interior of the camp teems with men who are at ease and who care for the animals, dress the wounded, repair the chariots, prepare the provisions—all of which can follow or precede a battle.

This is the ever renewed combat of light against darkness. Now, this combat is also the symbol of the beginning of things or, more exactly, it is the primordial combat that, by its constant renewal, causes the series of regenerations whose final goal is the return to the original Unity. The solar king is crowned with a war helmet, blue in color, which seems to signify that it is iron, the same nature as the iron symbolizing the sky.

Resting on a more or less historical basis is a teaching of natural fact symbolizing a cosmic, and at the same time, a vital function, and, probably, a secret of knowledge that is the door opening into the Temple.[12]

PLATE 93 • RIGHT AND LEFT

In the representation of the sacred theme (the principles) through the bas-reliefs, the parts of the body that are symmetrical are represented in profile; the parts of the body with asymmetric (left and right) organs are represented from the front. But when measures are given, or functions and states symbolized, all variations (positions, deformations, and so on) are acceptable. For example, the legs can be joined or taken as a single mass, as with a mummy, in order to express the idea of fixation, of death or inertia, as in the ithyphallic Amun (plate 93, no. 3), or they can be placed in front of one another to mark a state of movement, and in that case the left leg is in front. Thus, the striding figure (fig. 290) has a particular significance that must be interpreted along with his gestures, his attributes, his costume, and his color.

It is very important to note that the figures created by the Divine Verb and not procreated through woman *do not have navels*. For example, Tum, who comes forth from the primordial ocean and who is said to have been self-created, has no navel,[13] and the *kamutef* not only does not have a navel, but the phallus often occupies its place.[14]

---

[11] The king under the earth is related to the *am-dwat*, the subterranean world. See also the theme of Ramesses IX, chapter 37.

[12] The entire story is completed by the combat theme on the east wing of the pylon. My succinct interpretation will raise objections on the part of Egyptologists. I ask them to look at these things by relating them to the myth of the *am-dwat* of the Book of the Doors, etc., which will clarify, so to speak, the meaning of the dark battle of Kadesh. As for the designation of the Orientals as "Sethians," the philosophical reason for my characterizing them thus is confirmed by the word *Setiu*, used in the texts of the myth to designate the Asiatics or Orientals, and in the royal titles "the king vanquished the Setiu …," etc. Regarding the harnessed chariots, cf. plate 6 and chapter 27.

[13] Cf. plate 101, representation of Tum, and chapter 32, legend for plate 40, the Heliopolitan myth.

[14] Cf. plates 58 and 59 and chapter 40, the myth relating to the serpent Irta, primordial *neter* assimilated to the ithyphallic Amun of Luxor.

A single arm can be divided into two forearms, signifying a dualization (no. 3, from the west wall of room V). The example given here is part of a group of scenes that relate to the offering of the four cloths, which themselves are determined by a band that is divided in two. This characteristic gesture is particularly prominent in room V, where the theme of dualization is developed as much in the whole group of figurations as in the plan of the room itself, and corresponds to the symbolism of the place.[15]

The left and right arms are sometimes intentionally represented with two left hands or two right hands; the left receives, the right gives. Thus the king with the red crown represented in room XII on the west partition (no. 4) has two right hands, one to hold the ankh, the other to pour the libation on the three lotus flowers. In other cases the left arm terminates with a right hand, or vice versa, as can be seen in two registers on the north wall of room XII in two superimposed scenes that represent the entrance of the king.

On the second register (no. 5, above), the king, preceded by Iunmutef, is said to "enter" and to "make the offerings." He is active and holds the *mākes* staff in his right hand; the left hand holds the ankh and the white, horizontal (therefore inactive) club that passes behind his loincloth. Here the *mākes* staff is in action, whereas the power of the white club associated with the ankh is there, but remains passive.

On the first register (no. 5, below) the king is *passive* (summoned), although he makes the same gesture of entering and wears the same insignia. Here he holds the *mākes* staff in *the left hand on his right arm,* and the ankh along with the white club (always inactive and hidden) in *the right hand on his left arm.* The fact of holding the ankh and the white club in the right hand in this case confers on them an active character because of the ankh, the symbol of life. It is a question of an influence and not a formal action. The action of the *mākes* staff is stopped and the nonapplied power of the white club is activated. The reversal of the hands is not only motivated by the orientation of the gestures: there can be combinations of giving and receiving, or receiving and giving.

A *scepter of action,* such as that of the prefect (nos. 6 and 7), can only be carried by the right hand, which is the acting hand. If, however, the person invested with this power is seated, therefore arrested in his activity, and if he is not in a state of exercising his function, he can carry this scepter in his left hand. The intention of marking action by the right hand is emphasized by the two kings represented on the north and south doorposts of the east door of the hypostyle room. Each of them wears the crown that corresponds to his actual orientation: the king crowned in white (no. 7) holds the prefectorial scepter in his right hand and the ankh in the left, whereas the king facing him (no. 6) wears the *atef* crown in the red crown and holds the scepter of the prefect in a right hand at the end of his left arm, and the ankh in a left hand on his right arm.

The *scepter of the prefect* is held by the high dignitaries depicted in the tombs of all dynasties. Further, it is often part of the "friezes of objects" represented in the tombs, but since a scepter of this nature had never been found during excavations, it was difficult to know what material it was made of, and even its exact shape.

From its depictions, everything leads us to believe that this scepter was composed of a more or less long stem that opened out into a lotus or a blossoming papyrus, at the end of which was a piece that could be assumed to be cylindrical or curved slightly inward. The color is nearly always yellow, which causes us to imagine it as metal or perhaps as stuccoed-and-painted wood.

---

[15] Cf. chapters 18 and 39.

The friezes of objects usually contain only one of these scepters, and in the very rare cases in which several are found, they have different names. Its form and its names have led to the belief that this object was originally some sort of club that later became an insignia of nobility and had, moreover, a great importance in ritual.

The king actually carries this scepter in his right hand (plate 93, nos. 1 and 2)[16] when consecrating the "boxes for cloths." The arm raised above his head makes the gesture of striking. Now, the best known name of this insignia is *āb* or *āba*, from the Pyramid Texts, and this same root forms the verbs *āb*, "to offer," "to consecrate," and *āba*, "to command." This object is also qualified by the word *hwa*, the meaning of which is "to strike," which is understood through one of the Pyramid Texts that specifies, "he strikes with the *āba*."[17] It also bears the name of *kherp*, which signifies commandment, authority, supremacy. Finally, under the name of *sekhem*, it is part of the ritual objects of the temple and is particularly consecrated to Thoth and to Anubis.

The discovery of an *āba* scepter (fig. 292) in the tomb of Tutankhamun[18] is exceptionally important because it tells us about the precise form of this object. It is a wooden club, not cylindrical but flattened. It is covered with gold plating, which eliminates the idea of seeing it as a war club. From its name to its decoration and also its location in the tomb, this object is purely symbolic. Destined to "consecrate" by the ritual gesture of "striking" the offerings, and particularly the desert animals, it was found among the ritual offerings and vestments and carries carved on one of its sides precisely the animals it consecrates.

This is a marvelous example of the thinking of the Ancients, which is tangible throughout the ritual: the identification between the one who gives and the one who receives, between the object that strikes and what is struck, between the name of the thing and its activity.[19]

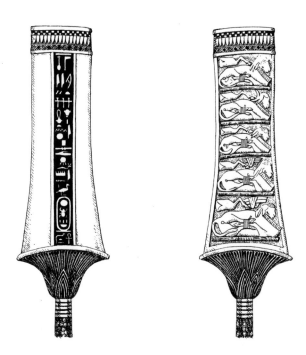

Fig. 292. The āba *scepter from the tomb of Tutankhamun*

---

[16] No. 1 comes from the east partition of room IV (cf. plate 31); no. 2 comes from room XII, south partition, register 3.

[17] For this summary concerning the *āba* scepters, cf. Jéquier, *Frises d'objets,* p. 181 et sqq.

[18] Cf. appendix, below.

[19] Cf. chapter 6, note 50, regarding the statement of problem 35.

GIVING AND RECEIVING,
RECEIVING AND GIVING

The fact of giving a functional meaning to each hand goes back to designating the orientations in the human body as parallel to those of the earth. The gesture thus takes on a significance that goes beyond the apparent action, and this is confirmed by which bas-reliefs are finished or unfinished. An orientation can be related to a figured symbol and the character of a function that will be either passive or active.

The position of a man with his back to the north and looking south (toward the equator) serves as a reference to the orientations. The spinal column belongs to the terrestrial axis. The North Pole, being the energetic inspiration, is that toward which the top of the spinal column should be turned, leaving materiality, the assimilative organs of the standing man, to the south. Then, the left is east and the right is west; the north, the head, will be the zenith; the feet, the south, will be the nadir. But in the head (the crown of the skull) the brain is the mirror that reverses consciousness, and in it everything is upside down: the homunculus of the fissure of Rolando has his head at the bottom, and the dominance of the hemispheres will be crossed with the corporeal effects.

The planet Earth, home of present humanity, serves as a reference for mankind through its movement as a body in the sky, and the vital functions in man are symbols for the vital functions of the planetary body that is the earth.

Reasonably, the orientations serve to designate sunrise and sunset, while the North and South Poles are the fixed points that belong to the terrestrial globe revolving around its axis. Seen from the North Pole, the earth turns from right to left, which makes the stars appear to rise from the left side. At first, there is no reason to conclude from this fact a difference in nature between left and right, since the diurnal rotation creates successive risings and settings of the stars for each part of the globe. The sun, for example, does not change; the terrestrial surface does not change, but, contrary to all reason, *the solar influence is not identical at the rising and the setting of the sun.* All of living nature experiences these differences, which are not only a rejoicing in the morning for animals and humans, and a sadness or a melancholy, a calm, at the hour of sunset. Certain animals, such as baboons, are particularly sensitive to these two moments. The life of insects is more revealing still and, even more than insects, plants instruct us about the fact that the light of the morning has nothing in common with that of the afternoon. The blue morning glory strongly desires the sun in the morning, as do the pink, white, or blue lotuses, and after one or two o'clock in the afternoon, the morning glories fade and the lotuses close. "Scientifically," however, it is difficult to notice a difference between the sun of ten o'clock and that of two o'clock. The temperature plays no role in these examples; the morning can be hot and the afternoon cool, animal and plant obey their rhythms. The different influence is therefore a functional effect (sunrise and sunset), not a quantitative one.

I have experimented in this way with milk drawn in the morning and milk drawn in the evening, as well as with particularly sensitive chemical reactions . . . there is no possible doubt: the morning gives that which the evening reabsorbs, in such a way that the earth and that which lives on it receives in the east and gives back in the west, and man, who is the living being incarnating the earth and its Universe, is the being who has these functions fixed in him. Thus his left hand is the one that receives and his right hand is the one that gives, while his brain acts oppositely to these orientations; it gives (concretizes) on the left, and receives (denies the concrete and spiritualizes) on the right.

Man is a totality, he summarizes in himself that which *gives,* the left side of the brain, and that which *receives,* also the left side of the body. Terrestrial nature has the same relation to the greater world as corporeal man has to his organ of reflection and thought. *Always there is a crossing; one affirms, the other denies what is affirmed.* This is the phenomenon of Life.

The pharaonic people unite left and east in a single word that designates the east, as the right side is designated by the west. And through a symbolic gesture their sculpture teaches us in a simple way that which would require a long explanation: on the left side the Mut bird has a claw that is sculpted (attached to the earth) and the animal is left without a body, while on the side of the setting sun, only the body exists without any attachment to the earth.

For the same reason, when one or another gesture of consecration is made with the right or left hand, it is prudent to think of the orientation rather than of the image to make this gesture more meaningful. But, in parallel with the diurnal cycle, there is the annual day for which midnight and noon are the winter and summer solstices, and the sunrise and sunset are the spring and autumn equinoxes.

There are still greater cycles, and these larger periods permit the subdivisions and the knowledge of influences hour by hour of one of our simple days, so that they give a certain schedule which, through a spoken symbolism, specifies extremely detailed nuances. As in the teachings of ancient China and India, these hours dominate the organs and functions of the human body. Perhaps now one can understand how this is possible and also understand how east and west, midday and midnight, can influence the part through the whole.

The Universe—I mean to say our Universe, the one to which current humanity has access—is entirely incarnate in man, in each of us, moving toward the Anthropocosmos, the one that has access to all.

—⁓—

He who gives can only take his gift within the Universe. He who receives adds to himself that which was taken elsewhere. That which was taken by the giver causes a disequilibrium. He who has received a surplus becomes the counterbalance for that which was impoverished.

Only the source of all things cannot be impoverished. To this source returns that which was impoverished and that which was enriched.

Disequilibrium is only in created things; equilibrium is only in the creative source. Disequilibrium is the cause of vital phenomena, it is what creates movement, as much in space as in genesis or time.

For forms, giving and receiving is the asymmetry that animates. Thus the soul is this mysterious power between symmetry and asymmetry, between giving and receiving.

The divine potter, Khnum, in forming the symmetrical vase on his wheel, encloses the soul that is between the formed and the unformed, between the gift of being and the body that receives it.

The monument will only be living if it is asymmetrical, in a rhythmic pulsation of increase and diminution, framing the abstraction, the irrational.

The asymptotic is a symbol of vital phenomena.

Royal, Cosmic Man is situated between being and nonbeing.

The canonical observance of the orientations in the gestures, left-right, east-west, north-south, proves that the Ancients identified the human with the earth, child of the sun. Man is the northern semi-axis of this earth, and woman is the southern semi-axis. The equator is the support, it corresponds to the principle of the Tree of Good and Evil of the Bible, the separation between that which *receives* (the North Pole) and that which *gives* (the South Pole that realizes, materializes).

Thus, to *receive* the light of the east (left side of a person) and to *give* at the end of the day (right side of a person) is intermingled with north and south, which is demonstrated by the inscriptions in the temple. There is, however, a difference in the nature of the gift. East and west belong to the activity of mankind, north and south are the natural states that all of nature undergoes, not only on earth but also throughout the Universe.

The circular (or comparable) curve, which draws the movement of all natural bodies back to itself, from celestial bodies down to electrons and atoms, is the effect of movement, and at each moment these bodies have a tendency to be projected in the direction of the tangent, from which comes the asymptotic character of the curve in general, the vital effect between that which attracts and that which projects, that which wants to *receive* and that which wants to *give*.

In physics as in metaphysics, the ritual gesture of "giving and receiving" has a cosmic significance giving to the offering and to the sacrifice a value that far surpasses the single moral intention.

APPENDIX:
THE ANNEX OF THE TOMB OF TUTANKHAMUN[20]

The scepter shown in figure 292 was found in this small chamber cut roughly into the rock, which opened on the antechamber of the tomb and was destined to serve as a storeroom.

The door had been walled up with blocks of limestone and plastered on the exterior. Its upper part carried numerous impressions of the four seals of the king and the royal necropolis, on which we can read, "The King of Upper and Lower Egypt, Neb-khepru-Re, who spent his life making images of the gods, that they might give him incense, libation, and offerings every day. Neb-khepru-Re, who made images of Osiris and built his house as in the beginning; Neb-khepru-Re—Anubis triumphant over the 'Nine Bows.' Their Overlord, Anubis, triumphant over the four captive peoples."[21]

On its lower part, an opening made by thieves has never been refilled. The disorder of the interior of this annex contrasted with the order and harmony that reigned in the interior treasury. It was a considerable and indescribable hodgepodge of the most varied objects, which seemed to have been treated in a most brutal fashion and bore all the marks of plundering. On one of the large curved boxes we can see the footprints of the last intruders.

It seems that the tomb had been violated on two occasions, a few years after the funerals of the king. The first incursion had been made by metal thieves who took all the easily transportable objects. A second theft—the time of which is impossible to specify—was carefully prepared and had for its objective precious oils and unguents contained in alabaster jars too heavy to be carried away. The thieves had brought goatskin bottles and leather bags (several of which were found in the descending entrance passage) in order to pour into them the contents of the jars, now empty, whose corks and lids were thrown onto the ground. The fingerprints of the thieves were still visible on the interior of the vases that had contained the viscous unguents. The oils and unctuous materials were stored in thirty-four alabaster vases that were remarkable for their cut and their various shapes (bowls, lion, ibex, and so on).

The jars and amphorae for wine bore labels in hieratic script that indicated the quality, the source, and the vintage date. In each of these containers there was still a small residue.

One hundred sixteen or more baskets had contained food, principally fruits and grains; in some in which there were bottles, there still remained some raisins.

All these objects were found in a jumble of beds (one of which was a folding camp bed), chairs, stools, cushions, pell-mell with the king's "ecclesiastical chair" and his footstool, a child's chair

[20] Adapted from Carter, *The Tomb of Tut-ankh-Amen*, vol. 3, chapter 3.
[21] Ibid., p. 100.

turned upside down, table-chests, ivory bedsteads, decorated cases encrusted with ivory, and a box for holding the king's headdresses.

Three small chests that had contained incense, gum, and antimony were—so say the labels on their covers—"the linen chests of His Majesty when he was a youth."[22] There were small jars of stoneware, of gold, and of silver, wrist and ankle bracelets of the child king, gaming boxes; an apparatus for making fire; two dalmatic "festive robes" in linen; a pair of gloves.

Two curious small wooden cases, one of which was in the form of a shrine, had apparently carried a metal cubit—taken by the thieves—which must have been, as far as can be estimated, "a unit something like 52.310 ms, having 7 palms of .07472 ms and 28 digits of .01868 ms [*sic*]."[23] A boat in alabaster, a vase in silver, gaming boxes with their pawns and dice.

Also present were a great number of offensive weapons, harpoons, bows, arrows, a boomerang; two unique kinds of scimitars in bronze, eight shields (four for actual use and four for ceremonies); a cuirass made of sheets of leather on a background of linen that was very deteriorated.

Of the purely ritual objects, there were sickled knives for grain harvesting in the Elysian Fields; various bronze amulets; a variety of wooden and stone utensils; some stone, earthenware, and gold amulets. Palettes of wood, stone, and glass. A large part of the group of wooden funerary barques and a large quantity of *ushabti* in boxes make up part of the series placed in the treasury.

There were ostrich-feather fans on the flabella and a *kherp* scepter.

Another very interesting and unique specimen discovered in this Annexe, was one of the king's sceptres. It is difficult to comprehend why such a sacred object should be in a store-room of this kind, and not where one would have expected it to be, among similar insignia in the Innermost Treasury. The only explanation that I can suggest is that, either the plunderers cast it there owing to some misgivings in stealing it, or that it belonged to a complete outfit which included the garments pertaining to religious ceremonies, such as the rites in which the King controlled the principle parts, that were originally deposited in one of the ornate caskets found in this chamber. The latter hypothesis is perhaps the most probable, since an adze of bronze inlaid with gold . . . that belonged to ceremonies performed in front of the dead, was also discovered among the objects strewn all over the floor. This kind of sceptre is known under several names, and, I believe, always as a staff or symbol of authority. As a *kherp*-sceptre, it was used in connection with offerings; this is indicated by the embossed decoration on one side of the "blade." It is about 21 inches in length, and is made of a thick sheet-gold, beaten on to a wooden core. It is embossed and inlaid; the tip, "capitulum," and the two ends of the shaft are richly embellished with (Egyptian) cloisonné-work. The gold and blue faience inscription reads: "The beautiful God, beloved, dazzling of face like the Aten when it shines, the Son of Amen, Tut-ankh-Amen," which is of interest, as it suggests a compromise between the Aten and Amen creeds.[24]

The presence of this scepter in this bewildering storeroom intrigued Howard Carter. The scepter seems to be explained by the fact that it was part of the offerings that it was destined to consecrate. This is the first time that it was found as a ritual object, and we see by the offerings sculpted on one of its faces its identification with the various names given to it.

[22] Ibid., p. 119.

[23] Ibid., p. 127.

[24] Ibid., pp. 133–34.

Chapter 42

THE ARCHITECTURAL STRUCTURE

—◦◦◦—

Plates 94–96

. . . the building can speak in all ways, through the material, the foundation, the plan, the elevation, the covering, the lighting, the orientation— not to mention the site. The building speaks the language that only spirit can understand; it is sacred writing.

(Chapter 25)

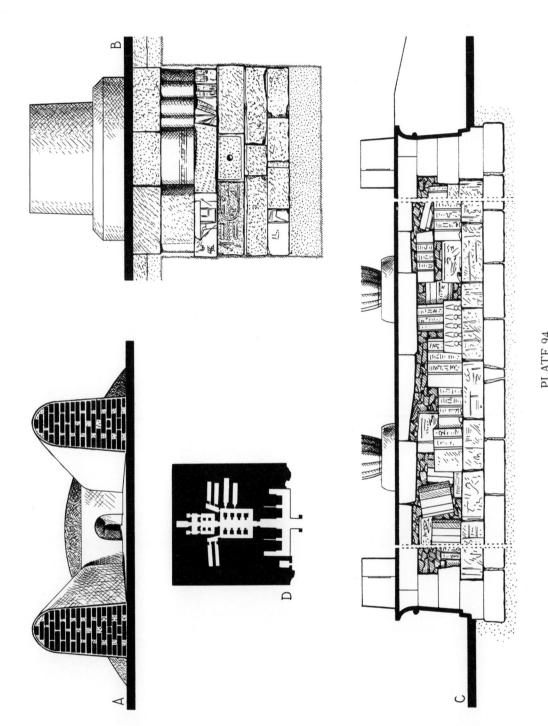

PLATE 94

The Various Foundations

*In man the absolute fixed salt of his being is
formed in the femur, the foundation and support
of the physical body.*

(Chapter 1)

PLATE 95

East Separating Wall, Nave of Luxor

Above all, it is to the monuments that the
archaeologist looks in order to draw near to . . .
the history of a past time. But, do we still know
how to read the architectural message?

(Chapter 25)

A

B

PLATE 96

The Actual and Symbolic Connections of the Blocks to the Bas-Reliefs

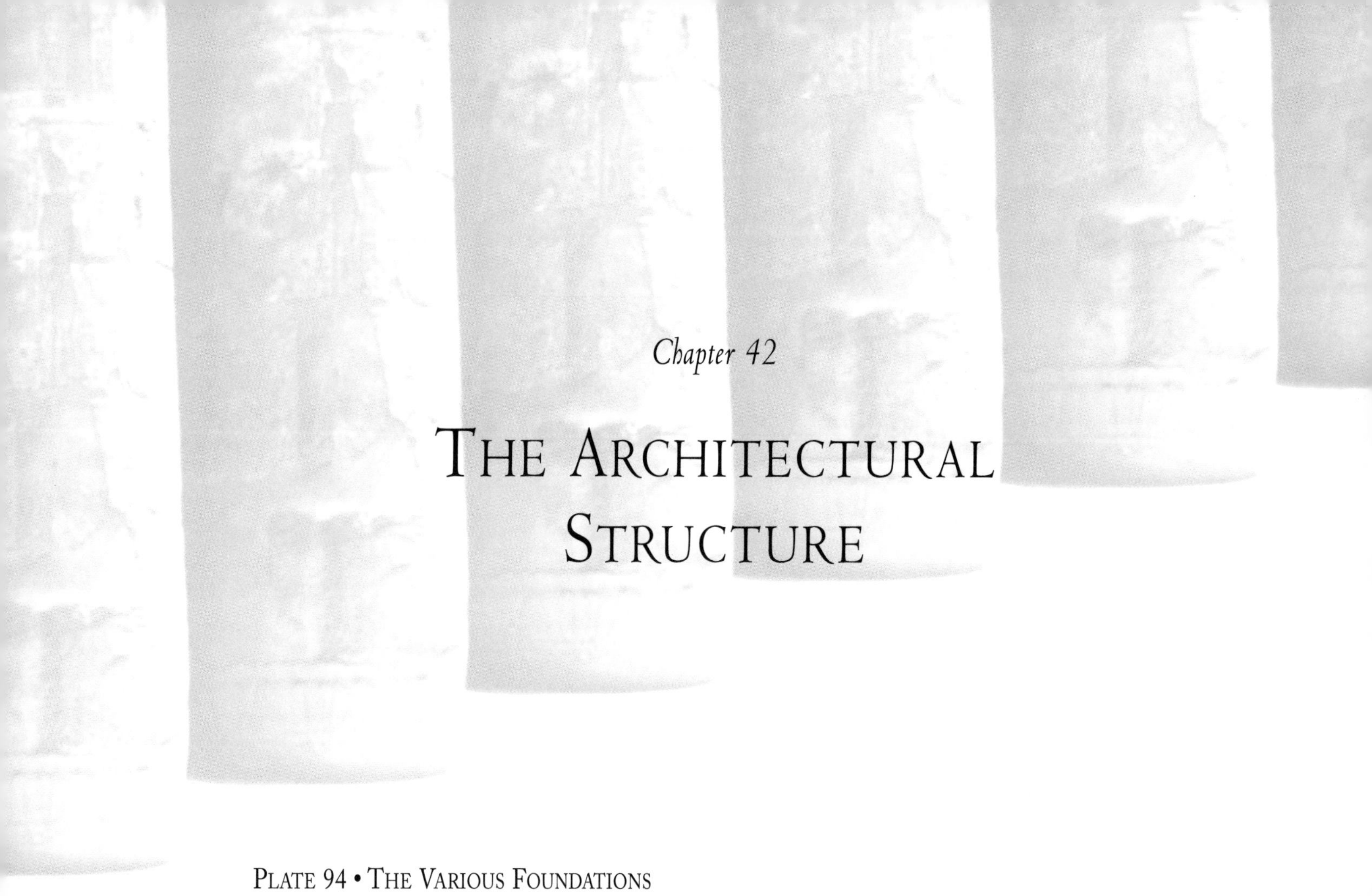

Chapter 42

THE ARCHITECTURAL
STRUCTURE

PLATE 94 • THE VARIOUS FOUNDATIONS

Pharaonic temples are constructed on different types of foundations, depending on the cause and purpose of the edifice. We give here several examples.

Plate 94A • Virgin Ground: The Original Temple of Medamud

This temple has been built on virgin ground with no foundation. It is made of two mounds of raw bricks on a natural knoll. The ground of black earth was prepared by the symbolic seeding of various materials, ash, resins, bitumen, natural salts, and other consecrated materials.[1]

Plate 94B • Seeding by the Preceding Monuments:
The Temple of Mentu at Karnak

The temple of Mentu was constructed on a platform covered with selected blocks from a "turned-under" temple, like generated seed that returns to earth. The choice of the stone blocks and their placement was made with care, giving, among others, some indications of the meaning of the preceding monument and the orientations of past and future temples. For example, as A. Varille has noted: "The southwest corner of the temple of Amun-Ra-Mentu is marked on the outside by a stone placed so as to support a block half embedded in the pedestal of the foundations. A fragment of a sandstone bas-relief with a cartouche of Amenhotep II was selected to play this role. It was intentionally placed upside down, facing south. It showed a bearded figure with a blue headdress surmounted by the hieroglyphic sign of the South."[2]

Another example of these seed-stones having been placed at chosen points is given in plate 94B, which shows the end of the foundation of a colonnade added by a Ptolemy to the north of the temple of Mentu and composed of five layers of blocks supporting a pavement and the colonnade.

---

[1] Cf. chapter 33, the foundation ritual described there; chapter 36, commentary on plate 50A; fig. 245; and chapter 21.

[2] Cf. Alexandre Varille, *Quelques caractéristiques du temple pharaonique* (Cairo: I.F.A.O., 1946), and *Le Musée vivant*, nos. 1 and 2 (1954), pp. 21–23.

In the lower layer a block has been reused showing only the foot of a figure facedown and another small foot, roughly carved, intentionally added afterward.

"At the third layer marking the northeast corner, there is a reused abacus with the title of 'Taharka, beloved of Mentu' at the north, and 'Taharka, beloved of Rattawi' at the east."[3] By means of this block and its inscription, Mentu and his feminine principle Rattawi are recalled in the foundation of the temple that is consecrated to them.

—⁓—

Some buildings are built on the raw brick of the preceding constructions. These bricks symbolize water, that is, the "mud of the waters," or the binding of the earth by water. The temples consecrated to Mentu (sign of Taurus) at both Medamud and Karnak provide several examples of this.

Plate 94C • A Temple Constructed on the Platform of a Tank Containing the Seeds

The temple of Mentu at Karnak has a foundation of the same type as that of the covered temple of Luxor. This tank plays the part of a "vase" that contains the root from which the new temple will "sprout" in a definitive "growth" from the seed deposited in this place.

The temple is built on the platform of a "tank" filled with stones from an earlier temple, placed in an only apparent disorder, for as one can observe, certain inscribed stones are related to the location in the temple constructed above them. These reused inscriptions are connected in such cases with the sacred meaning of this site.

For example, in the central part of sanctuary I of the temple of Luxor, there is a place that has no pavement; was this pavement destroyed? Or was there a ramp or a staircase rising toward the naos between the two end columns? The ritual including the chapter "mounting the staircase" suggests more this second hypothesis.

Desiring to know if the temple of Luxor, like that of Mentu, was constructed on the principle of the tank, C. Robichon made an investigation that allows the following observations:

1. Below the level of the pavement is a series of large blocks that alternate with the "chaos" of mixed sandstone and limestone blocks, all in disorder, as can be seen in the photographs.[4] There are thus three or four layers of blocks. Finally, below, a perfectly horizontal series of blocks could be seen, *which certainly represent the bottom of the tank.* The upper level of these blocks has been measured as 2.25 meters, about the upper level of the pavement. (This would represent the height of five courses of blocks each with a mean height of 45 centimeters including the pavestone, which could not be the case, given the large differences in the sizes of the materials used.)

2. A survey of two rectangular blocks located to the west shows that this apparent disorder has been made with great care. The upper stone is inclined to the north at about 9°36′. It has a width of 100.5 centimeters and a sort of procession in relief that is 53 centimeters wide. The gradient angle has been taken at "the largest gradient."

The block in the second course (from top to bottom) has a curved upper side, which makes it impossible to know its real north-south inclination. However, *its lateral edge is exactly on the axis of ankhs of room XII, which is also the central axis of the naos that formerly contained the gold statue of Amun. This is between the two columns of sanctuary I* (axis of Mut).[5]

---

[3] Ibid.

[4] Cf. plate 84.

[5] Cf. ibid. and chapter 15.

On this block there are three lines drawn north-south to 6 centimeters west of the axis of measures, and to 11.5 centimeters and 14.9 centimeters east of this same axis. The meaning of this east-west line remains to be clarified.

3. Under the east column there is a torus piece of about 18.5 centimeters in diameter laid flat horizontally and right side out. It is almost certainly the torus of a cornice. A little lower and in front of this torus there is a limestone rock stuck between two large blocks. It is placed backward and one of its flat surfaces shows an inscription of a very skilled carver.[6]

Figure 293. A reused piece of limestone under the naos of the sanctuary

In figure 293, under the sign of the mouth, *r*, which can signify "Verb" as in the fraction, or "emission," or a kind of "affirmation," is the group of signs *ht-ntr*, that is, the sanctuary determined by the symbol of the enclosed place. The group *tn*, which is found below it, specifies that it refers to "this sanctuary." The position of this block, exactly under the naos that contains the statue of the *neter* of this temple, cannot be accidental given its inscription.

The Egyptian temple is said "to be in the image of heaven." One of its names is *per*, written with the sign of the house. The particular name of the sanctuary is *r per*, signifying "that which appears, that which manifests the creative Verb here below." The temple, or sanctuary, is thus called *het neter*, which means "the place that limits, or defines, the principle, the *neter*."

Plate 94D • The Temple of Abu-Simbel, Hollowed out of Rock

The monument can be buried in earth or hollowed out of rock. Here, the earth and the rock are considered the matrix of the temple.

PLATE 95 • EAST SEPARATING WALL, THE NAVE OF LUXOR

This photograph is taken from a southern point looking north in order to show the construction of the east wall of the nave on a length of about 50 meters.[7]

Whereas the west wall of this nave is entirely solid, the east wall is "hollow," that is, composed of two facings of large blocks with an empty space between them. This construction demonstrates that if there were a "filling" of gravel, there would certainly not have been stones in the interior,

[6] Extract of a report [unpublished] by Lucie Lamy on the probing of sanctuary I of the temple of Luxor, September 1947.

[7] Compare with plate 4 showing the exterior surface of this wall.

which would make this wall very fragile. This shows that the Ancients, without being concerned with solidity, obeyed the symbolism.

With regard to the axes, we have already observed movement in the opening and closing of the colonnade and of these two walls of the nave. On the interior west partition, the procession of the barques comes from Karnak toward Luxor (solid wall), and to the east the procession returns toward the north to Karnak (hollow wall). The barque coming from Karnak (west partition) arrives therefore at Luxor in the evening to pass the night there (time of conception and of birth) and returns to Karnak (east partition) after the rebirth of the morning.

Finally, the exterior face of the west wall carries the representation of the cavalcade of Ramesses including the man riding sidesaddle (Sagittarius),[8] whereas the hollow wall of the east has retained its rough, that is, unfinished facade and therefore has neither bas-relief nor inscription.[9] We have already pointed out several times the primitive, unfinished character of the eastern side of this temple (room XII, chamber of Mut, and so on), while the west (Amunian) side shows a finished quality.

PLATE 96 • THE ACTUAL AND SYMBOLIC CONNECTIONS OF THE BLOCKS IN RELATION TO THE BAS-RELIEFS

In pharaonic architecture, as also in a great number of ancient monuments, the blocks of stone are frequently held together by notches intended to receive pieces of wood, stone, or metal called dovetails. In the pharaonic monuments, blocks in the same course can either not be linked by a dovetail (fig. 294A), or can carry only a drawing of the cavity intended to receive it (fig. 294B). In other cases, two blocks are theoretically linked, but the cavity of only half of the dovetail is hollowed and the other half is simply drawn (fig. 294C). Finally, complete cavities are found (fig. 294D) that sometimes still contain wooden dovetails. Here the goal of linking is purely symbolic because these weak connecting pieces would not be able to resist the least movement imposed by these blocks, which each weigh at least half a ton. Probings into the walls of the temple of Luxor have shown that *in the same wall* there are cavities that still contain their dovetails along with cavities that have never contained them, which proves that the Ancients did not grant any utilitarian purpose to these connecting pieces.

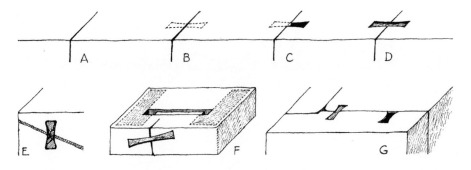

Fig. 294. Sketch of dovetails

On the east face of the throne of the seated colossus in the court of Ramesses, a cavity is hollowed out perpendicular to a vein that crosses the block of granite (figs. 294E and 295). The vein plays the role here of a joint between two stones that the dovetail is supposedly intended to link; for what reason then is the front of the cavity that receives it filled up with pieces of sandstone bound with mortar? These sandstone chips do not come from a later restoration since the decoration of the block of granite continues over these stones. We are certainly then dealing with a symbol!

Fig. 295. Eastern side of the throne of the east seated colossus in the court of Ramesses

It also happens that in the middle of one of the sides of a stone monolith there are cavities for dovetails, often of great size. Archaeologists have been able to ascertain that in numerous cases of this type, this dovetail was placed perpendicular to a break in the stone. At Karnak, the stones of the thresholds of the three doors of the court from the Middle Kingdom offer analogous cases: the stone of the second door is broken by a crack on the two sides of which are carved the two half-cavities destined to receive the dovetail (fig. 294F), while under the threshold of the first door, also a monolith, there is *no crack;* nevertheless, a long cavity characteristic of the dovetail has been carved there, which therefore has no practical utility.

Another case no less strange is met with in the temple of Luxor: the obelisk now in Paris rested on a granite pedestal, which is still in place, that has worshiping baboons on its north and south faces. This granite pedestal is placed on a second pedestal composed of several blocks of quartzite-bearing sandstone. On the north side, on its upper surface, a cavity has been hollowed out so that one of its extremities comes only up to the joint instead of crossing over it (fig. 294G, *right*). A dovetail of black granite is found in this cavity, the only example of this found until now. In contrast, alongside of this anomaly is the cavity for a dovetail that would sit astride both blocks (fig. 294G, *left*). Moreover, blocks have been found cut so that they contain a groove for a rope to fasten them together.[10]

It happens, finally, that the foundation courses of a pylon are linked by dovetails to the south, whereas they are not to the north, where they are simply drawn. It can also happen that on the same axis the stones of the last course of a loading dock can be linked in the direction opposite to the courses of the pylon: there is a reversal of orientations.

The upper parts of the cornices of a door, above the lintel, are often linked on one side and not the other, in relation to the orientation of that door.

—◠◠◠—

The dovetail is commonly regarded as a link reinforcing the union of two blocks of stone. Now, given the considerable number of irregularities that they present, these dovetails cannot in any way fulfill this goal. Their significance can only be symbolic: when, for example, the dovetail connects two blocks bearing figurations in which the hands are seen to be joined, or, in other cases, when these cuts are hollowed out on one block and only indicated on the neighboring block, when the symbolism of the figuration suggests a call for unification that is not yet accomplished (plates 96A and 96B).

—◠◠◠—

The bas-relief in plate 96B shows the single scene carved on an undecorated wall at Karnak. A priest, clothed in a panther skin, makes a libation with a ram-headed vase before the seated Amun, who holds the *was* scepter in his left hand along with an open lotus. The horizontal joint cuts the feet of the priest and fixes him in the earth. The vertical joint, crossing Amun's leg, separates the priest making the libation from Amun, who receives it. Now, the feet of Amun rest in the empty space, since the pedestal of the throne is not drawn.

On the upper part of the wall on which this scene is depicted, the dovetail—which in principle should connect the two blocks—is hollowed out on the block representing the terrestrial character of the priest, while the outline of it is simply drawn on the block of the aerial Amun (plate 96A).

---

[10] Cf. Robichon, Barguet, and Leclant, *Karnak-Nord IV*, fig. 59a and b.

Chapter 43

TRANSPARENCY AND TRANSPOSITION

―⁓―

Plates 97 and 98

*. . . the shape of the stone blocks: their joints,
overlappings, "transparencies" and "transpositions"
in the walls, comprise a subtle grammar in which
the finish of a carving or its rough aspect, the
absence of essential parts, . . . the reversal of right
and left . . . play the role of accents, declensions,
conjugations, and conjunctions.*

(Chapter 24)

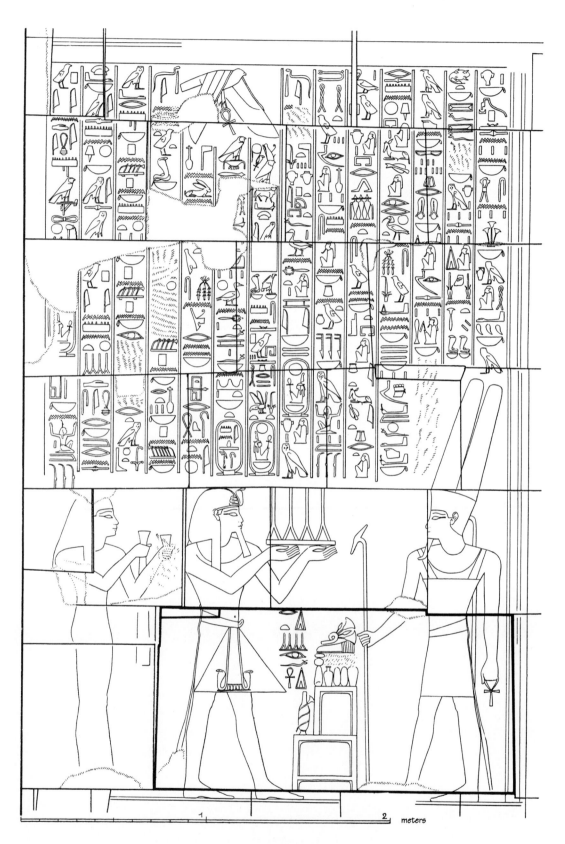

PLATE 97

South Wall of Room XII; the Cloths

In the "transparency," if the wall were of glass, we would be able to see, for example, a sign or figure drawn on the back side that would fill in a blank space left on the front side.

(Chapter 18)

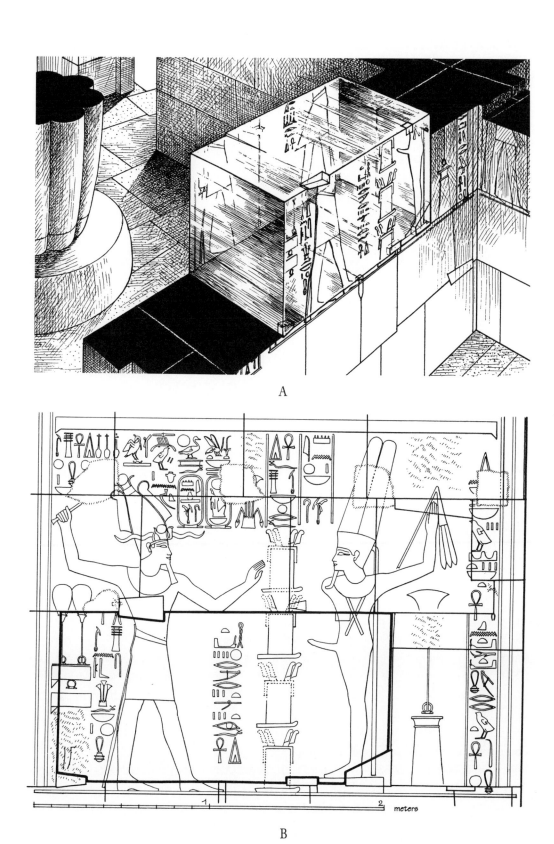

A

B

PLATE 98

North Wall of Room V; the Boxes for Cloths

Chapter 43

TRANSPARENCY AND TRANSPOSITION

The study of the installation of the stones of the wall that separates rooms XII and V allows verification of the fact that most of the scenes and inscriptions represented on one of the sides of this wall are in "transparency" with those of the other side. The study of the north wall of room V must therefore include the entire corresponding part of the south wall of room XII. We have already established two essential "transparencies" related to certain chapters of the "Ritual of Daily Worship." We will only recall them here.

On the first register, the tableaux are arranged so that the line of the base corresponds exactly with the level of the soles of the feet of the figures represented on both sides of the wall. The cloths represented in room XII are projected in room V into the "boxes for cloths" consecrated by the king.

On the upper register, the purifications with the red vases and the white vases are projected onto Amunet wearing the red crown and onto Mut wearing the white crown, respectively.[1] Finally, the offerings, which are only evoked in room XII, are represented in room V.

The middle register of room V (plate 75) corresponds to the upper part of the inscriptions of room XII. Whereas in room V the height of the lower tableau to just under the sky is exactly 2 meters, that of room XII measures 3.85 meters to under the sky, or 2 meters plus 1 mean fathom. This height of 1 fathom is occupied by the largest part of the inscriptions in room XII, which are thus projected onto the tableau of the presentation of the four calves of room V.

These texts are written in fourteen columns:

The seven columns inscribed from left to right above Amun are projected onto the four calves and the king on the opposite side of the wall; the three columns inscribed from right to left above the king and under the falcon that holds the key of life in its claws are projected in room V

---

[1] Cf. fig. 276. The offering of the cloths represented in room XII corresponds to chapter 49 of the Berlin Papyrus ritual concerning the white strip of cloth. The consecration of the boxes for cloths in room V corresponds to chapter 45 of this ritual, and the purifications with the red and white vases to chapters 46 and 47. In room V the offering of the cloths is depicted five times, which evokes a connection with chapters 49 to 53 of the ritual; the perfumes then correspond to chapters 54 and 55.

between the *was* and the axis of equilibrium of Amun (fig. 296); the four columns inscribed from right to left above the female *neter* in room XII correspond to Amunet carved on the side opposite (fig. 296).

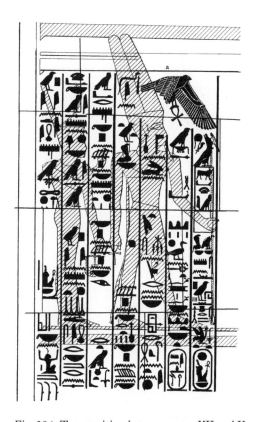

Fig. 296. Transposition between rooms XII and V

In black, room XII, the three columns of text of the king under the falcon, and the four columns of text of Renenutet (from right to left). *Hachures,* room V, second register, Amun and Amunet, who are found in front of the four calves.

The phrase beginning "*Neter nefer . . .*" is projected onto the face and body of Amun. Amunet and her red crown are entirely hidden by the text in transposition: "Thou appearest in her, thou art perfect in her, in this [her name] of the four cloths . . ." One can again observe that the words "thou receivest," in the second column of text of Renenutet, are projected into the two hands of Amunet, who holds the sign of the *sed* festival in her right hand. The end of the text mentions the gift of "millions of years."

The theme developed in room XII concerns the gift of cloths to Amun. To the left, the female *neter* who holds two strips of cloth in her hand is quite probably Renenutet. According to two passages from the Pyramid Texts concerning the offering of the cloths, she is connected to the strips of cloth that she offers, these cloths being themselves connected to the eye of Horus.

"I have clothed thee with the eye of Horus, this Renenutet . . . I have brought thee the eye of Horus which is in Tayt, this Renenutet . . . "[2] Let us remember that Tayt is also the cloth, the weaving, and

---

[2] Pyramid Texts, 1755 and 1794.

the *neter* of weaving,[3] and that she is determined by a serpent, as is the half-effaced name of the feminine *neter* represented in room XII. These are the words addressed by Renenutet to Amun:

"[1] Words spoken by Renenutet, mistress of . . . thou receivest this thy beautiful [strip of cloth], thou receivest [2] this thy *mār* cloth, thou receivest this thy *menkhet* cloth, thou receivest [this] eye [of Horus going out] from Nekhebet. [3] Thou appearest in her, thou art perfect in her, in this her name of the four *menkhet* cloths. She unites herself to thee in [4] this her name of *idmi* cloth."

The sentence inscribed in the third column, "Thou appearest in her [or through her], thou art perfect in her [or through her]," is normally related to the cloths that complete the clothing of the *neter*. These cloths—being both the *neter* who offers them and also the eye of Horus, the ultimate offering—signify more than a simple costume.

This third column of text is projected in room V onto Amunet, the feminine aspect of Amun, who wears the red crown, so that it is actually "in her" and "through her" that Amun appears in his sublime perfection.[4]

The three columns of text of the king consist of variations of his titulary. In transposition the first column corresponds to Amun's scepter in room V and is typically translated as follows: "The Horus-Ra, victorious bull, appearing in truth,[5] he of the two goddesses, who establishes the laws, pacifies the Two Lands, king of the South and of the North, Neb-maāt-re."

In the second column, the destroyed parts can be restored by means of analagous titulary encountered in the temple and generally following the golden Horus name.[6] "The golden Horus, great in power,[7] vanquisher of the Setiu,[8] son of Ra, of his belly, his 'magnet,' lord of all foreign countries, Amenhotep, prince of Thebes."

The third column, partially destroyed, gives an extremely rare variation of the titles beginning with *neter-nefer*. This anomaly makes the restoration of the text difficult. "*Neter-nefer* [realized entity] of existence? . . . who has [created] the white crown of the South, who has brought the red crown of the North into the world, who has raised up the lord[9] of the great house [*per-aā*] in order to reign[10] over that which the solar disk [Aten] encircles."

This variation of the royal title beginning with *neter-nefer* is projected on the Amun of room V. It offers a typical case of an apparently incomprehensible text that is explained on the opposite side of the wall.

We have just seen that Amun appears in Amunet (his feminine aspect) and is completed *in her* and *unites with her* "in this her name of the four cloths," and that she wears the red crown of Neith, the divinity of weaving, regent of the North. Moreover, the king is called "son of Ra, of his belly," and the incomprehensible text that refers to him as created by the white crown of the South and brought into the world by the red crown is clarified when we observe that actually these two crowns are projected by transposition onto Amun, who is only at this point one with his feminine aspect.

---

[3] Cf. chapters 39 and 18.

[4] Let us recall that "restoring to wholeness the eye of Horus" is the goal of the work of wisdom. "Weaving" is always meant in the sense of "rendering visible" and of linking the imponderable to a ponderable material.

[5] Or "appearing with the truth," that is, Maāt.

[6] For example, the doorposts of room V, plates 75 and 77.

[7] Or "strong of arm," "vigorous," etc.

[8] Or "who overthrows the Setiu," that is, the Asiatics.

[9] Or "the lady of the great house."

[10] Classically *ḥk* is always translated by "prince" or by "to reign." I have said elsewhere that the *ḥk* scepter implies the idea of ferment.

The white crown of the South is assimilated to the gestating Mut, regent of the South; the red crown is assimilated to Neith, divinity of weaving, regent of the North. Both are "in Amun," united with him, as this transposition shows us.

The text that Amun addresses to the king, his son, his creation, will confirm and justify this interpretation through the constant affirmation of not only the double character that governs this whole ensemble but also through the notion of unification, of connection, of "weaving" that is revealed in each phrase, and by the interpenetration of the texts and the figures represented on both sides of this wall.[11]

The seven columns of text inscribed above Amun in room XII are addressed to the king who makes an offering to him of the four cloths:

[1] Words spoken by [Amun-Ra] king of the *neters,* who is in the heart of his Apet: "My son, of my belly, the magnet, master of the Two Lands, Neb-maāt-re, my heart is in [2] gladness when I see thy realization.[12] I establish for thee thy annals[13] in millions of years.

[3] O Son . . . of my heart, issue of [myself],[14] I bequeath thee my seat, my throne, my inheritance, my property [that which is my own], [4] in order to perfect my house, my inheritance, and to make that which is glorious to him who put [thee] in the world. I give thee all the reunited [connected] lands[15] in thy fist.

[5] Thou hast seized the nine bows under thy sandals, I cause that they see thy majesty, [6] that thy dread, thy dignity[16] be in their hearts. I cause that the two goddesses scent[17] [7] thy face, that they dispense around thee their protection. I unite myself to thy members as . . .

Above the high plumes of Amun, in transparency, crossing the sky of the tableau of room V, the text leaves off unfinished with the letter *m* (the owl), which calls for something to follow it. But there is no place for the sentence to be finished on this side of the wall, and no "transparency" completes it on the other side of the wall.

The last words spoken by Amun present several particularities that are clearly related to the place in the temple in which they are inscribed. On the Man of the Temple, this wall corresponds to the top of the forehead, the base of the royal headband where the *wadjet* uraeus of the dual character rises up. Now, Amun speaks of the two *wadjet* goddesses determined by two raised cobras in two baskets; he makes them "scent" *(snsn)* the royal face by assuring him of their protection.

Finally, Amun says that he unites himself, joins himself, to the limbs of the king in the capacity of . . . of what? It is in this tableau that we must find the answer and the end of the sentence: it is Amun who must, as Amun-Ra, penetrate the king's limbs, after having bequeathed him all his

---

[11] Certain words written backward in the text support this constant crossing.

[12] *neferu,* here translated as "realization," also means "beauty," "energy," "perfection."

[13] *genwt,* "annals." The sign used to write this word also designates the bones and is then read *ks;* cf. vol. 1, fig. 167, no. 6.

[14] *per khnt,* "issue of myself," literally, "exiting from the front."

[15] This linkage implies a conjunction.

[16] *shfshf,* which some translate by "fright."

[17] *snsn,* literally "to scent," is customarily translated as a metaphor by "to embrace."

power, so that he might accomplish perfectly what has come from himself and what must return to him.[18]

The temple, the house, is the royal body, the manifestation of Amun, his inheritor, his son who, in perfecting himself through the gifts he has received, glorifies his father. . . . The king, after his realization, "returns to his father" after having acquired awareness thanks to the "weaving" of experience.

———⌇———

The principle of transparency, which must be understood as an "association of ideas," is also used in places other than in architecture, such as in papyri. We must not think of transparencies as only having the posing of an enigma as their goal. First of all, they allow an idea to be completed by developing it partly in the inscription of one room and partly in the neighboring room, each explanation having a point in common with the other. But observing these two images on both sides of a wall (or of a papyrus) also reverses the reading, as an image in a vertical reflection is reversed, and, in the case of architecture, the orientation comes into play.[19]

In addition to the development of a theme, there is then a more profound intention, which is to evoke the "turning around" of consciousness, such as occurs in the projection of the innate consciousness on the object of its (objectifying) reaction. This produces psychological and mental consciousness: the function of the object is in us, the (lunar) reflection of this function corporealizes the object for our consciousness (this is the weaving).

We find here again, as always, the care taken never to consider a notion in one sense only, nor to consider a definition in its schematic expression as an arrested function. Life is the effect of alternation. Any given moment must evoke its complementary moment; a science founded on invariable principles can only be speculative, therefore removed from the natural fact and knowledge of the secret of life.

This pharaonic discipline of thinking in the spirit of constant alternations poses the phenomenon as an illusion, and this way of saying it—which is comprehensible—is also more convincing than the simple affirmation of an illusory world justified by abstract reasoning.

Transparency, then, not only has the goal of completing an idea, but above all shows the phenomenen of *concretization* of the idea. This is simultaneously the *evocation* and the expression of its becoming.

Now, it is a universal principle that an energy, or activity, can only produce an effect through the resistance of its own nature, the cathodic effect.

———⌇———

Parallel with transparency, we also find in architectural "writing" the "transposition," which is an evocation. Here the issue is no longer that of container and the contents, the association of ideas, but of a function.

---

[18] In order to understand these sibylline texts, it would be good to place them in parallel with the Hermetic texts that name that which is designated by "Philosopher's Stone" as Man or the King, as well as the "Son of the Sun." Adepts are often given the title of "ordinary doctor of the king" or "extraordinary doctor of the king," according to their more or less complete knowledge of Hermetic secrets.

[19] Let us recall in this regard that the reading is always made face to face with the sign or image of the figure, that is to say, by going to meet it.

For example: an activity (a gesture) of a royal figure on one side of a wall is explained by a *was* scepter, the symbol-synthesis of this function, sculpted on the other side of this wall on the opposite face of the stone, and placed in such a way as to serve as the axis of stability or of movement of the figure by passing through the auditory center.[20]

This *was* scepter is also called "key of the Nile." This is true on the condition that it is understood in its actual significance. This staff is determined on the bottom by a small fork and on top by a short slanted branch. It has often been asked where this symbol comes from. I have claimed that it might refer to a growing branch: a stem going out from a trunk or from a larger branch, and dividing itself into two new branches[21] (fig. 297).

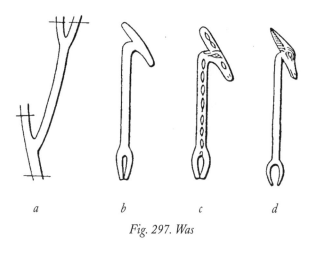

a   *b*   *c*   *d*

Fig. 297. Was

(a) Natural branching; *(b* and *c)* hieroglyphs of the Twelfth Dynasty; *(d) was* scepter of Ptolemaic era.

It is thus a matter of the rising of the sap (the primordial waters) undergoing the impulse of division, origin of all vegetation. This explanation was later confirmed by one of the *was* scepters found in the tomb of Tutankhamun, formed of a natural branch, just as it was cut from the tree, and entirely covered in pure gold leaf. We could not better verify the intention of giving a sacred character to this symbol. Moreover, this also confirms the natural origin of many symbolic figures and hieroglyphs, as well as the attributes given to the royal principle.

As for the *was* scepter, the vegetative dividing in two of the branch, the channel of the sap, in thus being defined, renders the object serving as the foundation for this symbol more explicit. The original branch from which the long stem comes out has an animal form considered by some to be the head of a donkey because of its long muzzle. In fact it is the eyes and the ears that complete the true meaning of this symbol. The eyes correspond to the small buds that will, for example, become branches. The ears have the same significance in the donkey and in the hare, the old Hermetic symbols. (For us, the symbol of the donkey goes back to the crèche at Bethlehem.)

---

[20] Cf. chapter 17, the transposition between rooms I and V, fig. 181, and between rooms I and VII, fig. 180.

[21] I have learned that Jéquier has had the same idea. Cf. *Frises d'objets*, p. 177.

Certain transpositions thus give the character of the *was* to a figure, and we then know what role he plays in the totality of the tableau, that is, in that chapter of the ritual. In one of the examples cited (fig. 181, transposition between rooms I and V), the *was* scepter in room V crosses the single arm (which splits into two forearms) of the king offering the cloths; on the other side, this *was* is projected onto the axis of equilibrium of the Amun in room I. In the other example (fig. 180, the transposition between rooms I and VII), there is also a projection of the *was* scepter held by Amun on one side of the wall onto the axis of equilibrium of the Amun represented on the other side. Now this Amun bears the title of *hek-was.t*, which is typically translated as "prince of Thebes." But since Thebes has the sign *was* for its symbol, the symbolic reading is: "Amun, ferment of the *waset*."

Chapter 44

SETH-HORUS

—◦◦◦—

Plates 99–101

All pharaonic Egypt, from
beginning to end and in all
its achievements, is but a
ritual gesture.

(Chapter 4)

meters   1   2   3

meters   10   20   30

PLATE 99

The Pylon and the West Wall of Room II; Animation

. . . the Temple becomes sacred when it is built from knowledge that includes all points of view: proportions and numbers, axes and orientations, choice of materials, harmony of figures, colors, light, foundation deposits, and so on. It is this harmonious synthesis that creates the Temple, not a vulgar sym-bolization of the sky by the roof, of the earth by the floor, and other playthings of a childish symbolism.

(Elements)

meters   1   2   3   4   5

meters   10   20   30   40   50

PLATE 100

The Pylon and the East Wall of Room VI; the Barque

You and I are not two. In the identity of form, in the origin and in the end, we are one.

I am responsible for your evil and your good, for your truth and your falsehood. I can do nothing to change you now, but I can improve you by improving myself.

(Introduction)

The Fire that separates (Seth) also contains the Fire that unifies (Horus)—Satan and Lucifer.

(Chapter 18)

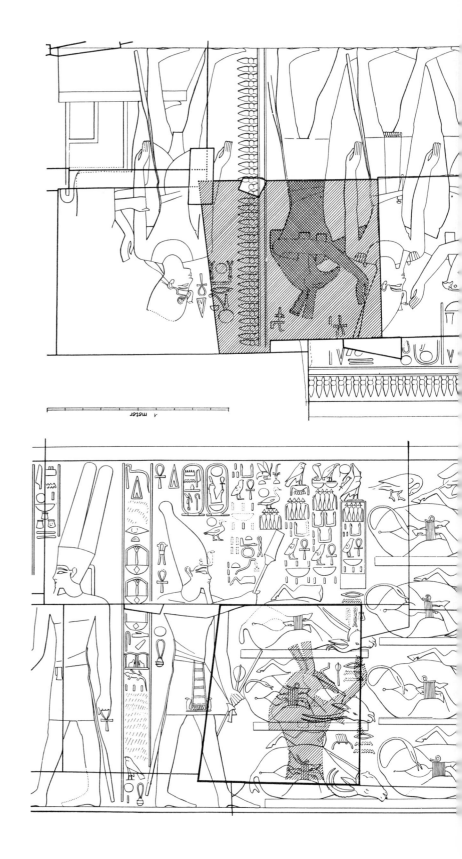

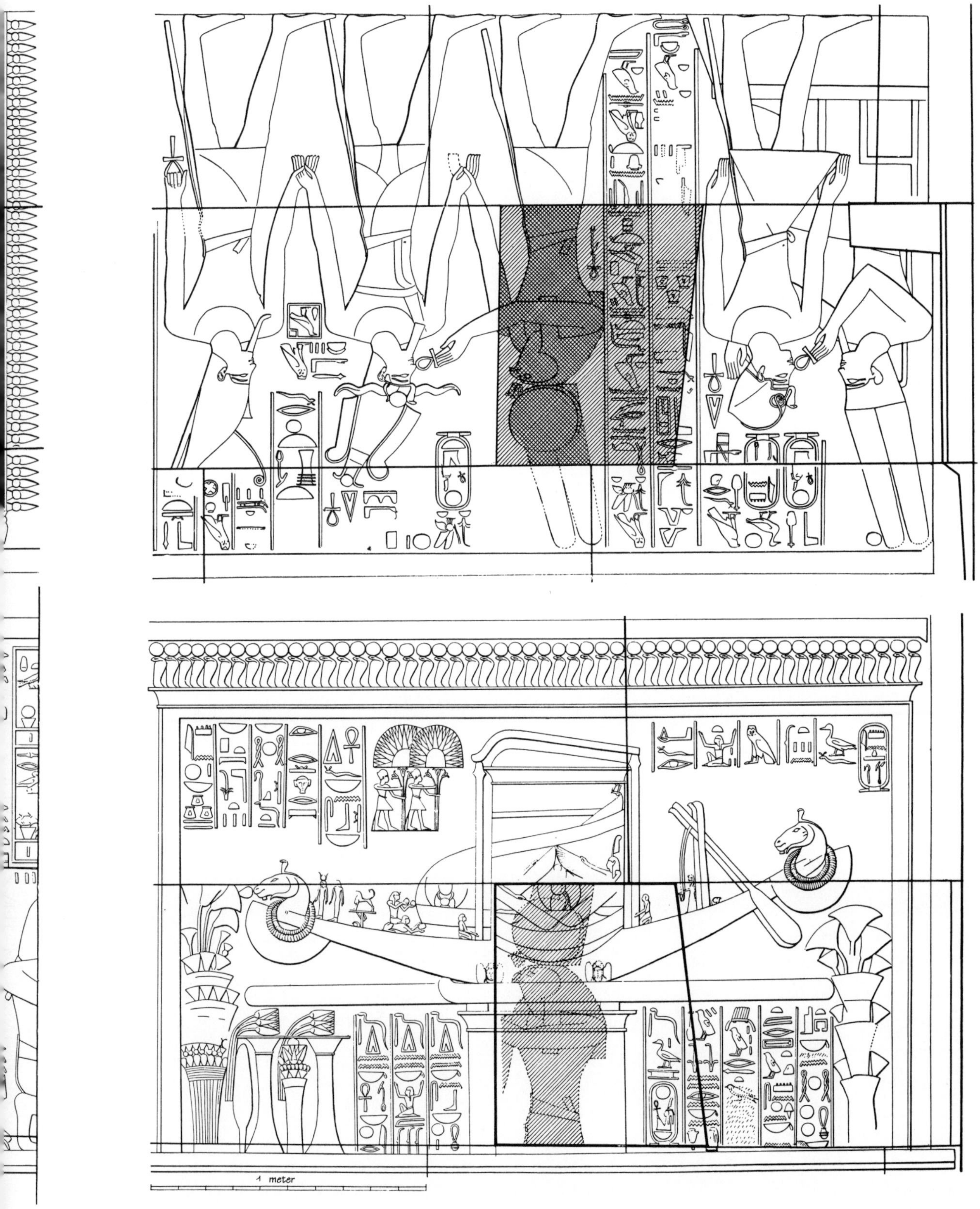

PLATE 101

Horus Born of Seth

Chapter 44

SETH-HORUS

THE REALIZERS OF THE PLAN: SUTI-HOR

Generally speaking, it is the large figurations that provide the theme and the texts that supply the functional details. The essential theme developed on the partitions of the wall separating rooms II and VI is the inversion of the spiritual state of the primary and original function, but in order to grasp it better, we must have a vision of the whole neighboring area of the temple.

Room II follows after room IX, which is called the "theogamy," or spiritual conception. The royal naming affirms everywhere that the king is the son of Amun, "of his belly." His spiritual conception is represented in room IX; the texts that accompany it describe how Amun manifests himself to the queen:

> Action of the Verb of Amun-Ra, master of the thrones of the Two Lands Khent-apet-f, after he had made his transformations [*kheperu*] in the majesty of this spouse [*hy*] the king of Upper and Lower Egypt Ra-men-kheperu [Tuthmosis IV] gifted with life.
>
> He found her lying in the depths of her palace. She awakened at the odor [*sty*] of the *neter*. She smiled before His Majesty. He came[1] to her at once. He made *hemed* toward her. He caused her to see him in his appearance as *neter* after he had come before her.[2]
>
> She rejoiced at the sight of his perfections [or of his beauties, *neferu*]. His love extended from one end to the other of his body. The palace overflowed in waves of the odor [*sty*] of the *neter*. All his "perfumes" were those of Punt.[3]

---

[1] *chem* = the idea of heat.

[2] The whole tableau shows a spiritual conception since Amun and Mut are located above the starry sky, and even Selkit and Neith, who support it, do not have their feet on the ground. The word *hemed* is translated as "to possess," "to copulate." These interpretations are dictated by the context, which supposes an act of conception. In fact, it is a question of an insemination, which becomes copulation in the anthropomorphized, mythic interpretation of a transcendental, creative gesture. At Deir el-Bahri this word is written *had*.

[3] Unpublished French translation by Alexandre Varille, 1949. Let us note that Punt is the "black country."

Queen Mutemwia cries out in the presence of the majesty of Amun and pronounces words. Then Amun announces to her the name of the future royal child, "since such is the sequence of the words that go out from thy mouth. . . ."

There is an insistence on the fact of creation by means of the Verb. It is the first words that are pronounced by the mother in childbirth that become the name of the child. Here they are cited at the conception, there being no distinction made in time between the conception and the delivery.

Next, in "transposition," Thoth confirms to the queen the future birth of this child in the barque of Mut, which Mutemwia (Mut in the barque) brings into the world in the presence of the *neters*.[4]

Finally, as all the texts affirm, the royal child is held in the arms of Mut, nourished by Neith, and nursed by the celestial cow. He will then be baptized in water by Tum and Mentu and will receive at this baptism his mystical names inscribed by Thoth and Seshat in the presence of Amun and the "souls of the North and of the South."

Also depicted in this room consecrated to the theogamy is the *sed* festival, the festival of renewal during which this ceremony takes place twice: clad in a tight costume, the king is first white in the southern pavilion then red in the northern pavilion. Now, it would seem that everything has been said and that the whole future life of the king has been described here, but in the neighboring chamber (room II) the whole ritual of the crowning is developed again.

This new chamber deals with a very special part of the ritual related to the purification of the king before he enters the sanctuary as priest-king.[5] In this place the king receives all the gifts of the powers of heaven from the North and from the South, and the two crowns from the hands of Seth and Horus. Presently, the east partition of this room II is partially destroyed, but the remaining elements allow us to suppose that its upper part completed that of the west wall (plate 99), and here is why.

On the upper register of the west wall of room II, the king is portrayed offering incense to the "great cycle of the *neters* of the North and of the South," as say the texts, but the legend that runs above these thirteen *neters* affirms that they come from the North (whereas they come from the South) and bring all their gifts in order to celebrate the festivals of renewal of the year and of the month. It is therefore very probable that on the east wall of this same room the *neters* coming from the South were found. At present there remains only the royal figure who makes exactly the same censing gesture with the same censer terminated by a hand that does not hold the standard vase bearing the flame, but a *chen* sign. Under this censer is inscribed the text that relates to this chapter of the ritual concerning the offering of incense to the "great cycle of the *neters*."[6]

In accepting this restoration, the "*neters* coming from the North" are drawn to the west and those from the South to the east, an orientation conforming to that of the crowns (fig. 287), and the two texts of the kings of the east and of the west complement each other.

To the west, only a single phrase is inscribed above the king: "Purified, the *neters* of the South and of the North who are those who come after [*imyu-khet*] Amun [in] his temple. Ah! . . ."

---

[4] Cf. fig. 223, the barque of Mut of room IV, in which the childbirth scene is projected in transposition. See also the black granite barque in which the queen is seated, originally from Luxor and now in the British Museum (ground floor, gallery 43).

[5] Cf. chapter 39, commentary on plate 75, the description of the daily ritual of divine worship.

[6] This text corresponds to chapter 43 of the Berlin ritual, for which Luxor gives only the essential phrases.

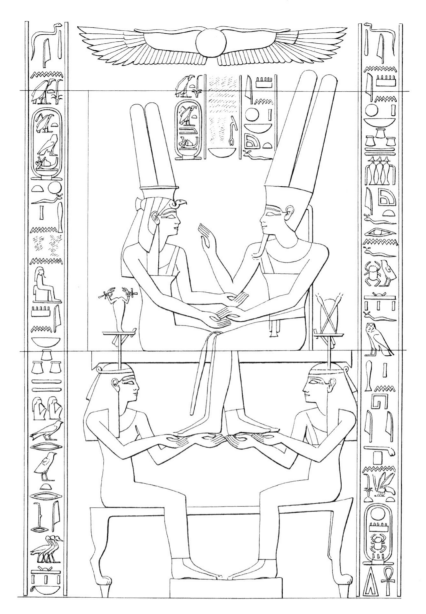

*Fig. 298. Scene of the theogamy, room IX, west wall, first register, central scene
(restored from the existing elements)*

Amun and Queen Mutemwia seated on the symbol of the sky, supported by Selkit wearing the emblem of the scorpion *(left)* and Neith with the two crossed arrows for her symbol *(right)*.

Right, the first of the four columns on which the "words spoken by Amun" are inscribed; *left,* the first of the five columns on which the exclamations of the queen and the answer of Amun are written. A horizontal joint of the stones coincides with the upper line of the sky supporting Amun and Mut.

This sentence requires some thought because the figuration does not at all show the *neters* "coming after" Amun, who is not depicted, but following Tum, master of Heliopolis, and proceeding toward the king, who offers incense. The literal meaning of *imyu-khet*[7] can be understood as "The *neters* of the South and of the North who come 'through' Amun, from whom they are born. . . ." Amun is indeed said to be the king and the father of all the *neters*.

We should not forget that the era of Amenhotep III falls during the precessional zodiacal sign of Aries, symbolized by Amun. It is a matter then of a *particular characteristic of the cosmic influence* that is taken to be the source of natural phenomena. In the same way Mentu symbolized the bull in the era ruled by the sign of Taurus.

To the east, the text inscribed under the censer completes the unfinished phrase of the west: "Purified the *neters* of the South and of the North . . . Amun [in] his temple. Ah! place your two hands on this sweet perfume.[8] It is the secretion of the *neter*, coming out of him . . . on the great perfume coming from the horizon. His perfume, toward you."[9]

What then is this "perfume" born of the divine secretion, this perfume that revivifies and purifies the *neters* and that is offered not with the censer but with the *chen* sign? This great perfume that comes from the eye of Horus, which comes out of the horizon? This *sty* perfume by which the queen was penetrated at the time of the royal conception?

The *chen* explains its implied meaning. The word *chen* is written by a hieroglyph representing a buckle attached to a length of string. The royal name is written in a similar loop, then called *ren* (cartouche), the name signifying the definition. The presentation of the *chen* with regard to the *sty* perfume, coming from the eye of Horus and the secretion of the *neter*, signifies the definition of what was, before the conception, abstract or spiritual.

With this perfume (we have seen it in regard to the "procession of the odor" in the sanctuary of the barque) we are dealing with the capture of the Fire. This Fire is an abstract soul that specifies; it is the particular hue seized or captured by Mut become Hathor in order to form the precious unguent that gives life.

The "*neters* coming from the North" portrayed on the west wall of room II hold in one hand the palm frond of the years, and in the other hold up the symbols of the pavilions of the *sed* festival. Most of these *neters* have had their names hammered out. The first is Tum, first of the Great Ennead of Heliopolis, the second is Ptah, great *neter* of Memphis, wrapped, standing in his naos and holding the *was* scepter in his hand. Among those behind him, one can recognize Horus (hieracocephalic) and Seth, master of the South, with large, cut ears. Here the spiritual aspect of the theme of the rites described in the lower registers is represented.

---

[7] *imyu-khet* is formed from two words the first of which means "between," "among," "that which is in" (Lefebvre, *Grammaire*, § 504), and the second, *khet*, implies an "idea of penetration" (§ 502). The group *imyu-khet* is sometimes translated by "the posterity," "the descendents" (§ 524).

[8] *sty nadjem*, sweet perfume; *sty*, perfume, is a word identical to that used to designate the "odor of the *neter*" that awakens the queen at the time of the royal spiritual conception; *nadjem*, written with the carob fruit, signifies "sweet," "agreeable."

[9] We can compare the Luxor text with chapter 43 of the Berlin ritual: "Words to be spoken: The *neters* of the South and of the North are purified, the great cycle of the *neters*, complete, which comes after Amun in his temple. Ah! Place your two hands on this perfume; it is pleasant; [it is] the secretion of the *neter*, coming out of him. Ah! Put your two hands on the great perfume coming from the eye of Horus, which revivifies the faces of the *neters* of the South and of the North, of the great cycle of the *neters*, complete, which comes after Amun in his temple. Ah! Put your two hands on the beneficent perfume coming from the horizon; its perfume comes toward you, the perfume of the eye of Horus, toward you." Cf. Moret, *Rituel du culte divin journalier*, pp. 166–67. We note that "the great cycle of the *neters*," *mi ked sen imyu khet Amun*, literally signifies "the great cycle of the *neters* according to their forms [or quality], which are in and through Amun."

The middle register confirms that the king receives the power of the "two *neters*," that is, of Seth and Horus, and that this is accomplished in the *per-dwat*. The *per-dwat* is a special chamber in which, before being able to officiate as priest, the king must be purified and invested with all the powers that are given to him by the two crowns and by the scepters. *Per-dwat* is written with the sign of the enclosure (the house) above a star. Now, if indeed the star is read *dwat*, another of its names is *sba*, which signifies "teaching" and "door" as well.[10]

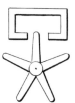

The king must always pass through the *per-dwat* before entering the sanctuary; should not this room II be named "chamber of the teaching"? Moreover, its location in the temple of Luxor corresponds to the jaw, one of the archaic names of which designates both the mandible and the two posts of a door.[11] Through its symbols, the west wall then evokes a door, an entrance, and this fact is confirmed by the architecture itself and by the arrangement of the tableaux.

Two blocks cut following the characteristic slope of a pylon[12] define, by the extension of their slopes to the line passing under the feet of the figures of the first register, the silhouette of a pylon ten times larger than the pylon built by Ramesses in the last stage of the construction of the temple.

In the ritual, the first scene of *per-dwat* is the double purification by Thoth and Horus, who pour a double stream onto the king. At Luxor this scene is located in the exact center of the first register; the king crowned with the diadem receives this purification made with ankhs forming a dome around him, and this scene is projected on the door *(sba)* of the ideal pylon defined by the reused stones traversing this wall. The traditional phrase is then pronounced four times by Thoth and by Horus: "Thy purification is my purification and vice versa."

Though the king looks toward the south, the tableaux that frame this first phase of the ritual must be read alternately in the two opposite directions to be in their proper order.

To the north, the king receives the two crowns from the hands of Seth and Horus in the palace.

To the south, the king accomplishes the "royal ascent toward the sanctuary," preceded by Mentu (the Innu of the South) and followed by Tum of Heliopolis (the Innu of the North); then he receives the influx of life, in the nape of the neck and by the nose, from the hands of the seated Amun who holds him "between his arms."

At the northern end, opposite the seated Amun, a bound figure seated on the throne holds the king by the left arm, and it is quite probable that this figure is Tuthmosis IV, the father of the king,[13] who is always present at the enthronement of his son.

Finally, under the aspect of a naked child holding the phoenix bird in a basket in his right hand, the prince is nourished at the breast by a female *neter*, followed by Khnum.

[10] Cf. I. Schwaller de Lubicz, *Her-Bak, Egyptian Initiate*, p. 107.

[11] Cf. vol. 1, fig. 167, no. 17.

[12] Cf. plate 67, and chapter 37.

[13] Cf. Moret, *Du Caractère religieux*, p. 80, fig. 12.

In front of the prince, held by "his father" (plates 99 and 101), one of the royal titles is *tit-Ra*, "image of Ra" or "emanation of Ra." The hieroglyphic group used to write this merits attention (fig. 299). In recalling that the pieces of the *wedjat* eye each represent one fraction of the *hekat* volume, the symbol *tit-Ra* forms the number 19 (sixty-fourths), the fundamental number governing the human canon. This play of numbers, which also recalls volume and signifies "in the image of Ra," evokes for us the formation of Adam "in the image of God" from the Mosaic Genesis.

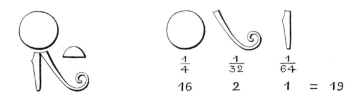

Fig. 299. Hieroglyphic group tit-Ra *and its decomposition into fractions of volume*

This decomposition recalls the destruction of the eye of Horus by Seth.

The development of the theme concerning the entrance into the Temple is given by the transpositions and transparencies of the key-stones that define the pylon in the wall itself, and confirm the idea of a passage through this wall. Actually, the two stones cut on a slope that give the proportions and measurements of the pylon have carved on their two sides, in rooms II and VI, representations that complement each other and conform to the myth.

In room II, these two stones depict Seth to the north and the hieracocephalic *neter* crowned by the solar disk and the plumes of Mentu to the south (plates 99 and 101). Now, in order to establish the correspondence between these two figurations and the pylon of Ramesses, the orientation of the crowns indicated throughout the temple and on the side of the pylon must be taken into account. Seth is master of the South and of the white crown; it is placed to the east (fig. 287), as the king crowned in white carved on the lintel of the door of the pylon (plate 10) also indicates. The red crown is located to the west (plate 9), which causes us to connect these two figurations with Seth and Horus, Suti-Hor, the two realizers of the plan. There is a reversal between right and left, but do not Suti-Hor say on their stele, "The director of Amun's works in Luxor, Suti [or] Hor [he says:] 'Whereas I am master in the west, he is master in the east [and vice versa]. We are to direct the great monuments in Apit, to the south of Thebes, city of Amun'"?[14]

Thus the ideal pylon evoked on the two partitions of the wall separating rooms II and VI is to be seen in reflection, exactly as the axis of Amun carved in the sanctuary of Amun's barque (room VI) is reflected in the repository of the interior face of the west wing of the pylon.[15] At this point the position of the crowns is reversed: the crown of the South is to the west, as the southern transposition stone corresponds to the west wing of the pylon (see plate 100, in which the walls of the chapels and the pylon are put together, the walls of the chapels being kept white and the mass of the pylon pictured in gray). The cornice on the pylon corresponds to the sky of the first register.

---

[14] Cf. chapter 26, the end of the text of the stele of Suti-Hor.

[15] Cf. plate 86, and chapter 40.

On this southern stone the solar disk of Mentu depicted in room II is projected in transposition into the naos of the barque of Amun-Ra depicted in room VI (plate 101). Now, the barque of Amun portrayed in sanctuary VI is veiled and allows only the winged scarabs to show, framed by two Maāts with their wings extended. It is necessary to go to the pylon, in the repository of Amun's barque, in order to know the content of its naos. There all the details are given: framed by two female deities with wings extended, a *neter* with a ram's head is seated on a lotus placed on the sign *mr* (the basin). Below, a hieracocephalic *neter* crowned with a solar disk is seated on the sign *mn* (checkerboard) framed by two Maāts (fig. 300).

The southern stone, cut following the same slope as the pylon and traversing the wall separating rooms II and VI, therefore reveals, by the transposition of the solar disk in the naos of the barque, the contents of this naos indicated by the pylon itself. In this transposition the winged scarab springs from the solar disk of Mentu, the feathers of which do not "traverse" the wall (plate 101).

On the northern stone, Seth is depicted on the wall on the side of room II, and his transposition on the opposite wall, in room VI, relates to the myth according to which Seth destroyed (decomposed) the eye of Horus. A thousand legends are related to the destruction and reconstitution of this eye, which is evoked by the cabala of numbers that we have just indicated. The fractions of the *hekat* volume are designated by the component parts of the *wedjat* eye, the healthy or reconstituted eye. We shall cite the following two fragments from these legends.

> "Seth found Horus sleeping in the mountain of the country of the Oasis and pulled his two eyes out of their sockets. The goddess Hathor, lady of the sycamore of the South, arrived and discovered Horus, who was stretched out helplessly on the mountain crying. She seized a gazelle and began to milk it. She said to Horus: 'Open thy eye so that I can put milk in it.' He opened his eye and she put milk in it; she did it for the right, she did it for the left, and she said to him: 'Open thy eye.' He opened it. She looked at it and observed that it was cured. . . ."
>
> It is important to know that the Egyptian name for the gazelle, given here as *ga-hes,* is a pun and can be understood as the injured sight.[16] There is a name for the antelope, which is *ma-hedj.* The Egyptians did not miss also making a play on the word from a religious text, chapter 112 of the Book of the Dead. It is the "Chapter of Knowing the Mysteries of Buto": "Do you know why the city of Buto has been given to Horus? You do not know it, but me, I know it: It is Ra who has given it to him as a compensation for the injury that he had experienced in his eye.[17] I know it. It is when Ra said to Horus: 'Let me then see thy eye concerning what has happened to it!' He looked at it and said: 'Look then at this line, thy hand covering thy good eye.' Then Horus looked at the line and said: 'I see it white, white.' And thus came the existence of the antelope [*ma-hedj*], which means 'white view.'"[18]

Tradition attributes to Seth the white crown, the domination of the Land of the South, and all the deserts and the animals of the desert, including the gazelle and the antelope, or more exactly, the oryx. Moreover, it is also said that these Sethian animals have "devoured" the eye of Horus and that is the reason that they are offered in sacrifice.

---

[16] Cf. Jean Capart, "Les Aventures d'Horus et de Seth," extract from the *Bulletin de la Classe des Lettres,* 5th series, 17 (9 Nov. 1931): 411–27. Cf. *Chronique d'Egypte* 8 (1933): 424–25.

[17] We see here the eye of Horus as being the eye of Ra, that is, the light of the eye, the sun Aten of the solar principle, Ra.

[18] Cf. Capart, "Les Aventures d'Horus et de Seth," p. 425.

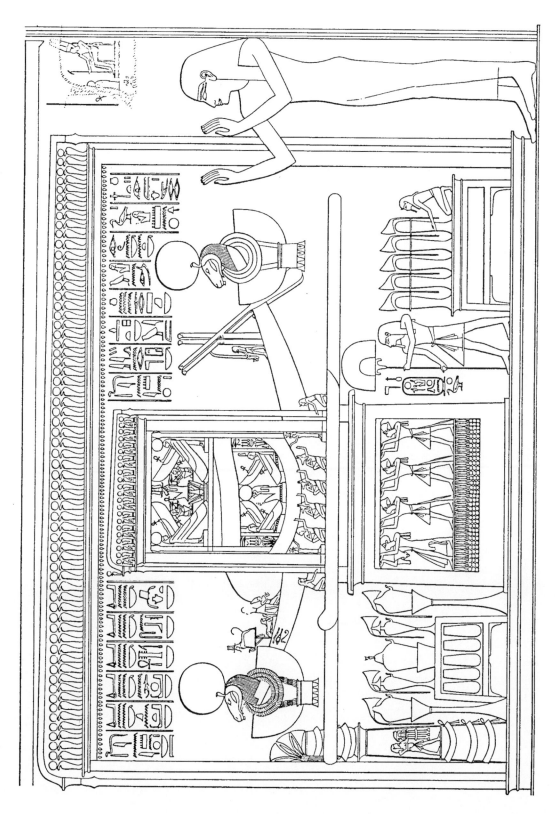

Fig. 300. Amun's Barque (restored from existing elements), repository of Ramesses II, west wall

The transposition of the northern stone between rooms II and VI is a synthesis of these variations of the myth and ritual, the goal of which is to reconstitute of the eye of Horus, which must be offered to the *neter* so that he can again be united with his soul each day with the appearance of Ra. Seth, portrayed in room II in the process of giving the king the white crown of the South, is projected by transposition into room VI onto the desert animals that are attributed to him: *ma-hedj*, the antelope-oryx, and *ga-hes*, the gazelle (plate 101).

The king shown in room VI wears the white crown and hold the *mākes* staff and the white *hedj* club in his hand, which he points toward the sacrificed animals, while he waves the *āba* scepter in his right hand to consecrate these offerings[19] (plate 101). Thus, the transposition from one room to another explains the myth.

CONCLUSION

Beyond all speculation and reasoned demonstration, there is the fact, the experience, that we live. Past experience makes us live, and life prepares us for future experience through antagonism contained in the seminal synthesis of the present moment. When it splits apart, we call this antagonism the opposites and give them all the names that designate everything that makes up our Universe: past and future, heaven and earth, good and evil.

In the Temple they are called Seth and Horus, in reference to the immanent possibilities that are, in the end, expressed in the combat of their natures.

They are the builders of the Temple, which is the tangible Universe, model of the temple conceived by man as the image of heaven.

Image of heaven: always Two, but then Two who search for each other, who come near to each other, in order to offer to the Being that animates us their own friendly go-between, so as to recover the Unity.

Eternal conflict in every creature, nameless anxiety in the mortal being who suffers the contradictory attraction of the two powers: the Horian power, immutable light, and the Scthian power of the atavisms and habits tied to the terrestrial form.

The secret vessel containing the two powers floats in the immaterial Waters of the cosmic ocean, Nun. This barque travels from the Fire of the east toward the Water of the west; in separating them by its movement, it also reunites them in the serenity of the culmination.

The naos is the image of that which manifests the opposites, but also the image of that which unifies them: movement, then the serenity of repose. The naos is the tabernacle, the sanctuary, the Ark of the Covenant, where the final death leads to the removal of antagonisms, the serenity of eternal life, there where the One is in the Other.

There is only inessential knowledge as long as the Same and the Other, Horus and Seth, combat each other, and Horus is but the memory of the Light in Seth, "fallen" into matter.

The ordinary definition of good and evil is subjective. Only illuminated beings and Spirit can say of what good consists, that is, of what leads toward deliverance from the mortal, which evil prevents. This is essential knowledge.

Designating Seth and Horus as being evil and good is reducing a universal principle to a personal opinion. The complements polarizing the specificity are the signature of each thing of which our human complex can have knowledge, this complementation being the architect of the Temple that is our world.

---

[19] Cf. fig. 292, the *āba* scepter covered in gold leaf and having carvings of sacrificial animals on one of its faces.

The essence of things is by this fact ternary because between One and Two lies the harmony that includes the "accords" and "discords" situated between these poles, separated by the harmony they create through their becoming and their affinity.

Now, if an object is only known through its complement, each of these complements evokes the other, and this general activity is the principle of the "inverse," in genetic phenomena as well as in mathematics. In genetics, one takes as extremes the two lineages, solar and lunar, transcribed into the colors red and white; the burning desert, dry and red, will call forth the *animals,* that is to say, that which is *animate,* designated as white, and this silvery white will in turn recall the tempered red.

This complementary activity is applied to all phenomena. The teaching of a law must be seen in these "symbols."

Characteristic of pharaonic teaching is the intermingling of *what makes* and *what is made,* identification of the gift with the one who receives this gift.

The weaving is also the cloth. The action from which an effect results is, potentially, this product. Spirit forms the body, of and through itself, therefore, the body is Spirit. One is abstract, the other concrete; one evokes the other, and in the inmost "esoteric" event, Two become One. Functionally, this is seeing the divinity in all things. This is also, in never opposing the divine to the natural, the absence of all philosophical conflict.

Knowing how to identify all thought and even all technique with theological expression represents the highest science. This makes of religious myth a very complex ensemble, but no more complex than the analysis of the transmutation of our airy, liquid, and solid food into thought. It would be absurd to see in this a physicochemical phenomenon and not a creative reality, a manifestation of the Original Verb, the Spirit, the Light; it is because of this that true science is necessarily theological. It is a serene science, because founded on the knowledge of the causal phenomenon, source of the laws that govern all phenomena.

Alternation is the pendulum of the life of apparent forms; the crossing is the equilibrium of a momentary death of the form, from which results a new polarized state. Its new crossing, or equilibrium, is life without death. This is said simply by the crossed scepters of the royal mummy. This is the law of the return in this Light that fills the absolute void, that reigns in the heavens of all nights, but is perceptible only because of the obstacle that opposes it there. This obstacle is Seth, the same light corporified, because only the Light can be opposed to the Light, can be *perceptible* to the Light. Thus "to corporify" is to make an obstacle to an activity through the same activity, and this occurs in all domains.

Is not wisdom then the law of non-willfulness of the sublime Lao-tzu? But for this it is necessary to know how to enter into the Temple, and also how to go out again.

Is not all of this illustrated by the fact of eating the bread and drinking the wine, these two substances rich in spirit, and by breathing the odor of the god in order to transmute it into the consciousness of the conflict and then into the consciousness of Being? The animal man eats; the human man transmutes; the superhuman man recognizes. This last is the Royal Man.

Let us call Spirit pure energy, but which is known to us only through polarization; let us call God consciousness, but which is known to us only through complementation; let us call Light the first phenomenon, but which is known to us only through shadows.

Let us call original scission the first act of becoming, but which is known to us only as separation. . . .

Let us change the names; we would not, for all that, be changing either the things or the functions.

Now, we cannot accept that the essences of that which we know would not have an absolute aspect: the *neters,* was this only a hypothesis of reference? They are the abstractions evoked by tangible things by virtue of that which we ourselves are, and that we know through the fact that only similar entities can recognize each other. We—mankind, the human species—are the reference for the knowledge of the world.

As for any observed or experienced phenomenon, let us look for the knowledge of it in ourselves and not outside of us through mechanical reasoning.

Thus, we can find the vital reason for the "function" because *only living humanity can reveal to us the law of a qualitative exaltation.*

Qualitative exaltation, this amplification of quality, is the desired fruit of the Seth-Horus drama, the survival beyond the Sethian body, the liberation of consciousness from physical contingencies; this is the story of all the "spiritual states" of which the traditions speak.

This qualitative exaltation that is the transmutation of nourishment into consciousness and thought can subsequently no longer be recognized by this same thought, which will consider it absurd.

. . . and the shadows no longer recognize the light from which they were born.

Man is the Temple where the mystery of the everyday is accomplished, the place of combat of the essential antagonisms, and, because of this, he is also the place of the revelation of the shadowless Light.

This is the soul of the pharaonic teaching, which believes only in this Irrational, which it never profanes and which it causes us to *hear* by means of harmony, whose laws ordain the Becoming and the Return.

This teaching tells us that proportion splits the elements and makes them appear in four and seven tones of this simultaneity that is the murmuring of the sistra, the Verb of the world.

It tells us that separating the Spirit from the body is the religion of death. To separate and split apart is to descend into transitory matter, is to remove ourselves far from the animating source of all. Not separating is pure love, it is the life of Horian Light, followed by those who have known how to avoid the Western way of the Osirian waters of rebirth.

Their reward is to emerge living from the Temple after having entered there by dying to illusion.

And now that the temple of Luxor has shown us the way to follow, let us begin to explore the deeper meaning of the teaching of the pharaonic sages.

THE UNITY

One sole Truth: Indivisible Unity.
One sole Reality: the Verb and its evolution in consciousness.
One sole universal morality: through Cosmic Man each is
bound to all, each is responsible for, or benefits from, the
good and evil deeds of all;
humanity is a whole united in the individual.
One sole Consciousness: Genesis.
One sole pure science: Numbers.
One sole expression: the Symbol.
One sole means: Harmony, which has its source in disorder
where the sundered parts rediscover one another,
naturally and of themselves, through affinity.
Spirit is at the beginning and the end of all form.
Form is the symbol of a function.
Wisdom is the perfect harmony of all the functions.

Appendix

COMPARISON OF PARTS AND CHAPTERS IN THE ENGLISH AND FRENCH EDITIONS

Note: volume 2 of the English edition combines volume 2 (the plates) with volume 3 (legends and commentaries on the plates) of the French edition.

LIST OF WORKS CITED

Note: Wherever possible, this list substitutes editions in English of sources referred to by the author. Additional works cited in the translation are also included.

Abellio, R. *La Bible, document chiffré, essai sur la restitution des clefs de la science numerale secrète.* Paris: Gallimard, 1950.

Angel, F. *Vie et moeurs des serpents.* Paris: Payot, 1950.

Antoniadi, E. M. *L'Astronomie égyptienne.* Paris: Gauthiers-Villars, 1934.

Arago, François. *Oeuvres complètes.* Paris: Gide, 1865.

Ariens Kappers, C. U., G. C. Huber, and E. C. Crosby. *The Comparative Anatomy of the Nervous System of Vertebrates, Including Man.* 2 vols. New York: Macmillan, 1936.

Barguet, P. "Le Rituel archaique de fondation des temples de Médinet Habou et de Louqsor." *Revue d'Egyptologie* 9 (1952).

Basil Valentine. *Chymische Schriften.* Hamburg, 1677.

Benoit, Jacques. "Hormones, determinisme du cycle sexuel saisonnier," and "Reproduction, caractères sexuels." *Traité de zoologie.* Vol. 15, *Oiseaux.* Paris: Masson, 1950.

Bernardi, Eduardi. *De ponderibus et mensuris antiquorum.* N.p., n.d.

Berthelot, Daniel. *La Physique et la métaphysique des théories d'Einstein.* Paris: Payot, 1922.

Bigourdan, G. *L'Astronomie.* Paris: Flammarion, 1917.

Blackman, A. M. *The Rock Tombs of Meir.* 6 vols. London: Egypt Exploration Society, 1914–53.

Borchardt, L. *Die Annalen und die zeitliche Feststellung des Alten Reichs der ägyptischen Geschichte.* Berlin, 1917.

Breasted, J. H. *The Edwin Smith Surgical Papyrus.* Chicago: Univ. of Chicago Press, 1930.

Brehm, A. E. *La Vie des animaux.* Vol. 3. Paris: Baillière, 1878–85.

Brugsch, H. *Nouvelles recherches sur la division de l'année des anciens Egyptiens.* Berlin, 1856.

Busquet, P., M.D. *Traité d'anatomie clinique médicale topographique.* Vol. 1. Paris: Baillière, 1927.

Capart, Jean. "Les Aventures d'Horus et de Seth." *Bulletin de la Classe des Lettres,* 5th series, 17 (9 Nov. 1931).

Carrel, Alexis *L'homme cet inconnu.* Paris: Plon, 1935.

Carter, Howard. *The Tomb of Tut-ankh-Amen.* London: Cassell, 1930.

Chassinat, Emile. *Le Temple d'Edfou.* 15 vols. Cairo: I.F.A.O., 1897–1985.

Clairaut, Alexis-Claude. *Eléments de géométrie.* Paris: Gauthier-Villars, 1920.

Cleomedes. *On the Orbits of the Heavenly Bodies.* Trans. T. L. Heath. In Morris R. Cohen and I. E. Drabkin. *A Source Book in Greek Science.* New York: McGraw-Hill, 1948.

Cossa, P. *La Cybernétique: Du cerveau humain aux cerveaux artificiels.* Paris: Masson, 1955.

———. *Physiopathologie du système nerveux.* Paris: Masson, 1950.

Daressy, Georges. *Le Temple du Louqsor.* Cairo: Imprimerie Nationale, 1893.

Decourt, J., and J. M. Doumic "Schéma anthropométrique appliqué à l'endocrinologie: Le Morphotype masculin." *La Semaine des Hôpitaux de Paris* 10, no. 7 (July 1950).

Déjérine, J. *Sémiologie des affections du système nerveux.* Paris: Masson, 1926.

Delmas, J., and G. Laux. *Système nerveux sympathique.* Paris: Masson, 1952.

Denicker, J. "Principaux caractères de l'homme moyen d'après Quetelet." Vol. 4. *Encyclopédie Française.*

Dezobry, L. C., and T. Bachelet. *Dictionnaire général de biographie et d'histoire de mythologie, de géographie ancienne et moderne comparé.* Paris: Delagrave, 1889.

Drioton, Etienne. "Médamoud, les inscriptions." *Rapports sur les fouilles de Médamoud 1925–*. Fouilles de l'I.F.A.O., rapports préliminaires. Vol. 4. Cairo, 1927.

Eliade, Mircea. *Patterns in Comparative Religion*. Trans. Rosemary Sheed. New York: Meridian, 1963.

Engelbach, H. *Introduction to Egyptian Archaeology*. Cairo: I.F.A.O., 1946.

Erman, A. *La Religion des Egyptiens*. Paris: Payot, 1937.

Erman, A., and H. Grapow. *Wörterbuch der ägyptischen Sprache*. Berlin: Akademie-Verlag, 1926–55.

Erman A., and H. Ranke. *La Civilisation égyptienne*. Paris: Payot, 1952.

Facsimile of the Rhind Mathematical Papyrus. London: British Museum, 1898.

Fabre, Jean-Henri. *Souvenirs entomologiques*. 5th series. Paris: Delagrave, 1922.

Gardiner, A. J. *Egyptian Grammar*. Oxford: Clarendon Press, 1927.

Gauthier, H. *Dictionnaire des noms géographiques contenus dans les textes hieroglyphiques*. 5 vols. Cairo: I.F.A.O., 1925.

Ghyka, Matila C. *L'Esthétique des proportions dans la nature et dans les arts*. Paris: Gallimard, 1927.

———. *The Geometry of Art and Life*. 1946. Reprint, New York: Dover, 1977.

———. *Le Nombre d'Or: Rites et rythmes pythagoriciens dans le développement de la civilisation occidentale*. 2 vols. Paris: Gallimard, 1931.

———. *Philosophie et mystique du nombre*. Paris: Payot, 1952.

———. *A Practical Handbook of Geometrical Composition and Design*. London: Alec Tiranti, 1952.

Gillain, O. *La Science égyptienne: l'Arithmétique au Moyen Empire*. Brussels: Fondation Egyptologique Reine Elisabeth, 1927.

Girard, M. P. S. "Mémoire sur le nilomètre d'Eléphantine." In *Description de l'Egypte*. Vol 1. Paris, 1809–1828.

Granet, Marcel. *La Civilisation chinoise*. Paris: Renaissance du Livre, 1929.

———. *La Pensée chinoise*. Paris: Renaissance du Livre, 1934.

Griaule, M. *Dieu d'eau, entretiens avec Ogotommeli*. Paris: Editions du Chêne, 1948.

Herodotus. *History*. Trans. George Rawlinson. New York: Appleton, 1866.

Hickmann, Hans. *Observations sur les survivances de la chironomie égyptienne dans le chant liturgique copte*. Annales du Service des Antiquités de l'Egypte 49. Cairo: I.F.A.O., 1949.

Hippocrates. 8 vols. Vol. 3. Trans. E. T. Withington. New York: Putnam's, 1927. Vol. 8. Loeb Classical Library. Cambridge: Harvard Univ. Press, 1995.

Hippocrates. *Oeuvres complètes*. Trans. Littré. Vol. 7. Paris: Baillière, 1851.

Hoefer, P. *Histoire des mathématiques*. Paris: Hachette, 1874.

Iversen, Erik. *Canon and Proportions in Egyptian Art*. London: Sidgwick and Jackson, 1955.

Jéquier, Gustave. *Les Frises d'objets des sarcophages du moyen empire*. Cairo: I.F.A.O., 1921.

Jomard, E. "Mémoire sur le système métrique des anciens Egyptiens." In *Description de l'Egypte*. Vol 1. Paris, 1809–1828.

Josephus. *Antiquities of the Jews*. In *The Complete Works of Josephus*. Trans. William Whiston. Grand Rapids, Mich.: Kregal Publications, 1981.

Keimer, Ludwig. *Die Gartenpflanzen im alten Ägypten*. 2 vols. Hamburg: Hoffmann und Campe, 1924.

Kramrisch, Stella. *The Hindu Temple*. 1946. Reprint, Delhi, India: Motilal Banarsidass, 1991.

Krappe, Alexander H. *La Genèse du mythe*. Paris: Payot, 1925.

Kraus, Paul. *Jābir ibn Hāyyan: Contribution à l'histoire des idées scientifiques dans l'Islam*. 2 vols. Mémoires présentés à l'Institut d'Egypte 44–45. Cairo: I.F.A.O., 1942.

Lacau, Pierre. *Inscriptions latines du temple de Louqsor*. Annales du Service des Antiquités de l'Egypte 34. Cairo: I.F.A.O.

———. *Le Plan du temple de Louqsor*. Mémoires de l'Académie des Inscriptions et Belles Lettres 18, no. 2, 1941.

Lamy, Lucie. *Egyptian Mysteries: New Light on Ancient Knowledge*. Trans. Deborah Lawlor. London: Thames and Hudson, 1981.

Lao-tzu. *Tao te Ching.* Trans. Frank J. MacHovec. Mount Vernon, N.Y.: Peter Pauper Press, 1962.

Laplace, Pierre-Simon. *Exposition du système du monde.* Vol. 6 of *Oeuvres complètes.* Paris, 1884.

Laville, C. "Numérations non décimales." *La Nature* (January 1953).

Lasteyrie, R. de. *L'Architecture religieuse en France à l'époque gothique.* Vol. 1. 1926.

Leclant, Jean. "Fouilles et travaux en Egypte." *Orientalia* 19 (1950).

———. "Fouilles et travaux en Egypte 1950–51." *Orientalia* 20, no. 4 (1951).

Lefebvre, Gustave. *Essai sur la médecine égyptienne de l'époque pharaonique.* Paris: Presses Universitaires, 1956.

———. *Grammaire de l'égyptien classique.* Cairo: I.F.A.O., 1955.

———. *Romans et contes égyptiens de l'époque pharaonique.* Paris: A. Maisonneuve, 1949.

———. *Tableau des parties du corps humain mentionées par les Egyptiens,* supplement aux Annales du Service des Antiquités de l'Egypte, notebook no. 17. Cairo: I.F.A.O., 1952.

Legrain, G. *Le Logement et le transfert des barques sacrées.* Bulletin de l'I.F.A.O. 13. Cairo, 1917.

Le Lionnais, F. *Great Currents of Mathematical Thought.* Trans. R. A. Hall and Howard G. Bergman. 2 vols. New York: Dover, 1971.

Longuet, Y. J. "Lésions et fractures des cinq dernières vertèbres cervicales." In *Encyclopédie médico-chirurgicale.*

———. "Lésions traumatiques du cuir chevelu." In *Encyclopédie médico-chirurgicale,* 15953.

———. "Lésions traumatiques fermées du rachis cervical." In *Encyclopédie médico-chirurgicale,* 15825.

MacHovec, Frank J., trans. *The Book of Tao.* Mount Vernon, N. Y.: Peter Pauper Press, 1962.

Manuscript 9512, Bibliothèque Nationale, Paris.

Mariette, Auguste. *Les Mastabas de l'Ancien Empire.* Paris: F. Vieweg, 1884.

Maspero, G. *Les Contes populaires de L'Egypte ancienne.* Paris: E. Guilmoto, 1911.

Meinertzhagen, R. *Nicoll's Birds of Egypt.* Vol 2. London: H. Rees, 1930.

Menod, G. H., trans. *Contes Khmers.* Högman, Mouans Sartoux, A.M.: Chitra Publications, n.d.

Merz, H. *Schéma d'anatomie topographique.* Paris: Doin, 1950.

Meyer, Eduard. *Chronologie égyptienne.* Trans. A. Moret. Annales du Musée Guimet 24. Paris: Leroux, 1912.

Michel, Paul-Henri. *De Pythagore à Euclide: Contribution à l'histoire des mathématiques préeuclidiennes.* Paris: Belles-Lettres, 1950.

Möller, G. *Hieratische Palaeographie.* Vol. 2. Leipzig, 1909.

Montet, Pierre. *Les Scènes de la vie privée dans les tombeaux égyptiens de l'Ancien Empire.* Strasbourg: Imprimerie Alsacienne, 1925.

Moret, Alexandre. *Du Caractère religieux de la royauté pharaonique.* Annales du Musée Guimet 15. Paris: Leroux, 1902.

———. *Le Rituel du culte divin journalier en Egypte.* Annales du Musée Guimet 14. Paris: Leroux, 1901.

Morgan, J. de. *Fouilles à Dahchour (mars–juin 1895).* Vienna: Adolphe Holzhausen, 1895.

———. *Fouilles à Dahchour en 1894–1895.* N.p., 1903.

Nasr, S. H. *Science and Civilization in Islam.* Cambridge: Harvard Univ. Press, 1968.

Neugebauer, O., and A. Sachs, eds. *Mathematical Cuneiform Texts.* New Haven: American Oriental Society, 1945.

Nicholson, G. *Dictionnaire pratique d'horticulture.* 5 vols. 1892–93.

Olivier, E., and A. Dufour. *Traité d'osteologie humaine.* Paris: Maloine, 1947.

Paracelsus. *Selected Writings.* Ed. Jolande Jacobi, trans. Norbert Guterman. Bollingen Series 28. Princeton: Princeton Univ. Press, 1979.

Pawlowski, G. de. *Voyage au pays de la quatrième dimension.* Paris: Eugène Fasquelle, 1923.

Peet, T. Eric. *The Rhind Mathematical Papyrus.* London: Hodder and Stoughton, 1923.

Perring, J. S. *The Pyramids of Gizeh.* London: J. Fraser, 1839–42.

Petit-Dutaillis, D. "Traumatismes cérébraux." In *Encyclopédie medico-chirurgicale.*

Petit-Dutaillis, D., and G. Guiot. "Fractures du crâne." In *Encyclopédie médico-chirurgicale.*

Petrie, Flinders. *Ancient Egypt*. London: Macmillan, 1932.

———. *Ancient Weights and Measures Illustrated by the Egyptian Collection in University College*. London, 1926.

Piankoff, Alexandre. *Les Deux Papyrus "mythologiques" de Her-Ouben au Musée du Caire*. Annales du Service des Antiquités de l'Egypte 49. Cairo: I.F.A.O., 1949.

Plato, *Timaeus*. Trans. B. Jowett. *The Dialogues of Plato*. Oxford: Clarendon Press, 1953.

Pliny. *Natural History*. Trans. H. Rackham. Loeb Classical Library. Cambridge: Harvard Univ. Press, 1938.

Quibell, J. E. *Hierakonpolis*. London: Egyptian Research Account, 1900.

Richer, P. *Canon des proportions du corps humain*. Paris: Delagrave, 1933.

Ricke, Herbert. *Bemerkungen zur ägyptischen Baukunst des Alten Reichs*. Vol. 1. Zurich: Borchardt Institut, 1944.

Rivet, P. *Cités Maya*. Paris: Albert Guillot, 1954.

Robichon, C., and A. Varille. *Description sommaire du temple primitif de Médamoud*. Recherches d'archéologie, de philologie et d'histoire 11. Cairo: I.F.A.O., 1940.

Robichon, C., P. Barguet, and J. Leclant. *Karnak-Nord IV*. Bulletin de l'I.F.A.O. 25. Cairo, 1954.

Rodet, L. "Les Prétendus problèmes d'algèbre du manuel du calculateur égyptien." *Journal asiatique* (1881).

Rouge, J. de. "Etude des monuments du massif de Karnak." *Mélanges archéologie égyptienne et assyrienne* 1 (1873).

Salmon, W., ed. *Bibliothèque des philosophes alchimiques ou hermétiques*. Paris: Cailleau, 1741.

Schack-Schackenburg, H. *Der Berliner Papyrus 6619*. *Zeitschrift für ägyptische Sprache*, no. 38.

Schwaller de Lubicz, Isha. *Her-Bak, Egyptian Initiate*. Trans. Ronald Fraser. 1967. Reprint, Rochester, Vt.: Inner Traditions, 1978.

———. *Her-Bak, Chick-Pea*. Trans. C. E. Sprague. 1954. Reprint, Rochester, Vt.: Inner Traditions, 1978.

Schwaller de Lubicz, R. A. *Nature Word*. Trans. Deborah Lawlor. Rochester, Vt.: Inner Traditions, 1990.

———. *Sacred Science: The King of Pharaonic Theocracy*. Trans. André and Goldian VandenBroeck. Rochester, Vt.: Inner Traditions, 1982.

———. *Symbol and the Symbolic*. Trans. Robert and Deborah Lawlor. 1978. Reprint, Rochester, Vt.: Inner Traditions, 1981.

———. *The Temple in Man*. Trans. Robert and Deborah Lawlor. 1977. Reprint, Rochester, Vt.: Inner Traditions, 1981.

Sethe, Kurt. *Die altägyptischen Pyramidentexte*. Leipzig: Hinrich, 1908–22.

Tannery, Paul. *Mémoires scientifiques*. 3 vols. Paris: Gauthier Villars, 1915.

Tardieu, G. and C. Tardieu. *Le Système nerveux végétatif*. Paris: Masson, 1948.

Testut, L., and O. Jacob. *Traité d'anatomie topographique*. 2 vols. Paris: Doin, 1914.

Theon of Smyrna. *Le Nombre de Platon*. Trans J. Dupuis. Paris: Hachette, 1892.

Theophrastus. *Enquiry into Plants*. Trans. Sir Arthur Hort. 2 vols. Loeb Classical Library. New York: Putnam's, 1916.

Thooris, A. *La Médecine morphologique*. Paris: Doin, 1937.

Thureau-Dangin, F. *Textes mathématiques babyloniens*. Leiden: E. J. Brill, 1938.

Vandervael, F. *Biométrie humaine*. 2nd ed. Paris: Masson, n.d.

Vandier, J. *La Religion égyptienne*. Paris: Presses Universitaires, 1949.

Varille, Alexandre. *A propos des Pyramides de Snefrou*. Cairo: Schindler, 1947.

———. *Hymne au Soleil des architects d'Amenophis III, Suti et Hor*. Bulletin de l'I.F.A.O. Cairo, 1942.

———. *Quelques caractéristiques du temple pharaonique*. Cairo: I.F.A.O., 1946.

Vyse. *Operations Carried on at the Pyramids of Gizeh in 1837*. London: J. Fraser, 1840-42.

Walle, B. van de, and J. Vergote. "Traduction des Hieroglyphes d'Horapollon." *Extrait de la Chronique d'Egypte*, no. 35 (January 1943).

Weill, Raymond. *Chronologie égyptienne*. Paris: Geuthner, 1926.

Wyzewa, Teodor de, trans. *La Légende dorée du Bienheureux Jacques de Voragine*. Paris: Perrin, 1910.

INDEX

Page numbers in italics refer to illustrations; suffix T designates a table.

23*n*.3; uniqueness of, 126

germ: from root minus one times root, 258; of the seed, 118; as surface, 117*n*.37; of the temple, Hindu, 499; of two (*see* two: square root of). *See also* seed

gestation, xxviii (Vol.1), 10, 15, 24, 56, 99, 101, 454, 457, 508, 675, 691*n*.8, 728*n*.9; and architecture, 578; universal, 53; world in, 509

gestures, 24, 77, 451, 674; of bent knee, 858; of consecration, 974; of the crossing, 478; divine, 127; as hieroglyph, 774; *hotep*, 818; magical, 34–35; as true symbol, 432; as vital movement, 75

ghosts, 21

Ghyka, Matila C., xvii (Vol. 1), 90, 90*n*.6, 326

gigantism, 664

Gillain, O., 150, 168, 272*n*.30

giving and receiving, 973–75

"Giving the House to Its Master," 669, *670, 671, 672, 673,* 727, 733. *See also* consecration of the temple

Giza, 295*n*.35, 496

Gley, E., 442

gluteal crease, 325, 328

gnomons, 94, 98, 141, 141*n*.31, 144; in Babylonian mathematics, 214–15, 218, 219; cubic, 314; and growth of cubes, 264–66; in proportional notation of angles, 193; of sundial, 304, 621; of sundials, 303

gnosticism, 9

God, 57; atheist's, 24; belief in, 22; Christian, personhood of, 23–24; and determinism, 69–70; and the irrational, 102

gods: Egyptian (*see* neters); Olympian, 10

gold, 108, 236*n*, 277, 732*n*.20

gold brick, 729*n*.15

golden proportion, xxii (Vol. 1), 82, 89, 239, 338, 341, 814; division of colossus no. 3, 626; in human canon, 313, 320, 325

Goneim, Zakaria, 560

Gospel, 505

graffiti: of figure in Mut's belly, 676; of restorers, 635

grain: measurement of, 110, 110*n*.29; as unit of measure, 277

granite, 518

grapes, 108

grapevine, 277

gravity, 81; *vs.* affinity, 63

gray matter, 434

Great Bear, *489,* 730, 732, 933, 940

Greeks, 7, 8, 130; and Babylonian calculation, 207; calendar, 318; and *daimons,* 10, 51*n*.5; Eleatic, dialectic mentality of, 211; on human proportion, 433; on infinity, 226; mathematics of, 126, 347; and metaphysics, 2, 27, 58; Mysteries, 457; Olympian gods of, 10; rationalism of, 75, 75*n;* science of, 83–84, 306; statuary, pro-

portions of, 311; unanswerable problems of, 23; and unity, 226, 256*n*.13

grid, 228; of Amun, *924-29. See also canevas*

growth, 356, 962; as function, 521; human laws of, 580; of the Man of the Temple, 581–87; organic, 356; Osirian *vs.* Horian, 619; by phi (φ) and square root of 2, *584;* and the pituitary gland, 662; of plants, 742

Gurob, 850

Habachi, Labib, 560

Hadrian, emperor, 635, 636

Haeckel, Ernst Heinrich, 32

Haggag, el-, Abu, 562

hairline, 328, 333. *See also* crown of the skull

half-tone, 112

Hambidge, 324, 326*n*.30, 814

Hammurabi, 207

Hamose, tomb of, 333

Hancock, Graham, xx (Vol. 1)

hands, 285; as measure, 845; mechanical claw, 414; right *vs.* left, 973, 974; severed, bas-relief of prisoners with, 561, 588; size of, 334*n*.47; as symbol, 22

hanging, death by, 454

Hap, *see* Apis

Hapi (Nile), 508

Hapu, 480, 734

hare: essential, 53–54; as Hermetic symbol, 1001; as symbol for 15th nome of Upper Egypt, 283; as symbol for *twnw,* 160*n*.62

harmonic, subcontrary to, 198, 198*n*.7

harmonic decomposition, 204, 828, 849, 858, 881

harmonic divisions of body, 331, *331*

harmonic mean, 200, 742

harmonic progression, 146

harmonic proportion, 173–75, 183, 188, 199, 200, 201, 227, 252, 253, 267*n*.24, 294, 319, 336, 342, 477, 828, 938*n*.17; and arithmetic proportion, 298; and newborns, 581

harmony, 15, 19–20, 26, 28, 44, 44*n*.17, 64, 64*n*.3, 103–6, 172, 273, 494, 1021; and absolute phi (φ), 229; in architecture of temple, 557; celestial, 273–75, 277; from disorder, 23; and form, 102, 125; intelligence of, 241; musical, 112–14, 250, 253–56, 271, 328, 328*n*.38, 880; and the passage from one to two, 234; and phi (φ), 233; rational, and irrational cause, 881; ratios of, 154; and the royal apron, 881–82, 883; and volumes, 125, 253–56

Harmya, 503

harpist: Bes as, *753, 759,* 760; in tomb of Ukhotep, 817

Harpocrates, *964*

harp of numbers, 240, *241*

Hathor, 108, 109, 289, 359, 359*n*.6, 455, 487, 487*n*.22, 509, *583,* 619*n*.12, 717, 719*n*.22, 835, 901, 1013; as mistress of

Cusae, 815; pentagon of, 510; symbol of, on king's stomach, 877, *877*

Hat-Hor, 710

Hatshepsut: chapel of, at Karnak, 729; obelisk of, 333

haty, 336, 378, 404–5, *423,* 563, 588, 733, 743; axis of (*see* axis of the hypostyle); of the temple, 632, *696,* 726, 732. *See also* hypostyle room

head, 448–57, 526; anatomy of, *696;* Aries assigned to, 775; and covered temple at Luxor, 433, *687,* 694*n*.12; gaping wounds to, 405–8, 409, 410–13; height of, 324; Hippocrates on lesions of, 407*n*.115; interior of, anatomical tems for, 385–98; of Man of the Temple, 588; seven orifices of, *378*

headband, 132, 433, 463*n*.10, 534; height of, 338; of Man of the Temple, 894 (*see also* temple of Apet of the South at Luxor: room V); royal (*see* royal headband)

hearing, 250

heart, 417, *423;* beats per minute, 931*n*.7; and *haty,* 404; hieroglyph of, 206; intelligence of, 2, 130*n*.6, 250, 507; muscles of, 405, *423;* sign of, 333

heat, 40, 43, 56*n*.11

Hebrew script, 72

hedj club, 669, 671, 1018

heels: of figure in chapel of Amun's barque, 669; and masonry joints, 675

height of child at birth, 238, 526, 580

Heisenberg, Werner Karl, 130*n*.7

hekat, 109, 110, 111T, 150, 152, 154, 253, 263, 403, 733*n*.23; scepter, 79, 80

heliocentric system, *vs.* geocentric system, 63*n*.2

Heliopolis, 495, 510, 770; creation mythology, 712, 713*n*.5; Ennead of, 237, 1013; Mystery of, 62*n*.1, 106, 126–27, 342, 717, 743, 769, 901, 950, 952, 968; revelation of, 89, 90; souls of, toes as, 429*n*.172; of the south (*see* Armant); temple of Ra at, 727; Tum of, 631

Heller, H. V., 312

hematomas, 398, 408, 424, 428; cerebral, 415, 744; of dura mater, 415; endocrinal, 393; of the interior capsule, 411

hemipenises, serpents', 469–470, *470*

hemoplegia, 378*n*.8, 414, 418; homolateral, 415

hemorrhages: from ears (otorrhea), 385, 398, 407, 410, 413, 415, 420, 422; from nose, 385, 398, 407, 413, 415, 419, 420, 422 (*see also* epistaxis); subarachnoid, 420; through mouth, 422

henbane, 412*n*.134

Henu the embalmer, 818, 819

henw, 110, 111T

Hephaestus, 768*n*.1, 859

heraldry and totemism, 64–68

Her-Bak, Chick-Pea (Isha Schwaller de Lubicz), xix (Vol. 1)